Footprint Peru

Ben Box and Steve Frankham
6th edition

"It is an image that is anyway a staple of Andean exploration: emerging out of the selva at midday after a long trip – the wide brown streets, with brown houses, everything brown and stark from the overhead sun – the gringo lumbering down the main street, silhouetted with his backpack, walking loose, already punch-drunk from his discoveries before he's even had a beer. It felt delirious and wonderful."

Hugh Thompson, *The White Rock*

❶ Máncora
Lively surfing spot with a long safe beach and holiday atmosphere

❷ Sicán
Last city of the Sicán culture amid ancient carob forests

❸ Kuélap
A pre-Columbian fortress, buried high in jungle-clad mountains

❹ Huaca de la Luna
Startling new murals inside a Moche pyramid

❺ Cañón del Pato
Thrill-a-minute bus ride through a spectacular, narrow pass

❻ Cordillera Blanca
Beautiful and terrifying, these mountains are the highest in Peru

❼ Chavín de Huantar
2500-year-old fortress temple; one of Peru's most important pre-Columbian sites

❽ Lima
Bold, brash and buzzing, with the best food and nightlife in the country

❾ Nazca Lines
Whales, spiders and humming birds, etched in the desert sand over 2500 years ago

Peru Highlights

See colour maps at back of book

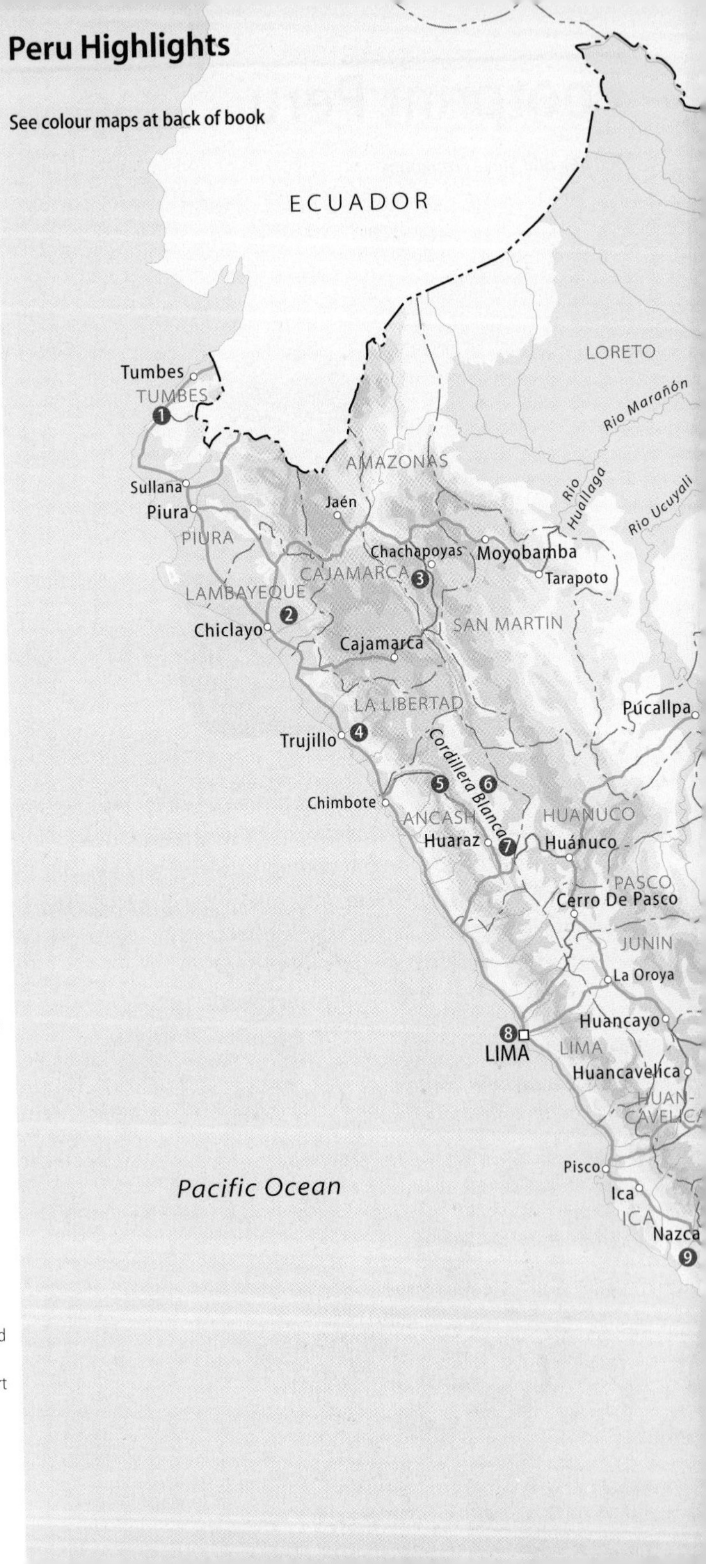

⑩ Ayacucho
The Holy Week celebrations in this colonial city are a sight to behold

⑪ Iquitos
An isolated city on the banks of the Amazon

⑫ Manu National Park
One of the largest protected areas of rainforest; home to jaguars and giant otters

⑬ Machu Picchu
Peru's number one attraction remains a special place

⑭ Choquequirao
A 'lost city' only reachable by some tough trekking

⑮ Cuzco
Gringo capital of South America and a fascinating place

⑯ Río Apurimac
The true source of the Amazon, offers amazing whitewater rafting

⑰ Colca Canyon
Come face-to-face with the condor, the largest bird of prey in the world

⑱ Lake Titicaca
Birthplace of the Inca Empire and home to communities unaffected by modern civilization

⑲ Santa Catalina Convent
This city within a city is the most enchanting colonial structure on the entire continent

Contents

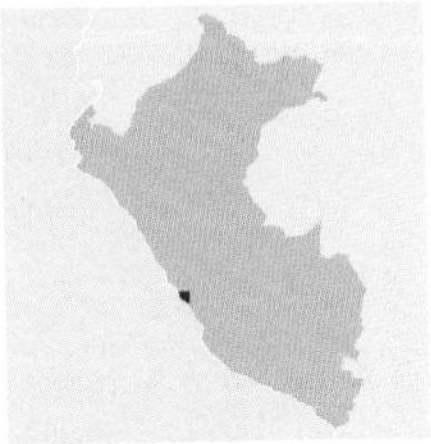

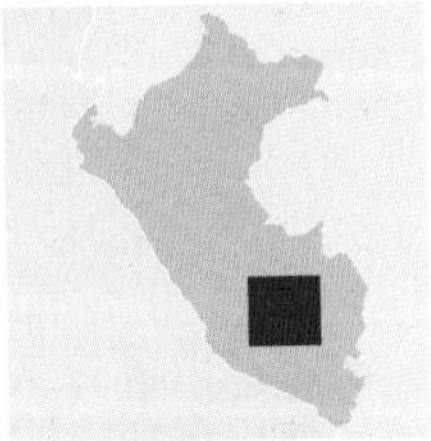

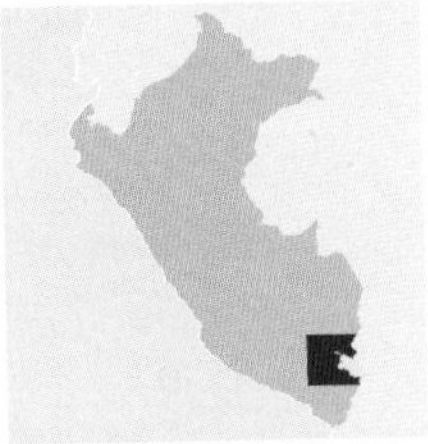

Arequipa

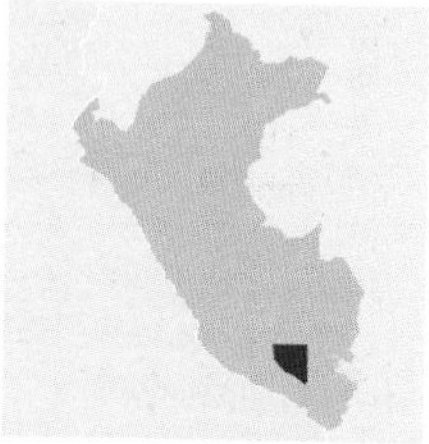

South Coast

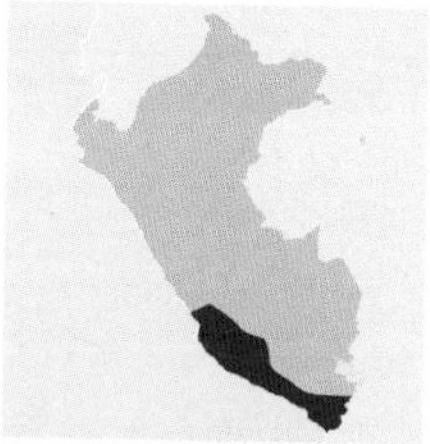

Cordilleras Blanca & Huayhuash

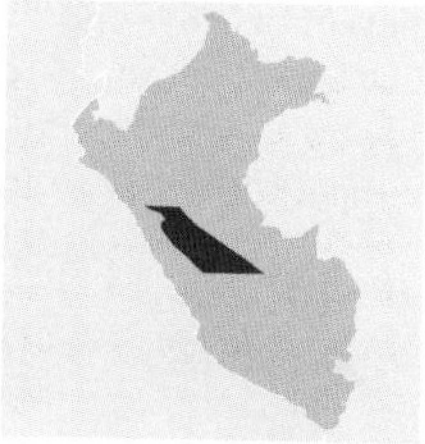

North Coast

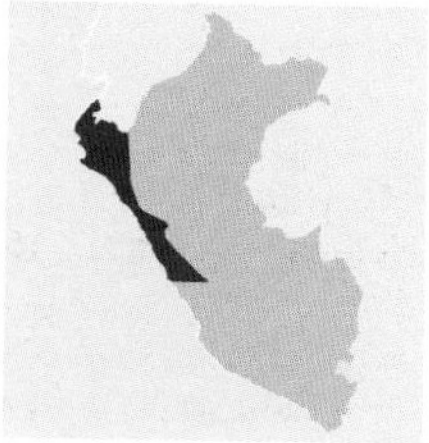

Northern Highlands

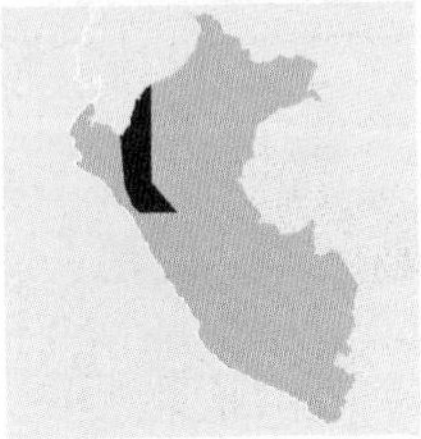

Central Highlands

Amazon Basin

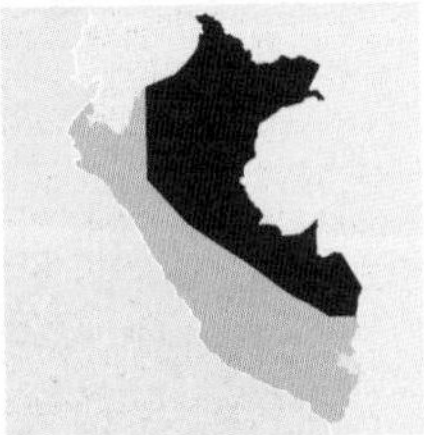

Background

Footnotes

Inside front cover

Inside back cover

Fiesta time

Dancers dress in garish, outlandish costumes and don elaborate masks.

Pisac market
Sunday is the day when the people of the highlands come down to sell their produce.

A foot in the door

Ever since the intrepid explorer Hiram Bingham first described Machu Picchu as a "wonderland", the fabled Inca city has become one of the most recognized images in the world. So much so that it virtually represents Peru, acting as a magnet for every visitor. But it's not even half the story. Peru has more ancient archaeological sites than any other country in South America, and more are being found all the time. One recent discovery, Caral, in the coastal desert, has turned the world of archaeology on its head and challenged accepted thinking on the entire theory of urban development.

There is much more to Peru than old stones, however. Of the 117 recognized life zones on the planet, Peru has 84, from mangroves to cloudforest, mist-fuelled oases in the desert to glacial lakes. It also has 28 out of 32 climate types. Amazingly, 60% of the country is jungle, even though less than 6% of its population lives there. The physical barrier of the Andes has prevented Peru from integrating the tropical lowlands, so much of its jungle remains intact and this vast green carpet is home to the greatest diversity of plants and wildlife on the planet. Not a year goes by without the recording of plants and animals previously unknown to science.

Peru is also a country of fiestas, and it would be an unusual visit to Peru that did not encounter at least one. Masks and costumes tell centuries-old stories and reveal an intense spirituality which enriches daily life. Christian saints are carried through the streets as if they were the Inca emperors' sacred remains. Pachamama – Mother Earth – is offered a drop of every drink and animal spirits and old combats come alive in masquerades. Peru is a wonderland, indeed, with the uncanny knack of springing new surprises at every turn.

10 Riches and rags

When the Spanish *conquistadores* arrived in Peru, they found immense displays of gold and silver, which they plundered with abandon. Such an experience could have made Peru secretive about its riches, but today there are many treasures for all to see. Lima and Cuzco house much of the wealth: Cuzco with its elegant Plaza de Armas and hotels and restaurants befitting a world-class tourist destination; Lima with its size, modernity and the gulf between rich and poor. But each is a world apart from the rest of the country. Elsewhere things are more intimate: general stores selling everything, unnamed restaurants offering *almuerzos*, every other house a speedy internet, dentist or optician. There are odd juxtapositions, too. The TV, which is never off, advertises goods that are out of the reach of many. In a busy street lined with smart shops a girl implores you to buy toilet paper. The top-of-the-range bus you travel on passes an old woman prodding a mixed herd of pigs, donkeys and goats along the road.

A busy street in Puno
One of the best places in Peru for buying llama and alpaca wool articles, which you may well need as it gets bitterly cold at night.

A land of sacrifice

It is easy to appreciate the pride that Peruvians take in their natural surroundings, the country's past achievements, its precolonial heritage and lasting traditions. You'll have no reluctance in sharing the reverence for snow-capped mountains, or marvelling at the grace of river dolphins. But the obvious attractions conceal a more ambiguous reality. The mountains and jungle hold mineral reserves, which may bring financial prosperity but with an inevitable environmental cost. Moreover, at the other end of the economic scale, when a pittance is paid for produce sweated from precipitous hillsides, it's not surprising that inequality breeds disillusion. In the 2006 elections, the despair of the poorest found a ready outlet in the campaign of radical nationalist Ollanta Humala, whose party now holds the largest number of seats in congress. President Alan García faces two major challenges: to gain the confidence of the indigenous population and the lowest paid, who would in the past have been expected to support his Apra party; and to dispel the memories of his earlier presidency, which left Peru economically ruined and in political chaos.

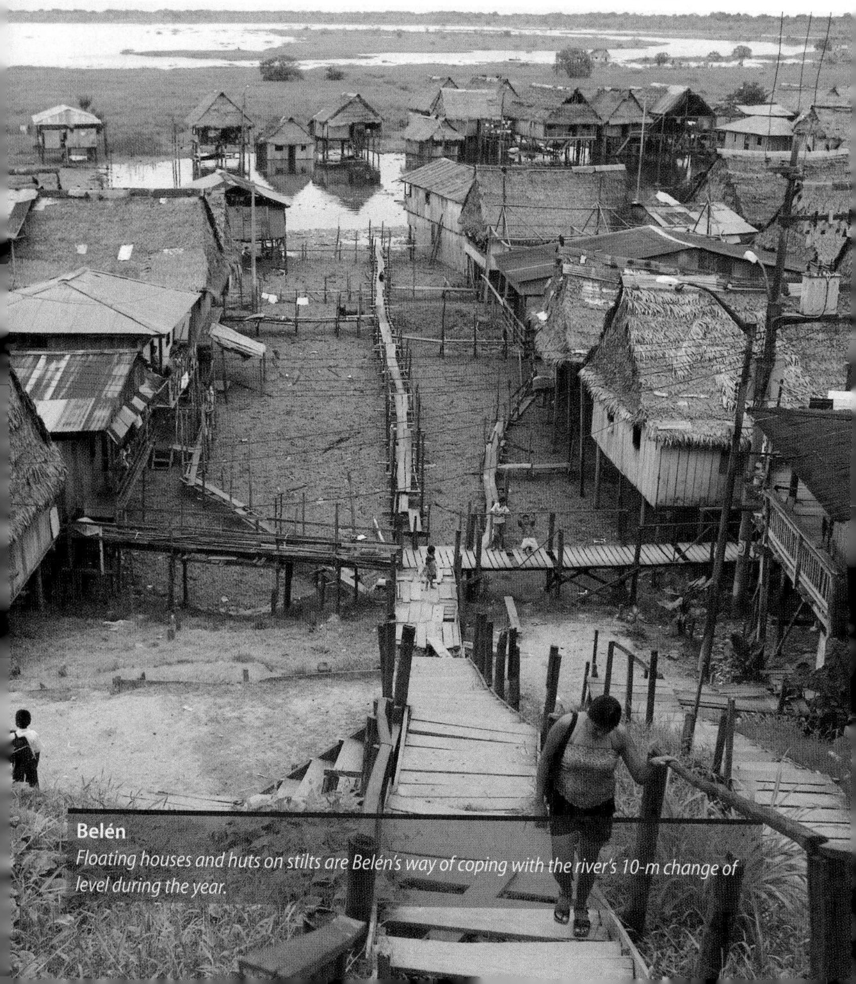

Belén
Floating houses and huts on stilts are Belén's way of coping with the river's 10-m change of level during the year.

1

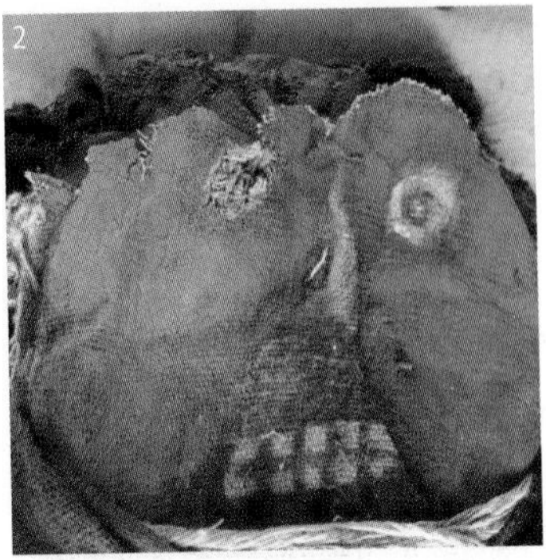
2

4

5

7

8

10

11

3

6

9

12

1 *As well as the capybara, the southern jungle is home to jaguar, puma, ocelot and tapir, 13 species of primate and many hundreds of bird species.* ➤➤ *See page 547.*

2 *The extreme dryness of the Nazca desert has preserved the textiles and ceramics in the mummies' tombs which have been excavated.* ➤➤ *See page 300.*

3 *At fiesta time the costumes often caricature the Spanish; in this way, the indigenous people mock those who erased their heritage.* ➤➤ *See page 599.*

4 *As casual as a coffee-break and as sacred as Communion, the chewing of coca leaves is an ancient ritual.* ➤➤ *See page 225.*

5 *The Cordillera Blanca has some of the best trekking and climbing in Peru, with a network of trails used by the local people.* ➤➤ *See page 325.*

6 *Huanchaco, near Trujillo, has long been a travellers' favourite for surfing, watching the fishermen on their reed boats and just hanging out.* ➤➤ *See page 392.*

7 *There is a tremendous feeling of awe on first witnessing the ancient citadel of Machu Picchu, especially if it comes at the end of a three-day pilgrimage.* ➤➤ *See page 190.*

8 *The highland people around the Titicaca basin have kept llamas for thousands of years.* ➤➤ *See page 568.*

9 *The staples of highland cooking, corn and potatoes are found in a remarkable variety of shapes, sizes and colours.* ➤➤ *See page 56.*

10 *Ancient weaving traditions have survived in the Andes since pre-Columbian times, when woven cloth was the most sought-after trading commodity.* ➤➤ *See page 592.*

11 *Fishermen on the Uros islands in Lake Titicaca build their boats from tortora reeds.* ➤➤ *See page 224.*

12 *Visitors flock to the beautiful Colca Canyon for a close encounter with the giant Andean condor.* ➤➤ *See page 266.*

14 Tales of the unexpected

At the end of the Inca Trail is the Intipinku, the Gate of the Sun. Through it you not only see Machu Picchu for the first time, but you are lead back through history to the cultures out of which the Inca civilization grew. The 2500-year-old fortress temple of Chavín de Huantar, in the lee of the snow-covered peaks of the Cordillera Blanca, represents one of the most influential societies of pre-Columbian times. The Nazca Lines, huge figures of animals and geometric patterns etched into the southern coastal desert between 200 BC and AD 600, are still puzzling scientists. Near the elegant colonial city of Trujillo, on Peru's northern coast, are Chan Chán, the largest adobe city in the world, and the massive adobe pyramids of Huaca del Sol and Huaca de la Luna. Further north still, the twin pyramid complex of Sipán has revealed some of the finest examples of pre-Columbian jewellery, pottery and textiles yet found on the continent. Also here are the mysterious and evocative ruins of Tucumé, a huge city of 26 pyramids, and Sicán, whose pyramids rise out of a forest of carob trees. In the northeast, where the Andean mountains drop to meet the vast Amazonian lowlands, the cities and cliffside tombs of the cloud people lie hidden in the forest. The most visited of these, Kuélap, is the greatest pre-Columbian fortress in the Americas.

Thrills, hills and Pacific breaks

Machu Picchu's near neighbour, Cuzco, is the gateway to living and natural history. Its festivals are a microcosm of 3000 others. It gives access to the

The Nazca area is dotted with over 100 cemeteries; mummies can still to be seen in a cemetery in the valley of Jumana.

The Peruvian jungles cover over half the country; less than 6% of its population lives here, but they are home to a diversity of life unequalled anywhere on Earth.

jungle reserves of Manu and Tambopata, where the tally of birds, mammals, reptiles, butterflies and plants has yet to be fully catalogued. Without doubt, Peru is the best place on earth for seeing jungle wildlife, but Cuzco is not the sole entry point. From the Amazon city of Iquitos you can go to Pacaya-Samiria on whose tracks and waterways you can watch Peru's wild heart to your own heart's content. In northern Peru, just as in Cuzco, the sporting possibilities are endless: hiking to ruined cities, whitewater rafting or biking down the highest mountains. Huaraz in the Cordillera Blanca is a mecca for climbers and there are fabulous treks in the Chachapoyas area. And, as everyone surely knows, Peru was the birth- place of surfing (in 2006 the women's world champion was, once again, a Peruvian).

Frozen in time

Look south beyond Cuzco, too, to the islands in the sparkling waters of Lake Titicaca, where communities preserve traditions untouched by modernity. In the magnificent city of Arequipa, watched over by volcanoes, the high walls of Santa Catalina convent hide a perfectly preserved miniature colonial town which was, until recently, closed to the outside world. Nearby are the Colca and Cotahuasi canyons, remarkable chasms twice as deep as the Grand Canyon, where you can trek along prehispanic agricultural terraces which are still in use, and look for mighty condors rising on the thermals.

The Inca Trail
It's a three- to four- day trek along the centuries-old highway that winds its way from the Sacred Valley to the ancient citadel of Machu Picchu.

Essentials

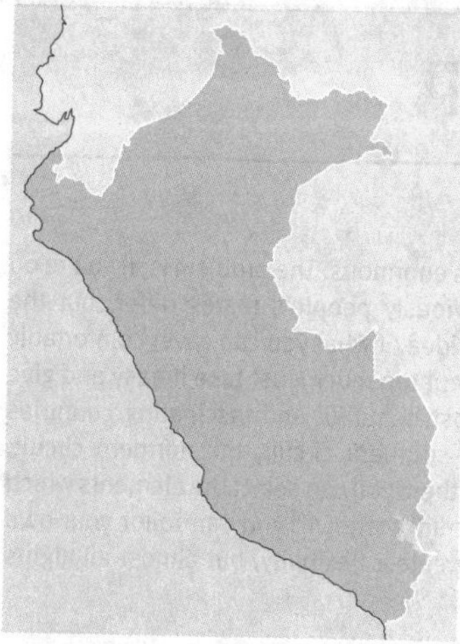

Footprint features

Planning your trip

Where to go

The variety which Peru can offer the visitor is enormous. The problem is, if you're on a tight schedule, how to fit it all in. Obviously people's tastes differ, but the suggested itineraries below should give an idea of what you can cover comfortably in the time available. Above all, don't attempt too much. Just take it easy and give yourself time to appreciate one of the most beautiful and fascinating countries on Earth. There are four main areas: the southern circuit, the northern circuit, the central highlands and the jungle. FroFm them you can select the elements which suit you best and, providing the transport links are OK, you can tailor your own itinerary. If short of time, flying gives the greatest flexibility, but almost all flights depart from Lima.

One to two weeks

While a one-week visit on its own to Peru would be very restrictive, there are certain places that fit neatly into seven days of travelling. **Southern Peru** offers a very rewarding short circuit covering the most important and popular sites in this part of the country. **Cuzco** and **Machu Picchu**, the crown jewels of the Inca Empire, frequently comprise a week (or less), but if you plan to hike the **Inca Trail** or any of the challenging alternatives, you need to consider two weeks in the region. Beautiful **Titicaca**, the highest navigable lake in the world, and the white city of **Arequipa** can be combined with Cuzco into a fortnight, using air, rail and road travel.

As an alternative to the highlands, try a week on the **southern coast**, taking in the **Paracas Peninsula** (near Pisco), with its marine birdlife, and the incredible **Nazca and Palpa Lines**.

Huaraz, in the **Cordillera Blanca**, is only seven hours by road from Lima and one of the world's premier high-altitude recreation areas, with unparalleled ease of access. A week's hiking or climbing in the Cordillera and neighbouring areas is a practical option. It can also easily be linked with the coastal archaeological sites near the colonial city of **Trujillo** (eg Chan Chán, the Huacas del Sol and de la Luna) and further north, around **Chiclayo** (eg Lambayeque with the Brüning and Sipán museums, Sipán itself, Túcume and Sicán), to fill two weeks. Alternatively, the **Cajamarca** area includes the pleasant city itself, plus thermal baths, archaeological and more recent historical sites and beautiful countryside. To get there quickly from Huaraz, you have to return to the coast for flights from Lima or bus services from Lima, Trujillo or Chiclayo.

Peru's **eastern jungle** includes zones with some of the highest levels of biodiversity in the world. There are two distinct areas with tourism development, north and southeast, and a central zone which has little infrastructure. The southeastern jungle contains the **Manu National Park** and the **Tambopata National Reserve**. These provide wonderful opportunities for watchers of birds, butterflies and animals and for plant lovers. A trip to the southeastern jungle is usually done as part of a visit to Cuzco, but can be an item on its own. Flying both ways to **Puerto Maldonado** is the only viable option if short of time. Going overland to the Amazon Basin is also possible. The adventurous way is from Cuzco to Puerto Maldonado (the most popular tours involve going one way by road, the other by air), but from Lima to the **central jungle**, via Tarma, is easy enough for people to do on a holiday weekend (and is therefore crowded at such times). The Amazonian city of **Iquitos** is the jumping-off point for the northern jungle, where there is a good network of jungle lodges on the river or its tributaries. Flying to Iquitos is one option, either from Lima, or from **Tarapoto**, which can be reached by a beautiful road which descends from the mountains just north of Chachapoyas. Alternatively, you can go overland to Pucallpa and then take a river boat downstream to Iquitos.

A trip to the **Central Andes** from Lima can be done fairly quickly, calling at **Huancayo, Huancavelica** and **Ayacucho** in a week to 10 days. Alternatively, the route from Cuzco to the Central Highlands is rewarding, but since there are no flights between Cuzco and Ayacucho, the only, if rather demanding option is by bus. Obviously the more time you allow, the greater the variety of sights you see, especially in the **Mantaro Valley** near Huancayo, and the places of historical interest around Ayacucho. These are also two of the best places for handicrafts.

At any time, a few extra days in **Lima** visiting its fascinating museums will give you an overview of what you'll be seeing later. And in the meanwhile, you can experience the capital's great nightlife.

Three to four weeks

Adding an extra week or two to the basic southern itinerary would allow you to see much more of Cuzco, especially the **Sacred Valley of the Incas.** You can also explore the **Colca** or **Cotahuasi Canyons** from Arequipa, or, from **Puno,** the shores and islands of Lake Titicaca.

Cajamarca gives access to the more remote **Chachapoyas** region, which contains a bewildering number of prehispanic archaeological sites. A week minimum here would be a good idea. Access by road is from the southwest through **Celendín.** There is also a more northerly road route to Chachapoyas from Chiclayo, where you should stop to see the nearby archaeological sites. You can break up a tour of archaeology and mountains with some surfing at **Puerto Chicama** (north of Trujillo) and there are many more beaches in the far north near **Piura** and Tumbes. **Tumbes** also has some wildlife parks, such as coastal mangroves, unlike those in other parts of the country.

If planning on spending more time in the Central Highlands, one variation is to travel overland from **Cerro de Pasco** via Oyón and Churín to **Huacho,** on the coast north of Lima. You would then be close to the recently discovered, intriguing city of **Caral.** Another good option is to combine the Central Highlands with the Cordillera Blanca, taking a series of buses between Huaraz and **Huánuco,** via La Unión and Huallanca. Finally, the **Cordillera Huayhuash** offers some rewarding long-distance, high-altitude trekking. It is most easily reached from Huaraz, via Chiquián, but should not be attempted unless you have a week to spare.

When to go

Climate

Peru's high season in the highlands is from May to September, when the weather is most stable for hiking and climbing. At this time the days are generally clear and sunny, though nights can be very cold at high altitude. During the wettest months in the highlands, November to April, some roads become impassable and hiking trails can be very muddy. April and May, at the tail end of the highland rainy season, is a beautiful time to see the Peruvian Andes, but the rain may linger, so be prepared. For a more detailed description of conditions in the Cordillera Blanca, see page 66.

On the coast, high seasons are September and Christmas to February. The summer months are from December to April, but from approximately May to October much of this area is covered with *la garúa*, a blanket of cloud and mist. At this time only the northern beaches near Tumbes are warm enough for pleasant swimming.

The best time to visit the jungle is during the dry season, from April to October. During the wet season, November to April, it is oppressively hot (40°C and above) and while it only rains for a few hours at a time, which is not enough to spoil your trip, it is enough to make some roads virtually impassable.

Festivals and events

Every bit as important as knowing where to go and what the weather will be like, is Peru's festival calendar. At any given time of the year there'll be a festival somewhere in the country, drawing people from miles around. Check the websites of **PromPerú** and **South American Explorers**, see Finding out more page 42. For a detailed list of local festival dates, see under each town in the travelling text. For a description of some of the main festivals and their historic roots, see under Culture, on page 598.

The high season for foreign tourism is June to September while national tourism peaks on certain holidays, Navidad, Semana Santa and Fiestas Patrias. Prices rise and accommodation and bus tickets are harder to come by. If you know when you will be travelling buy your ticket in advance.

Festivals Two of the major festival dates are **Carnaval**, which is held over the weekend before **Ash Wednesday**, and **Semana Santa** (Holy Week), which ends on **Easter Sunday**. Carnival is celebrated in most of the Andes and Semana Santa throughout Peru. Accommodation and transport is heavily booked at these times and prices rise considerably. Book tickets and make hotel bookings early.

Another important festival is **Fiesta de la Cruz**, held on **1 May** in much of the central and southern highlands and on the coast. In Cuzco, the entire month of **June** is one huge fiesta, culminating in **Inti Raymi**, on **24 June**, one of Peru's prime tourist attractions. This date is also celebrated for **San Juan** in the jungle lowlands. Many places on the coast celebrate **San Pedro y San Pablo** on the **29 June**, and Huaraz celebrates a week-long festival of Andinismo at the beginning of the month.

The two main festivals in Lima are **Santa Rosa de Lima**, on **30 August**, and **Señor de los Milagros**, held on several dates throughout **October**.

Another national festival is **Todos los Santos** (All Saints) on **1 November**, and on **8 December** is **Festividad de la Inmaculada Concepción**. See individual towns for local festival listings.

National holidays Apart from the festivals listed above, the main holidays are: **1 January**, New Year; **6 January**, *Bajada de Reyes*; **1 May**, Labour Day; **28-29 July**, Independence (Fiestas Patrias); **7 October**, Battle of Angamos; **24-25 December**, *Navidad*.

Most businesses such as banks, airline offices and tourist agencies close for the official holidays while supermarkets and street markets may be open. This depends a lot on where you are so ask around before the holiday. Sometimes holidays that fall during mid-week will be moved to the following Monday to make a long weekend. If you are going to spend a holiday in a certain area, find out what the local customs and events are. Often there are parades, processions, special types of food or certain traditions (like yellow underwear on New Year's Eve) that characterize the event.

Tour operators

UK and Ireland

Amazing Peru, 9 Alma Rd, Manchester M19 2FG, T0808-234 6805; Av Tullumayo 213, Cuzco, T084-262720, www.amazingperu.com. Professional and well-organized tours to Peru, with knowledgeable guides.
Andean Trails, The Clockhouse, Bonnington Mill Business Centre, 72 Newhaven Rd, Edinburgh, EH6 5QG, T0131-467 7086, www.andeantrails.co.uk. For mountain biking, trekking and other adventure tours.
Andes, 37a St Andrews St, Castle Douglas, Kirkcudbrightshire DG7 1EN, Scotland, T01556-503929, www.andes.org.uk. For climbing trips in Peru and all South America.
Audley Latin America, 6 Willows Gate, Stratton Audley, Oxfordshire OX27 9AU, T01869-276222, www.audleytravel.com.
Austral Tours, 20 Upper Tachbrook St, London SW1V 1SH, T020-7233 5384, www.latinamerica.co.uk.
Condor Journeys and Adventures, 2 Ferry Bank, Colintraive, Argyll PA22 3AR, T01700-841318, www.condorjourneys-adventures.com. Eco and adventure tourism with specially designed tours to suit your requirements.

Dragoman, Camp Green, Debenham, Stowmarket, Suffolk IP14 6LA, T01728-861133, www.dragoman.co.uk. Contact this outfit for overland camping and/or hotel journeys throughout both South and Central America.

Exodus Travels, Grange Mills, 9 Weir Rd, London SW12 0NE, T020-8675 5550, www.exodus.co.uk. Experienced in adventure travel, including cultural tours and trekking and biking holidays.

Explore, Nelson House, 55 Victoria Rd, Farnborough, Hampshire GU14 7PA, T0870-333 4002, www.explore. co.uk. Highly respected operator. They offer 2- to 5-week tours in more than 90 countries worldwide including Peru. Small groups. Well executed.

Galapagos Classic Cruises, 6 Keyes Rd, London NW2 3XA, T020 8933 0613, www.galapagoscruises.co.uk. This outfit offers good tailor-made tours.

Guerba Expeditions, Wessex House, 40 Station Rd, Westbury, Wiltshire BA13 3JN, T01373-826611, www.guerba.com. Specializes in adventure holidays, from trekking safaris to wilderness camping.

High Places, Globe Centre, Penistone Rd, Sheffield S6 3AE, T0845-257 7500, www.highplaces.co.uk. Trekking and mountaineering trips.

Journey Latin America, 12 & 13 Heathfield Terr, Chiswick, London W4 4JE, T020-8747 8315, and 12 St Ann's Sq, 2nd floor, Manchester M2 7HW, T0161-832 1441, www.journeylatinamerica.co.uk. The world's leading tailor-made specialist for Latin America, running escorted tours throughout the region, they also offer a wide range of flight options.

KE Adventure Travel, 32 Lake Rd, Keswick, Cumbria CA12 5DQ, T017687-73966, www.keadventure.com. Specialist in adventure tours, including 3-week cycling trips in and around Cuzco.

Kumuka Expeditions, 40 Earls Court Rd, London W8 6EJ, T0207-937 8855 , and Level 4, 46-48 York St, Sydney, NSW 2000, Australia, T1306-667277, www.kumuka.com. Overland tour operator for small groups, escorted or truck-based.

Last Frontiers, Fleet Marston Farm, Aylesbury, Buckinghamshire HP18 0QT,

T01296-653000, www.lastfrontiers.com. South American specialists offering tailor-made itineraries as well as discounted air fares and air passes.

Llama Travel, Oxford House, 49A Oxford Rd, London N4 3EY, T020 7263 3000, www.llama travel.com. Tours throughout Peru.

Naturetrek, Cheriton Mill, Cheriton, Alresford, Hampshire SO24 0NG, T01962-733051, www.naturetrek.co.uk. Birdwatching tours throughout the continent, also botany, natural history tours, treks and cruises.

New Worlds Ltd, Holly Cottage, Holt Rd, Cromer, Norfolk, NR27 9JN, T0800-1218104, www.newworlds.co.uk. Tailor-made trips to Peru.

Oasis Overland, The Marsh, Henstridge, Somerset, BA8 0TF, T01963-363400, www.oasisoverland.co.uk. Small group trips in Peru and overland trips across South America.

Select Latin Amercia (incorporating Galapagos Adventure Tours), 79 Maltings Pl, 169 Tower Bridge Rd, London SE1 3LJ, T020-7407 1478, www.selectlatinamerica.com. Quality tailor-made holidays and small group tours.

South American Experience, 47 Causton St, Pimlico, London, SW1P 4AT, T020-7976 5511, www.southamericanexperience.com. Apart from booking flights and accommodation, also offer tailor-made trips.

Steppes Latin America, 51 Castle St, Cirencester, Gloucestershire GL7 1QD, T01285-880980, www.steppes latinamerica.co.uk.

Sunvil Latin America, Sunvil House, Upper Sq, Old Isleworth, Middlesex TW7 7BJ, T020-8568 4499, www.sunvil.co.uk. Small groups or individual tours.

The Adventure Company, 15 Turk St, Alton GU34 1AG, T0870-794 1009, www.adventurecompany.co.uk.

Trailbreak, Unit 1, Bridge Farm, Reading Rd, Arborfield, Berkshire RG2 9HT, T0118-976 2491, www.trailbreak.co.uk. For mountain biking adventures.

Tribes Travel, 12 The Business Centre, Earl Soham, Woodbridge, Suffolk IP13 7SA, T01728-685971, www.tribes.co.uk. Tour company with an associated charitable foundation which aims to relieve poverty in indigenous communities.

Trips Worldwide, 14 Frederick Pl, Clifton, Bristol BS8 1AS, T0117-311 4400, www.tripsworldwide.co.uk. Tailor-made tours to South America.

Tucan Travel, 316 Uxbridge Rd, London W3 9QP, T020-8896 1600, www.tucantravel.com.

Veloso Tours, ground floor, 34 Warple Way, London W3 0RG, T020-8762 0616, www.veloso.com.

Continental Europe

South American Tours, Stephanstrasse 13, D-60313, Frankfurt/M, Germany, T+49-69-405 8970, www.southamericantours.de. For holidays, business travel, or special packages. Has own office at Av Miguel Dasso 117, piso 14, San Isidro, Lima, T01-422 7254, info@satperu.com.pe, and in New York, Tokyo, Quito, Rio de Janeiro, Santiago de Chile and Buenos Aires.

Nouveaux Mondes, Rte Suisse 7, CH-1295 Mies, Switzerland, T+41-22-950 9660, www.nouveauxmondes.com.

North America

4starSouthAmerica, in USA and Canada T1-800-747 4540, Europe T+49-(700)-4444 7827, UK T0800-011 2959; www.4starsouthamerica.com. Online tour operator. For flights in US T1-800-887 5686, www.4starflights.com.

Discover Latinamerica, 6205 Blue Lagoon Drive, suite 310, Miami, FL 33126, T305-266 5827, www.discoverlatinamerica.com.

eXito, 108 Rutgers St, Fort Collins, CO 80525, T1-800-655 4053, T970-482 3019 (worldwide), www.exito-travel.com.

GAP Adventures, 19 Charlotte St, Toronto, Ontario, M5V 2H5, T1-800-708 7761, www.gap.ca.

Ladatco Tours, 2200 S Dixie Highway, suite 704, Coconut Grove, FL 33133, T1-800-327 6162, www.ladatco.com. Based in Miami, run 'themed' explorer tours based around the Incas, mysticism, etc.

Lost World Adventures, 337 Shadowmoor Drive, Decatur, GA 30030, T800-999 0558, www.lostworld.com.

Myths and Mountains, 976 Tee Court, Incline Village, NV 89451, T775-832 5454, www.mythsandmountains.com.

Pedal Peru, PO Box 1921, Fraser, CO 80442, T1-800-708-8604, www.pedal peru.com. Multi-sport adventures.

Peru For Less, 450 Throckmorton, Suite 1110, Fort Worth, TX 761002, USA, T1-877 269 0309 (toll free), T020-3002 0571, www.peruforless.com; C Jorge Leguía 142, Miraflores, La Aurora,Lima, T01-272 0542. Tours to Peru at prices which aim to be the lowest outside Peru.

Peru Mountain Bike, in US T1-866 865 bike, in thr UK T0871-871 6759, in Peru, Av Arequipa 5241-504, Miraflores, Lima 18, T01-447 2057, www.perumountainbike.com.

Organizes mountain bike trips, working in conjunction with Peruvian companies in Huaraz, Caraz, Cuzco and Huancayo.

Puchka Peru, www.puchkaperu.com. Specializes in textiles, folk art and market tours.

South American Journeys, 9921 Cabanas Av, Tujunga, CA 91042, T1-800-884 7474, and Av La Marina 592, Iquitos, T094- 251078, www.southamericaexp.com. Small group tours off the beaten track, Peruvian guides, involvement in ecological projects.

Tambo Tours, 20919 Coral Bridge Lane, Suite 225-A, Spring, TX 77388, T1-888-2-GO-PERU (246-7378), T001-281 528 9448 (worldwide) www.2GOPERU.com. Long- established tour specialist with offices in Peru and USA. Customized trips to the Amazon and archaeological sites of Peru and Ecuador. Daily departures.

Tropical Nature Travel, PO Box 5276, Gainesville, FL 326270 5276, T1-877-827 8350, www.tropicalnaturetravel.com.

Wildland Adventures, 3516 NE 155 St, Seattle, WA 98155-7412, USA, T206-365 0686, T800-345 4453, www.wildland.com. Specializes in cultural and natural history tours to the Andes and Amazon.

South America

Kolibri Expeditions, contact Gunnar Engblom, Lima, T01-476 5016, www.kolibri expeditions.com. Trip reports, recent sightings, travel tips, travel partners, range extensions, identification help, www.birding-peru.com. **Birding Peru** e-group: birdingperu-subscribe@yahoo groups.com.

Aracari Travel Consulting, Av Pardo 610, suite 802, Miraflores, T01-242 6673, www.aracari.com. Regional tours throughout Peru.

Rest of the world

Adventure World, Level 20, 141 Walker St, North Sydney NSW 2060, T02-8913 0755 , and 197 St Georges Terrace, Perth 6000, T08-9226 4525, www.adventureworld.com.au. Escorted group tours, locally escorted tours and packages to Peru and all of Latin America.

Chimu Adventures, info@chimuadventures.com, www.chimuadventures.com. Web-based company offering discount tickets to Peru. They can organize Inca Trail permits in advance. As well as transport, accommodation and day tours.

Finding out more

Useful websites

www.aboutcusco.com, **www.cuscoon line.com**, **www.cuscoperu.com** and **www.cusco.net** Among many pages for Cuzco, in Spanish, English and other languages.

www.machu-picchu.info On Machu Picchu.

www.isidore-of-seville.com/machu Lots of links to sites about Macchu Picchu.

www.arequipa-tourism.com Site about Arequipa in Spanish and English.

www.yachay.com.pe/especiales/nasca Nazca lines (in Spanish).

www.andeanexplorer.com and **http://huaylas.com** For Huaraz and the Callejón de Huaylas, both available in English.

www.perunorte.com Northern Peru (La Libertad, Cajamarca and Lambayeque, in Spanish, English and German).

www.xanga.com/TrujilloPeru Mainly for the north of the country.

www.adonde.com and **www.perulinks.com/** General information, the latter in Spanish, English, French and German.

www.andeantravelweb.com/peru Andean adventure travel, with advice, links and more (English and Spanish).
www.conam.gob.pe National Environmental Commission (Spanish).
www.geocities.com/perutraveller/ English tourist information aimed at independent travellers.
www.perucultural.org.pe For information on cultural activities, museums and Peruvian pre-Columbian textiles (Spanish).
www.perurail.com PerúRail.
www.planeta.com Ron Mader's website which contains masses of useful information on ecotourism, conservation, travel, news, links, language schools and articles.
www.rree.gob.pe Ministry of Foreign Affairs, for consular information, etc.
www.terra.com.pe Click on Turismo to get to the travel page (in Spanish).
www.traficoperu.com On-line travel agent with lots of information (Spanish and English).
http://travel.peru.com/travel/english/ Peru.Com's travel page in English, or **http://travel.peru.com/travel/spanish** for the Spanish version).
www.yachay.com.pe Red Científica Peruana, click on Turismo to get to the travel page.

Language

The official language is **Spanish. Quechua,** an Andean language which predates the Incas, has been given some official status and there is much pride in its use, but despite the fact that it is spoken by millions of people in the sierra who have little or no knowledge of Spanish, it is not used in schools. Another important indigenous language is **Aymara,** used in the area around Lake Titicaca. The jungle is home to a plethora of languages but Spanish is spoken in all but the remotest areas. **English** is not spoken widely, except by those employed in the tourism industry (eg hotel, tour agency and airline staff). See page 618 for some basic Spanish for travellers.

Language courses are listed in the directories of cities and towns. **AmeriSpan** ⓘ *PO Box 58129, 117 South 17th St, 14th floor, Philadelphia PA 19103, USA, T1-800-879 6640 (USA and Canada), T215-751 1100 (worldwide), www.amerispan.com*, organizes programmes throughout Latin America from its North American and Guatemalan bases. They also have lots of information about travelling in the region. **Languages Abroad.com** ⓘ *386 Ontario St, Toronto, Ontario, Canada, M5A 2V7, T1-800-219 9924, in UK T0800-404 7738, www.languagesabroad.com*, offers Spanish and Portuguese programmes in every South American country except Colombia and Paraguay. They also have language immersion courses throughout the world. Similarly, there is **Cactus** ⓘ *4 Clarence House, 30-31 North St, Brighton BN1 1EB,*

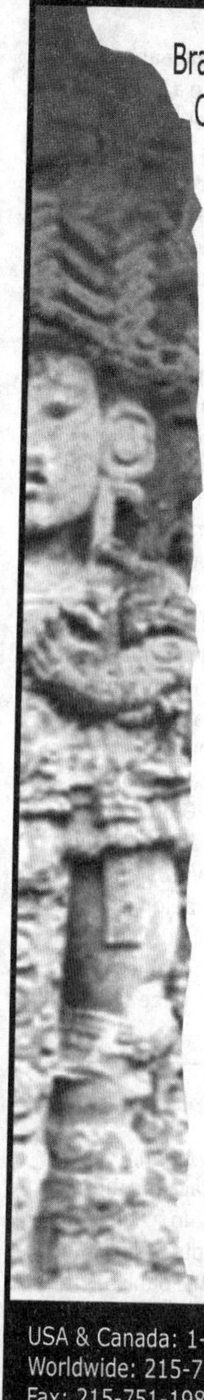

 To845-130 4775, www.cactuslanguage.com. **Spanish Abroad** ① *5112 N, 40th St, Suite 103, Phoenix, AZ 85018, USA, T1-888-722 7623, T1-602-778 6791 (worldwide), www.spanishabroad.com*. For a list of schools, see www.planeta.com/schoolist.html.

Disabled travellers

As with most underdeveloped countries, facilities for the disabled traveller are sadly lacking. Wheelchair ramps are a rare luxury and getting a wheelchair into a bathroom or toilet is well nigh impossible, except for some of the more upmarket hotels. The entrance to many cheap hotels is up a narrow flight of stairs. Pavements are often in a poor state of repair (even fully able people need to look out for uncovered manholes and other unexpected traps). Visually and hearing-impaired travellers are similarly poorly catered for as a rule, but experienced guides can often provide tours with individual attention. Disabled Peruvians obviously have to cope with these problems and mainly rely on the help of others to get on and off public transport and generally move around.

The Ministerio de la Mujer y Desarrollo Social (Ministry for Women and Social Development) incorporates a Consejo Nacional de Integración de la Persona con Discapacidad, CONADIS (National Council for the Integration of Disabled People, www.conadisperu.gob.pe – in Spanish). **CONADIS**, together with **PromPerú**, private business, **SATH** (see next paragraph) and **Kéroul** of Québec, has been involved in a project called **Peru: Towards an Accessible Tourism** and the *First Report on Accessibility in Peru for Tourists with Disabilities* was published in 2001. The report identifies many challenges in a number of major tourist sites. For instance, archaeological sites such as Machu Picchu and Chan Chán, being World Heritage sites, may not be altered for accessibility although the latter, apart from soft sand in places, is almost entirely accessible. Specially trained personnel, however, can provide assistance to those with disabilities in these cases. The project can be accessed through the PromPerú website; click on Turismo acesible/Accessible tourism.

Some travel companies are beginning to specialize in exciting holidays, tailor-made for individuals depending on their level of disability. The **Global Access Disabled Travel Network Site,** www.globalaccessnews.com, is dedicated to providing information for 'disabled adventurers' and includes a number of reviews and tips from members of the public. Another informative site, www.sath.org, belongs to the **Society for Accessible Travel and Hospitality,** and has lots of advice on how to travel with specific disabilities, plus listings and links. One company in Cuzco which offers tours for disabled people is **Apumayo,** see Cuzco Tours and activities, page 162.

Gay and lesbian travellers

Movemiento Homosexual de Lima (MHOL) ① *C Mcal Miller 828, Jesús María, T01-433 5519 (English from 1630 on), mhol@terra.com.pe*, is a great contact for the gay community in Lima. On-line resources for gay travellers in Peru are http://lima.queercity.info/index.html (a good site, in English, with lots of links and information), www.deambiente.com and www.gayperu.com (both in Spanish). The latter also has a **tour operator** ① *Larco 101, of 309, Miraflores, T01-447 3366, www.gayperu.com/travel*. In the Lima section we include the names of gay-friendly establishments. There are also gay-friendly places in Cuzco, but the scene is not very active there. This does not imply, however, that there is hostility towards gay and lesbian travellers. As a major tourist centre which welcomes a huge variety of visitors, Cuzco is probably more open than anywhere in Peru.

Student travellers

If you are in full-time education you will be entitled to an **International Student Identity Card**, which gives you special prices on all forms of transport (air, sea, rail, etc), and access to a variety of other concessions and services. If you need to find the location of your nearest ISIC office contact: **The ISIC Association** ⓘ *c/o IAS, Keizersgracht 174-176, 1016 DW Amsterdam, Holland, T+31-20-421 2800, www.istc.org.*

Students can obtain very few reductions in Peru with an international student card, except in and around Cuzco, at museums and Instituto Nacional de Cultura sites. To be any use in Peru, it must bear the owner's photograph. An ISIC card can be obtained in Lima from **Intej** ⓘ *Av San Martín 240, Barranco, T01-247 3230; also: Portal de Panes 123, of 107 (C Los Ruiseñores), T084-256367, Cuzco; Santo Domingo 123, of 307, p 3, T054-284756, Arequipa; Manuel María Izaga 176, T074-226789, Chiclayo; Calle Real 151, T064-218124, Huancayo; Jirón Pizarro 532, of 104, T044-201592, www.intej.org.*

Travelling with children

Travel with children can bring you into closer contact with local families and, generally, presents no special problems – in fact the path is often smoother for family groups. Officials tend to be more amenable where children are concerned and they are pleased if your child knows a little Spanish. **South American Explorers** in Lima, page 80, and Cuzco, page 135, can provide lots of useful information on travelling with children in Peru.

Getting from A to B involves a lot of time waiting for buses, trains, and especially for aeroplanes. You should take reading material with you. Train travel is limited to Cuzco–Machu Picchu, Cuzco–Puno and Huancayo–Huancavelica. The **PerúRail** services in the Cuzco region are comfortable, with tables between seats, so that games can be played. Elsewhere, you must be prepared for bus or more cramped *colectivo* travel.

On all long-distance buses you pay a **fare** for each seat, and there are no half-fares if the children occupy a seat each. For shorter trips it is cheaper, if less comfortable, to seat small children on your knee. On sightseeing tours you should *always* bargain for a family rate – often children can go free.

In all **hotels**, try to negotiate family rates. If charges are per person, always insist that two children will occupy one bed only, therefore counting as one tariff. You can almost always get a reduced rate at cheaper hotels.

Food can be a problem if the children are not adaptable. A small immersion heater and jug for making hot drinks is invaluable, but remember that electric current varies. In restaurants, you can normally buy children's helpings, or divide one full-size helping between two children.

Women travellers

Generally women travellers should find visiting Peru an enjoyable experience. However, machismo is alive and well here and you should be prepared for this and try not to over react. When you set out, err on the side of caution until your instincts have adjusted to the customs of a new culture.

It is easier for men to take the friendliness of locals at face value; women may be subject to much unwanted attention. To help minimize this, do not wear suggestive clothing and do not flirt. By wearing a wedding ring, carrying a photograph of your 'husband' and 'children', and saying that your 'husband' is close at hand, you may dissuade an aspiring suitor. If politeness fails, do not feel bad about showing offence and departing. When accepting a social invitation, make sure that someone knows the address and the time you left. Ask if you can bring a friend (even if you do not intend to do so).

If, as a single woman, you can befriend a local woman, you will learn much more about the country you are visiting as well as finding out how best to deal with the barrage of suggestive comments, whistles and hisses that will invariably come your way. Travelling with another *gringa* may not exempt you from this attention, but at least should give you moral support.

Unless actively avoiding foreigners like yourself, don't go too far from the beaten track. There is a very definite 'gringo trail' which you can join, or follow, if seeking company. This can be helpful when looking for safe accommodation, especially if arriving after dark (which is best avoided). Remember that for a single woman a taxi at night can be as dangerous as wandering around on her own. A good rule is always to act with confidence, as though you know where you are going, even if you do not. Someone who looks lost is more likely to attract unwanted attention.

Working in Peru

There are many opportunities for volunteer work in Peru (South American Explorers have an extensive database). Volunteers do not need a visa for Peru, but you must check with a Peruvian consulate that this applies to you. On **www.trabajovoluntario.org**, a site which offers volunteers and organizations to get in touch, you can browse for opportunities in Peru (in Spanish and English). Likewise, **www.volunteersouthamerica.net**, a continent-wide directory of low-cost to zero-cost programmes, offers several opportunities in Peru. In Cuzco, **Hope Foundation** (at Marani Hotel, see page 149) and **Amauta Spanish School** (see page 176) accept volunteers. **Socio Adventures** ⓘ *Casilla 431, Cajamarca, T076-831118, www.socioadventures.com,* incorporates building a cooking stove into a five-day trekking programme. For information outside Peru on voluntary work and working abroad, try **www.idealist.org** for non-profit and community organizations, volunteer opportunities and non-profit careers. There is some overlap between volunteering and gap year or career break tourism as many people who make this type of trip are going to do some form of work. There is an increasing amount of help for students on a gap year and the career-break market is growing fast. Here is a list of ideas: **www.gapyear.com, www.gap.org.uk** and **www.yearoutgroup.org** for that year away. For range of options, try **www.gvi.co.uk** (Global Vision International), or **www.i-to-i.com**. More specific (but not limited to South America) are **www.raleigh.org.uk** (Raleigh International), **www.handsupholidays.com** for project vacations, **www.madventurer.com** and **www.thepodsite.co.uk** (Personal Overseas Development), with projects only in Peru, and **www.teaching-abroad.co.uk** (Teaching and Projects Abroad), for more than teaching, including in Peru. The website **www.amerispan.com**, which is principally concerned with language learning and teaching, also has a comprehensive list of volunteer opportunities.

Before you travel

Visas and immigration

Tourist cards No visa is necessary for citizens of countries in the European Union, Asia, North and South America and the Caribbean, or for citizens of Andorra, Iceland, Liechteinstein, Norway, Switzerland, Australia, New Zealand and South Africa. A tourist card is free on flights arriving in Peru, or at border crossings for visits of up to 90 days. Insist on getting the full 90 days. The form is in duplicate, the original given up on arrival and the copy on departure, and may be renewed (see below). A new tourist card must be obtained for each re-entry or when an extension is given. If your tourist card is stolen or lost, get a new one at **Immigraciones** ⓘ *Av España 700 y Av Huaraz, Breña, Lima, Mon-Fri 0900-1330.*

Tourist visas For citizens of countries not listed above, tourist visas cost about US$38 or equivalent, for which you require a valid passport, a departure ticket from Peru (or a letter of guarantee from a travel agency), two colour passport photos, one application form and proof of economic solvency.

All foreigners should be able to produce on demand some recognizable means of identification, preferably a passport. You must present your passport when reserving tickets for internal, as well as, international travel. An alternative is to photocopy the important pages of your passport – including the immigration stamp, and have it legalized by a 'notario público' (US$1.50). This way you can avoid showing your passport. We have received no reports of travellers being asked for an onward ticket at the borders at Tacna, Aguas Verdes, La Tina, Yunguyo or Desaguadero. Travellers arriving by air are not asked for an onward flight ticket at Lima airport, but it is possible that you will not be allowed to board a plane in your home country without showing an onward ticket.

Renewals and extensions To extend a tourist card at Immigration in Lima (address above), go to the third floor and enter the long narrow hall with many 'teller' windows. Go to window No 5 and present your passport and tourist card. The official will give you a receipt for US$20 (the cost of a one-month extension) which you will pay at the Banco de la Nación on the same floor. Then go down to the first floor and buy form F007 for S/.24 (US$6.75). Fill out the form and return to window No 5 on the third floor. Give the official the paid receipt, the filled-out form, your passport and tourist card. Next, you will wait two minutes for your passport to be stamped and signed. **Note** three extensions like this are permitted, although it's unlikely that you will be allowed to buy more than one month at a time. Peruvian law states that a tourist can remain in the country for a maximum of six months, after which time you must leave. Crossing the border out of Peru and returning immediately is acceptable. You will then receive another 90 days and the process begins all over again.

If you let your tourist visa expire you can be subject to a fine of US$20 per day, but this is up to the discretion of the immigration official. You can extend your visa in Lima, Cuzco, Puno, Puerto Maldonado and Iquitos, but in the provinces it can take more time.

Business visas A visitor who is going to receive money from Peruvian sources, must have a business visa: requirements are a valid passport, two colour passport photos, return ticket and a letter from an employer or Chamber of Commerce stating the nature of business, length of stay and guarantee that any Peruvian taxes will be paid. The visa costs £21.60 (or equivalent) and allows the holder to stay 90 days in the country. On arrival business visitors must register with the **Dirección General de Contribuciones** for tax purposes.

Student visas To obtain a one-year student visa you must have: proof of adequate funds, affiliation to a Peruvian body, a letter of recommendation from your own and a Peruvian consul, a letter of moral and economic guarantee from a Peruvian citizen and four photographs (frontal and profile). You must also have a health check certificate which takes four weeks to get and costs US$10. Also, to obtain a student visa, if applying within Peru, you have to leave the country and collect it in La Paz, Arica or Guayaquil from Peruvian immigration (it costs US$20).

Peruvian embassies and consulates

Australia, 43 Culgoa Circuit, O'Malley, ACT 2606, Canberra, T61-2-6286 9507, www.embaperu.org.au. Consulate in Sydney.
Austria, Gottfried Keller-Gasse 2/1-2, 1030 Vienna, T713 4377, embajada@embaperuaustria.at.
Belgium, Ave de Tervuren 179, 1150 Brussels, T032-2-733 3185, comunicaciones@embassy-of-peru.be.
Canada, 130 Albert St, Suite 1901, Ottawa, Ontario K1P 5G4, T1-613-238 1777, emperuca@bellnet.ca. Consulates in Québec, Montréal, Toronto and Vancouver.
France, 50 Ave Kleber, 75116 Paris, T33-1-5370 4200, www.amb-perou.fr/.
Germany, Mohrenstrasse 42, 10117 Berlin, T49-30-206 4103, www.embaperu.de. Consulates in Bremen, Dusseldorf, Frankfurt, Hamburg, Hannover.
Israel, Medinat Hayehudim 60, Herzliya Pituach 46766, T972-9-957 8835, emperu@021.net.il
Italy, Via Francesco Siacci 2B, 2nd floor, 00197 Roma, T39-06-8069 1510, www.ambasciataperu.it. Consulates in Genoa, Milan and Turin.
Japan, 4-4-27 Higashi Shibuya-ku, Tokyo 150-0011, T81-3-3406 4243, embtokyo@embperujapan.org. Consulate General www.conpertokio.org/.
Netherlands, Nassauplein 4, 2585 EA, The Hague, T31-70-365 3500, info@embassyofperu.nl.
New Zealand, Level 8, 40 Mercer St, Cigna House, Wellington, T64-4-499 8087, embassy.peru@xtra.co.nz.
Norway, Consulate General, Munkendansveien 35, 0119 Oslo, T47-2-2323 7688, peru@via.no.
South Africa, Brooklyn Gardens, Velae St and Middel St, Block B, 1st floor, Nieuw Muckleneuk, 0181 Pretoria, T27-12- 346 8744, emperu@telkomsa.net.
Spain, C Príncipe de Vergara 36, 5to Derecha, 28001 Madrid, T34-91-431 4242, www.embajadaperu.es. Consulates in Barcelona, Bilbao, Sevilla, Valencia.
Sweden, Brunnsgatan 21 B, 111 38 Stockholm, T46-8-440 8740, www.webmakers/peru.
Switzerland, Thunstrasse No 36, CH-3005 Berne, T41-31-351 8555, lepruberna02@bluewin.ch. Consulates in Geneva and Zurich.
UK, 52 Sloane St, London SW1X 9SP, T020-7235 1917, www.peruembassy-uk.com.
USA, 1700 Massachusetts Av NW, Washington DC 20036, T1-202-833 9860, www.peruvianembassy.us. Consulates in Los Angeles, Miami, New York, Chicago, Houston, Boston, Denver, San Francisco.

Customs, duty free and export restrictions

When travelling into Peru you can bring 20 pack of cigarettes (400 cigarettes), 50 cigars or 500 g of tobacco, three litres of alcohol and new articles for personal use of gifts valued at up to US$300. There are certain items that cannot be brought in duty-free: these include computers (but laptops are OK). The value added tax for items that are not considered duty-free but are still intended for personal use is generally 20%. Personal items such as laptops, cameras, bicycles, hiking and climbing equipment and anything else necessary for adventure sports are exempt from taxes and should be regarded as personal effects that will not be sold or left in

Peru. All customs agents should be satisfied by this and allow you to pass. Anything that looks like it's being brought in for resale, however, could give you trouble.

It is illegal to take items of archaeological interest out of Peru. This means that any pre-Columbian pottery or Inca artefacts cannot leave Peru. If you are purchasing extremely good replicas make sure the pieces have the artist's name on them or that they have a tag which shows that they are not originals. It is very important to realize that no matter how simple it seems, there is no point in trying to take anything illegal out of the country – this includes drugs. The security personnel and customs officials are experts at their job, so save yourself the wasted time, money and energy of 10 years in jail.

Insurance

We strongly recommend that you invest in a good insurance policy which covers you for theft or loss of possessions and money, the cost of medical and dental treatment, cancellation of flights, delays in travel arrangements, accidents, missed departures, lost baggage, lost passport and personal liability and legal expenses. Also check on inclusion of 'dangerous activities' if you plan on doing any. These generally include climbing, diving, skiing, horse riding, parachuting, even trekking. You should always read the small print carefully. Not all policies cover ambulance, helicopter rescue or emergency flights home.

There are a variety of policies to choose from, so it's best to shop around. Your travel agent can advise on the best deals available. Reputable student travel organizations often offer good-value policies. Travellers from North America can try the **International Student Insurance Service (ISIS)**, which is available through **STA** ⓣ *T800-7814040, www.statravel.com*. Companies worth trying in Britain include **Direct Line Insurance** ⓣ *T0845-246 8704, http://uk.directline.com/travelling/index.htm*, and the **Flexicover Group** ⓣ *T0870-9909292, www.flexicover.net*. Some companies will not cover those over 65. The best policies for older travellers are through **Age Concern** ⓣ *T0800-009966, www.ageconcern.org.uk*.

Money

Currency → *In October 2006, the exchange rate was US$1 = S/. 3.39, 1 euro = S/.4.27.*

The **nuevo sol** (new sol, S/.) is the official currency of Peru. It is divided in 100 *céntimos* (cents) with coins valued at S/.5, S/.2, S/.1 and 50, 20, 10 and 5 *céntimo* pieces although the latter is being phased out as it is virtually worthless. A 1-céntimo coin also exists, but seems only to be given out in change when paying airport tax. Notes in circulation are S/.200, S/.100, S/.50, S/.20 and S/.10.

Prices of airline tickets, tour agency services, non-backpacker hotels and hostels, among others, are almost always quoted in dollars. You can pay in soles or dollars but it is generally easiest to pay dollars when the price is in dollars and in soles when the price is in soles. This will save you from losing on exchange rates. In major tourist centres such as Lima, Cuzco and Arequipa dollars are frequently accepted.

Almost no one, certainly not banks, will accept dollar bills that are ripped, taped, stapled or torn. Do not accept damaged dollars from anyone; simply tell them you would like another bill. Likewise, ask your bank at home to give you only nice, crisp, clean dollars and keep your dollars neat in your money belt or wallet so they don't accidentally tear.

Forgeries of dollars and soles are not uncommon. Always check the sol notes you have received, even at the bank. Money changers, especially at borders, mix fake notes with genuine bills when giving wads of soles for other currencies. Hold the bills

Money matters

Low-value US dollar bills should be carried for changing into soles if arriving in the country when banks or *casas de cambio* are closed. They are also useful for shopping. In larger establishments in cities which receive many tourists, dollars are accepted instead of soles. If you are travelling on the cheap it is essential to keep in funds; watch weekends and public holidays carefully and never run out of local currency. Take plenty of local currency, in small denominations, when making trips in the provinces. Try to break down notes whenever you can as there is a country-wide shortage of change (or so it seems) and it will make life simpler if you get change whenever you can. It is difficult to get change in shops and museums and sometimes impossible from street vendors or cab drivers.

up to the light to check the watermark and that the colours change according to the angle of the light. The line down the side of the bill in which the amount of the money is written should appear green, blue and pink at different angles; fake bills are only pink and have no hologram properties. There should be tiny pieces of thread in the paper (not glued on). Check to see that the faces are clear. Also, the paper should not feel smooth like a photocopy but rougher and fibrous. Try not to accept brand new notes, especially if changing on the street, slightly used notes are less likely to be forgeries. There are posters in public places explaining what to look for in forged sol notes. In parts of the country, forged one- and five-sol coins are in circulation. The fakes are slightly off-colour, the surface copper can be scratched off and they tend to bear a recent date.

Credit cards

Visa (by far the most widely accepted card in Peru), **MasterCard, Maestro, American Express** and **Diners Club** are all valid. There is often an 8-12% commission for all credit card charges. Often, it is cheaper to use your credit card to get money (dollars or soles) out of an ATM rather than to pay for your purchases. Of course, this depends on the interest rate for cash advances on your credit cards – ask your bank or card provider about this. Another option is to put extra money on your credit cards and use them as a bank card. Most banks are affiliated with Visa/Plus system; those that you will find in almost every town and city are **BCP** and **BBVA Continental. Interbank** ATMs accept Visa, Plus, MasterCard, Maestro, Cirrus and American Express. **Banco Weise Sudameris** (to merge with Scotiabank and become **BWS**) ATMs accept Visa, MasterCard, Maestro and Cirrus. There are also **Red Unicard** ATMs which accept Visa, Plus and MasterCard. Note that not every branch of each bank offers the same ATM services (even branches within the same city). Some ATMs incur a fee of US$1 per use. In comparison with widespread ATM use, businesses displaying credit card symbols may not accept foreign cards. Credit cards are not commonly accepted in smaller towns so go prepared with cash. Make sure you carry the phone numbers that you need in order to report your card lost or stolen. In addition, some travellers have reported problems with their credit cards being 'frozen' by their bank as soon as a charge from a foreign country occurs. To avoid this problem, notify your bank that you will be making charges in Peru (and other countries).

Credit card companies
American Express, Travex SA, Av Santa Cruz 621, Miraflores, Lima, T01-690 0900, info@travex.com.pe.
Diners Club, Canaval y Moreyra 535, San Isidro, T01-221 2050.
MasterCard, Porta 111, p 6, Miraflores, T01-311 6000, T0800-307 7309.
Visa Travel Assistance, T108 and ask the operator for a collect call (*por cobrar*) to T410-902 8022 (English), T581 0120/9754 (Spanish), or T420-937 8091.

Exchange

There are no restrictions on foreign exchange. Banks are the most discreet places to change traveller's cheques into soles. Some charge commission from 1-3%, some don't, and practice seems to vary from branch to branch, month to month. The services of the **BCP** have been repeatedly recommended. Changing dollars at a bank always gives a lower rate than with *cambistas* (street changers) or *casas de cambio* (exchange houses). Always count your money in the presence of the cashier.

In Lima and Cuzco, euros are as acceptable as US dollars for changing into soles. In other cities euros are less easy to change, but not impossible. Some street changers in Lima will exchange pounds sterling, but rates are poor. Other currencies carry high commission fees. For changing into or out of small amounts of dollars or euros cash, the street changers give the best rates, avoiding paperwork and queuing, but you should take care: check your soles before handing over your dollars, check their calculations, etc, and don't change money in crowded areas. If using their services think about taking a taxi after changing, to avoid being followed. Many street changers congregate near an office where the exchange 'wholesaler' operates; these will probably be offering better rates than elsewhere on the street.

Soles can be exchanged into dollars at the banks and exchange houses at Lima airport, and you can change soles for dollars with street changers and at any border. Dollars can also be bought at the various borders.

American Express will sell traveller's cheques to cardholders only, but will not exchange cheques into cash. Amex will hold mail for cardholders at the Lima branch only. They are also very efficient in replacing stolen cheques, though a police report is needed. Most of the main banks accept American Express traveller's cheques and **BCP** and **BSCH** accept Visa traveller's cheques. **Citibank** in Lima and some BSCH branches handle Citicorp cheques. Travellers have reported great difficulty in cashing traveller's cheques in the jungle area, even Iquitos, and other remote areas. Always sign traveller's cheques in blue or black ink or ballpen.

Cost of living

Living costs in the provinces are from 20-50% below those in Lima, although Cuzco is a little more expensive than other, less touristy provincial cities. For a lot of low-income Peruvians, many items are simply beyond their reach.

Cost of travelling

The approximate budget for travelling is US$25-35 per person per day for living comfortably, including transport, or US$12-15 a day for low-budget travel. Your budget will be higher the longer you stay in Lima and depending on how many flights you take between destinations. Accommodation rates range from US$3-4 per person for the most basic *alojamiento* to over US$150 for luxurious hotels in Lima and Cuzco. For the price of eating out, see page 57.

Getting there

Air

From Europe and Israel There are direct flights to **Lima** only from Amsterdam (**KLM** via Bonaire) and Madrid (**Iberia** and the no-frills **Air Madrid**). From London, Frankfurt, Rome, Milan, Lisbon or other European cities, connections must be made in Madrid, Caracas, Brazilian or US gateways. From Tel Aviv, make connections in either Madrid or Miami.

From North America Miami is the main gateway to Peru, together with Atlanta, Dallas, Houston, Los Angeles and New York. Airlines, not all direct, include **American, Continental, Delta, Lan, Copa** and **AeroMéxico**. Daily connections can be made from almost all major North American cities. From Toronto **Air Canada** flies to Lima, but not daily. From Vancouver, there are no direct flights or connections; fly via one of the above gateways.

From Australia and New Zealand There are no obvious connecting flights from either Australia or New Zealand to **Lima**. One option would be to go to Buenos Aires from Sydney or Auckland (flights twice a week with **Aerolíneas Argentinas**) and fly on from there (several daily flights). Alternatively, fly to Los Angeles and travel down from there.

From South Africa From Johannesburg, make connections in Buenos Aires or São Paulo.

From Latin America There are regular flights, in many cases daily, to Peru from most South American countries. The **Lan** group has the most routes to Lima within the continent. The **Taca** group also has quite extensive coverage, including to Central America and Mexico.

From Asia From Hong Kong, Seoul and Singapore, connections have to be made in Los Angeles. Make connections in Los Angeles or Miami if flying from Tokyo.

Baggage allowance

There is always a weight limit for your baggage, but there is no standard baggage allowance to Peru. If you fly via the USA you are allowed two pieces of luggage up to 32 kg per case. The American airlines are usually a bit more expensive but if you are travelling with a 40-kg bag of climbing gear, it may be worth looking into. On flights from Europe there is a weight allowance of 20 or 23 kg, although some carriers out of Europe use the two-piece system, but this may not apply it in both directions. At busy times of the year it can be very difficult and expensive to bring items such as bikes and surf boards along. Many airlines will let you pay a penalty for overweight baggage, but this usually depends on how full the flight is. Check first before you assume you can bring extra luggage. The weight limit for internal flights is often 20 kg per person, or less, so keep this in mind if you plan to take any internal flights.

Discount flight agents

Using the web for booking flights, hotels and other services directly is becoming an increasingly popular way of making holiday reservations. You can make some good deals this way. Be aware, though, that cutting out the travel agents is denying yourself the experience that they can give, not just in terms of the best flights to suit your itinerary, but also advice on documents, insurance and other matters before you set out, safety, routes, lodging and times of year to travel. A reputable agent will also be bonded to give you some protection if arrangements collapse while you are travelling.

UK and Ireland

STA Travel, T0870 160 5524, www.statravel.co.uk. They have 65 other branches in the UK, including many university campuses. Specialists in low-cost student/youth flights and tours, also good for student IDs and insurance.
Trailfinders, 194 Kensington High St, London, W8 7RG, T020-7938 3939, www.trailfinders.com. 18 branches in London and throughout the UK. Also one in Dublin.

North America

Air Brokers International, 685 Market St, Suite 400, San Francisco, CA94105, T01-800-883 3273, www.airbrokers.com. Consolidator and specialist on RTW and Circle Pacific tickets.
Discount Airfares Worldwide On-Line, www.etn.nl/discount.htm. A hub of consolidator and discount agent links.
STA Travel, 1-800-781-4040, www.statravel.com. Over 100 branches in the USA and Canada, including many university campuses.
Travel CUTS, in all major Canadian cities and on university and college campuses, T1-866-246-9762, www.travelcuts.com. Specialist in student discount fares, IDs and other travel services. Branches in other Canadian cities as well as California, USA.
Travelocity, www.travelocity.com. Online consolidator.

Australia and New Zealand

Flight Centre, with offices throughout Australia and other countries. In Australia call T133 133, or go to www.flightcentre.com.au. STA Travel, T134 STA, www.statravel.com.au; 208 Swanston St, Melbourne, VIC 3000, T03-9639 0599; five travel centres in Australia. In NZ: T0800-474400, www.statravel.co.nz, 130 Cuba St, Wellington, T04-385 0561. Also in major towns and university campuses.
Travel.com.au, 80 Clarence St, Sydney, NSW 2000, T1300 130 482, www.travel.com.au.

Prices and discounts

Most airlines offer discounted fares on scheduled flights through agencies who specialize in this type of fare. For a list of these agencies see above. The very busy seasons are 7 December to 15 January and 10 July to 10 September. If you intend travelling during those times, book as far ahead as possible. Between February and May and September to November special offers may be available. Examples of fares on scheduled airlines are: from the UK a return with flexible dates will cost about US$1215, but travelling over the Christmas/New Year period can see prices rise to over US$1600. The picture is the same from the USA: a low season return costs from US$670 from Miami, but high season is US$830-1000. From Los Angeles low season is US$820, high season US$1200. From Sydney, Australia, a low season return is US$2155, whereas a Christmas/New Year return will cost US$2515.

If you buy discounted air tickets always check the reservation with the airline concerned to make sure the flight still exists. Also remember the IATA airlines' schedules change in March and October each year, so if you're going to be away a long time it's best to leave return flight coupons open. In addition, check whether you are entitled to any refund or re-issued ticket if you lose, or have stolen, a discounted air ticket. Some airlines require the repurchase of a ticket before you can apply for a refund, which will not be given until after the validity of the original ticket has expired. Travel insurance in some cases covers lost tickets.

Departure information

Airlines recommend that you arrive at the airport three hours before international flights and two hours before domestic flights. Check-in for international flights closes one hour before departure, 30 minutes for domestic flights, after which you may not be permitted to board. Drivers of the cars entering the car park are subject to a document check.

Tax

There is a US$30.25 departure tax for international flights which is never included in the price of your ticket. It may be paid in dollars or soles. For national flights the airport tax is US$3.50-6, depending on airport, payable only in soles or dollars. When making a domestic connection in Lima, you are not required to pay airport tax. Contact airline personnel at baggage claim and they will escort you to your departure gate.

Tickets purchased in Peru also have the 19% state tax, but this will be included in the price of the ticket. It is very important to reconfirm your flights when flying internally in Peru or leaving the country (although practice varies with some international carriers). This is generally done 48-72 hours in advance and can be done by phoning or visiting the airline office directly or, sometimes, by going to a travel agent for which you may have to pay a service charge. If you do not reconfirm your internal or international flight, you may not get on the plane. See also Customs page 34.

Touching down

Airport information

All international flights arrive at **Jorge Chávez Airport**, located deep in the Lima district of Callao, 16 km from the centre of the city. The *aduana* (customs) process is relatively painless and efficient (a push-button, red light/green light system operates for customs baggage checks – see also Customs page 34). Once outside and past the gate separating arriving passengers from the general public, you're subject to the mob of taxi drivers all vying to offer you their services. Fares depend on where you pick up the taxi and your bargaining skills. For full details, see Lima page 123.

While Jorge Chávez airport has all the facilities one would expect at an international airport, it has been undergoing major remodelling. There are exchange facilities for cash in the international arrivals hall. ATMs accept American Express, Visa, MasterCard and the Plus, Cirrus and Maestro systems. There are also *casas de cambio* (money changing desks). Public telephones are everywhere in and around the airport. Internet facilities at US$3 per hour must be among the most expensive in the country. There are post offices, too. Branches of **City Café** have fast computers for internet access at US$1.75 per hour. The **Zeta** bookstalls have a good selection of English-language guidebooks. Information desks can be found in the national foyer and in the international foyer. There is also a helpful desk in the international arrivals hall, which can make hotel and transport reservations. They often say that cheaper hotels are full or unsafe and, if you allow them to make a choice for you, it will probably be more expensive than you want (they may get commission). Hotels in the immediate airport area are generally for short-stay couples and are not appealing, especially after a long-haul flight. The larger, more expensive hotels in Miraflores and San Isidro have their own buses at the airport, and charge for transfer. Several *hostales* also provide transport to and from the airport. See Lima listings for hotels near Jorge Chávez.

Tourist information

Tourism promotion and information is handled by **PromPerú** ⓘ *Edificio Mincetur, Calle Uno Oeste 50, piso 13, Urb Córpac, San Isidro, T01-224 3131, www.peru.org.pe, or www.peru.info*. They produce promotional material but offer no direct information service to individual tourists. The website does carry plenty of background and other

Touching down

Business hours **Shops** 0900 or 1000-1230 and 1500 or 1600-2000, or 1000-1900. In the main cities, supermarkets do not close for lunch, some in Lima open 24 hrs. Some are closed on Sat and most on Sun. **Banks** In Lima and Cuzco Mon-Fri 0945-1700, Sat 0945-1200 (not always). Outside Lima they generally close 1200-1500 for lunch. **Offices** Mon-Fri 0900-1700. Most close on Sat. **Government offices** Jan-Mar Mon-Fri 0830-1130; Apr-Dec Mon-Fri 0900-1230, 1500-1700, but these change frequently.
Electricity 220 volts AC, 60 cycles throughout the country, except Arequipa (50 cycles). Most 4- and 5-star hotels have 110 volts AC. Plugs are either American flat-pin or twin flat and round pin combined.
Emergency services
Ambulance T01-225 4040 in Lima. **Emergency medical attention** (SAMU) T117. **Fire service** T116.
International dialling code 51.
Official time 5 hrs behind GMT.
Police (PNP, Policía Nacional del Perú) T01-475 2995 in Lima. For emergencies nationwide T105.
Tourist Police Jr Moore 268, Magda lena, 38th block of Av Brasil, Lima, T01-460 1060, daily 24 hrs; for public enquiries, etc, Jr Pachitea at the corner of Belén, Lima, T01-424 2053. Come here if you have had property stolen. They are friendly, helpful and speak English and some German.
Tax General sales tax of 19% is automatically added to the bill.
Tourist Protection Bureau (Indecopi) 24-hr hotline for travellers' complaints T/F01-224 7888, outside Lima T0800-42579 (not from pay phones), tour@indecopi.gob.pe. This body (with offices, kiosks and information stands in every town) will help with complaints regarding customs, airlines, travel agencies, accommodation, restaurants, public authorities or if you have lost, or had stolen, documents.
Weights and measures
The metric system is compulsory.

information. PromPerú runs an information and assistance service, **i perú,** ⓘ *T01-574 8000 (24 hrs); main office Jorge Basadre 610, San Isidro, Lima, T01-421 1627, iperulima@promperu.gob.pe, Mon-Fri 0830-1830; there also a 24-hr office at Jorge Chávez airport*. There are also offices around the country; addresses are given in the text. Other offices in most towns, either run by the municipality, or independently, provide tourist information. Further information can obtained online from, **Cámara Nacional de Turismo (Canatur)** ⓘ *Alcanfores 680, Lima 18, T01-445 2615, www.go2peru.com*, the official travel planning website, with background details, bookings and practical information. **Indecopi** is the government-run consumer protection and tourist complaint bureau; see page 41. In overall charge of tourism is the **Ministerio de Comercio Exterior y Turismo** ⓘ *C Uno 50, Urb Córpac, San Isidro, Lima, T01-513 6100, www.mincetur.gob.pe.*

Outside Peru, tourist information can be obtained from Peruvian embassies and consulates, see page 34.

With regard to security, it is better to seek advice before you leave from your own consulate than from travel agencies. Before you travel you can contact the **British Foreign and Commonwealth Office** ⓘ *Travel Advice Unit, T0845-850 2829*. **Footprint** is a partner in the Foreign and Commonwealth Office's 'Know before you go' campaign www.fco.gov.uk/travel. **US State Department's Bureau of Consular Affairs** ⓘ *Overseas Citizens Services, T1-888-407 4747, www.travel.state.gov*. **Australian Department of Foreign Affairs** ⓘ *T61-2-6261 3305, www.smartraveller.gov.au/*.

South American Explorers ① *www.saexplorers.org*, a non-profit, educational organization, functions primarily as an information network for Peru and South America and is the most useful organization for travellers in the continent. They have offices in Lima, Cuzco, Quito, Buenos Aires and the USA. Full details are given in the Lima and Cuzco sections, see pages 80 and 135.

Useful organizations

Apavit (Asociación Peruana de Agencias de Viaje y Turismo), Antonio Roca 121, Santa Beatriz, Lima, T01-433 7610, www.apavitperu.org.

Apotur (Asociación Peruana de Operadores de Turismo), Daniel Olachea 199, Lima 11, T01-463 2828, www.apoturperu.org.

Aptae (Asociación Peruana de Operadores de Turismo de Aventura y Ecoturismo), Bolognesi 125, of 703, Miraflores, Lima 18, T01-447 8476, www.aptae.org.

Agotur (Asociación de Guías Oficiales de Turismo), La Venturosa 177, Surco, Lima, T01-448 5167, agoturlima@yahoo.com.

Local customs and laws

Codes of conduct

Politeness – even a little ceremoniousness – is much appreciated in Peruvian society. Men should always remove any headgear and say *con permiso* when entering offices, and shake hands with other men. Women or men meeting women usually greet each other with one kiss on the cheek. When introduced, Peruvians will probably expect to greet visitors in the same way. Always say *Buenos días* (until midday) or *Buenas tardes* and wait for a reply before proceeding further. Business cards are commonly used.

When dealing with officials, always remember to be friendly and courteous no matter how trying the circumstances. Never be impatient and do not criticize situations in public (the officials may know more English than you think and they can certainly interpret gestures and facial expressions). In some situations, however, politeness can be a liability. Most Peruvians are disorderly queuers. In commercial transactions (buying a meal, goods in a shop, etc) politeness should be accompanied by firmness, and always ask the price first.

Politeness should also be extended to street traders. Saying *no, gracias* with a smile is better than an arrogant dismissal. Whether you give money to beggars is a personal matter, but your decision should be influenced by whether a person is begging out of need or trying to cash in on the tourist trail. In the former case, local people giving may provide an indication. Giving money to children is a separate issue, upon which most agree: don't do it. There are occasions where giving some healthy food may be appropriate, but first inform yourself of local practice.

In Peru it is common for locals to throw their rubbish, paper, wrappers and bottles into the street. Sometimes when asking a local where the rubbish bin is, they will indicate to you that it is the street. This does not give you the right to apply the 'when in Rome' theory. There are rubbish bins in public areas in many centres and tourists should use them.

Dress

Most Latin Americans, if they can afford it, devote great care to their clothes and appearance. It is appreciated if visitors do likewise. How you dress is mostly how people will judge you. This is particularly important when dealing with officials. Women should pack at least one medium- to long-length skirt and men might want to consider bringing a smart sweater or jacket. Wool sweaters and shawls can be easily purchased in Peru and make good additions to your wardrobe.

In general, clothing is less formal in the tropical lowlands, where men and women do wear shorts. In the highlands, people are more conservative, though wearing shorts is acceptable on hiking trails. Men should not be seen bare-chested in populated areas.

Time-keeping

Peruvians, as with most Latin Americans, have a fairly relaxed attitude towards time. They will think nothing of arriving an hour or so late on social occasions. If you expect to meet someone more or less at an exact time, you can tell them that you want to meet *en punto* or specify *la hora inglesa* (English time).

Tipping

In most of the better restaurants a 10% service charge is included in the bill, but you can give an extra 5% as a tip if the service is good. The most basic restaurants do not include a tip in the bill, and tips are not expected. Taxi drivers are not tipped – bargain the price down, then pay extra for good service if you get it. Tip cloakroom attendants and hairdressers (very high class only), US$0.50-$1; railway or airport porters, US$0.50; car wash boys, US$0.30; car 'watch' boys, US$0.20. If going on a trek or tour it is customary to tip the guide, as well as the cook and porters.

Toilets

Most Peruvian toilets are adequate but the further you go from main population and tourist centres, the poorer the facilities, so you may require a strong stomach and the ability to hold your breath for a long time. Almost without exception used toilet paper or feminine hygiene products should not be flushed down the pan, but placed in the receptacle provided. This applies even in quite expensive hotels. Not doing so will block the pan or drain, which can be a considerable health risk. It is quite common for people to stand on the toilet seat, as they do in Asia.

Responsible tourism

Travel to the furthest corners of the globe is now commonplace and the mass movement of people for leisure and business is a major source of foreign exchange and economic development in many parts of South America. In some regions (such as Machu Picchu) it is probably the most significant economic activity.

The benefits of international travel are self-evident for both hosts and travellers – employment, increased understanding of different cultures, business and leisure opportunities. At the same time there is clearly a downside to the industry. Where visitor pressure is high and/or poorly regulated, adverse impacts on society and the natural environment may be apparent. Paradoxically, this is as true in undeveloped and pristine areas (where culture and the natural environment are less 'prepared' for even small numbers of visitors) as in major resort destinations.

The travel industry is growing rapidly and increasingly the impacts of this supposedly 'smokeless' industry are becoming apparent. Although these impacts can seem remote and unrelated to an individual trip or holiday, air travel is clearly implicated in global warming and damage to the ozone layer, and resort location and construction can destroy natural habitats and restrict traditional rights and activities. Nevertheless individual choice and awareness can make a difference in many instances (see box, next page) and, collectively, travellers can have a significant effect in shaping a more responsible and sustainable industry.

Of course travel can have beneficial impacts and this is something to which every traveller can contribute – many national parks are part funded by receipts from visitors. Similarly, travellers can promote patronage and protection of important

How big is your footprint?

1 Where possible choose a destination, tour operator or hotel with a proven ethical and environmental commitment – if in doubt, ask.
2 Spend money on locally produced (rather than imported) goods and services, buy directly from the producer or from a 'fair trade' shop, and use common sense when bargaining – your few dollars saved may be a week's salary to others.
3 Use water and electricity carefully – travellers may receive preferential supply while the needs of local communities are overlooked.
4 Learn about local etiquette and culture – consider local norms and behaviour and dress appropriately for local cultures and situations.
5 Protect wildlife and other natural resources – don't buy souvenirs or goods unless they are clearly sustainably produced and are not protected under CITES legislation.
6 Always ask before taking photographs or videos of people.
7 Consider staying in local accommodation rather than foreign-owned hotels – the economic benefits for host communities are far greater – and there are more opportunities to learn about local culture.
8 Make a voluntary contribution to Climate Care, www.co2.org, to counteract the pollution caused by tax-free fuel on your flight.

archaeological sites and heritage through their interest and contributions via entrance and performance fees. They can also support small-scale enterprises by staying in locally run hotels and hostels, eating in local restaurants and by purchasing local goods, supplies and arts and crafts.

In fact, since the early 1990s, there has been a phenomenal growth in tourism that promotes and supports the conservation of natural environments and is also fair and equitable to local communities. This 'ecotourism' segment, probably the fastest-growing sector of the travel industry, provides a vast and growing range of destinations and activities in South America. While the authenticity of some ecotourism operators' claims need to be interpreted with care, there is clearly both a huge demand for this type of activity and also significant opportunities to support worthwhile conservation and social development initiatives. If you are concerned about the application of the principles of ecotourism, in Peru as elsewhere, you need to make an informed choice by finding out in advance how establishments such as jungle lodges cope with waste and effluent disposal, whether they create the equivalent of 'monkey islands' by obtaining animals in the wild and putting them in the lodge's property, what their policy is towards employing and training local staff, and so on.

Organizations such as **Conservation International** ⓘ *T001-202-912 1000, www.ecotour.org*, the **International Ecotourism Society** ⓘ *T001-202-347 9203, www.ecotourism.org*, **Planeta** ⓘ *www.planeta.com* and **Tourism Concern** ⓘ *T+44-20-7133 3330, www.tourismconcern.org.uk*, have begun to develop and/or promote ecotourism projects and destinations and their websites are an excellent source of information and details initiatives throughout South America. Additionally, organizations such as **Earthwatch** ⓘ *T+44-1865-318838 or T978-461 0081 (in US), www.earthwatch.org*, and **Discovery Initiatives** ⓘ *T+44-1285-643333, www.discoveryinitiatives.com*, offer opportunities to participate directly in scientific research and development projects throughout the region.

South America offers unique and unforgettable experiences – often based on the natural environment, cultural heritage and local society. These are the reasons many of us choose to travel and why many more will want to do so in the future. Shouldn't we provide an opportunity for future travellers and hosts to enjoy the quality of experience and interaction that we take for granted?

Safety

The following notes on personal safety should not hide the fact that most Peruvians are hospitable and helpful. Peru is not a highly dangerous country to travel in, but it is by no means crime free. By being aware of the possible problems you may confront and by using a mixture of common sense and vigilance you can minimize the risks.

You need to take care everywhere but particularly in poor areas of cities, as this is where most theft takes place. While you should take local advice about being out at night, do not assume that daytime is safer than nighttime. If walking after dark, walk in the road, not on the pavement. You should also be on your guard during festivals, at markets and when streets are crowded. Care should be taken at all times and in most parts of Lima. Over the past couple of years there has been an alarming increase in aggressive assaults in centres along the Gringo Trail. Places like Arequipa, Puno and Cuzco have, at times, been plagued by waves of strangle muggings. Check with **South American Explorers** for a current summary of the situation and how to keep safe. A friendly attitude on your part, smiling even when you've thwarted a thief's attempt, can help you out of trouble. Be especially careful when using ATMs and when arriving at or leaving from bus and train stations, when you have a lot of important belongings with you. Do not set your bag down without putting your foot on it, even just to double check your tickets. Be wary of accepting food, drink, sweets or cigarettes from unknown people on buses or trains; they may be drugged.

Keep all documents secure and hide your main cash supply in different places or under your clothes. Keep cameras in bags, take spare spectacles and don't wear wrist-watches (even cheap ones have been ripped off arms!) or jewellery. If you wear a shoulder-bag, carry it in front of you. Small personal alarms are a good idea. Backpacks are vulnerable to slashers: a good idea is to cover the pack with a sack (a plastic one will also keep out rain and dust) with maybe a layer of wire netting between. Make photocopies of important documents and give them to family or friends. Alternatively send yourself an email containing all important details, addresses, etc which you can access in an emergency. It is best to leave any valuables you don't need in your hotel's safe-deposit box. But keep a record of what you have deposited. If you don't trust the hotel, lock everything in your pack and secure that in your room (some people take eyelet-screws for padlocking cupboards or drawers). If you lose your valuables, always report it to the police and note details of the report for insurance purposes.

If someone spits, smears mustard, or sprays paint or shampoo on to your clothes, walk on to a safe, private place to clean yourself up. Similarly, ignore strangers' remarks like 'what's that on your shoulder?' or 'have you seen that dirt on your shoe?'. Furthermore, don't bend over to pick up money or other items in the street. These are all ploys intended to distract your attention and make it easy for an accomplice to rob you. If someone follows you when you're in the street, let him catch up with you and 'give him the eye'. Ruses involving 'plainclothes policemen' are infrequent, but it is worth knowing that the real police only have the right to see your passport (not your money, tickets or hotel room).

Anyone found carrying even the smallest amount of an illegal drug is automatically assumed to be a trafficker. If arrested on any charge the wait for trial in prison can take up to a year and is particularly unpleasant. If you are asked by the narcotics police to go to the toilets to have your bags searched, insist on taking a witness. Tricks employed to get foreigners into trouble over drugs include slipping a packet of cocaine into the money you are exchanging, being invited to a party or somewhere involving a taxi ride, or simply being asked on the street if you want to buy cocaine. In all cases, a plain clothes 'policeman' will discover the planted cocaine – in your money or at your feet in the taxi – and will ask to see your passport and money. He will then return them, minus a large part of your cash. Beware also of thieves dressed as policemen asking for your passport and wanting to search for drugs; searching is only permitted if prior paperwork is done.

The activities of Sendero Luminoso and MRTA (Movimiento Revolucionario Túpac Amaru) appear to be a thing of the past, although it would be wrong to suggest that either organization is completely dead. In 2006 it was safe to travel to all parts of Peru, with the exception of the **Huallaga Valley**. This includes areas **near Tingo María**, as well as jungle areas **east of Ayacucho**. This is an important region for cocaine growing and trafficking, in which there remains some terrorist involvement. Keep yourself informed and always ask locals and other travellers about the conditions up ahead, especially if you are going off the beaten track. While in Lima or Cuzco, you can check in at **South American Explorers**, for latest travel updates (Lima T01-445 3306, Cuzco T084-245484).

The **tourist police** in Lima are excellent and you should report any incidents to them (see Emergencies, page 41). Double check that all reports written by the police actually state your complaint. There have been some mix-ups, and insurance companies seldom honour claims for 'lost' baggage. In the event of a vehicle accident in which anyone is injured, all drivers involved are automatically detained until blame has been established, and this does not usually take less than two weeks.

Never offer a bribe unless you are fully conversant with local customs. Wait until the official makes the suggestion, or offer money in some form which is apparently not bribery, eg 'In our country we have a system of on-the-spot fines (*multas de inmediato*). Is there a similar system here?' Do not assume that an official who accepts a bribe is prepared to do anything else that is illegal. You bribe him to persuade him to do his job, or to persuade him not to do it, or to do it more quickly, or more slowly. You do not bribe him to do something which is against the law. If an official suggests that a bribe must be paid before you can proceed on your way, be patient and he may relent.

Getting around

Although Peru's geography is dominated by the Andes, one of the world's major mountain ranges, great steps have been taken to improve major roads and enlarge the paved network linking the Pacific coast with the Highlands. This also means that there are various options, albeit on rougher roads, for the traveller wishing to go to northern Peru from the centre of the country (or vice versa), avoiding Lima. But it is worth taking some time to plan an overland journey in advance, checking which roads are finished, which have roadworks and which will be affected by the weather. The highland and jungle wet season, from mid-October to late March, can seriously hamper travel, so allow extra time if planning to go overland at this time. Peru also, unfortunately, suffers more than its fair share of natural disasters, such as the El Niño weather phenomenon. This can have dramatic effects on overland travel.

National air travel

If you only have a couple of weeks, travelling by air is the sensible option. It allows access to most major regions and means you can spend more time at your destination and less getting there. On the downside, though, you will see less of the country and will meet fewer people that if you travel overland.

The main national carriers serving the most travelled routes – Arequipa, Cajamarca, Chiclayo, Cuzco, Iquitos, Piura, Puerto Maldonado, Pucallpa, Tacna, Tarapoto, Trujillo and Tumbes – are **WayraPerú** and **Star Perú**. For destinations such as Ayacucho, Cajamarca, Iquitos, Pucallpa and Tacna, flights are offered by **Aero Cóndor** and **LC Busre. Lan,** part of the group formerly called **Lan Chile,** flies to many major cities and **Grupo Taca** (the Central American airline) offers service on the Lima-Cuzco route. These airlines generally cost the same, between US$69 and US$99 one-way anywhere in the country from Lima. Prices often increase at holiday times (Semana Santa, May Day, Inti Raymi, 28-29 July, Christmas and New Year), and for elections. During these times and the northern hemisphere summer seats can be hard to come by, especially on the Lima–Cuzco–Lima route, so book early. There are no deals for round trip tickets and prices can rise within four days of the flight. » *For contact details of National airlines, see Lima Transport, page 122.*

It is common for flight times to change, earlier or later, or be cancelled because of weather delays especially in the wet season. Do not be surprised or perturbed by this, often there is nothing the airline can do. Always give yourself an extra day between national and international flights to allow for any schedule changes. Flights are often overbooked so it is **very important** to reconfirm your tickets, as mentioned above, and be at the airport well in advance. By law, the clerk can start to sell reserved seats to stand-by travellers 30 minutes before the flight.

Internal flight prices are given in US dollars but can be paid in soles and the price should include the 19% general sales tax. Tickets are not interchangeable between companies but sometimes exceptions will be made in the case of cancellations. Do check with companies for special offers. If the price sounds too good to be true double check your ticket to make sure you are not being sold a ticket for Peruvian nationals; these tickets are often half price but you need to show Peruvian ID to get on the plane.

To save time and hassle, travel with carry-on luggage only (48 cm x 24 cm x 37 cm). This will guarantee that your luggage arrives at the airport when you do.

Domestic airlines A list of domestic airlines, with websites, is given under Lima, Transport, page 122.

Rail

Peru's national rail service was privatized in 1999. The lines of major interest to the traveller are Puno-Juliaca-Cuzco and Cuzco-Machu Picchu. They are operated by **PerúRail SA**, which provides luxury services and a backpacker train. For information, T084-238722, www.perurail.com. The other railway which carries passengers is the line from Lima to Huancayo, with a continuation to Huancavelica in the Central Highlands. The service from the capital to Huancayo runs on some holiday weekends through the year; check www.incasdelperu.com for the latest schedule. Huancayo-Huancavelica has daily passenger services. Train schedules may be cut in the rainy season.

River

On almost any trip to the Amazon Basin, a boat journey will be required at some point, either to get you to a jungle lodge, or to go between river ports. Motorized canoes with canopies usually take passengers to jungle lodges. They normally provide life jackets and have seats which are not very comfortable on long journeys, so a cushion may come in handy. Being open to the elements, the breeze can be a welcome relief from the heat and humidity in the daytime, but they can also be cold in the early morning and if there is any rain about it will blow into your face. Take a waterproof to keep you dry and warm. You sit very close to the water and you soon learn to respect the driver's mate's knowledge of the river.

Public river transport cannot be regarded as luxurious by any stretch of the imagination, although on the route from Iquitos to Brazil, some posh boats do run. Boats can be extremely uncomfortable, but with patience, perseverance and a strong stomach it is still far from impossible to travel this way. Accommodation is either in a cabin, frequently tiny and dirty, which will be more expensive than slinging your hammock in the general hammock area. If you choose to sleep in a hammock, hang it away from lightbulbs (they aren't switched off at night and attract all sorts of strange insects) and away from the engines, which usually emit noxious fumes and, of course, noise. Another useful tip is not to sling your hammock near the bottom of the stairwell on double-decked river boats, as this is where the cook slaughters the livestock every morning. Do try to find somewhere sheltered from the cold, damp night breeze. Take rope for hanging your hammock, plus string and sarongs for privacy. Use a double hammock of material (not string) for warmth; you may need a blanket as well. Boats have irregular schedules. Keep an eye on the departure notices (usually chalk boards) and look for a boat that other passengers have started to board. The captain will often let you embark a couple of days before departure. The captain, and only the captain, will take payment. You need to take: plenty of drinking water (the silt in the rivers will clog filters; purifying tablets may not kill giardia); decent food to relieve the appalling meals; eating utensils; plenty of prophylactic enteritis tablets; a bag to put your rubbish in (rather than doing as the other passengers do, ie chucking it all overboard); mosquito repellent and long-sleeved shirts and long trousers for after dusk. DEET is the best mosquito repellent but it will be washed directly into the river and it is lethal to most fish. Being able to speak Spanish is essential. Thieves are unscrupulous; do not leave anything out of sight, not even your shoes under your hammock at night. Women travellers can expect the usual unwanted attention, but it becomes more uncomfortable when confined to the small boat.

Road

Peru's road network is being upgraded and better roads mean better bus services and improved conditions for drivers. Peru, however, is no different from other Latin American countries in that travelling by road at night or in bad weather should be treated with great care. It is also true that there are many more unpaved than paved roads, so extended overland travel is not really an option if you only have a few weeks' holiday. Detailed accounts of major and minor road conditions are given in the travelling text.

The Pan-American Highway runs north-south through the coastal desert and is mostly in good condition. Also paved and well-maintained is the direct road which branches off the Pan-American at Pativilca and runs up to Huaraz and on to Caraz. The Northern route from Chiclayo through to Tarapoto is fully paved, as is the spur to Jaén. Cajamarca has a paved connection to the coast to serve the Yanacocha mining operation. The Central Highway from Lima to Huancayo is mostly paved. It continues (mostly paved) to Pucallpa in the Amazon Basin. There is also a paved road from La Oroya to Tarma and Satipo. South of Lima, there's the paved 'Liberatores' highway from Pisco to Ayacucho. From Nazca to Abancay and on to Cuzco is paved. This is now the main route from Lima to Cuzco. The main roads in and to the Sacred Valley from Cuzco are also paved. The Cuzco-Puno highway is fully paved and is a fast, comfortable journey to rival the train. The paved road continues along the south shore of Lake Titicaca to Desaguadero on the Bolivian border. From there the paving runs down the western slope of the Andes to Moquegua and the coast, one of the nicest highways in the country. Also in the south, the road which runs into the sierra to Arequipa is in good condition. From Arequipa the road to Puno is paved. Roads from Arequipa to Mollendo and Matarani are also excellent.

All other roads in the mountains are of dirt, some good, some very bad. Each year they are affected by heavy rain and mud slides, especially those on the eastern slopes of the mountains. Repairs can be delayed because of a shortage of funds. This makes for slow travel and frequent breakdowns. Note that some of these roads can be dangerous or impassable in the rainy season. Check beforehand with locals (not with bus companies, who only want to sell tickets) as accidents are common at these times.

Bus

Services along the coast to the north and south as well as inland to Huancayo, Ayacucho and Huaraz are very good. There are direct (*ejecutivo*) service buses to major centres (different companies use different titles for their top class or executive services, eg **Imperial, Ideal, Royal**). As well as *ejecutivo*, many bus companies have regular (local) service and the difference between the two is often great. Many buses have toilets, movies and reclining seats (*bus cama*); if any or all of these services are important to you, ask before you buy your ticket. **Ormeño** and **Cruz del Sur** are the two bus lines generally thought to have the best service with the most routes. *Cruz del Sur* accepts Visa cards and gives 10% discount to ISIC and Under26 cardholders (you may have to insist). **Civa** also offer extensive coverage throughout the nation, but are not in the same class as **Ormeño** and **Cruz del Sur**. There are many smaller but still excellent bus lines that run only to specific areas.

With the nicer companies or *ejecutivo* service you will get a receipt for your luggage, it will be locked under the bus and you shouldn't have to worry about it at stops because the storage is not usually opened. On local buses there will be lots of people getting on and off the buses, loading and unloading bags, so it's best to watch your luggage. It will provide you with a good excuse to get off the bus and stretch anyway. Do not put your day bag above your head inside the bus; keep it at your feet or beside you. It is too easy for someone to grab your bag and get off without your realizing. If you decide to get off the bus at a stop, take all your carry-on items with you. Tickets for *ejecutivo* service buses can cost up to double those of the local service buses. If you want to buy a return ticket from Lima, it is quite often cheaper to wait and buy the return portion when you arrive at your destination. This isn't the case always, but on the major lines things seem to cost more from the capital.

For long journeys be sure to take water and possibly a bit of food, although it is always possible to buy food at the stops along the way. See the warning under Safety, about not accepting food or drinks from fellow passengers. For mountain routes, have a blanket or at least a jacket handy as the temperature at night can drop quite low. Once you get off the beaten track, the quality of buses and roads deteriorates and you should stick to day buses. If your bus breaks down and you have to get on another bus, you will probably have to pay for the ticket, but keep your old ticket as some bus companies will give refunds. The back seats tend to be the most bumpy and the exhaust pipe is almost always on the left-hand side of the bus.

It is best to try to arrive at your destination during the day; it is safer and easier to find accommodation. Prices of tickets are raised 60-100% during Semana Santa (Easter), Fiestas Patrias (Independence Day – July 28 and 29), Navidad (Christmas) and special local events. Prices will usually go up a few days before the holiday and possibly remain higher a few days after. Tickets also sell out during these times so if travelling then, buy your ticket as soon as you know what day you want to travel.

Car

The main paved entry points for vehicles are as follows. From **Bolivia**: at Desaguadero and Yunguyo on the southeastern side of Lake Titicaca (there is also an unpaved crossing on the north shore between Moho and Puerto Acosta). From **Chile**: between Arica and Tacna. From **Ecuador**: at Aguas Verdes between Huaquillas and Zarumilla, between Macará and La Tina and at Balsas, between Jaén and Vilcabamba (another crossing, Alamor/Lalamor, is only possible by rowing boat). From **Brazil**: the crossing from Assis Brasil to Iñapari is unpaved and is only passable with ease in the dry season.

Toll roads in Peru include: Aguas Verdes–Tumbes, many on the Pan- American Highway between Tumbes and Lima, Pativilca–Huaraz, Lima–Pucusana, Ica–Nazca, Lima (highway around city), and Variante–Pacasmayo; these vary from US$1.50 to US$0.50. Ecuador to Chile/Bolivia on main roads comes to about US$20. Motorcycles are exempt from road tolls; use the extreme right-hand lane at toll gates.

You must have an international driving licence and be over 21 to drive in Peru. If bringing in your own vehicle you must provide proof of ownership. Officially you cannot enter Peru with a vehicle registered in someone else's name, but it is possible with a notarized letter of authorization and insurance documents stating that Peru is incorporated. On leaving Peru there is no check on the import of a vehicle as there is no evidence in your passport. There are two recognized documents for taking a vehicle into South America: a *carnet de passages* issued jointly by the **Fedération Internationale de l'Automobile** (FIA – Paris) and the **Alliance Internationale de Tourisme** (AIT-Geneva), and the *Libreta de Pasos por Aduana* issued by the **Federación Interamericana de Touring y Automóvil Clubs** (FITAC). Officially, Peru requires one or the other, but it is seldom asked for. Nevertheless, motorists seem to fare better with one than without it.

Insurance for the vehicle against accident, damage or theft is best arranged in the country of origin, but it is getting increasingly difficult to find agencies who offer this service. It is very expensive to insure against accident and theft, especially as you should take into account the value of the car increased by duties calculated in real (ie non-devaluing) terms. If the car is stolen or written off you will be required to pay very high import duty on its value. Get the legally required minimum cover, which is not expensive, as soon as you can, because if you should be involved in an accident and are uninsured, your car could be confiscated. If anyone is hurt, do not pick them up (you may become liable). Seek assistance from the nearest police station or hospital if you are able to do so.

The **Touring y Automóvil Club del Perú** ⓘ *Av César Vallejo 699, Lince, T01-221 2432, www.touringperu.com.pe*, offers help to tourists and particularly to members of the leading motoring associations. Good maps are available (see Maps, below).

Fuel 84 octane petrol/gasoline costs US$3.45/gallon; 90 octane, US$3.98; 95 octane, US$4.24; 97 octane, US$4.72. Diesel costs US$3.26. Unleaded fuel is available in large cities and along the Panamericana, but rarely in the highlands.

Car hire The minimum age for renting a car is 25. If renting a car, your home driving licence will be accepted for up to six months. Car hire companies are given in the text. Prices reflect high costs and accident rates. Hotels and tourist agencies will tell you where to find cheaper rates, but you will need to check that you have such basics as spare wheel, toolkit and functioning lights, etc.

Combis, colectivos and trucks

Combis operate between most small towns in the Andes on one- to three-hour journeys. This makes it possible, in many cases, just to turn up and travel within an hour or two. On rougher roads, combis are minibuses (invariably Japanese), while on better roads there are also slightly more expensive and much faster car *colectivos*. *Colectivos* usually charge twice the bus fare and leave only when full. They go almost anywhere in Peru. Most firms have offices. If you book one day in advance, they will pick you up at your hotel or in the main plaza. Trucks are not always much cheaper than buses. They charge avout 75% of the bus fare, but are wholly unpredictable. They are not recommended for long trips, and comfort depends on the load.

Hitchhiking

Hitchhiking in Peru is neither easy, owing to the lack of private vehicles, nor entirely risk-free. For obvious reasons, a lone female should not hitch by herself. Besides, you are more likely to get a lift if you are with a partner, be they male or female. The best combination is a male and female together. Positioning is also key. Freight traffic in Peru has to stop at the police *garitas* outside each town and these are the best places to try (also toll points, but these are further from towns).

Drivers usually ask for money but don't always expect to get it. In mountain and jungle areas you usually have to pay drivers of lorries, vans and even private cars; ask the driver first how much he is going to charge, and then recheck with the locals.

Motorcycling and cycling

Motorcycling The motorcycle should be off-road capable. A road bike can go most places an off-road bike can go. Get to know the bike before you go, ask the dealers in your country what goes wrong with it and arrange a link whereby you can get parts flown out to you. Get the book for international dealer coverage from your manufacturer, but don't rely on it. They frequently have few or no parts for modern, large machinery. An Abus D or chain will keep the bike secure. A cheap alarm gives you peace of mind if you leave the bike outside a hotel at night. Most hotels will allow you to bring the bike inside (see accommodation listings in the travelling text for details). Look for hotels that have a courtyard or more secure parking and never leave luggage on the bike overnight or whilst unattended. Passport, international driving licence and bike registration document are necessary. Riders fare much better with a *carnet de passages* than without it.

Cycling Unless you are planning a journey almost exclusively on paved roads – when a high-quality touring bike would suffice – a mountain bike is strongly recommended. The good-quality ones (and the cast-iron rule is **never** to skimp on quality), are incredibly tough and rugged, with low gear ratios for difficult terrain, wide tyres with plenty of tread for good road-holding, V brakes, sealed hubs and bottom bracket and a low centre of gravity for improved stability. A chrome-alloy frame is a desirable choice over aluminium as it can be welded if necessary. Although touring bikes, and to a lesser extent mountain bikes and spares are available in the larger cities, remember that most locally manufactured goods are shoddy and rarely last. (Shimano parts are generally the easiest to find.) Buy everything you possibly can before you leave home. *Richard's New Bicycle Book* (Pan, £12.99) makes useful reading for even the most mechanically minded (there is also *Richard's 21st century Bicycle Book*).

Remember that you can always stick your bike on a bus, canoe or plane to get yourself nearer to the heart of where you want your wheels to take you. This is especially useful when there are long stretches of major road ahead, where all that awaits you are hours of turbulence as the constant stream of heavy trucks and long-haul buses zoom by. It is possible to rent a bike for a few days, or join an organized tour for riding in the mountains. You should check, however, that the machine you are hiring is up to the conditions you will be encountering, or that the tour company is not a fly-by-night outfit without back-up, good bikes or maintenance

South American Explorers have valuable cycling information that is continuously updated. The **Expedition Advisory Centre** ⓘ *1, Kensington Gore, London SW7 2AR, T020-7591 3008, www.rgs.org*, administered by the Royal Geographical Society, has published a useful monograph entitled *Bicycle Expeditions*, by Paul Vickers. Published in March 1990, it can be downloaded from the RGS's website. Useful websites are **Bike South America** ⓘ *www.e-ddws.com/bsa/* and **Cyclo Accueil Cyclo** ⓘ *chez André Coadou, 35 A, rue de Larrey, 21000 Dijon, France, www.cci.asso.fr/cac/cac.htm*, an organization of long-haul tourers who open their homes for free to passing cyclists. » *See also mountain biking, page 62.*

Taxi

Taxi prices are fixed in urban areas and cost around US$0.75-1.20 for anywhere in the urban areas. In Lima prices range from US$1.50-3, but fares are not fixed. Some drivers work for companies that do have standard fares. Ask locals what the price should be and always set the price beforehand.

Taxis at airports are often a bit more expensive, but ask locals what the price should be as taxi drivers may try to charge you three times the correct price. Many taxi drivers work for commission from hotels and will try to convince you to go to that hotel. Feel free to choose your own hotel and go there. If you walk away from the Arrivals gate a bit, the fares should go down to a price that is reasonable.

Another common form of public transport is the *mototaxi*, or *motocarro*. This is a three-wheel motorcycle with an awning covering the double-seat behind the driver. In some places, like Iquitos and Tarapoto, they are ubiquitous and the only way to get around. Fares are about US$1.

Maps

It is a good idea to get as many as possible in your home country before leaving, especially if travelling by land. A recommended series of general maps is that published by **International Travel Map Productions (ITM)** ⓘ *345 West Broadway, Vancouver BC, V5Y 1P8, Canada, T604-879 3621, www.itmb.com*, compiled with historical notes by the late Kevin Healey. Relevant to this handbook are *South America North West* (1:4M) and *Amazon Basin* (1:4M). Another map series that has been mentioned is that of **New World Edition** ⓘ *Bertelsmann, Neumarkter Strasse 18, 81673 München, Germany: Südamerika Nord, Südamerika Sud* (both 1:4M).

Good maps are available from street sellers in the centre of Lima, or in better bookshops (published by **Lima 2000**, T01-440 3486, www.lima2000.com.pe, costing US$10, or US$14 in booklet form). Lima 2000's *Mapa Vial del Perú* (1:2,200,000) is probably the best and most correct road map available for the country. **Westermanns Monatshefte**; folio Ecuador, Peru, Bolivien has excellent maps of Peru, especially the archaeological sites. A cheaper, less accurate, and less discreet map is published by **Cartográfica Nacional** for US$3-4. The **Instituto Geográfico Nacional** in Lima sells a selection of good, accurate country and regional maps (see page 117). **South American Explorers**, who will give good advice on road conditions (see page 42), stock an excellent collection of country, regional and topographical maps. In the UK, **Stanfords** ⓘ *12-14 Longacre, London, WC2E 9LP, T020-78361321, www.stanfords.co.uk*, also branches in Manchester and Bristol, stocks an excellent range.

The **Touring and Automobile Club of Peru,** see page 51, sells a road map at US$5 (*Mapa Vial del Perú*, 1:3,000,000, Ed 1980) and route maps covering most of Peru (Hojas de Ruta, North, Centre and South, US$1.65 each). The *Guía Toyota* (Spanish), which is published annually, is one of the best guides for venturing off the beaten track.

Sleeping

Accommodation is plentiful throughout the price ranges and finding a hotel room to suit your budget should not present any problems, especially in the main tourist areas and larger towns and cities. The exception to this is during the Christmas and Easter holiday periods, Carnival, Cuzco in June and Independence celebrations at the end of July, when all hotels seem to be crowded. It's advisable to book in advance at these times and during school holidays and local festivals, see page 20.

Hotels, hostales, pensiones and hospedajes

There are many top-class hotels in Lima and Cuzco and in the main tourist centres, such as Arequipa, Iquitos and Trujillo. In less-visited places the choice of better-class hotels is more limited. Accommodation is more expensive in Lima, where good budget hotels tend to be busy. The best-value accommodation can be found in the busiest tourist centres, especially Cuzco, which is full of excellent-value hotels throughout the range. Accommodation also tends to be more expensive in jungle towns such as Iquitos and Puerto Maldonado and in the north compared with the south, especially on the coast. If you want a room with air conditioning expect to pay around 30% extra.

All hotels in the upper price brackets charge 19% general sales tax (IGV) and 10% service on top of prices (foreigners should not have to pay the sales tax on hotel rooms; neither tax is included in prices given in the accommodation listings, unless specified). The more expensive hotels also charge in dollars according to the parallel rate of exchange at midnight. For some suggestions, see www.hotelesenperu.com, with direct links to the hotels themselves.

By law all places that offer accommodation now have a plaque outside bearing the letters **H** (Hotel), **Hs** (Hostal), **HR** (Hotel Residencial) or **P** (Pensión) according to type. A hotel has 51 rooms or more, a hostal 50 or fewer, but the categories do not describe quality or facilities. Generally speaking, though, a *pensión* or *hospedaje* will be cheaper than a hotel or *hostal*. Most mid-range hotels have their own restaurants serving lunch and dinner, as well as breakfast. Many budget places serve breakfast – almost invariably continental breakfast. Most places are friendly and helpful, irrespective of the price, particularly smaller *pensiones* and *hospedajes*, which are often family-run and will treat you as another member of the family.

The cheapest (and often the nastiest) hotels can be found around bus and train stations. If you're just passing through and need a bed for the night, then they may be acceptable. The better-value accommodation is generally found on and around the main plaza (though not always).

A bed for the night

Prices given are for two people sharing a double room with bathroom (shower and toilet), unless the establishment charges per person. If travelling alone, it's usually cheaper to share with others in a room with three or four beds. Prices are for the busy seasons (May-September, Christmas-February and Holy Week). During the low season, when many places may be half empty, it's often possible to bargain the room rate down.

LL (over US$200), L (US$151-200), AL (US$101-150) and A (US$66-100) Hotels in these categories are usually only found in Lima and the main tourist centres. They should offer extensive leisure facilities (and superior business facilities in Lima), plus restaurants and bars and often a casino. Most will provide a safe box in each room. Credit cards are usually accepted.

B (US$46-65) and C (US$31-45) The better-value hotels in these categories provide more than the standard facilities and a fair degree of comfort. Most will include breakfast and many offer 'extras' such as cable TV, minibar, and tea- and coffee-making facilities. They may also provide tourist information and their own transport. Service is generally better and most accept credit cards. At the top end of the range, some may have a swimming pool, sauna and jacuzzi.

D (US$21-30) and E (US$12-20) Hotels in these categories range from very comfortable to functional, but there are some real bargains to be had. At these prices you should expect a reasonably sized, comfortable room with a/c (in tropical regions), your own bathroom, constant hot water, a towel, soap and toilet paper, TV, and a restaurant.

F (US$7-11) Usually in this range you can expect some degree of comfort and cleanliness, a private bathroom, possibly with hot water, and perhaps continental breakfast thrown in. Many of those catering for foreign tourists in the more popular regions offer excellent value for money and many have their own restaurant and offer services such as laundry, safe deposit box, money exchange and luggage store.

G (US$6 and under) Rooms at the upper end of this category may have a private bathroom, though this tends to be the exception rather than the rule. Breakfast is rarely included in the price. At the lower end of this price range rooms usually consist of little more than a bed and four walls, with barely enough room to swing a cat. If you're lucky you may have a window, a table and chair. Cheap places don't always supply soap, towels and toilet paper. In colder (higher) regions they may not supply enough blankets, so take your own or a sleeping bag.

The electric showers used in many hotels (basic up to mid-range) are a health and safety nightmare. Avoid touching any part of the shower while it is producing hot water and always get out before you switch it off.

At airports, bus or train stations, hotel representatives meet new arrivals and show them brochures of their properties. If not using their services when booking a hotel from an airport or station by phone, always talk to the hotel yourself; do not let anyone do it for you (except an accredited hotel booking service). You will be told the hotel of your choice is full and be directed to a more expensive one.

Youth hostels

The office of the Youth Hostel Association of Peru (**Asociación Peruana de Albergues Turísticos Juveniles** and **Administradora Peruana Hostelling International**) ⓘ *Av Casimiro Ulloa 328, Miraflores, Lima T01-446-5488, www.limahostell.com.pe/aphi/*, has information about youth hostels all around the world. For information about International Student Identity Cards (ISIC) and lists of discounts available to cardholders contact **Intej**, see Student travellers, page 31.

Camping

This normally presents no problems in Peru. There can, however, be problems with robbery when camping close to a small village. Avoid such a location, or ask permission to camp in a backyard or *chacra* (farmland). Most Peruvians are used to campers, but in some remote places, people have never seen a tent. Be casual about it, do not unpack all your gear, leave it inside your tent (especially at night) and never leave a tent unattended.

Obey the following rules for 'wild' camping: arrive in daylight and pitch your tent as it gets dark; ask permission to camp from the parish priest, the fire chief or the police, or a farmer regarding his own property; never ask a group of people – especially young people; never camp on a beach (because of sandflies and thieves). Also avoid camping at sea level, on riverbeds or on or below bluffs when El Niño rains are forecast as flash floods can occur; tidal waves may also follow earth tremors. If you can't get information from anyone, camp in a spot where you can't be seen from the nearest inhabited place, or road, and make sure no one saw you go there.

Camping gas in little blue bottles is available in the main cities. Those with stoves designed for lead-free gasoline should use *ron de quemar*, available from hardware shops (*ferreterías*). White gas is called *bencina*, also available from hardware stores. If you use a stove system that requires canisters make sure you dispose of the empty canisters properly; the same goes for all rubbish. Keep in mind as well that you are responsible for the trash that your group, guide or muledriver may drop and it is up to you to say something and pick up the rubbish. Often the rubbish that is on the trails is blamed on locals and this is not usually the case; low-impact travel is everyone's responsibility and while you are picking up your own trash, pick up other people's too.

Eating

Food

» *For a glossary of Peruvian food and drink terms, see page 624.*

Not surprisingly for a country with such a diversity of geography and climates, Peru boasts the continent's most extensive menu. Its cuisine varies from region to region, but basically can be divided into coastal, highland and tropical.

Coastal cuisine

With a coastline of more than 1800 km, the fruits of the se\a are almost limitless. Sea bass, flounder, salmon, red snapper, sole and shellfish are all in abundance. The best coastal dishes are those with seafood bases, with the most popular being the jewel in the culinary crown, *ceviche*. This delicious dish of raw white fish marinated in lemon juice, onion and hot peppers can be found in neighbouring countries, but Peruvian is best. Ask for 'sin picante' if you don't want it hot. Traditionally, *ceviche* is served with corn-on-the-cob, *cancha* (toasted corn), yucca and sweet potatoes. Another mouth-watering fish dish is *escabeche* – fish with onions, hot green pepper, red peppers, prawns (*langostinos*), cumin, hard-boiled eggs, olives, and sprinkled with cheese. For fish on its own, don't miss the excellent *corvina*, or white sea bass. You should also try *chupe de camarones*, which is a shrimp stew made with varying and somewhat surprising ingredients. Other fish dishes include *parihuela*, a popular bouillabaisse which includes *yuyo de mar*, a tangy seaweed, and *aguadito*, a thick rice and fish soup said to have rejuvenating powers.

Fish isn't just eaten on the coast. A favourite northern coastal dish is *seco de cabrito*, roasted kid (baby goat) served with beans and rice, or *seco de cordero* which uses lamb instead. Also good is *ají de gallina*, a rich and spicy creamed chicken, and duck is excellent. People on the coast are referred to as *criollos* (see page 587) and *criollo* cooking can be found throughout the country. Two popular examples are *cau cau*, made with tripe, potatoes, peppers and parsley, served with rice, and *anticuchos*, which are shish kebabs of beef heart with garlic, peppers, cumin seeds and vinegar.

Highland cuisine

The staples of highland cooking, corn and potatoes, date back to Inca times and are found in a remarkable variety of shapes, sizes and colours. Two good potato dishes are *causa* and *carapulca*. *Causa* is made with yellow potatoes, lemons, pepper, hard-boiled eggs, olives, lettuce, sweet cooked corn, sweet cooked potato, fresh cheese, and served with onion sauce. You will also find *causa* on coastal menus: the mashed potato is wrapped around the filling, which often contains crabmeat. Another potato dish is *papa a la huancaína*, which is topped with a spicy sauce made with milk and cheese. The most commonly eaten corn dishes are *choclo con queso*, corn on the cob with cheese, and *tamales*, boiled corn dumplings filled with meat and wrapped in a banana leaf.

Meat dishes are many and varied. *Ollucos con charqui* is a kind of potato with dried meat, *sancochado* is meat and all kinds of vegetables stewed together and seasoned with ground garlic and *lomo a la huancaína* is beef with egg and cheese sauce. A dish almost guaranteed to appear on every restaurant menu is *lomo saltado*, a kind of stir-fried beef with onions, vinegar, ginger, chilli, tomatoes and fried potatoes, served with rice. *Rocoto relleno* is spicy bell pepper stuffed with beef and vegetables, *palta rellena* is avocado filled with chicken or Russian salad, *estofado de carne* is a stew which often contains wine and *carne en adobo* is a cut and seasoned steak. Others include *fritos*, fried pork, usually eaten in the morning, *chicharrones*, deep fried chunks of pork ribs and chicken, and *lechón*, suckling pig. And not forgetting that popular childhood pet, *cuy* (guinea pig), which is considered a real delicacy.

Very filling and good value are the many soups on offer, such as *yacu-chupe*, a green soup which has a basis of potato, with cheese, garlic, coriander leaves, parsley, peppers, eggs, onions, and mint, and *sopa a la criolla* containing thin noodles, beef heart, bits of egg and vegetables and pleasantly spiced. And not to be outdone in the fish department, *trucha* (trout) is delicious, particularly from Lake Titicaca.

Tropical cuisine

The main ingredient in much jungle cuisine is fish, especially the succulent, dolphin-sized *paiche*, which comes with the delicious *palmito*, or palm-hearts, and the ever-present yucca and fried bananas. Other popular dishes include *sopa de motelo* (turtle soup), *sajino* (roast wild boar) and *lagarto* (caiman). *Juanes* are a jungle version of *tamales*, stuffed with chicken and rice. A common dish to start the day is *chapo*, banana porridge, delicious with evaporated milk.

Desserts and fruits

The Peruvian sweet tooth is evident in the huge number of desserts and confections from which to choose. These include: *cocada al horno* – coconut, with yolk of egg, sesame seed, wine and butter; *picarones* – frittered cassava flour and eggs fried in fat

Restaurant prices

The prices that are given for restaurants and other eateries throughout the guide refer to the cost of a two-course meal for one person, excluding tips or drinks.

TTT US$12 and over.

TT US$6-11.

T Under US$6.

and served with honey; *mazamorra morada* – purple maize, sweet potato starch, lemons, various dried fruits, sticks of ground cinnamon and cloves and perfumed pepper; *manjar blanco* – milk, sugar and eggs; *maná* – an almond paste with eggs, vanilla and milk; *alfajores* – shortbread biscuit with *manjar blanco*, pineapple, peanuts, etc; *pastelillos* – yuccas with sweet potato, sugar and anise fried in fat and powdered with sugar and served hot; and *zango de pasas*, made with maize, syrup, raisins and sugar. *Turrón*, the Lima nougat, is worth trying. *Tejas* are pieces of fruit or nut enveloped in *manjar blanco* and covered in chocolate or icing sugar – delicious.

The various Peruvian fruits are wonderful. They include bananas, the citrus fruits, pineapples, dates, avocados (*paltas*), eggfruit (*lúcuma*), the custard apple (*chirimoya* – the 'sweet of the gods' in Quechua) which can be as big as your head, quince, papaya, mango, guava, passion-fruit (*maracuyá*), prickly pear (*tuna*) and the soursop (*guanábana*). These should be tried as juices or ice cream – an unforgettable experience.

Eating out

The high-class hotels and restaurants serve international food and, on demand, some native dishes, but the best places to find native food at its best are the taverns (*chicherías*) and the local restaurants (*picanterías*).

Lunch is the main meal, and apart from the most exclusive places, most restaurants have one or two set lunch menus, called *menú ejecutivo* or *menú económico*. The set menu has the advantage of being served almost immediately and also usually **cheap**. The *menú ejecutivo* costs US$2 or more for a three-course meal with a soft drink and it offers greater choice and more interesting dishes than the *menú económico*, which costs US$1.50-2.50. Don't leave it too late, though, most Peruvians eat lunch around 1230-1400. There are many Chinese restaurants (*chifas*) in Peru which serve good food at reasonable prices. For really economically minded people the *comedores populares* found in the markets of most cities offer a standard three-course meal for as little as US$1 (but see Health, page 67).

For those who wish to eschew such good value, the menu is called *la carta*. An *à la carte* lunch or dinner costs US$5-8, but can go up to an **expensive** US$80 in a first-class restaurant, with drinks and wine included. Middle and high-class restaurants may add 10% service, but do include the 19% sales tax to the bill (which foreigners do have to pay). This is not shown on the price list or menu, so check in advance. Lower-class restaurants charge only tax, while cheap, local restaurants charge no taxes. Dinner in restaurants is normally about 1900 onwards, but choice may be more limited than lunchtime. Peruvians tend to ask guests for dinner at 2000.

The situation for **vegetarians** is improving, but slowly. In tourist centres you should have no problem finding a vegetarian restaurant (or a restaurant that has vegetarian options), especially Cuzco and Arequipa and, of course, Lima. Elsewhere, choice is limited and you may find that, as a non-meat eater, you are not understood. Vegetarians and people with allergies should be able to list (in Spanish) all the foods they cannot eat. By saying *no como carne* (I don't eat meat), people may assume that you eat chicken and eggs. If you do eat eggs, make sure they are cooked thoroughly. Restaurant staff will often bend over backwards to get you exactly what you want but you need to request it.

Drink

Peru's most famous drink is **pisco**, a grape brandy used in the wonderful pisco sour, a deceptively potent cocktail which also includes egg whites and lemon juice. The most renowned brands come from the Ica Valley. Other favourites are *chilcano*, a longer refreshing drink made with *guinda*, a local cherry brandy, and *algarrobina*, a sweet cocktail made with the syrup from the fruit of the carob tree, egg whites, evaporated milk, pisco and cinnamon.

Some Peruvian **wines** are good, others are acidic and poor. The best are the Ica wines Tacama and Ocucaje, and both come in red, white and rosé, sweet and dry varieties. They cost around US$5 a bottle, or more. Tacama Blancs de Blancs and brut Champagne have been recommended, also Gran Tinto Reserva Especial. Viña Santo Tomás, from Chincha, is reasonable and cheap, but Casapalca is not for the discerning palate.

Peruvian **beer** is good, especially the *Cusqueña* and *Arequipeña* brands (lager) and *Cusqueña Malta* and *Trujillo Malta* (porter). In Lima only *Cristal* and *Pilsener* (not related to true Pilsen) are readily available, others have to be sought out. Look out for the sweetish 'maltina' brown ale, which makes a change from the ubiquitous pilsner-type beers.

Chicha de jora is a strong but refreshing **maize beer**, usually homemade and not easy to come by, and *chicha morada* is a soft drink made with purple maize. **Coffee** in Peru is usually brought to the table in a small jug accompanied by a mug of hot water to which you add the coffee essence. If you want coffee with milk, a mug of milk is brought. The number of cafés serving good, fresh coffee is growing. There are many different kinds of herb **tea**: the commonest are *manzanilla* (camomile), *mate de coca* (frequently served in the highlands to stave off the discomforts of altitude sickness) and *hierbaluisa* (lemon grass).

Shopping

Almost everyone who visits Peru will end up buying a souvenir of some sort from the vast array of arts and crafts (*artesanía*) on offer. The best, and cheapest, place to shop for souvenirs, and pretty much anything else in Peru, is in the street markets which can be found absolutely everywhere. The country also has its share of shiny, modern shopping centres, especially in the capital, but remember that the high overheads are reflected in the prices.

What to buy

It is possible to find any kind of **handicraft** in the capital. The prices are often the same as in the highlands, and the quality is high. Good buys are: silver and gold handicrafts; hand-spun and hand-woven textiles; manufactured textiles in indigenous designs; llama and alpaca wool products such as ponchos, rugs, hats, blankets, slippers, coats and sweaters; **arpilleras** (appliqué pictures of Peruvian life), which are made with great skill and originality by women in the shanty towns; and fine leather products which are mostly handmade. Another good buy is **clothing** made from high-quality Pima cotton, grown in Peru.

The **mate burilado**, or engraved gourd found in every tourist shop, is cheap and one of the most genuine expressions of folk art in Peru. These are cheaper if bought in the villages of Cochas Grande or Cochas Chico near Huancayo in the Central Highlands. The Mantaro Valley is generally renowned for its folk culture, including all manner of *artesanía*, see Huancayo page 493.

Alpaca clothing, such as sweaters, hats and gloves, is cheaper in the sierra, especially in Puno. Another good source is Arequipa, where alpaca cloth for suits, coats, etc (mixed with 40% sheep's wool) can be bought cheaply from factories. However, although Lima is more expensive, it is often impossible to find the same quality of goods elsewhere. Genuine alpaca is odourless wet or dry, wet llama 'stinks'.

One of the best places in Peru to look for *artesanía* is Ayacucho in the Central Highlands. Here you'll find excellent woven textiles, as well as the beautifully intricate **retablos**, or Saint Mark's boxes, see page 595. Cuzco is one of the main weaving centres and a good place to shop for textiles, as well as excellent woodcarvings, see page 159. Also recommended for textiles is Cajamarca. The island of Taquile on Lake Titicaca is a good place to buy **ch'uspas** (bags for coca leaves), **chumpis** (belts) and **chullos** (knitted hats). For a more detailed look at Peruvian arts and crafts, see page 592.

Bargaining

Sooner or later almost everyone has to bargain in Peru. Only the rich and famous can afford to pay the prices quoted by taxi drivers, receptionists and self-proclaimed guides. The great majority of Peruvians are honest and extremely hard working, but their country is poor and often in turmoil, the future is uncertain and the overwhelming majority of people live below the poverty line. Foreigners are seen as rich, even if they are backpackers or students. In order to bring prices down, it is extremely helpful to speak at least some Spanish and/or to convince locals that you live, work or study in Peru and therefore know the real price. See page 123 for the box on bargaining for a taxi in the capital.

You will not have to bargain in restaurants, department stores, expensive hotels or airline offices. However, almost all the rest is negotiable. Almost all better-class hotels have 'corporate' rates. Just say that you work for some company, that you are a journalist (they never check ID), or you are a researcher. This way you can usually get a reduction. If you think a lower price is appropriate in a cheaper hotel, ask for 'una rebaja' or 'una rebajita, por favor'. You can negotiate the price of a tour booked through a travel agency, but not an aeroplane, bus or train ticket. In fact, you will probably get a better price directly from the airline ticket office.

Bargaining is expected when you are shopping for artwork, handicrafts, souvenirs, or even food in the market. Remember, though, that most of the handicrafts, including alpaca and woollen goods, are made by hand. Keep in mind, these people are making a living and the 50 centavos you save by bargaining may buy the seller two loaves of bread. You want the fair price not the lowest one, so bargain only when you feel you are being ripped off. Remember that some Peruvians are so desperate that they will have to sell you their goods at any price, in order to survive. Please, don't take advantage of it.

Sport and activities

The website www.ohperu.com/diversion/aventura.htm has a list of adventure sports specialists and associations.

Birdwatching

Peru is the number one country in the world for birds. Its varied geography and topography, and its wildernesses of so many different life zones have endowed Peru with the greatest biodiversity and variety of birds on Earth. Some 18.5% of all the bird species in the world and 45% of all neotropical birds occur in Peru. This is why Peru is the best destination for birds on the continent dubbed 'the bird continent' by professional birders.

A birding trip to Peru is possible during any month of the year, as birds breed all year round. There is, however, a definite peak in breeding activity – and consequently birdsong – just before the rains come in October, and this makes it rather easier to locate many birds between September and Christmas.

Rainwear is recommended for the mountains, especially during the rainy season between December and April. But in the tropical lowlands an umbrella is the way to go. Lightweight hiking boots are probably the best general footwear, but rubber boots are preferred by many neotropical birders for the lowland rainforests.

Apart from the usual binoculars, a telescope is helpful in many areas, whilst a tape recorder and shotgun microphone can be very useful for calling out skulking forest birds, although experience in using this type of equipment is recommended, particularly to limit disturbance to the birds.

If your experience of neotropical birding is limited, the potential number of species which may be seen on a three- or four-week trip can be daunting. A four-week trip can produce over 750 species, and some of the identifications can be tricky! You may want to take an experienced bird guide with you who can introduce you to, for example, the mysteries of foliage-gleaner and woodcreeper identification, or you may want to 'do it yourself' and identify the birds on your own. Books that cover the birds of Peru are listed on page 616.

Details of the following key sites are given in the main travelling text: **Paracas National Reserve** (page 288); **Lomas de Lachay** (page 376); **Huascarán Biosphere Reserve** (page 325); **Tambopata National Reserve** (page 553); **Iquitos** (page 532); **Manu Biosphere Reserve** (page 548). Some of the other birding hot-spots of Peru are listed below, but there are many more. A great three- to four-week combination is about 16 days in Manu, then two to three days in the highlands at Abra Málaga and two to three days in the Huascarán Biosphere Reserve. A trip into the Marañón Valley (Chiclayo-Cajamarca) can be substituted for Manu; this allows access to some of the most sought-after endemics, but would produce far fewer species. More information on the birds of Peru is given in the Flora and fauna section on page 611. Since 2004 **PromPerú** has been promoting birdwatching, through *Peru, a true paradise of birds*, with useful accompanying literature and lists of contacts. Special focus is being given to northern Peru, with its Tumbesian dry forest and Pacific slopes of the Andes, see for instance the Chaparrí Private Conservation Area, page 410, and the protected areas around Tumbes, page 430. See www.perubirdingroutes.com (Spanish and English).

Climbing and rock climbing

The attractions are obvious. The **Cordillera Blanca** is an ice climber's paradise. It takes just one or two days to reach the snowline on most mountains in this, the most intensive grouping of glaciated peaks in South America. The statistics are impressive: more than 50 summits between 5000 and 6000 m; over 20 surpassing 6000 m; 663 glaciers; and there are no peak fees (although at the time of writing, these were likely tobe introduced). It is not unusual for climbers to reach three or more 6000-m summits, climbed Alpine style, over a three-week trip. The degree of difficulty ranges from **Pisco** (5752 m), an excellent acclimatizer or novice's mountain (still demanding), to **Copa** (6173 m), of moderate difficulty, and the tremendous challenges of **Alpamayo** (5957 m), **Artesonraju** (6025 m), **Quitaraju** (6036 m) and **Ranrapalca** (6162 m). Huaraz, the main climbing centre of the Cordillera Blanca (see page 330), has a growing infrastructure and is home to the **Peruvian Mountain Guide Association** (see below).

The **Huayhuash** (see page 369) is a little more remote and Chiquián, northwest of the range, and Cajatambo to the south, have few facilities for climbers. It is possible to contact guides, *arrieros*, porters and cooks in Chiquián, although it is best to enquire in Huaraz first. Mules may need to be brought down from villages higher up. The Huayhuash has some of the most spectacular ice walls in Peru. The **Jirishancas** and **Yerupajas** (Grande and Chico) are the most popular and demanding.

The *cordilleras* **Vilcabamba** and **Vilcanota** (see page 211) have the enticing peaks of **Salkantay** (6271 m) and **Ausangate** (6398 m), but Cuzco is not developed for climbing. This is one of the genuine attractions of Peruvian Andinismo – there is always another mountain slightly more remote to feed the appetite. **Huagurunchu** (5730 m), for instance in the central Andes, is barely known and **Coropuna**, Peru's third highest at 6425 m, is hardly ever climbed.

Rock climbing In the *quebradas*, where the rock is most solid (frost-shattered higher up) this is becoming more popular, particularly in the **Quebrada de Llaca**, near Huaraz, and for beginners at **Monterrey** (see page 341). Other rock climbs in the Huaraz area are the boulders of Huanchac, the 'Sphinx', or Torre de Parón and routes in the Rurec Valley.

Technical equipment such as rope, harness, double boots, ice hammers, helmets, crampons, carabiners, pitons, chocks and ice screws can all be hired in Huaraz quite cheaply, but they can be of poor quality.

Founded in 1980, **Peruvian Mountain Guide Association (AGMP)** is housed in the Casa de Guías and is a member of the International Federation of Mountain Guides Association (IFMGA). It regulates and trains guides as well as the three classes of porter, which are: 1) those with some ice-climbing experience, who are most useful; 2) those who carry loads only on paths, who are less useful; and 3) *arrieros* (mule drivers), cooks and camp guardians. The AGMP also sets prices and organizes rescues, though don't rely on this. One criticism of the organization is that some of the guides only have experience on the most popular mountains such as Alpamayo and Huascarán and that its influence does not extend much beyond the Cordillera Blanca and Huayhuash. However, its continued development is a positive step.

Cultural tourism

This covers more esoteric pursuits such as archaeology and mystical tourism. Several of the tour operators listed on page 22 offer customized packages for special-interest groups. Local operators offering these more specialized tours are listed in the travelling text under the relevant location. Cultural tourism is a rapidly growing niche market. Under the umbrella heading *Turismo Vivencial*, **PromPerú** has a variety of interesting community-based tourism projects in archaeology, agro-tourism, education, jungle trips, llama trekking, nature tourism and traditional medicine; for details see Tourist information, page 40.

The **Instituto Nacional de Cultura**, in the Museo de la Nación, see page 91, should be contacted by archaeologists for permits and information. The **Museo Nacional de Antropología y Arqueología** in Pueblo Libre, see page 91, is the centre for archaeological investigation and the Museo de la Nación holds exhibitions.

Diving

Diving off the **Paracas peninsula** is rewarding, as is the warmer tropical ocean, with larger fish, off **Tumbes**. It is also practised in the **Bahía de Pucusana**. The best season for visibility is March to November because the rivers from the mountains don't deposit silt in the sea. See Lima page 119.

Kayaking

Peru offers outstanding whitewater kayaking for all standards of paddlers from novice to expert. Many first descents remain unattempted owing to logistical difficulties, though they are slowly being ticked off by a dedicated crew of local and internationally renowned kayakers. For the holiday paddler, you are probably best joining up with a raft company who will gladly carry all your gear (plus any non-paddling companions) and provide you with superb food whilst you enjoy the river from an unladen kayak. There is a surprising selection of latest-model kayaks available in Peru for hire from about US$10-20 a day.

For complete novices, some companies offer two- to three-day kayak courses on the **Urubamba** and **Apurímac** that can be booked locally. For expedition paddlers, bringing your own canoe is the best option though it is getting increasingly expensive to fly with your boats around Peru. A knowledge of Spanish is indispensable.

Mountain biking

With its amazing diversity of trails, tracks and rough roads, Peru is surely one of the last great mountain bike destinations yet to be fully discovered. Whether you are interested in a two-day downhill blast from the Andes to the Amazon jungle or an extended off-road journey, then Peru has some of the world's best biking opportunities. The problem is finding the routes as trail maps are virtually non-existent and the few main roads are often congested with traffic and far from fun to travel along. A few specialist agencies run by dedicated mountain bikers are now exploring the intricate web of paths, single tracks and dirt roads that criss-crosses the Andes, putting together exciting routes to suit everyone from the weekend warrior to the long-distance touring cyclist, the extreme downhiller to the casual day tripper.

If you are considering a dedicated cycling holiday, then it is best to bring your bike from home. It's pretty easy, just get a bike box from your local shop, deflate the tyres, take the pedals off and turn the handlebars. It is worth checking first that your airline is happy to take your bike: some are, some will want to charge. Make sure your bike is in good condition before you depart as spares and repairs are hard to come by, especially if your bike is very complicated (eg: XT V-brake blocks are virtually impossible to find and rear suspension/disc brakes parts are totally unavailable). A tip from a Peruvian mountain bike guide: take plenty of inner tubes, brake blocks, chain lube and a quick release seat. Leave all panniers at home and rely on the support vehicle whenever you get tired as there will be plenty more riding later.

If you are hiring a bike, be it for one-day or longer, the basic rule is you get what you pay for. For as little as US$5-10 a day you can get a cheap imitation of a mountain bike that will be fine on a paved road, but will almost certainly not stand up to the rigours of off-roading. For US$20-25 you should be able to find something half-decent with front shocks, V-brakes, helmet and gloves. You should check any hire bike thoroughly before riding it.

When signing up for a mountain bike trip, remember that you are in the Andes so if you are worried about your fitness and the altitude, make sure you get a predominantly downhill trip. Check there is a support vehicle available throughout the entire trip, not just dropping you off and meeting you at the end. Check the guide is carrying a first aid kit, at the very least a puncture repair kit (preferably a comprehensive tool kit) and is knowledgeable about bike mechanics. Bikes regularly go wrong, punctures are frequent and people do fall off, so it is essential that your guide/company provides this minimum cover.

On longer trips ask for detailed trip dossiers, describing the ups and downs and total distances of the routes, check how much is just dirt-road (suitable for just about anyone of reasonable fitness) and how much is single-track (often demanding considerable experience and fitness). Also it is good to know what support will be provided in the way of experienced bike guides, trained bike mechanics on hand, radio communications, spare bikes provided, cooking and dining facilities, toilet facilities, etc.

Parapenting and hang gliding

Vuelo libre is just taking off in Peru. Flying from the coastal cliffs is easy and the thermals are good. The **Callejón de Huaylas** is more risky owing to variable thermals, crosswinds and a lack of good landing sites, but there is a strong allure to flying at

6000 m in front of the glaciers of Huascarán. The area with the greatest potential is the **Sacred Valley** of Cuzco which has excellent launch sites, thermals and reasonable landing sites. The season in the sierra is May to October, with the best months being August and September. Some flights in Peru have exceeded 6500 m.

Rafting

Peru is rapidly becoming one of the world's premier destinations for whitewater rafting. Several of its rivers are rated in the world's top 10 and a rafting trip, be it for one or 10 days, is now high on any adventurer's 'must-do' list of activities while travelling in Peru. It is not just the adrenaline rush of big rapids that attract, it is the whole experience of accessing areas beyond the reach of motor vehicles, whether tackling sheer-sided, mile-deep canyons, travelling silently through pristine rainforest, or canoeing across the stark *altiplano*, high in the Andes.

Before you leap into the first raft that floats by, a word of warning and a bit of advice will help you ensure that your rafting 'trip of a lifetime' really is as safe, as environmentally friendly and as fun as you want it to be.

Basically, the very remoteness and amazing locations that make Peruvian whitewater rivers so attractive mean that dealing with an emergency (should it occur) can be difficult, if nigh-on impossible. As the sport of rafting has increased in popularity over the last few years, so too have the number of accidents (including fatalities); yet the rafting industry remains virtually unchecked. How then, do you ensure your safety on what are undoubtedly some of the best whitewater runs anywhere in South America, if not the whole world?

If you are looking to join a rafting expedition of some length, then it is definitely worth signing up in advance before you set foot in Peru. Some long expeditions have fewer than two or three scheduled departures a year and the companies that offer them only accept bookings well in advance as they are logistically extremely difficult to organize. For the popular day trips and expeditions on the Apurímac there are regular departures (the latter in the dry season only – see below). If you can spare a couple of days to wait for a departure then it is fine to book in Cuzco. It also gives you the chance to talk to the company which will be operating your tour and to meet the guides. There are day trip departures all year and frequent multi-day departures in the high season. Note that the difficulty of the sections changes between the dry and rainy season; some become extremely difficult or un-runable in the rainy season. The dry season is April/May to September (but can be as late as November), the rainy season is December to March. Err on the side of caution: if some companies are not running trips when the rivers are high, there must be a good reason for it. Seek more than one opinion on safety in the rainy season.

New legislation, yet to be fully implemented, demands that Class 4+ guides hold the internationally recognized qualifications of **Swift Water Rescue Technician** and hold current first aid certificates. All rafting equipment will be checked regularly to ensure it meets basic safety standards, eg life jackets that actually float, etc. At present there are a number of guides with the relevant qualifications, but you will only find them at companies who operate the longer, multi-day trips. Moreover, equipment standards in some of the companies are woefully low and it may prove difficult to enforce the new rules, should they be put in place, but at least it will be a step in the right direction.

At present (and probably in the foreseeable future), as with many of Peru's adventure options, it simply boils down to 'You get what you pay for'. Rafting is an inherently dangerous sport and doing it in Peru with the wrong operator can quite seriously endanger your life. If price is all that matters, bear in mind the following comments: the cheaper the price, the less you get, be it with safety cover, experience of guides, quality of equipment, quantity of food, emergency back up and environmental awareness.

Often on trips you will be required to show proof that your travel insurance will cover you for whitewater rafting (occasionally you may be asked to sign an insurance disclaimer). If you are unsure about it, and are planning to go rafting, it is worth checking with your insurance company before you leave, as some policies have an additional charge. Very few policies cover Grade 5 rafting – read the small print. When signing up you should ask about the experience and qualifications of the guides or even, if possible, meet them. At present there is no exam or qualification required to become a river guide (*conductor de río*), but certain things are essential of your guide. Firstly find out his command of English (or whatever language – there are a few German-speaking guides available), essential if you are going to understand his commands. Find out his experience. How many times has he done this particular stretch of river? Many Peruvian guides have worked overseas in the off-season, from Chile to Costa Rica, Europe and New Zealand. The more international experience your guide has, the more aware he will be of international safety practices. All guides should have some experience in rescue techniques. All guides must have knowledge of whitewater rescue and wilderness first aid. Ask when they last took a course and what level they are at.

Good equipment is essential for your safe enjoyment of your trip. If possible ask to see some of the gear provided. Basic essentials include self-bailing rafts for all but the calmest of rivers. Check how old your raft is and where it was made. Satellite phones are an essential piece of safety equipment on long trips in remote areas: does the company use them (they are not yet standard on the Apurímac)? Paddles should be of plastic and metal construction. Wooden paddles can snap, but a few companies use locally made ones which can be excellent, but expensive (in either case, losing a paddle should be of less importance to the company than the safety of the rafter). Helmets should always be provided and fit correctly (again, home-made fibreglass copies are an accident waiting to happen). Life jackets must be of a lifeguard-recognized quality and be replaced regularly as they have a tendency to lose their flotation. Locally made jackets look the business but, in fact, are very poor floaters. Does your company provide wetsuits (some of the rivers are surprisingly cold), or, at the very least, quality Splash jackets, as the wind can cause you to chill rapidly? On the longer trips, dry bags are provided – what state are these in? How old are they? Do they leak? There is nothing worse than a soggy sleeping bag at the end of a day's rafting. Are tents provided? And most importantly (for the jungle) do the zips on the mosquito net work and is it rain proof? Does the company provide mosquito netting dining tents? tables? chairs? These apparent excesses are very nice when camping for some time at the bottom of a sandfly-infested canyon!

Back onto first aid: ask to see the first aid kit and find out what is in there and, most importantly, do they know how to use it? When was it last checked? Updated? Pretty basic stuff, but if someone used all the *lomotil* you could come unstuck.

After a tough day on the river, the last thing you want to do is get sick from the food. Good, wholesome food is relatively cheap in Peru and can make all the difference on a long trip. Once again, you pay for what you get. Ask if there's a vegetarian option. On the food preparation, simple precautions will help you stay healthy. Are all vegetables soaked in iodine before serving? Do the cooks wash their hands and is there soap available for the clients? Are the plates, pots and cutlery washed in iodine or simply swilled in the river? (Stop and think how many villages up stream use that river as their main sewage outlet.) All are simple ways to avoid getting sick. On the Apurímac, the operator should provide a chemical toilet and remove all toilet paper and other rubbish. In the past, certain beaches have been subject to a completely uncaring attitude over toilet paper and human excrement. At the very least your company should provide a lighter for burning the paper and a trowel to go dig a hole. Simple rules to follow are always shit below the high-water mark so at least in the rainy season it will wash clean, always bury it good and deep and watch out when burning the paper so as not to start a fire. It is normal practice for guides to check the campsite on arrival to ensure it is clean and then again before leaving. If your company does not, make it your responsibility to encourage other members of the group to keep the campsites clean. Bottled gas is used for cooking; neither drift wood nor cut trees should be burnt.

Above all it is your safety on the river that is important. Some companies are now offering safety kayaks as standard as well as safety catarafts on certain rivers. This is definitely a step in the right direction but one that is open to misuse. Sometimes safety kayakers have little or no experience of what they are required to do and are merely along for the ride, sometimes they are asked to shoot video (rendering the safety cover useless). A safety cataraft is a powerful tool in the right hands, but weigh it down with equipment and it is of little use. All companies should carry at the very least a 'wrap kit' consisting of static ropes, carabiners, slings and pulleys should a raft unfortunately get stuck. But more importantly, do the guides know how to use it?

If all this doom and gloom has not put you off, you are now equipped to go out there and find the company that offers what you are looking for at a price you think is reasonable. Bear in mind a day's rafting in the USA can cost between US$75-120 for a basic one-day. In Peru you might get the same for just US$30 but ask yourself "What am I getting for so little?". After all, rafts and equipment cost the same, in fact more, in Peru.

Skiing

Without the aid of lifts, skiing in Peru is largely for the high-altitude enthusiast. **Pastoruri**, at 5000 m, has the only piste and holds a championship during **Semana del Andinismo** at the end of the November to June season. **Pisco, Vallunaraju** and **Caullaraju** are also used for skiing. **Huascarán** and **Copa** have been tackled by experienced ski-mountaineers and the eastern flank of **Coropuna** also has potential. There is, however, a high possibility of crevasses on Copa and Huascarán from November to March. Those thinking of skiing the more difficult peaks should have some technical climbing experience and a guide is recommended. The *Casa de Guías* has the names of people with skiing experience; they are not instructors but have taken groups to most peaks.

The extreme ski descent craze has hit the **Cordillera Blanca** and **Huayhuash** in a big way. Since **North Face Extreme** skied and snowboarded Artesonraju in the late 1990s, the flood gates have opened. There is practically no peak that is considered out of the question.

Surfing

Peru is a top, internationally renowned surfing destination. Its main draws are the variety of wave and the year-round action. Point Break, Left and Right Reef Break and waves up to 6 m can all be found during the seasons: September to February in the north; March to December in the south, though May is often ideal south of Lima.

Ocean swells are affected by two currents; the warm El Niño in the north and the cold Humboldt current in the south arriving from Antarctica. **Pimentel**, near Chiclayo, is the dividing point between these two effects but a wet suit is normally required anywhere south of Piura.

The biggest wave is at **Pico Alto** (sometimes 6 m in May), south of Lima, and the largest break is 800 m at **Chicama**, near Trujillo. There are more than 30 top surfing beaches. **North of Lima** these include: Chicama, Pacasmayo, Punta Tur, Punta Nonura, El Golf, Cabo Blanco, Los Organos and Máncora (all left break). **South of Lima** the best beaches are: Punta Hermosa, Punta Rocas (right break) and Pico Alto (right break, best in May), the pick of the bunch; Huaico/Santa Rosa (left break), Cabo Negro (left break), Sangallán (right break); El Olón, Piedras Negras and Caleta La Cruz, all near Ilo (the first two left, La Cruz right break).

International competitions are held at Pico Alto (Balin Open in May) and Punta Rocas (during the summer months). A surfing magazine, *Tablista*, is published bimonthly. Also lookout for the free *X3Mag* and, of course, Footprint's *Surfing the World*. Useful websites are www.peruazul. com.pe, www.bodyboardperu.com and www.wannasurf.com. See Lima page 119.

Swimming

Peru's Pacific coastline is more than 3000 km long. This desert shore is crossed by 52 rivers, which rush down from the Andes to create scores of fertile oases. The desert meets the ocean via hundreds of beaches ideal for lovers of watersports and fine seafood, as well as those who simply want to lie on the beach with a good book and soak up the sun after their adventures in Peru's highlands and rainforests. There are pristine stretches of fine white sand with palm tree backdrops, while other beaches are covered with round pebbles or surrounded by exotic mangroves. Not all beaches draw surfers to the powerful waves generated by the immense Pacific. Others offer calm waters ideal for swimming. The warmest water is to be found in northern Peru, southward from **Tumbes** on the Ecuadorean border. There are many bathing resorts near **Lima** (do not swim at, or even visit, these beaches alone); they are pretty quiet when the winter fog descends. In the main, though, sunny skies are guaranteed throughout the year right the way down to **Tacna** on the Chilean frontier. Note that the current off the coast can be very strong, making it too dangerous to swim in places; enquire locally.

Trekking

Peru has some outstanding circuits around the Nevados. The best known are the **Llanganuco to Santa Cruz** loop, see page 349, the **Ausangate circuit** and a strenuous trek around the **Huayhuash**, see page 370. For treks from Caraz, see page 348, for treks from Carhuaz, see page 344, and for information on trekking in the Cordillera Blanca and Huayhuash in general, see page 325. Other good areas are the **Colca Canyon**, the **Chincheros** area and the **upper Cañete valley**.

The other type of trekking for which Peru is justifiably renowned is walking among ruins, and, above all, for the **Inca Trail** (see page 194 and the comments on new regulations on this most popular of routes). However, there are many other walks of this type in a country rich in archaeological heritage. Some of the best are: the **valley of the Río Atuen** near Leymebamba and the entire **Chachapoyas region** (see page 455); the **Tantamayo** ruins above the Marañón; the **Cotahuasi canyon** (see page 276); and beyond Machu Picchu to **Vilcabamba** (see page 203) and **Choquequirao.** People tend to think of the Inca Trail to Machu Picchu as the only stretch of Inca roadway that can be walked. It is, however, a tiny fraction of the Incas' road network and vestiges of the Capaq Ñan (the Royal Road) can be found the length of the country. In places it is well preserved, still in use and makes for excellent trekking. In other parts it has been lost, but new interest in the road will, it is hoped, lead to its recognition as having supreme architectural and cultural value and make it accessible for walkers and Inca enthusiasts.

Most walking is on clear trails, well trodden by *campesinos* who populate most parts of the Peruvian Andes. If you camp on their land, ask permission first and, of course, do not leave any litter. Tents, sleeping bags, mats and stoves can easily be hired in Huaraz and Cuzco but check carefully for quality.

Trekking and climbing conditions and health May to September is the dry season in the Cordilleras. October, November and April can be fine, particularly for trekking. Most bad weather comes from the east and temperatures plummet around twilight. The optimum months for extreme ice climbing are from late May to mid-July. In early May there is a risk of avalanche from sheered neve ice layers. It is best to climb early in the day as the snow becomes slushy later on.

After July, successive hot sunny days will have melted some of the main support (compacted ice) particularly on north-facing slopes. On the other hand, high-altitude rock climbs are less troubled by ice after July. On south-facing slopes the ice and snow never consolidates quite as well.

Trekking and climbing companies show very little concern for their clients about acute mountain sickness, AMS (an exception is **Monttrek** in Huaraz). Almost every climb or trek in Peru is scheduled faster than the recommended 300 m per day, even the very popular Santa Cruz trek near Huaraz. Unlike Nepal, where everyone goes out of their way to prevent AMS in travellers, few ask whether you are acclimatized. You should be wary of agencies wanting to sell you trips with very fast ascents.

Spectator sports

Without a doubt, the most popular sport to watch is **football** (soccer). In Lima the rivalry between the two main clubs, **Alianza** and **La U** (Universitario) is legendary. Cuzco's top club is **Ciencianos**. Every village, it seems, has a football pitch, even if it means comandeering the only piece of flat land for the purpose.

Most spectator sports are represented in Lima, but nothing matches the attraction of football. There is, for instance, **horse racing** (information at www.peruhipico.com) and, throughout the country, great interest in the Peruvian *caballos de paso*, with their particular gait. Other equestrian activities are more participatory, such as riding in the sierra. **Bullfighting** is popular in Lima and there are two seasons, July and October to the first week in December.

Other sports that have a minority interest (in Peruvian terms) include cycling, tennis (www.tenisperu.com.pe), golf and rugby union (http://rugby7.com/peru.asp).

Health

→ *Hospitals/medical facilities are listed in the directory sections of each chapter sub-section.*

Local populations in South America are exposed to a range of health risks not encountered in the western world. Many of the diseases are major problems for the local poor communities. The risk to travellers is more remote but cannot be ignored. Obviously five-star travel is going to carry less risk than backpacking on a minimal budget. The health care in the region is varied. There are many excellent private and government clinics/hospitals. As with all medical care, first impressions count. If a facility is grubby, staff wear grey coats instead of white ones then be wary of the general standard of medicine and hygiene. A good tip is to contact the embassy or consulate on arrival and ask where the recommended clinics (those used by diplomats) are. Diseases you may be exposed to are caused by viruses, bacteria and parasites. Other health problems, such as altitude sickness, may affect you along the entire length of the Andes.

The greatest disease risk in tropical South America is caused by the greater volume of insect disease carriers in the shape of mosquitoes and sandflies. The parasitic diseases are many but the two key ones are **malaria** and South American trypanosomiasis (known as **Chagas Disease**). The key viral disease is **dengue fever,** which is transmitted by a mosquito that bites in the day. Bacterial diseases include **tuberculosis** (TB) and some causes of traveller's **diarrhoea.**

Before you go

Ideally, you should see your GP/practice nurse or travel clinic at least six weeks before your departure for general advice on travel risks, malaria and recommended vaccinations. Your local pharmacist can also be a good source of readily accessible advice. Make sure you have travel insurance, get a dental check (especially if you are going to be away for more than a month), know your own blood group and if you suffer a long-term condition such as diabetes or epilepsy make sure someone knows or that you have a Medic Alert bracelet/necklace with this information on it.

√ – O Rh positive

Recommended vaccinations

The following are commonly recommended for Peru. The final decision, however, should be based on a consultation with your GP or travel clinic: **Polio** Recommended if nil in last 10 years. **Tetanus** Recommended if nil in last 10 years (but after five doses you have had enough for life). **Typhoid** Recommended if nil in last three years. **Yellow fever** A yellow fever vaccination certificate is required if you are coming from infected areas of the world. If you are going to the Peruvian jungle, especially if you will be living rough, you should be vaccinated against yellow fever. Moreover, tours to Manu and Tambopata booked outside Peru state that a yellow fever vaccination certificate is required to be allowed to enter either region. **Rabies** Recommended if going to jungle and/or remote areas. **Hepatitis A** Recommended – the disease can be caught easily from food/water. Vaccination against cholera is not necessary.

A-Z of health risks

Altitude sickness

Acute mountain sickness (locally called *soroche*) can strike from about 3000 m upwards and in general is more likely to affect those who ascend rapidly (for example by plane) and those who over-exert themselves. Acute mountain sickness takes a few hours or days to come on and presents with heachache, lassitude, dizziness, loss of appetite, nausea and vomiting. Insomnia is common and often associated with a suffocating feeling when lying down in bed. You may notice that your breathing tends to wax and wane at night and your face is puffy in the mornings – this is all part of the syndrome. If the symptoms are mild, the treatment is rest and painkillers (preferably not aspirin-based) for the headaches. (*Sorojchi* pills, sold only by the Fasa chain of chemists, is claimed by many significantly to reduce the impacts of *soroche* – Ed.) Should the symptoms be severe and prolonged it is best to descend to a lower altitude immediately and reascend, if necessary, slowly and in stages. The symptoms disappear very quickly – even after a few hundred metres of descent.

The best way of preventing acute mountain sickness is a relatively slow ascent. When trekking to high altitude, some time spent walking at medium altitude, getting fit and acclimatizing is beneficial. When flying to places over 3000 m a few hours' rest and the avoidance of alcohol, cigarettes and heavy food will go a long way towards preventing acute mountain sickness.

Bites and stings

This is a very rare event indeed for travellers, but if you are unlucky (or careless) enough to be bitten by a venomous snake, spider, scorpion or sea creature, try to identify the culprit, without putting yourself in further danger (do not try to catch a live snake). Snake bites in particular are very frightening, but in fact rarely poisonous; even venomous snakes can bite without injecting venom. Victims should be taken to a hospital or a doctor without delay. It is not advised for travellers to carry snake bite antivenom as it can do more harm than good in inexperienced hands. Reassure and comfort the victim frequently. Immobilize the limb with a bandage or a splint and get the patient to lie still. Do not slash the bite area and try to suck out the poison. This also does more harm than good. You should apply a tourniquet in these circumstances, but only if you know how to. Do not attempt this if you are not experienced.

Certain tropical fish inject venom into bathers' feet when trodden on, which can be exceptionally painful. Wear plastic shoes if such creatures are reported. The pain can be relieved by immersing the foot in hot water (as hot as you can bear) for as long as the pain persists.

Chagas disease

The disease occurs throughout South America, affects locals more than travellers, but travellers can be exposed by sleeping in mud-constructed huts where the bug that carries the parasite bites and defecates on an exposed part of skin. You may notice nothing at all or a local swelling, with fever, tiredness and enlargement of lymph glands, spleen and liver. The seriousness of the parasite infection is caused by the long-term effects which include gross enlargement of the heart and/or guts. Early treatment is required with toxic drugs. To prevent the disease, always keep a light burning at night. Never scratch the bite, but swab it with disinfectant. Sleep under a permethrin-treated bed net and use insect repellents.

Dengue fever

This is a viral disease spread by mosquitoes that tend to bite during the day. The symptoms are fever and often intense joint pains; also some people develop a rash. Symptoms last about a week but it can take a few weeks to recover fully. Dengue can be difficult to distinguish from malaria as both diseases tend to occur in the same countries. There are no effective vaccines or antiviral drugs though, fortunately, travellers rarely develop the more severe forms of the disease (these can prove fatal). Rest, plenty of fluids and paracetamol (not aspirin) is the recommended treatment.

Diarrhoea and intestinal upset

Diarrhoea can refer either to loose stools or an increased frequency of bowel movement, both of which can be a nuisance. Symptoms should be relatively short-lived but if they persist beyond two weeks specialist medical attention should be sought. Also seek medical help if there is blood in the stools and/or fever.

Adults can use an antidiarrhoeal medication such as **loperamide** to control the symptoms but only for up to 24 hours. In addition keep well hydrated by drinking plenty of fluids and eat bland foods. Oral rehydration sachets taken after each loose stool are a useful way to keep well hydrated. These should always be used when treating children and the elderly.

Bacterial traveller's diarrhoea is the most common form. Ciproxin (Ciprofloxacin) is a useful antibiotic and can be obtained by private prescription in the UK. You need to take one 500 mg tablet when the diarrhoea starts. If there are so signs of improvement after 24 hours the diarrhoea is likely to be viral and not bacterial. If it is due to other organisms such as those causing giardia or amoebic dysentery, different antibiotics will be required.

The standard advice to prevent problems is to be careful with water and ice for drinking. Ask yourself where the water came from. If you have any doubts then boil it or filter and treat it. There are many filter/treatment devices now available on the market. Food can also transmit disease. Be wary of salads (what were they washed in, who handled them), re-heated foods or food that has been left out in the sun having been cooked earlier in the day. There is a simple adage that says wash it, peel it, boil it or forget it. Also be wary of unpasteurized dairy products as these can transmit a range of diseases.

Hepatitis

Hepatitis means inflammation of the liver. Viral causes of the disease can be acquired anywhere in the world. The most obvious symptom is a yellowing of your skin or the whites of your eyes. However, prior to this all that you may notice is itching and tiredness. Pre-travel hepatitis A vaccine is the best bet. Hepatitis B (for which there is a vaccine) is spread through blood and unprotected sexual intercourse, both of which can be avoided.

Leishmaniasis

A skin form of this disease occurs in Peru. If infected, you may notice a raised lump, which leads to a purplish discoloration on white skin and a possible ulcer. The parasite is transmitted by the bite of a sandfly. Sandflies do not fly very far and the greatest risk is at ground levels, so if you can sleep above ground, under a permethrin treated net, do so. In addition, use insect repellent. Seek advice for any persistent skin lesion or nasal symptom. Several weeks' treatment is required under specialist supervision. The drugs themselves are toxic but if not taken in sufficient amounts recurrence of the disease is more likely.

Leptospirosis

Various forms of leptospirosis occur throughout Latin America, transmitted by a bacterium which is excreted in rodent urine. Fresh water and moist soil harbour the organisms, which enter the body through cuts and scratches. If you suffer from any form of prolonged fever consult a doctor.

Malaria

Malaria can cause death within 24 hours and can start as something just resembling an attack of flu. You may feel tired, lethargic, headachy, feverish; or more seriously, develop fits, followed by coma and then death. Have a low index of suspicion because it is very easy to write off vague symptoms, which may actually be malaria. If you have a temperature, visit a doctor as soon as you can and ask for a malaria test. On your return home, if you suffer any of these symptoms, have a test as soon as possible. Even if a previous test proved negative, this could save your life.

Treatment is with drugs and may be oral or into a vein depending on the seriousness of the infection. Remember **ABCD: Awareness** (of whether the disease is present in the area you are travelling in), **Bite avoidance, Chemoprohylaxis, Diagnosis.**

To prevent mosquito bites wear clothes that cover arms and legs, use effective insect repellents in areas with known risks of insect-spread disease and use a mosquito net treated with an insecticide. Repellents containing 30-50% DEET (Di-ethyltoluamide) are recommended when visiting malaria endemic areas; lemon eucalyptus (Mosiguard) is a reasonable alternative. The key advice is to guard against contracting malaria by taking the correct anti-malarials and finishing the recommended course. If you are a popular target for insect bites or develop lumps quite soon after being bitten use antihistamine tablets and apply a cream such as hydrocortisone.

Remember that it is risky to buy medicine, and in particular anti-malarials, in some developing countries. These may be sub-standard or part of a trade in counterfeit drugs.

Rabies

Rabies is endemic throughout Latin America so be aware of the dangers of the bite from any animal. Rabies vaccination before travel can be considered but, if bitten, always seek urgent medical attention – whether or not you have been previously vaccinated – after first cleaning the wound and treating with an iodine-base disinfectant or alcohol.

Sun

Take good heed of advice regarding protection against the sun. Overexposure can lead to sunburn and, in the longer term, skin cancers and premature skin aging. The best advice is simply to avoid exposure to the sun by covering exposed skin, wearing a hat and staying out of the sun if possible, particularly between late morning and early afternoon. Apply a high-factor sunscreen (greater than SPF15) and also make sure it screens against UVB. A further danger in tropical climates is heat exhaustion or more seriously heatstroke. This can be avoided by good hydration, which means drinking water past the point of simply quenching thirst. Also when first exposed to tropical heat take time to acclimatize by avoiding strenuous activity in the middle of the day. If you cannot avoid heavy exercise it is also a good idea to increase salt intake.

Ticks

Ticks usually attach themselves to the lower parts of the body often when walking in areas where cattle have grazed. They take a while to attach themselves strongly, but swell up as they start to suck blood. The important thing is to remove them gently, so that they do not leave their head parts in your skin because this can cause a nasty allergic reaction some days later. Do not use petrol, vaseline, lighted cigarettes, etc to remove the tick, but, with a pair of tweezers remove the beast gently by gripping it at the attached (head) end and rock it out in very much the same way that a tooth is extracted. **Typhus**, carried by ticks, can also occur. There is usually a reaction at the site of the bite and a fever. Certain tropical flies which lay their eggs under the skin of sheep and cattle also occasionally do the same thing to humans with the unpleasant result that a maggot grows under the skin and pops up as a boil or pimple. The best way to remove these is to cover the boil with oil, vaseline or nail varnish so as to stop the maggot breathing, then to squeeze it out gently the next day.

Underwater health

If you plan to dive make sure that you are fit do so. The **British Sub-Aqua Club (BSAC)** ⓘ *Telford's Quay, South Pier Rd, Ellesmere Port, Cheshire CH65 4FL, UK, T01513-506200, www.bsac.com*, can put you in touch with doctors who will carry out medical examinations. Check that any dive company you use are reputable and have appropriate certification from the **Professional Association of Diving Instructors (PADI)** ⓘ *Unit 7, St Philips Central, Albert Rd, St Philips, Bristol, BS2 OTD, T0117-3007234, www.padi.com*.

Water

There are a number of ways of purifying water. Dirty water should first be strained through a filter bag and then boiled or treated. Bring water to a rolling boil for several minutes. There are sterilizing methods that can be used and products generally contain chlorine (eg Puritabs) or iodine (eg Pota Aqua) compounds. There are a number of water sterilizers now on the market available in personal and expedition size. Make sure you take the spare parts or spare chemicals with you and do not believe everything the manufacturers say.

Other diseases and risks

There are a range of other insect-borne diseases that are quite rare in travellers, but worth finding out about if going to particular destinations. Also remember that unprotected sex always carries a risk. You can lessen this by using condoms, a femidom or if you want to be completely safe, by avoiding sex altogether.

Further information

Websites

Centers for Disease Control and Prevention (USA), www.cdc.gov.
Fit for Travel (UK), www.fitfortravel.scot.nhs.uk. This site from Scotland provides a quick A-Z of vaccine and travel health advice requirements for each country.
Foreign and Commonwealth Office (FCO), UK, www.fco.gov.uk.
National Travel Health Network and Centre (NaTHNaC), www.nathnac.org/.
Prince Leopold Institute for Tropical Medicine, www.itg.be.
World Health Organisation, www.who.int.

Books

Dawood, R, editor, *Travellers' health*, 3rd ed, Oxford: Oxford University Press, 2002.
Warrell, David, and Sarah Anderson, editors, *Expedition Medicine*, The Royal Geographic Society, ISBN 1 86197 040-4.

Keeping in touch

Communications

Internet and email

You can find internet access everywhere. Centres with high tourism have internet cafés on every corner; many of them have **net2phone**. Internet cafés are incredibly cheap to use, normally about US$0.60-1 per hour. When they first open in the morning is often a good time to use cyber cafés, as they are less busy then. Access is generally quick. Internet access is more expensive in hotel business centres and in out-of-the-way places.

Post

The postal system is **Serpost**. Correo Central on the Plaza de Armas in Lima is the best place for postage (open Monday-Friday 0800-1800). Stamps, envelopes and cloth sacks (to send bigger parcels in) can all be bought there. Cuzco is also efficient for sending parcels. It costs US$1 to mail a letter up to 20 g anywhere in the Americas, US$1.50 to Europe and US$1.70 to Australia. You can also send letters *expreso* for about US$0.55, extra to the Americas, US$0.90 to the rest of the world. Don't put tape on envelopes or packages; wait until you get to the post office and use the glue they have. It is very expensive to mail large packages out of Peru so it is best not to plan to send things home from here. For emergency or important documents, **DHL** and **Federal Express** are also options in Lima.

To receive mail, letters can be sent to Poste Restante/General Delivery (*lista de correos*), your embassy, or, for cardholders, American Express offices. Members of the **South American Explorers** can have post and packages sent to them at either of the Peruvian offices. Try not to have articles sent by post to Peru – taxes can be 200% of the value.

Telephone → *International dialling code 51.*

The main service provider is **Telefónica**, www.telefonica.com.pe (or **Telser** in Cuzco) which has offices in all large and medium-sized towns. **Telefónica** offices are usually administrative and phones are provided on the street outside. Local, national and international calls can be made from public phone boxes with prepaid phone cards which can be bought at **Telefónica** offices or the many private phone offices. Also are cards for a number of other carriers for long distance calls. Their rates are very competitive and there are usually special offers. Not every phone takes cards;

Telefónica, for instance, has its own phones for its 147 service (national and international). The **SuperPlus 147** card for one long-distance call is very good value at S/.20 (US$5.70) for 48 minutes. You can also use coins to make calls: from public phones it costs US$1 per minute to North America, US$1.40 to Europe and US$1.50 to Australia and New Zealand. Collect calls are possible to almost anywhere by ringing the international operator (108). This is also the number for directory enquiries and for international direct options (they speak English). Your home telephone company can give you the number to call as well. **Net Phones** are popular; costs and service vary but can be as cheap as US$5 per hour to the USA. Calls to everywhere else are usually at least 50% more.

There are three mobile networks in Peru, **Telefónica Movistar, TIM** and **Bellsouth.** *Telefónica* has the most extensive network. Mobile phones brought into Peru which operate at 800 mhz may be activated at a **Telefónica** technical services office. **TIM** phones from Europe will operate in Peru, but calls cannot be diverted to another line if the phone number dialled is unanswered. **Bellsouth** uses TDMA technology and their technical staff would have to see a foreign phone to verify its compatibility. European mobiles are not compatible with **Bellsouth**. If you need to have a mobile phone, it's best to buy one locally. All three companies sell phones, which take prepaid cards, special offers start as low as US$45. All mobile phone numbers are prefixed by 9.

Media

Newspapers and magazines

Lima has several daily papers. The most informative are *El Comercio*, www.elcomercioperu.com.pe/, and *La República*, www.larepublica.com.pe. Also with an online edition is *Expreso*, www.expreso.com.pe. *Gestión*, www.gestion.com.pe/, is a business daily. Very popular are the sensationalist papers, written in raunchy slang and featuring acres of bare female flesh on their pages. The main provincial cities have at least one newspaper each. There are a number of websites which provide regular news updates, including www.terra.com.pe and www.peru.com.

The most widely read magazine is the weekly news magazine *Caretas*, which gives a very considered angle on current affairs and is often critical of government policy, www.caretas.com.pe. A bi-monthly magazine called *Rumbos*, www.rumbos delperu.com (Spanish, English and German), is a good all-round 'what's happening in Peru' magazine.

Radio and TV

Radio is far more important in imparting news to Peruvians than newspapers, partly due to the fact that limited plane routes make it difficult to get papers to much of the population on the same day. There are countless local and community radio stations which cover even the most far-flung places. The most popular stations are *Radioprogramas del Perú* (www.rpp.com.pe), which features round-the-clock news, and *Cadena Peruana de Noticias* (www.cpnradio.com.pe).

A shortwave (world band) radio offers a practical means to brush up on the language, keep abreast of current events, sample popular culture and absorb some of the richly varied regional music. International broadcasters such as the **BBC World Service**, the **Voice of America**, Boston- (Mass) based **Monitor Radio International** (operated by *Christian Science Monitor*) and the Quito-based Evangelical station, **HCJB**, keep the traveller informed in both English and Spanish.

Compact or miniature portables are recommended, with digital tuning and a full range of shortwave bands, as well as FM, long and medium wave. Advice on models (£150 for a decent one) and wavelengths can be found in the *Passport to World Band Radio* (International Broadcasting Services Ltd, USA, £11.55). Details of local stations are listed in *World Radio TV Handbook*, Wohlfarth Gert GmbH, £12 (www.amazon.co.uk prices). Both of these, free wavelength guides and selected radio sets are available from the **BBC World Service Bookshop** ⓘ *Bush House Arcade, Bush House, Strand, London WC2B 4PH, UK, T020-7557 2576.*

Many hotels include televisions in rooms, the more expensive the hotel, the more cable channels there will be on the set. There will almost certainly be US channels, often the BBC, Italian and occasionally German channels. You can find movies, sports, music, nature/discovery and news (CNN in both English and Spanish). Local channels include **América Televisión** (www.americatv.com.pe), **Cable Mágico** (www.cablemagico.com.pe), **Frecuencia Latina** (www.frecuencialatina.com.pe) and **24 Horas** (www.24horas.com.pe).

Lima

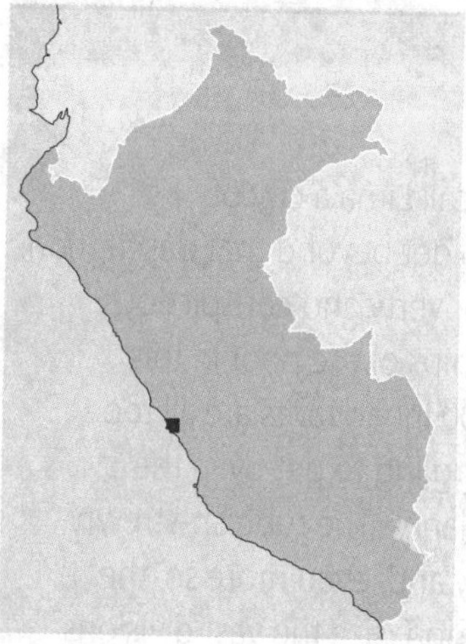

Footprint features

Introduction

The well-established cliché is to call Lima a city of contradictions, but it's difficult to get beyond that description. Here you'll encounter grinding poverty and conspicuous wealth in abundance. The hardships of the poor in this sprawling metropolis of 8,000,000 inhabitants are all too evident in the lives of those struggling to get by in the crowded streets and frantic bus lanes. The rubbish-strewn districts between airport and city and, even more so, the shanty towns on the outskirts emphasize the vast divisions within society. Most visitors, though, have the option of heading for Miraflores, San Isidro or Barranco, where smart restaurants and elegant hotels rub shoulders with pre-Inca pyramids, and neat parks and the cliff-top Larcomar shopping centre overlook the ocean. Lima's image as a place to avoid or quickly pass through is enhanced by the thick grey blanket of cloud that descends in May and hangs around for the next seven months. Wait until the blanket is pulled aside in November to reveal bright blue skies and suddenly all Limeños descend on the city's popular coastal resorts. Weekends then become a raucous mix of sun, sea, salsa and *ceviche*. Lima can also entertain, excite and inform. It boasts some of the finest historical monuments and museums in the country. The colonial centre, with its grand Plaza de Armas, fine churches and beautiful wooden balconies, is one of Peru's ten UNESCO World Heritage sites and strenuous efforts are being made to refurbish the historical districts. The city's cuisine has earned it the title 'Gastronomic Capital of the Americas' and the bars, discos and *peñas* of Barranco and Miraflores ring to the sounds of everything from techno to traditional music. Scratch beneath that coating of grime and decay and you'll find one of the most vibrant and hospitable cities anywhere.

★ Don't miss...

1. **Plaza de Armas** Step into the main square and try to imagine the days when it was the headquarters of Spain's South American empire, page 83.
2. **San Francisco** One of the city's original churches, with some beautiful decorations and a set of ghoulish catacombs, page 86.
3. **Larcomar** Looking for something contemporary? Here are shops, entertainment and watering holes carved out of the cliffs, page 93.
4. **Parque del Amor** One of Lima's most romantic places with its giant statue of lovers kissing and its view of the sea. If inspired to fly you can go parapenting nearby, page 93.
5. **Barranco** Another side of Lima and a must to visit for its nightlife and its fashionable modern art galleries, page 94.
6. **Pachacámac** Escape from the rush of the traffic at this vast pre-Columbian ceremonial centre, rescued from the desert sands. In the museum look for the statue that was the heart of the cult, page 98.
7. **Rosa Náutica** For the ultimate nostalgic dining experience, come to this restaurant on an old pier jutting into the Pacific, page 111.
8. **Petit Thouars market** Overload yourself with handicrafts in the largest concentration of ethnic goods in the country, page 118.

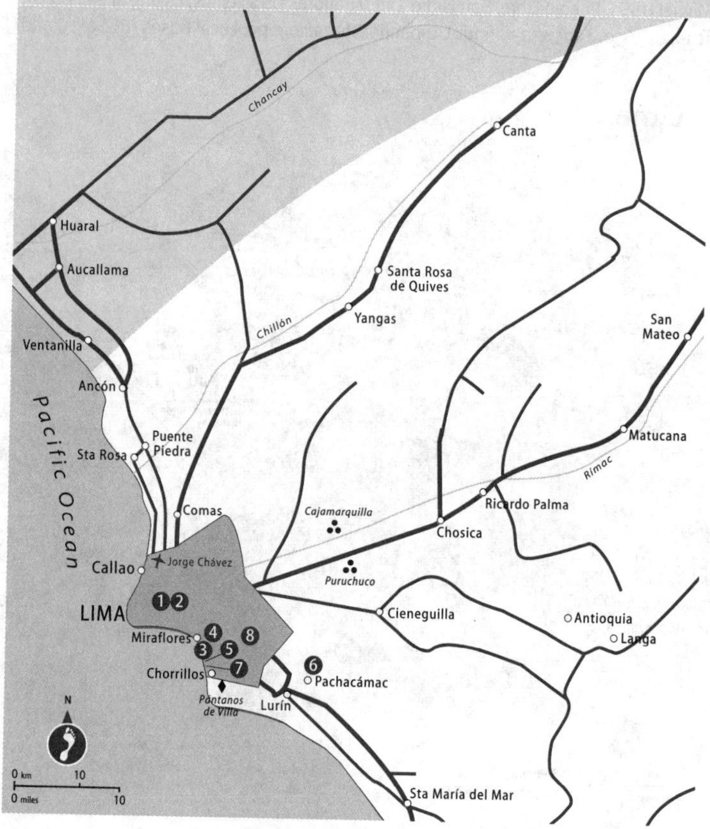

Ins and outs → *Phone code: 01. Colour map 5, A1. Population: 8,000,000.*

Getting there

All **international flights** land at Jorge Chávez Airport, some 16 km from the centre of the city. It is a little further to Miraflores and Barranco. Transport into town is easy if a bit expensive. Remise taxis (Mitsui or CMV) have representatives at desks outside International Arrivals and National Arrivals, US$7.25 to San Miguel, US$11.75 to the city centre, US$14.50 to San Isidro and Miraflores, US$17.50 to Barranco. This is the safest option, but also the most expensive. There are many taxi drivers offering their services outside Arrivals. **Taxi Green** has been recommended as reliable and economical. Regular taxis do not use meters, so make sure you fix the price before getting in and insist on being taken to the hotel of your choice, not the driver's. An illuminated sign outside the airport shows official taxi charges (eg US$10 to Miraflores) and there is usually a policeman monitoring the taxis. It helps to have exact change in soles to avoid having to break a large banknote along the way. If you are feeling confident and not too jet-lagged, go to the car park exit and find a taxi outside the perimeter, by the roundabout. They charge US$3-6 to the city centre. The security guards may help you find a taxi. All vehicles can enter the airport for 10 minutes at no charge. After that, it's S/.3.50 (US$1) per 30 minutes. Taxis that have been waiting for more than the allotted free time will try to make the passenger pay the toll upon leaving the airport. Always establish who will pay before getting in.

There is a bus service, **Urbanito,** from the airport to the centre, Breña and San Miguel US$3, Pueblo Libre, San Isidro and Miraflores US$5 (slow, calling at all hotels), T01-424 3650, T9957 3238 (mob), urbanito@terra.com.pe. Local buses (US$0.35) and

Lima

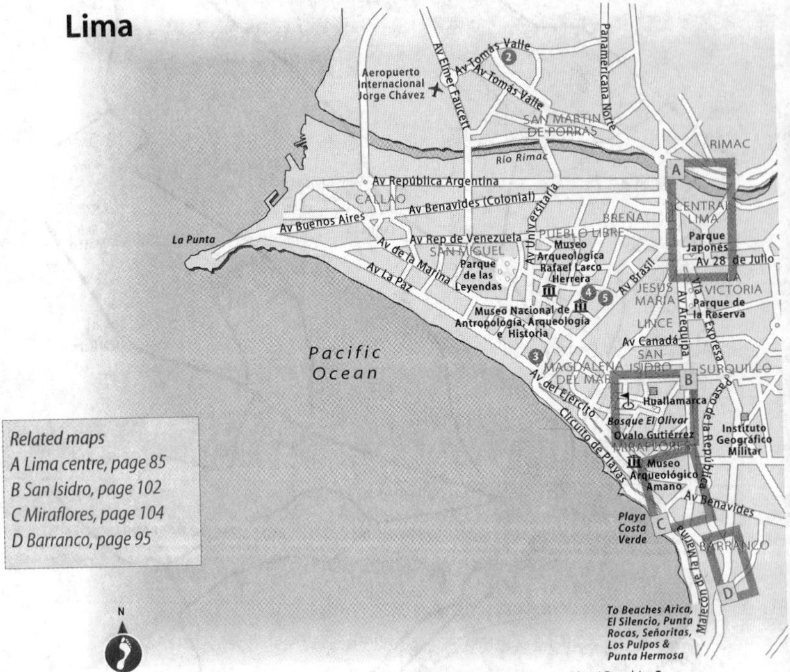

Sleeping
Guest House Marfil **5**
Hostal Bait Sababa **4**
Hostal Residencial Víctor **2**
Mami Panchita **3**

Arriving at night

Barring delays, there are usually no flight arrivals between 0100 and 0530. (There are money-changing facilities and information services to meet all flights.) However, as check-in time is supposed to be three hours before an international flight, and many flights depart from 0600 onwards, the airport starts to wake up between 0300 and 0400. No matter what time of night or day, though, there are people offering taxi rides into town and, as there are no hotels in the immediate vicinity of the airport, you must take some form of transport to get a bed and somewhere to stow your bags. Your best bet is to decide on a hotel before you even get to Lima. Most will arrange to pick you up from the airport, either free as part of the room rate, or for a fee of between US$12 and US$20 (depending on the category of hotel and how many people are in the vehicle). If you haven't arranged a room, don't leave the airport perimeter to find a public taxi or bus in the dark. The expensive *remise* services or the official taxis are the safest option. If you wish to stay in the airport until first light, the airport has seating areas and is safe.

colectivos run between the airport perimeter and the city centre and suburbs. Their routes are given on the front window: 'Tacna' is for the centre. Outside the pedestrian exit are the bus, *colectivo* and taxi stops, but there is more choice for buses at the roundabout by the car entrance. At busy times (which is any time other than very late at night or early morning) luggage may not be allowed on buses. Do not take the cheapest, stopping buses which go to the city centre along Avenida Faucett. They are frequently robbed. Pay a little more for a non-stopping bus.

The airport is the best and most cost-effective place to arrange car hire. The larger international chains – **Avis, Budget, Dollar, Hertz** – are usually cheaper and tend to have better-maintained vehicles than local firms.

If you arrive in Lima by **bus,** it is likely you'll pull into the main terminal at Jirón Carlos Zavala, just south of the historic centre of Lima. Take a taxi to your hotel even if it's close, as this area is not safe day or night. Some of the high-class bus companies have terminals in safer areas. » *For further details, see Transport page 122.*

Getting around

Downtown Lima can be explored on foot in the daytime, but take all the usual precautions. The central hotels are fairly close to the many of the tourist sites. At night taxis are a safer option. Many of the better hotels and restaurants are located in Miraflores and neighbouring San Isidro.

The streets of Lima

Several blocks, with their own names, make up a long street, which is called a *jirón* (often abbreviated to Jr). You will be greatly helped by corner signs which bear the name of both the *jirón* and the the block.

New and old names of streets are used interchangeably: remember that Colmena is also Nicolás de Piérola, Wilson is Inca Garcilaso de la Vega, and Carabaya is also Augusto N Wiese.

The Lima public transport system, at first glance very intimidating, is actually quite good. There are three different types of vehicle that will stop whenever flagged down: buses, combis, and *colectivos*. They can be distinguished by size; big and long, mid-size and mini-vans or cars, respectively. The flat-rate fare for the first two types of vehicle is US$0.35, the third costs a little more. On public holidays, Sunday and from 2400 to 0500 every night, a small charge is added to the fare. Always try to pay with change to avoid hassles, delays and dirty looks from the *cobrador* (driver's assistant). Routes on any public transport vehicle are posted on windscreens or written on the side. » *For further details, see Transport page 122.*

Best time to visit

Only 12° south of the equator, you would expect a tropical climate, but Lima has two distinct seasons. The winter is from May-November, when a damp *garúa* (sea mist) hangs over the city, making everything look greyer than it is already. It is damp and cold, 8° to 15°C. The sun breaks through around November and temperatures rise as high as 30°C. Note that the temperature in the coastal suburbs is lower than in the centre because of the sea's influence. You should protect yourself against the sun's rays when visiting the beaches around Lima, or elsewhere in Peru.

Tourist information

i perú has offices at **Jorge Chávez International Airport** ⓘ *T01-574 8000, daily 24 hrs*; at **Casa Basadre** ⓘ *Av Jorge Basadre 610, San Isidro, T01-421 1627, Mon-Fri 0830-1830*; and at **Larcomar shopping centre** ⓘ *Módulo 14, Plaza Gourmet, Miraflores, T01-445 9400, Mon-Fri 1200-2000*.

As an alternative, **Info Perú** ⓘ *Jr de la Unión (Belén) 1066, oficina 102, T01-424 7963, infoperu@qnet.com.pe, Mon-Fri 0930-1800, Sat 0930-1400*, is a very helpful office with lots of good advice; English and French spoken. Ask for the helpful free *Peru Guide*, published in English by **Lima Editora** (T01-444 0815), available at travel agencies or other tourist organizations.

A full-service travel agency rather than a tourist office, but highly recommended nonetheless, is **Fertur Perú** ⓘ *Jr Junín 211, Plaza de Armas, T01-427 2626, T427 1958; also at Schell 485, Miraflores, T01-242 1900, http://ferturperu.tripod.com, daily 0900-1900; in USA: T1-877 247 0055*. Run by Siduith Ferrer Herrera, it not only offers up-to-date, correct tourist information on a national level, but also great prices on national and international flights, discounts for those with ISIC and Youth cards and for **South American Explorers** members (of which she is one). Other services include flight reconfirmations, hotel reservations, transfers to and from the airport or bus stations and book exchange at the Junín branch.

South American Explorers ⓘ *Piura 135, Miraflores, T/F01-445 3306, T800 274 0568 (USA), www.saexplorers.org, Mon-Fri 0930-1700 (Wed until 2000) and Sat 0930-1300*. SAE is a non-profit educational organization which functions as a travel resource centre for South America and is widely recognized as the best place to get the most up-to-date information regarding everything from travel advice to volunteer opportunities. A yearly membership is currently US$50 per person and US$80 per couple. Services include access to member-written trip reports, a full map room for reference, an extensive library in English and a book exchange. Members can store luggage as well as valuables in their very secure deposit space. SAE sells official maps from the **Instituto Geográfico Nacional**, SAE-produced trekking maps, used equipment and a wide variety of Peruvian crafts. They host regular presentations on various topics ranging from jungle trips to freedom of the press. Discounts are available for students, volunteers and nationals. If you're looking to study Spanish in Peru, hoping to travel down the Amazon or in search of a quality Inca Trail tour company, they have the information you'll need to make it happen. South American Explorers, apart from the services mentioned above, is simply a great place to step out of the hustle and bustle of Lima and delight in the serenity of a cup of tea, a magazine and good conversation with a fellow traveller. SAE has other clubhouses in Cuzco, Quito (Ecuador), Buenos Aires (Argentina) and Ithaca, New York. Headquarters are located in the USA ⓘ *126 Indian Creek Rd, Ithaca, NY, 14850, T1-607 277 0488, www.saexplorers.org.*

Background

Lima, originally named *La Ciudad de Los Reyes*, the City of Kings, in honour of the Magi, was founded on Epiphany in 1535 by Francisco Pizarro. From then until the independence of the South American republics in the early 19th century, it was the chief city of Spanish South America. The name Lima, a corruption of the Quechua name *Rimac* (speaker), was not adopted until the end of the 16th century.

At the time of the Conquest, Lima was already an important commercial centre. It continued to grow throughout the colonial years and by 1610 the population was 26,000, of whom 10,000 were Spaniards. This was the time of greatest prosperity. The commercial centre of the city was just off the Plaza de Armas in the Calle de Mercaderes (first block of Jirón de la Unión) and was full of merchandise imported from Spain, Mexico and China. All the goods from the mother country arrived at the port of Callao, from where they were distributed all over Peru and as far away as Argentina.

At this time South American trade with Spain was controlled by a monopoly of Sevillian merchants and their Limeño counterparts who profited considerably. It wasn't until the end of the 18th century that free trade was established between Spain and her colonies, allowing Peru to enjoy a period of relative wealth. Much of this wealth was reinvested in the country, particularly in Lima where educational establishments benefited most of all.

After Francis Drake made a surprise attack on Callao on the night of 13 February 1579, plans were made to strengthen the city's defences against the threat from English pirates. However, an argument raged during the following century between Spain and Lima as to what form the defences should take and who should pay. Finally, it was agreed to encircle the city with a wall, which was completed by 1687.

Life for the white descendants of the Spaniards was good, although *criollos* (Spaniards born in the colonies) were not allowed to hold public office in Peru. The indigenous people and those of mixed blood were treated as lesser citizens. Their movements were strictly controlled. They weren't allowed to live in the city centre; only in areas allocated to them, referred to as *reducciones*.

There were few cities in the Old World that could rival Lima's wealth and luxury, until the terrible earthquake of 1746. The city's notable elegance was instantly reduced to dust. Only 20 of the 3000 houses were left standing and an estimated 4000 people were killed. Despite the efforts of the Viceroy, José Manso de Velasco, to rebuild the city, Lima never recovered her former glory. During the 19th century

Impressions of Lima

Ever since the earthquake of 1746 all but razed the city to the ground, descriptions of Lima have tended towards the unfavourable.

Take the German naturalist and traveller, Alexander Von Humboldt, for instance, who considered life in the city to be tedious with its lack of diversions, and described touring round the capital in 1802 thus: "The filthyness of the streets, strewn with dead dogs and donkeys, and the unevenness of the ground make it impossible to enjoy." Charles Darwin, who made a short visit in 1839 during his historic research trip on the *Beagle*, was no less graphic in his appraisal. He found it "in a wretched state of decay; the streets are nearly unpaved and heaps of filth are piled up in all directions where black vultures pick up bits of carrion."

Rather more complimentary was Jean Jacques Tschudi, the Swiss naturalist who made extensive explorations in Peru. He wrote: "The impression produced at first sight of Lima is by no means favourable, for the periphery, the quarter which the stranger first enters, contains none but old, dilapidated and dirty homes; but on approaching the vicinity of the principal square, the place improves so greatly that the miserable appearance it presents at first sight is easily forgotten."

The French feminist, Flora Tristan, who was Paul Gauguin's grandmother, came to Peru in 1834. She travelled extensively in the country and wrote a fascinating account of her experience, Peregrinaciones de una Paria, in which she painted Lima in a most favourable light: "The city has many beautiful monuments", she wrote: "The homes are neatly constructed, the streets well marked out, are long and wide." Paul Gauguin himself spent his formative years in Lima, where he was brought by his p arents who were fleeing Napoleon Bonaparte's France. Towards the end of his life Gauguin wrote a collection of memoirs in which he included his impressions of Lima.

man-made disasters rather than natural ones wreaked havoc on the capital and its people. The population dropped from 87,000 in 1810 to 53,000 in 1842, after the wars of Independence, and the city suffered considerable material damage during the Chilean occupation which followed the War of the Pacific.

Lima was built on both banks of the Rímac river. The walls erected at the end of the 17th century surrounded three sides while the Rímac bordered the fourth. By the time the North American railway engineer, Henry Meiggs, was contracted to demolish the city walls in 1870, Lima had already begun to spread outside the original limits. Meiggs reneged on his contract by leaving much of the wall intact in the poor area around Cercado, where the ruins can still be seen.

By the beginning of the 20th century the population had risen to 140,000 and the movement of people to the coastal areas meant that unskilled cheap labour was readily available for the increasing numbers of factories. Around this time, major improvements were made to the city's infrastructure in the shape of paved streets, modern sanitation, new markets and plazas. For the entertainment of the middle classes, a modern racetrack was opened in what is now the Campo de Marte, as well as the municipal theatre, the Teatro Segura. At the same time, the incumbent president, José Pardo, dramatically increased government expenditure on education, particularly in Lima.

Large-scale municipal improvements continued under the dictatorship of Augusto Leguía and the presidency of Oscar Benavides, who focused on education for the masses, housing facilities for workers and low-cost restaurants in the slum areas which were now growing up around Lima.

Lima, a city of over 8,000,000 people, continues to struggle to live up to its former reputation as the City of Kings. This has involved drastic changes in the last few years. The commercial heart has moved away from the centre of town and has taken root in more upmarket districts such as Miraflores and San Isidro. After suffering serious decline, the old centre is benefiting from great efforts to clean it up and is re-establishing itself as a place to visit. The city can, however, be seriously affected by smog at certain times of the year. It is also surrounded by *pueblos jóvenes*, or shanty settlements of squatters who have migrated from all parts of Peru looking for work and education (see box, page 97).

Sights

When Alberto Andrade Carmona became Mayor of Lima in 1995, he began a campaign to return the historic centre to its original beauty. This meant ejecting the ambulantes *(street sellers), cleaning the streets and pavements, and rehabilitating the Plaza de Armas and Plaza San Martín. He also mounted a security force called Serenazgo to enforce public safety and order, whose members are recognizable by their dark jump-suits, long night sticks and riot gear. The municipality of Lima has also begun a time-consuming balcony restoration project, soliciting businesses and citizens to take on the financial responsibility of a balcony in need. Although many buildings in the centre are not maintained, their architectural beauty and importance is still visible and worth seeing.* » *For Sleeping, Eating and other listings, see pages 100-130.*

Central Lima » *pp100-130.*

Plaza de Armas

One block south of the Río Rímac lies the Plaza de Armas, which has been declared a World Heritage site by UNESCO. The plaza used to be the city's most popular meeting point and main market. Before the building of the Acho bullring in the 1760s, bullfights were traditionally held here.

Around the great Plaza de Armas stand the **Palacio de Gobierno**, the **Cathedral**, the **Archbishop's Palace**, the **Municipalidad** and the **Club Unión**. In the centre of the plaza is a bronze fountain dating from 1650. The flower beds are planted with blooms whose colours reflect the city's celebrations, eg red and white at Independence in July, purple at El Señor de los Milagros in October.

Palacio de Gobierno

ⓘ *Plaza de Armas, www.peru.gob.pe/Palaciol/visitas.shtml. Tours in Spanish and English Mon-Fri 1400-1730, or 1100 for groups, 45 mins, free; book 2 days in advance at the Oficina de Turismo, of 201 (ask guard for directions); foreigners must take passport. Shorts may not be worn.*

The Government Palace stands on the site of the original palace built by Pizarro. When the Viceroyalty was founded, it became the official residence of the representative of the crown. Despite the opulent furnishings inside, the exterior remained a poor sight throughout colonial times, with shops lining the front facing the plaza. The façade was remodelled in the second half of the 19th century, then transformed in 1921, following a terrible fire. In 1937, the palace was totally rebuilt. The changing of the guard is at 1200.

The Cathedral

ⓘ *Plaza de Armas, T01-427 9647. Mon-Sat 0900-1630. All-inclusive entrance ticket is US$1.50.*

The Cathedral stands on the site of two previous buildings. The first, finished in 1555, was partly paid for by Francisca Pizarro on the condition that her father, the *Conquistador*, was buried there. A larger church, however, was soon required to complement the city's status as an archbishopric. In 1625, the three naves of the main building were completed while work continued on the towers and main door. The new building was reduced to rubble in the earthquake of 1746 and the existing church, completed in 1755, is a reconstruction on the lines of the original.

The interior is immediately impressive, with its massive columns and high nave. Also of note are the splendidly carved stalls (mid-17th century), the silver-covered altars surrounded by fine woodwork, mosaic-covered walls bearing the coats of arms of Lima and Pizarro and an allegory of Pizarro's commanders, the 'Thirteen men of Isla del Gallo'. The assumed remains of Francisco Pizarro lie in a small chapel, the first on the right of the entrance, in a glass coffin, though later research indicates that they reside in the crypt. There is a **Museo de Arte Religioso** in the cathedral, with free guided tours (English available, give tip), ask to see the picture restoration room.

Next to the cathedral is the **Archbishop's Palace**, rebuilt in 1924, with a superb wooden balcony.

Around the Municipalidad

Just behind the Municipalidad de Lima is **Pasaje Ribera el Viejo**, which has been restored and is now a pleasant place to hang out, with several good cafés with outdoor seating. The **Museo Filatélico** ⓘ *Central post office* (correos) *off Plaza de Armas, daily 0815-1300, 1400-1800, free*, contains an incomplete collection of Peruvian stamps and information on the Inca postal system. There is a stamp exchange in front of the museum every Saturday and Sunday, 0900-1300. You can buy stamps here as well, particularly commemorative issues.

Casa Aliaga ⓘ *Unión 224, T01-424 5110, tours only through Lima Tours*, is still occupied by the Aliaga family but has been opened to the public. It contains what is said to be the oldest ceiling in Lima and is furnished entirely in the colonial style. Don Jerónimo de Aliaga was one of the 13 commanders to arrive with Francisco Pizarro, all of whom were given land around the main square to build their own houses when Lima was founded in 1535.

Santo Domingo

ⓘ *Church and monastery on the first block of Jr Camaná, T01-427 6793. Mon-Sat 0900-1230, 1500-1800; Sun and holidays, mornings only. US$0.75.*

Built in 1549, the church is still as originally planned with a nave and two aisles covered by a vaulted ceiling, though the present ceiling dates from the 17th century. The cloister is one of the most attractive in the city and dates from 1603. The second cloister is much less elaborate. A chapel, dedicated to San Martín de Porres, one of Peru's most revered saints, leads off from a side corridor. Between the two cloisters is the Chapter House (1730), which was once the premises of the Universidad de San Marcos. Beneath the sacristy are the tombs of San Martín de Porres and Santa Rosa de Lima (see page 89). In 1669, Pope Clement presented the alabaster statue of Santa Rosa in front of the altar. The Basílica de La Veracruz is open at lunchtime. The main hall has some interesting relics.

Behind Santo Domingo is **Alameda Chabuca Granda**, named after one of Peru's greatest singers and composers. In the evening there are free art and music shows and you can sample food and sweets from all over Peru.

A couple of blocks beyond Santo Domingo is **Casa de Oquendo** or **Osambela** ⓘ *Conde de Superunda 298*. It is said that José de San Martín stayed here after proclaiming independence from Spain. The house is typical of Lima secular architecture with two patios and a broad staircase leading from the lower to the upper floor.

Lima centre

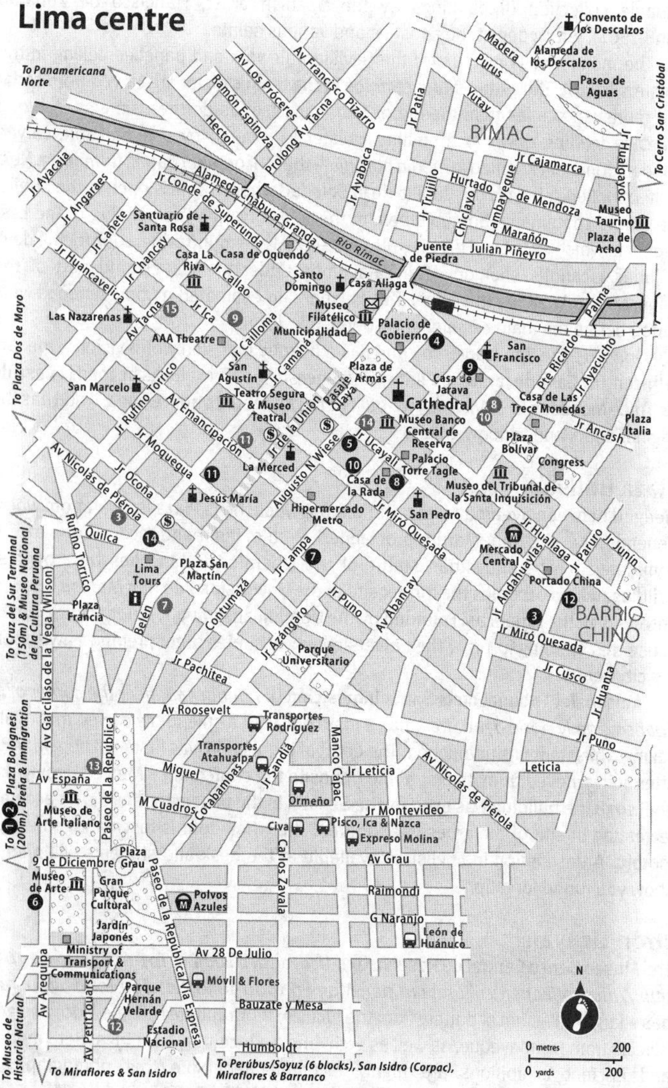

Sleeping
Familia Rodríguez **3**
Hostal Belén **7**
Hostal España **8**
Hostal Roma & Café Carrara **9**
Hostal San Francisco **10**
Kamana **11**
La Posada del Parque **12**
Lima Sheraton **13**
Maury **14**
Pensión Ibarra **15**

Eating
Azato **1**
Cordano **4**
El Maurito **5**
Govinda **6**
La Choza Náutica **2**
L'Eau Vive & Antaño **8**
Machu Picchu **9**
Manhattan **10**
Natur **11**
Neydi **7**
Salon Capon **12**
San Martín **14**
Wa Lok **3**

San Francisco and around

ⓘ *Church and monastery stand on the first block of Jr Lampa, corner of Ancash, T01-427 1381. Daily 0930-1730, guided tours only. US$1.50, US$0.50 children.*

The baroque church, which was finished in 1674, was one of the few edifices to withstand the 1746 earthquake. The nave and aisles are lavishly decorated in the Moorish, or Mudéjar, style. The choir, which dates from 1673, is notable for its beautifully carved seats in Nicaraguan hardwood and its Mudéjar ceiling. There is a valuable collection of paintings by the Spanish artist, Francisco de Zubarán (1598-1664), which depict the apostles and various saints.

The monastery is famous for the Sevillian tilework and panelled ceiling in the cloisters (1620). The 17th-century *retablos* in the main cloister are carved from cedar and represent scenes from the life of San Francisco, as do the paintings. A broad staircase leading down to a smaller cloister is covered by a remarkable carved wooden dome (nicknamed *la media naranja* – the half orange) dating from 1625. Next to this smaller cloister is the Capilla de la Soledad where a café is open to the public. The library contains 25,000 volumes. In the refectory, see the painting of the Last Supper in which Christ and his disciples are seated at a round table. Look for the devil at Judas Iscariot's shoulder. The catacombs under the church and part of the monastery are well worth seeing. This is where an estimated 25,000 Limeños were buried before the main cemetery was opened in 1808.

Opposite the San Francisco church is a historic mansion worth visiting, the late 16th-century **Casa de Jarava** or **Pilatos** ⓘ *Jr Ancash 390*. Two blocks beyond is **Casa de las Trece Monedas** ⓘ *Jr Ancash 536*, built in 1787 by counts from Genoa. It still has the original doors and window grilles.

Plaza Bolívar

Wedged between Avenida Abancay and Jirón Ayacucho is Plaza Bolívar, from where General José de San Martín proclaimed Peru's independence. The plaza is dominated by the equestrian statue of the Liberator. Behind lies the Congress building, which occupies the former site of the **Universidad de San Marcos**, the first university in the Americas. Founded by the Dominicans in 1551, students first began to use this building in 1574. The university now occupies other premises away from the city centre.

Museo del Tribunal de la Santa Inquisición ⓘ *Jr Junín 548, near the corner of Av Abancay, daily 0900-1700, free*, has a main hall with a splendidly carved mahogany ceiling which remains untouched. The Court of Inquisition was first held here in 1584, after being moved from its first home opposite the church of La Merced. From 1829 until 1938 the building was used by the Senate. In the basement there is an accurate recreation in situ of the gruesome tortures. The whole tour is fascinating, if a little morbid. A description in English is available at the desk and students will offer to show you round for a tip.

Jirón Ucayali

The **Museo Banco Central de Reserva** ⓘ *Jr Ucayali at Jr Lampa, T01-613 2000 ext 2655, http://museobcr.perucultural.org.pe/, Mon-Fri 1000-1630, Sat-Sun 1000-1300, free*, has a large collection of pottery from the Vicus or Piura culture (AD 500-600) and gold objects from Lambayeque, as well as 19th- and 20th-century paintings. Both modern and ancient exhibitions are highly recommended Note that photography is prohibited. It also contains the **Museo Numismático del Perú**.

The city's best surviving specimen of secular colonial architecture is **Palacio Torre Tagle** ⓘ *Jr Ucayali 363, access to the patio only Mon-Fri during working hours*, which was built in 1735 for Don José Bernardo de Tagle y Bracho, to whom King Philip V gave the title of First Marquis of Torre Tagle. The house remained in the family until it was acquired by the government in 1918. Today, it is still used by the Foreign Ministry, but

A fashion for passion

A unique form of women's dress worn by Lima's upper-class *mestizas* – women born in the colonies of Spanish origin – in the 18th century was the saya and *manto*. Both were of Moorish origin. The *saya* was an overskirt of dark silk, worn tight at the waist with either a narrow or wide bottom. The *manto* was like a thick black veil fastened by a band at the back of the waist where it joined the *saya*. It was brought over the shoulders and head and drawn over the face so closely that only a small, triangular space was left uncovered, sufficient for one eye to peep through. This earned them the title '*las tapadas*', or 'the covered ones'.

The fashion was created by Lima's mestizas in order to compete in the flirting stakes with their Spanish-born counterparts, whose tiny waists and coquettish fan-waving was turning men's heads. The *tapadas*, though veiled, were by no means modest. Their skirts were daringly short, revealing their appealingly tiny feet, and necklines plunged to scandalously low levels. The French feminist, Flora Tristan, was much taken with this brazen show. She commented: "I am sure it needs little imagination to appreciate the consequences of this time-honoured practice."

One consequence of this fashion, which ensured anonymity, was that Lima's *mestizas* could freely indulge in romantic trysts with their lovers. Often, however, they were content with some playful flirting – sometimes with their unwitting husbands. Another consequence of their anonymity was political. Many *tapadas* used their afternoon strolls to pass notes and messages to the organizers of the independence movement. This romantic and political intrigue usually took place on the Paseo de Aguas, a popular walkway of pools and gardens built by the Viceroy.

visitors are allowed to enter courtyards to inspect the fine, Moorish-influenced woodcarving in the balconies, the wrought ironwork and a 16th-century coach, complete with commode.

Opposite, **Casa de la Rada**, or **Goyoneche** ⓘ *Jr Ucayali 358*, is an extremely fine mid-18th-century town house in the French manner, which now belongs to a bank. The patio and first reception room are open occasionally to the public.

The church of **San Pedro** ⓘ *on the third block of Jr Ucayali, Mon-Sat 0930-1145, 1700-1800*, finished by Jesuits in 1638, has an unadorned façade, different from any other in the city. In one of the massive towers hangs a five-tonne bell called *La Abuelita* (the grandmother), first rung in 1590, which sounded the Declaration of Independence in 1821. The contrast between the sober exterior and sumptuous interior couldn't be more striking. The altars are marvellous, in particular the high altar, attributed to the skilled craftsman, Matías Maestro. The church also boasts Moorish-style balconies and rich, gilded woodcarvings in the choir and vestry, tiled throughout. The most important paintings in the church are hung near the main entrance. In the monastery, the sacristy is a beautiful example of 17th-century architecture. Also of note are La Capilla de Nuestra Señora de la O and the penitentiary. Several viceroys are buried below.

Jirón de la Unión

The Jirón de la Unión, the main shopping street, runs from the Plaza de Armas. It has been converted into a pedestrian precinct which teems with life in the evening. In the two blocks south of Jirón de la Unión, known as Calle Belén, several shops sell souvenirs and curios.

Guilt by inquisition

Established by Royal Decree in 1569, the Court of Inquisition was soon to prove a particularly cruel form of justice, even in the context of Spanish rule.

During its existence, the Church meted out many horrific tortures on innocent people. Among the most fashionable methods of making the accused confess their 'sins' were burning, dismemberment and asphyxiation, to name but a few. The most common form of punishment was public flogging, followed by exile and the not so appealing death by burning. Up until 1776, 86 people are recorded as having been burned alive and 458 excommunicated.

Given that no witnesses were called except the informer and that the accused were not allowed to know the identity of their accusers, this may have been less a test of religious conviction than a means of settling old scores. This Kafkaesque nightmare was then carried into the realms of surreal absurdity during the process of judgement. A statue of Christ was the final arbiter of guilt or innocence but had to express its belief in the prisoner's innocence with a shake of the head. Needless to say, not too many walked free.

The Inquisition was abolished by the Viceroy in 1813 but later reinstated before finally being proscribed in 1820.

La Merced ⓘ *Plazuela de la Merced, Unión y Miró Quesada, T01-427 8199, Mon-Sat 0800-1245, 1600-2000, Sun 0700-1300, 1600-2000; monastery 0800-1200 and 1500-1730 daily*, was the first church to be built in Lima, and it is said that it was the site where the first Mass took place. At Independence, the Virgin of La Merced was made a marshal of the Peruvian army. The restored colonial façade is a fine example of Baroque architecture. Inside are magnificent altars and some notable tilework on the walls. A door from the right of the nave leads into the monastery where you can see 18th-century religious paintings in the sacristy. The cloister dates from 1546.

A couple of blocks further on, the 18th-century **Jesús María** ⓘ *on the corner of Jr Moquegua and Jr Camaná, T01-427 6809, Mon-Sat 0900-1200, 1500-1700*, contains some of the finest paintings and gilded baroque altars in all of Lima.

South of Jirón de la Unión, the **Plaza San Martín** has a statue of the eponymous saint in the centre. The square has been restored and is now a nice place to relax.

San Agustín and around

The 1720 façade of **San Agustín** ⓘ *Corner of Jr Ica and Jr Camaná, west of the Plaza de Armas, T01-427 7548, 0830-1130, 1630-1900 (ring for entry)*, is a splendid example of Churrigueresque architecture. There are carved choir stalls and effigies, and a sculpture of Death, said to have frightened its maker into an early grave. Since being damaged in the last earthquake the church has been sensitively restored, but the sculpture of Death is in storage (to protect tourists of a more nervous disposition).

Museo Teatral ⓘ *Teatro Segura, Jr Huancavelica 265, T01-426 7189, 0900-1300, 1400-1700*, contains a collection of mementos and photographs of people who have appeared on the Lima stage.

AAA Theatre (Amateur Artists' Association) ⓘ *Jr Ica 323*, is in a lovely 18th-century house with an *azaguán*, a covered area between the door and patio, a common feature in houses of this period. Further along Ica is **Casa La Riva** ⓘ *Jr Ica 426*, which has an 18th-century porch and balconies, and a small gallery with some 20th-century paintings. It is run by the Entre Nous Society.

Las Nazarenas

ⓘ *Av Tacna, fourth block, T01-423 5718. Daily 0700-1200 and 1600-2000.*
This 18th-century church was built around an image of Christ crucified painted by a liberated slave in the mid-16th century. In the earthquake of 1655, the church collapsed but the painting on the wall remained intact. This was deemed a miracle and the painting became the most venerated image in Lima. Together with an oil copy of *El Señor de los Milagros* (Lord of Miracles), the image is encased in a gold frame and carried on a silver litter – the whole weighing nearly a ton – through the streets on 18, 19, and 28 October and again on 1 November (All Saints' Day). The whole city is decked out in purple. *El Comercio* newspaper and local pamphlets give details of times and routes.

Santuario de Santa Rosa

ⓘ *Av Tacna, first block, T01-425 1279. Daily 0930-1300, 1500-1800. Free.*
Santa Rosa is the first saint of the Americas and patron saint of Lima. Born on 20 April 1586, Rosa of Lima became a member of the third order of St Dominic and established an infirmary in her family home for destitute children and old people. She died at the age of 31 on 23 August 1617 and was beatified on 16 December 1668. Her day is 30 August. The small but graceful church was built in 1728 and contains the 'Little doctor' image of Jesus who helped Rosa cure the sick. Beyond the church is a sanctuary where she was born and lived. There is a tiny room where she would allow herself only two hours' sleep each night on a bed of two tree trunks with stones as pillows. A chapel was later built on the site.

The hermitage in the garden was built by Rosa herself and she would retire there to pray alone. The well, into which she threw the key to the padlocked chain around her waist, now receives thanksgivings and petitions for forgiveness from the faithful.

Southwest of the centre

Plaza Dos de Mayo is just over a kilometre west of the Plaza de Armas. About 1 km due south of this again is the circular **Plaza Bolognesi**, from which many major *avenidas* radiate.

San Marcelo ⓘ *Av de la Emancipación, fourth block*, is another church worth seeing for its two beautiful colonial doors. The interior is also remarkable, particularly the 18th-century gold-leaf high altar and pulpit and the religious paintings sited above attractive Sevillian tiles.

Museo Nacional de la Cultura Peruana ⓘ *Av Alfonso Ugarte 650, T01-423 5892, http://museodelacultura.perucultural.org.pe/, Tue-Fri 1000-1630, Sat 1000-1400, US$0.85, free guide in Spanish*, has an extraordinary mock Tiahuanaco façade and houses a rather disjointed collection of pre-Columbian and modern artefacts, including *mate burilado* (carved gourds), *retablos*, textiles, *keros* and *huacos* (pottery finds or artefacts). There are examples of ceramics and cloth from Amazonian tribes and a set of watercolours by Pancho Fierro, the 19th-century *costumbrista* artist.

South of the centre

South of the Plaza San Martín, the **Museo de Arte Italiano** ⓘ *Paseo de la República 250, T01-423 9932, Tue-Fri 0900-1900, Sat-Sun 1100-1700, US$1*, is in a wonderful neoclassical building, given by the Italian colony to Peru on the centenary of its independence. Note the remarkable mosaic murals on the outside. It consists of a large collection of Italian and other European works of art, including sculpture, lithographs and etchings. The museum now also houses the **Instituto de Arte Contemporáneo**, which has many exhibitions.

The **Gran Parque Cultural de Lima** (daily 0800-2030) was inaugurated in January 2000 by both the mayor of Lima, Alberto Andrade, and the then-president Alberto Fujimori. It has a medium-sized outdoor amphitheatre, Japanese garden, food court and children's activities. Relaxing strolls through this green, peaceful and safe oasis in the centre of Lima are recommended. Within the park is the **Museo de Arte** ⓘ *9 de Diciembre (Paseo Colón) 125, T01-423 4732, http://museoarte.peru cultural.org.pe/, Thu-Tue 1000-1700, US$3.65, free guide, signs in English*, which was built in 1868 as the Palacio de la Exposición. The building was designed by Alexandre Gustave Eiffel. There are more than 7000 exhibits, giving a chronological history of Peruvian cultures and art from the Paracas civilization up to today. They include excellent examples of 17th- and 18th-century Cuzco paintings, a beautiful display of carved furniture, heavy silver and jewelled stirrups and also pre-Columbian pottery. A *filmoteca* (cinema club) is on the premises and shows films almost every night; consult the local paper for details, or look in the museum itself.

Further southwest again is the **Museo de Historia Natural** ⓘ *Av Arenales 1256, Jesús María, T01-471 0117, Mon-Fri 0900-1500, Sat 0900-1700, Sun 0900-1300, US$1 (students US$0.50).* The museum belongs to the Universidad de San Marcos and its exhibits comprise Peruvian flora, birds, mammals, butterflies, insects, minerals and shells.

Northeast of the Plaza de Armas

From the Plaza de Armas, passing the Government Palace on the left, the **Desamparados Station** of the Central Railway lies straight ahead. The name, meaning 'the helpless ones', comes from the orphanage and church that used to be nearby.

Puente de Piedra, behind the Palacio de Gobierno, is a Roman-style stone bridge built in 1610. Until about 1870 it was the only bridge strong enough to take carriages across the river Rímac to the district of the same name. Though this part of the city enjoyed great popularity in colonial times, it can no longer be considered fashionable today.

Alameda de los Descalzos was designed in the early 17th century as a restful place to stroll and soon became one of the city's most popular meeting places. People of all social classes would gather here for their Sunday walk, some going up to the cross at the top of **Cerro San Cristóbal**. Today, however, you would be ill-advised to follow in their footsteps, as this is a dangerous area to wander around alone. Robberies are common in Rímac district and on Cerro San Cristóbal, so do not walk up; take a taxi (US$4.50). Worth visiting on the Alameda de los Descalzos, though, is the **Convento de los Descalzos** ⓘ *T01-481 0441, Wed-Mon 1000-1300, 1500-1800, US$1, by guided tour only, 45 mins in Spanish, worth it.* Founded in 1592, it now contains over 300 paintings of the Cuzco, Quito and Lima schools, which line the four main cloisters and two ornate chapels. The chapel of El Carmen was constructed in 1730 and is notable for its baroque gold-leaf altar. A small chapel dedicated to Nuestra Señora de la Rosa Mística has some fine Cuzqueña paintings. Opposite, in the chapel dedicated to La Señora de los Angeles, Admiral Grau made his last confession before the Battle of Angamos. The museum shows the life of the Franciscan friars during colonial and early republican periods. The cellar, infirmary, pharmacy and a typical cell have been restored. The library has not yet been incorporated into the tour (researchers may be permitted to see specific books on request). Near the Alameda is the **Paseo de Aguas**, which was also popular for a Sunday stroll in days gone by.

Tours in **Ofistur** combis ⓘ *every 15 mins, Sat and Sun 1000-2100, 1 hr, US$1.50*, depart from in front of Santo Domingo church. They go through the old *barrio* of Rímac and an improved ((but still rough) shanty town area up to the top of Cerro San Cristóbal for spectacular views over much of Lima. You pass the Inka Cola factory, too. Check the cloud level first, otherwise you will see very little.

Plaza de Acho, on Jr Hualgayoc, is the bullring, famous for once being the largest in the world and the first in Spanish America. It was inaugurated on 20 January 1766. Limeños have always been great enthusiasts of bullfighting and in 1798 a royal decree had to be passed forbidding fights on Sundays as people were failing to attend Mass. July is the month when the most famous fighters come from Spain for the Fiestas Patrias. The season also runs from October to the first week of December. Famous *toreros* practise in the Lima ring and fighting bulls are of Spanish stock. Next to the bullring is the **Museo Taurino** ⓘ *Hualgayoc 332, T01-482 3360, Mon-Fri 0800-1600, US$1, students US$0.50, photography US$2.* Apart from matadors' relics, the museum contains good collections of paintings and engravings, some of the latter by Goya. This, too, is in a dangerous area.

Barrio Chino

East of the historic centre of Lima in the district of Barrios Altos, next to the Mercado Central, is Lima's Chinatown (*barrio chino*). Peru is home to the largest population of first-generation Chinese in all of Latin America. Chinese people born in Peru (referred to as 'Tu-San') number more than a million. Some of the first immigrants arrived at the port of Callao in 1849 from the Chinese provinces of Canton and Fukien to work the coastal fields, replacing the black slaves given their freedom by then-president Ramón Castilla in 1851. More Chinese began to arrive, settling in the north in Chiclayo, Trujillo and the jungle town of Iquitos.

On the seventh block of Jirón Ucayali is the locally famous **Portada China**, the arch that stretches across the street and is the gateway to Chinatown. It was a gift from the Chinese government, officially inaugurated by Lima mayor Alberto Andrade in July 1997. ⏩ *For authentic Chinese cuisine in this area, see page 108.*

Museo de la Nación

ⓘ *Javier Prado Este 2465, San Borja, T01-476 9878. Tue-Sun 0900-1700, closed major public holidays; 4-hr tours are available. US$1.80, 50% discount with ISIC card. It is cold in the museum.*

This is the anthropological and archaeological museum for the exhibition and study of the art and history of the aboriginal races of Peru. There are good explanations in Spanish and English on Peruvian history, with ceramics, textiles and displays about many ruins in Peru. It is arranged so that you can follow the development of Peruvian pre-colonial history through to the time of the Incas. A visit is recommended before you go to see the archaeological sites themselves. There are displays on the tomb of the Señor de Sipán, artefacts from Batán Grande near Chiclayo (Sicán culture), reconstructions of the friezes found at Huaca La Luna and Huaca El Brujo, near Trujillo, and of Sechín and other sites. Also included is the **Museo Peruano de Ciencias de la Salud**, which has a collection of ceramics and mummies, plus an explanation of pre-Columbian lifestyle, divided into five sections: *micuy* (Quechua for food), *hampi* (medicine), *onccoy* (disease), *hampini* (healing) and *causay* (life). Temporary exhibitions are held in the basement, where there is also an Instituto de Cultura bookshop. The museum also has a cafetería.

To get to the museum from downtown Lima, take a combi with a window sticker that says 'Javier Prado/Aviación' from Av Garcilaso de la Vega. Get off at the 21st block of Javier Prado at Avenida Aviación. To get there from Miraflores, take a bus down Avenida Arequipa to Avenida Javier Prado (27th block), then take a bus with a window sticker saying 'Todo Javier Prado' or 'Aviación'. A taxi from down town Lima or from the centre of Miraflores costs US$2.

South and east of San Borja

South and east of San Borja are the districts of **Santiago de Surco** and **Monterrico**, upper and middle-class residential districts. Avenida Angamos Este and its continuation, Avenida Primavera, forms the boundary between San Borja and Surco. Primavera has become a new gastronomical centre in the city. ⏩ *For recommendations, see Eating, page 108.*

The **Museo de Oro del Perú y Armas del Mundo** ⓘ *Alonso de Molina 1100, Monterrico, T345 1271, 1130-1900, US$9*, has a huge, chaotic collection of gold and silver pieces, as well as exhibitions of textiles, weaponry and military uniforms. In 2001, a congressional committee, the **INC** (National Institute of Culture) and **Indecopi** (the Tourist Protection Bureau) declared that many of the metal objects, perhaps 98%, were fakes. If correct, that would represent fraud on a massive scale. The museum, nevertheless, remains on the tourist circuit.

Lima suburbs

» pp100-130.

Pueblo Libre

Museo Nacional de Antropología, Arqueología e Historia ⓘ *Plaza Bolívar, not to be confused with Plaza Bolívar in the centre, T01-463 5070, http://museonacional.perucultural.org.pe/, Tue-Sun 0930-1700, US$3.35, students US$1, guides available for groups*, is the original museum of archaeology and anthropology. On display are ceramics of the Chimú, Nazca, Mochica and Ichma (Pachacámac) cultures, various Inca curiosities, works of art and interesting textiles. The museum houses the Raimondi Stela and the Tello obelisk from Chavín (see page 362) and a reconstruction of one of the galleries there. It also has a model of Machu Picchu.

Next door is the **Museo Nacional de Historia** ⓘ *Plaza Bolívar, T01-463 2009, entry included in Antropología, Arqueología e Historia ticket*, housed in a mansion built by Viceroy Pezuela and occupied by San Martín (1821-1822) and Bolívar (1823-1826). The exhibits comprise colonial and early republican paintings, manuscripts, portraits, uniforms, etc. The paintings are mainly of historical episodes.

To get to both museums from the centre, take any public transport on Av Brasil with the window sticker 'Todo Brasil.' Get off at the 21st block and walk about five blocks down Vivanco. The museum will be on your left. From Miraflores, take bus SM 18 Carabayllo–Chorrillos, marked 'Bolívar, Arequipa, Larcomar', get out at block eight of Bolívar, by the Hospital Santa Rosa, and walk down Av San Martín five blocks till you see the 'blue line'; turn left. Taxi from downtown Lima US$2; from Miraflores US$2.

A very faded 'blue line' marked on the pavement links the Museo Nacional de Antropología, Arqueología e Historia to the **Museo Larco de Lima** (15 mins' walk) ⓘ *Av Bolívar 1515, T01-461 1312, www.museolarco.org, daily 0900-1800, US$7.55 (half price for students); texts in Spanish, English and French, guides, disabled access, no photography*. Located in an 18th-century mansion built on a seventh-century pre-Columbian pyramid, this museum houses the collection of the archaeologist Rafael Larco Herrera, which gives an excellent overview of the development of Peruvian cultures through their pottery. It has the world's largest collection of Moche, Sicán and Chimú pieces. There is a 'Gold and Silver of Ancient Peru' exhibition, a magnificent textile collection and a fascinating erotica section. Don't miss the storeroom with its vast array of pottery, unlike anything you'll see elsewhere. It is surrounded by beautiful gardens and has the **Café del Museo** (see Eating, page 109).

To get there, take any bus to the 15th block of Avenida Brasil. Then take a bus down Avenida Bolívar. Or, from Miraflores, take the SM 18 Carabayllo–Chorrillos, see above, to block 15 of Bolívar. A taxi from downtown, Miraflores or San Isidro takes 15 minutes and cost US$2.50.

The plain exterior of the church of **Santa María Magdalena**, on Jirón San Martín, conceals some fine ornamentation and art inside. **Parque de las Leyendas** ⓘ *La Mar, T01-464 4282, 0900-1730, US$2*, is arranged to represent the three regions of Peru: the coast, the mountainous sierra and the tropical jungles of the *selva*, with appropriate houses, animals and plants and a children's playground. It also contains a *huaca* from the Maranga culture, AD 500. The park gets very crowded at weekends. To get there from 24th block of Avenida de La Marina in San Miguel, take Avenida Parque Las

Leyendas. Bus 23 will get you there or take a *colectivo* from Avenida Abancay, or bus 135A or *colectivo* from Avenida La Vega. Just to the east of the park is the **Universidad Católica del Perú**.

San Isidro

The district of San Isidro combines some upscale residential areas, many of Lima's fanciest hotels and restaurants and important commercial zones with a huge golf course smack in the middle. Along Avenida La República is **El Olivar**, an old olive grove planted by the first Spaniards which has been turned into a beautiful park. It's definitely worth a stroll either by day or night.

Between San Isidro and Miraflores, is **Huallamarca** ⓘ *C Nicolás de Rivera 201 and Av Rosario, T01-222 4124, 0900-1700, closed Mon, US$1.75, take bus 1 from Av Tacna, or minibus 13 or 73 to Choquechaca, then walk.* This adobe pyramid of the Maranga culture is also known as the Pan de Azúcar and dates from about AD 100-500. There is a small site museum.

Miraflores

Miraflores, apart from being a nice residential part of Lima, is also home to a busy mercantile district full of fashionable shops, cafés, discos, fine restaurants and good hotels and guesthouses. As in the centre, there is a security force patrolling the streets, in trucks, on motorbikes or on foot.

In the centre of Miraflores is the beautiful **Parque Central de Miraflores** (aka **Parque Kennedy**) located between Avenida Larco and Avenida Oscar Benavides (locally known as Avenida Diagonal). This extremely well-kept park has a small open-air theatre with performances Thursday-Sunday, ranging from Afro-Peruvian music to rock'n'roll. Towards the bottom of the park is a nightly crafts market open from 1700 to 2300.

At the end of Avenida Larco and running along the promenade is the renovated **Parque Salazar** and the very modern shopping complex called **Centro Comercial Larcomar**. The shopping centre's terraces, which have been carved out of the cliff, contain expensive shops, hip cafés and restaurants, an open-air internet café and discos. The balustrades have a beautiful view of the ocean and the sunset. The 12-screen cinema is one of the best in Lima and even has a 'cine-bar' in the twelfth theatre. Don't forget to check out the Cosmic Bowling Alley with its black lights and fluorescent balls. A few hundred metres to the north is the renovated **Parque Champagnat** and then, across the bridge over the gorge, the famous **Parque del Amor** where on just about any night you'll see at least one wedding party taking photos of the newly married couple. Peruvians are nothing if not romantic.

The beach has a great view of the whole Lima coastline from Chorrillos to La Punta. **Rosa Náutica,** a very expensive restaurant/disco, see page 111, occupies a pier that juts out from the beach: a Lima dining institution for those willing to part with a nice chunk of cash.

The home of the author, poet and historian is now the **Museo Ricardo Palma** ⓘ *C General Suárez 189, T01-445 5836, Mon-Fri 0915-1245 and 1430-1700, small entrance fee; photography fee US$3.* Palma is one of Peru's most famous literary figures, best known for his work *Tradiciones Peruanas*, which covers the country's colonial period, see Literature page 599.

Huaca Pucllana ⓘ *at the intersection of C Borgoña y Tarapacá, near the 45th block of Av Arequipa, T01-445 8695, http://pucllana.perucultural.org.pe/, Wed-Mon 0900-1600, US$2, includes compulsory guide*, is a fifth- to eighth-century AD ceremonial and administrative centre of the pre-Inca Lima culture. The pyramid of small adobe bricks is 23 m high. Evidence of occupation of the site by the Wari culture was found in 2005. It has a site museum, alpacas, llamas, guinea pigs and a plant collection. See also Eating page 110.

Museo Arqueológico Amano ⓘ *C Retiro 160 near the 11th block of Av Angamos Oeste, T01-441 2909, open by appointment only Mon-Fri pm, free, photography prohibited*, is a very fine private collection of artefacts from the Chancay, Chimú and Nazca periods, owned by the late Mr Yoshitaro Amano. It boasts one of the most complete exhibits of Chancay weaving and is particularly interesting for pottery and pre-Columbian textiles, all superbly displayed and lit. To get there, take a bus or *colectivo* to the corner of Avenida Arequipa y Avenida Angamos and another one to the 11th block of Avenida Angamos Oeste. Alternatively a taxi from downtown costs US$2 or from Parque Kennedy US$1.

One of the best private collections of colonial paintings, silver, cloth and furniture in Peru is displayed in the **Poli Museum** ⓘ *Almte Cochrane 466, T01-422 2437, tours cost US$10 per person irrespective of the size of the group, allow 2 hrs, call in advance to arrange tours*. It also has a fine collection of pre-Columbian ceramics and gold, including material from Sipán. Guided tours are given in Spanish only and delivered rapidly by Sr Poli or his son, whose views are often contrary to long-held opinions about the symbolism of Peruvian cultures.

Barranco

South of Miraflores is Barranco, which was already a seaside resort by the end of the 17th century. During Spanish rule, it was a getaway for the rich who lived in or near the centre. Nowadays, Barranco is something of an intellectual haven, with artists' workshops and chic galleries.

No visit to Lima would be complete without a tour of Barranco's 'sights'.

The attractive public library, formerly the town hall, stands on the delightful plaza. Nearby is the interesting *bajada*, a steep path leading down to the beach, where many of Lima's artists live. The **Puente de los Suspiros** (Bridge of Sighs), leads towards the Malecón, with fine views of the bay.

Barranco is a quiet, sleepy suburb during the day but comes alive at night when the city's young flock here to party at weekends. Squeezed together into a few streets are dozens of good bars and restaurants.

An antique train that discontinued its Barranco-Lima service in 1965 now offers a pleasant, albeit very short ride (six blocks) down Avenida Pedro de Osma to the door of the museum of the same name. There is a video on board describing the train's history. It runs Tuesday-Sunday from 1000 to 1700, depending on the number of passengers. Tickets can be bought at the **Electricity Museum** ⓘ *Av Pedro de Osma 105, T01-477 6577, http://museoelectri.perucultural.org.pe/, US$0.70*.

Museo de Arte Colonial Pedro de Osma ⓘ *Av Pedro de Osma 421, T01-467 0915, open by appointment, US$3, bus 2, 54 or colectivo from Av Tacna*, has a private collection of colonial art of the Cuzco, Ayacucho and Arequipa schools. The number of visitors is limited to 10 at any one time.

Chorrillos

This district, beyond Barranco, has a redesigned, fashionable beachfront with mosaics and parks. It has always been a popular resort and is a good place to go to find fish restaurants. **Playa Herradura** is a little further on and is well-known for surfing. From Chorrillos you can get to some of the sites, such as Pachacámac and Pántanos de Villa, which are south of the city.

Lima beaches

Lima sits next to an open bay, with its two points at La Punta (Callao; see page 97) and Punta La Chira (Chorrillos). During the summer (December to March), beaches get very crowded on weekdays as much as at weekends, even though all the beaches lining the Lima coast have been declared unsuitable for swimming. Most beaches have very strong currents and extreme caution should be exercised.

Barranco

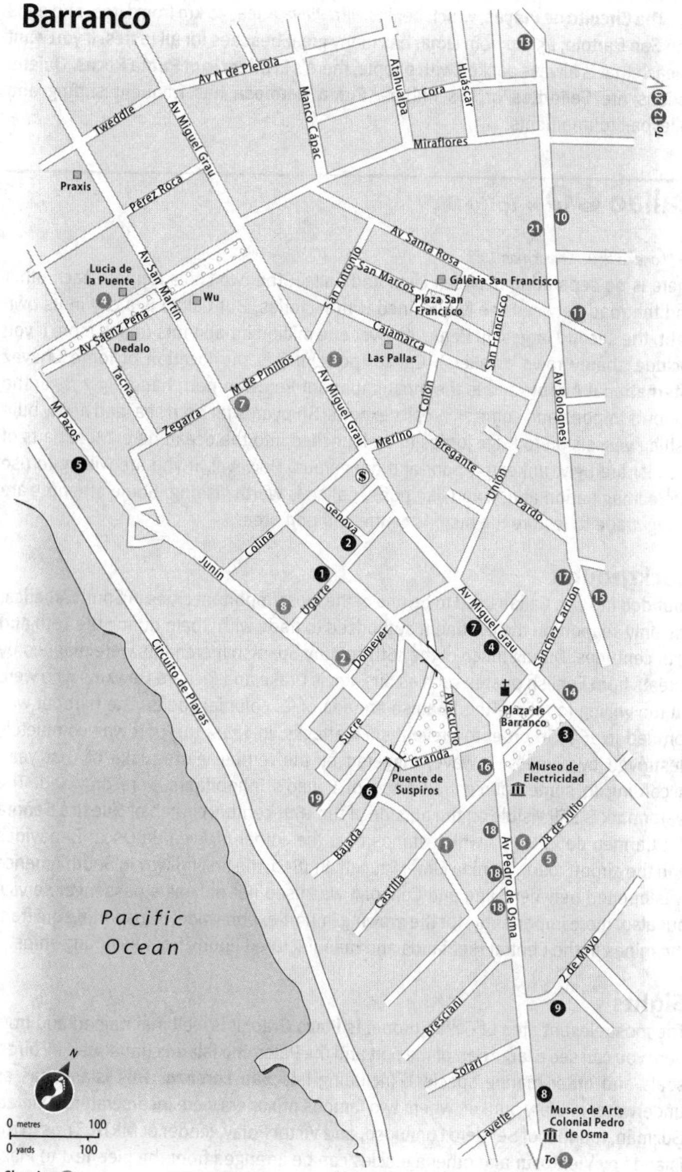

Sleeping
Barranco's Backpackers Inn **1**
Domeyer **2**
Hostal Gémina **3**
Hostal Los Girasoles **4**
La Quinta de Alison **5**
Mochileros Hostal **6**
Safe in Lima **9**
Suites California **7**
The Point **8**

Eating
Antica Trattoria **1**
Canta Rana **2**
El Hornito **3**
Festín **4**
La Costa Verde **5**
La Ermita **6**
Las Mesitas **7**
Manos Morenas **8**
Naylamp **9**

Bars & clubs
Bosa Nova **10**
De Rompe y Raja **11**
Del Carajo **12**
El Dragón **13**
El Ekeko & Las Terrazas **14**
La Candelaria **15**
La Estación de Barranco **16**
La Noche **17**
La Posada de Angel **18**
La Posada del Mirador **19**
Peña Poggi **20**
Sargento Pimienta **21**

Lifeguards are not always present. A stroll on the beach is pleasant during daylight hours but, when the sun goes down, the thieves come out and it becomes very dangerous. Needless to say, camping on the beach is a very idea.

The **Circuito de Playas**, which begins with Playa Arica, 30 km from Lima, and ends with San Bartolo, 45 km from Lima, has many great beaches for all tastes. If you want a beach that is always packed with people, there's **El Silencio** or **Punta Rocas**. Quieter options are **Señoritas** or **Los Pulpos**. **Punta Hermosa** has frequent surfing and volleyball tournaments.

Callao » *pp100-130.*

→ *Phone code: 01. Colour map 3, C3.*

There is no separation between Lima and Callao; the two cities run into each other and the road between the two is lined with factories. But Callao is a city in its own right, the second largest in Peru with over one million inhabitants (many more if you include shanty town dwellers). Callao (not Lima) is the location of **Jorge Chávez International Airport** and is the most important Peruvian port, handling 75% of the nation's imports and some 25% of its exports. Shipyards far from sea load newly built fishing vessels on to huge lorries to be launched into the ocean here. Most parts of the city are ugly, unkempt, poor and dangerous. However, if you are willing to use some imagination and, if you like ports, Callao is worth visiting. Some attempts are being made to restore the historic centre and port area.

Background

Founded in 1537, Callao used to be one of the most important cities in South America, the only seaport on the continent authorized to trade with Spain during the 16th and 17th centuries. During much of the 16th century Spanish merchants were plagued by threats from English pirates such as Sir Francis Drake and Richard Hawkins who were all too willing to relieve the Spanish armada of its colonial spoils. The harbour was fortified in 1639 in order to prevent such attacks. In 1746, the port was completely destroyed by a massive wave, triggered by the terrible earthquake of that year. According to some sources, all 6000 of Callao's inhabitants were drowned. The watermark is still visible on the outside of the 18th-century church of **Nuestra Señora del Carmen de la Legua** which stands near the corner of Avenida Oscar Benavides and the airport road, Avenida Elmer Faucett. In 1850, the first railway in South America was opened between Lima and Callao. It was used not only as a passenger service but also, more importantly, for the growing import-export trade, transporting ore from the mines in the Central Highlands and manufactured goods from incoming ships.

Sights

The most elegant area of Callao proper is **Plaza Grau**. It is well maintained and from here you can see a large part of the port and the **Palomino Islands** (inhabited by birds, seals and other marine species), including **Isla San Lorenzo**. This island has an underwater military bunker, where two famous prisoners were incarcerated, Abimael Guzmán, founder of Sendero Luminoso, and Víctor Polay, leader of MRTA. Trips to the islands by **Vientosur** and other agencies can be arranged from the pier next to Plaza Grau; ask around, as departures are mostly unscheduled.

Several houses surrounding the **Iglesia Matriz** have been restored, but generally the centre is in a state of permanent decay. **Museo Naval del Perú** ⓘ *Av Jorge Chávez 121, Plaza Grau, T01-429 4793, Tue-Sat 0900-1600, Sun 0900-1700, US$0.85*, has models of Peruvian and foreign ships, weapons, uniforms, torpedoes and other relics. There are also interesting photographs. It's recommended if you are in the area. **La Fortaleza Real Felipe** ⓘ *T01-429 0532, Tue-Sun 0900-1300, US$2 including*

Shanty towns

Known as *asentamientos humanos* or *pueblos jóvenes*, the shanty towns of Lima are monumental reminders of racial division and social inequality, and of the poverty in which more than half of the capital's population lives. Millions of people have no access to clean drinking water. Most of the Peruvians living in these settlements came from the provinces, escaping misery and the civil war of the 1980 and 1990s. They simply took the land on the hills surrounding Lima, only trying later to legalize their property.

There are old, 'established' shanty towns, like **Villa El Salvador**, with almost one million inhabitants, as well as new, rapidly expanding ones, like **Mi Perú** in Ventanilla, 20 km behind the Jorge Chávez airport. Some shanty towns, such as **Lurigancho** and **Canto Grande**, were controlled by Shining Path during the civil war. Others (around the Central Highway that leads towards the Andes) became famous for sheltering delinquents and drug addicts. There is even one shantytown housing Cuban exiles who escaped from the island looking for 'freedom' and a better life (now they wish they had stayed at home). Some settlements consist of bamboo shacks without roofs; others already have sound infrastructure, including markets, shops, even small restaurants and cafés.

Divisions in Peruvian society run very deep. Most of the shanty town dwellers don't even know of the existence of posh neighbourhoods like San Isidro and Miraflores. Needless to say, most inhabitants of the rich parts of Lima never visit shanty towns.

Some voyeuristic visitors feel a fascination for Lima's poorest districts. Villa El Salvador, one of the oldest and biggest shanty towns, is the only one that can be visited without much danger. The only safe way to travel is by hiring a taxi (round trip from Miraflores including an hour wait can be arranged for US$11.50). If you must go, travel only by day, wear modest clothes and, if you walk, stick to the main street. It is not recommended that you visit any other shanty towns. Almost without exception, they are dangerous, especially after dark. Every week, there are countless cases of robbery, stabbing, burglary and rape. Murder is not uncommon. Under no circumstances should you travel by public transport.

If you are planning to take a bus out of Lima, you will see many shanty towns along the highway.

guide, no cameras allowed, is an enormous Spanish castle standing in the heart of the city. It is still used by the Peruvian armed forces so you will have to negotiate entry with a lethargic guard. If you succeed, you will be provided with a military guide and the tour may take anything up to two hours. There are some interesting uniforms, arms and artefacts inside the castle, also plenty of cannons.

La Punta

Founded in 1555, La Punta is a green peninsula next to Callao. It has only 6800 permanent residents and enjoys the relaxed, nostalgic atmosphere of a beach resort, good local seafood restaurants, pleasant walks, friendly people and great views. It's an interesting place to come for lunch, but the ride back to Lima, even in a taxi, can be dangerous at night, as you have to drive through Callao proper.

La Punta's main artery, **Avenida Coronel Bolognesi**, is lined with impressive old villas. There is a well-maintained Malecón parallel to Bolognesi, a lovely walk and great views of the islands, sailing boats and Callao port. On the corner of El Malecón and Jirón García y García is the **Club de Regatas Lima**, with a nice café and view from the second floor (open sporadically). Nearby is the **Club de Regatas Unión**. Along El Malecón is a pebble beach, but the water is not very clean, due to the proximity of Callao port. **Plaza Grau** has been well restored, with a library inside the municipality building. It has no tourist pamphlets, but you can get information about the past and the present of La Punta there. At Plaza Grau bright pleasure boats, complete with life jackets, take trippers out to the end of La Punta beach and back. The journey takes about 25 minutes and costs US$1.

Around Lima » pp100-130.

Pántanos de Villa

ⓘ *Daily 0900-1700. US$1.55, guides available for groups of 15 (free).*

In the district of Chorrillos is the 396-ha wildlife sanctuary, Pántanos de Villa, an ecological wetland reserve with brackish water and abundant emergent vegetation. It provides the habitat for waterfowl typical of coastal Peru, including 17 species of migratory shorebirds. There are several species of fish, four types of reptile and over 50 species of water plants.

The visitors' centre has lots of information in Spanish. Allow up to two hours for a visit and take binoculars. Access is by the road which goes to the seaside district of La Villa; the nearest public transport stops about 1 km away, so it's best to take a taxi from Barranco, US$3.

Pachacámac

ⓘ *Lurín Valley, 31 km from Lima, T01-430 0168, http://pachacamac.perucultural.org.pe/. Daily 0900-1700; open on public holidays by appointment. US$1.65 including the small site museum.*

When the Spaniards arrived, Pachacámac was the largest city and ceremonial centre in coastal Peru. It was a vast complex of palaces and temple-pyramids, to which pilgrims paid homage, and where they obtained divinations from the oracle Pachacámac. A wooden statue of the god (a two-faced staff) is in the site museum. Hernando Pizarro came to Pachacámac in 1533, having been sent by his brother to speed the delivery of gold from the coast for Atahualpa's ransom. However, great disappointment awaited Pizarro as there was no store of riches. In their desperate search for the promised gold the Spaniards destroyed images, killed the priests and looted the temples. The ruins encircle the top of a low hill, whose crest was crowned with a **Temple of the Sun**, a large pyramid built in 1350 of sun-baked bricks, now partially restored. Slightly apart from the main group of buildings and hidden from view is the reconstructed **House of the Mamaconas**, where the 'chosen women' were taught to weave and spin fine cloth for the Inca and his court. Various other temples and palaces can be seen. Further to the north the Temple of Urpi-Huachac, who was reputed to be the wife of Pachacámac, is in a state of total ruin. The museum has a model of the city; there is also a café and toilets.

Cieneguilla

Cieneguilla, 20 km east of the centre of Lima, is a country town on the Lurín river, an easy escape from the city and its cloud cover. It is a popular place on Sunday, with restaurants with gardens and swimming, all of which open daily for lunch, recreation centres and cabins for longer stays. Take a combi running east on Avenida Prado Este. It takes around 30 to 45 minutes and costs US$0.50.

Puruchuco and around

In the eastern outskirts of Lima, near the stadium of La U football club, is **Puruchuco** ⓘ *End of Av Javier Prado Este, T01-494 2641, museopuruchuco.perucultural.org.pe. Tue-Fri 0830-1600, Sat and Sun 0900-1600. US$1.65*, the reconstructed palace of a pre-Inca Huacho noble. There is a very good site museum, Jiménez Borja, with ceramics and textiles from the lower Rímac or Lima valley (texts in Spanish and English). The palace is labyrinthine. This is also the site of a major archaeological find, announced in 2002. Under a shanty town called Túpac Amaru, over 2000 mummy bundles have been uncovered in an Inca cemetery known as **Puruchuco-Huaquerones**. The cemetery itself is not a new discovery, but the quantity and completeness of the mummies, plus the tens of thousands of accompanying objects, should reveal a wealth of information about the last century of Inca society before the Spanish conquest. It is clear that some of the mummies are of the Inca élite and all are well preserved. Archaeologists estimate that only 40% of the burials at the site have come to light. To see the tombs, ask the guards on Saturday morning if you can visit the archaeologists at work. The large adobe pre-Inca city of **Cajamarquilla** ⓘ *Daily 0900-1700. US$1.75*, can also be visited. The turnoff (left, at Huachipa) is about 6 km on from the Puruchuco turn. The site cannot be seen from the road; look for a sign 'Zona Arqueológica' in the middle of a brickyard. Keep on driving through the yard, and Cajamarquilla is at the end of an ill-kept dirt road.

Also in the eastern suburbs, the vintage car collection of Jorge Nicolini is open to the public as the **Museo del Automóvil Antiguo** ⓘ *Av La Molina cuadra 9, esquina Totoritas, Urb Sol La Molina, Lima 12, T01-368 0373, www.museodelautomovil nicolini.com*. Cars from 1901-1973 are on display. You can also visit the workshop where the cars are restored and can get involved in the restoration process.

Ancón

Ancón, 30 km northwest of Lima, is reached by a double-lane asphalted highway. In the 19th and early 20th centuries, this was the smart seaside resort in Peru, but has now been deserted by the wealthy and in summer is crowded with day trippers. It has a mix of elegant 19th-century houses with wooden balconies and modern apartment blocks. There are tennis courts and a yacht club. The beaches are very small and crowded during January-March holidays, but bathing is safe with no currents. Beyond Ancón is a **Chancay cemetery**, the source of much weaving and pottery, as seen in the Museo Amano (see page 94).

Canta → *Colour map 3, B4. Altitude: 2837 m.*

Canta is a popular small town on the fringes of the high Andes less than three hours from Lima by paved road. After 1½ hours, by which time the *garúa* has been left behind, you pass through **Santa Rosa de Quives**, the birthplace of the patron Saint of Lima. Her house and the adjoining sanctuary can be visited. After two hours the petrogylphs of **Checta** are reached. Numerous small, complex drawings cover the surface of boulders spread across a hillside 15-minutes' steep walk from the road. The path is marked.

Canta itself was founded by the Spanish in 1535. It lies on one of the initial main routes down from the mines of the sierra to Lima. It is not especially attractive, but there are good day walks and significant ruins nearby. On the main street is the **tourist office** ⓘ *T01-244 7013, Sat and Sun 1000-1600 only.*

The pre-Inca ruins of **Cantamarca** (3600 m) were probably built by the Chancay culture. They consist of large *chullpas* (burial towers) made from finely cut stone, many with roofs still supported by stone pillars. Take a steep trail from 5 km up the road to La Viuda. Allow two to three hours for the climb and carry water.

A few kilometres beyond Canta is Huaros (3587 m) from which a long day walk can be made to the **Parque Arqueológico de Huischo** and the **Bosque de Puyos Raimondis** (4050 m). Beyond Huaros the road continues to the beautiful Lake Chuchun below the 14 snow-capped peaks of the Cordillera de La Viuda.

Obrajillo

At weekends Limeños flock to this village set in beautiful countryside criss-crossed by fast-flowing streams. Eat in the main plaza or try the trout *chicharrones* and *pachamanca* at riverside restaurants. You can visit the waterfall (US$0.30), or go riding (US$4 per hour). A one-hour walk runs up the south side of the valley, on the opposite side to the waterfall, to **Santa Rosa de Acochaca** where there is a restaurant and shop. Returning on the opposite side of the valley a detour can be made to **San Miguel** (one hour), giving a bird's eye view of Obrajillo, before descending a steep path to the village (15 minutes).

Sleeping

All hotels in the upper price brackets charge 19% state tax (IVA) and a service charge on top of prices. In hotels foreigners pay no IVA and the amount of service charged is up to the hotel. Neither is included in prices below, unless indicated otherwise.

The central colonial heart of Lima is not as safe at night as the more upmarket areas of San Isidro, Miraflores or Barranco. If you are only staying a short time in the city and want to see the main sights, the centre is convenient, but do take care. San Isidro is the poshest district, while Miraflores has a good mix of places to stay, great ocean views, bookstores, restaurants and cinemas. From here you can commute to the centre by bus (30-45 mins) or by taxi (20-30 mins). Barranco, which is more bohemian, is a little further out.

Near the airport

There are lots of other places to stay on Av Tomás Valle, but they are almost without exception short stay and unsafe.

B-C Hostal Residencial Víctor, Manuel Mattos 325, Urb San Amadeo de Garagay, Lima 31, T01-567 5083, hostalvictor@terra.com.pe. 5 mins from the airport by taxi, or phone or email in advance for free pickup, large comfortable rooms, with bath, hot water, cable TV, free luggage store, free internet and 10% discount for Footprint book owners, American breakfast, evening meals can be ordered locally, mall with restaurants, fast food and gym nearby, very helpful, owner Víctor Melgar has a free reservation service for Peru and Bolivia. Recommended.

Central Lima *p83, map p85*

L Lima Sheraton, Paseo de la República 170, T01-315 5000, reservas@sheraton.com. pe. A 5-star hotel located on the edge of downtown Lima in an imposing building, with large casino on the ground floor. Gym, pool, tennis courts and shops, but the restaurants offer poor value. Check for special offers, as low as our **B** range.

B Maury, Jr Ucayali 201, T01-428 8188, hotmaury@amauta.rcp.net.pe. Breakfast included. The most luxurious hotel in the historic centre, fancy, secure and very clean.

B-C Kamana, Jr Camaná 547, T01-426 7204, www.hotelkamana.com. A comfortable, safe hotel with very friendly staff, TV, French and some English spoken, restaurant attached.

C Hostal La Posada del Parque, Parque Hernán Velarde 60, near 2nd block of Av Petit Thouars, Santa Beatriz, T01-433 2412, www.incacountry.com. A charmingly refurbished old house in a safe area, excellent bathrooms, cable TV, breakfast US$3 extra, airport transfer 24 hrs for US$14 for up to 3 passengers, no credit cards. The owners speak good English. Recommended as excellent value.

D Hostal Roma, Jr Ica 326, T/F01-427 7576, www.hostalroma.8m.com. With bathroom, **E** without bath, hot water all day, safe to leave luggage, basic but clean, often full, internet extra but good, motorcycle parking (**Roma Tours**, helpful for trips, reservations, flight confirmations, Errol Branca speaks English). Highly recommended.

E-F Hostal de las Artes, Jr Chota 1460, Breña, T01-433 0031, http://arteswelcome .tripod.com/. A nice colonial building with a small garden in one patio. Price is for room with bath; **F** without bath (no singles with bath), **G** per person in dormitory, Dutch-owned, English spoken, clean, safes in rooms and safe luggage store, gay and lesbian-friendly, solar hot water system, welcoming, book exchange, airport transfer US$12. Recommended.

E-F Hostal Iquique, Jr Iquique 758, Breña, T01-433 4724, http://barrioperu.terra.com.pe/hiquique. With bathroom, **F** without bath, clean but noisy and draughty, friendly, use of kitchen, warm water, storage facilities, rooms on the top floor at the back are best. Repeated recommendations.

F Hostal San Francisco, Jr Azángaro 125-127, T01-426 2735, hostalsf@lanpro.com.pe. Dormitories with and without bathrooms, new, safe, Italian/Peruvian owners, good service, internet and cafeteria.

G per person **Familia Rodríguez**, Av Nicolás de Piérola 730, 2nd floor, T01-423 6465, jotajot@ terra.com.pe. With breakfast, clean, friendly, popular, some rooms noisy, will store luggage, also has dormitory accommodation with only one bathroom (same price), transport to airport US$10 per person for 2 people, US$4 per person for 3 or more, good information, secure. Recommended.

G Hostal Belén, Belén 1049, just off San Martín, T01-427 8995. Discount for groups of 3 or more but give prior notice, Italian spoken, simple breakfast extra, hot water, basic, noisy, clean, friendly.

G Hostal España, Jr Azángaro 105, T01-427 9196, www.hotelespanaperu.com. **F** with private bath (3 rooms), **G** in the dorm. A fine old building, hot showers, friendly, English and French spoken, internet service, motorcycle parking, luggage store (free), laundry service, don't leave valuables in rooms, roof garden, good café, can be very busy.

G per person **Hostal Machu Picchu**, Av Juan Pablo Fernandini 1015 (block 10 of Av Brasil), Breña, T01-9794 4257. Family-run, rooms with shared bathroom only, hot water, cheap, kitchen facilities, cable TV, laundry service, excellent value.

G Pensión Ibarra, Av Tacna 359, 14th-16th floor, T/F01-427 8603 (no sign), pensionibarra@ekno.com. Breakfast US$2, discount for longer stay. Use of kitchen, balcony with views of the city, clean, friendly, very helpful owner, hot water, full board available (good small café next door).

Lima suburbs

Pueblo Libre *p92*

F per person **Guest House Marfil**, Parque Ayacucho 126, at the 3rd block of Bolívar, T01-261 1206, cosycoyllor@yahoo.com. Clean and friendly, English spoken, breakfast, kitchen facilities and laundry free of charge, internet service, Spanish classes can be arranged, family atmosphere. Recommended.

G Hostal Bait Sababa, Av San Martín 743, near the hospital, T01-261 4990, baitsababa@hotmail.com. In the home of a Jewish family who speak Spanish, English and Hebrew, very helpful, Fri evening meal provided, restaurants, laundry, internet and phone offices nearby.

San Isidro *p93, map p102*

LL Country Club, Los Eucaliptos 590, T01-611 9000, www.hotelcountry.com. An excellent hotel offering fine service and luxurious rooms with individual designs, thoroughly classically stylish. Safes in rooms, cable TV, free internet for guests, good bar and restaurant.

LL-L Swissôtel Lima, Vía Central, Centro Empresarial Real, T01-421 4400, reservations lima@swissotel.com. Beautiful hotel with excellent 5-star service, 2 superb restaurants including **Le Café**, swimming pool.

LL-AL Sonesta Posada del Inca El Olivar, Pancho Fierro 194, T01-712 6000, www.sonesta.com/peru_lima/. A luxurious hotel in a modern olive-green building , with a lawn in front and a park opposite, one of the top 5-star hotels in Lima. Rates vary according to season; look out for weekend deals. Many eating options, bar, garden, swimming pool, gym, quiet, popular with business visitors.

L Libertador San Isidro Golf, Los Eucaliptos 550, T01-442 1995, www.libertador.com.pe. Member of the **Libertador** group, overlooking the golf course, full facilities for business travellers, comfortable rooms, bar, gym, sauna, jacuzzi, fine service, good restaurant. Recommended. Head office at Las Begonias 441, of 240, T01-442 1995. Hotels also in Arequipa, Cuzco, Mancora, Puno, Tambopata, Trujillo, Valle del Colca, Urubamba and Valle Sagrado.

L-AL Sofitel Royal Park, Av Camino Real 1050, T01-215 1616, www.sofitel.com. Another excellent hotel with charming rooms, part of the French group, prices can be negotiated. Highly recommended.

A Garden Hotel, Rivera Navarrete 450, T01-442 1771, reservas@gardenhotel.com.pe. Includes breakfast and internet access. Good, large beds, shower, small restaurant, ideal for business visitors, travel agency, close to Ormeño bus terminal. Recommended.

C Sans Souci, Av Arequipa 2670, T01-422 6035, F441 7824. Breakfast included in the price. Clean, safe, friendly, good services and restaurant, garden, garage.

San Isidro

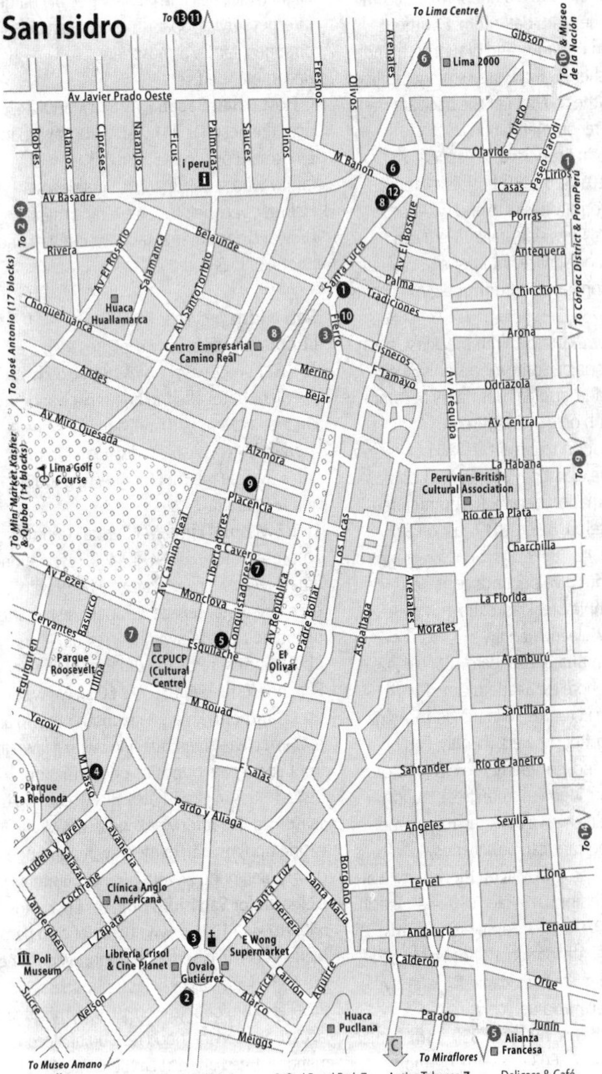

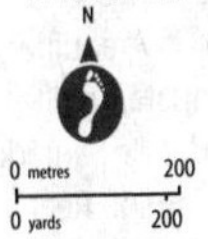

Sleeping
Albergue Juvenil Malka 1
Country Club & Le Perroquet 2
Garden 10
Home Perú 5
Hospedaje Elizabeth Ballon 9
Libertador 4
Sans Souci 6
Sofitel Royal Park 7
Sonesta Posada del Inca El Olivar 3
Swissôtel Lima 8

Eating
Alfresco 1
Antica Pizzería 13
Antica Taberna 7
Asia de Cuba 5
Bohemia 2
Café Olé & Pastelería Montserrat 10
Chez Philippe 11
chilis 3
Delicass & Café Positano 4
Fuji 14
Matsuei 6
News Café 8
Segundo Muelle 9
Valentino 12

E Hospedaje Elizabeth Ballon, Av del Parque Norte 265, San Isidro, T01-9980 07557, hospedajeebr@yahoo.fr. Family house in residential area 7 mins' walk from Cruz del Sur bus station. Shared or private bathrooms, TV room, laundry, luggage store, breakfast included, airport transfers US$13.

F per person **Albergue Juvenil Malka**, Los Lirios 165 (near 4th block of Av Javier Prado Este), T01-442 0162, hostelmalka @terra.com.pe. Youth hostel, 20% discount with ISIC card, dormitory style, 4-8 beds per room, English spoken, cable TV, laundry, kitchen, nice café, climbing wall. Highly recommended.

Miraflores *p93, map p104*

LL JW Marriott, Malecón de la Reserva 615, T01-217 7000, www.marriott.com. Buffet breakfast is included. Across from Larcomar shopping centre, wonderful views from its towers, pool, fitness centre and health club, two restaurants, tennis court.

LL Miraflores Park, Av Malecón de la Reserva 1035, T01-242 3000, www.mira -park.com. At the top of the range in Lima, an Orient Express hotel with excellent service and facilities, beautiful ocean views from the luxurious rooms. Check with the hotel for monthly offers. Highly recommended.

LL-L Apart Hotel Las Américas, C General Borgoño 116, T01-241 3350, aparthotel @hoteleslasamericas.com. Suites equipped with kitchenette, good café (**Café 21**), conveniently located at the corner of Av José Pardo.

L Las Américas, Av Benavides 415, T01-444 7272, hotel@hoteleslasamericas.com. In the same group as Apart Hotel Las Américas, this is a tall, silvery, glass-fronted building, 5-star, with a commercial centre, pool, gym and restaurant. Buffet breakfast is included.

L-AL Sol de Oro, Jr San Martín 305, T01-610 7000, www.soldeoro.com.pe. Price includes buffet breakfast. Secluded but convenient for the centre of Miraflores, very pleasant, with jacuzzi, sauna, room service, and laundry.

AL La Hacienda, 28 de Julio 511 y Av Larco, T01-213 1000, www.bwlahacienda.com. Breakfast included. English spoken, excellent service, free internet, casino.

AL-A Antigua Miraflores, Av Grau 350 at C Francia, T01-241 6116, www.peru-hotels -inns.com. A small hotel in a quiet but central location, with gym, cable TV and good restaurant. Has enjoyed a high reputation, but latest reports suggest a dip in standards.

AL-A La Paz Apart Hotel, Av La Paz 679, T01-242 9350, www.lapaz.com.pe. Apartments with bath, kitchen, lounge, cable TV, convenient, very clean and comfortable, helpful staff. Recommended.

AL-A Sonesta Posada del Inca, Alcanfores 329, T01-241 7688, www.sonesta.com/peru_ miraflores. A member of this recommended chain of hotels, 28 rooms in a mustard-coloured building, conveniently located, cable TV, a/c, restaurant.

A Ariosto, Av La Paz 769, T01-444 1414, www.hotelariosto.com.pe. Price includes buffet breakfast. A large, modern block of glass and concrete, with friendly staff, 24-hr medical assistance and all other services, travel agency and airport transfer. Recommended.

A Casa Andina, Av 28 de Julio 1088, T01-241 4050, www.casa-andina.com. One of another recommended chain of hotels. All have similar facilities and decor (others in the Cuzco area, Puno, Arequipa and Nazca). Very neat, with many useful touches, such as smoke detectors, emergency lighting and local maps given to all guests. Friendly service, comfortable beds, 10 mins free internet, a/c, fridge, safe, laundry service, deliveries from KFC, Burger King and Pizza Hut, buffet breakfast, other meals available. Discounts for internet booking.

A José Antonio, 28 de Julio 398, T01-445 7743, www.hotelesjoseantonio.com. This clean, friendly hotel and restaurant is good in all respects. Price includes buffet breakfast, huge rooms, large bathrooms with jacuzzis, cable TV, room service, helpful staff speak some English, internet, swimming pool, business facilties. Recommended.

B Alemán, Arequipa 4704, T01-445 6999, www.hotelaleman.com.pe/. No sign for this comfortable hotel, which is clean, friendly and quiet, with very good service. It has a garden, excellent breakfast is included in the price, free internet, enquire about laundry service.

B Colonial Inn, Comandante Espinar 310, T01-241 7471, coloinn@terra.com.pe. Price includes breakfast. A colonial-style hotel with excellent service, but it can be noisy from traffic, parking.

Miraflores

N

0 metres 50
0 yards 50

Sleeping

Albergue Turístico Juvenil Internacional **1** *D3*
Albergue Verde **5** *D2*
Alemán **32** *A3*
Antigua Miraflores **2** *B1*
Apart Hotel Las Américas **3** *A2*
Ariosto **4** *D2*
Casa Andina **43** *D2*
Casa de Baraybar **11** *A1*
Colonial Inn **6** *A2*
El Carmelo **7** *B1*
El Zaguán Lodging **40** *D3*
Eurobackpackers **39** *C1*
Explorer's House **37** *A1*
Flying Dog Backpackers **9** *C2*
Friend's House **10** *C1*
Friend's House 2 **8** *C1*
Hogar del Mochilero **36** *A1*
Home Perú **38** *A3*
Hospedaje Atahualpa **12** *A3*
Hospedaje José Luis **34** *D3*
Hostal El Patio **14** *C2*
Hostal Esperanza **15** *C3*
Hostal La Castellana **17** *C2*
Hostal Lucerna **18** *D1*
Hostal Señorial **19** *D1*
Hostal Torreblanca **31** *A1*
Huaychulo **16** *A2*
Inka Lodge **13** *A2*
José Antonio **21** *C1*
La Hacienda **22** *C1*
La Paz Apart Hotel **23** *C2*
Las Américas **24** *C2*
Lex Luthor's House **25** *C1*
Loki Backpackers **20** *B3*
Marriott **26** *D1*
Miraflores Park **42** *D1*
Pensión Yolanda **33** *B3*
Residencial El Castillo Inn **27** *C3*
San Antonio Abad **28** *D3*
Sipán **35** *D2*
Sol de Oro **29** *C1*
Sonesta Posada del Inca **30** *C2*
Stop & Drop **44** *B2*
Wayruro's Backpackers **45** *A2*

Eating

Astrid y Gaston **2** *C3*
C'est Si Bon **35** *A2*
Café Café **5** *B2*
Café de la Paz **6** *B2*
Café Voltaire **7** *B3*
Café Z **27** *B2*
Chef's Café **8** *C2*
Coco de Mer **9** *B1*
Cuarto y Mitad **41** *A2*
Dalmacia **38** *D1*
Dino's Pizza **34** *A2*
Dove Vai **10** *B2*
El Beduino **36** *D2*
El Kapallaq **43** *B3*
El Parquetito **12** *B2*
El Rincón Gaucho **37** *D1*
Haiti **13** *B3*
Heladeria 4D **14** *A3*
Il Postino **15** *C3*
La Gloria **16** *B3*
La Palachinke **17** *B2*
Las Brujas de Cachiche **4** *B1*
La Tiendecita Blanca **18** *B3*
La Tranquera **19** *B2*
La Trattoria **20** *B3*
Las Tejas **21** *C2*
Madre Natura **39** *A3*
Pardo's Chicken **22** *D2*
Pizza Street **23** *B2*
Ricota & Café Tarata **25** *C2*
San Antonio Café **33** *A3*
Sandwich.com **3** *B2*
Señorio de Sulco **40** *A1*
Sí Señor **28** *B1*
Super Rueda **26** *B2*
Tapas Bar **46** *B3*
Vivaldi **29** *B3*
Wa Lok **42** *A3*
Zugatti **30** *C2*

Bars & clubs

Media Naranja **31** *B2*
Murphys **32** *C2*
The Old Pub **45** *B2*
Voluntarios Pub **24** *B2*

B Hostal Esperanza, Esperanza 350, T01-444 2411, http://barrioperu.terra.com.pe/htlesperanza. Modern, convenient, good hot water, very helpful staff and manager, café, bar, secure, good value.

B Hostal La Castellana, Grimaldo del Solar 222, T01-444 4662, lacastellan@terra.com.pe. Pleasant, with a nice garden, safe, good value, but the restaurant is expensive, laundry, English spoken, special price for **South American Explorers** (SAE) members. Recommended.

B Hostal Lucerna, Las Dalias 276 (parallel with 12th block of Larco), T01-445 7321, hostallucerna@terra.com.pe. Friendly, safe, clean, quiet, cosy, excellent value, but breakfast, drinks and restaurant are expensive. Recommended.

B Hostal Torreblanca, Av José Pardo 1453, 1 block from the seafront, T01-447 0142, www.torreblancaperu.com. Includes breakfast and airport pickup. A caramel-coloured building on Plaza Centro América, at the quiet end of Miraflores. Bilingual receptionists, nice lounge, laundry, **A Fuego Lento** restaurant and bar, cosy rooms, will help with travel arrangements.

B San Antonio Abad, Ramón Ribeyro 301, T01-447 6766, www.hotelsanantonioabad.com. Clean, secure, quiet, good service, welcoming, tasty breakfasts, one free airport transfer with reservation. Frequently recommended.

B-C Hostal El Patio, Diez Canseco 341, T01-444 2107, www.hostalelpatio.net. Includes continental breakfast, reductions for long stays. The patio has a fountain, lots of flowers and bird cages; there are terraces for sitting outside. Very nice suites with big bathroom and kitchen, clean, comfortable standard rooms, gay-friendly, English and French spoken, convenient, very good value, airport pickup US$14.

C El Carmelo, Bolognesi 749, T01-446 0575, carmelo@amauta.rcp.net.pe. With bath and TV, in a great location a couple of blocks from the Parque del Amor, small restaurant downstairs serving *criolla* food and *ceviche*, price includes breakfast, good value and comfortable.

C Hostal Señorial, José Gonzales 567, T01-445 9724, senorial@viabcp.com. Includes buffet breakfast, comfortable, friendly, nice garden. Recommended.

C Huaychulo, Av 2 de Mayo 494, T01-242 8671, www.huaychulohotel.com. Secure, helpful, German owner-manager also speaks English, price includes continental breakfast, cable TV.

C Sipán, Paseo de la República 6171, T01-447 0884, www.hotelsipan.com. Breakfast is included in price. Very pleasant, a blue hotel in a residential area overlooking the Paseo, rooms with bath, cable TV, fridge, security box, internet and room service. Meals in the restaurant available if booked in advance. Free airport transfers available.

D Casa de Baraybar, Toribio Pacheco 216, T01-441 2160, www.casadebaraybar.com. One block from the ocean, extra long beds, breakfast included, TV, 24-hr room service, laundry, airport transfers free for stays of 3 nights or more. Bilingual staff, internet. Recommended.

D El Zaguán Lodging, Av Diez Canseco 736, T01-446 9356, www.elzaguanlodging.com. Price includes breakfast. No sign to this hotel that looks like a private residence near Parque Las Tradiciones, small, quiet and comfortable, with breakfast, internet, cable TV, cheaper with shared bath.

D **Hostal Mami Panchita**, Av Federico Gallessi 198, T01-263 7203, San Miguel, www.mamipanchita.com. Dutch- Peruvian owned, English, French, Dutch, Spanish and German spoken, includes breakfast and welcome drink, comfortable rooms with bath, hot water, living room and bar, patio, email service, book exchange, have their own **Raymi Travel agency** (good service), 15 mins from Miraflores, 20 mins from historic centre. Recommended. Several chicken places and *chifas* nearby around Mercado Magdalena.

D-E Home Perú, Av Arequipa 4501 (no sign), T01-241 9898, www.homeperu.com. In a 1920s mansion on the busy avenue, huge rooms, antiques in the public areas, with breakfast (cheaper without), rooms with and without bath, **E-F** per person with shared bath in group rooms. Welcoming and helpful, use of kitchen, luggage store, English spoken, laundry service, internet, near Plaza Vea hypermarket. Can help with bus and plane tickets, connected to other *hostales* in the country.

D-E per person **Hospedaje Atahualpa**, Atahualpa 646c, T01-447 6601. Cheaper without bath, including breakfast, long-stay rates available, parking, hot water, cooking and laundry, luggage store, taxi service.

E per person **Inka Lodge**, Elias Aguirre 278, T01-242 6989, www.inkalodge.com. Also with dorms (**F** per person), convenient, excellent breakfast included, internet, laundry, very helpful.

E per person **Hostal José Luis**, Francisco de Paula Ugarriza 727, San Antonio, T01-444 1015, www.hoteljoseluis.com. Price includes breakfast. Rooms with bath, hot water, safe, quiet, clean, internet, kitchen facilities, friendly, English spoken.

E Pensión Yolanda, Domingo Elias 230, T01-445 7565, pensionyolanda@hotmail.com or erwinpension@yahoo.com. Price includes breakfast. English and French spoken, family house, quiet, safe, laundry, book exchange, internet and luggage store. They have travel information, can reserve flights and hotels.

E per person **Residencial El Castillo Inn**, Diez Canseco 580, T01-446 9501. All rooms with private bath and hot water, in a family home where you can use the lounge, negotiate for longer stay.

E per person **Stop and Drop**, Berlín 168, p 2, T01-243 3101, www.stopandrop.com. **D** double rooms with private bath and breakfast. Backpacker hotel and guesthouse, also Spanish school. Bar, kitchen facilities, luggage store, laundry, TV, films, internet, games, comfortable beds, safe, hot showers 24 hrs, adventure sports and volunteer jobs. Airport pickup US$17.

E-F per person **Eurobackpackers**, Manco Cápac 471 (no sign, look for the cat with the world on his stick), T01-791 2945, www.eurobackpackers.com. Dorm and double rooms, basic breakfast included in price, family atmosphere, comfortable, safe, free internet. Good reputation but rooms downstairs are not as airy as those on 1st floor.

F per person **Albergue Turístico Juvenil Internacional**, Av Casimiro Ulloa 328, San Antonio between San Isidro and Miraflores, T01-446 5488, www.limahostell.com.pe. Youth hostel, dormitory accommodation, **D** in a double private room, US$2.50 discount for IHA card holders. Basic cafeteria for breakfasts, travel information, lounge with cable TV, laundry facilities, extra charge for use of minimal kitchen facilities, swimming pool often empty, clean and safe, situated in a nice villa. Recommended.

F per person **Albergue Verde**, Grimaldo del Solar 459, T01-445 3816, www.albergueverde.com. Nice small *hostal*, comfortable beds, **C** per person in double, friendly owner, Arturo Palmer, breakfast included, airport transfers US$15.

F per person **Explorer's House**, Av Alfredo León 158, T01-241 5002, explorers_house@yahoo.es. No sign, but plenty of indications of the house number, like a family home in a residential street. With breakfast, dormitory accommodation with shared bath, or double rooms with bath, hot water, use of kitchen, laundry service, Spanish classes, English spoken, TV lounge with DVD and video, very welcoming.

F per person **Flying Dog Backpackers**, Diez Canseco 117, T01-445 6745, www.flyingdog.esmartweb.com. Dormitories (some very small) or private rooms, shared bath (**D-E** in en suite rooms, with and without bath). This is a popular place so it's best to reserve through the web. Very central, comfortable, hot water, secure, friendly, free internet and local calls, lounge with DVD and videos, book exchange, kitchen facilities. Full transport information and tickets can be arranged.

F Friend's House, Jr Manco Cápac 368, T01-446 6248, friendshouse_peru@yahoo. Com.mx. Dormitory accommodation. Hot water, cable TV, use of kitchen and internet at no cost, book exchange, includes breakfast, very popular with backpackers, near Larcomar shopping centre, plenty of good information and help. Highly recommended. They have another branch at José Gonzales 427, T01-446 3521. **E** per person with bath, same facilities, except private rooms only and more like a family home. Neither branch is signed.

F per person **Hogar del Mochilero** (Backpacker's Home), Jr Cesareo Chacaltana 162, T01-446 3268, maurosilva@hotmail. com. Rooms for 5-6 people, with bath and hot water, internet access a little extra, pleasant, quiet, a short walk from all main facilities, airport transfer, use of kitchen, Mauro speaks English; he and his wife, Mila, are very helpful. Recommended.

F per person **Loki Backpackers** (formerly Incahaus), Av Larco 189, T01-242 4350, www.lokihostel.com. Restored house built in the 1920s, period details but with modern facilities. Right in the heart of Miraflores, the capital's sister to the party hostel of the same name in Cuzco, **D** in double room, good showers, with breakfast (cooked breakfast extra), Fri barbecues, use of kitchen, free internet, lockers, airport transfer extra.

F Wayruro's Backpackers, Enrique Palacios 900, T01-444 1564, www.wayruros.com. Bed and breakfast, comfortable dormitories, kitchen facilities, free tea and coffee, cheap bar, 24-hr hot water, laundry service, luggage storage, internet, TV, airport pickup.

G per person **Lex Luthor's House**, Porta 550 (look for the green lights), T01-242 7059, luthorshouse@hotmail.com. Breakfast included. Pleasant house, small and basic but clean, friendly, use of kitchen, good value.

Barranco *p94, map p95*

C Domeyer, C Domeyer 296, T01-247 1413, domeyerhostel@peru.com. Friendly, clean, hot water 24 hrs, laundry service, secure, welcomes gay and lesbian travellers.

C Hostal Gémina, Av Grau 620 in Galerías Gémina, T01-477 0712, hostalgemina @yahoo.com. A modern building whose exterior belies the interior with its old radios and sewing machines and its comfortable rooms. Price includes breakfast, with bath, hot water, TV, café, internet.

C per person **Suites California** (aka **Villa Barranquina**), Martínez Pinillos 129, corner with San Martín, T01-477 0772, hcalifor@viabcp.com. If you are looking for a flat, this would be a good choice. Fully equipped flatlets can sleep up to 4 (**D** per person), in a fascinating 1906 mansion, kitchen, lounge with sofa beds, bathroom, good bedrooms. Also has good restaurant and laundry services for guests.

D per person **Safe in Lima**, Alfredo Silva 150, T01-252 7330, www.safeinlima.com. A quiet,

comfortable Belgian-run guesthouse, very helpful with travel information, airport pick-up. Rooms have private bathroom, breakfast included. Also a tour operator, see page 122.
E La Quinta de Alison, Av 28 de Julio 281, T01-247 1515. Breakfast extra. A modern building with lovely rooms, TV and bath, hot water, some rooms with jacuzzi (extra), excellent value, parking. Recommended.
F per person **Barranco's Backpackers Inn**, Malecón Castilla 260, T01-247 1326, www.barrancobackpackers.com. Shared rooms, with lockers, hot water in bathrooms, breakfast included. If you want a private double room, the price is **D**. Kitchen, laundry service, internet access, modern.
F Hostal Los Girasoles, Av Saenz Peña 210, T01-247 6379, losgirasoles@hotmail.com. On a pleasant street near art galleries, simple rooms off a long corridor, some have TV, with bath and hot water, no breakfast.
F per person **Mochileros Hostal**, Av Pedro de Osma 135, 1 block from main plaza, T01-447 4506, backpackers@backpackersperu.com. Beautiful house, friendly English-speaking owner, huge shared rooms with lockers (**D** in double room), use of kitchen, good pub on the premises, a stone's throw from Barranco nightlife. Gay-friendly.
F per person **The Point**, Malecón Junín 300, T01-247 7997, www.thepointhostels.com. 80-year-old house with doubles and large dorms, all with shared bath. Very popular with backpackers (book in advance at weekends), breakfast included, internet, cable TV, laundry, kitchen facilities, welcomes gay travellers, party atmosphere. **Pointless Pub**, open from 2000, weekly barbecue, therapeutic massage, can arrange bungee jumping, flight tickets and volunteering. Airport pickup US$12.

Callao *p96*

It is not recommended that you sleep in the centre of Callao as it becomes a dangerous red-light district after sunset. There is, however, a safe place in La Punta:

La Punta *p97*

A-E La Punta, Jr Saenz Peña 486-490, La Punta, T/F01-429 1553, info@bed-and-breakfast-la-punta.com. Price includes breakfast, a variety of rooms in a recently restored 1930s mansion, with and without bath, spacious common rooms, patio, cable TV.

Around Lima

Canta *p99*

Arrive by lunchtime at weekends because all hotels fill up.
E Cancay Vento, T01-441 5733. Friendly, clean, hot water, big bathrooms, cable TV, swimming pool. Changes US$.
F Alborada, is the best of several more basic hotels here, hot water and TV.
F Hospedaje Casa Blanca, Arica 402, T01-526 0282. With bath, hot water, TV, clean.

Obrajillo *p100*

E Hostal Cabaña, Obrajillo, T01-244 7135, posadaobrajillo@hotmail.com. On the Canta side of the village. The best in town.
F Hostal Dodero, T01-244 7190, is the best of the *hostales* in Obrajillo.

Camping

Camping in Obrajillo is possible at the waterfall (US$3 per tent) and above Santa Rosa de Acochaca.

Eating

In restaurants, both foreigners and Peruvians have to pay 19% state tax (IVA) and the service charge.

Central Lima *p83, map p85*

Pasaje Olaya, on the Plaza de Armas between Jr de la Unión and Jr Carabaya, is a small pedestrian walkway with many nice restaurants frequented during lunch hours by executives. A bit on the pricey side but good. Other good places, though a little touristy, can be found in the passage behind the Municipalidad.

A variety of Lima's better-known restaurants and cafés have branches on **Av Primavera**: **Antica Pizzería** (no 275, T01-372 2698) and **Delicass** (no 654, T01-372 5203), both also in San Isidro; a branch of the **San Antonio Café** chain (see Miraflores, Cafés, page 112), and the main branch of **T'Anta** (see below).

TTT-TT **T'Anta**, Av Primavera 692, T01-372 3528, chacarilla@tanta.com.pe. Coffeeshop-cum-restaurant which specializes in the *novo andino* cuisine of Gastón Acurio (see **Astrid & Gastón**, page 110), excellent desserts too; other branches in Miraflores, San Isidro and central Lima.

TT **Antaño**, Ucayali 332, opposite the Torre Tagle Palace, T01-426 2372 . Good, typical Peruvian food, nice patio. Recommended.

TT **La Choza Náutica**, Jr Breña 204, close to Plaza Bolognesi, Breña. Good *ceviches* and friendly service in this old favourite.

TT **L'Eau Vive**, Ucayali 370, opposite the Torre Tagle Palace, T01-427 5612. Run by nuns, Mon-Sa, 1230-1500 and 1930-2130, fixed-price lunch menu, Peruvian-style in interior dining room, or à la carte in either of the dining rooms that open onto the patio, excellent, profits go to the poor, Ave Maria is sung nightly at 2100.

TT **Manhattan**, Jr Miró Quesada 259. Open Mon-Fri 0700-1900, low-end executive-type restaurant serving local and international food from US$5-10, good.

TT **Wa Lok**, Jr Paruro 864, Barrio Chino, T01-427 2656. Owner Liliana Com speaks fluent English and is very friendly. Highly recommended *chifa*.

TT-T **El Maurito**, Jr Ucayali 212, T01-426 2538. Serves Peruvian and international food, good *pisco sours*.

TT-T **San Martín**, Av Nicolás de Piérola 890, off Plaza San Martín. Typical Peruvian food from both coast and highlands, good value, reasonably cheap.

T **Azato**, Av Arica 298, 3 blocks from Plaza Bolognesi, Breña, T01-423 4369. Excellent and cheap Peruvian dishes.

T **Centro de Medicina Natural**, Jr Chota 1462. Next door to **Hostal de las Artes**, serving very good vegetarian.

T **Cordano**, Jr Ancash 202. Typical old Lima restaurant/watering hole, slow service and a bit grimy but full of character. Definitely worth the time it takes to drink a few beers.

T **Govinda**, Av Garcilaso de la Vega 1670, opposite Gran Parque de Lima. A good vegetarian restaurant which also sells natural products.

T **Kin Ten**, Ucayali y Paruro, Barrio Chino. Excellent vegetarian options at this *chifa*.

T **Machu Picchu**, near **Hostal Europa** at Jr Ancash 312. Huge portions, grimy bathrooms (to say the least), yet very popular, closed for breakfast.

T **Natur**, Moquegua 132, 1 block from Jr de la Unión, T01-427 8281. Vegetarian, the owner, Humberto Valdivia, is one of the **South American Explorers'** advisers, good for food and casual conversation.

T **Neydi**, Puno 367. Good, cheap seafood, open daily 1100-2000, popular.

T **Salon Capon**, Jr Paruro 819, Barrio Chino, is a highly recommended *chifa*. Has another branch in Larcomar shopping centre, Miraflores, which is TTT, elegant, equally recommended.

Cafés

Café Carrara, Jr Ica 330, attached to **Hostal Roma**. Open daily 0700-2200, multiple breakfast combinations, pancakes, sandwiches, nice ambience, good.

Lima suburbs

Pueblo Libre *p92*

TTT-TT **Café del Museo** at the Museo Larco, Av Bolívar 1515, Pueblo Libre, T01-461 1312, www.cafedelmuseo.com. Daily 0900-1800. Seating inside and on the terrace. Another Gastón Acurio restaurant, specially designed interior. Salads, fine Peruvian dishes, pastas and seafood, a tapas bar of traditional Peruvian foods, as well as snacks, desserts and cocktails. Highly regarded.

TT-T **Antigua Taberna Quierolo**, Av San Martín 1090, 1 block from the plaza with the Museo Nacional de Antropología y Arqueología. An atmospheric old bar with glass-fronted shelves of bottles, a marble bar and old photos. Has its own *bodega* next door. Serves simple lunches, sandwiches and snacks, good for wine, not open for dinner.

San Isidro *p93, map p102*

TTT **Alfresco**, Santa Lucía 295 (no sign), T01-422 8915. Best known for its tempting seafood and *ceviche*, also pastas and rice dishes, expensive wines. Has two dining rooms, an unfussy area at the front with white plastic furniture and a smarter room at the back.

¥¥¥ **Antica Pizzería**, Av 2 de Mayo 728, T01-222 8437. Very popular, great ambience, excellent food, Italian owner. Also **Antica Trattoria** in Barranco at Alfonso Ugarte 242, and an excellent bar, **Antica Taberna**, with a limited range of food at Conquistadores 605, San Isidro, very good value, fashionable, get there early for a seat.

¥¥¥ **Asia de Cuba**, Conquistadores 780, T01-222 4940, www.asiadecubaperu.com. A popular place serving a mix of Asian, Cuban and Peruvian dishes. It also has a reputation for its bar and nightclub; try the Martinis.

¥¥¥ **Matsuei**, C Manuel Bañon 260, T01-422 4323. Sushi bar and Japanese dishes, very popular, regarded as among the best Japanese food in Lima.

¥¥¥ **Valentino**, Manuel Bañon 215, T01-441 6174. One of Lima's best international restaurants, formal, so well known that it only needs a tiny brass sign.

¥¥ **Chez Philippe**, Av 2 de Mayo 748, T01-222 4953. Pizza, pasta and crêpes, wood oven, rustic decor (also own **Pizza B&B** in Huaraz).

¥¥ **Chilis**, Ovalo Gutiérrez. A branch of the American chain with a Peruvian twist, popular, like most of the places on the Ovalo.

¥¥ **Delicass**, Miguel Dasso 131. Great deli with imported meats and cheeses, good coffee, open late, slow service.

¥¥ **Segundo Muelle**, Av Conquistadores 490, T01-421 1206, and Av Canaval y Moreyra (aka Corpac) 605. Worth a visit for its excellent *ceviche* and other very good seafood dishes, popular with a youthful crowd.

¥ **MiniMarket**, Av Pexet 1472. Kosher products, excellent, cheap *chala* bread.

Cafés

Café Olé, Pancho Fierro 115 (1 block from Hotel El Olívar). Huge selection of entrées and desserts, also serves breakfasts and sandwiches, very smart with prices to match.

Café Positano/Café Luna, Miguel Dasso 147. Popular with politicians, café and bistro.

News Café, Av Santa Luisa 110. Another elegant café serving great salads and desserts, popular, in the upper price bracket.

Pastelería Montserrat, Av Santa Lucía 100 block, 2 doors from **Café Olé**. A much more simple place than its neighbour, for hot breads, cakes, pastries and coffee, smells very appetizing.

Miraflores *p93, map p104*

There are various small restaurants good for a cheap set meal along calles **Los Pinos** and **Schell**, at the bottom of Parque Kennedy.

Calle San Ramón, more commonly known as Pizza St (across from Parque Kennedy), is a pedestrian walkway lined with outdoor restaurants/bars/discos open until the small hours. It's a very popular place with good-natured touts trying to entice diners and drinkers with free offers.

¥¥¥ **Astrid y Gastón**, Cantuarias 175, T01-444 1496. Exceptional local/*novo andino* and international cuisine, one of the best in Lima, owners are Gastón Acurio and his wife Astrid. Also has a bar.

¥¥¥ **Café Voltaire**, Av 2 de Mayo 220. International cuisine with emphasis on French dishes, beautifully cooked food, pleasant ambience, good service, closed Sun.

¥¥¥ **Coco de Mer**, Av Grau 400, T01-243 0278, www.cocodemerlima.com. Run by Englishwoman Lucy Ralph, popular with foreigners because of its European feel. Mediterranean and Peruvian dishes, cocktails, events, open daily 1200 till whenever.

¥¥¥ **Cuarto y Mitad**, Av Espinar 798, T01-446 2988. This popular grill is close to the Ovalo Gutiérrez, it's one of places to go if you're looking for meat (beef or ostrich); they also serve seafood.

¥¥¥ **El Kapallaq**, Av Petit Thouars 4844, T01-444 4149. Prize-winning Peruvian restaurant specializing in seafood and fish, excellent *ceviches*. Open Mon-Fri 1200-1700 only.

¥¥¥ **El Rincón Gaucho**, Av Armendáriz 580, T01-447 4778. Good grill, renowned for its steaks.

¥¥¥ **El Señorío de Sulco**, Malecón Cisneros 1470, T01-441 0183, http://senoriodesulco.com. Overlooking a cliff-top park, with ocean views from upstairs. Forget the Footprint grading, this is a 'five-fork' restaurant which some believe is the best in Lima; all Peruvian food, à la carte and buffet, *piscos*, wines, piano music at night.

¥¥¥ **Fuji**, Paseo de la República 4090, T01-440 8531. Excellent Japanese restaurant, one of the best in Lima, authentic, with a separate menu for sushi.

¥¥¥ **Huaca Pucllana**, Gral Borgoña cuadra 8 s/n, alt cuadra 45 Av Arequipa, T01-445 4042. Open 1230-0030. Facing the archaeological site of the same name, contemporary Peruvian and fusion cooking, very good food in an unusual setting.

La Gloria, Atahualpa 201, T01-446 6504. Very smart, excellent international food and good service.

Las Brujas de Cachiche, Av Bolognesi 460, T01-447 1883. An old mansion converted into bars and dining rooms, almost Alpine in appearance. It specializes in traditional food (menu in Spanish and English), best *lomo saltado* in town, live *criollo* music.

Las Tejas, Diez Canseco 340. Open 1100-2300 daily, good, typical Peruvian food.

La Tranquera, Av Pardo 285. Argentine-owned steakhouse, ranch style, set back off the street, very good.

La Trattoria, Manuel Bonilla 106, 1 block from Parque Kennedy (no sign), T01-446 7002. The Italian cuisine is of a consistently high quality, very popular. It also serves a good cheesecake.

Rosa Náutica, T01-445 0149. Built on an old British-style pier, Lima Bay. Delightful opulence, finest fish cuisine, experience the atmosphere by buying an expensive beer in the bar at sunset. Daily 1230-2200.

Sí Señor, Bolognesi 706, T01-445 3789, www.sisenor.org. Mexican food, cheerful, lots of low-slung lights over the tables, interesting decor, good *fajitas*, huge portions.

Wa Lok, Av Angamos Oeste 703, T01-447 1280. A branch of the famous Barrio Chino *chifa*, also serving good food in a tasteful, modern setting.

Bohemia, Av Santa Cruz 805, Ovalo Gutiérrez. Large menu of international food, great salads and sandwiches. Also at Av El Polo 706, p 2, Surco, and at Pasaje Nicolás de Rivera 142, opposite the main post office near the Plaza de Armas, T01-427 5537.

Café Tarata, Pasaje Tarata 260. Good atmosphere, family run, good varied menu.

Dalmacia, San Fernando 401. Spanish-owned, casual gourmet restaurant serving tapas and main meals, excellent, seating on the terrace.

El Beduino, Av 28 de Julio 1301, T01-242 6642. Good, authentic Arabic food.

Il Postino, Colina 401, T01-446 8381. This is another restaurant serving great Italian food.

La Palachinke, Av Schell 120 at the bottom of Parque Kennedy. At the corner of the Diagonal, so very convenient, this place is recommended for its speciality pancakes.

Makoto Sushi Bar, Larcomar shopping centre, also Las Casas 145, San Isidro, T01-442 9183. Very good for Japanese food.

Ricota, Pasaje Tarata 248. Charming café on a walkway, huge menu, big portions.

Dino's Pizza, Av Cdte Espinar 374 and many other branches. Great pizza at a good price, delivery service.

El Parquetito, Diez Canseco 150. Seating outside by the park, or inside, serves breakfasts and has a good cheap menu.

Madre Natura, Chiclayo 815. Natural foods shop and eating place, highly recommended, closes at 2100.

Pardo's Chicken, Av Benavides 730. Chicken and chips, very good and popular (branches throughout Lima).

Sandwich.com, Av Diagonal 234. Good, cheap sandwiches with interesting combinations of fillings, both hot and cold, also fruits, puddings and drinks.

Super Rueda, Porta 133, also Av José Pardo 1224. Mexican food à la Peru, fast-food style, clean. Mon-Fri 0800-2400, Sat 0600-2400, Sun 1100-2300.

Cafés

Café Café, Martín Olaya 250, near the Parque Kennedy roundabout. Very popular, good atmosphere, over 100 different blends of coffee, good salads and sandwiches, very popular with well-to-do Limeños. Also in Larcomar, level 3, shop 2.

Café de la Paz, Lima 351, Parque Kennedy. Excellent café in the park; a nice place for an outdoor drink. Good cocktails but the meals are on the expensive side.

Café Zeta, Mcal Oscar R Benavides 598 y José Gálvez, past Parque Kennedy. American owned, excellent Peruvian coffee, teas, hot chocolate and excellent home-made cakes, cheap too. Interesting variety of seating.

C'est si bon, Av Cdte Espinar 663. Cakes by the slice or whole, arguably the best in Lima.

For an explanation of sleeping and eating price codes used in this guide, see inside the front cover. Other relevant information is found in Essentials, see pages 53-58.

Chef's Café, Av Larco 763. Nice place for a sandwich or coffee. Also has a little coffee cart in Parque Kennedy until 2200.

Dove Vai, Diagonal 228. A bright *heladería* in this block of eating places; try the *encanto* with lumps of chocolate brownie.

Haiti, Av Diagonal 160, Parque Kennedy. Open almost round the clock daily, great for people watching, good ice cream.

Heladería 4D, Angamos Oeste 408. Open 1000-0100 daily, Italian ice cream, at other locations throughout Lima.

La Tiendecita Blanca, Av Larco 111 on Parque Kennedy. One of Miraflores' oldest. Expensive, good people watching, very good cakes, European-style food and delicatessen under the **Café Suisse** brand.

Mi Abuela, Angamos 393. Open 0900-2100 for probably the best yoghurt in Lima and a large selection of natural foods.

San Antonio Café, Av Angamos Oeste 1494, also Vasco Núñez de Balboa 770, Rocca de Vergallo 201, Magdalena del Mar and Av Primavera 373, San Borja. A fashionable *pastelería* chain, serving good coffee, cakes and snacks, not too expensive.

Tapas Bar, Manuel Bonilla 103, T01-242 7922. Expensive but very good tapas bar behind huge wooden doors, extensive wine list, reserve a table at weekends.

Vivaldi, Av Ricardo Palma 260, 1 block from Parque Kennedy. A good but expensive café reminiscent of a gentleman's club, with dark wood and much newspaper reading. The group's international restaurant, **Vivaldi Gourmet**, is at Conquistadores 212, San Isidro.

Zugatti, Av Larco 361, across from Parque Kennedy. Good Italian *gelato*.

Barranco *p94, map p95*

Try the various small restaurants under the Bridge of Sighs and down towards the cliff tops, open late, great cheap Peruvian food (eg *anticuchos*). **La Ermita**, with the glass roof, has been recommended.

ΨΨΨ **Canta Rana**, Génova 101, T01-477 8934. Open daily 1200-1700, good *ceviche*, expensive, small portions.

ΨΨΨ **La Costa Verde**, on Barranquito beach, T01-441 3086. Excellent fish and wine, expensive but recommended as the best by Limeños, daily 1200-2400, Sun buffet.

ΨΨΨ **Manos Morenas**, Av Pedro de Osma 409, T01-467 0421. Open 1230-1630, 1900-2300. A popular Barranco establishment, serving pricey creole cuisine with excellent shows some evenings (cover charge for shows).

ΨΨΨ **Ñaylamp**, Av 2 de Mayo 239, T01-467 5011. Good seafood and *ceviche*, fashionable and expensive. The restaurant has a garden.

ΨΨ **Antica Trattoria**, Ugarte 242, T01-247 3443. In the same group as the **Antica Pizzería** in San Isidro, serving Italian and seafood dishes, wooden tables, stone floors and wooden barrels in the ceiling.

ΨΨ **El Hornito**, Av Grau 209, T01-477 2465. A pizzería which also serves creole food, in the heart of Barranco on corner of the main plaza.

ΨΨ **Festín**, Av Grau 323, T01-247 7218. Huge menu, typical and international food in a café-style environment.

ΨΨ **Las Mesitas**, Av Grau 341. Open 1200-0200. Traditional tea rooms-cum-restaurant serving creole food and old sweet dishes which you won't find anywhere else in Lima.

Chorrillos *p94*

ΨΨΨ **Costa Sur**, Av Chorrillos 180, T01-251 2497. Typical Peruvian dishes, good value, try the *causa* with crab. Recommended.

ΨΨΨ **El Hawaiano**, Av Guardia Civil 323, T01-467 0317, also at Rep de Panamá 258, Barranco. Two related seafood restaurants with an excellent daily buffet (US$16), lunch only, expensive but well worth it.

ΨΨ **Punta Arenas**, Santa Teresa 455, 1 block from the 1st block of Av Huaylas, T01-467 0053. Tasty seafood, popular, good value.

Callao *p96*

Ψ **Cevichería Mateo**, C Constitución 280. Worth trying as a good place for seafood.

Ψ **Leo**, Jr Adolfo King 182. A local place serving good food.

Around Lima

Pachacámac *p98*

ΨΨ **La Casa de Don Cucho**, in the Lurín valley; take a mototaxi from the ruins. The best of several local restaurants in the valley.

Canta *p99*

Ψ **La Casona**, just off the main street. Serves local trout in an interesting old building.

Ψ **Restaurant Cancay Vento**, in the hotel of the same name. It has an extensive menu.

Bars and clubs

Lima has an excellent nightlife, with many places to choose from, all with different styles and themes. Often there is a cover charge ranging from US$3-10 per person. Unfortunately, there are some nightclubs and bars that deny entrance to people solely on the basis of skin colour and assumed economic status. We only include here the names of establishments that do not practise this policy.

Central Lima *p83, map p85*

The centre of town, specifically **Jirón de la Unión**, has many discos. It's best to avoid the clubs on and around the intersection of Av Tacna, Av Piérola and Av de la Vega. These places can be rough and foreign visitors may receive unwanted attention.

720 Downtown, Av Uruguay 183. Exclusively gay, best in the centre, this is a rough neighbourhood so take a taxi to and from the club.

El Rincón Cervecero, Jr de la Unión (Belén) 1045. German pub without the beer, fun. Recommended.

Estadio Futbol Sports Bar, Av Nicolás de Piérola 926 on the Plaza San Martín, T01-428 8866. Beautiful bar with a disco on the bottom floor, international football theme, good international and creole food. Recommended.

Imperio, Jr Camaná 9th block. Exclusively gay, one of the older gay clubs in Lima, taxi recommended.

Piano Bar Munich, Jr de la Unión 1044 (basement). Small and fun.

Queirolo Bar, Jr Camaná 900 at Jr Quilca. A great place for soaking up genuine Lima atmosphere. Opposite is the Centre's version of **La Noche** (see Barranco clubs, below).

Lima suburbs

San Isidro *p93, map p102*

Palos de Moguer, Av Emilio Cavenecia 129, T01-221 8363. Brews 4 different kinds of beer, typical bar food.

Punto G, Av Conquistadores 512. Very popular, really small. Recommended.

Miraflores *p93, map p104*

Bars

Barcelona, Larcomar shopping centre, T01-445 4823. One of the best pubs in the city.

Barra Brava, Av Grau 192, T01-241 5840. Lots of fun, sports bar(ish).

The Clash Pub and Gallery, Psje Tello 269, Miraflores, T01-444 3376. Excellent drinks, friendly bar staff, and great decor, exclusively gay with shows and events.

Dionygreeks Pub, Av 2 de Mayo 385, T01-447 7958. Nice pub with Greek decor.

Media Naranja, C Schell 130, at the bottom of Parque Kennedy. Brazilian bar with typical drinks and food.

Murphys, C Schell 627, T01-242 1212. Irish pub, now doing food such as fish and chips. Look out for special events and happy hours.

The Old Pub, San Ramón 295 (Pizza St), T01-242 8155, n_ella@yahoo.com. Cosy, with live music most days, English spoken, darts.

Clubs

There are many discos on Pizza St.

Cocodrilo Verde, Francisco de Paula 226 near corner with Bellavista, Miraflores. Relaxed, stylish bar, slightly pricey but worth it for the Wed night jazz and live music at weekends, occasionally charges cover for music at weekends.

Santa Sede, Av 28 de Julio 441. Very popular, great music, fun crowd, gay-friendly. Recommended.

Satchmo, Av La Paz 538, T01-442 8425. Live jazz, creole and blues shows.

Teatriz, Larcomar shopping centre, T01-242 3084. Modern, expensive, very popular.

Voluntarios Pub, Independencia 131, T01-445 3939, www.voluntariospub.org. All staff are volunteers from non-profit organizations which benefit by receiving 90% of the profits made by the pub. Good atmosphere, music and drinks.

Barranco *p94, map p95*

Barranco is the capital of Lima nightlife.

Pasaje Sánchez Carrión, right off the main plaza, used to be the heart of it all. Watering holes and discos line both sides of this pedestrian walkway, but crowds and noise are driving people elsewhere. **Av Grau**, just across the street from the plaza, is also lined with bars, such as **El Ekeko** (no. 266) and **Las Terrazas** (no. 290). Many of the bars in this area turn into clubs as the evening goes on.

Bars

Bosa Nova, Bolognesi 660. Chilled student-style bar with good music.
El Dragón, N de Piérola 168, T01-797 1033, dragoncultural@hotmail.com. Popular bar and venue for music, theatre and art exhibitions.
El Grill de Costa Verde, part of the **Costa Verde** restaurant on Barranco beach. Young crowd, packed at weekends.
Juanitos, Av Grau, opposite the park. Barranco's oldest bar, a perfect place to start the evening.
La Noche, Bolognesi 307, at Pasaje Sánchez Carrión. A Lima institution with high-standard live music; Mon is jazz night, kicks off around 2200 (also in central Lima).
La Posada del Angel, 3 branches on Pedro de Osma between 164 and 222. These are popular bars serving snacks and meals.
La Posada del Mirador, near the Puente de los Suspiros (Bridge of Sighs). Beautiful view of the ocean, but you pay for the privilege.
Sargento Pimienta, Bolognesi 755. Live music, always a favourite with Limeños. Opposite is the relaxed **Trinidad**.

Entertainment

Cinemas

There are many good cinemas throughout the city. The newspaper *El Comercio* lists film information in the section called 'Luces'. Most films are in English with subtitles and cost US$2 in the centre and around US$4-5 in Miraflores. Many cinemas offer 2 seats for the price of 1 on Tue, or other special offers. Cinemas in the centre tend to have poor sound quality.

The best chains are **Cinemark**, **Cineplanet** and **UVK Multicines**. Others include: **Cine Roma**, C Teniente Fernández 242, 9th block of Av Arequipa, Santa Beatriz, T01-433 8618, and **Multicine Starvision El Pacífico**, on the Ovalo by Parque Kennedy, T01-445 6990, in Miraflores.

Cine Clubs include: **Cine Club Miraflores**, Av Larco 770, in the Miraflores Cultural Centre building, T01-446 2649, and **Filmoteca de Lima**, Av 9 de Diciembre 125 (better known as Colón), T01-331 0126.

Peñas

Central Lima *p83, map p85*
Las Brisas de Titicaca, Pasaje Wakuski 168, 1st block of Av Brasil near Plaza Bolognesi, T01-332 1881, www.brisasdeltiticaca.com. A Lima institution for folkloric music and dance, with workshops, restaurant and bar.

Miraflores *p93, map p104*
De Cajón, C Merino 2nd block, near 6th block of Av Del Ejército. Good *música negra*.
Sachun, Av Del Ejército 657, T01-441 0123. Great shows on Tue to Sat.

Barranco *p94, map p95*
Del Carajo, San Ambrosio 328, T01-247 7977. One of several *peñas* in Barranco. Traditional music, Thu-Sat from 2200.
De Rompe y Raja, Manuel Segura 127, T01-247 3271.
La Candelaria, Av Bolognesi 292, T01-247 1314. This is a good Barranco *peña*, Fri and Sat from 2130.
La Estación de Barranco, Pedro de Osma 112, T01-477 5030. Good, family-friendly atmosphere, varied shows.
Peña Poggi, Av Luna Pizarro 578, T01-247 5790. Over 30 years old, traditional. Recommended.

Theatre

There are many theatres in the city, some of which are related to cultural centres (see page 127). The press gives details of performances. Theatre and concert tickets can be booked through **Teleticket**, T01-610 8888, www.e-teleticket.com, Mon-Fri 0900-1900.
Teatro Segura, Jr Huancavelica 265, T01-427 9491. Most professional plays are staged here.

Festivals and events

17-18 Jan The Gran Serenata is performed by some of Peru's best musicians in the Plaza de Armas on the evening of the 17th. The following day is the anniversary of the founding of Lima.
Mar/Apr Semana Santa, or Holy Week, is a colourful spectacle with processions.
May The end of the month sees a **beer** festival which attracts many famous singers from Peru and some from abroad.
28-29 Jul **Independence** is celebrated with music and fireworks in the Plaza de Armas on the evening before.
30 Aug **Santa Rosa de Lima.**
Oct Month-long celebration of **Our Lord of the Miracles** with impressive processions (see Las Nazarenas church, page 89).
3 Nov **San Martín de Porres.**

Shopping

Art galleries

Many cultural centres (see page 127) have art galleries, cinemas and theatres.
Artco, Rouad y Paz Soldán 325, San Isidro, T01-221 3579, www.artcogaleria.com. Mon-Fri 1100-2000, Sat 1030-1330, 1530-1950.
Galería San Francisco, Plaza San Francisco 208, Barranco, T01-477 0537. A gallery in a pleasant building on a small plaza a little way from the centre of Barranco.
La Casa Azul, Alfonso Ugarte 150, Miraflores, T01-446 6380, T01-9807 1661. Marcia Moreno and Jorge Rengifo offer advice and sales of contemporary art and antique objects, handicrafts and furniture.
Lucia de la Puente, Paseo Sáenz Peña 206, Barranco, T01-477 9740, www.gluciadela puente.com. Mon-Sat 1100-2000. A gallery exhibiting modern non-Andean Peruvian art, also artwork for sale and a good small café.
Praxis, C San Martín 689, Barranco, T01-477 2822. Mon-Fri 0930-1330, 1700-2100, Sat 1700-2100. Art exhibitions and sales.
Wu, Paseo Sáenz Peña 129, Barranco, T01-247 4685. Mon-Fri 1000-1300, 1400-2000, Sat 1100-1300, 1630-2000. Artist Frances Wu's studio is also a gallery of engravings, etchings and other graphics, with an emphasis on Peruvian artists, including designs taken from engraved gourds.

Bookshops

Crisol, Ovalo Gutiérrez, Av Santa Cruz 816, San Isidro, T01-221 1010, Below **Cine Planet**. Large bookshop with café, titles in English, French and Spanish. Also in Jockey Plaza shopping centre, Av Javier Prado Este 4200, Surco, T01-436 004.
Ibero Librerías, Av Diagonal 500, T01-242 2798, Larco 199, T01-445 5520, Miraflores, and in Larcomar. Stocks **Footprint** titles as well as a wide range of other titles.
La Familia, Av Diagonal 382, T01-447 8353, and Schell 279, T01-444 3993, Miraflores. Has a good selection of books on a wide variety of topics, helpful staff. Other branches at **La Tertulia**, CCPUCP, Av Camino Real 1075, San Isidro, and in the **Jockey Plaza** and **El Polo** commercial centres in Surco.
Librería Cultura Peruana, José Gálvez 124, Miraflores. A wide selection of books on Peruvian culture, from art and archaeology to cooking.
Virrey. Chain with a great selection, but few in English. Branches at **Larcomar** shopping centre (local 210), Miraflores; **Pasaje Nicolás de Rivera**, central Lima behind the Municipalidad, T01-427 5080, and at Miguel Dasso 141, San Isidro (next door is **Librería Sur**, No 143).
Zeta, Av Cdte Espinar 219, T01-446 5139 and at the airport. Stocks **Footprint** titles and other guidebooks.

Magazines

Whether in downtown Lima or Miraflores, almost all street kiosks sell up-to-date magazines in English such as *Time*, *Newsweek*, *People* etc. For the most recently published magazines and newspapers, try Mallcco's, Av Larco 175, on the Parque

Kennedy roundabout, daily 0800-2100. It has a wide variety of magazines (expensive but the latest releases) and newspapers from England. In front of **Café Haiti** by Parque Kennedy, you'll often see the men with stacks of newspapers for sale. These are taken from incoming international flights so tend to be only a day or two old; bargain hard. **Hotel Sheraton** sells the *New York Times* and the *Wall Street Journal*. Many cafés have foreign newspapers to browse through while enjoying a cup of coffee or a sandwich.

Camping equipment

Camping gas (in small blue bottles) is available from any large hardware store or bigger supermarket, about US$3.

Alpamayo, Av Larco 345, Miraflores at Parque Kennedy, T01-445 1671. Sleeping mats, boots, rock shoes, climbing gear, water filters, tents, backpacks etc, very expensive but top-quality equipment. The owner speaks fluent English and offers good information.

Camping Center, Av Benavides 1620, Miraflores, T01-242 1779. Selection of tents, backpacks, stoves, camping and climbing gear.

El Mundo de las Maletas, Preciados 308, Higuereta-Surco, T01-449 7850. 0900-2200 daily for suitcase repairs.

Huantzan, Jr Tarapacá 384, Magdalena, T01-460 6101. Equipment sales and rentals, MSR stoves, backpacks, boots.

Mountain Worker, Centro Comercial Camino Real, level A, store 17, San Isidro, T01-813 8367. Quality camping gear for all types of weather, made-to-order products as well. Recommended.

Outdoor Peru, Centro Comercial Chacarilla, store 211, on Av Caminos del Inca 257, Surco, T01-372 0428. Decent selection.

Todo Camping, Av Angamos Oeste 350, Miraflores, near Av Arequipa, T01-447 6279. Sells 100% DEET, blue gas canisters, lots of accessories, tents, crampons and backpacks.

Handicrafts

Since so many artisans have come from the sierra to Lima, it is possible to find any kind of handicraft in the capital. The quality is high. Among the many items which can be bought here are silver and gold handicrafts, indigenous hand-spun and handwoven textiles and manufactured textiles in traditional designs. Although Lima is more expensive, it is often impossible to find the same quality of goods elsewhere. You can find llama and alpaca wool products such as ponchos, rugs, hats, blankets, slippers, coats, sweaters, etc. Note that genuine alpaca is odourless wet or dry, but wet llama stinks.

Lima is a good place to buy *arpilleras*, appliqué pictures of Peruvian life (originated in Chile with political designs). These are made with great skill by women in the shanty towns. The fine leather products on sale are mostly hand made. The *mate burilado*, or engraved gourd found in every tourist shop, is cheap and a genuine expression of folk art. These are cheaper in the villages near Huancayo (see page 489).

Alpaca and cotton

There are bargains in clothing made from high-quality Pima cotton.

Alpaca 111, Av Larco 671, Miraflores, T01-447 1623, www.alpaca111.com. High-quality alpaca, baby alpaca and vicuña items. Several other outlets including Larcomar and Museo Larco Herrera.

Alpaca 859, Av Larco 859, Miraflores. Excellent quality alpaca and baby alpaca products.

Alpaka Studio, Av Larco 1144, store 9, Miraflores. Fashionable alpaca garments.

Da Capo, Aramburú 920, dpto 402, San Isidro, T01-441 0714. Beautiful alpaca scarves and shawls in new designs.

La Casa de la Alpaca, Av La Paz 665, Miraflores, T01-447 6271. Open Mon-Fri 0930-2030.

Orígenes Andinos, Larcomar, Miraflores, T01-241 8472, www.origenesandinos.com. T-shirts and polo shirts made from Peruvian cotton with designs from the Nazca, Chimú, Moche, Mochica, Inca and other cultures.

Silvania Prints, Diez Canseco 337A, Miraflores. Sells modern silk-screen prints on Pima cotton with pre-Columbian designs.

Crafts

Agua y Tierra, Diez Canseco 298 y Alcanfores, Miraflores, T01-444 6980. Good for fine crafts and indigenous art.

Artesanía Santo Domingo, Plaza Santo Domingo, by the church of that name, in central Lima, T01-428 9860. Good Peruvian crafts.

Centro Comercial El Alamo, corner of La Paz y Diez Canseco, Miraflores. Artesanía shops with good choice.

Kuntur Wasi, Ocharan 182, Miraflores, T01-444 0557. English-speaking owner, very knowledgeable about Peruvian textiles, frequently has exhibitions of fine folk art and crafts.

La Casa de la Mujer Artesana, Juan Pablo Ferandini 1550, Av Brasil, cuadra 15, Pueblo Libre, T01-423 8840, F423 4031. A cooperative run by the **Movimiento Manuela Ramos**, excellent quality work mostly from *pueblos jóvenes*, Mon-Fri 0900-1300, 1400-1700.

Las Pallas, Cajamarca 212, 5th block of Av Grau, Barranco, T01-477 4629, Mon-Sat 0900-1900. Very high-quality handicrafts (textiles, ceramics, masks, etc); English, French and German spoken. The owner is Mari Solari.

Luz Hecho a Mano, Berlín 399, Miraflores, T01-446 7098, www.luzhechoamano.com. Lovely handmade bags, wallets and other leather goods including clothing, which last for years and can be custom-made.

Fine art

Dédalo, Paseo Sáenz Peña 295, Barranco, T01-477 0562. This is a labyrinthine shop selling modern designer crafts, furniture, jewellery and other items, but it is as good as a gallery. It also has a nice coffee shop and cinema shows.

Jewellery

C La Esperanza, in Miraflores, has become a new centre with dozens of shops offering gold and silverware at reasonable prices.

Ilaria, Av 2 de Mayo 308, San Isidro, T01-221 8575. Jewellery and silverware with interesting designs. There are other branches in Lima, Cuzco and Arequipa. Recommended.

Maps

Dress soberly and take your passport when going to these places (except **Lima 2000**).

Instituto Geográfico Nacional, Av Aramburú 1190, Surquillo, T01-475 3030, ext 119, www.ignperu.gob.pe. Mon-Fri 0800-1730. They have topographical maps of the whole country, mostly at 1:100,000, political and physical maps of all departments and satellite and aerial photographs. They also have a new series of tourist maps for trekking, eg of the Cordillera Blanca, the Cuzco area, etc.

Instituto Geológico Minero y Metalúrgico (Ingemmet), Av Canadá 1470, San Borja, T01-225 3128, www.ingemmet.gob.pe. Mon-Fri 0800-1300, 1400-1600. Sells a huge selection of geographic maps US$12-112. Also satellite, aeromagnetic, geochemical and departmental mining maps. Enquire about new digital products.

Lima 2000, Av Arequipa 2625, Lince (near the intersection with Av Javier Prado), T01-440 3486, www.lima2000.com.pe. Mon-Fri 0900-1300 and 1400-1800. They stock an excellent street map of Lima (the only one worth buying), US$10, or US$14 in booklet form. Provincial maps and a national road map, which is good for road conditions and distances, perfect for driving or cycling.

Ministerio de Transporte, Av 28 de Julio 800, central Lima, T01-433 7800, www.mtc.gob.pe. Mon-Fri 0800-1230, 1400-1600. Maps and plans of land communication routes, slow and bureaucratic service.

Servicio Aerofotográfico Nacional, Av Las Palmas s/n, Barranco, T01-477 3682, informes@sanperu.com. Mon-Fri 0800-1400. Aerial photographs from mid-1950s survey available, but they are expensive. Expect a waiting period as short as 1 day or as long as 2 weeks.

Markets

Central Lima *p83, map p85*

Polvos Azules, C García Naranjo, La Victoria, just off Av Grau in the centre of town. This is the official black market of Lima. The normal connotations of a black market do not apply here as this establishment is an accepted part of Lima society, condoned by the government and frequented by people of all economic backgrounds. It's good for cameras, hiking boots, music and personal stereos. This is not a safe area, so be alert and put your money in your front pockets.

Pueblo Libre *p92*
Feria Artesanal, Av La Marina y Av Sucre, is smaller than it used to be but is cheaper than Av Petit Thouars. Not safe.

Miraflores *p93, map p104*
Parque Kennedy hosts a daily crafts market 1700-2300. At **Av Petit Thouars** cuadras 51 a 54 (parallel to Av Arequipa, a few blocks from Parque Kennedy) you'll find an unnamed crafts market in a large courtyard and lots of small flags. This is the largest crafts arcade in Miraflores. From here to Av Ricardo Palma the street is lined with stalls; all are open 7 days a week until late(ish). **La Portada del Sol**, on cuadra 54 of Petit Thouars, has a small café with reasonable prices and good coffee.

Music

Music City, Av José Larco 459, Miraflores. Probably the best, but not the cheapest, place to buy CDs, no pirated material.

Photography

El Ojo Ajeno, 28 de Julio 547, T01-444 6999. Mon-Fri 0900-2100, Sat 0900-1800. A recommended photographic gallery.
Foto Magnum, Ocoña 190, central Lima, T01-427 1599. Mon-Fri 0900-2000. For film and accessories.
Laboratorio Color Profesional, Av Benavides 1171, Miraflores T01-446 7421. Mon-Fri 0900-1900, Sat 0930-1300. Professional-quality developing, fairly priced, touch-ups, repair services, excellent for slide developing, sells top-quality equipment, film and accessories, the best you'll find in Lima. Highly recommended.
Miranda's Photography, Jr Cusco 592, 445A, centre, T01-426 7920, T9706 9097 (mob), mirandas_photography@hotmail.com. Mon-Fri 1100-1800. Good for repairs.

Supermarkets

Lima has 4 main supermarket chains: **E Wong**, **Metro**, **Plaza Vea** and **Santa Isabel** (the last of these is usually smaller than the others). They are all well-stocked and carry a decent supply of imported goods (Marmite etc). **Santa Isabel** on Av Pardo in Miraflores is open 24 hrs. A new upmarket chain is **Vivanda**, with a branch at Benavides y Alcanfores in Miraflores.

Activities and tours

Cycling

Best Internacional, Av Comandante Espinar 2320, Miraflores, T01-446 4044, Mon-Sat 1000-1400, 1600-2000. Sells leisure and racing bikes, also repairs, parts and accessories.
Biclas, Av Conquistadores 641, San Isidro, T01-440 0890, Mon-Fri 1000-1300, 1600-2000, Sat 1000-1300. Knowledgeable staff, tours possible, good selection of bikes, repairs and accessories, cheap airline boxes for sale. Highly recommended.
BikeMavil, Av Aviación 4023, Surco, T01-449 8435. Mon-Sat 0930- 2100. Rental service, repairs, excursions, selection of mountain and racing bicycles.
Casa Okuyama, Manco Cápac 590, La Victoria, T01-330 9131. Mon-Fri 0900-1300, 1415-1800, Sat 0900-1300. Repairs, parts, try here for 28 inch tyres, excellent service.
Neuquén, Jr Paruro 875, El Cercado, T01-427 2379. For Shimano parts.
Peru Bike, Parque Nueva Castilla, Calle A, D-7, Surco, T01-449 5234, www.perubike.com. Experienced agency leading tours, specializing in the Andes, professional guiding. Also has a mountain bike school and a workshop.
Willy-Pro (Williams Arce), Av Javier Prado Este 3339, San Borja, T01-346 4082, Mon-Sat 0800-2000. Has a selection of specialized bikes, helpful staff.

Mountaineering and trekking clubs

Asociación de Andinismo de la Universidad de Lima, Universidad de Lima, Javier Prado Este s/n, T01-437 6767. Meetings Wed 1800-2000, climbing courses.
Club de Montañeros Américo Tordoya, Francisco Graña 378, Magdalena, T01-460 6101, http://es.geocities.com/clubamericotordoya/. Meetings Thu 2000,

contact Gonzalo Menacho. Climbing excursions ranging from easy to difficult.
Trekking and Backpacking Club, Jr Huáscar 1152, Jesús María, Lima 11, T01-423 2515, 9987 4193 (mob), www.angelfire.com/mi2/tebac. Señor Miguel Chiri Valle, treks arranged, including in the Cordillera Blanca.

Parapenting

From Lima, Pasamayo (430 m) is a good launch zone, as are the 80-m-high cliffs of the Costa Verde, which are suitable for beginners.
Fly Adventure, Jorge Chávez 658, Miraflores, T01-9816 5461 (Luis Munarriz), T9900 9150 (Eduardo Gómez). US$25 for 15-min tandem flight over the cliffs, 4 to 6-day courses US$250-350. Recommended.

Scuba diving

AquaSport, Av Conquistadores 645, San Isidro, T01-221 7270, www.aquasportperu.com. Owner is a CMAS instructor, gear for rent, tours and courses offered and quality equipment for sale.
Peru Divers, Av Huaylas 205, Chorrillos, T01-251 6231, www.perudivers.com. Open Mon-Fri 0900-1900, Sat 0900-1700. Owner Lucho Rodríguez is a certified PADI instructor who offers certification courses, tours and a wealth of good information.

Spectator sports

Matches and various athletic events take place at the National Stadium in the centre of the city, built on ground given by the British community on the 100th anniversary of Peru's declaration of independence.

Football

The local soccer derby is between **'La U'** (**Universitario**) and **Alianza Lima** (tickets US$2.50-25). Matches are also played at Alianza's stadium in the district of La Victoria and Universi tario's new stadium in the La Molina district.

Horse racing

Jockey Club of Peru (Hipódromo de Monterrico) has horse races every Tue and Thu 1900, Sat and Sun 1400. Bets start at US$0.75. For information about Peruvian Paso horses contact the **Asociación Nacional de Caballos de Paso**, T01-447 6331.

Surfing

Focus, Leonardo Da Vinci 208, San Borja, T01-475 8459. Shaping factory which makes some decent boards, knowledgeable about local spots and conditions, one of the better surf shops in Peru, rents boards.
Klimax, José Gonzales 488, Miraflores, T01-447 1685. Sells new and second-hand boards, knowledgeable.
Wayo Whiler, Av 28 de Julio 287, Barranco, T01-247 6343, www.wayowhilar.com.pe. Makes all kinds of boards, sells clothing and materials, rentals and repairs, email in advance to have a board ready for when you arrive, can also organize excursions and runs a surf school with his brother (US$100 per month).

Tour operators

Lima is bursting at the seams with tour and travel agencies. Some are good and reliable, many are not. If possible, use agencies in or close to the area you wish to visit and always shop around. Bargaining ability is a plus. See also **Fertur Perú**, page 80.

We have received complaints about agencies, or their representatives, at bus offices or the airport arranging tours and collecting money for companies that either do not exist or which fall far short of what is paid for. Do not conduct business anywhere other than in the agency's office and insist on a written contract.
Andean Tours, Schell 319 of 304-305, Miraflores, T01-444 8665, www.andean-tours.com. Recommended for bespoke arrangements.
AQP, Los Castaños 347, San Isidro, T01-222 3312, www.saaqp.com.pe. Comprehensive service, with tours offered throughout the country.
Aracari Travel Consulting, Av Pardo 610, suite 802, Miraflores, T01-242 6673, www.aracari.com. Regional tours throughout Peru, also themed and activity tours, has a very good reputation.
Class Adventure Travel, San Martín 800, Miraflores, T01-444 1652, www.cat-travel.com. Dutch-owned and run; one of the best. CAT

has offices in several Latin countries and offers tailor-made travel solutions throughout the continent. For local contact details, information and bookings, visit the website.

Coltur, Av Reducto 1255, Miraflores, T01-615 5555, www.coltur.com.pe. Very helpful, experienced and well-organized for tours throughout the country.

Cóndor Travel, Mayor Armando Blondet 249, San Isidro, T01-615 3000, www.condor travel.com.pe. Also has branches in Cuzco, Arequipa and Puno, and others in Ecuador, Bolivia and Chile for tours throughout the Andes.

Dasatariq, Jr Francisco Bolognesi 510, Miraflores, T01-447 7772, www.dasatariq.com. Also in Cuzco. A well-organized company with a good reputation and helpful staff.

Domiruth Travel Services, Jr Rio de Janeiro 216-218, Miraflores, T01-610 6000, www.domiruth.com. pe. Tours throughout Peru, from the mystical to adventure travel.

EcoAndes Travel, Av Larco 1150, of 704, T01-214 8029, www.ecoandestravel.com. Peruvian branch of this Ecuadorean company, with classic tours and a wide range of adventure tours and expeditions. Also has an office in Cuzco.

Explorandes, C San Fernando 320, T01-445 0532, www.explorandes.com. Award-winning company with a wide range of adventure and cultural tours throughout Peru. Offices in Cuzco page 164 and Huaraz page 342.

Hada Tours, 2 de Mayo 529, Miraflores, T01-446 8157, www.hada tours.com.pe. Over 20 years of experience.

Highland Peru Tours, Av Pardo 231, Miraflores, T01-242 6292, www.highlandperu.com.

InkaNatura Travel, Manuel Bañón 461, San Isidro, Lima 27, T01-440 2022, www.inka natura.com. Also in Cuzco, Chiclayo and with properties in the southeastern jungle, offers good tours with knowledgeable guides, emphasis on sustainable tourism and conservation.

Karlop Andean Trek, T01-9622 0714, karlop_36@hotmail.com. For adventure tours with Carlos Pacheco Ramos to the heart of Peru, eg Choquequirao, 7 days, 6 nights overland, US$260. Previously recommended in Abancay.

Kinjyo Travel, Las Camelias 228, p 2, San Isidro, T01-212 7070, also office in Cuzco, www.kinjyotravel.com.

Lima Tours, Jr Belén 1040, central Lima, T01-619 6900, www.limatours.com.pe. Recommended for tours in the capital and around the country.

Marilí Tours, Diez Canseco 392, p 2, T01-242 9567, www.marilitours.com.pe. Tours of all types, including adventure and ecological, within Peru and outside.

Masi Travel Sudamérica, Porta 350, Miraflores, T01-446 9094, www.masi travel.com. Tours throughout Peru, plenty of information on the website. Contact Verónika Reategui for an efficient service.

Peru Expeditions, Av Arequipa 5241-504, Lima 18, T01-447 2057, www.Peru-exped itions.com. Specializing in expeditions in 4WD vehicles and Andes crossings.

Peru For Less, C Jorge Leguía 142, Miraflores, La Aurora, T01-272 0542; and 450 Throckmorton, Suite 1110, Fort Worth, TX 761002, USA, T1-877 269 0309 (toll free), T020-3002 0571, www.peruforless.com. A US-based company offering packages to Peru and other South American countries.

Peru Travel Bureau, Sebastián Tellería 45, San Isidro, T01-222 1909, www.ptb.com.pe. Recommended.

Roma Tours, Jr Ica 330, next to Hostal Roma, T/F01-427 7572, dantereyes @hotmail. com. Good, reliable. Dante Reyes is very friendly and speaks English.

Rutas del Peru SAC, Av Enrique Palacios 1110, Miraflores, T01-444 5405, www.rutasdelperu.com. Tailor-made trips and overland expeditions in trucks.

Safe in Lima, Alfredo Silva 150, Barranco, T01-252 7330, www.safeinlima.com. Belgian-owned and run, specializes in tailor-made trips and Lima city tours, very reliable. For details of the hostel, see Sleeping page 107.

South American Destination, Av Larco 345, of 1106, Miraflores, T01-241 1594, www.southamericandestination.net.

Victor's Travel Service, Jr de la Unión (Belén) 1068, T01-431 4195, victortravel @terra.com.pe. Hotel reservations (no commission, free pickup), free maps of Lima and Peru, Mon-Sat 0900-1800, very helpful.

Viracocha, Av Vasco Núñez de Balboa 191, Miraflores, T01-445 3986, peruviantours. @viracocha.com.pe. Very helpful, especially with flights; cultural and mystical tours, also hiking, rafting and birdwatching.

Private guides

The Ministry of Industry, Tourism, Integration and International Business certifies guides and can provide a list. Most are members of **AGOTUR** (Asociación de Guías Oficiales de Turismo), La Venturosa 177, Surco, T01-448 5167, agoturlima @yahoo.com. Always book well in advance. Most guides speak English or another language in addition to Spanish.

Escorted Economic Overland Peru, T/F01-567 5107, victormelgar777@ yahoo.com, is run by an experienced tour guide, Víctor Melgar. He'll escort individuals, families and groups throughout Peru and Bolivia, safely and economically. He also runs **Hostal Víctor**, see Sleeping, page 100.

Transport

Air

For information on international flights, see Essentials, page 38. For domestic flights, see Essentials, page 47, and under the relevant destinations. Call T01-511 6055 or consult www.lap.com.pe for arrival and departure information. For all other information see Ins and outs page 79.

Airline offices

Domestic Aero Cóndor, C Juan de Arona 781, San Isidro, T01-614 6000, www.aerocondor.com.pe, flights to Andahuaylas, Arequipa, Ayacucho, Cajamarca, Cuzco, Iquitos, Piura, Puerto Maldonado, Tacna, Tumbes and over the Nazca Lines. **Lan**, Av José Pardo 513, Miraflores, T01-213 8200, www.lan.com, flights to Arequipa, Chiclayo, Cuzco, Iquitos, Juliaca, Piura, Puerto Maldonado, Tacna, Tarapoto and Trujillo. **LC Busre**, Los Tulipanes 218, Urb San Eugenio, Lima 14, T01-619 1300, www.lcbusre.com.pe, flights to Ayacucho, Cajamarca, Huánuco, Iquitos and Pucallpa. **Star Perú**, Av José Pardo 485, Miraflores, T01-705 9000, www.star peru.com, to Arequipa, Chiclayo, Cuzco, Iquitos, Juliaca, Pucallpa, Tarapoto and Trujillo. **Taca Perú**, Av Comandante Espinar 331, Miraflores, T01-511 8222, www.grupo taca.com, flights between Lima, Arequipa and Cuzco. **Wayra Perú**, Av Javier Prado Oeste 2501, Lima 17, T01-261 4400, www.wayra.com.pe, flights to Arequipa, Iquitos, Pucallpa, Tacna, Talara, Tarapoto, Trujillo and Tumbes.

International Aerolíneas Argentinas, Carnaval y Moreyra 370, p 1, San Isidro, T01-513 6565, ventasperu@aerolineas argentinas.com.pe. **Air France-KLM**, Av Alvarez Calderón 185, p 6, San Isidro, T01-213 0200, reservations.peru @klm.com. **Air Madrid**, Av José Pardo 269, Miraflores, T01-214 1040, for reservations, www.airmadrid.com. **Alitalia**, Pardo 601, of 804 , Miraflores, T01-444 9285, www.alitalia.com.pe. **American Airlines**, Av Canaval y Moreyra 390, San Isidro, and in Hotel Las Américas, Av Benavides y Av Larco, Miraflores, T01-211 7000, www.aa.com. **Avianca**, Av José Pardo 140, Miraflores, T01-445 6895, T0800-51936, www.avianca.com. **Continental**, 147 Via Principal 110 of 101, Edificio Real 5, San Isidro, and in the Hotel Marriott, Av Larco 1325, Miraflores, T01-712 9230, or 0800-70030, www.continental.com. **Copa**, Canaval y Moreyra y Los Halcones, Centro Empresarial Torre Chocavento

How not to be taken for a ride

When the city of Lima tried to introduce meters in taxis, it failed. Almost anyone who puts a small sticker behind the windscreen can pass as a cabbie. Official taxis were simply too expensive and despised by the locals and by now they have almost disappeared. If you flag down a taxi in Miraflores, you will be asked (depending on your language skills) to pay up to S/.25 (almost US$7) to go to the city centre. Some locals and ex-pats pay only S/.7 (about US$2). A reasonable price is between S/.8 and S/.12 (US$2.25-3.35), depending on the destination. Bargaining is done in a friendly, almost joking fashion and always before you enter the taxi. If you don't speak Spanish, use your fingers (one for each sol) and smile. Despite the hardship, Peruvians have a great sense of humour. When you have some cash to spare and if you like the driver – some of them are professional people just trying to make extra money – contract him by the hour for the current rate of S/.15 (US$4.15).

of 105, T01-610 0810, www.copaair.com. **Delta**, C Victor Belaúnde 147, San Isidro, T01-211 9211, www.delta.com. **Iberia**, Av Camino Real 390, p 9, San Isidro, T01-411 7800, www.iberia.com. **Lacsa**, Av 2 de Mayo 755, Miraflores, T01-444 7818, www.taca.com. **Lan**, see Domestic airlines, above. **Lloyd Aéreo Boliviano**, Av José Pardo 231, Miraflores, T01-241 5210, www.labairlines.com.bo. **Lufthansa**, Av Jorge Basadre 1330, San Isidro, T01-442 4455, www.lufthansa.com. **Taca Perú**, see Domestic airlines, above. **Tame**, Av La Paz 1631, Miraflores, T01-422 6600, www.tame.com.ec. **Varig**, Av Camino Real 456, p 8, San Isidro, T01-221 0275, www.varig.com.

Bus

Although Lima is home to a seemingly never-ending list of bus companies, only a small percentage can actually be recommended.

Local

Vía Expresa Lima's only urban freeway runs from Plaza Grau in the city centre to the northern tip of the district of Barranco. This six-lane thoroughfare, locally known as 'El Zanjón' ('the ditch'), with a separate bus lane in the middle, is the fastest way to cross the city. From Plaza Grau the 8 stops in order are: Av México, Av Canadá, Av Javier Prado, Corpac, Av Aramburú, Av Angamos, Av Ricardo Palma, for Parque Kennedy, Av Benavides. Buses downtown for the Vía Expresa can be caught on Av Tacna, Av Wilson (aka Garcilaso de la Vega), Av Bolivia and Av Alfonso Ugarte. These buses are the target of pickpockets who sometimes work in groups. If you're standing in the aisle, be extra careful.

To Miraflores Av Arequipa runs 52 blocks between the downtown Lima area and Parque Kennedy in Miraflores. There is no shortage of public transport on this avenue; they have 'Todo Arequipa' on the windscreen. When heading towards downtown from Miraflores the window sticker should say 'Wilson/Tacna'. To get to Parque Kennedy from downtown look for 'Larco/Schell/Miraflores', 'Chorrillos/Huaylas' or 'Barranco/Ayacucho'.

To Callao At least 20 mins from central Lima by *colectivos*, US$0.30, bus US$0.25, taxi US$3-4 to the centre or Miraflores. Do not take a bus back to Lima after dark.

To Pachacámac If you plan to take public transport, go to the Pan-American Highway (southbound) and take a combi with window sticker 'Pachacámac/ Lurín' (US$0.85). Let the driver know you want to get off at the ruins. A taxi will cost approximately US$4.30, but if you don't ask the driver to wait for you (an extra cost), finding another to take you back to Lima may be a bit tricky. For organized tours contact a tour operator.

To Canta and beyond 100 km, 3 hrs by bus, US$2. **Trans El Chaparito** (Av G Unger 601, San Martín de Porres, Lima) and **Trans Cueva Santa** (Av G Unger 369) offer an hourly service between them at weekends and every 2 hrs on weekdays. Cueva Santa buses from Lima continue to **Huaros**, **Laguna Chuchun** and **La Viuda**. A few combis run to **La Viuda** daily from Canta, 3 hrs, US$2. To **Obrajillo** from Canta, 5 km, 10 mins, US$0.50; combis leave when full. To **Huallay** and **Cerro de Pasco** from Canta, only occasional vehicles cross the La Viuda pass (4500 m).

Long distance

There is no central bus station. All companies leave from their own terminals. Some are in San Isidro, but many are in an area around Av Carlos Zavala, which is very unsafe at any time of day but much more so at night. You are strongly advised to take a taxi to and from these terminals. Make sure you see your gear being stored on the correct bus as the place is always very busy. 'Mistakes', intentional or innocent, are not uncommon.

The following is a list of the companies repeatedly recommended for either their service or their professionalism. Note that some less-reputable companies are included simply because they're the only ones with buses to certain destinations. It's best to buy tickets as early as possible before travelling to ensure the level of service that you want. Most offer daily service. Confirm that the bus leaves from same place that the ticket was purchased. For prices and approximate duration of trip, refer to the destination.

Cruz del Sur, Jr Quilca 531, central Lima, T01-431 5125, www.cruzdelsur.com.pe, has routes to many destinations in Peru with *Ideal* ('ee-de-al') service, meaning quite comfortable buses and periodic stops for food and bathroom breaks, a cheap option with a quality company. The website accepts Visa bookings without surcharge. Destinations include **Ica**, **Arequipa**, **Cuzco**, **Puno**, **Chiclayo**, **Trujillo**, **Chincha**, **Camaná**, **Ilo**, **Moquegua**, **Pisco** and **Juliaca**.

The other **Cruz del Sur** terminal is at Av Javier Prado Este 1109, San Isidro, T01-225 6163. This offers the *Imperial* service (luxury buses, more expensive and direct, with no chance of passengers in the aisle) and *Cruzero* service (super-luxury) to **Tumbes**, **Sullana**, **Huancayo**, **Piura**, **Chiclayo**, **Trujillo**, **Huaraz**, **Jauja**, **Camaná**, **Arequipa** (with *Ideal* transfer to La Paz), **Moquegua**, **Ilo**, **Tacna** and **Cuzco**. *Imperial* buses stop at the central terminal when going north and *Ideal* buses stop at the Javier Prado terminal when going south.

Most **Ormeño** services depart from and arrive at Av Carlos Zavala 177, central Lima, T01-427 5679, www.grupo-ormeno.com: *Expreso Ancash* to the **Huaraz** area, *Expreso Continental* to the **north**, *Expreso San Cristóbal* to the **southeast** and *Expreso Chinchano* to the **south coast** and **Arequipa**. Ormeño also offers *Royal Class* and *Business Class* services to certain destinations. These buses are very comfortable with bathrooms. They arrive and depart from Av Javier Prado Este 1059, La Victoria, T01-472 5000, although *Business* buses stop at both terminals. Javier Prado is the best place to buy any **Ormeño** ticket.

Other companies include: **Transportes Atahualpa**, Jr Sandia 266, central Lima, T01-428 7732, direct to **Cajamarca** continuing to **Celendín**. **Transportes Chanchamayo**, Av Manco Cápac 1052, La Victoria, T01-265 6850, to **Tarma**, **San Ramón** and **La Merced**. **CIVA**, Paseo de La República 569-571, La Victoria, T01-330 4080, terminal at Av 28 de Julio y Paseo de La República, T01-332 5236, www.civa.com.pe, to all parts of the country with various levels of service, but mixed reports about this company. **Ittsa**, Paseo de la República 815, T01-423 5232, excellent, very secure services to the **north**, to **Trujillo**, **Chiclayo** and **Piura**. **Transportes León de Huánuco**, Av 28 de Julio 1520, La Victoria, T01-424 3893, daily to **Huánuco**, **Tingo María** and **Pucallpa**. **Línea**, José Gálvez 999, T01-424 0836, www.transporteslinea.com.pe. **Móvil Tours**,

If arriving in Lima by bus from the north and heading for the airport, you do not need to go into the centre: ask to be let out at 'Fiori' (look for the sign on top of a building on the left-hand side of the highway). This is by the junction of the Panamericana and Av Tomás Valle, which leads almost to Jorge Chávez. Take a taxi from Fiori.

Av Paseo de La República 749, central Lima near the national stadium, T01-332 0024, www.moviltours.com.pe, recommended service to **Huaraz** (*bus cama* at 1300, 2200, standard at 0800, 2100, lots of leg room, comfortable), **Chiclayo** and **Chachapoyas** should you want to go straight through. (Móvil has a second terminal at Los Olivos, very close to the airport, handy for those who are short of time for a bus connection after landing in Lima. **Oltursa**, Bauzate y Meza 644, T01-431 2395 and Aramburu 1160, San Isidro, T01-225 4499, www.oltursa.com.pe, a highly reputable company offering top-end services to **Arequipa** and destinations in **northern Peru**, mainly at night. **PerúBus/Soyuz**, Av México 333, La Victoria, T01-266 1515, www.soyuz.com.pe, to **Ica** every 8 mins, well-organized, few stops, luggage stowed safely. **Rodríguez**, Av Roosevelt 393, central Lima, T01-428 0506, good company with various levels of bus service to **Huaraz**, **Caraz**, **Yungay**, **Carhuaz**. (You are recommended to arrive in Huaraz and then use local transport to points beyond.) **Tepsa**, Av Javier Prado Este 1091, La Victoria, T01-470 6666, www.tepsa.com.pe, also at Lampa 1237-41, Lima 1, T01-477 5642, services to the north as far as **Tumbes** and the south to **Tacna**. (Tepsa also shares Terminal Delta Norte on the Panamericana Norte, with **Cruz del Sur** and **Línea**, at Av Alfredo Mendiola 5100, Urb Industrial Infantas, Los Olivos, T01-593 9000.) **Wari**, Av Luna Pizarro 343, La Victoria, and Av Los Héroes 811, San Juan de Miraflores, T01-330 3543, www.expresowari.com.pe, to **Ayacucho** and **Cuzco** via **Abancay**.

International

Ormeño, Av Javier Prado 1059, La Victoria, T01-472 1710, to **Guayaquil** (29 hrs, with a change of bus at the border, US$50), **Quito** (38 hrs), **Cali** (56 hrs), **Bogotá** (70 hrs), **Caracas** (100 hrs), **Santiago** (54 hrs), **Mendoza** (78 hrs), **Buenos Aires** (90 hrs). There is a baggage allowance of max 20 kg per person; depending on the destination, extra weight penalties are US$1-3 per kg. **El Rápido**, Av Rivera Navarrete 2650, Lince, T01-422 9508, to **Argentina** and **Uruguay**.

For international services, it's cheaper to take a bus to the border, cross and then catch another bus to your final destination. The week before and after 28 Jul (Peruvian Independence Day) and Semana Santa (Holy Week) are the busiest times of the year. Bus tickets out of Lima are extremely hard to come by unless purchased in advance. Expect prices to double during these period and check in earlier than normal to avoid possible problems.

Car

Most rental companies have an office at the airport, where you can arrange everything and pick up and leave the car. It's recommended to test-drive the car before signing the contract, as quality varies. **Avis Rent A Car**, Av Javier Prado Este 5235, T01-434 1111, www.avis.com. **Budget Car Rental**, Canaval y Moreyra 569, San Isidro, T01-442 8703, www.budget.com. **Hertz** (Inka's), Av Cantuarias 160, Miraflores, T01-445 5716, www.hertz.com.pe. **National**, Av Costanera 1380, San Miguel, T01-578 7878 , www.nationalcar.com. **Paz Rent A Car**, Av Diez Canseco 319, oficina 15, Miraflores, T01-446 4395, T9993 9853 (mob), pazrent@latinmail.com.

Taxi

Conventional taxis operate without meters so agree the fare before you get in. Tips are not expected. As driving a taxi in Lima (or anywhere in Peru) simply requires a windscreen sticker saying 'Taxi', they come in all colours and sizes. By law, though, all must have the vehicle's registration number painted on the side. If it does not, don't take it. Yellow taxis are usually the safest since they have a number, the driver's name and radio contact. A large number of taxis are also white. Daewoo Tico were most common, but they are regarded as unsuitable for the rigours of Lima traffic and are being phased out. Choose something more substantial and always use the seatbelt.

The following are taxi fares for some of the more common routes, give or take a sol.

From downtown Lima To Parque Kennedy (Miraflores), US$2; Museo de la Nación, US$2; South American Explorers, US$2; Archaeology Museum, US$2; Immigration, US$1.15; Barranco, US$3.

From Miraflores (Parque Kennedy)
To Museo de la Nación, US$2; Archaeology Museum, US$3; Immigration, US$2.

Official taxi companies, registered with the Municipality of Lima are without a doubt the safest option but cost much more than just picking one up in the street; hourly rates possible: **Taxi América**, T01-265 1960; **Moli Taxi**, T01-479 0030; **Taxi Real**, T01-470 6263; **Taxi Seguro**, T01-241 9292; **Taxi Tata**, T01-274 5151; **TCAM**, run by Carlos Astacio, T01-983 9305, safe, reliable.

Private drivers
Recommended, knowledgeable drivers include: **César A Canales N**, T01-436 6184, T9687 3310 (mob), or through **Home Perú**, only speaks Spanish, reliable; **Hugo Casanova Morella**, T01-485 7708 (he lives in La Victoria), for city tours, travel to airport, etc; **Mónica Velásquez Carlich**, T01-425 5087, T01-9943 0796 (mob), vc_monica @hotmail.com, airport pickups, tours, speaks some English, many recommendations.

Taxi colectivos
Regular private cars acting as taxis (*colectivos*) charge US$0.50. They are a faster, more comfortable option than municipal public transport, but they are no safer. There are three routes: 1 between Av Arequipa and Av Tacna, which runs from Miraflores to the centre of Lima; 2 between Plaza San Martín and Callao; 3 between the Vía Expresa and the district of Chorrillos. Look for the coloured sticker posted on the windscreen. These cars will stop at any time to pick people up. When full (usually five or six people) they will only stop to let some- one off, then the process begins again to fill the empty space.

Train

At the time of going to press, service on the **Central Railway** to **Huancayo** was running only on special occasions, such as Bank Holiday weekend, see page 487.

Directory

Banks
BCP, Jr Lampa 499, central Lima, Av Pardo 425 and Av Larco at Pasaje Tarata, Miraflores, Av Pardo y Aliaga at Av Camino Real, San Isidro. Mon-Fri 0900-1800, Sat 0930-1230. Accepts and sells American Express TCs only, accepts Visa card and branches have Visa/Plus ATM.
Banco de Comercio, Av Pardo 272 and Av Larco 265, Miraflores, Jr Lampa 560, central Lima (main branch). Mon-Fri 0900-1800, Sat 0930-1200. Changes and sells American Express TCs only, ATM accepts Visa/Plus.
BBVA Continental, corner of Av Larco and Av Benavides and corner of Av Larco and Pasaje Tarata, Miraflores, Jr Cusco 286, central Lima near Plaza San Martín. Mon-Fri 0900-1800, Sat 0930-1230. TCs (American Express). Visa/Plus ATM.
Banco Financiero, Av Ricardo Palma 278, near Parque Kennedy (main branch). Mon-Fri 0900-1800, Sat 0930-1230. TCs (American Express), ATM for Visa/Plus.
Banco Santander Central Hispano (BSCH), Av Pardo 482 and Av Larco 479, Miraflores, Av Augusto Tamayo 120, San Isidro (main branch). Mon-Fri 0900-1800, Sat 0930-1230. TCs (Visa and Citicorp). Red Unicard ATM for Visa/Plus and MasterCard.
Banco Wiese Sudameris, Av Diagonal 176 on Parque Kennedy, Av José Pardo 697, Miraflores, Av Alfonso Ugarte 1292, Breña, Miguel Dasso 286, San Isidro. Mon-Fri 0915-1800, Sat 0930-1230. TCs (American Express only), ATM for Visa, MasterCard, Maestro and Cirrus.
Citibank, in all **Blockbuster** stores, and at Av 28 de Julio 886, Av Benavides 23rd block and Av Emilio Cavenecia 175, Miraflores, Av Las Flores 205 and in Centro Comercial Camino Real, Av Camino Real 348, San Isidro. **Blockbuster**, Sat and Sun 1000-1900. changes and sells Citicorp cheques.
Interbank, Jr de la Unión 600, central Lima (main branch). Mon-Fri 0900-1800. Also Av Pardo 413, Av Larco 690 and in Larcomar, Miraflores, Av Grau 300, Barranco, Av Pezet 1405 and Av Pardo y Aliaga 634, San Isidro. Accepts and sells American Express TCs only, ATM for Visa/Plus, MasterCard, Maestro,

Cirrus and AmEx. You can also get good rates of exchange at supermarkets such as **Wong**, **Metro** and **Santa Isabel**.
Cajero GlobalNet ATM, Diez Canseco y Av La Paz, Miraflores. Claims to take all cards; also has phones for international calls.

Casas de cambio

There are many *casas de cambio* on and around Jr Ocoña off the Plaza San Martín. On the corner of Ocoña and Jr Camaná you'll no doubt see the large concentration of *cambistas* (street changers) with huge wads of dollars, euros and soles in one hand and a calculator in the other. They should be avoided. Changing money on the street should only be done with official street changers wearing an identity card with a photo. Keep in mind that this card doesn't *automatically* mean that they are legitimate but most likely you won't have a problem. Around Parque Kennedy and down Av Larco in Miraflores are dozens of official *cambistas* with ID photo cards attached to their usually blue, sometimes green vests. There are also those who are independent and are dressed in street clothes, but it's safer to do business with an official money changer. There are a few places on Jr de la Unión at Plaza San Martín that will accept worn, ripped and old note, but the exchange rate will be terrible. There are also several *cambios* and *cambistas* on Av José Pardo, Miraflores.

A repeatedly recommended *casa de cambio* is **LAC Dolar**, Jr Camaná 779, 1 block from Plaza San Martín, p 2, T01-428 8127, also at Av La Paz 211, Miraflores, T01-242 4069. Mon-Sat 0930-1800, good rates, very helpful, safe, fast, reliable, 2% commission on cash and TCs (Amex, Citicorp, Thomas Cook, Visa), will come to your hotel if you're in a group. Another recommended *casa de cambio* is **Virgen P Socorro**, Jr Ocoña 184, T01-428 7748. Daily 0830-2000, safe, reliable and friendly.
American Express, Travex SA, Av Santa Cruz 621, Miraflores, T01-710 3900, info@travex.com.pe, Mon-Fri 0830-1730, Sat 0900-1300. Replaces lost or stolen Amex cheques of any currency in the world. Can purchase Amex cheques with Amex card only. Or branches of **Viajes Falabella**, eg Jr Belén 630, T01-428 9779, or Av Larco 747-753, Miraflores, T01-444 4239, lgutierrez@viajesfalabella.com.pe.
MasterCard, Porta 111, p 6, Miraflores, T01-311 6000.
Moneygram, Ocharan 260, Miraflores, T01-447 4044. Safe and reliable agency for sending and receiving money. Locations throughout Lima and the provinces. Exchanges most world currencies and TCs.
Western Union, Av Petit Thouars 3595, San Isidro, T01-422 0036, main branch. Av Larco 826, Miraflores, T01-241 1220 (also **TNT** office). Jr Carabaya 693, central Lima, T01-428 7624.

Cultural centres

Alianza Francesa, Av Arequipa 4595, Miraflores, T01-446 5524, www.alianzafrancesalima.edu.pe. Various cultural activities, also has a library.
British Council, Torre Parque Mar, p 22, Av José Larco 1301, T01-617 3060, www.britishcouncil.org/peru.htm.
CCPUCP (cultural centre of the Universidad Católica), Camino Real 1075, San Isidro, T01-616 1616, http://cultural.pucp.edu.pe. One of the best in Lima, with an excellent theatre (tickets US$7.15), European art films (US$1.45 Mon-Wed), galleries, good café and a bookshop selling art and literature titles. Recommended.
Centro Cultural de España, Natalio Sánchez 181-85, Santa Beatriz, T01-330 0412. Has an art gallery and a cinema.
Centro Cultural Peruano Japonés, Av Gregorio Escobedo 803, Jesús María, T01-463 0606, postmast@apjp.org.pe. Has a concert hall, cinema, galleries, museum of Japonese immigration, cheap and excellent restaurant, lots of activities. Recommended.
Goethe Institute, Jr Nasca 722, Jesús María, T01-433 3180, www.goethe.de/hn/lim/deindex.htm. 0800-2000 Mon-Fri, library, German papers.
Instituto Cultural Peruano-Norteamericano, Jr Cusco 446, central Lima, T01-428 3530, with library. Main branch at Av Angamos Oeste 120, Miraflores, T01-242 6300, www.icpna.edu.pe. Theatre productions and modern dance performances are just a couple of the activities the ICPNA offers. See also Language schools below.

Doctors

For hospitals, see page 128.
Recommendations for doctors and dentists, are available from your consulate.
Backpackers Medical Care, Dr Jorge Bazan, T01-9735 2668, backpackersmc@yahoo.com. About US$13 per consultation, speaks English, frequently recommended.

Embassies and consulates

Australia, Av Víctor Belaúnde 147, Vía Principal 155, ed 3, of 1301, San Isidro, T01-222 8281, info.peru@austrade.gov.au.
Austria, Av Central 643, p 5, San Isidro, T01-442 0503.
Belgian Consulate, Angamos Oeste 392, Miraflores, T01-422 8231.
Bolivian Consulate, Los Castaños 235, San Isidro, T01-442 3836, postmast@emboli.org.pe. Daily 0900-1330, 24 hrs for visas (except those requiring clearance from La Paz).
Brazilian Consulate, José Pardo 850, Miraflores, T01-421 5650, Mon-Fri 0930-1300.
Canada, Libertad 130, Miraflores, T01-444 4015, lima@dfait-maeci.gc.ca.
Chilean Consulate, Javier Prado Oeste 790, San Isidro, T01-611 2211, embchile@mail.cosapidata.com.pe. Open 0900-1300, need appointment.
Colombian Consulate, Av Jorge Basadre 1580, San Isidro, T01-441 0530. Mon-Fri 0800-1400.
Ecuadorean Consulate, Las Palmeras 356, San Isidro (6th block of Av Javier Prado Oeste), T01-440 9991, embjecua@amauta.Rcp.net.pe.
Finland, Av Víctor Belaúnde 147, Torre Real Tres of 502, Centro Empresarial Real, San Isidro, T01-222 4466.
France, Arequipa 3415, San Isidro, T01-215 8400, FRANCE.EMBAJADA@com putextos.com.pe.
Germany, Av Arequipa 4202, Miraflores, T01-212 5016, F422 6475; emergency number T9927 8338.
Israel, Natalio Sánchez 125, p 6, Santa Beatriz, T01-433 4431.
Italy, Av G Escobedo 298, Jesús María, T01-463 2727.
Japan, Av San Felipe 356, Jesús María, T01-463 0000.
Netherlands Consulate, Torre Parque Mar, Av José Larco 1301, p 13, Miraflores, T01-213 9800, info@nlgovlim.com, open Mon-Fri 0900-1200.
New Zealand Consulate, Av Camino Real 390, Torre Central, p 17 (Casilla 3553), San Isidro, T01-221 2833, reya@nzlatam.com. Open Mon-Fri 0830-1300, 1400-1700.
Spain, Jorge Basadre 498, San Isidro, T01-212 5155, open 0900-1300.
Sweden, La Santa María 130, San Isidro, T01-442 8905, konslima@terra.com.pe.
Switzerland, Av Salaverry 3240, Magdalena, Lima 17, T01-264 0305, embsuiza@correo.tnet.com.pe.
UK, Torre Parque Mar, Av Larco 1301, p 22, T01-617 3000, www.britishembassy.gov.uk/peru. Apr-Nov Mon-Thu 1300-2130, Fri 1300-1830; Dec-Apr Mon and Fri 1300-1830, Tue-Thu 1300-2130, good for security information and newspapers.
USA, Av Encalada block 17, Surco, T01-434 3000, for emergencies after hours T434 3032, http://lima.usembassy.gov. The Consulate is in the same building.

Hospitals and clinics

Clínica Anglo Americano, Av Salazar 3rd block, San Isidro, a few blocks from Ovalo Gutiérrez, T01-221 3656. Stocks yellow fever and tetanus vaccines. Dr Luis Manuel Valdez recommended.
Clínica Internacional, Jr Washington 1471 y Paseo Colón (9 de Diciembre), downtown Lima, T01-433 4306. Good, clean and professional, consultations up to US$35, no inoculations.
Instituto Médico Lince, León Velarde 221, near 17th and 18th blocks of Av Arenales, Lince, T01-471 2238. Dr Alejandro Bussalleu Rivera speaks English, good for stomach problems, about US$28 for initial consultation. Repeatedly recommended.
Instituto de Ginecología y Reproducción, Av Manuel Urbina 1045, Monterrico, T01-434 2650. Recommended gynaecologists are **Dra Alicia García** and **Dr Ladislao Prasak**.
Instituto de Medicina Tropical, Av Honorio Delgado near the Pan-American Highway in the Cayetano Heredia Hospital, San Martín de Porres, T01-482 3903.
Clínica del Niño, Av Brasil 600 at 1st block of Av 28 de Julio, Breña, T01-330 0066, www.isn.gob.pe. Gives yellow fever vaccination, US$20.

Centro Anti-Rabia de Lima, Jr Austria 1300, Breña, T01-425 6313. Mon-Sat 0830-1830. Consultation is about US$2.50.
Clínica Padre Luis Tezza, Av El Polo 570, Monterrico, T01-610 5050, www.clinica tezza.com.pe. Clinic specializing in a wide variety of illnesses/disorders etc, expensive; for stomach or intestinal problems, ask for Dr Raúl Morales (speaks some English, US$28 for first consultation).
Clínica Ricardo Palma, Av Javier Prado Este 1066, San Isidro, T01-224 2224, www.crp.com.pe. For general medical consultations, English spoken.
Clínica Santa Teresa, Av Los Halcones 410, Surquillo, T01-221 2027, stateresa@terra.com.pe. Dr José Luis Calderón, general practitioner. Good.
International Chiropractors Center, Av Santa Cruz 555, Miraflores, T01-221 4764.
International Health Department, at Jorge Chávez airport, T01-517 1845. Open 24 hrs a day for vaccinations.

Internet
Lima is completely inundated with internet cafés, so you will have no problem finding one regardless of where you are. An hour will cost you approximately S./2-3 (US$0.60-0.90). In Miraflores, cafés are usually open till 2400.

Language schools
Conexus, Av Paseo de la República 3195, of 1002, San Isidro, T01-421 5642, www.conexusinstitute.com. Reasonably priced and effective.
El Sol School of Languages, Grimaldo del Solar 469, Miraflores, T01-242 7763, www.elsol.idiomasperu.com. US$15 per hr for private tuition, also small groups US$11 per hr. Family homestays and volunteer programmes available.
ESIT Idiomas de Lima, Av Javier Prado Este 4457, Surco, Lima 33, T01-434 1060, www.esit-peru.com.
Instituto Cultural Peruano-Norte-americano, see Cultural centres. Classes Mon-Fri 0900-1100, US$80 per month, no private classes.
Instituto de Idiomas (Pontífica Universidad Católica del Perú), Av Camino Real 1037, San Isidro, T01-442 8761. Classes Mon-Fri 1100-1300, private lessons possible.

There are also numerous independent teachers (enquire about rates): **Srta Susy Arteaga**, T01-534 9289, T9989 7271 (mob), susyarteaga@hotmail.com or susyarteaga@yahoo.com; **Srta Patty Félix**, T01-521 2559, patty_fel24@yahoo.com; **Sra Lourdes Gálvez**, T01-435 3910, also Quechua; **Sr Mariano** and **Sr Dante Herrera**, T01-275 6460, peruidiomas@LatinMail.com; **Sra Georgelina Sadastizágal**, T01-275 6460, peruidiomas@LatinMail.com; **Luis Villanueva**, T01-247 7054, www.ac spanishclasses.com, flexible, reliable, helpful.

Laundry
There are *lavanderías* (laundromats) all over Lima. Some charge by piece (expensive), others by weight. Many have a self-service option. Next-day service is the norm if you've left laundry for them to wash. Most of the hotels in the higher price range offer laundry but tend to be very expensive.
Cisne Blanco, Av Santa Cruz 1318, Miraflores, T01-221 5234.
Lavva Queen, Av Larco 1158, Miraflores, T01-444 8520.
Laverap, Schell 601, Miraflores, T01-241 0759; Av Pardo y Aliaga 590, T01-422 1618, San Isidro. You can wash your own clothes or leave them to be picked up (more expensive).
Martinizing Dry Cleaning, Av Espinar 270, T01-446 2406, and Av Benavides 1763, T01-447 5547 in Miraflores, Av Dos de Mayo 1225, T01-440 2911, San Isidro. Probably the best, but very expensive.
Presto, Av Benavides 433, Miraflores, T01-242 9910. Good, reliable.

Pharmacies
When possible it is recommended to use pharmacy chains as they are modern, well-stocked, safe and very professional. They can be found in or next to supermarkets, sometimes attached to fuel station mini-marts and pretty much everywhere else. Some offer 24-hr delivery service. Try **Boticas Fasa**, T01-619 0000 for delivery, www.boticasfasa.com.pe; **Farmacia Deza**, Av Conquistadores 1144, San Isidro, same as Pharmax, open 24 hrs; **Pharmax**, Av Salaverry 3100, San Isidro, Centro Comercial El Polo, Monterrico (near the US embassy), pharmacy/hypermarket, with imported goods (Jewish food products sometimes

available at Av Salaverry branch, which is open 24 hrs); **Superfarma**, T01-267 9000 for delivery, servicioalcliente @superfarma.com.

Post

The central post office is on Jr Camaná 195 in the centre of Lima near the Plaza de Armas. Hours are Mon-Fri 0730-1900 and Sat 0730-1600. Poste restante is in the same building but is considered unreliable. In Miraflores the main post office is on Av Petit Thouars 5201 (same hrs). There are many more small branches scattered around Lima, but they are less reliable. When receiving parcels weighing more than 1 kg from other countries, they will be automatically sent to one of Lima's two customs post offices: C Teodoro Cárdenas 267, Santa Beatriz (12th block of Av Arequipa); and Av Tomás Valle, Los Olivos (near the Panamerican Highway). Bring your passport and a lot of patience as the process can take a long time. Long trousers must be worn when going to these offices.

For express service, there are a few companies to choose from: **DHL**, Los Castaños 225, San Isidro, T01-215 7500; **UPS**, Av del Ejército 2107, San Isidro, T01-264 0105; **Federal Express**, Av Jorge Chávez 475, T01-242 2280, Miraflores, and C José Olaya 260, Miraflores.

Prison visits

Visits to the **Establecimiento Penitenciario de Mujeres Chorrillos Santa Mónica** (women's prison) in the district of Chorrillos are easy and much appreciated by the inmates, both Peruvian and foreign. You must bring your passport and give the name of someone you're visiting (for the current list, check with your embassy for prisoners from your own country, or ask at **South American Explorers**, who have full details). You are permitted to bring food (up to 1 kg of fruit, but none that ferments), toiletries, magazines, books etc. Visiting times are 0900-1300 and 1400-1600 on Sat for men and Wed and Sun for women. Shoes that have any kind of heel are not permitted (nor are boots) and women must wear skirts below the knee which, if you don't have one, can be rented across the street from the prison. Men must wear long trousers. Visits are also possible to the men's prisons of **Callao** and **Lurigancho**.

Telephone

Easiest to use are the many independent phone offices, *locutorios*, all over the city, which take phone cards. Cards can be purchased in the *locutorios* or in the street nearby. There are payphones all over the city; some accept coins, some only phone cards and some both.

Useful addresses

Immigration, Av España 700 y Jr Huaraz, Breña, open 0900-1330. Visa extensions on 3rd floor given the same day, usually within 30 mins (expensive). Provides new entry stamps if passport is lost or stolen.
Intej, Av San Martín 240, Barranco, T01-247 3230. They can extend student cards, change flight itineraries bought with student cards.
National Library, Av Abancay 4th block, with Jr Miró Quesada, T01-428 7690. Mon-Sat 0800-2000, Sun 0830-1330.
Peruvian Touring and Automobile Club: Av César Vallejo 699, Lince, T01-221 2432, www.touringperu.com.pe. Offers help to tourists and particularly to members of the leading motoring associations. Good maps of whole country, regional routes and the South American sections of the Pan-American Highway available (US$5).
Tourist Police, administrative office at Jr Moore 268, Magdalena at the 38th block of Av Brasil, T01-460 1060, open daily 24 hrs; for public enquiries etc, Jr Pachitea at the corner of Belén (Jr de la Unión), Lima, T01-424 2053. They are friendly and very helpful, English spoken. It is recommended to visit if you have had property stolen.
Voluntary organizations in and around Lima often welcome volunteers. Some will ask interested parties to show up when they can, others might ask for a commitment of at least 3 months. **South American Explorers** is the best place to find out about volunteer opportunities.

Cuzco & the Sacred Valley

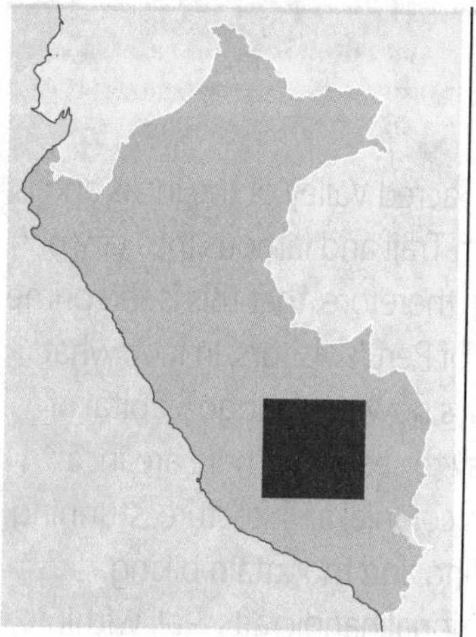

Footprint features

Introduction

Cuzco stands at the head of the Sacred Valley of the Incas and is the jumping-off point for the Inca Trail and famous Inca city of Machu Picchu. It's not surprising, therefore, that this is the prime destination for the vast majority of Peru's visitors. In fact, what was once an ancient Inca capital is now the 'gringo' capital of the entire continent. And it's easy to see why. There are Inca ruins aplenty, as well as fabulous colonial architecture, stunning scenery, great trekking, river rafting and mountain biking, beautiful textiles and other traditional handicrafts – all within easy reach of the nearest cappuccino or comfy hotel room.

The Spaniards transformed the centre of a magnificent Inca civilization into a jewel of colonial achievement. Yet the city today is not some dead monument; its history breathes through the stones. The Quechua people bring the city to life, with a combination of prehispanic and Christian beliefs, and every visitor is made welcome.

Starting your visit to the Cuzco region outside the city has many advantages. Staying a day or two in the valley of the Urubamba river will give you time to acclimatize to the shortage of oxygen at these altitudes. And, as nowhere is very far from the city, you can easily nip into town for any necessities. At Ollantaytambo and Pisac you will see Inca ruins and terraced hillsides without the overlay of the Spanish conquest. Then, when you are fit and ready, you can make your own assault on Cuzco and all its churches, museums, pubs, clubs and shops, not to mention the many festivals which are held throughout the year. If city life is not for you, there is no shortage of adventure. The huge influx of visitors has encouraged the opening of new trails, some for walking, some for biking, the latest hot spot being the 'lost city' of Choquequirao.

★ Don't miss...

1 **Church of San Blas** The carved pulpit is remarkable and you can get your fill of traditional crafts in the surrounding streets, page 141.
2 **Inca stonework** The Stone of 12 Angles on Calle Hatun Rumiyoc is the best example, page 142.
3 **Pisac** Walk up to the ruins; it's a stiff climb, but not only are the Inca ruins worth the effort, as you go higher the views of the Urubamba valley just get better and better, page 178.
4 **Moray** In the hills above the Urubamba, three large depressions, converted into terraced crop laboratories show to perfection the Incas' thorough understanding of their environment, page 182.
5 **Machu Picchu** Find the time to peer into corners, investigate angles of stones, the weight of lintels, the outlook of windows. See how rocks and openings align themselves with peaks across the valley, page 191.
6 **Andahuaylillas** Visit the Sistine Chapel of the Andes and, nearby, the equally remarkable church at Huaro. For the best view, take a strong torch as they are poorly lit, page 211.
7 **Choquequirao** The newest addition to the 'lost cities trail', is only reached by adventurous trekking, page 215.

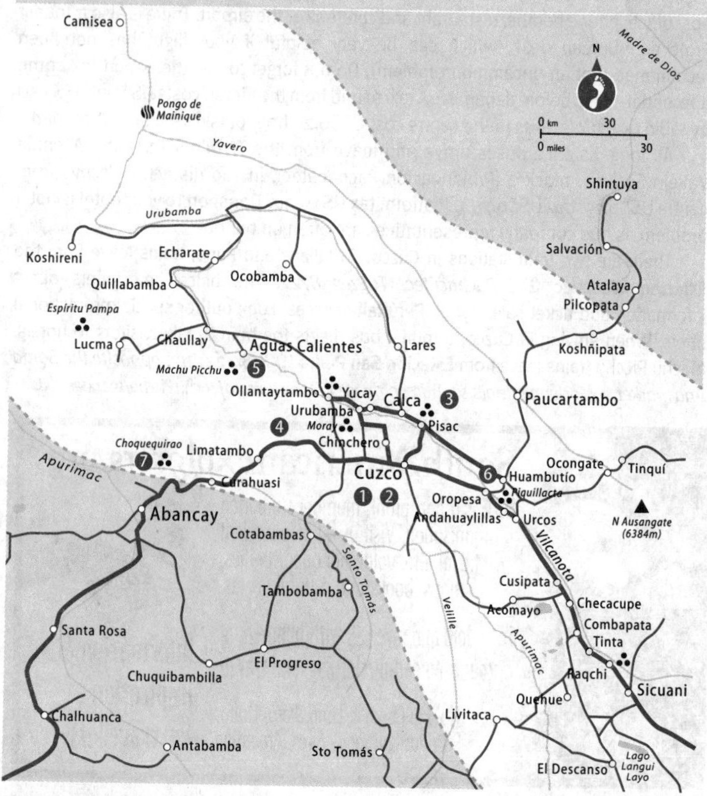

Cuzco city

→ *Colour map 5, A5.* *Population 275,000. Altitude 3310 m.*

Since there are so many sights to see in Cuzco city, not even the most ardent tourist would be able to visit them all. For those with limited time, or for those who want a whistle-stop tour, a list of must-sees would comprise: the combination of Inca and colonial architecture at Qoricancha; the huge Inca ceremonial centre of Sacsayhuaman; the paintings of the Last Supper and the 1650 earthquake in the cathedral; the main altar of La Compañía de Jesús; the pulpit of San Blas; the high choir at San Francisco; the monstrance at La Merced; and the view from San Cristóbal. If you have the energy, catch a taxi up to the White Christ and watch the sunset as you look out upon one of the most fascinating cities in the world. If you visit one museum make it the Museo Inka; it has the most comprehensive collection. ▸▸ *For Sleeping, Eating and other listings, see pages 144-177.*

Ins and outs

Getting there

Most travellers arriving from Lima will do so by air. No flights arrive in Cuzco at night. The airport is at Quispiquilla, near the bus terminal, 1.6 km southeast of the centre. Airport information T084-222611/601. You can book a hotel at the airport through a travel agency, but this is not really necessary. Many representatives of hotels and travel agencies operate at the airport, offering transport to the hotel with which they are associated. Take your time to choose your hotel, at the price you can afford. There is a post office, phone booths, restaurant and cafeteria at the airport. There is also a Tourist Protection Bureau desk, which can be very helpful if your flight has not been reconfirmed (not an uncommon problem). Do not forget to pay the airport tax at the appropriate desk before departure. A taxi to and from the airport costs US$1-2 (US$3.50 by radio taxi). *Colectivos* to the centre cost US$0.20 from outside the airport car park.

All long-distance buses arrive and leave from the Terminal Terrestre, Avenida Vallejo Santoni, block 2 (Prolongación Pachacútec), in Ttio district. *Colectivo* from centre US$0.15, taxi US$0.75-1. Platform tax US$0.30. Transport to your hotel is not a problem as bus company representatives are often on hand.

There are two train stations in Cuzco. To Juliaca and Puno, trains leave from the **Estación Wanchac** ⓘ *C Pachacútec, T084-238722*. The office here offers direct information and ticket sales for all **PerúRail** services. Look out for special promotional offers. When arriving in Cuzco, a tourist bus meets the train to take visitors to hotels. Machu Picchu trains leave from **Estación San Pedro** ⓘ *T084-221313, opposite the Santa Ana market.* ▸▸ *For further details, see Transport, page 173. For trains to Machu Picchu, see page 208.*

Getting around

The centre of Cuzco is small and is easily explored on foot. Bear in mind, however, that at this altitude walking up some of the city's steep cobbled streets may leave you out of breath, so you'll need to take your time. It is even possible to walk up to Sacsayhuaman, but a better idea is to take a combi to Tambo Machay and walk back downhill to town via Qenqo and Sacsayhuaman. Combis are the main form of public transport in the city: well- organized, cheap and safe. Taxis are also cheap and recommended when arriving by air, train or bus. If you wish to explore this area on your own, Road Map (*Hoja de ruta*) No 10 is excellent. You can get it from the **Automóvil y Touring Club del Perú**, see page 174. There are very few good maps of Cuzco available. ▸▸ *For further details, see Transport, page 122.*

Motorists beware; many streets end in flights of steps not marked as such.

Tourist information

Official **tourist office** ⓘ *Portal Mantas 117-A, next to La Merced church, T084-263176, daily 0800-2000*. There are also **i perú** tourist information desks ⓘ *airport, T084-237364, daily 0600-1300; Av Sol 103, of 102, Galerías Turísticas, T084-234498, daily 0830-1930*. **Dirección Regional de Turismo** ⓘ *Av de la Cultura 734, 3 piso, T084-223701, Mon-Fri 0800-1300*. See box, page 136, for OFEC offices and INC office for Machu Picchu. **South American Explorers** ⓘ *Cusco Clubhouse, Choquechaca 188, No 4, T084-245484, www.saexplorers.org, Mon-Fri 0930-1700, Sat 0930-1300*, is an excellent resource for the traveller, only a couple of minutes' walk from the Plaza de Armas. Great information on the Cuzco area, along with an extensive English-language library, expedition reports, maps, weekly events, flight confirmations, free internet for members, phone and mail service and equipment storage. They have a recycling centre, practical advice on responsible tourism and a volunteer resource centre. Their leaflet *Enjoy Cusco Safely* is invaluable (for more advice see page 45). They are also in Lima, see page 78.

Safety

If you need a *denuncia* (a report for insurance purposes, available from the Banco de la Nación), the **tourist police** ⓘ *C Saphi 510, T084-249654*, will type it out. Always go to the police when robbed, even though it will take a bit of time. Police patrol the streets, trains and stations, but one should still be vigilant. On no account walk back to your hotel after dark from a bar or club, as muggings do occur. For safety's sake, pay the US$1 taxi fare, but not just any taxi. Ask the club's doorman to get a licensed taxi for you (see Taxis, page 174). Other areas in which to take care include Santa Ana market, the San Cristóbal area and at out-of-the-way ruins. **Indecopi** (Tourist Protection Bureau) ⓘ *Portal Carrizos, Plaza de Armas, toll free T0800-42579 (24-hour hotline, not available from pay phones); head office Av Sol 8212B, p 2, T084-252987, mmarroquin@indecopi. gob.pe*, protects the consumer rights of all tourists and helps with any problems or complaints. It can be helpful in dealing with tour agencies, hotels or restaurants.

Permission to enter

A combined entry ticket to most of the sites of main historical and cultural interest in and around Cuzco, called the **Boleto Turístico General** (BTG), costs US$21 (S/.70) and is valid for 10 days, or US$12 (S/.40) for two days (either just the museums, or just the archaeological sites). It is payable in soles only. It permits entrance to: Santa Catalina convent and art museum, Museo de Sitio Qoricancha (but not Qoricancha itself), Museo Histórico Regional (Casa Garcilaso), Museo Palacio Municipal de Arte Contemporáneo, Museo de Arte Popular, Centro Qosqo de Arte Nativo, Monumento Pachacútec; the archaeological sites of Sacsayhuaman, Qenqo, Puka Pukara, Tambo Machay, Pisac, Ollantaytambo, Chinchero, Tipón and Piquillacta.

The BTG can be bought at the **OFEC office** (Casa Garcilaso), Plaza Regocijo, esquina C Garcilaso, T084-226919, Mon-Sat 0800-1600, Sun 0800-1200, or Av Sol 103, T084-227037, Mon-Fri 0800-1800, Sat 0830-1230, or at any of the sites included in the ticket. There is a 50% discount for students with a green ISIC card, which is only available at the OFEC office (Casa Garcilaso) upon presentation of the student card. Take your ISIC card when visiting the sites, as some may ask to see it.

All sites are very crowded on Sundays but many churches are closed to visitors on Sundays. Be aware too that 'official' opening times are unreliable. Photography is not allowed in the churches and museums.

On the back of the BTG is a map of the centre of Cuzco with the main sites of interest clearly marked. It also includes a map of the tourist routes from Cuzco to the Sacred Valley following the Río Urubamba towards Machu Picchu, as well as the southeastern area of Cuzco on the road to Puno.

Entrance tickets for the cathedral, Museo de Arte Religioso, Museo Inka (Palacio del Almirante), Santo Domingo/Qoricancha and La Merced can be bought separately, or some of them on a joint ticket covering the cathedral, San Blas, Museo de Arte Religioso and La Compañía for US$10 (S/.35). Machu Picchu ruins and Inca Trail entrance tickets are sold at the **Instituto Nacional de Cultura** (INC), San Bernardo s/n between Mantas and Almagro, T084-236061, Mon-Fri 0900- 1300, 1600-1800, Sat 0900-1100.

Background

The ancient Inca capital is said to have been founded around AD 1100. According to the central Inca creation myth, the Sun sent his son, Manco Cápac, and the Moon sent her daughter, Mama Ocllo, to spread culture and enlighten- ment throughout the dark, barbaric lands. They emerged from the icy depths of Lake Titicaca and began their journey in search of a place where they could found their kingdom. They were ordered to head north from the lake until a golden staff they carried could be plunged into the ground for its entire length. The soil of the *altiplano* was so thin that they had to travel as far as the valley of Cuzco where, on the mountain of Huanacauri, the staff fully disappeared and the soil was found to be suitably fertile. This was the sign they were looking for. They named this place Cuzco, meaning 'navel of the earth' according to popular legend (there is no linguistic basis for this).

Today, the city's beauty cannot be overstated. It is a fascinating mix of Inca and colonial Spanish architecture: churches, monasteries and convents and pre-Columbian ruins are interspersed with hotels, bars and restaurants that have sprung up to cater for the hundreds of thousands of tourists. Almost every central street has remains of Inca walls, arches and doorways and many are lined with Inca stonework, now serving as the foundations for more modern dwellings.

Cuzco has developed into a major commercial centre of 275,000 inhabitants, most of whom are Quechua. The city council has designated the Quechua name, Qosqo, as the official spelling. Despite its growth, however, the city is still laid out much as it was in Inca times. The Incas conceived their capital in the shape of a puma and this can be seen from above, with the Río Tullumayo forming the spine, Sacsayhuaman the head, and the main city centre the body. The best place for an overall view of the Cuzco Valley is from the puma's head – the top of the hill of Sacsayhuaman.

Sights

Plaza de Armas and around

The heart of the city in Inca days was *Huacaypata* (the place of tears) and *Cusipata* (the place of happiness), divided by a channel of the Río Saphi. Today, Huacaypata is the Plaza de Armas and Cusipata is Plaza Regocijo. This was the great civic square of the Incas, flanked by their palaces, and was a place of solemn parades and great assemblies. Each territory conquered by the Incas had some of its soil taken to Cuzco to be mingled symbolically with the soil of the Huacaypata, as a token of its incorporation into the empire. As well as the many great ceremonies, the plaza has also seen its share of executions, among them the last Inca, Túpac Amaru, the rebel *conquistador*, Diego de Almagro the Younger, and the 18th-century indigenous leader, Túpac Amaru II.

On the northeast side of the square, the early 17th-century baroque **cathedral** ⓘ *Mon-Wed, Fri and Sat 1000-1130, 1400-1730, Thu and Sun 1400-1730 only, US$3; daily 0500-1000 for worshippers, Quechua Mass at 0500-0600,* forms part of a three-church complex: the cathedral itself, **Iglesia Jesús y María** (1733) on the left as you look at it and **El Triunfo** (1533) on the right. There are two entrances; the cathedral doors are used during Mass but the tourist entrance is on the left-hand side through Iglesia Jesús y María. The cathedral itself was built on the site of the Palace of Inca Wiracocha (*Kiswarcancha*) using stones from Sacsayhuaman.

The gleaming, renovated gilded main altar of the **Iglesia Jesús y María** draws the eyes to the end of the church. However, take the time to look up at the colourful murals which have been partially restored. The two gaudy, mirror-encrusted altars towards the front of the church are also hard to miss.

Walking through into the cathedral's transept, the oldest surviving painting in Cuzco can be seen. It depicts the 1650 earthquake. It also shows how, within only one century, the Spaniards had already divided the main plaza in two. *El Señor de los Temblores* (The Lord of the Earthquakes) can be seen being paraded around the Plaza de Armas, while fire rages through the colonial buildings with their typical red-tiled roofs. Much of modern-day Cuzco was built after this event. The choir stalls, by a 17th-century Spanish priest, are a magnificent example of colonial baroque art (80 saints and virgins are exquisitely represented), as is the elaborate pulpit. On the left is the solid-silver high altar. At the far right-hand end of the cathedral is an interesting local painting of the Last Supper (there is another in the Museo de Arte Religioso, see page 141). But this is the Last Supper with a difference, for Jesus is about to tuck into a plate of *cuy*, washed down with a glass of *chicha*!

Entering **El Triunfo** there is a stark contrast between the dark, heavy atmosphere of the cathedral and the light, simple structure of this serene church. Built on the site of *Suntur Huasi* (The Roundhouse), El Triunfo was the first Christian church in Cuzco. The name *El Triunfo* (The Triumph) came from the Spanish victory over an indigenous rebellion in 1536. It was here that the Spaniards congregated, hiding from Manco Inca who had besieged the city, almost taking it from the invaders. The Spaniards claim to have witnessed two miracles here in their hour of need. First, they were visited by the Virgin of the Descent, who helped put out the flames devouring the thatched roofs, then came the equestrian saint, James the Greater, who helped kill many indigenous

Cuzco

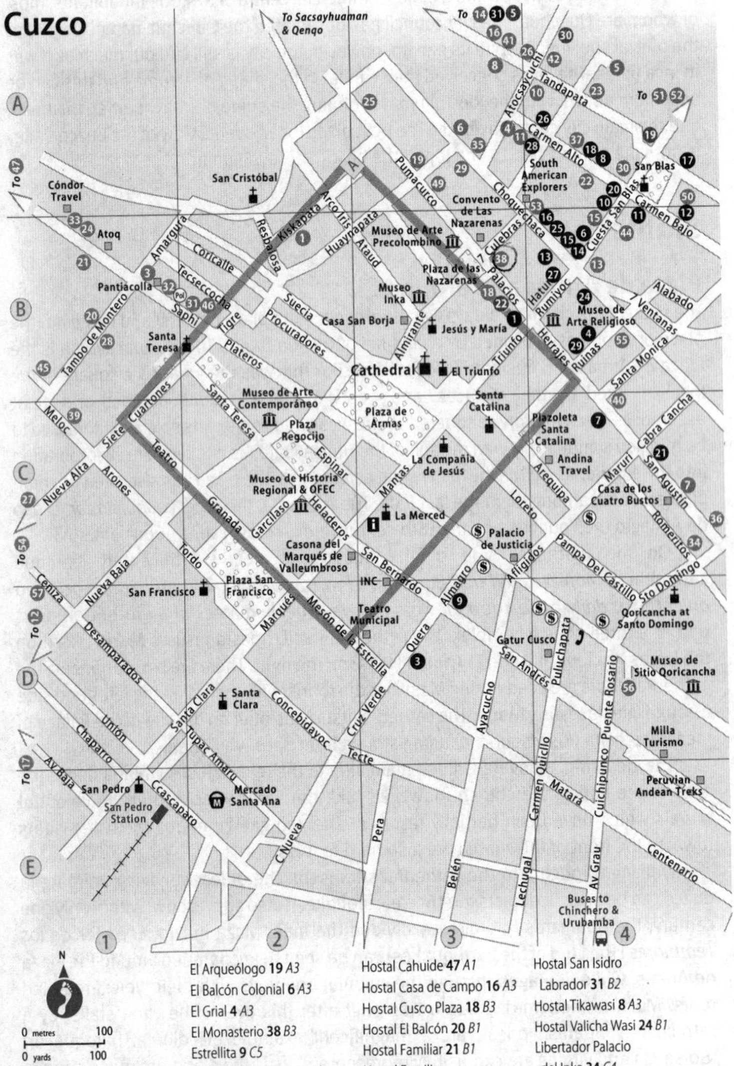

Sleeping

Albergue Casa Campesina & Store of Weavers **2** *C5*
Albergue Municipal **1** *B2*
Blue House **5** *A4*
Casa Andina Koricancha **7** *C4*
Casa Andina Private Collection Cusco **36** *C5*
Casa Andina San Blas **43** *B5*
Casa Elena **53** *A4*
Casa San Blas **44** *B4*
Chaska Wasi **3** *B1*
Cusco Plaza 2 **32** *B1*
El Arqueólogo **19** *A3*
El Balcón Colonial **6** *A3*
El Grial **4** *A3*
El Monasterio **38** *B3*
Estrellita **9** *C5*
Hospedaje El Artesano de San Blas **51** *A5*
Hospedaje Familiar Inti Quilla **10** *A4*
Hospedaje Inka **52** *A5*
Hospedaje Jhuno **11** *A3*
Hospedaje Killipata **45** *B1*
Hospedaje Plaza de San Blas **50** *A4*
Hospedaje Turístico San Blas **13** *B4*
Hostal Amaru **15** *B4*
Hostal Andenes de Saphi **33** *B1*
Hostal Cahuide **47** *A1*
Hostal Casa de Campo **16** *A3*
Hostal Cusco Plaza **18** *B3*
Hostal El Balcón **20** *B1*
Hostal Familiar **21** *B1*
Hostal Familiar Carmen Alto **22** *A4*
Hostal Familiar Mirador del Inka **23** *A4*
Hostal Kuntur Wasi **14** *A3*
Hostal Loki **54** *C1*
Hostal Luzerna **17** *D1*
Hostal María Esther **25** *A3*
Hostal Pakcha Real **26** *A4*
Hostal Pumacurco **49** *A3*
Hostal Qorichaska **27** *C1*
Hostal Rickch'airy **28** *B1*
Hostal Rumi Punku **29** *A3*
Hostal Sambleño **30** *A4*
Hostal San Isidro Labrador **31** *B2*
Hostal Tikawasi **8** *A3*
Hostal Valicha Wasi **24** *B1*
Libertador Palacio del Inka **34** *C4*
Los Apus Hostal y Mirador **35** *A3*
Maison de la Jeunesse **56** *D4*
Marani **37** *A4*
Niños **39** *C1*
Niños 2 **12** *D1*
Novotel **40** *C4*
Pensión Alemana **41** *A3*
Posada del Sol **42** *A4*
Renacimiento **57** *D1*
Residencial Torre Dorada **58** *E6*
Ruinas **55** *B4*

people. The two divinities are said to have led to the Spanish victory; not only was it the triumph of the Spaniards over the Incas, but also of the Catholic faith over the indigenous religion. The fine granite altar of El Triunfo is a welcome relief from the usual gilding. Here, the statue of the Virgin of the Descent resides and, above her, is a wooden cross known as the Cross of Conquest, said to be the first Christian cross on Inca land brought from Spain.

On the southeast side of the plaza is the beautiful church of **La Compañía de Jesús**, built on the site of the Palace of the Serpents (*Amarucancha*, residence of the Inca Huayna Cápac). The original church was destroyed in the earthquake of 1650 and the present-day building took 17 years to construct. It was inaugurated in 1668. The altarpiece is resplendent in gold leaf: it stands 21 m high and 12 m wide. It is carved in the baroque style, but the indigenous artists felt that this was too simple to please the gods and added their own intricacies. Gold leaf abounds in the many *retablos* and on the carved pulpit.

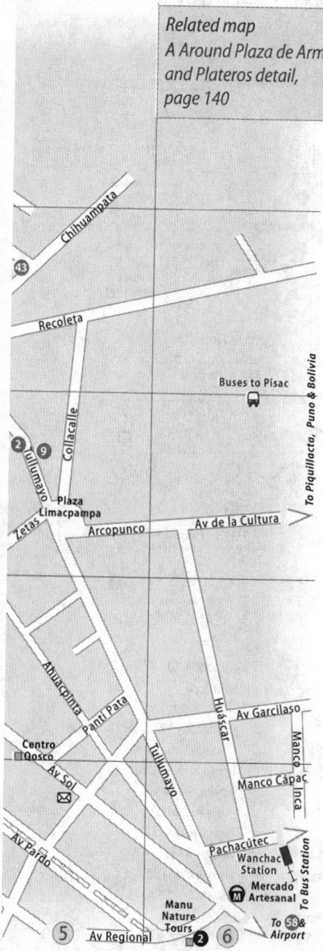

Suecia II **46** *B2*

Eating
A Mi Manera **1** *B3*
Baco **4** *B4*
Café Cultural Ritual **15** *B4*
Café Manu **2** *E6*
Chifa Sipan **3** *D3*
Chocolate **16** *B4*
El Encuentro **24** *B4*
Granja Heidi **6** *B4*
Gypsy Pub **18** *A4*
Inca Food **25** *B4*
Inkafe **13** *B4*
Inkanato **7** *C4*
Jack's Café **14** *B4*
Kachivache **26** *A4*
La Bodega **8** *A4*
La Bodeguita Cubana **27** *B4*
Los Toldos **9** *D3*
Macondo **10** *A4*
Moni **21** *C4*
Mundo Hemp **28** *A4*
Muse **17** *A4*
Pachapapa **11** *B4*
Panadería El Buen Pastor **20** *A4*
Velluto **31** *A3*
Witches Garden **12** *A4*
Yanapay **29** *B4*

Bars & clubs
Bar 7 **5** *A3*
Km 0 (Arte y Tapas) **19** *A4*
Mandela's Bar **22** *B3*
Siete Angelitos **30** *A4*

North and northeast of the Plaza de Armas

Palacio del Almirante, just north of the Plaza de Armas, is one of Cuzco's most impressive colonial buildings and houses the interesting **Museo Inka** ① *Cuesta del Almirante 103, T084-237380, Mon-Fri 0800-1730 (Sat till 1700), US$2.40,* which exhibits the development of culture in the region from pre-Inca, through Inca times to the present day. The museum has a good combination of textiles, ceramics, metalwork, jewellery, architecture, technology, photographs, 3-D displays and a section on coca. There is an excellent collection of miniature turquoise figures and other objects made as offerings to the gods. The display of skulls, deliberately deformed by trepanning is fascinating, as is the full-size tomb complete with mummies stuck in urns. Note the pillar on the balcony over the door, showing a bearded man from inside and a naked woman from the outside. During the high season, local Quechuan weavers can be seen working and selling in the courtyard. The weavings are for sale; expensive but high quality.

Two blocks northeast of Plaza de Armas, the **Palacio Arzobispal** was built on the site of the palace occupied in 1400 by the Inca Roca and was formerly the home of the Marqueses de Buena Vista. It contains the

Around Plaza de Armas

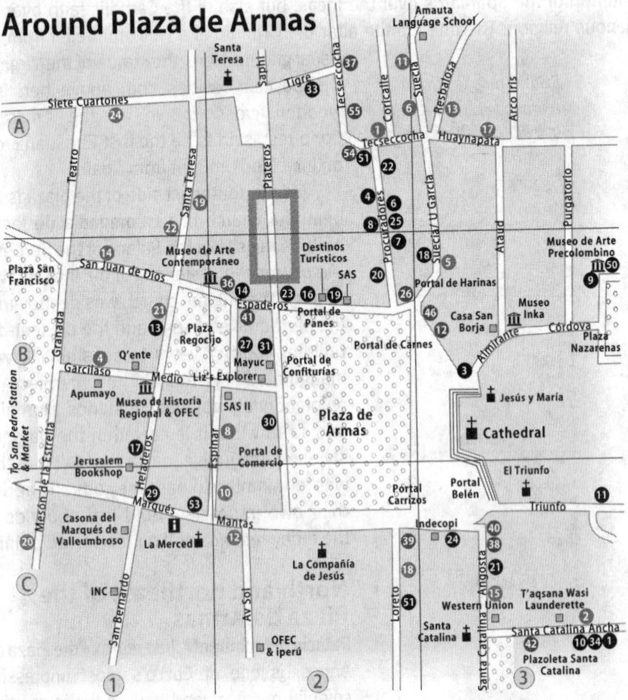

Plateros detail

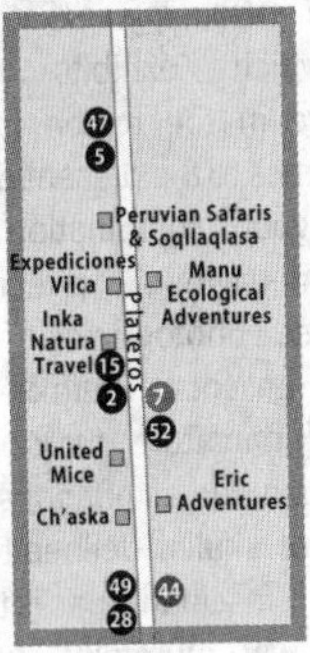

Sleeping

Casa Andina Catedral **15** *C3*
Casa Andina Plaza **10** *C2*
Del Prado Inn **5** *B3*
El Procurador del Cusco **1** *A2*
Emperador Plaza **2** *C3*
Hostal Corihuasi **6** *A3*
Hostal Q'Awarina **11** *A2*
Hostal Qosqo **12** *C2*
Hostal Resbalosa **13** *A3*
Hostal Royal Frankenstein**14** *B1*
Hostal Turístico Plateros **7** *Plateros detail*
Marqueses **4** *B1*
Munay Wasi **17** *A3*
Pensión Loreto **18** *C2*
Picoaga **19** *A1*
Royal Inka I **21** *B1*
Royal Inka II **22** *A1*
Sonesta Posada del Inca Cusco **8** *B2*
The Point **20** *C1*
Tumi I **24** *A1*

Eating

Al Grano **1** *C3*
Amaru **2** *Plateros detail*
A Mi Manera **11** *C3*
Ayllu **3** *B3*
Café Halliy **5** *Plateros detail*
Chez Maggy Clave de Do **6** *A2*
Chez Maggy El Corsario **7** *B2*
Chez Maggy La Antigua **8** *A2*
Cicciolina **11** *C3*
Dolce Vita **10** *C3*
El Encuentro **34** *C3*
El Fogón **47** *Plateros detail*
El Molino **15** *Plateros detail*
El Truco & Taberna del Truco **13** *B1*
Fallen Angel **9** *B3*
Incanto & Greens Organic **21** *C3*
Inka Grill **16** *B2*
Kapaj Ñan **22** *A2*
Kintaro **17** *B1*
Kusikuy **18** *B3*
La Biondet **29** *C1*
La Retama **19** *B2*
La Tertulia **20** *B2*
Los Candiles & Café Amaru **49** *Plateros detail*
MAP Café **50** *B3*
Mía Pizza **4** *A2*
Pachacútec Grill & Bar **23** *B2*
Paititi **24** *C3*
Paloma Imbil **25** *A2*
Pizzería Marengo **27** *B2*
Pomodoro **51** *C2*
Pucará **28** *Plateros detail*
Real McCoy **52** *Plateros detail*
Trotamundos **30** *B2*
Tunupa & Cross Keys Pub **31** *B2*
Tupananchis **53** *C1*
Varayoc **14** *B2*
Víctor Victoria **33** *A2*
Yaku Mama **51** *A2*

Bars & clubs

Big Blue Martini **54** *A2*
Blueberry Lounge **12** *B3*
Corruption **55** *A2*
El Garabato Video Music Club **41** *B2*
Extreme **46** *B3*
Kamikaze **36** *B2*
Los Perros **37** *A2*
Mama Africa **26** *B2*
Norton Rat's Tavern **39** *C2*
Paddy Flaherty's **40** *C3*
Rosie O'Grady's & Sky Travel **42** *C3*
Ukuku's **44** *Plateros detail*
Uptown **38** *C3*

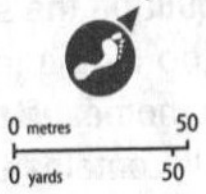

Museo de Arte Religioso ⓘ *Hatun Rumiyoc y Herrajes, Mon-Sat 0830-1130, 1500-1800, US$3, US$1.50 for students*, which has a fine collection of colonial paintings, furniture and mirrors. The Spanish tiles are said to be over 100 years old and each carved wooden door has a different design. The collection includes the paintings by the indigenous master, **Diego Quispe Tito**, of a 17th-century Corpus Christi procession that used to hang in the church of Santa Ana. They now hang in the two rooms at the back of the second smaller courtyard (see Fine art and sculpture, page 604). The throne in the old dining room is 300 years old and was taken up to Sacsayhuaman for the Pope to sit on when he visited in 1986.

In the Casa Cabrera, on the northwest side of the plaza, is the beautiful **Museo de Arte Precolombino** ⓘ *Plaza de las Nazarenas 231, T084-233210, 0900-2200, US$6, US$3 with student card; under same auspices as the Larco Museum in Lima*. Set around a spacious courtyard, it is dedicated to the work of the great artists of pre-Colombian Peru. Within the expertly lit and well-organized galleries are many superb examples of pottery, metalwork (largely in gold and silver) and wood carvings. There are some vividly rendered animistic designs, giving an insight into the way Peru's ancient peoples viewed their world and the creatures that inhabited it. Most of the pieces originate from the Moche, Chimú, Paracas, Nazca and Inca empires, with explanations in English and Spanish. The museum has shops, such as **Alpaca 111** and **H Stern**, and the **MAP Café**, see Eating, page 155.

Convento de las Nazarenas, on Plaza de las Nazarenas, is now an annex of **El Monasterio** hotel, see page 147. You can see the Inca-colonial doorway with a mermaid motif, but ask permission to view the lovely 18th-century frescos inside. **El Monasterio** itself is well worth a visit – ask at reception if you can have a wander. Built in 1595 on the site of an Inca palace, it was originally the **Seminary of San Antonio Abad** (a Peruvian National Historical Landmark). One of its most remarkable features is the baroque chapel, constructed after the 1650 earthquake. If you are not disturbing mealtimes, check out the dining room. This is where the monks used to sing.

San Blas

The San Blas district, called **Tococache** in Inca times, has been put on the tourist map by the large number of shops and galleries which sell local carvings, ceramics and paintings, see page 159. Even though it's a bit of climb from the Plaza de Armas, it has also become a popular place to stay and eat, with lots of choice and nothing too expensive. The **church of San Blas** ⓘ *Carmen Bajo, 0800-1130, 1400-1730, closed Thu mornings, US$3, US$1.50 for students*, is a simple rectangular adobe building whose walls were reinforced with stone after the 1650 and 1950 earthquakes. It houses one of the most famous pieces of wood carving found in the Americas, a beautiful mestizo pulpit carved from a single cedar trunk.

East and southeast of the Plaza de Armas

The magnificent church, convent and museum of **Santa Catalina** ⓘ *Arequipa at Santa Catalina Angosta, Sat-Thu 0900-1200, 1300-1700, Fri 0900-1200, 1300-1600, entrance with BTG visitors' ticket, guided tours by English-speaking students (tip is expected), church daily 0700-0800*, is built upon the foundations of the *Acllahuasi* (House of the Chosen Women), whose nobility, virtue and beauty permitted them to be prepared for ceremonial and domestic duties – some were chosen to bear the Inca king's children. Today the convent is a closed order where the nuns have no contact with the outside world. The church has an ornate, gilded altarpiece and a beautifully carved pulpit. The museum has a wonderful collection of Cuzqueño school paintings spanning the decades of Spanish rule – a good guide can point out how the style changes from the heavy European influence to the more indigenous style.

Much original Inca stonework can be seen in the streets, particularly in the **Callejón Loreto**, running southeast past La Compañía de Jesús from the main plaza. The walls of the *Acllahuasi* are on one side, and of the *Amarucancha* on the other. There are also Inca remains in Calle San Agustín, east of the plaza. The famous **Stone of 12 Angles** is in Calle Hatun Rumiyoc, halfway along its second block, on the right-hand side going away from the plaza. The finest stonework is in the celebrated curved wall beneath the west end of Santo Domingo. This was rebuilt after the 1950 earthquake, when a niche that once contained a shrine was found at the inner top of the wall. Excavations have revealed Inca baths below here, and more Inca retaining walls. Another superb stretch of late-Inca stonework is in **Calle Ahuacpinta**, outside Qoricancha, to the east or left as you enter. True Inca stonework is wider at the base than at the top and features ever-smaller stones as the walls rise. Doorways and niches are trapezoidal. The Incas clearly learnt that the combination of these four techniques helped their structures to withstand earthquakes. This explains why, in two huge earthquakes (1650 and 1950), Inca walls stayed standing while colonial buildings tumbled down.

Qoricancha at Santo Domingo

ⓘ *Mon-Sat 0800-1700, Sun 1400-1600 (except holidays), US$1.50 (not on the BTG visitor ticket). There are guides outside who charge around US$2-3.*

This is one of the most fascinating sights in Cuzco. Behind the walls of the Catholic church are remains of what was once the centre of the vast Inca society. The Golden Palace and Temple of the Sun was a complex filled with such fabulous treasures of gold and silver it took the Spanish three months to melt it all down. The Solar Garden contained life-sized gold sculptures of men, women, children, animals, insects and flowers, placed in homage to the Sun God. On the walls were more than 700 gold sheets weighing about 2 kg each. The *conquistadores* sent these back intact to prove to the King of Spain how rich their discovery was. There would also have been a large solar disc in the shape of a round face with rays and flames. This disc has never been found.

The first Inca, Manco Cápac, is said to have built the temple when he left Lake Titicaca and founded Cuzco with Mama Ocllo. However, it was the ninth Inca, Pachacútec, who transformed it. When the Spaniards arrived, the complex was awarded to Juan Pizarro, the younger brother of Francisco. He in turn willed it to the Dominicans who ripped much of it down to build their church.

Walk first into the courtyard then turn around to face the door you just passed through. Behind and to the left of the paintings (representing the life of Santo Domingo Guzmán) is Santo Domingo. This was where the Temple of the Sun stood, a massive structure 80 m wide, 20 m deep and 7 m in height. Only the curved wall of the western end still exists and will be seen (complete with a large crack from the 1950 earthquake), when you later walk left through to the lookout over the Solar Garden. Still in the baroque cloister, close by and facing the way you came in, turn left and cross to the remains of the Temple of the Moon, identifiable by a series of niches. Beyond this is the so-called Temple of Venus and the Stars. Stars were special deities used to predict weather, wealth and crops. In the Temple of Lightning on the other side of the courtyard is a stone. Stand on this and you will appreciate how good the Incas were as stonemasons: all three windows are in perfect alignment.

Museo de Sitio Qoricancha ⓘ *Mon-Sat 0900-1200, 1300-1700, Sun 0800-1400, entrance by the BTG visitor ticket, or US$2, guided tour in Spanish, but please give a tip*, formerly the Museo Arqueológico, is now housed in an underground site on Avenida Sol, in the gardens below Santo Domingo. It contains a limited collection of pre-Columbian artefacts, a few Spanish paintings of imitation Inca royalty, dating from the 18th century, and photos of the excavation of Qoricancha.

South and southwest of the Plaza de Armas

Originally built in 1534, the church of **La Merced** ⓘ *C Márquez, monastery and museum 1430-1700, church Mon-Sat 0830-1200, 1530-1730, US$0.85*, was razed in the 1650 earthquake and rebuilt by indigenous stonemasons in the late 17th century. The high altar is neoclassical with six gilded columns. There are a further 12 altars. Inside the church are buried Gonzalo Pizarro, half-brother of Francisco, and the two Almagros, father and son. Attached is a very fine monastery. The first cloister is the most beautiful, with its two floors, archways and pillars. The pictures on the first floor depict the Saints of the Order (those of the second floor have been removed for restoration).

Museo Histórico Regional ⓘ *Casa Garcilaso, C Garcilaso y Heladeros, daily 0730-1730, entrance with BTG visitors' ticket, guide recommended,* shows the evolution of the Cuzqueño school of painting. It also contains Inca agricultural implements, a mummy from Nazca, complete with 1 m-long hair, colonial furniture and paintings, a small photographic exhibition of the 1950 earthquake and mementos of more recent times.

Three blocks southwest of the Plaza de Armas, the austere church of **San Francisco** ⓘ *Plaza San Francisco, daily 0600-0800, 1800-2000,* reflects many indigenous influences, but it has a wonderful monastery, cloister and choir. Although at the time of writing the monastery was not officially open to the public, it is possible to visit. Approach the door to the left of the church and knock on it. The cloister is the oldest in the city, built in the Renaissance style, but with diverse influences. The ground floor has several crypts containing human bones. The high choir contains 92 carvings of martyrs and saints.

West and northwest of the Plaza de Armas

Above Cuzco, on the road up to Sacsayhuaman, is the church of **San Cristóbal**, built to honourhis patron saint by Cristóbal Paullu Inca. The church's atrium has been restored and there is access to the Sacsayhuaman Archaeological Park (see below). North of San Cristóbal, you can see the 11 doorway-sized niches of the great Inca wall of the **Palacio de Colcampata**, which was the residence of Manco Inca before he rebelled against the Spanish and fled to Vilcabamba. **Cristo Blanco**, arms outstretched and brilliantly illuminated at night, stands over the town and is clearly visible if you look north from the Plaza de Armas. He was given to the city as a mark of gratitude by Palestinian refugees in 1944. A quick glance in the local telephone directory reveals there is still a large Arab population in Cuzco.

Sacsayhuaman

ⓘ *Daily 0700-1730. You can get in earlier if you wish; definitely try to get there before 1200 when the tour groups arrive. Entrance by BTG visitors' ticket. Free student guides are available, but you should give them a tip. Lights to illuminate the site at night, which is a 30-min walk from the town centre; walk up Pumacurco from Plaza de las Nazarenas. Taxi US$1.50.*

There are some magnificent Inca walls in the ruined ceremonial centre of Sacsayhuaman, on a hill in the northern outskirts. The Inca stonework is hugely impressive. The massive rocks weighing up to 130 tons are fitted together with absolute perfection. Three walls run parallel for over 360 m and there are 21 bastions.

Sacsayhuaman was thought for centuries to be a fortress, but the layout and architecture suggest a great sanctuary and temple to the Sun, rising opposite the place previously believed to be the Inca's throne – which was probably an altar, carved out of the solid rock. Broad steps lead to the altar from either side. Zigzags in the boulders round the 'throne' are apparently '*chicha* grooves', channels down which maize beer flowed during festivals. Up the hill is an ancient quarry, the Rodadero, now used by children as a rock slide. Near it are many seats cut perfectly into the smooth rock.

The hieratic, rather than the military, hypothesis was supported by the discovery in 1982 of the graves of priests, who would have been unlikely to be buried in a fortress. The precise functions of the site, however, will probably continue to be a matter of dispute, as very few clues remain, due to its steady destruction.

The site survived the first years of the conquest. Pizarro's troops had entered Cuzco unopposed in 1533 and lived safely at Sacsayhuaman, until the rebellion of Manco Inca, in 1536, caught them off guard. The bitter struggle that ensued became the decisive military action of the conquest, for Manco's failure to hold Sacsayhuaman cost him the war, and the empire. The destruction of the hilltop site began after the defeat of Manco's rebellion. The outer walls still stand, but the complex of towers and buildings was razed to the ground. From then until the 1930s, Sacsayhuaman served as a kind of unofficial quarry of pre-cut stone for the inhabitants of Cuzco.

Other sites near Cuzco

Along the road from Sacsayhuaman to Pisac, past a radio station at 3600 m, is the temple and amphitheatre of **Qenqo**. These are not exactly ruins, but are the finest examples of Inca stone carving *in situ*, especially inside the large hollowed-out stone that houses an altar. The rock is criss-crossed by zigzag channels that give the place its name and which served to course *chicha*, or perhaps sacrificial blood, for purposes of divination. The open space that many refer to as the 'plaza' or 'amphitheatre' was used for ceremonies. The 19 trapezoidal niches, which are partially destroyed, held idols and mummies.

Known as an Inca fortress, **Puka Pukara** ⓘ *about 6 km from Qenqo*, whose name translates as 'Red Fort', was more likely to have been a *tambo*, a kind of post-house where travellers were lodged and goods and animals were housed temporarily. It is worth seeing for the views alone.

A few hundred metres up the road is the spring shrine of **Tambo Machay**, still in excellent condition. There are many opinions as to the function of this place. Some say it was a resting place for the Incas and others that it was used by Inca Yupanqui as a hunting place. There are three ceremonial water fountains built on different levels. It is possible that the site was a centre of a water cult. Water still flows via a hidden channel out of the masonry wall, straight into a rock pool, traditionally known as the Inca's bath.

It is possible to walk from Sacsayhuaman to Tambo Machay, via Qenqo, then **Cusilluchayoc** (Templo de los Monos, or Monkey Temple), an area of rocks and galleries with the remains of a fountain, then on a section of the Incas' Cuzco–Pisac road to **Laqo** (Templo de la Luna, or Temple of the Moon), with sculptures in caves and an observatory, Chilcapuquio and Puka Pukara.

Taking a guide to the sites mentioned above is a good idea and you should visit in the morning for the best photographs. Carry your multi-site ticket as there are roving ticket inspectors. You can visit the sites on foot. It's a pleasant walk through the countryside requiring half a day or more, though remember to take water and sun protection, and watch out for dogs. An alternative is to take the Pisac bus up to Tambo Machay (which costs US$0.35) and walk back. Another excellent way to see the ruins is on horseback, arranged at travel agencies. An organized tour (with guide) will go to all the sites for US$6 per person, not including entrance fees. A taxi will charge US$15-20 for three to four people. Some of these ruins are included in the many City Tours available (see page 162).

Sleeping

You should book more expensive hotels well in advance through the internet or a good travel agency, particularly for the week or so around **Inti Raymi** (page 159), when prices are much higher. Hotel prices, especially in the mid to upper categories, are often lower when booked through tour agencies. When there are fewer tourists hotels may drop their prices by as much as half. Be wary of unlicensed hotel agents for mid-priced hotels, who are often misleading about details; their local nickname is *jalagringos* (gringo pullers), or *piratas* (pirates). Taxis and tourist minibuses meet arriving trains and take you to the hotel of your choice for US$0.75-1, but be insistent.

It is cold at night in Cuzco and many hotels do not have heating. It is worth asking for an *estufa*, a heater, which some places will provide for an extra charge. When staying in the big, popular hotels, allow plenty of time to check out if you have a plane or train to catch: front desks can be very busy. Assume that hotels have free luggage storage and 24-hr hot water in pre-heated tanks, unless otherwise stated. The city can suffer from water shortages. Cuzco's low-power electric showers often do a poor job of heating the very cold water and their safety is sometimes questionable.

Perurooms SAC, Las Acacias 502, Lima 18, T01-447 4630, www.perurooms.com. Helps travellers to select and book hotel rooms (3- to 4-star) in Cuzco and throughout Peru.

Plaza de Armas and around

p83, map p140

AL Picoaga, Santa Teresa 344 (2 blocks from the Plaza de Armas), T084-252330, www.picoagahotel.com. Price includes buffet breakfast. Originally the home of the Marqués de Picoaga, this beautiful colonial building has large original bedrooms set around a shady courtyard and a modern section, with a/c, at the back. Cable TV, minibar and safe. Pleasant staff. Recommended.

AL Ruinas, Ruinas 472, T084-260644, www.hotelruinas.com. A comfortable hotel conveniently located close to the plaza, good facilities (TV, minibar, etc) and comfortable beds, a little expensive, with a 0900 check-out, but helpful staff, price includes buffet breakfast.

AL Sonesta Posada del Inca Cusco, Portal Espinar 108, T084-227061, www.sonesta.com. Price includes buffet breakfast. Warmly decorated rooms with heating, safe and cable TV. Some rooms on 3rd floor have view of the plaza. Very helpful staff who speak English, restaurant serves Andean food, excellent service, business centre available.

A Casa Andina Plaza, Portal Espinar 142, T084-231733, www.casa-andina.com. 1 block from the plaza, this hotel has 40 rooms with cable TV, bath, safe deposit box, heating, duvets on the beds, wi-fi internet, ATM, restaurant and all the features common to this bright, cheerful chain. Equally recommendable are the **Casa Andina Koricancha**, San Agustín 371, T084-252633, the **Casa Andina Catedral**, Santa Catalina Angosta 149, T084-233661, and the **Casa Andina San Blas**, Chihuampata 278, San Blas, T084-263694, all of which are in the same vein and price range (but the last 3 do not have an ATM).

A Del Prado Inn, Suecia 310, T084-224442, www.delpradoinn.com. A very smart hotel just off the plaza. 24-hr room service available, and closed-circuit TV in the public areas for additional security. Suites with jacuzzi cost US$130.

A Royal Inka I, Plaza Regocijo 299, T084-231067, royalin@speedy.com.pe. Price includes buffet breakfast. Bedrooms, with cable TV and heating, are set in a colonial house around a shady central patio. Tranquil atmosphere, bar, restaurant with set menu. Recommended.

A Royal Inka II, close by, on Santa Teresa, same phone and email. More modern and expensive but the price includes buffet breakfast, saunas and jacuzzi (massage US$25). The colonial façade hides a modern building, the rooms of which open out onto a huge atrium dominated by an incongruous, 3-storey high mural. All rooms have cable TV and heating. Free bus for guests to Pisac at 1000 daily, returning at 1800.

A-C Hotel Marqueses, Garcilaso 256, T084-264249, marqueses@sastravel peru.com. Restored in Spanish colonial style, with suitable artwork and 2 lovely courtyards. Prices include buffet breakfast. Some rooms have bath, others are a little dark. Discounts on **SAS** tours (see Activities and tours, page 162).

B Emperador Plaza, Santa Catalina Ancha 377, T084-227412, emperador@terra.com.pe. Price includes buffet breakfast. A modern, light, airy hotel with friendly and helpful English-speaking staff. Cable TV, hairdryer, gas-heated showers and electric radiators.

B-C Hostal Qosqo, Portal Mantas 115, near the Plaza de Armas, T084-252513. Bargain hard for a discount. Price includes continental breakfast, a heater and cable TV. The state of decor and quality of mattress varies from room to room but most stay here for its proximity to the plaza. Clean, friendly and helpful.

C Hostal Corihuasi, C Suecia 561, T084-232233, www.corihuasi.com. Price includes continental breakfast and airport pickup. A tough climb up from the northernmost corner of the Plaza de Armas, tranquil, popular with tour groups. Friendly, some rooms with good views, cable TV, solar heating. Recommended.

C Pensión Loreto, Pasaje Loreto 115, Plaza de Armas (it shares the same entrance as **Norton's Rat** pub), T084-226352, www.hloreto.com. Price includes continental breakfast and a heater for the spacious rooms with original Inca walls. Great location; they will serve you breakfast in bed. Laundry service, will help organize travel services including guides and taxis, free airport pickup.

D Hostal Q'Awarina, at the top of Suecia 575, T084-228130. Price includes continental breakfast, heating US$2, TV extra. No laundry service. Rooms are good, ask for those with a view. Lovely living room with views across the city; the breakfast area upstairs is even better. Good value.

D-E Hostal Turístico Plateros, Plateros 348, T084-236878, plateroshostal@hotmail.com. Price includes continental breakfast. Clean, good value *hostal* in a great location, pleasant communal area with cable TV. The best rooms overlook the street.

E Hostal Resbalosa, Resbalosa 494, T084-224839. Breakfast is US$1.45 extra; laundry costs US$0.75 per kg. Superb views of the Plaza de Armas from a sunny terrace. Owner Georgina is very hospitable. Best rooms have a view (US$1.45 extra), others may be pokey. The electric showers are reportedly cool, but most guests love this place; it's often full.

E Hostal Royal Frankenstein, San Juan de Dios 260, 2 blocks from the Plaza de Armas, T084-236999, ludwig_roth@hotmail. com. This unforgettable place, with its ghoulish theme, has good services: fully equipped kitchen (just US$0.30 a day), cable TV in the living room, safe, laundry facilities, excellent mattresses but few rooms have outside windows. German owner. Recommended.

E-F El Procurador del Cusco, Coricalle 440, Prolongación Procuradores, at the end of Procuradores, T084-243559. **G** per person without bathroom, price includes use of the basic kitchen (no fridge) and laundry area. Basic rooms and the beds somewhat hard, but upstairs is better. Staff are very friendly and helpful, good value. Recommended.

F Munay Wasi, Huaynapata 253, not far from the Plaza de Armas, T084-223661. Price includes hot drinks and laundry facilities. Quiet, but run-down colonial house, with basic, clean rooms, friendly and helpful.

F The Point, Mesón de la Estrella 172, T084-252266, www.thepointhostels.com. Latest addition to the Point's stable. Price is per person in dormitory, also has doubles (**E**), includes breakfast, free internet, good beds, hot showers, clean, nice atmosphere.

F Tumi 1, Siete Cuartones 245, 2 blocks from Plaza de Armas, T084-244413. Price includes use of the kitchen and laundry area; free book exchange, laundry service US$0.85. Colonial house, clean rooms around a sunny courtyard, all with shared bath. Facilities are basic and you have to pay for more than one shower a day, friendly, popular, good value; bargain for longer stays.

North and northeast of the Plaza de Armas *p139, map p138*

LL El Monasterio, Palacios 136, T084-241777, www.monasterio.orientexpress.com. This 5-star, beautifully restored Seminary of San Antonio Abad is central and quite simply the best hotel in town for historical interest; it is worth a visit even if you cannot afford the price tag (see page 141). Soft Gregorian chants follow you as you wander through the baroque chapel, tranquil courtyards and charming cloisters, admiring the excellent collection of religious paintings. Rooms have all facilities, including cable TV, some even offer an oxygen-enriched atmosphere to help clients acclimatize, for an additional fee of US$25. Staff, who all speak English, are very helpful and attentive. The price includes a great buffet breakfast (US$19 to non- residents) which will fill you up for the rest of the day. The restaurant serves lunch and dinner à la carte. Recommended.

LL Novotel, San Agustín 239, T084-881030, www.novotel.cusco.com.pe. 4-star, US$50 cheaper (US$180 as opposed to US$230) in modern section; price includes buffet breakfast. Converted from the home of *conquistador* Miguel Sánchez Ponce, it was remodelled after the 1650 earthquake with lovely stone archways and paintings of the saints on the grand stairway. Beautiful courtyard, roofed in glass, with sofas, coffee tables and pot plants around the central stone fountain. The modern 5-storey rear extension has excellent airy and bright rooms. Rooms in the colonial section are not much different but have high, beamed ceilings and huge beds. There are 2 restaurants and a French chef.

A El Arqueólogo, Pumacurco 408, T084-232569, www.hotelarqueologo.com. Price includes buffet breakfast. Services include oxygen, a library and hot drinks. A colonial building on Inca foundations, this has rustic but stylish decor. Lovely sunny garden with comfy chairs and a small restaurant that serves interesting Peruvian food and fondue. French and English spoken. Recommended. Also has **Vida Tours**, at this address, T084-227750, www.vidatours.com. Traditional and adventure tourism.

A-B Hostal Cusco Plaza 1, Plaza Nazarenas 181 (opposite **El Monasterio**), T084-246161, www.cuscoplazahotels.com. Price includes continental breakfast. Situated on a lovely small plaza in the town centre, clean rooms all with cable TV. Room 303 has the best view.

B Hostal Rumi Punku, Choquechaca 339, T084-221102, www.rumipunku.com. A genuine Inca doorway leads to the sunny, tranquil courtyard of this 3-star *hostal*. 20 large, clean, comfortable rooms, helpful staff and safe. Highly recommended.

D Casa Elena, Choquechaca 162, T084-241202, www.geocities.com/casa_elena. French/Peruvian hostel, very comfortable and friendly, breakfast included. Highly recommended.

D Hostal María Esther, Pumacurco 516, T084-224382. Price includes continental breakfast; heating extra. This very friendly, helpful place has a lovely garden, a lounge with sofas and a variety of rooms. There is also car parking. Recommended.

E El Balcón Colonial, Choquechaca 350, T084-238129, balconcolonial@hotmail.com. Continental breakfast extra, use of the kitchen US$1 per day and laundry US$0.70 per kg. Accommodation for 11 people in this family house. Basic rooms with foam mattresses but the hospitality is exceptional. Free airport pickup.

F Hostal Pumacurco, Pumacurco 336, Interior 329, T084-243347 (3 mins from the Plaza de Armas). Some large rooms in the restored part of a colonial house. Clean, secure and laundry facilities. Owner Betty is very friendly and helpful.

San Blas *p141, map p138*

A Casa San Blas, Tocuyeros 566, just off Cuesta San Blas, T/F084-237900, www.casasanblas.com. A new 'boutique' hotel with bright, airy rooms decorated with traditional textiles. Breakfast and internet are included. Pleasant balcony with good views, very attentive service.

A Los Apus Hotel y Mirador, Atocsaycuchi 515 y Choquechaca esq Choquechaque, T084-264243, www.losapushotel.com. Price includes buffet breakfast and airport pickup; laundry US$1 per kg. Swiss-owned, very clean and smart with beamed bedrooms fitted with cable TV and real radiators!

B Hostal Casa de Campo, Tandapata 296-B (at the end of the street), T084-244404, www.hotelcasadecampo.com. Price (10% discount for Footprint readers) includes continental breakfast and free airport/rail/ bus transfer with reservations. Bedrooms have fabulous views but it's quite a climb to get to them! Safe deposit box, laundry service, meals on request and a sun terrace. Dutch and English spoken; take a taxi there after dark.

C Pensión Alemana, Tandapata 260, T084-226861. Price includes American breakfast; laundry and heating extra. Car parking available. Swiss-owned, modern European decor with a comfy lounge area, free internet, lovely garden with patio furniture. Recommended.

D El Grial, Atocsaycuchi 594, T084-223012, www.cusco-peru.de. With continental breakfast, hot water, cable TV. A charming hotel, in traditional style, spacious and clean, some shared bathrooms, books in English, German and French, videos to watch, free internet, tours arranged, discounts at neighbouring language school.

D Hospedaje Turístico San Blas, Cuesta San Blas 526, T084-225781, sanblascusco@yahoo.com. Price includes continental breakfast; heaters are extra. Cable TV in the comfortable, covered courtyard. Well-decorated bedrooms, charming for a basic *hostal*.

D Hostal Amaru, Cuesta San Blas 541, T084-225933, www.cusco.net/amaru (**E** without bathroom). Price includes breakfast and airport/train/bus pickup. Services include oxygen, kitchen for use in the evenings only, laundry and free book exchange. Rooms around a pretty colonial courtyard, good beds, pleasant, relaxing, some Inca walls. Rooms in the first courtyard are best. Recommended. Also has **E Hostal Anita**, with bath, safe, quiet, good American breakfast.

D Hostal Kuntur Wasi, Tandapata 352-A, T084-227570. **F** without bath, services include a safe, use of the kitchen (for US$0.60 a day) and laundry. Great views from the terrace where you can breakfast. Very welcoming, helpful owners; a very pleasant place to stay.

D Marani, Carmen Alto 194, T084-249462, www.hostalmarani.com. Breakfasts available. Book exchange and information on Andean life and culture. Large rooms with heaps of character, set around a courtyard. The **Hope Foundation** (www.stichtinghope.org) is run from here: Walter Meekes and his wife, Tineke, have built 20 schools in poor mountain villages and *barrios*, established a programme to teach teachers and set up a 30-bed burns unit in Cuzco general hospital. Good value, a great cause and highly recommended.

D Posada del Sol, Atocsaycuchi 296, T084-246394. Includes American breakfast, heater and airport pickup. Cheerfully decorated, sun terrace with great views, fantastic showers. Use of kitchen, laundry service; food is available. Cannot be reached by taxi. Recommended.

E Hostal Pakcha Real, Tandapata 300, T084-237484, pakcharealhostal@hotmail.com. Price includes airport/train/bus pickup; rooms with bath; breakfast, heaters and use of kitchen extra. Family-run with the comforts of home. Laundry service, spotless rooms, friendly and relaxed, but confirm booking if arriving late.

E-F Hospedaje Jhuno, Carmen Alto 281, T084-233579. A small family-run *hospedaje*, clean rooms, family lounge. Breakfast is not included but guests can use the tiny kitchen.

E-F Hospedaje Plaza de San Blas, Plazoleta San Blas 630, T084-235358, psanblas@corihuasi.com. Colourful, welcoming and a great location. Price includes continental breakfast. The 4-bed family room has a balcony and overlooks the *plazoleta*.

E-F Hostal Familiar Mirador del Inka, Tandapata 160, off Plaza San Blas, T084-261384, miradordelinka@latinmail.com. This *hostal* was redeveloped in a very stylish way, with its Inca foundations and white colonial walls. Bedrooms with bath are spacious and some have great views. The owner's son Edwin runs trekking trips and has an agency on site.

E-F Hostal Sambleño, Carmen Alto 114, T084-262979. A lovely jumble of staircases overlooks a central courtyard. Rooms of varying quality, breakfast available, laundry service. Beds are comfortable, showers are electric.

F Hostal Familiar Carmen Alto, Carmen Alto 197, first on the right down steps (no sign), T084-224367. If there's no answer when ringing the bell, go to the shop next door, it's run by the same family. Basic rooms with great character (in one case, constructed around a huge tree). Tranquil, family-run, use of kitchen and washing machine. Carmen will make you a very good breakfast for US$2. All rooms with shared bath, electric showers. Recommended.

F Hostal Tikawasi, Tandapata 491, T084-231609, tikawasi@hotmail.com. Price includes breakfast and all rooms are heated. A family-run *hostal* with a lovely garden overlooking the city. Very stylish, softly lit rooms, great views. Comfortable beds and spotless bathrooms make this a good choice.

G The Blue House, Kiskapata 291 (there are 2 Kiskapatas – this one runs parallel to and above Tandapata), T084-242407. Price per person. Snug little *hostal*, excellent value, with reductions for longer stays. Breakfast is included, DVD room, shared kitchen and great views with a small park in front.

G Hospedaje El Artesano de San Blas, Suytucato 790, T084-263968, manosandinas@yahoo.com. Many clean, bright and airy rooms. As with the **Hospedaje Inka**, you need to walk up from San Blas.

G Hospedaje Familiar Inti Quilla, Atocsaycuchi 281, T084-252659. Breakfast not included and no facilities for making food. Colourful rooms around a little courtyard, quiet (on pedestrian street so taxis cannot drop you at the door). Good value.

G Hospedaje Inka, Suytuccato 848, T084-231995. Taxis leave you at Plaza San Blas, walk steeply uphill for 5-10 mins, or phone the *hostal*. Price includes bath and breakfast. Wonderful views, spacious rooms, very helpful owner, Américo.

East and southeast of the Plaza de Armas *p141, map 138*

LL Libertador Palacio del Inka, in the Casa de los Cuatro Bustos, at Plazoleta Santo Domingo 259, T084-231961, www.libertador.com.pe. This splendid 5-star, award-winning hotel is built on Inca ruins (the walls can be seen in the restaurant and bar) and is set around courtyards. It has 254 well-appointed rooms; the attention to detail is so great there are even Nazca Lines drawn in the sand of the ashtrays! Enjoy Andean music and dance over dinner in the excellent **Inti Raymi** restaurant. Recommended.

AL Casa Andina Private Collection Cusco, Plazoleta de Limacpampa Chico 473, T084-232610, www.casa-andina.com. In a 16th-century mansion with 3 courtyards, this hotel is one of the recommended Casa Andina chain's upmarket establishments, with even higher standards of services and comfort than those listed above. It has all the main facilities, plus a gourmet restaurant serving local cuisine and a bar with an extensive *pisco* collection.

E Maison de la Jeunesse (affiliated to Hostelling International), Av Sol, Cuadra 5, Pasaje Grace, Edificio San Jorge (down a small side street opposite Qoricancha), T084-235617, www.hostellingcusco.com.

Price includes breakfast. Very friendly hostel with a selection of dormitories and private rooms. TV and video room, cooking facilities and very hot water.

F **Albergue Casa Campesina**, Av Tullumayo 274, T084-233466, ccamp@apu.cbc.org.pe. Price includes breakfast, shared bathrooms only. A lovely place, set up to support the work of the **Casa Campesina** organization (www.cbc.org.pe/casacamp/), which is linked to local *campesina* communities. On the same site is the **Store of the Weavers** (see Shopping, page 161). The money that people pay for accommodation goes to this good cause. 23% discount for **SAE** members.

F **Estrellita**, Av Tullumayo 445, parte Alta, T084-234134. Price includes breakfast and tea and coffee all day. TV, video and old stereo in the tiny communal sitting area, basic kitchen for guests. Rooms are multiples with shared bath, plus 2 with private bath. Basic but excellent value. It is about a 15-min walk from the centre. When you arrive ring the bell several times and wait; you will be given your own keys when you register. Safe parking for cars and bikes. Recommended.

West and northwest of the Plaza de Armas *p143, map 138*

A **Cusco Plaza 2**, Saphi 486, T084-263000, www.cuscoplazahotels.com. Under same management as the **Cusco Plaza 1** (see page 148). The 24 nicely decorated rooms are set around 3 charming covered patios. Price includes American breakfast, and all rooms have cable TV and heating.

B **Hostal Andenes de Saphi**, Saphi 848, T084-227561, www.andenesdesaphi.com. Price includes continental breakfast and all rooms have heaters. Very friendly little hostel with a cosmopolitan atmosphere. Each room is decorated in a different style; the 4-bed family room is very nice. Lovely entertainment/games room, and a small but pleasant garden.

B **Hostal El Balcón**, Tambo de Montero 222, T084-236738, balcon1@terra.com.pe. Price includes breakfast. Lovingly restored 1630 colonial house with rooms set around a beautiful garden, homely atmosphere. Ask for a TV if you want one. Restaurant and kitchen for guests, laundry service. Recommended.

C **Hostal Cahuide**, Saphi 845, T084-222771, F248262. Price (negotiate for a discount, especially for longer stays) includes American breakfast. Cable TV in all rooms, ask for a heater. A modern hotel with 1970s furniture, plain white walls and comfortable beds. Helpful staff.

C **Hostal San Isidro Labrador**, Saphi 440, T084-226241, labrador@qnet.com.pe. Continental breakfast included in the price. Very pleasant 3-star hotel with elegant but simple decor, colonial arches and lovely patios. Plenty of hot water and heating. Recommended.

C **Niños Hotel**, Meloc 442, T084-231424, www.ninoshotel.com. Price does not include the excellent breakfast, which costs US$1.70-2.50. Services include the cafeteria and laundry service (US$1.15 per kg), Dutch, English, German and French spoken. Spotless, beautiful rooms in a 17th-century colonial house funding a fantastic charity established by Dutch couple, Titus and Jolande Bovenberg. Also has **Niños 2**, on C Fierro, a little further from the centre, 20 nicely decorated, clean and airy rooms, surrounding the central courtyard.

C **Renacimiento**, Ceniza 331, T084-226951, www.cuscoapart.com. 1-2-bedroom self-contained apartments in beautifully renovated 18th-century building, traditional style around courtyard with balconies, 4 blocks from Plaza de Armas along San Juan de Dios. Discounts for long stays.

C-D **Hostal Valicha Wasi**, Saphi 766, T084-242002, www.hostalvalichawasi.com. In a restored building with small courtyard. Quiet, very helpful staff, clean rooms, breakfast included, internet, tours can be arranged.

E **Hostal Familiar**, Saphi 661, T084-239353. Popular *hostal* in a colonial house 3 blocks from the central plaza. Most beds are comfy, hot water erratic. Luggage deposit costs US$2.85 a day for a big pack.

E **Hostal Qorichaska**, Nueva Alta 458, T084-228974, qorichaska77@yahoo.com. Price includes continental breakfast, use of the well-equipped kitchen, internet and safe. Laundry service. Rooms in this colonial house are clean and sunny; ask for the older rooms which are bigger and have traditional balconies. Friendly and recommended.

E **Hostal Rickch'airy**, Tambo de Montero 219, T084-236606. **G** without bath. Backpackers' haunt with views from the garden. Owner Leo has tourist information and will collect guests from the station. 15 new rooms with bath in **D**. Mixed reports.

E Hostel Loki, Cuesta Santa Ana 601, T084-243705, www.lokihostel.com. (**F** per person). Huge, ultra-funky new hostel in a restored viceroy's residence on the super-steep Cuesta Santa Ana. Dorms and rooms are set around a beautiful courtyard, and the view alone makes the climb well worth the effort. The beds have comfortable duvets, there's plenty of hot water, free internet access and lots of chill-out areas. A great place to meet other travellers.

E Suecia II, Tecseccocha 465 (no bell – knock!), T084-239757 (it is wise to book ahead). **G** without bath, breakfast US$1.40. Rooms are set around a glass-covered colonial courtyard and are warm. Beds have thick foam mattresses, but no seats on the toilets, water not always hot or bath- rooms clean, can be noisy and the luggage store is closed at night, otherwise OK.

F Albergue Municipal, Kiskapata 240, near San Cristóbal, T084-252506, albergue@municusco.gob. Private rooms with double beds and dormitories in this very clean, helpful youth hostel. Nice communal area with cable TV and video. No rooms have bath. Great views, cafeteria and laundry facilities (laundry service US$0.75 per kg). Showers are electric, but there is no kitchen.

F Chaska Wasi, Amargura 130 (there is no sign), T084-622831. Pay US$3 extra for cable TV and American breakfast. Use of basic kitchen (there is no fridge), laundry service. Family house with character, hard beds (singles only), good showers, excellent value for its location.

F Hospedaje Killipata, Killichapata 238, just off Tambo de Montero, T084-236668, www.geocities.com/killipata. Very clean, family-run lodging with good showers, hot water and fully equipped kitchen – it even has a pizza oven. Recommended.

F Hostal Luzerna, Av Baja 205, near San Pedro train station (take a taxi at night), T084-232762. Price includes breakfast. A nice family-run *hostal*, hot water, good beds, clean, safe to leave luggage. Recommended.

Away from the centre

A The Garden House, Urb Larapa Grande B-6, T084-271117, www.cuscohouse.com. Set in a large garden and orchard with views of the city, 7 rooms with bath and breakfast, sitting rooms, dining room and bar, internet, activities can be arranged, airport pickup.

B Residencial Torre Dorada, C los Cipreses N–5, Residencial Huancaro, T084-241698, www.torredorada.com.pe. In a tranquil suburb to the west of the airport, this sparklingly clean modern hotel makes up in service for anything it might lose in location. Good size rooms with very comfortable beds, heating and plenty of hot water in the well-appointed en-suite bathrooms. Buffet breakfast is included, as is free transportation to and from the airport/bus/train station, and daily to the historical centre of Cuzco. Internet access is also available. An excellent option for people looking to stay in a quieter part of town. Highly recommended.

Eating

Plaza de Armas and around

p83, map p140

TTT Cicciolina , Triunfo 393, 2nd floor, T084-239510, cicciolinacuzco@yahoo.com. Sophisticated restaurant focusing largely on Italian/Mediterranean cuisine. Antipasti, salads and bruschettas are all excellent. Main dishes range from hand-made pasta, through excellent steaks to Moroccan lamb tagine. It also has a tapas bar and a boutique bakery; the kitchens are open to view. The impressive wine list draws from across the globe but the emphasis is on Latin American produce. Good atmosphere, fine decor and great for treat. Ask about their **Open Air Restaurant in Cuzco** scheme: a gourmet picnic will be taken to the location of your choice, with chef, waiters and all the trimmings (best for groups).

TTT El Truco, Plaza Regocijo 261. Excellent local and international dishes, used a lot by tour groups, buffet lunch 1200-1500, nightly folk music at 2045, next door is **Taberna del Truco**, which is open 0900-0100.

TTT Incanto, Santa Catalina Angosta 135, T084-254753, incanto@cuscorestaurants.com. Under same ownership as **Inka Grill** and with the same standards, this new restaurant has Inca stone work and serves pastas, grilled meats, pizzas, desserts, accompanied by an extensive wine list. Open daily 1100-2400. There is also a Peruvian delicatessen on the premises. Upstairs is the new venture of **Greens Organic** (formerly in San Blas), exclusively organic ingredients in fusion cuisine and a fresh daily buffet.

ƔƔƔ Inka Grill, Portal de Panes 115, T084-262992, www.inkagrillcusco.com. 1100-2300 daily. According to many the best food in town is served here, specializing in *novo andino* cuisine (the use of native ingredients and 'rescued' recipes) and innovative dishes, also home-made pastas, wide vegetarian selection, live music, excellent coffee and home-made pastries 'to go'. A good place to spoil yourself, recommended.

ƔƔƔ La Retama, Portal de Panes 123, 2nd floor, T084-226372. Excellent *novo andino* food and service. We recommend the mouth-watering trout sashimi as a starter, followed by steak. There is also a balcony, an enthusiastic music and dance group and art exhibitions.

ƔƔƔ Pachacútec Grill and Bar, Portal de Panes 105. International cuisine including seafood and Italian specialities, also features folk music shows nightly.

ƔƔƔ Paititi, Portal Carrizos 270. Live music and good atmosphere in a setting with Inca masonry. Excellent pizzas but the restaurant can get very busy.

ƔƔƔ Pomodoro, Loreto 125, T084-221397. Almost certainly the best Italian food in Cuzco, hidden down Calle Loreto just behind **Norton Rat's Tavern**. The owner describes his restaurant as a bastion of 'slow food', with all pasta and pizza hand made on the spot. Don't expect speed, but the wait is worth it. Superb.

ƔƔƔ Tunupa, Portal Confiturías 233, 2nd floor (same entrance as **Cross Keys**). One of the finest restaurants on the plaza (often used by tour groups). Also has the longest (glassed-in) balcony but this is narrow and best for couples only. Food is international, traditional and *novo andino*; the wine list is limited. Also an excellent buffet for US$15 including a *pisco sour* and a hot drink. In the evenings there is an excellent group playing 16th- and 17th-century-style Cuzqueñan music of their own composition, accompanied by dancers. Recommended.

ƔƔƔ Tupananchis, Portal Mantas 180, T084-976 4494, tupananchis_rest_cusco@hotmail.com. Tasty, beautifully presented *novo andino* and fusion cuisine in a smart, sophisticated atmosphere. Try the alpaca curry, river fish ceviche or stuffed chicken supreme. There is a café next door. Highly recommended.

ƔƔ Al Grano, Santa Catalina Ancha 398, T084-228032, 1000-2100, closed on Sun. Lunchtime menu US$2.15 is a good option if you are fed up with other menus. Evening serves 5 authentic Asian dishes for US$5.50, menu changes daily. Without doubt some of the best coffee in town, vegetarian choices and breakfasts, including 'Full English'. Recommended.

ƔƔ A Mi Manera, corner of Triunfo and Palacios. Great-tasting food and good value if you ask for a set menu (not often advertised).

ƔƔ Baco, Ruinas 465, T084-242808, bacorestaurante@yahoo.com. New wine bar and bistro-style restaurant with same owner as **Cicciolina**. Specializes in *degustación* meals for groups, with barbecued and grilled meats, vegetarian dishes, interesting pizzas, and good wines. Unpretentious but comfortable, with a wide range of prices.

ƔƔ Kintaro, Heladeros 149. 1200-2200, closed Sun. Excellent home-made food, set menu (1200-1500) particularly good value at US$3, run by its Japanese owner. Low-fat food is said to be good for high altitude.

ƔƔ Kusikuy, Suecia 339, T084-292870. Mon-Sat 0800-2300. Some say this serves the best *cuy* (guinea pig, US$10.90) in town and the owners say if you give them an hour's warning they will produce their absolute best. Many other typical Cuzco dishes on the menu. Set lunch is unbeatable value at only US$2. Good service, live music, highly recommended.

ƔƔ Pizzería Marengo, Plaza Regocijo 246, T084-264151. Excellent pizzas for US$7-8 per person. Ask for a table in the back room next to the cosy clay oven and watch your food being prepared (eating indoors will also keep you from the street vendors). Also does deliveries.

ƔƔ Varayoc, Espaderos 142, T084-232404. Open daily 0800-2400. Swiss-owned restaurant including Peruvian ingredients (the only place in Cuzco that serves cheese fondue). Also has a variety of pastas, good desserts, 'tea time' beverage and pastry for US$2.80 accompanied by Andean harp music. Pleasant, literary atmosphere.

ƔƔ-Ɣ Yanapay, Ruinas 415, p 2, T255134. A good café serving breakfast, lunch and dinner. It is run by a charity which supports children's homes; head office at Av Alta 466, T084-245779, www.aldeayanapay.org. They welcome volunteers.

¶ **El Encuentro**, Santa Catalina Ancha 384, T084-247977, and Choquechaca 136, T084-225496. One of the best-value eateries, 3 courses of good healthy food and a drink will set you back US$1.35, very busy at lunchtime.
¶ **Víctor Victoria**, Tigre 130. Israeli and local dishes, highly recommended for breakfast, good value.

Procuradores and Plateros

These 2 streets lead off the northwest side of the Plaza de Armas. Procuradores, or **Gringo Alley** as the locals call it, is good for a value feed; its menus take the hungry backpacker from Mexico to Italy, Spain and Turkey. None is dreadful, many are very good indeed, especially for the price. Parallel with Gringo Alley, Plateros also has good-value places to eat. It is also lined with a great many tour operators, so you can wander up and down checking what deals are on offer.
¶¶ **Kapaj Ñan**, Procuradores 398, kapajnan@hotmail.com. Attentive service, an interesting mix of Peruvian, Asian and Italian cuisine. This one's a rustic, cosy little hole-in-the-wall and very different from the Gringo Alley standard.
¶¶ **Pucará**, Plateros 309. 1230-2200, closed Sun. Peruvian and international food. Japanese owner does very good US$2 set lunch, pleasant atmosphere. Recommended.
¶¶ **The Real McCoy**, Plateros 326, p 2, T084-261111, therealmccoycafelounge@yahoo.com. A fabulous retreat for homesick Brits and Aussies. The equal best greasy-spoon brekkie in town (the other being **Jack's Café**). There's a good-value breakfast buffet (US$2), with PG Tips and Heinz Baked Beans. On offer for dinner are some English classics: roast beef with Yorkshire pudding, etc. Finish it all off with banoffee pie or apple crumble with custard and cream.
¶ **Chez Maggy**, a long-established group with 3 branches: La Antigua (the original) at Procuradores 365 and, on the same street, **El Corsario**, No 344, and **Clave de Do**, No 374, (opens at 0700 for buffet breakfast).
¶ **El Fogón**, Plateros 365. Huge local *menú del día* for US$1.80, good solid food at reasonable prices. Very popular with locals and increasingly so with travellers.
¶ **El Molino**, Plateros 339. Snug little place that serves excellent pizza.
¶ **Los Candiles**, Plateros 323. Good set lunch for US$2.50.
¶ **Mía Pizza**, Procuradores 379. Good range of cheap menus, including a good curry.
¶ **Paloma Imbil**, Procuradores 362. The *rollo mixto*, US$3, comes in delicious home-baked bread. Has doner kebabs. For vegetarians the *rollo de falafel y queso* is a tasty option.

Cafés, delis and panaderías

Amaru, Plateros 325, 2nd floor, T084-246976. Limitless coffee, tea, great bread and juices served, even on non-buffet breakfasts (US$1.15 for simple). Colonial balcony; also a pub serving pizzas etc. Recommended.
Ayllu, Portal de Carnes 208, to the left of the cathedral. Probably one of the oldest cafés in Cuzco and a great place to go. Fantastic breakfasts (have the special fruit salad, US$2.30), sandwiches, coffee and classical music as well as wonderful apple pastries. The *ponche con pisco* is an excellent way to end a cold evening. Very much a local venue with superb service.
Café Halliy, Plateros 363. Popular meeting place, especially for breakfast, good for comments on guides, has good snacks and *copa Halliy* (fruit, muesli, yoghurt, honey and chocolate cake), also serves vegetarian dishes.
Dolce Vita, Santa Catalina Ancha 366 (with another branch on Márquez), 1000-2100. At just US$0.30 per delicious Italian scoop, this *heladería* is an absolute must.
La Bondiet, corner of Av Márquez and Heladeros. Clean, simple and inexpensive café with a huge selection of sweet and savoury pastries and decent sandwiches. Good juices and the coffee's OK.
La Tertulia, Procuradores 50, 2nd floor. Breakfast, served 0630-1300, includes muesli, bread, yoghurt, eggs, juice and coffee, eat as much as you like for US$3, superb value, vegetarian buffet daily 1800-2200, set dinner and salad bar for US$3.50, also fondue and gourmet meals, book exchange, newspapers, classical music.
Trotamundos, Portal Comercio 177, 2nd floor. Mon-Sat 0800-2400. One of the most pleasant cafés in the plaza if a bit pricey. Has a balcony overlooking the plaza and a warm atmosphere especially at night with its open fire. Good coffees and cakes, safe salads, *brochetas*, sandwiches and pancakes as well as 4 computers with internet access.
Yaku Mama, Procuradores 397. Good for breakfast; unlimited fruit and coffee.

North and northeast of the Plaza de Armas *p139, map p138*

TTT Fallen Angel, Plazoleta Nazarenas 221, T084-258184, contacto@fallenangelin cusco.com. This is the art gallery of Andrés Zúniga, like nowhere else ("completely OTT") in that it just happens to serve great food in an original *conquistador* residence. The menu features steaks and some innovative pasta dishes. Cocktails are excellent. Live DJ at night. Regular parties/fashion shows are always events to remember. The gallery in the patio exhibits clothing designed by Norma Peña. Free wireless internet connection. Mon-Sat 1100 till whenever (bar closes at midnight, kitchen at 2300), Tue and Sun opens at 1500. Always phone to reserve.

TTT MAP Café, Plaza de las Nazarenas 231, a glass structure in the **Museo de Arte Precolombino**, T084-242476, www.map-cafe.com. Operates as a café 1000-1830 and a restaurant 1830-2200. Serves excellent Peruvian-Andean cuisine and international food, with an innovative children's menu. It has a very good list of wines and *piscos*. After your museum visit, this is an ideal place for tea or coffee or a sophisticated meal.

TT Inca Food, Choquechaca 152, 2nd floor. Charmingly decorated, overlooking the street, well-prepared and presented food, including *novo andino* dishes, very helpful, good value.

T Café Cultural Ritual, Choquechaca 140. Good value and tasty vegetarian *menú*, including some decent Indian dishes (the veggie curry is good), for US$2.20.

Cafés, delis and panaderías

Chocolate, Choquechaca 162, T974 9343 (mob). Good for coffee and cakes but the real highlights are the fresh gourmet chocolates (up to European standards).

San Blas *p141, map p138*

TT La Bodega, Carmen Alto 146. Snug Dutch- and Peruvian-owned café/restaurant serving hot chocolate by candlelight in the after-noons, evening meals – dishes come with side trip to salad bar, American breakfast and a US$1.50 lunch menu. Highly recommended.

TT Macondo, Cuesta San Blas 571, T084-229415. Bit pricier than others in this range but fantastic. A casual, cosy, arty and comfortable restaurant which has been redecorated under a change of ownership. Serves an exotic menu with jungle and *novo andino* food. It also has an art gallery. Popular, and a steep 3-block walk from the plaza.

TT Jack's Café, on the corner of Choquechaca and San Blas. T084-806960. Opens at 0630 for great-value English breakfast. Excellent varied menu with generous portions, all in a light and relaxed atmosphere. Fabulous American-style pancakes and freshly ground local coffee. Lunchtime can be very busy.

TT Pachapapa, Plazoleta San Blas 120, opposite church of San Blas, T084-241318, www.cuscorestaurants.com/pachapapa. Open 1130-2200. A beautiful patio restaurant in a wonderful old colonial house, with resident harp player. Under same ownership as **Inka Grill**. Very good Cuzqueña dishes, including *pachamanca* (previous reservation required for 6 people). At night, diners can sit in their own private colonial dining room. Recommended.

TT Witches Garden, Carmen Bajo 169, just off Plazoleta San Blas, T084-244077, www.witches garden.net. Good *novo andino*, Quebecois and international cuisine served in this warmly decorated little restaurant; the chicken and beef dishes, the Montreal Classic Combo and the desserts are recommended. Theres TV and video, with a selection of movies, available for patrons. French-Canadian owned.

TT-T La Bodeguita Cubana, Hatunrumiyoc 487, p 2. Specializes in Cuban food, but they also have other dishes, such as pizza, pastas, Peruvian food and soups, and breakfasts. Caribbean drinks, as well.

TT-T Mundo Hemp, Qanchipata 596, www.mundohemp.com. Foccacia bread, interesting savoury pancakes, quiche and good fresh juices. Nice atmosphere with a beautiful sunny courtyard, lots of cushions inside, a colourful place and great for chilling out, but the food's overpriced for what you get. Also has a shop selling a range of hemp products.

T Granja Heidi, Cuesta San Blas 525, T084-238383. US$3 gets you an excellent 3- or 4-course *menú del día* in a clean and relaxed environment. There are usually vegetarian options; superb yoghurt.

T Gypsy Pub, Carmen Alto 162-C. Comfortable bar/restaurant a little further down the street from **La Bodega**. Good *menú del día* for US$2 and the chicken is some of the best in Cuzco.

¶ **Inkafe**, Choquechaca 131-A, T084-258073. Good coffee, set breakfasts and good-value lunch menus. Range of sandwiches in French bread and good desserts.

¶ **Kachivache**, Carmen Alto 260, T084-265143, kachivache_peru@yahoo.es. Tasty Spanish cuisine, bruschettas, sandwiches and grilled meats, vegetarian options available. Prices are very reasonable. Relaxed, light and airy – a good spot for a leisurely lunch.

Cafés, delis and panaderías

The Muse, Tandapata 682, Plazoleta San Blas. Funky little café with a cosy feel and great views over the plaza. Fresh coffee, good food, including vegetarian lasagne, chicken curry, carrot cake and the best smoothies in town. There's often live music in the afternoons/evenings with no cover charge. English owner Clair is very helpful. The Muse will refill water bottles for a small charge in an attempt to minimize plastic waste in Cuzco.

Panadería El Buen Pastor, Cuesta San Blas 579. Very good bread and pastries, the proceeds from which go to a charity for orphans and street children. Very popular with backpackers. Recommended.

Velluto, Tandapata 700, T084-240966. A great place for crêpes, savoury and sweet.

East and southeast of the Plaza de Armas *p141, map p138*

¶¶ **Inkanato**, San Agustín 280, T084-222926, www.perou.net. Good food, staff dressed in Inca outfits and dishes made only with ingredients known in Inca times, calls itself a 'living museum'.

¶¶ **Los Toldos**, Almagro 171 y San Andrés 219. If you're feeling peckish, on a budget and fancy being served by waiters in a bow tie, try their great chicken *brocheta*. Comes with fries, a trip to the salad bar and is enough for 2 people at just US$2.30. Also *trattoria* with home-made pasta and pizza, delivery T084-229829.

¶ **Chifa Sipan**, Quera 251 (better than their other branch for tourists in Plateros). Owner Carlos may not sound Chinese but he is and joins in the cooking at this excellent restaurant. There is no great ambience but it's busy at lunchtimes with locals, which speaks volumes. Skip to the back of the menu for their better deals.

South and southwest of the Plaza de Armas *p142, map 138*

¶ **Santa Ana market**, to eat really cheaply, and if your stomach is acclimatized to South American food, head for the market 5 blocks southwest of the Plaza de Armas at Túpac Amaru and eat at one of the many stalls. Food will cost no more than US$0.70 and 3-fruit juices are just US$0.45! Otherwise, look for the set *menús*, usually served 1200-1500, although they are no good for vegetarians.

Cafés, delis and panaderías

Café Manu, Av Pardo 1046. Good coffee and good food too in a jungle decor. It would be a sin to miss one of their liqueur coffees.

Moni, San Agustín 311, T084-231029, www.moni-cusco.com. Peruvian/English-owned, good fresh food and breakfast, British music, magazines, bright, clean and comfy.

Bars and clubs

Maps p138 and p140

Bars

Bar 7, Tandapata 690, San Blas, T084-506472. Good food and drinks in a trendy bar which specializes in local ingredients.

Big Blue Martini, Tecseccocha 148, T084-248839. Sophisticated, split-level sofa bar with funky lighting, very good cocktails, food and a lively music scene. There are jazz sessions on Thu, and a guest DJ on the decks on Sat .

Blueberry Lounge, Portal de Carnes 235, T084-249458, www.cuscorestaurants.com/blueberry. Dark, moody and sophisticated, this is a slice of London's Soho on the Plaza de Armas. There's a good menu, featuring American gourmet fast food.

Cross Keys Pub, Portal Confiturías 233 (upstairs). 1100-0130. Run by Barry Walker of **Manu Expeditions**, a Mancunian and ornithologist. Darts, cable sports, pool, bar meals, happy hours 1830-1930 and 2130-2230, plus daily half-price specials Sun-Wed, great *pisco sours*, very popular, loud and raucous, great atmosphere.

Km 0 (Arte y Tapas), Tandapata 100, San Blas. Lovely Mediterranean-themed bar tucked in behind San Blas. Good snacks and tapas (of course), affordable, and with live music every night (around 2200 – lots of acoustic guitar, etc).

Los Perros Bar, Tecseccocha 436, above Gringo Alley (Procuradores). A great place to chill on comfy couches listening to excellent music. There's a book exchange, English and other magazines and board games. Opens 1100 for coffee and pastries; kitchen opens at 1300; very good vegetarian lunch. Occasionally hosts live music and special events.

Mandela's Bar, Palacios 121, 3rd floor, T084-222424, www.mandelasbar.com. Cutting-edge bar/restaurant with an African theme. Good atmosphere, live music on Thu, Fri, Sat; lots of space to spread out and relax. Serves breakfast, lunch and drinks in the evening, also Sun barbecues and special events all year. Proceeds of Wed pub quiz go to street children. The food is a Cuzqueña/South African mix. Great 360º panorama from the rooftop.

Norton Rat's Tavern, Loreto 115, 2nd floor, on the plaza but has a side entrance off a road to the left of La Compañía (same entrance as **Hostal Loreto**), T084-246204, nortonrats@yahoo.com. Pleasant pub with a pool table, dart board, cable TV and lots of pictures of motorbikes! Owner Jeffrey Powers loves the machines and can provide information for bikers. There's a balcony which offers great views of the Plaza de Armas. Also has a juice bar serving Amazonian specials. Happy hour 1900-2100 every night with other daily specials.

Paddy Flaherty's, C Triunfo 124, corner of the plaza, 1300-0100. An Irish theme pub, deservedly popular. Good seating and great food – the jacket potatoes, shepherd's pie and baguettes are all highly recommended.

Rosie O'Grady's, at Santa Catalina Ancha 360, T084-247935. Open 1100 till late (food served till midnight, happy hours 1300-1400, 1800-1900, 2300-2330). Has good music, tasty food. English and Russian spoken.

Siete Angelitos, Siete Angelitos 638. Tiny hole in the wall bar, just a couple of rooms really, but spectacular cocktails and good food (especially the pasta dishes and steaks), a friendly owner by the name of Walter and an awesome atmosphere when things get going. Often hosts guest DJs, ranging from Latin to trance. Happy hour 2000-2200.

Clubs

Before your evening meal don't turn down flyers being handed out around the Plaza de Armas. Each coupon not only gives you free entry, it is worth a *cuba libre*. On the back of this tour you will be able to check out which club most suits your tastes. Sadly, the free entry-and-drink system doesn't appear to apply to Peruvians who are invariably asked to pay, even if their tourist companions get in for free. This discrimination should be discouraged. Also note that free drinks are made with the cheapest, least healthy alcohol; always watch your drink being made and obviously never leave it unattended. If you fancy learning a few Latin dance steps before hitting the dancefloor, many of the clubs offer free lessons. Ask at the door for details or look out for flyers.

Corruption, Tecseccocha. Wide range of music, very in vogue with Israeli backpackers. A good alternative to the scene on the plaza.

El Garabato Video Music Club, Espaderos 132, 3rd floor. Daily 1600-0300. Dance area, lounge for chilling, bar with saddles for stools, tastefully decorated in a colonial setting, with live shows 2300-0300 (all sorts of styles) and a large screen showing music videos. Recommended.

Extreme, on Suecia, next door to **Magtas Bar**. An old Cuzco staple. Movies are shown late afternoon and early evening, but after midnight this place really gets going with an eclectic range of music, from 60s' and 70s' rock and pop to techno and trance. This place seems to give out more free drinks than most, so it's a good option for kicking off a big night on the town!

Kamikaze, plaza Regocijo 274, T084-233865. Peña at 2200, good old traditional rock music, candle-lit cavern atmosphere, entry US$2.50 but usually you don't have to pay.

Mama Africa, Portal de Harinas, 2nd floor. Cool music and clubbers' spot. Serves good food from a varied menu, happy hour till 2300, good value.

Ukuku's, Plateros 316. US$1.35 entry or free with a pass. This is somewhat different to the other clubs as every night there is a live band that might play anything from rock to salsa. The DJ then plays a mixture of Peruvian and international music but the emphasis is on local. It has a good mix of *cuzqueños* and tourists. Happy hour 0730-0930.

Uptown, Portal Belén 115, 2nd floor. Formerly **Mama América**, with a dancefloor and a large video screen. The music is middle of the road, from local music through 70s' classics to the latest releases.

Entertainment

Maps p138 and p140

Centro Qosqo de Arte Nativo, Av Sol 604, T084-227901. There's a regular nightly folklore show here 1900-2030, entrance on the BTG visitors' ticket.

Teatro Inti Raymi, Saphi 605. Music nightly at 1845, US$4.50 entry and well worth it.

Teatro Municipal, C Mesón de la Estrella 149 (T084-227321 for information 0900-1300 and 1500-1900). This is a venue for plays, dancing and shows, mostly Thu-Sun. Ask for their programmes. They also run classes in music and dancing Jan-Mar which are great value.

Festivals and events

Maps p138 and p140

20 Jan A procession of saints in the San Sebastián district of Cuzco.

Feb/Mar **Carnival** in Cuzco is a messy affair with flour, water, cacti, rotton fruit and manure thrown about in the streets. Be prepared.

Mar/Apr Easter Mon sees the procession of **El Señor de los Temblores** (Lord of the Earthquakes), starting at 1600 outside the cathedral. A large crucifix is paraded through the streets, returning to the plaza de Armas around 2000 to bless the tens of thousands of people who have assembled there.

2-3 May The **Vigil of the Cross** takes place at all mountaintops with crosses on them, is a boisterous affair.

Jun **Corpus Christi**, on the Thu after Trinity Sunday, when all the statues of the Virgin and of saints from Cuzco's churches are paraded through the streets to the cathedral. This is a colourful event. The Plaza de Armas is surrounded by tables with women selling *cuy* (guinea pig) and a mixed grill called *chiriuchu* (*cuy*, chicken, tortillas, fish eggs, water-weeds, maize, cheese and sausage) and lots of Cusqueña beer.

Early Jun 2 weeks before Inti Raymi (see below) is the highly recommended **Cusqueña Beer Festival**, held near the rail station, which boasts a great variety of Latin American music. The whole event is well-organized and great fun.

Jun is **Qoyllur Rit'i** (Snow Star Festival), held at a 4700-m glacier north of Ocongate (Ausangate), 150 km southeast of Cuzco. It has its final day 58 days after Easter Sun. To get there involves a 2-hr walk up from the nearest road at Mawayani, beyond Ocongate, then it's a further exhausting climb up to the glacier. It's a good idea to take a tent, food and plenty of warm clothing. Many trucks leave Cuzco, from Limacpampa, in the days prior to the full moon in mid-Jun; prices from US$2 upwards. This is a very rough and dusty overnight journey lasting 14 hrs, requiring warm clothing and coca leaves to fend off cold and exhaustion. Several agencies offer tours, see page 162.

24 Jun **Inti Raymi**, the Inca festival of the winter solstice (see box, page 159), where locals outnumber tourists, is enacted at the fortress of Sacsayhuaman. The spectacle starts at 1000 at the Qoricancha (crowds line the streets and jostle for space to watch), then proceeds to the Plaza de Armas.

From there performers and spectators go to Sacsayhuaman for the main event, which starts at 1300. It lasts 2½ hrs and is in Quechua. Locals make a great day of it, watching the ritual from the hillsides and cooking potatoes in pits in the ground. Tickets for the stands can be bought in advance from the **Emufec** office, Santa Catalina Ancha 325 (opposite the Complejo Policial), and cost US$35. Standing places on the ruins are free but get there at about 1030 as even reserved seats fill up quickly, and defend your space. Travel agents can arrange the whole day for you, with meeting points, transport, reserved seats and packed lunch. Don't believe anyone who tries to persuade you to buy a ticket for the right to film or take photos. On the night before **Inti Raymi**, the Plaza de Armas is crowded with processions and food stalls. Try to arrive in Cuzco 15 days before Inti Raymi. The atmosphere in the town during the build up is fantastic and something is always going on (festivals, parades, etc).

Last Sun in Aug The **Huarachicoy Festival** at Sacsayhuaman is a spectacular re-enactment of the Inca manhood rite, performed in dazzling costumes by boys of a local school.

8 Sep **Day of the Virgin**, when there's a colourful procession of masked dancers from the church of Almudena, at the southwest edge of Cuzco, near Belén, to the Plaza de San Francisco. There is also a fair at Almudena, and a bull fight the following day.

8 Dec **Cuzco Day**, when churches and museums close at 1200.

The festival of Inti Raymi

The sun was the principal object of Inca worship and at their winter solstice, in June, the Incas honoured the solar deity with a great celebration known as Inti Raymi, the sun festival. The Spanish suppressed the Inca religion, and the last royal Inti Raymi was celebrated in 1535.

However, in 1944, a group of Cuzco intellectuals, inspired by the contemporary 'indigenist' movement, revived the old ceremony in the form of a pageant, putting it together from chronicles and historical documents. The event caught the public imagination, and it has been celebrated every year since then on 24 Jun, now a Cuzco public holiday. Hundreds of local men and women play the parts of Inca priests, nobles, chosen women, soldiers (played by the local army garrison), runners, and the like. The coveted part of the Inca emperor Pachacuti is won by audition, and the event is organized by the municipal authorities.

It begins around 1000 at the Qoricancha (page 142) – the former sun temple of Cuzco – and winds its way up the main avenue into the Plaza de Armas, accompanied by songs, ringing declarations and the occasional drink of *chicha*. At the main plaza, Cuzco's presiding mayor is whisked back to Inca times, to receive Pachacuti's blessing and a stern lecture on good government. Climbing through Plaza Nazarenas and up Pumacurcu, the procession reaches the ruins of Sacsayhuaman at about 1400, where scores of thousands of people are gathered on the ancient stones.

Before Pachacuti arrives the *Sinchi* (Pachacuti's chief general) ushers in contingents from the four *Suyus* (regions) of the Inca empire. Much of the ceremony is based around alternating action between these four groups of players. A *Chaski* (messenger) enters to announce the imminent arrival of the Inca and his *Coya* (queen). Men sweep the ground before him and women scatter flowers. The Inka takes the stage alone and has a dialogue with the sun. Then he receives reports from the governors of the four *Suyus*. This is followed by a drink of the sacred *chicha*, the re-lighting of the sacred fire of the empire, the sacrifice (faked) of a llama and the reading of auguries in its entrails. Finally the ritual eating of *sankhu* (corn paste mixed with the victim's blood) ends the ceremonies. The Inca gives a last message to his assembled children, and departs. The music and dancing continues until nightfall. See also Festivals and events, page 158.

24 Dec Santuranticuy, 'the buying of saints'. This is a huge celebration of Christmas shopping with a big crafts market in the Plaza de Armas, which is very noisy until the early hours of the 25th.

Shopping

Maps p138 and p140

Arts and crafts

Cuzco has some of the best craft shopping in all Peru. In the Plaza San Blas and the surrounding area, authentic Cuzco crafts still survive and woodworkers can be seen in almost any street. A market is held on Sat. The main market for artisans' stalls is at the bottom of Av Sol (the **Cholitas de los Andes** stall, No 96, sells textiles made by unsupported mothers). There are also small markets of 10 or so permament stalls dotted around the city which offer goods made from alpaca as well as modern materials. For example, at **Feria Artesanal Tesores del Inka**, Plateros 334 (open 0900-2300), the first stall in the doorway will tailor-make reversible fleeces in 2 colours for US$10.

Cuzco is also the weaving centre of Peru and excellent textiles can be found at good value; but watch out for sharp practices when buying gold and silver objects and jewellery. Note that much of the wood used for picture frames, etc, is *cedro*, a rare timber not extracted by sustainable means.

Agua y Tierra, Plazoleta Nazarenas 167, and also at Cuesta San Blas 595, T084-226951. Excellent quality crafts from lowland rainforest communities, largely the Shipibo and Ashaninka tribes from the Selva Central whose work is considered to be among the finest in the Amazon Basin.

Alpaca 111, Plaza Regocijo 202, T084-243233. High-quality alpaca clothing, with shops also in hotels **Monasterio**, **Libertador** and **Machu Picchu Sanctuary Lodge**, the **Museo de Arte Precolombino** and at the airport.

Alpaca 3, Ruinas 472. Quality alpaca items.

Andean Spirit, Hatun Rumiyoc 487-B, T084-232962. Potter Lucho Soler claims to use traditional Inca methods in his work. Whether this is true or not the ceramics on display are excellent.

Arte Vivo del Cusco al Mundo, on the right-hand side in Capilla San Ignacio, Plaza de Armas. Open 1030-1300, 1530-2100. The outlet for 2 cooperatives of weavers.

Away, Procuradores 361, T084-229465. Sells blankets, leather goods and handmade shoes, prices from US$15-40 for a pair, allow 2 days delivery for your own design.

Calas, Siete Angelitos 619-B, San Blas. Handmade silver jewellery in interesting designs and alpaca goods from the community of Pitumarca.

Carlos Chaquiras, Triunfo 375 y Portal Comercio 107, T084-227470, www.carlos chaquiras.com. 1000-1930. Very upmarket jewellery, with lots of Inca figures, among other designs, enhanced with semi-precious stones and shells. Also at Av Berriozabal s/n, Urubamba, T084-201266.

Center for Traditional Textiles of Cusco, Av Sol 603, T084-228117, www.textiles cusco.org. A non-profit organization that promotes the weaving traditions of the area. Tours of workshops in Chinchero and beyond can de arranged, also weaving classes. In the Cuzco outlet you can watch weavers at work. Excellent quality textiles at prices reflecting the fact that over 50% goes direct to the weaver. Recommended.

Cuzmar II, Portal Mantas 118T. For good quality alpaca items (English spoken).

Ilaria, Portal Carrizos 258, T084-246253, and in hotels **Monasterio**, **Libertador** and at the airport. Branches of the recommended jewellery and silver stores from Lima.

Inkantations, Choquechaca 200. Radical baskets made from natural materials in all sorts of weird and wonderful shapes. Also ceramics and Andean weavings. Interesting and original.

Josefina Olivera, Portal Comercio 173, Plaza de Armas. She sells old ponchos and antique *mantas* (shawls), without the usual haggling. Her prices are high, but it is worth it to save pieces being cut up to make other items, open daily 1100-2100.

La Casa de la Llama, Palacio 121, www.llamactiva.com. A smart establishment with a variety of excellent quality, well-designed llama wool sweaters, scarves and llama-leather bags. They also sell alpaca goods; compare prices with elsewhere.

La Mamita, Portal de Carnes 244, Plaza de Armas, sells the ceramics of **Seminario-Behar** (see page 181), plus cotton, basketry, jewellery, etc.

La Pérez, Urb Mateo Pumacahua 598, Huanchac, T084-232186. A big cooperative with a good selection. They will arrange a free pickup from your hotel.

Maky Artesanías, Carmen Alto 101, T084-653643. A great place to buy individually designed ceramics. Ask for discounts if buying several pieces.

Mon Repos, Portal de Panes 139, Plaza de Armas, T084-251600. High-quality alpaca clothing, expensive, but nicely presented and with a wide selection.

Mullu, Triunfo 120, T084-229831. Contemporary silver jewellery with semi-precious stones and cotton clothing with interesting designs, open Mon-Sat 1000-2100.

Pedazo de Arte, Plateros 334B. A tasteful collection of Andean handicrafts, many designed by Japanese owner Miki Suzuki.

Primitiva, Hatun Rumiyoc 495, T084-993 3693, San Blas, www.coscio.com. Excellent Peruvian contemporary art gallery, largely featuring the work of Federico Coscio.

Spondylus, Cuesta San Blas 505 y Plazoleta San Blas 617, T084-226929, spondylus cusco@mixmail.com. Interesting jewellery in gold and silver, also using semi-precious stones and shells. They also sell T-shirts featuring Inca and pre-Inca designs.

Store of the Weavers (Asociación Central de Artesanos y Artesanas del Sur Andino Inkakunaq Ruwaynin), Av Tullumayo 274, T084-233466/227656, www.cbc.org.pe/tejidosandinos. A store administered by 6 local weaving communities, some of whose residents you can see working on site. All profits go to the weavers themselves. Most of the work utilizes traditional dyes and the fine quality of the *mantas* and other textiles on sale makes this store well worth a visit.
Taki Museo de Música de los Andes, Hatunrumiyoq 487-5. Shop and workshop selling and displaying musical instruments, knowledgeable owner, who is an ethnomusicologist. Recommended.

Books

Centro de Estudios Regionales Andinos Bartolomé de las Casas, Av Tullumayo 465, T084-233472, www.cbc.org.pe. Mon-Sat 1100-1400, 1600-1900. Good books on Peruvian history, archaeology, etc. Head office is at Pampa de La Alianza 164, T084-245415.
Jerusalem, Heladeros 143, T084-235408. English books, guidebooks, music, postcards, book exchange (3 for 1).
SBS (Special Book Services), Av Sol 781-A, opposite the post office, T084-248106.
The Sun, Plazoleta Limacpampa Chico 471. This café/restaurant has the best book exchange, 1 for 1, maintained by an Australian.

Camping equipment

There are several places on Plateros which rent out equipment but check it carefully as it is common for parts to be missing. An example of prices per day: tent US$3-5, sleeping bag US$2 (down), US$1.50 (synthetic), stove US$1. A deposit of US$100 is asked, plus credit card, passport or plane ticket. Wherever you hire equipment, check the stoves carefully. White gas (*bencina*) costs US$1.50 per litre and can be bought at hardware stores, but check the purity. Stove spirit (*alcohol para quemar*) is available at pharmacies. Blue gas canisters, costing US$5, can be found at some hardware stores and at shops which rent gear. You can also rent equipment through travel agencies.
Edson Zuñiga Huillca, Mercado Rosaspata, Jr Abel Landeo P-1, T084-802831, 993 7243 (mob). Three mins from Plaza de Armas, for repair of camping equipment and footwear, also equipment rental, open 24 hrs a day, 7 days a week, English and Italian spoken.
Soqllaq'asa Camping Service, Plateros 365 No 2F, T084-252560. Owned by English-speaking Sra Luzmila Bellota Miranda, recommended for equipment hire, from down sleeping bags (US$2 per day) to gas stoves (US$1 per day) and **ThermaRest** mats (US$1 per day); pots, pans, plates, cups and cutlery are all provided free by the friendly staff. They also buy and sell camping gear and make alpaca jackets, open Mon-Sat 0900-1300, 1600-2030, Sun 1800-2030.
Tatoo, Plazoleta Las Nazarenas 211, T084-245314, www.tatoo.ws. High-quality hiking, climbing and camping gear, not cheap, European prices in fact, but western brand names: Colombia, Gore-Tex, Polartec etc. The house brand, Tatoo, produces good trousers, thermals, fleeces and jackets. Imported hiking boots. Another branch in the Larcomar shopping centre in Lima.

Food

Casa Ecológica Cusco, Triunfo 393, www.casaecologicacusco.com. Organic foods, wild honey, coffee, granola. Casa Ecológica also offers natural medicines, indigenous art and weavings. They claim to pay fair prices when dealing with local suppliers.
La Cholita, Portal Espinar 142-B and at airport. Extra-special chocolates made with local ingredients.

Markets

San Jerónimo, just out of town, is the wholesale Sat morning fruit and vegetable market, but food just as good and not much more expensive (and washed) can be bought at the markets in town: **Huanchac**, Av Garcilaso (not C Garcilaso), or **Santa Ana**, opposite Estación San Pedro, which sells a variety of goods. The best value is at closing time or in the rain. Take care after dark. Sacks to cover rucksacks are available in the market for US$0.75. Both Huanchac and Santa Ana open every day from 0700.

El Molino, under the Puente Grau, is for contraband goods brought in from abroad without duty or tax being paid, but it is tolerated by the authorities. Everything from computers to hi-fis, personal stereos to trekking boots, cheap camera film to wine can be bought here (take a taxi for US$0.60).

It is clean and safe (but take the usual common sense precautions about valuables) and is open daily 0600-2030.

Supermarkets

La Canasta, Av La Cultura 2000 block. Very well stocked, takes credit cards, ATM outside.
D'Dinos Market, Av La Cultura 2003, T084-252656. Open 24-hrs, well supplied, takes credit cards.
Dimart, Matará 271, and Av La Cultura 742. Daily 0700-2200, credit cards accepted.
El Pepito, Plaza San Francisco, Mon-Sat 0900-2000, closed lunchtime. Sells a wide variety of imported goods and also has a delicatessen, stocks multi-packs of food (eg chocolate bars) much cheaper than other shops, a good bargain for trekking supplies.

Activities and tours

Maps p138 and p140

There are a million and one tour operators in Cuzco, most of whom are packed into the Plaza de Armas. The sheer number and variety of tours on offer is bewildering and prices for the same tour can vary dramatically. You should only deal directly with the agencies and seek advice from visitors returning from trips for the latest information. Agencies listed below are included under the field in which they are best known and for which they receive consistent recommendations. City tours cost about US$6 and last 4 hrs; check what sites are included (usually too few) and that the guide is experienced. Beware of tours which stop for long lunches at pricey hotels. Check if there are cancellation fees. Students will normally receive a discount on production of an ISIC card.

Inca Trail and general tours

Only a restricted number of agencies are licensed to operate Inca Trail trips. A full list will be found on the **INC** website, www.inc-cusco.gob.pe: click on Sistema de Reservas RCI and go to Agencias de Turismo Autorizadas. (INRENA, Av José Gabriel Cosio 308, Urb Magisterial, 1 etapa, T084-229297, www.inrena.gob.pe, will verify operating permits.) Other agencies will sell Inca Trail trips, but pass clients on to the operating agency in a pooling system. This can cause confusion and booking problems at busy times.

Inclusion in our list does not guarantee that the company is licensed to operate the Inca Trail (2006). All those listed below have been recommended for their services (except for any reservations noted). Many agencies, and the alternatives they offer, can be found in the trip reports in the **South America Explorers'** clubhouse at Choquechaca 188 (for members only).
Andean Adventures, Urb Lucrepata E-13, T084-263498, www.andeanadventures peru.com. An experienced outfit offering cultural trips and ecotourism. Tailor-made tours of the region as well as treks to Machu Picchu.
Andina Travel, Plazoleta Santa Catalina 219, T084-251892, www.andinatravel.com. Agency specializing in trekking and biking. One of the company's specialities is the Lares Valley programme, which works together with some of the valley's traditional weaving communities and provides employment for village residents – many trekking variations are possible in this area.
Apu Expediciones, T084-969 8311, www.apuexpediciones.com. Operator with many years experience in adventure and cultural travel. Deals with customers mostly on-line.
Big Foot, Triunfo 392 (of 213), T084-238568, www.bigfootcusco.com. Specialists in tailor-made hiking trips, especially in the remote corners of the Vilcabamba and Vilcanota mountains. Also the more conventional Inca Trail routes.
Ch'aska, Plateros 325, 2nd floor, T084-240424, www.chaskatours.com. Dutch-Peruvian company that has quickly acquired a solid reputation offering cultural, adventure, nature and esoteric tours. They specialize in the Inca Trail, but also llama treks to Lares and recommended trips to Choquequirao and beyond.
Cóndor Travel, C Saphi 848-A, T084-225961, www.condortravel.com.pe (for flights diviajes@condortravel.com.pe). A high-quality, exclusive agency that will organize trips throughout Peru and the rest of the world. They have a specialized section for adventure travel and are an excellent port of call if looking for international flight tickets. They are representatives for several inter national airlines and have many programmes to complement business trips and conferences.
Destinos Turísticos, Portal de Panes 123, of 101-102, Plaza de Armas, T084-228168,

www.destinosturisticosperu.com. The owner speaks Spanish, English, Dutch and Portuguese and specializes in package tours from economic to 5-star budgets. Individuals are welcome to come in for advice on booking jungle trips to renting mountain bikes. Ask in advance if you require guides with specific languages. Very informative and helpful.

Ecotrek Peru, Totorapaccha 769, T084-247286, T084-972 7237 (mob), www.ecotrekperu.com. Scot and long-time Cuzco resident Fiona Cameron runs this environmentally friendly tour agency, Ecotrek, offering a wide range of adventures through their excellent website, specializing in little visited areas such as the Pongo de Mainique and Espíritu Pampa/Vilcabamba Vieja. Fiona's partner, David Ugarte, is a mountain biking specialist and will tailor 2-wheeled adventures as required. David speaks fluent English, has a degree in tourism, and is great fun to hang out with. He can be contacted direct on T084-974 4810 (mob). Both David and Fiona pride themselves on fair treatment of local staff and communities. Tour prices (mid-range) are dependent on group numbers and type of service required. Fiona also manufactures a range of organic soaps.

Enigma, Jr Clorinda Matto de Turner 100, Magisterio 1a etapa, T084-222155, www.enigmaperu.com. Adventure tour agency run by Spaniard Silvia Rico Coll. Has an excellent reputation for well- organized and innovative trekking expeditions. In addition to the regular Inca Trail, she offers, for example, a 7-day programme to the remote and beautiful Laguna Sibinacocha, in the Vilcanota Mountains, or a 3 night trek into the Lares Valley. Set departures and fixed prices on some routes, but on the more remote excursions prices depend on group numbers. Also cultural tours to traditional weaving communities, Ayahuasca therapy and can arrange climbing and biking itineraries on demand.

Explorandes, Av Garcilaso 316-A (not to be confused with C Garcilaso in the centre),

Explorandes, Av Garcilaso 316-A (not to be confused with C Garcilaso in the centre), T084-238380, www.explorandes.com. Experienced high-end adventure company. Their main office is in Lima, but trips can be arranged from Cuzco. Vast range of trips available in both Peru and Ecuador, easily booked through their well-organized website. Also arranges tours across Peru for lovers of orchids, ceramics or textiles. Award-winning environmental practices.

Flamenco Travels, Portal de Confiturias 265, oficina 3, info@ponyexpeditions.com. Associated with **Pony 's Expeditions** of Caraz (Cordillera Blanca). They run the Classic Inka Trail pooled trek at US$275, with daily departures (average of 8-10 people). Also the 5-day Salkantay trek at US$275.

Galacruises Expeditions, N22-118, 9 de Octubre y Veintimilla, Edificio El Trebol, T0059-2-504002, www.galacruises.com. Trips to Peru, Bolivia, Ecuador, and the Galápagos.

Gatur Cusco, Puluchapata 140 (a small street off Av Sol 3rd block), T084-223496, www.gaturcusco.com. Esoteric, ecotourism, and general tours. Owner Dr José (Pepe) Altamirano is knowledgeable in Andean folk traditions. Excellent conventional tours, bilingual guides and transportation, very helpful. Guides speak English, French, Spanish and German. They can also book internal flights.

Hiking Peru, Portal de Panes 109, office 6, T084-247942/965 1414 (mob), www.hikingperu.com. Concentrates on the less-beaten paths, eg 8-day treks to Espíritu Pampa, 7 days/6 nights around Ausangate, Lares Valley Trek, also with 4 clients US$175 (but is licensed for the Inca Trail).

Inca Explorers, Ruinas 427, T084-241070, www.incaexplorers.com. Specialist trekking agency with a good reputation for small group expeditions executed in socially and environmentally responsible manner. More demanding, adventurous trips include a 2-week hike in the Cordillera Vilcanota (passing Nevado Ausangate), and Choquequirao to Espíritu Pampa, again for 2 weeks.

Inka Legacy Tours, San Isidro F-7, T084-807750, 968 3767 (mob), info@inkalegacytours.com. Good customized tours, attentive service, flexible, ask for Antonia Graneros.

Liz's Explorer, Medio 114B, T084-246619, www.lizexplorer.com. For the Inca Trail and other trips. Liz gives a clearly laid out list of what is and what is not included. Down sleeping bags are US$2.50 per day extra, fibre bags US$2. If you need a guide who speaks a language other than English let her know in advance. Also city tours and the Sacred Valley. Feedback on trip is good, less so for the office.

Machete Tours, Tecseccocha 161, T084-224829, T963 1662 (mob), www.machetetours.com. Founded by born-and-bred jungle hand Ronaldo and his Danish partner Tina, **Machete** offer many innovative trekking trips, for example a complete 9-day traverse of the Cordillera Vilcabamba from the Apurímac Canyon and Choquequirao across the range to Machu Picchu itself. They also offer expeditions to Espíritu Pampa, Ausangate and the Inca Trail. They have a new rainforest lodge on the remote Río Blanco, south of the Manu Biosphere Reserve and have set up a series of camps deep in the forest. These jungle trips are focused

more on hiking and rustic 'adventure' than those of the classic Manu operators. Not all of the guides speak English so check this before trip details are confirmed. Eric is a recommended guide for Choquequirao.
Manu Nature Tours, Av Pardo 1046, T084-252721, www.manuperu.com. Owned by Boris Gómez Luna, English spoken.
Oropéndola Tours EIRL, Calle 7 Cuartones, 284 interior 3-D, T084-9668 5990, www.oropendolaperu.org. English-, Spanish- and Japanese-speaking guides specializing in Manu National Park, as well as birdwatching, nature and cultural experience tours.
Peruvian Andean Treks, Av Pardo 705, T084-225701, www.andeantreks.com. Mon-Fri 0900-1300, 1500-1800, Sat

0900-1300. Manager Tom Hendrickson uses high-quality equipment and satellite phones. His 7-day/6-night Vilcanota Llama Trek to Ausangate includes a collapsible pressure chamber for altitude sickness. Tom also organizes interesting extended trekking itineraries, for example an 18-day trip connecting Machu Picchu, Vitcos and Choquequirao.

Peru Treks and Adventures, Garcilaso 265 of 11 (2nd floor), 2 blocks from main square, T084-505863, www.perutreks.com. Trekking agency set up by Englishman Mike Weston and his wife Koqui González. They pride themselves on good treatment of porters and support staff and have been consistently recommended for their professionalism and customer care. A portion of profits goes to

community projects (school supplies and clothing accepted at office). Treks offered include Salkantay, the Lares Valley and Vilcabamba Vieja. Mike also runs the **Andean Travel Web**, www.andeantravel web.com, which focuses on sustainable tourism in the region.

Peru Unknown SRL, Av Tacna 166 Wanchaq, T084-249739, www.peruunknown.com. Tailor-made trips around Cuzco and southern Peru.

Q'ente, Garcilaso 210, int 210b, T084-222535, www.qente.com. Their Inca Trail service is recommended. They will organize private treks to Salkantay, Ausangate, Choquequirao, Vilcabamba and Q'eros. Prices depend on group size. Sacred Valley Tours, also day tours to Piquillacta and Tipón, and Moras and Moray. Horse riding to local ruins costs US$35 for 4-5 hrs. Very good, especially with children.

SAS Travel, Portal de Panes 143, T084-237292/255205 (staff in a 2nd office at Medio 137, mainly deal with jungle information and only speak Spanish), www.sastravel.com. Discount for SAE members and students. Inca Trail 4-day/3-night excludes sleeping bags (can rent down bags for US$12, fibre bags for US$8), the bus down from Machu Picchu to Aguas Calientes and lunch on the last day. SAS has its own hostel in Aguas Calientes – if clients wish to stay in Aguas after the trail and return the next morning this can be arranged. SAS offers a variety of alternatives to the classic Inca Trail. Before setting off you are told everything that is included and given advice on what personal items should be taken. Also Manu, mountain bike, horse riding and rafting trips can be organized. All guides speak English (some better than others). They can book internal flights at much cheaper rates than booking from overseas. For many years SAS has enjoyed a solid reputation for its services, but in 2005-2006 reports have been increasingly mixed.

Sky Travel, Santa Catalina Ancha 366, interior 3-C (down alleyway next to **Rosie**

O'Grady's pub), T084-261818, www.skyperu.com. English spoken. General tours around city and Sacred Valley. Prides itself on leaving 30 mins before other groups, thus reaching sights and the lunch spot (!) before anyone else. 4-day/3-night Inca Trail in good-sized double tents and a dinner tent. Continuing with the theme of concern for food, the group is asked what it would like on the menu 2 days before departure. Other trips include Vilcabamba and Ausangate (trekking only).

Tambo Tours, 20919 Coral Bridge Lane, Suite 225-A, Spring, TX, 77388, USA, T 1-888-2-GO-PERU (246-7378), T001-281 528 9448, www.2GOPERU.com. Long-established adventure and tour specialist with offices in Peru and USA. Customized trips to the Amazon and archaeological sites of Peru, including Machu Picchu.

Tanit Trails, Pasaje Las Dalias 2E Mariscal Gamarra 1a Etapa, T084-234591, www.tanittrails.com. Tailor-made adventure trips, including mountain biking, trekking, rafting, horse riding and fishing.

Trekperu, Ricaldo Palma N-9, Santa Mónica, T084-252899, www.trekperu.com. Experienced trek operator as well as other adventure sports and mountain biking. Offers 'culturally sensitive' tours. 5-day/4-night Cuzco Biking Adventure visits Tipón ruins, Huacarpa Lake, Ninamarca burial towers, Paucartambo, Tres Cruces (superb views over Manu) as well as Pisac and Cuzco. Includes support vehicle and good camping gear. Need sleeping bag.

Tucan Travel, T084-241123, cuzco@tucan travel.com. Offer adventure tours and overland expeditions.

United Mice, Plateros 351y Triunfo 392, T084-221139, www.unitedmice.com. Inca Trail and alternatives via Salkantay and Santa Teresa. Good English-speaking guides; Salustio speaks Italian and Portuguese. Discount with student card, good food and equipment. Also city tours in Spanish and English, Sacred Valley Tours in Spanish and English. They offer treks to Choquequirao for 5 days/4 nights.

Wayki Trek, Procuradores 3512nd floor, T084-224092, www.waykitrek.net. Budget travel agency, recommended for their Inca Trail service. Owner Leo grew up in the countryside near Ollantaytambo and knows the area very well. They run treks to several almost unknown Inca sites. Leo offers many interesting variations on the 'classic' Inca Trail and runs a programme where clients can visit porters communities before starting treks. Wayki also run treks to Ausangate, Salkantay and Choquequirao.

Mountain biking

Cuzco offers a multitude of rides to suit all abilities. All ideally require a guide as its very easy to get lost in the Andes. Some options are: a half-day tour of nearby **Inca ruins** (Tambo Machay, Qenqo and Sacsayhuaman); don't forget your combined entrance ticket. **Chinchero-Moray-Maras-Las Salinas-Urubamba**: one of the finest one-day trips in Peru, best done with a guide. **Lares Valley**, which offers some incredible down- and uphill options on 2- to 3-day circuits including a relaxing soak in the beautiful Lares hot springs. Various descents from the sierra to the jungle: **Abra Málaga**: from 4200 m, an 80-km descent to the jungle;

Tres Cruces to Manu, a 250-km, beautiful dirt road ride offering big climbs and an even bigger (2-day) descent; and **Cuzco-Puerto Maldonado**, possibly the greatest Trans-Andean Challenge on a bike: 550 km of hard work up to 4700 m and down to 230 m on one of the roughest roads there is (with the odd full-on single track thrown in).

Rafting

The Cuzco region is probably the 'rafting capital' of Peru, with more whitewater runs on offer than anywhere else in the country. When looking for an operator please consider more than just the price of your tour. Competition between companies in Cuzco is intense and price wars can lead to compromises in safety as corners are cut or less experienced (and therefore cheaper) guides are hired. Similarly, bargaining the price down, will have the same effect. A 1-day trip should cost a minimum of US$30, and a 3-day trip to the Apurímac not less than US$250. Consider the quality of safety equipment (lifejackets, etc) and the number and experience of rescue kayakers and support staff. On a large and potentially dangerous river like the Apurímac and when any of the rivers is high (fatalities have occurred, most recently in 2006), this can make all the difference. See Rafting, page 63, for more advice.

Urubamba Perhaps the most popular day run in the whole country, but sadly one heavily affected in parts by pollution both from Cuzco and from the towns of the Sacred Valley. Clean-up campaigns are organized periodically, but they just touch the surface of the problem. There are various stretches of rafting on the river, from grade 1 to grade 5+. Some are available all year, others depend on the season. Ask a reputable operator for recommendations to suit your ability and always heed advice if the river is running high.

Apurímac Technically the true source of the Amazon (see page 269), the Apurímac cuts a 2000-m deep gorge through incredible desert scenery and offers probably some of the finest whitewater rafting sections on the planet. Some are rarely run, such as **The Abyss** or **Choquequirao** (consult an agency which caters for experts), but most popular for a multi-day trip is **Puente Hualpapacha- Punte Cunyac** (May-Nov, Grade 4-5): 3 days (better in 4) of non-stop whitewater through an awesome gorge just 5 hrs drive from Cuzco. Again, book with the experts to get you through rapids with names like *U-first*, *Toothache* and *Last laugh*.

Amazonas Explorer, Av Collasuyo 910, Miravalle, PO Box 722, T084-252846 T084-976 5448 (mob), www.amazonas-explorer.com. Experts in rafting, hiking and biking; used by BBC. English owner Paul Cripps has great experience, but takes most bookings from overseas (in England, T01437-891743). However, he may be able to arrange a trip for travellers in Cuzco. Rafting includes Río Apurímac and Río Tambopata including Lake Titicaca and Cuzco, with all transfers from Lima. Also 5-day/4-night Inca Trail trip of the highest quality, and alternatives to the Inca Trail and Choquequirao to Vitcos. Amazonas offer an excellent variation of the Ausangate Circuit, featuring an extension to the little visited Laguna Singrenacocha and an opportunity for ice-climbers to tackle the remote Campa Peak with experienced guides. Multi-activity and family trips are a speciality, catering for all ages, but juniors in particular. All options are at the higher end of the market and are highly recommended.

Apumayo, Av Garcilaso 316, Wanchaq, T084-246018, www.apumayo.com. Mon-Sat 0900-1300, 1600-2000. Urubamba and Apurímac rafting; Inca Trail trekking. Also mountain biking, eg Maras and Moray in Sacred Valley, or 5-day epic biking from Cuzco to Quillabamba. This company also offers tours for disabled people, including rafting.

Atoq, C Saphi 704, T084-253902, www.atoqoffroad.com. Specialists in innovative biking trips, from novice level to hardcore suicidal! Road and single-track tours range from day trips to multi-week expeditions. Professional guides and excellent equipment.

Camp Expeditions, Triunfo 392, T084-489859, www.campexpedition.com. All sorts of adventure tours, but specialists in climbing, for which they are recommended as most reliable, and trekking.

The Climbing Room, Cuesta Santa Ana 549, T084-994 1844, pukyocusco@yahoo.com. They have a new climbing cave open to the public for training and workshops. They also have information about climbing and bouldering in the area, and can organize private climbing and canyoning trips. Phone or email in advance.

Eric Adventures, Plateros 324, T084-234764, www.ericadventures.com. Specialize in adventure activities: rafting, kayaking, canyoning, hydrospeed, mountain biking, plus the Inca Trail. They clearly explain what equipment is included in their prices and what you will need to bring. They also rent motorcross bikes. Prices are more expensive if you book by email, you can get huge discounts if you book in the office. A popular company.

Land of the Inkas with Instinct Tour Operator, Av de la Cultura 1318 Wanchaq, T084-233451, www.landoftheinkas.com. Run by the very experienced Juan and Benjamín Muñiz, this company now largely operates through web-based bookings, arranging both multi-week expeditions and shorter adventures for those already in the Cuzco area. **Instinct** offers activities as diverse as surf safaris on Peru's north coast to multi-day horseriding tours in the Sacred Valley.

Manu Expeditions, Humberto Vidal Unda G-5, 2a Etapa, Urb Magisterial, T084-226671, www.ManuExpeditions. com. As well as Manu trips (see page 548), also runs tailor-made bird trips in cloud- and rainforest around Cuzco and Peru, as well as butterfly watching, and has horse riding and a 9-day/8-night trip to Machu Picchu along a different route from the Inca Trail, rejoining at Sun Gate. Barry runs horse-supported treks to Choquequirao, starting from Huancacalle. Highly recommended.

Mayuc Ecological Tourism Adventure Travel, Portal Confiturías 211, Plaza de Armas, T084-232666, www.mayuc.com. One of the longest-running river rafting adventure companies in Cuzco. Rafting on the Ríos Urubamba and Apurímac. **Mayuc** now have a permanent lodge, **Casa Cusi**, on the upper Urubamba, which forms the basis of 2-day, Class III-IV trips in the area. Other tours include Inca Trail and Salkantay.

The Medina Brothers, contact Christian or Alain Medina on T084-225163 or 084-965 3485/969 1670(mob). Friendly family-run rafting company with good equipment and plenty of experience. They usually focus on day rafting trips in the Sacred Valley, but services are tailored to the needs of the client. Reasonable prices dependent on client numbers. Recommended.

Swissraft-Peru, Plateros 369, T084-264124, www.swissraft-peru.com. This company runs rafting tours on the Apurímac and Urubamba rivers. Equipment is of good quality.

Terra Explorer Peru, T084-237352, www.terraexplorerperu.com. Offers a wide range of trips from high-end rafting in the Sacred Valley and expeditions to the Colca and Cotahuasi canyons, trekking the Inca Trail and others, mountain biking, kayaking (including on Lake Titicaca) and jungle trips. All guides are bilingual. Linked with **Q'awana Lodge** at Huarán, page 185.

Paragliding, ballooning and bungee

Magnificent scenery, soaring close to snow-capped mountains makes this an awesome experience. 45 km from Cuzco is **Cerro Sacro** (3797 m) on the Pampa de Chincheros with 550 m clearance at take-off. It is the launch site for cross-country flights over the Sacred Valley, Sacsayhuaman and Cuzco. Particularly good for parapenting is the **Mirador de Urubamba**, 38 km from Cuzco, at 3650 m, with 800-m clearance and views over Pisac. Note that the Sacred Valley offers exciting but challenging paragliding so if wind conditions are bad, flights may be delayed till the following day. Beware pilots offering suspiciously cheap flights; their experience and equipment is unlikely to be appropriate for the Sacred Valley's conditions.

The Adventure Valley, Portal de Panes 123, Plaza de Armas T084-240835, www.actionvalleytrips.com. For bungee jumping (US$59), the Superman jump

(US$59 or US$100 for both), climbing wall, etc. They can arrange transport.

Globos de los Andes, Arequipa 271, T084-232352, www.globosperu.com. Hot-air ballooning in the Sacred Valley and expeditions with balloons and 4WD lasting several days.

Richard Pethigal, T084-993 7333 (mob), www.cloudwalkerparagliding.com. Richard offers a condor's-eye view of the Sacred Valley. May-Sep he runs half-day tandem paraglider flights from Cuzco. He is a very experienced pilot, the only one with an international licence in Cuzco, and uses high-quality equipment. He charges US$70 for a 15-30 min flight. Longer cross-country flights and flights from El Misti (Arequipa) can be arranged.

Shamanic and other cultural tours

Among the many forms of spiritual tourism offered in the Cuzco region, one that attracts much attention is shamanic and drug experiences. (The following list is not restricted to this type of tourism.) San Pedro and Ayahuasca have been used since before Inca times, mostly as a sacred healing experience. The plants are prepared with special treatments for curative purposes; they have never been considered a drug. If you choose to experience these incredible healing/teaching plants, only do so under the guidance of a reputable agency or shaman and always have a friend with you who is not partaking. If the medicine is not prepared correctly, it can be highly toxic and, in rare cases, severely dangerous. Never buy tours off the streets, never buy from someone who is not recommended and never try to prepare the plants yourself.

Another Planet, Triunfo 120, T084-242714, www.anotherplanetperu.net. Run by Lesley Myburgh, who operates all kinds of adventure tours and conventional tours in and around Cuzco, but specializes in jungle trips anywhere in Peru. Lesley is an expert in San Pedro cactus preparation and she arranges San Pedro sessions for healing at physical, emotional and spiritual levels in the beautiful garden of her guesthouse, **La Casa de la Gringa**, Pasñapacana y Tandapata 148, San Blas, T084-241168, 965 2006 (mob). This a good place to stay if you are looking for this kind of experience. **Inca Planet Mystical Tours**, at the same address and in same family (Mark Myburgh), www.inkaplanetcusco.com, is another tour operator.

Milla Tourism, Av Pardo 689 y Portal Comercio 195 on the plaza, T084-231710, www.millaturismo.com. Mon-Fri 0800-1300, 1500-1900, Sat 0800-1300. Mystical tours to Cuzco's Inca ceremonial sites such as Pumamarca and the Temple of the Moon. Also private tours arranged to Moray agricultural terracing and Maras salt mines in Sacred Valley. Guide speaks only basic English. They also arrange cultural and environmental lectures and courses.

Eleana Molina, T084-975 1791, misticanativa@yahoo.com. For Ayahuasca ceremonies.

Mystic Inca Trail, Unidad Vecinal de Santiago, bloque 9, dpto 301, T084-221358, ivanndp@terra.com.pe. Specializes in tours of sacred Inca sites and the study of Andean spirituality. This takes 10 days but it is possible to have shorter 'experiences'.

Tours to Manu Biosphere Reserve

There are many operators in Cuzco offering trips to Manu. For full details of these operators and the tours on offer, see page 560.

Private guides

As most of the sights do not have any information or signs in English, a good guide can really improve your visit. Either arrange this before you set out or grab one of those hanging around the sights' entrances (this is much easier to do in the low season). A tip is expected at the end of the tour. All of those listed are bilingual. Set prices: City tour US$15-20 per day; Urubamba/Sacred Valley US$25-30, Machu Picchu and other ruins US$40-50 per day.

Boris Cárdenas, boriscar@telser.com.pe. Esoteric and cultural tours.

José Cuba and Alejandra Cuba, Urb Santa Rosa R Gibaja 182, Urb Santa Rosa R Gibaja 182, T084-226179, T968 5187 (mob), ale17ch1@yahoo.com. Both speak English, Alejandra also speaks German and French, very good tours.

Miguel Angel Jove Mamani, T084-245670, 974 0143 (mob), miguelj24@hotmail.com. Recommended by South American Explorers.

Percy Salas Alfaro, c/o Munditur, T084-240287, 962 1152 (mob), smunditur@hotmail.com. Serious, friendly, English-speaking.

Roger Valencia Espinoza, José Gabriel Cosio 307, T084-251278, 977 0973 (mob), vroger@qenqo.rcp.net.pe. Offers adventure trips.

Victoria Morales Condori, T084-224877, kuntur01@yahoo.com.mx.

Transport

Maps p138 and p140

Air

Airline offices Aero Cóndor, at the airport, T084-252774. **LAB**, Santa Catalina Angosta 160, T084-222990. **Lan**, Av Sol 627-B, T084-225552. **Star Perú**, Av Sol 679, of 1, T084-234060. **Taca**, Av Sol 602, T084-249921, good service.

Bus

Local Combis run 0500-2200 or 2300, US$0.15, to all parts of the city, including the bus and train stations and the airport, but are not allowed within 2 blocks of the Plaza de Armas. Stops are signed and the driver's assistant calls out the names of stops. By law all passengers are insured. After 2200 combis may not run their full route; demand to be taken to your stop, or better still, use a taxi late at night.

El Tranvía de Cusco is actually a motor coach which runs on the route of the original Cuzco tramway system. The route starts in the Plaza de Armas (except on Sun morning) and ends at the Sacsayhuaman Archaeological Park. There is a 10-min stop at the mirador by the Cristo Blanco before descending to the Plaza de Armas. Departures start at 1000 daily, 1 hr 20 mins, with explanations of the city's history, architecture, customs, etc; US$2, US$1.40 for students with ID. For group reservations, T084-740640.

Long distance All direct buses to **Lima** (18-20 hrs) go via **Abancay**, 195 km, 5 hrs (longer in the rainy season), and **Nazca**, on the Panamerican Highway. This route is paved, but floods in the wet season can damage sections of the highway. If prone to car sickness, be prepared on the road to Abancay, there are many, many curves, but the scenery is magnificent (it also happens to be a great route for cycling). At Abancay, the road forks, the other branch going to **Andahuaylas**, a further 138 km, 10-11 hrs from Cuzco, and **Ayacucho** in the Central Highlands, another 261 km, 20 hrs from Cuzco. On both routes at night, take a blanket or sleeping bag to ward off the cold. All buses leave daily from the Terminal Terrestre.

Molina, who also have an office on Av Pachacútec, just past the railway station, has buses on both routes. They run 3 services a day to **Lima** via **Abancay** and **Nazca**, and 1, at 1900, to **Abancay** and **Andahuaylas**; Wari leaves at 0800, 1400, 1600 and 1700 to **Abancay**, **Nazca** and **Lima**. **Cruz del Sur**'s cheaper *Ideal* service leaves for **Lima** via Abancay at 1430, while their more comfortable *Imperial* service departs at 1530 and 1830. **San Jerónimo** and **Los Chankas** have buses to **Abancay**, **Andahuaylas** and **Ayacucho**, San Jerónimo at 1830. **Turismo Ampay** goes to Abancay at 0630, 1300 and 2000, **Turismo Abancay** at 0630, 1300 and 2000, and **Expreso Huamanga** at 1600. **Bredde** has 5 buses a day to Abancay. Fares to **Abancay** US$3.40, **Andahuaylas** US$6, **Ayacucho** US$12, **Nazca** US$17-20, **Lima** US$20 (**Cruz del Sur**, *Ideal* class) to US$32 (**Cruz del Sur**, *Imperial* class). In Cuzco you may be told that there are no buses in the day from Abancay to Andahuaylas; this is not so – **Señor de Huanca** does so. If you leave Cuzco before 0730, with luck you'll make the onward connection at 1300, which is worth it for the scenery.

To **Lake Titicaca and Bolivia**: To **Juliaca**, 344 km, 6 hrs, US$3-4. The road is fully paved, but after heavy rain buses may not run. To **Puno**, 44 km from Juliaca, US$4.50-6; there is a good service with **Ormeño**at 0900, US$10, 6 hrs. This service continues to **La Paz**, Bolivia. **First Class**, Av Sol 930, have a service at 0800, calling at Andahuaylillas church, Raqchi and Pucará en route (lunch, but not entrance tickets, is included), US$25. Travel agencies sell this ticket. Other services are run by **Tour Perú** and **Libertad** (at night), US$8.60, 6½-8 hrs. **Tour Perú** also offers a direct service to **La Paz**, US$15.

To **Arequipa**, 521 km, **Cruz del Sur** use the direct paved route via Juliaca and have an *Imperial* service at 2000, 10 hrs, US$15. **Ormeño**'s fare is US$18. Other buses join the new Juliaca–Arequipa road at Imata, 10-12 hrs, US$7.75 (eg **Carhuamayo**, 3 a day). To **Tacna**, **San Martín**, T084-805729, at 1430, US$15.

Car

Avis, Av El Sol 808 and at the airport, T084-248800, avis-cusco@terra.com.pe. **Touring y Automóvil Club del Perú**, Av Sol 349, T084-224561, cusco@touringperu.com.pe. A good source of information on motoring, car hire and mechanics (membership is US$45 per year).

Taxi

Taxis have fixed prices: in the centre US$0.60 (US$0.85 after dark); and to the suburbs US$0.85-1.55 (touts at the airport and train station will always ask much higher fares). In town it is advisable to take municipality-authorized taxis which have a blue sticket on the windscreen. Safer still are licensed taxis, which have a sign with the company's name on the roof, not just a sticker in the window. These taxis are summoned by phone and are more expensive, in the centre US$1-1.25 (**Ocarina** T084-247080, **Aló Cusco** T084-222222, radio taxi T084-222000).

Taxi trips to **Sacsayhuaman** cost US$10; to the ruins of **Tambo Machay** US$15-20 (3-4 people); a whole-day trip costs US$40-70. For US$50 a taxi can be hired for a whole day (ideally Sun) to take you to **Chinchero**, **Maras**, **Urubamba**, **Ollantaytambo**, **Calca**, **Lamay**, **Coya**, **Pisac**, **Tambo Machay**, **Qenqo** and **Sacsayhuaman**.

To organize your own **Sacred Valley** transport, try one of these taxi drivers, recommended by **South America Explorers**: **Manuel Calanche**, T084-227368, T969 5402 (mob); **Carlos Hinojosa**, T084-251160; **Ferdinand Pinares**, Yuracpunco 155, Tahuantinsuyo, T084-225914, T968 1519 (mob), speaks English, French and Spanish; **Eduardo**, T084-231809, speaks English. Also recommended are: **Angel Marcavillaca Palomino**, Av Regional 877, T084-251822, amarcavillaca@yahoo.com, helpful, patient, reasonable prices; **Movilidad Inmediata**, T962 3821 (mob), runs local tours with an English-speaking guide. **Angel Salazar**, Marcavalle I-4 Huanchac, T084-224679 (to leave messages), is English-speaking and arranges good tours, very knowledgeable and enthusiastic; **Milton Velásquez**, T084-222638, T968 0730 (mob), is also an anthropologist and tour guide and speaks English.

Train

All details of the train services out of Cuzco can be found on www.perurail.com. For trains to Aguas Calientes for Machu Picchu, see page 208. The train to **Juliaca** and **Puno** leaves at 0800, on Mon, Wed and Sat, arriving in Puno at 1730 (sit on the left for the best views). The train makes a stop to view the scenery at La Raya. Trains return from Puno on Mon, Wed and Sat at 0800, arriving in Cuzco at 1730. Fares: tourist/backpacker class, US$19 (drinks and snacks extra), 1st class US$130, includes lunch, afternoon tea, entertainment, luxury seating (recommended).

Tickets can be bought up to 5 days in advance, cash only (dollars accepted). The ticket office at Wanchac station is open Mon-Fri 0800-1700, Sat 0900-1200. Tickets sell out quickly and there are queues from 0400 before holidays in the dry season. In the low season tickets to Puno can be bought on the day of departure. You can buy tickets through a travel agent, but check the date and seat number. Meals are served on the train. Always check whether the train is running, especially in the rainy season, when services might be cancelled.

Directory

Maps p138 and p140

Banks All the banks along Av Sol have ATMs from which you can withdraw dollars or soles at any hour. Whether you use the counter or an ATM, choose your time carefully as there can be long queues at both. Most banks are closed 1300-1600. **BCP**, Av Sol 189. Gives cash advances on Visa and changes TCs to soles with no commission, 3% to dollars. It has an ATM for Visa. It also handles Amex. **Interbank**, Av Sol y Puluchapata. Charges no commission on TCs and has a Visa ATM which gives dollars as well as soles. Accepts Visa, Plus, Amex, Maestro, Cirrus and MasterCard. Next door is **Banco Continental**, also has a Visa ATM but charges up to US$4 commission on TCs. **BSCH**, Av Sol 459. Changes Amex TCs at reasonable rates. Has Red Unicard ATM for Visa/Plus and MasterCard. **Banco Latino**, Almagro 125 y Av Sol 395. Has ATMs for MasterCard. **Banco Wiese**, Maruri between Pampa del Castillo and Pomeritos. Gives cash advances on MasterCard, Maestro, Cirrus and Visa, in dollars. Emergency number for lost or stolen Visa cards, 0800-1330.

As well as the ATMs in banks (most of which have 24-hr police protection), there are ATMs on the Plaza de Armas at the entrance to Inka Grill, Portal de Panes, Incanto (Santa Catalina Angosta 135, for Citibank), Supermercado Gato's, Portal Belén, and the entrance to Cross Keys and Tunupa, Portal de Confiturías. There are other ATMs on Av la Cultura, beside Supermercado Dimart and beside Supermercado La Canasta. **Western Union** at Santa Catalina Ancha 165, T084-233727. Money transfers in 10 mins; also at **DHL**, see below.

Many travel agencies and *casas de cambio* change dollars. Some of them change TCs as well, but charge 4-5% commission. There are many *cambios* on the west side of the Plaza de Armas (eg Portal Comercio Nos 107 and 148) and on the west side of Av Sol, most change TCs (best rates in the *cambios* at the top of Av Sol). **LAC Dólar**, Av Sol 150, T084-257762, Mon-Sat 0900-2000, with delivery service to central hotels, cash and TCs, is recommended. The street changers hang around Av Sol, blocks 2-3, every day and are a pleasure to do business with. Some of them will also change TCs. In banks and on the street check the notes.

Clinics and doctors Clínica **Panamericana**, Av Infancia 508, Wanchac, T084-249494, T965 1552 (mob). 24-hr emergency and medical attention. **Clínica Pardo**, Av de la Cultura 710, T084-240387, www.clinicapardo.com. 24-hr emergency and hospitalization/medical attention, international department, trained bilingual personnel, handles complete medical assistance coverage with international insurance companies, free ambulance service, visit to hotel, discount in pharmacy, dental service, X-rays, laboratory, full medical specialization. The most highly recommeded clinic in Cuzco. Director is Dr Alcides Vargas. **Clínica Paredes**, C Lechugal 405, T084-225265. Offers a wide range of medical attention. Director is Dr Milagros Paredes, whose speciality is gynaecology. Recommended. **Hospital Regional**, Av de la Cultura, T084-227661, emergencies T084-223691. **Dr Ilya Gomon**, Av de la Cultura, Edif Santa Fe, oficina 207, T084-965 1906 (mob). Canadian chiropractor, good, reasonable prices, available for hotel or home visits. **Dr Gilbert Espejo** and **Dr Boris Espejo Muñoz**, both in the Centro Comercial Cusco, oficina 7, T084-228074 and T084-231918 respectively. If you need a yellow fever vaccination (for the jungle lowlands, or for travel to Bolivia or Brazil where it is required), it is available at the paediatric department of the **Hospital Antonio Lorena**, Plazoleta Belén 1358, T084-226511, from 0830 on Mon, Wed and Fri; they are free and include the international vaccination certificate.

Dentists Dr Eduardo Franco, Av de la Cultura, Edif Santa Fe, oficina 310, T084-242207, T965 0179 (mob). 24-hr.

Embassies and consulates **Belgium**, Av Sol 954, T084-221098. Mon-Fri 0900-1300, 1500-1700. **France**, Jorge Escobar, C Micaela Bastidas 101, 4th floor, T084- 233610. **Germany**, Sra Maria-Sophia Júrgens de Hermoza, San Agustín 307, T084-235459, Casilla Postal 1128, Correo Central. Mon-Fri, 1000-1200, appointments may be made by phone, it also has a book exchange. **Ireland**, Charlie Donovan, Santa Catalina Ancha 360 (Rosie O'Grady's), T084-243514. **Italy**, Sr Fedos Rubatto, Av Garcilaso 700, T084-224398. Mon-Fri 0900-1200, 1500-1700. **Netherlands**, Sra Marcela Alarco, Av El Sol 954, T084-224322, marcela_alarco@yahoo.com. Mon-Fri 0900-1500. **Spain**, Sra Juana María Lambarri, T965 0106 (mob). **UK**, Barry Walker, Av Pardo 895, T084-239974, bwalker@amauta.rcp.net.pe. **US Agent**, Dra Olga Villagarcía, Apdo 949, Cuzco, T084-222183, or at the Binational Center (ICPNA), Av Tullumayo 125, Wanchac.

Internet You can't walk for 2 mins in Cuzco without running into an internet café, and new places are opening all the time. Most have similar rates, around US$0.60 per hr, although if you look hard enough you can find cheaper places. The main difference between cafés is the speed of internet connection and the facilities on offer. The better places have scanners, webcams and CD burners, among other gadgets, and staff in these establishments can be very knowledgeable.

Language classes Academia **Latinoamericana de Español**, Av El Sol 580, T084-243364, www.latinoschools.com. Professionally run with experienced staff. Many activities per week, including dance lessons and excursions to sites of historical and cultural interest. Good for homestay. Private classes US$350 for 20 hrs, groups, with a maximum of 4 students US$265, again for 20 hrs: thorough if traditional tuition. **Acupari**, San Agustín 307, T084-242970. The German-Peruvian Cultural Association, Spanish classes are run here. **Amauta**, PO Box 1164, Suecia 480, T084-241422, www.amautaspanish.com. Spanish classes, individual or in small groups, also Quechua classes and workshops in Peruvian cuisine, dance and music, US$10.50 per hr individual, but cheaper and possibly accommodation on site, as well as a free internet café for students, and can arrange excursions and can help find voluntary work. They also have a school in Urubamba and can arrange courses in the Manu rainforest, in conjunction with Pantiacolla Tours. **Amigos Spanish School**, Zaguán del Cielo B-23, T084-242292, www.spanishcusco.com. Profits from this school support a foundation for disadvantaged children. Private lessons for US$8 per hr, US$108 for 20 hrs of classes in a group. Homestays available, many recommendations. **La Casona de la Esquina**, Purgatorio 395, corner with Huaynapata, T084-235830, www.spanishlessons.com.pe. US$5 per hr for one-to-one classes. Recommended. **Cusco Spanish School**, Garcilaso 265, oficina 6 (2nd floor), T084-226928, www.cuscospanishschool.com. US$175 for 20 hrs of private classes, cheaper in groups. School offers homestays, optional activities including dance and music classes, cookery courses, ceramics, Quechua, hiking and volunteer programmes. They also offer courses on a hacienda at Cusipata in the Vilcanota Valley, east of Cuzco. **Excel**, Cruz Verde 336, T084-235298, www.Excel-spanishlanguageprograms-peru.org. Very professional, US$7 per hr for private one-to-one lessons. US$229 for 20 hrs with 2 people, or US$227 with homestay and one-to-one tuition for 20 hrs. **Mundo Verde**, C Nueva Alta 432-A, T084-221287, www.mundoverdespanish.com. Spanish lessons with the option to study in the rainforest and the possibility of working on environmental and social projects while studying. US$250 for 20 hrs tuition with homestay. **San Blas Spanish School**, Tandapata 688, T084-247898, www.spanishschoolperu.com. Groups, with 4 clients maximum, US$90 for 20 hrs tuition; US$130 for the same thing one-to-one.

Laundry There are several cheap laundries on Procuradores, and also on Suecia and Tecseccocha. **Adonai**, Choquechaca 216-A, San Blas. Good hole-in-the-wall laundry, US$0.60 per kg for wash and dry, friendly and usually reliable, small book exchange. **Dana's Laundry**, Nueva Baja y Unión. US$2.10 per kg, takes about 6 hrs. **Lavandería**, Saphi 578. 0800-2000 Mon-Sat, 0800-1300 Sun. Good, fast service, US$1 per kg. String markers will be attached to clothes if they have no label. **Lavandería Louis**, Choquechaca 264, San Blas. US$0.85 per kg, fresh, clean, good value. **Lavandería T'aqsana Wasi**, Santa Catalina Ancha 345. Same-day service, they also iron clothes, US$2 per kg, good service, speak English, German, Italian and French, Mon-Fri 0900-2030, Sat 0900-1900. **Splendid Laundry Service**, Carmen Alto 195. Very good, US$0.75 per kg, laundry sometimes available after only 3-4 hrs.

Massage and therapies **Casa de la serenidad**, Pumacurco 636, T084-233670, www.shamanspirit.net. A shamanic therapy centre run by a Swiss-American healer and Reiki Master who uses medicinal 'power' plants. It also has bed and breakfast and has received very good reports. **Healing Hands**, based at Loki Hostel. Angela is a Reiki, Shiatsu and CranioSacral Therapist. Very relaxing and recommended, track Angela down at Loki or drop her line at faeryamanita@hotmail.com.

Post **Central office**, Av Sol at the bottom end of block 5, T084-225232. Mon-Sat 0730-2000, 0800-1400 Sun and holidays. Poste restante is free and helpful. Sending packages from Cuzco is not cheap. **DHL**, Av Sol 627, T084-244167. For sending packages or money overseas.

Telephone There are independent phone offices in the centre. **Telefónica**, Av del Sol 386, T084-241111. For telephone and fax, Mon-Sat 0700-2300, 0700-1200 Sun and holidays.

Useful addresses **Immigration** Av Sol, block 6, close to post office, T084-222740. Mon-Fri 0800-1300. Reported as not very helpful. **Perú Verde** Ricaldo Palma J-1, Santa Mónica, T084-226392, www.peruverde.org. For information and free video shows about Manu National Park and Tambopata National Reserve. They are friendly and have information on programmes and research in the jungle area of Madre de Dios.

The Urubamba Valley

The Río Urubamba cuts its way through fields and rocky gorges beneath the high peaks of the Cordillera. Brown hills, covered in wheat fields, separate Cuzco from this beautiful high valley, which stretches from Sicuani (on the railway to Puno) to the gorge of Torontoi, 600 m lower, to the northwest of Cuzco. That the river was of great significance to the Incas can be seen in the number of strategic sites they built above it; Pisac, Ollantaytambo and Machu Picchu among them. Upstream from Pisac, the river is usually called the Vilcanota; downstream it is the Urubamba.

▸▸ *For Sleeping, Eating and other listings, see pages 184-190.*

Ins and outs

Getting there The road from Cuzco which runs past Sacsayhuaman and on to Tambo Machay (see page 143) climbs up to a pass, then continues over the pampa before descending into the densely populated Urubamba Valley. This road then crosses the Río Urubamba by a bridge at Pisac and follows the north bank to the end of the paved road at Ollantaytambo. It passes through Calca, Yucay and Urubamba, which can also be reached from Cuzco by the beautiful, direct road through Chinchero, see page 182.

▸▸ *For further details see Cuzco Tour operators, page 162, and Transport, page 189.*

Getting around Paved roads, plentiful transport and a good selection of hotels and eating places make this a straighforward place to explore. You can choose either a quick visit from the city or, better still, linger for a few days. Don't hurry; most organized tours are too fast. Explore it on foot, by bike or on horseback. Using public transport and staying overnight in the Valley allows much more time to see the ruins and markets.

Best time to to visit April to May or October to November. The high season is from June to September, but the rainy season, December to March, is cheaper and pleasant enough.

Pisac

▸▸ *pp184-190. Colour map 5, A5.*

Only 30 km north of Cuzco is the little village of Pisac, which is well worth a visit for its superb Inca ruins, perched precariously on the mountain, above the town. They are considered to be among the very finest Inca ruins in the valley. Strangely, however, most visitors don't come to Pisac for the ruins. Instead, they come in droves for its Sunday morning market and growing number of shopping outlets. Pisac is usually visited as part of a tour from Cuzco but this often allows only 1½ hours here, not enough time to take in the ruins and splendid scenery.

Pisac village and market

The market contains sections for the tourist and for the local community. Traditionally, Sunday is the day when the people of the highlands come down to sell their produce (potatoes, corn, beans, vegetables, weavings, pottery, etc). These are traded for essentials such as salt, sugar, rice, noodles, fruit, medicines, plastic goods and tools. The market comes to life after the arrival of tourist buses around 1000, and is usually over by 1500. However, there is also an important ceremony every Sunday, in which the *Varayocs* (village mayors) from the surrounding and highland villages participate in a Quechua Catholic mass in **Pisac church**. It is a good example of the merging of, and respect for, different religious cultures. This aspect of the traditional Pisac Sunday market is still celebrated at 1100 sharp. Pisac has other, somewhat less crowded, less expensive markets on Tuesday and Thursday morning; in each case, it's best to get there before 0900.

On the plaza, which has several large *pisonay* trees, are the church and a small interesting **Museo Folklórico**. The town, with its narrow streets, is worth strolling around, and while you're doing so, look for the fine façade at Grau 485. There are many souvenir shops on Bolognesi.

Inca ruins

ⓘ *Daily 0700-1730. If you go early (before 1000) you'll have the ruins to yourself. Entry is by BTG visitors' ticket (see box, page 136). Guides charge US$5, but the wardens on site are very helpful and don't charge anything to give out information.*
The ruins of Inca Pisac stand on a spur between the Río Urubamba to the south and the smaller Chongo to the east. It provides an ideal vantage point over the flat plain of the Urubamba, the terraces below and the terraced hillsides. This is one of the largest Inca ruins in the vicinity of Cuzco and it clearly had defensive, religious and agricultural functions, as well as being an Inca country estate.

To appreciate the site fully, allow five or six hours on foot. Even if going by car, do not rush as there is a lot to see and a lot of walking to do. Walking up, although tiring, is recommended for the views and location. It's at least one hour uphill all the way, but the descent takes 30 minutes. Horses are available for US$3 per person. Road transport approaches from the Kanchiracay end. The drive up from town takes about 20 minutes. Combis charge US$0.60 per person and taxis US$3 one way up to the ruins from near the bridge. Then you can walk back down (if you want the taxi to take you back down negotiate a fare and pickup time). Overnight parking is allowed in the car park.

The walk up to the ruins begins from the plaza, passing the Centro de Salud and a control post. The path goes through working terraces, giving the ruins a context. The first group of buildings is **Pisaqa**, with a fine curving wall. Climb up to the central part of the ruins, the **Intihuatana** group of temples and rock outcrops in the most magnificent Inca masonry. Here are the **Reloj Solar** (Hitching Post of the Sun) – now closed because thieves stole a piece from it – palaces of the moon and stars, solstice markers, baths and water channels. From Intihuatana, a path leads around the hillside through a tunnel to **Q'Allaqasa** (military area). Across the valley at this point, a large area of Inca tombs in holes in the hillside can be seen. The end of the site is **Kanchiracay**, where the agricultural workers were housed. At dusk you will hear, if not see, the *pisaca* (partridges), after which the place is named, and you may see deer too.

Pisac to Urubamba

» *pp184-190.*

Calca and around

Near **Lamay**, the second village on the road from Pisac towards Urubamba, are warm springs, which are highly regarded locally for their medicinal properties. **Calca**, 18 km beyond Pisac at 2900 m, is a busy hub in the valley, with a plaza which is divided into two parts. Look out for the *api* sellers with their bicycles loaded with a steaming kettle and assortment of bottles, glasses and tubs. There are mineral baths at **Machacancha**, 8 km east of Calca. These springs are indoors, pleasantly warm and will open at night for groups. They are half an hour by taxi from town. About 3 km beyond Machacancha are the Inca ruins of **Arquasmarca**.

The ruins of a small Inca town, **Huchuy Cuzco**, are reached across the Río Urubamba and after a stiff three- to four-hour climb. Huchuy Cuzco (also spelt Qosqo), which in Quechua means 'Little Cuzco', was originally called Kakya Qawani, 'from where the lightning can be seen'. It is dramatically located on a flat esplanade almost 600 m above the villages of Lamay and Calca in the Sacred Valley. The views are magnificent. The ruins themselves consist of extensive agricultural terraces with high retaining walls and several buildings made from finely wrought stonework and adobe mud bricks.

A market for beads

The huge variety of multicoloured beads on sale in the markets are commonly called Inca beads, although this is, in fact, something of a misnomer. The Incas were highly talented potters and decorated their ware with detailed geometric motifs, but they are not known to have made ceramic beads. These attractive items have become popular relatively recently.

They used to be rolled individually by hand and were very time- consuming to produce. Now, in a major concession to consumerism, they are machine-made and produced in quantity, then hand-painted and glazed.

Today, the beads are produced in countless, often family-run, workshops in Cuzco and Pisac. Some are made into earrings, necklaces and bracelets, other are sold loose.

The easiest route to the site follows the steep trail behind the village of Lamay, which is reached by crossing the bridge over the river. There is also a clearly marked trail from the village of Calca. Another longer route leads to Huchuy Cuzco from Tambo Machay near Cuzco, a magnificent one- or two-day trek along the route once taken by the Inca from his capital to his country estate at Huchuy Cuzco; some sections of the original Inca highway remain intact.

Valle de Lares

To the north of Urubamba and Calca, beyond the great peaks that tower above the Sacred Valley, lies the valley of **Lares**, an area famed for its traditional Quechua communities and strong weaving traditions. The mountainous territory that lies between these two valleys and, indeed, the valleys themselves offers a great deal for the ambitious trekker. The entire Urubamba range is threaded with tracks and the remains of ancient Inca trails and, as you might expect, the variety of trekking routes is almost endless. One of these options is presented below.

The four-day trek from **Huarán** (6 km west of Calca) to **Yanahuara** (beyond Urubamba on the road to Ollantaytambo) goes via the village of Lares through ancient native forests and past some of the Cordillera Urubamba's greatest snow peaks, their waters feeding jewelled lakes and cascades below. It provides an insight into the communities that inhabit this rugged and challenging land. Halfway you can have a good soak in the hot springs at Lares. Many of the locals may offer to sell weavings or *mantas* along the route, at prices a fraction of those in Cuzco. Remember if you bargain that many of these works take weeks, or perhaps a month or more to complete, so always give a fair price; at least here all the money goes to the weavers themselves.

Lares is also a perfect example of Peru's fabulous mountain biking opportunities and it has something for everyone, suiting all levels of daring and technical ability. In two days you can freewheel from chilly mountain passes, past llamas and traditional Quechua communities, on unpaved but drivable roads, or down technical single-track routes following old Inca trails and through precipitous canyons alongside rushing mountain torrents. The area is slowly being 'discovered' by Cuzco agencies and many offer trekking and cycling tours, often as an alternative to the Inca Trail. » *For further details see Cuzco Activities and tours, page 162.*

Yucay

A few kilometres east of Urubamba, Yucay has two large, grassy plazas divided by the restored colonial church of **Santiago Apóstol**, with its oil paintings and fine altars. On the opposite side from Plaza Manco II is the **adobe palace** built for Sayri Túpac (Manco's son) when he emerged from Vilcabamba in 1558.

Urubamba and around » pp184-190.

Urubamba → *Colour map 2, B2. Altitude: 2863 m.*

Like many places along the valley, Urubamba has a fine setting, with views of the Chicón snow-capped peaks and glaciers, and enjoys a mild climate. The main plaza, with a fountain capped by a maize cob, is surrounded by buildings painted blue. Calle Berriózabal, on the west edge of town, is lined with pisonay trees. The large market square is one block west of the main plaza. The main road skirts the town and the bridge for the road to Chinchero is just to the east of town.

Seminario-Behar Ceramic Studio ⓘ *C Berriózabal 111, a right turning off the main road to Ollantaytambo, T084-201002, kupa@terra.com.pe, open every day, just ring the bell,* founded in 1980, is located in the beautiful grounds of the former **Hostal Urpihuasi**. Pablo Seminario has investigated the techniques and designs of pre-Columbian Peruvian cultures and has created a style with strong links to the past. Each piece is handmade and painted, using ancient glazes and minerals, and is then fired in reproduction pre-Columbian kilns. The resulting pieces are very attractive. Reservations to visit the studio and a personal appointment with the artists (Pablo and Marilú) are welcomed.

Urubamba

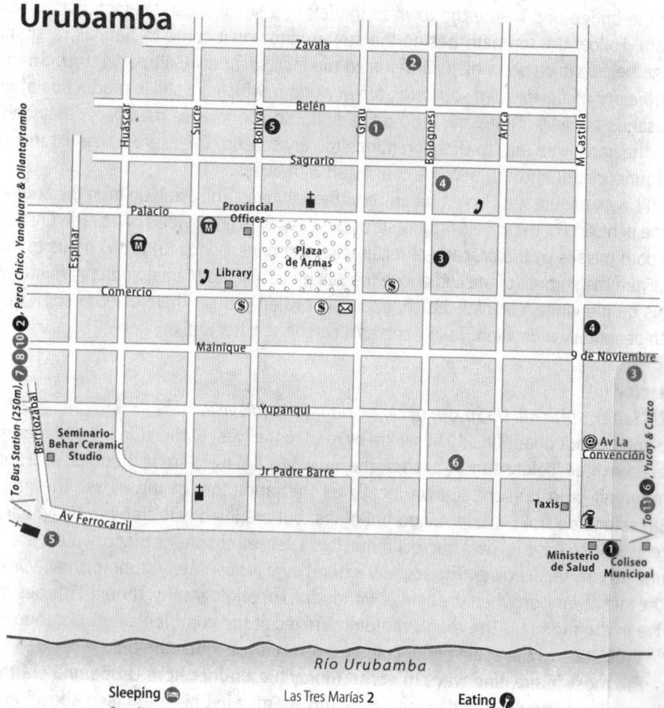

Sleeping
Capulí 1
Hospedaje Perla de Vilcanota 3
Hostal Urubamba 4
K'uychi Rumi 8
Las Chullpas 10
Las Tres Marías 2
Libertador Tambo del Inca 5
Mach'a Wasi 6
San Agustín Urubamba 11
Sol y Luna 7

Eating
El Fogón 1
La Casa de la Abuela 5
Pintacha 3
Pizzonay 4
Quinta los Geranios 6
Tunupa 2

Chinchero → *Colour map 2, B3. Altitude: 3762 m.*

ⓘ *Daily 0700-1730. Can be visited on the BTG visitors' ticket (see page 136).*

Chinchero is northwest from Cuzco, just off a direct road to Urubamba. The streets of the village wind up from the lower sections, where transport stops, to the **plaza** which is reached through an archway. The great square appears to be stepped, with a magnificent Inca wall separating the two levels. Let into the wall is a row of trapezoidal niches, each much taller than a man. From the lower section, which is paved, another arch leads to an upper terrace, upon which the Spaniards built an attractive **church**. The ceiling, beams and walls are covered in beautiful floral and religious designs. The altar, too, is fine. The church is open on Sunday for mass and at festivals. Opposite the church is a small local museum. Excavations have revealed many Inca walls and terraces.

Chinchero attracts few tourists, except on Sunday. The local produce **market** on Sunday morning is fascinating and very colourful, and best before the tour groups arrive. It's on your left as you come into town. There's also a small handicraft market on Sunday, up by the church. The town celebrates the **Day of the Virgin**, on 8 September.

Salinas

Five kilometres west of Urubamba is the village of **Tarabamba** (Km 77 on the Sacred Valley road), where a bridge crosses the Río Urubamba. If you turn right after the bridge you'll come to **Pichingoto**, a tumbled-down village built under an overhanging cliff. Just over the bridge and before the town to the left of a small, walled cemetery is a salt stream. Follow the footpath beside the stream and you'll come to **Salinas**, a small village below which are a mass of terraced pre-Inca *salineras* (salt pans) ⓘ *US$1.50, payable at whichever point you enter, top or bottom*, which are still in production after thousands of years. There are 3200 pools and 480 cooperative members. They only work the pans from May to October, during the dry season. These are now a fixture on the tourist circuit and can become congested with buses.

It's a 45-minute walk from Urubamba to the salt pans. The climb up from the bridge, on the right side of the valley, is fairly steep but easy, with great views of Nevado Chicón. The path passes by the cascade of rectangular salt pans, taking up to 1½ hours to the top. From the summit of the cliff above the salt pans, walk to **Maras**, about 45 minutes. Focus on the white, colonial church, and visit it when you get there ⓘ *US$1.50*; it has been beautifully renovated. Take water as it can be very hot and dry here.

Moray

ⓘ *US$1.80, students US$0.90; allow an hour for a full visit.*

This remote but beautiful site lies 9 km by road to the west of the little town of Maras. There are three 'colosseums', used by the Incas, according to some theories, as a sort of open-air crop nursery, known locally as the laboratory of the Incas. The great depressions do not contain ruined buildings, but are lined with fine terracing. Each level is said to have its own microclimate. It is a very atmospheric place, which, some claim, has mystical power. The scenery around here is absolutely stunning, especially in the late afternoon when the light is wonderful. For photography, though, it's best to arrive in the morning. The road eventually arrives at the guardian's hut, but there is little indication of the scale of the colosseums until you reach the rim.

The most interesting ways to get to Moray are on foot from Urubamba via the *salineras* (see above), or a day-long cycle trip, starting in Chinchero (see above) and ending at the foot of the *salineras* (a challenging descent; go with a specialist agency or guide). ▸▸ *See also Chinchero Transport, page 189.*

Ollantaytambo

» pp184-190. Colour map 2, A2.

→ *Altitude: 2800 m.*

The attractive little town of Ollantaytambo, at the foot of some spectacular Inca ruins and terraces, is built directly on top of the original Inca town, or Llacta. The Inca *canchas* (blocks of houses) are almost entirely intact and can be clearly seen. It's an impressive sight and one that shouldn't be missed, even though many people only visit the ruins above the town.

Ins and outs

Getting there Ollantaytambo can be reached by bus from Cuzco, Urubamba and Chinchero. It is also one of the principal stations for catching then train to Machu Picchu; see page 207 for details. You won't be allowed on the station unless you have previously bought a ticket for the train; the gates are locked and only those with tickets can enter. » *See also Transport page 190.*

Getting around Entering Ollantaytambo from Urubamba, the road is built along the long **Wall of 100 Niches**. Note the inclination of the wall towards the road. Since it was the Incas' practice to build with the walls leaning towards the interiors of the buildings, it has been deduced that the road, much narrower then, was built inside a succession of buildings. The road leads into the main plaza, where public transport congregates in the centre. The original Inca town is behind the north side of the plaza. The road from the northwest corner of the plaza looks up to the Inca temple, but to get there you have to cross the bridge over the river and go down to the colonial church with its *recinto* (enclosure). Beyond is a grand plaza (and car park) with a market and entrances to the archaeological site.

The fortress

ⓘ *Daily 0700-1730. Admission is by BTG visitors' ticket (see page 136), which can be bought at the site. Guides at the entrance charge US$2. Allow 2-3 hrs to explore the ruins fully.*

When Manco Inca decided to rebel against the Spaniards in 1536, he fell back to Ollantaytambo from Calca to stage one of the greatest acts of resistance to the *conquistadores*. Hernando Pizarro led his troops to the foot of the Inca's stronghold and, on seeing how well-manned and fortified the place was, described it as "a thing of horror". Under fierce fire, Pizarro's men failed to capture Manco and retreated to Cuzco, but Manco could not press home any advantage. In 1537, feeling vulnerable to further attacks, he left Ollantaytambo for Vilcabamba.

When you visit Ollantaytambo you will be confronted by a series of 16 massive, stepped terraces of the very finest stonework, after crossing the great high-walled trapezoidal esplanade known as *Mañariki*. Beyond these imposing terraces lies the so-called **Temple of Ten Niches**, a funeral chamber once dedicated to the worship of Pachacútec's royal household. Immediately above this are six monolithic upright blocks of rose-coloured rhyolite, the remains of what is popularly called the **Temple of the Sun**. The dark grey stone is embellished today with bright orange lichen.

> *If possible arrive very early, 0700, before the tourists. Avoid Sun afternoons, when tour groups from Pisac descend in their hundreds.*

You can either descend by the route you came up, or follow the terracing round to the left (as you face the town) and work your way down to the **Valley of the Patacancha**. Here are more Inca ruins in the small area between the town and the temple fortress, behind the church. Most impressive is the **Baño de la Ñusta** (Bath of the Princess), a grey granite rock, about waist high, beneath which is the bath itself. The front of the boulder, over which the water falls, was delicately finished with a three-stepped pyramid, making a relief arch over the pool.

The town

If you are visiting Ollantaytambo, begin your tour at **El Museo Catcco** (Centro Andino de Tecnología Tradicional y Cultural de las Comunidades de Ollantaytambo) ⓘ *Casa Horno, Patacalle, 1 block from the plaza, T084-204024, www.ollantaytambo.org, daily 0900-1900, US$1.50 requested as a donation*, which houses a fine ethnographical collection. Its information centre gives tips on day-hikes, things to see and places to dine and stay. Local guides are available for tours of the town and surrounding areas. Outside the museum, **Catcco** runs non-profit cultural programmes, temporary exhibitions, concerts and lectures. Also on site is a ceramics workshop, a textile revitalization programme and an educational theatre project. Ceramics and textiles are sold in the museum shop. The museum has internet access. Note the canal down the middle of the street outside the museum.

A two-dimensional **'pyramid'** has been identified on the west side of the main ruins of Ollantaytambo. Its discoverers, Fernando and Edgar Elorietta, claim it is the real Pacaritambo, from where the four original Inca brothers emerged to found their empire (this alternative Inca creation myth, the Inn of Origin, tells of four brothers and four sisters emerging from a cave in a cliff). Whether this is the case or not, it is still a first-class piece of engineering with great terraced fields and a fine 750-m wall creating the optical illusion of a pyramid. The wall is aligned with the rays of the winter solstice, on 21 June. People gather at mid-winter dawn to watch this event. The mysterious 'pyramid', which covers 50 to 60 ha, can be seen properly from the other side of the river. This is a pleasant, easy one-hour walk, west from the Puente Inca, just outside the town. You'll also be rewarded with great views of the Sacred Valley and the river, with the snowy peaks of the Verónica massif as a backdrop.

Around Ollantaytambo

The stone quarries of **Cachiccata** are some 9 km from Ollantaytambo. Standing to the left of the six monolithic blocks of the Temple of the Sun, you can see them, looking west-southwest across the valley. The stones that the Inca masons chose here had to be quarried, hewn into a rough shape and hauled across the valley floor and up to the temple by means of a ramp, which can still be seen. Between the ruins and the quarries more than 50 enormous stones that never reached their destination lie abandoned. They are know as the '*las piedras cansadas*', or 'the tired stones'. It takes about a day to walk to the Inca quarries on the opposite of the river and return to Ollantaytambo.

At **Pinkuylluna Hill**, on the western edge of Ollantaytambo, is an impressive collection of storehouses, or *qolqas*, sometimes referred to as prisons. It's a relatively straightforward climb up the mountain, although there are some difficult stretches. Allow two to three hours going up. The path is difficult to make out, so it's best not to go on your own.

Sleeping

Pisac *p178*

A Royal Inca Pisac, Carretera Ruinas Km 1.5, T084-203064, www.royalinkahotel.com/hpisac.html. In the same chain as the **Royal Incas I and II** in Cuzco, this hotel can be reached by the hotels' own bus service. It is a short distance out of town, on the road that goes up to the ruins, a taxi ride after dark. Price includes taxes and breakfast. Camping is available for US$5 per person. A guide for the ruins can be provided. The rooms are comfortable, in a number of blocks in the grounds of a converted hacienda. There is a pool, sauna and jacuzzi (US$7), tennis court, horse riding and bicycle rental. The restaurant is good and there is a bar. The hotel is popular with day-trippers from Cuzco. Staff are very helpful and accommodating.

D-E Pisaq, at the corner of Pardo on the Plaza, Casilla Postal 1179, Cuzco, T084-203062, www.hotelpisaq.com. Bright and charming local decor and a pleasant atmosphere at this hotel, with private and shared bathrooms, hot water, sauna and massage. Good breakfast, basic, clean and friendly. The restaurant serves meals using local ingredients, some nights pizza is served, café.

F Residencial Beho, Intihuatana 642, 50 m up the hill from the plaza, T/F084-203001. Ask for a room in the main building. They serve a good breakfast for US$1. The *hostal* has a shop selling local handicrafts including masks. The owner's son will act as a guide to the ruins at the weekend.

G Hospedaje Familiar Kinsa Ccocha, on the plaza. The rooms are basic and none has bath. Price per person; you pay less if you don't use hot water.

G Parador, on the plaza, T084-203061. Price per person. All rooms share bathrooms, which have hot water. Breakfast is not included, but the restaurant serves other meals.

Pisac to Urubamba *p179*

AL Sonesta Posadas del Inca, Plaza Manco II de Yucay 123, Yucay, T084-201107, T01-7126060 (Lima) www.sonestaperu.com. A converted 300-year-old monastery is now a hotel which is like a little village with plazas, lovely gardens, a chapel and 69 comfortable, heated rooms. The price includes buffet breakfast, but not taxes. The restaurant serves an excellent buffet lunch. Lots of activities can be arranged, canoeing, horse riding, mountain biking, etc. There is a conference centre. Highly recommended.

A La Casona de Yucay, Plaza Manco II 104, Yucay, T084-201116, www.lacasonade yucay.com. This colonial house was where Simón Bolívar stayed during his liberation campaign in 1824. The price includes taxes and breakfast. The rooms have heating and, outside, there are 2 patios and gardens. **Don Manuel** restaurant is good, also has bar. Helpful staff, although front-of-house is not so good.

A Q'awana Lodge, Km 60.5, Huarán, T084-812409, www.munaycha.com. Country lodge with a rustic atmosphere, rooms and lovely terrace overlooking the Urubamba river. Includes breakfast. The restaurant serves Andean and international cuisine and has a good reputation. Adventure trips can be arranged.

C-D Hostal Y'Llary, on the plaza, Yucay, T084-201112. The price includes bathroom and breakfast, nice garden.

G Hostal Jerseyhuasi, Lamay, beside the springs. A nice little place, price includes breakfast, with generous portions of good food at other meals, clean and comfortable rooms. They also have camping possibilities.

Urubamba *p181, map p181*

AL Casa Andina Private Collection Sacred Valley, 5º paradero, Yanahuara, between Urubamba and Ollantaytambo, T084-976 5501, www.casa-andina.com. In its own 3-ha estate, with all the facilities associated with this chain, plus a gym, organic garden and restaurant with *novo andino* cuisine. Adventure activities can be arranged here. It also has a spa offering a range of massages and treatments and a planetarium and observatory, showing the Inca view of the night sky (US$10).

AL Libertador Valle Sagrado Lodge, 5º paradero, Yanahuara, T084-961 3316, http://en.vallesagradolodge.com/about/. Affiliated to the Libertador group, a colonial- style hotel with 16 rooms in extensive grounds. Libertador's **Tambo del Inka** in Urubamba (formerly the Incaland Hotel and Conference Center) is under renovation until 2007.

AL **San Agustín Monasterio de la Recoleta**, Jr Recoleta s/n, T084-201004, www.hotelessanagustin.com.pe. In a converted monastery (the earliest in Cuzco), this new hotel has suites and standard rooms with heating, TV and all facilities, **San Isidro** restaurant.

AL **San Agustín Urubamba**, Ctra Cuzco–Pisac Km 69, T084-201444, www.hotelessanagustin.com.pe. An upgraded hot el in a lovely setting just out of Urubamba, with suites and standard rooms, pool, sauna, massage and jacuzzi, **Naranjachayoc's** restaurant and bar.

AL **Sol y Luna**, west of town, T084-201620, www.hotelsolyluna.com. Attractive bungalows set off the main road in lovely gardens, pool, excellent buffet in restaurant, French-Swiss owned. Has **Viento Sur** adventure travel agency, for horse riding, mountain biking, trekking and paragliding, www.aventurasvientosur.com.

A **K'uychi Rumi**, Km 73.5 on the road to Ollantaytambo, 3 km from town, T084-201169, www.urubamba.com. 6 cottages for rent with 2 bedrooms, fully equipped, fireplace, terrace and balcony, surrounded by gardens. Price is for 1-2 people, each house can accommodate 6.

D **Las Tres Marías**, Zavala 307, T084-201004 (Cuzco T084-225252). Beautiful gardens, hot water, welcoming. Recommended.

D **Mach'a Wasi**, Jr Padre Barre, T084-201612, www.machawasi.com. An attractive guesthouse with comfortable rooms, under new ownership, solar-heated water, totally non-smoking, delicious breakfast extra (vegans catered for), safe, lovely garden, laundry. Mountain bike tours and treks can be arranged. Recommended.

E **Las Chullpas**, 3 km west of town in the Pumahuanca Valley, T084-201568, or 969 5030, www.uhupi.com/chullpas. Price per person. Very peaceful, includes excellent breakfast, vegetarian meals, English and German spoken, Spanish classes, natural medicine, treks, horse riding, mountain biking, camping US$3 with hot shower. Mototaxi from town US$0.85, taxi (ask for Querocancha) US$2.

G **Capulí**, Grau 222. With bath, hot water and TV. Price per person, cheaper with shared bath.

G **Hospedaje Perla de Vilcanota**, 9 de Noviembre, T084-201135. Price is per bed, without bath, but shared bathrooms have hot water; some rooms are even cheaper.

G **Hostal Urubamba**, Bolognesi 605. Basic but pleasant rooms with bath and cold water, cheaper without bath.

Chinchero *p182*

G **Hotel Restaurant Antabaraj**, just beyond ticket control, T084-306002 (Patricia Cagigao), antabaraj@hotmail.com. Basic rooms, take sleeping bag, kitchen facilities, good views, food at reasonable prices.

Ollantaytambo *p183*

A **Ñustayoc Mountain Lodge and Resort**, 5 km west of Ollantaytambo, just before Chillca and the start of the Inca Trail, T084-204098, www.nustayoclodge.com. Large and somewhat rambling lodge in a wonderful location with great views of the snowy Verónica massif and other peaks. Lovely flower-filled garden and grounds. Nicely decorated, spacious rooms, all with private bath. Price includes continental breakfast served in the large restaurant area.

C **Pakaritampu**, C Ferrocarril s/n, T084- 204020, www.pakaritampu.com. The price includes breakfast and taxes. This modern, 3-star hotel has 20 rooms with bath and views. It is owned by a former Peruvian women's volleyball star. There is a TV room, restaurant and bar, internet service for guests, laundry, safe and room service. Adventure sports such as rafting, climbing, trekking, mountain biking and horse riding can be arranged. Meals are extra: buffet US$13, dinner US$12-15. Excellent quality and service.

D **Albergue Kapuly**, at the end of the station road, T084-204017. Prices are lower in the off season. A quiet place with spacious rooms, some with and some without bath. The garden is nice and the price includes a good continental breakfast.

D **El Albergue Ollantaytambo**, within the railway station gates, T084-204014, www.rumbosperu.com/elalbergue/. Owned by North American Wendy Weeks, the *albergue* has 8 rooms with shared bathrooms. Price (per person) includes breakfast; box lunch costs US$4, full dinner US$7 on request. The rooms are full of character and are set in buildings around a courtyard and lovely gardens. Great showers (24 hrs a day) and a eucalyptus steam sauna (US$5). The whole place is charming, relaxing and homely. See the office-cum-shop-cum-exhibition where interesting handicrafts can be bought. Also for sale is Wendy's digestif, *compuesto matacuy*. It's very convenient for the Machu Picchu train and good place for information. Private transport can be arranged to the salt mines, Moray, Abra Málaga for birdwatching and taxi transfers to the airport. Highly recommended.

D Hostal Munay Tika, on the road to the station, T084-204111, munaytika@latin mail.com. Price includes breakfast and bath. Dinner is served by arrangement. To use the sauna costs US$5 with prior notice. Also has a nice garden. Recommended. It also has a complex of beautiful cabins (**D**), 2 km west of town (mototaxi US$0.60), set among extensive flower beds and with wonderful views down the valley. Ask at the hotel.

F Hostal Chaskawasi, Chaupicalle (also C Taypi) north of the plaza, T084-208085, anna_machupicchu@hotmail.com. A *hostal* snuggled away in the small alleys behind the plaza. Owner Anna is very friendly.

F Hostal La Ñusta, C Ocobamba, T084-204035. Ask about accommodation in the shop/restaurant of the same name on the plaza or in the **Gran Tunupa** restaurant. This is a decent although uninspiring budget option. Proprietor Rubén Ponce loves to share his knowledge of the ruins with guests. You get a good view of the ruins from the balcony. See page 188, for the restaurant.

F Hostal Ollanta, on the south side of the plaza, T084-204116. Basic and clean, but with a great location. All rooms with shared bath.

F Las Orquídeas, near start of the road to the station, T084-204032. A good choice. Price includes breakfast, and meals are available; may be used by tour groups.

G Hostal Chuza, just below the main plaza in town, T084-204113. Very clean and friendly with safe motorcycle parking. They have a TV in the front room for guests and one of the rooms features a wonderful view of the ruins with the Nevado de Verónica framed perfectly behind – a wonderful sight to wake up to in the morning. Recommended.

G Hostal KB, between the main plaza and the ruins, T084-204091. A basic *hostal* with shower included. It's very friendly, clean and the flower-filled garden is pleasant.

G Hostal Tambo, just walk up the street called Lari that heads north from the plaza. After 20 m or so you'll see an unmarked blue door on the left-hand side... bang on the door! If this doesn't work keep walking, turn left down the first small alley and bang on that blue door instead! Once past this unassuming exterior you emerge into a mini Garden of Eden, full of fruit trees, flowers, dogs, cats and domesticated parrots in the trees. There's no hot water and only 3 basic rooms (price per person), but the family is very friendly and the Señora is a character.

Eating

Pisac *p178*

ΨΨ-Ψ Miski Mijuna Wasi, on the Plaza de Armas, T084-203266, MARICUCHA103@ hotmail.com. Serves very tasty local food, typical and *novo andino*, also international dishes. Has a *pastelería* also.

ΨΨ-Ψ Mullu, Mcal Castilla 375, T084-208182. Tue-Sun 0900-1900. Café/restaurant related to the Mullu store in Cuzco, also has a gallery promoting local artists.

Ψ Doña Clorinda, on the plaza opposite the church, doesn't look very inviting but cooks tasty food, including vegetarian options. A very friendly place.

Cafés

Bakery, Av Mcal Castilla 372, sells excellent cheese and onion *empanadas* for US$0.25, suitable for vegetarians, and good whole-meal bread. The oven is tremendous.

Ulrike's Café, Plaza de Armas 828, T084-203195, ulrikescafe@terra.com.pe. This comfortable café is renowned for its apple crumble with ice cream, to say nothing of great coffee, smoothies and a wide range of international cuisine. A good place to chill after a hard day exploring the market and ruins.

Pisac to Urubamba *p179*

ΨΨ Allpamanka, Yucay. In an attractive old colonial house, offers a wide-ranging menu and is cheaper than nearby hotel restaurants.

Urubamba *p181, map p181*

ΨΨΨ Tunupa, Km 77, on left side of the road on the riverbank, in a renovated colonial hacienda (same ownership as Tunupa in

Cuzco), zappa@terra.com.pe. Excellent food served indoors or outdoors, bar, lounge, library, chapel, gardens, stables and an alpaca-jewellery shop. Outstanding exhibition of pre-Columbian objects and colonial paintings. **Seminario**'s ceramics feature in the decor. People on valley tours are served a varied buffet including *novo andino* cuisine; buffet lunch US$14, 1200-1500. Dinner (1800-2030) is à la carte.

🍴🍴 **El Fogón**, Parque Pintacha, T084-201534. Traditional Peruvian food, large servings, nice atmosphere. Recommended.

🍴🍴 **El Maizal**, on the road before the bridge, T084-201454. Country-style restaurant with a good reputation, buffet service with a variety of typical *novo andino* dishes, plus international choices, beautiful gardens with native flowers and fruit trees. Recommended (they also have a hotel of the same name).

🍴🍴 **La Casa de la Abuela**, Bolívar 272, 2 blocks up from the Plaza de Armas, T084-622975. Excellent restaurant with rooms grouped around a small courtyard. The trout is fantastic and food is served with baskets of roasted potatoes and salad. Recommended.

🍴🍴 **Quinta los Geranios**, on the main road before the bridge, T084-201043. Regional dishes, excellent lunch with more than enough food, average price US$13.

🍴 **Pintacha**, Bolognesi 523. Pub/café serving sandwiches, burgers, coffees, teas and drinks. Games and book exchange, cosy, open till late.

🍴 **Pizzonay**, Av Mcal Castilla, 2nd block. Pizzas, excellent spinach ravioli (not so good lasagne). Mulled wine served in a small restaurant with nice decor. Clean, good value. Recommended.

Ollantaytambo *p183*

🍴🍴 **Fortaleza**, 2 branches, one on Plaza Ruinas, the other on north side of the main plaza. Basic but good food, breakfasts, pizza and pasta – all the gringo favourites are on offer, as well as some more local dishes.

🍴🍴 **Gran Tunupa**, corner of Cocobamba and Bentinerio, right-hand side between the plaza and the bridge. Nice view and reasonable food but the pizzas suffer from the usual Peruvian lack of tomato sauce.

🍴🍴 **Il Cappuccino**, just before the bridge on the right-hand side. Offers the best cappuccino in town, great coffee generally, also café latte and espresso. Good continental and American breakfasts. Slightly more sophisticated ambience and service in comparison with many other establishments in town. Also run **Kusicoyllor**, Plaza Ruinas, for pizza, pasta and good coffee.

🍴🍴 **Mayupata**, Jr Convención s/n, across the bridge on the way to the ruins, on the left, T084-204083 (Cuzco). Serving international choices and a selection of Peruvian dishes, desserts, sandwiches and coffee. It opens at 0600 for breakfast, and serves lunch and dinner. The bar has a fireplace; river view, relaxing atmosphere.

🍴 **Alcázar Café**, C del Medio s/n, 50 m from the plaza, T084-204034, alcazar@ollantaytambo.org. Vegetarian restaurant, also offering fish and meat dishes, pasta specialities. Offers excursions to traditional Andean communities.

🍴 **Bahía**, on the east side of the plaza. Very friendly, vegetarian dishes served on request.

🍴 **La Ñusta**, on the plaza, same owner as *hostal*. Popular, good food, snacks available.

Bars and clubs

Urubamba *p181, map p181*

Tequila, Av Mcal Castilla 3rd block. The door is always closed so you must ring the bell. Disco, drinks, good coffee, open till late.

Festivals and events

Pisac *p178*

15 Jul A local fiesta in Pisac.

Pisac to Urubamba *p179*

15-16 Aug Fiesta de la Virgen Asunta, Coya.
15 Aug Lamay hosts a festival.

Urubamba *p181, map p181*

May and Jun Harvest months, with many processions following mysterious ancient schedules.

1st week of Jun Urubamba's main festival, El Señor de Torrechayoc.

Ollantaytambo *p183*

6 Jan Bajada de Reyes Magos (the Magi), with traditional dancing, a bull fight, local food and a fair.

End May-early Jun Pentecost, 50 days after Easter, is the **Fiesta del Señor de Choquekillca**, patron saint of Ollantaytambo.

There are several days of dancing, weddings, processions, masses, feasting and drinking (the last opportunity to see traditional *cuzqueño* dancing).

29 Jun Following **Inti Raymi** in Cuzco, there is a colourful festival, the **Ollanta-Raymi**, at which the Quechua drama, *Ollantay*, is re-enacted.

29 Oct **Aniversario de Ollantaytambo**, a festival with dancing in traditional costume and many local delicacies for sale.

Activities and tours

Urubamba *p181, map p181*

Agrotourism

Chichubamba, Casa de ProPerú, Jr Rejachayoc, Urubamba, T084-201562, www.agrotourismsacredvalley.com. A community tourism project which lets visitors take part in a number of traditional activities (culinary, horticulture, textiles, ceramics, beekeeping, etc, US$3 pp, cheaper for groups), hiking US$10, lodging **E** per person and local meals. It's about 10 mins' walk from Urubamba; follow the signs.

Horse riding

Perol Chico, 5 km from Urubamba at Km 77, T084-962 4475 (mob), office T054-213386, www.perolchico.com. Owned and operated by Eduard van Brunschot Vega (Dutch/Peruvian), 1- to 14-day trips out of Urubamba, good horses, riding is Peruvian Paso style; 1-day trip to Moray and the salt pans costs US$110 (minimum 2 people, starting in Cuzco). Recommended.

Trekking

Haku Trek, contact Javier Saldívar or Yeral Quillahuman, T084-961 3001 (mob), www.hakutrek.com. A new cooperative tourism project in the Chicón valley (the mountain valley above Urubamba), run by residents of the community. 3 different hiking trips are offered: two 1-day hiking options (US$20 per person including food and accommodation) and a third, 2-day hike up to the Chicón Glacier itself (US$45 all inclusive). Hikes are based at a simple, but beautifully located eco-lodge in the valley and profits are used to fund reforestation of native forest in the area.

Transport

To organize your own Sacred Valley transport, try one of the taxi drivers listed on page 174.

Pisac *p178*

Bus

From Cuzco From C Puputi on the outskirts of Cuzco, near the Clorindo Matto de Turner school and Av de la Cultura. 32 km, 1 hr, US$0.85. *Colectivos*, minibuses and buses leave when full, between 0600 and 1600; also trucks and pickups. Buses returning from Pisac are often full. The last one back leaves around 2000. Taxis charge about US$20 for the round trip. To **Pisac**, **Calca** (18 km beyond Pisac) and **Urubamba**, buses leave from Av Tullumayo 800 block, Huanchac, US$1.

Urubamba *p181, map p181*

Bus

The bus and combi terminal is just west of town on the main road. To **Calca**, **Pisac** (US$0.80, 1 hr) and **Cuzco** (2 hrs, US$1), from 0530 onwards. Also buses to Cuzco via **Chinchero**, same fare.

Colectivos to **Cuzco** can be caught outside the terminal and on the main road, US$1.15. Combis run to **Ollantaytambo**, 45 mins, US$0.30. There are also buses from here to **Quillabamba**.

Train

See page 208 for the Sacred Valley Railway from Urubamba to **Aguas Calientes**.

Chinchero *p182*

Bus from Cuzco Combis and *colectivos* for Chinchero leave from 300 block of Av Grau, **Cuzco**, 1 block before crossing the bridge. 23 km, 45 mins, US$0.45; and for **Urubamba** a further 25 km, 45 mins, US$0.45 (or US$1 Cuzco-Urubamba direct, US$1.15 for a seat in a *colectivo*).

To Maras There is public transport from Chinchero to Maras and regular pickup trucks which carry people and produce in and out. Transport stops running between 1700 and 1800; it costs between US$0.60 and US$1. If you cannot get transport to Maras, take any combi going between Urubamba and Chinchero, get out at the junction for Maras and walk from there.

It's 4 km to Maras; once through the village, bear left a little, and ask directions to Moray. Hitching back to **Urubamba** is quite easy, but there are no hotels at all in the area, so take care not to be stranded. **Taxis** wait at the Maras/Moray junction on the Urubamba/Chinchero road. They charge US$20 to go to Salinas and then on to Moray, with a 1 hr wait at each.

Ollantaytambo *p183*

Bus

There is a direct bus service to Ollantaytambo from Av Grau, **Cuzco**, at 0745 and 1945 direct (or catch a bus to Urubamba from Av Grau). From Ollantaytambo to Cuzco at 0715 and 1945; the fare is US$2.85.

Train See page 208. The station is 10-15 mins walk from the plaza (turn left at the sign that says 'Centro de Salud' between the Plaza de Armas and the ruins). There are *colectivos* at the plaza for the station when trains are due. Also, a bus leaves the station at 0900 for **Urubamba** (US$0.30) and **Chinchero** (US$1).

Directory

Pisac *p178*

Banks If you need to change money, there is a shop on M Castilla, heading away from the plaza, near where the road bends; it will change TCs.

Internet and telephone On the same side of the plaza as the museum is the municipal building with a computer centre (internet for US$0.75 per hr, closed Sun morning); also a public phone booth.

Pisac to Urubamba *p179*

Internet In **Calca**, the municipal library has internet connection. In **Yucay**, there are several places.

Urubamba *p181, map p181*

Banks Banks in the town centre on Comercio. ATM on the main road not far from the bridge. **Internet** Connections, corner of Av M Castilla and Av La Convención. **Post** Serpost, post office, Plaza de Armas. **Telephone** There are several phone booths around the centre. The one outside **Hostal Urubamba** makes international calls.

Ollantaytambo *p183*

Banks ATM in **Hostal Sauce**, C Ventiderio 248, between the Plaza and Av Ferrocarril. **Internet** Several places in town, US$0.30 for 30 mins.

Machu Picchu and the Inca Trails

There is a tremendous feeling of awe on first witnessing this incredible sight. The ancient citadel of Machu Picchu, 42 km from Ollantaytambo by rail, straddles the saddle of a high mountain with steep terraced slopes falling away to the fast-flowing Río Urubamba snaking its hairpin course far below in the valley floor. Towering overhead is Huayna Picchu, and green jungle peaks provide the backdrop for the whole majestic scene.

If you take the Inca Trail to Machu Picchu, following in the footsteps of its creators, you are making a true pilgrimage and the sweat and struggle is all worth it when you set your eyes on this mystical site at sunrise from the Inca sun gate above the ruins. That way you see Machu Picchu in its proper context. Afterwards you can recover in Aguas Calientes and soothe those aching limbs in the hot springs. The introduction of new regulations for walking the Inca Trail in 2001 opened up additional options for trekking to Machu Picchu, some shorter, some longer than the old route. So if you fancy widening the perspective of how the Incas walked to their sacred city, ask your chosen tour operator to show you the alternatives. ▸▸ *For Sleeping, Eating and other listings, see pages 203-209.*

Ins and outs

Getting there There are two ways to get to Machu Picchu. The easy way is by train from Cuzco, Ollantaytambo or Urubamba, with a bus ride for the final climb from the rail terminus at Aguas Calientes to the ruins (see Transport, page 207, for the timetables). The walk up from Aguas Calientes takes 1½ to two hours, following the Inca path. Walking down to Aguas Calientes, if staying the night there, takes between 30 minutes and one hour. The ruins are quieter after 1530, but don't forget that the last bus down from the ruins leaves at 1730.

The strenuous, but most rewarding way to Machu Picchu is to hike one of the Inca Trails, the 'classic' example of which is described in its own section (see page 194).

Visitor information Tickets for Machu Picchu must be purchased in advance from the **Instituto Nacional de Cultura** (INC) ⓘ *Av Pachacútec cuadra 1, Aguas Calientes, www.inc-cusco.gob.pe, or in Cuzco (see page 136)*, which also gives permission to enter the ruins before 0630 to watch the sunrise over the Andes, which is a spectacular experience. The INC website publishes the regulations and lists of licensed tour operators and guides (see Inca Trail and general tours, page 162). The agency officially responsible for the site is **Unidad Gestión de Machu Picchu** ⓘ *C Garcilaso 223, Cuzco, T084-242103*. It is an excellent source of information on Machu Picchu and this is the place to which any complaints or observations should be directed. **i perú** ⓘ *in the INC office, as above, of 4, T084-211104, can provide general information.*

Machu Picchu ruins ▸▸ *pp203-209. Colour map 2, A2.*

→ *Altitude: 2380 m.*

ⓘ *Daily 0700-1730. Entrance fee is US$36, to be purchased in advance from the INC, see above. It is possible to pay in dollars, but only clean, undamaged notes will be accepted. You cannot take backpacks into Machu Picchu; leave them at the entrance for US$0.50. Guides are available at the site, they are often very knowledgeable and worthwhile, and charge US$15 for 2½ hrs.*

For centuries Machu Picchu was buried in jungle, until Hiram Bingham stumbled upon it in July 1911. It was then explored by an archaeological expedition sent by Yale University. Machu Picchu was a stunning find. The only major Inca site to escape 400 years of looting and destruction, it was remarkably well preserved. And it was no ordinary Inca settlement. It sat in an inaccessible location above the Urubamba Gorge, and contained so many fine buildings that people have puzzled over its meaning ever since.

Once you have passed through the ticket gate you follow a path to a small complex of buildings which now acts as the **main entrance** (1) to the ruins. It is set at the eastern end of the extensive **terracing** (2) which must have supplied the crops for the city. Above this point, turning back on yourself, is the final stretch of the Inca Trail leading down from **Intipunku** (Sun Gate), see page 197. From a promontory here, on which stands the building called the **Watchman's Hut** (3), you get the perfect view of the city (the one you've seen on all the postcards), laid out before you with Huayna Picchu rising above the furthest extremity. Go round the promontory and head south for the **Intipata** (Inca bridge), see page 193. The main path into the ruins comes to a **dry moat** (4) that cuts right across the site. At the moat you can either climb the long staircase which goes to the upper reaches of the city, or you can enter the city by the baths and Temple of the Sun.

The more strenuous way into the city is by the former route, which takes you past quarries on your left as you look down to the Urubamba on the west flank of the mountain. To your right are roofless buildings where you can see in close up the general construction methods used in the city. Proceeding along this level, above the main plazas, you reach the **Temple of the Three Windows** (5) and the **Principal Temple** (6), which has a smaller building called the **Sacristy** (7). The two main buildings are three-sided and were clearly of great importance, given the fine stonework involved. The wall with the three windows is built onto a single rock, one of the many instances in the city where the architects did not merely put their construction on a convenient piece of land. They used and fashioned its features to suit their concept of how the city should be tied to the mountain, its forces and the alignment of its stones to the

Machu Picchu

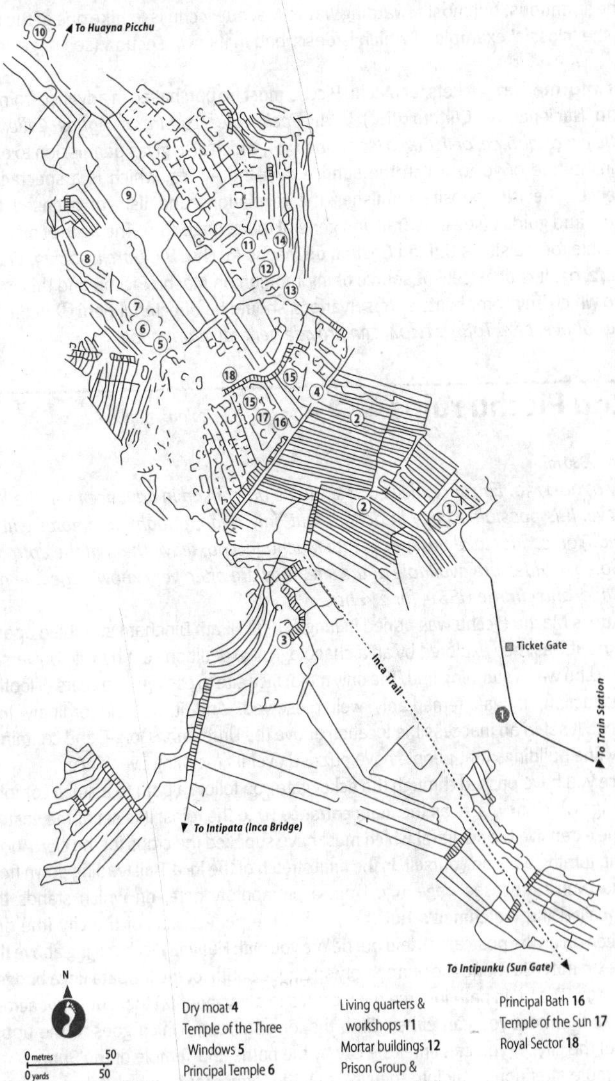

Main entrance **1**
Terracing **2**
Watchman's Hut **3**
Dry moat **4**
Temple of the Three Windows **5**
Principal Temple **6**
Sacristy **7**
Intihuatana **8**
Main Plaza **9**
Sacred Rock **10**
Living quarters & workshops **11**
Mortar buildings **12**
Prison Group & Condor Temple **13**
Intimachay **14**
Ceremonial baths or Fountains **15**
Principal Bath **16**
Temple of the Sun **17**
Royal Sector **18**

Sleeping
Machu Picchu Sanctuary Lodge **1**

surrounding peaks. In the Principal Temple, a diamond-shaped stone in the floor is said to depict the constellation of the Southern Cross.

Continue on the path behind the Sacristy to reach the **Intihuatana** (8), the 'hitching-post of the sun'. The name comes from the theory that such carved rocks (*gnomons*), found at all major Inca sites, were the point to which the sun was symbolically 'tied' at the winter solstice, before being freed to rise again on its annual ascent towards the summer solstice. The steps, angles and planes of this sculpted block appear to indicate a purpose beyond simple decoration, and researchers have sought the trajectory of each alignment. Whatever the motivation behind this magnificent carving, it is undoubtedly one of the highlights of Machu Picchu.

Climb down from the Intihuatana's mound to the **Main Plaza** (9). Beyond its northern end is a small plaza with open-sided buildings on two sides and on the third, the **Sacred Rock** (10). The outline of this gigantic, flat stone echoes that of the mountains behind it. From here you can proceed to the entrance to the trail to Huayna Picchu (see below). Returning to the Main Plaza and heading southeast you pass, on your left, several groups of closely packed buildings which have been taken to be **living quarters** and **Workshops** (11), **Mortar Buildings** (12)(look for the house with two discs let into the floor) and the **Prison Group** (13), one of whose constructions is known as the **Condor Temple**. Also in this area is a cave called **Intimachay** (14).

A short distance from the Condor Temple is the lower end of a series of **ceremonial baths** (15) or fountains. They were probably used for ritual bathing and the water still flows down them today. The uppermost, **Principal Bath** (16), is the most elaborate. Next to it is the **Temple of the Sun** (17), or Torreón. This singular building has one straight wall from which another wall curves around and back to meet the straight one, but for the doorway. From above it looks like an incomplete letter P. It is another example of the architecture being at one with its environment as the interior is taken up by the partly worked summit of the outcrop onto which the building is placed. All indications are that this temple was used for astronomical purposes. Underneath the Torreón a cave-like opening has been formed by an oblique gash in the rock. Fine masonry has been added to the opposing wall, making a second side of a triangle, which contrasts with the rough edge of the split rock. But the blocks of masonry appear to have been slotted behind another sculpted piece of natural stone, which has been cut into a four-stepped buttress. Immediately behind this is a two-stepped buttress. This strange combination of the natural and the man-made has been called the Tomb or Palace of the Princess. Across the stairway from the complex which includes the Torreón is the group of buildings known as the **Royal Sector** (18).

The famous Inca bridge – **Intipata** – is about 30 minutes along a well-marked trail south of the Royal Sector. The bridge, which is actually a couple of logs, is spectacularly sited, carved into a vertiginous cliff-face. The walk is well worth it for the fine views, but the bridge itself is closed to visitors. Not only is it in a poor state of repair, but the path before it has collapsed.

> *Camping is not allowed at Intipunku, nor anywhere else at the site; guards may confiscate your tent. There is a free campsite down beside the rail tracks at Puente Ruinas station.*

Huayna Picchu

ⓘ *Access daily 0700-1300, with the latest return time being 1500.*

Synonymous with the ruins themselves is Huayna Picchu, the verdant mountain overlooking the site. There are also ruins on the mountain itself, and steps to the top for a superlative view of the whole magnificent scene, but this is not for those with vertigo. The climb takes up to 90 minutes but the steps are dangerous after bad weather and you shouldn't leave the path. You must register at a hut at the beginning of the trail. The other trail to Huayna Picchu, down near the Urubamba, is via the Temple of the Moon: two caves, one above the other, with superb Inca niches inside, sadly blemished by graffiti. To reach the **Temple of the Moon** from the path to Huayna Picchu, take the marked trail to the left; it is in good shape. It descends further than you think it should. After the Temple you may proceed to Huayna Picchu, but this path is overgrown, slippery when wet and has a crooked ladder on an exposed part about 10 minutes before the top (not for the faint-hearted). It is safer to return to the main trail to Huayna Picchu, but this adds about 30 minutes to the climb. The round trip takes about four hours.

The Inca Trail » pp203-209.

The wonder of Machu Picchu has been well documented over the years. Equally impressive is the centuries-old Inca Trail that winds its way from the Sacred Valley near Ollantaytambo, taking three to four days. What makes this hike so special is the stunning combination of Inca ruins, unforgettable views, magnificent mountains, exotic vegetation and extraordinary ecological variety. The government acknowledged all this in 1981 by including the trail in a 325 sq-km national park, the Machu Picchu Historical Sanctuary. Machu Picchu itself cannot be understood without the Inca Trail. Its principal sites are ceremonial in character, apparently in ascending hierarchical order. This Inca province was a unique area of elite access. The trail is essentially a work of spiritual art, like a Gothic cathedral, and walking it was formerly an act of devotion.

Ins and outs

Entrance tickets and tours An entrance ticket for the trail or its variations must be bought at the **Instituto Nacional de Cultura (INC)** office in Cuzco; no tickets are sold at the entrance gates. Furthermore, tickets are only sold on presentation of a letter from a licensed tour operator on behalf of the visitor. There is a 50% discount for students, but note that officials are very strict, only an ISIC card will be accepted as proof of status. Tickets are checked at Km 82, Huayllabamba and Wiñay-Wayna.

On all hiking trails (Km 82 or Km 88 to Machu Picchu, Salkantay to Machu Picchu, and Km 82 or Km 88 to Machu Picchu via Km 104) adults must pay US$60, students and children under 15 US$30. On the **Camino Real de los Inkas** from Km 104 to Wiñay-Wayna and Machu Picchu (see page 198) the fee is US$30 per adult, US$15 for students and children; Salkantay to Huayllabamba and Km 88 is US$30. The **Salkantay trek** (see page

Inca Trail

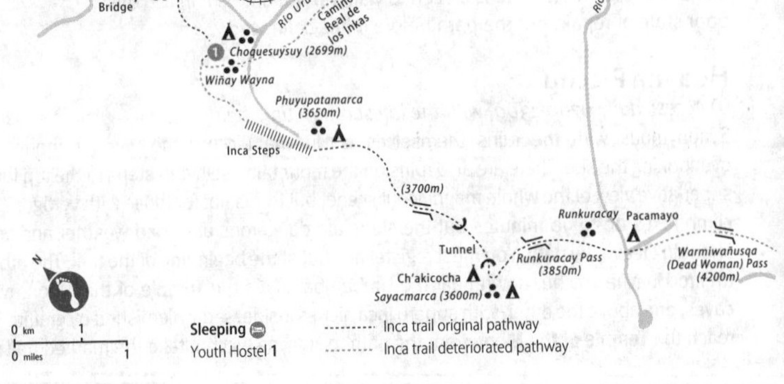

198) which used not to be subject to a charge now has a US$36 trekking fee. It is likely that the Instituto Nacional de Cultura will introduce charges on more trails in 2006-2007, further eroding the scope for independent trekking in this region.

Travel agencies in Cuzco arrange transport to the start, equipment, food, etc, for an all-in price. Prices vary from about US$200 to US$300 per person for a four-day, three-night trek (similar prices are charged for the Salkantay trek). Remember that you get what you pay for, but also bear in mind that the cheaper the price the more corners may be cut and the less attention paid to the environment and the porters. This respect is, after all, the goal of the 2001 legislation.

There is a quota for agencies and groups to use the Trail, but some agencies make block bookings way in advance of departure dates. This makes it much harder for other agencies to guarantee their clients places on the Trail. Consequently, current advice is to book your preferred dates as early as possible, even up to a year in advance, then confirm nearer the time. There have been many instances of disappointed trekkers whose bookings did not materialize: don't wait till the last minute and always check your operator's cancellation charges.

You can save a bit of money by arranging your own transport back to Ollantaytambo in advance, either for the last day of your tour, or by staying an extra night in Aguas Calientes and taking the early morning train, then a bus back to Cuzco. If you take your own tent and sleeping gear, some agencies give a discount. Make sure your return ticket for the tourist train to Cuzco has your name on it, otherwise you have to pay for any changes.

Advice and information Although security has improved in recent years, it's still best to leave all your valuables in Cuzco and keep everything else inside your tent, even your shoes. Avoid the July/August high season and the rainy season from November to April (note that this can change, so check in advance). In the wet it is cloudy and the paths are very muddy and difficult. Also watch out for coral snakes in this area (black, red, yellow bands). Please remove all your rubbish, including toilet paper, or use the pits provided. Do not light open fires as they can get out of control. The **Annual Inca Trail Clean-up** takes place usually in September. Many agencies and organizations are involved and volunteers should contact **South American Explorers** in Cuzco (see page 135) for full details of ways to help.

Guidelines for the treatment of porters can be found on the website of the now defunct **Inka Porter Project**, www.peruweb.org/porters/. If you feel that your porters have been neglected or abused on the trek, express this to your agency, inform the **South American Explorers** and please also drop us a line at Footprint (go to www.footprintbooks.com or send us a letter to our Bath address in the UK). We read all your letters and agencies who repeatedly mistreat porters will be removed from our publications.

Equipment It is cold at night and weather conditions change rapidly, so it is important to take strong footwear, rain gear and warm clothing (this includes long johns if you want to sleep rather than freeze at night): dress in layers. Also

Inca Trail regulations

The year 2001 signalled the beginning of strict new rules on the Inca Trail; tourists should be aware of the following regulations:

- All agencies must have a licence to work in the area.
- Groups of up to seven independent travellers who do not wish to use a tour operator are allowed to hike the trail accompanied by an independent, licensed guide, as long as they do not employ any other support staff, such as porters or cooks.
- A maximum of 500 visitors per day are allowed on the trail.
- Operators pay US$12.15 for each porter and other trail staff; porters are not permitted to carry more than 25 kg (although less scrupulous agencies often find ways to circumvent this requirement).
- Littering is banned. Plastic water bottles may not be carried on the trail; only canteens are permitted.
- Pets and pack animals are prohibited, although llamas are allowed as far as the first pass.
- Groups have to use approved campsites; on the routes from Km 82, Km 88 and Salkantay, the campsites may be changed with prior authorization.
- The Inca Trail is closed each February for maintenance.

take food, water, water purification tablets, insect repellent, sunscreen, a hat and sunglasses, a supply of plastic bags, coverings, a good sleeping bag, a torch and a stove for preparing hot food and drink to ward off the cold at night. It is worth paying extra to hire a down sleeping bag if you haven't brought your own. A paraffin (kerosene) stove is preferable, as fuel can be bought in small quantities in markets.

A tent is essential, but if you're hiring one in Cuzco, check carefully for leaks. Caves marked on some maps are little better than overhangs and are not sufficient shelter to sleep in. You could also take a first-aid kit; if you don't need it, the porters probably will, given their rather basic footwear. It is forbidden to use trekking poles because the metal tips are damaging the trail. Instead, buy a carved wooden stick on sale in the main plaza in Ollantaytambo or at the trail head. Many will need this for the steep descents on the path.

You are not allowed to walk back along the Inca Trail, though you can pay US$6 at Intipunku to go as far as Wiñay-Wayna.

All the necessary equipment can be rented in Cuzco, see page 161. Good maps of the trail and area can be bought from **South American Explorers** in Lima or Cuzco, see pages 78 and 135. If you have any doubts about carrying your own pack, porters/guides are available through Cuzco agencies. Always carry a day-pack, though, with water and snacks, in case you walk at faster or slower than the porters. Take around US$30 extra per person for tips and for a drink at the end of the trail.

The trek

Day 1 The trek to the sacred site begins either at Km 82, **Piscacucho**, or at Km 88, **Qorihuayrachina**, at 2600 m. In order to reach Km 82, hikers are transported by their tour operator in a minibus on the road that goes to Quillabamba. From Piri onwardS the road follows the riverbank and ends at Km 82, where there is a bridge. You can depart as early as you like and arrive at Km 82 faster than going by train. The Inca Trail equipment, food, fuel and field personnel reach Km 82 (depending on the tour operator's logistics) for the Inrena staff to weigh each bundle before the group arrives. When several groups are leaving on the same day, it is more convenient to arrive early.

Km 88 can only be reached by train, subject to schedule and baggage limitations. The train goes slower than a bus, but you start your walk nearer to Llaqtapata and Huayllabamba.

The first ruin is **Llaqtapata**, near Km 88, the utilitarian centre of a large settlement of farming terraces which probably supplied the other Inca Trail sites. From here, it is a relatively easy three-hour walk to the village of **Huayllabamba**. Note that the route from Km 82 goes via **Cusichaca**, the valley in which Ann Kendall worked, rather than Llaqtapata.

A series of gentle climbs and descents leads along the Río Cusichaca, the ideal introduction to the trail. The village is a popular camping spot for tour groups, so it's a better idea to continue for about an hour up to the next site, **Llulluchayoc** – 'three white stones' – which is a patch of green beside a fast-flowing stream. It's a steep climb but you're pretty much guaranteed a decent pitch for the night. If you're feeling really energetic, you can go on to the next camping spot, a perfectly flat meadow, called **Llulluchapampa**. This means a punishing 1½-hour ascent through cloudforest, but it does leave you with a much easier second day. There's also the advantage of relative isolation and a magnificent view back down the valley.

Day 2 For most people the second day is by far the toughest. It's a steep climb to the meadow, followed by an exhausting 2½-hour haul up to the first pass – aptly named **Warmiwañusqa** (Dead Woman) – at 4200 m. The feeling of relief on reaching the top is immense. After a well-earned break it's a sharp descent on a treacherous path down to the Pacamayo Valley, where there are a few flat camping spots near a stream if you're too weary to continue.

Day 2/3 If you're feeling energetic, you can proceed to the second pass. Halfway up comes the ruin of **Runkuracay**, which was probably an Inca *tambo* (post-house). Camping is no longer permitted here. A steep climb up an Inca staircase leads to the next pass, at 3850 m, with spectacular views of Pumasillo (6246 m) and the Vilcabamba range. The trail descends to **Sayacmarca** (Inaccessible town), a spectacular site over the Aobamba Valley. Just below Sayacmarca lies **Conchamarca** (Shell town), a small group of buildings standing on rounded terraces.

Day 3 A blissfully gentle two-hour climb on a stone highway, leads through an Inca tunnel and along the enchanted fringes of the cloudforest, to the third pass. This is the most rewarding part of the trail, with spectacular views of the entire Vilcabamba range. Then it's down to the extensive ruins of **Phuyupatamarca** (Cloud-level town), at 3650 m, where Inca observation platforms offer awesome views of nearby Salkantay (6270 m) and surrounding peaks. There is a 'tourist bathroom' here, where water can be collected, but purify it before drinking.

From here, an Inca stairway of white granite plunges more than 1000 m to the spectacularly sited and impressive ruins of **Wiñay-Wayna** (Forever Young), offering views of agricultural terraces at **Intipata** (Sun place). A trail, not easily visible, goes from Wiñay-Wayna to the terracing. There is a youth hostel at Wiñay-Wayna (see Sleeping, page 204) and there are spaces for a few tents, but they get snapped up quickly. After Wiñay-Wayna there is no water, and no place to camp, until Machu Picchu. A gate by Wiñay-Wayna is locked between 1530 and 0500, preventing access to the path to Machu Picchu at night.

Day 4 From Wiñay-Wayna it is a gentle hour's walk through another type of forest, with larger trees and giant ferns, to a steep Inca staircase which leads up to **Intipunku** (Sun gate), where you look down, at last, upon Machu Picchu, basking in all her glory. Your aching muscles will be quickly forgotten and even the presence of the functional hotel building cannot detract from one of the most magical sights in all the Americas.

Camino Real de los Inkas

The Inca Trail from Km 104 This short Inca Trail is used by those who don't want to endure the full hike. It starts at Km 104, where a footbridge gives access to the ruins of **Chachabamba** and the trail ascends to the main trail at Wiñay-Wayna. Half way up is a good view of the ruins of **Choquesuysuy**. The first part is a steady, continuous three-hour ascent (take water) and the trail is narrow and exposed in parts. About 15 minutes before Wiñay-Wayna is a waterfall where fresh water can be obtained (best to purify it before drinking).

Salkantay treks

Four hours' drive west of Cuzco is **Mollepata**, starting point for two major alternatives to the 'classic' Inca Trail. The road from Cuzco is good-quality tarmac until the turn off just beyond Limatambo, in the Río Colorado valley floor. A dirt road then winds steeply up to Mollepata. Both treks pass beneath the magnificent glacial bulk of **Salkantay**, at 6271 m the loftiest peak of the Vilcabamba range.

Santa Teresa trek The first four-day trek takes the northwestern pass under Salkantay, leading into the high jungles of the Santa Teresa valley and eventually down to the town of Santa Teresa itself at the confluence with the Río Urubamba, from where Aguas Calientes and Machu Picchu are accessible. **Cruzpata** (3100 m) is the starting point for the trek, which goes via **Soraypampa** and **Salkantay Pampa**, the 4500-m **Huamantay Pass**, the villages of **Chaullay** and **Colcanpampa** and the meeting of the Río Totora with the Quebrada Chalán to form the **Río Santa Teresa**. After the village of **La Playa** you can choose to go to the Hidroeléctrica railway station, via the ruins of **Patallacta**, or to the village of Santa Teresa. The restrictions on the Inca Trail quickly turned the Santa Teresa Trek into the most popular alternative to the 'classic' Trail, but in 2006 the **INC** got wise to this and introduced new rules: this trek may now only be done with an agency and trekkers are charged US$36. At the time of writing the permit was being applied haphazardly.

High Inca Trail The second route, often referred to as the High Inca Trail, follows the same route up to the base of Salkantay before turning east across the **Inca Chiriasca Pass** at approximately 4900 m. This route then descends via **Sisaypampa**, from where you trek to **Pampacahuana**, an outstanding Inca ruin. The remains of an Inca road then go down to the singular Inca ruins of **Paucarcancha**. Paucarcancha is also an important camping site on the Ancascocha trek, described below. On the third day you join the 'classic' Inca Trail at **Huayllabamba** (see page 197), before continuing to Machu Picchu. Because the route follows the Km 88 trail in its second half, permits are required and thus booking in advance is highly recommended. It is not possible to trek this route without a registered Peruvian guide. There is an obligatory change from animals to porters before you reach Huayllabamba.

If you don't want to join up with the classic Inca Trail, an alternative is to go to Huayllabamba, then down to Km 88, from where you can take the train to Aguas Calientes, or back to Cuzco. There is an entrance fee of US$30 for this hike, but it does not include the entrance to Machu Picchu. If you combine this route with the short Inca Trail from Km 104, you have to pay the US$30 trail fee (see above for full details on prices).

Ancascocha

Named after a tiny but beautifully situated community in the Cordillera Vilcabamba's remote eastern fringe, this is a little-known, but worthy addition to the growing list of alternative Inca Trails. It starts in the village of Huarocondo (near the Cuzco-Aguas Calientes rilway line). Crossing three fairly steep passes, it offers fabulous views of some of the region's best-known snow peaks, Salkantay and La Verónica foremost among them. An added bonus is the impressive Nevado Huayanay, which towers above a landscape laced with icy lakes and cascades. Along with the natural attractions you'll pass interesting ruins, fragmented sections of Inca trail and friendly pastoral communities. Ancascocha can easily be combined with the classic Inca Trail (given the timely reservation of permits), or longer routes into the heart of the Vilcabamba range. For those with more limited time, transport direct to either Aguas Calientes or Cuzco can be obtained from the trail's end. The Ancascocha trail finishes at several points: you can link up with the Salkantay treks at Paucarcancha; you can link up with the Inca Trail at Huayllabamba and continue to Machu Picchu; or you can end up at Km 88 or Km 82 on the railway line.

Aguas Calientes » *pp203-209. Colour map 2, A2.*

→ *Phone code: 084.*

Only 1.5 km back along the railway from Puente Ruinas, this is a popular resting place for those recovering from the rigours of the Inca Trail. It is named Aguas Calientes (or just Aguas) after the hot springs above the town. It is also called the town of Machu Picchu. Most activity is centred around the old railway station, on the plaza, or on Avenida Pachacútec, which leads from the plaza to the **thermal baths** ⓘ *10 mins' walk from town, daily 0500-2030. US$3.15.* They consist of a rather smelly communal pool, 10 minutes' walk from the town. You can rent towels and bathing costumes for US$0.65 at several places on the road to the baths. There are basic toilets and changing facilities and showers. Take soap and shampoo and keep an eye on your valuables. The new **Museo Manuel Chávez Ballon** ⓘ *Carretera Hiram Bingham, Wed-Sun 0900-1600, US$6,* displays objects found at Machu Picchu.

The town of Aguas Calientes/Machu Picchu is twinned with Haworth, the birthplace of the Brontë sisters, www.haworth-village.org.uk.

Beyond Machu Picchu » *pp203-209.*

The lower reaches of the Río Urubamba beyond Machu Picchu are the gateway to regions that are very different from the highlands of Cuzco, yet intimately linked to it by history. The most important town is Quillabamba, from where you can set out to the mysterious last stronghold of the Incas, Vilcabamba, or to the Pongo de Mainique, frequently described as one of the most beautiful places on earth.

Ins and outs

As no trains run beyond Aguas Calientes, the only route to Quillabamba is by road from Cuzco via Ollantaytambo. Beyond here, there are buses to Ivochote, for boats down river, and to Huancacalle for the hike to Vilcabamba. After leaving Ollantaytambo, the road passes through Peña, a place of great beauty. Once out of **Peña**, the road climbs on endless zigzags, offering breathtaking views, to reach the **Abra Málaga Pass**, just below the beautiful glaciated peak of Verónica. At Chaullay, the road meets the old railway to Quillabamba, Machu Picchu and Cuzco and continues up the east bank of the river.

Quillabamba and around → *Colour map 2, A2.*

La Ciudad de Eterno Verano (The City of Eternal Summer), as it is known, was once a prosperous town from the sale of coffee. It has now become the overnighting spot for people going to Vilcabamba, Espíritu Pampa and the Pongo de Mainique. This delightful market town survives on the export of fruit, coffee, honey and other produce to Cuzco. The tourist season is from June to July, when Peruvian holidaymakers descend on the place. Although Quillabamba has plenty to offer, it's normally overlooked because of the incredibly bumpy, but beautiful ride to get there.

For the weary traveller one of the biggest attractions, about 1.5 km from Quillabamba, is **Sambaray** ⓘ *US$0.20, transport by combi costs US$0.20, taxi US$0.60*, a recreation area with an outdoor swimming pool, restaurant, volleyball and football field. As Sambaray is situated on the Río Alto Urubamba, you can also swim in the river, or, if you're feeling brave, tube down it. Ask locals for the best place

Aguas Calientes

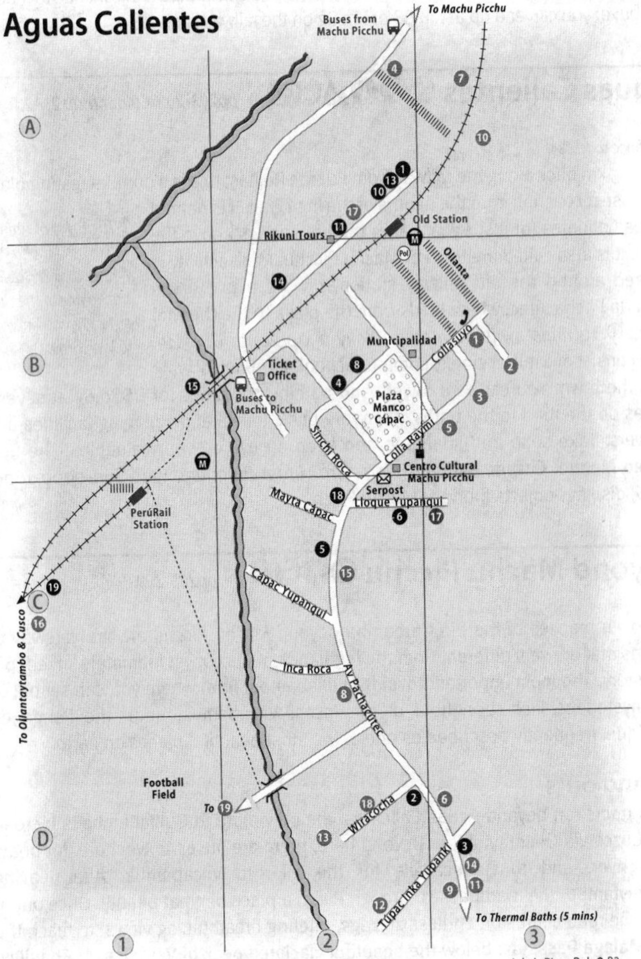

Sleeping
Gringo Bill's (Hostal Q'oñi Unu) **3** *B3*
Hatuchay Tower **4** *A2*
Hospedaje Inca Tambo **1** *B3*
Hospedaje Las Bromelias **5** *B3*
Hospedaje Quilla **6** *D3*
Hostal Continental **7** *A3*
Hostal Don Guiller & Pizzería El Candamo **8** *C2*
Hostal Ima Sumac **9** *D3*
Hostal Los Caminantes **10** *A3*
Hostal Pachakúteq **11** *D3*
Hostal Samana Wasi **12** *D2*
Hostal Wiracocha Inn **13** *D2*
Jardín Real **18** *D2*
La Cabaña **14** *D3*
Las Orquídeas **19** *D2*
Machu Picchu Inn **15** *C2*
Machu Picchu Pueblo **16** *C1*
Presidente & Hostal Machu Picchu **17** *A2*
Rupa Wasi **2** *B3*

Eating
Aiko **1** *A2*
Café Inkaterra **19** *C1*
Clave de Sol **2** *D2*
Govinda **3** *D3*
Illary **4** *B2*
Inca Wasi **5** *C2*
Indio Feliz **6** *C2*
Inka's Pizza Pub **8** *B2*
La Chosa Pizzería **10** *A2*
Las Qenas **11** *A2*
Pizzería Samana Wasi 1 **13** *A2*
Pizzería Samana Wasi 2 **14** *B2*
Pueblo Viejo **18** *C2*
Toto's House **15** *B1*

Bars & clubs
Waisicha Pub **17** *C3*

to start, as the river can be quite rapid. **Siete Tinajas** (Seven Small Baths) is a beautiful waterfall some 45 minutes by combi from town (take the bus from Paradero El Grifo, US$1). It is well worth the trip for the photos, although be careful when climbing to the top, as it can be very slippery.

Pongo de Mainique and beyond

Before the Río Urubamba enters the vast plain of the Amazon Basin it carves its way through one last wall of foothills and the result is spectacular. The Pongo de Mainique is a sheer rainforest canyon, hundreds of metres deep with the Urubamba surging through its centre and many small waterfalls tumbling in on either side. The Machiguenga people who live in the area believe this to be a portal to the afterlife. They are, however, very private people and do not take kindly to uninvited strangers; if you wish to visit them on their reserve take someone who has contact with them.

To get to the Pongo de Mainique, take a bus from Quillabamba's northern bus 'terminal' (a dusty outdoor affair with many food stalls and the occasional ticket booth) to **Ivochote**, via a new road into the jungle. The road can be in terrible condition in places. En route you'll pass **Kiteni**, a rapidly expanding jungle town. Ivochote is the end of the road, literally, but it develops a party atmosphere on Saturday, which is market day in the jungle. Due to the **Camisea Natural Gas Project** downriver, boat traffic is fairly intense. *Lanchas* (boats) head downstream early in the morning on most days during the dry season. In the wet season (roughly December to April) the river may be too dangerous to navigate, especially the rapids in the Pongo itself. Depending on your bargaining ability, passage downriver to the Pongo or to the **Casa de los Ugarte** (see Sleeping, page 203) will set you back between US$6 and US$8.50, providing the captain has trading business downstream. Hiring a boat independently will cost a lot

Vilcabamba

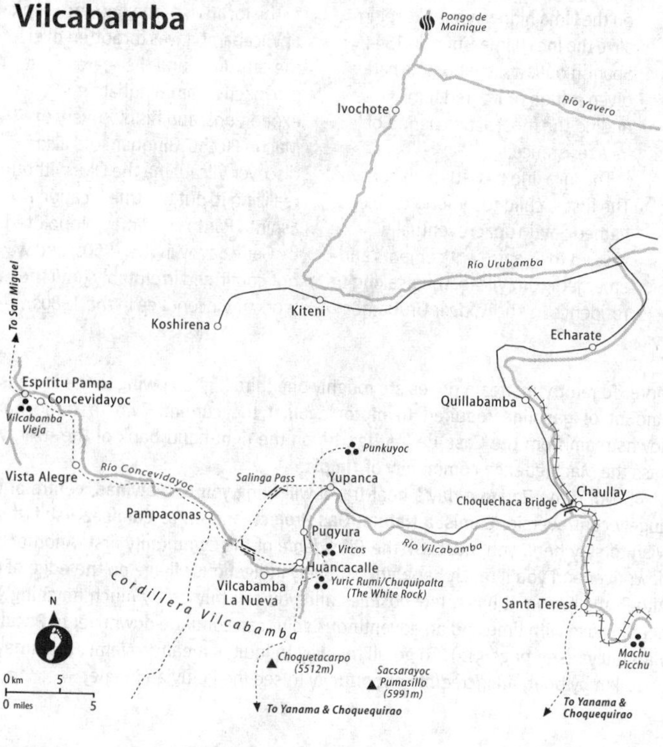

The last Incas of Vilcabamba

After Pizarro killed Atahualpa in 1532, the Inca empire disintegrated rapidly, and it is often thought that native resistance ended there. But, in fact, it continued for 40 more years, beginning with Manco, a teenage half-brother of Atahualpa.

In 1536, Manco escaped from the Spanish and returned to lead a massive army against them. He besieged Cuzco and Lima simultaneously, and came close to dislodging the Spaniards from Peru. Spanish reinforcements arrived and Manco fled to Vilcabamba, a mountainous forest region west of Cuzco that was remote, but still fairly close to the Inca capital, which he always dreamed of recapturing.

The Spanish chased Manco deep into Vilcabamba but he managed to elude them and continued his guerrilla war, raiding Spanish commerce on the Lima highway, and keeping alive the Inca flame. Then, in 1544, Spanish outlaws to whom he had given refuge murdered him, ending the most active period of Inca resistance.

The Inca line passed to his sons. The first, a child too young to rule named Sayri Túpac, eventually yielded to Spanish enticements and emerged from Vilcabamba, taking up residence in Yucay, near Urubamba in 1558. He died mysteriously – possibly poisoned – three years later.

His brother Titu Cusi, who was still in Vilcabamba, now took up the Inca mantle. Astute and determined, he resumed raiding and fomenting rebellion against the Spanish. But in 1570, Titu Cusi fell ill and died. A Spanish priest was accused of murdering him. Anti-Spanish resentment erupted, and the priest and a Spanish viceregal envoy were killed. The Spanish Viceroy reacted immediately, and the Spanish invaded Vilcabamba for the third and last time in 1572.

A third brother, Túpac Amaru, was now in charge. He lacked his brother's experience and acuity, and his destiny was to be the sacrificial last Inca. The Spanish overran the Inca's jungle capital, and dragged him back to Cuzco in chains. There, Túpac Amaru, the last Inca, was publicly executed in Cuzco's main plaza.

The location of the neo-Inca capital of Vilcabamba was forgotten over the centuries, and the search for it provoked Hiram Bingham's expeditions, and his discovery of Machu Picchu. Bingham did also discover Vilcabama the Old, without realizing it, but the true location at Espíritu Pampa was only pinpointed by Gene Savoy in the 1960s, and was not confirmed irrefutably until the work of Vincent Lee in the 1980s.

more. To return upstream prices are roughly one third higher, owing to the increased amount of gasoline required to motor against the current. Two to three hours downstream from the **Casa de los Ugarte,** on the right-hand bank of the river, you pass the Machiguenga community of **Timpia**.

Beyond the Pongo a day's boat travel will bring you to **Malvinas,** centre of the hugely controversial **Camisea Natural Gas Project,** and on to **Camisea** itself. If you wish to stay here, you must ask the *Presidente* of the community first. Another day downriver and you'll reach **Sepahua,** a largely indigenous village on the edge of the Alto Purus region. It has a few *hostales* and you can buy pretty much anything you need. Those with time and an adventurous spirit can continue downriver to **Pucallpa** via Atalaya (see page 512). To go all the way to Iquitos means, overall, a journey of 2500 km by boat, an incredible opportunity to see the Peruvian jungle.

Huancacalle and around

At **Chaullay**, the historic **Choquechaca Bridge**, built on Inca foundations, allows drivers to cross the river to Huancacalle, a two-street village (no restaurants, but a few shops) between four and seven hours from Quillabamba. Huancacalle is the best base for exploring the nearby Inca ruins of Vitcos and is the starting point for the trek to Espíritu Pampa. At **Vitcos** is the palace of the last four Inca rulers from 1536 to 1572, and **Yurac Rumi**, the sacred White Rock of the Incas (also referred to as **Chuquipalta**). The White Rock, once the most sacred site in South America, is very large (8 m high and 20 m wide), with intricate and elaborate carvings. Lichens now cover its whiteness.

You can also hike up to **Vilcabamba La Nueva** from Huancacalle. It's a three-hour walk through beautiful countryside with Inca ruins dotted around. There is a missionary building run by Italians, with electricity and running water, where you may be able to spend the night.

Huancacalle to Espíritu Pampa → *Colour map 2, A1.*

In 1536, three years after the fall of the Inca Empire to the Spanish *conquistadores*, Manco Inca led a rebellion against the conquerors. Retiring from Cuzco when Spanish reinforcements arrived, Manco and his followers fell back to the remote triangle of Vilcabamba, where they maintained the Inca traditions, religion and government outside the reach of the Spanish authorities. Centuries after the eventual Spanish crushing of Inca resistance, it was difficult to locate and identify Manco's capital of Vilcabamba. See box, above.

The trek to Espíritu Pampa from Huancacalle takes three days, but would be a more comfortable undertaking in four. Espíritu Pampa itself is quite a large site, and further groups of buildings may still be awaiting discovery in the densely forested mountains surrounding the valley. Give yourself at least a day at the site to soak up the atmosphere before continuing a further six hours to Chanquiri, the starting point for transport to Kiteni and Quillabamba. The best time of year is from May to November, possibly December. Outside this period it is very dangerous, as the trails are very narrow and can be thick with mud and very slippery. Insect repellent is essential; there are millions of mosquitoes. Also take pain-killers and other basic medicines; these will be much appreciated by the local people should you need to take advantage of their hospitality.

An excellent guide is Jesús Castillo Alveres who can be contacted through the **Hospedaje Sixpac Manco** in Huancacalle (see page 206). Many members of the Cobos family (see page 206) also guide. A good rate of pay for guides/mule drivers is US$5 per day, plus US$5 per mule or horse used. Before you leave be very clear about your exact itinerary and expectations; some guides have been known to leave clients in Espíritu Pampa, half a day's hike from the roadhead in Chanquiri. Always provide sufficient food and a waterproof tent by way of accommodation for your guide on the trail. If you enjoy your trip, give your guide a tip; it will be appreciated. Remember, *arrieros* (mule drivers) based in Huancacalle have to walk all the way back along the route, a journey of at least 2½ days, and for this they don't charge. Always take all plastic and non-biodegradable rubbish back to Cuzco for more efficient disposal. All supplies must be brought from Huancacalle as even basic supplies are scarce on the trail.

Sleeping

Machu Picchu ruins *p191, map p192*

L Machu Picchu Sanctuary Lodge, under the same management as the **Hotel Monasterio** in Cuzco, T084-211039, www.sanctuarylodge.net. This hotel, at the entrance to the ruins, has some environmentally friendly features and will accept American Express TCs at the official rate. The rooms are comfortable, the service is good and the staff helpful. Electricity and water are available 24 hrs a day. Food in the restaurant is well cooked and presented; the restaurant is for residents only in the evening, but the buffet lunch is open to all. The hotel is usually fully booked well in advance; if struggling for a booking try Sun night as other tourists find Pisac market a greater attraction.

The Inca Trail *p197*

G **Youth Hostel**, at Wiñay-Wayna, price per person, with bunk beds, showers and a small restaurant. It is often fully booked. You can sleep on the floor of the restaurant more cheaply, but it is open for diners until 2300. There are also spaces for a few tents, but they get snapped up quickly too. The hostel's door is closed at 1730.

Salkantay treks *p198*

G per person **Hospedaje Mollepata**, Mollepata, T084-832103/832045, or Cuzco 245449. Just above the plaza, behind the solid, elegant church. Hot water electric shower, nice courtyard with café and **ÑanTika** restaurant attached. Swings in the courtyard a real bonus!

Aguas Calientes *p199, map p200*

Some hotels in Aguas Calientes have increased their prices in response to the rising costs of train services and excursions on the Inca Trail. Bargain hard for good-value accommodation and book in advance from Cuzco.

L **Hatuchay Tower**, Ctra Puente Ruinas block 4, T084-211201. This smart, modern hotel is below the old station. Buffet breakfast and all taxes are included. There are standard rooms and luxury suites with hot water.

L **Machu Picchu Pueblo Hotel**, Km 110, T084-211122. Reservations: Jr Andalucía 174, San Isidro, Lima, T01-610 0404; in Cuzco at Plaza las Nazarenas 211, T084-245314, www.inkaterra.com. Beautiful colonial-style bungalows have been built in a village compound surrounded by cloudforest 5 mins' walk along the railway from the town. The hotel has lovely gardens in which there are many species of birds, butterflies and orchids. There is a pool, an expensive restaurant, but also a **campsite** with hot showers at good rates. It offers tours to Machu Picchu, several guided walks on the property and to local beauty spots. The buffet breakfasts for US$12 are great. It also has the **Café Inkaterra** by the railway line. The hotel is involved in a project to rehabilitate spectacled bears and release them back into the wild. Recommended, but there are a lot of steps between the public areas and rooms.

A **Machu Picchu Inn**, Av Pachacútec 101, T084-211057, mapiinn@peruhotel.com.pe. The price includes bathroom and breakfast. A modern hotel, with a functional atmosphere.

B **Presidente**, at the old station, T084-211034 (Cuzco T084-244598), presidente@terra.com.pe. Next to **Hostal Machu Picchu**, see page below, this is the more upmarket half of the establishment. Rooms without river view are cheaper, but the price includes breakfast and taxes. There seems to be only minimal difference between this and **Machu Picchu**, which represents much better value for money.

C **Gringo Bill's (Hostal Q'oñi Unu)**, Colla Raymi 104, T084-211046, gringobills@yahoo.com. Price includes bathroom and continental breakfast. An Aguas Calientes institution, it's friendly, relaxed, with a lot of coming and going, hot water, good beds, luggage store, laundry and money exchange. Good but expensive meals are served in **Villa Margarita** restaurant; breakfast starts at 0530 and they offer a US$4 packed lunch to take up to the ruins.

C **Hostal Pachakúteq**, up the hill beyond Hostal La Cabaña, T084-211061. Rooms with bathroom and 24-hr hot water. Good breakfast is included, quiet, family-run. Recommended.

C **La Cabaña**, Av Pachacútec M20-3, T084-211048. Price includes bathroom and continental breakfast. Rooms have hot water. There is a café, laundry service and a DVD player and TV (with a good selection of movies) for clients in the lounge. The staff are helpful and can provide information on interesting local walks. The hotel is popular with groups.

D **Hostal Ima Sumac**, Av Pachacútec 173, T084-211021. 5 mins before the baths, so quite a climb up from the station. Some of the rooms smell a little damp, but are generally of a reasonable standard; they exchange money.

D **Hostal Machu Picchu**, at the old station, T084-211212. Price includes breakfast and taxes. A clean, functional establishment, which is quiet and friendly (especially Wilber, the owner's son). There is hot water, a nice balcony over the Urubamba, a grocery store and travel information is available. Recommended.

D Rupa Wasi, C Huanacaure 180, T084-211101, http://perucuzco.com/rupawasi/lodge_english.htm. Rustic and charming 'eco-lodge', located up a small alley off Collasuyo. The lodge and its owners have a very laid-back, comfortable style, and there are great views from the balconies of the first-floor rooms. This lodge is slowly adding to its environmentally friendly credentials with purified water available (so you don't have to buy more plastic) and an organic garden and rainwater collector in the pipeline. Great breakfasts for US$3.

D-E Jardín Real, C Wiracocha 7, T084-211234, jardinrealhotel@hotmail.com. A clean, modern hotel with good hot water. At the unofficial price this hotel represents great value, so bargain hard. Same owner as **Pizzería Los Jardines** on Pachacútec.

E Hospedaje Quilla, Av Pachacútec, T084-211009, between Wiracocha and Túpac Inka Yupanki. Price includes breakfast, bath and hot water. They rent bathing gear for the hot springs if you arrive without your costume and towel.

E Hostal Continental, near the old train station, T084-211065. Very clean rooms with good beds, hot showers. This *hostal* was closed for renovation at the time of writing.

E Hostal Don Guiller, Av Pachacútec 136, T084-211145. Price includes breakfast. Rooms have bath and hot water. In the same building is the **Pizzería El Candamo**.

E Hostal Wiracocha Inn, C Wiracocha, T084-211088. Rooms with bath and hot water. Breakfast included. There is a small garden at this very friendly and helpful *hostal*. It's popular particularly with European groups.

E Las Orquídeas, Urb Las Orquideas A-8, T084-211171. From Av Pachacútec, cross the bridge over the river to the football pitch and follow the small dirt path on the right. Rooms have bath and hot water and are clean. This is a quiet, pleasant place away from the main part of town.

E-F Hospedaje Inca Tambo, C Huana-caure s/n, T084-211135, hostalinkatambo@ latin mail.com. Basic but clean, situated just below **Rupa Wasi** (above); negotiate.

E-F Hospedaje Las Bromelias, Colla Raymi, T084-211145. Just off the plaza before Gringo Bill's, this is a small place which has rooms with bath and hot water. Accommodation is cheaper without bath.

F Hostal Los Caminantes, Av Imperio de los Incas 140, by the railway just beyond the old station, T084-211007. Price per person for a room with bathroom. Hot water but breakfast extra. Basic but friendly and clean.

G Hostal Samana Wasi, C Túpac Inka Yupanki, T084-211170, quillavane@hotmail.com. Price includes bath and 24-hr hot water. There are cheaper rooms without bath at this friendly, pleasant place.

Camping

The only official campsite is in a field by the river, just below Puente Ruinas station. Do not leave your tent and belongings unattended.

Quillabamba *p199*

E Hostal Quillabamba, Prolongación y M Grau, just behind the main market, T084-281369, hostalquillabamba@latinmail.com. Highly kitsch design, one of the largest hostels in Quillabamba, all rooms have private bath, TV (local channels only) and telephone, swimming pool (which occasionally has water in it), restaurant, parking. Less appealing is the small zoo. They also have a cockfighting school for the championship, which is held every year in late Jul.

F Hostal Alto Urubamba, Jr 2 de Mayo 333, T084-281131, altourub@ec-red.com. Rooms with shared bath cheaper. Spotlessly clean, pleasant hotel, 1 block from the Plaza de Armas. Staff are friendly and knowledge-able. Small local restaurant attached and there are great views over the town from the roof. Highly recommended.

F Hostal Don Carlos, Jr Libertad 566, T084-281371. Clean and simple, all rooms have private shower with generally hot water. There is a bar and restaurant.

Pongo de Mainique and beyond *p201*

G Hostal Pongo de Mainique, Ivochote, just behind **G Señor de Huanca**, Ivochote, on the right once over the footbridge. The former is the nicer of the 2 *hostales*, although both are basic.

For an explanation of sleeping and eating price codes used in this guide, see inside the front cover. Other relevant information is found in Essentials, pages 53-58.

G Hostal La Casa de los Ugarte, just beyond the Pongo, on the left bank of the river (if heading downstream). The small hacienda of Ida and Abel Ugarte. They are very helpful and will let you camp on their land for a small fee. They have a modest general store and basic supplies, fruit and very fresh eggs are available. The forest behind the hacienda is rich in wildlife and the family may be able to arrange expeditions in the jungle, given time to make the arrangements.
G Hostal Vanessa, Sepahua. On the main street close to the port, very pleasant.

Huancacalle and around *p203*

Villagers will accept travellers in their very basic homes (take a sleeping bag).
G Sixpac Manco, managed by the Cobos family, this hostel is fairly comfortable and has good beds.

Eating

Aguas Calientes *p199, map p200*

Pizza seems to be the most common dish in town, but many of the pizzerías serve other types of food as well. The old station and Av Pachútec are lined with eating places. At the station (where staff will try to entice you into their restaurant), are, among others: **Aiko**, which is recommended; **La Chosa Pizzería**, with pleasant atmosphere, good value; **Las Quenas**, which is a café and a baggage store (US$0.30 per locker); and 2 branches of **Pizzería Samana Wasi**. See under Sleeping, above.
Café Inkaterra, on the railway, just below the **Machu Picchu Pueblo Hotel**. US$15 for a great lunch buffet with scenic views of the river.
Indio Feliz, C Lloque Yupanqui, T084-211090. Great French cuisine, excellent value and service, set 3-course meal for US$10, good *pisco sours*. Highly recommended.
Inka's Pizza Pub, on the plaza. Good pizzas, changes money and accepts TCs. Next door is **Illary**, which is popular.
Inca Wasi, Av Pachacútec. A very good place to eat.
Pueblo Viejo, Av Pachacútec, near the plaza. Good food in a spacious but warm environment. Price includes salad bar.
Toto's House, Av Imperio de los Incas, on the railway line. Same owners as **Pueblo Viejo**. Good value and quality *menú*.
Clave de Sol, Av Pachacútec 156. Same owner as **Chez Maggy** in Cuzco, serving Italian food for about US$4, changes money, also has a vegetarian menu, open 1200-1500, 1800-whenever.
Govinda, Av Pachacútec y Túpac Inka Yupanki. Vegetarian restaurant with a cheap set lunch. Recommended.

Quillabamba *p199*

Quillabamba's a great place for freshly squeezed fruit juices – head for the 2nd floor in the main market. **Gabbi's Juice Stall**, on the far right-hand side, is especially good.
El Gordito, on Espinar. A good place for chicken.
Pizzería Venecia, Jr Libertad 461, on the Plaza de Armas, T084-281582. Decent pizza, delivery available.
Pub Don Sebas, Jr Espinar 235 on Plaza de Armas. Good, great sandwiches, run by Karen Molero who is very friendly and always ready for a chat.

Bars and clubs

Aguas Calientes *p199, map p200*

Waisicha Pub, C Lloque Yupanqui. For good music and atmosphere.

Activities and tours

Aguas Calientes *p199, map p200*

Horacio Edwin Rodríguez, of Centro Andino Machu Picchu, T084-975 1377 (mob), www.centroandinomachupicchu.com. Speaks English and Spanish, tours of the site, also specializes in astrological topics.
Rikuni Tours, at the old station, Av Imperio de los Incas 123, Aguas Calientes, T084-211036, rikuni@chaski.unsaac.edu.pe. Nydia is very helpful. They change money, have a postal service and sell postcards, maps and books (expensive).
Tambo Tours, 20919 Coral Bridge Lane, Suite 225-A, Spring, TX, 77388, USA, T 1-888-2-GO-PERU (246-7378) T001-281 528 9448, www.2GOPERU.com. See page 168.
Ecotrek Peru, Pongo de Mainique, see page 163, run tours in the region.

Transport

Aguas Calientes *p199, map p200*
Bus
To **Machu Picchu** every 30 mins from 0630 to 1300, US$12 return, US$6 single, valid for 48 hrs. Buses return from the ruins 1200-1730. It is also possible to take a bus down 0700-0900. The ticket office is opposite the bus stop, which is 50 m from the railway station. Tickets can also be bought in advance at **Consetur**, Santa Catalina Ancha, Cuzco, which saves queuing when you arrive in Aguas Calientes.

Train
See box, page 208.

Quillabamba *p199*
Bus
Most buses leave **Cuzco** for Quillabamba from the Terminal Terrestre de Santiago between 1800 and 2000. Journey time is about 8 hrs, although expect 14 hrs or more in the rainy season, because of landslides. 4 bus companies on this route are: **Valle de los Incas**, T084-244787, **Ben Hur**, T084-229193, **Ampay**, T084-245734, and **Selva Sur**, T084-247975. **Selva Sur** has 2 buses on the route, one of which is quite comfortable, with good reclining seats, perhaps the best bus for the journey. Buy tickets in advance, US$4. Ampay also runs from **Ollantaytambo** to Quillabamba. The bus station in Quillabamba is on Av 28 de Julio and buses depart for **Cuzco** daily, with buses leaving in the morning around 0700 and evening. There are extra services at weekends.

From **Quillabamba** buses take 10 hrs to reach **Ivochote** and cost around US$4. Ask locals for their opinions on the best companies for this route. Buses (combis) leave Quillabamba for **Huancacalle** daily from Jr San Martín, near Plaza Grau, at 0900

Travelling by train to Machu Picchu

There are two classes of tourist train: **Vistadome** and **Backpacker**. Note that timetables and prices are subject to frequent change. Tickets for all trains should be bought at Wanchac station in Cuzco, Av Pachacútec, or via PerúRail's website, www.perurail.com. Services other than those listed here are run entirely at the discretion of PerúRail.

PerúRail trains leave from San Pedro station in Cusco and pass through Poroy and Ollantaytambo en route to Aguas Calientes (the official name of this station is Machu Picchu).

From Cuzco

Vistadome (US$66 single, US$113 return) departs San Pedro station daily at 0600 and 0700, arriving Aguas Calientes (Machu Picchu) at 0940 and 1100. It returns from Machu Picchu at 1530 and 1700, reaching Cuzco at 1920 and 2125.

Backpacker (US$46 single, US$73 return) departs San Pedro station daily at 0615 reaching Aguas Calientes at 1015. It returns at 1555, getting to Cuzco at 2020. If you do not want to arrive in Cuzco in the dark (especially if you have no hotel booked), ask to get off the train at Poroy and take a bus from there. This saves about an hour.

Hiram Bingham (US$535 return) is a super-luxury train with dining car and bar. It leaves Poroy (west of Cuzco) at 0900 with brunch on board, reaching Aguas Calientes at 1230. It leaves Aguas Calientes at 1800, cocktails, dinner and live entertainment on board, arriving in Poroy at 2125 with a bus service back to Cuzco hotels. The cost includes all meals, buses and entry to the ruins.

From Urubamba

Sacred Valley Railway Vistadome (US$46 single, US$77 return) departs Urubamba at 0610, reaching Aguas Calientes at 0820. The return service leaves at 1645, reaching Urubamba at 1915. You must reserve seats 10 days in advance. Several hotels in Urubamba and Yucay offer free transport to and from the station in Urubamba. (Always check in advance that this train is running; it was not in Aug 2006, but the PerúRail website includes it.)

and 1200, US$2.50. The journey takes 4-7 hrs. On Fri they go all the way to **Vilcabamba La Nueva**.

Pongo de Mainique and beyond *p201*

Boat

For boats beyond Ivochote, you may have to wait a few days for a boat downstream, but try to get as far as Bajo Pongo or **Timpia**, 4 hrs, US$10. It's a further 4 hrs, US$10 to **Camisea**. After **Sepahua** boats are larger, boats more frequent and distances greater. To **Atalaya** you can take an express, 10 hrs, US$15, or a delivery boat, up to 2 days. From here boats go to **Pucallpa**.

Espíritu Pampa *p203*

From Chanquiri, at the end of the Espíritu Pampa trail, trucks and buses leave for **Kiteni** and **Quillabamba**, Wed and Sun, 8-12 hrs, US$2.50.

Directory

Aguas Calientes *p199, map p200*

Banks There are several ATMs in town.

Internet Many internet shops, average price US$1 per hr; slow connection.

Post Serpost agencies, just off the plaza, between the Centro Cultural Machu Picchu and Galería de Arte Tunupa, and on the

Ollantaytambo Vistadome (US$46 single, US$77 return) leaves Ollantaytambo at 0705, 1030 and 1455, and returning from Aguas Calientes at 0835, 1320 and 1645; journey time 1 hr 20 mins. Tickets include food in the price. These trains have toilets, video, snacks and drinks for sale.

Ollantaytambo Backpacker Shuttle (US$57 return; no one-way tickets) only runs 1 Apr to 31 Oct, departing at 0905, arriving at 1100, returning from Aguas Calientes at 1620, reaching Ollantaytambo at 1800. Seats can be reserved even if you're not returning the same day.

There is also a cheap, unscheduled Backpacker train from Ollantaytambo (US$20 single, US$40 return), leaving at 2000, arriving in Aguas Calientes at 2120, returning from Aguas at 0545 the following morning and arriving in Ollantaytambo at 0740. Tickets can be bought 1-2 days in advance (and they sell out fast); but check on the train's existence at the time of travel as it is not included on regular timetables. Note that, if you use this service, you will have to spend two nights in Aguas Calientes if you want to see Machu Picchu.

Local trains

Tourists are not permitted to travel on the local train from Cuzco to Machu Picchu, but you can board the local train from the station at Hidroeléctrica. This can be combined with local buses and walking for a cheap route to Machu Picchu as follows: take a bus from Cuzco towards Quillabamba at 1900, US$4. Get out at Santa María where minibuses wait to go to Santa Teresa, 2 hrs, US$1.50. You reach Santa Teresa by sunrise in time to buy breakfast. Walk 6 km to the Central Hidroeléctrica on a nice, flat road or hitch a ride on a workers' truck, US$0.60. From the Hidroeléctrica train station it's 40 mins on the local train to Aguas Calientes at 1520 (US$1.50 for tourists), or you can walk along the railway in 2-3 hrs. To return, leave Aguas Calientes at 0600 to walk to Santa Teresa, where you catch the 1000 bus to Santa María, arriving at 1200. At 1300 take a bus to Cuzco, arriving around 1900-2000. Or take the local train from Aguas Calientes to Santa Teresa at 1210, stay in a hostal, then take the 1000 bus to Santa María.

railway line. **Telephone** Oficina on C Collasuyo, and there are plenty of phone booths around town. The town has electricity 24 hrs a day.

Quillabamba *p199*
Banks BCP, Jr Libertad, good for TCs. Banco Continental, Av F Bolognesi, accepts Visa and Cirrus. **Internet** Ciber Master, Jr Espinar, plaza.

East of Cuzco

Along or near the main road from Cuzco to Lake Titicaca and Peru's major southern city, Arequipa, are a number of archaeological sites, some fascinating colonial churches, beautiful lakes and the majestic Ausangate massif, where you can do some serious high-altitude trekking. Off this route is also the gateway to Peru's southeastern jungle in the Department of Madre de Dios. ▸▸ *For Sleeping, Eating and other listings, see pages 213-214.*

Ins and outs

A paved road runs southeast from Cuzco to Sicuani, at the southeastern edge of the Department of Cuzco. It continues to Puno, on the shores of Lake Titicaca, then on to the border with Bolivia. Combis run every 15 to 20 minutes between Cuzco and Sicuani, and more frequently to the villages and towns in between.

To Huambutío and Paucartambo

Tipón ruins ⓘ *between Saylla and Oropesa, US$1.80, also on the BTG visitors' ticket, see page 136*, are extensive and include baths, terraces, irrigation systems and a temple complex, accessible from a path leading from just above the last terrace, all in a fine setting. From Tipón village it's an hour's climb to the ruins; or take a taxi. At the Tipón ruins, if you head to the left at the back, there is a trail round to where you will see more small ruins. From there you will find an amazing Inca road with a deep irrigation channel, which can be followed to Cerro Pachatusan. Nearby, **Oropesa** is known as the national capital of bread; try the delicious circular loaves.

At **Huambutío**, north of Huacarpay, the road divides: northwest to Pisac (see page 178) and north to Paucartambo, on the eastern slope of the Andes. The road from Huambutío northwest to Pisac (about 20 km) is unpaved and poor. This is an access road for the first river-rafting section on the Río Urubamba, which also connects with another rafting route from Piñipampa. In the rainy season, and for less experienced rafters, the Huambutío (Piñipampa) to Pisac river section is safer to run. The rafting trip is 30 to 35 km long with spectacular views of the Urubamba valley that are not seen in a conventional valley tour. This part of the river offers views of the **Sanctuary of El Señor de Huanca**, an image painted on a rock around which the church has been built. The rock and surroundings date back to pre-Inca times as a *huaca*, or sacred place. The month of pilgrimage to El Señor de Huanca is September, with the 14th being the main day.

Paucartambo

This once remote town, 80 km east of Cuzco, is on the road to Pilcopata, Atalaya and Shintuya. This is now the overland route used by tour companies from Cuzco into Manu National Park (see page 548). Consequently, it has become a popular tourist destination. It has a famous 17th-century stone bridge, built on the orders of King Carlos III of Spain. From Paucartambo, in the dry season, you can go 44 km to **Tres Cruces**, along the Pilcopata road, turning left after 25 km. Tres Cruces gives a wonderful view of the sunrise in June and July: peculiar climactic conditions make it appear as if three suns are rising. Tour operators in Cuzco, see page 162, can arrange transport and lodging.

Piquillacta Archaeological Park

ⓘ *Daily 0700-1730, US$1.80 or by BTG visitors' ticket, see page 136. Buses to Urcos from Av Huáscar, Cuzco drop you at the north side entrance, though this is not the official entry.*
The Piquillacta Archaeological Park is 30 km southeast of Cuzco, with an area of 3421 ha. Its nucleus is the remains of a lake, the Laguna de Huacarpay, around which are many pre-Columbian archaeological remains, the principal of which are Piquillacta and Rumicolca. The lake is a favourite birdwatching destination and it's good to hike or cycle round it. The Huari ruins of **Piquillacta** (which translates as the City of Fleas) are large, with some reconstruction in progress. It was an administrative centre at the southern end of the Huari Empire. The whole site is surrounded by a wall, encompassing many enclosed compounds with buildings of over one storey; it appears that the walls were plastered and finished with a layer of lime.

The huge gateway of **Rumicolca** is on the right of the main road to Sicuani, shortly after the turn-off to Piquillacta. You can walk around it for free. This was a Huari aqueduct, built across this narrow stretch of the valley, which the Incas clad in fine stonework to create this gateway. If you look at the top you can see the original walls, four tiers high.

Andahuaylillas

Continuing southeast towards Urcos you reach Andahuaylillas, 32 km from Cuzco, with a fascinating 17th-century church. This is a simple structure, but it has been referred to as the Andean Sistine Chapel because of its beautiful frescoes, and internal architecture. Go in and wait for your eyes to adjust to the darkness, in order to see, on the right of the splendid door, the path to heaven, which is narrow and thorny, and, on the left, the way to hell, which is wide and littered with flowers. Above is the high choir, built in local wood, where there are two organs. The carved ceiling is painted, too. The main altar is gilded in 24-carat gold leaf and has symbols from both the Quechua and Christian religions. Ask for Sr Eulogio; he is a good guide, but speaks Spanish only.

Huaro and Urcos

At the quiet village of Huaro, the church on the ugly plaza is stunning inside. The walls are plastered with frescoes used to evangelize the illiterate. Grinning skeletons compete with dragons and devils ushering the living into the afterlife and punishing them thereafter. They are now mostly in a sad state of repair. Beyond Huaro is **Urcos**. There are lodgings here, but they're basic to say the least. A spectacular road from Urcos crosses the Eastern Cordillera to Puerto Maldonado in the jungle (see page 551).

Cordillera Vilcanota → *Colour map 2, B4.*

East of Cuzco lies the **Cordillera Vilcanota**, the greatest concentration of mountains and glaciers in southern Peru. With at least four great peaks towering above 6000 m in densely packed icy masses, this area is reminiscent of the Cordillera Huayhuash further to the north. Viewed from the ruins of Sacsayhuaman above Cuzco, **Ausangate**, at 6384 m the range's loftiest member, is impressive even from a distance of nearly 100 km, but in the Vilcanota mountains Ausangate is just the beginning. Unlike both the Cordilleras of Vilcabamba and Urubamba, which plunge precipitously from sheer glaciers into lush subtropical valleys, the Vilcanota rises from the northern *altiplano*; treks into the region rarely, if ever, drop below 4000 m. Life is harsh for the communities who live in the shadow of these great peaks. Knowledge of Spanish is often limited or non-existent and the people's respect for ancient ways and the power of the *apus* (mountain spirits), runs strong. Survival is eked from a meagre diet of potatoes, *cuy* (guinea pig) and the meat and wool of the large herds of domesticated llamas and alpacas that roam the valleys.

The road to Puerto Maldonado Some 82 km from Urcos, at the base of Nevado Ausangate, is the town of **Ocongate**, which has two hotels on the Plaza de Armas. The small town of **Tinqui**, further east, is the traditional starting point for treks into the region and is a good place to find local guides and *arrieros* (mule drivers). Forty-seven kilometers after passing the snow-line **Hualla-Hualla pass**, at 4820 m, the super-hot thermal baths of **Marcapata** ⓘ *173 km from Urcos, US$0.10*, provide a relaxing break. Beyond this point, what is arguably the most spectacular road in Peru descends the eastern flank of the Andes towards Puerto Maldonado (see page 552).

Ausangate circuit This is the most popular trekking route and involves four-to-six days of fairly tough hiking around the peak itself, featuring icy mountain vistas, high passes (including two over 5000 m) and some beautiful turquoise lakes. As an added bonus, there are two geothermal springs, **Upis** and **Pacchanta**, to thaw out in at the beginning and end! In addition to 'The Circuit' there is a great variety of other options, including treks around the range's northern peaks and routes to the magnificent **Laguna Sibinacocha**, a stunning 15-km long lake set at 4800 m in remote territory to the east of Ausangate.

A standard fee for locals hired independently is US$7 per day for an *arriero* a US$6 per horse per day. You are also expected to provide sufficient food and a tent fo the *arriero*. Tiofilo is a recommended guide/*arriero* who can contacted through Tinqui's radio station, located just of the town's main plaza. The **IGN** 1:100,000 Ocongate map (available at **South American Explorers** in Cuzco) covers all trekking areas described below and is fairly accurate. Note that as you leave Tinqui you will be charged a community fee for using the Ausangate trail; at the time of writing this was S/.10 per person (US$3).

Acomayo and the Inca bridge

Between Cusipata and **Checacupe** a road branches west, soon becoming a dirt road. At the first fork, just before a beautiful mountain lake, **Lago Pomancanchi**, turn right to travel past a small community and on to **Acomayo**, a pretty village which has a chapel with mural paintings of the 14 Incas. From Acomayo, you can walk to the canyons of the upper Apurímac, vast beyond imagination, and to Inca ruins in astonishing locations.

If you turn left at Lago Pomancanchi the road passes three more beautiful lakes. Stop awhile by the fourth. Set against the pale green grass banks, serene waters reflect the red soil of the hills behind. The only sound is the occasional splash and hoot of a white-beaked Andean coot. The air is thin, clear and crisp.

The road continues to **Yanaoca**, where you'll find basic accommodation and restaurants. From here it is possible to continue on to Sicuani, but a side trip to **Qeswachaka** and the grass Inca bridge 30 km away is well worth the effort. Turn right just before you leave the village to join a road which, at times, is very rough. The way is marked with kilometre signs and you must turn right just after Km 22 where another road begins, marked with a Km 0. You will find steps down to the bridge shortly before Km 31, two bends from the bright orange road bridge. The footbridge has been rebuilt every year for the past 400 years during a three-day festival. This starts on 10 June and is celebrated by the three communities who use the bridge. It is built entirely of *pajabrava* grass, woven and spliced to make six sturdy cables which are strung across the 15-m chasm. The work lasts five months, after which the fibres deteriorate and you should not attempt to cross.

Raqchi → *Colour map 2, B4.*

ⓘ *Entrance to the site is US$1.80. There is a basic shop at the site.*

About 120 km southeast of Cuzco, in a fertile tributary valley of the Vilcanota, is the colonial village of **San Pedro de Cacha**, which stands within one of the most important archaeological sites in Peru, Raqchi. A few hundred metres beyond the village are the principal remains, the once great **Temple of Viracocha**, the pan-Andean creator of all living creatures. This is one of the only remaining examples of a two-storey building of Inca architecture. It was 90 m long and 15 m high and was probably the largest roofed building ever built by the Incas. Above walls of finely dressed masonry 3-4 m high rise the remains of another 5-6 m high wall of adobe brickwork of which only isolated sections remain. Similarly, of the 22 outer columns, which supported great sloping roofs, just one or two remain complete, the others being in various states of preservation. There are numerous other constructions, including *acllahuasi* (houses of chosen women), granaries, reservoirs, baths and fountains. The burial site includes round *chullpa* tombs of the sort found around Lake Titicaca. Much of it was damaged and demolished in search of treasure during or after the Spanish conquest.

Sicuani → *Phone code: 084. Colour map 2, B4. Altitude: 3690 m.*

Sicuani is an important agricultural centre and an excellent place for items of llama and alpaca wool and skins. They are sold at the railway station and at the excellent Sunday morning market. Around the plaza are several shops selling local hats. For places between Sicuani and Juliaca, see page 236.

Sleeping

Andahuaylillas *p211*

F La Casa del Sol, close to the central plaza on Garcilaso. Relaxing, clean and bright *hostal*. Well-decorated rooms set around a courtyard, this is excellent value. Owned by Dr Gladys Oblitas, the *hostal* funds her project to provide medical services to poor *campesinos*. While staying you can take a course or take part in workshops on natural and alternative medicine.

Cordillera Vilcanota *p211*

G Ausangate, Tinqui, very basic but warm, friendly atmosphere. Sr Crispin (or Cayetano), the owner, is knowledgeable and can arrange guides, mules, etc. He and his brothers can be contacted in Cuzco on F084-227768. All have been recommended as reliable sources of trekking and climbing information, for arranging trips and for being very safety conscious.
G Hostal Tinqui Guide, on the right-hand side as you enter the village, friendly, meals available, owner arranges guides and horses.

Acomayo and the Inca bridge *p212*

There are many places to camp wild by the lakes. Take warm clothing for night time and plenty of water. At **Qeswachaca** there's good camping downstream, but take water.

Sicuani *p212*

F Hotel Obada, Jr Tacna 104, T084-351214. At the new end of the bridge, close to the centre of town. Has seen better days. There are large, clean rooms with hot showers.
F Royal Inti, Av Centenario 116, T084-352730, on the west side of the old pedestrian bridge across the river. Modern, clean and friendly.
F Samariy, Av Centenario 138 (next to Royal Inti), T084-352518. Offers good-value rooms with bathrooms.
G per person **José's Hostal**, Av Arequipa 143, T084-351254. Rooms with bath, clean and good.

Eating

Sicuani *p212*

El Fogón, C Zevallos, the main drag down from the plaza, smart, painted pink, on the left heading down. Serves up good chicken and chips for US$1.70.
Mijuna Wasi, Jr Tacna 146 . Closed Sun. One of several *picanterías* which prepares typical dishes such as *adobo* served with huge glasses of *chicha* in a dilapidated but atmospheric courtyard. Recommended.
Pizzería Bon Vino, 2 de Mayo 129, 2nd floor, off the east side of the plaza, is good for an Italian meal.

Festivals and events

Paucartambo *p210*

15-17 Jul The Fiesta of the Virgen del Carmen is a major attraction and well worth seeing. Masked dancers enact rituals and folk tales in the streets.

Acomayo and the Inca bridge *p212*

10 Jun A 3-day festival is celebrated for the rebuilding of the grass Inca footbridge at Qeswachaka.

Raqchi *p212*

24-29 Jun Start of the **Wiracocha** festivities in San Pedro and neighbouring San Pablo. Dancers come to Raqchi from all over Peru and through music and dance they illustrate everything from the ploughing of fields to bull fights. This leads into the feast of **San Pedro and San Pablo** on 29 Jun.

Transport

Paucartambo *p210*

Private car hire for a round trip from Cuzco on 15-17 Jul costs US$30. Tour operators in Cuzco can arrange this. A minibus leaves for Paucartambo from Av Huáscar in Cuzco, every other day, US$4.50, 3-4 hrs; alternate days Paucartambo–Cuzco. Trucks and a private bus leave from the Coliseo, behind Hospital Segura in Cuzco, 5 hrs, US$2.50.

Andahuaylillas *p211*

To Andahuaylillas take a taxi, or the **Oropesa** bus from Av Huáscar in Cuzco, via Tipón, Piquillacta and Rumicolca.

Huaro and Urcos *p211*

Transportes Vilcanota depart from the terminal on Av de la Cultura, Cuzco, at the Paradero Hospital Regional (on a side street), and run to **San Jerónimo**, **Saylla**, **Huasao**,

Tipón, Oropesa, Piquillacta/ Huacarpay, Andahuaylillas and on to **Urcos**. These buses run 0500-2100, fare US$0.75 to Urcos.

Cordillera Vilcanota *p211*
Buses leave for **Tinqui** from C Tomasatito Condemayta, near the Coliseo Cerrado in Cuzco, Mon-Sat 1000, 6-7 hrs, US$3.50.

Acomayo and the Inca bridge *p212*
To get to **Acomayo**, take a combi from Cuzco to Sicuani (US$1.25, 1½ hrs), then a truck or bus to Acomayo (3 hrs, US$1). Alternatively, get off at Checacupe and take a truck on to Acomayo. To visit the 4 beautiful mountain lakes and Inca bridge, it would be worthwhile renting a 4WD for 2 days. Giving locals a lift is both fun and helpful – they will make sure you take the right road. Alternatively, hire a vehicle with a driver. It is just as feasible by combi, if you have more time. The bridge can also be reached from **Combapata** on the main Cuzco–Sicuani road. Combis and *colectivos* leave for the 30-km trip when full from the plaza for **Yanaoca** (US$0.50). Then hitchhike to **Quehue** (no accommodation), a 1½-hr walk from Qeswachaka, or to **Qeswachaka** itself, on the road to Livitaca. Be prepared for long waits on this road. On Wed and Sat there are direct buses to **Livitaca** from Cuzco with the **Warari** and **Olivares** companies which pass the site, returning on Mon and Thu.

Raqchi *p212*
There are frequent combis to and from **Cuzco** on the Sicuani route, or you can take the train.

Sicuani *p212*
Combis run every 15-20 mins between **Cuzco** and Sicuani (137 km, US$1.25). It is 250 km to **Puno**. 38 km beyond the town is La Raya pass (4321 m), the highest on this route, which marks the divide between Cuzco Department and the *altiplano* which stretches to Lake Titicaca. It is impossible to buy unleaded petrol in this town.

West of Cuzco

West of Cuzco is the road to Abancay (195 km from Cuzco), where the principal overland route to Lima, via Nazca, heads west and another road continues through the highlands to Ayacucho. There are enough Inca sites on or near this road in the Department of Cuzco to remind us that the empire's influence spread to all four cardinal points. Add to this some magnificent scenery, especially in the canyon of the Río Apurímac, and you have the makings of some fascinating excursions away from the centre. One, to the ruins of Choquequirao, is a tough but rewarding trip; getting there requires an expedition of four days or more. » *For Sleeping, Eating and other listings, see page 216.*

Anta to Curahuasi → *Colour map 2, B2.*

The Cuzco–Machu Picchu train follows the road west from the city through the Anta canyon for 10 km, and then, at a sharp angle, the Urubamba canyon, and descends along the river valley, flanked by high cliffs and peaks. In the town of **Anta**, felt trilby hats are on sale.

Some 76 km from Cuzco, beyond Anta on the Abancay road, and 2 km before Limatambo, are the ruins of **Tarahuasi** ⓘ *US$1.80*. A few hundred metres from the road there is a very well-preserved Inca temple platform, with 28 tall niches, and a long stretch of fine polygonal masonry. The ruins are impressive, enhanced by the orange lichen which give the walls a beautiful honey colour. It was near here that the *conquistadores*, en route to the Inca capital of Cuzco, suffered what could have been a major setback. Had it not been for the arrival of Spanish reinforcements, they may well have been routed by the Inca army at Vilcaconga.

One hundred kilometres from Cuzco along the Abancay road is the exciting descent into the **Apurímac Canyon**, near the former Inca suspension bridge that inspired Thornton Wilder's *The Bridge of San Luis Rey* (see Books page 615). The bridge itself was made of rope and was where the royal Inca road crossed the river. When the *conquistadores* reached this point on the march to Cuzco, they found the bridge destroyed. But luck was again on their side since, it being the dry season, the normally fierce Apurímac was low enough for the men and horses to ford. In colonial times the bridge was rebuilt several times, but it no longer exists.

Choquequirao → *Colour map 2, B2.*

ⓘ *Entry US$3.35.*

Choquequirao is another 'lost city of the Incas', built on a ridge spur almost 1600 m above the Apurímac. Its Inca name is unknown, but research has shown that it was built during the reign of Inca Pachacútec. Although only 30% has been uncovered, it is believed to be a larger site than Machu Picchu, but with fewer buildings. The stonework is different from the classic Inca construction and masonry, simply because the preferred granite and andesite are not found in this region. A number of high-profile explorers and archaeologists, including Hiram Bingham, researched the site, but its importance has only recently been recognized. And now tourists are venturing in there, too. The introduction of regulations to cut congestion on the Inca Trail promoted Choquequirao as a replacement for the traditional hike. At the time of writing the authorites had not increased the entry cost or imposed rules to prevent independent trekking.

The main features of Choquequirao include the **Lower Plaza**, considered by most experts to be the focal point of the city. Three of the main buildings were two-storey structures. The **Upper Plaza**, reached by a huge set of steps or terraces, has what are possibly ritual baths. A beautiful set of slightly curved agricultural terraces run for over 300 m east-northeast of the Lower Plaza. The **usnu** is a levelled hilltop platform, ringed with stones and giving awesome 360° views. Perhaps it was a ceremonial site, or was used for solar and astronomical observations. The Ridge Group, still shrouded in vegetation, is a large collection of buildings some 50 to 100 m below the *usnu*. Unrestored, with some significant hall-like structures, this whole area makes for great exploring. The **Outlier Building**, isolated and surrounded on three sides by sheer drops of over 1.5 km into the Apurímac Canyon, possesses some of the finest stonework within Choquequirao. The significance of this building's isolation from other structures remains a mystery, like so many other questions regarding the Incas and their society. **Capuliyoc**, nearly 500 m below the Lower Plaza, is a great set of agricultural terraces, visible on the approach from the far side of the valley. These terraces enabled the Incas to cultivate plants from a significantly warmer climate in close geographical proximity to their ridge-top home. Recently uncovered are further terraces decorated with llamas in white stone; ask if they are open to the public.

Cachora to Choquequirao There are three ways to reach Choquequirao; none is a gentle stroll. The shortest way is from **Cachora,** a village in a magnificent location on the south side of the Apurímac, reached by a side road from the Cuzco–Abancay highway, near Saywite (see page 503). It is four hours by bus from Cuzco to the turn-off, then a two-hour descent from the road to Cachora (from 3695 m to 2875 m). Combis run from Abancay to Cachora. Accommodation, guides (Celestino Peña is the official guide) and mules are available in Cachora (about US$12 a day for guide and mule).

From Cachora take the road heading down, out of the village, through lush cultivated countryside and meadows. There are many trails close to the village; if uncertain of the trail, ask. After 15 minutes, a sign for Choquequirao points to a left-hand path, initially following the course of a small stream. Follow the trail and cross a footbridge to the other side of a large stream. From here the trail becomes more obvious, with few trails diverging from the main route. After 9 km, two to 2½ hours from the start of the trek, is the wonderful mirador (viewpoint) of **Capuliyoc,** at 2800 m, with fantastic vistas of the Apurímac Canyon and the snowy Vilcabamba range across the river (this also makes a great day-hike from Cachora). With a pair of binoculars it's just possible to recognize

Choquequirao, etched into the forested hills to the west. Condors are sometimes seen in this area. Beyond Capuliyoc the trail begins to descend towards the river. Further down the valley lies **Cocamasana**, a rest spot with a rough covered roof. From this point the river is clearly visible. At Km 16 is **Chiquisca** (1930 m), a lovely wooded spot; if you don't want to continue any further on the first day, this is a good campsite, but ask permission of the local family. Another one-hour descent leads to the suspension bridge crossing the Río Apurímac. On the other side the path ascends very steeply for 1½ hours. **Santa Rosa**, a good area for camping, again near the property of a local family, is just after the Km 21 sign. Clean water is available. If this area is occupied, another larger site is available 10 minutes further up the hill. Ask residents for directions. From Santa Rosa continue uphill on a steep zigzag for two hours to the mirador of **Marampata**, from where the trail flattens out towards Choquequirao. After 1½ hours on this flatter trail you enter some beautiful stretches of cloudforest, before a final short climb and arrival at Choquequirao itself. If coming from Santa Rosa you should have the afternoon free to explore the complex, but you could easily allow an extra day here. To return to Cachora, simply retrace the route, possibly camping at Chiquisca, which would nicely break the two-day return trek.

Other treks The second and third routes take a minimum of eight days and require thorough preparation. Both cross the watershed of the Cordillera Vilcabamba between the Urubamba and Apurímac rivers. The second hike uses the same route from Cachora as the first trek, then continues from Choquequirao to the **Yanama** river valley before continuing to **Santa Teresa** or **Machu Picchu** itself. The third route splits from the second in the Yanama valley and goes to **Huancacalle** (see page 203), via the pass of **Choquetacarpo**, 4600 m high. From Huancacalle it's possible to continue on to **Espíritu Pampa** on the edge of the rainforest (see page 203). Either route can be undertaken in reverse. Both pass the mines of La Victoria and both involve an incredible number of strenuous ascents and descents. En route you are rewarded with fabulous views of the Sacsarayoc massif (also called Pumasillo), Salkantay, other snow peaks, and the deep canyons of the Río Blanco and the Apurímac. You will also see condors and meet very friendly people, but the highlight is Choquequirao itself.

Sleeping

Anta to Curahuasi *p214*

G **Hostal Central**, Jirón Jaquijahuanca 714, Anta. A basic, friendly place with motorbike parking; beware of water shortages.

G **Hostal Rivera**, near the river, at Limatambo. An old stone house built round a courtyard, clean, quiet and full of character.

G **Hostal San Cristóbal**, Curahuasi. Clean, nice decor, pleasant courtyard, shared bath, cold shower (new bathroom block being built).

Camping in Curahuasi is possible on the football pitch, but ask the police for permission.

Choquequirao *p215*

G per person **La Casona de Ocampo**, San Martín 122, Cachora, T084-237514, lacasonadeocampo@yahoo.es. With hot shower all day, free camping, owner Carlos Robles is very friendly and knowledgeable, rents camping equipment, organizes treks to Choquequirao and beyond.

Eating

Anta to Curahuasi *p214*

La Amistad, Curahuasi.The best restaurant in town, popular, with good food and moderate prices, but has poor service.

Restaurant, Limatambo, hidden from the road by trees, is a good option.

Tres de Mayo, Anta. Very good and popular, with top service.

Transport

Choquequirao *p215*

From Cachora to **Abancay**, buses at 0630 and 1100, 2 hrs, US$1.50; also *colectivo* taxis.

Lake Titicaca

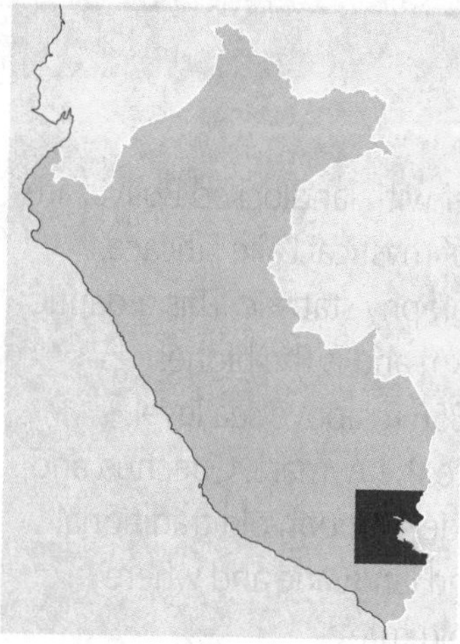

Footprint features

Introduction

Straddling Peru's southern border with landlocked Bolivia are the deep, sapphire-blue waters of mystical Lake Titicaca, everyone's favourite school geography statistic. This gigantic inland sea covers up to 8500 sq km and is the highest navigable lake in the world, at 3856 m above sea level. Its shores and islands are home to the Aymara, Quechua and Uros peoples. Here you can wander through old traditional villages where Spanish is a second language and where ancient myths and beliefs still hold true.

The main town on the lake is Puno, where chilled travellers gather to stock up on warm woollies to keep the cold at bay. The high-altitude town is the departure point for the islands of Taquile and Amantaní, as well as the floating reed islands of Los Uros. But while the latter may not be to everyone's taste, having acquired a reputation for tourism overkill, a trip to Taquile and Amantaní provides a real insight into traditional Andean life, especially during one of the festivals. Apart from the obvious attraction of the lake's islands, Puno is also well placed to visit the remarkable funeral towers of Sillustani. Even if you're feeling a bit ruined-out by this stage in your Peruvian odyssey, Sillustani is well worth the effort. For community-based tourism, the Capachica Peninsula is similar to the islands, but quieter, and you don't have to take a boat to get there. When it is time to move on, there is the beautiful train ride from Puno to Cuzco, and the opportunity to reach the parts of Peru that other travellers rarely get to, by exploring the remote eastern shore of the lake, an area that is only just beginning to welcome curious visitors.

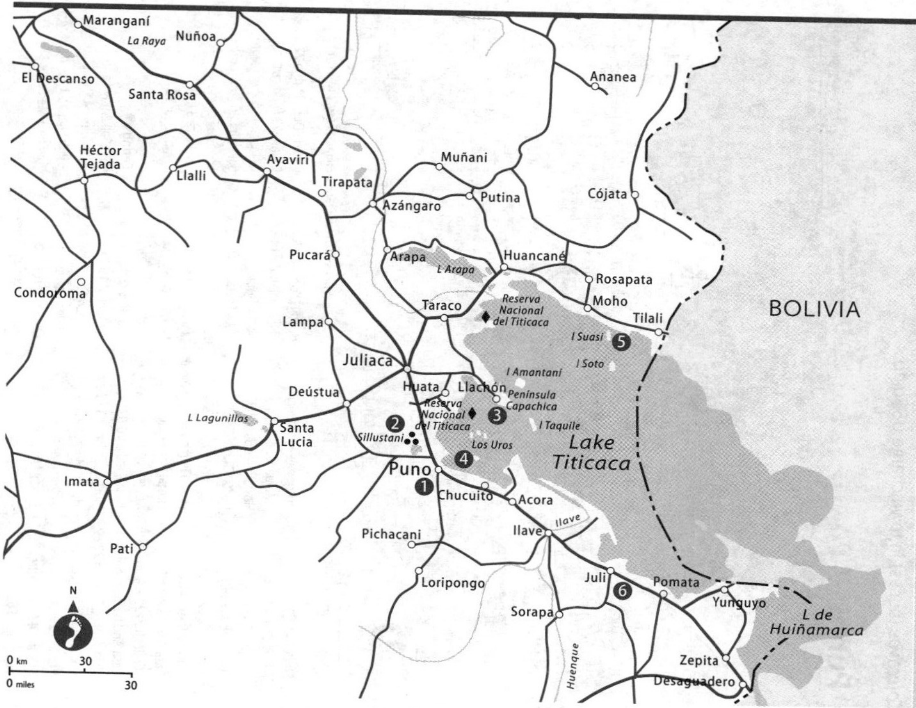

★ Don't miss...

1. **The Yavari** This museum ship, moored near one of Puno's upmarket hotels, is a reminder of how shipping once was on Titicaca, page 222.
2. **Sillustani** Wonder at the architectural quality of the funerary towers, emphasized all the more by the barrenness of the surroundings, page 222.
3. **Capachica** Community tourism has made a great start at the charming villages on this peninsula, which still gives access to some of the lake's better-known attractions, page 223.
4. **Fiesta de la Virgen de la Candelaria** Of the umpteen festivals around the lake, this is deservedly the most famous and one of the best ways to immerse yourself in the extensive folklore of the region, page 231.
5. **Suasi** Watch the sun set from the summit of this island hideaway, whose only building is a hotel, page 238.
6. **Juli and Pomata** These two towns on the western shore have some of the most beautiful churches of the region. They make a good day out from Puno, page 242.

Puno and the islands

→ Colour map 6, B2.

On the northwest shore of Lake Titicaca, at 3855 m, Puno is a major folklore centre and a great place to buy handicrafts, particularly those amazingly tactile alpaca jumpers and hats. It also has a rich tradition of music and dance and is a good place to enjoy a number of Andean festivals, some wild, some solemn. Puno is capital of its department and, while it isn't the most attractive of cities, it has a certain vitality, helped by the fact there is a large student population. ▸▸ *For Sleeping, Eating and other listings, see pages 227-234.*

Ins and outs

Getting there The railway station for trains from Cuzco is quite central and within walking distance of the centre, but if you've got heavy bags, it's a good idea to hire a three-wheel cycle cart, *trici-taxi*, which costs about US$0.35 per km per person. The train halts for guests at the hotels **Libertador** and **Sonesta**. The bus station and the depots for local buses are further away, southeast of the centre, but *trici-taxis* and conventional taxis serve this area.

Getting around The centre of town is easy to walk around, but as said above, a *trici-taxi* can make life a lot easier, even if this is not your first stop at high altitude. *Colectivos* (buses) in town charge US$0.20.

Puno

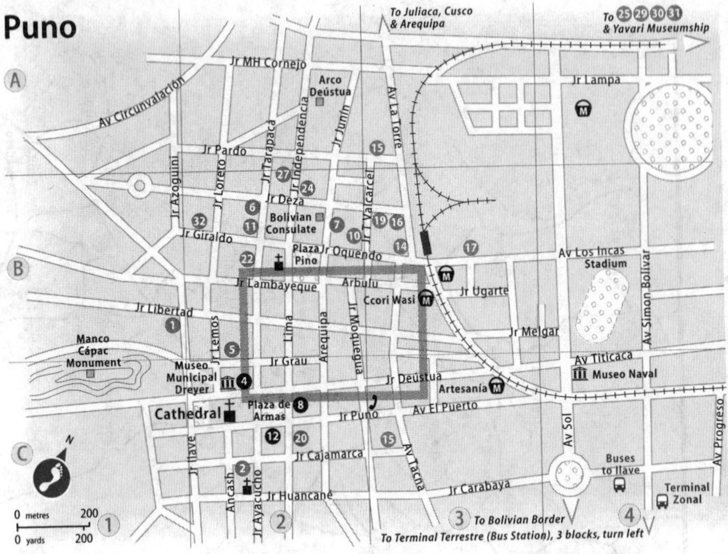

Sleeping
Albergue Juvenil Virgen de Copacabana **1** *B1*
Balsa Inn **2** *C2*
Camino Real **24** *B2*
Casa Andina Private Collection **25** *A4*
Casa Andina Plaza **5** *B2*
Casa Andina Tikarani **27** *B2*
Colón Inn 3 *Puno centre*
Eco Inn **29** *A4*
El Buho **4** *Puno centre*
Ferrocarril **16** *B3*
Hospedaje Residencial Margarita **6** *B2*
Hostal Arequipa **7** *B2*
Hostal Don Julio **28** *Puno centre*
Hostal Europa **8** *Puno centre*
Hostal Hacienda **9** *Puno centre*
Hostal Italia **10** *B2*
Hostal Los Pinos **11** *B2*
Hostal Monterrey **12** *Puno centre*
Hostal Nesther **13** *Puno centre*
Hostal Q'oñiwasi & Hostal Ilampu **14** *B3*
Hostal Rubi 'Los Portales' **15** *C3*
Joya del Titicaca **33** *Puno centre*
Libertador Isla Esteves **30** *A4*
Los Uros & Hostal Imperial **19** *B3*
Manco Cápac Inn **20** *Puno centre*
Ollanta Inn **17** *B3*
Plaza Mayor **21** *Puno centre*
Posada Don Giorgio **22** *B2*
Pukara **23** *Puno centre*
Qelqatani **18** *Puno centre*
Sillustani **26** *Puno centre*
Sonesta Posada del Inca **31** *A4*
Tambo Real **32** *B2*

Eating
Apu Salkantay, Lago de Flores & Pub Ekeko's **1** *Puno centre*
Cafetería Mercedes **3** *Puno centre*

Best time to visit Being so high up, Puno gets bitterly cold at night, especially in June-August, when the temperature at night can plummet to -25°C. Days are bright and the midday sun is hot, but you can never be quite sure what weather is going to come off the lake. The first two weeks in February, when the Fiesta de la Candelaria takes place, and 4-5 November, the pageant of the emergence of the founding Incas, are good times to visit, but crowded, too.

Tourist information **i perú** ⓘ *Lima y Deústua, T051-365088, near Plaza de Armas, Mon-Sun 0830-1930*. They are friendly and helpful with general information and they provide all maps and information free. The **Dircetur** office is at ⓘ *Ayacucho 682, T051-364976, puno@mincetur.gob.pe*. Puno is gaining a reputation for scams; keep your wits about you and don't be fooled by changes to prices or menu items in restaurants, by claims that entry tickets have expired or that your return boat ticket is in fact a single. Note also that some hotels are full of dubious street tour sellers. Others are linked to tour operators which may or may not belong to them, so are not above pressurized tour selling (see Tour operators, page 232).

Puno »pp227-234.

Puno sits on a bay at the northwest end of the lake. The Bahía de Puno is only 3 m deep and a channel is dredged to the exit into the open water of Titicaca. The port and lakeside quarters are several blocks from the centre, whose focus is the Plaza de Armas. The impressive baroque exterior of the **cathedral** ⓘ *0800-1200, 1500-1700*, completed in 1657, belies an austere interior. Just across the street from the cathedral is the famous **Balcony of the Conde de Lemos,** on the corner of Deústua and Conde de Lemos, where Peru's Viceroy stayed. Also here is the **Museo Municipal Carlos Dreyer** ⓘ *Conde de Lemos 289, Mon-Fri 0730-1330, US$1*. The museum combines municipal collections with the private collection of pre-Columbian artefacts bequeathed to the city by their owner, Sr Carlos Dreyer. In the same block is the **Casa del Corregidor** ⓘ *Deústua 576, T051-351921, www.casadelcorregidor.com.pe, Tue-Fri 1000-2200, closed for lunch on Sat*. One of Puno's oldest buildings, it has been converted into Puno's most important cultural centre, check website for exhibitons. It also has a great café (see page 230).

A short walk up Independencia leads to the **Arco Deústua**, a monument to those killed in the battles of Junín and Ayacucho. Nearby, is a mirador giving fine views over the town, the port and also the lake beyond. The walk from Jirón Cornejo following the Stations of the Cross up a nearby hill, with fine views of Lake Titicaca,

Puno centre

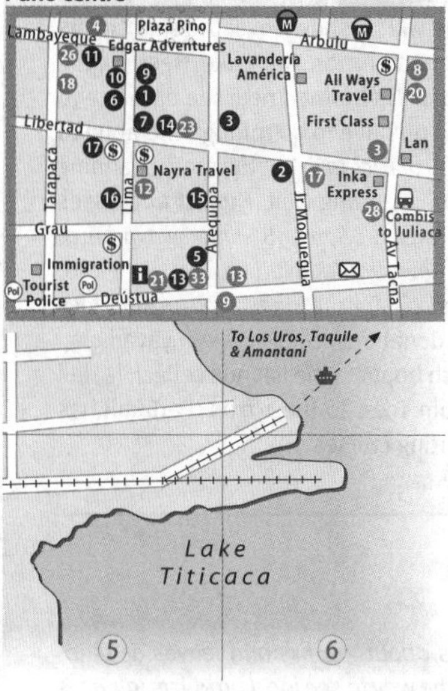

Casa del Corregidor **4** *C2*
Chifa Fon Seng **5** *Puno centre*
Don Piero **6** *Puno centre*
El Dorado **7** *Puno centre*
Fontana **9** *Puno centre*
Govinda **13** *Puno centre*
IncAbar **10** *Puno centre*
Keros **11** *Puno centre*
La Cayma **15** *Puno centre*
La Plaza **12** *C2*
Mojsa **8** *C2*
Pizzería El Buho **14** *Puno centre*
Remembranzas **2** *Puno centre*
Ricos Pan **16** *Puno centre*
Vida Natural **17** *Puno centre*

Bars & clubs
Café Concert **20** *C2*

has been recommended, but be careful and don't go alone. The same applies to all the hills around Puno: Huajsapata is known for music and folklore gatherings; Azoguine and Cancharani are higher, with good views and sacred associations. To get to Azoguine you go through Barrio Las Cruces, which is very dangerous.

On the way from the centre to the port is the **Museo Naval** ⓘ *Av El Puerto y Av Sol, Mon-Fri 0900-1700, Sat and Sun 0900-1300*. Here you can find a small exhibit on navigating on Lake Titicaca. A new **Malecón Bahía de los Incas**, near the port, is a pleasant place for a stroll with views of the lake. The bay by Puno is noticeably polluted. Not for the first time, plans were announced in 2005 for the construction of a badly needed sewage treatment plant.

The **MN Yavari** ⓘ *0800-1715, then illuminated till 2230 for 'Happy Hour' run by Hotel Posada del Inca, entry free in daytime, but donations of US$6 encouraged*, is the oldest ship on Lake Titicaca. It was restored in the port of Puno and turned into a museum, before being moved to its present location in 2002. The iron-hulled ship, now painted in her original livery of black, white and red, was built in England in 1862 and, together with her twin, the *Yapura* (now the Peruvian Navy's Hospital ship and called the *BAP Puno*), was shipped in kit form to Arica. From Arica, the two ships went by rail to Tacna from where the 2766 pieces were carried by mule to Lake Titicaca. The journey took six years. The *Yavari* was eventually launched on Christmas Day 1870 and on 14 June 1871 sailed on her maiden voyage. From after the War of the Pacific until the nationalization of the Railways and Lake Fleet in 1975, the *Yavari* was operated as a passenger/cargo vessel by the London-based Peruvian Corporation. The ship was bought in 1987 and is being restored by an Anglo-Peruvian Association. Visitors are very welcome on board the *Yavari* and will be shown over the ship and its exhibition of archival documentation and memorabilia on the Lake Fleet by the Captain, Carlos Saavedra, or a volunteer. The *Yavari* is berthed near the entrance to the **Sonesta Posada del Inca Hotel** (see below). You have to go through the hotel to get to the ship. To get there you can go by taxi, bus or *trici-taxi*, but the most charming way is by boat from the port, about US$2 return, including wait. **Project addresses** ⓘ *61 Mexfield Rd, London, SW15 2RG, England, T44-20 8874 0583, info@yavari.org; in Lima: Giselle Guldentops, T01-9998 5071, yavari.gulden@dwp. net; in Puno: Asociación Yavari, c/o Capitán Carlos Saavedra, T051-369329, carlosalberto@* yavari.org. For general information, volunteering, donations, etc, visit www.yavari.org.

In the harbour, moored at the jetty near which boats to the islands collect, is Hull (UK)-built **MS Ollanta**, which sailed the lake from 1926 to the 1970s. **PerúRail** has restored the vessel with a view eventually to starting cruises.

Around Puno »pp227-234.

Sillustani → Colour map 6, B2.

ⓘ *US$1.65. Take an organized tour, which lasts about 3-4 hrs and leaves at 1430, US$6.30. Tours usually stop at a Colla house on the way to see local products, alpacas and guinea pigs. Alternatively, take a Juliaca bus to the Sillustani turn-off (US$0.35); from here a 15-km paved road runs across the altiplano to the ruins. Moto-taxis and some combis run to Atuncolla (4 km away with a lovely colonial church), US$0.40, or US$0.85 to Sillustani (out of season you may have to walk the 4 km from Atuncolla). Go early to avoid tour groups at the site. A taxi from Puno costs about US$12, including wait. Camping possible outside the museum (tip the guardian).*

A highly recommended trip is to the *chullpas* (pre-Columbian funeral towers) of Sillustani in a beautiful setting on a peninsula in **Lago Umayo** (3890 m), 32 km from Puno on an excellent road. According to expert John Hemming, these are burial towers of the Aymara-speaking Colla tribe and most of them date from the period of Inca occupation in the 15th century. As Hemming also states: "The engineering involved in

Sacred lake

Lake Titicaca has played a dominant role in Andean beliefs for over two millennia. This, the highest navigable body of water in the world, is the most sacred lake in the Andes.

From the lake's profound, icy depths emerged the Inca creator deity, Viracocha. Legend has it that the sun god had his children, Manco Cápac and his sister, Mama Ocllo, spring from the its waters to found Cusco and the Inca dynasty.

The name Titicaca derives from the word *titi*, an Aymara mountain cat and the Quechua word *caca* meaning rock. The rock refers to the Sacred Rock on the Isla del Sol (on the Bolivian side) which was worshipped by the pre-Inca people on the island. The mountain cat inhabited the shores of the lake and is said to have visited the Isla del Sol occasionally.

The link between the rock and the cat comes from the legend that the ancient indigenous people saw the eyes of a mountain cat gleaming in the Sacred Rock and so named it Titicaca, or Rock of the Mountain Cat. It was this that gave rise to the idea of the sun having its home there.

The *titi* has characteristics – such as its aquatic ability and the brilliance of its eyes – that conceptually link it with a mythological flying feline called *ccoa*. The role of the *ccoa* was (and in some parts still is) important throughout the Andes. It is believed to have thrown lightning from its eyes, urinated rain (hence the expression), spit hail and roared thunder. It was generally associated with the gods that coolled the weather.

Among indigenous people today the *ccoa* is believed to be one of the mountain god's servants and lives in the mountains. It is closely involved in their daily life and is considered the most feared of the spirits as it uses lightning and hail.

their construction is more complex than anything the Incas built – it is defeating archaeologists' attempts to rebuild the tallest 'lizard' *chullpa*. Two are unfinished: one with a ramp still in place to raise blocks; the other with cut stones ready to go onto a very ambitious corbelled false dome. A series of stone circles to the east of the site are now thought to be the bases of domed thatch or peat living huts, rather than having any religious meaning. The quarry near the towers is also worth seeing." Other Inca remains can be seen in the shape of square buildings, a temple of the Sun and a temple of the Moon. Underground burials at the site predating the Colla have been found from the Pukara and Tiahuanaco periods.

There is a museum, and handicraft sellers in traditional costume wait at the exit. Guides are also available here. Photographers will find the afternoon light best, though this is when the wind is at its strongest and can kick up a mini-sandstorm. It's also best not to wear contact lenses. The scenery is barren, but nonetheless impressive. The island in Lago Umayo is a nature reserve. On the lake before the ruins there are flamingos and ducks. Take warm clothing, water and sun protection.

Capachica Peninsula

The pretty farming villages of **Llachón**, **Santa María** and **Ccotos**, at the eastern end of the Península de Capachica, have become a focus of community-based tourism. The sandy beaches, pre-Inca terracing and trees and flowers dotted around, make the peninsula a charming place to visit. You'll be welcomed with a necklace of cantuta flowers and then invited to share in local activities; 70% of all produce served is from the residents' farms. The peninsula is also good for hiking and mountain-biking and sailing boats can be hired. After all that activity, take in the sunset from the **Auki Carus** hill; reckoned to be better even than from Taquile. Neither Taquile nor Amantaní are far away. **Capachica** is the main town and crossroads of the peninsula. It has a colourful Sunday market, two very basic *hospedajes* and simple *comedores*. Nearby is Playa Chifrón, popular with locals. Throughout the peninsula the dress of the local women is very colourful, with four-cornered hats called *monteros*, matching waistcoats and colourful *polleras*.

There are currently six different community-tourism organizations, each with a dozen or more families and links to different tour operators in Puno, Cuzco or abroad. Families offer accommodation on a rotational basis, see page 229. The atmosphere is pleasant and low key. The peninsula is a great place to start a visit to Lake Titicaca, especially if you are flying in. It is closer to come here directly from Juliaca and you can go to the islands or to Puno by boat.

Other sights

Another place where *chullpas* can be seen is **Cutimbo**, 34 km south of Puno in the district of Pichacani, between Puno and Laraqueri on the old road to Moquegua. Here the funeral towers are round and square and stand on a table-top mountain. There are rock paintings on the mountainside. A road goes part of the way up. A taxi there costs US$19, including wait, three hours.

Some 8 km from Puno, just off the Puno-Juliaca road, is **Fundo Chincheros** ① *T051-355694, www.casadelcorregidor.com.pe, or go to Jr Deústua 572, for more information, US$7.50 includes guided tour; US$15 for half-day stays including lunch (available for groups of 5 or more)*, an old hacienda recently opened to the public. The colonial house with its own chapel is in the middle of fields. Llamas, alpacas and vicuñas are on site as well as horses for riding. The wild flowers, cactus and views make this a worth while trip.

The islands »pp227-234.

Los Uros → *Colour map 6, B2.*

① *Entry US$0.60*

Of the estimated 32 floating islands, only about 15 are regularly visited by tourists, and today we can talk about two kinds of Uros people; those close to the city of Puno and easily accessible to tourism, and those on islands which remain relatively isolated. The Uros' islanders fish, hunt birds and live off the lake plants, most important of which are the totora reeds they use for their boats, houses and the very foundations of their islands (see box, page 226). Their diet is very rich in fats. This, plus the high red corpuscle content, leads to the saying that they have black blood. On those more far-flung islands, reached via narrow channels through the reed beds, the Uros do not like to be photographed and continue to lead relatively traditional lives outside the monetary economy. They hunt and fish and still depend on trade with the mainland for other essentials.

! There is no drinking water on the floating islands and you need to be careful where you walk, as the surface can be unsteady underfoot.

Visitors to the floating islands encounter more women than men. These women wait every day for the tour boats to sell their handicrafts. The few men one does see might be building or repairing boats or fixing their nets. The rest are to be found out on the lake, hunting and fishing. The Uros cannot live from tourism alone, and the extra income they glean from tourists merely supplements their more traditional activities.

Many tourists find that, although the people are friendly, they are very poor and a few subject visitors to a hard-sell approach for handicrafts. The islands visited by tour boats are little more than 'floating souvenir stalls'. All the same, this form of tourism on the Uros Islands is now well-established and, whether it has done irreparable harm or will ultimately prove beneficial, it takes place in superb surroundings.

A lasting tradition

One of the most enduring textile traditions in Peru is found among the people of Taquile. Each family possesses at least four different types of costume: for work, leisure, weddings and festivals.

For weddings, which all take place on 3 May, when the planet Venus – Hatun Chaska – is visible, the bridegroom wears a red poncho provided by the best man. As a single man he wore a half red, half white cap, but to signify his married status he wears a long red hat and a wide red wedding belt, or *chumpi*. His bag for coca leaves, *ch'uspa*, is also filled.

The bride wears a wide red hat (*montera*) and her hands are covered with a ritual cloth (*katana-oncoma*). A *quincha*, a small white cloth symbolizing purity, is hidden in her skirt. With her red wedding blouse, or *gonna*, she wears a gathered skirt or *pollera*, made from 20 different layers of brightly coloured cloth. She also wears a belt (*faja*) and black cloak known as a *chukoo*.

The wool used for weaving is usually spun by the women, but on Taquile men spin wool, as well as knitting their conical hats (*chullos*). In fact, only the men on Taquile know how to knit. By the age of 10, a boy can knit his own Chullo Santa María, which is white-tipped to show single status. When he marries, or moves in with a woman, he adopts the red-tipped *chullo*, which is exclusive to the island. Today, much of the wool for knitting is bought ready-spun from factories in Arequipa.

Taquile

Isla Taquile, some 45 km from Puno, has numerous pre-Inca and Inca ruins, and Inca terracing. At the highest point is a ruin from which to view the sunset (the path is signed). The island is quiet and hospitable, but at the height of the season and at Sunday lunchtime it gets busy and touristy (about 50 boats a day in high season).

The island is only about 1 km wide and 6-7 km long. On the north side of the island is the warmest part of Lake Titicaca. Ask for the (unmarked) **museum of traditional costumes** ⓘ *on the plaza, free*, and also where you can see and photograph local weaving. There is a co-operative shop on the plaza that sells exceptional woollen goods which are not cheap, but of very fine quality. They are cheaper in the market at Puno. You need to spend a night on Taquile to appreciate fully its beauty and, therefore, it may be better to travel independently and go at your own pace.

Every Sunday, the island's four *suyos* (districts) coordinate their activities with a reunion in the main plaza after Quechua mass. Numerous **festivals** take place on the island (see page 231), with many dances in between. Weddings are celebrated each May and August. The priest comes from Puno and there is a week-long party. The book, *Encuentro con los hijos del sol/Encounter with the Children of the Sun/Rencontre avec les fils du soleil*, by Christian Nonis of the Colón Inn, has been recommended.

The influx of tourists unfortunately prompts persistent requests by children for sweets or to have their photo taken. They whisper, quite politely, *caramelo* (sweet) or *foto* (photo). When you arrive, boys tie friendship bracelets to your wrist, or give you *muña* (a herb used for infusions) for a sol. Recordings of traditional music have been made and are on sale as an additional source of income for the islanders. Buy their handicrafts instead of handing out sweets indiscriminately. Gifts of fruit, sugar, salt, spices, torches/flashlights (there is no electricity), moisturizer or sun block (the children suffer sore cheeks) are appreciated.

You are advised to take with you some food, particularly fruit, bread and vegetables, water, plenty of small-value notes, candles and a torch/flashlight. Take

Like the fish and birds of the water

Titicaca's waters nourished great civilizations like the Tiahuanaco and Pukará and drew the Incas south in search of new lands and the origin of their own creation legend. But very little is known about a third people who made Titicaca their home. They were the Uros, the people of the floating islands. The ephemeral nature of their totora reed constructions and the watery world they inhabit make archaeological study impossible, and only their myths remain to teach us something of their history.

In their oral histories, the Uros say that their forefathers came from the south. We cannot know with any certainty when the Uros first arrived at Lake Titicaca, but it is thought that a great drought around 1200 AD provoked a series of massive migrations of entire peoples across the *altiplano*. In a scenario similar to the one predicted for many parts of the world in the 21st century, conflicts arose as competition increased for water and fertile land.

The Uros found the fertile shores of the great lake occupied by other, much larger ethnic groups. According to Uro tradition, facing inevitable defeat by their more established rivals, the Uros escaped to the reed beds. It is said that they hid in the water among the reeds. Tired and cold, they cut the *totora* and, by binding the reeds together, made a number of rafts on which they slept.

Legend has it that when the Inca Pachacútec arrived to conquer the lake region he asked the Uros who they were. These people who had hunted and fished in the same way for generations replied as they always had, saying: "We are the founders of the world, the first inhabitants of the planet. Our blood is black and we cannot drown. We are like the fish and birds of the water".

With the arrival of the Spanish in the 16th century, the Uros isolated themselves even more from the mainland. Persecuted by the invaders, they began to meld themselves more than ever to their lake environment and their only outside contact was with other ethnic groups onshore, with whom they exchanged fish and birds for agricultural products.

Recalling their childhood, some old Uros islanders still remember when the first tourists arrived. Fearing that the Spanish had returned, their grandparents told them to run and hide.

Times have changed on some of the floating islands. There the Uros smile, pose for photographs, and then ask for a tip. After generations of intermarriage with their Aymara neighbours, what was once one of South America's most ancient tribal groups is in fact now ethnically extinct. The last Uro died in 1959, and the Uros' language died with her.

precautions against sunburn and seasickness. If staying the night, take warm clothes, a sleeping bag and a hot water bottle. The same applies to Amantaní. Tourism to both islands is community based: the less you pay, the smaller the amount that goes to the islanders. Bear this in mind when you shop around for a good-value tour (there is not much variation at the lower end of the price range).

There are two main entry points. The Puerto Principal at the south end has a very steep climb up many steps; the northern entry is longer but more gradual (remember you are at 3800 m). Visitors pay US$0.60 to land. Plentiful accommodation can be found in private houses and, on arrival, you are greeted by a *jefe de alojamiento*, who oversees where you are going to stay. There used to be a system of assigning accommodation to visitors by rota, but this has fallen into disuse. You can either say where you are going, if you (or your guide) know where you want to stay, or the *jefe* can find you a room. Guides have been instrumental in this change as large groups wish to stay close together, rather than be separated. See Sleeping, below.

Amantaní → *Colour map 6, B2.*

Another island well worth visiting is Amantaní. It is very beautiful and peaceful, and many say is less spoiled, more genuine and friendlier than Taquile (about 10 boats visit a day in high season). Visitors pay US$0.60 to land. There are six villages and ruins on both of the island's peaks, **Pacha Tata** and **Pacha Mama**, from which there are excellent views. There are also temples and on the shore there is a throne carved out of stone, the **Inkatiana**. It is rather eroded from flooding. It's a 30-minute walk west of **El Pueblo**, the village on the north end. Turn right down the steep slope after the last house on the right.

Several fiestas are celebrated on Amantaní (see page 231) and islanders arrange dances for tour groups (independent travellers can join in); visitors dress up in local clothes and join the dances. Small shops sell water and snacks, but are more expensive than those in Puno.

The residents make beautiful textiles and sell them at the **Artesanía Cooperativa**, at the east end of El Pueblo. They also make basketwork and stoneware. The people are Quechua speakers, but understand Spanish.

Anapia and Yuspique

In the Peruvian part of the Lago Menor are the islands of Anapia, a friendly, Aymara-speaking community, and Yuspique, on which are ruins and vicuñas. The community has organized committees for tourism, motor boats, sailing boats and accommodation with families (**All Ways Travel** arranges tours, see Activities and tours, page 232). This is part of **PromPerú's Al Tur** 'Turismo Vivencial' scheme. Visitors are involved with community projects during their visit and there is always a celebration at the end of the stay. It's highly worthwhile. On the island ask for José Flores, who is very knowledgeable about Anapia's history, flora and fauna. He sometimes acts as a guide. » *See Transport, page 234, on how to get to the islands in the lake.*

Sleeping

Puno *p221, map p220*

Check if breakfast is included in the price. Puno sometimes suffers from power and water shortages.

AL Libertador Isla Esteves, on an island linked by a causeway 5 km northeast of Puno (taxi US$3, or red *colectivo* No 16, or white Nos 24 and 33), T051-367780, www.libertador.com.pe. Built on a Tiahuanaco-period site, the hotel is spacious with good views. Bar, good restaurant, disco, good service, electricity and hot water all day, parking.

AL-A Sonesta Posada del Inka, Av Sesquicentenario 610, Huaje, 5 km from Puno on the lakeshore (same transport as for **Libertador Isla Esteves**), T051-364111, www.sonesta.com/peru_puno/. 62 large rooms with heating, in similar vein to other hotels in this group but with local touches, such as the textile decorations and the Andean menu in the **Inkafé** restaurant. Has facilities for the disabled, fine views, attractive, good service, folklore shows.

A Casa Andina Private Collection Puno, Av Sesquicentenario 1970, Huaje, T051-363992, www.casa-andina.com. A new addition in 2006 to this recommended chain, in its more luxurious range, on the lakeshore.

A Eco Inn, Av Chulluni 195, Huaje (same transport as for **Libertador Isla Esteves**), T051-365525, www.ecoinnpuno.com. Price includes taxes and buffet breakfast. Comfortable, brightly decorated rooms with bath, safe, luggage store, internet, parking, nice view of the lake from the front. Has alpacas in the grounds.

A-B Plaza Mayor, Deústua 342, T051-366089, www.plazamayorhotel.com.

Price includes buffet breakfast. Comfortable, well appointed and decorated, very close to the plaza. The rooms have good big beds, hot water and TV. There is a laundry, safe and a restaurant serving local and European food. Recommended.

A-B Qelqatani, Tarapacá 355, T051-366172, www.qelqatani.com. A hotel in colonial style, central, very clean, a good option in this price range.

B Balsa Inn, Cajamarca 555, T051-363144, www.hotelbalsainn.com. With breakfast (no other meals except for groups by arrangement). See the Nativity collection on display; comfortable lobby. Rooms are comfy, too, with big bathrooms, hot water, TV, safe, heating. Very helpful.

B Casa Andina Plaza, Jr Grau 270, T051-367520, www.casa-andina.com. Price includes breakfast and 10% service. One of this chain's modern hotels, a block from the plaza, rooms with bath, TV and heating, non-smoking rooms, clean, safe and central. Business centre with internet for guests, parking.

B Casa Andina Tikarani, Independencia 185, T051-367803, www.casa-andina.com. Similar in most respects to the **Casa Andina Plaza**, but further from the centre.

B Colón Inn, Tacna 290, T051-351432, www.coloninn.com. Price includes tax and buffet breakfast. Colonial style, good rooms with hot shower, good service, safe, internet for guests, restaurant **Sol Naciente** and pizzería **Europa**, the Belgian manager Christian Nonis is well known, especially for his work on behalf of the people on Taquile island. Recommended.

B El Buho, Lambayeque 142, T/F051-366122, www.hotelbuho.com. Breakfast included. Hot water, nicely decorated rooms with heaters, TV, restaurant, safe, special discount to **Footprint** readers, travel agency for excursions and flight reconfirmations. Recommended.

B Hostal Hacienda, Jr Deústua 297, T/F051-356109, haciendahostal@hotmail.com. Price includes breakfast. Refurbished colonial house, comfortable rooms with bath and hot water, TV, café. Rooms facing the front have private balconies. Recommended.

B Sillustani, Jr Lambayeque 195, T051-351881, www.sillustani.com. Price includes breakfast and taxes. Hot water, cable TV, safety deposit, heaters, internet, very good.

B Tambo Real, Jr Santiago Giraldo 362, T051-366060, www.tamborealtitikaka.com. A few blocks from the Plaza de Armas, clean, bright rooms, price includes breakfast, family-owned, professional and helpful staff.

C Camino Real, Deza 328, T051-367296, www.caminoreal-turistico.com. Good central hotel, price includes buffet breakfast, cable TV, 24-hour room service, internet. Recommended.

C Ferrocarril, Av La Torre 185, T051-351752, www.hotelferrocarril.com. This place is over 100 years old, by the train stations, price includes breakfast, central heating throughout the hotel is a big plus, parking space also available.

C Hostal Italia, Teodoro Valcarcel 122, T051-367706, www.hotelitaliaperu.com. 2 blocks from the station. With good breakfast, cheaper in low season. Good, safe, hot water, good food, free tea and coffee, small rooms, staff helpful, internet. Recommended.

C Hostal Pukara, Jr Libertad 328, T/F051-368448, pukara@terra.com.pe. Includes good American breakfast. Popular, with bath, hot water and heating. English spoken, central, quiet, free coca tea in evening. Recommended.

C Joya del Titicaca, Arequipa 522, T051-351823, www.joyadeltiticaca.com. Price includes good breakfast in upstairs room with great views, served early for those leaving on buses or boats. Helpful staff, ask for hot water.

D Posada Don Giorgio, Tarapacá 238, T051-363648, dongiorgio@titicacalake.com. Breakfast included. Large, comfortable, pleasantly decorated rooms with bath, hot water, TV, parking US$1.50 extra.

D Hostal Imperial, Teodoro Valcarcel 145, T051-352386, imperial_hostal_puno@yahoo.com. **E-F** (low season), breakfast extra, US$1.85 (good coffee). With good shower, hot water, helpful, stores luggage, comfortable if basic, safe, ask for extra blanket if cold.

D Hostal Monterrey, Lima 441, T051-351691, monterreytours@hotmail.com. Price includes breakfast and cable TV. **F** without bath, better rooms with good showers, hot water, restaurant, laundry, secure for luggage, motorcycle parking US$0.50.

D-E Hostal Don Julio, Tacna 336, T051-363358, hostaldonjulio@hotmail.com. Very clean, hot water, price includes full breakfast, some staff speak English.

D-E Hostal Rubi 'Los Portales', Jr Cajamarca 152-154, T/F051-353384, www.mancocapacinn.com. Breakfast US$2 extra, hot water, safe, TV, good, tours arranged. Recommended.

D-E Manco Cápac Inn, Av Tacna 227, T051-352985, www.mancocapacinn.com. With bath and hot water, luggage store, safe, average breakfast extra, as are heating and cable TV.

E Hospedaje Residencial Margarita, Jr Tarapacá 130, T051-352820, hostalmargarita@hotmail.com. Large building, family atmosphere, hot water most of the day, stores luggage, tours can be arranged. Recommended.

E Los Uros, Teodoro Valcarcel 135, T051-352141, huros@speedy.com.pe. Cheaper without bath. Hot water, plenty of blankets, breakfast is available (at extra cost), quiet at the back, good value. They make a small charge to leave luggage, laundry, often full, changes TCs a reasonable rate. Recommended.

E-F Hostal Arequipa, Arequipa 153, T051-352071, hotelarequipa@speedy.com.pe. With bath, hot water, will change TCs at good rates, stores luggage, secure, arranges tours to the islands, also has parking space.

E-F Hostal Los Pinos, Tarapacá 182, T/F051-367398, hostalpinos@hotmail.com. Cheaper without bath. Family-run, electric showers, without breakfast, clean, safe, luggage store, laundry facilities, helpful, cheap tours organized. Recommended.

E-F Hostal Nesther, Deústua 268, T051-363308. Also has triples, with bath, hot water, clean. Recommended.

E-F Hostal Q'oñiwasi, Av La Torre 119, opposite the rail station, T051-365784, qoniwasi@mundomail.net. **E** without bath and in low season. Heating is extra, but hot water available all day, laundry facilities and service, luggage store, breakfast extra from 0600-0900, lunch on request, safe, very helpful. Recommended.

E-F Ollanta Inn, Jr Ilo E-1, 2a cuadra Jr Los Incas, T051-366743. New, just behind station, hot water 24 hrs, pleasant, clean, helpful owner, fan heater and TV extra, breakfast is also extra but is good.

F Hostal Europa, Alfonso Ugarte 112, near the train station, T051-353026, hostaleuropa@hotmail.com. Very popular, cheaper without bath, luggage may be stored, but don't leave your valuables in the room, hot water sometimes, garage space for motorcycles.

F Hostal Illampu, Av La Torre 137-interior 9, T051-353284, illampu97@hotmail.com. With bath and warm water, breakfast and TV extra. Has a café, laundry, safe, exchanges money, arranges excursions (ask for Santiago).

Youth hostel

G per person **Albergue Juvenil Virgen de Copacabana**, llave 228, T051-T363766, hostelling_virgen_copacabana@yahoo.com. Entrance is down a passageway. Hot water in bathrooms, but cleanliness not of the highest order, unhelpful staff, will wash your clothes for a reasonable fee, full breakfast for US$1.30.

Around Puno *p222*

Llachón community phone T051-832323.

F Primo Flores, near church and bus stop in Llachón, T051-968 0040 (mob), primopuno@yahoo.es. Rustic family accommodation, includes breakfast, other meals on request US$2.50, knowledgeable and friendly. Sr Flores is the head of one of the community tourism groups.

F Valentín Quispe is the organizer of tourism in Llachón. He offers lodging and meals (breakfast US$1.20, other meals US$2). To contact Don Valentín, T051-982 1392 (mob), llachon@yahoo.com, or visit www.titicaca-peru.com/capachicae.htm.

Another family is that of **Tomás Cahui Coila**, Centro Turístico Santa María Llachón, T051-992 3595 (mob). All hosts in Llachón can arrange boat transport to Amantaní. There is a campsite towards the end of the peninsula, mostly used by tour groups. See Transport, below.

The islands *p224*

Taquile The average rate for a bed is US$3 per person, without any meals (see Eating, below). Several families now have sizeable *alojamientos* (eg **Pedro Huille**, on the track up from the north entry, with showers, proper loos, no sign).

Instead of staying in the busy part around the main square, the Huayllano community, on the south side of the island,

For an explanation of sleeping and eating price codes used in this guide, see inside the front cover. Other relevant information is found in Essentials, pages 53-58.

is hosting visitors. Contact **Alipio Huata Cruz**, T051-952 4650 (mob, you can leave a voicemail that he will retrieve from Puno as there is no reception on the island) or you can arrange a visit with **All Ways Travel** (see Tour operators, below).

Amantaní Ask your boat owner where you can stay; families living close to the port tend to receive tour company business and more tourists. Accommodation is US$6 per person. This includes 3 meals of remarkable similarity and generally poor quality (take bread and fruit). It's good value for visitors, but the prices have been forced down to unrealistically low levels, from which the islanders benefit hardly at all. Some contacts for accommodation are:

Hospedaje Jorge Wasi, basic, but nice family, great view of lake from room.

Ambrosio Mamani, j.mamani.cari@eudora mail.com, skipper of the *Barco Atlántico*, good lodging and food.

Familia Victoriano Calsin Quispe, Casilla 312, T051-360220 (Irma) or T051-363320 (Puno contact).

Eating

Puno *p221, map p220*

Very cheap places on Jr Deústua serve lunch or dinner. There are many places on Lima, too many to list here, which cater for the tourist market, they usually have good atmosphere and very good food.

IncAbar, Lima 356-A. Open for breakfast, lunch and dinner, interesting dishes in creative sauces, fish, pastas, curries, café and couch bar, nice decor.

Internacional, Moquegua 201. Very popular, excellent trout, good pizzas, service variable.

La Plaza, Puno 425, Plaza de Armas. Good food, including fish.

Mojsa, Lima 635 p 2, Plaza de Armas, T051-363182. Good international and *novo andino* dishes, also has an arts and crafts shop. Recommended.

Apu Salkantay, Lima 357 and in 400 block. Wide menu of meats, fish (more expensive), pastas, sandwiches, pizza, coffee, popular.

Don Piero, Lima 360. Huge meals, live music, try their 'pollo coca-cola' (chicken in a sweet and sour sauce), slow service, popular, tax extra.

El Dorado, Lima 371. Good for local fish, large portions.

Fontana, Lima 339. Pizzería and trattoria, good food.

Keros, Lambayeque 131. Fancy, expensive bar/restaurant catering for the tourist market, mostly Peruvian food, good service, pleasant surroundings, good drinks.

La Casona, Lima 521. Good for typical food, also Italian and pizzas.

La Caywa Andean Cuisine Bar, Jr Arequipa 410. T051-351490. Open 1000-2200. Typical and international. New, recommended.

Lago de Flores, Lima 357. Local dishes and pizza, very good food, open fire in the shape of a pizza oven keeps diners warm.

Pizzería El Buho, Lima 349 and at Jr Libertad 386. Excellent pizza, lively atmosphere, open 1800 onwards, pizzas US$2.35-3.

Adventista, Jr Deza 349. Good, closed after lunch.

Chifa Fon Seng, Arequipa 552. Good food, service and value, Chinese, popular.

Chifa Nan Hua, Arequipa 167, 1 block from Plaza de Armas. Tasty, big portions of Chinese food.

Govinda, Deústua 312. Cheap vegetarian lunch menus, closes at 2000.

Remembranzas, Jr Moquegua 200. Pizzas as well as local food. Open 0630-2200.

Vida Natural, Libertad 449. Open for breakfast, salads, fruits, yoghurts.

Cafés

Cafetería Mercedes, Jr Arequipa 351. Good menú US$1.50, also breads, cakes, snacks, juices and tea.

Casa del Corregidor, Deústua 576, aptdo 2, T051-355694. In restored 17th-century building, sandwiches, good snacks, coffee, good music, great atmosphere, nice surroundings with patio.

Panadería Una, Lima 317 and Arequipa 144. For croissants, fresh bread and cakes.

Ricos Pan, Jr Lima 424. Café and bakery, great cakes, excellent coffees, juices and pastries, good breakfasts and other dishes, reasonable prices, great place to relax, open 0600-2300, closed Sun. Branches of their panadería at Av Titicaca 155 and Moquegua 330.

The islands *p224*

Taquile There are many small restaurants around the plaza and on the track to the Puerto Principal (eg Gerardo Hualta's **La Flor**

de Cantuta, on the steps; **El Inca** on the main plaza). Meals are generally fish (the island has a trout farm), rice and chips, tortilla and *fiambre* – a local stew. Meat is rarely available and drinks often run out. Breakfast consists of pancakes and bread. Shops on the plaza sell film, postcards, water, chocolate bars and dry goods.

Amantaní There is one restaurant, **Samariy**.

Bars and clubs

Puno *p221, map p220*

Café Concert, Jr Lima 723. Open daily 2000-2300.

Dómino, Libertad 443. 'Megadisco', happy hour Mon-Thu 2000-2130, good.

Peña Hostería, Lima 501. Good music, also restaurant with good value set menu. Recommended.

Pub Ekeko's, Jr Lima 355, p 2. Live music every night, happy hour 2000-2200.

Festivals and events

Puno *p221, map p220*

It is difficult to find a month in Puno without some sort of celebration.

Feb The very colourful **Fiesta de la Virgen de la Candelaria** takes place during the first 2 weeks in Feb. Bands and dancers from all the local towns compete in this *Diablada*, or Devil Dance, with the climax coming on Sun. The festival is famous for its elaborate and grotesque masks, which depict characters in local legends as well as caricatures of former landowners and mine bosses. The festivities are better at night on the streets than the official functions in the stadium. Check in advance on the actual date because Candelaria may be moved if pre-Lenten carnival coincides with it. This festival is great fun and shouldn't be missed if you're in the vicinity around this time.

Mar/Apr On **Good Fri** there's a candlelit procession through darkened streets, with bands, dignatories and statues of Jesus.

3 May **Invención de la Cruz**, an exhibition of local art.

29 Jun San Pedro, is a colourful festival of with a procession at Zepita (see page 243).

20 Jul Another colourful Puno festival.

5 Nov There's an impressive pageant dedicated to the **founding of Puno** and the emergence of **Manco Cápac** and Mama Ocllo from the waters of Lake Titicaca. The royal couple sail from a point on the lake (it varies annually) and arrive at the port between 0900 and 1000. The procession from the lake moves up Av Titicaca to the stadium where a ceremony takes place with dancers from local towns and villages. If you buy an entrance ticket, US$0.60, you can watch from the top tier as the float carrying the Incas, followed by the local dancing groups, enters the stadium. Many of the groups continue dancing outside. This is not the best time to visit Taquile and Amantaní since many of their inhabitants are at the festival. This date coincides with the anniversary of the founding of Puno, celebrated with parades at night and a full military parade on the Sun.

The islands *p224*

Taquile

The principal festival days are: **Mar/Apr** (Semana Santa); **2 -7 Jun**; **Mid-Jul** (Fiesta de Santiago, held over 2 weeks); **1-2 Aug**.

Amantaní

15 Jan (or thereabouts) **Fiesta de la Tierra** Santa, or **Pago a la Tierra** is celebrated on both hills. The festivities have been reported as spectacular, very colourful, musical and hard-drinking.

9 Apr **Aniversario del Consejo** (of the local council), which might not be as boring as it sounds.

Shopping

Puno *p221, map p220*

The markets between Av Los Incas and Arbulu (Ccori Wasi) and on the railway between Av Libertad and Av El Puerto are two of the best places in Peru (or Bolivia) for **llama and alpaca wool** articles, but bargain for a good price when buying in quantity (and you will!), especially in the afternoon. In the covered part of the market (bounded by Arbulu, Arequipa, Oquendo and Tacna) mostly **foodstuffs** are sold (good cheeses), but there are also model **reed boats**, attractive **carved stone amulets** and Ekekos (**household goods**). This central market covers a large area and on Sat it expands down to the stadium (mostly fruit and vegetables) and along Av Bolívar (potatoes

Pot luck

One of the most intriguing items for sale in Andean markets is Ekeko, the god of good fortune and plenty and one of the most enduring and endearing of the Aymara gods and folk legends.

He is a cheery, avuncular little chap, with a happy face to make children laugh, a pot belly, because of his predilection for food, and short legs so he can't run away. His image, usually in plaster of Paris, is laden with sacks of grain, sweets, household tools, baskets, utensils, suitcases, confetti and streamers, rice, noodles and other essentials. Dangling from his lower lip is the ubiquitous lit cigarette. Believers say that these little statues only bring luck if they are received as gifts, and not purchased.

and grains). You will be hassled on the street and outside restaurants to buy woollen goods, so take care.

Alpaca 111, Lima 343, T051-366050, www.alpaca111.com. A very good-quality alpaca shop at the high end of the price range.

Alpaca's, Lima 394. T051-363551, alpacas @terra.com.pe. Another expensive, high-quality alpaca store.

Cooperación Artesanal Ichuña, Jr Libertad 113, www.ichunia.org. The outlet for a cooperative of about 100 women from Ichuña, 90 km southwest of Puno, selling handwoven textiles made of alpaca wool.

Activities and tours

Puno *p221, map p220*

Agencies organize trips to the Uros floating islands and the islands of Taquile and Amantaní, as well as to Sillustani, and other places. Make sure that you settle all details before embarking on the tour. Alternatively, you can easily go down to the lake and make your own arrangements with the boatmen. Watch out for the many unofficial street tour sellers – or *jalagringos* – who offer hotels and tours at different rates, depending on how wealthy you look. Once you realize they have charged more than the going rate, they'll be gone. They are everywhere: train station, bus offices, airport and hotels. Ask to see their guide's ID card. Only use agencies with named premises and compare prices.

Tour operators

The following have been recommended as reliable and helpful and offer good value:

All Ways Travel, Tacna 234, T/F051-355552, www.titicacaperu.com. Also in Casa del Corregidor, Deústua 576. Very helpful, kind and attentive to visitors' needs. Reliable, staff speak German, French, English and Italian. They offer a unique cultural tour to the islands of Anapia and Yuspique in Lake Wiñaymarka, beyond the straits of Tiquina, 'The Treasuer of Wiñaymarka', departures Thu and Sun. You can contribute to owner Víctor Lazo's educational project by donating children's books for schools. They also have a speed boat for 40 passengers. Also doing an alternative visit to Taquile where you go to the south of the island to visit the Huayllano community, this is a lot less touristy then the regular Taquile visit.

Arcobaleno, Jr Lambayeque 175, T/F051-351052, www.titicacalake.com. Local tours, Western Union representative and agent for **Crillon Tours** of La Paz, Bolivia.

Edgar Adventures, Jr Lima 328, T/F051-353444 , www.edgaradventures.com. Run by Edgar Apaza and Norka Flórez who speak English, German and French, very helpful.

Ecoturismo Aventura, Jr Lima 458, T051-355785. Very helpful.

Käfer Viajes, Arequipa 179, T051-354742, www.kafer-titicaca.com. Efficient and helpful.

Kontiki Tours, Jr Melgar 188. T051-355887, www.kontikiperu.com. Receptive tour agency specializing in special interest excursions. Recommended.

Nayra Travel, Jr Lima 419, of 105. T051-337934, www.nayratravel.com. Small but very helpful staff, offering local tours.

Pirámide Tours, Jr Rosendo Huirse 130, T051-366107, www.titikakalake.com. Out of the ordinary and classic tours, flexible, personalized service, modern fast launches, very helpful, but works only via internet and overseas clients.

Titikaka Explorers, Av La Torre 339-4, T051-355219, peru-titikaka@hotmail.com. Good service, helpful.

Transport

Puno *p221, map p220*

Air

The nearest airport is at Juliaca. **Airline offices**: Lan, Tacna y Libertad, T051-367227.

Boat

Boats to the islands leave from the terminal in the harbour; *trici-taxi* from centre, US$1.

Bus

All long-distance buses, except some Cuzco services and buses to La Paz (see below), leave from the new Terminal Terrestre, which is between Av Simón Bolívar and the lake, southeast of the centre. It has a tourist office, snack bars and toilets. Platform tax US$0.30. Bus prices to Cuzco and La Paz have seasonal variations.

Daily buses to **Arequipa**, 5-6 hrs via **Juliaca**, 297 km by paved road, US$4.50-6 (**Cruz del Sur**, **Best Way**, **Destinos**, **Julsa**, **Señor de Milagros**, or **Sur Oriente**, most have a morning and evening bus – better quality buses go at night). To **Moquegua**, US$4.50-6, and **Tacna**, US$10. To **Lima**, 1011 km, 19 hrs, US$21-25, all buses go through **Arequipa**, *bus cama* (requires transfer in Arequipa) US$30; **Ormeño** T051-368176. **Ormeño** has a service to **La Paz** (Bolivia), as does **Litoral** (cheaper).

Small buses and *colectivos* for **Juliaca**, **Ilave** and towns on the lake shore between Puno and Desaguadero, including **Yunguyo**, leave from Av Bolívar between Jrs Carabaya and Palma. To **Juliaca**, 44 km, 45 mins, US$0.85. For **Yunguyo** and the **Bolivian border**, see page 243.

To **Cuzco**, 388 km, 5 hrs. If you wish to travel by bus and cannot get on a direct bus, it is no problem to take separate buses to Juliaca, then to Sicuani, then to Cuzco, but obviously this takes longer. Do not take night buses to Cuzco: in 2005-2006 robberies were still being reported. **Tour Perú**, 0830, 2000; **Libertad**, 4 a day, **Cisnes**, 2 a day, and others, US$4.50-6. **First Class** and **Inka Express** both at 0830 arriving 1800, US$20, 10 hrs, daily. This service, while higher in price than the *turismo* train or other buses, leaves a little later and is comfortable, with a good lunch stop and visits to Pukará, La Raya, Raqchi and Andahuaylillas en route. This option is popular so book in advance, especially in high season.

Bus companies Cisnes, at Terminal, T051-368674. **First Class**, Jr Tacna 280, T051-365192, firstclass@terra.com.pe. **Inka Express**, Jr Tacna 314-B, T051-365654. **Julsa**, T051-369447. **Libertad**, at Terminal, T051-363694. **Ormeño** T051-368176. **Sur Oriente**, T051-368133. **Tour Perú**, T051-352991, tourperu@mixmail.com.

Train

The railway runs from Puno to **Juliaca** (44 km), where it divides, to **Cuzco** (381 km) and **Arequipa** (279 km; no passenger service, 2006). To **Cuzco** on Mon, Wed and Sat at 0800 (sometimes Fri in high season), arriving in Juliaca at 0910 and in Cuzco at about 1800 (try to sit on the right-hand side for the views). The train stops at **La Raya**. In the high season (Jun especially), tickets sell well in advance. In the wet season services may be cancelled for short periods. Always check, www.perurail.com. **Puno-Cuzco** fares, turismo/backpacker, US$16.66; first class, US$119 including lunch, afternoon tea, entertainment and luxury seating (recommended). The ticket office is open from 0630-1030, Mon-Sun. Tickets can be bought in advance, or 1 hr before departure if there are any left. The station is well-guarded by police and sealed off to those without tickets.

Around Puno *p222*

Only one weekly public boat from **Llachón** to Puno, Fri 0900, returning to Llachón Sat 1000. The daily 0800 boat from Amantantí can drop you off at **Colata** (at the tip of the peninsula), a 1-hr walk from Llachón, or a minibus ride to Capachica; confirm details in advance. Returning to Puno, you can try to flag down the boat from Amantaní which passes Colata between 0830 and 0930. All fares US$3 one way. Combis from Puno to **Capachica**, several departures 0700-1200, 1½ hrs, US$1; from Capachica to **Juliaca**, US$0.80, leave when full from the plaza (likewise to Puno). Capachica to Llachón, buses and combis leave plaza when full,

30 mins, US$0.30. Tour operators in Puno arrange visits, about US$25 per person staying overnight, in groups of 10-15.

The islands *p224*

Motorboats charge US$3 per person to take tourists to the **Uros** islands for a 2-hr excursion. Boats leave from the harbour in Puno about every 30 mins from about 0630 till 1000, or whenever there are 10 or more people to fill the boat. The earlier you go the better, to beat the crowds of tourists. Almost any agency going to the other islands in the lake will stop first at Los Uros. Just to Los Uros, agencies charge US$6.

Boats leave Puno harbour for **Taquile** daily at 0700 and 0800, returning 1430 and 1500, US$3 one way. The journey takes 3 hrs. This doesn't leave enough time to appreciate the island fully in one day. Organized tours can be arranged for about US$10-16 per person, but only give you about 2 hrs on the island. Make sure you and the boatman know exactly what you are paying for.

Boats for **Amantaní** from the harbour in Puno leave at 0815 daily, and return to Puno at 0800 the following day. The trip costs US$4.50 one way. The journey takes 4-5 hrs – take water. A 1-day trip is not possible as the boats do not always return on the same day. Several tour operators in Puno offer 2- to 3-day excursions to Amantaní, Taquile and a visit to the floating islands. These cost from US$12 per person upwards, including meals, depending on the season and size of group. This gives you 1 night on Amantaní and 3 or 4 hrs on Taquile. There is little difference in price visiting the islands independently or on a tour, but going independently means that the islanders get all the proceeds, with no commission paid to Puno tour companies, you can stay as many nights as you wish and you will be able to explore the islands at your own pace. When not taking a tour, do not buy your boat ticket from anyone other than the boat operator at the harbour, do not believe anyone who says you can only visit the islands on a tour and do not be pressurized by touts. If you wish to visit both Taquile and Amantaní, it is better to go to Amantaní first. From there boats go to Taquile at around 0800, costing US$2.50 per person. There is no regular service – boats leave if there are enough passengers. You can then take the 1430 or 1500 boat from Taquile to Puno.

To visit **Anapia** independently, buses Sun, Tue, Thu, US$3 one way. Or take a *colectivo* from Yunguyo to Tinicachi and alight at Punta Hermosa, just after Unacachi. Boats to Anapia leave Punta Hermosa on Sun and Thu at 1300 (they leave Anapia for Yunguyo market on the same days at 0630). It's 2 hrs each way by boat.

Directory

Puno *p221, map p220*

Banks BCP, Lima 510. Changes TCs before 1300 without commission, cash advance on Visa and Visa ATM. **Banco Continental**, Lima 444-411, Visa ATM. **Banco Wiese Sudameris**, Lima with Deústua, MasterCard ATM. **Interbank**, Lima 444, changes TCs morning and afternoon, 0.5% commission, Visa ATM. For cash go to the *cambios*, the travel agencies or the better hotels. Best rates with money changers on Jr Lima, many on 400 block, and on Tacna near the market, eg Arbulu y Tacna. Check your Peruvian soles carefully. Exchange rates from soles to bolivianos and vice versa are sometimes better in Puno than in Yunguyo; check with other travellers. **Consulates** Bolivia, Jr Arequipa 136, T051-351251. Issues a visa on the spot, US$10, Mon-Fri 0830-1400. **Internet** There are offices everywhere in the centre, upstairs and down. Average price is US$0.30-0.45/hr; many have overnights. **Laundry** Don Marcelo, head office at Ayacucho 651, T051-352444, has agencies in several places in the centre, including on Lima 427, and will collect and deliver laundry. US$1.50 per kg, good service. **Lavandería América**, Moquegua 175, T051-351642. Also had a good service, US$1.50. **Post** Jr Moquegua 267. **Telephone** Telefónica at Puno y Moquegua for local and international calls. Another phone office is at Lima 489. **Useful addresses** Immigration, Ayacucho 280, T051-357103. For renewing entry stamps, etc. The process is very slow and you must fill in 2 application forms at a bank, but there's nothing else to pay. **Indecopi**, Lima y Fermín Arbulú, p 2, T/F051-366138, odipun@indecopi.gob.pe. The office of the tourist protection bureau.

Juliaca to the northeastern shore

The opposite shores of Lake Titicaca are quite different. Between Puno and Desaguadero at the lake's southeastern tip, the plain is intensively worked. The tin roofs of the communities glint everywhere in the sun. Heading north from Puno, the road crosses a range of hills to another coastal plain, which leads to Juliaca. North of Puno is the first sector (29,150 ha) of the Reserva Nacional del Titicaca. The smaller, Ramis sector (7030 ha) is northeast of Juliaca, at the outflow of the Río Ramis which floods in the wet season. The reserve protects extensive totora reed beds in which thousands of birds live. On the flat, windy altiplano between Juliaca and Huancané (see below) you will see small, square houses with conical roofs, all made of blocks of earth, putukus de champa. *After Huancané, the lakeshore becomes mountainous, with cliffs, bays and fabulous vistas over the water.* ▸▸ *For Sleeping, Eating and other listings, see pages 239-241.*

Ins and outs

Heading north and west, Juliaca is a major transport hub for paved roads to Cuzco and Arequipa and also has the only airport in the region. Transport along the north shore is less frequent, but that should not discourage you from travelling here. For

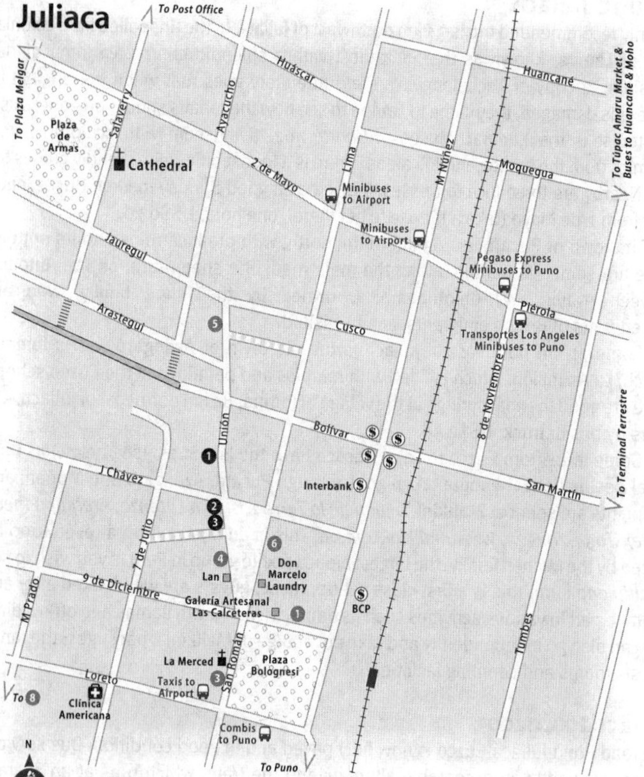

 information in Spanish, see www.juliacavirtual.com. **Dircetur** regional tourist office ⓘ *Jr Noriega 191, p 3, T051-321839.*

Juliaca → *Colour map 6, B2. Population: 134,700. Altitude: 3825 m.*

As the commercial focus of an area bounded by Puno, Arequipa and the jungle, Juliaca has grown very fast into a chaotic place with a large impermanent population, lots of contraband and more tricitaxis (*taxicholos*) than cars. Monday, market day, is the most disorganized of all. On the positive side, Juliaca provides access to the north side of the Lake as well as various other worthwhile attractions. It is less of a tourist town than Puno and is an alternative base for independent travellers who want to explore Titicaca beyond the gringo trail. It's freezing cold at night, so make sure you're wrapped up well in your recently purchased alpaca clothing.

You can buy wool and alpaca goods at the large Sunday **market**, La Dominical, near the exit to Cuzco. Another good place to find cheap alpaca sweaters is the **Galería Artesanal Las Calceteras**, on Plaza Bolognesi. **Túpac Amaru market**, on Moquegua, seven blocks east of the railway line, is a cheap black market. Everything is great value. The **Plaza de Armas** is mostly lined with modern buildings. On it stands the grey-stone cathedral, Santa Catalina, sombre inside and lit by candles and the yellow light through the windows. If you're unlucky enough to fall ill here, there's a first-class hospital run by the Seventh Day Adventists.

Around Juliaca

A highly recommended trip is 34 km northwest of Juliaca to the unspoiled little colonial town of **Lampa**, known as the 'Pink City', with a splendid church, La Inmaculada, containing a copy of Michelangelo's *Pietà* (the story goes that when the original in Rome was damaged, they came to Lampa to see how the repairs should be done). Also of interest is the **Kampac Museo** ⓘ *Ugarte 462*, a museum with sculptures and ceramics from the Lampa and Juli areas. There is a tourist office with friendly guides for free. Nearby are three Inca fortresses. It also has a good Sunday market. Buses leave daily from 2 de Mayo (take a tricycle to get there), one hour, US$0.70.

The town of **Pucará** lies 63 km to the north, with pre-Inca ruins and its pottery. There are some restaurants along the main road. The sheep farm of San Antonio, between Ayaviri and Chiquibambilla, owned by the Prime family, who are descendants of British emigrants, can be visited.

Some 71 km northeast of Juliaca is the old town of **Azángaro** with a famous church, La Asunción, which is filled with *retablos* and paintings of the Cuzco school. There are good thermal springs at the village of **Putina**, 84 km northeast of Juliaca, 5½ hours by bus or truck, US$2.50.

Some tours from Cuzco to Lake Titicaca have the Isla Suasi (see below) as their initial destination. The route taken goes through Pucará, Azángaro and Muñani and two nights are spent at **Mallkini** ⓘ *Juan de la Torre 101, San Lorenzo, Arequipa (head office), T054-202525, www.mallkini.com.pe.* This is an alpaca farm at over 4000 m, owned by the Michell family, the largest alpaca textile group in Peru. If you wish to see an *altiplano* farm, this is a first-class set-up, rustic, guests are well-looked after and can take part in various activities such as riding, trekking with llamas and off-roading. You can also go independently and take advantage of Mallkini's packages; the ranch has six rooms and camping facilities.

Juliaca to Cuzco

The road Puno-Juliaca-Cuzco is now fully paved and in good condition. Bus services are consequently an acceptable alternative to the train, which runs at an average altitude of 3500 m. There is much to see on the way, but neither the daytime buses nor the trains make frequent stops. You would have to be using your own transport, or taking buses from town to town to sample what the places en route have to offer. The

Mother Earth

Pachamama, or Mother Earth, occupies a very privileged place in Aymara culture because she is the generative source of life. The Aymara believe that man was created from the land, and thus he is fraternally tied to all the living beings that share the earth. According to them, the earth is our mother, and it is on the basis of this understanding that all of human society is organized, always maintaining the cosmic norms and laws.

Women's and men's relationship with nature is what the Aymara call ecology, harmony and equilibrium. The Aymara furthermore believe that private land ownership is a social sin because the land is for everyone. It is meant to be shared and not only used for the benefit of a few.

Vicenta Mamani Bernabé of the Andean Regional Superior Institute of Theological Studies states: "Land is life because it produces all that we need to live. Water emanates from the land as if from the veins of a human body, there is also the natural wealth of minerals, and pasture grows from it to feed the animals. Therefore, for the Aymaras, the Pachamama is sacred and since we are her children, we are also sacred. No one can replace the earth, she is not meant to be exploited, or to be converted into merchandise. Our duty is to respect and care for the earth. This is what white people today are just beginning to realize, and it is called ecology. Respect for the Pachamama is respect for ourselves as she is life. Today, she is threatened with death and must be liberated for the sake of her children's liberation."

road climbs steadily after Juliaca, passing Pucará (see above) then running through the villages of Ayaviri and Santa Rosa (where knitted alpaca ponchos and pullovers and miniature llamas are sold, rooms are available). It then rises further, up to the pass at La Raya. **Ayaviri** is a lively town with a daily market. In the pleasant plaza are two puya raimondi plants.

The road and railway cross the *altiplano*, climbing to **La Raya**, the highest pass on the line; 210 km from Puno, at 4321 m. Up on the heights breathing may be a little difficult, but the descent along the Río Vilcanota is rapid. To the right of **Aguas Calientes**, 9 km from La Raya, are steaming pools of hot water. The temperature of the springs is 40°C, and they show beautiful deposits of red ferro-oxide. Several communal bathing pools and a block of changing rooms have been opened. Entrance US$0.15. At **Maranganí**, the river is wider and the fields greener, with groves of eucalyptus trees. At Km 147, next to a colonial house, is the **Maranganí Fábrica Tejidos** ① *T084-352215*, a textile manufacturer using alpaca wool. Although little more than 10 years old, some of the machines are much older than that and all use punch cards (no computerization here). The textiles are exported all over the world. The administrator, Sr Walter Chung Valdez, is happy to show interested travellers around.

The Vilcanota plunges into a gorge, but the train winds above it and round the side of the mountain. At **Huambutío** the railway turns left to follow the Río Huatanay on the final stretch to Cuzco. The Vilcanota here widens into the great Urubamba canyon, flanked on both sides by high cliffs, on its way to join the Ucayali, a tributary of the Amazon. For more information about places between La Raya and Cuzco, see page 209.

The northeast coast of Lake Titicaca

The crossing from Peru to Bolivia via Huancané and Moho is the most remote, but nevertheless a highly recommended route between the two countries. As the road leaves Juliaca, it crosses a single-track bridge, which can get congested if opposing drivers do

LAMPA

 not give way. To Huancané the road is paved across the *altiplano*. The road then deteriorates, badly in places, although work has started (2005) to widen and improve it.

Huancané (56 km from Juliaca, altitude 3825 m) is known as *tierra de chirihuanos*, for the wind instrument (like a *zampoña*) that is played here. It has a massive adobe church by a nice plaza. The town suffers from water shortages. There are good birdwatching possibilities 10 km southwest of town where the road crosses the Río Ramis, part of the Reserva Nacional del Titicaca. Ten kilometres east of Huancané, 1 km off the road to Moho, is the small town **Vilque Chico**, from where a road goes northeast to Cojata on the Bolivian border (Ulla Ulla on the Bolivian side). Several undeveloped archaeological sites can be visited from here; **Cotañi** with one *chullpa* is one hour's walk away and the more extensive **Quiñalata**, two hours' walking; ask for directions or hire a taxi in town. There are no lodgings in Vilque Chico, only a couple of very basic eateries. Combi from Huancané US$0.30, 15 minutes. Past Vilque Chico, the views are especially beautiful.

At Jipata, the road splits, giving two ways of getting to **Moho** (40 km; public phones 051-832300/01/02): inland, over the hills, the route the buses take as it is shorter; or clinging to the lakeshore, with lots of bends, but beautiful views. Moho is known as the 'Garden of the Altiplano'. Maximizing the climatic benefits of the lake, they grow roses and many other flowers. The plaza has rose bushes, topiary hedges and a colourful fountain. The large, green Consejo Municipal is totally out of keeping with the rest of the plaza. Buses for Juliaca collect on the plaza. The main fiesta in honour of Señor de la Exaltación is held 13-16 September, celebrated with dances, bands, bullfights, etc. On a ridge top, two hours' climb from Moho is **Merka Marka** or 'old city', an impressive, undeveloped pre-Inca archaeological site, with gorgeous views of the lake and the *altiplano*, all the way to the glaciers on the Cordillera Apolobamba.

Conima, a pleasant small town in a lovely setting overlooking the lake, has a nice plaza with a fountain, colouful flower beds and an old stone church tower. The main fiesta, San Miguel Arcángel, runs from 28-30 September. A 30-minute walk through worked fields leads down to a nice beach. Nearby is the Península de Huata with a stone monolith on the rigetop. **Cambria**, a village 2 km north of Conima is the access point for **Isla Suasi**, the only tourist project on the north shore. A fine, get-away-from-it-all hotel is the only house on this tiny, tranquil island. The microclimate allows for beautiful terraced gardens, which are at their best from January to March. The non-native eucalyptus trees are being replaced by native varieties. You can take a community rowing boat around the island to see birds (US$1.50) or paddle yourself in one of the hotel's canoes. The island has six vicuñas, a small herd of alpacas and various domestic animals. The sunsets from the highest point are out of this world. See Sleeping and Transport, below.

To Bolivia

The last Peruvian settlement before the border is **Tilali**, a small town with a large Plaza de Armas with topiary. It is a very sleepy place except on Wednesday and Saturday, market days at the border. There are a couple of basic, cheap *hospedajes* on or near the plaza. The main fiesta in honour of Virgen de los Remedios is held from 19-21 November.

Border crossing There is a Peruvian customs post 2 km past Tilali but no immigration service here, so you must get your exit stamp ahead of time in Puno. The border is a further 2-km steep climb along a very poor dirt track. An obelisk marks the international frontier at Cerro Janko Janko, on a promontory high above the lake with magnificent views. Here are hundreds of small stone storerooms, deserted except during the busy Wednesday and Saturday smugglers' market. From the border it is about 10 km to **Puerto Acosta**, Bolivia, where you must get a preliminary entry stamp at the police station on the plaza. Get the definitive entry stamp at Migración in La

Paz. Despite its name, Puerto Acosta is not right on the lake. It is a nice town with a large plaza and several simple places to stay and eat.

Transport across this border is difficult and unreliable. Walking 10 to 15 km with all your luggage at 3800 m above sea level may be necessary. **Note** Bolivian time is one hour ahead of Peru. » *For Transport details, see page 241.*

Rinconada

At 5200 m, Rinconada is a cold, isolated town near Ananea and Culijón mountain. Its population of about 25,000 is involved entirely in gold mining and the mines are all under a glacier. A glacier lake below the town is marred by the rock and sand dug out of the mines. You can see all the processes in extracting, refining and selling the gold (which can be found pretty cheaply in the local shops). There is no infrastructure for tourists: there are four or five basic *hostales*, countless basic restaurants serving good food and, apart from gold, shops sell mainly mining equipment. Wrap up warm as it is cold by day and bitter at night (it is hard to sleep in the thin air).

Sleeping

Juliaca *p236, map p235*

There are water problems in town, especially in the dry season. There are many cheap hotels near the corner of Núñez and Cusco.

A **Suites Don Carlos**, Jr M Prado 335, on the outskirts of town, T051-321571, www.hoteles doncarlos.com. 45 rooms, including a presidential suite. Prices include taxes, good facilities, quite central, continental breakfast US$6.50, lunch/dinner US$13.

B-C **Royal Inn**, San Román 158, T051-321561, www.royalinnhoteles.com. Decent accommodation with hot water, jacuzzi, TV, heaters in rooms, safe, laundry, good restaurant **La Fonda del Royal**. Recommended as good value.

C **Don Carlos**, Jr 9 de Diciembre 114, Plaza Bolognesi, T051-323600, www.hoteles doncarlos.com. Breakfast and taxes included. Owned by the same group as the **Suites**. Comfortable, modern facilities, hot water, TV, heater, good service, restaurant and room service. Recommended.

D **Karlo's Hostal**, Unión 317, T051-321817, lanzap@hotmail.com. Comfortable, firm beds, hot water, TV, laundry, restaurant, overpriced.

E **Hostal Luquini**, San Brasesco 409, T051-321510. Comfortable, reliable hot water in morning only, helpful staff, patio, good value, motorcycle parking. Recommended.

F **Hostal Sakura**, San Román 133, T051-322072. Rooms with bath and hot water, TV extra. Also has rooms without bath, **G**. Breakfast is extra.

Around Juliaca *p236*

G **Hostal La Casona**, on the main plaza in **Lampa**, T051-360228, mariaelenafd@ hotmail.com. Recently opened, refurbished old house, clean. Recommended.

Juliaca to Cuzco *p236*

G **Paraíso**, Jr Leoncio Prado 254 (about 3 blocks from the plaza), Ayaviri, T051-863024. Hot showers, clean, friendly.

The northeast coast of Lake Titicaca *p237*

L **Hotel Isla Suasi**, T051-962 2709, Casa Andina Private Collection hotel, www.casa-andina.com. Price is full board. Facilities are spacious, comfortable and solar-powered. Rooms have bath and hot water and hot water bottles are put between your sheets at bedtime, very attentive service. The food is excellent and innovative (Andean *nouvelle cuisine*), lots of vegetables, all locally produced. Internet access US$20 per hr (!), canoes. Spa planned (2005). Warmly recommended.

F **Hotel Moho**, at the Consejo Municipal, Plaza de Armas, Moho. Modern, becoming run down, some rooms small, solar heated water (best shower in the early afternoon), friendly.

G **Hospedaje Huancané**, Jr Lima 309 at Plaza de Armas, Huancané (no phone). Basic, shared bath, cold water, nice courtyard, friendly. A couple of other places at the entrance to town from Juliaca.

G **Hostal Moheño**, Arequipa behind the church, Moho. Shared bath, cold water, very basic, friendly.

G **Hotel Don Raúl**, at a corner shop on the Plaza de Armas (no sign), Conima. Basic but reasonably clean and friendly, shared crouch toilet, no running water.

Eating

Juliaca *p236, map p235*

ŦŦ-Ŧ **Trujillo**, San Román 163. Extensive menu, daily specials, US$3-5.50 for mains.

ŦŦ-Ŧ **La Fonda del Royal**, Hotel Royal Inn, San Román158. US$3-5 for very good, varied food.

Ŧ **Asador**, Unión 119. Chicken, grill and pizza, pleasant atmosphere.

Ŧ **Ricos Pan**, San Román y Chávez. A good bakery with café, very popular. Recommended.

Juliaca to Cuzco *p236*

Ŧ **Restaurante La Mundial**, Jr Tacna 465, Ayaviri, T051-863375. Serves cheap local food, including lamb, a speciality, friendly place.

The northeast coast of Lake Titicaca *p237*

All the main towns along this route have simple *comedores*.

Festivals and events

Juliaca *p236, map p235*

Feb/Mar **Carnival** is unusually celebrated on the week starting Ash Wed, with over 50 groups dancing *morenada* and *diablada*.

23-24 Sep **Virgen de las Mercedes** is celebrated with brass bands, *morenada* and fireworks (*castillos*).

Transport

Juliaca *p236, map p235*

Air

There are daily flights to/from Lima (2¼ hrs) with Lan, via **Arequipa** (30 mins), or Cuzco, and StarPerú once a day via Arequipa. Beware overcharging for transport from Juliaca airport. If you have little luggage, combis stop just outside the airport parking area, US$0.15 to centre. Taxi from Plaza Bolognesi, US$1.75. Tourist buses run direct from Puno to the airport and vice versa; US$3.50 per person, 1 hr. You can book ahead with **Rossy Tours** T051-366709. Rosa has minibuses and will drop you off/pick you up at your hotel for US$3.50. Also taxis, US$11.75. If taking a public *colectivo* from Puno to Juliaca for a flight, allow plenty of time, as the drivers travel around town looking for more passengers.

Airline offices Lan, San Román 125, T051-322228 (airport 324448), Mon-Fri 0800-1900, Sat and Sun 0800-1800. **StarPerú**, San Román 175, T051-327478.

Bus

The Terminal Terrestre is at Jr Mantaro y San Agustín: go down San Martín 10 blocks and cross Av Circunvalación. Lots of companies serve **Arequipa** (4 hrs, US$3), **Lima** (US$17-43) and **Cuzco** (6 hrs, US$3-4). **Cruz del Sur, Julsa, Ormeño**. To **Cuzco**, 344 km, 5-6 hrs, with **Tour Perú**, day and night buses, prices as from Puno (see page 233 for warning about night buses to Cuzco). **First Class** and **Inka Express** have pPullman tourist buses which stop for sightseeing and lunch, with guide, see under Puno. The road is paved and in good condition. Buses from Puno will stop in Juliaca on the way to Cuzco. To **Puno**, 44 km, 1 hr, US$0.60; small buses leave from Piérola y 18 de Noviembre, 2 companies, **Pegaso Express** and **Los Angeles**. Combis to Puno leave from another Terminal Terrestre on Plaza Bolognesi, also US$0.85. Buses to **Capachica** for Llachón from Cerro Colorado Market, leave when full 0500-1700, 1½ hrs, US$0.80. To **Puerto Maldonado**, 18 hrs, US$15, along a rough but dramatic road via the San Gabán gorge with **Transportes Madre de Dios** and **Tahuamanu**. The journey takes much longer in the wet season.

Bus companies Cruz del Sur, T051-322011. **First Class**, www.firstclassperu.com. **Inka Express**, inkaex@yahoo.com. **Julsa**, T051-331952. **Ormeño**, T051-326994. **Tour Perú**, tourperu@mixmail.com.

Train

The station at Juliaca is the junction for services between **Arequipa** (no passenger services in 2006), **Puno** and **Cuzco**. See under Puno (page 233) and Cuzco (page 175) for more information. Fares to Cuzco are the same as for Puno, but no tickets are sold in

Juliaca. You can get on the train in Juliaca but only if you have purchased your ticket in advance in Puno. "At Juliaca, the track runs down the middle of the main market street, which is hurriedly cleared as the train approaches and rebuilt as soon as it passes, great place for camera shots" (Martin Steer).

The northeast coast of Lake Titicaca *p237*

Bus From **Juliaca**: combis to **Huancané** (on the north side of Lake Titicaca), 51 km, 40 mins, from Grifo San Juan del Oro, Sucre y Ballón, US$0.45, 1 hr. From Hunacané, combis leave for Juliaca when full throughout the day. Buses to **Moho**, 31 km beyond Huancané, from Moquegua y Ballón, past Túpac Amaru market, 4 daily, 2-2½ hrs, US$1.50. From Moho to Juliaca, buses leave at 0130, 0800 and 1300 daily. Buses to **Conima**, Municipal bus Mon 1300, Thu 1300, Sun 0800, 2½-3 hrs, US$1.80. Buses to **Tilali**, **Transportes Lucero**, 1 or 2 daily in early morning, **Aguila del Sur**, 1 daily in morning, both from Circunvalación y Lambayeque, 4 hrs, US$2.50. Also several buses around 2000 Tue and Fri from Jr Huancané y El Maestro, but usually crowded with *contrabandistas* and reported unsafe at night. For **Isla Suasi**: take a Tilali or Conima bus and alight in Cambría, about 20 mins past Moho (walk down to the shore and take a rowing boat to Suasi, 10 mins, US$1.50 per person). Private boats from Puno to **Isla Suasi** are expensive and take 4-6 hrs (2½ hrs by fast boat, US$450 up to 15 passengers), but you can call at the islands or Llachón en route. A car for 4 people will cost US$75.

To Bolivia *p238*

Bus Transport to the border from Juliaca is abundant on Tue and Fri starting 2000, but it is not considered safe: buses are very crowded, you arrive in the middle of the night, there is nowhere to stay and it is bitterly cold. The best option is to take an early morning bus from Juliaca to Tilali which, on Wed and Sat, usually goes on to the border. Confirm all details in advance in Juliaca. It is very difficult to get transport from Tilali to the border on other days. You can try to arrange a private vehicle, but there are few in town. It is even more difficult to arrange transport from Tilali all the way to Puerto Acosta; expect to pay about US$25 if you can find something.

From the border to Puerto Acosta, you can try to get a ride (45 mins) with the trucks returning to La Paz on market days. Daily buses from Puerto Acosta to La Paz at about 1400, more frequent service on Sun, 5 hrs, US$3.75. If you are in a hurry and miss the bus, ask the truck to drop you off 25 km further in Escoma, from where there are frequent minivans to La Paz. Travelling from Bolivia to Peru is equally challenging. Buses leave La Paz for Puerto Acosta at 0600 daily, from Reyes Cardona 772, Cancha Tejar (cemetary district), T02-238 2239. Transport past Puerto Acosta only operates on market days and is mostly cargo lorries. There are daily buses from Tilali to Juliaca, departing around 0100, plus a morning bus (about 0800-1000) on Sun, Tue and Fri.

Rinconada

Bus Buses leave Juliaca at 0600-0700, taking 5-6 hrs, and the road is deteriorates after Huancané. Buses return from Rinconada at 0500-0700, taking about 30 mins less on the downhill journey; US$3.50 one way.

Directory

Juliaca *p236, map p235*

Banks **Interbank**, M Núñez 231. With Red Activa 24 ATM for Visa/Plus, MasterCard/Cirrus and Amex. **BCP**, M Núñez entre Chávez y 9 de Diciembre, changes cash and TCs but has no ATM. Many *cambios* and street changers at Núñez y Bolívar, cash US dollars and soles. **Milenium**, Bolívar y Núñez, change bolivianos, but don't always have small bills. **Internet** There are many places in the centre, all charging US$0.30 per hr.

The southwestern shore and into Bolivia

The road from Puno towards Bolivia runs along the western shore of Lake Titicaca, so the villages described below are easily reached by frequent public transport. Anybody interested in religious architecture should go from Puno to visit these villages. They are all on the main road except Zepita, which is beyond the turn-off to Yunguyo, see page 243. ▸▸ *For Sleeping, Eating and other listings, see pages 243-246.*

Chucuito

An Inca sundial can be seen near the village of Chucuito (19 km), which has an interesting church, **La Asunción**, and houses with carved stone doorways. Visits to Chucuito usually include the Templo de la Fertilidad, **Inca Uyo**, which boasts many phalli and other fertility symbols. The authenticity and original location of these objects is the subject of debate. The locals tend to expect a tip for every and any thing. Nearby, are cave paintings at **Chichiflope**.

Ilave

On the road to Juli is Ilave, where the old road for Tacna branches off. It is typical of a gaunt *altiplano* town, with a good Sunday market where you can buy woven goods. This town received a lot of press in 2004 when the local population lynched the corrupt mayor and besieged the police station. This also blocked all land transport to and from Bolivia.

Juli

The main road then bypasses the little town of Juli, 83 km southeast, which has some fine examples of religious architecture in its four churches. **San Pedro** on the plaza, designated as the cathedral, has been extensively restored. It contains a series of paintings of saints, with the Via Crucis scenes in the same frame, and gilt side altars above which some of the arches have baroque designs. No opening hours are displayed. **San Juan Letrán** ⓘ *mornings only, US$1.15*, has two sets of 17th-century paintings of the lives of St John the Baptist and of St Teresa, contained in sumptuous gilded frames. San Juan is a museum. It also has intricate mestizo carving in pink stone. A long flight of shallow steps leads past the Centro Comunal and schools to the **church of Santa Cruz**, which is closed to visitors, but there is a view of the lake from the plaza in front. The fourth church, **La Asunción** ⓘ *US$0.85*, is also a museum. The great nave is empty, but its walls are lined with colonial paintings with no labels. The original painting on the walls of the transept is fading. Its fine bell tower was damaged by earthquake or lightning. Outside is an archway and atrium which date from the early 17th century. Needlework, other weavings, handicrafts and antiques are offered for sale in town. Near Juli is a small colony of flamingoes. Many other birds can be seen from the road.

Pomata

A further 20 km along the lake is Pomata (US$0.45 from Juli), whose **church of Santiago Apóstol** ⓘ *0700-1200, 1330-1600, free, but give a donation and a tip to the guardian*, is built of red sandstone (1532, started by the Jesuits, finished by the Dominicans). If the *colectivo* does not enter town, get out by the barracks (*cuartel*) and walk up. It stands on a promontory above the main road and has wonderful carvings in Andean mestizo baroque of vases full of tropical plants, flowers and animals in the window frames, lintels and cornices. The windows and font are of alabaster. The beautiful interior contains statues, painted columns, a Spanish tiled floor, paintings of the Cuzqueña school and a cupola decorated with figures whose florid, stylized bodies have linked arms. Beneath the Altar of El Señor del Sepulcro is an altarpiece covered in all the tools used in the construction. At **Zepita**, near Desaguadero, the 18th-century Dominican church is also worth a visit.

Border with Bolivia

There are two principal routes across the border, both of which are fairly straightforward. The one listed first is by far the more popular of the two. There is a third and rarely travelled route (see under Juliaca, above) and, finally, it is possible to cross the border by hydrofoil or catamaran as part of a tour. Peruvian time is one hour behind Bolivian time.

Puno to La Paz via Yunguyo and Copacabana The road is paved from Puno to Yunguyo (the border) and the scenery is interesting. The views are also good on the Bolivian side. The Peruvian immigration office is five minutes' drive from Yunguyo and 100 m from the Bolivian post. It is open 24 hours a day (but Bolivian immigration is only open 0830-1930). When leaving you must get an exit stamp before crossing the border and a tourist visa on the other side. A 90-day visa is normally given when entering Peru (30 days for Bolivia). Be aware of corruption at customs and look out for official or unofficial people trying to charge you a fee on either side of the border (say that you know it is illegal and ask why only gringos are approached to pay the 'embarkation tax').

The Bolivian border town of **Copacabana** is famous for its Dark Virgin of the Lake, La Virgen de Candelaria. From the town, excursions can be made to Isla del Sol and Isla de la Luna on Lake Titicaca. There is a wide variety of hotels, restaurants and other services. All road transport from Copacabana to La Paz has to take the ferry across the Straits of Tiquina.

Puno to La Paz via Desaguadero When leaving Peru for Bolivia, this is the most direct road route, which continues 41 km beyond the turn-off to Yunguyo, all paved for the 150 km to the border. Desaguadero is a scruffy, unscrupulous place, with poor restaurants and dubious accommodation. Tuesday and Friday are *feria* days, busy with locals and their contraband. There is no need to stop over in Desaguadero as all roads to it are paved and if you leave La Paz, Moquegua or Puno early enough you should be at your destination before nightfall.

Peruvian immigration is beside the bridge. It is open 0830-1230 and 1400-2000. Bolivian immigration is open the same hours, except closes at 2100. Both offices are usually closed for dinner around 1830-1900. A 30-day visa is normally given on entering Bolivia, ask for more if you need it, or get an extension in La Paz. Into Bolivia, the road to Guaqui (22 km) and on to La Paz is paved. This particular border crossing allows you to stop at the archaeological site of **Tiahuanaco** ⓘ *US$2.10*, en route. It is possible to do a round trip to the site from Puno in about 12-13 hours. Take an early *colectivo* to Desaguadero, cross the border and take another *colectivo* towards La Paz. Pay the full fare, but ask to be let out at the junction for Tiahuanaco; walk or hitch the 1.5 km to the ruins.

Sleeping

Chucuito *p242*

A Taypikala Hotel & Spa, 18 km south of Puno on the road to Desaguadero, T051-369689, www.taypikala.com. Built in 'inka' style with lots of indoor plants, new-age feel, lovely gardens, most rooms have a view of the lake. Good restaurant, bar, spa, store, disco, medition room, popular with tour groups.

E per person **Albergue Juvenil Las Cabañas**, T051-351276, www.chucuito.com. Great wee cottages, meals, will collect you from Puno if you phone in advance. A very good choice.

Juli *p242*
G per person **Hostal San Pedro**, main plaza. Basic, cold water, shared bath, restaurant.

Border with Bolivia *p243*
There is also accommodation on the Bolivian side. Most places have rooms for sleeping and lock-ups to store your bags.
E-G Hostal Corona, Av Panamericana 248, Desaguadero, T851120. The best hotel of a poor lot, cheaper without bath, TV, hot water, parking, luggage store, no meals.
G San Carlos, Desaguadero. Without bath, extra for hot shower, basic, tiny rooms.
G Hostal Isabel, San Francisco 110, Plaza de Armas, Yunguyo, T051-856019. Price per person. Shared bathroom, hot water, good value, will change money and arrange transport.

Eating

Border with Bolivia *p243*
There are several restaurants in Desaguadero, mostly *pollerías*. On the Peruvian side **Panamericano, Así Es Mi Tierra** and **Perú Criollo** advertise a bit more variety.

Activities and tours

Crillon Tours, PO Box 4785, Av Camacho 1223, La Paz, Bolivia, T591-2-2337533, www.titicaca.com.
Transturin, C Alfredo Ascarrunz 2518, PO Box 5311, La Paz, Bolivia, T591-2- 2422222, www.travelbolivia.com.

Transport

Ilave *p242*
Many buses and *colectivos* go to Ilave from Puno, US$1.40.

Juli *p242*
Colectivos from Puno to Juli cost US$1. They stop in the main plaza before going to the *paradero* outside market, at Ilave 349, from where they return to Puno.

Border with Bolivia *p243*
Puno to La Paz via Yunguyo and Copacabana In Puno 3 companies sell bus tickets for the direct route from Puno to La Paz, taking 6-8 hrs (the fare does not include the Tiquina ferry crossing, US$0.25): **Colectur**, Tacna 221, T051-352302, 0730, US$6.50, combines with **Galería** in Bolivia; **Panamericano**, Tacna 245, T051-354001, 0730, US$7.35, combines with **Diana Tours**; **Tour Perú** (see page 233), 0800, US$8.75, combines with **Combi Tour** (fares rise at holiday times). They stop at the borders and 1 hr for lunch in Copacabana, arriving in La Paz at about 1700. Passengers change buses at Copacabana and it seems that the Bolivian bus may not be of the company indicated and may not be of the same standard as the Peruvian bus. This can cause discomfort and delays. You only need to change money into bolivianos for lunch on this route. Bus fare Puno-Copacabana US$4.40-5.80. There are minibuses and *combis* from the Terminal Zonal in Puno to Yunguyo 0600-1900,

INTENSIVE TITICACA
NEW
Discover the Hidden Pre-Inca treasures in the Southern part of Lake Titicaca, unknown today for the traditional Tourism. Nature, Adventure & Mysticism:
Pariti Island & Local Museum, Urus Iruitos Floating Islands & Quewaya Sustainable Tourism Project, Kalauta Island & Largest Lake Necropolis.
COMPLETE PERU - BOLIVIA DAILY TITICACA CRUISES
Puno / Juli / Sun & Moon Islands / Urus Iruitos Authentic Floating Islands / Andean Roots Eco-Village - Huatajata / La Paz or vice versa
Crillon Tours s.a. Bolivia since 1958
Bolivian and Regional Programs
• LA PAZ, BOLIVIA: P.O. Box 4785 / Av. Camacho 1223 / Phone: (591-2) 2337533 or 2339047 Fax: (591-2) 211-6481 E-mail: titicaca@entelnet.bo - andes@entelnet.bo
• USA INF. OFFICE: 1450 South Bayshore Dr. Suite 815 Miami, / Fl 33131 / Phone: (305) 358-5353 Toll Free 1-888-Titicaca / Fax: (305) 372-0054 / E-mail: darius@titicaca.com
Urus Iruitos Floating Islands & Sustainable Tourism Project
Inca Utama Hotel & SPA (Hutajata) *****
Posada del Inca Ecolodge Sun Island
Andean Roots - Eco Village
www.titicaca.com

2½ hrs, US$1.80. From Yunguyo to the border (Kasani), *colectivos* charge US$0.25 per person. From the border it is a 20-min drive to Copacabana. *Colectivos* and minibuses leave from just outside Bolivian immigration, US$0.50 per person. A taxi from Yunguyo to Copacabana costs about US$1.50 per person. Entering Peru, don't take a taxi Yunguyo-Puno without checking its reliability first, the driver may pick up an accomplice to rob passengers.

Puno to La Paz via Desaguadero

Trici-taxis carry people and their baggage around for US$0.30, but they'll probably ask for more at some point in the ride. To Desaguadero, from the Terminal Zonal in **Puno**, *combis* and minibuses hourly 0600-1900, 2½ hrs, US$1.80. The last bus from the border to Puno leaves at 1930. Taxis between Puno and Desaguadero charge US$30, 1½ hrs. There are minibuses to **La Paz** (105 km from Desaguadero), 1½ hrs, US$1.50. The last one leaves at 1700, though buses may leave later if there are enough passengers. See page 311 for the road from **Moquegua**. **Mily Tours**, Av Panamericana 321, run *colectivos* to Moquegua, US$10, 3½ hrs. Several bus companies do the route for US$6, 4 hrs (Ormeño US$11.75), continuing to **Arequipa**.

To La Paz by hydrofoil or catamaran

There are luxury services from Puno to La Paz by **Crillon Tours** hydrofoil and **Transturin**'s catamarans. **Crillon Tours** services can be booked at their office at **Arcobaleno Tours** (see page 232), or all Puno travel agents have details, or their head office at Av Camacho 1223, La Paz, T591 2-233 7533, www.titicaca.com. The Puno office will take care of all documentation for crossing the border into Bolivia. The main itinerary is: Puno-Copacabana by bus or hydrofoil; Copacabana-Isla del Sol-Huatajata (Bolivia) by hydrofoil; Huatajata-La Paz by bus; 13 hrs. Visits to their establishments can be incorporated into Crillon's tours covering many options. **Crillon** also has a sustainable tourism project with Urus-Iruitos people from the Río Desaguadero area which will be of great interest to anyone who has visited the Urus of the bay of Puno.

Similar services, by more leisurely catamaran, are run by **Transturin**, whose dock is at Chúa, Bolivia. Bookings can be made through **Transturin**'s offices in La Paz, C Alfredo Ascarrunz 2518, Sopocachi, T591 2-242 2222, www.travelbolivia. com (this office offers economical, last-minute bookings, 24 and 48 hrs in advance). The main route is Puno to Copacabana by bus, Copacabana to the Isla del Sol (including a land tour) and on to Chúa by catamaran, then bus to La Paz. The trip can be done in one day, or with a night on board the catamaran, moored at the Isla del Sol. It is also possible to go Puno (depart 0630)-Isla del Sol-Puno (arrive 1930). Transturin also run buses between Puno and La Paz, with no change of bus at the border.

Directory

Border with Bolivia *p243*

Banks Good rates are available for dollars or bolivianos at the two *casas de cambio* in the main plaza in Yunguyo, cash only. TCs can be exchanged but rates poor. It is better to change money (even bolivianos) on the Peruvian side in Desaguadero.

Consulates **Bolivian Consulate**, Jr Grau 339, T051-856032, near the main plaza in Yunguyo. Mon-Fri 0830-1500, for those who need a visa. Some nationalities have to pay, the fee varies per nationality.

Arequipa

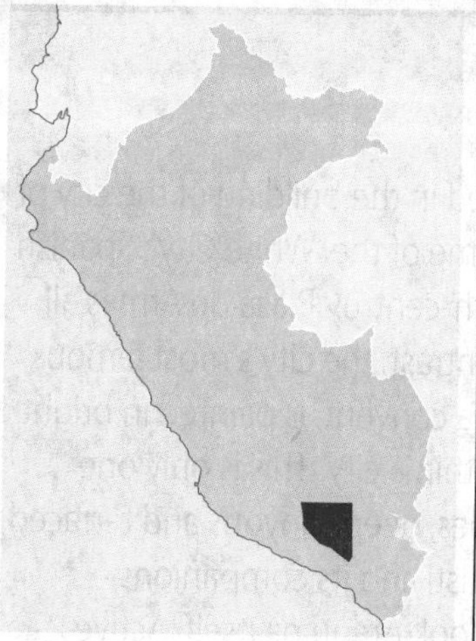

Footprint features

Introduction

The distinctive volcanic sillar used in the building of the city of Arequipa, has given it its nickname of the 'White City'. Spanish churches, mansions and the 19th-centruy Plaza de Armas all shine with this stonework. In contrast, the city's most famous colonial jewel, the Santa Catalina convent, is painted in bright colours, a gorgeous little city within a city. This is only one attraction in a region of volcanoes, deep canyons and terraced valleys. The perfect cone of El Misti and its companions Chachani and Pichu-Pichu overlook Arequipa itself. Active Sabancaya and frequent earth tremors are reminders that this is a very unstable region.

Two famous canyons are within relatively easy reach. To arrive at these great gorges, you must take rough roads at high altitudes. Cotahuasi Canyon is the deepest in the world at 3354 m, but it has not yet achieved the same popularity as its neighbour, Colca. And it was only recently that the ancient peoples here, the Cabana and Collagua, had their villages and farms exposed to the gaze of tourism. There is excellent trekking and riding on the terraces of Colca, accommodation is improving all the time and the calendar is full of festivals. Above all, Colca also happens to be the best place in the whole world to get close-up view of the majestic condor rising on the morning thermals. On the *altiplanos* of this region there are herds of alpaca and vicuña and, at the World Heritage site of Toro Muerto, the largest field of petroglyphs in the world.

There's an individual feeling to this southwestern corner of Peru which, in part, stems from the stubborn pride of its people who have continuously attempted to gain more independence from Lima. Fellow Peruvians will jokingly refer to this region as the 'Independent Republic of Arequipa'.

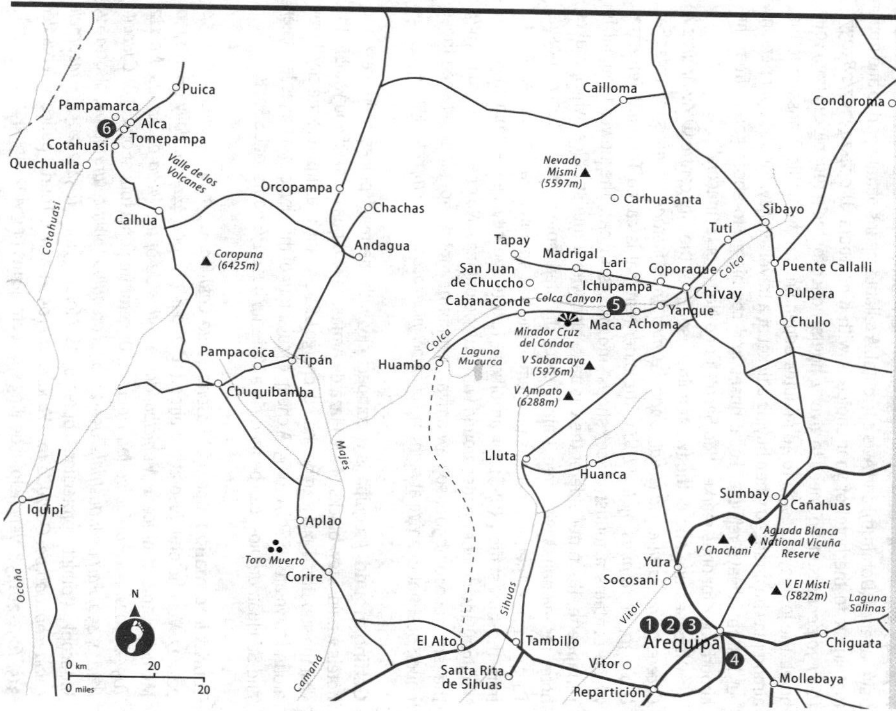

★ Don't miss...

1 **Santa Catalina Convent** The beauty and variety of flowers in vases and the touching quality of some of the rooms in this city in miniature make it a must on anyone's itinerary, page 252.

2 **Museo Santuarios Andinos** This is the home of Juanita (when she is not jet-setting off on some foreign exhibition) and other mummies, victims sacrificed in the highest Andes, page 253.

3 **Yanahuara** Before it gets dark, you should go to the mirador at this city suburb to see the setting sun light up El Misti volcano, page 254.

4 **Molino de Sabandía** Leave the city and pass Inca terraces and views of the volcanoes on the way to the first stone mill in the area, a relaxing half-day out of the city, page 254.

5 **Colca Canyon** Try to catch one of the festivals in the villages and experience the traditional way of life that extends throughout the entire canyon, page 266.

6 **Cotahuasi Canyon** Take a trip to the deepest canyon in the world, more adventurous than Colca because it has not yet acquired major tourist status, page 276.

Arequipa

→ *Phone code: 054. Colour map 5, C6. Altitude: 2380 m.*

The city of Arequipa stands in a beautiful valley at the foot of El Misti volcano, a snow-capped, perfect cone, 5822 m high, guarded on either side by the mountains Chachani (6057 m), and Pichu-Pichu (5669 m). The city was re-founded on 15 August 1540 by an emissary of Pizarro, but it had previously been occupied by Aymara Indians and the Incas. It has since grown into a magnificent city – fine Spanish buildings and many old and interesting churches built of sillar, a pearly white volcanic material were almost exclusively used in the construction of Arequipa – exuding an air of intellectual rigour and political passion. Among its famous sons and daughters are former President Fernando Belaúnde Terry and the novelist and failed presidential candidate, Mario Vargas Llosa (see page 252). Now, Arequipa is the main commercial centre for the south and its fiercely proud people resent the general tendency to believe that everything is run from Lima. » *For Sleeping, Eating and other listings, see pages 256-266.*

Ins and outs

Getting there Aeropuerto Rodríguez Ballón ⓘ *7 km from town, information T054-443464*, has two desks offering hotel reservations and free transport to town, a travel agency (Domiruth) and Avis car rental. A reliable means of transport to and from the airport to the hotel of your choice is with **King Tours** ⓘ *054-243357/283037, US$1.30 per person*. You need to give 24 hours' notice for the return pickup from your hotel. The journey takes 30 to 40 minutes depending on the traffic. Transport to the airport may be arranged when buying a ticket at a travel agency, for US$1 per person, but it's not always reliable. Local buses and combis go to about 500 m from the airport, look for ones marked 'Río Seco', 'Cono-Norte' or 'Zamacola'.

All buses use one of the two terminals south of the city centre ⓘ *Av Andrés A Cáceres s/n, Parque Industrial, opposite Inca Tops factory; 15 mins by colectivo US$0.30, or 10 mins by taxi US$1*. The older terminal is called **Terminal Terrestre,** which contains a tourist office, shops and places to eat. The newer terminal is **Terrapuerto,** the other side of the car park, also with a tourist office (which makes hotel reservations, with free transfers to affiliated hotels, and its own *hostal*, T054-421375). Theft is a serious problem in the bus station area. Take a taxi to and from the bus station (US$1 for an official taxi to the city centre from inside the terminal) and do not wander around with your belongings. No one is allowed to enter the terminal 2100-0500, so new arrivals cannot be met by hoteliers between those hours; best not to arrive at night. » *For further information, see Transport, page 264.*

Getting around Arequipa is a compact city with the main places of interest and hotels within a few blocks of the Plaza de Armas. Take a bus or taxi if you want to the visit the suburbs. Taxis (can be shared) charge US$4-5 from the airport to the city. Fares around town are US$0.70-0.85. A cheap circular tour of the city, down Calles Jerusalén and San Juan de Dios, can be made in a Vallecito bus: 1½ hours for US$0.30.

Tourist information i perú ⓘ *Casona Santa Catalina, C Santa Catalina 210, T054-221227*. Very helpful. Also at the airport ⓘ *2nd floor, T054-444564, daily 0630-1730*. **Municipal tourist office** ⓘ *Municipalidad, south side of the Plaza de Armas, No 112, T054-211021, www.arequipa-tourism.com*. **Dircetur** (regional tourist office) ⓘ *C Jacinto Ibáñez, 450, Parque Industrial, T054-213044, arequipa @mincetur.gob.pe*, 0800-1615. **Indecopi** (tourist protection bureau) ⓘ *Moral 316, T054-212054, mcornejo @indecopi.gob.pe; Quezada 104, Yanahuara, T054-270181*. **Tourist police** ⓘ *Jerusalén 315, T054-201258*, very helpful dealing with complaints or giving directions.

Security There was an increase in street crime in Arequipa in 2005-2006, with many reports of taxi drivers in collusion with criminals to rob both tourists and locals. Theft can be a problem in the market area, especially after dark, in the park at Selva Alegre and on Calles San Juan de Dios and Alvarez Thomas. Be very cautious walking south of the Plaza de Armas area at night. The police are conspicuous, friendly, courteous and efficient, but their resources are limited.

Arequipa

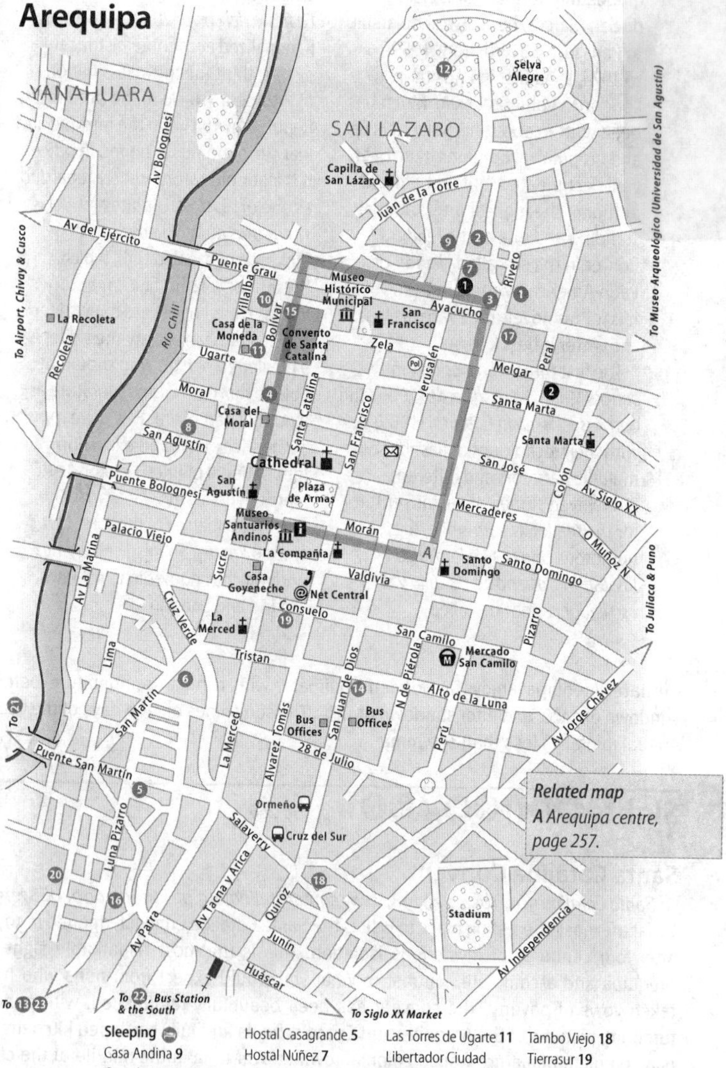

Related map
A Arequipa centre, page 257.

Sleeping
Casa Andina 9
Casa de Mi Abuela 2
Colonial House Inn II 1
El Indio Dormido 22
Home Sweet Home 3
Hostal Bolívar 4
Hostal Casagrande 5
Hostal Núñez 7
Hostal Rivero 17
Hostal Tumi de Oro 8
La Casa de Avila 6
La Casa de Tintin 13
La Estación 21
La Hostería 10
Las Torres de Ugarte 11
Libertador Ciudad Blanca 12
Miamaka 14
Piccola Daniela 15
Point Hostel 20
Posada El Castillo 23
Queen's Villa 16
Tambo Viejo 18
Tierrasur 19

Eating
La Quinta 1
Nómadas 2

Mario Vargas Llosa

The best known of Peru's writers, Mario Vargas Llosa, was born in 1936 in Arequipa and educated in Cochabamba (Bolivia), from where his family moved to Piura. After graduating from the Universidad de San Marcos, he won a scholarship to Paris in 1958 and, from 1959 to 1974, lived first in Paris then in London in voluntary exile. Much has been written about his personal life, and his political opinions have been well documented, but, as befits an author of the highest international standing and one of the leading figures in the so-called 'Boom' of Latin American writers in the 1960s, it is for his novels that Vargas Llosa the writer is best known.

The first three – *La ciudad y los perros* (1963), *La casa verde* (1966) and *Conversación en la Catedral* (1969) – with their techniques of flashback, multiple narrators and different interwoven stories, are an adventure for the reader. Mean-while, the humorous books, like *Pantaleón y las visitadoras* and *La tía Julia y el escribidor* cannot be called lightweight. *La guerra del fin del mundo* marked a change to a more direct style and an intensification of Vargas Llosa's exploration of the role of fiction as a human necessity, extending also to political ideologies. *La fiesta del chivo* (2000) is another fictionalized account of historical events, this time the assassination of President Trujillo of the Dominican Republic in 1961 and the intrigue and fear surrounding his period in office. It is a gripping story, widely regarded as one of his best. His latest novel is *Travesuras de la niña mala* (2006 – Mischiefs of the Bad Girl), which the author calls his first 'love story'. Vargas Llosa has always maintained that in Peruvian society the writer is a privileged person who should be able to mix politics and literature as a normal part of life. This drive for authenticity led to his excursion into national politics. He stood as a presidential candidate in 1990, losing to Alberto Fujimori. He has since taken up Spanish citizenship and now has homes in Lima, Paris, Madrid and London.

Climate Arequipa enjoys a wonderful climate, with a mean temperature before sundown of 23°C, and after sundown of 14°C. The sun shines on 360 days of the year. Annual rainfall is less than 150 mm.

Sights » pp256-266.

Santa Catalina Convent

Santa Catalina 301, T054-229798, www.santacatalina.org.pe, 0900-1600, US$7.25. By far the most interesting place to visit is the Santa Catalina Convent, opened in 1970 after four centuries of mysterious isolation. This is the most remarkable sight in Arequipa and a complete contrast to what you would expect from nuns who had taken vows of poverty. The convent has been beautifully refurbished, with period furniture, pictures of the Arequipa and Cuzco schools and fully equipped kitchens. It is a complete miniature walled colonial town of over 2 ha in the middle of the city. About 450 nuns lived here in total seclusion, except for their women servants.

The few remaining nuns have retreated to one section of the convent, allowing visitors to see a maze of cobbled streets and plazas bright with geraniums and other flowers, cloisters and buttressed houses. These have been restored and painted in white, orange, deep red and blue. There are tours of 1½ hours; there's no set price and many of the guides speak English or German (a tip of US$2.85 is expected). There is a good café, which sells cakes made by the nuns and a special blend of tea.

Around the centre

The elegant **Plaza de Armas**, beautifully laid out with palm trees, gardens and fountain, is faced on three sides by arcaded colonial buildings (rebuilt after an earthquake in 1863) with many restaurants, and on the fourth by the massive **cathedral**. The cathedral was founded in 1612 and largely rebuilt in the 19th century. It is remarkable for having its façade along the whole length of the church and takes up one full side of the plaza. Inside is a fine Belgian organ and elaborately carved wooden pulpit. Despite improved building techniques, the June 2001 earthquake famously caused one of the cathedral's twin towers to collapse. Repairs were completed in 2003. The entrance to the cathedral is on the plaza. Behind is an alley, Pasaje Catedral, with handicraft shops and places for tourists to eat.

A visit to the church and cloister of **La Compañía** at General Morán y Alvarez Thomas, is recommended. The main façade (1698) and side portal (1654) are striking examples of the florid Andean mestizo style. There are two adjoining cloisters now given over to attractive shops. Also of note is the **Capilla Real** (Royal Chapel) ⓘ *Mon-Fri 0900-1130, 1500-1730, US$0.65*, to the left of the sanctuary, and its San Ignacio chapel with a beautiful polychrome cupola. The stark cloister is impressive.

Also worth seeing, west of the plaza, are the recently restored church of **San Agustín** ⓘ *San Agustín y Sucre, Mon-Sat 0800-1200, 1700-1900*, and **La Casona Chávez de la Rosa** ⓘ *San Agustín 104*, part of the Universidad San Agustín, which holds art and photography exhibitions.

Firmly established as one of the major sites in Arequipa, **Museo Santuarios Andinos** ⓘ *La Merced 110, T054-215013/200345, www.ucsm.edu.pe/santury, Mon-Sat 0900-1800, Sun 0900-1500, US$5, discount with student card*, contains the frozen mummies recently found on Ampato volcano. The mummy known as 'Juanita' is particularly fascinating (see page 267). From January to April, Juanita is often jetting round the world, and is replaced by other child sacrifices unearthed in the mountains. Admission to the museum includes a 20-minute video of the discovery in English, followed by an hour-long guided tour in English, French, German, Italian or Spanish (tip the guide).

Museo de Arte Textil ⓘ *Patio del Ekeko, Mercaderes 141, Mon-Sat 1000-2030, Sun 1000-1530*, has an interesting collection of textiles and shows short documentaries about Arequipa. The 16th-century church of **San Francisco** also has a convent and library and opposite is the interesting **Museo Histórico Municipal** ⓘ *Plaza San Francisco 407, Mon-Fri 0900-1700, US$0.50*, with much war memorabilia.

Arequipa is said to have the best-preserved colonial architecture in Peru, apart from Cuzco. Several fine seignorial houses with large carved tympanums over the entrances can be seen in the city centre. Thanks to their being one-storey structures, they have mostly withstood the earthquakes which regularly pound this city. They are distinguished by their small patios with no galleries, flat roofs and small windows, disguised by superimposed lintels or heavy grilles.

One of the best examples is the 18th-century **Casa Tristán del Pozo**, better known as the **Gibbs-Ricketts house** ⓘ *San Francisco 108, Mon-Sat 0915-1245, 1600-1800*, with its fine portal and puma-head waterspouts. It is now the main office of Banco Continental. Other good examples are the **Casa del Moral**, or Williams house ⓘ *C Moral 318 y Bolívar, Mon-Sat 0900-1700, Sun 0900-1300, US$1.80 or US$1 for students*, with a museum, in the Banco Industrial. **Casa de la Moneda** ⓘ *Ugarte y Villalba*, is behind Santa Catalina convent. **Casa Goyeneche** ⓘ *La Merced 201 y Palacio Viejo*, is now an office of the Banco Central de la Reserva. Ask to see the courtyard and fine period rooms. In the next block south is the early 17th-century church of **La Merced** ⓘ *La Merced 303*.

The church of **Santo Domingo** ⓘ *Santo Domingo y Piérola*in 1936 , dates from the 17th century. In its fine door, an indigenous face can be seen amid the flowers and grapes. The central **San Camilo market** ⓘ *between Perú, San Camilo, Piérola and Alto de la Luna*, is worth visiting, as is the **Siglo XX market**, to the east of the rail station.

La Recoleta

ⓘ *Jr Recoleta 117, T054-270966, Mon-Sat 0900-1200, 1500-1700, US$1.50.*
La Recoleta, a Franciscan monastery built in 1647, stands on the other side of the river. It contains several cloisters, a religious art museum, a pre-Columbian museum, two rooms dedicated to the Amazon rainforest, a library with 20,000 volumes including many rarities, and is well worth visiting.

San Lázaro

The oldest district in the city is San Lázaro, a collection of tiny climbing streets and houses quite close to the Hotel Libertador, where you can find the ancient **Capilla de San Lázaro**. At **Selva Alegre** there is a shady park in front of the **Hotel Libertador**, which is within easy walking distance of all the famous churches and main plaza (but see page 251). East of San Lázaro, the **archaeological museum** ⓘ *Av Independencia between La Salle and Santa Rosa, apply to Dr E Linares, the Director, T054-229719, Mon-Fri 0800-1300, US$1*, is at the Universidad de San Agustín. It has a good collection of ceramics and mummies.

Around Arequipa

Northwest

Some 2 km northwest of the city is the district is **Yanahuara**, where there is a 1750 mestizo-style church (opens 1500), with a magnificent churrigueresque façade, all in sillar. The church stands on a plaza, at the end of which is a mirador, through whose arches there is a fine view of El Misti with the city at its feet. There's live music at **Peña El Moro**, on Parque Principal. A score of *picanterías* specialize in piquant foods such as *rocoto relleno* (hot stuffed peppers), *cuy chactado* (seared guinea-pig), *papas con ocopa* (boiled potatoes with a hot spicy yellow sauce) and *adobo* (pork stew).

Churches are usually open 0700-0900 and 1800-2000.

In the hillside suburb of **Cayma**, 3 km northwest of the city, is a delightful 18th-century church ⓘ *open until 1700*, and many old buildings associated with Bolívar and Garcilaso de la Vega. Many local buses go to Cayma.

Beyond the airport, at **Las Canteras de Sillar**, you can see the quarries where the sillar blocks are cut for buildings in the city. They are worth a brief visit if passing, but not a special detour.

Southeast

Tingo has a very small lake and three swimming pools. You should visit on Sunday for local food such as *anticuchos* and *buñuelos*. (Take bus 7, US$0.20.) Three kilometres past Tingo, beside the Sabandía river on the Huasacache road, is **La Mansión del Fundador** ⓘ *0900-1700, US$2.50*, with a cafeteria and bar. Originally built by the founder of Arequipa, Don Garcí Manuel de Carbajal, in 1540, it has been open to the public since 1897 and restored as a museum with original furnishings and paintings. Nearby is the **Mirador Sachaca** ⓘ *US$0.35; take a bus marked 'Sachaca' from C La Merced*. It has fine panoramic views, best between 0630 and 0730 before the smog obscures the view. In the district of Sachaca, 4 km from the centre, is the **Palacio Goyeneche**.

Molino de Sabandía ⓘ *US$1.50, ring the bell for admission*, is 8 km from Arequipa. A round trip by taxi costs US$4. This was the first stone mill in the area, built in 1621. It has been fully restored and the guardian diverts water to run the grinding stones when visitors arrive. The well-kept grounds have old willow trees and the surrounding countryside is pleasant; a worthwhile trip. Adjoining Sabandía is **Yumina**, with many Inca terraces which are still in use and between Sabandía and Arequipa is **Paucarpata**, with an old church and views of terraces, El Misti and Chachani. The **thermal baths of Jesús** ⓘ *0500-1230*, are 30 minutes by car, on the slopes of Pichu-Pichu.

Yura → *Colour map 5, C6.*

Yura, is a pleasant town, 29 km from Arequipa in a small, interesting valley on the west slopes of Chachani. It is popular with Arequipeños for its **thermal baths** ⓘ *Tue-Sat until 1500, US$2*. A bus leaves from Calle San Juan de Dios in Arequipa, every three hours (US$0.40); alight on the main road by the **Yura Tourist Hotel**, which serves meals, and then walk down to the river. The first set of baths contains four small pools which are not suitable for swimming; follow the river to the next one, which is bigger. Note that the water is not very hot. To return to Arequipa, catch a *colectivo* on the main road by the hotel.

El Misti and Chachani → *Colour map 5, C6.*

At 5822 m, El Misti volcano offers a relatively straightforward opportunity to scale a high peak. There are three routes for climbing the volcano; all take two days.

The northeast route starts from the Aguada Blanca reservoir, reached by 4WD, from where a four-hour hike takes you to the Monte Blanco camp at 4800 m. Then it's a five- to six-hour ascent to the top. Two hours takes you back down to the trail.

The southwest route involves taking a 4WD vehicle to the trailhead at Pastores (3400 m), followed by a hike of five to six hours to a camp at 4700 m. A five-hour climb takes you to the summit, before a three-hour descent to the trail.

A southern route (Grau) also starts at 3400 m, with a camp at 4610 m, followed by a five-hour hike to the summit and a two-hour descent.

In all cases contact an experienced guiding agency in Arequipa. Be prepared for early starts and climbing on loose scree. Take plenty of water, food and protection against the weather. Favoured months are May to September.

In recent years climbing the peak of **Chachani**, just to the northwest of El Misti, has also become popular. In the January to April rainy season, when El Misti has a full covering of snow, they say he is wearing his poncho. But in recent years the sight of snow crowning El Misti's summit has become increasingly rare, especially in the drier winter months. Chachani, in contrast, still retains its icy covering, though this too is fast disappearing. The fact that Chachani tops the magic 6000-m mark (6057 m) has led to a growing number of climbers on the mountain.

Remember that both summits are at very high altitude and that this, combined with climbing on scree and sometimes ice, makes it hard going for the untrained; take your time to acclimatize. Proper equipment (crampons, walking pick, etc) is required on Chachani and recent reports of armed hold-ups make it inadvisable for you to climb alone; join a group or take a guide. Further information is available from travel agencies and professional guides; see Climbing page 262 for details. For a description of **Nevado Mismi**, see page 269.

Laguna Salinas

In this area, it is possible to see many of the specialities which inhabit the arid scrub and Polylepis woodland of the Andean west slope. The best road for birdwatching is the one heading east of Arequipa to Laguna Salinas. This large salt lake regularly holds three species of flamingo: Chilean, Andean and puna. It is also a good place to see Andean avocet and puna plover. In the dry season, you may have to hike out towards the middle of the lake, but do not forget your sunglasses as the glare from the salt is fierce. Between Arequipa and Laguna Salinas, birding the Polylepis-clad slopes and arid scrub can reveal various earthcreepers and canasteros not found elsewhere; this is one of only two places for tamarugo conebill.

Sleeping

Maps p251 and p257

L-AL LibertadorCiudad Blanca, Plaza Simón Bolívar, Selva Alegre, T054-215110, www.libertador. com.pe. Safe, large comfortable rooms, good service, swimming pool (cold), gardens, good meals, pub-style bar, cocktail lounge, squash court. Recommended.

A Sonesta Posada del Inca, Portal de Flores 116, T054-215530, www.sonesta.com. On the Plaza de Armas, all the services associated with this chain, **Inkafé café and** bar with good views, restaurant, tiny outdoor pool, business centre with internet. Price rises to **AL** at Christmas time.

A Hostal Casagrande, Luna Pizarro 202, Vallecito, T054-222031, www.aqplink.com /hostal/casagrande.html. Includes taxes, small, cosy, well-furnished, quiet, friendly, good services and restaurant. Recommended.

A-B Casa Andina, C Jerusalén 603, T054-202070, www.casa-andina.com. Part of the attractive Casa Andina chain, with breakfast, comfortable and colourful, central, modern, good restaurant, safe, cable TV, phones, friendly staff, car parking.

B La Posada del Monasterio, Santa Catalina 300, T/F054-405726, www.posada delmonasterio.com.pe. Colonial building opposite Santa Catalina, breakfast included, furnished with antiques, garden. Has a pleasant atmosphere.

C Casa de Mi Abuela, Jerusalén 606, T054-241206, www.lacasademiabuela.com. Very clean, friendly, safe, hot water, laundry, cable TV, swimming pool, rooms at the back are quieter and overlook the garden (but the room at the very back beyond the garden is dark and has no hot water), **E** without bathroom, self-catering if desired, English spoken, internet access US$3 per hr, tours and transport organized in own agency (**Giardino**, T054-221345, www.giardino tours.com), which has good information (expensive), small library of European books, breakfast or evening snacks on patio or in beautiful garden, parking, **B** for apartment for 4, lots of tour groups. Recommended.

C Hostal de la Fuente, Urb Campiña Paisajista D-14A, San Lázaro, T054-203996, delafuente_hostal@hotmail.com. In a residential district 4 blocks from the Plaza de Armas, comfortable rooms, with bath, 24-hrs hot water, cable TV, internet, laundry, café, bar, safe boxes.

C Hostal Solar, Ayacucho 108, T/F054-241793, solar@star.com.pe. Nice colonial building, TV, bath, hot water, includes good breakfast served in nice patio, sun lounge on roof, very secure, quiet.

C Queen's Villa, Luna Pizarro 512, Vallecito, T054-235233, jrowlands@terra.com.pe. With bath, hot water, breakfast, safe, parking, laundry.

C Tierrasur, Consuelo 210, T054-227132, www.tierrasur.com. Modern 3-star, convenient for centre, clean, comfortable, safe, very helpful staff, English spoken, gym. Recommended.

C-D Posada el Castillo, Pasaje Campos 105, Vallecito, T054-201828, www.posadael castillo.com. Newly built Dutch-owned hotel in colonial style 15 mins walk south of Plaza de Armas. Variety of rooms and suites, some with balcony and view of El Misti, free internet, TV, pool, wonderful breakfast, laundry. Recommended.

D Casa de Melgar, Melgar 108, T/F054-222459, www.lacasademelgar.com. Excellent rooms, all different, delightful 18th- century building, with bathroom, hot water all day (solar panel), safe, clean, friendly, nice courtyard, good breakfast in café open in the morning and 1730-2100, book exchange, luggage store. Can arrange good taxi tours with driver, Angel. Recommended.

D Hostal Bolívar, Bolívar 202, T054-200280, www.hostalbolivar.com. Colonial-style, cable TV, internet and fax service, breakfast served in patio. Recommended.

D La Casa de Avila, San Martín 116, T054 213177, www.casadeavila.com. All rooms with bathroom and hot water, price includes good breakfast, spacious, courtyard, guests' kitchen, internet, can arrange airport/bus station pickup, Spanish courses (which are recommended) and other activities.

D **La Casa de Margott**, Jerusalén 304, T054-229517, lacasademargotthostal @hotmail.com. Bright with a massive palm tree in patio, spotless, small bar/café, new, cable TV, phone, security box, bathroom. Recommended.

Arequipa centre

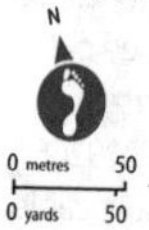

Sleeping
Casa de Melgar **1**
Casablanca Hostal **7**
Colonial House Inn **2**
Hospedaje El Caminante Class **4**
Hostal La Reyna **6**
Hostal Posada Santa Catalina **10**
Hostal Regis **9**
Hostal Solar **11**
La Casa de Margott **3**
La Casita de Ugarte **12**
La Fiorentina **13**
La Posada del Cacique **19**
La Posada del Fraile **20**
La Posada del Monasterio **14**
Lluvia de Oro **15**
Los Balcones de Moral y Santa Catalina **16**
Sonesta Posada del Inca **18**

Eating
Ary Quepay **2**
Bóveda San Agustín **4**
Café Capriccio **5**
Café El Buho **6**
Café Manolo **7**
Café Valenzuela **1**
Cioccolata **8**
El Turko **13**
El Turko II **14**
Fez **9**
La Canasta **17**
La Casita de José Antonio **18**
Lakshmivan **19**
Le Café Art Montreal **10**
Mandala **21**
Pizzería Los Leños **22**
Pushkin **24**
Salchichería Alemana **11**
Sonccollay **28**
Tacos y Tequila **12**
Zig Zag **25**
Zig Zag Crêperie **26**
Zun Zun **15**

Bars & clubs
Blue Margarita **33**
Farren's **34**
Forum & Dejá Vu **30**
Las Quenas **36**

D **La Casa de Tintin**, Urbanización San Isidro F1, Vallecito, T054-284700, www.hoteltintin.com. 15 mins' walk, 5 mins by taxi from the Plaza de Armas. Belgian/Peruvian owned, hot water, cable TV, garden, terrace, sauna, laundry service, restaurant, café, bar, internet, mountain bike hire, pleasant and comfortable, breakfast included. Recommended.

D **La Hostería**, Bolívar 405, T/F054-289269, lahosteria@terra.com.pe. Small, friendly, comfortable and attractive. Recommended.

D **Los Balcones de Moral y Santa Catalina**, Moral 217, T054-201291, losbalcones@hotmail.com. Convenient, 1 block from Plaza de Armas and close to Santa Catalina, large rooms, comfortable beds, with bath, hot water, laundry, café, tourist information.

D **Miamaka**, San Juan de Dios 402, T054-241496, hotel_miamaka@terra.com.pe. Excellent service and well-decorated, cable TV, helpful, English spoken. Recommended, but not the safest area.

D-E **Casablanca Hostal**, Puente Bolognesi 104, a few m from the Plaza de Armas, T054-221327, www.casablancahostal.com. Super stylish hostal, lovely minimalist rooms in a colonial building. Ambient lighting, most rooms with private bath (hot water) and balcony. Has the atmosphere of an exclusive docklands apartment. Family suite available.

D-E **La Posada del Fraile**, Santa Catalina 103, T054-282006, posadadelfraile@hotmail.com. Cheaper without breakfast, with bath, clean, safe, well-furnished, very central.

E **Home Sweet Home**, Rivero 509A, T054-405982, www.homesweethome-peru.com. Run by María and daughter Cathy, who runs a travel agency and speaks Spanish, English, Italian, French, very helpful, warm and inviting atmosphere, substantial fresh breakfast included. Private or shared bath, hot water all day, simple rooms.

E **Hospedaje El Caminante Class**, Santa Catalina 207-A, 2nd floor, T054-203444. With bathroom, cheaper without, hot water, TV, clean, laundry service and facilities, sun terrace, very helpful owners. Recommended.

E **Hostal Núñez**, Jerusalén 528, T054-233268, hostal_nunez@terra.com.pe. With bathroom, cheaper without, hot water, small rooms but comfortable, TV, laundry, safe, good value, helpful, breakfast on roof terrace overlooking the city.

E Hostal Regis, Ugarte 202, T054-226111. Colonial house, French-style interior, clean, hot water all day, cooking and laundry facilities (good laundry service), sun terrace with good views, safe deposit, luggage store, video rental, tours arranged, but poor breakfast.

E Hostal Tumi de Oro, San Agustín 311A, 2½ blocks from the Plaza de Armas, T/F054- 281319. With bathroom, French and English spoken, hot water, roof terrace, book exchange, tea/coffee facilities, safe. Recommended.

E La Estación, Loreto 419, Umacollo, T054-273852, www.backpackerperu.com. Unusual dormitory accommodation in two train carriages, includes breakfast, hot water, restaurant next door, friendly, clean and fresh. 10 mins' walk from Plaza, ask directions for 'el Ovalo del Vallecito', English spoken.

E La Posada del Cacique, Puente Grau 219, T054-202170, posadadelcacique@yahoo.es. Old house with tall ceilings, teeny patio, sun terrace, friendly, good hot water, English spoken, family atmosphere, **F** without bath, also dorm accommodation, safe storage facilities, breakfast available, laundry service, will pick up from terminal. Recommended.

E Las Torres de Ugarte, Ugarte 401-A, T/F054-283532, hostaltorresdeugarte@star.com.pe. Next to Santa Catalina convent, occasional hot water, cable TV, roof terrace, laundry service, parking, safe, luggage store, helpful staff, price includes breakfast served in a sunny room. Recommended.

E Lluvia de Oro, Jerusalén 308, T054-214252, lluvia_de_oro@hotmail.com. Cheaper without bath, English-speaking, breakfast US$2, good views, laundry service, friendly. Recommended.

E-G Tambo Viejo, Av Malecón Socabaya 107, IV Centenario, 5 blocks south of the plaza near the rail station, T054-288195, www.tamboviejo.com. 5 blocks south of the plaza near the rail station. Rooms vary and range from double with bath to dormitory, quiet, English and Dutch spoken, walled garden, hot water, breakfast extra, expensive laundry service, cable TV, safe deposit, coffee shop, bar, book exchange (2 for 1), money changed, tourist information for guests, use of kitchen, internet, phone for international calls, bike rental, popular with young travellers, luggage store extra, tours and volcano climbs arranged. For a small fee, you can use the facilities if passing through. Telephone the hostel and they will pick you up free of charge from 0500-2100 as it's some distance from centre and not the safest area.

F Casa Itzhak, Av Parra 97, T054-204596, 994 6643 (mob). With and without bath, includes breakfast, cable TV, laundry service, restaurant, free transport to bus station, very helpful.

F Colonial House Inn, Puente Grau 114, T/F054-223533, colonialhouseinn@hotmail.com. Hot water, quieter rooms at the back, laundry facilities and service, kitchen facilities, roof terrace, good choice of breakfasts, owners speak English. Same owners run **Colonial House Inn II**, Rivero 504, which is more modern and nicer.

F Hostal La Reyna, Zela 209, T054-286578, hostalreyna@yahoo.com. With or without bath, two more expensive rooms at the top of the house (very good), hot water 24 hrs, clean, can be noisy because of location, the daughter speaks English, laundry, breakfast for US$1.15, rooftop seating, can arrange Spanish classes, will store luggage and arrange trips to the Colca Canyon and volcanoes, especially Misti and Chachani a bit chaotic, but recommended nonetheless). Do not believe taxi drivers who say the hotel is closed or full; ring the doorbell and check for yourself.

F Hostal Rivero, Rivero 420, T054-229266. Cheaper with shared bath, hot water, cable TV extra, medical assistance, laundry facilities, very helpful, good value.

F Hostal Posada Santa Catalina, Santa Catalina 500, T054-243705. Comfortable rooms arranged around a courtyard, roof terrace with great views, charming and helpful staff. Can arrange trips and accommodation in other cities.

F Piccola Daniela, Bolivar 400, T054-405727, piccoladanielaaqp@hotmail.com. Includes breakfast, **F** without bath, good value, cable TV, hot water, tiny patio, no English.

F per person **The Point Hostel**, Av Lima 515, Vallecito, T054-286920, www.thepointhostels.com. In a relaxed suburb, free airport/bus station pickup. Nice building with big garden, great place to meet other travellers, lots of services (free internet, laundry, DVDs etc) and a big party pad. Other **Points** are located in Lima and Cuzco.

G per person **El Indio Dormido**, Av Andrés Avelino Cáceres B-9, T054-427401, the_sleeping_indian@ yahoo.com Close to bus terminal, free transport to centre, some rooms with bath, comfortable beds, **F**, TV, clean, very helpful.

G **Fiorella**, Octavio Muñoz Nájar 262, T054-226078. Family stay, cheap, a bit out of town, phone to ask if she has a room available.

G **La Casita de Ugarte**, Ugarte 212, T054-204363. English/Peruvian run, large basic rooms, colonial building, good value.

G **La Fiorentina**, Puente Grau 110, T054-202571. Cheaper without bath, hot water, comfortable, ask for a good room, family atmosphere, tours arranged, laundry facilities, use of kitchen extra.

Eating

Maps p251 and p257

Several restaurants overlook the Plaza de Armas; their staff may pounce on you good-naturedly as you pass. For typical Arequipeño food, head to Av Arancota, in the Tingo District, by the Río Chili. **La Cecilia** is highly recommended. Typical Arequipeño food is also available at the San Camilo market. A good local speciality is Mejía cheese. You should also try the queso helado, which is frozen fresh milk mixed with sugar and a sprinkling of cinnamon. The local chocolate is excellent: **La Ibérica**, in Patio del Ekeko, Mercaderes 141, is top quality, but expensive. The toffee and the fruit drinks called papayada and tumbada are also local specialities in the market and restaurants. Try **Casa Tropical**, on the first block of Rivero for a huge selection.

TTT **La Quinta**, Jerusalén 522. Excellent food, large portions of local food but limited menu, some vegetarian dishes, attentive service, quiet garden, aimed primarily at the tourist market.

TTT **Tradición Arequipeña**, Av Dolores 111, Paucarpata, T054-246467. Restaurant serving excellent food, popular with tourists and locals alike, also dance hall. There are many other restaurants and discos on this avenue, some distance from the centre.

TT **Ary Quepay**, Jerusalén 502. Excellent local meat and vegetarian dishes, 1000-2400, very touristy, but fun.

TT **Café-Restaurante Bóveda San Agustín**, Portal San Agustín 127-129. Attractive, good value breakfasts and lunches, evening specials, opens at 0700.

TT **El Turko II**, San Francisco 315. Excellent Turkish, local and international food, has a lovely courtyard. Recommended.

TT **La Casita de José Antonio**, Plaza San Francisco 401 y Zela. Cevichería, fish and seafood, lunchtime only.

TT **Nómadas**, Melgar 306. Swiss and South American owned, breakfasts, wide menu including vegetarian, sandwiches.

TT **Pizzería Los Leños**, Jerusalén 407. Excellent, good atmosphere, evenings only, popular, especially with tourists.

TT **Sonccollay**, Portal de San Agustin 149. Serving 'Inca and Pre-Inca' dishes, this restaurant gives a new twist to 'traditional' food. Stone-cooked alpaca steaks and meats are a speciality. Hosted by an entertaining owner, plenty of home-made *chicha*.

TT **Zig Zag**, Zela 210. In a colonial house, European (including Swiss) and local dishes, excellent meats include ostrich and alpaca, top class.

TT **Zig Zag Crêperie**, Santa Catalina 208. Excellent crepes, good value set lunch, also snacks, cocktails, coffee.

T **Café El Buho**, in Casona Chávez de la Rosa (UNSA), San Agustín. Evenings only. Recommended.

T **El Turko**, San Francisco 216. Kebabs, coffee, breakfasts, good sandwiches, 0700-2200.

T **Fez**, San Francisco 229. Delicious falafel, Middle Eastern fast food and coffee, friendly, courtyard. Same company as **El Turko**.

T **Lakshmivan**, Jerusalén 402. Vegetarian, set lunch for US$1.25, pleasant courtyard, good value and healthy, but slow service.

T **Mandala**, Jerusalén 207, mandala26@ correoweb.com. Good value vegetarian, breakfast, 3 set menus for lunch, buffet, dinner, friendly staff. Recommended.

T **Tacos y Tequila**, Ugarte 112. All the Mexican regulars, tacos, burritos, enchiladas, quesadillas, as vegetarian or carnivorous as you like. Cheap, and you can even wear a big hat and pretend to be in *The Good, the Bad and the Ugly* – which one are you?

Cafés

Café Capriccio, Mercaderes 121. Not that cheap, but excellent coffee, cakes etc.

Café Manolo, Mercaderes 107 and 113. Great cakes and coffee, also cheap lunches, pastas, sandwiches and juices.
Café Valenzuela, Moran 114. Fantastic coffee, locals' favourite.
Cioccolata, Mercaderes 120. Among the best for cakes, nicely decorated.
La Canasta, Jerusalén 115. Bakes excellent baguettes twice daily, also serves breakfast and delicious apple and brazil nut pastries.
Pushkin, Ugarte 121B. Good for set breakfasts, crêpes, burgers, very friendly, pleasant.
Salchichería Alemana, San Francisco 137. More sausages than you can wave a knackwurst at, plus some very good empanadas and sandwiches. Good value and popular.
Zun Zun, San Francisco 304, T054-283086. Best bagels (with cream cheese!) in town, pastries, burritos and excellent coffee. Fresh fruit juices and smoothies, very friendly owner and staff. Free internet for customers.

Bars and clubs

Maps p251 and p257
There are many good dancing spots on Av Ejército in Yanahuara, but most night-owls head to Av Dolores, a short taxi ride away (US$1), which can get rowdy.
Try **Salsodromo** for salsa, or **Cajuma** and **Siomama**.
Blue Margarita, Melgar 119. Large club with several areas, good mix of music.
Déjà Vu, San Francisco 319-B. Café, restaurant and bar, good food, relaxing terrace, DJ evenings and live music, shows movies, 2000-2400. Recommended.
Farren's, Pasaje La Catedral. Friendly Irish bar with local and imported (expensive) beer.
Forum, San Francisco 317. Rock café, live music Thu-Sat 1800-0400, disco, pool tables, US$5 cover if band is playing, includes 1 drink, drinks US$1.50.
La Quinta, Jerusalén 522. For *peña* folklore music, weekends mainly, US$1.50 cover.
Las Quenas, Santa Catalina 302. For *peña* music, Mon-Fri 2100.
Le Café Art Montreal, Ugarte 210. Atmospheric Canadian-run jazz/blues restaurant/bar with live music Wed and Sat.
Siwara, Santa Catalina 210. Trendy hangout, lively in the evenings, good food, and some live music.

Festivals and events

Maps p251 and p257
6 Jan El Día de los Reyes in the district of Tiabaya is traditionally celebrated by shaking the fruit from pear trees.
10 Jan Sor Ana de Los Angeles y Monteagudo, a festival for the patron saint of Santa Catalina monastery.
2-3 Feb Fiesta de la Virgen de la Candelaria is celebrated in the churches of Cayma, Characato, Chiguata and Chapi with masses, processions of the Virgin through the streets, and fireworks.
3 Mar Fiesta de La Amargura is a movable feast in Paucarpata, during which the Passion Play is enacted in the main plaza. **Domingo de Cuaresma**, in the district of Tiabaya, is also dedicated to Jesus Christ. Residents gather in the plaza and carry the cross from there up to a nearby hilltop, crossing the Río Chili.
Mar/Apr Semana Santa celebrations in Arequipa are carried out Sevillano style, with the townsfolk turned out in traditional mourning dress. There are huge processions every night, culminating in the burning of an effigy of Judas on **Easter Sun** in the main plazas of Cayma and Yanahuara, and the reading of his 'will', containing criticisms of the city authorities. Afterwards, people retire to the *picanterías* to partake of a little Adobo a la Antaño with some *pan de tres puntas*.
1 May Fiesta de la Virgen de Chapi is a great pilgrimage to the sanctuary of Chapi and one of the most important religious ceremonies in the region.
May Known as the **Month of the Crosses**, during May there are ceremonies on hilltops throughout the city.
15 May The popular fiesta of **San Isidro Labrador** takes place in Sachaca, Chuquibamba and other towns and villages in the valley, and lasts for 7 days.
13 Jun A remembrance of **San Antonio de Padua**, patron of hopeless cases, is held in the churches of Tingo Grande and San Francisco, among others.
29 Jun In Yanahuara, the **Fiesta de San Juan**, the local patron saint, is held with mass and fireworks.
6-31 Aug Fiesta Artesanal del Fundo del Fierro, a sale and exhibition of artesanía from all parts of Peru, taking place near Plaza San

Ancient apparel

Four thousand years before the Spanish *conquistadores* set foot on Peruvian soil, the indigenous peoples excelled at the textile arts. Cotton was cultivated on the arid coast but, up on the high Andean plain, there was a ready supply of fibre in the shape of the native camelids – llamas, alpacas, vicuñas and guanacos. Alpacas and llamas were domesticated as early as 4000 BC and the wild camelids (guanacos and vicuñas) were used as clothing even further back, by hunters who roamed the bleak, high Andean plateau. By 1500-1000 BC llamas were being used for ritual burial offerings, indicating their prestige.

Camelid fibre is easy to spin and dye and allowed the ancient weavers to develop extraordinarily fine spinning techniques. The pre-Columbian peoples prized the silky soft fibre of the alpaca, in particular. Living at altitudes of 4000 m, where temperatures can drop to -15°C, these animals have developed a coat that not only has thermal properties but is also soft and resistant. Production of alpaca fibre remains low because more than 75% of Peru's alpacas are in the hands of small breeders and peasant communities who still herd and manage their animals in much the same way as their ancestors.

Francisco. At the same time, 6-17 Aug is the celebration of the **city's anniversary**; various events are held, including music, dancing and exhibitions. On the eve of the actual day, the 15th, there is a splendid firework display in the Plaza de Armas and a decorated float parade. For a short time it feels like Rio Carnival with music everywhere, no space to move and parties continuing till morning. There is also a mass ascent of El Misti from the Plaza de Armas. It is virtually impossible to find a hotel room during the celebrations.

30 Aug El Día de Santa Rosa is celebrated in the churches of Tomilla, Cayma and Huancarqui in the Majes Valley.

Nov In Arequipa, this is the month of the traditional **guaguas**, which are *bizcochos* (sponge cakes) filled with *manjar* (caramel made from boiling milk and sugar).

Shopping

Maps p251 and p257

Alpaca goods, textiles and clothing

Arequipa is an excellent place to buy top-quality alpaca knitwear.

Alpaca 21, Jerusalén 115, of 125, T054-213425. Recommended.

Casa Secchi, Av Víctor Andrés Belaunde 124, in Umacollo (near the aeroplane statue). This shop sells good clothing, arts and crafts.

Colca Trading Company, Santa Catalina 300B, T054-242088 (Lima 01-254 1885), colcatradingperu@yahoo.com. Sells a wide variety of naturally coloured cotton and alpaca clothing for adults and children.

Incalpaca, parent company of Alpaca 111 (www.alpaca111.com), Av.Juan Bustamante de la Fuente s/n, Tahuaycani, T054-251025, in outskirts (large store with some good bargains and a small zoo of camelids), also in Claustros del Compañía, local 18, T205931, www.incalpaca.com.

Michell y Cia, Juan de la Torre 101, T054-202525, www.michell.com.pe. Factory outlet, excellent place for alpaca yarn in huge variety of colours, also a clearance room for baby and adlult alpaca yarn is sold. They also sell other types of wool. Alpaca garments also for sale. 1920s machinery on display.

Millma's, Pasaje Catedral 117 and 112 opposite, millmas@hotmail.com. 100% baby alpaca goods, run by Peruvian family high quality, beautiful designs, good prices.

Patio del Ekeko, Mercaderes 141, T054-215861, www.patiodelekeko.com, is a shopping and entertainment and cultural centre. Shops include **Alpaca 111** for alpaca and vicuña (recommended for high-quality alpaca and wool products), **Ilaria** for fine jewellery and silverware, **La Ibérica** for chocolates and **Artesanías del Ekeko**. There is also the **Café del Ekeko**, which has internet, as well as sandwiches, desserts, coffee and a bar (**Centro del Pisco**), and **Museo de Arte Textil** (see Sights page 252).

Sombrería El Triunfino, N de Piérola 329-331. A good selection of hats, but pricey.

Bookshops

For international magazines, look along San Francisco, between Mercaderes and San José.

Librería El Lector, San Francisco 221. Wide selection, including of Peruvian authors, book exchange in various languages.

Librerías San Francisco has branches at Portal de Flores 138, San Francisco 102-106 and 133-135. Books on Arequipa and Peru, some in English.

SBS Book Service, San Francisco 125. Has a good selection of travel books etc.

Handicrafts

Arequipa is noted for its leather work. The main street of saddlers and leather workers is Puente Bolognesi. The handicraft shop in the old prison opposite San Francisco is particularly good for bags. There are markets which are good for general handicrafts. The covered market opposite the Teatro Municipal on Mercaderes is recommended for knitted goods, bags, etc. Also worth a try is the market around Valdivia and Nicolas de Piérola. The large **Fundo del Fierro** handicraft market behind the old prison on Plaza San Francisco is also worth a visit. Shop 14 sells alpaca-wool handicrafts from Callalli in the Colca Canyon.

Photography

Try **Foto Esparza**, Mercaderes 321-A-6132-2, T054-992783 (home 054-253125) for repairs; **Foto Mundo Color**, San Francisco 218-A, for prints (US$3.50 for 24) and the shop at Palacio Viejo 105 for Fuji slide film.

Supermarkets

El Super, on the south side of Plaza del Armas. Buy supplies for trekking here.

▲ Activities and tours

Maps p251 and p257

Climbing and trekking

Recommended climbing guides include **Julver Castro** at **Mountrekk**, T054-601833, julver_mountrekk@hotmail.com, an experienced guide, and **Jörg Krosel**, T054-997971, joergkrosel@hotmail.com.

Colca Trek, Jerusalén 401 B, T054-206217, www.trekinperu.com. Run by the English-speaking Vlado Soto, this company is recommended for climbing, trekking and mountain biking in the Colca Canyon. Vlado is one of the best guides for the Cotahuasi Canyon. He also rents equipment and has topographical maps. Recommended.

Naturaleza Activa, Santa Catalina 211, T054-695793, naturactiva@yahoo.com. Experienced guides, knowledgeable, climbing and trekking. Good quality mountain biking and safety equipment. They also offer paragliding and rafting trips.

Selern Services, Urb Puerta Verde F13, José LB y Rivero, Arequipa, T054-348685, www.selernexpediciones.com. Trekking in Colca and Cotahuasi canyons, adventure tourism, volcano and rock climbing.

Volcanyon Travel, C Villalba 414, T054-205078, mario-ortiz@terra.com.pe. Trekking and some mountain bike tours in the Colca Canyon, also volcano climbing.

Carlos Zárate Aventuras, Santa Catalina 204, of 3, T054-202461/263107, www.zarate advenures.com. Run by Carlos Zárate of the Mountaineering Club of Peru. Good family- run business that always works with qualified mountain guides. A specialist in mountaineering and exploring, with a great deal of information and advice and some equipment rental. Carlos also runs trips to the source of the Amazon, Nevado Mismi, as well as trekking in the Cotahuasi canyon and climbing tougher peaks such as Coropuna.

Guides

Gerardo J Pinto Abraca, geratour@yahoo.com For general tours, speaks good English, helpful, lots of information.

Holley's Unusual Excursions, T/F054-258459 (home) daily 1700-0700, or all day Sat and Sun, or Mon-Fri 0800-1600 T054-222525 and leave a message, angocho@terra.com.pe. Expat Anthony Holley runs trips in his Land Rover to El Misti, Toro Muerto, the desert and coast.

Richard Saraya Chambi, PP JJ San José, Manzana T, Cote 6, Comité 10, Distrito de Tiabaya, T054-488063, sacgra@yahoo.com. Reliable, trustworthy, helpful, for tours to Colca, El Misti, etc.

Rafting

Río Chili (year round, Grade 2-4): just outside Arequipa but highly water dependent and relying on dam releases to make it worthwhile. A fun half-day out if need a break from the heat.

Río Colca (Jun, Grade 4-5): possibly even harder than the Cotahuasi, this rarely run expedition river has had its fair share of casualties in the past. Be prepared for rocks falling off the cliffs almost continuously, sandflies, storms and out of this world whitewater. Recent seismic activity around Arequipa has caused major changes to several rapids; definitely book with the local experts.

Río Cotahuasi (May-Jun, Grade 4-5): this is a total expedition, including a long drive in past Corupuna mountain, a two-day trek around the spectacular Sipia Falls (where the river drops 150 m into an impenetrable gorge), followed by six days of non-stop technical whitewater. The scenery is out of this world, including pre-Inca Huari culture terracing and ruins all in an incredibly deep desert canyon. Probably the best whitewater river on offer in Peru, only a handful of operators offer this trip and only one or two depart each year. Book early only with companies who have the experience.

Río Majes (all year, Grade 2-3): where the Colca emerges from its gorge it becomes the Río Majes and some day trips can be organized directly from Arequipa. Good fresh water shrimp make up for the pretty average whitewater.

Cusipata, Jerusalén 408, T054-203966, www.cusipata.com. Recommended as the best local operator, run 6-day trips on the Río Colca. May-Dec, Río Chili 1-day kayak courses, also trekking and mountain bike tours.

Tour operators

These agencies have been recommended as helpful and reliable. Most run tours to the Colca Canyon (page 266). Many agencies on Jerusalén, Santa Catalina and around Plaza de Armas sell air, train and bus tickets and offer tours of Colca, Cotahuasi, Toro Muerto, Campiña and the city. Prices vary greatly so shop around. As a general rule, you get what you pay for, so check details of the the cheapest of tours carefully and make sure that there are enough people for the tour to run. Many tourists prefer to contract tours through their hotel. If a travel agency puts you in touch with a guide, make sure he or she is official. It is not advisable to book tours to Machu Picchu here; make all these arrangements in Cuzco.

A I Travel Tours, Santa Catalina 203, of 1, T054-222052, www.aitraveltours.com. Peruvian-Dutch tour operator. Tours and trekking to Colca Canyon, as well as tours throughout Peru for groups and individuals. Book exchange.

Eco Tours, Jerusalén 409, T054-202562, ecotours@terra.com.pe. Regular and adventure tours, recommended for Colca tours, Spanish lessons, accommodation arranged.

Illary Tours, Santa Catalina 205, T054-220844, illarytours@hotmail.com. English-speaking guides. Daily 0800-1300, 1500-1930. Good for 'classical' tours in the Colca region, straightforward and friendly. Teresa is a good source of information.
Peru Adventure Tours, Jerusalén 410, T054-221658, www.peruadventures tours.com. Downhill mountain biking, start at 0700 with 4WD 3-hr trip into Misti and Chachani mountains, stopping along the way for sightseeing. Cycle ride starts at Azufrero (5000 m), finishing in Arequipa at 1600. All equipment, oxygen and snack provided. English-speaking guide.
Pablo Tour, Jerusalén 400-AB-1, T054- 203737, www.pablo tour.com. Family-run agency that owns several *hostales* in Cabaconde (**Valle del Fuego** etc; page 274); they know the area well. Free tourist information, sells topographical maps, hotel and bus reservations. Son Edwin Junco Cabrera can usually be found in the office, T054-961 1241 (mob), he speaks fluent French and English. The family are keen to promote 'mixed adventure tours': several days exploring the region with combinations of biking (safety equipment provided), horse riding, trekking and rafting – many options available. Good for a challenge!
Santa Catalina Tours, Santa Catalina 219-223, T054-216994. Offer unique tours of Collagua communities in the Colca Canyon. Daily 0800-1900. Recommended.
Transcontinential Arequipa, Puente Bolognesi 132, oficina 5, T054- 213843, transcontinental-aqp@terra.com.pe. Cultural and wildlife tours in the Colca Canyon.

Transport

Maps p251 and p257

Air

Several flights daily to and from **Lima**, with Lan, Aero Cóndor, Star Perú, Taca and Wayra Perú. Lan also to **Juliaca** and **Cuzco**.

Airline offices Most tour agencies sell air tickets. Prices are quoted in dollars but payment is in soles so check exchange rate carefully. **A&R**, Moral 212, T054-285050, Iberia representative, reconfirmation and sales. **Lan**, Santa Catalina 118-C, T054-201100. **Servicios Aéreos AQP**, Santa Catalina 210, T054-281800, www.saaqp. Com.pe, for private hire and tourist flights to the Colca Canyon and around the country. **Star Perú**, Santa Catalina 105a, T054-221896. **Taca**, Av Cayma 636 y Av Ejército, p 1 Banco Wiese Sudameris, T0800-18222. **WayraPerú**, Portal de San Agustín 113, T054-222627.

Bus

For details of the terminals, see Ins and outs, page 250. A terminal tax of US$0.30 must be paid on entry to the platform. Check which terminal your bus will leave from as it may not depart from the terminal where you bought your ticket. All the bus companies have their offices in the **Terminal Terrestre** and several also have offices in **Terrapuerto**. Some tour operators also make bus reservations for a small fee.

To **Lima**, 1011 km, 16-18 hrs, 'normal' service US$8.70, 'imperial' US$17.40 (video, toilet, meals, comfortable seats, blankets), 'crucero' US$23-29 several daily. **Enlaces** (T054-430333, office only in Terrapuerto), **Tepsa** (T054-424135), **Cruz del Sur** (T054-217728) and **Ormeño** (T054-424187) are recommended (prices quoted are for Cruz del Sur). The road is paved but drifting sand and breakdowns may prolong the trip. Buses will stop at the major cities en route, but not always Pisco. The desert scenery is stunning.

To **Nazca**, 566 km, 9 hrs, US$7.25-10 (US$30 on Ormeño Royal service), several buses daily, mostly at night and most buses continue to Lima. Beware, some bus companies to Nazca charge the Lima fare. To **Moquegua**, 213 km, 3 hrs, US$3-5.85, several buses and *colectivos* daily. To **Tacna**, 320 km, 6-7 hrs, US$7-11, several buses daily, most with **Flores**.

To **Cuzco**, all buses now go via Juliaca or Puno, US$15-18, 10 hrs. Most companies use double-decker buses (toilet, TV, hostess, etc), eg **Enlaces, Cruz del Sur, Cial** and **Ormeño**, running one morning and, some companies, one afternoon bus. There is a new, quick paved road to **Juliaca**, via Yura and Santa Lucía, cutting the Arequipa–Juliaca journey time to 4 hrs, US$3, and **Puno**, 6 hrs, US$4.50-6. Most buses and *colectivos* continue to Puno. **Sur Oriente** and **Julsa** are recommended.

Transportes Milagros, La Reyna (recommended) and **Andalucia** have 7 departures daily from Arequipa to **Chivay** (for the Colca Canyon) continuing to

Cabanaconde; a further 75 km, 2 hrs, US$1. **La Reyna** has the quickest service at about 6 hrs, US$3.85; others US$3. Buy a ticket in advance to ensure a seat (many agencies can buy them for you for a fee).

Car and taxi

Car hire Avis, Palacio Viejo 214, T054-282519, or at the airport T054-443576. **Transjesa**, Urb Guardia Civil III Etapa E-6, Paucarpata, T054-460403, www.planet.com/transjesa. Also at the airport. Good value and new vehicles. **Genesis**, Jerusalén y Puente Grau, T054-202033. Rents 4x4s in good condition, can also arrange drivers. Owner of **Hostal Reyna**, see Sleeping, can arrange cars, vans and 4x4s with drivers. Recommended.

Radio taxis: **Nova Taxi**, T054-252511; **Taxi 21**, T054-212121; **Telemóvil**, T054-221515; **Taxitur**, T054- 422323; **Henry Málaga**, T054-655095, Spanish only.

Train

The railway goes from Arequipa to Juliaca, where it divides, one line going north to Cuzco, the other south to Puno. With the opening of the new Arequipa–Juliaca highway, the decreased demand for rail travel has led to the suspension of regular passenger services on this route. **PerúRail**, www.perurail.com, runs trains for private charter for groups of over 40.

Directory

Maps p251 and p257

Banks **ATM Globalnet** cash machines everywhere, eg on the Plaza, at **i perú** offices. Many give cash in soles or US$ and they accept a wide range of cards: Visa, Plus, Diners Club, Amex, Maestro, Cirrus and many Peruvian cards. **Interbank**, Mercaderes 217. MasterCard representative and ATM, also Visa and AmEx, US$5 commission on TCs. **BCP**, San Juan de Dios 125, also at Santo Domingo y Jerusalén. Accepts Visa Card (has ATM) and gives good rates, no commission. Recommended. **BBV Continental**, San Francisco 108. Visa ATM, US$12 commission on TCs. **BSCH**, C Jeru-salén. Changes Visa and Citicorp TCs, low rates, has Visa and MasterCard ATM. **Banco Wiese**, Mercaderes 410. Change money at cambios on Jerusalén and San Juan de Dios, and several travel agencies. **Sergio A del Carpio D**, Jerusalén 126, T054-242987, good rates for dollars. **Via Tours**, Santo Domingo 114, good rates. **Casa de Cambio**, San Juan de Dios 109, T054-282528, good rates. It is almost impossible to change TCs on Sat afternoon or Sun; try to find a sympathetic street changer. Better rates for cash dollars in banks and casas de cambio. **Consulates** **Bolivia**, Rivero 408, of 6, T054-213391. Mon-Fri 0900-1400, 24 hrs for visa (except those needing clearance from La Paz), go early. **Chile**, Mercaderes 212, p 4, Of 401-402, Galerías Gameza, T/F054-233556, entrance to lift 30m down passageway down Mercaderes on left. Mon-Fri 0900-1300, present passport 0900-1100 if you need a visa. **Italy**, La Salle D-5, T054-221444, 1130-1300; in the afternoon T054-254686 (home). **Netherlands**, Centro Comercial Cayma, of 36, 054-271607, conshonlaqp @star.com.pe. Mon-Fri 0900-1300, 1630-1830. **Spain**, Ugarte 218, p 2, T054-205747 (home T054-224915). Mon-Fri 1100-1300, Sat 0900-1300. **Sweden**, Av Villa Hermosa 803, Cerro Colorado, T054-259847. Mon-Fri 0830-1300, 1500-1730. **Switzerland**, Av Miguel Forga 348, Parque Industrial, T054-232723. **UK**, Mr Roberts, Tacna y Arica 156, T054-241340, gerencia@grupo roberts.com. Mon-Fri 0830-1230, 1500-1830, reported as very friendly and helpful. **Cultural centres** **Alianza Francesa**, Santa Catalina 208, T054-215579, www.afarequipa.org.pe. **Instituto Cultural Peruano-Norte Americano**, Casa de los Mendiburo, Melgar 109, T054-891020, www.ccpna.edu.pe, has an English library. **Instituto Cultural Peruano Alemán**, Ugarte 207, T054-218567, icpa@terra.com.pe. **Instituto Nacional de Cultura**, Alameda San Lázaro 120, T054-213171. **Hospitals and clinics** **Regional Honorio Delgado**, Av A Carrión s/n, T054-238465 /233812/231818 (inoculations). **Central del Sur**, Filtro y Peral s/n, T054-214430 in emergency. **Clínica Arequipa SA**, esq Puente Grau y Av Bolognesi, T054-253424 /416. Fast and efficient with English-speaking doctors and all hospital facilities, consultation US$18, plus US$4 for sample analysis, around US$7 for a course of antibiotics. **Paz Holandesa**, Av Jorge Chávez 527, T/F054-206720, www.pazholandesa.com. Dutch foundation with a travel clinic for tourists. Dutch and

English spoken, 24-hr service. Highly recommended. **Internet** Internet cafés are everywhere, often charging less than US$0.50 per hr. Best services are constantly changing, so hunt around. **Chips Internet**, San Francisco 202-A, chips@chips.com.pe. Good computers, helpful, international calls. Another next to the **i perú** office, Santa Catalina 210. Big screens, skype, international calls plus CD burning, good service.
Language courses Centro de Intercambio Cultural Arequipa (CEICA), Urb Universitaria G-9, T/F054-231759, www.ceica-peru.com. Individual classes US$6 per hr, US$4.50 for groups, rooms with families, with board (US$70 per week) or without (US$30), also excursions. **Escuela de Español Ari Quipay (EDEAQ)**, T054-257358, 999 2995 (mob), www.edeaq.com. Peruvian-Swiss run, experienced, multilingual staff, recognized by Ministry of Education, in a colonial house near the Plaza de Armas, one-to-one and group classes, home stay available. **Silvana Cornejo**, 7 de Junio 118, Cerrito Los Alvarez, Cerro Colorado, T054-254985, silvanacornejo @yahoo.com. US$6 per hr, negotiable for group, recommended. Her sister Roxanna charges US$3 per hr. **Liz and Edwin Pérez**, T054- 264068, edwinett @mixmail.com. US$5 per hr one-to-one tuition, will go to your hotel. Classes also available at the **Instituto Peruano-Norte Americano** (US$10 per hr) and **Instituto Cultural Peruano Alemán** (US$4 per hr). **Carlos Rojas Núñez**, Filtro 405, T054-285061, carlrojas @mixmail.com. Private or group lessons for all levels, encourages conversation, knowledgeable on culture and politics. Recommended. **Laundry** Don Marcelo, T054-421411 (morning), T054- 229245 (afternoon). Delivery service. **Lavandería Quick Laundry**, Santa Catalina 312, T054-205503. Fast, reliable and friendly, clothes ironed and bagged. **Magic Laundry**, Jerusalén 404B and La Merced 125. Coin- operated, open daily. **Pharmacy** Farmacia Libertad, Piérola 108. Owner speaks English. **Post** Central office is at Moral 118, opposite Hotel Crismar, Mon-Sat 0800-2000, Sun 0800-1400. DHL, Santa Catalina 115, T054-234288, for sending documents and money. Western Union representative. **Telephone** Alvarez Thomas y Palacio Viejo. *Locutorios* and internet cafés offer international calls from US$0.25 per min. **Useful addresses** Ambulance: San Miguel, T054-283330 (24 hrs).

Colca Canyon

→ *Colour map 5, B6.*

Twice as deep as the Grand Canyon and once thought to be the deepest canyon in the world (until the nearby Cotahuasi Canyon was found to be all of 163 m deeper), the Colca Canyon is an area of astounding beauty. Giant amphitheatres of pre-Inca terracing become narrow, precipitous gorges, and in the background looms the grey, smoking mass of Sabancaya, one of the most active volcanoes in the Americas, and its more docile neighbour, Ampato (6288 m). Unspoiled Andean villages lie on both sides of the canyon, inhabited by the Cabana and Collagua peoples. The Río Colca snakes its way through the length of this massive gorge, 3500 m above sea level at Chivay (the canyon's main town) falling to 2200 m at Cabanaconde, at the far end of the canyon. Now, the Colca Canyon is best known for its associations with some rather large birds. Visitors flock here for a close encounter with the giant Andean condor at the aptly named Cruz del Cóndor and for many, this is the final destination in the canyon. Rather than hurrying back to Arequipa, continue to Cabanconde, as good a base for exploring as Chivay, with many new options opening up. ▸▸ *For Sleeping, Eating and other listings, see pages 273-276.*

Ins and outs

Getting there and around Most buses from Arequipa take the new road via Yura and Cañahuas, following the railway, which is being developed as a route to Cuzco. This is longer, but quicker, than the old route through Cayma. In the rainy season it is better to travel by day as the road can get icy and slippery at night. Buses all leave

Appeasing the gods

To the Incas, Nevado Ampato was a sacred god who brought life-giving water and good harvests and, as such, claimed the highest tribute: human sacrifice.

In September 1995, Johan Reinhard of Chicago's Field Museum of Natural History, accompanied by Peruvian climber, Miguel Zárate, whose brother, Carlos is a well-known mountain guide, were climbing Ampato when they made a startling discovery. At about 6000 m they found the perfectly preserved mummified body of an Inca girl, wrapped tightly in textiles. They concluded that she had been ritually sacrificed and buried on the summit.

Mummies of Inca human sacrifices had been found before on Andean summits, but the girl from Ampato, nicknamed Juanita, is the first frozen Inca female to be unearthed and her body may be the best preserved of any found in the Americas from pre-Columbian times. The intact tissues and organs of naturally mummified, frozen bodies are a storehouse of biological information. Studies reveal how she died, where she came from, who her living relatives are and even yield insights about the Inca diet.

Juanita's clothes are no less remarkable. The richly patterned, dazzling textiles will serve as the model for future depictions of the way noble Inca women dressed. Her *lliclla* – a bright red and white shawl beneath the outer wrappings – has been declared "the finest Inca woman's textile in the world".

Ampato was described as one of the principal deities in the Colca Canyon region. The Incas appeased the mountain gods with the sacrifice of children. The Cabana and Collagua people even bound their children's heads to make them look like the mountains from which they believed they were descended.

A subsequent ascent of Ampato revealed a further two mummies at the summit. One is a young girl and the other, though badly charred by lightning, is believed to be a boy. If so, it may mean that these children were ritually sacrificed together in a symbolic marriage.

Nowadays, villages in the Colca continue to make offerings to the mountain gods for water and good harvests, but thankfully the gods have modified their tastes, now preferring *chicha* to children.

from the main terminal in Arequipa (see page 250) but you can get your ticket the previous day at the bus company offices in Calle San Juan de Dios, or reservations through some of the tourist agencies on Santa Catalina and Jerusalén. Buses and *colectivos* run from Chivay to the villages in the canyon. And, naturally, there numerous trekking possibilities to consider. ⏩ *For further details, see Transport, page 275.*

Entry ticket A fee of US$10 is charged for a tourist ticket (usually valid for up to a week) granting entrance to the Cruz del Cóndor, trekking and tourist areas in the Colca and valley of the volcanoes, plus Nevado Mismi and the Aguada Blanca y Salinas reserve. This cost is not included in agency prices and most visitors buy the ticket at a checkpoint before entering Chivay. Keep the ticket with you while in the Colca area

Best time to visit From January to April is the rainy season, but this makes the area green, with lots of flowers. This is not the best time to see condors. May to December is the dry, cold season when there is more chance of seeing the birds.

Chivay and around pp273-276.

Chivay is the gateway to the canyon and the overnight stopping point for two-day tours run by agencies in Arequipa. There is a road bridge over the river here (others are at Yanque and Lari).

Arequipa to Chivay → *Colour map 5, B/C6.*

From Arequipa there are two routes to Chivay, the first village on the edge of the Canyon: the old route, via the suburb of **Cayma**, and the new route following the railway, through **Yura**, which is longer but quicker. It can be cold, reaching 4825 m on the Pata Pampa pass, north of Cañahuas, but the views are worth it. Cyclists should use the Yura road, as it's in better condition and has less of a climb at the start.

The old dirt route runs north from Arequipa, over the *altiplano*. About an hour out of Arequipa is the **Aguada Blanca National Vicuña Reserve**. If you're lucky, you can see herds of these rare and timid camelids near the road. If taking a bus to the reserve to vicuña-watch, there should be enough traffic on the road to be able to hitch a ride back to Arequipa in the evening. This route affords fine views of the volcanoes Misti, Chachani, Ampato and the active Sabancaya.

All the churches in the Colca valley are being renovated with EU funds. Lari and Yanque had been completed in 2006.

From Chivay, a road heads northeast to **Tuti** (for the start of the Nevado Mismi trek, see page 269), where there is a small handicrafts shop, and **Sibayo**, with a pensión and grocery store. A long circuit back to Arequipa heads south from Sibayo, passing through **Puente Callalli** (where Arequipa buses can sometimes be caught for Cuzco), **Chullo** and **Sumbay**. This is a little-travelled road, but the views of fine landscapes with vicuña, llamas, alpacas and Andean duck are superb. Another road from Sibayo goes northwest, following the northern side of the Colca mountain range to **Cailloma**, **Orcopampa** and **Andagua** (see page 277). Water from the Colca river has been diverted through a series of tunnels and canals to the desert between Repartición and Camaná, to irrigate the Majes pampa.

Chivay → *Colour map 5, B6. Altitude 3600 m.*

There is a very helpful **tourist office** in the Municipalidad on the west side of the plaza which gives away a useful map of the valley. The tourist police, also on the plaza, can give advice about locally trained guides. A reconstructed *chullpa* on the hilltop across Puente Inca gives good views over the town. The **Maria Reiche Planetarium and Observatory** ⓘ *Casa Andina hotel, 6 blocks west of the Plaza between Huayna Capac and Garcilazo (www.casa-andina.com), US$6, discounts for students*, makes the most of the Colca's clear Southern Hemisphere skies with a powerful telescope and two 55-minute presentations per day at 1830 (Spanish) and 1930 (English).

The hot springs of **La Calera** ⓘ *US$3*, are 4 km from Chivay. To get there take one of the regular *colectivos* (US$0.25) from beside the market or it's a pleasant hour-long walk. There are several large hot pools and showers but only two pools are usually open to tourists. The hot springs are highly recommended after a hard day's trekking, with good facilities and a beautiful setting. A small cultural museum on site is included in the price. From La Calera you can trek through the Canocota canyon to Canocota (four to five hours); alternatively take a *colectivo* to Canocota and hike to La Calera; it's a beautiful trip, but ask directions.

From Chivay you can hike to **Coporaque** (1¾ hours) and **Ichupampa** (a further 1½ hours). Half an hour above Coporaque are interesting **cliff tombs** and, just beyond the

The name Colca derives from the Inca practice of storing harvested crops in sealed vaults, called colcas, which were carved into the canyon walls.

village, are the Huari ruins of **Ullu Ullu**. West beyond Ichupampa are **Lari**, **Madrigal** (where a footbridge connects to Maca) and **Tapay** (connected by a footbridge to Cabanaconde). Between Coporaque and Ichupampa, foot and road bridges cross the river to **Yanque** (one hour), from where it's an 8-km hike back to Chivay. Follow the road or you'll end up lost in a maze of terraced fields. If you feel too tired to walk back to Chivay, catch a *colectivo* from the plaza in Yanque for US$0.25.

Nevado Mismi: trek to the source of the Amazon

Although not the greatest mountain in the region, **Nevado Mismi**, a rugged 5597-m peak roughly 15 km north of Ichupampa and the Río Colca, is special for a couple of reasons that might be worth remembering at 0300, when it's -15°C and you're huddled inside a sleeping bag, counting the hours to daylight.

First, it provides an adventurous trek to the source of what, in terms of volume, number and scale of tributaries, perhaps even legendary status, is the greatest river system on the planet (see box, page 270). Below the mountain to the east, tropical forest stretches uninterrupted to the Atlantic Ocean. Second, the region's extreme remoteness means that wildlife, extinct in other parts of the Andes, is present here. It's not unusual to see vicuñas, viscachas, many species of Andean water birds and, perhaps, the occasional condor in the mountains to the north of Tuti. Pumas and the spectacularly rare Andean mountain cat, prey on the tough herbivores of these undeveloped hills. Cultural aspects long vanished elsewhere also cling to existence close to the Amazon's beginning. The area north of the Colca Canyon has some of Peru's last traditional llama- and alpaca-herding communities. Living a nomadic existence, these remarkable folk live a life dedicated to the needs of their animals and the growth of the tough grasses that form their staple diet.

On a practical level, this is one of harder areas in the Peruvian Andes to get to with public transport, so a professional guide or, at a bare minimum, a local *arriero* (mule driver) is highly recommended. Several established agencies in Arequipa offer itineraries in the area. Carlos Zarate (see page 262) is very knowledgeable regarding the region's possibilities and has backed up TV companies in the zone. Without a guide you must be totally self-sufficient. There are many interesting hiking routes in this region. A good one requiring four to five days is outlined below. Make sure you're well acclimatized before you start treks in the area; much of the land lies at 5000 m or higher and you must be prepared for rapidly changing weather conditions.

Day 1 With Chivay as a starting point it's fairly easy to hire a taxi as far as **Tuti**, a pleasant rural community and a good spot to begin your trek. Beyond Tuti the road continues a few kilometres to the northeast before one branch turns to the north, gaining height in switchbacks on the route towards Mismi and the Amazon source. The route, now mainly heading northwest, passes some beautiful alpine lakes, excellent for bird watching, and the lovely 17th-century church and colonial *reduction* of **Ran Ran**, before emerging onto the bare moonscape of the *altiplano*. At **Aquenta**, 4800 m, there's a site with good water where it's possible to camp for the first night. If required, a 4WD can reach just beyond this point, as far as the **Carhuasanta** valley in the dry season. In the rainy season the entire region becomes a mud bath and vehicular access is practically impossible.

Day 2 Crossing into the Carhuasanta valley and following the stream south to its source, takes you to the Amazon watershed. Carhuasanta is a beautiful, windswept and empty valley, stained with the reds and browns of metals and other minerals. Scrambling up some boulders brings you to the base of a dark cliff, where the source itself is marked with a cross carved into the rock. This is the place where the ice melts and the water's journey of over 6000 km begins. For real perfectionists the small **Laguna McIntyre**, and indeed the summit of Mismi itself, lie only a couple hundred metres higher. Glacial retreat

A source of controversy

So, how do we know that the source of the Amazon is on Nevado Mismi? In 1971 a *National Geographic*-sponsored expedition, led by acclaimed explorer Loren McIntyre was the first to speculate that this might be longest of the river's many tributaries. Unfortunately, McIntyre possessed neither the technology nor the resources to prove this beyond doubt. In 1985/86 an 11-man international team set out to prove the river's length and kayak it from the source to the mouth. Dogged by accidents, illness and a leadership crisis, only four of the 11 made it to the Atlantic six months later, among them American journalist Joe Kane, author of the highly entertaining account, *Running the Amazon*. In 2000, Andrew Pietowski led a 22-man *National Geographic* expedition and confirmed Nevado Mismi as the source, using state-of- the-art GPS technology, also giving the length of the river at 6275 km.

means that, for most of the year, crampons aren't necessary. Give yourself a couple of days to explore the picturesque vicinity of the source and summit of Mismi but remember that nights spent here above 5000 m are truly chilling. From this point onwards you can either retrace your steps via Tuti and Chivay, or, in a couple more days, complete a circuit of Mismi, crossing the 5200-m **Apacheta pass** (and the Atlantic/Pacific watershed) and descending via the Qollpa/Callumayo valley to Lari and the Colca Canyon. On this far side of Apacheta you will encounter the remains of an Inca, possibly pre-Inca highway.

Chivay to Cabanaconde » *pp273-276.*

From Chivay, the main road goes west along the Colca Canyon. The first village, after 8 km, is **Yanque,** where there's an interesting church and a bridge to the villages on the other side (see page 268). Beside the renovated Inca bridge, a 20-minute walk from Yanque plaza, is a large, warm thermal swimming pool ⓘ *US$0.75*. The next village after Yanque is **Achoma,** 30 minutes from Chivay along the Cabanaconde road. There is an old settlement where you can camp. The road continues to **Maca**, which barely survived an earthquake in November 1991. Then comes the tiny village of **Pinchollo,** with a basic *hostal* on the plaza (a room full of beds and one shared bathroom). There are no restaurants but you can eat at the *comedor popular*. You can walk from here to the **Sabancaya** geyser in approximately seven hours. Boys will offer to guide you there. For information, ask for Eduardo, who acts as a guide. He lives next to the plaza.

Cruz del Cóndor » *See Ins and outs, page 266, for entry fees.*

From Pinchollo the road winds its way on to the Mirador, or Cruz del Cóndor at the deepest point of the canyon. The view from here is wonderful but people don't come for the view. This is where the immense Andean vulture, the condor, can be seen rising on the morning thermals. The reason this particular spot is so unique is that the condors swoop by in startling close up, so close, in fact, that you feel you can reach out and touch them. It is a breathtaking and very humbling experience.

The best time to arrive in the morning is a matter of some dispute, although the consensus is around 0900. Arrive by 0800 for a good spot, any earlier and you may be faced with a long, chilly wait; this may be unavoidable if you're travelling by public transport, as buses from Chivay stop here very briefly. To get to the Mirador from Cabanaconde, take one of the return buses which set off at around 0730, and ask to be dropped off at the Mirador, just in time for the morning performance. Or you can walk along the road, which takes about three hours. Horses can be hired to save you the walk; arrange the night before in Cabanaconde.

The condors fly off to look for carrion on the higher slopes of the surrounding peaks at 0900-1000. The condors can also be seen returning from a hard day's food searching at around 1600-1800. Just below the Mirador is a rocky outcrop, which allows a more peaceful viewing but take great care on the loose scree (or you'll end up on the menu). Binoculars are recommended. Snacks and drinks are available but camping here is officially forbidden, although if you ask the tourist police in Chivay, they may help.

Unfortunately, the peace of the Cruz del Cóndor has been disrupted by road-building projects, ironically to improve access for tourist buses. The projects have been carried out without an environmental impact assessment and have been decried by locals and tour operators alike. For now, it's not known what consequences the bulldozers and explosives blasts will have on future condor populations, but it is feared that the birds' breeding cycles may have been badly effected by the disturbances.

Cabanaconde → *Colour map 5, B5*.

From the Mirador it is a 20-minute bus ride to this friendly village at 3287 m, the last in the Colca Canyon. To walk from the Mirador to Cabanaconde, follow the road until Cabanaconde is in sight, then turn off the road 50 m after a small reservoir down a walled track. After about 1 km turn left on to an old Inca road and continue down to rejoin the road into Cabanaconde.

The indigenous people of this part of the canyon are **Cabanas**. Cabanaconde plaza is brimming with life. Women squat on their haunches, selling bruised fruit and a few knobbly root crops. Their distinctive flower-patterned hats, voluminous skirts and intricately embroidered blouses bring a splash of colour to the uniform brown adobe buildings. Children tend sheep, goats and llamas; old men lead burdened mules while pigs laze in the sun and chickens peck at the ground. At dusk, large groups of animals wander back into the village to the corrals adjoining most houses.

The views into the canyon are excellent and condors can be seen from the hill just west of the village, a 15-minute walk from the plaza. From here, you'll also see the amazing terraces to the south of the village, arguably the most attractive in the valley. The hill is surrounded by a 2-km-long Huari wall, which is 6 m high and 4 m wide in places. It also encompasses the village football field where it is possible to see condors overflying a late-afternoon game.

Cabanaconde suffered badly during an earthquake in April 1998. In 2006, recovery and reconstruction were close to completion and the village now provides an excellent base for visiting the region. Interesting trekking and climbing lies all around the village, and local guides are beginning to see new opportunities for biking and horse riding in this amazing landscape. Many locals are keen to encourage respectful tourism in the area. There's a tourist information office attended by friendly locals willing to give plenty of advice, if not maps. It's a good place to find trekking guides and muleteers.

It takes two days to walk from Chivay to **Cabanaconde** (70 km) but you can camp along the route. You will have to walk all day in the sun – there is no shade – so you'll need plenty of drinking water and sun block. Mule hire is US$30 a day including guide (ask if they have a saddle). You can hike for three days through the local villages and return by bus as an alternative to a two-day tour.

Trekking from Cabanaconde

There are many hikes in the area. Make sure to take enough water as it gets very hot and there is not a lot of water available. Sun protection is also a must. Some treks are impossible if it rains heavily in the wet season, but most of the time the rainy season is dry; check beforehand. Ask locals for directions as there are hundreds of confusing paths going into the canyon. Buy food for longer hikes in Arequipa. Topographical maps are available at the **Instituto Geográfico Militar** in Lima (IGM 1:100,000 Huambo and Chivay sheets give the best coverage), from **Colca Trek** or **Pablo Tour** in Arequipa (see page 263), and good information can be obtained from **South American Explorers.**

Two hours below Cabanaconde is **Sangalle**, a beautiful oasis of palm trees and swimming areas, where there are three campsites with basic bungalows and toilets. The three sites from top to bottom are: **Eden**, US$3, the first site you come too, nice huts; **Oasis Paradise**, US$5, but often free entry if you stay at Valle del Fuego, run by Pablo Tour, lots of space; finally, closest to the river is the new **El Paradaiso**, US$6, cheaper out of season, the most aesthetically pleasing site, pools and waterfalls built into huge natural boulders. It takes up to 4½ hours to climb back up but horses can be hired to carry your bag, US$5.85; ask for the best route in both directions.

A popular hike from Cabanconde involves walking east on the Chivay road to the **Mirador de Tapay** (before Cruz del Cóndor), then descending to the river on a steep track (four hours, take care). Cross the bridge to the north bank. At the village of **San Juan de Chuccho** you can stay and eat at a basic family hostel, of which there are several. **Hostal Roy** and **Casa de Rebelino** (**G**) are both good and US$2 will buy you a decent meal. From here pass **Tapay,** where it is also possible to camp and the small villages of Malata and Cosnirhua, all the time heading west along the north side of the Río Colca; take a guide or ask local directions as there are many different trails. After about three hours' walking, cross another bridge to reach **Sangalle** on the south bank of the Río Colca, follow signs to the oasis, spend the night and return to Cabanconde on the third day. This route is offered by many Arequipa and local agencies. More good hiking and a further extension of this 'Oasis' trek heads up a **Quebrada** to the north-northwest, leading to an impressive waterfall above the settlement of **Fure** (accommodation available, **G**). Again, ask locally for details.

A longer hike from Cabanaconde goes to **Chachas** and takes four or five days. Follow a small path to the west, descending slowly into the canyon (three hours); ask locals for directions to **Choco**. Cross the Río Colca by the Puente Colgado (an Inca bridge) and ascend to Choco, 2473 m (five to six hours). From Choco climb high above the village to the pass at 4500 m and then down to Chachas, at 3100 m (eight to 12 hours). There is a minibus daily at 1300 from Chachas to **Andagua** in the valley of the volcanoes (see page 277). Otherwise it is a day's hike. This is a superb walk through untouched areas and villages but you'll need all camping equipment, food and plenty of water, as there is hardly any on this trek.

Trekking around Cabanaconde

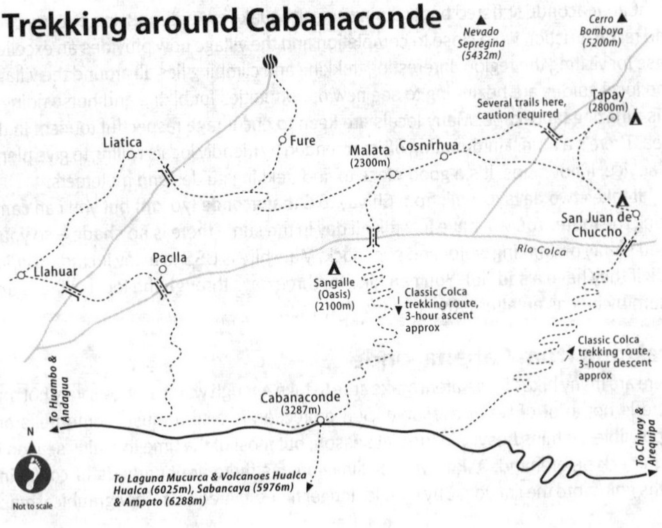

South of Cabanaconde

Fifteen kilometres to the south on rough trails is **Laguna Mucurca**, an 8-km long lake that offers good birdwatching, especially in June to October when its resident group of flamingos are present; please don't disturb their feeding. Reigning supreme above the lake is the volcanic chain of **Ampato** (6288 m), **Sabancaya** (5976 m – caution required, this is the most active volcano in Peru) and **Hualca Hualca** (6025 m, the most northerly of the three). A minimum of two days is required to make the most of this area and qualified guides are essential if you want to climb any of the peaks, all of which were sacred *Apus*, or gods, for the Incas.

Sleeping

Chivay and around *p268*

Ask if your hotel can provide heating. Many of the better hotels are used by tour groups. There are several other hotels and family homes where you can stay; ask around.

AL Parador del Colca, T054-288440, www.paradordelcolca.com. 3½ km from Yanque, 10 km from Chivay, owned by Orient Express. Built of local materials, with solar power, on an old estate, the hotel offers lots of activities; comfortable cabin-like suites, typical food and home-grown vegetables, meals extra. Recommended.

A Colca Lodge, between Coporaque and Ichupampa, T054-202587/203604, www.colca-lodge.com). Very pleasant and relaxing, safe, heating, restaurant with good buffet, TV and DVD players. Beautiful hot springs by the river, trekking, cycling, riding, rafting, spend at least a day there to make the most of what's on offer. A good spot for families and children. Recommended.

A Estancia Pozo del Cielo, over the Puente Inca from Chivay amid pre-Inca terraces, T054-531041, www.pozodelcielo.com.pe. Very comfortable, friendly, warm rooms, good views, good service and restaurant. Recommended.

B Casa Andina, Huayna Cápac s/n, T054-531020, www.casa-andina.com. Attractive cabins with hot showers and a cosy bar/dining area, another member of this recommended hotel chain, heating, internet, parking. Also here (not directly owned by Casa Andina) is the Maria Reiche Planetarium and Observatory; see page 268.

C Colca Inn, Salaverry 307, T054-531111, www.hotelcolcainn.com. A good mid-range option, modern, spick and span, hot water, with a decent restaurant.

D Hostal Posada Chivay, Salaverry 325, T054-531032, posadachivay@hotmail.com. Central, clean and friendly, good rooms, hot water, breakfast included.

D Tradición Colca, on main road, Yanque. Reservations: C Argentina 108, Urb Fecia JL Bustamante y Rivero, Arequipa, T054-424926, 935 7117 (mob), www.tradicioncolca.com. Price is per unit, **E** in low season and includes breakfast, with gardens, spa, restaurant, bar, games room, also backpackers' rooms; they also have a travel agency. Recommended.

D Wasi Kolping, 10 blocks south of the town, opposite the Plaza de Toros, T054-521076. Comfortable cabins with hot shower, very clean and quiet, good views.

E La Casa de Lucila, M Grau 131, T054-607086. With bath, comfortable, coffee, guides available.

E La Pascana, Calle Siglo XX 106, T054-531190, hrlapascana@hotmail.com. On the northwest corner of the Plaza. Excellent value with spacious en-suite rooms, spotless showers with hot water, most rooms overlooking a pleasant garden. Price includes breakfast, there is parking space and a good restaurant.

E-F Hospedaje Restaurant Los Portales, Arequipa 603, T054-521101. Good-value accommodation, though beds have rather floppy mattresses, breakfast included in the price. Clean restaurant downstairs.

F Hostal Anita, on the north side of the plaza, T054-531114. Clean, with bathroom, rooms look onto a small garden, friendly. Recommended.

F La Casa de la Bella Flor, Cusco 303, Yanque, T054-280454. Charming small lodge run by Sra Hilde Checca, flower-filled garden, tasteful rooms, good meals (also open to non-residents), Hilde's uncle, Gregorio, guides visitors to pre-Columbian sites.

G Hospedaje Jessy, Zarumilla 218, 1 block from market. Simple, clean, excellent showers, cheaper without bath, helpful, with parking.

G per person **Rumi Wasi**, C Sucre 714, 6 blocks from plaza (3 mins' walk), T054-531146. Good rooms, breakfast included, hot water, bike hire, helpful.

Cabanaconde *p271*

B Kuntur Wassi, C Cruz Blanca s/n, on the hill above the plaza, T054-812166, kunturwassi@terra.com.pe, or waltertinta @hotmail.com. Excellent 3-star hotel with parking, breakfast included and fine traditional meals on request. Creative design with rooms spaced between rock gardens and waterfalls. 'Viewing tower' and conference centre above. Good views of the valley everywhere, and owners Walter and María very welcoming. Recommended.

E Posada del Conde, C San Pedro a couple of blocks from the plaza, T054-440197, pdelconde@yahoo.com. Very smart, cheaper in low season, rooms with private hot shower, excellent value but can be a bit noisy, very good restaurant. Booking advised.

E-F Hostal Valle del Fuego, 1 and 2 blocks from the plaza on C Grau, T054-830032, www.pablotour.com. Good rooms with comfortable beds, all with private bath and hot water, plus free laundry facilities. They have 2 places, both with restaurants serving meals for around US$3. The Junco family, Pablo, Edwin and Jamil, among others, are a wealth of information having built up a small family 'empire', including the Arequipa agency **Pablo Tour**, the **Oasis Paradise** in Sangalle (discounts for clients of Valle del Fuego) and a new bar, the **Casa de Pablo Club** (see below) at the end of the street. They usually meet the incoming buses. Good value choice for backbackers, but keep in mind the 'family' nature of the business.

G Virgen del Carmen, 5 blocks from the plaza. Clean, hot showers, friendly, may offer you a welcoming glass of *chicha*. Recommended.

Eating

Chivay and around *p268*

There are several good, attractively decorated restaurants in Chivay, both cosy and friendly. They serve good value set meals for around US$3 with a choice of dishes. Not all restaurants are open at night.

ΨΨ-Ψ Fonda del Cazador, on the north side of the plaza, serves delicious alpaca steaks.

ΨΨ-Ψ Lobos Pizzería, on the plaza. Good pizzas and pasta, fast service, bar, popular.

ΨΨ-Ψ Los Sismos, by the petrol station. Alsoserves great alpaca steaks, often has live folklore shows.

ΨΨ-Ψ Witete, Siglo XX 328. Good international food and some local dishes.

ΨΨ-Ψ McElroy's Irish Pub, on the plaza. Bar run by a Peruvian and an Irishman, warm, friendly, good selection of drinks (including – sometimes – expensive Guinness), pizza, pasta, sandwiches and music. Mountain bikes for hire. Accepts Visa.

Ψ La Pascana, near the Plaza de Armas. Good value, tasty local food. Also has good lodging in our **D** range.

Cabanaconde *p271*

Both hotels **Posada del Conde** and **Kuntur Wasi** offer excellent food (ΨΨ), although they might need some advance notice. There are several basic restaurants around the plaza (Ψ).

ΨΨ-Ψ Casa de Pablo Club, Calle Grau. Jamil Junco has now opened this comfortable bar just beyond **Valle del Fuego**. Excellent fresh juices and pisco sour, cable TV (football!), small book exchange and equipment hire.

Ψ Don Piero, signposted just off main plaza. Excellent choice and good information.

Ψ Limeño, just to the north of the Plaza. Excellent value breakfasts, friendly service.

Ψ Rancho del Colca, on the plaza. Serves mainly vegetarian food.

Festivals and events

20-25 Jan This is a region of wild and frequent festivals. **El Día de San Sebastián** is celebrated over 5 days in Pinchollo.

2-3 Feb **Virgen de la Candelaria** is celebrated in the towns of Chivay and Cabanaconde, with dancing in the plaza, and over 5 days in Maca and Tapay.

Mar/Apr **Semana Santa** is celebrated with particular gusto in the villages of the Colca Canyon.

27 Apr Celebration of the apostle **Santiago**.

Apr/May Many festivals are held in the Colca canyon at this time of year. **La Cruz de Piedra** is celebrated over 5 days in May in the main plaza in Tuti, near Chivay.

13 Jun **San Antonio** is celebrated in the

villages of Maca, Callalli and Yanque.

14 Jun In Sibayo and Ichupampa the **Fiesta de San Juan** is held over 5 days.

21 Jun Anniversary of the district of Chivay in Cailloma.

14-17 Jul **Fiesta de la Virgen del Carmen** is held in Cabanaconde and Pampacolca, when folk dancing takes place in the streets. Of particular interest is the dance of **Los Turcos**, which represents the indigenous peoples' struggle against the conquistadors. This fiesta is also held in the churches of Yura, Carmen Alto, Congata, Tingo Grande and the Convent of Santa Teresa in Arequipa city.

25 Jul **Fiesta de Santiago Apostol** in Coporaque and Madrigal, in the canyon.

26 Jul-2 Aug Various religious ceremonies, accompanied by dancing, are held in honour of the **Virgen Santa Ana** in Maca.

15 Aug In Chivay, fiesta of the **Virgen de la Asunta**, the town's patron saint, lasts 8 days.

Sep In Tisco, the fiesta of the **Virgen de la Natividad** is held over 5 days.

8 Dec The fiesta of the **Inmaculada Concepción** is held in Chivay and Yanque. Groups of musicians and dancers present the traditional dance, the **Witite**, lasting 5 days.

25 Dec In Yanque, the **Witite** is held over 6 days.

Activities and tours

Travel agencies in Arequipa (see page 263) arrange a one-day tour to the **Cruz del Cóndor** for US$20-25. They leave Arequipa at 0400, arriving at the Cruz del Cóndor at 0800-0900, followed by an expensive lunch stop at Chivay and back to Arequipa by 2100. For many, especially for those with altitude problems, this is too much to fit into one day (the only advantage is that you don't have to sleep at high altitude). It's also more dangerous since drivers get tired on the way back. Two-day tours start at US$25-30 per person with an overnight stop in Chivay; more expensive tours range from US$45 to US$90 with accommodation at the top of the range. You should allow at least 2-3 days, more if you are planning to do some trekking in the Colca Canyon.

Travel agents frequently work together in a 'pooling' system to fill buses (even the more expensive agencies may not have their own transport) and there are lots of touts. This can mean that a busload of tourists will come from different agencies, all paying different prices, but all expecting the same level of service. On occasion the company providing the transport may not have the same high standards as the operator through whom the tour was booked.

Note Don't forget that the compulsory entry ticket (see Ins and outs, page 266) is rarely include in agency prices.

Chivay and around *p268*

Ampato Adventure Sports, Plaza de Armas (close to **Lobos Pizzería**), Chivay, T054-531073, www.ampatocolca.com. Offer information and rent good mountain bikes.

Colca-Turismo, Av Salaverry 321, Chivay, 054-503368, and guide **Zacarías Ocsa Osca**, zacariasocsa@hotmail.com, seem to offer a professional service.

Cabanaconde *p271*

Henry López Junco, is a guide in Cabanaconde, T054-280367. US$7.15 per day for 2 people.

Transport

Chivay and around *p268*

Transportes Milagros, La Reyna (recommended) and **Andalucia** from Arequipa to Chivay (see page 264) continue to **Cabanaconde**, 7 daily, 75 km, 2 hrs, US$1. Buses return to **Arequipa** from the new bus station in Chivay, three blocks from the main plaza, next to the stadium. For **Cruz del Cóndor** catch the 0500 Cabanaconde bus from Chivay, which stops briefly at the Mirador at 0700 (if this doesn't seem likely, ask), US$0.75. Buses run infrequently in each direction, fewer on Sun. You could also try hitching a lift with a tour bus.

Combis and *colectivos* leave from the new terminal in Chivay to any village in the area including **Achoma** (every ½ hr), **Maca** (every hr), **Ichupampa** (every hr) and **Puente Callalli** (every hr); ask the drivers for details.

It is difficult to go to **Cuzco** from Chivay: you can take a *colectivo* to Puente Callalli, but the police there are unwilling to let passengers wait for a passing Cuzco-bound bus, which may not stop anyway. Best to go back to Arequipa.

Cabanaconde *p271*
See under Chivay for buses on the Arequipa–Chivay–Cabanaconde route. **Milagros, Andalucía** and **La Reyna** buses leave Cabanaconde for **Arequipa** between 0730 and 1500, always from the Plaza de Armas, US$4.50 (usually a wait in Chivay).

Directory

Chivay and around *p268*
Banks TCs and credit cards are seldom accepted so take plenty of cash in soles, not dollars.

Cotahuasi Canyon

→ *Colour map 5, B5.*

A road heads northwest off the Panamericana between Camaná and Repartición towards Corire, Aplao and the Cotahuasi Canyon. It passes the Toro Muerto petroglyphs and traverses the western slopes of Nevado Coropuna, Peru's third highest peak at 6425 m, before winding down into Cotahuasi. Considered one of the most beautiful canyons in the world, as well as the deepest (about 1850 m deeper than the Grand Canyon in the USA), Cotahuasi has several traditional communities where ancient customs persist. The river, cutting its way through steep walls, is the focus of some tremendous scenery and top-quality rafting or kayaking. Once part of an Inca route from the coast to Cuzco, it is now a great place for hiking, with no end of ruins, hot springs, cascades and rivers to explore. » *For Sleeping, Eating and other listings, see pages 279-280.*

Ins and outs

The only way into the canyon is by road; there are bus services from Arequipa. Tour operators run to Toro Muerto and can arrange trips to Cotahuasi. Accommodation and services are basic. A website with pictures and some information on Cotahuasi is www.lared.net.pe/cotahuasi. The most knowledgeable contact for trekking and exploring is Vlado Soto of **Colca Trek**, see page 262.

Background

The canyon, in the northwest of the Department of Arequipa, has been cut by the Río Cotahuasi, whose waters are formed by the Río Huayllapaña flowing from the north, above Pampamarca, and the Río Huarcaya from the west, above Tomepampa. The river cuts its way westwards and then southwards through the deepest parts of the canyon, below Quechualla. It flows into the Pacific as the Río Ocuña, having joined with the Río Marán along the way. At its deepest, at Ninochaca (just below the village of Quechualla), the canyon is 3354 m deep, 163 m deeper than the Colca Canyon and the deepest in the world. From this point the only way down the canyon is by kayak and it is through kayakers' reports since 1994 that the area has come to the notice of tourists. It was declared a Zona de Reserva Turística in 1988 and there is pressure to make parts of it into a national park. The vertiginous gradient of the canyon walls and the aridity of its climate allow little agriculture but there are several charming citrus-growing villages downstream, among them **Chaupa, Velinga** and **Quechualla**.

In Inca times the road linking Puerto Inca on the Pacific coast and Cuzco ran along much of the canyon's course. It was used for taking fish to the ancient Inca capital. Parts of the road are still intact and there are numerous remains of *andenes*, or terraces, which supported settlement along the route. There are also Huari and other pre-Inca ruins.

Northeast from Arequipa » pp279-280.

Toro Muerto

The world's largest field of petroglyphs at Toro Muerto is near **Corire**. There are several restaurants around the plaza in Corire and a **BCP**. You can make a return day trip from Arequipa, if you leave really early, but it's better to allow two days, or combine it with a trip to the Cotahuasi Canyon.

To reach the petroglyphs, there's a turn-off on the right heading back out of Corire; it's about a one-hour walk. Alternatively, ask to be let off the bus at the big sign to 'Toro Muerto' beside a small church. A track leads through the fields; at the end, turn right. Ask directions en route. Just before the site is a tiny settlement of wattle and daub huts. From here follow the most worn track, which veers right between the hills. There are two signposts on the track leading into the desert valley.

The higher you go, the more interesting the petroglyphs, though many have been ruined by graffiti. The designs range from simple llamas to elaborate human figures and animals. The sheer scale of the site is awe-inspiring (it's on the UNESCO World Heritage list) and the view back down the arid desert valley against the backdrop of the distant lush, green irrigated fields is wonderful. Go early to allow several hours to appreciate the place fully and take plenty of water and protection against the fierce sun, including sunglasses. Also take insect repellent if crossing the fields on foot. A guide is recommended if you're short of time because they take you to some of the more interesting carvings.

Towards the Valle de los Volcanes

A road goes north from **Aplao** on the Cotahuasi road to **Andagua**, a village lying at the head of the Valley of the Volcanoes. No fuel is available here. **Transportes Reyna**'s Arequipa–Andagua bus goes on to **Orcopampa**, from which the thermal springs of Huancarama can be visited.

From Andagua there is a road to **Chachas**, a picturesque little village on the edge of a lake. The area is heavily cultivated and there are perfect views of the valley from the top of the hill above Chachas. It is possible to hike from Chachas to Choco and on to Cabanaconde via the Río Colca in four or five days (see page 272). If you have a 4WD vehicle, this is a superb area for driving some rough roads: for instance, a circuit: Arequipa–Aplao–Andagua–Orcopamba–Cailloma–Chivay–Arequipa.

Cotahuasi and around » pp279-280.

Cotahuasi → *Population: 3200. Altitude: 2600 m.*

Cotahuasi town nestles in a sheltered hanging valley beneath Cerro Huinao, several kilometres away from the erosive action of the Río Cotahuasi. Though above the citrus zone itself, it has fertile, irrigated environs. The name Cotahuasi derives from the Quechua words 'Cota' (union) and 'Huasi' (house), literally translating as united house or close-knit community.

It is a peaceful, colonial town of narrow streets and whitewashed houses with gently subsiding balconies. The main street, Jirón Arequipa, becomes a part of the plaza on busy Sunday mornings. The only traffic seen is the occasional glimpse of the mayor's car, the odd tractor and the infrequent comings and goings of the two buses and occasional combi (see Transport page 280).

From Cotahuasi, routes split in a 'Y': southwest along the Río Cotahuasi to the Cataratas de Sipia, Quechualla and beyond; north up the Río Huayllapaña to Pampamarca, and northeast to Tomepampa, Alca, Puica and its environs. You can purchase expensive fuel in these places. It is possible to raft or kayak from a point on the

 Upper Cotahuasi, just past the town, almost to the Pacific, a descent of 2300 m (boats are usually taken out of the water at the village of Iquipi). The season is May to June; rapids class four to five; some portaging is unavoidable. ▸▸ *For further details, see Rafting, page 262.*

Around Cotahuasi

Pampamarca, two bumpy hours by combi north of Cotahuasi, is a quaint, small village well-known for rugmaking. It is set on a plateau at 3200 m. From here, you can trek up to the **Bosque de Piedras** (three hours), to the hot springs of **Josla** (3½ km), or down to the 50-m waterfall of **Uskuni** (under an hour). There's a mirador with beautiful views of the waterfall and the valley (15 minutes). Ask at the Municipio for directions. Some local women can prepare food given warning; ask for Señora Julia to the right of the Municipio. There are also a few rudimentary shops.

Following the Río Cotahuasi to the northeast up the valley, you come to the villages of **Tomepampa** (10 km), the hotsprings of **Luicho** (18 km) and **Alca** (20 km), all connected by buses and combis from Cotahuasi. Tomepampa is a neat little hamlet at 2700 m, with painted houses and a handsome chapel. A day's walk beyond Tomepampa is the spectacular rock forest of **Santo Santo**. The recently rehabilitated and attractive hotsprings of **Luicho** ⓘ *24 hrs, US1.50*, are a short walk from the road, across a bridge. The small village of Alca has one *hostal* (see Sleeping, page 279), Above Alca are the small ruins of Kallak, Tiknay and a 'stone library' of rock formations. Head out of Alca by climbing the stone stairs for the village of Cahuana.

Puica is the last village of any significance in the valley, hanging on a hillside at nearly 3700 m and connected to Alca by combi (three hours, US$1.50). Though facilities are basic, it's an ideal springboard for nearby attractions: for Churca and a vast prairie of Puya Raimondi cacti; the Ocoruro geysers; the ruins of Maucallacta; and the Laguna de Igma. Horses can be hired for US$3 a day, and locals can act as guides. Puica's fiesta is on the 28 July.

About 4 km out of Cotahuasi on the road to Tomepampa, a bridge crosses over to **Taurisma**, from where it's a two-hour walk northeast to the village and pre-Inca ruins of **Huaynacotas**. At the village of **Toro** you can find the thermals springs of Sirhua and Siringay. There are ruins nearby and, from the village, you get fantastic views of the Solimana glacier. To get to Toro, take a combi from Cotahuasi back up the main road towards Chuquibamba, then fork west (around two hours).

Trekking in the Cotahuasi Canyon

One of the main treks in the region follows the Inca trade road from Cotahuasi to **Quechualla** (two days each way).

The path starts next to the football pitch beside the airstrip in Cotahuasi. It heads downhill to **Piro**, which is almost a satellite of Cotahuasi and the gateway to the canyon (the path heads round to the right of the village, just above it). The path then crosses the river twice as it follows its course to **Sipia** (three hours), near which are the tremendously powerful, 150-m-high **Cataratas de Sipia**. Climb to the bluff just beyond the mouth of the black hole and you'll have a superb view downriver. Take extreme care near the falls, if it is windy. Water is a problem further down the canyon, so if continuing, fill up your water bottles near the falls. You can get to within an hour's walk of the Cataratas by combi from Cotahuasi; they leave 0600 and 1930, return 0900 and 1400. It's best to visit at midday. A road is being built from this point to the falls, and may be complete by the time you read this.

The next three-hour stretch to **Chaupo** is not for those of a nervous disposition as the path is barely etched into the canyon wall, 400 m above the river in places. The towering cliffs are magnificent reds and browns and dissected by near vertical water channels. You can camp at Chaupo, which lies on the pampa, 100 m above the river. Water is available, but ask permission.

Next is **Velinga**, a village which was almost wiped out by Chagas disease. Now only six families remain. Take the path down to the river before the village and cross over the bridge to the right bank. Half a kilometre further on you may need to wade for about 15 m at the foot of a cliff to regain the path. Stay on the same side of the river. If it rains, Quechualla can be cut off for days, as sections of river become too deep and treacherous to wade through (eg just past Velinga).

Before Quechualla are the extensive ruins of **Huña**. They are dilapidated but the remains of terraces and houses give a good idea of the importance of this route in pre-Columbian times. There is an almost intact 100-m stretch of Inca road above a bend in the river on the approach to Quechualla. It can be a bit scary in parts but the alternative is to wade waist deep through the river.

Quechualla is a charming village and administrative capital of the district and, although it is populated by only eight families, it is the administrative capital of the district. It sits up on a cliff above the river. The church and school overlook the wooden bridge and the short climb up to the citrus groves. Trellised vines provide some welcome shade in the street. You may be able to sleep in the schoolhouse; ask Señor Carmelo Velásquez Gálvez for permission. Below the village, on the opposite side of the river, are the ruined terraces of **Maucullachta**. A 16-km hike continues to the ruins of **Marpa**, which are in better condition. The canyon walls, however, are too steep to continue along the river. You need to climb 8 km, on a path at right angles to the river, to Huachuy, then descend a further 8 km to the ruins near the river. There is no water en route; allow four more days to get there.

Sleeping

Toro Muerto *p277*

F Hostal Willys, Av Progreso before the Plaza de Armas, Corire, T054-472046. It is clean and helpful.

F El Mirador, Lima 304, Chuquibamba, T054-489279. New, good showers, clean, friendly owner, good views, use of kitchen.

G Hostal Rodríguez, on main plaza in Chuquibamba, T054-489206. Primitive.

Towards the Valle de los Volcanes *p277*

There are several hotels in **Andagua**; Casa Grande is recommended. On the plaza, Restaurant Sarita will cook good, cheap meals for you. In **Chacas**, a woman in the village will let you sleep in a spare room next to her house; she also provides an evening meal. The cost is not fixed and is left up to you – around US$2 per person should be OK.

Cotahuasi *p277*

F Hostal Alcalá II, Arequipa 116, T054-581090. Run by same family as Hostal Alcalá in Alca. New, very good, 24-hr hot showers, excellent beds, doubles and triples, friendly, a bit small. Recommended.

G Alojamiento Chávez, Jr Cabildo 125, T0554-581029. Has basic rooms around a pleasant, flower-filled courtyard, friendly, Sr José Chávez is helpful on places to visit.

G Hostal Fany Luz, Independencia 117, T054-581002. Opposite **Hostal Villa**, basic but amenable, with shared hot showers, double room available with cold water only.

G Hostal Villa, Independencia 118, just off the plaza, T054-581018. Basic, shared bathroom is miles from the rooms.

Around Cotahuasi *p278*

F-G Hostal Alcalá, Alca, T054-280224. One of the best *hostales* in the valley. 2 bedrooms with private showers, others shared, very clean, plenty of hot water, restaurant, good food. Prices vary, sometimes wildly, according to season and demand.

G Hospedaje Primavera, C Unión, Tomepampa, T054-280356. On the main street, accommodation with the local school teacher, Señora Irma Sanabria, with hot water and pretty rooms.

G Hostal Uskuni, the only *hostal* in Pampamarca, off the main square, T054-812189, uskuni@aedes.com.pe. Run by the Vargas family, very basic, cold water, friendly.

G Wasi Punko. Simple accommodation near the turn off for the Luicho baths.

The Municipio in **Puica** has decrepit rooms for guests and can give information, T054-280458. Better accommodation is with the Señora who runs the shop opposite the Municipio, 3 rooms, shared cold water baths, nice views.

Eating

Toro Muerto *p277*

Recommended restaurants in Corire include **El Fogón** and **La Sirena,** both on Av Progreso. Try the local speciality of *camarones* from the Río Majes.

Cotahuasi *p277*

Three small restaurants/bars on Jr Arequipa offer basic fare; the best is **BuenSabor,** opposite **Hostal Alcalá II.** There are many well-stocked *tiendas*, selling fruit, vegetables and local wine.

El Pionero, Jr Centenario. Clean, good *menú*.

Las Quenas and **Las Delicias**, both on main square, have decent menus.

Transport

Toro Muerto *p277*

To reach the petroglyphs take the **Empresa Del Carpio** bus to **Corire** from Arequipa main terminal (hourly from 0500, 3-4 hrs, US$3) and ask to be let out at the beginning of the track to Toro Muerto. You can also hire a taxi from the plaza in Corire to the petroglyphs, US$6-10, including a 2-hr wait.

Towards the Valle de los Volcanes *p277*

La Reyna services from Arequipa to **Andagua** continue to **Orcopampa**. Buses return from Andagua to **Arequipa** early afternoon, arriving in the very early morning but you can sleep on the bus until daybreak. There is a daily minibus service Chacas to **Andagua** at 1300 and a truck at around 1000, usually on Sat, Tue and Thu; ask the locals when it's leaving.

Cotahuasi and around *p277*

Alex and La Reyna buses leave Alca for **Arequipa** around 1400 daily. They depart from the plaza in Cotahuasi at 1530 (**Alex**) and 1600 (**La Reyna**), 11-12 hrs, US$9. All companies stop for refreshments in **Chuquibamba**, about halfway to Arequipa. There are also combis between Cotahuasi and Alca.

Directory

Cotahuasi *p277*

There is no place to change money. The PNP are on the plaza; it is advisable to register with them on arrival and before leaving. Some survey maps are available in the **Municipalidad** and **PNP**; ask for Richard Posso, T054-581012. They may let you make photocopies at the shop on the corner of the plaza and Arequipa. Sr Chávez has photocopies of the sheets covering Cotahuasi and surroundings.

South Coast

Footprint features

Introduction

The Pan-American Highway runs all the way south from Lima to the Chilean border and the desert coast has some distinctive attractions. The most famous and, perhaps, the strangest are the enigmatic Nazca Lines, whose origin and function continue to puzzle scientists. More designs on the desert, plus tomb finds at neighbouring Palpa are casting new light on the mystery. Paracas peninsula is one of the world's great marine bird reserves and was home to one of Peru's most important ancient civilizations. As you bob in a boat to the Ballestas Islands to watch the seabirds, look for the giant Candelabra, drawn on the cliffs by unknown hands.

Further south, the Ica Valley, with its wonderful climate, is home to that equally wonderful grape brandy known as *pisco*. South of Nazca, on a small bay, is Puerto Inca, the seaport and fishing harbour for Cuzco in pre-colonial times. The road from here through the canyons to the sierra was a major Inca artery. That route may have fallen into disuse, but new roads are making it much easier to climb up from the coast with its ramshackle fishing villages and brief flashes of green irrigated valleys. One is the newly paved highway from Nazca to Abancay which passes the Pampas Galeras vicuña reserve. Further south the stunning road from the port of Ilo to Lake Titicaca can be picked up in the oasis town of Moquegua.

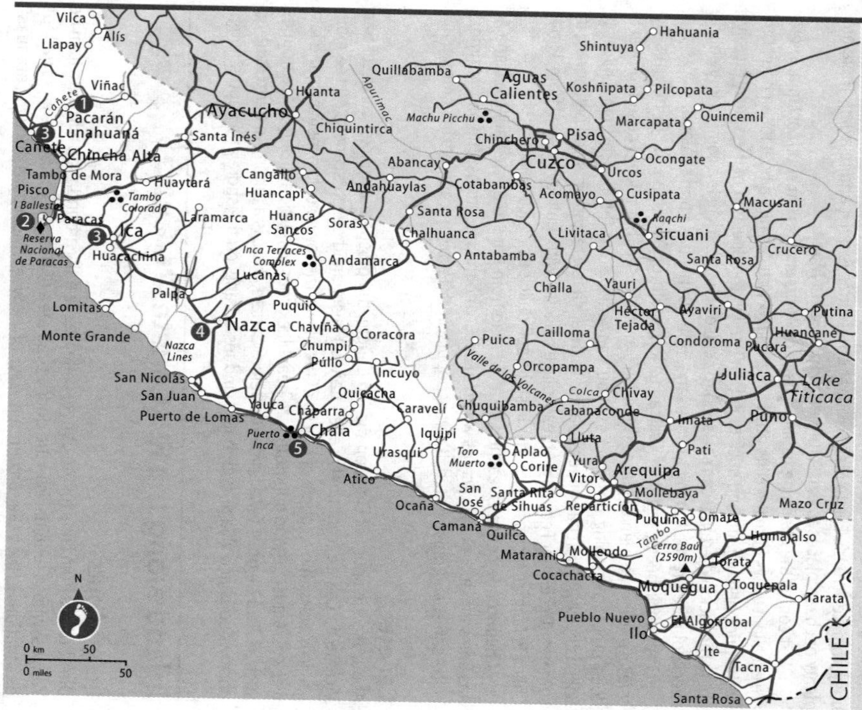

★ Don't miss...

1 **Cañete Valley** For some real off-the-beaten track adventure follow the Río Cañete towards the sierra to tiny villages, secret valleys and some of the most breathtaking scenery in Peru, page 285.

2 **Ballestas Islands** Visit the 'guano' producers of the Paracas National Reserve. Cormorants, boobies, pelicans and terns as well as penguins and sea lions inhabit the rocks and arches of the islands, page 289.

3 **Bodegas** Sample table wines, sweet wines and, above all, *pisco* at one of the wineries in the river valleys south of Lima. The owners are usually pretty generous with their measures, pages 285 and 297.

4 **Nazca Lines** From a small plane, take a gods' eye view of the lines etched in the desert, one of the great archaeological enigmas, page 301.

5 **Puerto Inca** On the barren Pacific coast are the ruins of Cuzco's port, from where runners carried fresh fish to the Inca's table, page 310.

Lima to Pisco

South to Cañete

» pp290-295. Colour map 5, A1/2.

The first 60 km south from Lima are dotted with a series of seaside resort towns and clubs that come alive in the summer months of December to March. Note that most beaches have very strong currents and can be dangerous if swimming. If you're unsure, ask the locals. The first popular beach is **El Silencio**, at Km 34, which is good for a day trip from Lima. The beach is lined with *cebicherías*, all offering fresh seafood, but go early to get an umbrella and lounge chair (you will be expected to buy food or drinks if using these facilities). Just before El Silencio is a spectacular rock formation a short distance out to sea consisting of two islands known as **La Ballena** (the whale). The next notable beach is **Punta Hermosa** at Km 39, which is a popular summer retreat for Limeños. There are many summer houses here and some nice hostels for those looking to soak up some sun or to surf. Fresh seafood restaurants line the boardwalk of Punta Hermosa. The next beach from Punta Hermosa is **Punta Negra**, Km 47, a popular spot for surfers, well-known for having the most consistent surfing break south of Lima. **San Bartolo** is 49 km south from Lima. It is very busy from New Year's Eve to March, but at other times is quiet and relaxing. There are plenty of cheap places to eat. A further 2 km is **Santa María**.

If driving south from Lima, you can make a detour to visit the ruins of Pachacámac on the way, see page 98.

Next comes the charming fishing village of **Pucusana**, 60 km south of Lima. There are excellent views from the cliffs above the village. You can hire a boat for an hour, but fix the price beforehand and stick to it. Don't sail in the direction of the smelly factory, but to the rocks where you can see seabirds close at hand. There is a compulsory police checkpoint before the turning to Pucusana. **Hotel Bahía** has good seafood.

The small beach resort of **Chilca**, 14 km south of Pucusana, is 30 minutes by *colectivo* from the market place. There isn't much to see, but a long, deserted beach does present camping possibilities. You can walk along the beach from Chilca to Salinas (5 km), which has mineral baths. There are a few restaurants and pensiones. In summer (December-February), these places fill up with holidaymakers from Lima. Chilca is famous for its figs; roadside stalls sell delicious fig ice cream.

Chepeconde beach is reached by a dirt road from Km 120 of the Panamericana. It has fine sand and rocky outcrops which divide it into three sections. The northernmost is the safest and most visited. It's very popular with Peruvian campers in summer.

Cañete

About 150 km south of Lima, on the Río Cañete, the prosperous market centre of **San Vicente de Cañete** (commonly called **Cañete**) is set amid desert scenery. All the main services are within a couple of blocks of the plaza. The town hosts a festival in the last week of August, a good opportunity to hear black coastal music and see dance troupes such as Perú Negro. A few kilometres before Cañete, there is a turning to **Cerro Azul**, an uncrowded beach village, with hotels and restaurants on the shore and good surfing.

Inland along the Río Cañete

» pp290-295.

Ins and outs

Direct buses from Lima for the Cañete valley leave daily around 1500 with **San Juan de Yauyos**, whose terminal is in the dodgy Grau area of the city. The buses go to various destinations in the valley on different days of the week. Most pass through **Catahuasi**, the stop for Tupe, and on Thursday go direct to **Laraos**. Otherwise go to Cañete and ask about the service with **ETAS/Angoma** (see page 294) to **Huancayo**, via **Catahuasi**, **Chavín**, **Yauyos** and **Llapay**. ▸▸ *For further details, see Transport, page 294. For ETAS services in the opposite direction, see page 494.*

Quebrada de Lunahuaná → *Phone code: 01. Colour map 5, A2.*

From Cañete, a paved road runs inland, mostly beside the Río Cañete, through **Imperial**, which has a market on Saturday, Sunday and Monday (good for every type of household item), and Nuevo Imperial to the **Quebrada de Lunahuaná**.

Lunahuaná consists of a town and several districts (*anexos*) strung along the valley. They are totally dependent on the Río Cañete for irrigation and for the tourist attractions of rafting and kayaking. Beyond the reach of the water, the surrounding countryside is completely barren but not without its own appeal. In early morning and at dusk the hills are painted in infinite shades of grey, pink and brown, framed by the clear blue sky, fertile green valley and rushing water.

Eight kilometres before Lunahuaná is **Incawasi**, the ruins of an Inca city. A new road cuts right through the middle of the site, which dominates the valley and *quebradas* that run down into it. Incawasi is said to have been a replica of Cuzco, with its divided trapezoidal plaza. The site was built outside the fertile zone of the valley and its rough walls blend in perfectly with the barren hills.

Paullo is the first *anexo* reached after Incawasi. Here stand the ruins of the first church of Lunahuaná. In summer, when the river is high, rafting trips start from just below the plaza. In the low river season a temporary footbridge crosses the river to **Lúcumo**. Two kilometres further on is **San Jerónimo**, the area's whitewater rafting centre; there are several agencies to choose from (see Activities and tours, page 294). Other adventure tourism activities include paragliding and there is an artificial wall for climbing. At San Jerónimo, a poor but dramatic dirt road runs 40 km up to the small Andean village of **Viñac** (3190 m).

Lunahuaná town (40 km from Cañete) has an 18th-century church on the plaza. Opposite the west door, at the top of the plaza, are the Banco de la Nación and Municipalidad. There are several restaurants in town and in the surrounding *anexos*, some offering rafting. After the town of Lunahuaná (40 km from Cañete), the road continues unpaved to Huancayo up in the sierra, see page 487. Beyond **Condoray** and **Uchupampa** it crosses the Río Cañete to **Catapalla**. A little further on is a *puente colgante* (suspension bridge). Across the road bridge turn right to the village or left to the pre-Inca remains of **Cantagallo**. The site is not signposted; ask directions. Miguel Casas Sánchez in Catapalla can guide to these ruins.

Bodegas

It is interesting to visit the *bodegas* (wine cellars) in the valley and try the wine. The best known is **Los Reyes** (T01-284 1206) in Condoray, where you can try *pisco*, wine, manzanilla and *arope* (a grape juice concentrate). A good time to visit is during February and March when you can see the traditional methods of treading the grapes by foot to the beat of the drum. Other *bodegas* in Condoray include: **Viña Santa María** (T01-437 8892), beside Hostal Río Alto; **Del Valle**, by La Laguna restaurant, and **Viñas del Sur** (T01-437 3187). Also try **El Olimpo** (T01-460 7698) in Uchupampa, beside the Hotel Embassy and *bodegas* **Reina de Lunahuaná**, in Catapalla, a five-minute walk from the suspension bridge. This last is the most rustic and authentic *bodega* in the valley and produces an excellent *pisco*. It offers a free tour and has a restaurant, open at weekends. Recommended.

Cañete Valley

Beyond Lunahuaná the road ascending the Cañete Valley leaves the narrow flood plain and runs through a series of *retama*-lined gorges. It passes through **Pacarán**,

 Catahuasi (for access to Tupe, see below) and **San Lorenzo de Putinza** before entering the **Reserva Paisajística Nor Yauyos-Cochas**. The market town of **Yauyos**, with basic accommodation, is 5 km off this road. The next village is **Llapay**, a good base for exploring the area. There is a basic *hostal* with a restaurant here and you may be able to catch transport to other villages with workers from the **Instituto Valle Grande AECI**. If you have your own car, you can go wherever you want, but the roads are poor and you should seek the advice of someone who knows the region well. The people are friendly but you need to speak Spanish. Two hours' walk west from Llapay (one hour by car) is the village of **Carania**, from where a further two hours' trekking leads to the pre-Inca ruins of **Huamanmarca**.

Further upstream, the valley narrows to an exceptionally tight canyon, with a hairy road squeezed between nothing but rock and rushing water. At **Alís** the road forks: north, following the Río Cañete deeper into the reserve to **Huancaya** and **Vilca**, and east, where a steep climb leads to mine workings near the 4600-m pass, beyond which the road drops to Huancayo.

North of Alís, the upper valley is one of the most beautiful and amazing of all Peru's coastal river valleys, on a par with the Colca Valley. Above Huancaya the river passes through high Andean terrain and descends through a seemingly endless series of incredibly attractive, absolutely clear, turquoise pools and lakes, interrupted by cascades and whitewater rapids. In some pools, huge clumps of tortora reed sway gently and in all there are prolific numbers of trout and abundant birdlife. Large parts of the valley are inaccessible in this section but marvellous day walks can be made upriver from Huancaya and 30 km further on at **Vilca**. At both there are also attractive old colonial bridges across the river.

Culturally, the valley is fascinating for its dying indigenous languages and perhaps the best pre-Columbian terracing anywhere in Peru. **Tupe**, reached on a six-hour walk from Catahuasi, is home to the Jaqaru people, distant cousins to the Aymara of Bolivia and southern Peru. Astonishingly, the Jaqaru have managed to keep alive their traditions and language, which may be the key to unravelling the ultimate origins of the Aymara languages. Tupe's older women still wear traditional red and black dress, though a modern tartan-style variant is taking over among most younger women. Dark red headscarves also abound, and for festivals they still wear *tupus* (traditional dress pins), identical to those depicted on colonial drawings of Inca women's dress. The village is overlooked by the almost sheer rock-face of Tupinachaka, complete with ancient rock paintings.

Laraos is also a linguistic final refuge. A very few aged speakers of the local form of Quechua are to be found in a beautiful, old village of steep streets. Some houses here have the same structure as the reconstructed Inca houses at Machu Picchu, with steeply sloping thatched roofs much longer and lower on one side than on the other. Good times to visit are for the *fiestas* at Carnival (beware the water bombs and flour or talcum powder attacks!), for the irrigation channel cleaning in May, or for the town *fiesta* in August. The valley's sides are covered with *andenes* in a sweeping curve of several kilometres. There are scenic hikes further up the valley beyond the seasonal lake below the village. Laraos is a 1½-hour walk from Llapay, or there is a daily combi from Llapay at 1100.

Pisco and around

» pp290-295.

Chincha Alta → *Colour map 5, A2. Population: 110,016.*

Some 35 km north of Pisco, near Chincha Baja, is **Tambo de Mora**, the old port, with nearby archaeological sites at Huaca de Tambo de Mora, La Centinela, Chinchaycama and Huaca Alvarado. **Chincha** itself is a fast-growing town where the negro/criollo culture is still alive (for more details, see pages 587 and 596). It is a good place to sample locally produce wine and *pisco*. One of the best *bodegas* is the 100-year-old **Naldo Navarro** ⓘ *Pasaje Santa Rosa, Sunampe, 100 m west of the Panamericana, free guided tours, including tasting*. Other *bodegas* also have guided tours and the third Saturday in September is national *pisco* day.

Pisco → *Phone code: 056. Colour map 5, B2. Population: 82,250.*

Despite being christened as San Clemente de Macera by the Spanish in 1640, the town had already been unofficially named after the famous local brandy and would always be known as Pisco. Now the largest port between Callao and Matarani, 237 km south of Lima, it serves a large agricultural hinterland. The town is small and compact. All you want to do and see is contained within a 300-m radius of the quiet Plaza de Armas, with its equestrian statue of San Martín.

The town was originally divided into two: **Pisco Pueblo**, with its colonial-style homes, patios and gardens; and **Pisco Puerto**, which, apart from fisheries, has been replaced as a port by the deep-water Puerto General San Martín, beyond Paracas. The two have now expanded into one fairly unattractive town. If the wind is in the wrong direction, the smell of fish can be pretty bad. In Pisco Pueblo, half a block west of the Plaza de Armas, at San Martín 132 is the **Club Social Pisco**, the HQ of San Martín after he had landed at Paracas Bay. There is an old Jesuit church on San Francisco, one block from the plaza, separated from the Municipalidad by a park. The newer **cathedral** is on the main plaza. Avenida San Martín runs from the Plaza de Armas to the sea.

It is not recommended to walk on or near **Pisco Playa** at night, as there are many reports of tourists being robbed while walking to the beach; take taxi or mototaxi. It is best not to carry important items such as plane tickets, passports, flashy toys, etc, while out at night.

Inland from Pisco

From the Pan-American Highway near Pisco, a paved road runs 317 km up to Ayacucho in the sierra, with a branch to Huancavelica. At Castrovirreyna the road reaches 4600 m. The scenery on this journey is superb.

One of the best-preserved Inca ruins in coastal Peru is **Tambo Colorado** ⓘ *48 km from Pisco, US$1.50; buses and colectivos from Pisco pass right through the site, taxi US$25; tours US$10-15 with guide, minimum 2 people*. It includes buildings where the Inca and his retinue would have stayed. Many of the walls retain their original colours. On the other side of the road is the public plaza and the garrison and messengers' quarters. The caretaker will act as a guide and has a small collection of items found on the site. Wait at his house for transport back to Pisco.

At **Huaytará**, four hours by bus from Pisco, the whole side of the church is a perfectly preserved Inca wall with niches and trapezoidal doorways. Twenty minutes from town are the ruins of Incahuasi with thermal baths. On 24 June is the **Fiesta of San Juan Bautista**.

Paracas Peninsula and the Ballestas Islands

▸▸ *pp290-295. Colour map 5, B2.*

Fifteen kilometres down the coast from Pisco Puerto is the bay of Paracas sheltered by the Paracas Peninsula. It is named after the Paracas winds – sandstorms that can last for three days, especially in August. The wind gets up every afternoon, peaking at around 1500. The whole peninsula, a large area of coast to the south and the Ballestas Islands are all part of a national reserve, created in 1975, which covers a total of 335,000 ha on land and sea. It is one of the most important marine reserves in the world, with the highest concentration of marine birds. The region is also economically important, being a major producer of guano (see page 289).

Ins and outs

Getting there and around Most visitors explore the reserve on an organized tour from Pisco but, if you're travelling independently, it can be reached along the coast road from Pisco and San Andrés, passing the fishing port and a large proportion of Peru's fishmeal industry. Alternatively, go down the Pan-American Highway for 14½ km beyond the Pisco turning and take the road to Paracas across the desert. After 11 km turn left along the coast road and, 1 km further on, fork right to Paracas village. Return to the main road for the entrance to the reserve (entry fee US$1.50), where you can ask for a map.

From the park entrance, it takes about 50 minutes to get to Lagunilla by private transport, 45 minutes to La Mina and an hour to Mirador de los Lobos. Make sure your car is in good condition, never leave it unattended and travel in a group as robbery has been a problem in the past. » *For details of tours, see Activities and tours, page 294.*

Paracas National Reserve

The entrance to the reserve is just south of the village of Paracas at the **Julio Tello Site Museum** ⓘ *daily 0900-1700, museum entry fee US$2*. The museum also has a shop which sells guidebooks, film and drinks, and a visitors' centre, with information in Spanish only. The exhibits are from the burial sites discovered in 1925 under the Paracas desert by the Peruvian archaeologist, Julio C Tello (see page 290). However, the best examples of textiles and funerary bundles can be found in Lima at the Museo de la Nación and at the archaeological museum, Pueblo Libre (see pages 91 and 92).

A network of good dirt roads, reasonably well-signed, crosses the peninsula. Details of walking routes are available from the visitors' centre or ask for the 'Hoja 28-K' map at **Instituto Geográfico Nacional** in Lima. It is not safe to walk alone and it is easy to get lost in the hot, wide desert area. The wildlife on view includes a wide variety of sea mammals and rare and exotic birds. Condors can even be seen in February and March from the rough road between Paracas and Laguna Grande. These massive vultures feed on the ready supply of sea lion carcasses. Rather more delicate are the flamingos which feed in Paracas bay. The closest you can get to the birds is a *mirador*, a short walk from the museum, from where they can be seen well only with binoculars. Note that from January to March the birds head for the sierra.

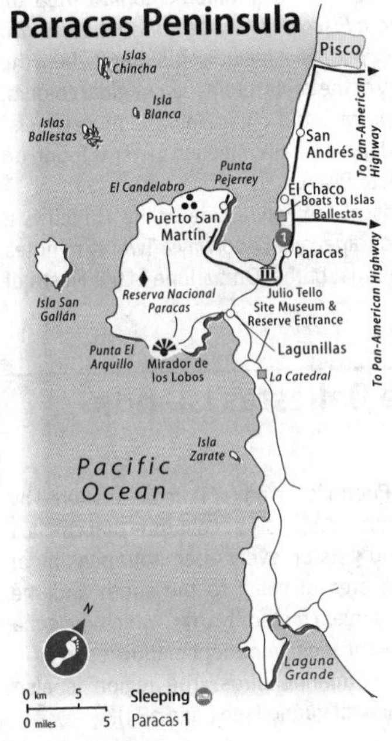

The tiny fishing village of **Lagunilla** is 5 km from the museum across the neck of the peninsula. It has beaches which are free from sting rays, but not very clean, and eating places which tend to be overpriced. Six kilometres southeast is **La Catedral**, a rock formation in the cliffs that some guides may tell you was the location for filming *Planet of the Apes*. Nearby, a monument marks the spot where San Martín landed in Peru, on 8 September 1820, after liberating Argentina. Soon after, a shipload of British troops, led by Lord Cochrane, arrived to help the General plan his strategy to break the Spanish stranglehold in the region.

Heading west from Lagunilla 6 km around the peninsula, you reach **Mirador de los Lobos** at Punta El Arquillo, which

An economic mess

The islands lying off the coast of Peru are the breeding grounds for millions of sea birds, whose droppings have accumulated over the centuries. These piles of mineral-rich excrement were turned into piles of cash during the last century.

Though the ancient Peruvians knew of the benefits of guano – the name given to the natural fertilizer – and used it on their crops, it wasn't until 1840 that vast deposits of the stuff were exploited for commercial purposes. It was at this time that Peru first began to trade abroad, particularly with France and England. Almost simultaneously, guano began to replace rare metals as the country's main export.

However, with the economy heavily based on the sales of bird droppings, Peru was caught in a vicious circle of borrowing money on future sales, then having to repay loans at vastly inflated rates. This unhealthy state of affairs was exacerbated in 1864 when Spain, in a petulant show of aggression towards her ex-colony, decided to occupy the guano islands of Chincha, to the south of Lima, thereby leaving the Peruvian government really up to its neck in it.

The main producers of guano are the guanay cormorant and the Peruvian booby. They gather in colonies on the islands, attracted by the huge shoals of anchovy which feed on the plankton in the cold water of the Humboldt current.

looks down on a raucous mob of sea lions. On the north side of the peninsula, about 14 km from the entrance, a pre-Columbian drawing known as **El Candelabro** (the candelabra) is traced into the hillside. At least 50 m long, it is best seen from the sea. Approaching it by land is not a good idea as disturbance of the sand around it is beginning to destroy the monument; some idiots have even driven over it. There are differing theories as to its exact purpose. Some believe it to be linked to the Nazca Lines (see page 301), 200 km to the south, others that it is related to the Southern Cross constellation and was used to help guide ancient sailors. Still others contend that it represents the cactus used by the ancient high priests for its hallucinogenic powers. A few cruel cynics have even suggested – God forfend – that it was the work of some opportunistic local guides.

Ballestas Islands

The Ballestas islands, dubbed the poor man's Galápagos by many, are nonetheless spectacular in their own right and well worth visiting. They are eroded into numerous arches and caves, hence their name – *ballesta* means bow, as in archery. These arches provide shelter for thousands of seabirds, some of which are very rare, and countless sea lions. A former guano factory can be seen on one of the islands and several others have installations. The book *Las Aves del Departamento de Lima* by Maria Koepcke is useful.

Boat trips to the islands leave from the jetty at **El Chaco**, a beach and fishing port by Paracas village. They usually depart at 0730, returning at 1100 to avoid rougher seas in the afternoon; tours may be cancelled entirely if the sea is too choppy. Most boats are speedboats with life jackets, but some are very crowded. Wear warm clothing, but also take protection against the sun and wear sunglasses. You will see, close up, sea lions, guano birds, pelicans, penguins and, if you're lucky, dolphins

It is said that the graceful red and white flamingos of the Paracas Peninsula inspired General San Martín to design Peru's red and white flag of independence.

Textiles and trepanation

The Paracas Necropolis culture, which inhabited this region between 1300 BC and AD 200, is renowned for its finely woven textiles, in particular *mantos*, large decorated cloths, embroidered with anthropomorphic, zoomorphic and geometric designs. These *mantos* were used to wrap mummified bodies in their funerary bundles. Their discovery by anthropologists and archaeologists provided vital clues to this civilization. The bodies were often found to have trepanned skulls. Trepanation was a form of brain surgery performed by the Paracas people in which metal plates were inserted to replace broken sections of skull – a common injury among warring factions at that time. In addition, the Paracas culture practised the intentional deformation of infants' skulls for aesthetic reasons.

swimming in the bay. The boats pass Puerto San Martín and the Candelabra (see above) en route to the islands but they do not go to see the flamingos and few tours include Isla San Gallán, where there are thousands of sea lions.

Sleeping

South to Cañete *p284*

Many hotels advertise that they have swimming pools. If they do indeed have them, they are only unlikely to be full during the summer, Dec-Mar/Apr.

Punta Hermosa

D-E **Casa Barco**, Av Punta Hermosa 340, T01-230 7081, www.casabarco.com. This is a funky little hostel with a pool, decorated with great art work, very clean and offers rooms with views and cable TV (**B**). It's a short walk from where buses drop passengers off.

E **La Rotunda**, Av Bolognesi 592, T01-440 2529. This is a quaint little hostel above a restaurant of the same name. Large rooms, great views, above the boardwalk, cable TV.

E-F **La Isla**, T01-230 7146. Also right on the boardwalk, not as charming as the others, but cheaper in a dorm. Breakfast is included.

Punta Negra

E **Hostal Hamacas**, T01-231 5498, surfresortperu@terra.com.pe. Right on the beach, but the lodgings are basic.

San Bartolo

C **Hostal 110**, next door to **Posada del Mirador** (see below), Malecón San Martín. Rents apartments and rooms with great views, some with chimney, all with fridge, pool, very comfortable.

D **Posada del Mirador**, Malecón San Martín 105, T01-430 7822, or 9648 8169 (mob). Price is for a bungalow only; **A** with full board.

D per person **Casa Resort Peñascal**, Av Las Palmeras 258, T01-430 7436, www.surfpenascal.com. Price is for full board, including welcome drink, hot water and laundry; surf specials available. Relaxing spot, with balconies overlooking the surf – a good place to chill for a couple of days.

Pucusana

E-F **El Mirador – Centro Turístico Belvedere**, T01-430 9228, elmiradordepucusana@hotmail.com. Owned by hospitable Adolfo del Campo, on hill overlooking the village and harbour, a cheap haven for travellers. Adolfo cooks whatever is available when the boats come in.

Cerro Azul

C **Las Palmeras**, on the beach, T01-284 6005. Said to be the best in town, with TV and pool.

Cañete *p284*

E **Hostal Colibrí**, Urb Los Libertadores, Mz A, Lote 9, T01-581 1309. A clean hotel. The basic rooms have TV.

E Hostal Edwar's, Benavides 150, T01-581 3632. Clean, friendly, rooms with TV and bath, quieter rooms at the back.
E Hostal Rec, Urb Los Libertadores, Mz A, Lote 7, T01-581 2623. A comfortable hotel with wooden floors and cable TV.
F Hostal San Francisco, Santa Rosa 739, 2 blocks north of the plaza, T01-581 2409. Rooms with bathroom, clean, friendly, quiet. Recommended.

Quebrada de Lunahuaná *p285*

B El Refugio, Viñac, T01-421 6952 in Lima, ventasyreservas@refugiosdelperu.com. A beautiful lodge with fantastic views down the Viñac valley, excellent full board, log fires, jacuzzi. Trekking, horse riding and mountain biking available. A great place to escape from Lima for a couple of days.
B Regina, Condoray, T/F01-472 2370. Price drops to **D** in low season. Hot water, TV, swimming pool, cafetería, attractive, with good views over the valley.
C Embassy Jardín, Uchupampa, T01-472 3525. Price is **D** in low season. All facilities, restaurants, disco, gardens, rafting, large property, good, popular with families. In same group but slightly more expensive is Embassy Río, same phone, riverside location.
C Río Alto, just outside Lunahuaná, T01-284 1125, www.rioaltohotel.com. Rooms with bathroom or bungalows for 7, hot water. Also pool, restaurant, disco, rafting, very nice.
E El Refugio, Jr Bolognesi 179, Lunahauná, T01-284 1020. A nice, serviceable *hostal* near the plaza, with TV, clean.
F Hostal Casuarinas, Grau 295, Lunahuaná, T01-284 1045. Near the plaza, a clean, basic *hostal*, with TV, bath and hot water.
F Hostal Lunahuaná, Lunahuaná, T01-284 1089. At the southern entrance to the village, friendly, clean, hot water and private bath, good value. Recommended.

Cañete Valley *p285*

G Familia Torres, Huancaya, T01-534 5860 (Lima). Accommodation and meals, basic but clean and friendly.
G Hostal Llapay, Llapay. Basic, very friendly, with restaurant. They will open the door even if you arrive in the middle of the night.

There is a basic *hospedaje* in **Vilca** (**G**) and a municipal hotel with a restaurant in **Laraos** (**G** per person) that is basic but good; pay a little bit extra for a hot shower. In **Tupe** formal accommodation and restaurants hardly exist, but there is a very basic municipal *hostal*, and you should always be able to find someone willing to put you up and cook you a basic meal. Alternatively there are flat grazing areas with streams both immediately below and above the village where a tent could be pitched.

Chincha Alta *p286*

B Hacienda San José, 9 km south of town in El Carmen district, turn off at Km 203, T056-221458, hsanjose@terra.com.pe (or book in Lima at Juan Fanning 328, of 202, Miraflores, T01-444 5242). Price is for full board (cheaper Mon-Thu). A 17th-century sugar and cotton estate ranch-house, with beautiful buildings, pool, garden, small church, colonial crafts. Tunnels run from the basement and are believed to link up with Tambo de Mora in order to facilitate the contraband trade in black slaves from Africa. The catacombs, where many of those slaves were interred, can be visited, US$3 per person. Criollo shows and buffet lunches are extra. Take a taxi for US$4 or 20-min *colectivo* for US$.30. It is very busy at weekends.
D El Valle, Panamericana, in Chincha itself, T056-262556. A central hotel with the excellent **Palacio de los Mariscos** restaurant.
F Hostal La Rueda, Santo Domingo 228, near the plaza. The *hostal* is rustic, breakfast is extra, hot showers, small pool, lounge.
F-G Sotelo, Benavides 260, T056-261681. A basic hotel; rooms without bath are cheaper.

Pisco *p286, map p292*

The town is full at weekends with visitors from Lima. Mosquitoes are a problem at night in the summer.
C Hostal Villa Manuelita, San Fransisco 227, T056-535218, hostalvillamanuelita @hotmail.com. Very charming, elegantly decorated colonial mansion with cafeteria and restaurant. All rooms with private bath, cable TV, fan. Helpful staff, tranquil patios and warm atmosphere. Recommended.

For an explanation of sleeping and eating price codes used in this guide, see inside the front cover. Other relevant information is found in Essentials, pages 53-58.

C **Las Olas**, Av Miguel Grau 156, Pisco Playa, T056-532315, www.lasolasperu.com. This modern hotel on the beach, 10 minutes from Pisco Pueblo, is clean and would be a great choice for lounging by the pool. Some rooms with ocean view, games room, buffet breakfast. IYH card discount. Recommended.

D **Hostal Candelabro**, Callao y Pedemonte, T056-532620. TV, fridge, fax service, hot water, café, bar on roof, laundry, safe, clean.

D **Regidor**, Arequipa 201, T/F056-535220, regidor@mail.cosapidata.com.pe. With bath, TV, fan, jacuzzi, café and restaurant, sauna, very good, price negotiable at quiet times.

E **Embassy**, Jr Comercio just off the Plaza de Armas, T056-535215. With bathroom, clean, noisy, nice bar on roof, has disco, trips to Ballestas Islands, under the same ownership as **Embassy Suites** on Bolognesi and the **Embassy Beach**.

E **Hostal Los Inkas Inn**, Prol Barrio Nuevo Mz M Lt 14, Urb San Isidro, T056-536634, los_inkas_inn@hotmail.com. 5 blocks from the Plaza de Armas. Comfortable and straightforward. The pool may not always be full but there is internet, cafetería, sauna, laundry services and garage. Single and double/twin rooms with bath and cable TV, and **F** dorms with shared bathrooms. Tours can be arranged.

E **Posada Hispana Hotel**, Bolognesi 236, T056-536363, www.posadahispana.com. Rooms each with terrace and bathroom, with breakfast, also rooms with shared bath (**G** per person), hot water, TV, can accommodate groups, comfortable, clean, safe, information service, email, laundry facilities, luggage store, English, French, Italian and Catalan spoken. Recommended.

E **Hostal San Isidro**, San Clemente 103, T/F056-536471, www.hostalsanisidro.com. With bath, **F** without, hot water, safe, clean and welcoming, very nice pool and cafeteria, free laundry facilities, use of kitchen, but no fridge, games room, English spoken, parking. Arranges dune buggy tours. Recommended.

F **El Condado**, Arequipa 136, Plazuela Belén, T056-533623, hostalcondado@hotmail.com. Hot water, cable TV, laundry, expensive breakfast available, tours to Ballestas arranged. Good if a bit noisy.

F **Hostal Belén**, Arequipa 128, Plazuela Belén, T056-533046. Near three other hotels on the same plaza, all with the same feel: basic and a bit outdated, with hot water. The rooms in the new Belén annex are much better and the hotel is safe and clean, can book tours.

F **Hostal La Portada**, Alipio Ponce 250, T056-532098, hostallaportada@terra.com.

Pisco

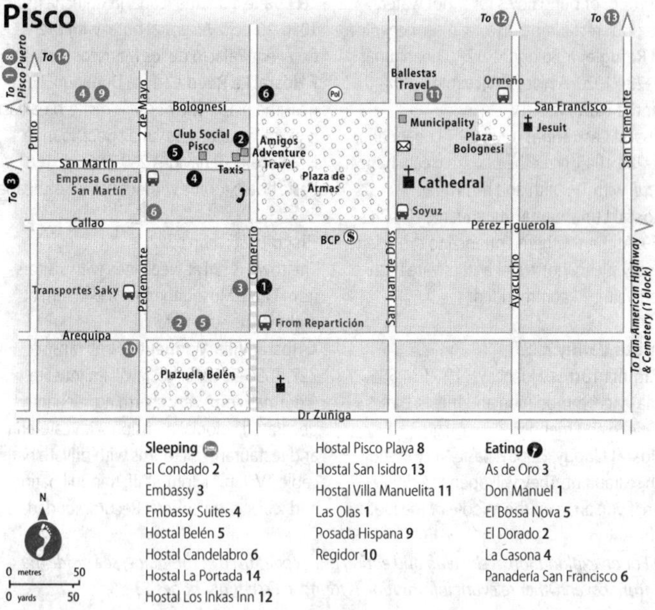

Sleeping
El Condado 2
Embassy 3
Embassy Suites 4
Hostal Belén 5
Hostal Candelabro 6
Hostal La Portada 14
Hostal Los Inkas Inn 12
Hostal Pisco Playa 8
Hostal San Isidro 13
Hostal Villa Manuelita 11
Las Olas 1
Posada Hispana 9
Regidor 10

Eating
As de Oro 3
Don Manuel 1
El Bossa Nova 5
El Dorado 2
La Casona 4
Panadería San Francisco 6

Clean, free coffee, hot water, bath, cable TV, laundry, friendly staff. Recommended.
G per person **Hostal Pisco Playa** (Youth Hostel), Jr José Balta 639, Pisco Playa, T056-532492. Quite nice, clean, kitchen, washing facilities, breakfast US$1.50.

Paracas Peninsula *p287, map p288*
AL-A Paracas, T056-545100, hparacas @terra.com.pe. Bungalows on the beach, suites in **L** range, fine grounds facing the bay. Good food, not cheap, with buffet lunch on Sun US$25. It is a good centre for excursions to the peninsula and flights over Nazca. It also houses the Masson ceramics collection, which is worth seeing. Tennis courts and an open-air pool (US$2 for non-residents). Dune-buggy trips of 2 hrs can be arranged for US$25 per person, good fun. TCs can be changed here at good rates. Next door is the **Hostería Paracas**, Av Paracas 169, reasonably priced, comfortable.
B-C El Mirador, at the turn-off to El Chaco, T056-545086, reserves@elmiradorhotel.com. Reservations in Lima, T01-241 6803 . Hot water, good service, boat trips arranged, meals available, sometimes full board only.
C El Chorito, across the plaza from El Amigo, T056-545045. Nice rooms, ask for a view. El Chorito restaurant is very good.
E Alojamiento El Amigo, on the plaza. 5 rooms, nice terrace and good view from 1st floor, with bathroom.
F Hostal Los Frayles, Av Paracas Mz D, Lote 5, P2, T056-545141. Good value, nice terrace, no TV.

Eating

Cañete *p284*
The followin are all in Cañete, where there are also several good Chinese restaurants near the plaza. Try **Panadería Valentino** for baked empanadas and sweet treats.
¥ **Cevichería Muelle 56**, Bolognesi 156. A recommended restaurant serving seafood specialities.
¥ **El Piloto**, Km 137 on the Panamerican Highway just before entering Cañete. This is a great restaurant serving fresh seafood and other Peruvian dishes, guaranteed to satisfy.
¥ **Magdalena**, Bolognesi 135. Serves a good *menú*, including dishes such as pork cooked in wine and butter beans.
¥ **Marinas Chicken** on 2 de Mayo, 2 blocks from the plaza. A welcoming restaurant with great chicken and other Peruvian food.

Quebrada de Lunahuaná *p285*
¥¥-¥ **El Pueblo**, Grau 406, Lunahuaná. Specializes in *camerones*. The *chupe de camerones* is recommended.
¥¥-¥ **Pizzería de Camerones**, Condoray. As the name suggests, serves huge pizzas covered in shrimp, open at weekends only.
¥¥-¥ **Refugio de Santiago**, Paullo. Excellent restaurant with a fine view, herb garden and orchard. Try the *criollo* buffet. Sat and Sun only.
¥ **Cremoladas Josefina**, Jita. Delicious, refreshing *cremoladas* of crushed ice (boiled water used) mixed with fruit pulp; grape and *lúcuma* varieties are especially good.

Pisco *p286, map p292*
There are restaurants on the pedestrianized block of Comercio and along San Martín. Seafood restaurants can be found on the shore between Pisco and San Andrés and in San Andrés itself (buses from Plaza Belén).
¥¥-¥ **As de Oro**, San Martín 472, T056-532010. Good food at decent prices, closed Mon. Doubles as a disco and karaoke bar on Sat.
¥¥-¥ **El Bossa Nova**, San Martín 176, p 2, T056-807388. This café/bar is a stylish place for an espresso or your favorite trago. Good night and day.
¥¥-¥ **La Casona Restaurant and Churrascaría**, San Martín between Plaza and 2 de Mayo. Specializes in grilled meats, large portions, good value.
¥ **Don Manuel**, Comercio 187. US$2-4 for a main dish.
¥ **El Dorado**, main plaza opposite the cathedral. Good-value local dishes, popular.

Cafés
Panadería/Café San Fransisco, on the main Plaza. Has great *empanadas* and baked goods, with a restaurant next door, cheap.

Festivals and events

Quebrada de Lunahuaná *p285*
Feb Festival of adventure sports.
Mar Fiesta de la Vendimia, the grape harvest festival on the 1st weekend.
Late Sep/early Oct The lively **Fiesta del Níspero** (medlar fruit harvesting festival).

Cañete Valley *p285*
2 Feb Tupe's main annual festival celebrates the **Virgen de la Candelaria**.
17 Jul **Festival Nor-Yauyina** held in Llapay, attended by many people including Limeños.

Chincha Alta *p286*
Among other things (olives, for one) Chincha is famous for its many festivals.
6 Jan **Celebración del Nacimiento de la Beata Melchorita Saravia**.
End Feb **Verano Negro**, or Black Summer. During this time the black culture of the area, repressed for so many centuries, is freely expressed in the dancing competitions, though black participation in the festival is still somewhat limited.
Mar **Festival de la Vendimia**, grape harvest festival is celebrated in the 2nd week.
Mid-Jul **Festival de la Virgen del Carmen**.
Late Oct/earlyNov **Tourist Week**.
Nov **Festival de Danzas Negras**, held in the black community of El Carmen, 10 km south.
4 Dec **Peregrinación a la Ermita de la Beata Melchorita**.

Pisco *p286, map p292*
End Jun **Fiesta de San Pedro**.
Sep **Tourist Week** in the 2nd week.
21 Nov The grandly titled **Peregrinación a la Hermita de la Beata de Humay**.

Activities and tours

South to Cañete *p284*
Peru Adventure Lodge, Manzana Ñ, Lote1, Urb La Planicie, Punta Hermosa, T01-230 8351, www.peruadventure.com. Offers accommodation, surfing, spearfishing, fossil hunting and more.
Surf Perú Surfcamp, Lote 27 y 28, Urb La Planicie, Punta Hermosa, T01-230 7421, www.peru-surf.com. Opposite Pico Alto, surfing, classes and equipment rental, bungalows and bunk rooms, hot water, all meals available, airport transfers, internet, living room with cable TV.

Quebrada de Lunahuaná *p285*
Several places in **San Jerónimo** and **Paullo** offer rafting and kayaking. In Nov-Apr, when the river is high (highest from Dec), whitewater rafting is at levels 4-5. May-Oct is the low-water season when only boat trips are possible (levels 1-2). There's excellent kayaking 2½ hrs upriver. Rafting costs US$15 per person for 1½ hrs. Annual championships and a festival of adventure sports are held every Feb.

Pisco *p286, map p292*
Tours to the **Ballestas Islands** cost US$10 per person, and to the **Paracas Peninsula** US$20 per person, but are a lot cheaper out of season. Beware scams; only book tours in company offices not in hotels, nor on the street. The main hotels will also arrange tours. Operators usually visit Ballestas in the morning and the Reserve in the afternoon.
Amigos Adventure Travel Agency, Jr Progreso 167, p 2, T056-311984, amigos _adventures @hotmail.com. Tours to Ballestas Islands and Paracas Reserve, sandboarding, English, Italian, French, Dutch and Hebrew spoken. Recommended.
Ballestas Travel Service, San Francisco 249, T056-535564. Recommended.
Blue Sea Tours, C Chosica 320, San Andrés, Pisco; also at El Chaco, near Paracas. Tours to the Ballestas Islands. Guides Jorge Espejo and Hubert Van Lomoen (speaks Dutch) are frequently recommended and there is no time limit on tours.
Zarcillo Connection, Callao 137, suite B-21, T056-536543, www.zarcilloconnections.net, www.zarcillotravel.com. For Paracas National Reserve, Tambo Colorado, trekking and tours to Ica, Chincha and the Nazca Lines and surrounding sites. Also has its own hotel, **Zarcillo Paradise II**, on Paracas Bay. Recommended.

Paracas Peninsula and Ballestas Islands *p287, map p288*
Most operators are based in Pisco (see above). **Hotel Paracas** (see Sleeping) also runs a tour to the islands and reserve, 0900-1700, US$18 in its own speed boat.

Transport

Cañete *p284*
The main bus stop in San Vicente de Cañete is on the highway; wait for the service you want going north or south and hope there are free seats. To **Lima**, frequent, with **Soyuz/PerúBus** (2 de Mayo block 7 y Panamericana), 2 hrs, US$2.45. To **Pisco**, 2 hrs, US$1.50.

To **Huancaya** direct, Sat night only, but a more frequent service is planned, following road improvements in 2006. Other options include taking a bus to Yauyos or Alís and looking for onward traffic from there.

To **Huancayo**, via the Cañete Valley, with ETAS/Angoma (opposite the AEDO service station), T01-287 8831, T9771 1254, US$7.55.

Quebrada de Lunahuaná

To reach **Lunahuaná**, take a taxi from Cañete (US$1.20 from the Panamericana, US$0.90 from centre), or a *colectivo* from 2 de Mayo block 1 (US$0.75) to **Imperial** and then a *colectivo* from Av La Mar, 30 mins, US$0.90, or combi, 45 mins, US$0.75; for **Condoray** or **Uchupampa**, take a taxi, US$1-2. **Turismo Viñac**, Av La Mar, runs from Imperial to **Viñac**, Mon, Wed, Sat, 5 hrs, US$3.50. You can get from Lunahuaná to **Yauyos** in the upper Cañete Valley, daily 1900-2200; ask for the shop where the bus stops and get the shopkeeper to stop the bus.

Cañete Valley *p285*

Bus services through the valley are provided by **San Juan de Yauyos** to and from **Lima**, and by ETAS/Angoma in **Cañete** and **Huancayo**. If you visit **Laraos**, you may be lucky and get a direct bus back to Lima from Laraos itself (usually Thu, about 1000) but on other days your best bet is to hitch or hike back down to **Llapay** for the ETAS bus from Huancayo as it passes through. A bus goes from Yauyos at 0100-0230, passing **Llapay** 0200-0400 en route to **Huancayo**. There may also be a few buses a week from Huancayo to Yauyos with **San Juan de Yauyos**. There is little regular traffic north of Alís to **Huancaya** and **Vilca**.

Pisco and around *p286, map p292*

All the bus terminals are in the centre near the Plaza de Armas. However, if arriving by bus, make sure it is going into town and will not leave you at the Repartición right on the Panamericana, which is 5 km from the centre, a 10-min taxi (US$1) or mototaxi ride (US$0.50), and not a particularly safe area after dark. Transport from the Repartición stops at Hostal Comercio by Plaza Belén. If staying by the beach, it will cost US$0.50 to get to the Plaza de Armas, but drivers try to charge US$1.50.

Local To **Tambo Colorado**, 0800 from near the Plaza (ask for directions), US$1.60, 3 hrs; also *colectivos*, US$1.20 per person. Get off 20 mins after the stop at Humay. Return by bus to Pisco in the afternoon. To **Huaytará**, US$2.25 (rising to US$5.50 for the San Juan Bautista festival!); also **Molina** buses from Lima, 6 hrs.

Long distance To **Lima**, 242 km, 3-4 hrs, US$4 with **Ormeño** (San Francisco, 1 block from the plaza), **San Martín** (San Martín 199) and **Soyuz**, Callao on the Plaza (US$0.30 taxi ride to Panamericana to catch the bus). Buses leave almost hourly 0715-1800. Also *colectivos*. To **Ayacucho**, 317 km, 8-10 hrs, US$7.55-15.15, several buses daily from San Clemente 10 km north on Panamericana Sur, take a *colectivo* (20 mins), book in advance to ensure seat and take warm clothing as it gets cold at night. The road is completely paved. To **Huancavelica**, 269 km, 12-14 hrs, US$7, with **Oropesa** (Conde de la Monclova 637) coming from Ica. To **Ica**, 70 km, 45 mins, US$0.90; with **Ormeño** and **Saky** (Pedemonte y Arequipa). To **Nazca**, 210 km, 3 hrs, US$5, via Ica, at 0830 with **Oropesa** and 3 daily with **Ormeño**. To **Arequipa**, US$12, 10-12 hrs, 2 buses daily.

Paracas Peninsula and Ballestas Islands *p287, map p288*

A taxi from Pisco to **Paracas** costs about US$2.50-3. Combis to/from **El Chaco** beach (marked 'Chaco-Paracas-Museo') leave when full, US$0.50, 25 mins; the last one returns at around 2200. There is no public transport on the peninsula, although **Ormeño** passes by the **Hotel Paracas** at 1630, US$15, en route to Nazca (compared with US$6 on the same Royal Class bus from Ica).

Directory

Pisco *p286, map p292*

Banks ATMs at banks on Plaza de Armas, mostly Visa. **BCP** on the Plaza de Armas, gives good rates for AmEx TCs and cash, Visa ATM. Also on Plaza is **Interbank**, for MasterCard. **Doctor** Dr Carlos Alfonso Bonilla Flores, at C San Francisco 219, doesn't speak English but is very helpful and will make hotel visits. **Internet** In the town centre. **Telephone** On the Plaza de Armas between Av San Martín y Callao.

Ica and around

➔ *Phone code: 056. Colour map 5, B2. Population: 161,406. Altitude: 410 m.*

Ica is Peru's main wine centre. The city is on the Río Ica, which is almost permanently dry and rubbish-strewn but the waters of the Choclacocha and Orococha lakes at 4570 m are tunnelled for 9 km from the Andes into the Ica valley and irrigate 30,000 ha of land. As well as wine, the city is also famous for its tejas, *a local sweet of* manjarblanco. *Most travellers spend little time in Ica itself, preferring to stay at the oasis at Huacachina. Here you will find a lake surrounded by towering sand dunes, which are great for racing up and down on dune buggies and learning the skills of sandboarding. Increasingly popular are trips into the desert to experience the mysteries of this barren landscape.*

▸▸ *For Sleeping, Eating and other listings, see pages 298-300.*

Ins and outs

Getting there and around Buses from Lima travel along the Av Municipalidad nearly into the centre of town. Most hotels, though, are on the far side of the Plaza de Armas. Most bus offices are on Lambayeque blocks 1 and 2 and Salaverry block 3. Look after your bags when transferring between buses to or from Nazca, Pisco or Lima; pickpockets and bagsnatchers operate here. Ica is much more spread out than Pisco. You will need a taxi to get around especially if you intend to visit the *bodegas*.

Tourist information Regional information is available from **Dircetur** ① *Av Grau 148, T056-238710, www.mincetur.gob.pe*, and agencies. Also try **Touring y Automóvil Club del Perú** ① *Fermín Tangüis 102, San Miguel, T056-219393, www.touringperu.com.pe.*

Ica

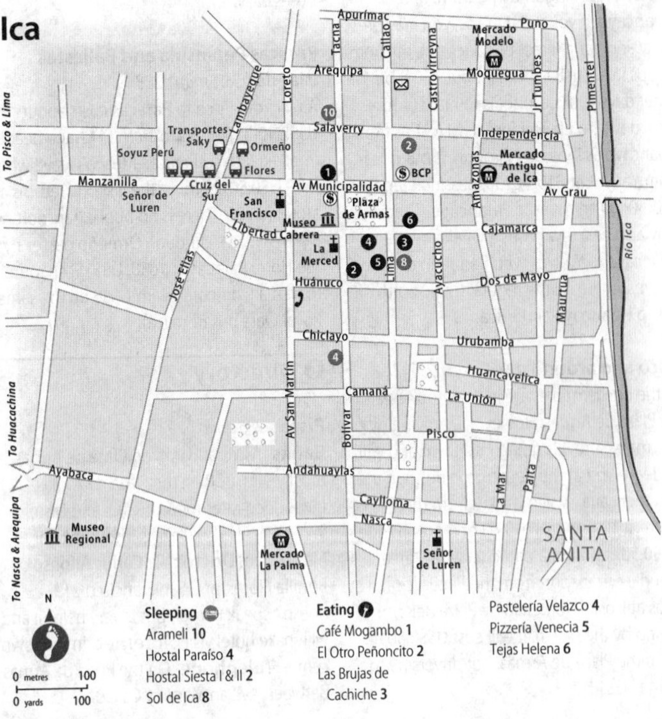

Sleeping
Arameli 10
Hostal Paraíso 4
Hostal Siesta I & II 2
Sol de Ica 8

Eating
Café Mogambo 1
El Otro Peñoncito 2
Las Brujas de Cachiche 3
Pastelería Velazco 4
Pizzería Venecia 5
Tejas Helena 6

Pisco: a history in the making

A visit to Peru would not be complete without savouring a *pisco sour*. Peruvians are mighty proud of their national tipple, which has turned out to be one of the few positive results of conquest.

Peru was the first conquered territory in Spanish America to produce wines and brandies. The cultivation of grapes began with the import of vinestalks from the Canary Islands which were planted on the outskirts of Lima. The crop later reached Cuzco and Ayacucho in the Andes but it was in Ica that the enterprise really took off, owing to the region's exceptional climate.

A hundred years after the conquest, the wine and *pisco* trade had grown considerably. Ica sent its wine to Huamanga, Cuzco, Lima and Callao. And ships left from Pisco for ports in Central America, as well as Valparaíso and Buenos Aires.

Royal bans tried to halt the expansion of Peruvian vineyards because it endangered the Spanish wine industry. In 1629, the prohibition included the transport of Peruvian wines aboard Atlantic-bound ships. But despite the restrictions, the industry continued to expand during the 17th and 18th centuries.

Though a few firms utilize modern procedures to manufacture and market larger quantities, *pisco* is still mostly made by small, independent producers using traditional techniques. The grapes are crushed by foot and the fermented grape juice is emptied into traditional Peruvian stills, called *falcas*, which are crucial to the process of true *pisco* production. More conventional wineries still rely on wood from the carob tree, a slow-burning fuel whose constant source of heat makes for a finer flavour, rather like food cooked over a charcoal fire.

Another important factor in *pisco* production is the type of grape. The unscented Quebranta, brought to the Americas by the Spaniards, lends its unique characteristics to the making of renowned 'pure' *pisco*. There are also fragrant *piscos* from Moscatel and Albilla varieties, 'creole' *piscos* made with prime fragrant grapes and 'green' *piscos* made with partially fermented grape juice.

The Ica valley is still Peru's foremost producer of *pisco*, followed by the valleys of Pisco, Chincha, Lunahuaná and Moquegua. Other centres include Vitor in Arequipa, Locumba in Tacna and Surco in Lima.

Sights

San Jerónimo church, at Cajamarca 262, has a fine mural behind the altar. Southwest of the centre is the **Museo Regional** ⓘ *Mon-Sat 0800-1900, Sat, Sun and hols 0900-1800, US$3.35, US$1.20 for photos, bus 17 from the Plaza de Armas (US$0.50)*. It houses mummies, ceramics, textiles and trepanned skulls from the Paracas, Nazca and Inca cultures. There's a well-displayed collection of Inca counting strings (*quipus*) and clothes made of feathers. It also has informative displays with maps of all sites in the department. Behind the building is a scale model of the Nazca Lines with an observation tower. The kiosk outside sells copies of motifs from ceramics and textiles.

Bodega El Carmen is on the right-hand side when arriving from Lima. This *pisco* distillery has an ancient grape press made from a huge tree trunk and is worth a visit.

Bodegas around Ica

Ten kilometres outside Ica, in the district of Subtanjalla, is **Bodega El Catador** ⓘ *T056-403295, daily 1000-1800, good tours in Spanish, take a combi from the second block of Moquegua, 20 mins, US$0.40, taxi, 10 mins, US$1.50*. It has a shop selling home-made wines and *pisco*, plus traditional handicrafts associated with winemaking. There is also a restaurant-bar serving lunch, with dancing and music in the evening. The best time to visit is during harvest – late February to early April – when wine and *pisco* tasting is usually possible. Try Cachina, a very young white wine 'with a strong yeasty taste', which is drunk about two weeks after the grape harvest. Nearby is **Bodega Alvarez**, whose owner, Umberto Alvarez, is very hospitable. Ask about their *pisco de mosto verde* and the rarer, more expensive, *pisco de limón*, which will set you back US$40 per bottle.

In **Ocucaje**, 30 km south of Ica, Señor Luis Chipana's *bodega* ⓘ *Mon-Fri 0900-1200, 1400-1700, Sat 0900-1200*, makes a very good, strong Moscatel, sold in unlabelled bottles. He is always short of bottles so it's best to take your own. A visit is recommended, but you'll need good Spanish. Señor Chipana lives on the main plaza beside his *bodega*; ask for him in the bar on the plaza. The town is a popular excursion from Ica for tours of the **Ocucaje winery** ⓘ *Ctra Panamericana Sur, Km 335.5, T056-837065, www.ocucaje.com*, which makes wines and *pisco*. There is a hotel at the winery (see Sleeping, page 298), which also has a collection of fossilized whale and other sea creatures' bones in the garden. The winery's restaurant has a limited menu but serves good food.

Huacachina

This attractive oasis and summer resort is 5 km from Ica, set around a palm-fringed lake and amid impressive sand dunes. Its green sulphur waters are said to possess curative properties and attract thousands of visitors. Increasingly, the resort has become a hang-out for people seeking a change from the archaeology and chill of the Andes. Plenty of cheap hostels and bars have opened, playing pop and grunge as opposed to pan-pipe music. Paddleboats can be rented for US$3 for 30 minutes of boating around the lake. Sandboarding on the dunes has become a major pastime here, attracting fans from Europe and elsewhere. Board hire is US$1.50 per hour. Dune buggies also do white-knuckle, rollercoaster tours for US$12, or you can hire a buggy and scare yourself for US$6 per person for three to four hours. In the town is the **Biblioteca de Abraham Valdelomar** ⓘ *Mon-Sat 0900-1300, 1500-1800, take a taxi from Ica for US$1*, which is open to the public.

Sleeping

Ica *p297, map p296*
Hotels are fully booked during the harvest festival and prices rise greatly.
A Las Dunas, Av La Angostura 400, T056-256224, www.lasdunashotel.com. (Lima office: Malecón Armendáriz 193, Miraflores, Lima, T01-241 8000.) Prices don't include service, about 20% cheaper on weekdays, meals extra. Complete resort with restaurant, swimming pool, water slide, horse riding and other activities. Also has its own airstrip for flights over the Nazca Lines, with **Aerocondor**, 50 mins (see page 309). Recommended.
C Sol de Ica, Lima 265, 1 block from Plaza de Armas, T056-236168. Clean rooms, reasonably comfortable, breakfast extra, swimming pool, tour agency.
D-E Hostal Siesta I, Independencia 160, T056-233249. With bathroom, hot water, friendly owner, but very noisy. Also Siesta II, T056-234633, which is similar.
E Princess, Urb Santa María D-103, T/F056-215421, www.geocities.com/hotel_ princess. A mototaxi ride from the main plaza, small rooms, with hot water, TV, pool, tourist information, helpful, peaceful neighbour-hood, clean, good.
E-F Arameli, Tacna 239 T056-239107. One block from the Plaza de Armas, this clean hotel has cable TV and is a nice place to stay, good value.
G Hostal Paraíso, Bolívar 418, T056-227582. Clean, quiet but thin walls, basic.

Around Ica *p297*
A Hacienda Ocucaje, Ctra Panamericana Sur Km 334, Ocucaje, T056-837049 (in Lima T01-444 4059), www.hotelocucaje.com.

A lovely ex-hacienda, with good rooms, cheaper mid-week, restaurant and bar, pool, sauna and activities, sandboarding, visits to fossils at Cerro Blanco and to *bodegas*, flights over Nazca Lines can be arranged.

Huacachina *p298*
Huacachina is less stressful than Ica.
B **Hotel Mossone**, at the eastern end of the lake, T056-213660, reserva@derrama.org.pe. An elegant hacienda-like hotel to relax at, full board available, with bath, pool (open to non-residents for US$4 including snacks, US$15 including meals), bicycles and sandboards for guests' use. End the day with a Perú libre in the majestic bar/restaurant with a fantastic view over the lake.
C **Hostería Suiza**, Malecón 264, T056-238762, hostesuiza@terra.com.pe. Nice airy house with a huge terrace overlooking the lake, lovely grounds, quiet, friendly, clean, includes breakfast, safe parking. Recommended.
F **Casita de Arena**, T056-215274, casadearena@hotmail.com. Basic rooms, **G** without bath, bar, small pool, laundry facilities, board hire, popular with backpackers, can be noisy, check your bill and change carefully, don't leave valuables unattended.
F **Hostal Rocha**, T056-222256. Rooms with bath (**G** without), hot water, family run, kitchen and laundry facilities, board hire, small pool and nice grounds, popular with backpackers, but a bit run-down.
G **Hostal del Barco**, Balneario de Huacachina 180. A very relaxed place with hammocks on the front terrace, basic rooms, bar, use of kitchen, can arrange tours.
G **Hostal Salvatierra**, T056-232352. Though not on the waterfront, this is a charming *hostal* in a grand old building. It has a great pool, relaxing courtyard, all rooms with private bathroom, rents sandboards at a good price. Good value.
G **Hostal Titanic**, T056-229003. Small rooms, pool, café, clothes washing, board hire, good value for lodging and set meals.

Eating

Ica *p297, map p296*
There's a good restaurant at the Ormeño bus terminal.
TTT **Las Dunas Resort Hotel**, La Angostura 400, T056-256224. The resort serves great buffet lunches and has a nice restaurant, pricey but worth it.
TT-T **El Otro Peñoncito**, Bolívar 255. Set lunch in a pleasant atmosphere, friendly, clean, good toilets.
TT-T **Chifa Karaoke Central**, Urb Los Viñedos de Santa María E-25, T056-221294. Excellent Chinese food.
TT-T **Las Brujas de Cachiche**, Cajamarca 118. Serves local dishes such as *chicharrones con pallares* (butter beans).
TT-T **Pizzería Venecia**, Lima 252. Best in town!

Cafés
Café Mogambo, Tacna 125. Good breakfast.
Pastelería Velazco, on Plaza de Armas. Clean, good service, great caffeinated drinks. Recommended.
Tejas Helena, Cajamarca 137. This is the place for the best *tejas*.
Tejas Ruthy, Cajamarca 122. Also sells good *tejas* and they are a bit cheaper.

Huacachina *p298*
TT-T **La Sirena**. This is the best place to eat. The big *corvina* fish steaks are excellent, also serves good sandwiches.
TT-T **Morrón**, beside the lake. Also good, but it's closed in the evening.

Festivals and events

Ica *p297, map p296*
Early Mar Festival Internacional de la Vendimia (wine harvest festival) and the Concurso Nacional de Marinera.
Early May Fiesta de la Cruz in the 1st week.
Late May Día Internacional del Pisco celebrated on 3rd Sun.
Jun Ica Week is the 3rd week.
End Sep Tourist Week.
Early Oct The image of El Señor de Luren, in a fine church in Parque Luren, draws pilgrims from all Peru, and there are all-night processions throughout the first fortnight.

Activities and tours

Ica *p297, map p296*
Lima travel agencies (see page 119) arrange 3-day, 2-night tours of 'La Ruta del Pisco' including accommodation, transport from Lima and visits to *bodegas*, from US$70-100; additional options to Nazca or Paracas.

Ica Desert Trip, icadeserttrip@yahoo.es. Robert Penny Cabrera (speaks English) offers 1-, 2- and 3-day off-road trips into the desert, focusing on archaeology, geology, etc. US$50 per person per day (max 4 people), contact by email in advance. Take toilet paper, a long shirt and trousers for day and something warm for the evenings. Recommended but "not for the faint-hearted".

Huacachina *p298*
Hostales will help their guests arrange tours. **Desert Adventures**, T01-981 69352, desertadventures@hotmail.com. Frequently recommended for sandboarding and trips into the desert, US$10 for 2-hr trip, French, English and Spanish spoken.

Transport

Ica *p297, map p296*
Most bus offices are on Lambayeque blocks 1 and 2 and Salaverry block 3. **Ormeño** is at Lambayeque 180. To **Pisco** (70 km), 45 mins, US$0.90 with **Saky** buses from opposite the Ormeño terminal, leaving every 30 mins; they go to the centre of Pisco and are careful with baggage. To **Lima** (302 km), 4 hrs, US$5-10, several daily including **Soyuz** (Av Manzanilla 130) every 8 mins, 0600-2200, and **Flores** (see page 122). To **Nazca**, 140 km, 2 hrs, minimum US$1.50; several buses and *colectivos* daily, including **Ormeño**, Flores, 4 daily, and **Cueva** (José Elias y Huánuco), hourly on the hour 0600-2200. To **Arequipa** the route goes via Nazca (see page 309), US$15-25; most reliable buses with **Ormeño, Cruz del Sur** and **Flores**.

Directory

Ica *p297, map p296*
Banks Avoid changing TCs if possible as commission is high. If you need to, though, BCP is reasonable. **Post** At Callao y Moquegua. **Telephone** At Av San Martín y Huánuco.

Nazca and around

→ *Phone code: 056. Colour map 5, B3. Population: over 50,000. Altitude: 598 m.*

Set in a green valley surrounded by mountains, Nazca would be just like any other anonymous desert oasis (the sun blazes for much of the year by day and the nights are crisp) were it not for the 'discovery' of a series of strange lines etched on the plains to the north. Tourists in their thousands now flock to the town to fly over the famous Nazca Lines, whose precise purpose still remains a mystery. Overlooking the town, 10 km southeast, is Cerro Blanco (2078 m), the highest sand dune in the world; it's popular for sandboarding and paragliding. ▸▸ *For Sleeping, Eating and other listings, see pages 305-310.*

Ins and outs

Getting there and around There is no central bus station in Nazca, but offices are at the western end of town, close to the Panamericana Sur after it has crossed the Río Tierras Blancas. Most of the hotels are on Jirón Lima and around the Plaza de Armas, within easy walking distance of the bus stations. A taxi to the airport for sightseeing flights costs US$1.35; bus, US$0.10. Do not pay attention to people selling tours or hotel rooms on the street, especially near bus stations; head straight to a hotel and find an official agency to handle your flights and tours. Taxi drivers usually act as guides, but most speak only Spanish. It is not dangerous to visit the outlying sites with a trustworthy person but do not take just any taxi on the plaza, as they are unreliable and can lead to robbery. Taxis will charge from US $4-6 per hour to wait for you at the sites and bring you back to the city. ▸▸ *For more information, see Activities and tours, page 308, and Transport, page 309.*

Sights

As most of Nazca's attractions lie on the outskirts, the town itself is quite functional. In 2006 it was in the process of being renovated and its streets paved. The large **Museo Antonini** ⓘ *Av de la Cultura 600, at the eastern end of Jr Lima, ring the bell to get in,*

T056-523444, cahuachi@terra.com.pe, daily 0900-1900, US$3, including a local guide, US$1.50 extra to use a camera, is worth a visit for a perspective on the area. A video is shown in the Conference Room. It is a 10-minute walk from the plaza, or a short taxi ride. It houses the discoveries of Professor Orefici and his team from the huge pre-Inca city at Cahuachi (see page 304), which, Orefici believes, holds the key to the Nazca Lines. Many tombs survived the *huaqueros* and there are displays of mummies, ceramics, textiles, amazing *antaras* (panpipes) and photos of the excavations and the Lines. Recommended.

The **Maria Reiche Planetarium** ⓘ *Hotel Nasca Lines, T056-522293, shows at 1900 and 2100 nightly, US$6 (half price for students)*, was opened in May 2000 in honour of Maria Reiche (see page 302). Stimulating lectures are given every night about the Nazca Lines, based on Reiche's theories, which cover archaeology and astronomy. The show lasts about 45 minutes (commentary in English), after which visitors are able to look at the moon, planets and stars through sophisticated telescopes.

Nazca Lines → *Colour map 5, B3.*

Cut into the stony desert are large numbers of lines, not only parallels and geometrical figures, but also a killer whale, a monkey, birds (one with a wing span of over 100 m), a spider and a tree. The lines, which can best be appreciated from the air, are located above the Ingenio valley on the Pampa de San José, about 22 km north of Nazca, and across the Ingenio river, on the plain around Palpa. The Pan-American Highway passes close to, even through, the Lines.

Background

The Nazca Lines were etched on the Pampa sands by the Nazca people. It's estimated that they were begun around 400 BC and continued to be made for perhaps another thousand years. Since they were first spotted from the air 70 years ago, their meaning, function and origin have tormented scientists around the world. Dr Paul Kosok, a North American scientist, gave the first explanation in 1941, when he observed a line pointing towards the place where the sun would have risen on the midwinter solstice in ancient Nazca times. So impressed was he, that he described the Nazca pampa as "the biggest astronomy book in the world".

By the 1950s Maria Reiche (see page 302), inspired by Kosok, was mapping the area and discovered giant animals too vast to be appreciated from the ground. Her many years of research led her to the conclusion that the Lines were a huge astronomical calendar. (Reiche's book, *Mystery on the Desert*, is on sale for US$10 (proceeds to conservation work) in Nazca.)

There are those who disagree with the German mathematician's hypothesis. The International Explorers Society, for example, was convinced that the desert artists would not have drawn something they themselves could not see. They set out to prove that the ancient Peruvians could fly, based on the fact that the lines are best seen from the air, and that there are pieces of ancient local pottery and tapestry showing balloonists as well as local legends of flying men. In 1975, they made a hot-air balloon of cloth and reed, called it *Condor I* and attempted to fly it for 15 minutes over the pampa. Unfortunately for them, the flight lasted only 60 seconds, thereby leaving the issue unresolved.

Some of the competing theories as to the function of the Nazca lines are rather far-fetched. Erich Von Daniken, in his book *Chariots of the Gods*, posited that the pampa was an extraterrestrial landing strip. This idea, however, only succeeded in drawing to the site thousands of visitors who tore across the lines on motorbikes, four-wheel drives, horses and whatever else they could get their hands on, leaving an indelible mark. It is now an offence to walk or drive on the pampa, punishable by heavy

Guardian of the lines

The greatest contribution to our awareness of the lines is that of Maria Reiche, who lived and worked on the Pampa for over 50 years. The young German mathematician arrived in Peru in the early 1930s and would dedicate the rest of her life to removing centuries of windswept debris and painstaking survey work. She even used to sleep on the Pampa.

Maria Reiche's years of meticulous measurement and study of the lines led her to the conclusion that they represented a huge astronomical calendar. She also used her mathematical knowledge to determine how the many drawings and symbols could have been created with such precise symmetry. She suggested that those responsible for the lines used long cords attached to stakes in the ground. The figures were drawn by means of a series of circular arcs of different radius. Reiche also contended that they used a standard unit of measurement of 1.30 m, or the distance between the fingertips of a person's extended arms.

As well as the anthropomorphic and zoomorphic drawings, there are a great many geometric figures. Reiche believed these to be a symbolic form of writing associated with the movements of the stars. In this way, the lines could have been used as a kind of calendar that not only recorded celestial events but also had a practical day-to-day function such as indicating the times for harvest, fishing and festivals.

Whatever the real purpose of the Nazca lines, one fact remains indisputable: that their status as one of the country's major tourist attractions is largely due to the selfless work of Maria Reiche, the unofficial guardian of the lines. Maria Reiche died in June 1998.

fine or imprisonment (undeterred, trucks avoiding a toll post near the lines have driven over the site; just one of many threats to this remarkable plain).

Other theories are that the Nazca designs were part of a giant running track (George A Von Breunig – 1980; also proposed by the English astronomer Alan Sawyer). Another suggestion is that they represent weaving patterns and yarns (Henri Stirlin), or that the plain is a map demonstrating the Tiahuanaco Empire (Zsoltan Zelko). Dr Johan Reinhard brings together ethnographic, historical and archaeological data, including the current use of straight lines in Chile and Bolivia, to suggest that the Lines conform to fertility practices throughout the Andes.

Recent research The BBC series *Ancient Voices* pointed to yet another theory. The clues to the function of the lines are found in the highly advanced pottery and textiles of the ancient Nazcans. Some pots and tapestries show a flying being emitting discharge from its nose and mouth. This is believed to portray the flight of the shaman. The shaman consumes certain psycho-active drugs that convince him he can fly and so enter the real world of spirits in order to rid sick people of evil spirits. In this way, the lines were not designed to be seen physically from above, but from the mind's eye of the flying shaman. This also explains the presence of incongruous creatures such as a monkey or killer whale. They were chosen because they possess the qualities admired and needed by the shaman in his spirit journeys.

But this does not explain the spectacular geometric figures. These straight lines are a feature of ancient Peruvian ritual behaviour, much like ley lines in Europe. They represent invisible paths of perceived energy. The Pampa's most remarkable features are the trapezoids, which are thought to have been ritual spaces where offerings were made to the gods, in the hope of favours in return.

Scientists have discovered evidence of a terrible 40-year drought around AD 550 or 600. This coincides not only with the abandonment of the nearby Cahuachi temples (see page 304) but also with a period of increased bloody warfare and increased line-making in the desert sands. This would seem to indicate that the Nazcans grew increasingly desperate in the face of continued drought, abandoned traditional religious practices and, instead, made more and more sacrificial offerings to the gods.

The results of eight years' work by Peruvian archaeologist Johny Isla and Markus Reindel of the Swiss-Liechtenstein Foundation threw new light on the Lines in 2002. Their findings tie together some of the earlier ideas and discredit both the astronomical calendar and extraterrestrial theories. Working at La Muña and Los Molinos, near Palpa (see page 304) with photogrammetry (mapping using aerial photographs), they have deduced that the lines on both the Palpa and Nazca plains are offerings dedicated to the worship of water and fertility. These two elements were of paramount importance to the coastal people in this arid environment; they expressed their adoration not only in the desert, but also on their ceramics and on the engraved stones of the Paracas culture (see page 290). Isla and Reindel believe that the Palpa lines predate those at Nazca and that the lines and drawings themselves are scaled-up versions of the Paracas drawings, made at a time when the Nazca people were becoming independent of Paracas. In addition, objects in the shape of drops of water, whales and chillies, found in grave sites, are repeated in the desert. In 2005, drawings similar to those at Palpa were uncovered by the Paracas winds near the Río Ingenio in Nazca. This new research proposes the theory that the Nazca culture succumbed not to drought, but to heavy rainfall, probably during an El Niño event.

Viewing and understanding the Nazca Lines

In 1976 Maria Reiche had a 12-m **Mirador** put up at her own expense, 17 km north of Nazca. From here three of the huge designs can be seen – the Hands, the Lizard and the Tree, although some travellers suggest the view from the hill 500 m back to Nazca is better. The Mirador is included on some arranged tours but enquire with your agency to be sure. If you're travelling independently, go early as the site gets very hot; better still, take a taxi (US$4-6 per hour) and arrive at 0745 before the tour buses; make sure it will wait for you and take you back.

In January 1994 Maria Reiche also opened a small **museum** ⓘ *5 km from Nazca, Km 416, US$1; take micro from in front of Ormeño terminal, US$0.70*. Viktoria Nikitzhi, a colleague of Maria Reiche, gives one-hour lectures about the Nazca Lines at **Dr Maria Reiche Center** ⓘ *Av de los Espinales 300, 1 block from Ormeño bus stop, T056-969 9419, viktorianikitzki@hotmail.com*. She also organizes tours in June and December to see the sun at the solstice striking the Lines (phone in advance to confirm times) and has many original documents and objects; see also the Planetarium, page 301. » *For details of aerial tours over the Lines, see Activities and tours, page 308.*

Around Nazca » *pp305-310.*

Palpa → *Population: 15,000.*

Known as the 'Capital de la Naranja' (the Capital of Oranges), Palpa is a hospitable town 43 km northwest of Nazca, 97 km south of Ica. The climate is hot and dry (average annual temperature 21.4°C) and the main crops, besides oranges, are other fruits (eg plums, bananas) and cotton. There is also fishing for shrimp in the river.

The Plaza de Armas, on which the Municipalidad and church stand, is bordered by arches. Also on the plaza is the **Municipal Museum** ⓘ *daily 0900-1700, free*, which contains aerial photos of the area, models and ceramics. Information is displayed in English and Spanish. Some colonial-style buildings survive. There are no travel agencies in town.

Around Palpa

There are several archaeological sites, of different periods, not far from Palpa. The **Ciudad Perdida de Hualluri**, on the west side of the Panamericana Sur, 16 km from Palpa, 5 km from the Highway (Distrito Santa Cruz), is a ruined pre-Inca city. At the entrance to the site is a *huarango* tree which is over 1000 years old. In Sector Sacramento, 2 km from the Highway, is the **Puente Colgante del Inca**, built during the reign of Pachacútec. At **Chichictara** is a vast area of petroglyphs thought to date from the Formative Period, 3000 to 500 BC (Chavín and Paracas cultures).

On the desert near Palpa there are drawings similar to those found at Nazca: a sun dial, the Reloj Solar, measuring 150 m across, a whale (35 m), a pelican (45 m), the so-called Familia Real, a man, woman and child (30 m tall) and another 1000 or so lines and figures. Two Nazca culture centres have been excavated at **La Muña**, which has the largest Nazca tombs, and **Los Molinos**. Ceramics, necklaces, spondylus sea shells and gold objects have been found, despite earlier sacking by grave robbers. Los Molinos is a monumental complex where more burials have been uncovered. See page 303 for the relationship of these markings on the desert with those at Nazca. For further information, visit the Consejo Municipal in Palpa or ask tour operators in Nazca, see page 309.

West of Nazca

The Nazca area is dotted with over 100 cemeteries and the dry, humidity-free climate has preserved perfectly invaluable tapestries, cloth and mummies. A good cemetery, with mummies still to be seen, is in the valley of **Jumana**, one hour west of Nazca in the river bed. Gold mining is one of the main local industries and a cemetery tour usually includes a visit to a small family processing shop where old-fashioned techniques are still used. Some tours also include a visit to the studio of local potter, Señor Andrés Calle Benavides, who makes Nazca reproductions. He is very friendly and takes time to explain the techniques he uses, although his small gallery is a bit on the expensive side. Anyone interested in pre-Columbian ceramics is welcome to make an appointment to visit him independently. He is very knowledgeable on the coastal desert cultures.

West of the Nazca Lines, **Cahuachi** comprises some 30 pyramids and is believed to have been a sacred centre for the exclusive use of artists and priests whose symbols were given expression in the lines on the desert. A site called 'El Estaquería', with a series of wooden pillars, is thought to have been a place of mummification, where dead bodies were dried. Tours of the ruins of Cahuachi cost US$10 per person, minimum two people; some include a visit to the **Museo Antonini** (see page 300).

East of Nazca

The ruins of **Paredones** ⓘ *just east of Nazca on the Puquio road, US$3, ticket also includes Acueducto Ocongalla, Cantalloc, El Telar and Las Agujas, taxi US$10 round-trip or tour US$10 per person*, also called Cacsamarca, are Inca on a pre-Inca base. They are not well-preserved but the cool, underground aqueducts, or *puquios*, built 300 BC to AD 700, still provide water for the local people: 33 aqueducts irrigate 20 ha each and, to this day, local farmers have the job of cleaning the section for which their group has been responsible for as long as they can remember. The aqueducts are beautifully built and even have S-bends to slow down the flow of water.

Up to one hour on foot from Paredones, through Buena Fe, are markings on the valley floor at **Cantalloc**. These consist of a triangle pointing to a hill and a *tela* (cloth) with a spiral depicting the threads; climb the mountain to see better examples. There are also aqueducts here. Visits to Catalloc are best done with a guide, or by car. A round-trip by taxi (with a wait at the site) will cost US$7; arranged tours cost US$10 per person, minimum two people.

South of Nazca

Some 30 km south of Nazca on the Panamericana Sur, then a further 12 km left off the highway (unsigned) is the cemetery site of **Chauchilla**. Grave-robbing *huaqueros* have ransacked the tombs and left remains all over the place: bones, skulls, mummies and pottery shards litter the desert. A tour is worthwhile and takes about two hours. It should cost about US$10 per person, plus the cost of entrance to the cemetery, with a minimum of two people. The area has been cordoned off and has clean bathrooms. There are other cemeteries in the vicinity. Some, like **Poroma**, have been so desecrated that there is nothing left to see.

Ninety kilometres south of Nazca is **Sacaco**, which has a museum built over the fossilized remains of a whale excavated in the desert. The keeper lives in a house nearby and is helpful. To get there, take a morning bus from Calle Bolognesi in Nazca (check times in advance) towards Chala (see page 309); ask the driver where to get off and be ready for a 2-km walk in the sun. Return to the Pan-American Highway no later than 1800 for a bus back. Do not go two to three days after a new moon as a vicious wind blows at this time.

Nazca to Cuzco

The highway from Nazca to Cuzco is paved and safe; fuel is available in Puquio and Chalhuanca. Two hours out of Nazca (80 km) is the **Reserva Nacional Pampas Galeras** at 4100 m. The Reserve covers 12,000 ha and contains 8000 vicuñas. Shearing takes place May to October and is celebrated during a three-day annual round-up and shearing ceremony in June, known as the *chaccu*. At Km 89 is the Reserve office and a free museum containing stuffed Andean animals.

At Km 155 is **Puquio**, a small highland town at 3200 m from which the impressive Inca terraces at Andamarca and the sierra towards Cotahuasi to the south are accessible. The principal fiesta is on 7 October. There is a **Banco de la Nación** on the Plaza de Armas, open weekdays 0800-1730 and Saturday morning. Combis depart from Puquio when full for the journey to the steep terraced valley of **Andamarca** (3450 m), 3 hours, US$2. The Incas' complex underground drainage system has survived and has ensured that the Andamarca terraces have remained the most extensively and continuously used agricultural terraces anywhere in Peru since Inca times. They are at their greenest and most beautiful in May and June, covered with traditional crops such as quinua, maize, kiwicha and alfalfa. The nearby village of Sondondo was the birthplace of the great Inca chronicler Guaman Poma (see page 601).

After another 185 km **Chalhuanca** is reached. There are wonderful views on this stretch, with lots of small villages, valleys and alpacas. Across the river from Chalhuanca in the village of **Chiquinga**, where a beautiful 17th-century church with extensive frescos is being restored. A further 5 km and 200 m above the valley floor are the new thermal baths (478°C) of **Pinahuacho** ⓘ *US$0.70, taxi from Chalhuanca US$4, including a 1-hr wait.*

Sleeping

Nazca *p300, map p306*

Those arriving by bus should beware being told that the hotel of their choice is closed, or full. Go to the hotel and find out for sure.

L Cantayo, 5 km east of town, T056-522264, www.hotelcantayo.com. In a beautiful renovated hacienda with pool, spa, horse-riding, restaurant and gardens.

AL-A Maison Suisse, opposite the airport, T/F05-522434, www.aeroica.net. Nice, comfortable, safe car park, expensive restaurant, pool, suites with jacuzzi, accepts AmEx, shows video of Nazca Lines. Also has camping facilities. Ask for packages, including flights over Nazca Lines.

A Casa Andina, Jr Bolognesi 367, T056-523563, www.casa-andina.com. Part of chain of hotels, offering standardized services in distinctive style. Bright, modern decor, clean, a/c, pool, friendly staff, TV, internet, restaurant.

A Nasca Lines, Jr Bolognesi, T056-522293, reservanasca@derramajae.org.pe. Large remodelled hotel with a/c, comfortable, rooms with private patio, hot water, peaceful, price includes American breakfast, restaurant, good but expensive meals, safe car park, pool (US$4.50 for non-guests, or free if having lunch), they can arrange package tours which include 2-3 nights at the hotel plus a flight over the lines and a desert trip: enquire about the price. Recommended.

B Majoro, Panamericana Sur Km 452, T056-522490, www.hotelmajoro.com. A charming old hacienda at Majoro about 5 km from town past the airstrip, beautiful gardens, pool, restaurant, quiet and homely, attentive service, serene surroundings, good arrangements for flights and tours.

B Nido del Cóndor, opposite the airport, Panamericana Sur Km 447, T056-522424, contanas@terra.com.pe. Large rooms, hot water, good restaurant, bar, shop, videos, swimming pool, camping US$3, parking, English, Italian German spoken, free pickup from town, reservation advised.

C-D Alegría, Jr Lima 166, T056-522702, www.nazcaperu.com. Continental breakfast and tax included. Rooms with bathroom, carpet and a/c, rooms with shared bath G per person, hot water, cafeteria, pool, garden, English, Hebrew, Italian and German spoken, laundry facilities, safe luggage deposit, book exchange, email facilities for US$2 per hr, netphone also US$2, free video on the lines at 2100, very popular. Recommended. Efraín Alegría also runs a tour agency and guests are encouraged to buy tours (see page 309), flights and bus tickets arranged. Don't listen to anyone who says that Alegría is closed, or full, and no longer runs tours; if you phone or email the hotel they will pick you up at the bus station free of charge day or night (1 hr free internet use to those who email in advance).

D Paredones Inn, Jr Arica 115, T056-522181, paredoneshotel@terra.com. One block from the Plaza de Armas, nice, ample rooms with cable TV, clean bathrooms, modern, great views from rooftop terrace, laundry service, bar, suites with jacuzzi, helpful staff. Good.

E Hostal Internacional, Av Maria Reiche 112, T056-522744, hostalinternacional @hotmail.com. With bathroom, hot water, garage, café and very nice bungalows.

E Hostal Las Líneas, Jr Arica 299, T056-522488. Cheaper without bath, clean, spacious, restaurant. Recommended, but ask for a room away from the street.

Nazca

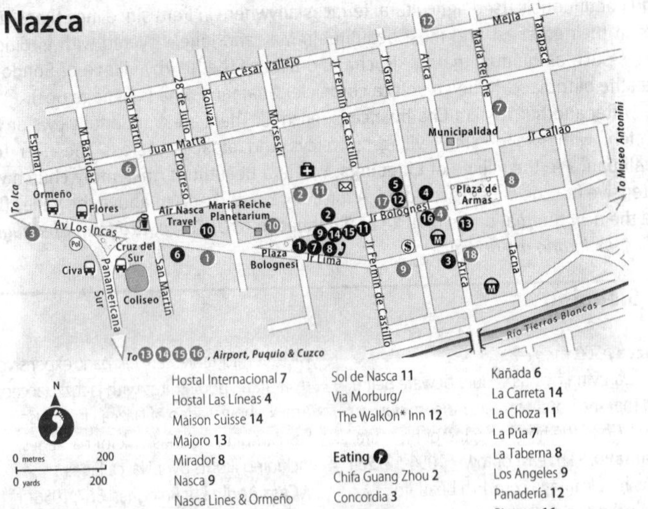

Sleeping
Alegría 1
Casa Andina 17
Estrella del Sur 2
Hostal Alegría 3
Hostal Internacional 7
Hostal Las Líneas 4
Maison Suisse 14
Majoro 13
Mirador 8
Nasca 9
Nasca Lines & Ormeño Royal Class Buses 10
Nido del Cóndor 15
Paredones Inn 18
Posada Guadalupe 6
Rancho Park 16
Sol de Nasca 11
Via Morburg/ The WalkOn* Inn 12

Eating
Chifa Guang Zhou 2
Concordia 3
El Portón 1
El Puquio 4
Fuente de Soda Jumbory 5
Grumpys 15
Kañada 6
La Carreta 14
La Choza 11
La Púa 7
La Taberna 8
Los Angeles 9
Panadería 12
Picantes 16
Plaza Mayor 13
Rico Pollo 10

E Mirador, Tacna 436, T056-523121. On main plaza, comfortable rooms with shower, cheaper with shared bath, hot water, good breakfast, TV downstairs, modern, clean. Recommended.

E Nasca, C Lima 438, T/F056-522085. **F** without bathroom, hot water, noisy, clean, nice lawn area, new annex at the back, clothes washing facilities, luggage store, safe motorcycle parking.

F Estrella del Sur, Callao 568, T056-522106. Small, rooms with shower, cable TV, price includes breakfast.

F Hostal Alegría, Av Los Incas 117, opposite Ormeño bus terminal, T056-522497. More basic than Alegría (above) with which it is unrelated, **F** without bathroom, hot water, clean, hammocks, nice gardens, camping permitted, restaurant.

F Via Morburg/The WalkOn Inn, JM Mejía 108, 3 blocks from Plaza de Armas, T/F056-522566, www.walkoninn.com. Under new management, rooms with bathroom, hot water, family feel, small swimming pool, TV room, excellent and cheap restaurant on top floor for breakfast and salads, very helpful staff, internet, luggage store, works with **Nasca Trails** for flights and tours, information given. Recommended.

F Posada Guadalupe, San Martín 225, T056-522249. Family-run, basic rooms, **G** without bath, hot water, good breakfast, relaxing (touts who try to sell tours are nothing to do with hotel).

F Rancho Park, on Panamericana 1 km from town towards the airport, T056-521153. Hotel on farmland with two swimming pools (one for children), entry to pools US$1, popular at weekends, good restaurant.

F Sol de Nasca, Callao 586, T056-522730. Rooms with and without hot showers, TV, also has a restaurant, pleasant, don't leave valuables in luggage store; tours booked here are expensive.

Palpa *p303*

G San Francisco, 2 blocks from the plaza in Palpa. Other hotels include the **Palpa**. There are also several *pensiones*, including **El Sol**, which is not recommended.

Puerto de Lomas *p310*

D Hostal Capricho de Verano, T056-210282. Beautifully situated on the cliffs, bungalows with bathroom, clean, very friendly, special rates for young travellers. Recommended.

Nazca to Cuzco *p305*

F Hostal Jousef, Ayacucho 246, Puquio, T066-407415. New, clean, hot water, private bath, TV, clothes washing possible. Recommended.

F Hostal Los Andes, 9 de Diciembre 286, Puquio, T066-452323. The best alternative, in an older house, hot water, private bath.

F Hostal Zegara, Panamericana 241, Chalhuanca, T083-832047. Quite basic, dirty, hot water, TV, reasonable restaurant.

Eating

Nazca *p300, map p306*

There are many restaurants near the Plaza de Armas and along Bolognesi as well.

ŸŸ-Ÿ Concordia, Lima 594. Good, also rents bikes at US$1 an hr.

ŸŸ-Ÿ El Portón, Moresky 120, in front of **Hotel Nasca Lines**. A popular stopover with tours, and well worth the visit. Specializes in Peruvian food, has a great indoor/outdoor setting with wood decor. Can cater to large groups with advanced notice.

ŸŸ-Ÿ El Puquio, Bolognesi 50 m from plaza. Good food, especially pastas, pleasant atmsophere, good for drinks, popular.

ŸŸ-Ÿ La Carreta, Bolognesi, next door to **Los Angeles**. New, look for *novo andino* dishes using traditional Andean ingredients, rustic, lively atmosphere, stage for live music. Good.

ŸŸ-Ÿ La Choza, Bolognesi 290. Nice atmosphere with woven chairs and thatched roof, all types of food, live music at night.

ŸŸ-Ÿ La Taberna, Jr Lima 321, T056-521411. Excellent food, live music, popular with gringos, it's worth a look just for the graffiti on the walls.

ŸŸ-Ÿ Plaza Mayor, on the Plaza. Specializes in barbecue of all types, roasted chicken, steaks, anticuchos and great salads. Large portions, nice staff. Highly recommended.

Ÿ Chifa Guang Zhou, Bolognesi 297, T056-522036. Very good Peruvian/Chinese food.

Ÿ Kañada, Lima 160, nazcanada@yahoo.com. Cheap *menú*, excellent *pisco sours*, nice wines, popular, display of local artists' work, email service, English spoken, owner Juan Carlos Fraola is very helpful.

¥ **La Púa**, Jr Lima, next to **La Taberna**. Great espresso, also serves pizzas, pastas and sandwiches, good, courtesy *pisco sour*.
¥ **Los Angeles**, Bolognesi 266. Good, cheap, try *sopa criolla*, and chocolate cake.
¥ **Rico Pollo** opposite **Hotel Alegría**. Good local restaurant with great chicken dishes, cheap.

Cafés

Fuente de Soda Jumbory, near the cinema. Good *almuerzo*.
The Grumpys, Bolognesi 282. Really friendly, salads, fish and chicken dishes, cocktails.
Panadería, Bolognesi 387.
Picante's, Av Bolognesi 464. Delicious real coffee and cakes. Owner, Percy Pizzaro, is knowledgeable about the Nazca Lines.

Palpa *p303*

¥ **Claudia**, Grau 291. Good for *camarones*.

Nazca to Cuzco *p305*

¥ **La Estancia**, Colón 109, Puquio. Serves typical local dishes such as *olluquito* and *ccapchi* (a curd and *huacatay* sauce served cold with boiled potatoes). The owner, Laura, is a good source of local information. Opens for breakfast.

Festivals and events

Nazca *p300, map p306*

29 Aug-10 Sep Festival de la Virgen de la Guadelupe.

Palpa *p303*

Mar/Apr Fiesta de la Ciruela y Vendimia (plum and wine harvest festival).
Last week of Jul The town's Tourist Week.
30 Jul-17 Aug Fiesta de la Naranja is part of the main fiesta; 15 Aug is the main day.

Shopping

Nazca *p300, map p306*

There is a market at Lima y Grau; the **Mercado Central** is between Arica and Tacna.

Activities and tours

Nazca *p301, map p306*

All guides must be approved by the Ministry of Tourism and should have an official identity card. More and more touts (*jaladores*) operate at popular hotels and the bus terminals using false ID cards and fake hotel and tour brochures. They are all rip-off merchants who overcharge and mislead those who arrive by bus. Only conduct business with agencies at their office, or phone or email the company you want to deal with in advance. Some hotels are not above pressurizing guests to buy tours at inflated prices.

Aerial tours

Flights over the Nazca Lines last 30-40 mins and are controlled by air traffic personnel at the airport, just south of town. Small planes take 3-5 passengers. The price for a flight is US$50 per person (special deals are sometimes available; touts charge more; shorter flights on sale for US$25). You also have to pay US$3 airport tax. It is best to organize and reserve a flight direct with the airlines at the airport rather then through an agency or tout. The companies listed below are well-established and recommended; there are others.

Flights are bumpy and many people are airsick, so it may be best avoid food and drink. Best times to fly are 0800-1000 and 1500-1630 when there is less turbulence and better light (assuming there is no fog, in which case chaos may ensue).

Aerocóndor, based at **Hostal Nido del Cóndor**, Panamericana Sur Km 447, T056-521168, www.aerocondor.com.pe. They offer flights over the lines in a 1-day tour from Lima with lunch in Nazca; or flights from Ica. Offices in Lima T01-614 6014, and in Ica at **Hotel Las Dunas**, Av Angostura 400, T056-256230.
Aero Ica, in Jr Lima and at the airport, T01-446 3026 (Lima), www.aeroica.net. Make sure you clarify everything before getting on the plane and ask for a receipt. Also offers full-day packages from Ica and Lima with lunch at **Maison Suisse** plus flight over the lines, but book 48 hrs in advance.
Alas Peruanas, T056-522444, www.alasperuanas.com. (experienced pilots fluent in English). Often include other features in their 35-min flight over the Lines, such as the spiral ventilation holes of the aqueducts. Also 1-hr flights over the Palpa and Llipata areas (US$75 per person,

minimum 3). They can organize flights from Pisco (US$140), Ica (US$130) and Lima (US$326). All flights include the BBC film. Can be booked at **Hotel Alegría** (see page 306).

Helinka, Av Libertadores 799, San Isidro, Lima 27, T01-222 7575, www.helinka.net. View the Lines by helicopter, expensive.

Tour operators

Air Nasca Travel, Jr Lima 185, T056-521027, guide Susi recommended. Very helpful and friendly staff, very competitive prices. Can do all types of tours around Nazca, Ica, Paracas and Pisco. Recommended.

Alegría Tours, Lima 168, T056-522444 (24 hrs), www.nazcaperu.com. Run by Efraín Alegría (see Sleeping, page 306). Inclusive tours to Palpa, Puerto Inca, Sacaco and the San Fernando Reserve, also to Chauchilla, Cantalloc, Ica, Paracas and the Ballestas Islands. Often recommended. Guides with radio contact and maps can be provided for hikes to nearby sites. They have guides who speak English, German, French and Italian. Birdwatching in the high Andes, visits to Pampas Galeras vicuña reserve, the village of Andamarca and downhill mountain biking trips. Also sandboarding on Cerro Blanco. Alegría runs a bus from Nazca to Pisco daily 1000 (from Pisco's, Plaza de Armas), via Ica, Huacachina and *bodegas*. Bus and flight tickets can be arranged, as well as packages to other parts of Peru. Ask Efraín Alegría to arrange a taxi for you to one of the sites outside Nazca (eg US$50 to Sacaco, 30 mins at site).

Jesús Erazo Buitrón, Juan Matta 1110, T056-523005. Very knowledgeable. He speaks a little English and his Spanish is easy to follow. Recommended.

Fernández family, who run the **Hotel Nasca**, also run local tours. Ask for the hotel owners and speak to them direct. They will arrange taxis to outlying sites.

Nanasca Tours, Jr Lima 160, T/F056-522917, 962 2054 (mob), nanascatours@yahoo.com. Very helpful.

Nasca Trails, Bolognesi 550, T056-522858, nascatrails@terra.com.pe. Juan Tohalino Vera speaks English, French, German and Italian.

Félix Quispe Sarmiento, El Nativo de Nazca, Fedeyogin5@hotmail.com. He has his own museum, **Hantun Nazca**, Panamericana Sur 447 and works with the Instituto Nacional de Cultura. Tours off the beaten track, can arrange flights, knowledgeable, ask for him at **Kañada** restaurant. Recommended.

Transport

Nazca *p300, map p306*

Bus

Local To **Palpa**, *colectivos* leave when full, 20 mins, US$0.75. *Colectivos* to **Chala**, 2 hrs, daily in the morning, US$3.50 per person.

Long distance To **Ica**, 2 hrs, US$1.50, 4 daily, with both **Ormeño** and **Flores**. To **Pisco**, 210 km, with **Ormeño**, 3 daily, 3 hrs, US$5, also Royal Class via **Paracas**, 2¾ hrs, 1330, US$12. Note that buses to Pisco don't go into the centre, but stop 5 km outside town; change to a *colectivo*.

To **Lima** (446 km), 6 hrs, several buses and *colectivos* daily. Recommended companies include: **Ormeño**,T056-522058, Royal Class from Hotel Nasca Lines, Jr Bolognesi, at 0530 and 1330, US$21.50, normal service from Av Los Incas, 6 a day, US$12.50; **Civa**, Av Guardia Civil, T056-523019, normal service at 2300, US$6; **Cruz del Sur**, Av Guardia Civil 290, T056-523713, 4 daily, US$6 (Cruzero US$20). Note that **Ormeño's** Royal Class arrives in Santa Catalina, a much safer area of Lima.

To **Arequipa**, 565 km, 9 hrs, with **Ormeño**, 1530, 2000, 2400, from Av Los Incas, US$10, or with Royal Class at 2100, US$20, 8 hrs; **Cruz del Sur** has 4 buses daily 1900-2400, US$10-US$27; **Civa**, at 1100, US$20, 8 hrs. Delays are possible out of Nazca because of drifting sand across the road or mudslides in the rainy season. Travel in daylight.

To **Puerto de Lomas**, 1½ hrs, US$1.75.

To **Cuzco**, 659 km, 14 hrs, via **Chalhuanca** and **Abancay**, with **Expreso Wari**, 6 daily on the Lima–Nazca–Abancay–Cuzco route, normal US$17, or Imperial US$20 (bus may run if not enough passengers). Their offices are at the exit from Nazca on the road to Puquio. Nazca to **Puquio**, combis, 4 hrs, US$3, and *colectivos*, 3 hrs, US$4.50. Most depart, in both directions, in the early morning from the market. They will drop visitors off at the **Pampas Galeras** vicuña reserve en route, 2 hrs, US$1.50 by combi, or 1½ hrs, US$2.50 by *colectivo*. Also buses to Cuzco via Arequipa with **Ormeño**, US$27, and **Cruz del Sur**, 2015 Imperial and 2100 Ideal, US$27.

Directory

Nazca *p300, map p306*
Banks BCP, Lima y Grau, changes cash and Visa TCs at decent rates, also cash advance on Visa, Visa ATM. Some street changers will change TCs, but at 8% commission.
Hospital Callao entre Morsesky y Castillo. Open 24 hours. **Internet** Many places on Jr Bolognesi. Facilities at Hotel Alegría and Casa Andina. **Post** Fermín de Castillo 379, T056-522016. Also at Hotel Alegría. **Police** Av Los Incas, T056-522105, T105 for emergencies.
Telephone Telefónica for international calls with coins on Plaza Bolognesi. Also on Plaza de Armas and at Lima 359.

Nazca to Chile

From Nazca to the Chilean border the coastal desert continues, broken by the occasional irrigation scheme. In places the dunes are otherwordly. There are a few ports, old ones such as Puerto Inca, which served Imperial Cuzco, and new ones like Matarani. If you head south on the Panamericana, instead of turning off at the junction to Arequipa and the sierra, you reach the fruitful valley of Moquegua. This town has many historical associations and is the start of a great road up to Lake Titicaca. On the border with Chile is the city of Tacna, seemingly a long way from anywhere else in Peru. ▸▸ *For Sleeping, Eating and other listings, see pages 317-320.*

South of Nazca ▸▸ *pp317-320.*

Lying on the coast, 98 km from Nazca and 7 km off the Pan-American Highway, is **Puerto de Lomas**, a fishing village with safe beaches which are popular in February and March. From here, the Panamericana heads south through the **Yauca Valley**, which is almost entirely devoted to olive trees; have a few *soles* ready to buy some when the bus stops.

Chala and Puerto Inca → *Phone code: 054.*

Chala, 173 km from Nazca, is a friendly fishing village with nice beaches, although it is only safe to swim near the harbour. The town has expanded greatly in recent years on the back of gold-mining in the nearby hills. It now consists of **Chala Sur**, where the fishing pier, better hotels and restaurants are located; and **Chala Norte**, a bit seedier, where buses stop and miners congregate around video bars. Fresh fish is available in the morning and it may be possible to go out with the local fishermen. There are dozens of restaurants, most catering for passing buses. Try *chicharrones de pulpo* (octopus) and *lenguado* (fried fish). **Chala Viejo** is a separate village, 11 km inland.

Ten kilometres north of Chala are the large pre-Columbian ruins of **Puerto Inca** on the coast in a beautiful bay. On its discovery in the 1950s, the site was misunderstood and thus neglected but it is now recognized that this was the port for Cuzco. The site is in excellent condition: drying and store houses can be seen as holes in the ground (be careful where you walk); there's a cemetery on the right side of the bay and a temple of resurrection on the hill; the Inca road from the coast to Cuzco is also clearly visible. The road was 240 km long and had a staging post every 7 km; with a change of runner at every post, fish for the Inca's table and messages could be sent to Cuzco in 24 hours.

The water in the two small bays is usually calm and clear and the fishing and diving are excellent. In winter, though, coastal fog can take away much of the bay's atmosphere. There is a good two-hour walk back from Puerto Inca to Chala. Take one of the paths going up behind the ruins on the south side of the bay and swing slightly inland to cross a deep *quebrada*. The path then continues through spectacular rock formations with dramatic views of the coast towards the Panamerica.

Camaná heading inland → *Phone code 054. Population 40,000.*

South of Chala the Pan-American Highway passes **Atico**, where there is a basic *hostal*, and **Ocaña** before reaching **Camaná**, 222 km south of Chala and 5 km inland from the sea. It has a modern church and plaza, as well as a short pedestrian boulevard. There is an archaeology museum at **La Inmaculada** high school ⓘ *Av Samuel Pastor 1201, north end of town, free but contributions appreciated*. It's a small well-presented collection of ceramics and textiles, including Nazca, Tiahuanaco, Wari and Inca. There are few other attractions in the town itself but various beaches to the south are visited by *arequipeños* from January to March. Camaná has a range of hotels, restaurants and other services; bus agencies are concentrated on the 300 block of Av Lima.

The Pan-American Highway swings inland from Camaná to **El Alto** where a road branches left off the Pan-American Highway and leads to **Corire**, **Aplao** and the valley of the Río Majes (see page 277). The Panamericana, meanwhile, runs along the top of a plateau with strange ash-grey sand dunes. These are unique in appearance and formation. All are crescent shaped and of varying sizes, from 6 to 30 m across and from 2 to 5 m high, with the points of the crescent on the leeward side. The sand is slowly blown up the convex side, drifts down into the concave side, moving the dunes about 15 m a year. If plans to extend the Majes project are completed, the irrigation of a further 60,000 ha of land will destroy a large portion of these unique sand dunes.

Mollendo → *Phone code: 054. Colour map 6, C1. Population: 30,000.*

Since Matarani, 14½ km to the northwest, has replaced it as a port, Mollendo depends partly upon the summer attraction of its beaches. Hotels can be full during the high season, which starts on 6 January, the first day of summer and anniversary of the district, and lasts until March. Out of season Mollendo is pleasant and tranquil. The town has lots of character, with an abandoned castle perched high on bluffs above the sea, brightly painted old wooden houses, a wrought-iron market and many well-maintained parks. People are friendly and the authorities are trying to foster tourism. A new tourist/fishing pier was under construction in 2006.

Playa Catarindo, in a small bay 2 km north of town, is reportedly good for bathing. There are many others but mind the powerful undertow. Three sandy beaches stretch south of town, of which the small one nearest town is the safest for swimming. The swimming pool on the beach is open January to March. Out of season the beaches are littered with rubbish.

On the coast, a few kilometres southeast by road is a national reserve based around lagoons at **Mejía** ⓘ *visitors centre at entrance, T054-835001, daily 0700-1700, US$1.50; US$0.40 by colectivo from Mollendo*. Part of the Ramsar Convention on Wetlands, the reserve has 92 resident species of birds and 83 visiting species. Arrive early in the morning to see the birdlife at its best. A 7½-km trail runs parallel to the wild seashore; it can be flooded so be prepared to wade and take insect repellent, hat, sun screen, water, etc.

The road out of Mollendo goes through the fertile **Valle de Tambo**, which is full of rice paddies, sugar cane and fields of peppers and onions. Tambo is famous for its *alfajores de Tambo*, small round pastries filled with cane syrup or *manjar blanco*. The very best are made in **La Curva**, 10 km from Mollendo, eg at **Alfajorería Vildoso**, Calle Las Mercedes 121. Take any combi toward Cocachacras and ask for directions.

Moquegua and around » *pp317-320.*

→ *Phone code: 053. Colour map 6, C2. Population: 110,000. Altitude: 1412 m.*

Moquegua is a peaceful town in the narrow valley of the Moquegua River and enjoys a sub-tropical climate. Strategically placed near the intersection of the Panamericana and the paved road to Lake Titicaca and Bolivia, it offers a full range of services and is a more tranquil alternative to Tacna for breaking a journey through this area. The town was formerly known as Santa Catalina de Guadalcazar but reverted to its original name, which means 'silent place' in Quechua. This could be due to the rather taciturn nature of its inhabitants. The Inca Emperor, Mayta Capac, sent his captains to carry out a pacifying occupation of the fertile valleys around Moquegua. They founded two settlements, Moquegua and Cuchuna, which is thought to be the site of present-day Torata. Today, most of the valley below the city grows grapes and the upper part grows avocados (*paltas*), wheat, maize, potatoes, some cotton and fruits. Northeast from Moquegua is Cuajone, one of the most important copper mines in Peru.

Ins and outs

Getting there and around There is no bus station. All bus companies are on Avenida Ejército, two blocks north of the market, at Grau, except **Ormeño,** which is on Avenida La Paz casi Balta. The road into town runs along Avenida La Paz. It joins the main street (Avenida Balta) at the large roundabout. Avenida Balta runs two blocks north of the Plaza de Armas. On Saturday nights Jirón Moquegua, west from the plaza to Jirón Piura, becomes the centre of activity in this compact town. Taxi in town costs US$0.60 or US$0.85 outside the city.

Tourist information Information is available from the **municipal office** ⓘ *Ayacucho y Ancash on the plaza, Mon-Fri 0800-1600.* Pamphlets and useful information about the archeological sites are available from **Museo Contisuyo** (see page 312).

Sights

Moquegua is not a pretty sight from the Pan-American Highway, but the old centre, a few blocks above Avenida Balta, is well worth a look for its quiet, winding cobbled streets and historic buildings. The **Plaza de Armas,** with its mix of ruined and preserved churches, colonial and republican façades and fine trees, is one of the most interesting small-town plazas in the country. The fountain is said to have been designed by Eiffel, though there is some debate on the matter. **Museo Contisuyo** ⓘ *Plaza de Armas, T053-461844, http://bruceowen.com/contisuyo/MuseoE.html, Wed-Mon 0800-1300, 1430-1730, Tue 0800-1200, 1600-2000, US$0.45,* is within the ruins of the Iglesia

Moquegua

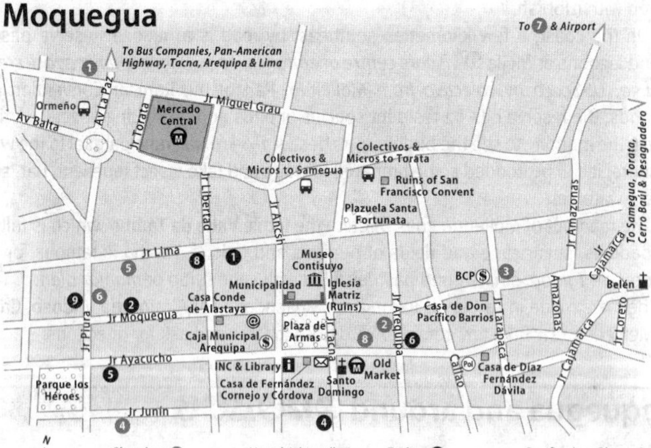

Sleeping
Alameda 4
Arequipa 2
El Mirador 7
Hospedaje Cornejo 3
Hostal Adrianella 1
Hostal Carrera 5
Hostal Piura 6
Hostal Plaza 8

Eating
Bar Bandido 2
Chifa Fong Mey 1
La Oficina 6
Moraly 8
Panificadora Obrero 9
Panificadora Victoria 4
Pizzería Casa Vieja 5

Matriz, which was rebuilt after many earthquakes over the centuries, but finally left as a ruin in 1868. It covers the cultures which thrived in the Moquegua and Ilo valleys, including the Huari, Tiahuanaco, Chiribaya and Estuquiña, who were conquered by the Incas. Artefacts from the area are well-displayed and all the exhibits are explained in Spanish and English.

The decadent statuary of the fountain in front of the **Santo Domingo** church is seen by some as a challenge to the traditional Catholic religious iconography inside, where the body of the city's saint, Fortunata, lies in a glass-sided casket. She died in the 17th century but her hair and nails are reputed to continue to grow miraculously. The old market beside Santo Domingo has a fine entrance but not much inside.

The roofs of many of the old houses in Moquegua are built with sugar-cane thatch and clay and are of an unusual design, with semi-rounded gables, a little reminiscent of 18th-century Dutch gables. This type of construction is called *mojinete* and is also found in the Valle de Tambo. The houses' sculpted door surrounds are particularly notable, as are the balconies, for example on 700 block of Moquegua.

There are several interesting colonial houses which make a good, short walking tour. Some are private, but the owners may allow entry. **Casa de Regidor Perpetuo de La Ciudad** or **Casa Conde de Alastaya**, at Jirón Moquegua 404-414, is an 18th-century house, although just the portal remains after the 2001 earthquake. **Casa de Fernández Cornejo y Córdova** (La Casa Tradicional de Moquegua) at Jirón Ayacucho 540, beside the post office on the plaza, has a fine 18th-century wooden balcony; visitors are welcome. Also on the south side of the Plaza is the office of the **INC** (corner of Ancash); a museum of regional ethnography is being established. **Casa de Díaz Fernández Dávila**, Jirón Ayacucho 828, has a collapsed interior but baroque elements can be seen in the ornate portal. Also worth seeing is **Casa de Don Pacífico Barrios** at Jirón Moquegua 820-848 and, opposite, the façade at No 831. On Jirón Lima, between Callao and Tacna, are the ruins of the convent of San Francisco. There is little to see and nothing inside except an open-air church with an awning roof.

Moquegua is famous for its *pisco*; **Biondi** is the best known brand. Outside town in the direction of the airport are some interesting *bodegas*, such as **Bodega Villegas** at the corner of Jirón Ayacucho and Puno. You can also find wine from Omate in town.

To the southeast of town is the **Chen Chen** archaeological site, a Tiahuanaco settlement with remains of houses, a cemetery and geoglyphs carved into a hillside. **Samegua**, 4½ km from Moquegua, is known as 'avocado town', with many restaurants. To get there take a micro from Avenida Balta, between Tacna and Ancash; 10 minutes.

Omate → *Population: 3000. Altitude: 2160 m.*

Omate is a small town, 146 km north of Moquegua on an unpaved road and 129 km south of Arequipa (five hours). The town is important for its famed **Semana Santa processions**. It is also known for growing grapes, *damascos* and other fruits, and for its shrimp farms. Nearby are the thermal baths at **Ulucán**.

Torata and around

Torata is 24 km northeast of Moquegua. It's a quiet, small town with a shaded plaza. Above the town, on a hill are two crosses and the Huari ruins of **Torata Alta**, a 30-minute walk away. The ruins are in a poor state but you can get an idea of the shape and size of the houses from the low surviving walls. The site enjoys good views over to **Cerro Baúl**, 2590 m, which can be combined with the ruins at Torata to make a full day's excursion. The mountain is like a *tepuy*, with sheer sides and flat top, hence its name, which means trunk. Covering the entire summit, which is 1½ km long and 200 m wide, are hundreds of modern arrangements of stones and miniature houses, which, together with looting, are destroying the original look of the place. In the seventh century AD Cerro Baúl was a Huari citadel; there are extensive Huari ruins at the end nearest the path. The mountain became famous in legend as the place of refuge for the Cochunas, who resisted the peaceful invasion of the Incas and whose children regularly made nocturnal food raids into the Inca camps below. The Cochunas were eventually starved off the mountain.

To get to Torata, take a micro or *colectivo* from Avenida Balta in Moquegua, between Jirón Arequipa y Tacna, US$1.70, 30 minutes. To reach Cerro Baúl get off at the crossroads at the top of the pass beneath the northern end of the mountain. The path leads up the gradual slope from the road. There is a steep section for the last 200 m, on which cement steps have been built. It takes an hour or so from the road to the top. The path leads to a Christian shrine (two crosses). Take water and sun protection.

Moquegua to Desaguadero

The Carretera Binacional, from Ilo on the coast to La Paz, has a breathtaking stretch from Moquegua to Desaguadero at the southeastern end of Lake Titicaca. It skirts Cerro Baúl and climbs through zones of ancient terraces at Camata to its highest point at 4755 m. At 4610 m is lonely **Restaurant Humajalso**. On the *altiplano* there are herds of llamas and alpacas, watery *bofedales*, lakes with waterfowl, strange mountain formations and snow-covered peaks. At **Mazo Cruz** there is a PNP checkpoint where all documents and bags are checked. As you approach Desaguadero, the Cordillera Real of Bolivia comes into view. The road is fully paved but should only be taken in daylight.

Ilo → *Phone code: 053. Population: 65,000.*

Located near the mouth of the Río Osmore, 90 km southwest of Moquegua (two hours by bus), Ilo is the southernmost port of Peru. It hopes to become the Pacific terminus of the **Vía bi-oceánica** connecting Peru, Bolivia, Paraguay and Brazil, once the paving of this route is complete. Ilo is a functional place with air pollution from a copper smelter. It has a *malecón* (oceanfront promenade) but few other attractions. At **Algarrobal** along the road to Moquegua is an archaeological site of the Chiribaya culture with on-site museum. A coastal road (an alternative to the Panamericana), served by buses, runs northwest to Mollendo (unpaved, 3½ hours) and southeast to Tacna (paved, 2½ hours; customs checkpoint at Vila Vila).

Tacna and around » pp317-320.

→ *Phone code: 052. Colour map 6, C2. Population: 174,366. Altitude: 550 m.*

Tacna was in Chilean hands from 1880 to 1929, when its people voted by plebiscite to return to Peru. It is an important commercial centre and has a free-trade zone. There are good schools, housing estates, a stadium to seat 10,000 people, an airport, many military posts and a hospital. Chileans cross the border for cheap medical and dental treatment, to shop and to play the slot machines. Around the city the desert is gradually being irrigated. The local economy includes olive groves, vineyards and fishing. The waters of **Laguna Aricota**, 80 km north, are now being tapped for further irrigation and hydroelectric power for industry.

Ins and outs

Getting there Tacna is 156 km south of Moquegua by the Pan-American Highway, 36 km from the Chilean frontier and 56 km from the international port of Arica, to which there is a railway. It is 1292 km from Lima by road. As this is the nearest town to Chile, transport links are good. The airport (T052-314503) is at Km 5 on the Panamericana Sur, on the way to the border. A taxi from the airport to town and the bus terminal costs US$2-3. It is also possible to take a taxi from the airport to Arica, US$30, but the cheapest way is either to take a taxi to Tacna bus station, then take a *colectivo* (see page 320), or to call the bus terminal and request a *colectivo* to pick you up on its way to the border, US$4. » *For further details, see Transport, page 319.*

Getting around Many hotels, restaurants and cafés are in the city centre, within easy walking distance. Otherwise the town is quite spread out and you will need to catch a bus or taxi to see much. City bus costs US$0.15; taxi minimum US$0.60.

Tourist information A city map and regional information is available from **Dirección Regional de Comercio Exterior y Turismo** (DIRCETUR) ⓘ *Blondell 50, p3-4, T052-422784, www.mincetur.gob.pe /regiones/tacna, Mon-Fri 0730-1515; also at the Centro Cultural Miculla, corner Blondell y Francisco Lazo, Mon-Fri 0800-1300, Spanish only.* There are also helpful, friendly information booths at the **Terminal Terrestre Nacional** ⓘ *T052-427007, daily 0600-2200*; and at the **Terminal Internacional** ⓘ *Mon-Fri 0800-1500, Sat 0800-1200*, both of which can provide a city map and a list of official taxi rates to different destinations. There's no tourist information at the airport.

Safety The city centre is generally safe and pleasant, but be careful outside banks and *cambios* and watch for pickpockets in markets. Drug smuggling is rife in this border area, so only ever transport your own possessions. If they are just passing through, visitors can leave their bags with the **Tourist Police** ⓘ *Jr Callao 103, next to the Comisaría Central, T052-414141 ext 245*; who will also escort groups on request.

Sights

The **cathedral**, designed by Eiffel, faces the **Plaza de Armas**, which contains huge bronze statues of Admiral Grau and Colonel Bolognesi. They stand at either end of the **Arca de los Héroes**, the triumphal arch which is the symbol of the city. The bronze fountain in the plaza is said to be a duplicate of the one in the Place de la Concorde (Paris) and was also designed by Eiffel.

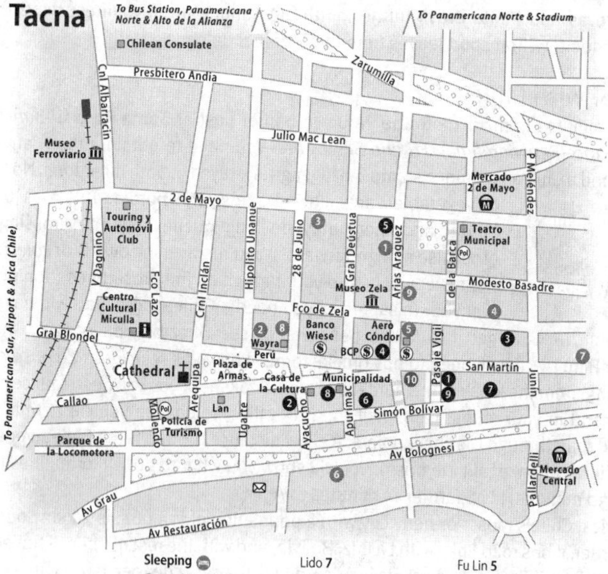

Sleeping
Copacabana **1**
Dorado **5**
El Mesón **2**
Gran Hotel Tacna **6**
Hostal Anturio **8**
Hostal Bon Ami **3**
Hostal HC **4**
Lido **7**
Maximo's **9**

Eating
Club La Unión **1**
Cusqueñita **3**
Da Vinci **4**
El Sabor Criollo **2**
Fu Lin **5**
Il Pomodoro **6**
Koyuki **7**
La Espiga **8**
Verdi **9**

Bars & clubs
Genova **10**

N

0 metres 400
0 yards 400

Parque de la Locomotora, on Avenida Grau near the city centre, has a British-built locomotive, which was used in the War of the Pacific. There is also a very good railway museum further north at the station: **Museo Ferroviario** ⓘ *Coronel Albarracín, daily 0700-1700, US$0.30; ring the bell by the gate on Jr 2 de Mayo for entry*. The **Teatro Municipal** ⓘ *Pasaje Calderón de la Barca y 2 de Mayo, knock on second door on 2 de Mayo, free*, built in the 1870s, is well preserved and worth a visit. There are occasional performances, enquire in advance. The house of Francisco Zela, who gave the 'Cry of Independence' on 20 July 1811 now houses the **Museo de Zela** ⓘ *Zela 542, Mon-Sat 0830-1230, 1530-1900, free*. At Bolognesi 721 is **Feria Caplina**, a shopping mall-cum-market selling jewellery, musical instruments but mostly clothes. **Mercado Central** is at Bolognesi y Pallardelli.

Some 8 km above the city, just off the Panamericana Norte, is the Campo de la Alianza, scene of a battle between Peru and Chile in 1880.

Around Tacna

To the northeast is the fruit growing valley of the **Río Caplina**, known as Valle Viejo, where *tacneños* go for *comida típica* at weekends. It is 23 km to the thermal baths at **Calientes** ⓘ *open 24 hrs, US$1 for pool, US$2.50 per person for tubs*, which has clean individual hot tubs and a tepid outdoor pool, popular with locals and crowded at weekends. There's a restaurant and simple accommodation (D) on site. One hour's walk through the desert from Calientes is the archeological site of **Miculla** ⓘ *daily 24 hrs, entry US$0.30*, set in the rocky valley of the Río Palca. Many excellent petroglyphs from various periods may be seen as well as two rope suspension bridges over the river (rebuilt with a steel cable core) and a fragment of ancient road. It's a good spot for stargazing at night from June to September. There is a caretaker at the entrance but the site itself is vast and desolate; do not take valuables nor go alone.

Along the Tacna seashore are several fishing villages and beaches, popular with locals from January to March. **Playa Los Palos** to the south, as well as **Pozo Redondo**, **Tres Cuevas** and **Punta Brava** further north, are among the favourites; beware of strong undertow. Transport leaves from the Terminal Bolognesi.

Border with Chile

It is 30 minutes from Tacna to the Peruvian border post at **Santa Rosa** ⓘ *Sun-Thu 0800-2300 (Peruvian time), Fri and Sat 24 hrs*. You need to obtain a Peruvian exit stamp and a Chilean entrance stamp. All luggage is x-rayed in both directions. No fruit or vegetables are allowed across the border. This is a busy border and there may be long queues but the crossing is otherwise straightforward. If you're travelling by bus or *colectivo*, the driver will hustle you through all the procedures (don't give him your passport). If you need a Chilean visa, you will have to get it in Tacna beforehand (see Directory, page 320). Those leaving Peru by car will need to buy official forms, known as *relaciones de pasajeros* (US$0.45) from the kiosk at the border or from a bookshop; you will need four copies. Next, hand in your tourist card, visit the PNP office, return the vehicle permit and finally depart through the checkpoints. A short distance beyond is the Chilean post at **Chacalluta**, where again the bus driver will show you what to do. All formalities take about 30 minutes. It's a further 15 minutes to Arica.

Peruvian time is 1 hr behind Chilean time Mar-Oct; 2 hrs behind Sep/Oct-Feb/Mar (varies annually).

Arica, Chile's most northerly city with a population of 174,064, is 20 km south of the border. It has road links with La Paz, Bolivia, and with the rest of Chile. If travelling onwards into Chile, buy bus tickets in Arica, where they are cheaper than in Tacna. It is a good starting place for visits to Andean national parks, such as Lauca and has a wide selection of hotels and restaurants. Tourist information is available from **Sernatur** ⓘ *San Marcos 101, T058-252054*, in a kiosk next to the Casa de la Cultura.

Sleeping

Chala *p310*

All the better hotels are in Chala Sur.

D Turistas, Chala Sur, T054-551111. With breakfast and bath (**E** without), large rooms, good beds, friendly, hot water, restaurant, sea view, showing its age but best in town.

F Hostal Evertyth, Chala Sur, T054-551095. Clean, with bath, cold water, simple, friendly, rooms facing the ocean, secure parking.

F Hostal Camino Real, Chala Norte near bus agencies. Cold water, private bath, **G** with shared bath, new in 2005, decent, good value.

G Hostal 2 de Enero, 2 de Enero, 2 blocks from the Panamericana. Shared bath, cold water, small rooms, basic, clean and friendly.

Puerto Inca *p310*

B Puerto Inka, signposted 2 km along a side road from Km 610 on the Panamericana, T054-551055, www.puertoinka.com.pe. A great place to relax, with bungalows on a superb beach, boats and diving equipment for hire, disco, hammocks, recommended but used by tour groups and busy in summer, low season discounts. Price reflects the location. Camping US$3 per person.

Mollendo *p311*

Low season prices are given below, they increase by 50% or more Jan-Mar.

D La Villa, Av Mcal Castilla 366, away from centre, T/F054-525700. Grand old wooden house in front with modern comfortable rooms at back. Restaurant and bar, nice terrace and small pool, parking.

E Hostal Cabaña, Comercio 240, T054-534571. A wooden building with huge balconies, rooms with bath, hot water, faded glory but still OK.

E Hostal California, Blondel 541, T054-533675. With private electric shower, **F** with shared bath, breakfast available, family run, friendly, best rooms at top.

E Hostal D'Manuel, Deán Valdivia 416, T054-535511. With bath, solar hot water best during daytime, modern, good value.

Moquegua *p311, map p312*

B-C El Mirador, Alto de la Villa, 10 mins by taxi from centre, T053-461765, www.derrama.org.pe. Rooms and bungalows, includes breakfast, restaurant, pool (US$1.50 for non-guests), great views, starting to show its age but still best in town.

D Alameda, Junín 322, T053-463971. Includes breakfast, large comfortable rooms, friendly service.

E Arequipa, Jr Arequipa 360, T053-461338, javierhotelarequipa@hotmail.com. Clean, hot water sometimes, pleasant.

E Hostal Adrianella, Miguel Grau 239, T/F053-463469. Hot water, TV, safe, helpful, close to market and buses, adequate.

E Hostal Piura, Piura 225, T053-463974. With bath, hot water, small comfortable rooms, TV, friendly.

E Hostal Plaza, Ayacucho 675, T053-461612. Modern and comfortable, realtively new, good value.

F Hostal Carrera, Jr Lima 320, T053-462113. With bath (**G** shared bath), solar hot water in shared showers only – best in afternoon, small patio, clean, friendly, good value, laundry facilities on roof.

G Hospedaje Cornejo, Tarapacá 281-A, T053-507681. With bath, electric shower, basic but clean.

Tacna *p314, map p315*

There are a great many hotels and rooms are usually easy to find, except perhaps before Christmas. There are several simple places by the bus terminals, but it makes more sense to stay in the centre.

B Gran Hotel Tacna, Av Bolognesi 300, T052-424193, www.derrama.org.pe. Includes breakfast, internet in rooms US$1/hr, pool gardens, 2 pools (open to non-guests who spend min US$8 in restaurant or bar), safe car park, English spoken.

C Dorado, Arias Araguez 145, T052-415741, www.doradohotel.com. Includes breakfast, restaurant, modern and comfortable.

D Maximo's, Arias Araguez 281, T052-242604, www.maximoshotel.com. With breakfast, modern rooms with frigo-bar, wireless internet, sauna.

E Copacabana, Arias Araguez 281 y 2 de Mayo, T052-421721, www.copahotel.com. Includes breakfast, good rooms.

E El Mesón, Unánue 175, T052-425841, www.mesonhotel.com. With breakfast, TV, central, modern, comfortable, safe, wireless internet in rooms. Recommended.

E **Hostal Anturio**, 28 de Julio 194 y Zela, T052-244258, www.anturiohostaltacna.com. Cafeteria downstairs, breakfast extra, clean, modern and good value.

F **Hostal Bon Ami**, 2 de Mayo 445, T052-244847. Private bath, cheaper with shared bath, solar hot water best in afternoon, simple but clean and adequate, secure.

E **Hostal HC**, Zela 734, T052-242042. Hot water, TV, discounts available, laundry service, nice and clean, friendly, family run, good value. Recommended.

E **Lido**, San Martín 876-A, near Plaza de Armas, T052-577001. With hot showers, no breakfast, simple but OK.

Eating

Mollendo *p311*

Several restaurants including **Cevichería Teo**, Comercio 208, excellent, cheap set meals. Others can be found on Comercio (eg **Marco Antonio**, plus several *chifas* and *pollerías*).

Heladería Venezia, Comercio 118. Ice cream made on the premises.

Moquegua *p311, map p312*

The best-known local dish is *cuy chactado*, pan-fried guinea pig. Two famous places to try it are **Samagua** and **Los Angeles**, both a few kilometres out of town (taxi US$0.50, or combi, 10 mins), with several restaurants in each town. *Damascos*, a type of small, yellow plum, can be found both stewed and *remojado*, steeped in *pisco* (delicious). *Chicha de jora* and *chicha de maíz morado* (from malted purple maize) can be found in the market; the latter is served with most *menús* at lunchtime. Local spirits and other liqueurs can be bought at **La Tranquita**, Piura 148 (no sign). All foodstuffs can be bought at the market (bounded by Grau, Torata, Av Balta and Libertad) and the streets around.

ΨΨ **El Bosque**, Av 25 de Noviembre s/n, beyond La Villa bridge., T053-462245. Typical dishes including *cuy*, *lomito saltado*, fish, meat dishes and *chifa*. Recommended.

ΨΨ-Ψ **Bar Bandido**, Jr Moquegua 333. European-style bar serving spirits, pizzas, wood oven, opens 1930, rock music, videos.

ΨΨ-Ψ **Pizzería Casa Vieja**, Moquegua 326. Mon-Sat 1830-2300, pizza and Italian dishes.

Ψ **Chifa Fong Mey**, Jr Lima 434. closed Tue midday, set lunch and Chinese à la carte.

Ψ **La Oficina**, Ayacucho 707. Lunches, juices, snacks, breakfast. Recommended.

Ψ **Moraly**, Lima 398 y Libertad. Good-sized portions, moderate prices, best in town, *menú del día* US$1.75, good lunches, Mon-Sat 1000-2200, Sun 1000-1600.

Ψ **Panificadora Victoria**, Tacna 525 y Junín. Good bread and sweets.

Tacna *p314, map p315*

ΨΨ **DaVinci**, San Martín 596 y Arias Araguez. Mon-Sat 1100-2300, pizza and other dishes, nice atmosphere, **Leonardo** bar upstairs Tue-Sat 2000-0200.

ΨΨ **Il Pomodoro**, Bolívar 524 y Apurimac. Closed Sun evening and Mon midday, upscale Italian, set lunch Tue-Fri, pricey à la carte in the evening, attentive service.

ΨΨ **Salón Chino**, Bolívar 659 y Pasaje Vigil. 1200-0100, extensive Chinese menu, popular with locals.

Ψ **Club La Unión**, San Martín 705 y Pasaje Vigil. Set lunch featuring mostly international dishes, chifa at night.

Ψ **Cusqueñita**, Zela 747. 1100-1600, excellent 4-course lunch, large portions, good value, variety of choices. Recommended.

Ψ **El Sabor Criollo**, Ayacucho No 86-C. One of three popular lunchtime eateries, all in a row.

Ψ **Epicentro**, Pasaje Vigil y San Martín. Inexpensive set lunch and à la carte, popular.

Ψ **Fu-Lin**, Arias Araguez 396 y 2 de Mayo. Mon-Sat 0930-1600, vegetarian Chinese.

Ψ **Koyuki**, Bolívar 718. Generous set lunch daily, seafood and other à la carte in the evening, closed Sun evening. Several other popular lunch places on the same block.

Ψ **La Espiga**, San Martín 431. Good bakery.

Ψ **Verdi**, Pasaje Vigil 57. Simple place for set lunch, excellent *empanadas* and sweets.

Bars and clubs

Mollendo *p311*

El Observatorio, Comercio y Deán Valdivia. A massive semi-open-air disco, "has to be seen to be believed", no cover charge.

Tacna *p314, map p315*

Genova, Av San Martín 649 y Pasaje Libertad. Mon-Sat 1100-0200, Sun 1200-2300, trendy bar/café/restaurant with sidewalk seating.

Jethro's Pub, Arias Araguez 131 y San Martín. Popular.

Festivals and events

Moquegua *p311, map p312*
14 Oct Santa Fortunata.
25 Nov Día de Santa Catalina, anniversary of the founding of the colonial city.

Tacna *p314, map p315*
Jun 23-24 Noche de San Juan y Caravana al Valle Viejo combines the Christian festival with a tribute to the *pachamama*.
Aug 28 Reincorporación de Tacna al Perú, week-long celebrations with parades, cultural events and a fair.

Activities and tours

Moquegua *p311, map p312*
Ledelca Tours, Ayacucho 625, T053-463890, opposite Santo Domingo. For city tours and trips to *bodegas* and archaeological sites.

Transport

Chala *p310*
Buses stop in **Chala Norte**, a 10-min walk from the Chala Sur hotels. Night buses from Lima arrive 0600-0700; there are others in the early evening. To **Lima**, 9 hrs, US$11, with **Flores**, 6 daily from 1200, *bus cama* at 2215; also 6 daily with **Cruz del Sur**, 1330 and late at night. To **Arequipa**, 7½ hrs, US$6, with **Flores, Llamosa** and **Caminos del Inca**, all around 2000; also **Caminos del Inca** at 1330. To **Puerto Inca**, get a *colectivo* just north of the town as far as the turn-off for Puerto Inca, Km 610, about US$1 per person, beware overcharging; a taxi costs US$5.

Mollendo *p311*
Bus station at north end of town, usage fee US$0.30, taxi from centre US$0.60. To **Arequipa**, 129 km, buses and *colectivos* daily, 2½ hrs, US$2. To **Moquegua**, 156 km, 2 hrs, US$2-3, buses and *colectivos* daily. No direct service to Lima or Tacna (315 km): for **Lima**, take an Arequipa-bound bus to '48', on the Pan-American Highway, 1½ hrs, US$1.50; buses pass frequently en route to Lima, 13 hrs, US$11. To **Moquegua** or **Tacna** take a *colectivo* from the obelisk at the top end of Av Mcal Castilla to **Cocachacra**, 40 min, US$1; then another to **El Fiscal**, 20 min, US$0.60; catch a southbound bus from there.

Moquegua *p311, map p312*
Flores, Av del Ejército y Andrés Aurelio Cáceres, has frequent service throughout the region. To **Lima**, many companies, 15 hrs, US$15-$30. Bus service hourly throughout the day to the following: **Tacna**, 2½ hrs, US$3; **Arequipa**, 3½ hrs, US$5.50; **Ilo**, 1½ hrs, US$2. *Colectivos* for the above destinations leave when full from corner of Av del Ejército and Andrés Aurelio Cáceres, they charge almost double the bus fare – negotiate. To **Lake Titicaca** region, **San Martín-Nobleza** is recommended: to **Desaguadero** and **Puno**, 4 a day, 6 hrs, US$7.50; the 2130 bus continues to **Cuzco**; to Cuzco direct at 1100, 13 hrs, US$13.50. **Mily Tours**, Av del Ejército 32-B, T053-464000, *colectivos* to **Desaguadero**, 4 hrs, US$15. To **Mollendo**, no direct service, take an Arequipa-bound bus to El Fiscal, see Mollendo Transport, above.

Tacna *p314, map p315*
Local To **Calientes**, take Ruta 12 minibus from the Centro Comercial Tacnacentro, Av Leguía cuadra 9, every 15 mins throughout the day, 45 mins to Calientes, US$0.60. For **Miculla**, get off at the fork 2 km before Calientes and walk 2 km along a paved road to the archaeological site. Taxis charge US$12 to both sites with 1-hr wait.

Air
To **Lima**, 1½ hrs, some via Arequipa, daily with **Aero Cóndor** (Arias Araguez 135, T052-248187), **Lan** (San Martín 259, T052-428346), **Wayra Perú** (28 de Julio 102, T052-426642).

Bus
There are 4 main bus terminals. The stations for **international** (Arica) and for **domestic** services (both called **Manuel A Odria**, T052-427007) are on Hipólito Unánue, 1 km from the plaza (*colectivo* US$0.25, taxi US$0.60 min). Local tax US$0.30, baggage store, easy connections to the border, Arequipa or Lima. Tickets can be purchased several days before departure. Beware of touts selling tickets at inflated prices; only buy tickets at company offices. **Terminal Bolognesi**, Av Circunvalación y Unánue, 2 blocks from the national terminal, serves beaches and rural destinations within the Department of Tacna. **Terminal Collasuyo**, Av Internacional, Altos de la Alianza, T052-312538; buses for Desaguadero, Puno

and Cuzco; taxi to the centre US$0.75. Also a couple of private terminals: **Flores Hermanos**, Av Saucini behind the Terminal Nacional, T052-426691, for services to Ilo; buses for Moquegua and Arequipa also stop here after leaving the national terminal. **Ormeño** has its terminal on Arias Araguez by the petrol station.

Heading north, note that luggage is checked at a customs complex at **Tomasiri**, 35 km north of Tacna, whether you have been out of the country or not. There is also a police control 10 km after the **Camiara** bridge (near a military base), just before the Tacna/Moquegua departmental border, 59 km from Tacna, 61 km from Moquegua.

To **Moquegua**, 159 km, hourly with **Flores**, US$3, 2½ hrs. There are no direct buses to **Mollendo**, so catch one of the frequent buses to **El Fiscal** (US$4, 4 hrs, see Mollendo Transport, above), then a *colectivo* to Mollendo. To **Arequipa**, 6 hrs, US$7 (US$11 non-stop), several buses daily with **Flores**. To **Nazca**, 793 km, 12 hrs, about US$3 less than to Lima, several buses daily, en route for Lima. Several companies daily to **Lima**, 1239 km, 21-26 hrs, regular US$15-20, *bus cama* US$30-40, all leave after midday.

To **Desaguadero** and **Puno**, 395 km, from Terminal Collasuyo, **San Martín-Nobleza** (T052-952 4252) is recommended, 4 daily, US$8, 8-10 hrs, the 1900 bus continues to **Juliaca** and **Cuzco**; to Cuzco direct at 0830, US$15, 15 hrs, or change in Moquegua. Bus travel to **La Paz**, 10-11 hrs, via either Arica and Tambo Quemado or Desaguadero. The latter is cheaper and involves one less border, but there are delays at the checkpoints.

To **Arica**, 56 km, 1-2 hrs, depending on waiting time at the border; buses charge US$1.80 and *colectivo* taxis US$3.60 per person. All leave from the international terminal in Tacna throughout the day. *Colectivos* only leave when full. As you approach the terminal you will be grabbed by a driver or his agent and told that the car is "just about to leave". This is hard to verify as you may not see the *colectivo* until you have filled in the paperwork. It is best to deal with the company's office, rather than a driver/agent. Either way, at the company's office your passport will be taken from you and the details filled out on a Chilean entry form. You can change your remaining *soles* at the bus terminal while this is being done. It is 30 mins to the Peruvian border post at **Santa Rosa** (see page 316), plus 30 mins for all formalities and a further 15 mins to Arica's bus terminal. A Chilean driver is more likely to take you to any address in Arica.

Train

The station is on Av Albaracín y 2 de Mayo, ticket office daily 0800-0900 and 1430-1600; for the morning train it's best to buy tickets the day before as they sell out. *Autoferro* to **Arica**, Mon-Sat 0545 and 1600 (returning from Arica at 0900 and 1800 Peruvian time), US$1.50, 1½ hrs, customs and immigration at railway stations.

Directory

Moquegua *p311, map p312*
Banks BCP, esq Moquegua y Tarapacá, the only bank that changes TCs, will advance money on Visa. Daily 0915-1315, 1630-1830, Telebanco 24 Horas ATM (Visa). Street changers at the **Mercado Central**. **Internet** Many places all over town, US$0.30 per hr. **Post** On the Plaza de Armas in a colonial house. **Telephone** Phone offices all over town.

Tacna *p314, map p315*
Banks BCP, San Martín 574, no commission for TCs (AmEx, Citicorp) into soles. Similarly at **Banco Wiese**, San Martín 476. **Interbank**, San Martín 646, has ATM for Visa/Plus, MasterCard/Cirrus and Amex. Several *casas de cambio* at San Martín y Arias Araguez and at the international bus terminal, all offering good rates for US$; also euros, *pesos chilenos* (best rates) and *bolivianos*. Street changers stand outside the **Municipalidad**. **Car hire** Explorer Tacna Rent a Car, T052-421753, explorer tacna@viabcp.com. **Consulates** **Bolivia**, Av Bolognesi 1751 y Piura, T052-2245121. Mon-Fri 0900-1500. **Chile**, Presbítero Andía block 1, T052-423063. Mon-Fri 0800-1300, closed hols. **Internet** All over the centre, average US$0.30 per hr. **Laundry** Lavandería Tacna, Zela 374. US$1.50 per kg, Mon-Sat 0800-1300, 1500-2000. **Post** Av Bolognesi 361. Mon-Sat 0800-2000. **Telephone** Public *cabinas* everywhere. **Useful addresses** Touring y Automóvil Club del Perú, Av 2 de Mayo 67, T052-244237, tacna@touringperu.com.pe.

Cordilleras Blanca & Huayhuash

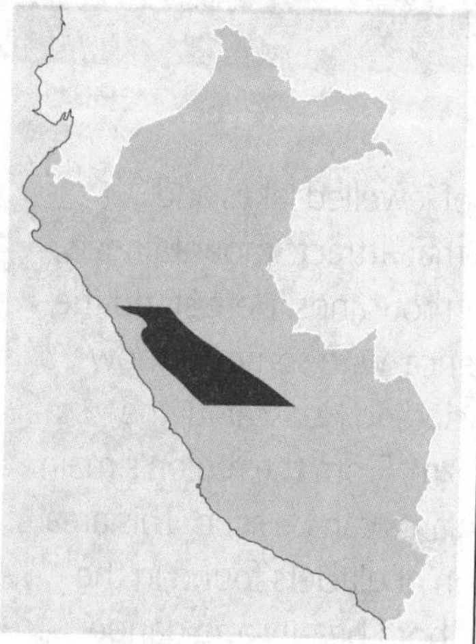

Footprint features

Introduction

The Cordillera Blanca is a region of jewelled lakes and sparkling white mountain peaks that attracts mountaineers, hikers, cyclists and rafters in their thousands. Here stand the highest mountains in South America, with some 30 snow-crested peaks of over 6000 m, including Huascarán, the highest mountain in Peru at 6768 m. From the region's main centre, Huaraz, several of these giants can be seen. This area contains the largest concentration of glaciers found in the world's tropical zone: a source of both beauty and danger.

The turquoise-coloured lakes (*cochas*) which form in the terminal moraines are the jewels of the Andes and you should hike up to at least one during your stay. Laguna Churup is a day's walk from Huaraz, Lago Parón is close to Caraz, while the beautiful twin lakes of Llanganuco are within easy reach of Yungay and are on the route of the long-distance Santa Cruz trek. The tranquility of these glacial lakes masks a frightening history. They have caused much death and destruction when dykes have broken, sending tons of water hurtling down the canyons, wiping out everything in their path. The levels of some have been artificially lowered for flood control and to feed the huge Cañón del Pato dam. Earthquakes, too, have scarred the high valleys and the mass grave which was once the old town of Yungay is a very humbling place.

Southeast of Huaraz, the Cordillera Huayhuash is an area that more than equals the Cordillera Blanca in beauty and majesty. It is rapidly gaining a reputation among long-distance trekkers and climbers. Even the archaeologist is catered for here in the shape of the ruins of Chavín de Huantar. This fortress-temple belonged to one of the earliest and most influential cultures in pre-Inca Peru and it has some fine carvings and stonework.

★ Don't miss...

1 **Yungay** Besides its typical market on a Thursday, Yungay's *campo santo* is a poignant memorial to the devastating power of the mountains, page 345.
2 **Llanganuco lakes** Take time to study the bark of the *quenoal* trees (polylepis), like shreds of the finest paper, against the blue of the water, page 346.
3 **Llanganuco to Santa Cruz trek** To visit the Cordillera Blanca without doing just one of the fantastic treks on offer is really missing the point of coming here at all, page 349.
4 **Puya Raimondi** There are many plants in the mountains, but keep an eye out for these remarkable bromeliads with their century-long lifespan, page 355.
5 **Chavín de Huantar** Don't leave without visiting the 2500 year-old fortress temple; either take a tour, or hike three days from Olleros, page 362.
6 **Huayhuash circuit** You need stamina for this trek through majestic mountain scenery, page 370.

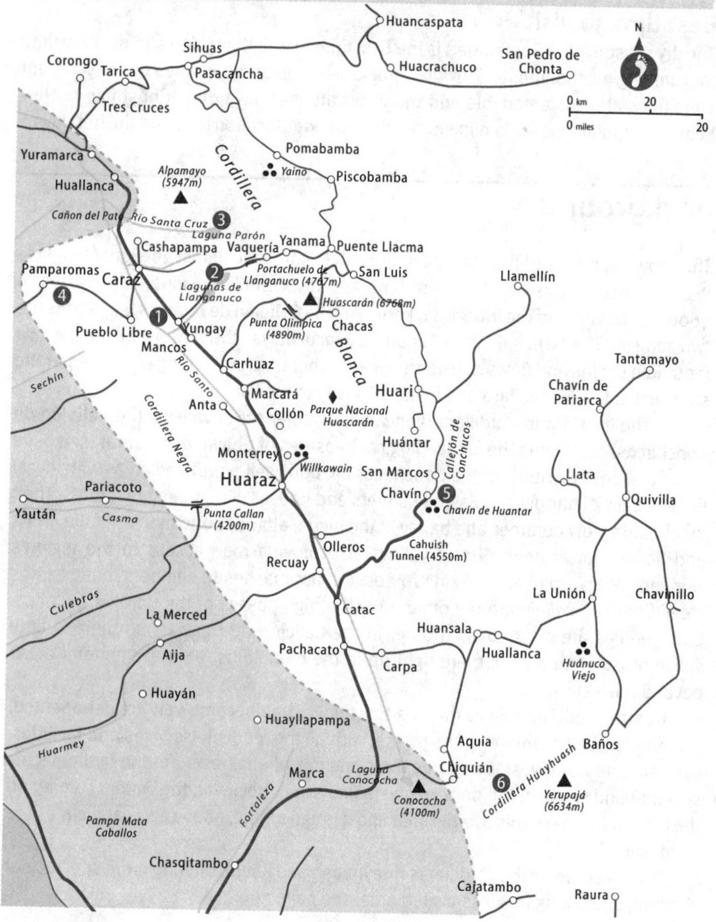

Ins and outs → *Colour map 3, B3.*

Getting there

There are three main routes to reach the Cordillera Blanca. Probably the easiest is the paved road which branches east off the Pan-American Highway north of Pativilca, 187 km from Lima, see page 378. Further north, a second route is via the Callán pass from Casma to Huaraz, see page 379, a rough but beautiful trip through the heart of the Cordillera Negra. The third alternative is from Chimbote to Caraz via the Cañón del Pato, see page 381, also a very scenic journey, with magnificent views of this spectacular canyon. The main access to the Cordillera Huayhuash is from Huaraz. Cajatambo, the southern access point, can be reached from Lima by bus and the area can also be reached by bus on the Huánuco–La Unión–Huaraz route ▸▸ *For further details, see Transport, page 342.*

Getting around

In the Cordillera Blanca minibuses run between most of the towns on a regular basis, while more remote places have less frequent services. Several roads are being improved to cope with mining traffic. Of course, on some routes, you can always walk!

Best time to visit

The dry season (May-September) is the best time to visit the region and the only time for climbing most summits. Trekking is also possible at other times of the year, but conditions are less amenable and the views are less rewarding. Christmas to New Year is a popular time for foreigners seeking an exotic location to spend the holidays.

Background

The snow-capped Cordillera Blanca runs north to south for almost 200 km. Alongside it to the west lies its alter ego, the bare and dry **Cordillera Negra**, which rises to 4600 m. The valley of the **Río Santa**, known as the **Callejón de Huaylas**, separates the two ranges. The Santa rises in **Laguna Conococha**, at the south end of the two mountain chains and flows due north between them, before turning west to enter the spectacular **Cañón del Pato** and making its way to the Pacific.

To the east of the Cordillera Blanca lies another set of valleys, the **Callejón de Conchucos**, containing the archaeological treasures of **Chavín de Huantar**, see page 363. Callejones de Huaylas and Conchucos are both well-populated areas with lovely little villages of narrow cobblestone streets and houses with odd-angled roofs. Their inhabitants grow potatoes and barley at the higher altitudes and maize, alfalfa, fruits and flowers lower down. These valleys also provide road access to the region's wonders. Many excellent trekking routes and approaches to climbers' base camps cross from one *callejón* to the other, over the high passes of the Cordillera Blanca. Communities are close to each other in the Callejón de Huaylas, so there is little sense of isolation until you are right up in the mountains, or in the remoter areas beyond this valley.

Huaraz, undoubtedly at the heart of things, has become very tourist-oriented, catering for the adventure sports market with all the requisite services and facilities. Only an hour northwest, **Caraz** has the same mix of engineers (for the hydroelectric scheme) and tourism, but on a much smaller scale. However, the waters coming off the mountains make this a fertile area and it is agriculture, above all, that dictates the pace of life.

Further south lie the cordilleras Huayhuash and Raura, offering more spectacular climbing and hiking in a less-visited area, see page 369.

Huascarán National Park

Established in July 1975, the park encompasses the entire Cordillera Blanca above 4000 m. It covers a total area of 3400 sq km: 180 km from north to south and 20 km from east to west. It is a UNESCO World Biosphere Reserve and part of the World Heritage Trust. The park's objectives are to protect the unique flora, fauna, geology, archaeological sites and extraordinary scenic beauty of the Cordillera. Please make every attempt to help by taking all your rubbish away with you when camping; there have been more than enough complaints that campsites are dirty and toilet pits foul.

Park administration is at Jirón Federico Sal y Rosas 555, by Plazuela Belén, Huaraz, T043-422086. Open Monday-Friday 0830-1300, 1430-1700. Fees for visiting the national park are collected at rangers posts at **Quebrada Llanganuco** (see page 346) and **Huascarán** (see page 349) for the Llanganuco to Santa Cruz trek, at **Collón** on the way up the Quebrada Ishinca (see page 332) and at **Pitec** (see page 332). It costs US$1.25 for a day visit. For visits of up to seven days (ie for trekking and climbing trips) a permit costing US$20 (in late 2006) must be bought. If you stay longer than seven days, you will need another permit.

Stop press: in September 2006 it was reported that **INRENA** (the National Institute for Natural Resources, www.inrena.gob.pe) had announced new regulations governing the national park. Similar to rules governing the Inca Trails at Machu Picchu, local guides will be mandatory for everywhere except designated 'Recreation Zones' (areas accessible by car) and climbers attempting difficult climbing routes will have to be accompanied by a local climbing guide. At the time of writing these regulations had not been instituted, nor the cost of permits announced, but anyone wishing to trek or climb independently should make enquiries before setting out.

Trekking and climbing

The Cordillera Blanca offers the most popular – and some of the best – trekking and climbing in Peru, with a network of trails used by the local people and some less well-defined mountaineers' routes. There are numerous possibilities for day hikes, trekking and climbing. Of these, only a very few routes are currently used by most visitors, and so they have accumulated rubbish and other signs of impact. While these favourite treks – notably Santa Cruz–Llanganuco (see page 349) and the Alpamayo circuit (see page 351) – are undeniably interesting, you should consider the various excellent alternatives if you want to enjoy a less-crowded experience and help conserve the area's great natural beauty. For details of access and permits, see box, above.

Trekking options

The many other options include: **Laguna Parón,** with its impressive cirque of surrounding summits (access from Caraz, see page 347); **Hualcayán to Pomabamba,** traversing the northern end of the Cordillera Blanca with fine views of Alpamayo and many other peaks (access from Caraz; see page 351); **Laguna 69** at the end of Llanganuco valley (access from Yungay; see page 346); the **Ulta Valley** and **Laguna Auquiscocha,** between the massifs of Huascarán, Ulta and Hualcán (access from Carhuaz, see page 344); to name but a few. There remains a good deal to be discovered in the area and your creativity in choosing a route is certain to be rewarded.

Mining in the mountains

The Department of Ancash contains important mineral deposits including copper, zinc, silver, gold and perhaps uranium (the latter is not discussed openly). In the Cordillera Negra alone, 12,000 different sites have been prospected. An open pit mine and smelter, 12 km north of Huaraz, has brought major changes to the Callejón de Huaylas. The US/ Canadian consortium operating the mine promised to minimize environmental impact, yet there are conflicting claims as to the extent of environmental damage. There has, however, been undeniable impact on some of the finest natural areas of the Peruvian Andes. Mining companies have built their own neighbourhoods and camps, while many new roads continue to be made by and for the mines.

Similar developments are taking place east of San Marcos, near Chavín in the Callejón de Conchucos, where a huge underground mine and concentrator at Antamina has come on stream. Hundreds of kilometres of good roads, thousands of jobs for Peruvians and a resident ex-pat community near Huaraz have undoubtedly had a significant effect on the local economy.

In the Cordillera Huayhuash, a Japanese corporation has a major mining project in the vicinity of Pocpa and Laguna Jahuacocha, the jewel of the entire region. Other mines are under consideration and some local residents have proposed the creation of a Huayhuash National Park to protect the region's unique natural beauty, as well as its economically important tourist potential.

There are two traditional trekking routes in the **Huayhuash**: a complete loop around the range (see page 370); and a half-circuit, starting from the trail head at Cuartel Huain and ending in Cajatambo. These are but two of very many excellent options and hikers are urged to be creative in choosing their routes and campsites, both to enjoy more pristine surroundings and to allow over-used areas to recover.

Advice to climbers

The height of the mountains in the Cordillera Blanca and nearby ranges and their location in the tropics create conditions different from the Alps or even the Himalayas. Fierce sun makes the mountain snow porous and the glaciers move more rapidly. Deglaciation is rapidly changing the face of the Cordillera, so older maps do not provide a reliable indication of the extent of glaciers and snow fields (according to some studies 15% of the range's glaciers have disappeared since the 1970s); local experience is important. Climbers should not assume that their experience on other ranges will be sufficient for the Cordillera Blanca and first-timers here should take a guide for safety.

The British Embassy advises climbers to take at least six days for acclimatization, to move in groups of four or more, reporting to a reliable fellow climber, an agency, your hotel or embassy before departing, giving the date at which a search should begin, and leaving the telephone number of your Embassy with money.

The **Policía Nacional de Perú** ⓘ *T043-393333/393300, usam@pnp.gob.pe*, has a 35-member rescue team in Yungay, with 24-hour phone service and vhf/uhf radio dispatch. They have two helicopters and trained search-and-rescue dogs. At present, they will rescue anyone – climbers, trekkers, tourists – without asking for cash up front; insured climbers will be billed but rescues are currently free for uninsured climbers, although this policy is likely to change. PNP will only take the injured person as far as Huaraz hospital, from where additional costly medical evacuation may be required. It therefore remains imperative that all climbers carry adequate insurance; it cannot be purchased locally. Be well-prepared before setting out on a climb. Wait or cancel your trip when weather conditions are bad. Every year climbers are killed through failing to take weather conditions seriously. Climb only when and where you have sufficient experience.

Advice to hikers and trekkers

Most circuits can be hiked in five days. Although the trails are easily followed, they are rugged and the passes are very high – between 4000 and nearly 5000 m – so you should be fit and properly acclimatized to the altitude, and carry all necessary equipment. In the Cordillera Huayhuash you must be entirely self-sufficient. Evacuation in the event of illness or accident may require several days. Essential items are a tent, warm sleeping bag, stove and protection against wind and rain (climatic conditions are quite unreliable here and you cannot rule out rain and hail storms even in the dry season). Trekking with mules or donkeys demands less stamina, since equipment is carried for you. Nobody should trek entirely on their own. Something as minor as a sprained ankle can become a disaster if there is no one to assist you or go for help. As with the British Embassy advice to climbers above, you should always inform trusted friends or associates where you plan to hike and the latest date you plan to return.

Safety and conduct

Before heading out on any route, trekkers and climbers must always enquire locally about public safety. Following hold-ups of trekking parties in the Cordillera Huayhuash in 2003 and 2004, the local communities agreed to provide an armed escort for all groups hiking in the area. In 2006 the system was working well. Each community charges a separate fee for this service, the total at the time of writing being in the region of US$30-35 per person. The fee was still being finalized at the time of going to press, so enquire in Huaraz and Chiquián about specific payments before embarking on the trek. The Cordillera Blanca is generally quite safe, but muggings have taken place on the way to Laguna Churup, to the Mirador Rataquena above Huaraz, the Mirador above Monterrey, and at Wilkawain. The eastern side of the Huayhuash/Raura range, in the Department of Huánuco, has a reputation for more aggressive behaviour; be especially cautious in this area.

On all treks in this area, respect the locals' property, leave no rubbish behind, do not give sweets or money to children who beg (a serious problem on popular routes) and remember your cooking utensils, tent, etc, would be very expensive for a *campesino*, so be sensitive and responsible. Do not leave your gear unattended at any time and stow everything in your tent overnight. Some camping areas in the Huayhuash have recently begun charging a small fee for trekkers; insist on an official receipt.

You will encounter many cattle with dogs guarding them; it's best to give both a wide berth. Carrying a walking stick or crouching to pick up a stone will usually discourage the canines but throwing stones has been known to provoke an attack.

Rubbish is a significant problem at the usual campsites and you should personally pack out everything you bring in; you cannot trust muleteers in this regard. Much of the area is above the tree line; the remainder has been badly deforested. Make sure you have a reliable stove and enough fuel for cooking and resist the temptation to use what little firewood remains. Camp fires spreading out of control have caused huge damage in critical areas of the Andes. Improper disposal of human waste is also a problem. Use great care in this fragile environment.

Hiring guides and muleteers

The **Dirección de Turismo** issues qualified guides and *arrieros* (muleteers) with a photo ID. Always check for this when making arrangements; note down the name and card number in case you should have any complaints. Prices for specific

Climbing Pisco... or not quite *Touching the Void*

If you spend any serious time in Huaraz – in Café Andino or a dozen other places – and you possess even the mildest interest in mountains, you'll quickly get used to the climbing scene, to the lingo and to the casually thrown words drifting over the cappuccinos, and last but not least, to designer stubble and sporty guys in Gore-Tex jackets. Great peaks and some of the world's best climbing are seemingly close enough to touch. Joe Simpson's legendary and inspiring story of adventure and survival in the Cordillera Huayhuash is hard to ignore from this proximity, but not everyone possesses the 'luck' of Joe Simpson. These are among some of the world's mightiest and least predictable mountains and underestimating these climbs has become as common as pizza.

I'm a fit and enthusiastic trekker, but not really a technical climber so, on the rare occasions when I don crampons and ice-axe, it's usually just for a challenge and for the pleasure of getting up high among the ice-bound peaks. On this occasion, however, pleasure is, perhaps, not the first term I'd use to describe the terror which bolted me to a small ice cliff on the so-called 'easy' Pisco. I fought with exhaustion as I tried not to look down at the huge drop below. A few minutes later, freezing tears of frustration battled with embarrassment, then anger at myself, which faded once more as I reached the summit. Sunrise illuminated mighty peaks like sharks' teeth. Clouds lay like a fluffy carpet far below and seemed to curve with the expanse of the earth. The north face of Huandoy turned orange. I could barely stand-up, but it was worth it: fabulous memories created on the spot and the photos weren't bad either.

Another side of the story: one of my happy-go-lucky climbing buddies, who'd helped drag me up Pisco, offered to help find three Americans lost on the face of 6025-m Artesonraju (which the fraternity also calls 'easy'). My friend, not much over 20 and a bit of a party monster from Northern England, was successful in his mission, helping the rescue group find the bodies and pull the frozen remains off the mountain. He didn't party afterwards though, summing it up pretty concisely: "I don't know mate, I don't want to climb anymore. I just want to go home, see my girlfriend, my family. It's just all totally screwed up, ya know?" He took the first flight home he could get.

Somebody told me once that the better climber you are, the more dangerous it becomes. Don't get me wrong, I'd never advise experienced climbers NOT to climb here, just don't be deceived by these peaks, no matter how simple you think they might be, and no matter how good a climber you are.

Steve Frankham

services are set, so enquire before hiring someone. You should also make your priorities clear to the muleteer in advance of the trek (pace, choice of route, campsites, etc) or else you will be led around with the line, 'all the gringos do this'. Some guides speak English and are friendly but lack technical expertise; others have expertise but lack communicative ability. You may have to choose between the former and the latter. Avoid 'private' guides who seek you out on the street.

Prices in 2006 for both Cordilleras Blanco and Huayhuash were as follows: *arriero*, US$10 per day; donkey or mule US$4-5 per day; trekking guides US$40-50 per day (more for foreign guides); climbing guides US$70-120 per day (more for foreign guides), depending on the difficulty of the peak; cooks US$25-30 per day. You are required to provide or pay for food and shelter for all porters, guides, cooks and *arrieros*. Tour operators in Huaraz (see page 340) offer 11-day treks in the Huayhuash for US$350 including guide/cook, food, equipment, mules and driver, and public transport. The operators in Caraz (see page 359) also offer treks in the Huayhuash. Tours without guide cost US$160 per person: you have to cook your own food and feed the mule driver, do your own setting up of tents, etc.

For the Cordillera Huayhuash treks, it is sometimes a problem in the high climbing/trekking season to hire mules straightaway. This is because all the ones at the northern end are kept at Llamac and Pocpa and it may take a day to bring the mules to your starting point. The muleteers are a mixed bunch, ranging from excellent to irresponsible. Get a recommendation from someone who has recently returned from a trek; otherwise call ahead to **Hostal San Miguel** or ask at **Restaurant Yerupajá** or **Panadería Santa Rosa** (see Chiquián Sleeping and Eating, page 372).

Mountain shelters

Refugios have been built at Pisco (4700 m), Huascarán (4800 m) and Ishinka (4300 m and 4700 m). They are operated by **Organización Mato Grosso** ⓘ *Huaraz (Marcará), T043-443061, www.rirugi-omg.org, US$30 per person including breakfast and supper*, and are open in high season only,

Provisions and equipment

Huaraz is the region's supply centre and all but the most specialized items may be obtained here (see page 339). Check all camping and climbing equipment very carefully before hiring or buying it. Hired gear is of variable quality and most is second hand, left behind by others. Also note that some items may not be available, so it's best to bring your own. All prices are standard, but not cheap, and all require payment in advance, passport or air ticket as deposit and will only give 50% of your money back if you return gear early. Many trekking agencies sell camping gaz cartridges. White gas (*bencina*) is available from *ferreterías*, but shop around to avoid overcharging. It should cost about US$1 per litre. If you require freeze-dried meals, these should be brought from abroad.

In the Huayhuash, Chiquián's shops are usually well stocked with basic supplies, including locally produced butter and cheese, although prices may be a bit higher here. Almost nothing is available in the hamlets along the route, but fresh trout may be purchased by some of the lakes and a very few items (mostly beer, soft drinks and potatoes) might be purchased in Llamac, Pocpa, Carhuacocha, Huayllapa and Pacllón. Take coins and small notes as there is seldom any change. Bring a fishing line and lure to supplement your diet.

Maps and information

Casa de Guías ⓘ *Plaza Ginebra 28-g, Huaraz, T043-421811, casa_de_guias @hotmail.com, Mon-Sat 0900-1300, 1600-2000*, is the climbers' and hikers' meeting place. It has information, books, maps, arrangements for guides, *arrieros*, mules, etc. There is a noticeboard, postcards and posters for sale. The Casa de Guías has a full list of all members of the **Asociación de Guías de Montaña del Perú (AGMP)** throughout the country. A great site for trekking is www.huaylas.com.

A good tourist map of the Callejón de Huaylas and Cordillera Huayhuash, by **Felipe Díaz**, is available in many shops in the region and at **Casa de Guías** in Huaraz (see above); it's not accurate enough for hiking the less-travelled trails. **Alpenvereinskarte Cordillera Blanca Nord 0/3a** and **Alpenvereinskarte Cordillera Blanca Süd 0/3b at 1:100,000** are easily the best maps of the Cordillera Blanca; they are available in Huaraz for US$12 each (also in Lima). Stocks locally are small, so it's best to get it before you arrive. **Instituto Geográfico Nacional** has mapped the area with its 1:100,000 topographical series. These are more useful to the mountaineer than hiker, however, since the trails marked are confusing and inaccurate. **South American Explorers** publishes a good map with additional notes on the popular Llanganuco to Santa Cruz loop. See also page 370 for a recommended Cordillera Huayhuash map. ⏩ *For guide books, see Books page 615.*

Huaraz and around

→ *Phone code 043. Colour map 3, B3.*

The main town in the valley, with a population of 80,000, Huaraz is expanding rapidly as a major tourist centre but it is also a busy commercial hub, especially on market days (Monday and Thursday). The region is both a prime destination for hikers and international climbers, as well as a vacation haven for Peruvian urbanites seeking clean mountain air and a glimpse of the glaciers. School groups flock to the city from mid-September to mid-December (the 'época de promociones colegiales'). The city was half destroyed in the earthquake of May 1970 so don't expect red-tiled roofs or overhanging eaves. What the reconstructed city lacks in colonial charm, it makes up for with its spectacular setting at 3091 m between the mountains of the cordilleras Blanca and Negra. The peaks of Huamashraju, Churup, Rima Rima and Vallunaraju loom so close as to seem almost a part of the architecture while, in the distance, the giants Huascarán and Huandoy can be seen. ⏩ *For Sleeping, Eating and other listings, see pages 333-343.*

Ins and outs

Getting there and around The bus offices are in the centre of town and are conveniently close to many of the hotels and hostels. The city is small enough to get around by foot, providing sensible precautions are taken, especially at night. Huaraz has its share of crime, especially since the arrival of mining in the area (see box, page 326) and during the high tourist season. On no account should women go to surrounding districts and sites alone. ⏩ *For safety while trekking or climbing, see page 327.*

Tourist information Information is provided by **iPerú** ⓘ *Luzuriaga on Plaza de Armas, T043-428812, iperuhuaraz@promperu.gob.pe, Mon-Sat 0800-1830, Sun 0800-1400.* On the second floor of same building, **Policía de Turismo** ⓘ *T043-421341, ext 315, Mon-Fri 0900-1300, 1600-1900, Sat 0900-1300*, is the place to report all crimes and mistreatment by tour operators, hotels, etc.

Sights

The **Plaza de Armas** has been rebuilt, with a towering white statue of Christ, and a new cathedral is being constructed. **Museo Arqueológico de Ancash** ⓘ *Instituto Nacional de Cultura, Plaza de Armas, daily 0800-2000, US$1.80*, contains stone monoliths and *huacos* (pottery artefacts) from the Recuay and other cultures. The exhibits are well labelled and laid out. The **Sala de Cultura SUNARP** ⓘ *Av Centenario 530, Independencia, T043-421301, Mon-Fri 1700-2000, Sat 0900-1300, free*, often has interesting art and photography exhibitions by local artists.

The main thoroughfare, **Avenida Luzuriaga**, is bursting at the seams with travel agencies, climbing equipment hire shops, restaurants, cafés and bars. Within a block or two you can find a less frantic ambience, but a good alternative for those seeking peace and quiet is the **La Soledad** neighbourhood, six blocks uphill from the Plaza de Armas on Avenida Sucre. Here, along Sucre as well as Jirón Amadeo Figueroa, every second house seems to rent rooms, most without signs. We list but a few, see page 333. There are several decent neighbourhood eateries nearby, plus many shops, internet cafés and other facilities.

Huaraz

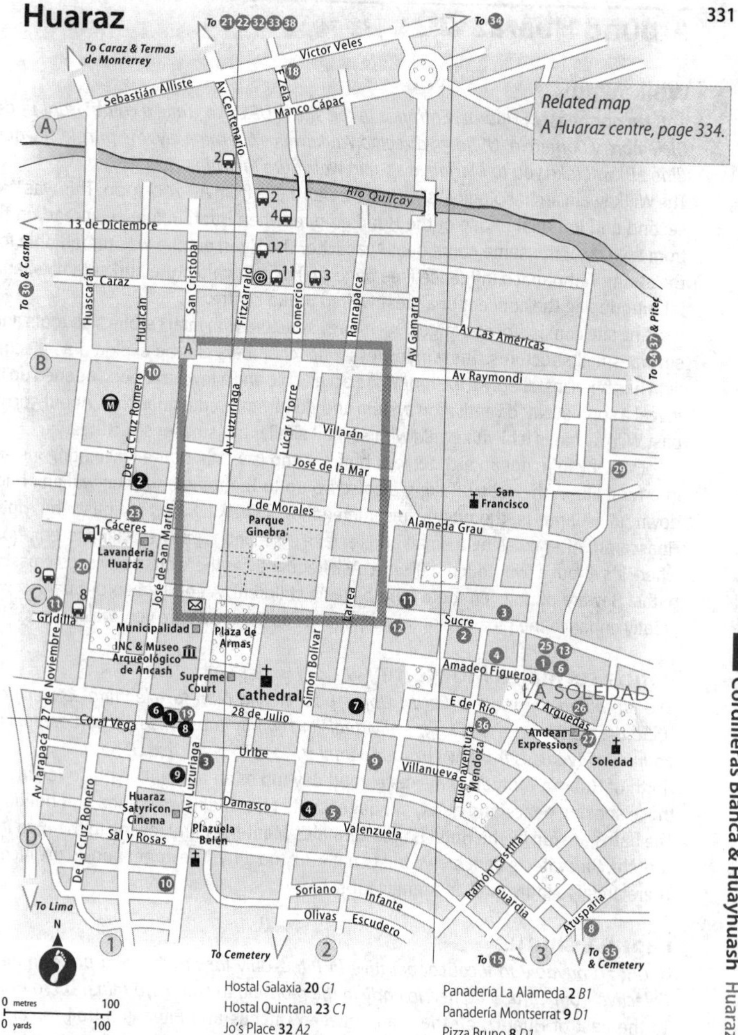

Sleeping
Albergue Churup **1** *C3*
Alojamiento El Jacal **2** *C3*
Alojamiento Marilia **3** *C3*
Alojamiento Nemy's **4** *C3*
Alojamiento Norma **5** *D2*
Alojamiento Soledad **6** *C3*
Andino Club **8** *D3*
Angeles Inn & Sol Andino **9** *D2*
Apu Wasi **15** *D3*
Backpackers **10** *B1*
Casa de Jaimes **11** *C1*
Casa Jansy's **12** *C2*
Edward's Inn **30** *B1*
Hatun Wasi **21** *A1*
Hostal Alfredo **22** *A2*
Hostal Colomba **18** *A2*
Hostal Continental **19** *C1*
Hostal Galaxia **20** *C1*
Hostal Quintana **23** *C1*
Jo's Place **32** *A2*
La Cabaña **25** *C3*
La Casa de Zarela **26** *C3*
La Estancia **33** *A2*
Lazy Dog **24** *B3*
Lodging Casa Sucre **13** *C3*
Lodging House Ezama **34** *A3*
Olaza Guesthouse **27** *D3*
Pastoruri **38** *A2*
San Sebastián **29** *B3*
Steels **35** *D3*
Way Inn **36** *C3*
Way Inn Lodge **37** *B3*

Eating
Café El Centro **1** *C1*
California Café **6** *C1*
Encuentro **7** *C2*
Huaraz Querido **4** *D2*
Panadería La Alameda **2** *B1*
Panadería Montserrat **9** *D1*
Pizza Bruno **8** *D1*

Bars & clubs
Chacraraju/Chill-out **11** *C2*
Extreme **3** *D1*
La Cascada **10** *D1*

Transport
Chavín Express **1** *C1*
Combis to Caraz **2** *A1, A2*
Combis to Llupa (for Laguna Churup) **3** *B2*
Combis to Wilcawain **4** *A2*
Terminal Terrestre Transportistas Zona Sur **8** *C1*
Trans Huandoy **12** *A2*
Trans Rodríguez **9** *C1*
Virgen de Guadalupe **11** *B2*

Around Huaraz » p333-343.

Willkawain

ⓘ 8 km northeast of Huaraz. Entrance to the site is US$1.50. Take a combi from 13 de Diciembre y Comercio, US$0.55 direct to Willkawain. Alternatively, the purple city bus (line 2B) will take you to Marian, a 15-min walk from the ruins.

The Willkawain archaeological site near Huaraz dates from AD 700-1000. This was the second and imperial phase of the Huari empire, when Huari influence spread north from the city of the same name near Ayacucho. The Huari empire was remarkable for the strong Tiahuanaco influence (see page 571) in its architecture and ceramics, and for introducing the concept of a great walled urban centre.

The site consists of one large three-storey structure with intact stone slab roofs and several small structures. The windowless inner chambers can be explored as electric light has been installed. All the rooms are accessible and a few have been opened up to reveal a sophisticated ventilation system and skilful stone craftsmanship. About 500 m past Willkawain is **Ichiwillkawain** with several similar but smaller structures.

Even if you're not an archaeology buff, the trip is worth it for a fascinating insight into rural life in the valley. Taking a *colectivo* up to the ruins and then walking back down to Huaraz is thoroughly recommended. If walking up, go past the **Hotel Huascarán**. After crossing a small bridge, take a second right (well-signposted), from where it's about a two-hour uphill walk. Ask frequently as there are many criss-crossing paths. Beware of dogs en route (and begging children). A good grasp of Spanish will greatly enhance the pleasure of this experience as the locals are very welcoming.

Baños Termales Monterrey → *Colour map 3, B3.*

ⓘ 6 km along the road to Caraz. Upper pool closed Mon for cleaning. Lower pool US$0.85, upper pool US$1.35, individual and family tubs US$1.35 per person for 20 mins. City buses from Av Luzuriaga until 1900, US$0.22. Taxi US$2-3.

North of Huaraz, Monterrey makes a good day trip or an alternative place to stay for those seeking peace and quiet, although it gets crowded at weekends and holidays. The baths are run by the **Hotel Baños Termales Monterrey** and, owing to the high iron content, the water is dark brown but usually not too dirty. The upper pool is the nicest. There are also individual and family tubs.

Laguna Churup

ⓘ US$20 payable to local cooperative in Pitec, only for groups with pack animals. Colectivo from Caraz y Comercio early in the morning to Llupa, 40 mins, US$0.60.

To the east of Huaraz, off the road between Unchus and Pitec is a trail to Laguna Churup, which makes a good one-day excursion from Huaraz. The trail starts at **Llupa**, from where it's a one-hour hike to the National Park ranger post at **Pitec**. From there, it's a further three hours up to the lake, which is surrounded by high mountains. The last part involves scrambling over rocks (dangerous when raining). It's about three hours back to Llupa, where *colectivos* run until about 1800.

From **Pitec** there are three-day hikes up the Quebrada Quillcayhuanca to Cayesh or to Lagunas Tullpacocha and Cuchilacocha. From the latter you can cross a pass to the Cojup Valley (see page 333 below) and descend to Llupa (a further two days). You have to pay a national park entrance fee in Pitec to do these treks.

Quebrada Ishinca

A good place for acclimatization and trekking at high altitude is the Ishinca hut at 4350 m in the Quebrada Ishinca. To get there, take a bus towards Paltay and then a *colectivo* to **Collón**; a taxi from Huaraz costs US$20. From Collón it's a nice four-hour walk to the hut; donkeys can be arranged in Collón, ask for Lorenzo. To sleep at the hut costs US$10, breakfast and dinner are US$10 each; you can also camp here. It's very popular with climbers. The easiest nearby climbs are Urus, 5420 m, and Ishinca, 5530 m. It is also possible to make a circuit back to Huaraz via Quebrada Cojup in three days, going over 5000 m. This is a good trek with great views.

Punta Callan

ⓘ *A taxi to Punta Callan will cost about US$25 and take about one hour, or take a Casma bus and get off at the pass.*

This walk in the Cordillera Negra makes an excellent day trip from Huaraz, with superb views of almost the whole of the Cordillera Blanca and some nice rural scenery. It is best to leave Huaraz early in the morning, ideally about 0800, for the best light on the mountains. From the pass at 4200 m, walk northwards (the right-hand side of the road) to a small hill of 4600 m for the best views. Then head directly back down to Huaraz, which you'll see in the valley below you. Follow various trails and farm tracks, with several routes being possible. It takes about four hours' walking to reach the first places where you'll get return minibus transport. Add another hour or so to walk all the way back to Huaraz.

Sleeping

Huaraz *p330, maps p331 and p334*

Hotels are plentiful (there are many more than those listed below) but fill up rapidly during the high season (May-Sep), especially during public holidays and special events (such as the **Semana de Andinismo** in Jun) when prices rise. Lodging in private homes is common during these periods. Avoid touts at bus stations offering rooms and tours.

AL Andino Club, Pedro Cochachín 357, some way southeast from the centre (take a taxi after dark), T043-421662, www.hotelandino.com. Good international standard hotel with restaurant, free internet for guests, lift, safe parking, Swiss run, and friendly. 2nd, 3rd and 4th floor rooms have balconies and views of Huascarán. Newly built section has suites and an apartment, which boast personal saunas, among other facilities. Not surprisingly these are more expensive. Recommended.

AL-A Pastoruri, Jr Corongo 145, across the bridge, several blocks north of the river, T043-427018, www.pastoruri hotel.com. New 3-star business-style hotel with well-equipped, internet-enabled, spacious rooms and big bathrooms. Suites have jacuzzis into the bargain. Breakfast and use of the top-floor gym is included in the price.

A Hostal Colomba, Francisco de Zela 278, on Centenario across the river, T043-421501, www.huarazhotelcolomba.com. Lovely old hacienda, family-run, fabulous garden, safe car parking, gym and well-equipped rooms with cable TV, comfortable beds and internet access. All bathrooms have tub and jacuzzi.

B San Sebastián, Jr Italia 1124, T043-426960, www.hotelhuaraz.com. Elegant, modern hotel, comfortable beds with duvets, parking available, internet connection in rooms. Very helpful, buffet breakfast included, good views. Junior suites **A**. Recommended.

C **Hostal Alfredo**, Av Centenario 184, T043-4211632, www.hostalalfredo.com. Variety of rooms and suites, refurbished in 2006, TV, phones, room service 0600-2400, jacuzzi, bath with hydro massage, internet, tourist information, English and German spoken. Cafeteria with local and international food.

C **Steel Guest House**, Alejandro Maguiña 1467, T043 429709, www.steelguest.com. Comfortable guesthouse under new management. Excellent view of the major peaks from the roof terrace, although its location (close to **Andino Club**) entails a fair walk from the centre; a taxi is recommended late at night. Small but comfortable rooms with TV and private bathroom, a sauna, kitchen for guests, internet access, good value. Table football, a full size pool table,

Huaraz centre

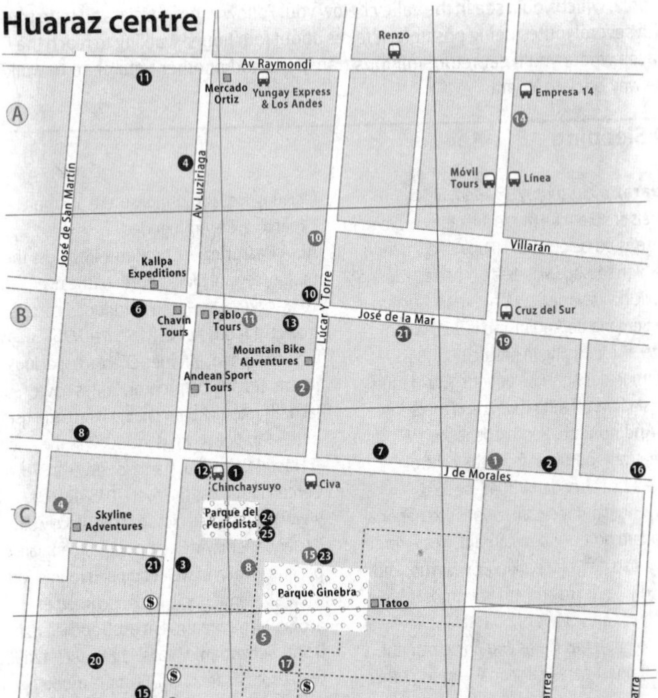

0 metres 20
0 yards 20

Sleeping
Alpes Andes & Casa de Guías **15** *C2*
Cayesh Guesthouse **1** *C3*
Familia Meza & Café Andino **2** *B2*
Hostal Estoico **4** *C1*
Hostal Gyula **5** *D2*
Hostal Montañero & Tour agency **8** *C2*
Hostal Tany **10** *B2*
Oscar's Hostal **11** *B2*
Schatzi **14** *A3*

Eating
Bistro de los Andes **2** *C3*
Cafetería y Juguería **22** *D3*
Chifa Jim Hua **3** *C1*
Chili Heaven **23** *C2*
Crêperie Patrick **4** *A1*
El Horno **24** *C2*
Encuentro **25** *C2*
Fuente de Salud **6** *B1*
La Placita: Rinconcito Minero, El Querubín & Vagamundo **7** *C2*
Las Puyas **8** *C1*
Las Tulpas y Chimichurri **1** *C2*
Monte Rosa **10** *B2*
Monttrek Pizza Pub & Trekking agency **21** *C1*
Pachamama **20** *D1*
Pepe's Place **11** *A1*
Piccolo **12** *C1*
Pizza B&B **13** *B2*
Pizzería Landauro **14** *D2*
Sabor Salud **15** *D1*
Siam de Los Andes **16** *C3*

Bars & clubs
13 Buhos **19** *B3*
Amadeus **17** *D2*
Makondo's **19** *B3*
Monttrek Disco **18** *D2*
Taberna Tambo **21** *B2*

plus a TV lounge with DVDs make this a good place to recuperate after a tough adventure in the mountains.

D **Albergue Churup**, Jr Figueroa 1257, T043-422584, www.churup.com. Price includes breakfast and bath, **F** in dormitory without breakfast, hot water, nice fire in the attractive sitting room on 4th floor, internet (including wireless) access in the private rooms, cafeteria, use of kitchen, sauna and massage room, roof terrace, lots of information, luggage store, laundry, book exchange, English spoken, Spanish classes, extremely helpful. Recommended.

D **Apu Wasi**, Jr Federico Sal y Rosas 820, T043-426035, h_apuwasi@yahoo.com. Modern but simple hotel. All rooms have TV, private bathrooms and very comfortable beds. Standard price includes a basic breakfast. Discounts for longer stays.

D **Hostal Montañero**, Plaza Ginebra 30-B, T/F043-426386, www.trekkingperu.com. Price includes breakfast. Hot water, comfortable, clean, friendly and a good contact point for quality mountain and trekking guides. Also climbing equipment rental and sales.

D **Olaza Guesthouse**, J Argüedas 1242, T043-422529, www.andeanexplorer.com. Run by Tito Olaza and recently upgraded with minimalist but very comfortable rooms. Safe, stylish, luggage stored, nice terrace with views, breakfast included. Pickup from bus station with room reservation. Downstairs there's an office for **Mountain Bike Adventures** (see page 340), run by Julio Olaza. They have a second office closer to the centre at Jr Lúcar y Torre 530.

D-E **Alojamiento Soledad**, Jr Amadeo Figueroa 1267, T043-421196, ghsoledad @hotmail.com. Price includes breakfast and bath, some hard beds, hot water, kitchen, use of internet, family-run and friendly, secure, trekking information given. Higher prices in high season.

E **Angeles Inn**, Av Gamarra 815, T043-422205, solandperu@yahoo.com. No sign, look for **Sol Andino** travel agency in same building (www.solandino.com). Kitchen and laundry facilities, small garden, hot water. Owners Max and Saul Angeles are official guides, helpful with trekking and climbing, equipment hire.

E **Edward's Inn**, Bolognesi 121, T/F043-422692, www.edwardsinn.com. Cheaper without bath, clean, nice garden, laundry, friendly, breakfast extra, insist on proper rates in low season, popular. Edward speaks English and has 30 years' experience trekking, climbing and guiding in the area. He also rents gear. Highly recommended.

E **La Casa de Zarela**, J Arguedas 1263, T043-421694, www.lacasadezarela.com. With bath, hot water, breakfast available, use of kitchen, laundry facilities, owner Zarela, who speaks English, organizes groups and is very knowledgeable, stores luggage, has a nice terrace.

E **Schatzi**, Bolívar 419, near Raimondi, T043-423074, www.schatzihostal.com. Clean and welcoming, nice courtyard, rooms with bathroom, hot water, breakfast (extra) served in the café in front. Limited facilities for the price.

E-F **Hostal Galaxia**, Jr de la Cruz Romero 638, T043-422230. Cheaper without bathroom, hot water, rooftop café, laundry facilities, basic, friendly. Rooms clean but in need of redecoration at the time of writing.

E-F **Hatun Wasi**, Jr Daniel Villayzán 268, T043-425055, www.hatunwasi.net. New hotel opened by a friendly family, next door to **Jo's Place**. Clean, spacious rooms, all with private bathroom and hot water. Also has a very pleasant roof terrace, ideal for breakfasts, with great views of the Cordillera.

E-F **The Way Inn Hostel**, Jr Buenaventura Mendoza 821, near Parque Fap, www.thewayinn.com. Run by Alex and Bruni. Dorms and private rooms available; all mattresses are orthopaedic. Fully functioning kitchen (including oven and fridge), huge video library, laundry facilities, camping equipment for hire, free information on treks, places to eat, hanging out/etc, sauna and steam room. Good place to meet other travellers. Also see **The Way Inn Lodge** under the same management (above).

F **Alojamiento Marilia**, Sucre 1123, T043-428160, alojamaril@latinmail.com. Good views, modern, clean rooms with bath, **G** without bath, also dormitories, hot water, breakfast available, kitchen facilities, luggage store, knowledgeable, friendly owners.

For an explanation of sleeping and eating price codes used in this guide, see inside the front cover. Other relevant information is found in Essentials, pages 53-58.

F **Alojamiento Nemy's**, Jr Figueroa 1135, T043-422949. Secure, hot shower, breakfast US$2.40, good for climbers, luggage store. Recommended.

F **Alojamiento Norma**, Pasaje Valenzuela 837 (Hostal 'NG' on the sign), near Plaza Belén, T043-421831, www.residencialng.com. G per person, includes breakfast, cheaper without bathroom, hot water, good value, friendly. Recommended.

F **Familia Meza**, Lúcar y Torre 538, T043-426367, familiameza_lodging@hotmail.com. Shared bath, hot water, use of kitchen and laundry facilities, terrace with view, popular with trekkers, mountaineers and bikers.

F **Hostal Estoico**, San Martín 635, T043-422371. Cheaper without bathroom, friendly, clean, safe, hot water, laundry facilities, good value. Recommended.

F **Hostal Gyula**, Parque Ginebra 632, opposite the Casa de Guías, T043-421567, hostal_gyula_inn@yahoo.com. With bathroom, hot water, cheaper in dorm-style rooms, very friendly and helpful, information on tours, stores luggage. Noisy at weekends.

F **Hostal Quintana**, Jr Mcal A Cáceres 411, T043-426060, www.geocities.com/hostal_quintana/. Cheaper without bathroom, hot shower, laundry facilities, clean, basic, stores luggage, breakfast extra, friendly, popular with trekkers. **Mountclimb** climbing and rental agency next door is owned by the same family. Recommended.

F **Hostal Tany**, Lúcar y Torre 468A, T043-422534. With bathroom, cheaper without, hot water, clean, friendly but rather old fashioned, money exchange, tours, café/restaurant.

F **Jo's Place**, Jr Daniel Villayzan 276, T043-425505, www.josplacehuaraz.com. Safe, hot water at night, kitchen facilities, mountain views, garden, terrace, warm atmosphere, English owner Jo and his very partner Vickie are good sources of information with plenty of advice on trekking and climbing in the area. Popular meeting point for climbers. Highly recommended.

F **La Cabaña**, Jr Sucre 1224, T043-423428, www.huaraz.com/lacabana. Shared and double rooms, hot showers, cable TV, small breakfast included, laundry, kitchen, computer, DVD, very friendly, popular, safe for parking, bikes and luggage, English and French spoken, very good value.

F **Lodging Caroline** , Urb Avitentel Mz D – Lt 1, T043-422588. Price includes breakfast, free pickup from bus station (phone in advance), hot water, kitchen facilities, tourist information and guides, laundry, very helpful. Frequently recommended.

F **Lodging Casa Sucre**, Sucre 1240, T043-422264, filibertor@terra.com.pe. Private house, with bath, kitchen, laundry facilities, friendly, clean, hot water, English, French and German spoken. Mountaineering guide, Filiberto Rurush, can be contacted here.

F **Oscar's Hostal**, La Mar 624, T/F043-422720, cvmonical@hotmail.com. With bathroom, hot water, cheap breakfast next door, good beds, helpful, cheaper in low season. Recommended.

F-G **Alojamiento El Jacal**, Jr Sucre 1044, T043-424612, reservaseljacal@yahoo.es. With or without shower, hot water, nice family, use of kitchen, internet, garden, luggage store, laundry, good value, popular.

F-G **Casa Jansy's**, Jr Sucre 948. Hot water, meals, laundry, owner Jesús Rivera Lúcar is a mountain guide. Recommended.

F-G per person **Cayesh Guesthouse**, Jr Julián de Morales 867, T043-428821, www.cayesh.net. Comfortable new hostel with good location, efficient solar hot water system, kitchen and TV lounge with over 250 DVDs. Owner is an enthusiastic climber and happy to provide advice on potential routes in the Cordilleras.

G per person **Casa de Jaimes**, Alberto Gridilla 267, T043-422281, www.casajaimes.com. Friendly and cheap. 1 hr free internet use per day, laundry facilities and cheap laundry service, has maps and books of the region, equipment rental, use of kitchen, popular with Israelis. Noisy but recommended.

G **Hostal Continental**, 28 de Julio 586, nr Plaza de Armas, T043-424171. With bath, clean, hot water, friendly, cafeteria serving good breakfasts. Recommended but avoid the rooms overlooking the street as there are 2 noisy *peñas* nearby.

G **La Estancia**, Jr Huaylas 162, Centenario, T043-423183. With shared shower only, luggage store, safe motorcycle parking, pleasant garden, good value.

G per person **Backpackers**, Av Raimondi 510, T043-429101, http://huaraz.com/backpackers. Breakfast not included. Spacious, hot showers, good views, very friendly, a real bargain.

G per person **Casa de Familia Gómez Díaz**, Jr Eulogio del Río 1983, T043-423224. Hot water, quiet, family atmosphere, good beds.
G per person **Lodging House Ezama**, Mariano Melgar 623, Independencia, T043-423490, 15 mins' walk from Plaza de Armas (US$0.50 by taxi). Light, spacious rooms, hot water, safe, helpful.

Youth hostels
G per person **Alojamiento Alpes Andes**, at **Casa de Guías**, Plaza Ginebra 28-g, T043- 421811, casa_de_guias@hotmail.com. Member of the Peruvian Youth Hostel Association, 1 dormitory with 14 beds and another with 6 beds, hot water, with very good restaurant (open 0700-1100, 1700-2300), laundry, free luggage store, the owner Sr López speaks English, French and German and is very helpful, he is the mountain guides administrator.
G per person **Albergue El Tambo**, Confraternidad Internacional Interior 122-B, T043-425114, marielafm@yahoo.com. Shared bath, free coffee and tea, laundry service, use of kitchen and pizza oven, book exchange, luggage store, safe, owner Mariela is very helpful and bakes delicious chocolates enhanced with coca extract. A real bargain but a little difficult to find down a back alley just to the south of Av Raymondi.

Around Huaraz *p332*
A-C The Lazy Dog Inn, 3.1 km past the town of Marian, close to the Quebrada Cojup and the boundary of Huascarán National Park, T043-9789330, www.thelazydoginn.com. Eco-tourism lodge built with local materials, manpower and support. Actively involved in community projects. Beautifully designed in warm colours, each room with its own design. The lodge is constructed with adobe bricks and features water recycling systems and composting toilets. Great location gives access to several fabulous, little-visited mountain valleys. Friendly owners Wayne and Diana can organize horse-riding and hiking trips into the mountains. Excellent home cooking on request. 30 mins' drive from Huaraz (US$8-10 by taxi).
B El Patio, Av Monterrey, 250 m downhill from the Monterrey baths, T043-424965, www.elpatio.com.pe. Very classy hotel with lovely gardens and comfortable rooms, some with balconies; also a couple of bungalows (**A**). Meals on request, bar, friendly, colonial-style. Recommended.
C-D Baños Termales Monterrey, Av Monterrey, at the top of the hill in Monterrey, T/F043-427690, realhotelmonterrey @yahoo.com. Slightly run down but classic old spa, beautiful garden and use of pools, restaurant, bar. Good location for walking. There is a rock face behind the hotel which is used for climbing practice. Very good value.
D The Way Inn Lodge, www.theway inn.com. Excellent lodge located at 3712 m, close to the border of Huascarán National Park. Dorm rooms and camping **F** and **G** respectively; accommodation includes an excellent breakfast. 60% of vegetables are grown on site and the lodge is aiming to be as self-sustaining as possible. Many activities available, from paragliding to yoga classes and mountain biking. Good place to chill and acclimatize yourself for the mountains.
E El Nogal, Jr Los Libertadores 106, close to El Patio and the **Baños Termales Monterrey**, T043-425929. New friendly hotel with good-value, pleasant rooms, especially on 2nd floor.

Eating

Huaraz *p330, maps p331 and p334*
For local dishes, such as *pachamanca*, go to C José Olaya at the weekend, where stalls are set up.
TTT **Crêperie Patrick**, Luzuriaga 422. Tasty crêpes, fish, quiche, spaghetti and good wine.
TTT **Huaraz Querido**, Bolívar 981. Excellent *cevichería*.
TTT **Monte Rosa**, J de la Mar 661. 1000-2300. Pizzería, also fondue and other Swiss dishes. Swiss owner is Victorinox representative, offering knives for sale and repair also Suunto (altimeters, GPS), mountain gear and excellent postcards. Rents snowboards and skis and has climbing and trekking books.
TTT **Pizza Bruno**, Luzuriaga 834. 1600-2300. Excellent pizzas, crêpes and pastries, good service. French owner Bruno Reviron also has a 4WD with driver for hire.
TTT **Siam de Los Andes**, Gamarra corner J de Morales. Authentic Thai cuisine, not cheap, but tasty and with a wide range of dishes, as mild or spicy as you desire. There is a nice fireplace, too. Recommended.

ŸŸ **Alpes Andes**, Plaza Ginebra in Casa de Guías. Muesli, yoghurt etc in the morning, pastas and pizzas in the evening.

ŸŸ **Bistro de los Andes**, J de Morales 823 and Plaza de Armas 2nd floor, T/F043-426249 /429556. Good food, owner speaks English, French and German. Plaza branch has a nice panoramic view of the plaza. Very wide range of dishes including breakfasts, meats, pastas and curries – even Peruvian dishes if you look hard enough. Recommended.

ŸŸ **Chilli Heaven**, Parque Ginebra, just up from the Casa de Guías. Great curries, Indian, Thai, or otherwise and filling burritos, chillies – the works. In fact anyone who appreciates a bit of spice will enjoy this snug new, very popular restaurant and its wares. Good pizza and the desserts are mouth-watering as well.

ŸŸ **El Horno, Pizzería Grill**, Parque del Periodista, T043-424617. Good atmosphere, fine grilled meats and nice location overlooking the Parque del Periodista.

ŸŸ **El Rinconcito Minero**, J de Morales 757. Breakfast, good value at lunchtime (including vegetarian), coffee and snacks, popular for good food and service, also has a video bar.

ŸŸ **Fuente de Salud**, J de la Mar 562. Vegetarian, also meat and pasta dishes, good soups, excellent fruit salads and smoothies, breakfasts. Recommended.

ŸŸ **Monttrek Pizza Pub**, Luzuriaga 646 (upstairs from the agency). Good pizzas and pastas, indoor climbing wall, shows videos.

ŸŸ **Pachamama**, San Martín 687. Bar, café and restaurant, concerts, art gallery, garden, nice place to relax, good toilets, pool table and table-tennis, information on treks, Swiss-owned. Recommended.

ŸŸ **Pepe's Place**, Raymondi 624, good pizza, chicken, meat, warm atmosphere, run by Pepe from Residencial Cataluña.

ŸŸ **Piccolo**, J de Morales 632. Pizzería, very popular with gringos.

ŸŸ **Pizza B&B**, La Mar beside laundry of same name. Pizza is excellent, as is their dessert specialty *tarte flambée*, wood oven, pleasant decor and atmosphere, attentive service. Recommended.

ŸŸ **Pizzería Landauro**, Sucre, on corner of Plaza de Armas. Good for pizzas, nice vibe.

ŸŸ **Sabor Salud**, Luzuriaga 672, upstairs. Restaurant and pizzería specializing in vegetarian and Italian food.

ŸŸ-Ÿ **Chifa Jim Hua**, Luzuriaga 645, upstairs. Large, tasty portions, *menú* US$1.15 and a wide variety of other Peruvian-Chinese dishes. Mon-Sat 0900-1500, 1800-2400, Sun 1800-2200.

ŸŸ-Ÿ **Encuentro**, Parque Ginebra, off Luzuriaga cuadra 6. Opens 0700 for breakfast, serves good lunches and dinners, very busy, try the fillet mignon. Recommended.

Ÿ **El Querubín**, J de Morales 767. Clean, friendly, good breakfast and set meals (high season only), also vegetarian, snacks and à la carte, very good, decorated with nice regional paintings. Recommended.

Ÿ **Las Puyas**, Morales 535. Popular with gringos, serves an excellent *sopa criolla* and very good trout, also serves breakfast.

Ÿ **Vegetarian Food**, Sucre y Av Bolívar. Excellent vegetarian, 3-course meal US$1.

Cafés

Café Andino, Lúcar y Torre 538, T043-421203, cafeandino@hotmail.com. American-run café and book exchange, great coffee and food, including very good curries, extensive lending library in many languages, a nice place to relax and write postcards, great atmosphere, and a good meeting place. The café's owner, Chris, organizes treks in cordilleras Blanca and Huayhuash, lots of advice offered. Recommended.

Café El Centro, 28 de Julio 592. Good breakfast for US$1.30-2, great chocolate cake and apple pie.

Cafetería y Juguería, Sucre 806. Cheap café just above the Plaza. Serves excellent yogurt and honey drinks, among other treats.

California Café, Jr 28 de Julio 562, T043-428354. A rival to **Café Andino** in all but the view, California offers perhaps the best breakfast in town, great coffee and chocolate cake that can only be described as dangerous! Oh yes, and there's a book exchange, library, games and some comfortable sofas into the bargain.

Comedor 14, San Martín 525. Good-value breakfasts, sandwiches, teas, etc.

Las Tulpas y Chimichurri, J de Morales 756, between Luzuriaga y Bolívar. Open 0730-2300, nice garden. Good breakfasts and good value lunchtime menu, keen to promote Peruvian cuisine with Western standards of presentation. Good fish, excellent *lomo saltado*. Recommended.

Panadería Ancash, Raymondi cuadra 7. Different types of bread, including integral, cakes, ice cream.
Panadería La Alameda, Juan de La Cruz Romero 523 near market. Excellent bread and sweets.
Panadería Montserrat, Av Luzuriaga 928, T043-426260. Bakery and café, pleasant atmosphere, lots of cakes and *empanadas*, sausage rolls etc. Good for a snack.
Panadería Robles, Bolívar 479. Sells good bread that keeps well on treks.
Samuels, José de la Mar y Luzuriaga. Great ice cream.

Around Huaraz *p332*
There are several country-style restaurants in Monterrey which are popular with locals and busy at weekends, serving trout, *pachamanca* and other regional specialities. There are several cheaper restaurants and stands along Av Monterrey.
TT El Cortijo, Monterrey, along the Huaraz–Caraz road at Km 6.5. Serves very good food, eg chicken and barley stew, and *anticuchos*.

Bars and clubs

Huaraz *p330, maps p331 and p334*
13 Buhos Bar, José de la Mar 2nd floor, just above Makondo's. Funky, popular bar with good range of tunes, snacks and plenty of games. Owner is Lucho, tall in reality and big on personality… with a hat like Indian Jones.
Amadeus, Parque Ginebra, bar-disco.
Chacraraju/Chill-out Bar, Jr Sucre 959, next of the agency of the same name. Good pizzas, good atmosphere, and, on occasion, a good DJ or two.
Extreme, Jr Gabino Uribe near Luzuriaga. Upstairs bar, popular with gringos. 1900-0200.
La Cascada, Luzuriaga 1276, disco tavern.
Makondo's, José de la Mar opposite Cruz del Sur bus station. Disco, bar and nightclub, safe, popular.
Monttrek Disco, Sucre just off Plaza de Armas, in a converted cinema, reasonable prices.
Taberna Tambo, José de la Mar 776, daily 1000-1600 and 2000 till late. Folk music and disco. Full-on, non-stop dance mecca. Very popular with both locals and gringos, although the music can lack variety.
Vagamundo, J de Morales 753. Popular bar with snacks and football tables.

Entertainment

Huaraz *p330, maps p331 and p334*
Cinema
Huaraz Satyricon, Luzuriaga 1036, T043-9557343. American-run café and movie theatre, big screen, comfortable sofas, chocolate chip cookies and falafel sandwiches, US$1.20. Movies range from 1960s' classics to cutting-edge Latin American, plus occasional showings of *Touching the Void*, the film set and partially shot in the Huayhuash.

Festivals and events

Huaraz *p330, maps p331 and p334*
Mar/Apr Semana Santa (Holy Week) is widely celebrated and always colourful and lively.
3 May El Señor de la Soledad, the town's patron saint's day, marks the start of a week of parades, dancing, music, fireworks and much drinking.
Jun Semana del Andinismo is an international climbing and skiing week.
Last week of Jun San Juan and San Pedro are celebrated throughout the region. On the eve of San Juan fires are lit throughout the valley to burn the chaff from the harvest. The following day the valley is thick with smoke.

Shopping

Huaraz *p330, maps p331 and p334*
Climbing and trekking equipment
For equipment rental, see Activities and tours, below.
Tatoo, on Parque Ginebra, T043-422966, www.tatoo.ws. Good shop for climbing and outdoor clothes and gear, locally produced and international brands.

Food and drink
The central market offers a wide variety of canned and dry goods, including nuts and dried fruit, as well as fresh fruit and vegetables. Be sure to check expiry dates. Also be sure to leave all valuables in a safe place when shopping in the market; pickpockets abound.
Ortiz, Luzuriaga 401 corner Raymondi. A well-stocked supermarket with a good selection of items, but expensive.
Rosa Rosita, Jr San Martín, ½ block from Morales. Local cheese and *manjarblanco*.

Handicrafts

Local sweaters, hats, gloves, ceramics and wall hangings can be bought from stalls on Pasaje Mcal Cáceres just off Luzuriaga, in the stalls off Luzuriaga between Morales and Sucre, on Bolívar cuadra 6 and elsewhere.

Andean Expressions, Jr J Arguedas 1246, near La Soledad church, T043-422951, olaza@qnet.com.pe 0800-2200, run by Lucho, Mauro and Beto Olaza, and recommended for hand-printed T-shirts and sweatshirts with unusual motifs.

La Perla, Sr Enrique Salazar Salas, Jr San Martín 574. Handmade cowboy-style boots can be made to fit in 3 days for about US$80.

Shumaq Maki, Lucar y Torre next to **Café Andino**. Good quality crafts.

Photography

Foto Galería Andes, at Pasaje Cayetano Requena, near the market. Good for camera repairs. Sells professional photos of the Cordillera Blanca.

Activities and tours

Huaraz *p330, maps p331 and p334*

Huaraz is overflowing with agencies and quality varies. Try to get a recommendation from someone who has recently returned from a tour, climb or trek. All agencies run conventional tours to **Llanganuco**, **Pastoruri** (both US$10 per person, both very long days) and **Chavín** (8-10 hrs, US$6-10 per person), entry tickets not included. Many hire equipment and also offer climbing and trekking tours and ski instruction. **Note** Tour agencies shouldn't recommend Pastoruri as a first trip. It's best to go to Llanganuco first to acclimatize.

Equipment hire

For general information, see page 329.

The **Casa de Guías** (see page 329) rents equipment and sells dried food. The following agencies are also recommended for hiring gear: **Andean Kingdom**; **Andean Sport Tours**; **Galaxia Expeditions**, **Monttrek**; **Kallpa** (see page 340 for their addresses). Also try **Skyline**, T043-427097, www.sladventureschool.com; **Montañero**, Parque Ginebra 30-B, T043-426386, andeway@terra.com.pe, and **MountClimb**, Jr Mcal Cáceres 421, T043-426060, mount climb@yahoo.com.

Horseriding

Sr Robinson Ayala Gride, T043-423813. Contact him well in advance for half-day trips (enquire at **El Cortijo** restaurant, page 339). He is a master *paso* rider.

Posada de Yungar, at Yungar (about 20 km on the Carhuaz road), T043-421267, 967 9836 (mob). Swiss run.

Ask for José Flores or Gustavo Soto. US$4.50 per hr on nice horses; good 4-hr trip in the Cordillera Negra with fabulous views.

Mountain biking

The Callejón de Huaylas offers superb variety for mountain bikers, from one-day routes to popular attractions to longer trails through agricultural land, over bridges and into traditional villages. More demanding are the routes over the Cordillera Negra to the Pacific coast and, toughest of the lot, the energy-sapping, highly exhilarating climbs over 5000-m passes beneath the snow peaks of the Cordillera Blanca.

A typical circuit is Huaraz–Recuay–Chavín–Huari–San Luis–Chacas–Punta Olímpica which lasts two days; or returning through Quebrada Llanganuco, lasting 6 days. Camping gear is needed. Local tour and trekking agencies can supply bikes, guides and full back-up, including driving you up some of the steepest bits if your leg muscles can't cope.

Mountain Bike Adventures, Lúcar y Torre 530, T043-424259, www.chakinaniperu.com. Contact Julio Olaza. US$20 for 5 hrs, various routes. Julio speaks excellent English and also runs a book exchange, sells topo maps and climbing books. Recommended for its two-wheeled exploits and excellent standard of equipment.

Mountain guides

For further information, visit the **Casa de Guías** (see page 329). The guides listed below are not necessarily members of AGMP but are recommended for their mountaineering expertise.

Ted Alexander, Skyline Adventures, T043-427097, www.sladventureschool.com. American Outward Bound instructor, very knowledgeable, lots of information.

Koky Castañeda, La Casa de Zarela, T043-421694 (or through **Café Andino**). Speaks English and French, AGMP certified.

Aritza Monasterio, through **Casa de Guías**. Speaks English, Spanish and Euskerra.
Augusto Ortega, Jr San Martín 1004, T043-424888. The only Peruvian to have climbed Everest.
Filiberto Rurush Paucar, Lodging Casa Sucre, Sucre 1240, T043-422264. Speaks English, Spanish and Quechua.
Hugo and César Sifuentes Maguiña, Siex (Sifuentes Expeditions), Jr Huaylas 139, T043-426529, www.siexperu.org. César speaks English and a little French.

Parapenting and hang gliding

Launch sites near Huaraz are the Puca Ventana near the Mirador, or from Churup-Pitec.

River rafting and canoeing

Rafting on the Río Santa is available (US$15 for half a day), year round, Grade 2-3, not particularly special whitewater, but in a pretty setting. Most agencies provide food, transport, mules and guides. Prices tend to be 20% less during low season, Oct-Apr.
Ario Ferri, T043-961 3058/963 5920 (mob, between 1800-2000), www.yurakyaku.com, www.naturavive.com, or contact through **Café Andino**. Multilingual rafting guide and certified kayak instructor. Also a well-regarded climbing and hiking guide.

Trekking and climbing

Trekking tours cost US$40-70 per person per day; climbing US$90-140 per person per day. Prices vary a great deal. Ask tour agencies, independent guides and the **Casa de Guías** about rock-climbing courses at Monterrey (behind **Hotel Baños Termales Monterrey**, see page 332), Chancos, Recuay and Huanchac (30 mins' walk from Huaraz), and about ice climbing on Vallanaraju and Pastoruri (for example). Jatun Machay in the Cordillera Negra is another fabulous spot for rock climbing and bouldering, be it at beginner level or if you are an experienced climber looking for a serious challenge.
Active Peru, Av Gamarra 699, T043-423339, www.activeperu.com. Friendly agency offering the classic treks, climbing, plus the standard tours to Chavín, Pastoruri and Llanganuco, among others.
Andean Kingdom, Luzuriaga 522, www.andeankingdom.com. Free information, maps, climbing wall, rock and ice climbing, including multi-day courses, treks, equipment rental, very helpful, English and some Hebrew spoken, can be very busy. The company is building a lodge near the excellent rock climbing site of Hatun Machay in the Cordillera Negra. They should be moving to a new Huaraz office for 2007: Jr San Martín 613, p 2, T043-425555.
Andean Sport Tours, Luzuriaga 571, T043-421612. Have a basic practice wall behind the office. They also organize mountain bike tours, ski instruction and river rafting.
Andeno Viaggio, Av Luzuriaga 627, T043-428047, www.andenoviaggio.com. Offers the usual range of day tours (Llanganuco, Pastoruri, Chavin) plus trekking and climbing, reputable.
Andescamp, Malecón Sur 310 (Río Quillkay), T043-428214, www.andescamp.com. Popular new agency, especially with budget travellers. Frank Beteta states that he uses only qualified guides for climbing trips. There's also a great variety of treks on offer, from the 9-12 day Huayhuash circuit to

Olleros to Chavín over 3 days, plus rafting, paragliding and more.

Chacraraju Expeditions, Jr José de Sucre No.959, T043-426172, www.chacraraju expedition.com. Tours and equipment for hire, plus a small climbing wall and the aptly named **Chill-out Bar** next door.

Cordillera Blanca Adventures, run by the Mejía Romero family, T043-424352. Experienced, quality climbing and trekking trips, good guides and equipment.

Explorandes, Av Centenario 489, T043-421960, postmast@exploran.com.pe.

Galaxia Expeditions, Jr Mariscal Cáceres 428, T043-425691, galaxia_expeditions @hotmail.com. Reputable agency with the usual range of tours, equipment hire, etc.

Huascarán, Jr Figueroa 1257 (below **Albergue Churup**), T043-424504, peru huascaran@yahoo.com. Contact Pablo Tinoco Depaz. 4-day Santa Cruz trip recommended. Good food and equipment, professional and friendly service, free loan of waterproofs and *pisco sour* on last evening. Recommended.

Kallpa, José de la Mar y Luzuriaga, p 2, T043-427868, www.peruviantrek.com. Organizes treks, rents gear, arranges *arrieros* and mules, very helpful.

Montañero, Parque Ginebra 30-B, T043-426386, www.trekkingperu.com. Run by veteran mountain guide Selio Villón, German, French and English spoken.

Monttrek, Luzuriaga 646, upstairs, T043-421124, F426976. Good trekking and climbing information, advice and maps, ice and rock climbing courses (at Monterrey), tours to Laguna Churup and the 'spectacular' Luna Llena tour; they also hire out mountain bikes, run ski instruction and trips, and river rafting. Helpful, conscientious guides. Next door in the Pizzería is a climbing wall, good maps, videos and slide shows. For new routes and maps contact Porfirio Cacha Macedo, 'Pocho', at **Monttrek** or at Jr Corongo 307, T423930.

Peruvian Andes Adventures, José Olaya 532, T043-421864, www.peruvianandes.com, www.perutrekkingclimbing.com. Run by Hisao and Eli Morales, with an agency in New Zealand, professional, registered mountain and trekking guides. All equipment and services for treks of 3-15 days, climbing technical and non-technical peaks, or just day walks. Vegetarians catered for.

Trekking guides

Max and Saul Angeles, T043-422205 (Sol Andino travel agency), speaks some English, knows the Huayhuash well.

Christopher Benway, La Cima Logistics, T043-421203, cafeandino@hotmail.com. Organizes treks in the Huayhuash. Chris is the owner of **Café Andino**, so usually easy to track down, plus very friendly and helpful.

Vladimiro and Máximo Hinostrosa, at **Mountain Shop Chacraraju**, T043-969 2395, trekking guides with knowledge of the entire region.

Tjen Verheye, Jr Carlos Valenzuela 911, T043-422569, is Belgian and speaks Dutch, French, German and reasonable English, runs trekking and conventional tours and is knowledgeable about the Chavín culture.

Genaro Yanac Olivera, T043-422825, speaks good English and some German, also a climbing guide.

Tour operators

It is difficult and pricey to purchase airline tickets in Huaraz. Best to do so in Lima.

Chavín Tours, Luzuriaga 502, T043-421578, F424801. Local tours, long-standing agency.

Pablo Tours, Luzuriaga 501, T043-421142. Local tours, with many years of operation.

Transport

Huaraz *p330, maps p331 and p334*

Bus

Many bus companies have offices selling tickets in the centre, but buses leave from the edge of the centre. Several buses and minivans run daily, 0500-2000, to **Caraz**, 1¼ hrs, US$1.35, stopping at all the places in between. They depart from the parking area under the bridge on Fitzcarrald and from the open space beside the bridge on the other side of the river (beware of thieves here).

To **Chavín**, 110 km, 2 hrs (sit on left side for best views), US$3. Service provided by **Chavín Express**, Mcal Cáceres 338, T043-424652, 3 a day, Sun 1500, and by **Trans Río Mosna**, Tarapacá 576, T043-426632, daily 0700 and 1300. Both have buses that go on to **Huari**, 6 hrs, US$5, and **Llamellín**, 8 hrs, US$7.

To **Chacas** (US$3.75) and **San Luis** (US$5.75), at 0700 with **Virgen de Guadalupe**, Caraz 607. **Renzo**, Raymondi 821, T043-424915, runs to Chacas and San Luis (0615

Mon-Sat, 0645 Sun), **Yanama, Piscobamba** and **Pomabamba** (0630, best). Los Andes, same office as Yungay Express, T043-427362, daily 0630 to **Yungay**, US$0.75, **Lagunas de Llanganuco**, US$3.45, **Yanama**, US$3.45, **Piscobamba**, US$5.20 and **Pomabamba**, US$6 (8 hrs). This route also served by **Copa**, J de Morales y Lúcar y Torre, daily 0630 and 1430; **Transvir**, Caraz y Comercio, daily 1400 (continuing to **Sihuas**), and **La Perla de Alta Mayo**, daily 0630, 8hrs to Pomabamba, US$6. To **Sihuas**, also **Chavín Express**, Tue and Fri 0800; **Perú Andino**, 1 a week, 8 hrs, US$7.

Colectivos to **Recuay**, US$0.45, **Ticapampa** and **Catac**, US$0.55, leave daily 0500-2100, from Gridilla, just off Tarapacá (Terminal Terrestre Transportistas Zona Sur).

To **Chiquián** for the Cordillera Huayhuash, 120 km, 3½ hrs: **El Rápido**, at Bolognesi 216, T043-422887, at 1345, and **Chiquián Tours**, on Tarapacá behind the market.

To **Huallanca** (Huánuco), along a paved road through Conococha, Chiquián and Aquia to Huansala, then good dirt road to Huallanca and **La Unión**. Departs Huaraz 0800, 1300, 1500, 6 hrs, with **Trans El Rápido**, Bolognesi 216, T043-422887. Also **Virgen de Guadalupe**, Caraz 607, to **La Unión**, US$4.35 at 0700.

To **Lima**, 420 km, 7-8 hrs, US$6-14. The road is in good condition. There is a large selection of buses to Lima, both ordinary service and luxury coaches, with departures throughout the day. Many of the companies have their offices along Av Raymondi and on Jr Lúcar y Torre. Some recommended companies are: **Cruz del Sur**, Bolívar y José de la Mar, T043-423969; **Transportes Rodríguez**, Tarapacá 622, T043-421353; **Civa**, Morales opposite Lúcar y Torre; **Móvil Tours**, Bolívar 452, T043-422555; **Empresa 14**, Fitzcarrald 216, T043-421282, terminal at Bolívar 407.

To **Casma** via the Callán pass and Pariacoto, 150 km, 7 hrs, US$6, the lower section of the road is very poor, landslides and closures are common (sit on the left for best views, as long as you don't mind precipices): **Transportes Huandoy**, Fitzcarrald 261, T043-427507 (terminal at Caraz 820), daily 0800, 1000 and 1300; **Yungay Express**, Raymondi 744, T043-424377, 3 a day, continuing to **Chimbote**, 185 km. To **Chimbote** via Caraz and the Cañón del Pato (sit on the right for the most exciting views; see page), with **Yungay Express**, daily, US$7, 10 hrs. Other companies go to **Chimbote** , US$6, 7 hrs, via **Pativilca**, 160 km, 4 hrs, US$3.50, and most continue to **Trujillo**, 8-9 hrs, US$8.60; all buses depart at night: **Chinchaysuyo**, J de Morales 650, T043-426417; **Línea**, Simón Bolívar 450, T043-426666; **Empresa 14** and **Móvil Tours**, addresses above.

Taxi

The standard fare for a taxi in town is about US$0.60, US$0.70 at night. The fare to Monterrey or Huanchac is US$1.45. Radio taxis T043-421482 or T043-422512.

Directory

Huaraz *p330, maps p331 and p334*

Banks BBVA, on the Plaza de Armas, cash withdrawals in soles and US$. **BCP**, on the Plaza de Armas, closed 1300- 1630, changes cash, 3.25% commission on TCs into soles, good rates, 5% commission charged on TCs into dollars, cash advance on Visa, very long queues, 2 ATMs (Visa). **Interbank**, on Plaza de Armas, cash and TCs (no commission into soles), MasterCard ATM. **Banco Wiese**, Sucre 766, changes cash and cheques. **Casa de Cambio Oh Na Nay**, across the street from Interbank, good rates for US$, but poor for other currencies. There are several other *casas de cambio* and many street changers (be careful) on Luzuriaga. **Internet** Ubiquitous, US$0.30 per hr. Cafés usually offer video phones, scanning, CD burning and printing services. Since equipment is constantly changing it is best to find your own favourite spot; you should have plenty of choice. Phonecalls to Europe or North America are sometimes possible from US$0.15 per min. **Laundry** B & B, La Mar 674. US$1.20 per kg, special machine for down garments and sleeping bags, French run. Recommended. **Huaraz**, on the plaza on Mcal Cáceres, next to Galaxia Mountain Shop. **Lavandería Liz**, Bolívar 711, US$2 per kg, also at the **Casa de Guías** (see page 329). **Laundry Express** at JM Expediciones, between Luzuriaga and Plaza Ginebra. **Takshar**, Jr Bolívar 617, next-day service, US$1 per kg. **Post** Serpost is on Luzuriaga 702, daily 0800-2000. **Telephone Telefónica**, Sucre y Bolívar, corner of Plaza de Armas. National and international phone and fax, daily 0700-2300. Private calling centres along Luzuriaga. Many coin phones.

North from Huaraz

The road north out of Huaraz goes through the beautiful Callejón de Huaylas, giving access to some wonderful treks which go up into, or over the mountains of the Cordillera Blanca. Caraz, the focus of the northern end of the valley, is less hectic than Huaraz, but is just as good a place to stay. It is definitely worth spending some time in this area. » For Sleeping, Eating and other listings, see pages 355-360.

Huaraz to Caraz » pp355-360. Colour map 3, B2/3.

There are frequent small buses running up and down the Callejón from Huaraz and in between the towns en route. The main road north from Huaraz through the **Callejón de Huaylas** goes to **Taricá** (not to be confused with Tarica at the north end of the Cordillera Blanca), where there is a home pottery industry. Good-value purchases can be made from Francisco Zargosa Cordero.

Marcará and the Huandoy valley

The next town is **Marcará**, 26 km from Huaraz (one hour, US$0.45), where there are a couple of hotels, basic restaurants and shops. Pick-ups and *colectivos* go east from Marcará along a branch road 3 km to **Chancos**, a little settlement with hot baths. There is an uninviting lukewarm pool (US$0.45) here, as well as some none-too-clean private tubs (US$0.90) and very popular natural steam baths in caves (US$1.35 per person). The caves are interesting and worth a try, with locked changing rooms (cave 5 is the smallest and hottest). Just before the hot springs, on the left-hand side of the road, is a very good 10-m climbing wall (free), with bolts and anchor chains in place. There is accommodation in the shape of two very basic *alojamientos* and there are also several basic restaurants and food stalls.

From Chancos the road and transport continue to **Vicos**, 3 km further up the Huandoy valley. Vicos is 7 km from Marcará (US$0.30) in superb surroundings, with views of Nevados Tocllaraju and Ranrapalca. To hike from Chancos to Vicos takes about two hours up the valley through farmland. A trail leads from Vicos to Laguna Lejíacocha, taking four hours. There are archaeological sites nearby at **Copa**, **Kekepampa** and **Joncopampa**. The last named is considered to be second only to Chavín in the region. From Vicos, cross the river on a footbridge, and it's about one hour further to Joncopampa. From Vicos, you can also walk through the Quebrada Honda, over the Portachuelo de Honda pass at 4750 m, to **Chacas**, an excellent, not difficult hike, which takes about four days.

Carhuaz → Colour map 3, B2.

Carhuaz, a friendly, quiet mountain town with a pleasant plaza with tall palm trees and lovely rose bushes is 7 km further on from Marcará. There is very good trekking in the neighbourhood (outlined below). There's a market on Wednesday and another larger market on Sunday, when *campesinos* bring their produce to town. Good peaches are grown locally, among other crops. The locals are renowned for their lively celebrations, hence the town's nickname, '*Carhuaz alegría*'.

Treks from Carhuaz

Trek 1: to Yanama The trek up to the **Ulta valley** over the Punta Yanayacu pass to Yanama is little used but offers impressive views of Huascarán and other peaks. It takes three days. If you catch a truck up the valley to where the road begins to zig-zag up to the pass, it will shorten the trek by one day (see Transport, page 359). If not, start hiking from Shilla, 13 km east of Carhuaz, or from Huaypan. There are combis to Shilla when full (early morning) from Jirón 9 de Diciembre y La Merced, one block northeast of the plaza in Carhuaz, US$0.30. A taxi to Shilla costs US$3 (sharing possible). Return transport to Carhuaz is scarce. Combis go to Huaypan on Wednesday and Sunday only, US$0.50, one hour.

Trek 2: to hot springs Seven kilometres east of Carhuaz, near the village of Hualcán, are the **Baños de Pariacaca**, which were badly damaged by a landslide in 1993. The hot springs can be seen bubbling between the rocks by the river's edge and there are some small rock pools in which the enthusiastic can bathe. From the plaza in Carhuaz follow Comercio to the top of the hill, turn right as far as Cinco esquinas (five corners), turn left and follow the road uphill. When you reach the bridge, cross it left to Hualcán and ask directions from there. There is transport to Hualcán leaving from the plaza in Carhuaz on Wednesday and Sunday.

Trek 3: to Laguna 513 Half an hour beyond Baños de Pariacaca (see Trek 2 above) is the village of **Pariacaca** (no facilities) from where a trail continues into the mountains. In three hours you can reach **Laguna Rajupaquinan** and, 45 minutes beyond, the imaginatively named **Laguna 513**, with beautiful views of the surrounding peaks. If you continue, you will see the Auquiscocha lakes which you can reach in another three hours. Laguna 513 can also be reached directly from Hualcán in about four hours, along the north side of the river. This latter trail has fewer rocks to negotiate. Make sure to take adequate gear and a map if you plan to go beyond Pariacaca.

Mancos and around → *Colour map 3, B2.*

From Carhuaz it is a further 14 km to Mancos, at the foot of Huascarán. (From here, climbers can go to **Musho** to reach the base camp.) You can also do a strenuous 30-km, one-day walk from Mancos which gives great views of Huascarán. Follow the road east and take the branch for Tumpa, about 13 km away; ask directions as the road branches several times. Continue north to Musho for about 1 km, then descend via Arhuay to **Ranrahirca**, which is between Mancos and Yungay on the main road. There are daily *colectivos* from Mancos to Musho; transport to Ranrahirca and Arhuay is on Wednesday and Sunday only.

Cueva Guitarreros is a cave, west of Mancos in the Cordillera Negra, which contains rock paintings dating back some 12,000 years. Access is either through Mancos, from where it is about 30 minutes' walk along an overgrown trail (with many spines!), or through Tingua and Shupluy further south, from where it takes about one hour. The thermal springs at **Chirpas**, which have a high lithium content (used in the treatment of manic depression), are near the caves. There are good views of Huascarán from this area.

Yungay → *Colour map 3, A2. Altitude 2500 m.*

Yungay is 8 km north of Mancos on the main road. The original town of Yungay was completely buried during the 1970 earthquake by a massive mudslide, caused when a piece of Huascarán's glacier was prised loose by the quake and came hurtling towards the town. It was a hideous tragedy in which 20,000 people lost their lives. The earthquake and its aftermath are remembered by many residents of the Callejón de Huaylas and the scars remain part of the local psyche.

The original site of Yungay, known as **Yungay Viejo** ⓘ *off the Huaraz–Yungay road, officially open daily 0800-1800, US$0.75*, has been consecrated as a *camposanto* (cemetery). It is a haunting place, with flower beds and paths covering the eight to 12 m of soil under which the old town lies. Of the four palm trees from the old Plaza de Armas that protrude through the landslide, only one remains alive. Five pine trees and a monument mark the site where five policemen died. Nearby, on top of a hill, is the old cemetery with a large statue of Christ, where a handful of residents managed to escape the disaster. Many of the town's children also escaped as they were in the stadium watching the circus. There are a few monuments marking the site of former homes. There's a café, toilets and shops at the main entrance.

The **new settlement** is on a hillside just north of the old town, and is growing gradually. It has a pleasant modern plaza and a concrete market, busiest on Wednesday and Sunday, which is good for stocking up on supplies for hiking. The predominant colour in the town is *celeste* (sky blue). One part of town is called the **Barrio Ruso**, where typical, Russian wooden houses, erected temporarily in the 1970s as a gift from the USSR, are still in use. For information, visit the **tourist office** ⓘ *on the corner of the Plaza de Armas, Mon-Fri 0800-1300, 1400-1800.*

Around Yungay

A day walk from Yungay to **Mirador de Atma** gives beautiful views of Huascarán, Huandoy and the Santa valley. From town, follow a dirt road east for 3 km (about one hour). You can return via the Quebrada Ancash road which runs further north, between the Río Ancash and Cerro Pan de Azúcar. This will bring you to the Yungay–Caraz road about 1 km north of Yungay. It is about a three-hour round trip.

Matacoto, 6 km from Yungay in the Cordillera Negra at 3000 m, has excellent views of Huascarán, Huandoy and other major peaks. The turnoff is at Huarazcucho (Km 251), 3 km south of new Yungay. It is another 3 km from here, across the bridge over the Río Santa to Matacoto. (Matacoto can also be reached in three hours from Mancos.) *Colectivos* from Yungay run daily 0700-1300, US$0.30; taxis charge US$2.

Laguna 69 can also be visited in a day from Yungay. Take a combi from Yungay past the Llanganuco lakes (see below; US$2.45-3). After about 90 minutes get off the bus at a bend called Curva Pisco. Keep to the right of the river along the valley bottom. You will see the gentle zigzags going up to the right to a col with a small lake. Pass this and you come to a large plateau: keep to the right-hand side. There is a signpost in the middle pointing right to a glacier and straight ahead to Laguna 69, heading to a large wall of rock. The path zigzags steeply up to the left of this rock face to the lake, near glaciers and the snow line. It takes three to four hours for the 7-km hike and 750-m climb and some two to three hours to walk back down to the road. There are superb views of waterfalls, glaciers and Huascarán. A new trail now leads from Laguna 69 to the Refugio Perú or Pisco Base Camp, taking about two to three hours. Ask the combi to return for you at about 1630, the latest time to get back to Yungay for a combi back to Huaraz.

Lagunas de Llanganuco

The Lagunas de Llanganuco are two lakes nestling 1000 m below the snowline beneath Huascarán and Huandoy. From Yungay, the first you come to is **Laguna Chinancocha** at 3850 m, followed by **Laguna Orconcocha** at 3863 m. The story goes that in times gone by, when the water levels were higher, the day's snow melt and rainfall would raise Orconcocha sufficiently for it to flow into Chinancocha each evening; by dawn they had separated again. Hence the lakes' other names: Laguna Macho (male – Orconcocha) and Laguna Hembra (female – Chinancocha). A nature trail, **Sendero María Josefa** (sign on the road), leads for 1½ hours to the western end of Chinancocha where there is a control post, descriptive trail and boat trips on the lake (a popular area for day trippers). Walk along the road beside the lake to its far eastern end for peace and quiet among the *quenoal* trees. These trees (polylepis, or

According to legend, the rise and fall of the waters in Lagunas de Llanganuco is also related to the tears of Huáscar and Huandy, the prince and princess of enemy tribes whose forbidden love was discovered, causing them to be turned into the mountains Huascarán and Huandoy.

paper bark) are the symbol of the Huascarán national park and provide shelter for 75% of the birdlife found in the park. The lakes themselves are superb areas for observing water birds, with yellow-billed, blue and mountain ducks commonly seen, as well as Andean geese, puna ibis and a variety of gulls. Hunting birds such as caracas and American kestrels make an appearance. If you're lucky, you may even catch a glimpse of the rare torrent duck, swimming up grade 5 rapids in classic style.

This trek can also be done as a day trip from Huaraz by taking the 0700 combi to Yungay.

Caraz and around

» *pp355-360.*

→ *Altitude: 2290 m. Colour map 3, A2.*

The pleasant town of Caraz is a good centre for walking and the access point for many excellent treks and climbs. It is increasingly popular with visitors as a more tranquil alternative to Huaraz. In July and August the town has splendid views of Huandoy and Huascarán from its lovely plaza, which is filled with jacarandas, rose bushes and palms. In other months, the mountains are often shrouded in cloud. Caraz has a milder climate than Huaraz and is more suited to day trips. The sweet-toothed will enjoy the locally produced *manjar blanco*, from which the town derives its nickname, '*Caraz dulzura*'. Market days are Wednesday and Sunday. The **tourist office** ⓘ *Plaza de Armas, T043-391029, Mon-Fri 0745-1300, 1430-1700*, has limited information.

The ruins of **Tunshukaiko** are 1 km from the Plaza de Armas, in the suburb of Cruz Viva. This is a poor area so be discreet with cameras etc. There are seven platforms from the Huaraz culture, dating from around 2000-1800 BC, between the Galgada and Chavín periods. Recent excavations have uncovered structures 300 m in diameter, 25 m high. They are on a promontory with a panoramic view of the farms, fields,

Sleeping
Alojamiento Caballero 1
Caraz Dulzura 12
Casa de Campo 8
Chamanna 17
Chavín 3
Cordillera Blanca 2
Familia Aguilar 4
Hostal La Casona 5
La Alameda 13
La Perla de los Andes 6
La Perla de los Andes Annex 7
Los Pinos 9
O'Pal Inn 14
Ramírez 10
Regina & Huandoy 11
Tunshukaiko 15
Villa Huandy 16

Eating
El Mirador 4
El Turista 5
Esmeralda 6
Heladería Caraz Dulzura 2
Jeny 7
La Punta Grande 9
Oasis 3
Panificadora La Alameda 8

Bars & clubs
El Tabasco Taberna 11
Taberna Disco Huandy 12

Transport
Chinchaysuyo 3
Combis to Huallanca 2
Coop Ancash 5
El Huaralino 6
Expreso Ancash 1
Móvil 7
Transportes Rodríguez 8
Yungay Express 10

 eucalyptus and other trees between the Cordilleras Blanca and Negra. To get there, from the plaza in Caraz follow San Martín uphill, turn left on 28 de Julio, continue about 400 m past the bridge over the Río Llullán. Look for a wide track between houses on your left (about 300 m before the turnoff for Lago Parón); ask the way.

Five kilometres north of **Cashapampa** (see page 349), or a one- to 1½-hour hike, are the small, clean hot-baths of **Huancarhuaz**. These have been improved, with an outdoor pool, US$0.30, and individual baths, US$0.60. *Colectivos* from Santa Cruz y Grau in Caraz go to Cashapampa and continue to Huancarhuaz.

Cañón del Pato

The road out of the Callejón de Huaylas heads north from Caraz, en route to Chimbote on the coast. After some 30 km the road enters the very narrow and spectacular **Cañón del Pato**. You pass under tremendous walls of bare rock and through 35 tunnels, but the flow of the river has been greatly reduced by the hydroelectric scheme, which takes the water into the mountain at the Bocatoma.

The canyon can be visited on a half-day trip from Caraz. Take a microbus from near the market towards Yuramarca, see Transport page 342. Sit in the front or on the right for great views. Get off at Huallanca and get on the next bus going back, sitting in the front or on the left. Ask the driver to drop you off at the yellow footbridge where the canyon is narrowest (ask for Cañón del Pato). Walk back north through one small tunnel. In the second tunnel, take the first side tunnel to the right that leads to a very precarious footpath that goes along the edge of the canyon at its narrowest point. Walking back south you come to a dam and the hydroelectric plant with water pouring over the dam wall. Pick up another bus going back to Caraz. Take great care on the path in the canyon and in the tunnels as they are narrow and have no places to retreat if a large vehicle comes through. Take a torch. The trip is best at midday when the sun shines directly into the gorge.

Treks from Caraz in the Cordillera Blanca

Cerro San Juan

This is a six- to seven-hour walk with views of Huandoy and Huascarán. It follows the foothills of the Cordillera Blanca, south from Caraz. Leave town on Bolognesi, continuing up to 28 de Julio; turn right, go past the **2 de Mayo (Markham) High School** and climb Cerro San Juan; about 45 minutes. Continue south to the main local summit in an area known as **Ticrapa** (two hours). Head down to **Pata-Pata**, from where a track goes down beside the Río Ancash to **Puente Ancash** on the Caraz–Yungay road (two to three hours), where you can take transport back to Caraz. The hike can be done the other way by getting out of a combi from Huaraz or Caraz at Puente Ancash. The tourist office and **Pony's Expeditions** (see page 359) have a map of this trek.

Some of these treks can also be done by transport. Pony's Expeditions (page 359) has a bulletin board where people who want to share transport leave their name and contact details.

Laguna Parón

From Caraz a narrow, rough road goes east 32 km to Laguna Parón, in a cirque surrounded by several, massive snow-capped peaks, including Huandoy, Pirámide Garcilazo and Caraz. The water level has been lowered to protect Caraz, and the water from the lake is used for the Cañón del Pato hydroelectric scheme. The gorge leading to it is spectacular.

It is a long days' trek from Caraz for acclimatized hikers (25 km) up to the lake at 4150 m, or a four- to five-hour walk from the village of **Parón**, which can be reached by combi. Where possible follow the walking trail which is much shorter than the road. By climbing up the slippery moraine to the south of the lake towards Huandoy, you get a fine view of Artesonraju. Camping is possible next to the **Duke Energy** refuge. A trail follows the north shore of the lake to a base camp on the north side of the inflow, about two hours past the refuge. Beyond this point, the trail divides: one branch goes towards **Pirámide Garcilazo** (5885 m) and **Pisco** (5752 m); another to **Laguna Artesoncocha** at the base of an enormous glacier, and a third towards **Artesonraju** (6025 m). You will need a map if you are going past Laguna Parón.

There are camping possibilities along these trails. Try to find shelter in the *quenoal* stands or behind a ridge, as the wind can be very strong and the nights are cold. The views are magnificent as you are always surrounded by many beautiful peaks. When you ford a river, remember that the flow increases in the afternoon with the meltdown, so make sure you can get back to your camp early. On the route to Artesonraju there is a morraine camp, just before reaching the glacier.

A taxi from Caraz to Laguna Parón costs US$25 for four, with two hours' wait. **Pony's Expeditions** (Caraz) have a pool of well-trained drivers that make daily departures to Parón at 0800, US$25 for four, including a one-hour visit to the lake and a one-hour walk downhill to the bridge, where the driver will pick up the group. Extra hours cost US$3. You can also hire a bicycle (US$15) and use these transport services one-way (US$6) and cycle back down.

Santa Cruz valley

This loop is one of the finest and most heavily used walks in the Cordillera Blanca. It usually takes three to five days depending on your starting point. It is considered easier in the opposite direction (Santa Cruz to Llanganuco), requiring four to five days, depending where you finish. **Please take all your rubbish with you**.

Day 1 Caraz to Llamacorral (3850 m) Taking a combi to **Cashapampa** covers the first 600 m and one hour, 20 minutes of the trip (see Transport, page 359). Services in Cashapampa include shops, campsites and transport; *arrieros* and their mules can be hired. (In 2006 fees were US$ 8-10 per day for an *arriero* US$ 4 per day for a mule, plus half fee for return days. You also pay for food and tent if hired in Cashapampa.) A recommended *arriero* is **Mellan Leiva Pariachi** (Caserío de Shuyo, Cashapampa). From here it's a 10-km, 900-m climb to the Llamacorral campsite (four hours).

Day 2 Llamacorral to Taullipampa (4250 m) This is an easy day, perfect for acclimatizing (a total of 12 km, climbing about 400 m). The trail leads to the Ichiccocha and Jatuncocha lakes, both providing shelter for many water birds and exotic plants. Beyond the lakes there is a *quisuar* forest, providing perfect shade for lunch. A side trip to the north (left) of the main valley takes a series of switchbacks to the famous **Alpamayo Base Camp** (see page 353). After 45 minutes and climbing some 200 m, the circle of glaciers and snow peaks comes into full view. Go no further unless you plan to camp here. If returning to the main trail, look on the left of the trail (east) for a tiny path that will take you to **Taullipampa**, the next campsite. It's only 3 km to the camp, which is one of the most beautiful in the whole region, surrounded by snow peaks, a silent river and incredible plants.

Day 3 Taullipampa to Huaripampa (3750 m) Make an early start for the **Punta Unión Pass**, the highest point on the trail, at 4750 m. The 4-km trail makes a series of switchbacks, but at a gentle pace you will reach this point in two to three hours. From the campsite the pass seems to be just a notch on the rock ridge right of Taulliraju (5850 m) but once there, the view is a 360° panorama of the snow peaks. The descent starts steeply, then traverses the granite slabs close to the ridge, before another series of switchbacks drive to the far left of the valley to descend on the lake below, another nice spot for lunch. Now the trail becomes slippery, crossing grass-like meadows towards **Quebrada Huaripampa**. After about two hours, a granite tower on your left is your sign to look for the bridge to cross the river. Now, with the river on your right, you will soon reach the **Quebrada Paría**. This is a good campsite, with great views of Paría mountain. It's usually crowded in July and August so, for more privacy, continue 2 km down the valley to camp at **Quenoapampa**. This is a spot at the end of the *quenoal* forest. For most travellers, the next campsite, some 3 km away, known as **Cachina Pampa** (3750 m), is a better option as it makes a shorter fourth day to catch the early buses back to Yungay. Total distance from the pass is 9 km, some three to four hours, descending 1000 m.

Day 4 For those who have only four days, the exit is at **Vaquería**, a group of houses at the side of the Yanama to Yungay road. Descend for 4 km in about one hour to the bridge on your right, climb to the left until you meet the fork to Colcabamba, take the right path steeply upwards and after 1½ hours you will meet the road.

If making a five-day trek, at Vaquería, continue along the road for some 4 km to a green meadow, a toilet block (or what is left of it) and a huge rock forming a sort of cave (**Pampa Machay**, 4000 m). This is a good campsite. If you have energy enough, and want to gain on the next day, continue by taking the first short cut on the right. Walk uphill across the trail through bushes to the **Paccha Pampa** campsite, named after the waterfalls by the campsite.

Treks from Yungay & Caraz

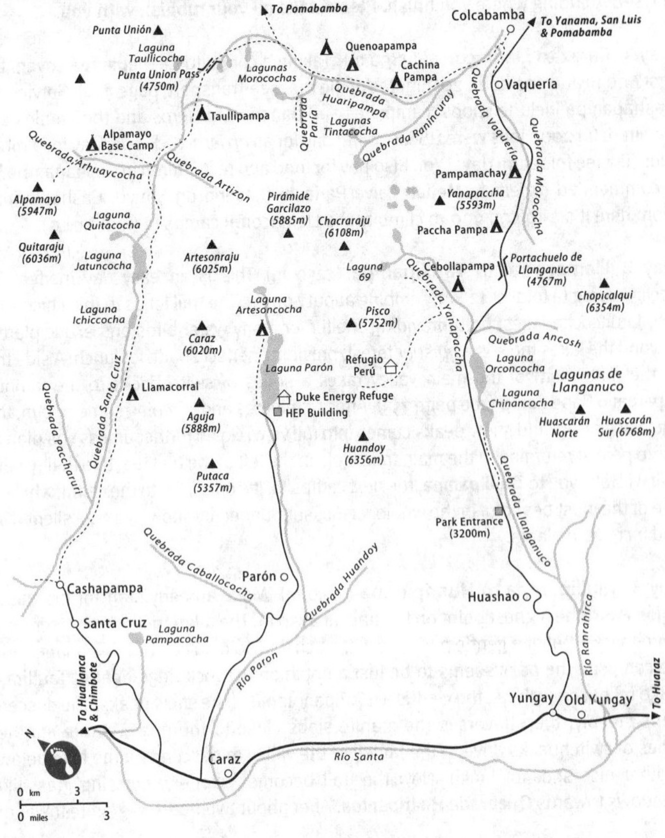

Day 5 Portachuelo to Llanganuco lakes (3850 m) A final climb reaches the Portachuelo pass at 4767 m, in about two hours. You can see, on a clear day, more snow peaks than on any of the previous days, including the twin peaks of Huascarán, four summits of Huandoy, two of Pisco, two of Chacraraju, three of Yanapaccha and the giant Chopicalqui. The trail to the lakes starts on the south (left) of the pass, then after 5 km you reach the area of **Cebollapampa**, a popular campsite for climbers going to Cerro Pisco. At this point, cars are available to take you back to Yungay. If you wish, pause on the way down at the Llanganuco lakes (see page 346).

Alpamayo North trek

This difficult but spectacular trek can begin from either **Cashapampa** (see page 349), or from the more remote, smaller community of **Hualcayan**. Starting the trek from Hualcayan avoids several hours' fairly pleasant hike along the base of the mountains from Cashapampa, but supplies in this village are very limited and it may take more time to organize *arrieros*. Once on the trek you can either hike directly across the range to **Pomabamba** (as described below – allow at least 7 days), returning to Huaraz by bus, or extend the trek into a circuit of Alpamayo returning from Huilca via the Yanta Quenua and Santa Cruz valleys. For this second option allow at least 12 days. Do not underestimate either route. They take in spectacular, constantly changing mountain vistas, including picture-postcard views of Alpamayo, Quitaraju and the Pucajirca range. They cross three major, very steep mountain passes over 4700 m, plus an assortment of smaller challenges.

Day 1 Cashapampa to Hualcayan (4-4½ hours) After 20 minutes' hiking north along the main route from Cashapampa, the **Baños Termales Huancarhuas** come into view in the valley below. These are passed after one- to 1½ hours of easy walking, first crossing a rushing stream in the valley floor. Beyond the baths the route climbs gently uphill, following the trail beneath the mountains. You pass through traditional villages and fields. Cacti, spider plants, bromeliads and flowers are everywhere, not to mention the ubiquitous stands of eucalyptus. Views of the Cordillera Negra include a rich agricultural tapestry of small holdings and villages. After about three hours, the trail turns a little to the north, crossing a steep *quebrada*, just before a final one-hour steep climb to **Hualcayan** (3139 m). If you ask politely, you may be able to camp next to the football pitch and beneath the ancient terraces that rise above the village. US$1.50 per person was the community charge for park entry and trail maintenance in 2006. A receipt was given by Sr Irazmo Ramírez. Note that Park entry fees were fluctuating quite dramatically in 2006, so adjustments to these fees are not out of the question.

Day 2 Hualcayan to Huishcash (2½ hours) Heading east into the mountains you quickly leave the 'road', following a zigzag trail as it climbs steeply, heading towards a waterfall. A red signpost showing a trekking figure confirms you're on the correct route. Quickly gaining height, the trail keeps to the south of the waterfall for the first hour before crossing an adobe bridge to the north bank above the cascade. Views of the Cañón del Pato below, not to mention the Cordillera Negra across the valley, become increasingly more impressive as you climb above Hualcayan. After two hours, the path begins taking a more direct route, slowly climbing north towards a small patch of polylepis woodland. A red sign board marks the limit of Parque Nacional Huscarán at 3710 m. Thirty minutes later, heading north, you begin crossing a large landslide area and just beyond that you reach the beautiful remnant of polylepis woodland just mentioned. Beyond the forest there's an open pasture area, which makes a good stopping point for lunch and also a very good camping spot. (Note that the next potential campsite is by Laguna Cullicocha (see below), 3½ hours away: very high and cold.) If you decide to stay at **Huishcash** you could explore **Laguna Yanacocha**, 1.65 km away; a sign just beyond Huishcash points the way.

Day 3 Huishcash to Quebrada Vientunan (5½-6 hours) At the sign to Laguna Yanacocha, walk up the winding trail heading away from the direction in which the sign is pointing, straight up the hill in front of you. Fifteen minutes later you cross a small stream on an adobe bridge passing a small 'walking man' trail sign. This sign also names this pampa as Huishcash (4220 m), as well as listing various prohibitions: no fires, no fishing, no booze, no rubbish etc. Some 1½ hours after the Huishcash lunch/camping spot, a sign indicates 2.7 km to Laguna Cullicocha and, in another direction, 7 km to Laguna Yanacocha. On the left is a black, canyon-like feature, full of dense native vegetation below, but barren on exposed ridges and faces. Not far beyond the last signpost the path runs just to the left, underneath a black hill on top of the pass and in between the two black mountains above the dark valley. Lots of polylepis woodland covers the inaccessible parts of this gorge.

Roughly 3½ hours after leaving Huishcash you come to the water pumping micro-hydro station and the potential campsite in front of **Laguna Cullicocha**. This station is always manned, at the time of writing by the very friendly guard called Elvis (ayrton2805@hotmail.com). Before arriving at the station, follow the steep right-hand side of the gorge, passing (but not following) a water drainage channel. The campsite itself is set in a landscape of smooth sculpted rocks backed by spectacular views of the Laguna Cullicocha and, behind the lake, the icy walls of the Santa Cruz massif: **Santa Cruz Norte** (5829 m), **Chico** (5800 m) and **Santa Cruz Grande** (6241 m, also referred to as **Pucaraju**). The rocks and high altitude make for an uncomfortable campsite but, if you are very polite, the pumping station attendant may let you stay in the station's spare accommodation. The next good campsite is a couple of hours' hike further, on the far side of one of the trek's major passes.

Head north, following trail markers just to the west of the Cullicocha pumping station, with great views again of the Santa Cruz mountains and the lakes below. After about 15 minutes the trail begins to swing more to the east towards Santa Cruz Norte and begins to zigzag higher above the lakes towards the pass. Thirty to 40 minutes after the station, the route starts to turn north through a jagged rocky area, heading up towards the pass. From here you have a good view down into the glacial moraine of Santa Cruz. Fifty minutes after Cullicocha, a knife-edge ridge on the top of the first pass, **Osoruri** (4860 m), is reached. A great vista of the mountains of the **Milluacocha** massif opens up, with the trail twisting into the valley below you on your right. Condors may be seen here. Between Osoruri and Nevado Milluacocha the valley of the **Quebrada Alpamayo** plunges beneath you, its floor around 1700 m below. Turning east-northeast you descend into the steep, bowl-like valley, underneath the next pass, **Punta Vientunan**. This, with shelter and water, is as good a campsite as any.

Alpamayo North trek

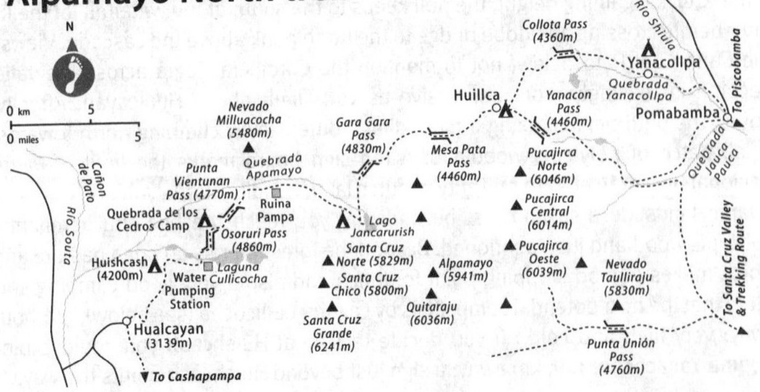

Day 4 Vientunan to Alpamayo (6-7 hours) Climb steeply in switchbacks on the far wall of the valley to reach the next pass, **Punta Vientunan** (4770 m). Before climbing, at the bottom of the valley, a sign points to Ruina Pampa, 5.2 km away. You reach the pass after a little more than an hour's climb. A very long descent follows Vientunan Pass, at least 1¼ hours of knee stress, before beginning to approach the bottom of the Quebrada Alpamayo. A few traditional houses mark a small settlement and, on the far side of the valley, an extensive area of terraces hints at a long history of habitation. A red signpost gives the distance to the base camp at **Nevado Alpamayo** as 10.5 km to the east up the valley, and the distance to the Ruinas de Auquis Puquio as 13 km to the west. Take the east route up the valley deeper into the heart of the mountains. The valley floor soon begins to open up, passing the unrestored walls of **Ruina Pampa** (another potential camping spot) and continuing along the valley's right-hand side fairly constantly for around 10 km until reaching an official camping spot, marked by another red/orange board. Surrounded by magnificent mountains on all sides, the site is positioned just before the turn to the south where the valley swings towards Lago Jancarurish and the glacial moraines. In good weather the classic northwest face of **Alpamayo** is visible, but for the best views of the mountain, leave yourself some time the following day and ascend the moraine to the south.

Day 5 Alpamayo viewpoint (optional) Heading south up the valley, a brief climb to the summit of the moraine affords fabulous views of the turquoise **Lago Jancarurish**, vast cliffs and a spectacular cascade pouring from Alpamayo and its glacier above. Glance to the west and you'll find views of **Santa Cruz** and her sister peaks, perhaps from their most striking angle. Hiking further up the valley on the right-hand side will bring you to the climbers' base camp, and the beauty and potential risk that the world of ice and snow entails.

Day 6 Alpamayo to Huillca (6½-7 hours) From the official campsite near Lago Jancarurish, cross to the north side of the Quebrada Alpamayo, then bear left, heading north towards the Gara Gara pass, but zigzagging up on the left-hand (west) side of the valley. The initial climb is steep but offers increasingly panoramic views of the surrounding peaks, including **Quitaraju** to the south, an impressive mountain often hidden by rocky outcrops from the valley floor. After about an hour of climbing, the trail leads into a flatter valley, with a small lake on its right-hand side. Beyond this flatter section, the final push up to the pass is a steep scree slope, almost a scramble in the last moments. It should take a couple of hours to reach the chilly, windswept **Gara Gara** pass (4830 m). There's not a lot of room to manoeuvre up there, but with awe-inspiring peaks all around, Gara Gara offers perhaps the most jaw-dropping vista on the trek.

On the far side of the pass, descend roughly east-to-northeast, following the trail down through steep rocky ground. This valley appears to have a slightly wetter climate than Quebrada Alpamayo, with cushion mosses and many flowers. A couple of small ruins are passed in the higher sections of the valley. The descent from the pass is fairly steep for the first 45 minutes, then flattens out into a damp puna environment, with thick ichu grass everywhere and occasional boggy patches. Follow the left flank of the valley to the northeast. A couple of hours after the pass, the trail reasserts its easterly course, crossing to the right-hand side of the valley and climbing towards the small Mesapata pass. At the same time the Quebrada Mayobamba swings sharply to the north, away from your route. After another hour (5 hours after starting out) you reach the summit of **Mesapata** (4460 m), to be rewarded by yet another imposing range, the ice-bound peaks of the **Pucajirca** massif. Below you lies the **Quebrada Tayapampa** and, on the river's left-hand bank, a rough road heading northeast. Descend into the valley and follow the road until it crosses the river and opens up into the wide valley of **Huillca**. Here you'll find a traditional, almost totally self-sufficient settlement of three Quechua families, all carving a rugged existence from animal herding, with large groups of pigs, alpacas and horses. With permission from these families, it's possible to camp on the eastern side of the valley, beyond the Yanta Quenua stream. The inhabitants of the valley are often interested in trading food (cooked potatoes, eggs etc) for products difficult to obtain locally: matches, lighters, pens etc. Always treat the inhabitants of this valley, and their extraordinary culture, with respect. At the same make sure you store all valuables inside your tent.

At Huillca, you have the choice of either continuing east to the far side of the mountains and **Pomabamba** (described in detail below), or turning southeast up the **Yanta Quenua** valley. This route, if followed for a couple of days over the 4610-m Yanacon pass, then through the Quebradas Yanajanca and Tuctubamba will bring you to the classic Santa Cruz trekking route (see page 349), close to the small Laguna Huecrucocha. Heading west from here will lead you in two or three days over the spectacular Punta Unión pass (see page 349) and through the Santa Cruz valley, completing what's generally termed the **Alpamayo Circuit**.

Day 7 Huillca to Quebrada Yanajanca (5-6 hours) The trail to Pomabamba starts in the Huillca valley's southeast corner, zigzagging up the hill to the northeast before swinging more to the north. The top of the first pass is reached after around 50 minutes, the route commanding spectacular views of the Pucajirca snow peaks and passing through a small patch of polylepis woodland. Reaching the top of the pass (there's no name on the Alpenverin Map, but let's call it **Punta Shuitucocha** for clarity) you are presented with a view of a second valley to the east. This valley has two lakes, the more southerly, larger of which is **Laguna Shuitucocha**. The trail now follows a route between the two lakes, then up the hill to the far side, taking a generally east-northeastly course along the left-hand edge of the hills. After around 2½ hours you'll reach the bleak 4360-m **Collota** pass, crowned by a large cross.

A steep descent to the east leads towards a trail/rough road. A long descent down this valley on the left (north) bank leads into a lush, jungle-like landscape. The valley becomes increasingly heavily populated, the trail crossing over onto the right bank of the river, passing some small shops, before re-crossing the river and heading through the main part of the **Yanacollpa** village. Some families in the village and slightly beyond it will allow you to camp or rent a room for a small fee. Keep a close eye on your gear when staying close to the village.

Day 8 Yanacollpa to Pomabamba Just a few hours' trek this morning, first crossing the river, following its course down the right-hand bank of the Yanacollpa until it meets the Río Shiula, then following the water downstream to the southeast to your destination. Make certain that just before **Pomabamba** you cross the river to the north side; this route will take you right into the town centre. If you want to relax after trek, there are some good thermal baths close to Pomabamba (see page 365).

Cordillera Negra

Torreón Andino

West of Caraz is **Huata** at 2700 m, where there is a religious sanctuary and a dirty hotel (F); a truck leaves from Caraz market daily at 1000. Some 6 km down a track off the Caraz–Huata road are the Inca ruins of **Chonta**. From Huata you can climb to the **Quebrada de Cochacocha** (3500 m), at the top of which is the Inca ruin of Cantu (excellent views), and on to the Inca lookout, **Torreón Andino** (5006 m). Take water, food and tent with you. Allow three days for the hike, as there are lagoons near the peak. Refer to the late Professor Bernardino Aguilar Prieto's *Torreón Andino Information* book before climbing it.

A blooming century

The giant Puya Raimondi, named after Antonio Raimondi, the Italian scholar who discovered it, is a rare species, considered to be one of the oldest plants in the world.

Often mistakenly referred to as a cactus, it is actually the largest member of the bromeliad family and is found in only a few isolated areas of the Andes. One of these areas is the Huascarán National Park, particularly the Ingenio and Queshque gorges, the high plateaus of Cajamarquilla, along the route leading to Pastoruri in the Pachacoto gorge and by the road from Caraz to Pamparomas.

At its base, the Puya forms a rosette of long, spiked, waxy leaves, 2 m in diameter. The distinctive phallic spike of the plant can reach a height of 12 m during the flowering process. This takes its entire lifespan – an incredible 100 years – after which time the plant withers and dies.

As the final flowering begins, usually during May for mature plants, the spike is covered in flowers. As many as 20,000 blooms can decorate a single plant. During this season, groups of Puya Raimondi will bloom together, creating a spectacular picture against the dramatic backdrop of the Cordillera Blanca.

Pueblo Libre

A good day hike from Caraz with nice views of the Cordillera Blanca is to Pueblo Libre. Follow Jirón D Villar west across the Río Santa bridge and turn south to **Tunaspampa**, an interesting desert area with cacti and hummingbirds. Continue through the villages of Shingal, Tocash and Rinconada on to **Pueblo Libre**. It is about a four-hour round trip, or you can take a *colectivo* back to Caraz.

Winchos

Beyond Pueblo Libre, the road continues via Pamparomas and Moro to join the coastal highway between Casma and Chimbote. After 45 km (two hours) a large stand of Puya Raimondi (see above) can be seen at a place called **Winchos**, with views stretching 145 km, east to the Cordillera Blanca and west to the Pacific. The flowers are usually in bloom in May or October. 'Wincho' is the local name for the giant hummingbird, Patagona gigas, which has an 18-cm wingspan.

There are two possible routes by public transport from Caraz to the puyas at Winchos: Caraz–Huata–El Cruce (from where it's a 2-km walk to the puyas), continuing to Pamparomas; or Caraz–Pueblo Libre–Huashtacruz–El Paso (from where it's a 15-minute walk to the puyas), continuing to El Cruce and Pamparomas. On the return to Caraz, you will have to walk 2 km to El Cruce to be sure to catch the returning transport between 1230 and 1300. This will not give you too much time at the puyas. Increasingly popular alternatives are to rent a bicycle (US$15), which you can take on public transport to the puyas (departing at 0900; see Transport, page 359) and then ride back to Caraz in about four to five hours. Or form a group and hire a car which will wait for you; a board at **Pony's Expeditions** (see page 359) has offers of shared transport.

Sleeping

Huandoy Valley *p344*
There are homestay opportunities in **Vicos**, contact the **Mountain Institute** in Huaraz, Ricardo Palma 100, Pedregal Alto, T043-423446, www.mountain.org.

Carhuaz *p344*
B-C El Abuelo, Jr 9 de Diciembre y Tumbes, T043-394149, www.elabuelohostal.com. Modern, pricey 3-star, comfortable, with cafeteria and parking. Ask at **Heladería El**

Abuelo on main plaza. Knowledgeable owner, Felipe Díaz, is the publisher of a useful tourist map of the *cordilleras* Blanca and Huayhuash, available widely in the area.
C per person **Casa de Pocha**, 1½ km out of town towards Hualcán, ask directions in town, T043-961 3058 (mob, 1800-2000), lacasadepocha@ yahoo.com. Advance bookings required. Nice country setting, price includes breakfast and dinner, solar- and wind-powered electricity, hot water, sauna and pool, home-produced food (vegetarian available), horses for hire, Spanish, Quechua, Portuguese, English, French and Italian spoken. Good base for hiking. Recommended.
D COMTUCAR, 200 m south of town on main road to Huaraz, T043-394051, www.qnet.com.pe/carhuaz. Includes breakfast, restaurant, pool, sauna, gardens.
F Hostal Señor de Luren, Buin 549, 30 m from Plaza de Armas. Hot water, TV, safe motorcycle parking, very friendly.

Four family-run *hospedajes* (**F**) have been built as part of a community development project. All have private bath and hot water. The better two are the modern **Hospedaje Robri**, Jr Comercio 935, T043-394505, and **Alojamiento Las Torresitas**, Jr Amazonas 603, T043-394213. The latter is a nice place with friendly *señora* and pretty courtyard. Rooms with TV and bath. Breakfast negotiable.
G Hostal La Merced, Ucayali 724, T043-394241 (in Lima T01-442 3201). 'Like going back to the 1950s', clean, friendly, hot water (usually), some rooms with private bathroom, luggage store.

Mancos and around *p345*

There's a nice dorm at **La Casita de mi Abuela**, Barrio Huascarán, Pukio, Jr Comercio 110, and **La Plazza**, on the Plaza de Armas, can provide meals. Also some basic shops and restaurants.

Yungay *p345*

F per person **COMTURY**, Complejo Turístico Yungay, Prolongación 2 de Mayo 1019, 2½ km south of the new town, 700 m east of the main road in Aura, the only part of old Yungay that survived, T043-969 1698 (mob). Nice bungalows with space for up to 10, in a pleasant country setting, hot water, fireplace, friendly, restaurant with regional specialities, camping possible.
F Hostal Gledel, Av Arias Grazziani, north past the plaza, T043-393048, rugamboa@viabcp.com. Owned by Sra Gamboa, who is hospitable and a good cook, very clean but tiny rooms, shared bathroom, warm water, no towels or soap, cheap meals prepared on request, nice courtyard.
F Hostal Las Rosas, T043-393073. Clean and friendly, with hot water.
F Hostal Sol de Oro, Santo Domingo 07, T043-393116. Private bath, hot water, comfortable and good value. The best in town.
F Hostal Yungay, Jr Santo Domingo on the plaza, T043-393053. A clean, basic *hostal*, with private bath, electric shower and small rooms.
G Complejo Turístico Huascarán, Leoncio Prado s/n, T043-393023. With private bath, hot water and parking, modern but uninspiring.
G Hostal Mery, 28 de julio s/n. Simple but OK, hot water, the rooms at the front can be noisy.

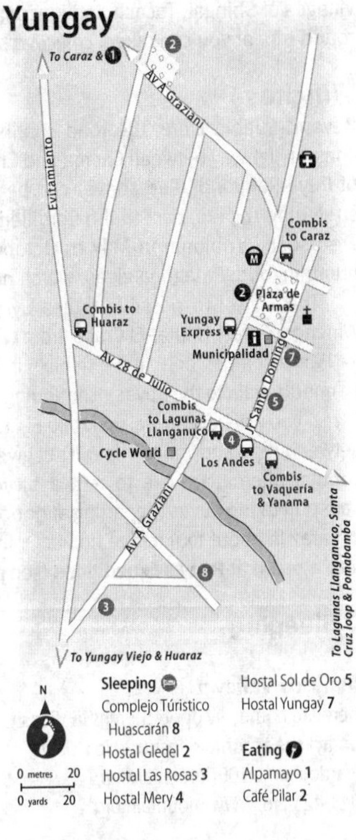

Caraz and around *p347, map p347*

B-C O'Pal Inn, 3 km south of Caraz, T/F043-391015, www.opalsierraresort.com. This scenic hotel is outside town, set back from road. Bungalows and rooms, which have private bath, in a country setting, swimming pool. Recommended.

D Chamanna, Av Nueva Victoria 185, 25 mins walk from centre, T043-978 4841/953 5279 (mob), www.chamanna.com. Clean cabañas in a beautiful garden, hot water, secure, excellent French and international cuisine in pricey restaurant. Recommended.

D-F Los Pinos, Parque San Martín 103, 5 blocks from plaza, T043-391130, lospinos @apuaventura.com. Rooms with and without private bath, hot water, airy and comfortable, garden open to all travellers, camping US$2.50, use of internet US$0.50 per hr, use of kitchen US$3, laundry service, clean, safe, book exchange, information and travel agency **Apu-Aventura** (see page 359). Breakfast and dinner are available, bar with movies every night. Recommended.

E Caraz Dulzura, Sáenz Peña 212, about 10 blocks from the town centre, T043-391523, hostalcarazdulzura@hotmail.com. Modern building in an old street, 6 double rooms, hot water, with bathroom and TV, comfortable, great service, very helpful owner (Carlos), clean and airy rooms, breakfast included, very good food available. Recommended.

E Casa de Campo, 28 de Julio 201, at the top of San Martín, T043-391319/01-9876 9638 (mob), tinebethdepe@hotmail.com. Interesting arty place with friendly owners. Sports training, cycling and Swedish massage are among the activities offered; breakfast is included. Owner Christine spent much of her life growing up in the pre-glasnost Soviet block.

E La Perla de los Andes, Plaza de Armas 179, T/F043-392007. Comfortable rooms with bath, hot water, TV, helpful, fair restaurant. Has a large new, cheaper annex 1 block up San Martín. Recommended.

E Tunshukaiko, Jr Melgar 114, T043-392212. Private bath, hot water, balconies, nice garden, sitting room with fireplace.

E Villa Huandy, by Puente Llullan just before Tunshukaiko ruins, T043-391104, ocanadav@qnet.com.pe. Modern and spacious, balconies, swimming pool, parking, restauarnt, far from centre.

E-F La Alameda, Av Noé Bazán Peralta 262, T043-391177, jtorres@viabcp.com.pe. Hot water. Comfortable or cheaper rooms, breakfast, parking, gardens. Recommended.

F Chavín, San Martín 1135 just off the plaza, T043-391171, hostalcahvin66@hotmail.com. With bathroom, warm water, good service but a bit grubby and dark, breakfast extra, guiding service, tourist information, owner can arrange transport to Lago Parón.

F Cordillera Blanca, Grau 903, T043-391938. Modern concrete building opposite market, rooms with private bath, hot water and TV.

F Huandoy, Los Olivos s/n, T043-391441. Private bath, hot water, modern, good value.

F Regina, Los Olivos s/n y Gálvez, south end of town, 1 block west of road to Yungay, T043-391520. Modern, with bathroom, hot water, clean, quiet, good value.

G Alojamiento Caballero, D Villar 485, T043-391637, or ask at **Pony's Expeditions** . Shared bathroom, hot water, washing facilities, stores luggage, basic, family run.

G Familia Aguilar, San Martín 1143, next to Chavín, T043-391161. Basic, one room with bath, otherwise shared bathroom.

G Hostal La Casona, Raymondi 319, 1 block east from the plaza, T043-391334. Most rooms without bathroom; a couple of more expensive rooms have bath, hot water, clean, lovely little patio, basic but good.

G per person **Ramírez**, D Villar 407. Basic, clean, shared bathroom, limited hot water.

Eating

Carhuaz *p344*

El Abuelo, Plaza de Armas, T043-394149. Local and international fare. Produce from their garden, including natural ice cream.

La Bicharra, just north of Carhuaz on main road, T043-978 0893 (mob). Innovative North African/Peruvian cooking, lunch only, busy at weekends, check if they are open Mon-Fri.

La Cabaña, at Acopampa, 3 km south of town. Specialities are regional dishes, including *cuy*. Nice garden, friendly owner.

Yungay *p345*

Alpamayo, Av Arias Grazziani s/n, at the northern entrance to town. Best in town serving excellent value local dishes such as trout, *cuy*, *tamales* and *pachamanca* at weekends. Open lunch only.

Ÿ **Café Pilar**, on the main plaza. Good for juices, cakes and snacks.

Around Yungay *p346*
The only tourism infrastructure in **Matacota** is the **Almawasi** restaurant, serving European home cooking at reasonable prices on a breathtaking terrace facing the snow peaks.

Caraz and around *p347, map p347*
ŸŸ-Ÿ **La Punta Grande**, D Villar 595, 10 mins' walk from centre. Best place for local dishes, good, open for lunch only till 1700.
Ÿ **El Mirador**, Sucre 1202 on the plaza. Nice view from terrace, set lunch and BBQ chicken at night.
Ÿ **Esmeralda**, Av Alfonso Ugarte 404. Good set meal, breakfast, friendly, recommended.
Ÿ **Heladería Caraz Dulzura**, D Villar on the plaza, next to **Perla de los Andes**. Excellent home made ice cream, good value meals, pastries.
Ÿ **Jeny**, Daniel Villar on the plaza between cathedral and phone office. Good food at reasonable prices, also *pollería*.
Ÿ **Oasis**, Raymondi, just off the plaza. Meals for about US$1-1.50, also has rooms (**E**).

Cafés
Good *manjar blanco* is sold by the Lúcar family, Villa Luisa brand, in a house next to the phone office on Raymondi.
Café de Rat, Sucre 1266, above **Pony's Expeditions**. Serves breakfast, vegetarian and meat dishes, pizzas, drinks and snacks, darts, travel books, nice vibe, recommended.
El Turista, San Martín 1117. Open in morning and evening only. Small, popular for breakfast; ham omelettes and ham sandwiches are specialities.
Establo La Alameda, D Villar 420. Excellent *manjar blanco*, cakes and sweets.
Panificadora La Alameda, D Villar y San Martín. Very good bread and pastries, ice cream, popular with locals.

Bars and clubs

Caraz and around *p347, map p347*
El Tabasco Taberna, 3 blocks from the plaza. Disco, latin and other music
Taberna Disco Huandy, Mcal Cáceres 119. Reasonable prices, good atmosphere, young crowd, Latin music. Fri and Sat only .

Festivals and events

Carhuaz *p344*
14-24 Sep Fiesta in honour of the **Vírgen de las Mercedes**, rated as the best in the region.

Yungay *p345, map p356*
28 Oct The anniversary of the founding of the town: parades, fireworks and dances.

Caraz and around *p347, map p347*
20 Jan Virgen de Chiquinquirá.
Mar/Apr Semana Santa (Holy Week) features processions and streets carpeted with flower petals.
Last week in Jul Semana Turística, with sports festivals, canoeing, parasailing and folkloric events.

Shopping

Caraz and around *p347*
Shop for camping supplies, such as fresh food, in the market. Some dried camping food is available from **Pony's Expeditions**, who also sell camping gas.

Activities and tours

Yungay *p345, map p356*
Cycle World, Arias Graziani 3ra cuadra, near bridge at south end of Yungay, T043-303109. Bike rentals at US$10/day including helmet and gloves. For US$3 a combi will take you and your rented bike to Llanganuco. The ride down is beautiful and exhilarating, but cold. Recommended.

Caraz and around *p347, map p347*
Horse riding
La Alameda, 4 km south of Caraz, 5 mins by combi towards Yungay, T043-391935. A variety of horse riding routes through fields, across the Río Santa and in to the Cordillera Negra to give fine views of the peaks, US$5 per hr, with guide. Horses for both novice and experienced riders are available.

Mountain biking
Llanganuco is a popular one-day ride from Caraz, as is **Lago Parón**, the **Cañón del Pato** and the Puya Raimondii plants at **Winchus**. The **Santa Cruz Valley** forms part of another long circuit.

Parasailing
Parasailing is practised 9 km on the road to Huaraz but you must supply your own equipment. **Cayasbamba**, near Caraz, is a good launch site at 3000 m. Those who need a few lessons, should contact Alex, owner of **The Way Inn Hostel** and **The Way Inn Lodge**, see page 335 for details.

Tour operators
Apu-Aventura, based at Hotel Los Pinos (see page 357), www.apuaventura.com. Adventure sports and equipment rental.
Pony's Expeditions, Sucre 1266, near the Plaza de Armas, T/F043-391642, www.ponyexpeditions.com. Mon-Sat 0800-2200. English, French and Quechua spoken, reliable information about the area. Owners Alberto and Aidé Cafferata are very knowledgeable about treks and climbs. They arrange local tours, trekking and transport (US$30 for up 4 people) for day excursions, maps and books for sale, also equipment for hire, mountain bike rental (US$15 for a full day). Possible to pay for services with Visa. Highly recommended.

Trekking
Mariano Araya is a trekking guide who is also keen on photography and archaeology. Ask at the municipality.

Transport

Carhuaz *p344*
All transport leaves from the main plaza. To **Huaraz**, *colectivos* and buses 0500-2000, US$0.75, 40 mins. To **Caraz**, 0500-2000, US$0.75, 1 hr. Buses from Huaraz to **Chacas** in the Cordillera Blanca (see page 342), 87 km, 4-5 hrs, US$3.75, pass through Carhuaz about 40 mins after leaving Huaraz. The road works its way up the Ulta valley to **Punta Olímpica** from where there are excellent views. The dirt road is not in a very good condition owing to landslides every year (in the wet season it can be closed). The trucks continue to **San Luis**, a further 10 km, 1½ hrs. In addition, Trans Huandoy does the return trip from Carhuaz to **Chacas**, Thu only, US$6 one way, 5 hrs.

Yungay *p345, map p356*
Most transport leaves from Jr 28 de Julio. Buses, *colectivos* run all day to **Caraz**, 12 km, US$0.30, and to **Huaraz**, 54 km, 1½ hrs, US$1. To **Lagunas Llanganuco**, combis leave when full, especially 0700-0900, from Av 28 de Julio 1 block from the plaza, 1 hr, US$1.50; otherwise it's US$9 to hire a vehicle (or US$12 with 2 hrs wait). To **Yanama**, via the Portachuelo de Llanganuco Pass, 4767 m, 3½ hrs, US$3; stopping at María Huayta, after 2 hrs, US$2. To **Pomabamba**, via Piscobamba, **Trans Los Andes**, daily 0700-0730 (this is the only company with a ticket office in Yungay); **Transvir** and **La Perla de Altamayo** buses from Huaraz, 0730, stop if they have room, 6-7 hrs, US$6. After passing the Llanganuco lakes and crossing the Portachuelo the buses descend to Puente Llacma, where it is possible to pick up buses and combis heading south to San Luis, Chacas and Huari.

Caraz and around *p347, map p347*
Local To **Huaraz**, frequent combis, daily 0400-2000, 1¼ hrs, US$1.35, the road is in good condition. They leave from a terminal on the way out of town, where the south end of Sucre meets the highway. By combi to **Yungay**, 12 km, 15 mins, US$0.30. To the village of **Parón** (for trekking in Laguna Parón area) combis leave from the corner Santa Cruz and Grau by the market, Mon-Sat 0400 and 1300, Sun 0300 and 1300, 1 hr, US$1.20; they return from Parón at 0600 and 1400. To **Cashapampa** (Quebrada Santa Cruz) buses from Santa Cruz y Grau, hourly 0600-1530, 2 hrs, US$1.50; taxis charge US$7.55. To **Huallanca** (Caraz) and **Yuramarca** for the Cañón del Pato (see page), combis and cars leave from Córdova y La Mar, 0700-1730, US$1.50. Combis to **Hualcayan** for the Alpamayo Valley trek leave from Santa Cruz y Grau, 0400, 0700, 1100 and 1300, US$2.45, 2 hrs. To **Huata** for the Cordillera Negra, combis and cars leave from the Parque del Maestro (Córdova y Santa Cruz), 0700, 1000, 1200, 1 hr. For the Puya Raimondi at **Winchos**, take a combi from Grau y Ugarte around 0900 to **Pamparomas**, 2 hrs, US$2, or hire a combi for US$42.50 for 8 people, plus US$7.20 for a guide.
Long distance Most Lima–Huaraz buses continue to Caraz. To **Lima**, 470 km, via Huaraz and Pativilca; several companies on D Villar and Jr Córdova, daily, 10-11 hrs, US$7: **El Huaralino, Expreso Ancash**, T043-391509, **Móvil, Rodríguez**, T043-391184.

To **Chimbote**, with Yungay Express (D Villar 318), via Cañón del Pato, 0830, US$6.60, 8 hrs; sit on the right for best views. To **Trujillo**, via Huaraz and Pativilca, with Chinchaysuyo (Córdova 830, T791930), daily 1845, US$9.10, 11-12 hrs, stops in Casma (US$7.60) and Chimbote (US$7.60).

Directory

Caraz and around *p347, map p347*
Banks BCP, D Villar 217, cash and TCs at good rates, also cash advances against Visa, Mon-Fri 0930- 1600, Sat 1000-1300. Importaciones América, Sucre 721, T043-391479, offers good rates and service, open weekends and evenings. For large amounts of cash, however, it is better to exchange in Huaraz. **Internet** There are many places around the plaza and throughout town, US$0.30. **Post** At San Martín 909. **Telephone** International and national phone and fax service at Raymondi y Sucre. Also several others, eg at Sucre y Santa Cruz, and on Plaza de Armas next to **Jeny**. Collect calls can only be made from private lines. Note that very few of the coin boxes take phone cards.

Eastern flank of the Cordillera Blanca

A trip to Chavín de Huantar is a must if you are in the area, as it is one of the most important archaeological sites in the country. At the height of its power, Chavín's influence was felt over a vast area. Along the east side of the Cordillera Blanca, which is known as the Callejón de Conchucos, runs a good, but narrow, dirt road, subject to rapid deterioration when it rains. The region has seen fewer foreign tourists than the Callejón de Huaylas, so some discretion, as well as responsible behaviour, is called for. ›› *For Sleeping, Eating and other listings, see pages 366-369.*

Ins and outs

Many people only go as far as Chavín de Huantar, taking a tour with a Huaraz company. If you decide to go north from Chavín all, or part way up the eastern side of the Cordillera Blanca, note that public transport is less frequent and less reliable here than in the Callejón de Huaylas, with some towns getting only two buses per week, direct from Lima. Private vehicles, usually large trucks, are few and far between, although there are some buses running across the passes back to the Callejón de Huaylas. ›› *For further details, see Transport page 368.*

Huaraz to Chavín ›› *pp355-360.*

Olleros and around

The main road south to Pativilca passes the turn-off for **Olleros** at 3450 m, the starting point for the spectacular three-day hike to Chavín, along a pre-Columbian trail (see below). Some basic meals and food supplies are available here. An alternative trek from Olleros is to **Quebrada Rurec** via **Huaripampa**, a small village with a few *bodegas* that will sell or prepare food. Public transport is available to Huaripampa. There are granite walls of up to 600 m at Rurec, the highest in the Cordillera Blanca, which are recommended for rock climbing. The trek itself is also worthwhile.

Further south on the main road (27 km, 30 minutes from Huaraz) is **Recuay,** one of the few provincial capitals to have survived the 1970 earthquake and retained its colonial features. There is a sizeable cave with stalagmites and stalagtites on the main road (entry free). On 11-16 September the town celebrates the **Festividad Señor de Burgos de Recuay.**

Olleros to Chavín trek

The trek begins at the village of **Canrey Chico** and follows an impressive pre-Inca road with several unexplored ruins along the way. There are combis to Canrey Chico from Parque PIP or Avenida Tarapacá in Huaraz, starting early, but with no reliable schedule (US$1.50); better to take a taxi, 30 minutes, US$4.

This lovely and relatively easy three- to four-day trek has become less popular with agencies and groups in recent times, perhaps because of persistent begging on the Chavín side. Hence there is is an opportunity for independent trekkers to fill the gap and try to remedy the social situation. Never give money, medicines or sweets, which will do more harm than good. Consider sharing other food, if you feel it is appropriate, otherwise offer only a polite smile. There are also dogs along the route, generally raucous but inoffensive. The route follows the south (right) shores of the Río Negro, Quebrada Uquián, Quebrada Shongo, and Quebrada Huachecsa all the way to the Chavín archaeologic site.

Numbers in the text refer to numbers on the map, below.

The route When you reach **Canrey Chico** (1), turn right to keep on the road which follows the Río Negro. Keep the river on the left. The track is perfectly clear and there is a large Parque Nacional Huascarán sign. At this point a track branches off to the left into the **Quebrada Rurec** (see above); continue straight ahead. A small sign marks the intersection (2). **Quebrada Uquian** (3) becomes flatter here and the river more sinuous. By some stone corrals, you see a lateral morraine on your right, evidence of old glacial activity. To avoid the boggy valley floor, you can climb along the crest of the morraine (4) to more corrals and straw-thatched stone huts. Here you begin to see the large flat top of the valley.

Sacrapampa (5), marked with a large sign, is a convenient spot to camp before starting the climb to the pass. At the top of the valley, it divides into four valleys. The path swings right to avoid the marsh then heads up the second valley on the left, often with a ridge between the path and the river, to the highest point. It is quite easy to lose the track here, but keep heading in the direction of the pass and you'll pick it up eventually. It's a slow, gradual climb to the pass. There are stone cairns and several small ponds at **Punta Yanashallash** (6; 4700 m), and great views of the surrounding summits. The trail then follows the ancient road over impressive zigzags making light work of what would otherwise be a difficult 400-m descent.

Shongo (7), also called Shongopampa and marked with a large sign, is a good camping spot; the last before entering populated areas where begging is a problem. At **Lluchucaca** (8; bare cliff) the trail crosses a narrow ledge. This is safe in dry weather but can be avoided by descending to the river. Fifteen minutes ahead is a wooden

Olleros to Chavín trek

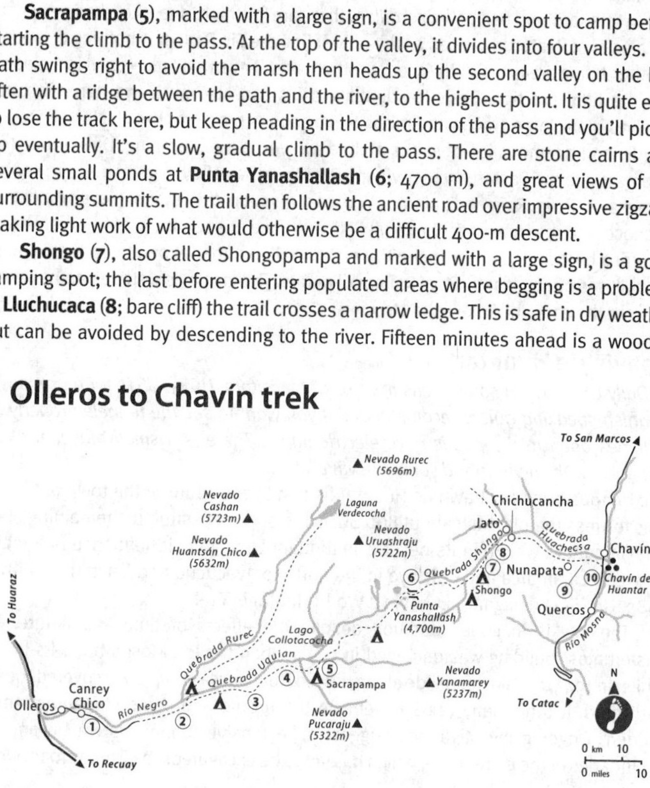

 bridge over Quebrada Shongo. Cross to the north side if you wish to make a side-trip to Jato and explore the valleys up from there. Otherwise, stay on the south side of Quebrada Shongo and follow the trail through the hamlet of **Chichucancha**. Head down into the **Quebrada Huachecsa (9)** till you reach Punta Huancayo where you can see the ruins of **Chavín de Huantar (10)**. Go through the village of Nueva Florida to reach the road. The town of Chavín is on the left and the archaeological ruins are straight ahead (see page 362).

If cycling through the Cahuish tunnel, make sure you have a strong light so that trucks and buses can see you.

Catac to Chavín → *Colour map 3, B3.*

The main road continues 11 km south from Recuay to **Catac**, where a road branches east for Chavín (all paved). From Catac to Chavín is a magnificent, scenic journey, if frightening at times. Beyond Laguna Querococha, there are good views of the Yanamarey peaks and, at the top of the route, the road is cut through a huge rock face, entering the **Cahuish tunnel** at 4550 m . The road through the tunnel is one lane, with a concrete surface, covered with wet sand. A small stream, up to 30-cm deep, runs inside. On the other side the road descends into the Tambillo Valley, then the Río Mosna gorge before reaching Chavín.

A good spot to see Puya Raimondi plants is the Queshque Gorge. Follow the Río Queshque from Catac; it's easy to find.

Southern Cordillera Blanca

Several kilometres south of Catac is **Pachacoto** from where a road goes to **Huallanca** (Huánuco) on the other side of the Cordillera Blanca (133 km, 4½ hours; see page 522), not to be confused with the town of the same name by the Cañón del Pato. Buses to Huallanca no longer take this route but go on the paved road via Chiquián.

In this southern part of the *cordillera* there are few high, snow-covered peaks, but the glacier of **Pastoruri** is used as the only skiing area in Peru. It is nothing compared to other skiing areas in South America – there aren't even ski lifts – but it is a place to get in a little practice. Basic ice-climbing skills can also be learnt here. Pastoruri receives many large groups and rubbish is a serious problem. The glacier is receding rapidly and a famous ice cave has melted away to almost nothing. Daily tours from Huaraz run to the Pastoruri valley via the **Pumapampa valley**, a good place to see the impressive Puya Raimondi plants. You can hike up the 14-km gravel road from Pachacoto to the Huascarán National Park entrance at 4200 m, in 2½ hours. There's an office here and you can spend the night. Walking up the road beyond this point, you will see more gigantic Puya Raimondi plants. The glacier is a steep one-hour walk up from the car park. Take extra clothing.

Chavín de Huantar → *Colour map 3, B3.*

ⓘ *Daily 0800-1700; some areas are closed to visitors. US$3, US$5 for a group with Spanish-speaking guide; recommended if you want to see the tunnels properly. All galleries open to the public have electric lights. There is a small museum at the entrance, with carvings and some Chavín pottery.*

The famous ruins of Chavín de Huantar lie just to the south of the town of Chavín. This fortress temple, built about 800 BC, is the only large structure remaining of the Chavín culture which, in its heyday, is thought to have held influence in a region between Cajamarca and Chiclayo in the north to Ayacucho and Ica in the south. In 1985, UNESCO designated Chavín a World Heritage Site.

The site is in good condition despite the effects of time and nature. The easternmost building was damaged in 1993, when the Río Mosna burst its banks, while, in 1945, a major landslide along the Río Huachecsa completely covered the site with mud. It took many years to remove the rubble and some structures remain hidden. Ongoing investigations suggest an extensive tunnel system beyond the boundaries of the current site, which has yet to be excavated. The Huaraz road, which

The stone gods of Chavín

Archaeologists have learnt very little about the Chavín culture, whose architecture and sculpture had a strong impact on the artistic and cultural development of a large part of the coast and central highlands of Peru. Based on physical evidence from the study of this 17-acre site, the temple of Chavín de Huantar is thought to have been a major ceremonial centre.

What first strikes visitors upon arrival at Chavín is the quality of the stonework. The sculptures have three functions: architectural, ornamental and cultist. Examples include the Lanzón, the Tello obelisk and the Raimondi stela; the latter two currently grace the Museo Nacional de Antropología, Arqueología e Historia in Lima (see page 92).

At 5 m high, the **Lanzón** is the crowning glory of the Chavín religion and stands at the heart of the underground complex. Its Spanish name comes from the lance-, or dagger-like shape of the monolith which appears to be stuck in the ground. Carved into the top of the head are thin, grooved channels; some speculate that animals, or even humans, may have been sacrificed to this god. Others suggest that the Lanzón was merely the dominant figure for worship.

Named after the Peruvian scientist, Julius C Tello, the **Tello obelisk** belongs to the earliest period of occupation of Chavín (ca 100 BC). It represents a complex deity – perhaps a caiman-alligator – connected with the earth, water and all the living elements of nature. Carved on the body are the people, birds, serpents and felines that the divine beast has consumed.

The **Raimondi stela** was named after the Italian naturalist, who also gave his name to the famous plant (see page 355), not to mention a fair percentage of the streets in the region. It shows a feline anthropomorphic divinity standing with open arms and holding some sort of staff in each hand.

Together, the figures carved on the stones at Chavín indicate that the resident cult was based principally on the feline, or jaguar, and secondarily on serpents and birds.

cuts across this area, may have to be moved to the other side of the valley some time in the future in order for excavations to continue.

The main attractions are the marvellous carved stone heads, the designs in relief of symbolic figures (see box above) and the many tunnels and culverts which form an extensive labyrinth throughout the interior of the structures. The carvings are in excellent condition, though many of the best sculptures are in Huaraz and Lima. The famous Lanzón dagger-shaped stone monolith of 800 BC is found inside one of the temple tunnels. Excavations in 2001 uncovered a collection of 20 *pututos* (wind instruments) dating from the site's origins.

Day tours from Huaraz are offered by many agencies; it's a long but worthwhile trip, but check how many hours you get at the site. In high season, the site is busy with tourists all day through. You will receive an information leaflet in Spanish at the entrance. The guard also sells other reference material including *Chavín de Huantar* by Willhelm and Nancy Hoogendoorn, an English/Spanish guide to the ruins which includes a description of each building and an historical overview.

Chavín → *Colour map 3, B3. Altitude: 3160 m.*

The town of Chavín is the commercial centre for the nearby potato- and corn-growing area. The local *fiesta* takes place on 13-20 July. It has a pleasant plaza with palm and pine trees, and several good, simple hotels and restaurants. The shops are well stocked with basic supplies, and carved stone replicas are produced for the tourist trade. There is also a small market. Gasoline is available at the north end of town but there is nowhere to change money. Now that the road from Huaraz is fully paved, the trip to Chavín takes about two hours, short enough for a day trip. Sadly, perhaps because it has been flooded by tour groups, Chavín has become increasingly uncomfortable for gringos, with overcharging, begging and hostile stares. The **Baños Termales de Chavín** ⓘ *Quercos, Km 68, 2 km south of Chavín, US$0.60*, are hot sulphur baths, consisting of one small, quite cool pool and four individual baths in a pleasant setting by the Río Mosna. You may have to queue and clean the bath yourself. Camping is possible here.

Callejón de Conchucos » *pp355-360.*

The road north from Chavín descends into the dry Mosna river canyon. This is the start of the route to Pomabamba and beyond. If you plan to travel in this area, allow plenty of time, especially in the rainy season, as the bus service is infrequent.

San Marcos → *Altitude 2960 m.*

After 8 km is San Marcos, a small, friendly town with a nice plaza and a fancy modern church. It is known as 'City of the Magnolias', but there are few in evidence around the town. Gasoline is available 24 hours. Combis run from San Marcos to the large Canadian-run mine, high on the puna, at **Antamina**, two hours. (Unfortunately, the impressive mine road from Antamina, via Huallanca (Huánuco), to Conococha is privately owned and it is not possible to travel direct from Chavín to Huallanca without returning to Huaraz at present.)

Twenty kilometres beyond San Marcos, at the junction of the Huari and Mosna rivers, is the village of **Pomachaca** (Las Tunas), where a road branches northeast to **Llamellín**. The main road continues north and climbs, criss-crossing the Huari river amid dry hills, to reach Huari 12 km further on.

Huari and around → *Colour map 3, B2. Altitude 3150 m.*

The town, perched on a hillside at 3150 m, has steep streets with good views of the mountains. The Plaza de Armas and cathedral are modern, having been rebuilt after the 1970 earthquake. It has a small fruit and vegetable market, which is quite busy on Sunday, and well-stocked shops. The water supply can be intermittent. The local *fiesta* of **Nuestra Señora del Rosario** is held during the first two weeks of October.

There is a spectacular two- to three-day walk from Huari to Chacas via **Laguna Purhuay**. The route is clearly shown on the IGM map, sheet 19. The walking is very easy, crossing over a 4500-m pass and through the beautiful Purhuay valley, at 3500 m. The valley has its own microclimate and the animals, insects and flowers are more like those found in a tropical jungle. At the northern end of Purhuay there's a *quenoal* forest. There's plenty of running water and lots of good places for camping.

A day walk to Laguna Purhuay can be done by those who don't want the longer walk to Chacas, but there is not really enough time to walk the steep paths that go round and above the lake. To get to Laguna Purhuay, climb the stairs at the end of Jirón Luzuriaga in Huari to the main road; turn north, and walk for about 3 km to the village of **Acopalca**, which has a fish farm where you can buy trout. Turn left after crossing the bridge (ask directions), from where it's a 1½-hour walk up to the lake. The path to Chacas forks left just before the lake, while another good trail crosses the outflow and climbs above the eastern shore to a lookout, where it divides: the left fork descends to the inflow, which is a narrow gorge called La Cola (the tail); the right fork climbs to the village of Cachitzin (no facilities). There are no good trails along the shore of the lake.

Chacas → *Colour map 3, A3. Altitude 3360 m.*

Ten kilometres south of San Luis, off the main road, is Chacas, with its fine church. The local *fiesta patronal* is in mid-August, with bullfights, a famous *carrera de cintas* (belt race) and fireworks. There are a few basic shops, restaurants, a small market and two or three basic *hostals*, including **Hostal de Pilar**. Seek out the **Taller Don Bosco**, a woodcarving workshop run by an Italian priest.

It is a two-day hike from Chacas to **Marcará** (see page 344) via the Quebradas Juytush and Honda (lots of condors to be seen). The latter is known as the 'Paraíso de las Cascadas' because it contains at least seven waterfalls.

San Luis and around → *Colour map 3, A3. Altitude 3130 m.*

From Huari the road climbs to the Huachacocha pass at 4350 m and descends to San Luis at 3130 m. There is basic and cheap accommodation at **Hostal Rotta**, also a few basic restaurants, shops and a market. To continue north from San Luis, you may have to hire a minibus (US$15 for the vehicle) to take you the 28 km to **Puente Llacma**, the junction of the roads for Yanama and Pomabamba, from where you can hitchhike. The road which branches left at Puente Llacma goes to **Yanama**, 45 km from San Luis, at 3400 m. The village is beautifully surrounded by snow-capped peaks. A day's hike to the ruins above the town affords superb views. There are lodgings and food is available. From Yanama, you can return to Huaraz via Yungay (see page 345).

Piscobamba → *Colour map 3, A3. Altitude 3290 m.*

A large sanctuary to **Nuestro Señor de Pumayukay**, built by Italian priests, is a 15-minute ride from San Luis towards Pomabamba and then a turn-off to the east. The main road through the Callejón de Conchucos continues north for 62 km to **Piscobamba** ('pampa of the birds', from the quechua 'Pishco Pampa'). It has a pleasant plaza and spectacular views across the heavily wooded valley to the Cordillera Blanca, stretching from the Alpamayo massif in the north to beyond Huascarán in the south. Hostales **San Pedro** and **Yomara** are both basic. There are also a few shops and small restaurants.

Pomabamba → *Colour map 3, A3. Altitude 2950 m.*

Known as 'City of the Cedars', though only two very old specimens remain in the centre of the plaza, surrounded by roses and jacarandas, Pomabamba ('pampa of the pumas', quechua 'Puma Pampa') is 22 km beyond Piscobamba. The main plaza has been rebuilt (2006) and there is a small museum and tourist office at Huaraz 515, with variable opening hours. A five-minute walk down a steep path from the plaza and across the river are very hot natural springs and three different bathing establishments, all with private baths (US$0.30 per person, no time limit). Ask for the baths to be cleaned before you use them. The main festival is 24 June.

Treks from Pomabamba

Several good walks into the Cordillera Blanca start from near Pomabamba. You can hike up either the Yanacollpa or Jancapampa valleys, from where you can go on, if you're fit enough, to **Nevado Alpamayo**, dubbed 'the most beautiful mountain in the world', with an incredible glacier. A complete description of this route is given on page 351.

For the less energetic, a good day trip can be made to the quite extensive, though sadly dilapidated, Huari ruins of **Yaino**, on top of a very steep mountain and visible from the main plaza of Pomabamba. The walls are beautifully built and there are two very large buildings, a square one and a circular one. The site commands excellent views of the many peaks of the Cordillera. To get there take a combi to Huaychó, one hour, US$1. Take the path to Garhuay (two hours), a set of smaller Huari ruins, and continue upwards to Yaino (two hours). An alternative return route is to walk down to Huayllan, on the Pomabamba–Huaychó road, and catch a combi (30 minutes). Take food and lots of water, as you can get very dehydrated by climbing and perspiring in the thin dry air. It's also very cold when the sun goes in, so take warm, waterproof clothes.

Another good day walk leaves Pomabamba for the Inca Road: climb from the **Curayacu** fountain to the hamlet of **Cushurú** and then up along the ridge on your right. You can follow the road south and return to Pomabamba via Pajash. There are several unexplored ruins along the Inca Road. To the north is **Mesa Rumi**, two hours, a remarkably precise and unique metre-square block of Inca stone with ceremonial holes in its upper surface.

A shorter walk (three to four hours) begins from the bridge over the river and runs up a side valley, past a trout farm, to the beautiful **Jancapampa** valley below the Alpamayo massif. Camping is possible there.

To Sihuas and beyond → *Colour map 3, A2. Altitude 2730 m.*

From Pomabamba a dusty road runs up the wooded valley crossing the puna at **Palo Seco**, 23 km. The road then descends steeply into the desert-like Sihuas valley, passing through the village of **Sicsibamba**. The valley is crossed half an hour below Sihuas.

The small town of Sihuas itself is divided into three sections spreading over a kilometre up the valley. The lowest district is the oldest with a fine colonial interior to the church. All the bus company offices, hotels and restaurants are in the middle district. The town is a major connection point between the Callejón de Conchucos, Callejón de Huaylas, the upper Marañón and the coast but although you may stopover while travelling between these areas, there is little to do in the immediate surrounding area. The town suffers from water shortages.

From Sihuas it is now possible to travel, via Huancaspata, Tayabamba, Retamas and Chahual, to **Huamachuco** along a road which is very poor in places and involves crossing the river Marañón twice. The building of a new bridge over the river means that it is now possible to travel by public transport all the way from Cuzco to Quito through the Andes, without going down to the Pacific Lowlands. The journey is best undertaken in this direction (south–north) though the road may be almost impassable in the wet season. A detour up the Marañón Valley leads to **Huacrachuco**, where there are several basic *hostales*. The significant Inca ruins of **Mamahuagay** are nearby and a five-day walk down to Uchiza in the Huallaga valley can be made.

Sleeping

Olleros *p360*
D **Altas Montañas**, at edge of Olleros, T043-722569, altasmont@yahoo.es. Small 3-star lodge, Belgian-run, with hot showers, good breakfast included, dinner available, bar, birdwatching, guided treks, information, laundry, recommended for start or end of trek to Chavín, phone 24 hours in advance, preferably at 2000, to arrange free pickup from Huaraz.

Chavín *p363, map p367*
E **La Casona**, Wiracocha 130, Plaza de Armas, T043-454048, lacasonachavin@peru.com. In an old house with attractive courtyard, private bathroom, cheaper with shared bath, insufficient hot water, friendly, one room with a double bed, motorcycle parking.
E **R'ickay**, on 17 de Enero 172N (north), T043-454027, 01-9657 4013 (mob). Set around two patios, modern, pricey, all rooms with private bathroom and TV, hot water, restaurant (see below).
F **Hostal Chavín**, Jr San Martín 141-151, half a block from the plaza, T/F043-454055. Set around a pleasant courtyard, **G** without bath, hot water, provides breakfast for groups, best of the more basic hotels, friendly and helpful, but poor beds.
E **Inca**, Wiracocha 160, T043-454021. In a renovated house, garden, friendly.

Camping at Chavín de Huantar is possible for vehicles, with permission from the guard.

San Marcos *p364*

A per person **Konchukos Tambo**, 2 km from San Marcos, T043-454630, www.perunature.com, chavin@rainforest.com.pe. A new lodge in the Conchucos valley, about 12 km from Chavín. Price includes full board and transport from Huaraz. Bungalow complex, rooms with stove, bath and hot water. Gardens, dining room and bar. Activities include visits to Chavín, hikes, textile demonstrations, horse riding, biking and fishing. Run by **Rainforest Expeditions**, who also run **Posada Amazonas**, see page 559.

G **La Rinconada**, La Merced 325. Best of the several basic *hostales*.

Huari *p364*

G **Añaños**, Alvarez 437, next to the market. Very basic but clean.

G **El Dorado**, Bolívar 341. Basic, comfortable, sunny patio, shared bathroom, hot water.

San Luis and around *p365*

F **Hostal El Pino**, Yanama. The best place to stay in Yanama, clean, with good views and a small restaurant. Recommended.

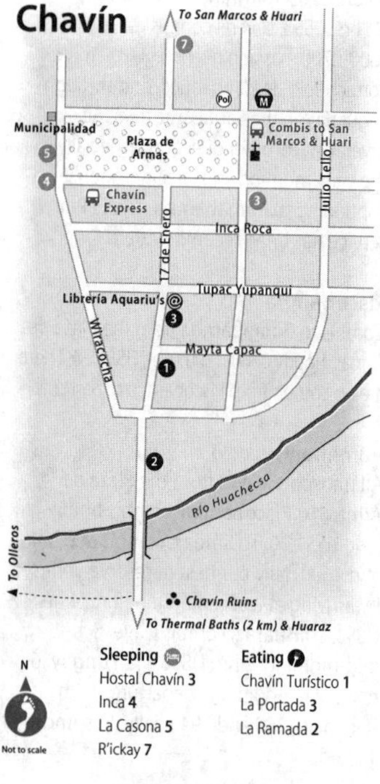

Pomabamba *p365*

F **Albergue Turístico Vía**, Jr Primavera 323, T043-741052, verladicho@hotmail.com. Family run, breakfast available, rooms with bath and shared bath, cold water, friendly and helpful. Also private bath-house at thermal baths.

G **Anny**, Jr Moquegua y Jorge Gálvez, barrio El Convento, T043-751125. Some rooms with private bath, cold water.

G **Hostal Estrada Vidal**, Huaraz 209, T043-804615. Run by friendly Sra Estrada Vidal, rustic, rooms around a pleasant courtyard, clean, cold water, good value. Recommended.

G **Hostal Pomabamba**, Jr Huamachuco 338 on Plaza de Armas, T043-751276. With private bath, even cheaper without, cold water, basic but OK.

To Sihuas and beyond *p366*

F **Hostal Liliana**, Jr Ramón Castilla y Ricardo Palma, T043-741125. In a newer building, large rooms some with bath, G without bath, basic but OK.

G **Hostal Don César**, Av 28 de Julio 309, T043-741044. With shared bath, neither clean nor friendly, very basic.

Eating

Chavín *p363*

In the better restaurants, specialities include rabbit stew, trout *ceviche* and *llunca*, a solid, wheat-based soup.

¶¶ **R'ickay**, see Sleeping, above. Pasta and pizza dishes in the evenings.

¶¶-¶ **Chavín Turístico**, 17 de Enero. Overpriced and mediocre *menú*, but good à la carte, delicious apple pie, clean, nice courtyard. Beware overcharging.

¶¶-¶ **La Portada**, 17 de Enero. In an old house with tables set around a garden.

¶ **La Ramada**, 17 de Enero. Regional dishes, also trout and set lunch.

San Marcos *p364*

Las Magnolias and Crillón Chico, in the main plaza, are the best of several basic, cheap restaurants.

Huari *p364*

¶ **Centro Virgen del Rosario**, San Martín by Parque Vigíl. Serves coffee, sweets and snacks, very clean and friendly, open evenings and Sun, run by an Italian nun and her students.

🍴 **Los Angeles**, Ancash 669, off the main plaza. Mainly chicken, popular.

🍴 **Rinconcito Huaracino**, Bolívar 530. Good *menú*, open till 2100.

Pomabamba *p365*

There is a limited choice of places to eat and most close by 2100.

🍴 **Davis-David**, Huaraz 269. Offers the best *menú* and can prepare soups to order.

🍴 **Las Piedras**, Jr Arica 350. *Menú* and à la carte, including trout.

🍴 **Los Cedros**, Huaraz 531. Good for breakfast.

Sihuas and beyond *p366*

🍴 **Chosas Nauticas** is a basic *comedor*, also good for breakfast. There are other similar places in town.

Transport

Chavín *p363, map p367*

Bus

It is much easier to get to Chavín than to leave the place by bus. All buses to Huaraz originate in Huari or beyond. They pass through Chavín at irregular hours and may not have seats available. Buying a ticket at an agency in Chavín does not guarantee you will get a seat or even a bus. To **Huaraz**, 110 km, 2 hrs, US$3. **Chavín Express** passes through around 1200, 1600 and 1700 daily; **Río Mosna** around 0430, 1600, 1800, 2000, and 2200 daily. All schedules are subject to change during road construction and improvements in the area.

To **Lima**, 438 km, 12 hrs, US$9, with **Trans El Solitario** and **Perú Andino** daily. Most companies use older, uncomfortable buses and many locals prefer to travel first to Huaraz and then take one of the more reputable companies from there (see page 342).

To other destinations in the Callejón de Conchucos it is necessary either to use buses coming from Huaraz or Lima, or to hop on and off combis which run between each town. Combis to **San Marcos**, every 20 mins from the Plaza de Armas, 25 mins, US$0.50; to **Huari**, 2 hrs , US$1.50. There are buses during the day from Lima and Huaraz, which go on to Huari, with some going on to **San Luis**, a further 61 km, 3 hrs; **Piscobamba**, a further 62 km, 3 hrs; and **Pomabamba**, a further 22 km, 1 hr; try **El Solitario**, which passes through Chavín at 1800. Other buses from Huaraz and Lima terminate in **Llamellín**, 120 km, 4 hrs, US$3.

Huari *p364*

Bus

Bus companies have their offices around Parque Vigil. To **Huaraz**, 5-6 hrs, US$3.75; departures through the day. To **San Luis**, Tue and Sat, 0600 with **El Solitario**, 0830 with **Perú Andino**. Buses heading north pass through Huari 2200-2400, but not every day. To **Lima**, 13 hrs, US$10, with **Turismo Huari** on Sun, Wed and Fri 0630, or with **Perú Andino** on Sun and Wed 0800. On Mon, Tue and Sat buses bound for Lima originating further north pass Huari 1000-1200.

San Luis and around *p365*

Bus

From San Luis to **Chavín** Wed and Sun, 5 hrs, US$6. To **Huaraz**, via Yanama and the pass at 4730 m under Huascarán, 8 hrs, but public transport is scarce on this route (**Virgen de Guadalupe** and **Renzo** buses go to Huaraz via Chacas). From Yanama to **Yungay**, 3½ hrs, US$3, several combis daily 0600-0700, passing over the 4767 m Portachuelo de Llanganuco and through Vaquería (on the Santa Cruz trek). Also several in the other direction, especially in the early morning and late afternoon, continuing to **Pomabamba**. The **El Pino** service has been recommended.

Piscobamba *p365*

Combis to **Pomabamba** from the Plaza de Armas, hourly 0700-1800, 1 hr, US$1.20. There are no combis from Piscobamba to San Luis.

Pomabamba *p365*

All transport leaves from the Plaza de Armas. To **Piscobamba**, combis hourly, 1 hr, US$1.20. To **Sihuas**, combis at 0200 and 1600 daily but best to reserve your seat by arriving at least an hour before, 4 hrs, US$3. To **Huaraz**, combis leave mid-morning, 7 hrs, US$6, via **Yungay**, 6 hrs, US$6. Additional departures with **Renzo** at 1300 and 1945 daily; **Los Andes** at 1945 daily.

To **Lima**, 18 hrs, US$11, via **San Luis** (4 hrs, US$3), **Huari** (6 hrs, US$4.50) and **Chavín** (9 hrs, US$6), with El Solitario, Sun, Mon and Thu 0800. To **Lima**, 16 hrs, US$11, via **Yungay** and **Huaraz** with La Perla del Alto Mayo, Wed, Thu, Sat, Sun.

Sihuas and beyond *p366*
To **Pomabamba**, combis daily at around 0700 and 1100, 4 hrs, US$3; no office, be out on the street early to get a seat. To **Huaraz**, via Huallanca, with **Transvir**, daily 0830, 8 hrs, US$7; **Trans Chavín Express**, Wed and Sat, and **Perú Andino**, Tue 1100, 8 hrs, US$7. To **Tayabamba**, for the Marañón route north to Huamachuco and Cajamarca, with **Andía** (en route from Lima) Mon, Wed and Sat 0100-0200, or **La Perla del Alto Mayo** (also from Lima), Wed and Sat 0000-0200; also twice a week with **Garrincha** and once a week with **San Antonio de Padua**; all 7-8 hrs, US$6, the beginning of a long wild ride. To **Huacrachuco, Trans Andina**, daily 1000. To **Chimbote**, **La Perla de Alta Mayo** Tue, Thu and Sun, 10 hrs, US$9. To **Lima** via Chimbote, with **Andía** daily around 0200-0500, 17 hrs, US$9; confirm all times locally. To **Trujillo** via Chimbote, Garrincha Mon and Thu 2200, 12 hrs, US$12.50.

Directory

Chavín *p363, map p367*
Internet At Librería Aquarius, 17 de Enero y Túpac Yupanqui, US$1 per hr. **Post** At 17 de Enero 365N (north). 0630-2200.
Telephone Pay phones all over town.

Huari *p364*
Post Luzuriaga 324 by Parque Vigíl.
Telephone Libertad 940. 0700-2200 daily.

Cordilleras Huayhuash and Raura

→ *Colour map 3, B3/4.*

Lying south of the Cordillera Blanca, the Cordillera Huayhuash has been dubbed the 'Himalayas of America' and is perhaps the most spectacular in Peru for its massive ice faces which seem to rise sheer out of the contrasting green of the puna. Azure trout-filled lakes are interwoven with deep quebradas and high pastures around the hem of the range. You may see tropical parakeets in the bottom of the gorges and condors circling the peaks.

Although the area may well have been inhabited for thousands of years, the Huayhuash only became known to the outside world following a plane crash on the southeast face of Jirishanca in 1954. Since then, the number of visitors has grown steadily, with a hiatus during the era of insurgency in the 1980s. The mountain range's renown increased following Joe Simpson and Simon Yates' near-tragic climbing expedition in 1985, as recounted in Simpson's book and the subsequent hit film, Touching the Void. *Although less touristy than some popular routes in the Cordillera Blanca, it nonetheless receives significant numbers of trekkers and climbers every year.*

The area is rugged and traditional, with local villagers generally surviving as herdsmen, tending flocks of cattle, sheep and alpacas. Having said that, tourism, large-scale mining interests and the relentless advance of paved roads has significantly affected the area, its people and environment, not always for the better.

▸▸ *For Sleeping, Eating and other listings, see page 372.*

Ins and outs

Getting there Both the Huayhuash and Raura ranges can be approached from **Chiquián** in the north; from **Oyón,** with links to Cerro de Pasco to the southeast; from **Churín** in the south, or from **Cajatambo** to the southwest. Coming from Huaraz, the road is now paved beyond Chiquián as far as **Huansala**, on the road to Huallanca (Huánuco). Whereas only five years ago it was necessary to hike from Chiquián through semi-desert canyons for a couple of days before reaching the peaks, now you can drive directly to the base of the cordillera and the trailhead close to the settlements of **Matacancha** and **Rondoy**. In the south, surfaced roads from Cajatambo now push as far as the breathtaking **Punta Cuyoc**, situated between the Cordilleras Huayhuash and Raura.

Trekking Trekking in the Cordillera Huayhuash is generally considered difficult and certainly requires stamina, with up to eight passes over 4600 m, depending on the route. Ten to 12 days are required for the complete loop, but the trails are good and most gradients are relatively gentle. Moreover, due to the improving road access (see below), many Huaraz-based tour agencies (see page 340) now offer shortened eight-day itineraries.

Safety and practicalities The roads and increasing popularity have brought significant waste disposal issues, and, as mentioned earlier in the chapter, problems with aggressive behaviour and armed robbery in 2004. As of 2006 local communities now provide an armed escort service for all trekking groups in between camping areas on the entire circuit. Each community charges an obligatory fee for protection on its land before handing responsibility over to the next village. Make sure you hang on to **all** receipts/tickets and know exactly what you are paying for. At the time of publication the 'protection fee' amounted to around US$30 per person when combining fees for the entire circuit. Obtain full details on arrival in the area.

Maps The 2nd edition of Brad Johnson's 1:50,000 topographic map (revised 2004) is highly recommended, if not essential, for adventures in the Huayhuash. It can be obtained internationally through map specialists such as **Stanfords** in London, several locations in Huaraz (eg **Café Andino**; see page 338), or from branches of **South American Explorers** in Lima and Cuzco.

Chiquián → *Phone code: 043. Altitude: 3400 m.*

Chiquián is a little town of narrow streets and overhanging eaves. An interesting feature is a public television mounted in a box on a pedestal which sits proudly in the Plaza de Armas, around which folks gather every evening. There is a Semana Turística during the first week of July and the local fiesta is celebrated on 30 August in honour of Santa Rosa.

Cajatambo → *Phone code: 043. Altitude: 3380 m.*

The southern approach to the Cordillera Huayhuash is a small, developing market town, with a beautiful 18th-century church and a lovely plaza. Note that the road out of Cajatambo is not for the fainthearted. For the first three to four hours it is no more than a bus-width, clinging to the cliff edge.

Huayhuash Circuit

The trail head is at **Cuartel Huain** (1), between Matacancha and the **Punta Cacanan** pass (the continental divide at 4700 m). This northernmost point on the trek gives access to the village of **Janca**, to **Laguna Mitucocha** (2) and to the eastern flank of the Cordillera. A very steep short cut on scree takes you through the gap in the northern spur of the range above Matacancha and Janca village on the other side. This could save two or three hours.

Figures in the text and on the map indicate the most usual camping sites.

The eastern side of the Cordillera is a chain of passes, lakes and stunning views of **Jirishanca Chico, Yerupajá Chico, Yerupajá** (Peru's second highest peak at 6634 m) and **Siulá Grande.** From Janca, a small side valley leads off **Quebrada Mitucocha** to

Punta Carhuac (4650 m) and beyond to **Laguna Carhuacocha**, with magnificent camping (3) and views. Following on from there are **Punta Carnicero** (4600 m) – a section of Inca road and petroglyphs are found nearby – the twin lakes of **Azulcocha** and **Atoqshaico** (just beyond the pass) and **Huayhuash village** (4 – one house).

This is the regular route, but a new route is also open, following round Laguna Carhaucocha, passing Laguna Siulá and emerging on the regular route just before Huayhuash village. This trail has gained popularity thanks to *Touching the Void*; there are no maps and it is for experienced trekkers only. A guide is recommended as the weather can change very suddenly.

The next pass, **Portachuelo Huayhuash** (4750 m, the continental divide), overlooks the superb southward line of pyramidal peaks and rounded ice caps of the **Cordillera Raura**. A path leads from **Laguna Viconga** below (5 – near the dam), over a pass and hugs the western flank of the Raura all the way to **Oyón**. (**Transportes Javier** run a daily bus from **Raura** to Cerro de Pasco, seven hours, US$5.50; there are also daily buses from Oyón.) Four hours away from Oyón is **Churín**, which boasts the 'best thermal baths in Peru'. There is also a small thermal pool 1 km past the outflow of Viconga, along the trail to Cajatambo. Note that water is released from the Viconga dam daily 0500-1100, and you cannot ford the outflow during this time. If you are bailing out at **Cajatambo** (6), it is downhill all the way from Laguna Viconga, apart from a short sting in the tail at the end.

Those continuing the circuit must cross the **Punto Cuyoc** (5000 m), sometimes snowbound, with outstanding 360° views. This is the highpoint of the circuit in every sense of the word. There follows a long, gentle descent into the **Quebrada Huanacpatay** (6 on the full circuit) and an optional one-day side trip up the valley of the **Río Huayllapa** to **Laguna Jurau** and **Laguna Sarapococha**, both beautiful lakes.

The route continues downhill to the village of **Huayllapa** (with shop and basic lodging and meals); just before town it turns north to begin climbing to the **Tapush Pass** (4800 m) below the summit of **Diablo Mudo** (also known as **Suerococha**), via **Huatac** (7).

Cordilleras Huayhuash & Raura

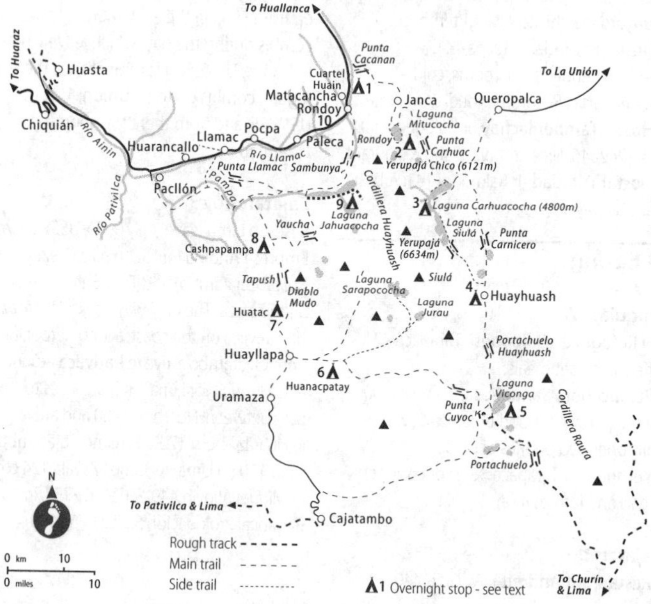

After the pass you reach **Cashpapampa** (8), from where you head east to the **Yaucha Pass** (4800 m, outstanding views), then north, by way of the **Quebrada Huacrish**, to **Laguna Jahuacocha**, which lies beneath **Yerupajá** and *nevados* **Jirishanca** and **Rondoy**. The lake offers the most idyllic campsite (9) in the Cordillera. It can also be reached from **Llamac**, by crossing over the Punta Llamac pass at 4300 m, southeast of that town: first head southwest along a path just beneath the cemetery and zig-zag up above the town. Llamac is also used as a starting point for the trek. You can camp on the football pitch (US$1.50 per night) and drinking water is available from the water source which is 200 m on the trail north to Pocpa; ask locals.

The 4800-m **Sambunya pass**, beneath Rondoy, leads to the descent to the town of **Rondoy** (10), Matacancha and the trail head.

Sleeping

Chiquián *p370*

F Gran Hotel Huayhuash, Figueredo esquina 28 de Julio, T043-747049. Private bathroom, hot water, TV, restaurant, laundry, parking, modern, great views.

F Hostal San Miguel, Jr Comercio 233, T043-747001. Nice courtyard and garden, clean, many rooms, popular.

G per person **Los Nogales de Chiquián**, Jr Comercio 1301, T043-747121 (in Lima T01-460 8037), hotel_nogales_chiquian @yahoo.com.pe. With bath, cheaper without, hot water, cable TV, cafetería, parking. Recommended.

Cajatambo *p370*

G Hostal Cajatambo, on the plaza. Basic, cheap, not for the squeamish as the courtyard is a chicken slaughterhouse.

G Hostal Miranda, Jr Tacna 141. Homely, friendly, small rooms, cold shower, basic. Recommended.

G Hostal Tambomachay, Jr Bolognesi 110, T043-242046. Nice courtyard and restaurant.

G Hostal Trinidad, Jr Raimondi 141. A basic place to stay.

Eating

Chiquián *p370*

El Refugio de Bolognesi, Tarapacá 471. Offers basic set meals.

Panificadora Santa Rosa, Comercio 900, on the plaza. For good bread and sweets, coin-operated phones and fax.

Yerupajá, Jr Tarapacá 351. For basic set meals and information.

Cajatambo *p370*

Restaurant Andreita, Av Grau 440.

Activities and tours

Chiquián *p370*

Sr Delao Callupe is a guide for the Huayhuash. Ask for him in Chiquián.

Transport

Chiquián *p370*

To **Huaraz**, **Chiquián Tours** leave from the plaza daily 0500, US$1.75; **El Rápido**, T043-747049, leaves from Jr Figueredo 216, daily 0500 and 1330, US$3.65. Also *colectivo* Chiquián–Huaraz 1500, 3 hrs, US$2.45 per person. To **Llamac**, 0900 and 1700 (returning 0800 and 1200), 1½ hrs, US$2; book as early as possible. Llamac to Huaraz, with a change in Chiquián, 1130, arrive 1630.

There is also a connection from Chiquián to **Huallanca** (Huánuco) with buses coming up from Lima in the early morning and combis during the day, which leave when full, 3 hrs, US$2.50. From Huallanca there are regular combis on to **La Unión**, 1 hr, US$0.75, and from there transport to **Huánuco**.

Cajatambo *p370*

Buses to **Lima** leave daily 0600, US$8.80, with **Empresa Andina** (office on plaza next to Hostal Cajatambo) and **Tour Bello**, one block off the plaza. The only way back to **Huaraz** is via Pativilca on the coast, a long detour. Buses from Cajatambo arrive in **Pativilca** around midday; wait for Lima–Huaraz buses to pass between 1330 and 1400 and arrive in Huaraz about 1700. **Turismo Cajatambo**, Jr Grau 120 (in Lima, Av Carlos Zavala 124 corner of Miguel Aljovin 449, T01-426 7238, in Barranca, Prologación Sáenz Peña 139).

North Coast

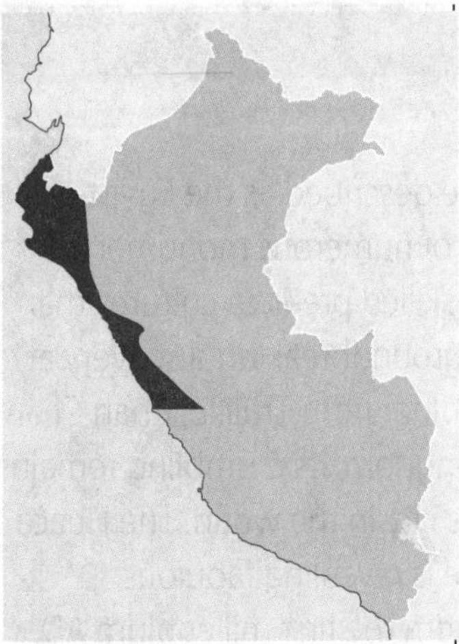

Footprint features

Introduction

Peru's north coast could well be described as the Egypt of South America. This is a region of numerous monumental ruins, built by the many highly skilled pre-Inca cultures that once thrived here. The recent, groundbreaking discovery at Caral is now open to visitors. Not far from Trujillo, Chan Chán was the capital of the Chimú Kingdom; its crumbling remains still represent the largest adobe city in the world. The Huaca de la Luna of the Moche empire is revealing fabulous, multicoloured friezes of gods from the first millennium AD. Further north, near Chiclayo, the adobe brick pyramids of Túcume, Sipán and Sicán rise massively from the coastal plains. The wealth from some of their tombs is now displayed in new, state-of-the-art museums.

But it's not all pyramids and royal tombs. The elegant city of Trujillo is one of the finest examples of colonial architecture in the country. There are charming towns such as Huanchaco, with its bizarre-looking reed-fishing rafts, and Chulucanas, with its famous pottery. Lambayeque Department has umpteen festivals; you can visit witchdoctors or simply buy their potions; up and down the coast the seafood is wonderful and the hospitality unrivalled. In addition, the northern seaboard enjoys a rain-free climate all year, and sports Peru's finest beaches for bathing and surfing. Around Tumbes, the most northerly provincial capital, three reserves protect mangroves, equatorial dry scrub and rainforest, each of which contains endangered species, ranging from crocodiles to eagles.

★ Don't miss...

1 **Caral** A city, 4600 years old, whose peace-loving inhabitants seem to have upset all previous theories of urban archaeology, page 378.
2 **Trujillo** See the Sunday morning flag-raising ceremony in the Plaza Mayor, surrounded by colonial buildings, page 386.
3 **Huanchaco** Ride the waves on the totora-reed boats-cum-surfboards, known as 'little horses', page 392.
4 **El Brujo** Bones and pottery shards crunch under your feet as you explore this mysterious archaeological complex, page 394.
5 **Lambayeque** The Brüning and Royal Tombs of Sipán museums, two ultra-modern settings for some of Peru's richest historical finds, page 406.
6 **Máncora** Great beaches, good surfing, a lively party scene at weekends, just the place for a break on the long haul up the Panamericana, page 428.

Lima to Chimbote

Between Lima and Pativilca there is a narrow belt of coastal land deposited at the mouths of the rivers and, from Pativilca to the mouth of the Río Santa, north of Chimbote, the Andes come down to the sea. The Pan-American Highway parallels the coast all the way to the far north, and feeder roads branch from it up the various valleys. » *For Sleeping, Eating and other listings, see pages 382-386.*

Pasamayo sand dune

Just north of Ancón, see page 99, the Pasamayo sand dune, stretching for 20 km, comes right down to the seashore. The old road which snakes above the sea is spectacular, but is now closed except to commercial traffic and buses. The new toll road (US$0.85), which goes right over the top, is safe and gives spectacular views over the nearby coast and valleys.

Chancay Valley → *Colour map 3, C3.*

Though the Chancay Culture once extended across many valleys to the north of Lima and much evidence of ceramic artefacts can be seen in museums, there are no significant remains in the valley. There are, however, two curiosities to distract the traveller. As the old coastal road descends into the valley a complex of strange, decorated, conical structures made of adobe comes in to view (Km 63). **Eco Truly Park** ⓘ *Eco Truly Tours, Javier Prado Este 185, Lima, T01-421 0016, www.ecotrulypark.org, complex tour, 1 hr, US$2.50*, is run by the Hare Krishna movement and consists of a temple complex, vegetarian restaurant, organic farm and rustic accommodation for visitors in the *trulys* (conical constructions, G). Mediation, t'ai chi and other courses are run regularly. **Chancay 'castle'** ⓘ *entrance and tour US$1.50*, built by a bohemian descendant of the last viceroy in the 1920s, is located on the cliff tops in Chancay town. Once visited by the elite of Lima, it is now a decaying recreational centre with restaurants, bars, pools and a museum containing many Chancay culture artefacts.

Just inland from the coastal town of Chancay is **Huaral**, which gives access to the Chancay Valley, up which are the extraordinary, little-visited ruins of **Chiprac**, **Rupac** and **Añay**. Chiprac is a 2½-hour climb from **Huascoy** (see below). The Salvador family has accommodation and Carlos is a recommended guide for the ruins, though a guide is not strictly necessary. It is a good day's walk there and back with time to take photographs and eat. Huascoy celebrates the **Fiesta de San Cristóbal** in the week before Independence (28 July), with a procession, masses, dancing, fireworks and football matches. **Rupac** is best reached from La Florida. Its ruins are the best preserved of the group, though less extensive than Chiprac. All the ruins have complete roofs, which is unique in Peru. For **Añay**, go to Huaral as for the other ruins, then get transport to Huayopampa (basic accommodation) or La Perla from where the ruins can easily be reached. Get a guide to take you there from either village.

Loma de Lachay National Reserve

ⓘ *Daily 0900-1800, US$1.50, Lima-Huacho buses drop off/pick up from Km 83.*
One kilometre north of the southern turn-off to Sayán is a sandy track signposted to the **Loma de Lachay** (5070 ha). It is 4 km, a one-hour walk, up to the guard post.

This small reserve is a typical example of 'loma' habitat, and it holds several important species. Loma vegetation is formed during the winter months, when fog caused by the Humboldt Current drives inland, rises and condenses, and forms a dew on the surrounding landscape. This dew is sufficient to sustain the seasonal loma or 'fog vegetation' that is the home of birds such as the endemic Raimondi's yellow-finch and thick-billed miner. Within just 5 km the landscape changes from barren desert to a green carpet, resonating with the sound of birdcalls. In September and October the plants are in bloom and very beautiful. There is a visitors' centre, trails and picnic areas. Camping is permitted at the visitors' centre in the heart of the reserve, 2 km beyond the guard post, US$3 for up to three days, bring all food and water, especially in the dry season (January-March). The reserve is very popular with Lima residents at the weekend.

Huacho → *Colour map 3, B3. Population: 35,900.*

At Km 101 is Huacho, where you can turn off the Pan-American and head west to Puerto Huacho, which is the outlet for cotton and sugar grown in the rich Huaura Valley. There are cotton-seed oil and other factories. The port and sea are sometimes alive with huge jellyfish. There are several basic hotels at Huacho (none at the port). A turn-off at Km 135 leads to **El Paraíso**, where endless, empty beaches and calm, clear waters attract campers in summer. There is good fishing and windsurfing. Birdwatchers should go to the nearby lagoon, formed by run-off from an irrigation project, where over 100 species have been recorded.

Huacho to Churín

The journey inland from Huacho, up the Huaura Valley, is spectacular. **Sayán**, 30 km inland, is an attractive agricultural town at the base of the Andean foothills. It would be a nicer place to stay en route to Churín than the coastal towns, if there were more choice in the way of hotels. Combis go every half hour to Huacho from Avenida Balta. Buses from Lima for Churín stop at the bridge.

Churín → *Colour map 3, B3. Population: 2000. Altitude: 2080 m.*

Beyond Sayán the road follows the Huaura Valley which narrows almost to a gorge before climbing steeply to Churín, one of Peru's best-known spas, with hot, sulphurous springs which are used to cure a number of ailments. The climate is dry, temperatures ranging from 10°C to 32°C. The area is famous for cheese, yoghurt and other natural products. Churín is very popular with Limeños. Accommodation and buses are fully booked at holiday times.

A highly recommended excursion can be made up a side valley, 5 km below Churín, to **Huancahuasi**. The new Huancahuasi baths include a pool that ex-President Fujimori swam in (hot, US$0.70 per person), while on the opposite side of the river the new **Picoy** baths include excellent private pools carved out of the rock (hot, US$0.30 per person). Snacks such as *pachamanca* are available at riverside stalls. The trip includes a stop-off at Picoy, which has a remarkable colonial church with a highly carved façade, and at **Chiuchin**. **Chiuchin baths** ⓘ *US$30 per person for pool; US$0.50 per person for private baths*, are now rather neglected and run down. Combis leave from beside the church in Churín for the two-hour trip 0800-0900, returning 1500-1700. A round trip costs US$3.

Huacho to Barranca

The town of **Huaura**, on the north bank of the Río Huaura, has grown little over the last 200 years but remains hugely significant in the annals of Peruvian Independence. It was here that General San Martín first proclaimed the country's independence from Spain, eight months prior to the official declaration of Independence in Lima. The house with the balcony from which he made the proclamation is now a small museum ⓘ *0900-1700, US$0.75*. Stand on the balcony yourself and re-enact the declaration.

The road passes from the valley of Mazo through the irrigated valley of San Felipe. There is more desert and then the cotton-fields of San Nicolás lead to **Supe** at Km 187, and nearby Puerto Supe, a busy port shipping fishmeal, cotton, sugar and minerals. At **El Aspero**, near Supe, is one of the earliest prehistoric sites in Peru, see page 568.

At **Barranca** (Km 195), 1 km below the town, lies the long, sandy Chorrillos beach, which is windy but popular with surfers. Banco de la Nación accepts traveller's cheques, but at poor rates.

Caral

ⓘ *Visitors must report to the tourist post in the car park. US$3, US$1 with student card, plus US$6 per group for a guide (Spanish only) if required. For details contact Proyecto Especial Caral, Unión 1040, Lima 1, T01-332 5380, www.caralperu.gob.pe. Camping is permitted (small fee) at the house of archaeologists working on the site; bring all food.*

A few kilometres before Barranca, a turning to the right (east) leads to Caral, a city 20 km from the coast whose date (3200-3000 BC) and monumental construction are overturning many of the accepted theories of Peruvian archaeology. It appears to be easily the oldest city-state in South America. Tours operate from Lima, see page 384.

▸▸ *See also Transport, page 384.*

The dry, desert site lies on the southern fringes of the Supe Valley, along whose flanks there are many more unexcavated ruins. Caral covers 66 ha and contains eight significant pyramidal structures. To date seven have been excavated by archaeologists from the University of San Marcos, Lima. One remains unexcavated, a rounded mound of stone and sand showing no discernible sign of its likely inner contents. The seven pyramids investigated reveal a stone and mortar construction with a yellow and white wash being the most common finish, small areas of which remain visible. Archaeologists are undertaking careful renovation upon the existing foundations to re-establish the pyramidal tiers. It is possible to walk around and, in some cases, up on to the pyramids. A viewpoint provides a panorama across the whole site. **Pirámide de Anfiteatro** (11 m high), on the north side of the small pyramid, is a large amphitheatre from which a series of ceremonial rooms rise. **Pirámide de la Huanca** (12 m high) is constructed in three tiers with a 23-step staircase leading up to the ceremonial platform. It takes its name from the large stone obelisk (*huanca*) in the centre of the plaza, which it overlooks. The residence of the elite, a complex of well-built adobe rooms, abuts the pyramid. **Pirámide de la Galería** (the gallery pyramid, 17 m high) has a nearly 7-m-wide stairway leading up to a room sunk into the ceremonial platform lined with huarango wood and containing eight huge whalebone vertebrate seats. **Pirámide Menor** (7.5 m high) is the smallest of the pyramids. **Pirámide Mayor** (the great pyramid, 153.5 by 110 by 28 m) is the largest pyramid with a sunken circular plaza on its south side. Two *lanzones* (obelisk-sized stones) frame the two entrances to the plaza and a further *lanzón* sits atop the pyramid which is reached by an impressive 9-m-wide stairway from the plaza. **Pirámide de la Cantera** (the quarry pyramid, 13.5 m high) is the only pyramid partly straddling a rock outcrop, much of which was used in its construction. A 4.2-m-wide stairway with 32 steps ascends to the summit, on which is a round, walk-in altar with an outer wall 8 m in diameter and an inner wall 3.7 m in diameter, inside which there was a central fireplace. In addition, there is a long building containing 18 internal niches along each facing wall. **El Templo de Altar Circular** (4 m high) consists of at least 13 rooms in at least two groupings. Inside one square room there is a 2.7-m-diameter walk-in altar with a central fireplace. Some later adobe ruins of the Chancay era fringe the site. Detailed, illustrated Spanish/English information panels are located around the site, which is well organized, criss-crossed by paths which must be adhered to. Allow at least two hours to fully visit the site.

Pativilca to Huaraz

The straggling town of Pativilca (Km 203), has a small museum and a good, cheap restaurant, **Cornejo.** Just beyond town, a good paved road turns east for Huaraz in the Cordillera Blanca, see page 330.

The road at first climbs gradually from the coast. At Km 48, just west of the town of **Chasquitambo (Restaurante Delicias)** it reaches Rumi Siki (Rump Rock), with unusual rock formations, including the one that gives the site its name. Beyond this point, the grade is steeper and at Km 120 the chilly pass at 4080 m is reached. Shortly after, **Laguna Conococha** comes into view, where the Río Santa rises. Delicious trout is available in Conococha village. A dirt road branches off from Conococha to

Chiquián (see page 370) and the Cordilleras Huayhuash and Raura to the southeast. After crossing a high plateau the main road descends gradually for 47 km until **Catac** (see page 362), where another road branches east to Chavín and on to the Callejón de Conchucos (see page 364). Huaraz is 36 km further on and the road then continues north through the Callejón de Huaylas.

Four kilometres beyond the turn-off to Huaraz, beside the highway, are the well-preserved ruins of the Chimú temple of **Paramonga** ⓘ *US$1.20, no buses run to the ruins, only to the port (about 15 mins from Barranca), a taxi from Paramonga and return after waiting costs US$4.50, otherwise take a Barranca-Paramonga port bus, then it's a 3-km walk.* Set on high ground with a view of the ocean, the fortress-like mound is reinforced by eight quadrangular walls rising in tiers to the top of the hill. It is well worth visiting. The town of Paramonga is a small port, 3 km off the Pan-American Highway, 4 km from the ruins and 205 km from Lima.

Between Pativilca and Chimbote the mountains come down to the sea. The road passes by a few very small protected harbours in tiny rock-encircled bays – **Puerto Huarmey, Puerto Casma** and **Vesique**. Between Paramonga and Huarmey there are restaurants at Km 223 and 248.

Casma to Huaraz via Pariacoto → *Colour map 3, B2.*

Casma, largely destroyed by the 1970 earthquake, has since been rebuilt, partly with Chilean help. It has a pleasant Plaza de Armas, several parks and two markets including a good food market. Sechín ruins are only 5 km away and it is a much nicer place to stay than Chimbote. The weather is usually sunny, hence its title Ciudad del Sol Eterno (City of Eternal Sun).

From Casma a road runs inland over the **Callán Pass** (4224 m) 150 km to Huaraz. It's a difficult but beautiful trip, and worth taking in daylight. Few buses take this route, so check before leaving (see Transport, page 385).

From Casma the first 30 km are paved, then a good dirt road follows for 30 km to **Pariacoto**. From here to the pass the road is rough, with landslides in the rainy season, but once the Cordillera Negra has been crossed, the wide, gravel road is better with spectacular views of the Cordillera Blanca. To catch the best views, before the Cordillera Blanca becomes covered in cloud (usually in the afternoon), take the earliest bus possible. Sit on the right-hand side of the bus.

Sechín → *Colour map 3, B2.*

ⓘ *Daily 0800-1800, www.xanga.com/sechin, US$1.50, children half price; the ticket is also valid for the museum and Pañamarca (see page 381). Frequent* colectivos *leave early in the morning from in front of the market in Casma, US$0.30 per person; otherwise take a moto-taxi for US$1 per person.*

Casma

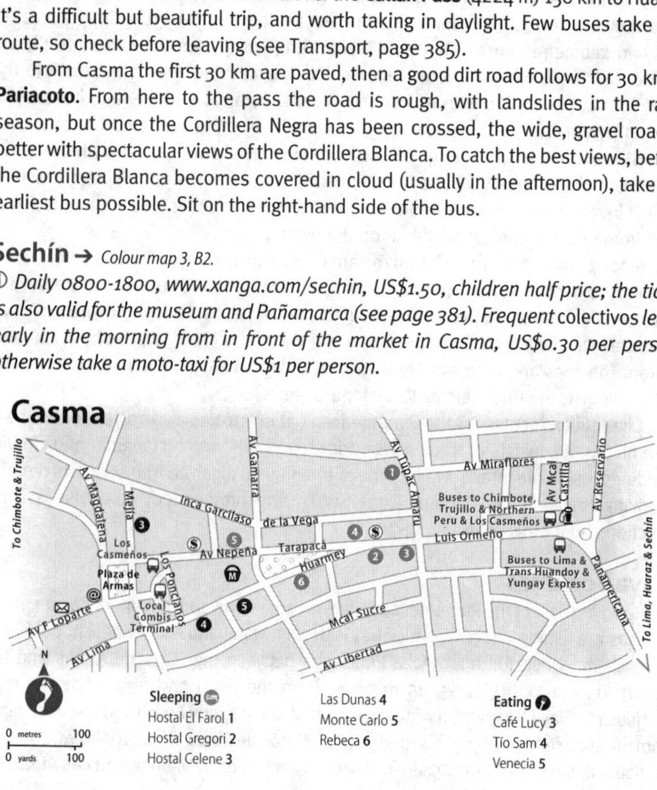

This is one of the most important ruins on the Peruvian coast. It consists of a large square temple completely faced with carved stone monoliths – probably over 500 of them – representing two lines of warriors marching towards the principal entrance from opposite sides. Between each warrior are carvings of men being eviscerated, heads with blood gushing from eyes or mouths, dismembered legs, arms, torsos, ears, eyes and vertebrae.

The mural is thought to narrate the results of a battle, with the fates of the conquerors and the conquered graphically depicted. The style is unique in Peru for its naturalistic vigour. The importance of the site lies in the fact that it is one of the oldest centres in the country to demonstrate the development of warlike activity and the extent to which extreme violence was a part of life.

Within the stone temple is an earlier, pre-ceramic mud temple with painted walls. The complex as a whole forms a temple-palace associated with the development of the local pre-Chavín Sechín culture, dating from about 1600 BC. Three sides of the large stone temple have been excavated and restored. You cannot see the adobe buildings inside the stone walls, which belong to an earlier period. They were later covered up and used as a base for a second storey which, unfortunately, has been completely destroyed.

Some experts think the temple and surroundings were buried on purpose. Others believe it was engulfed by natural disaster. The latter theory is supported by finds of human skeletons. Tombs have been found in front and at the same level as the temple. A wall of a large adobe building under excavation runs round the sides and back of the temple.

There is an attractive, shady picnic garden. Photography is best around midday. **Max Uhle Museum** by the ruins has an interesting display of Sechín artefacts and a replica of the façade of the inner adobe temple. If you need a guide ask in advance for Wilder León or Carlos Cuy, who speaks English and French. Outside the museum is a map showing the location of the different archaeological sites in the Casma area.

Two kilometres further along is **Sechín Alto**, two pyramids of the late Chavín period, but these have not yet been extensively excavated. Follow the track to the west (left) at the Km 4 post past the first, smaller pyramid and the farm house. The second pyramid is huge, measuring 300 x 250 x 25 m, covering 50 ha, and once consisted of three levels. Though most of the stone façade has turned to rubble, small sections of the exterior wall and huge entrance stones on the north side are visible. Recent investigations have uncovered some storage chambers and adobe platforms built from unusual conical adobes atop the pyramid.

Among numerous other sites in the area, there are two of particular interest, but a mototaxi is needed to visit them. At Km 15 on the Pariacoto road there are several lines and figures etched in the desert surface, as at Nazca. Though nowhere near as impressive as the Nazca Lines, the figure of a 'warrior' is clearly visible from a nearby hilltop. The lines are up to 25 m long, 20 cm wide and have been dated to 1000 BC. Archaeologists are uncertain as to their purpose.

Chanquillo, located off the Panamericana at Km 361, is a 2300-year-old fortress on a hilltop. It consists of three concentric stone walls with rectangular and circular buildings inside the interior wall. Some of the original algarrob tree supports remain. If driving there off the Panamericana, 4WD is recommended, otherwise ask for directions from other roads.

Playa Tortugas

Located 2 km east of the Pan-American Highway at Km 391, 18 km north of Casma, Playa Tortugas is a fishing village on a nice bay with calm water and a rocky beach. *Colectivos* leave Casma when full from Plaza Poncianos between the Plaza de Armas and the market, 0500-2000, US$0.75, 15 minutes. From the north end of the bay the road continues to **Playa Huayuna**, a windy, closed bay with a sandy beach and a scallop farm. From the south end of Tortugas a road goes to **Rincón de Piños**, a beach with wild surf. To the south of Casma, at Km 345, are the sandy beaches of **La Gramita** and **Las Aldas**.

Chimbote → *Phone code: 043. Colour map 3, A2. Population: 296,600.*

Not only is Chimbote Peru's largest fishing port, it is also the smelliest city in the country, with the powerful stench of the fishmeal plant permeating every nook and cranny, and one of the least desirable places, with an palpable sense of danger lurking around every corner. There are no tourist attractions as such, although it has a spacious **Plaza de Armas** with the cathedral and the modern Municipal building, which has a small **art gallery** ⓘ *0900-2000*. The best thing about the place is the Terminal Terrestre, 4 km south of the centre on Avenida Meiggs. When transferring from Trujillo, Huaraz, Casma or Lima, there is no need to leave the bus station.

The Nepeña Valley

About 25 km south of Chimbote, at Km 405 on the Pan-American Highway, a paved road leads east to the Nepeña Valley, where several pre-Columbian ruins including Cerro Blanco, Pañamarca and Paredones can be found. The valley is dominated by the vast San Jacinto sugar plantation. The village of Capellanía is 11 km from the crossroads. Just beyond are the ruins of **Pañamarca**. The site includes a two-storey stone structure, built on a hill, dating from the formative period (2000 BC-AD 100) and many adobe structures from the Moche period, including three pyramids. Remains of polychromatic murals and animal sculptures can also be seen. Twenty kilometres from Pañamarca, via the villages of San Jacinto and Moro, is the site of **Paredones**, a large stone structure, with 4-m-high granite walls and a very impressive gateway known as 'Portada de Paredones' or 'Puerta del Sol'. It is believed to have been a Chavín palace.

Chimbote to Huaraz

The route from Chimbote to Huaraz passes through the **Santa Valley** and the spectacular Cañón del Pato, one of the most thrilling bus trips in all of Peru. Just north of the smelly port, a road branches northeast off the Pan-American Highway and, joining another road from the town of Santa, goes up the Santa Valley following the route, including tunnels, of

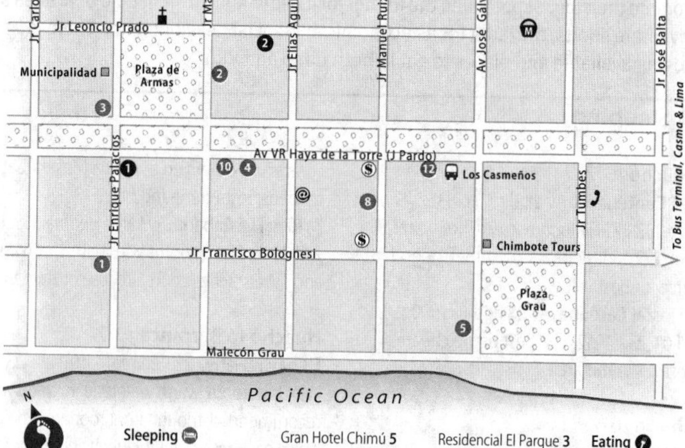

Sleeping
Cantón & Chifa Cantón 1
D'Carlo 2
Felic 4
Gran Hotel Chimú 5
Hostal Karol Inn & Chifa Jin Lon 8
Ivansino Inn 12
Residencial El Parque 3
San Felipe 10
Tany 11

Eating
Aquarius 1
Recutecu 2

 the old **Santa Corporation Railway**. This used to run as far as **Huallanca** (Ancash – not to be confused with the town of the same name southeast of Huaraz), 140 km up the valley, but the track was largely destroyed by the 1970 earthquake. At Chuquicara, three hours from Chimbote, some 60 km before Huallanca, is **Restaurante Rosales**, a good place to stop for a meal (US$1-1.30 – you can sleep here, too, but it's very rough). The road from Chimbote to Chuquicara is paved, but after that it becomes a track, very bumpy, stony and dusty (hard driving). The road goes between barren hills and passes poor mining camps. The geology is fantastic, with ravines, whorls, faults and strata at all angles to each other. The varying colours of the rock are also amazing. At the next village, **Yuramarca**, there is lodging, places to eat, fuel and a police station.

Chimbote is not safe by day or night. Travellers are often attacked and robbed here. Take extra precautions. Although it's small enough to walk around, don't; take a taxi, except for going out to eat near your hotel. On no account walk from the bus station to town.

At Huallanca is an impressive hydroelectric plant, built into a mountain, which cannot be visited. There is accommodation at the **Hotel Huascarán**, which is good and friendly; also **Koki's Hostal**. Fuel is available. Everything closes early.

At the top of the valley by the hydroelectric centre, the road turns right to go through the **Cañón del Pato**. After this point the road is fully paved. Soon you reach the Callejón de Huaylas and the road south to Caraz and Huaraz (see page 348).

An alternative road for cyclists (and vehicles with a permit) is the private road known as the 'Brasileños', used by the Brazilian company Odebrecht which has built a water channel for the Chavimochic irrigation scheme from the Río Santa to the coast. Permits are available (US$6.50) from the company HQ in San José de Virú, or from the guardian at the gate on Sunday. The turn-off is 35 km north of the Santa turning, 15 km south of the bridge in Chao, at Km 482 on the Pan-American Highway. It is a good all-weather road to Tanguche, 22 km from the turn-off, where it continues up the north bank of the Río Santa, crosses a bridge 28 km from Tanguche, to meet up with the public road.

North of Chimbote

The highway crosses the valleys of Chao and Virú and, after 137 km, reach the first great city of Northern Peru, Trujillo. The Virú Valley contains the largest single sand dune in South America, known as **Pur Pur**. Between Virú and Trujillo the desert is being turned 'green' with asparagus and other crops, thanks to the huge Chavimochic project. It is hard to believe that the irrigated land was once as lifeless as the desert that surrounds it. For different reasons, both Virú and Chavimochic are proposing to promote their tourist potential, the former for its little-known archaeological sites and adventure sports, the latter for its economic and social developments. There is basic lodging available and places to eat in both Chao and Virú.

Sleeping

Huacho *p377*

D-E Centenario, Av 28 de Julio 836, T01-232 3731. Modern, clean, hot water, with outdoor pool, café, internet, negotiate price for best value.

F Hostal Carolina, Av 28 de Julio 590, T/F01-232 4952. The best of the cheaper *hostales* in this area.

Churín *p377*

Prices double at holiday periods.

D Las Termas, Av Larco Herrera 411, T01-237 3094. Has rooms with a pool in the town centre and others up at the La Meseta baths, gardens, restaurant and bar.

F Hostal La Cabaña, Av Larco Herrera 368, T01-237 3023. Clean, rooms with bath, hot water and TV, attractive courtyard, use of kitchen.

Huacho to Barranca *p377*

E Chavín, Gálvez 222, Barranca, T01-235 2358. With bathroom, warm water, clean, good value, recommended, though front rooms are noisy; it also has a restaurant for lunch and dinner (try *arroz con conchas*), breakfast bar and café opens onto the street by the main entrance.

G **Jefferson**, Lima 946, Barranca, T01-235 2184. Clean, friendly.

Pativilca to Huaraz *p378*

D **La Posada de Huarmey**, Panamericana 293, Huarmey, T043-600330. Small, with bath, TV, hot water, clean, good service, restaurant, noisy from road traffic.

Casma to Huaraz via Pariacoto *p379, map p379*

Most of the following hotels in Casma are on the Panamericana so rooms at the back will be quieter. The Panamericana is divided into 3 sections: Av Luis Ormeño, Av Tarapacá and Av Nepeña, which leads to the plaza.

D **Hostal El Farol**, Túpac Amaru 450, Casma, T043-711064, hostalfaro@yahoo.com. Ask for the cheaper rate in the low season, with bathroom, breakfast extra, hot water, swimming pool, good restaurant, pleasant garden setting surrounded by a wall, parking, good local information.

F **Gregori**, Luis Ormeño 530, Casma, T043-711073. Cheaper without bathroom, clean, friendly, café downstairs.

F **Monte Carlo**, Nepeña 370, Casma, T043-711421. Clean, friendly, TV, internet, laundry, good value.

F **Hostal Celene** Ormeño 595, Casma, T043-711065. Large rooms in a clean and friendly *hostal*.

F **Rebeca**, Huarmey 377, Casma, T043-711258. Modern, hot water only at night, good.

G **Alojamiento Sáenz Peña**, Gonzalo Salazar, cuadra 5, Pariacoto. Basic.

G **Hostal Eddier**, on the plaza in Pariacoto. Basic but nice.

G **Las Dunas**, Ormeño 505, Casma, T/F043-711057. A converted, upgraded and enlarged family home, friendly.

Playa Tortugas *p380*

D **Las Terrazas**, T043-961 9042, www.lasterrazas.com. Open Nov-Apr, with restaurant.

D **Hotel Farol Beach Inn**, sister to the one in Casma, open all year.

Chimbote *p381, map p381*

There are plenty of hotels in Chimbote so it is often possible to negotiate a lower rate. The main street, Av Victor Raul Haya de la Torre, is commonly known as José Pardo.

B **Cantón**, Bolognesi 498, T043-344388. The most modern, luxury hotel in the city, has a good but pricey *chifa* restaurant.

C **Gran Hotel Chimú**, José Gálvez 109, T/F043-321741. Price includes breakfast, minibar, safe parking.

C **Ivansino Inn**, Haya de la Torre 738, T043-321811, ivansino@hotmail.com. Includes breakfast, comfortable, clean, modern, cable TV, minibar.

D **D'Carlo**, Villavicencio 376, on the plaza, T/F043-321047. Spacious, friendly, TV, minibar, restaurant.

D **San Felipe**, Haya de la Torre 514, T043-323401. With bathroom, hot water, clean, friendly, comfortable, restaurant.

E **Felic**, Haya de la Torre 552, T043-325901. Cheaper without bathroom, clean, quiet. Recommended.

E **Hostal Karol Inn**, Manuel Ruiz 277, T/F043-321216. Clean, with bathroom, hot water, a good place to stay, family-run, laundry service, cafeteria.

E **Residencial El Parque**, E Palacios 309, on the main plaza, T043-323963. A converted old home, with bathroom, hot water, clean, nice, secure, friendly, no breakfast.

F **Tany**, Palacios 553, T/F043-323411. Clean, friendly, TV, includes breakfast, good value.

F-G **Hostal El Ensueño**, Sáenz Peña 268, 2 blocks from Plaza Central, T043-328662. Cheaper rooms without bath, very good, safe, welcoming.

North of Chimbote *p382*

G **La Posada**, Carretera Virú con Panamericana. Price per person. Simple, with cold water; cheap, good restaurant downstairs.

Eating

Huacho *p377*

D'Coco, Túpac Amaru 156. Serves very good soups and steaks. Try the delicious local speciality *salchicha huachana*, scrambled egg and sausage meat.

Huacho to Churín *p377*

Jalisco, Balta 342, Sayán. The best place to eat, sometimes has local river shrimp and wine on the menu.

Churín *p377*
Churín is full of restaurants and cafés offering healthy portions and a wide range of *dulces* (desserts). Local delicacies include honey, *alfajores*, flavoured *manjar blanca*, cheeses and *calabaza* (a delicious pudding made from squash).

Huacho to Barranca *p377*
ΨΨ-Ψ **Tacu Tato**, on Chorrillos beach. Has won national prizes for its *tacu tacu*, a Peruvian seafood paella.
Ψ **Cevichería Fujino**, Arica 210, Barranca. Good for fish. Try the *tamales*.

Casma to Huaraz via Pariacoto
p379, map p379
In Casma, there are several cheap restaurants on Huarmey. The famous locally made ice cream, Caribe, includes some delicious flavours such as *lúcuma* and *maracuyá*. Available at the *panadería* at Ormeño 545.
Ψ **Tío Sam**, Huarmey 138, Casma. Decorated with photos of Sechín, this restaurant specializes in excellent fresh fish dishes, such as *lenguado sudado*.
Ψ **Venecia**, Huarmey 204, Casma. Serves local dishes such as goat stew, popular with locals.

Cafés
Café Lucy, Mejía 150, Casma. Opens early for breakfast, which includes fried fish and soups.

Playa Tortugas *p380*
ΨΨ-Ψ **Costa Azul**, on the seafront as you enter the settlement. One of the best seafood restaurants for fried fish or ceviche.

Chimbote *p381, map p381*
There are several cheap restaurants on Haya de la Torre by the plaza.
Ψ **Aquarius**, Haya de la Torre 360. A vegetarian restaurant in the centre.
Ψ **Chifa Jin Lon**, adjoining **Hostal Karol Inn**. Well-prepared Chinese food, popular and convenient.
Ψ **Las Flores**, Jr Enrique Palacios, 2 blocks west of the plaza. Open 24 hrs, serves good food for breakfast.
Ψ **Recutecu**, L Prado 556. Good set lunch with a wide choice.

Cafés and panaderías
Delca, Haya de la Torre 568, excellent bakery.

Activities and tours

Casma to Huaraz via Pariacoto
p379, map p379
Sechín Tours, in **Hostal Monte Carlo**, Casma, T043-711421. Organizes tours in the local area. The guide, Renato, only speaks Spanish but has knowledge of local ruins and can be contacted on T043-712528, renatotours@yahoo.com. US$3 per hr, including mototaxi.

Transport

Chancay Valley *p376*
Take a bus to **Huaral** from Plaza de Acho, by the bullring, in Lima (beware of thieves). Then take the Juan Batista bus, on Tue and Fri, to **Huascoy**, US$2, 2 km beyond San Juan, which is up beyond Acos, at 3500 m.

Huacho *p377*
Litsa runs every 30 mins Lima-Huacho, from 0445 to 2045, 2½ hrs, US$2. Also Comité 18, daily *colectivos*, US$2.50. Buses north usually arrive full. They can be caught at the roundabout on the Pan-American. There are regular combis to **Sayán**. There is a toll post at El Paraíso Huacho, US$0.75 for cars.

Churín *p377*
Trans Estrella Polar, Espadín and **Beteta** each have several buses a day to **Lima**, 4-5 hrs, US$5. Some buses from Lima continue to **Oyón**, 1 hr. From Oyón it is possible to continue over the sierras to **Cerro de Pasco** on a very rough high-altitude road, **Trans Javier**, 0800, 5 hrs, US$3.50.

Huacho to Barranca *p377*
From **Lima** to Barranca takes 3½ hrs, US$3. Several bus companies serve the Lima-Barranca route such as **Trans América** and **Trans Paramonga**. To continue to **Huaraz** or northern coastal cities, take a *colectivo* to the service station (el grifo) at the northern end of Pativilca, where buses from Lima with space stop. There are also *colectivos* to **Huarmey**, 1¼ hrs, US$2, from where it is also possible to continue northward.

Caral *p378*
Caral is best visited from Barranca or Supe. *Colectivos* leave from Av Lima, 2 blocks from

the market, in Barranca for the village of Caral from 0700, 1½ hrs, US$1.50. The ruins are 25 km along a rough road which runs up the Supe valley following the route of an old railway for much of the way. A path leads from the road across the valley to the ruins, though the river may be impassable when the rains fall in the Andes (Dec-Mar), 30 mins. The *colectivos* can also be picked up in Supe or at the signposted turn-off to the ruins on the Panamericana at Km 185, if they have room (there is some confusion with the km posts along this section of the Panamericana). Alternatively, a taxi in Barranca or Supe may be prepared to take you, US$20, including a 2-hr wait while you visit the ruins. Caral can also be approached from the south along a rough road, 28 km, passing through the **Granja Toshi** chicken farm. There is no regular transport but it may be possible to hire one of the taxis waiting at the Km 160 turn-off on the Panamericana, 2 hrs, US$20, including a 2-hr wait. This route is unsigned but may be the only way to reach the ruins in the rainy season.

Casma to Huaraz via Pariacoto

p379, map p379

There are half-hourly buses from **Lima** to Chimbote which can drop you off in Casma, 370 km, 6 hrs, US$5. If going to **Lima** many of the buses from Trujillo and Chimbote stop briefly opposite the petrol station, block 1 of Ormeño or, if they have small offices, along blocks 1-5 of Av Ormeño. To **Chimbote**, 55 km, it is easiest to take a **Los Casmeños** *colectivo*, huge old Dodge cars, which depart when full from in front of the petrol station, block 1 of Ormeño, or from Plaza Poncianos, 45 mins, US$1.20. To **Trujillo** it is best to go first to Chimbote bus station and then take an **América Express** bus (see Chimbote page 376). To **Huaraz** (150 km), via Pariacoto, buses come from Chimbote, 6-7 hrs, US$4.25 (for a description of the route see above). **Transportes Huandoy**, Ormeño 166, T043-712336, departs at 0700, 1100 and 1400, while **Yungay Express**, Ormeño 158, departs at 0600, 0800 and 1400. Most Huaraz buses go via Pativilca, which is further but the road is better, 6 hrs, US$5, **Móvil Tours** and **Trans Chinchaysuyo**, all run at night.

Chimbote *p381, map p381*

Bus

Under no circumstances, walk the 4 km from the bus station to the city centre. Some buses to/from places north of Chimbote stop in the centre, but not in a safe area. Likewise *colectivo* taxis from Casma, drop passengers near the market; ask to be let out at the bus terminal. Always go to the terminal even though there are no hotels nearby: a *colectivo* to town costs US$0.30, taxi US$1. If arriving from Caraz via the Cañón del Pato there is usually time to make a connection to **Casma** or **Trujillo/Huanchaco** and avoid overnighting in Chimbote. If travelling to **Caraz**, however, overnighting in Chimbote is almost unavoidable. Casma is near enough to stay in but you will need to buy your Caraz ticket the day before; the bus station is on the Casma side of Chimbote.

From **Lima** to Chimbote, 420 km, 6 hrs, US$7-9. Buses depart every 30 mins, **Trans Isla Blanca** has the most frequent service, **Línea** (T043-322416), **ECS** (T043-318132) and **Oltursa** (T043-328275). To **Trujillo**, 130 km, 2 hrs, US$1.20, **América Express** have buses every 20 mins until 2100, after which you must hope for Lima buses passing through with space. To **Huaraz** most companies, with the best buses, go the 'long way round', ie down the Panamericana to Pativilca, then up the paved highway, 7 hrs, US$8.45. The best companies are **Móvil Tours**, T043-353616, and **Chinchaysuyo**; both start in Trujillo, their buses continue on to **Caraz**. To **Huaraz** via Pariacoto, 7 hrs, US$5.50, **Trans Huandoy** (Etseturh, T043-354024), at 0600, 1000 and 1300, 7 hrs, US$5.50, and **Yungay Express** at 0500, 0700 and 1300. See above for a description of this route. To **Caraz** via Cañón del Pato, 7-8 hrs, US$7, **Yungay Express** at 0830 (for a description of this route see above). To guarantee a seat on this bus if coming from Trujillo or Casma, T043-321235 the evening before and they will meet your incoming bus and transfer you. To **Sihuas**, 10 hrs, US$7, **Trans Andino** is the only company with a daytime bus at 0800 on Wed, Fri and Sun.

Taxi

Radio taxis from T043-334433.

Directory

Casma to Huaraz via Pariacoto
p379, map p379
Banks Good rates for cash and TCs, no commission, at BCP, Bolívar 111, Casma. Dollars can be changed in Casma at Ormeño 529 and Nepeña 384. **Internet** Café on west side of plaza, Casma. 0900-2100. **Post** Fernando Loparte, ½ block from Plaza de Armas, Casma.

Chimbote *p381, map p381*
Banks **BCP** and **Interbank**, both on Bolognesi and M Ruiz. For TCs and cash. **Casa Arroyo**, M Ruiz 292. For cash only. There are other casas and street changers along M Ruiz between Bolognesi and VR Haya de la Torre. **Internet** At Palacios 518, Aguirre 278 and J.Pardo 660. **Post** Serpost, Av J Pardo 294. **Telephone** Telefónica main office, Tumbes 356. National and international fax and phone. Also at Haya de la Torre 420 and M Ruiz 253.

Trujillo and around

Trujillo, capital of the Department of La Libertad, disputes the title of second city of Peru with Arequipa. Founded by Diego de Almagro in 1534 as an express assignment ordered by Francisco Pizarro, the city was named after the latter's native town in Spain. There is enough here to hold the attention for several days. The area abounds in pre-Columbian sites, there are beaches and good surfing within easy reach and the city itself still has many old churches and graceful colonial homes, built during the reigns of the viceroys.

Perhaps Trujillo's greatest attractions are the impressive Pre-Inca ruins which surround it: the Moche pyramids of Huaca del Sol and de la Luna, Chan Chán and the more distant El Brujo. All can be reached by public transport, but if that sounds complicated, there are many tours available. You need at least an hour to gain a full explanation of Chan Chán and Huaca La Luna, but many tours only allow 20 minutes each. If you are all ruined-out, just a few minutes up the coast from Trujillo is the seaside town of Huanchaco, long a favourite of travellers for surfing, watching the fishermen on their reed boats and just hanging out. » For Sleeping, Eating and other listings, see pages 394-404.

Trujillo

» pp394-404. Colour map 3, A1.

→ *Phone code: 044. Population: 850,000.*

Ins and outs

Getting there The airport is to the west of town. You will enter town along Avenida Mansiche. There is no central bus terminal and none of the bus stations is in the centre. They are spread out on three sides the city, beyond the inner ring road, Avenida España. Plenty of taxis and *colectivos* can be found at the terminals to get you to your hotel. Insist on being taken to the hotel of your choice. Taxi drivers constantly say your hotel is too far/close, expensive/cheap, noisy/boring. They want to take you to the most distant/expensive/remote place to increase fare/commission/ overcharging possibilities. » See Transport page 402 for more details.

The very centre of Trujillo has confusing double street names; the smaller printed name is the one generally shown on maps, and in general use.

Getting around With its compact colonial centre and mild, spring-like climate, Trujillo is best explored on foot. However, should you need a taxi, there are plenty of them. Always use official taxis, which are mainly yellow. The major sites outside the city, Chan Chán, the Moche pyramids and Huanchaco beach are easily reached by public transport or taxi/*colectivo*, but care is needed when walking around. Beware of overcharging, check fares with locals. A taxi can be hired from in front of the **Hotel Libertador** for US$7 an hour about the same rate as a tour with an independent guide or travel agent for one to two people. A number of recommended guides run expert tours to these and other places.

Tourist information i perú ⓘ *Municipalidad, Pizarro 402, p 2, Plaza Mayor, T044-294561, iperutrujillo@promperu.gob.pe, Mon-Sat 0800-1900, Sun 0800-1400.* Take care anywhere beyond the inner ring road, Avenida España, as well as obvious places around bus stops and terminals, and at ATMs. Tourists may be approached by vendors selling *huacos* and necklaces from the Chimú period. The export of these items is strictly illegal if they are genuine, but they almost certainly aren't.

Sights

Plaza Mayor The focal point is the pleasant and spacious Plaza Mayor (used more commonly than Plaza de Armas here). The prominent sculpture represents agriculture, commerce, education, art, slavery, action and liberation, crowned by a young man holding a torch depicting Liberty. Fronting it is the **cathedral**, dating from 1666, with its museum of religious paintings and sculptures next door. Also on the plaza are the **Hotel Libertador**, the colonial-style Sociedad de Beneficencia Pública de Trujillo and the Municipalidad.

The **Universidad de La Libertad**, second only to that of San Marcos at Lima, was founded in 1824. Two beautiful colonial mansions on the plaza have been taken over. The Banco Central de Reserva is in the colonial-style **Casa Urquiaga** (or **Calonge**), ⓘ *Pizarro 446, Mon-Fri, 0900-1500, Sat-Sun 1000-1330, free guided tour lasts 30 mins, take passport or photocopy*. It contains valuable pre-Columbian ceramics. The other is **Casa Bracamonte** (or **Lizarzaburu**), at Independencia 441, with occasional exhibits. Opposite the cathedral on Independencia is the **Casa Garci Olguín** (Caja Nor Perú), recently restored but boasting the oldest façade in the city, baroque and rococo features and Moorish-style murals. The buildings that surround the plaza, and many others in the vicinity, are painted in bright pastel colours. Street lamps are on brackets, adding to the charm of the centre.

North and east of the Plaza Mayor In **San Francisco** ⓘ *on the corner of Gamarra and Independencia, 0800-1200, 1600-2000*, is the pulpit which survived the earthquake of Saint Valentine's Day in 1619. It has three golden altars and others inside. **Casa Ganoza Chopitea** ⓘ *Independencia 630 opposite San Francisco church, Mon-Fri 0915-1230, 1430-1630*, is architecturally the most representative house in the city and considered the most outstanding of the viceroyalty. It combines baroque and rococo styles (it is due to be restored as a cultural centre). Continuing up Independencia you come to the **Museo del Juguete** ⓘ *Independencia 705 y Junín, Mon-Sat 1000-1800, US$0.85, children US$0.30*, the toy museum, which contains examples from prehistoric times to 1950, collected by painter Gerardo Chávez. Downstairs is the **Espacio Cultural Angelmira** ⓘ *daily 0900-2300*, with a café bar. It's worth a visit. Turn off Independencia to **Santa Clara** ⓘ *Sun only*, on the fourth block of Junín. The next cross street is Pizarro. Turn left to **Plazuela El Recreo** at the north end of Pizarro. It was known as El Estanque during the colonial period as it housed a pool from which the city's water was distributed. A marble fountain by Eiffel now stands in the square, transferred from the Plaza de Armas, fronted by restaurants.

If you head back to the Plaza de Armas, you pass the spacious 18th-century **Palacoio Iturregui**, now occupied by the **Club Central** ⓘ *Jr Pizarro 688, Mon-Sun 1100-1800*. To enter the patio is free, but to see more of the palace and the ceramics collection costs US$1.45. This exclusive social centre of Trujillo houses a private collection of ceramics. **Casa de la Emancipación** ⓘ *Jr Pizarro 610, Banco Continental, Mon-Sat 0915-1230, 1600-1830*, is where independence from Spain was planned and was the first seat of government and congress in Peru. The first room on the right as you go in displays plans and the history of the building. There are exhibits on the life of the poet César Vallejo and Bishop Martínez Compañón (1737-1797), whose tours took him all

Trujillo

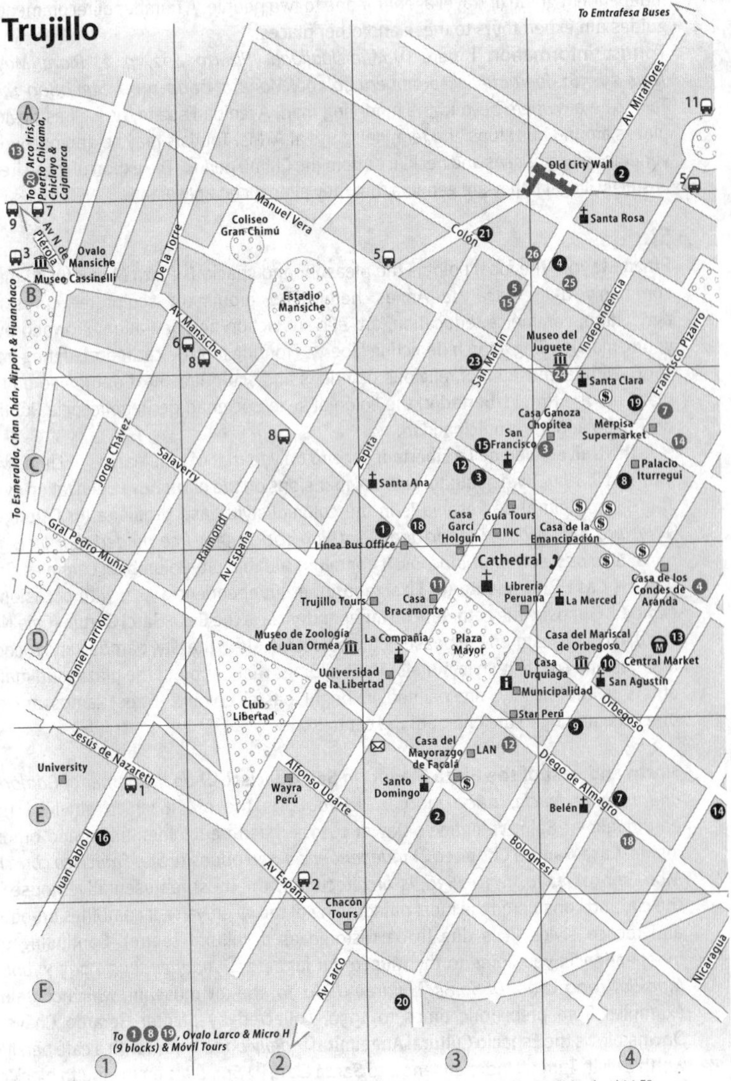

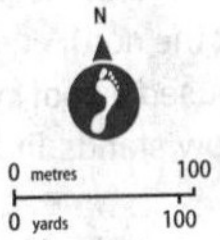

Sleeping
Almagro **18** *E4*
Casa de Clara **9** *F6*
Chan Chán Inn **2** *A5*
Colonial **3** *C4*
Continental **4** *D4*
El Gran Marqués **19** *F1*
Gran Bolívar **6** *B5*
Hostal Americano **7** *C4*
Hostería El Sol **20** *A1*
Libertador **11** *D3*
Los Conquistadores **12** *E3*
Malibu Hostal **8** *F1*
Primavera **13** *A1*
Residencial Vanini **1** *F1*
Saint Germain **14** *C4*
San Martín **15** *B3*
Turismo **17** *D5*

Eating
ABC **1** *C3*
Asturias **19** *C4*
Café Amaretto **3** *C3*
Café Santo Domingo **2** *E3*
Demarco **19** *C4*
Dulcería Doña Carmen **4** *B4*
El Chileno **7** *E4*
El Mochica **9** *E4*
El Sol **8** *C4*
Juguería San Agustín **10** *D4*
La Casona **23** *B3*
Milenium **12** *C3*
Oviedo **19** *C4*
Panadería José Antonio **13** *D4*
Panadería Sandoval **14** *E5*
Parnasillo **15** *C3*
Pizzería Pizzanino **16** *E1*
Rincón de Vallejo **18** *C3*
Romano **19** *C4*
Romano-Rincón Criollo **20** *F3*
Sal y Pimienta **21** *B3*

Bars & clubs
Bar/Café Juguete **24** *C4*
Bar/Café Stradivarius **25** *B4*
Canana **5** *B3*
El Estubo **26** *B4*

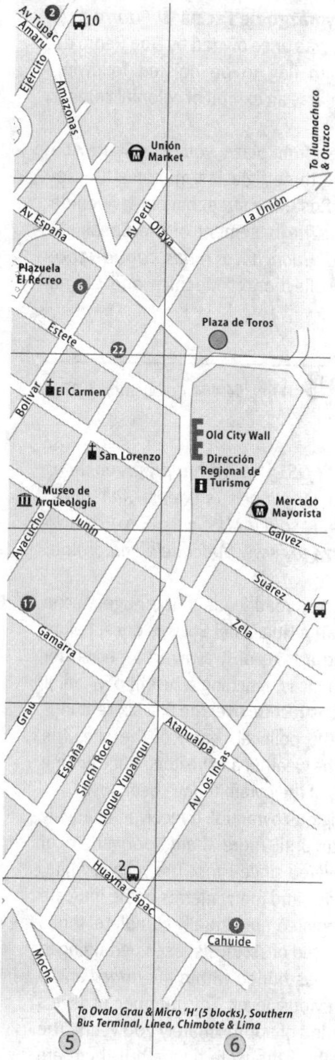

Taverna Chelsea **22** *B5*

Buses

Buses to Huaca del Sol y de la Luna **4** *D6*
Chinchaysuyo **6** *B2*
Combi A & Micro H to Chan Chán & Huanchaco **1** *E1*
Combi A to Chan Chán & Huanchaco **2** *E2 & E5*
Combis A & B & Micros B, H & 'H Corazón' to Chan Chán & Huanchaco **3** *B1*
Combi B and Micro B to Chan Chán & Huanchaco **5** *A3 & B5*
El Dorado **7** *B1*
ITTSA **8** *B2 & C2*
Oltursa & Flores **10** *A5*
Ormeño **11** *A5*
Turismo Díaz **9** *B1*

round northern Peru. There are watercolours of life in the 18th century. Before you arrive back at the plaza you come to the 17th-century church of **La Merced** ⓘ *Pizarro 550, 0800-1200, 1600-2000, free*, with picturesque moulded figures below the dome, has been restored. It has a mock rococo organ above the choir stalls and *retablos* from the 17th century which, unusually, are still visible, painted on the walls, from the time before free-standing altars were used.

If you leave the plaza on Orbegoso, the **Casa del Mariscal de Orbegoso** ⓘ *Orbegoso 553, daily from 0930, free, take passport or photocopy*, is at the first junction. It was named after the ex-President, General Luis José de Orbegoso, is the Museo de la República, owned by Banco de Crédito. It holds temporary exhibitions and cultural events most Thursday evenings. Opposite is **San Agustín** ⓘ *Bolívar 508, 0800-1200, 1600-2000*. Turn up Bolívar and go one block right for the **Museo de Arqueología** ⓘ *Casa Risco, Junín 682 y Ayacucho, T044-249322, www.unitru.edu.pe/cultural/arq (mainly in Spanish), Mon 0900-1445, Tue-Fri 0900- 1300, 1500-1900, Sat and Sun 0930-1600. US$1.50, guided tours in Spanish available*. It houses a large collection of thematic exhibits from prehispanic cultures of the area. Further up Bolívar is the church and monastery of **El Carmen** ⓘ *Colón y Bolívar, church and pinacoteca open Mon-Sat 0900-1300, US$0.85, the church is open for mass Sun 0700-0730*. Described as the 'most valuable jewel of colonial art in Trujillo', El Carmen has five gilt altars, balconies and religious paintings. Next door is the Pinacoteca Carmelita, with more paintings. It includes a room on picture restoration.

South and west of the Plaza Mayor The **Museo de Zoología de Juan Ormea** ⓘ *Jr San Martín 368, Mon-Fri 0800-1900, Sat 0800-1300, US$0.60*, has interesting displays of Peruvian animals. **La Compañía**, the former Jesuit church near Plaza de Armas, is now an auditorium for cultural events. Other churches in this area are **Santo Domingo** ⓘ *on the 4th block of Bolognesi*, and **Belén** ⓘ *on the 6th block of Almagro*. The **Casa del Mayorazgo de Facalá** ⓘ *Pizarro 314, Mon-Fri 0915-1230*, which is now the **Banco Wiese**, was once owned by Don Pedro de Tinoco whose wife embroidered the first Peruvian flag to be hoisted following Trujillo's independence from Spanish rule in 1820. It has an exhibit of colonial coins.

Northwest of the Plaza Mayor Heading northwest from plaza, you pass **Santa Ana** ⓘ *on the 2nd block of Mcal Orbegoso*, one of the three 'iglesias menores' (lesser churches). The others were San Lorenzo and Santa Rosa. The street becomes Avenida Mansiche which leads to the routes out of town. The basement of the **Cassinelli** garage ⓘ *on the fork of the Pan-American and Huanchaco roads, 0900-1300, 1500-1900, US$1.50*, contains a superb private collection of Mochica and Chimú pottery and is highly recommended.

Around Trujillo

» *pp394-404. Colour map 3, A1.*

Huacas del Sol and de la Luna

ⓘ *0830-1600 (last entry, but site open till sunset), US$3.50, with a professional or student guide, some of whom speak European languages (students half price, children US$0.40). A booklet in English or Spanish is sold for US$2.85. See Proyecto Huaca de la Luna, Jr Junín 682, Trujillo, T044-297430, www.huacadelaluna.org.pe; also www.huacas.com.*

A few kilometres south of Trujillo a new 3.2-km access road leads to the huge Moche pyramids, the Huaca del Sol and Huaca de la Luna. The Huaca del Sol was once, before the Spanish diverted the nearby river and washed a third of it away in a search for treasure, the largest man-made structure in the Americas, reaching a height of 45 m. It consisted of seven levels, with 11 or 12 phases of construction over the first six centuries AD. Built from 143 million adobe bricks, it was the political centre of the site. The ceremonial platforms have been further eroded by the weather and visitors, but climbing on them is now prohibited. Today, about two-thirds of the pyramid have been lost.

The Huaca de la Luna, 500 m away, was a 'religious pyramid'. It received relatively little attention compared to its larger neighbour until more than 8000 sq m of remarkable mural paintings and reliefs were uncovered since 1990. The yellow, white, red and black paint has faded little over the centuries and many metres of the intricate geometric patterns and fearsome feline deities depicted are virtually complete. It has now been established that the pyramid once consisted of six levels, each pertaining to a different ruler-priest. When each priest died he was buried within the *huaca* and a new level was built covering up entirely the previous level. The number of levels suggests that there were six ruler-priests over a period of approximately 200 years. The highest mural is a 'serpent' which runs the length of the wall, beneath it there are repeated motifs of 'felines' holding decapitated heads of warriors, then repeated motifs of 'fishermen' holding fish against a bright blue background and, next, huge 'spider/crab' motifs. The bottom two levels show dancers or officials grimly holding hands and, below them, victorious warriors following naked prisoners past scenes of combat and two complex scenes, similar to those at Huaca Cao Viejo at El Brujo (see page 394). Combined with intricate, brightly painted two-dimensional motifs in the sacrificial area atop the *huaca*, Huaca de la Luna is now a truly significant site well worth visiting. The project was awarded an EU prize as the best in Latin America in 2006; the money will go towards a new site museum.

Between the two *huacas* lie the remains of a once sizeable settlement, now mainly lost beneath the sands, though excavations are taking place.

The visitor's centre (T044-834901) has a café showing videos and a souvenir shop selling attractive ceramics, T-shirts, woven bags, wooden boxes, etc. In an outside patio craftsmen reproduce ceramics in designs from northern Peru. Also good toilets.

Chan Chán → *Colour map 3, A1.*

ⓘ *A ticket which covers the entrance fees for Chan Chán, the site museum, as well as Huaca El Dragón and Huaca La Esmeralda (for 2 days) costs US$3.50 (half price for students with an official ISIC card; tickets can be bought at any of the sites, except La Esmeralda). A guide at the site costs US$5.80 per hr (the price is the same for a small group); recommended so you don't miss anything. A map and leaflet in English is on sale for US$0.75. Robberies have occurred on the dirt track from turn-off to the site (20 mins), even on the track from the site museum and the main palace complex. It is best to go in a group. If alone, contact the Tourist Police in Trujillo to arrange for a policeman to accompany you (there should be no charge). On no account walk the 4 km to the site, or on Buenos Aires beach, near Chan Chán, as there is serious danger of robbery, and of being attacked by dogs.*

This crumbling imperial city of the Chimú is the largest adobe city in the world and lies about 5 km from Trujillo. Heavy rain and flooding in 1925 and 1983 damaged much of the ruins and, although they are still standing, eight palaces are closed to visitors. Thankfully, UNESCO donated US$100,000 and protection work ensured that the 1998 El Niño had little effect. Conservation work has uncovered more friezes since then.

The ruins consist of nine great compounds built by Chimú kings. The 9-m-high perimeter walls surrounded sacred enclosures with usually only one narrow entrance. Inside, rows of storerooms contained the agricultural wealth of the kingdom, which stretched 1000 km along the coast from near Guayaquil, in Ecuador, to beyond Paramonga.

Most of the compounds contain a huge walk-in well which tapped the ground water, raised to a high level by irrigation higher up the valley. Each compound also included a platform mound which was the burial place of the king, with his women and his treasure, presumably maintained as a memorial. The Incas almost certainly copied this system and transported it to Cuzco where the last Incas continued building huge enclosures. The Chimú surrendered to the Incas around 1471 after 11 years of siege and threats to cut the irrigation canals.

Sometimes a singer waits in the Plaza Principal of the Ciudadela to show the perfect acoustics of the square (she expects a tip).

The dilapidated city walls enclose an area of 28 sq km containing the remains of palaces, temples, workshops, streets, houses, gardens and a canal. Canals up to

Around Trujillo

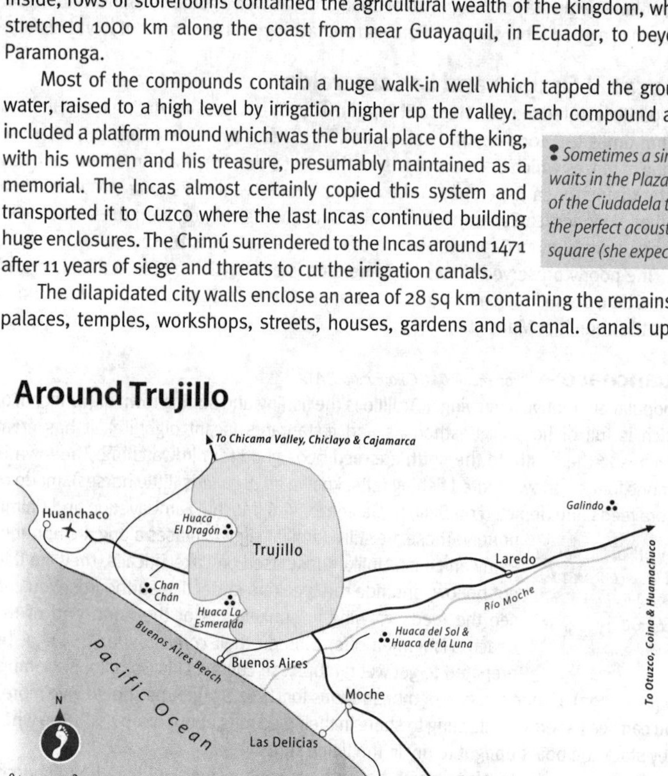

Absolute power

Chimú was a despotic state which based its power on wars of conquest. Rigid social stratification existed and power rested in the hands of the great lords. These lords were followed in the social scale by a group of urban courtiers who enjoyed a certain amount of economic power. At the bottom were the peasants and prisoners for sacrifice. The Chimú economy was based on agriculture supplemented by fishing, hunting and craft production. They were renowned metalsmiths, who, like the Moche, alloyed and plated copper with gold and silver. The burial mounds of the Chimú nobles at Chan Chán were despoiled of all their gold and silver statuettes and ornaments by the Spaniards.

74 km long kept the city supplied with water. What is left of the adobe walls bears well-preserved moulded decorations showing small figures of fish, birds and various geometric motifs. Painted designs have been found on pottery unearthed from the debris of a city ravaged by floods, earthquakes and *huaqueros*.

The **Ciudadela of Tschudi** ⓘ *daily 0900-1630 (but it may be covered up if rain is expected); arrive well before 1600 as you need more than 30 mins to see the site and will not be allowed in much after that*, is a 20-minute walk from the main road and has been restored. The site museum on the main road, 100 m before the turn-off, has a son-et-lumière display of the growth of Chan Chán as well as objects found in the area. It also has a good table showing Peruvian archaeology in the context of world history.

Huacas El Dragón and La Esmeralda

The partly restored temple, **Huaca El Dragón** ⓘ *daily 0900-1630*, dating from Huari to Chimú times (AD 1000-1470), is also known as **Huaca Arco Iris** (rainbow), after the shape of friezes which decorate it. It is on the west side of the Pan-American Highway in the district of La Esperanza. Take a combi from Avenida España y Manuel Vera marked 'Arco Iris/La Esperanza', from the Ovalo Mansiche, or, if on the east side of the city, from Huayna Cápac y Avenida Los Incas; a taxi costs US$2.

The poorly preserved **Huaca La Esmeralda** is at Mansiche, between Trujillo and Chan Chán, behind the church (not a safe area). Buses to Chan Chán and Huanchaco pass the church at Mansiche.

Huanchaco → *Phone code: 044. Colour map 3, A1.*

A popular alternative to staying in Trujillo is the fishing and surfing town of Huanchaco, which is full of hotels, guesthouses and restaurants (scant nightlife). It has great beaches to the south; to the north are reed beds good for birdwatching. The town is famous for its narrow pointed fishing rafts, known as *caballitos* (little horses), made of totora reeds and depicted on Salinar, Gallinazo, Virú, Moche, Lambayeque and Chimú pottery. These are still a familiar sight in places along the northern Peruvian coast. Unlike those used on Lake Titicaca, they are flat, not hollow, and ride the breakers rather like surfboards. You can see the reeds growing in sunken pits at the north end of the beach. Fishermen offer trips on their *caballitos* for US$1.50, be prepared to get wet (groups can contact Luis Gordillo, El Mambo, T044-461092). Fishermen give demonstrations for US$2.85 (groups should give more). You can see fishermen returning to shore in their reed rafts about 0800 and 1600 when they stack the boats upright to dry in the fierce sun.

The strength of the sun is deceptive. A cool breeze off the sea reduces the temperature, but you can still be badly sunburned.

The town, now developed with beach houses, is overlooked by a huge **church**, one of the oldest in Peru, from the belfry of which are extensive views. The **pier**

Masters of sculpture

One of the most remarkable pre-Inca civilizations was that of the Moche people, who evolved during the first century AD and lasted until around AD 750. Though these early Peruvians had no written language, they left a vivid artistic record of their life and culture in beautifully modelled and painted ceramics.

Compared with the empires of their successors, the Chimú and Inca, the realm of the Moche was very small, covering less than 250 miles of coast from the valleys of Lambayeque to Nepeña, south of present-day Chimbote. Though a seemingly inhospitable stretch of coast, the Moche harnessed rivers spilling from the Andean cordillera, channelling them into a network of irrigation canals that watered the arid coastal valleys. The resultant lush fields produced plentiful crops, which, along with the sea's bountiful harvest of fish and seafood, gave the Moche a rich and varied diet. With the leisure allowed by such abundant food, Moche craftsmen invented new techniques to produce their artistic masterpieces. It is these ancient pottery vessels that have made the greatest contribution to our understanding of this great civilization.

These masters of sculpture used clay to bring to life animals, plants and anthropomorphic deities and demons. They recreated hunting and fishing scenes, combat rituals, elaborate ceremonies and sexual intercourse (sometimes with contraception). They depicted the power of their rulers as well as the plight of their sick and invalid.

The violence and death of war is a common theme in their work; prisoners of war are apparently brought before congregations where their throats are cut and their blood offered to those present. Decapitation and dismemberment are also shown.

Moche potters were amazingly skilled at reproducing facial features, specializing in the subtle nuances of individual personality. In addition to these three-dimensional sculptures, the Moche potter was skilled at decorating vessels with low-relief designs. Among the most popular scenes are skeletal death figures holding hands while dancing in long processions to the accompaniment of musicians. The potters also developed a technique of painting scenes on ceramic vessels. Over a period of several centuries the painters became increasingly skillful at depicting complex and lively scenes with multiple figures. Because of their complexity and detail, these scenes are of vital importance in reconstructing Moche life.

The early introduction of moulds and stamps brought efficiency to the production of Moche ceramics. By pressing moist clay into the halves of a mould, it was possible to produce an object much more rapidly than by hand. Similarly, the use of stamps facilitated the decoration of ceramic vessels with elaborate low-relief designs. Mould-making technology thus resulted in many duplications of individual pieces. Since there were almost no unique ceramic objects, elaborate ceramics became more widely available and less effective as a sign of power, wealth and social status of the élite.

Although among the most sophisticated potters in Spanish America, the Moche did not use ceramics for ordinary tableware. Neither do their ceramics show many everyday activities, such as farming, cooking and pottery making. This is because Moche art expresses the religious and supernatural aspects of their culture and nothing of everyday life is illustrated for its own sake. See also under History, on page 571.

 ⓘ *US$0.20*, also gives good views. Drivers should note that the municipality charges US$0.55 per vehicle to enter town in summer; in winter is very quiet.

Chicama Valley

North of Trujillo is the sugar estate of **Hacienda Cartavio**, in the Chicama Valley (43 km). The plant includes a distillery and rum factory. Visits are possible by appointment only. One of the biggest sugar estates in the world, also in the Chicama Valley, is the **Casa Grande cooperative**. It covers over 6000 ha and employs 4000 members. Visits (guided) are only possible before 1200; many buses and combis go there from the Santa Cruz terminal in Trujillo, US$0.75.

El Brujo → *Colour map 3, A1.*

ⓘ*US$3.50, students half price, see www.xanga.com/ElBrujoPeru.*

Sixty kilometres north of Trujillo, is considered one of the most important archaeological sites on the entire north coast. The complex, covering 2 sq km, consists of Huacas Prieta, Cortada and Cao Viejo. This complex is collectively known as El Brujo and was a ceremonial centre for perhaps 10 cultures, including the Moche.

Huaca Cortada (or El Brujo) has a wall decorated with high-relief, stylized figures. **Huaca Prieta** is, in effect, a giant rubbish tip dating back 5000 years, which once housed the very first settlers to this area. **Huaca Cao Viejo** has extensive friezes, polychrome reliefs up to 90 m long, 4 m high and on five different levels, representing warriors, prisoners, sacrificer gods, combat and more complex scenes, with a total of seven colours in reliefs. The mummy of a tattooed woman, dating from 450 AD, has also been found (see *National Geographic*, June 2006). In front of Cao Viejo are the remains of one of the oldest Spanish churches in the region. It was common practice for the Spaniards to build their churches near these ancient sites in order to counteract their religious importance. The excavations will last many years at the site, which was opened to the public in 2006. Photography is allowed. There are exhibitions in the Chan Chán site museum, Banco Wiese and Museo de la Nación in Lima.

North of Chicama

Seventy kilometres north of Trujillo, Puerto Malabrigo (Chicama) is a real surfers' hang-out, as it's the best surf beach in Peru, claiming that it has the longest left-hand point-break in the world. There are several basic places to stay and eat. Combis and *colectivos* go there from the Santa Cruz terminal in Trujillo. Pacasmayo, port for the next oasis north, is 102 km north of Trujillo, and is the main road connection from the coast to Cajamarca. The paved 180 km road to Cajamarca branches off the Pan-American Highway soon after it crosses the Río Jequetepeque.

A few kilometres northwest on the other side of Río Jequetepeque are the ruins of Pacatnamú, comparable in size to Chan Chán. It consists of pyramids, cemetery and living quarters of nobles and fishermen, possibly initiated in the Chavín period. There is evidence also of Moche and Chimú occupation. No explanations at the site. To get there, take a taxi bus to Guadalupe, 10 km from the ruins, and a taxi is possible from there for US$20. Micros run in summer.

Where the Pan-American Highway crosses the Jequetepeque are the well-signed ruins of Farfán, separate from those of Pacatnamú, but probably of the same period. It has yielded important Inca burials in recent years. For web information, search 'Carol Mackey+Farfan' for various sites and articles.

Sleeping

Trujillo *p386, map p388*

AL Libertador, Independencia 485 on Plaza de Armas, T044-232741, trujillo@libertador.com.pe. Price includes tax, pool (can be used by non-guests if they buy a drink), cafeteria and restaurant, continental breakfast US$5, excellent buffet lunch on Sun. Recommended.

A El Gran Marqués, Díaz de Cienfuegos 145-147, Urb La Merced, T/F044-249366,

Huanchaco

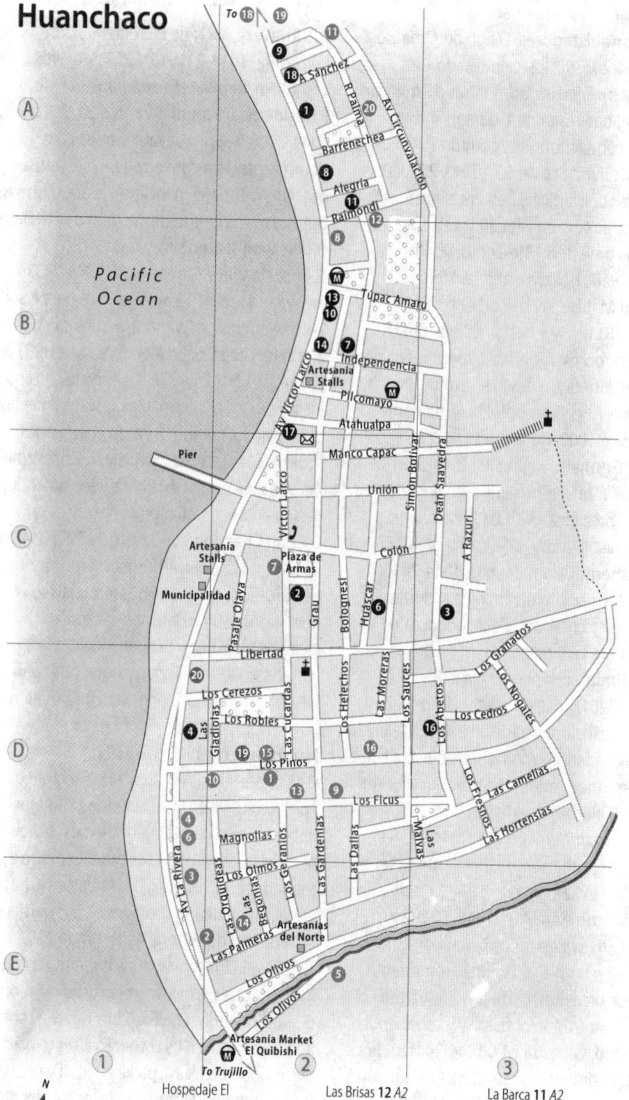

0 metres 100

0 yards 100

Sleeping

Caballito de Totora **6** *D1*
Casa Hospedaje Los Ficus **13** *D2*
Cherry's **16** *D2*
El Malecón **3** *E1*
Golden Club **4** *D1*
Hospedaje El Boquerón **20** *A2*
Hospedaje Huankarute **2** *E1*
Hospedaje My Friend **1** *D2*
Hostal Bracamonte **5** *E2*
Hostal Huanchaco **7** *C2*
Hostal Ilablo **14** *E2*
Hostal Los Esteros **8** *B2*
Hostal Solange **9** *D2*
Hostal Sol y Mar **10** *D2*
Huanchaco Inn **15** *D2*
Huanchaco's Garden **11** *A2*
Las Brisas **12** *A2*
Las Palmeras **18** *A2*
Naylamp **19** *A2*

Eating

Big Ben **1** *A2*
Casa Tere **2** *C2*
Chelita **3** *C3*
Club Colonial **4** *D1*
El Caribe **17** *B2*
El Mochica **14** *B2*
El Mococho **7** *B2*
Estrella Marina **10** *B2*
La Barca **11** *A2*
La Charapita **6** *C2*
Los Herrajes **8** *A2*
Lucho del Mar **13** *B2*
Otro Cosa **9** *A2*
Piccolo **16** *D3*
Sabes? **18** *A2*

Bars & clubs

La Tribu **19** *D2*
Nutrias **20** *D1*
Xeros **20** *D1*

www.elgranmarques.com. Price includes tax and breakfast, modern, free internet connection in rooms, pool, sauna, jacuzzi, restaurant. Recommended.

A Los Conquistadores, Diego de Almagro 586, T044-203350, losconquistadores@viabcp.com. Price includes tax and American breakfast, bar, restaurant, garage and internet connection, very comfortable.

B Gran Bolívar, Bolívar 957, T044-222090, www.granbolivarhotel.net. Price includes breakfast, airport transfer and welcome drink, in converted 18th-century house, internet, café, bar, gym and parking.

C Hostal Malibú, Av Larco 1471-1474, T044-284811, www.hostalmalibu.com. Variety of rooms, restaurant, room service, mini-bar, laundry, massage, currency exchange. Also sister hotel of same name at Av Larco 1000, Huanchaco.

C Saint Germain, Junín 585, T044-208102, www.perunorte.com/saintgermain. Price includes breakfast. With bath, hot water, TV, internet, laundry, safe, parking.

D Continental, Gamarra 663, T044-241607, F249881. Opposite the market, includes good buffet breakfast, clean, good, safe, the staff are very helpful.

D-E Colonial, Independencia 618, T044-258261, hostcolonialtruji@hotmail.com. Price includes basic breakfast. Clean, attractive, friendly, rooms are a bit small, hot showers, good restaurant, especially for the set lunch. Recommended.

E Almagro, Jr Almagro 748, T044-223845. New hotel with cable TV, hot water, cafetería (breakfast extra), good.

E San Martín, San Martín 749, T/F044-252311, www.deperu.com/sanmartin. Good value, with bath and TV, small restaurant, good for breakfast, clean but noisy from neighbouring establishments. Recommended.

E Turismo, Gamarra 747, T044-244181. Price includes continental breakfast. Central hotel with good services, cable TV, restaurant, parking and travel agency.

F Hostal Americano, Pizarro 764, T044-241361. A vast, rambling old building, which is getting run-down, rooms without bathrooms are noisy and very basic, most rooms don't have window (Nos 134 and 137 and those either side of 303 have windows, balconies and good views), cold water only, friendly staff, but mixed reports.

F Hostería El Sol, Brillantes 224, Urb Santa Inés, T044-231933, near bus terminals on Av Nicolás de Piérola. With hot shower, restaurant, all meals available for US$2.60.

F Primavera, Av N de Piérola 872, Urb Primavera, T044-231915, F257399. With bathroom, hot water, restaurant, bar, pool.

F Residencial Vanini, Av Larco 237, T044-200878, enriqueva@hotmail.com. Youth hostel in a converted private house, outside Av España in location, a good option but not in the centre, some rooms with bath, others with shared shower.

G Casa de Clara, Cahuide 495, T044-243347, www.xanga.com/TrujilloPeru. Price per person. With bath, cheaper without, groups can be accommodated, good food (breakfast US$0.90, lunch US$1.50, dinner US$2), very helpful and friendly, loads of information available, meeting place and lots going on, many languages spoken (see Clara Luz Bravo and Michael White, Activities and tours page 400). Recommended. Restaurants and fast internet nearby.

G Chan Chán Inn, Av Ejército 307, T/F044-294281, mocheperu@hotmail.com. Price per person. Close to several bus terminals so very noisy from 0500 till late at night, price includes breakfast (cheaper without), popular with backpackers, luggage store, café, laundry, internet, money exchange and information.

Huanchaco *p392, map p395*

C Las Palmeras, Av Larco 1150, sector Los Tumbos, T044-461199, www.laspalmerasdehuanchaco.com. One of the best hotels in town, rooms with terrace more expensive than those with view of pool; bath, TV, hot water, small dining room, pool and gardens.

D Caballito de Totora, Av La Rivera 219, T/F044-461154, www.caballitodetotora.com. Includes taxes, **E** in low season, surfers' room **G**, pool, friendly, English, Portuguese, French and Italian spoken by owner Elvira, nice garden, clean, good breakfast, parking, good value. Recommended. Elvira and Walter are friendly and knowledgeable and offer a discount to *Footprint Peru* owners in low season (after Easter to 24 Dec, except Jul national holidays).

D Hospedaje Huankarute, La Rivera 233, T044-461705, www.huanchaco.com/huankarute. On the seafront, with small pool, bar, sun terrace, friendly; some rooms larger, more luxurious and more expensive. Recommended.

D Hostal Bracamonte, Los Olivos 503, T044-461162, www.hostalbracamonte.com. Comfortable, good (chalets with private bathroom **C**), you can camp on the grass (US$4.25), pool, secure, good restaurant, English spoken, internet US$0.65/hr. Highly recommended.

D Hostal Huanchaco, Av Larco 287 on the plaza, T044-461272, www.huanchaco hostal.com. With bath, breakfast extra, TV, hot water, **G** per person for room without bath, clean and friendly, pool, car park, cafeteria with home-made cakes and other good meals, video, pool table, back door is ½ block from beach. Recommended.

D Hostal Sol y Mar, La Rivera 400, T044-461120, www.ctsolymar.cjb.net. Breakfast extra, expanding, friendly owner is a doctor. With pool, restaurant and garden. Recommended.

D-E El Malecón, Av La Rivera 225, T044-461275. Overlooking the sea, some rooms with terrace, clean, hot water, TV, café, friendly staff.

E Hostal Los Esteros, Av Larco 618, T044-461300, huanchacoesteros@yahoo.com. Bathroom, hot water, cable TV, restaurant, friendly, safe car and motorcycle parking, can arrange surfing and *caballitos de totora* trips.

E Huanchaco Inn, Los Pinos 528, T044-461158, www.huanchacoinn.com. Rooms with and without bath, new and still expanding, hot water, cable TV, internet cabins, use of kitchen, laundry service, small pool.

E Las Brisas, Raymondi 146, T044-461186, lasbrisas@hotmail.com. 20 rooms with bathroom, hot water, cafeteria, cable TV, comfy.

F Ñaylamp, Prolongación Víctor Larco 1420, northern end of the seafront in El Boquerón, T044-461022, www.hostalnaylamp.com. Rooms set around a courtyard, a little more expensive in the new wing, dorms too (**G** per person), hammocks, nice garden, kitchen, very clean, with bath, hot water 24 hrs, camping US$2.45 with own tent, US$3 with hired tent, laundry facilities, safe, good views of the sunset from the campsite and terrace restaurant, Italian food, good breakfasts. Recommended.

G Casa Hospedaje Los Ficus, Los Ficus 516, T044-461719, www.huanchaco.net/ losficus. With bath, breakfast and laundry extra. Family-run, hot water, use of kitchen. Recommended.

G Cherry's, Los Pinos 448, T044-461837, juancarlos160@yahoo.es. Price per person. Owner Juan Carlos speaks English, cheaper without bath, hot water, use of kitchen, it has a shop, bar, internet with good machines, even a small swimming pool.

G Golden Club, Av La Rivera 217, T044-461306. Price per person. 5 rooms, gym, pool, popular with surfers, laid-back atmosphere, excellent value, rooms on 2nd floor available for monthly rent (US$300). Recommended.

G Hospedaje El Boquerón, R Palma 330, T044-461968, maznaran@hotmail.com. One block from beach, a modern house with shared bathrooms, hot water, fully equipped kitchen, laundry facilities and service, clean, friendly landlady speaks French.

G Hospedaje My Friend, Los Pinos 533, T044-461080, magowave@hotmail.com. Popular new place with surfers and foreigners, good for meeting others and for a meal in the restaurant (closed 1500-1900), with bath and hot water, TV room. Tours arranged.

G Hostal Ilablo, La Orquídeas 339, T044-9579753. Hot water, roof terrace, popular with backpackers.

G Hostal Solange, Los Ficus 484, 1 block from the beach, T044-461410, hsolange@yahoo.es. With bathroom, hot water, good food, laundry facilities, limited use of kitchen, very helpful. Highly recommended.

G Huanchaco's Garden, Av Circunvalación 440, El Boquerón, T044-461194, www.huan chacogarden.com. Price per person. Family-run, bungalows, cable TV, also camping, hot water, use of kitchen, free luggage store, friendly and helpful, garden with 2 pools (1 for children), internet US$0.65, parking, laundry. Frequently recommended.

G Sra Mabel Díaz de Aguilar, Túpac Amaru 248, T044-461232, mabel _minerva@hotmail.com. Price per person. Near the football ground. Shared bath, hot water, Sra Mabel speaks English, very friendly.

North of Chicama *p394*

D-E Hotel Chiacama Beach, Puerto Malabrigo, T044-576130, www.chicamabeach.com. A new hotel, with pool, some rooms with balconies overlooking the sea, friendly.

G Panamericano, Leoncio Prado 18, Pacasmayo, T044-522521. With private cold shower, small, basic, friendly, safe, reasonable restaurant downstairs.

G San Francisco, Leoncio Prado 21, Pacasmayo, T044-522021. Basic, but cleaner than the Panamericano which is opposite, OK.

Eating

Trujillo *p386, map p388*

It's difficult to find a meal before 0800. A speciality is *shambar*, a thick minestrone made with gammon, served on Mon. There are 5 cheap seafood restaurants at **Plazuela El Recreo**, at the end of Pizarro. For really cheap meals try the **central market** at Grau y Ayacucho.

¥¥ **Demarco**, Pizarro 725. Good food and excellent desserts at this place in a cluster of restaurants in the centre.

¥¥ **El Mochica**, Bolívar 462. Typical restaurant with a good reputation, the food is good and, on special occasions, there's live music. There is another branch on the road to Las Delicias beach and another in Huanchaco.

¥¥ **Pizzería Pizzanino**, Av Juan Pablo II 183, Urb San Andrés, opposite the university, T044-263105. Recommended for pizzas, also pasta, meats and desserts, open in evenings.

¥¥ **Romano**, Pizarro 747. International food, good *menús*, breakfasts, coffee, milkshakes and cakes, but slow service and poor salads.

¥¥ **Romano-Rincón Criollo**, Estados Unidos 162, Urb El Recreo, a 10-min walk from the centre, T044-244207. Specializes in northern Peruvian cuisine and has a good-value lunch menu for US$2 in smart surroundings.

¥ **ABC**, Orbegoso 290 y San Martín. Good for chicken, open in the evening only.

¥ **Asturias**, Pizarro 741. Nice café with excellent meals, good juices and snacks.

¥ **Café Oviedo**, Pizarro 737. With vegetarian options, good salads, helpful.

¥ **Café Santo Domingo**, Av Larco 268. Popular with locals in the morning.

¥ **El Sol**, Pizarro 660. The original and best vegetarian, cheap set meals, also serves other dishes.

¥ **Juguería San Agustín**, Bolívar 526. Good juices, good *menú*, popular, excellent value.

¥ **La Casona**, San Martín 677. Their set lunch menu is popular with locals.

¥ **Milenium**, Gamarra 316. A cheap vegetarian place.

¥ **Parnasillo**, Gamarra 353, T/F044-234715. Hotel and restaurant school, good set menu US$1.70 and US$2.25, served Mon-Sat 1300-1530, but small portions.

¥ **Rincón de Vallejo**, Orbegoso 303. Good set menu, typical dishes, very crowded at peak times.

¥ **Sal y Pimienta**, Colón 201. Very popular for lunch, US$1 and US$1.85, close to buses for Huanchaco and Chan Chán.

Cafés

Café Amaretto, Gamarra 368. Good selection of coffees, brilliant cakes, sweets, snacks and drinks.

Dulcería Doña Carmen, San Martín 814. Serves local 'sweet' specialities such as *alfajores, budín, king kong*, etc.

El Chileno, Ayacucho 408. Café and ice cream parlour, popular.

Fitopán, Bolívar 406. Good selection of breads, also has a small cafeteria for lunch, very popular.

Panadería José Antonio, Ayacucho 561-65, in the Mercado Central. Another good bakery.

Panadería Sandoval, Orbegoso 822. Good bread selection.

Huanchaco *p392, map p395*

There are about 30 restaurants on the beachfront. Many close in the low season.

¥¥¥ **Big Ben**, Av Larco 836, near A Sánchez, T044-461869. Seafood and international menu, à la carte only, most expensive but very good. Daily 1130-1730.

¥¥¥ **Club Colonial**, La Rivera 171, on the beachfront, T044-461015. A smart restaurant and bar, open in the evenings, Belgian owner.

¥¥¥ **El Mochica**, Av Larco 552, T044-293441. Same owners and quality as this restaurant in Trujillo, very nice dining area and panorama. Daily 0900-1800.

¥¥¥ **El Mococho**, Bolognesi 535. Said to be one of the best seafood restaurants, expensive, caters for groups.

¥¥ **El Caribe**, just around the corner from Pisagua at Atahualpa 291. Another good seafood and fish place.

¥¥ **Estrella Marina**, Av Larco, next door to Lucho del Mar. Great value for fish.

¥¥ **La Barca**, Raimondi 111, T044-461855. Very good seafood, well-run, popular, but loud music or TV usually playing.

¥¥ **Los Herrajes**, Av Larco 712. Excellent seafood and nice sea-view terrace. In low season only open at weekends and on holidays.

¥¥ **Lucho del Mar**, Av Larco. On seafront road, serves excellent sea food.

¥¥ **Sabes?**, Av Larco 920, T044-461555, ysabes@yahoo.com. Pub with food, internet café, popular, owned by an American tour guide.

ΨΨ-Ψ Otra Cosa, Av Larco 921, T044-461346, www.otracosa. info. A vegetarian restaurant overlooking the sea (fair trade and organic produce), with Dutch owners, also has a volunteering agency, internet, massage, Spanish lessons, book exchange, movies, tourist information and surfing services. Open Wed-Sun 0900-2000. Recommended.

Ψ Casa Tere, Av Larco 280, Plaza de Armas. For best pizzas in town, also pastas, burgers and breakfasts.

Ψ Chelita, Deán Saavedra 270. Good-value *menú*, fish dishes are best, very popular.

Ψ La Charapita, Huáscar 162. Modest but very popular restaurant serving large portions.

Ψ Piccolo, Los Abetos 142, 5 blocks from the plaza. Cheap, friendly, live folk music weekend evenings, excellent, surf and art shop.

Bars and clubs

Trujillo *p386, map p388*

Bar/Café Juguete, Junín y Independencia. An old-style café serving good coffee. Open to midnight.

Bar/Café Stradivarius, Colón 327. An attractive café with sofas, open in the evenings only.

Canana, San Martín 788, T044-232503. Bars and restaurant, disco, live music at weekends (US$1.50-3 depending on the show), video screens (also has travel agency). Recommended, but take care on leaving.

El Estubo, San Martin 380. A new club playing a wide genre of sounds and attracting a mixed crowd.

Taverna Chelsea, Estete 675, T044-257032. Bar, restaurant, live salsa at weekends (US$4 entry), exclusive and lively. Recommended.

Huanchaco *p392, map p395*

On Av La Rivera, block 5, there are several lively bars with music such as **Nutrias** and **Xeros**. They open late in the summer.

La Tribu, Los Pinos 540. Galería, café and bar, opens 1900, unpretentious and popular, live music Thu. The owner is a sculptor, his workshop is worth seeing.

Festivals and events

Trujillo *p386, map p388*

End Jan The National Marinera Contest lasts 2 weeks and consists of hundreds of couples competing in 6 categories, from children to seniors (see page 598). This event is organized by the Club Libertad and has taken place since 1960.

19-22 Mar Feria de San José, an important festival held in Las Delicias.

18 Jun Festival de la Música.

Last week of Sep Festival Internacional de la Primavera, www.tuprimaveraentrujillo.com. Organized by the Club de Leones, it is a celebration of the arrival of spring and has grown over the years to become one of Peru's most important tourist events. The final parade (*corso*) has plenty to enjoy, with many local dancers, dog owners' clubs, schools parades and so on. Those who are strongly opposed to beauty pageants may want to give it a miss as there are floats with beauty queens from South and North America participating. Other days feature cultural events (some charitable), and, above all, Trujillo's famous **Caballos de Paso**, a fine breed of horses with a tripping gait that has made them renowned worldwide. These horses, a Spanish legacy, have been immortalized in Peruvian waltzes. Riders still compete in their own form of the Marinera dance and buyers from around the world congregate to see them shown at the Spring Festival (see www.rcp.net.pe/rcp/caballos).

Huanchaco *p392, map p395*

1st week of May Festival del Mar, a celebration of the disembarkation of Taycanamo, the leader of the Chimú period. A procession is made in *totora* boats.

30 Jun San Pedro, patron saint of fishermen. His statue is taken out to sea on a huge *totora*-reed boat.

There are also surf competitions and Carnival and New Year are especially popular.

Shopping

Trujillo *p386, map p388*

Bookshops

Librería Adriatica, Jr Junín 565, T044-291569, libreria@adriaticaperu.com. A very good bookshop, stocks Footprint.

Librería Peruana, Pizarro 505, just off the Plaza Mayor. Has the best selection in town, ask for Sra Inés Guerra de Guijón.

Camera repairs

Fotolab, Av España 2755, T044-295590. Hugo Guevara repairs all makes, film developing.
Fotovisión Para Tí, Pizarro 523, also repairs cameras.

Handicrafts

APIAT, Av España near Zela, open daily 0900-2300, Sun 0900-1400. The largest crafts market in Trujillo, selling ceramics, wood-carvings, totora boats, etc, and kiosks selling shoes and leather goods at competitive prices.
Artesanía del Norte, Independencia 616. A branch of the shop which can be found in Huanchaco.
Liga de Artesanos, Colón 423.
Los Tallanes, San Martín 455: For souvenirs, artworks and antiques.

Leather and shoes

Trujillo is renowned for its leather and shoe industry. Prices for shoes are very attractive, but sizes over European 42 are hard to find. Try on both sides of block 18 of **Av España**, or **Alameda del Calzado**, Av España, block 20.

Markets

Mercado Central, Gamarra, Ayacucho and Pasaje San Agustín. **Mercado Mayorista** between Sinchi Roca and Av Los Incas (not a safe zone).

Supermarkets

Merpisa, Junín y Pizarro and Av Larco y Los Angeles. Best choice for food at competitive prices.

Huanchaco *p392, map p395*

The main *artesanía* market, **El Quibishi**, is at the entrance to Huanchaco at the southern end of the beach and is divided into handicraft stalls and a food section. Some stalls also on the seafront adjoining the Municipalidad, **El Erizo**, and in Av Larco, block 2, **Takaynamo**. **Artesanías del Norte**, Los Olivos 504, T044-461220, marycortijo@usa.net. Sells mostly items of her own design, using prehispanic methods and motifs, primarily ceramics, but also cotton and alpaca goods and hand-painted products in wood. Food in the shops is a bit more expensive than Trujillo. There is a small fresh food market on Pilcomayo, ½ block from Deán Saavedra.

Activities and tours

Trujillo *p386, map p388*

Caballos de paso

La Asociación de Criadores de Caballos de Paso Peruanos, www.ancpcpp.org.pe, has an enclosure with plots for each member's house and stables on the Vía de Evitamiento, just north of its junction with Av Larco. Owners may be prepared to show visitors around.
El Palmar, stables, on the Vía de Evitamiento near **Hotel El Golf**, charges US$12 per person to see and maybe ride the horses at its stables. Book the day before at the office on Pizarro, on the Plaza Mayor.
For group visits to **Manucci** stables, just south of the Huaca del Sol, and **Vásquez Nacarino** at Paijan, contact Clara Bravo and Michael White, see Tour guides, page 401.

Cycling

Bicycle Tours, Bolognesi 350, T044-993 9064 (mob), peruguide@hotmail.com.

Sandboarding

Sandboarding is possible on large dunes near Simbal, 1 hr up the Moche Valley, about US$10 with agencies, including board.

Swimming

Academia Berendson, Bolognesi 231, heated pool. There's an outdoor swimming pool next to Mansiche stadium, where buses leave for Chan Chán and Huanchaco. Daily 0900-1300 and 1600-1800, entry US$0.50.

Tour operators

Prices vary and competition is fierce so shop around for the best deal. Average tour costs are: to **Chan Chán**, **El Dragón** and **Huanchaco**, 3 hrs, US$8.50 per person, not including entrances. To **Huaca del Sol** and **Huaca de la Luna**, 2 hrs for US$7 per person. To **El Brujo**, US$17 per person. **City tours** cost US$5.65 per person (minimum of 2 people; discounts for 4 or more). Few agencies run tours on Sun and often only at fixed times on other days. Check exactly which sites are included in the tour, if transport, entry and guide are included and whether guides speak anything other than Spanish.
Chacón Tours, Av España 106-112, T044-255212. Open Sat afternoon and Sun

morning. Recommended.

Guía Tours, Independencia 580, T044-234856, guiatour@amauta.rcp.net.pe. Also Western Union agent. Recommended.

Tesores del Perú, Pizarro 575, of 03, T044-582381, oscarcampos10@hotmail.com. Oscar Campos Santa María organizes custom-made tours at affordable prices to archaeological sites, as far as Lambayeque.

Trujillo Tours, San Martín y Almagro 301, T044-257518, ttours@pol.com.pe. Work with Lima Tours.

Tour guides

Many hotels work on a commission basis with taxi drivers and travel agencies. If you decide on a guide, make your own direct approach. The tourist police (see Directory, below) has a list of official guides; average cost is US$7 per hr. Beware of cowboy outfits herding up tourists around the plazas and bus terminals for rapid, poorly translated tours. Also beware of scammers offering surfing or salsa lessons and party invitations.

Clara Luz Bravo Díaz, Cahuide 495, Urb Santa María, T044-243347, www.xanga.com/TrujilloPeru. An experienced tourist guide, who speaks Spanish, German and understands Italian. She takes tourists on extended circuits of the region and is good for information (archaeological tour US$16 for 6 hrs, city tour US$7 per person, US$53 per car to El Brujo, with extension to Sipán, Brüning Museum and Túcume possible – tours in Lambayeque involve public transport, not inlcuded in cost). Clara works with English chartered accountant **Michael White** (same address, microbewhite@yahoo.com) who speaks German, French and Italian and provides transport. He is very knowledgeable about tourist sites. They run tours any day of the week; 24-hr attention. They can also arrange tours to see and possibly ride *caballos de paso*.

Laura Durán, T044-281590, lauraduran@yahoo.com. Speaks English, German and some Hebrew, lots of information, very accommodating.

Zaby Miranda Acosta, T01-9966 6421, zabymiranda@hotmail.com. Speaks German and Italian.

José Ocas Cuenca, Túpac Amaru 596, Villa del Mar, T044-583556, jocas_cuenca@hotmail.com. Speaks English, German and French, very knowledgeable, plays an ancient flute.

Oscar and Gustavo Prada Marga, Miguel Grau 169, Villa del Mar, or at Chan Chán.

Jannet Rojas Sánchez, Alto Mochica Mz Q 19, Trujillo, T044-934 4844, jannarojas@hotmail.com. Speaks English, enthusiastic, works independently and for **Guía Tours**.

Celio Eduardo Roldán, celioroldan@hotmail.com. Helpful and informative taxi driver.

José Soto Ríos, Atahualpa 514, dpto 3, T044-251489. He speaks English and French.

Huanchaco *p392, map p395*

Picolo, Los Abetos 142. Instruction, rent wet suits and boards, owner is a local champion.

The Wave, Av Larco 525. Staff speak English.

Un Lugar, Bolognesi 457, T044-957 7170, unlugarsurfingschool@hotmail.com. Ask for English-speaking Juan Carlos. Yenth Ccora, Av Larco 468, T044-940 3871, ycc_mar@hotmail.com. Surf school and surf equipment manufacture, repair and rental.

Transport

Trujillo *p386, map p388*

Air

Airport T044-464013. There are daily flights to and from **Lima** with Lan, Star Perú (also to **Chiclayo**) and WayraPerú (also to **Talara** and **Tumbes**). Taxi to airport costs US$4; or take a bus or *colectivo* to Huanchaco, get out at airport turn-off then walk 2 km (US$0.25).

Airline offices Lan, Pizarro 340-42, T044-221469. **Star Perú**, Almagro 539, of 102, T044-293392, 0900-1930. **WayraPerú**, Jr Alfonso Ugarte 310, T044-200434.

Bus

Local Micros (small buses with 25 or more seats) and combis (up to 15 passengers), on all routes, cost US$0.15-0.30; *colectivos* (cars carrying 6 passengers), US$0.25, tend to run on main avenues starting from Av España. None is allowed inside an area bounded by Av Los Incas in the east to Ovalo Mansiche in the west and the north and south perimeters of Av España.

Long distance Concentrations of companies are around Avs Ejército/ Amazonas/Túpac Amaru; on Av Nicolás de Piérola, blocks 10-13 for northbound buses; and on Av La Marina, between Ovalos Grau and La Marina, for southbound buses. The better bus companies maintain their own terminals. To and from **Lima**, 561 km on a good road, 8 hrs in the better class buses, average fare US$14.30-18.50 in luxury classes, 10 hrs in the cheaper buses, US$7.15-11.50. There are many bus companies doing this route, among those recommended are: **Ormeño**, 3 levels of service, 5 daily; **Cruz del Sur**; **Turismo Días**, leaves at 2230; **Línea**, 3 levels of service, recommended, also to **Chimbote**, US$2.20, hourly, **Huaraz**, 2100, 9 hrs, US$8.65, Cajamarca 5 a day, US$4.25-10, **Chiclayo**, US$3.35, and **Piura**, 2300, US$7. Also Flores, **Ittsa** and **Móvil Tours**. **Oltursa** offers a *bus cama* service to Lima, with full reclining seats, a/c, heating, meals and drinks, depart at 2200, with connection at Lima for Arequipa. Small **Pakatnamú** buses leave when full, 0400-2100, from Av N de Piérola 1092, to **Pacasmayo**, 102 km, 1¼ hrs, US$2.

To **Chiclayo**, another 118 km, 3 hrs from Trujillo, US$2.85, several companies. Among the best are **Emtrafesa**, on the ½-hr every hr; to **Piura**, 278 km beyond Chiclayo, 6 hrs, US$7 (Ittsa's 1330 bus is a good choice); and **Tumbes**, a further 282 km, US$7.15, 8 hrs. Other companies include: **Transportes El Dorado**, leave at 1245, 2220 to **Piura** and **Sullana**, US$4.30/5.75; and **Olano, Civa, Ormeño**, US$8.60; **Ormeño** also has US$14.35 (2215) and US$8.65 (1915) services to Tumbes. **Móvil**'s **Lima-Chiclayo-Chachapoyas** service passes through Trujillo at 1600 and Chiclayo at 2000 (US$11.50). Direct buses to **Huaraz**, 319 km, via Chimbote and Casma (169 km), with **Móvil** and **Línea**, 8 hrs, US$8.60 special. Also **Chinchaysuyo**, at 2030; US$7.15, 10 hrs.

There are several buses and *colectivos* to **Chimbote**, with **América Express** from Lloque 162, 135 km, 2 hrs, US$2.20, departures every 30 mins from 0530 (ticket sales from 0500); then change at Chimbote (see above – leave Trujillo before 0600 to make a connection with the 0830 Cañón del Pato service (see Chimbote Transport, page 385); **Línea**'s 0600 bus also makes the connection). Ask Clara Bravo and Michael White (see Tour guides, page 401) about transport to Caraz avoiding Chimbote (a worthwhile trip via the Brasileños road and Cañón del Pato). To **Cajamarca**, 300 km, 7-8 hrs, US$4.55-10: with **Línea**, best at 1030; **Emtrafesa**, at 2200, and **Tur Díaz** 4 a day. To **Huamachuco**, 170 km, 6 hrs, US$4.55-5.50, **Trans Gran Turismo**, 4 a day; **Trans Horna**, 4 a day; **Turismo Negreiros**, 0900, 1300, recommended. To **Tarapoto**, via Moyobamba, **Turismo Tarapoto**, at 2230, US$14.30, and **Ejetur**, at 1100 and 1315, US$15, also to Yurimaguas at 0900, US$20, and to Jaén at 1600, US$7.50. To **Sihuas** with **Trans Garrincha**, Sat and Tue 1900, US$12.50, 12 hrs on a very rough road. From the Santa Cruz terminal at Av Santa Cruz y Av América Sur, microbuses, combis and *colectivos* depart for **Puerto Malabrigo/ Puerto Chicama**, **Cartavio**, **Casagrande**, **Paijan**, **Ascope**, **Chao** and **Virú**.

Bus companies América Express, Lloque 162. **Cruz del Sur**, Amazonas 437 near Av Ejército, T044-261801. **Ejetur** Av N de Piérola 1238, T044-222228. **Emtrafesa**, Av Túpac Amaru 285, T044-471521. **Flores**, Av Ejército 350, T044-208250. **Ittsa**, Av Mansiche 145, T044-251415; No 431 for northern destinations, T044-222541. **Línea**, Av América Sur

2857, T044-297000, ticket office at Orbegoso 300, T044-255181. **Móvil Tours**, Av América Sur 3959 – Ovalo Larco, T044-286538. **Oltursa**, Av Ejército 342, T044-263055. **Ormeño**, Av Ejército 233, T044-259782. **Pakatnamú**, Av N de Piérola 1092, T044-206564. **Trans Garrincha**, Prolongación Vallejo 1250, T044-214025. **Trans Gran Turismo**, Prolongación Vallejo 1368, T044-425391. **Trans Horna**, Av N de Piérola 1279, T044-294880. **Transportes El Dorado**, Nicolás de Piérola (Av América Norte) opposite Díaz, T044-291778. **Turismo Días**, Nicolás de Piérola 1079 on Panamericana Norte, T044-201237. Turismo Negreiros, Prolongación Vallejo block 13. **Turismo Tarapoto**, Av N de Piérola 1239, T044-470318.

Taxi

Taxis charge US$0.55 within Av España and US$0.70 within the Av América ring road (drivers may ask for more at night). To Chan Chán US$3 per car, to the airport is US$4; to Huanchaco, US$3-5.

Huacas del Sol and de la Luna *p390*

The road to the site is paved. A taxi to the site costs US$2 (there are plenty at the site for the return). *Colectivos* (blue and yellow) every 15 mins to the visitors' centre, US$0.30. They are most safely caught at the Ovalo Grau; less safe stops at Huayna Cápac blocks 5 and 6, southeast of Av Los Incas, and Suárez y Los Incas. On the return go to Ovalo Grau for onward connections, or you can get out at Huayna Cápac y Los Incas. If you want a walk take any Moche *colectivo* or bus and ask to get off at the turn-off to the Huacas. It's about an hour's interesting walk through farmland beside irrigation canals, but don't walk after dusk.

Chan Chán *p391*

Take any transport between Trujillo and Huanchaco (see next paragraph) and ask to get out at the turn-off to Chan Chán, US$0.25. A taxi is US$3 from Trujillo to the ruins, US$0.85 from museum to ruins, US$1.85 to Huanchaco.

Huanchaco *p392, map p395*

2 combi routes (A and B) run between Trujillo and Huanchaco. 3 micros run between Trujillo and Huanchaco: **micro B** (also known as Mercado Mayorista), **micro H** (UPAO) and **micro H-Corazón** (with red heart, Mercado Hermelinda). Combis run 0500-2030, micros 0630-2030, every 5-10 mins. Fare is US$0.35 for the 20-min journey. The easiest place to pick up any of these combis or micros is Ovalo Mansiche, 3 blocks northwest of Av España in front of the Cassinelli museum. In Trujillo, **combi A** takes a route on the south side of Av España, before heading up Av Los Incas. **Combi B** takes the northerly side of Av España. From Huanchaco to the **Línea, Móvil Tours** and southern bus terminals, take micro H. It also goes to Ovalo Grau where you can catch buses to the **Huacas del Sol y de la Luna**. For **Cruz del Sur, Ormeño, Flores, Oltursa**, etc, take combi or micro B from Huanchaco. There are also *colectivos* and taxis Trujillo-Huanchaco, minimum fare US$3, more likely US$4-5.

El Brujo *p394*

The complex can be reached by taking one of the regular buses from **Trujillo** to **Chocope**, US$0.55, and then a *colectivo* (every 30 mins) to **Magdalena de Cao**, US$0.45, then a mototaxi or taxi to the site, including wait, US$4.50, or a 5-km walk to the site. Alternatively take a tour with an agency from Trujillo, US$10 per person.

North of Chicama *p394*

Pacasmayo-Cajamarca bus US$4.30, 5 hrs; to Chiclayo US$1.70, 2 hrs.

Directory

Trujillo *p386, map p388*

Banks BCP, Gamarra 562. No commission on cash into soles, but US$12 fee on TCs or changing into dollars, cash advance on Visa card, ATM (Visa). **Interbank**, Pizarro y Gamarra. Good rates for cash, no commission on Amex TCs into soles, reasonable rate, Visa cash advance, quick service, also has Visa, MasterCard and Maestro ATMs (doesn't close for lunch). **Banco Wiese Sudameris**, Pizarro 314, Casa de Mayorazgo de Facalá. Good rates for Amex TCs, 2% commission into soles or dollars, ATM for Visa/Plus. **BBV Continental**, Pizarro 620. Amex TCs and Visa card accepted, US$10 commission up to US$500. Note that banks close 1300-1615. There is little difference between the rates for cash dollars given by banks and street changers, *casas de cambio* and travel agencies. There are many *casas de cambio* and street changers on the plazoleta opposite the Casa de Condes de Aranda and all along the 600 block of Bolívar. Western Union, Almagro 581, España y Huayna Cápac, see also *Guía Tours*, above. **Cultural centres** Alianza Francesa, San Martín 858-62, T044-231232, www.ucv.edu.pe/ alianzafrancesa-trujillo. Instituto de Cultura Peruano Norte-americano, Av Venezuela 125, Urb El Recreo, T044-232512, www.elcultural.com.pe.

Consulates UK, Honorary Consul, Mr Winston Barber, Jesús de Nazareth 312, T044-235548, winstonbarber@ terra.com.pe. Mon-Fri 0900-1700. **Doctors** Dr César Aníbal Calderón Alfaro, T044-255591, 948 2466 (mob). Understands English.

Hospitals Hospital Belén, Bolívar 350, T044-245281, emergency entrance from Bolognesi. Clínica Peruano Americana, Av Mansiche 702, T044-231261. English spoken, good. Clínica Sánchez Ferrer, Los Laureles 436, Urb California, T044-284889.

Immigration Av Larco 1220, Urb Los Pinos. Mon-Fri 0815-1230, 1500-1630. Gives 30-day visa extensions, US$20 (proof of funds and onward ticket required), plus US$0.80 for *formulario* in Banco de la Nación (fixers on the street will charge more).

Internet There are internet offices all over the centre, mostly on Pizarro blocks 1 and 6, and Av España blocks 1 and 8.

Laundry American dry cleaners, Bolognesi 782, US$1.45 wash only, ironing extra. 24-hr service. Aquarelas, Bolívar 355, laundry and dry cleaner. Lavandería y Tintorería Luxor, Grau 637. 0800-2000, cheap, charges per item, next day service. **Pharmacies** Several pharmacy chains in the centre (on Pizarro and Gamarra) and others on either side of Belén hospital on Bolognesi. Farmacia La Libertad, Bolívar 498. Old-fashioned, but good stock at competitive prices.

Post Independencia 286 y Bolognesi. 0800-2000, Sun 0900-1300, stamps only on special request. DHL, Almagro 579.

Telephone Telefónica, headquarters at Bolívar 658. Private call centre at Pizarro 561, Ayacucho 625, Gamarra 450, others on 5th block of Orbegoso and Av España 1530.

Tourist police Independencia 630, Casa Ganoza Chopitea, T044-291705, policia_turismo_tru@hotmail.com. Mon-Sat 0800-2000. They provide useful information.

Useful addresses Touring and Automobile Club, Av Argentina 258, Urb El Recreo, T044-290736, trujillo@touring peru.com.pe. Gobierno Regional de La Libertad, Los Brillantes 6550, Urb Santa Inés, T044-231791. For information on rural tourism in the department. Instituto Nacional de Cultura, Independencia 572. The Indecopi tourist complaints office, Jr Bolivia 251, Urb El Recreo, T044-295733.

Huanchaco *p392, map p395*

Banks BBV ATM just south of pier next to Municipalidad. **Health** Centro de Salud, Jr Atahualpa 128, T044-461547. **Internet** Many places on Los Pinos, Deán Saavedra and La Rivera, as well as in hostales. **Post office** Grau y Manco Capac, Mon-Sat 1300-1800.

Chiclayo and around

Chiclayo, founded by Spanish priests in the 1560s as a rural Indian village, has long since outgrown other towns of the Lambayeque Department. Sandwiched between the Pacific Ocean and the Andes, Lambayeque is one of Peru's principal agricultural regions, and its chief producer of rice and sugar cane. It is also the outlet for produce from the northern jungle, which comes by road over the comparatively low Porculla Pass. Chiclayo is the major commercial hub of the zone, but also boasts distinctive cuisine and musical tradition (Marinera, Tondero and Afro-Peruvian rhythms), a famous witchdoctors' market and an unparalleled archaeological and ethnographic heritage. The area is also growing in importance as a birdwatching destination. Chiclayo is dubbed 'The Capital of Friendship', and while that tag could equally apply to most of the north coast of Peru, there is an earthiness and vivacity about its citizens that definitely sets it apart. ▸▸ *For Sleeping, Eating and other listings, see pages 413-418.*

Ins and outs

Getting there José Abelardo Quiñones González airport is 1 km from the town centre; taxi from centre costs US$2. There is no bus terminal; most buses stop outside their offices, many on or around Bolognesi, which is south of the centre. Confusingly many of the buses leaving for the surrounding area are to the north of the centre.

Getting around Calle Balta is the main street but the markets and most of the hotels and restaurants are spread out over about five blocks from the Plaza de Armas. Mototaxis are cheap. They cost US$0.50 anywhere in city, but are not allowed in the very centre. The surrounding area is well served by public transport.

Tourist information **Centro de Información Turística** ⓘ *Sáenz Peña 838, T074-238112.* There are kiosks on the plaza and outside **El Rancho.** For information on birdwatching sites, visit www.darwinnet.org/VICNO/birding_main.htm.

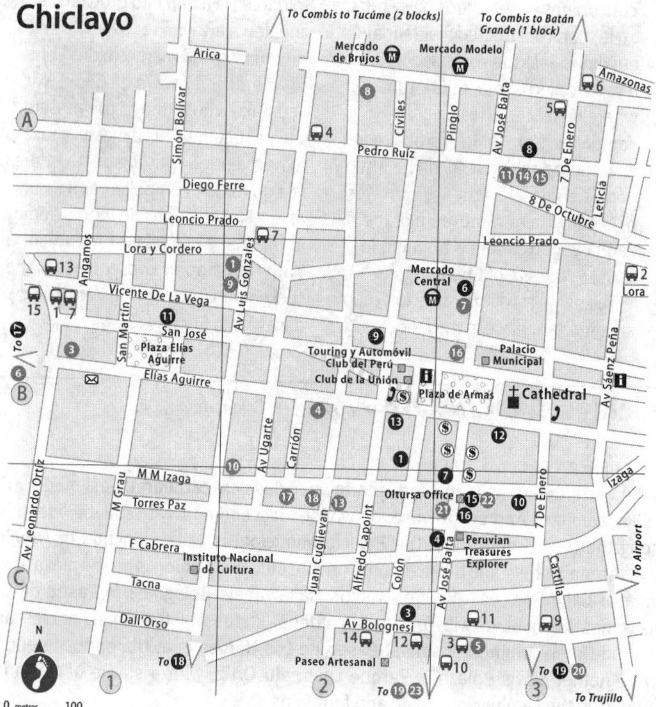

0 metres 100
0 yards 100

Sleeping
Adriático 7 *B3*
América 1 *B2*
Costa del Sol 21 *C3*
El Sol 3 *B1*
Europa 4 *B2*
Garza 5 *C3*
Gran Chiclayo 6 *B1*
Hospedaje San Eduardo 20 *C3*
Hostal San José 8 *A2*
Hostal Santa Victoria 19 *C2*
Hostal Sicán 17 *C2*
Inca 10 *B2*
Kalu 11 *A3*
Las Musas 23 *C2*
Mochicas 13 *C2*
Paracas 14 *A3*
Paraíso 15 *A3*
Pirámide Real 22 *C3*
Royal 16 *B3*
Santa Rosa 9 *B2*
Sol Radiante 18 *C2*

Eating
Boulevar 1 *B2*
Café Astoria 3 *C2*
D'Onofrio 4 *C3*
El Huaralino 18 *C1*
Govinda 6 *B3*
Hebrón 7 *C3*
Kaprichos 8 *A3*
La Fiesta 17 *B1*
La Panadería 9 *B2*
La Parra 10 *C3*
La Plazuela 11 *B1*
Las Américas 12 *B3*
Mi Tía 13 *B2*
Roma 15 *C3*
Romana 16 *C3*
Tradiciones 19 *C3*

Transport
Brüning Express to Lambayeque 1 *B1*
Buses to Chonoyape 2 *B3*
Civa 3 *C3*
Colectivos to Lambayeque 4 *A2*
Colectivos to Monsefú 5 *A3*
Colectivos to Puerto Etén 6 *A3*
Combis to Pimentel 7 *A2, B1*
Cruz del Sur 9 *C3*
Emtrafesa 10 *C3*
Flores/Cial 11 *C3*
Línea 12 *C2*
Oltursa 13 *B1*
Tepsa 14 *C2*
Transportes Chiclayo 15 *B1*

Legend of Ñaylamp

Like much else along this stretch of the Peruvian coast, the exact origin of the people's forebears is something of a mystery. The Spaniard, Cabello de Balboa, in 1578, is said to be the first outsider to hear of a local folk legend referring to a person named Ñaylamp who arrived on the coast of Lambayeque along with his court, his servants and his many concubines in numerous balsa rafts.

He then constructed residential buildings near the coast and a temple called Chota, or Chotuna, where he placed an idol called Yampallec, from which Lambayeque is supposed to derive its name. (At Cerro Cerrillos – Reque – 15 km west of Chiclayo, a new museum of the Lambeyeque culture is opening in 2006, at the site of Chota.)

The name Ñaylamp came to occupy an important place in the religious imagery of later civilizations through the designs of *tumis*, or ceremonial knives, funerary masks and countless other objects. In the ancient Muchik language spoken by the Moche, *ñam* means bird and *lá* means water, and the figures on Moche ceramics, jewellery and temple walls often have bird-like features and eyes shaped like wings. On his death, the people were told that Ñaylamp had grown wings and flown away.

Ñaylamp had many children but only three are known of: Cium, Nor and Cala, who founded the present site of Túcume. This dynasty is said to have ended with the death of the last governor, Fempellec, as a result of his illicit relationship with a demon in the shape of a beautiful woman. With catastrophic consequences, she tricked him into moving Yampallec a way from Chota.

Chiclayo » pp413-418. Colour map 1, C2.

→ *Phone code: 074. Population: 411,536.*

On the Plaza de Armas is the 19th-century neoclassical **cathedral**, designed by the English architect Andrew Townsend, whose descendants can still be identified among the town's principals. The **Palacio Municipal** is at the junction of Avenida Balta, the main street and the plaza. The private **Club de la Unión** is on the plaza at the corner of Calle San José. Where Avenida Balta meets Bolognesi, a **Paseo de Las Musas** has been built, with pleasant gardens, statues of the Greek muses and imitation Greek columns. A similar **Paseo de Los Héroes** is at the opposite end of town. Another newish plaza is **Parque Leonardo Ortiz**, with a statue of Ñaylamp, buildings in the Lambayeque style and fountains.

Around Chiclayo » pp413-418.

Lambayeque → *Colour map 2, C2.*

Twelve kilometres northwest from Chiclayo is the quiet town of Lambayeque. Its narrow streets are lined by colonial and republican houses, many retaining their distinctive wooden balconies and wrought-iron grille-work over the windows. For some fine examples, head along Calle 8 de Octubre: at No 410 is the opulent **Casona Iturregui Aguilarte** and, at No 328, **Casona Cuneo** is the only decorated façade in the town. Opposite is **Casona Descalzi**, perhaps the best preserved of all Lambayeque's colonial houses. Calle 2 de Mayo is also a good source of colonial and republican architecture, especially **Casa de la Logia o Montjoy,** whose 64-m balcony is said to be the longest in the colonial Americas.

Also of interest is the 16th-century **Complejo Religioso Monumental de San Pedro** and the baroque church of the same name which stands on the Plaza de Armas 27 de Diciembre. The French neo-baroque **Palacio Municipal** is also on the plaza.

The reason most people come to visit is to see the two museums: the longer-established and highly recommended Brüning Archaeological Museum, located in an impressive modern building, and the new Museo de las Tumbas Reales de Sipán. The **Brüning Archaeological Museum** ⓘ *daily 0900-1700, US$3.50, a guided tour costs an extra US$2.85, most exhibits labelled in English*, specializes in Mochica, Lambayeque/Sicán and Chimú cultures, and has a fine collection of Lambayeque gold. A board outside shows Peruvian cultures in relation to each other.

Three blocks east, the **Museo de las Tumbas Reales de Sipán** ⓘ *T074-283978, http://sipan.perucultural.org.pe, Tue-Sat 0900-1700, US$9, a guide is advisable as no explanations are in English; bags and cameras must be left at the entrance*, is shaped like a pyramid. The magnificent treasure from the tomb of 'The Old Lord of Sipán', found at Sipán in 1987, and a replica of the Lord of Sipán's tomb are displayed here (see page 409). A ramp from the main entrance takes visitors to the third floor, from where you descend, mirroring the sequence of the archaeologists' discoveries. This museum is frequently recommended and is judged to be one of the best in the world.

Mórrope → *Colour map 2, C2.*

At Mórrope, on the Pan-American Highway north of Chiclayo (20 km beyond Lambayeque), craftsmen still produce pottery for the towns of northern Peru using

Chiclayo area

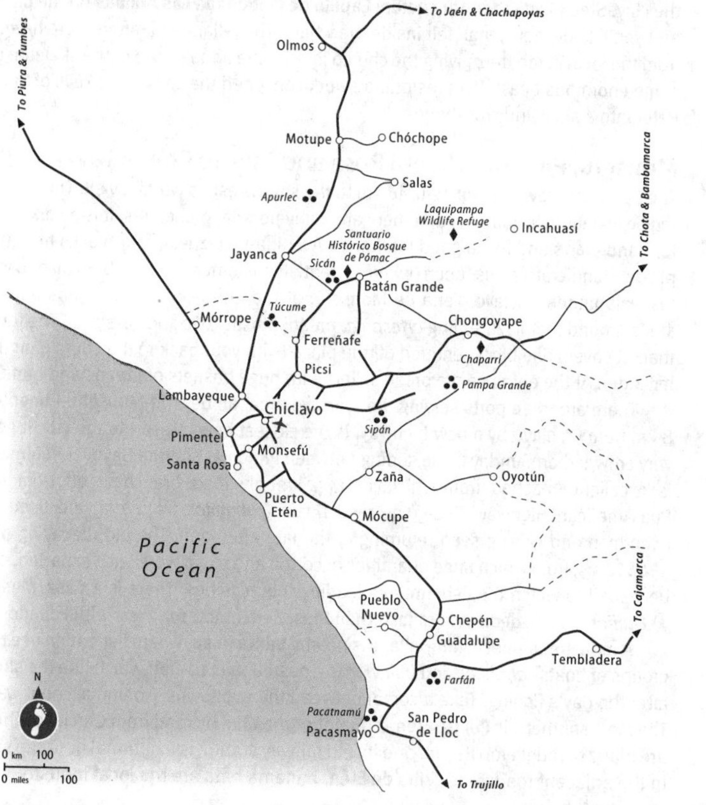

Old Lord of Sipán

The excavations at Sipán by the archaeologist Walter Alva have already revealed a huge number of riches in the shape of 'El Señor de Sipán'. This well-documented discovery was followed by an equally astounding find dating from AD 100. The tomb of the 'Old Lord of Sipán', as it has come to be known, predates the original Lord of Sipán by some 200 years, and could well be an ancestor of his.

Some of the finest examples of Moche craftsmanship have been found in the tomb of the Old Lord. One object in particular is remarkable; a crab deity with a human head and legs and the carapace, legs and claws of a crab. The gilded piece is over half a metre tall – unprecedented for a Moche figurine. This crab-like figure has been called Ulluchu Man, because the banner on which it was mounted yielded some of the first samples yet found of this ancient fruit.

The ulluchu fruit usually appears in scenes relating to war and the ritual offering of a prisoner's blood. One theory is that the ulluchu is part of the papaya family and has anticoagulant properties which are useful to prevent clotting before a man's blood is offered.

prehispanic techniques. Using a *paletín* (paddle) the potter manipulates the coil of clay into shape. Sometimes the *paletín* has a pattern on it, which is transferred onto the clay. Step inside the 16th-century **Capilla de la Ramada Las Animas** on the plaza and you'll know how Jonah felt inside the whale. The pillars and rafters were hewed from the local carob tree, giving the church interior the appearance of the skeleton of some enormous beast. Poor restoration work converted the crown and keys of Saint Peter into a skull and crossbones.

Monsefú, Pimentel, Santa Rosa and Puerto Etén → *Colour map 2, C2.*

The traditional town of **Monsefú**, 16 km to the southwest, is worth a visit. The town's **music** is nationally famous, and there are many popular orchestras. It is also known for **handicrafts** and has a good **market** on Avenida Venezuela, four blocks from the plaza. Handicraft stalls open when potential customers arrive. See also Local festivals under Chiclayo. **Feria de Monsefú**, at the end of September, has market stalls around the plaza selling *artesanía*, bread, plastic toys and ceramics. The town market covers one block, entered off the plaza (with your back to the church, on the left side). At the entrance are bread sellers with huge baskets of breads and buns.

There are three ports serving the Chiclayo area, all beyond Monsefú. **Pimentel**, 8 km from Chiclayo by a new highway, is the closest beach resort to the city. It gets very crowded on Sundays. The surfing between Pimentel and the Bayovar Peninsula is excellent, reached from Chiclayo (14.5 km) by road branching off from the Pan-American Highway. Sea-going reed boats (*caballitos de totora*) are used by fishermen and can be seen returning in the late afternoon. The old, decaying **pier** ⓘ *US$0.25*, from which huge quantities of cotton and sugar were once exported, can be visited to watch the fishermen unloading their catches. There is a **Casa/Museo** ⓘ *Quiñones 448*, dedicated to **José Quiñones**, hero of the 1942 war with Ecuador.

A more traditional fishing village is nearby **Santa Rosa**, where fishermen use two groups of boats *caballitos* and *bolicheros* – pastel-painted craft which line the shore after the day's fishing. Take a combi between the two towns – on no account walk. The most southerly is **Puerto Etén**, a quaint port 24 km by road from Chiclayo. There are plans to redevelop its pier and its old railway station is a national heritage site. In the adjacent roadstead, **Villa de Etén**, panama hats are the local industry.

Zaña and Chepén → *Colour map 2, C2.*

The ruined Spanish town of **Zaña** (also spelt Saña), lies 51 km south of Chiclayo. Zaña was destroyed by floods in 1726, and sacked by English pirates on more than one occasion. The ruins of five colonial churches and the convents of San Agustín, La Merced and San Francisco bear witness to the former splendour of this town which, at one time, was destined to become the country's capital. Further south, on the Pan-American Highway to Trujillo, lies **Chepén**. The town itself is not particularly fascinating but **Cerro Chepén**, towering over it, is the site of an ancient fortress from the Middle Horizon (late Moche/Huari). The fortress contains the ruins of what may be a palace, surrounded by other buildings. The as yet unexcavated site could have been the main station in a chain of lookout posts along the north coast. Take any Trujillo bus, US$1.10.

Sipán → *Colour map 2, C2.*

ⓘ *Site is open 0800-1600 and the museum 0800-1700. Entrance for the tombs and museum is US$2, students half price. A guide at the site costs US$2.85 (may not speak English). Small boys offer to guide you (other kids hang around the handicraft stalls and pester for a tip for doing nothing). Allow about 3-4 hrs. Take mosquito repellent.*

At this imposing twin-pyramid complex 35 km southeast of Chiclayo, excavations since 1987 in one of the three crumbling pyramids have brought to light a cache of funerary objects considered to rank among the finest examples of pre-Columbian art.

The Peruvian archaeologist Walter Alva, leader of the dig, continues to probe the immense mound that has revealed no less than 12 royal tombs filled with 1800-year-old offerings worked in precious metals, stone, pottery and textiles of the Moche culture (circa AD 1-750). In the most extravagant Moche tomb discovered, **El Señor de Sipán**, a priest was found clad in gold (ear ornaments, breast plate, etc), with turquoise and other valuables. A site museum was opened in 1992 featuring photos and maps of excavations, technical displays and replicas of some finds (it is due for redevelopment).

In another tomb were found the remnants of what is thought to have been a priest, sacrificed llama and a dog, together with copper decorations. In 1989 another richly appointed, unlooted tomb contained even older metal and ceramic artefacts associated with what was probably a high-ranking shaman or spiritual leader, called **'The Old Lord of Sipán'**.

Three tombs are on display, containing replicas of the original finds. Replicas of the Old Lord and the Priest are awaited. You can wander around the previously excavated areas of the Huaca Rajada to get an idea of the construction of the burial mound and adjacent pyramids. For a good view, climb the large pyramid across from the excavated Huaca Rajada. There is a path, but it looks as though it should be closed off to prevent erosion of the pyramid.

Around Sipán

Twenty-five kilometres from Sipán is **Pampa Grande**, a Mochica settlement dating from circa AD 550. This was the largest Moche complex 1400 years ago, at which time as many as 10,000 people may have lived here. Pampa Grande was a ceremonial centre, possibly including ritual offering of human blood as represented in the Sipán exhibits. These were presided over by a lord who also directed production and distribution, including precious materials to the artisans. Some experts believe that a prolonged drought around AD 562-594 displaced large groups of Moche people living to the south who moved to Pampa Grande, which become the centre of a state holding sway over the Lambayeque and Jequetepeque valleys.

The reason for the downfall of this once-powerful city remains in dispute. The structures associated with the rich and powerful ruling class appear to have been selectively burned and then abandoned leading some to conclude that a peasant revolution may have been the cause. Others (eg Moseley) believe that an earthquake, El Niño events and drought combined to lead to the demise of the Moche.

A minor road runs to Chongoyape, a pleasant old town 70 km to the east (3 km before the city, turn left/west to the Chavín petroglyphs of Cerro Mulato). Nearby are the vast Taymi and Pampa Grande pre-Columbian and modern irrigation systems (the modern are also called Taymi). Also near Chongoyape are the aqueduct of Racarrumi, the hill fort of Mal Paso and the ruins of Majín (12-14 pyramids). In the district of Chongoyape is the **Chaparrí Private Conservation Area** ⓘ *Comunidad Campesina Muchik Santa Catalina de Chongoyape, visits by prior arrangement only.* This community-owned project (the first of its kind in Peru) covers over 36,000 ha, extending from 1540 to 1350 m above sea level. The variety of habitats, including dry desert forest, harbours many bird and mammal species, some of which are extremely rare. Notable birds are the white-winged guan and the Peruvian plantcutter, while there are also spectacled bears, Sechuran fox, puma and other cats. Small numbers of visitors are accommodated in a secluded lodge beside a river.

Túcume → *Colour map 1, C2.*

ⓘ *0800-1700, museum 0800-1600, US$2, guides charge US$2.85.*
About 35 km north of Chiclayo, beside the old Panamericana to Piura, lie the ruins of this vast city built over a thousand years ago. This mysterious and evocative site is worth visiting around sundown, not only to avoid the fierce heat, but to add to the eerie thrill that the place induces. It may be difficult to persuade anyone to accompany you, though, as local people are very superstitious.

A short climb to the two *miradores* on **Cerro La Raya**, or **El Purgatorio**, as it is also known, offers an unparallelled panoramic vista of 26 major pyramids, platform mounds, walled citadels and residential compounds flanking a ceremonial centre and ancient cemeteries. The entire complex covers well over 200 ha and measures 1.7 km from east to west and 2 km from north to south. One of the pyramids, Huaca Larga, where excavations were undertaken from 1987-1892, is the longest adobe structure in the world, measuring 700 m long, 280 m wide and over 30 m high.

There is no evidence of occupation of Túcume previous to the Sicán, or Lambayeque people (see below) who developed the site between AD 1050/1100 and 1375 until the Chimú came, saw and conquered the region, establishing a short reign until the arrival of the Incas around 1470. The Incas built on top of the existing structure of **Huaca Larga** using stone from Cerro La Raya. Among the tombs excavated so far is one dating from the Inca period. It is thought to be that of a warrior, judging by the many battle scars. The body is heavily adorned and was interred along with two male compatriots and no less than 19 females aged between 10 and 30. Beside the Huaca Larga is the shrine known as the Templo de la Piedra Sagrada (Temple of the Sacred Stone), which was clearly very holy to the Lambayeque, Chimú and Incas.

Among the other pyramids which make up this huge complex are: **Huaca El Mirador, Huaca Las Estacas, Huaca Pintada** and **Huaca de las Balsas**, which is thought to have housed people of elevated status such as priests.

Excavations at the site, led by the late Norwegian explorer-archaeologist, Thor Heyerdahl of *Kon-Tiki* fame, challenge many conventional views of ancient Peruvian culture. Some suspect that it will prove to be a civilization centre greater than Chan Chán. There is also evidence, including art and remains of navigation gear, that the people of Túcume were intrepid seafarers. A five-year excavation project was undertaken by Thor Heyerdahl, since when there has been no further excavation work for lack of funds.

The **site museum**, with three halls, is built from adobe and mezquite logs in prehispanic style. The collections show architectural reconstructions, photographs and drawings, highlighting the finds, which include weaving paraphernalia, a ceremonial oar and a fabulous bas relief and mural depicting maritime scenes suggesting former sea trade and interregional contact. Traditional dishes and drinks are available.

The town of Túcume is a 15-minute walk from the site, or a US$0.85 mototaxi ride. On the plaza is the interesting **San Pedro Church**, a mixture of baroque, churri-

A tale of demons and fish

Just one of the many legends that abound in this part of Northern Peru pertains to the hill which dominates the pyramids at Túcume and the precise origin of its name. The hill is known locally as 'El Purgatorio' (Purgatory), or more commonly, Cerro La Raya (Ray Hill).

The former name derives from the conquering Spaniards' attempts to convert the indigenous people to the Christian faith. The Spanish invaders encountered fierce local resistance to their religion and came up with the idea of convincing the people of Túcume that the hill was, in fact, purgatory. They told the locals that there lived on the hill a demon who would punish anyone not accepting the Roman Catholic faith.

In order to lend some credence to this tale, a group of Spaniards set out one dark, moonless night and built a huge bonfire at the foot of 'El Purgatorio', giving it the appearance of an erupting volcano and frightening the townsfolk half to death. Thus they came to accept the Spaniards' assertion that any unbelievers or sinners would be thrown alive into the flames of this diabolical fire.

As if that wasn't enough to terrify the local populace, the Spanish also concocted the fiendish tale of 'El Carretón', or wagon. This was an enormous wagon pulled by four great horses which supposedly would speed forth from the bowels of 'El Purgatorio' on the darkest of nights. Driven by a dandily dressed demon boss, and carrying his equally dandy demon buddies, this hellish vehicle careered round the town of Túcume making a fearsome racket. Any poor unbelievers or sinners unfortunate enough to be found wandering the streets would immediately be carted off and thrown into the flames of purgatory.

The alternative name of Cerro La Raya refers to the local legend of a Manta Ray that lived in a nearby lake. The local children constantly tormented the fish by throwing stones at it, so, to escape this torment, the poor creature decided to move to the hill and become part of it. The lake then disappeared and ever since, the hill has been enchanted.

gueresque and neoclassical styles. There are no hotels in town. The surrounding countryside is pleasant for walks and swimming in the river. The present site of the town is not the original one but dates from 1720. Local legend has it that the town was moved following an apparition of the Virgin. The icon of the Virgin mysteriously disappeared but was later seen on top of Cerro Cueto, having her long hair combed by a native girl while gazing over pasture lands below. This was taken as a sign to relocate the church and the rest of the town with it. » *See Festivals and events page 415.*

Ferreñafe and Sicán → *Colour map 1, C2.*

The colonial town of Ferreñafe, 18 km northeast of Chiclayo, is worth a visit, especially for the **Museo Nacional Sicán** ⓘ *T074-286469, Tue-Sat 0900-1700, US$2 plus US$4 per guide (Spanish only)*. This excellent new museum is designed to house objects of the Sicán (Lambayeque) culture from near Batán Grande (fascinating exhibits, knowledgeable staff, but little English spoken). There is a helpful **Mincetur tourist office** ⓘ *T074-282843, citesipan@mincetur.gob.pe*, on the Plaza de Armas.

The entrance to **El Santuario Histórico Bosque de Pómac**, which includes the ruins of **Sicán**, lies 16 km beyond Ferreñafe along the road to Batán Grande. Visiting the sanctuary is not easy because of the very arid conditions, lack of marked trails and distances involved which mean that walking around the site is only for the intrepid and well prepared: it is 10 km to the nearest *huaca* (pyramid). At the **visitors' centre** ⓘ *T074-963 2390, bosquepomac@ecoportal.zzn.com, 0700-1600, a guide (Spanish only) can be hired with transport, US$3 with motorbike and US$7 with mototaxi, which includes the entrance fee*. The two-hour tour of the area includes a mirador over the forest, some of the most ancient *algarrobo* (carob) trees and at least two *huacas*. Food and drinks are available at the centre and camping is permitted. Sicán has revealed several sumptuous tombs dating to the middle Sicán period, AD 900-1100. The ruins comprise some 34 adobe pyramids, arranged around a huge plaza, measuring 500 by 250 m. They range in size with the largest reaching 40 m in height and approximately 100 m square. The site as a whole covers 45 sq km. A visit to the mirador affords a beautiful view across the emerald green tops of the algarrobo forest with the enormous pyramids dramatically breaking through. The two main tombs discovered were located either side of the entrance ramp leading up the south face of **Huaca de Loro**. In one tomb 20 bodies were excavated and nearly a tonne of metal and other objects unearthed. There is nothing to see on the ground now both sites are completely overgrown with scrub. Here some of the best examples of pre-Columbian gold artefacts were found, notably the oldest *tumi* (ceremonial knife) unearthed in Peru. *Tumis* so commonly found in other cultures are all later which suggests that they were copied from Sicán. A Sicán *tumi* can be identified from the particularly feline, slanted form of the eyes, reflecting the iconografic representation of their principal deity. Many gold objects have been removed to private collections, such as the Gold Museum in Lima, but many are in the new Museo Nacional Sicán in Ferreñafe (see page 411). The *huacas* were badly eroded by the rains of the 1998 El Niño and are now semi-protected by flimsy corrugated-iron 'roofs'.

Professor Izumi Shimada has worked here for more than 15 years researching a culture which has, to a large extent, been forgotten. It now seems that the origins of the Sicán culture lie with the Mochica (Muchik), though there are clear influences of other contemporary cultures: Wari and Pachacámac. Recent research suggests that when the Mochica religio-political centre based around Huaca Fortaleza, Pampagrande, collapsed in AD 700-750 the population was displaced. It moved 30 km north to Poma on the banks of Río La Leche, which was not then a dry river. The resulting culture extended across the Motupe valley to the north, La Leche valley, and Zaña and Lambeyeque valleys to the south. It is known today as the Sicán culture (some refer to it as Lambayeque), which reached its height in AD 900-1100. The city was probably moved to a new site at Túcume, 6 km west, following 30 years of severe drought and then a devastating El Niño-related flood in AD 1050-1100. These events appear to have provoked a rebellion in which many of the remaining temples atop the pyramids were burnt and destroyed. At the new Túcume site the Sicán culture continued to flourish for another 300 years until conquest by the Chimú.

Historical Sanctuary Bosque de Pómac, established in 2001, covers 5887 ha of algarrobo forest either side of the river La Leche which remains dry most years. It is the largest intact algarrobo forest in the world, containing trees up to 1000 years old. Despite the dry, scrubby terrain the tree tops shimmer emerald green and there is prolific birdlife (47 species) as well as numerous reptiles and mammals, including an endangered species of wild cat.

Laquipampa Wildlife Refuge ⓘ *zr_laquipampa@inrena.gob.pe*, covering 8329 ha, is situated in a green and fertile high Andean valley. It is the habitat of the rare and critically endangered white-winged guan (*Penelope albipennis*), the bearded guan and many other birds endemic to the Tumbesian zone, also the spectacled bear and rare flora in a dry forest belt ranging from 500-2500 m. It lies two hours beyond Sicán; take a passing bus for Incahuasi. A captive breeding centre for the white-winged guan has been set up north of Olmos (see below), www.pavaaliblanca.org.

North to Piura

Sixty kilometres north of Chiclayo, beside the old Panamericana, is the site of **Apurlec**. It comprises a stone wall surrounding a hill and pyramids dating from the Tiahuanaco period, as well as irrigation canals and reservoirs. The system was enlarged during Moche, Chimú and Inca occupation of the site. The ruins are overgrown, but climb the Cerro Viejo to get an idea of the size. To get there from Chiclayo, take a bus from Pedro Ruiz block 5. The bus continues to Motupe (10 km).

Further north on the old Pan-American Highway, 885 km from Lima, is the peaceful town of **Olmos**. During the last week of June the **Festival de Limón** is celebrated here. At Olmos, a road runs east over the Porculla Pass for Jaén and Bagua, see page 475. The old Pan-American Highway continues from Olmos to Cruz de Caña and on to Piura.

At Lambayeque the new Pan-American Highway, which is in good condition, branches off the old road and drives 190 km straight across the Sechura Desert to Piura. There is also a coast road, narrow and scenic, between Lambayeque and Piura, via Bayovar and the town of **Sechura**. The fine 17th-century cathedral has a lovely west front which has been under renovation for a long time and is normally closed to the public. There is a restaurant at the junction to Bayovar, where you can sleep.

Sechura Desert → *Colour map 1, B2.*

A large area of shifting sands separates the cities of Chiclayo and Piura. Water for irrigation comes from the Chira and Piura rivers, and from the Olmos and Tinajones irrigation projects which bring water from the Amazon watershed by means of tunnels (one over 16 km long) through the Andes to the Pacific coast.

The northern river – the Chira – usually has a superabundance of water. Along its irrigated banks large crops of Tangüis cotton are grown. A dam has been built at Poechos on the Chira to divert water to the Piura valley. In its upper course the Piura – whose flow is far less dependable – is mostly used to grow subsistence food crops, but around Piura, when there is enough water, the hardy long-staple Pima cotton is planted.

In the 1870s, the government of Manuel Pardo decreed that all native cotton, including kapok, should be destroyed because it was believed that it gave parasites to the favoured, imported varieties. This was not the case and the value of Peruvian cotton is now recognized. It grows on a tall bush, unlike the short, Egyptian variety, and comes in seven colours, each of which was given a name by the Moche.

Solo cyclists should not cross the Sechura Desert as muggings have occurred. Take the safer, inland route. There are several restaurants between Km 845 and 848, and another midway between Mórrope and Piura, but there are no hotels. Do not camp out if possible, though heading south, strong headwinds may make camping unavoidable.

Sleeping

Chiclayo *p406, map p405*

There are several cheap hotels on Av Balta, near the bus offices, which range from basic to hygienically challenged. Most have only cold water. There are other cheap hotels near the Mercado Modelo, especially on Arica.

A Gran Hotel Chiclayo, Villareal 115, T074-234911, granhotel1@terra.com.pe. Refurbished to a high standard, price includes taxes and breakfast, pool, jacuzzi, entertainments, restaurant, safe car park, changes dollars, casino. Recommended.

A-B Garza, Bolognesi 756, T074-228172, www.garzahotel.com. Excellent bar and restaurant, a/c, pool, car park, tourist office in lobby provides maps, information in English, vehicle hire. Highly recommended; it is close to the bus stations so there is activity at all hours.

A-C Inca, Av L González 622, T074-235931, pewww.incahotel.com. Recently refurbished, with TV and a/c, more expensive with jacuzzi, restaurant, garage, comfortable and helpful.

B Costa del Sol, Balta 399, T074-227272, www.costadelsolperu.com. New, smart, direct dial telephones, TV, minibar, non-smoking rooms, small pool, sauna, jacuzzi. **Páprika** restaurant, good value Sun buffets US$7.50, vegetarian options.

B Las Musas, Los Faiques 101, by Parque Las Musas, T074-239885, reservaslasmusas@hotmail.com. Quiet area, large rooms, bathtubs, TV, minibar, affable service, internet available, tours arranged. Recommended.
D América, Av L González 943, T074-229305, americahotel@latinmail.com. Comfortable, friendly, breakfast included, restaurant, good value (except for the expensive laundry). Recommended.
D Hostal Santa Victoria, La Florida 586, Urb Santa Victoria, T074-225074. Hot water, restaurant, free parking, dollars exchanged, very good, 15-20 mins' walk from the centre.
D-E El Sol, Elías Aguirre 119, T074-232120, hotelvicus@hotmail.com. Price includes taxes, big rooms with bath, hot water, restaurant, pool by the car park, TV lounge, clean, good value.
E Kalu, Pedro Ruiz 1038, T/F074-229293, HOTELKALU@terra.com.pe. Near the Mercado Modelo. Comfortable, with bath and TV, laundry, safe, good.
E Mochicas, Torres Paz 429, T074-237217, mochcas1@hotmail.com. Fan, TV, helpful, good service.
E Paracas, Pedro Ruiz 1046, T074-221611. Near the Mercado Modelo. With bathroom, TV, good value. Recommended.
E Paraíso, Pedro Ruíz 1064, T/F074-222070, hotelparaiso@terra.com.pe. Also near the Mercado Modelo, also comfortable and well appointed, but can be noisy. Recommended.
E Pirámide Real, MM Izaga 726, T074- 224036. Compact but spotless, good value, very central.
E Santa Rosa, L González 927, T074-224411. With bathroom, clean, laundry service, international phone service, breakfast downstairs in snack bar. Good value, but check bill carefully.
E-G Europa, Elías Aguirre 466, T074-237919, hoteleuropachiclayo@terra.com.pe. With bath (cheaper without; single rooms can be small), hot water, restaurant, good value.
F Hospedaje San Eduardo, 7 de Enero 235, Urb San Eduardo, T074-209423. A 10-min walk from the centre; no sign other than a little notice in the window. Family-run, large rooms, quiet, safe, cable TV, hot water.
F Hostal Sicán, Izaga 356, T074-237618. With breakfast, bath, hot water, cable TV, clean, comfortable but some rooms are gloomy, welcoming and trustworthy. Recommended.
F Sol Radiante, Izaga 392, T074-237858, robertoiza@mixmail.com. With bath and TV, cold water, comfortable, pleasant, but noisy at the front.
G Adriático, Av Balta 1009. Price per person. The best of a bad bunch on Av Balta, fairly clean but basic, with cold water.
G Hostal San José, on Juan Cuglievan 1370, 1 block from Mercado Modelo, T074-273394. Basic, clean, acceptable, but cold water.
G Royal, San José 787, on the plaza, T074-233421. With bathroom, a big, rambling old building, a bit seedy and run down, rooms on the street have a balcony but are noisy.

Around Chiclayo *p406*

There are several **F** options in Lambayeque, including **Hostal Karla**, Av Huamachuco 758, Lambayeque, T074-282930 (opposite the museum); **Jopami**, Grau 143, Lambayeque, T074-282367; and **Lambayeque**, Tarapacá 261, Lambayeque, T074-283474.
G Hotel Puente Azul, outside Chepén on the Panamericana. Pleasant, clean, with bath and cold water. The restaurant is open in the afternoon only, not for dinner.
G La Posada Norteña, Panamericana Norte Km 780, Lambayeque, T074-282602. Price per person. With bath, quiet, safe, clean, cold water, more expensive with TV.

Eating

Chiclayo *p406, map p405*

Local specialities include *ceviche* and *chingurito* (a *ceviche* of strips of dried guitar fish, which is chewy but good). For delicious and cheap *ceviche*, go to the Nativo stall in the Mercado Central, a local favourite. *Cabrito* is a spiced stew of kid goat. *Arroz con pato* is a paella-like duck casserole. *Humitas* are *tamal*-like fritters of green corn. King kong is a baked pastry layered with candied fruit and milk caramel, appealing to those with a very sweet tooth (San Roque is the best brand). *Chicha* is the fermented maize drink with delicious fruit variations.
ΨΨΨ **El Huaralino**, La Libertad 155, Santa Victoria. Serves a wide variety of international and creole dishes.
ΨΨΨ **La Fiesta**, Av Salaverry 1820 in 3 de Octubre suburb, T074-201970. Local specialities, first class.

Hebrón, Balta 605. For more upmarket than average chicken, but also local food, salads and *parrilla*. Also does an excellent breakfast and a good buffet at weekends.
Kaprichos, Pedro Ruiz 1059, T232721. Chinese, delicious, huge portions.
Las Américas, Aguirre 824. Daily 0700-0200, good service. Recommended.
Roma, Izaga 706. Wide choice of dishes; also has a bar.
Romana, Balta 512,T223598. First-class food, usually good breakfast, popular with locals.
Tradiciones, 7 de Enero Sur 105, T074-221192. Daily 0900-1700. Good variety of local dishes, including *ceviche*, and drinks, nice atmosphere and garden, good service.
Boulevar, Colón, entre Izaga y Aguirre. Good, friendly, *menú* and à la carte.
Govinda, Balta 1029. Good vegetarian. Daily 0800-2000.
Café Astoria, Bolognesi 627. Daily 0800-1200, 1530-2100 for breakfast, and a good-value *menú*.
La Parra, Izaga 752. Chinese and creole, *parrillada*, very good, large portions.
La Plazuela, San José 299, Plaza Elías Aguirre. Good food, seats outside.
Mi Tía, Aguirre 650, just off the plaza. Huge portions, great-value *menú*, very popular at lunchtime, but poor breakfasts, otherwise recommended.

Cafés

D'Onofrio, Balta y Torres Paz. For great ice cream.
Greycy, Elias Aguirre y Lapoint. Also serves good ice cream.
La Panadería, Lapoint 847. Good choice of breads, including integral, also snacks and soft drinks.

Around Chiclayo *p406*

El Cántaro, on the 1st block of 2 de Mayo, Lambayeque. Serves excellent traditional local dishes cooked by Juanita.
El Flamenco, Atahualpa 159, opposite Museo Brüning, Lambayeque. Excellent restaurant with set menu.
La Cabaña, on the 4th block of Calle Libertad, Lambayeque. Good for *ceviche*.
La Huaca, on the 3rd block of Calle Junín, Lambayeque. Also good for *ceviche*.

Festivals and events

Around Chiclayo *p406*

6 Jan Among the many festivals held in and around the city is **Reyes Magos** in Mórrope, Illimo and other towns. This is a recreation of a medieval pageant in which pre-Columbian deities become the Wise Men.
4 Feb **Túcume devil dances.**
Feb Túcume celebrates the **Fiesta de la Purísima Concepción**, the town's Patron Saint, 8 days prior to Carnival in Feb, with music, dancing, fireworks, cockfights, sports events and, of course, much eating and drinking. During the **Dance of the Devils** (which is common in northern Peru), the participants wear horned masks, forked tails and long capes and are said to represent the diabolical drunken Spanish priests from colonial times. It also features a song and dance dedicated to the native girl who was seen combing the Virgin's hair.
14 Mar **Festividad Señor Cautivo**, Monsefú.
Mar/Apr **Holy Week**, many villages have traditional Easter celebrations and processions.
1 May **Fiesta de la Cruz** is held in Pimentel.
Last week of Jun **Festividad de San Pedro** in Morrope.
1st week of Jun **Divine Child of the Miracle**, in Villa de Etén.
27-31 Jul **Fexticum**, in Monsefú, with traditional foods, drink, handicrafts, music and dance.
5 Aug **Pilgrimage** from the mountain shrine of Chalpón to Motupe, 90 km north of Chiclayo; the cross is brought down from a cave and carried in procession through the village.
24 Sep **Virgen de las Mercedes** in Incahuasi, 12 hrs by truck east of Chiclayo. The local people still sing in the ancient Mochica language in this post-harvest festival.
Dec **At Christmas and New Year**, processions and children dancers (*pastorcitos* and *seranitas*) can be seen in many villages, eg Ferreñafe, Mochumi and Mórrope.

Shopping

Chiclayo *p406, map p405*

Markets

Mercado Modelo, 5 blocks north of the main plaza on Balta. This is one of northern Peru's liveliest and largest daily markets. Don't miss the colourful fruits, handicrafts

stalls (see Monsefú) and the well-organized section of ritual paraphernalia used by traditional curers and diviners (*curanderos*), which is just off C Arica on the south side. It is filled with herbal medicines, folk charms, curing potions, and exotic objects used by *curanderos* and *brujos* to cure all manner of real and imagined illnesses. The stallholders are generally very friendly and will explain the uses of such items as monkey claws, dried foetuses and dragon's blood. As in all markets, take good care of your belongings.
Mercado Central, in the city centre, is smaller than the Mercado Modelo.
Paseo de Artesanías, 18 de Abril at the end of Colón. Stalls sell woodwork, basketwork and other handicrafts in a quiet, peaceful, custom-built open-air arcade.

Activities and tours

Chiclayo *p406, map p405*
Expect to pay US$18-25 per person for a 3-hr tour to Sipán, and US$25-35 per person for Túcume and Lambayaque (5 hrs). Brüning Museum, Sipán and Túcume, however, can easily be done by public transport. Sicán, which has less frequent public transport, is US$45-55 per person for a full-day tour including Ferreñafe and Pómac. To Zaña and the coastal towns is US$35-55 per person. These prices are based on 2 people; there are discounts for larger groups.
Indiana Tours, Colón 556, T074-222991, www.indianatoursperu.com. Daily tours to nearby archaeological sites and museums and a variety of other daily and extended excursions with 4WD vehicles, as well as reservations for national flights and hotels. English and Italian spoken and Footprint users welcome. Recommended.
Inkanatura Travel, Gran Hotel Chiclayo, see page 413, T074-209948, www.inkanatura.com, postmaster@inkanatura.com.pe. Also at Manuel Bañón 461, San Isidro, Lima, T01-4402022, and Plateros 361, Cuzco, T084-255255. Archaeological and cultural programmes, wildlife tours, catamaran trips and jungle walks.
Peruvian Treasures Explorer, Balta 398, T074-233435. Archaeological tours, helpful.
Tambo Tours, USA and Peru, www.2GOPERU.com. See page 168.

Transport

Chiclayo *p406, map p405*

Air

Flights to and from **Lima** and **Piura** with **Lan**, daily, and **Star Perú**, except Sun (Av Bolognesi 316, T074-271173).

Bus

To **Lima**, 770 km, US$12 and US$22 for bus cama: **Civa**, **Cruz del Sur** (*bus cama*; has the only daytime service at 0800, US$22); **Ormeño**, *especial* and *bus cama* (US$20); **Línea**, *especial* and *bus cama* service (recommended); **Móvil** (goes as far as Tarapoto); **Oltursa**, full range of services; **Tepsa**, **Transportes Chiclayo**. Most companies leave from 1900 onwards. To **Trujillo**, 209 km, with **Línea** and **Emtrafesa**, almost hourly from 0530-2015, US$3.35. To **Piura**, US$3.65, **Línea** and **Trans Chiclayo** leave hourly throughout the day; also **Emtrafesa** and buses from the **Cial/Flores** terminal on Bolognesi 751, and **Turismo Tarapoto**. To **Sullana**, US$4.35. To **Tumbes**, US$5.75, 9-10 hrs; with **Cial**, or **Transportes Chiclayo**; **Oltursa** has an overnight service which leaves at 2015 and arrives at 0530 (this is a good bus to take for crossing to Ecuador the next day), seats can be reserved, unlike other companies which tend to arrive full from Lima late at night.

Many buses go on to the **Ecuadorean border** at **Aguas Verdes**, while Ormeño goes direct to **Guayaquil** (daily 0200) and **Quito** (Tue 0100). It's possible to get a substantial discount on the fare to the border: go to the *Salida* on Elías Aguirre (mototaxi drivers know where it is), be there by 1900. All buses stop here after leaving their terminals to try and fill empty seats. Bear in mind that the cheapest buses may not be the most secure. Direct bus to **Cajamarca**, 260 km, 6 hrs; with **Línea**, 1315, US$5.65, 2200, US$8.45, *bus cama* at 2245 US$7.60; many others from Tepsa terminal, eg **El Cumbe**, 4 a day, **Días**, 3 a day, **Mendoza**, 2 a day, all US$4.55. To **Chachapoyas**, 230 km, US$6-10.60: with **Civa** at 1730 daily, 10-11 hrs; **Móvil** at 2000; **Turismo Kuélap**, in Tepsa station, 1830 daily. To **Jaén**, US$4.35- 6.15: with **Línea** at 1300 and 2300, 8 hrs; **Móvil**, 1400 and 2300 daily; **Turismo Jaén**, in Tepsa station, 7 a day. To **Tarapoto**, 18 hrs,

US$11.50, with **Ejetur**, **Turismo Tarapoto** and **Móvil**, at 1830. To **Huancabamba**, with **Etipthsa**, on Mon and Fri from the Tepsa terminal at 1700, 12 hrs, US$8.65.

Bus companies Civa, Av Bolognesi 714, T074-223434; **Cruz del Sur**, Bolognesi 888, T074-225508; **Días**, T074-224448; **Ejetur**, Bolognesi 536, T074-209829; **El Cumbe**, T074-272245; **Emtrafesa**, Av Balta 110, T074-234291; **Etipthsa**, T074-229217; **Flores**, T074-239579; **Línea**, Bolognesi 638, T074-222221; **Móvil**, Bolognesi 195, T074-271940; **Oltursa**, ticket office at Balta e Izaga, T074-237789, terminal at Vicente de la Vega 101, T074-225611; **Ormeño**, Haya de la Torre 242 (2 blocks south of Bolognesi), T074-234206; **Tepsa**, Bolognesi 504-36 y Colón, T074-236981; **Transportes Chiclayo**, Av L Ortiz 010, T074-237984; **Turismo Tarapoto**, T074-490332; **Turismo Tarapoto**, Bolognesi 751, T074-490332.

Around Chiclayo *p406*

For **Lambayeque**, *colectivos* from Chiclayo; US$0.45, 25 mins. They leave from Pedro Ruiz at the junction with Av Ugarte. Also **Brüning Express** combis from Vicente de la Vega between Angamos and Av L Ortiz, every 15 mins, US$0.20.

From **Monsefú** combis to Chiclayo cost US$0.45; from Chiclayo they leave from Amazonas y 7 de Enero, beyond the Mercado Modelo. *Colectivos* to Monsefú leave from 7 de Enero y Arica.

The ports of **Pimentel**, **Santa Rosa** and **Puerto Etén** can all be visited on a pleasant half-day trip from Chiclayo. Combis leave from Vicente de la Vega 200 to Pimentel; others leave from González y L Prado. Both take 20 mins, US$0.25. *Colectivos* to Etén leave from 7 de Enero y Arica.

Buses to **Sipán** leave from Terminal Este Sur-Nor Este on C Nicolás de Piérola, east of the city (take a taxi there, US$1; it can be a dangerous area), US$0.45, 1 hr. *Colectivos* leave from 5-6 blocks east of Mercado Modelo (take care here, too). The way to the village is well signed through fields of sugar cane. Once you get to the village, the signs end: turn left, then right and go through the village to get to the site.

Buses from Chiclayo to **Chongoyape** leave from the corner of Leoncio Prado and Sáenz Peña; US$1, 1½ hrs.

For **Túcume** combis go from Chiclayo, Angamos y Manuel Pardo, US$0.70, 45 mins. A combi from Túcume to the village of **Come** passes the ruins hourly. You cannot miss the town of Túcume with its huge sign. Soon after the sign take a right turn on the paved road which leads to the museum and site. Don't be fooled by the pyramid close to the sign; it's part of the group, but some distance from the entrance. A combi from Túcume to **Lambayeque** is US$0.35 and takes 25 mins.

Colectivos from Chiclayo to **Ferreñafe** leave every few mins from 8 de Octubre y Sáenz Peña, 15 mins, U$0.30, but only run to Ferreñafe town centre so take a mototaxi on to the museum, 5 mins, US$0.50. Alternatively, combis for Batán Grande depart from the Terminal Nor-Este, in Av N de Piérola in Chiclayo, and pass the museum every 15-20 mins, 20 mins, US$0.50.

Directory

Chiclayo *p406, map p405*

Banks Banking hrs 0915-1315, 1630-1830, Sat 0930-1230. You may have to wait for a while in the banks. It's much quicker and easier to use the ATMs. Beware of counterfeit bills, especially among street changers on the 6th block of Balta, on Plaza de Armas and 7th block of MM Izaga. BCP, Balta 630, no commission on Amex TCs for US$100 or more (US$12 commission if less), cash on Visa, also Telebanco 24 Horas ATM for Visa. Opposite, at Balta 625, is Banco Wiese Sudameris, changes Amex TCs, cash advance on Visa card, ATM for Visa/Plus. Banco Santander, Izaga y Balta, changes Amex TCs. Interbank, on the Plaza de Armas, no commission on TCs, OK rate, good rates for cash, Visa cash advance, MasterCard and Visa ATM. Western Union and DHL are both at Tumi Tours, Elías Aguirre 560, also both at Cruz del Sur. **Cultural centres** Alianza Francesa, Cuglievan 644, T074-237571, www.universidadperu.com/alianza-francesa-de-chiclayo.php. Instituto de Cultura Peruano- Norteamericana, Av MM Izaga 807, T074-231241, icpnachi@mail.udep.edu.pe. Instituto Nacional de la Cultura, Av L González 375, T074- 237261. Has occasional poetry readings, information on local archaeological sites, lectures, etc. **Internet** Lots of places, particularly on San José and Elías Aguirre, average price US$0.60 per hr. **Post** On the first block of Aguirre, 6 blocks from the plaza. **Telephone** Telefónica, headquarters at Aguirre 919; bank of phone booths on 7th block of 7 de Enero behind cathedral for international and collect calls. Phone card sellers hang around here. **Tourist police** Av Sáenz Peña 830, T074- 236700, ext 311, 24 hrs a day, are very help- ful and may store luggage and take you to the sites themselves. **Useful addresses** Ambulance: Max Salud, 7 de Enero 185, T074-234032, maxsalud@telematic.edu.com. Touring y Automóvil Club del Perú, San José 728, T074-231821, chiclayo@touringperu.com.pe. Also has a travel agency selling air tickets. Indecopi, Av Balta 506, T074-209021, ctejada@indecopi.gob.pe, Mon-Fri 0800-1300, 1630-1930, for complaints and tourist protection.

Piura and around

A proud and historic city, 264 km from Chiclayo, Piura was founded as San Miguel at Tangarará in 1532, three years before Lima, by the conquistadores *left behind by Pizarro. It was relocated, first as Pirwa, then with its current name, in 1534. There are two well-kept parks, Cortés and Pizarro (with a statue of the* conquistador, *also called Plaza de las Tres Culturas), and public gardens. Old buildings are kept in repair and new buildings blend with the Spanish style of the old city. Close to the city are interesting towns on the coast and others specializing in handicrafts. Further afield is the culturally fascinating area of Las Guaringas and the more prosaic route to Ecuador through Sullana.* » *For Sleeping, Eating and other listings, see pages 423-427.*

Ins and outs

Getting there A taxi to the airport costs US$1.85 by day, more by night. Most bus companies are on Avenida Sánchez Cerro, blocks 11, 12 and 13 in the northwest of the town. There are some hotels in this area, but for central ones take a taxi.

Getting around From the Plaza de Armas, some of the hotels and bus companies are too far to walk, but many of the sights and places to stay can be reached on foot. Three bridges cross the Río Piura to Castilla, the oldest from Calle Huancavelica (Puente San Miguel), another from Calle Sánchez Cerro and the newest from Avenida Panamericana Norte, west of town. A fourth bridge was lost in El Niño of 1997-1998. Taxis in town charge US$1, mototaxis US$0.50. Transport to nearby towns is easy to find, likewise buses going to Sullana and on to Ecuador. For Las Guaringas, expect a long journey.

Tourist information Information at the **tourist office** ⓘ *Ayacucho 377, T073-310772. Daily 0900-1900. See www.munipiura.gob.pe/turismo/ in Spanish for lots of information and links.*

Best time to visit The winter climate, May to September, is very pleasant although nights can be cold and the wind piercing, while December to March is very hot. It is extremely difficult to find a room in the last week of July because of Independence festivities. The city suffers from water shortages.

Piura

» *pp423-427. Colour map 1, B1.*

→ *Phone code: 073. Population: 324,500.*

Standing on the **Plaza de Armas** is the **cathedral**, with gold-covered altar and paintings by Ignacio Merino. A few blocks away at Lima y Callao is the **San Francisco** church, where the city's independence from Spain was declared on 4 January 1821, nearly eight months before Lima. The church was being completely rebuilt in 2002.

The church of **María Auxiliadora** stands on a small plaza on Libertad, near Avenida Sánchez Cerro. Across the plaza is the **Museo de Arte Religioso**. **San Sebastián**, on Tacna y Moquegua, is also worth seeing. The birthplace of Admiral Miguel Grau, hero of the War of the Pacific with Chile, is **Casa Museo Grau** ⓘ *Jr Tacna 662, opposite the Centro Cívico, Mon-Fri 0800-1300, 1530-1800, free*. It has been opened as a museum and contains a model of the *Huáscar*, the largest Peruvian warship in the War of the Pacific, which was built in Britain. It also contains interesting old photographs.

The **Museo Municipal Vicús** ⓘ *Sullana, near Huánuco, Mon-Sat 0800-2200, Sun 0800-1200*, includes 60 gold artefacts from the local Vicus culture. It also has an art section. Local craftwork is sold at the **Mercado Modelo**. The market on Sánchez Cerro is good for fruit.

Around Piura

» *pp423-427.*

Catacaos is a small town famous for its *chicha* (maize beer) – though be careful as the quality is not always reliable – and *picanterías*, which are local restaurants, some with music. The village is also noted for its *artesanía* such as tooled leather, gold and silver filigree jewellery, wooden articles and straw hats, though prices are relatively high and streets are lined with shops, including some jewellers more suited to a shopping mall. Inside the large church are vivid murals and, in 2000, a miracle was said to have occurred when an image of Christ appeared in the paintwork on an exterior wall. The village is also renowned for its celebrations in **Holy Week**, Good Friday especially (when all of Piura seems to be there). There is a procession at 1800 and the town centre is closed to traffic.

Two kilometres south of Catacaos is the Narihualá archaeological site. It includes a large adobe pyramid, 40 m high, from the Tallán culture which populated the Chira and Piura valleys before it was conquered by the Chimús.

The port for the area is **Paita**, 50 km from Piura. It exports cotton, cotton seed, wool and flax. It is a very old fishing port built on a small beach, flanked on three sides by a towering, sandy bluff and connected with Piura and Sullana by paved highways. Several colonial buildings survive, but they are in poor condition. Bolívar's mistress, Manuela Sáenz, lived the last 24 years of her life in Paita, after being exiled from Quito. She supported herself until her death in 1856 by weaving and embroidering and making candy after refusing the fortune left her by her husband. The house can be visited if you ask the people living in it, but there's not much to see. It is on the main road into town, after the market, just before and overlooking a petrol station. Fishing and fishmeal are prosperous industries.

On a bluff looming over Paita is a small colonial **fortress** built to repel pirates. Paita was a port of call for Spanish shipping en route from Lima to Panama and Mexico. It was a frequent target for attack, from Drake (1579) to Anson (1741).

Twenty-five kilometres up the coast is **Colán**, reached by driving down a large, sandy bluff (turn off at Km 989). Near the base is a striking and lonely colonial church, with breathtaking architecture and beautiful paintings in good condition. It is claimed by some to be the oldest church in Peru, if not in South America. The key-holder can be found by asking in the adjoining village of San Lucas de Colán. The seafront houses in the holiday resort stand on wooden stilts and are surrounded by palms. The seawater is clear and warm (but beware of stingrays – drag your feet when entering the water) and sunsets are spectacular; the town has excellent seafood restaurants. By public transport, go to Paita and change buses there.

Fifty kilometres northeast of Piura and 10 km off the old Pan-American Highway is the small town of **Chulucanas**, centre of the lemon- and orange-growing area. An ancient pottery technique has been discovered and revived here since the 1960s. The local potters formerly produced only large, utilitarian terracotta pots, until the 1960s when graverobbers brought to light examples of pottery from the Vicus and Tallane cultures dating from the second half of the first millennium BC. A group of Quechua pottery specialists researched and experimented with forms and techniques based on the pre-Columbian finds. These produce a very subtle and unusual effect. At first, the potters imitated the forms of the Vicus pieces but gradually they began to develop their own stylized figures. The most popular form is now the Chichera, a fat lady who makes and sells *chicha*. The most highly prized pieces are signed and sold in galleries and shops in Lima and abroad. Excellent ceramics can also be bought in the town, at a shop on the plaza and three others are within one block.

Huancabamba and Las Guaringas

▸▸ *pp423-427. Colour map 1, B2.*

From Chulucanas the paved road heads southeast. A turn-off east to Morropán leads to a dirt road to **Canchaque**, a delightfully situated small centre for coffee, sugar-cane and fruit production (basic lodging). The difficult and tiring road, impossible for ordinary vehicles in the wet season, continues over a pass in the Andes of more than 3000 m for 69 km to Huancabamba. This very pretty town in a wonderful setting hosts a tourist week in early July and the Virgen del Carmen festival in mid-July. It has three claims to fame. First, the predominance of European features, due to the fact that it was an important Spanish settlement in colonial times. Second, it is called *la ciudad que camina*, 'the walking town', as it is built on irregularly slipping strata causing much subsidence. Evidence for this includes the fall of the bridge over the Río Huancabamba.

The third, and by far the most remarkable claim to fame, is that Huancabamba is the base for reaching **Las Guaringas**, a series of lakes at about 4000 m. Around here live the most famous witch doctors of Peru, to whom sick people flock from all over the country and abroad. The shamanic ceremony is definitely off the gringo trail and is an unforgettable trip. To take part in the ceremony, arrive in town and prepare to be approached almost immediately by a shaman's 'agent'. As dodgy as this sounds, this person can help you by doing all preparations. Go to the tourist centre in the plaza beforehand and double check if the agent's witch doctor is trustworthy. You'll then hop in a van, travel to the doctor's house, agree on a price and commence the ceremony immediately. It is an outdoor affair involving light hallucinogenic San Pedro cactus juice that is quite vile. The ceremony lasts all night and participants dance, reveal and predict the future. The entire ceremony is very mellow and most witch doctors have the disposition of concerned uncles. A spartan meal is provided so bring snacks. The next day involves a three-hour horse ride to a high mountain lagoon where near-skinny dipping and more ceremonies take place. You're back in Huancabamba (tired and cold) by late afternoon.

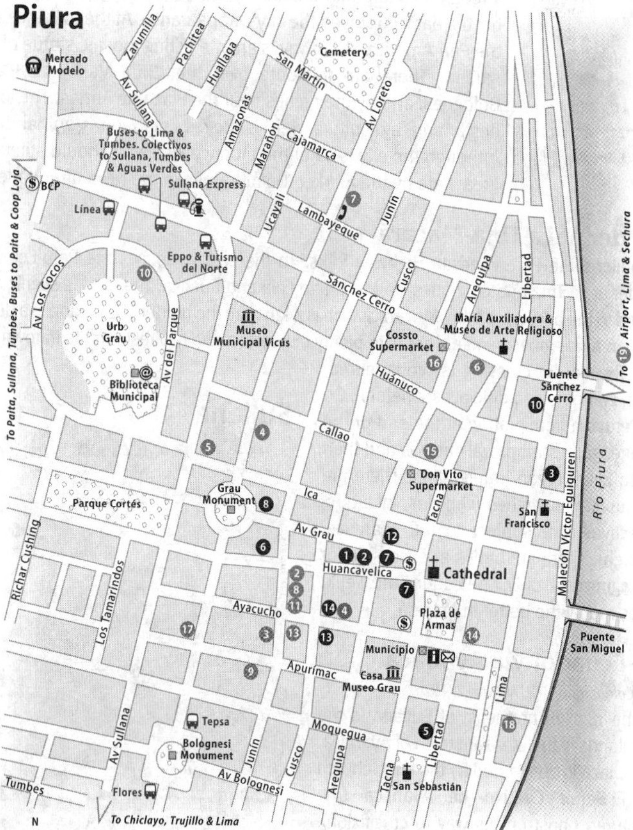

0 metres 100

0 yards 100

Sleeping
California 2
Continental 3
Costa del Sol 4
El Almirante 5
El Sol 6
Esmeralda 7
Hospedaje Aruba 8
Hostal Los Jardines 10
Hostal Moon Night 11
La Capullana 13
Los Portales 14
Oriental 15
Pacífico 9
Perú 16
San Jorge 17
San Miguel 18
Vicús 19

Eating
Alex Chopp's 1
Brosti Chopp 2
Carburmer 5
Chalán del Norte 7
D'Pauli 3
El Chalán de la Grau 8
Ganímedes 10
Italia 12
La Carreta 6
Las Tradiciones Piuranas & Piura Tours 13
Picantería Los Santitos 5
Romano 14

Bars & clubs
Bloom Moon 4
Café R&B Zelada 4

Horses to the lakes can be hired for US$5. There are also trips to the village of **San Antonio** below Lago Carmen, and the village of **Salalá** below Lago Shumbe. Ignacio León, who owns a *bodega* opposite **Hotel El Dorado** (see Sleeping, page 424), runs an early pickup service to the outlying villages and takes trips at negotiable prices.

Sullana to Ecuador » pp423-427.

Sullana → *Colour map 1, B1. Population: 147,361.*

Sullana, 39 km north of Piura, is built on a bluff over the fertile Chira valley and is a busy, modern place. Avenida José de Lama, once a dusty, linear market, has a green, shady park with benches along the centre. Many of the bus companies have their offices along this avenue. San Martín is the main commercial street. Parks and monuments were added in 1994 to 1995, and have greatly improved the city's appearance. At the entrance, on the Pan-American Highway is an interesting mosaic statue of an iguana. There are lookouts over the Chira Valley at Plaza Bolognesi and by the arches near the Plaza de Armas. The local fiesta and agricultural fair is **Reyes**, held on 5-29 January. Although the city is safer than it once was, you should still take great care by the market. Do not arrive in the town after dark.

The more frequently used route to the border is the coastal road which goes from Sullana north-west towards the Talara oilfields and then follows the coastline to Máncora and Tumbes, see page 428.

Border at La Tina-Macará

At Sullana the Pan-American Highway forks. To the east it crosses the Peru-Ecuador border at La Tina and continues via Macará to Loja and Cuenca. The road is scenic and paved to the border, 128 km. **Macará**, which is 4 km from the border in Ecuador, is a dusty town in a rice-growing area. There are plenty of hotels and a few restaurants in town.

The border crossing is problem-free, open 24 hours and officials are helpful. Go to Peruvian immigration at the end of the bridge, get a stamp, walk across and then go to Ecuadorean immigration. There are no customs searches (vehicles, including *colectivos*, are subject to full searches, though). There are banks at each side for changing cash only, open during the week; rates are a little better in Macará.

To Ecuador via Ayabaca

→ *Colour map 1, B2. Altitude 2710 m.*

Some 182 km northeast of Sullana in the highlands is the pleasant town of Ayabaca. The plaza is dominated by the large church of **El Señor Cautivo de Ayabaca** (the captured Christ on his way to crucifixion). Many devotees make pilgrimages to his shrine, the most famous in northern Peru, especially on 12 October.

Northeast of Ayabaca is the 1200-ha **Bosque de Cuyas** nature reserve which protects a remnant of cloudforest. One hundred and twenty-one species of bird have been identified here. It is run by **Naturaleza y Cultura Internacional**

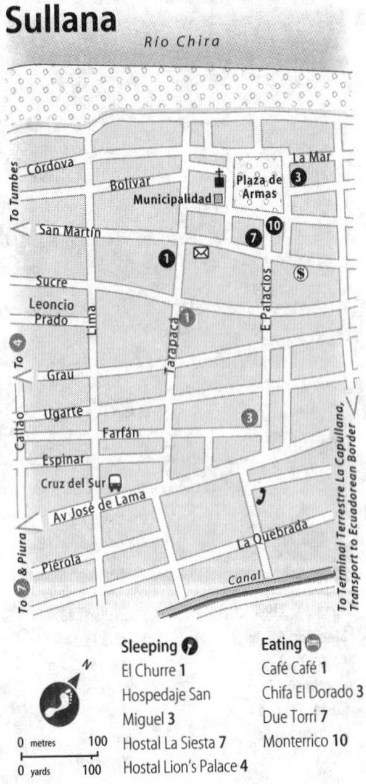

ⓘ *T073-502431, Sullana, ayabaca@natureandculture.org; Ayabaca contact Angel Seminario, T073-471108*. Access is along a road north which starts at **Los Cocos**, 5 km from Ayabaca on the road to Espíndola. **Aypate**, an impressive archaeological site on a mountain-top, is part of what is believed to have been an important Inca settlement. Only two of over 100 ha have been cleared. The *usnu* (platform) and temple of the sun are especially beautiful and a mirador gives wonderful views. Access is along a poor road (impassable in the rainy season) from Yanchalá. Pickups from Ayabaca charge US$45 return with several hours' wait. It's a 20-minute walk from the end of the vehicle road to the ruins. There are cheaper ways to get there: a shared taxi to Yanchalá or Hualcuy from Prado y Bolognesi near the Ayabaca market, followed by three- or five-hour trails (but there were safety problems here in 2006). Make local enquiries before setting out. There is no lodging at Aypate but the caretakers may offer basic hospitality or you can camp. Take food, water and warm clothing.

A rough road with great views goes via Yanchalá (34 km), Samanguilla (49 km), and El Toldo (57 km) to **Espíndola** (64 km; 2280 m), a tiny frontier village with a satellite phone, a simple *comedor* and no other services; accommodation may be arranged in private homes. Near Samanguilla and El Toldo are the **Samanga** petroglyphs. A very poor road continues 2 km to the small international bridge over the Río Espíndola for Peruvian immigration, open 24 hours (ask in the village for the officer if the post is unmanned). There are no services or *cambios* at the bridge. An equally poor road climbs steeply 1 km to the Ecuadorean hamlet of El Salado on the Jimbura-Zumba road. Ecuadorean immigration is at the entrance to Jimbura, 4 km from El Salado, open 24 hours. There is one basic *residencial* in Jimbura and a place to eat, shopkeepers change soles at poor rates. There is regular transport from Jimbura to Loja via Amaluza, which has places to eat and stay and buses to Loja (US$4.75, five hours) and Quito (US$18, 16 hours).

Border at Alamor → *Colour map 1, B2.*

Colectivos run from Sullana for three dusty, bumpy hours to Alamor, a rather remote, but official border crossing west of La Tina (US$3, or US$18 for whole car). A rowing boat crosses the Río Lalamor to Lalamor in Ecuador (US$0.20), or you can wade across. Peruvian immigration is a short walk from the ferry and there are money changers offering regular rates. On the Ecuadorean side immigration is by the church, a long walk from the crossing (ask directions). Officials on both sides have to leave their post once a fortnight to register their documents. If you are unlucky enough to arrive on one of these days, you can't cross because you cannot get the right stamps. From Lalamor trucks run to the riverside town of **Zapotillo** (21 km, dirt, 40 minutes, US$1), also on the border, but not an official crossing. Best hotel is **Los Charanes**; several restaurants. A paved road goes to Macará.

Sleeping

Piura *p419, map p421*

A Costa del Sol, Loreto 399, T/F073- 302864, www.costadelsolperu.com. Luxury, pool, casino, internet facilities, restaurant.

A Los Portales, Libertad 875, Plaza de Armas, T073-321161, www.hoteleslos portales.com. Price includes breakfast, tax and welcome cocktail. This ex-government hotel, in the Country Club group, has been attractively refurbished and is the city's social centre, elegant, a/c, hot water, pleasant terrace and patio, nice pool.

D Esmeralda, Loreto 235, T/F073-331205, www.hotelesmeralda. com.pe. With bathroom, hot water, fan (**C** with a/c and breakfast), clean, comfortable, good, restaurant.

D San Miguel, Lima 1007, Plaza Pizarro, T073-305122. Modern, comfortable, with bath, TV, café.

D Vicús, Av Guardia Civil B-3, in Castilla 2 blocks across the river on the Sánchez Cerro bridge, T073-343201. With bathroom, hot water, fan, clean, quiet, parking.

E El Almirante, Ica 860, T/F073- 335239. With bathroom, fan, clean, modern, owner is knowledgeable about the area (see page 422).

E El Sol, Sánchez Cerro 411, T073-324461. With bathroom, hot water, small pool, snack bar, parking, accepts dollars cash or TCs but won't change them. Recommended.

E Perú, Arequipa 476, T073-333919. With bathroom and fan, clean, safe, friendly, laundry service, cold water, modern small rooms, all meals in restaurant extra.

E San Jorge, Jr Loreto 960, T073-327514. With bathroom and fan, cheaper without cable TV, hot water, clean but a little overpriced.

F La Capullana, Junín 925, T073-321239. With bath, some cheaper single rooms, welcoming.

F Continental, Junín 924, T073-334531. Some rooms with bathroom, clean, comfortable, no breakfast.

F Hostal Los Jardines, Av Los Cocos 436, T073-326590. With bath, hot water, TV, laundry, parking, good value.

F Pacífico, Apurímac 717, T073-303061. With bath, hot water and fan, simple and clean, good value.

F-G Hostal Moon Night, Junín 899, T073-336174. Comfortable, modern, spacious, cheaper without bath/TV, clean, good value.

G California, Junín 835, upstairs, T073-328789. Price per person. Shared bath, own water tank, mosquito netting on windows, roof terrace, clean, brightly decorated, friendly owner. Recommended (some rooms rented by the hour, though).

G Hospedaje Aruba, Junín 851, T073-303067. Small rooms but clean and comfortable, shared bath, fan on request, very friendly. Recommended.

G Oriental, Callao 446, T073-304011. Cheaper without bathroom and fan, clean, good value but very noisy, TV in reception.

Around Piura *p419*

A Bocatoma Resort, Av Costanera Norte, Colán, T074-997 0100, www.bocatoma.com. Prices rise in high season and there is a variety of cabins and offers. Cabins on a spit of land between the occean and lagoons, with restaurant, pool and sports facilities.

A Hotel Sol de Colán, on the promenade, Colán, T073-321784, deltareps@terra.com.pe. With pool, bar, games room, restaurant and bungalow accommodation with en-suite facilities.

E Frente al Mar, Colán, T073-615465. Owner Alfred Leigh is of English descent, 4 rooms, damp, sea terrace, friendly. Its seafood restaurant is quite cheap and will cook vegetarian pasta if you wish.

F El Faro, Junín 322, Paita, T073-611076. Small and clean.

F Las Brisas, Av Ugarte, Paita. The best, with bathroom but little cold water, safe.

G El Mundo, on 300 block of Bolívar, Paita. Not bad but some rooms rented by the hour.

Huancabamba and Las Guaringas *p420*

G Hotel El Dorado, on the main plaza, Huancabamba. Good, clean hotel, informative owner, with restaurant.

G Hotel San José, Salalá. Very basic, take your own food.

Sullana to Ecuador *p422, map p422*

At the border of La Tina-Macará, there is one *hospedaje* and several eating places on the road down to the bridge. At Suyo (a pretty place), 1½ hrs from Sullana , there are 2 *hospedajes*.

B-C Hostal La Siesta, Av Panamericana 400, Sullana, T/F073-502264, at the entrance to town. Hot water, fan, cable TV, cheaper with cold water, pool, restaurant, laundry.

E El Churre, Tarapacá 501, Sullana, T/F073-507006. With bath, TV, laundry, café. Recommended.

F Hostal Lion's Palace, Grau 1030, Sullana, T073-502587. With bathroom, fan, patio, pleasant, quiet, no breakfast.

F-G Hospedaje San Miguel, C J Farfán 204, Sullana, T073-502789. Cheaper without bathroom, all rooms open off a central passageway, basic, helpful, good showers, staff will spray rooms against mosquitoes, cafeteria.

To Ecuador via Ayabaca *p422*

E Hotel de Turistas Samanga, Tacna y Grau, Plaza de Armas, Ayabaca, T073-471049. With bath, hot water, a bit run-down but still best in town.

F Hostal Oro Verde, Salavery 381, 1 block from plaza, Ayabaca, T073-499830, adac1277@hotmail.com. Cheaper with shared bath, limited hot water (best in morning), meals on request, family-run, good value, noise every night from nearby disco.

G Hospedaje Plaza, Cáceres at Plaza de Armas, Ayabaca, T073-471085. Shared bath, electric shower, basic and friendly.

Eating

Piura *p419, map p421*

Piura's special dishes include *majado de yuca* (manioc root with pork); *seco de chavelo* (beef and plantain stew); and *carne seca* (sun-dried meat). Its best-known sweet is the delicious *natilla*, made mostly of goats' milk and molasses. The local drink is *pipa fría*, chilled coconut juice drunk from the nut with a straw.

TTT **Carburmer**, Libertad 1014, T073-332380. Very good lunches and dinners, also pizza.

TTT **Picantería Los Santitos**, in the same precinct and same phone as **Carburmer**. Lunch only, wide range of traditional dishes in a renovated colonial house.

TT **Alex Chopp's**, Huancavelica 538, T073-322568. A la carte dishes, seafood, fish, chicken and meats, beer, popular at lunchtime.

TT **Brosti Chopp**, Arequipa 780, T073-303753. Similar to **Alex Chopp's**, but with lunch menu for US$1.45.

TT **La Carreta**, Huancavelica 726, T073-304231. One of the most popular places for roast chicken.

TT **Las Tradiciones Piuranas**, Ayacucho 579, T073-803084. Regional specialities, also an art gallery.

TT **Romano**, Ayacucho 580. Popular with locals, extensive menu, excellent set meal for US$1.55. Highly recommended.

T **Ganímedes**, Lima 440, T073-329176. A good vegetarian restaurant, very popular set lunch, à la carte is slow but well worth it, try the excellent yoghurt and fruit.

Cafés

Chalán del Norte, Tacna 520, Plaza de Armas, Grau 173 and 452 (Chalán de la Grau). Several branches of this popular chain, for good sweets, cakes and ice cream.

D'Pauli, Lima 541. Also for sweets, cakes and ice cream, good.

Italia, Grau 172. For breakfasts, snacks, desserts and juices.

Around Piura *p419*

TT-T **La Chayo**, San Francisco 439, Catacaos, T073-370121. Recommended for its local dishes and *chicha*. There are several other places to eat on and close to C San Francisco.

T **Chifa Hong Kong**, Junín 358, Paita. Considered by locals to offer really authentic Chinese food.

T **Club Liberal building**, 2nd floor, Jorge Chávez 161, Paita. This serves good fish, seafood and crêpes, and is good value.

Huancabamba and Las Guaringas *p420*

Local specialities include *rompope*, a rich and strong drink made of egg, spices and *cañazo* (sugar-cane spirit), roast *cuy* (guinea-pig) and local cheeses.

Sullana to Ecuador *p422, map p422*

T **Café Café**, Tarapacá 484, Sullana. Sandwiches, *tamales*, lunch menu US$1, juices and drinks.

T **Chifa El Dorado**, on the plaza, Sullana. One of the more authentic of several *chifas*.

T **Due Torri**, E Palacios 122, Sullana. Italian and regional, popular with locals.

T **Monterrico**, Plaza de Armas, Sullana. Set menu for US$1, popular.

To Ecuador via Ayabaca *p422*

TT **El Carbón**, Tacna 1 block from Plaza de Armas, Ayabaca. Peruvian and international dishes, upscale for where it is, pleasant atmosphere.

There are other limited eating places.

Bars and clubs

Piura *p419, map p421*

Many of the nightspots are concentrated on Ayacucho, and some of them are also restaurants. **Bloom Moon**, Ayacucho 522. **Café R & B Zelada**, Ayacucho 562.

Festivals and events

Piura *p419, map p421*

26-28 Jul Festival Internacional de Tunas.

27 Aug-2 Sep Semana Turística de Piura, tourism week.

7 Oct Festival Nacional de Marinera y Tondero, celebrating local dances.

Activities and tours

Piura *p419, map p421*

Piura Tours, C Ayacucho 585, T073-328873, piuratours@mail.udep.edu.pe. The manager Mario speaks very good English.

Transport

Piura *p419, map p421*

Air

Capitán Guillermo Concha airport is in Castilla, 10 mins from the centre by taxi (US$1). It has gift shops and 2 car rental agencies. Airport tax US$3.50. Two daily flights with **Lan** (T073-302145) to **Lima** (US$111) via Chiclayo.

Bus

Most companies are on Av Sánchez Cerro, blocks 11, 12 and 13 (see www.munipiura.gob.pe/turismo/transporte.shtml). To **Lima**, 1038 km, 14-16 hrs, from US$7 (eg **Tepsa**), on the Panamericana Norte. Most buses stop at the major cities on route; **Flores**, **Ittsa**, **Línea**, **Tepsa**. To **Chiclayo**, 190 km, 3 hrs, US$3.65, several buses daily. To **Trujillo**, 7 hrs, 487 km, US$7, several daily. To travel by day change in Chiclayo. To **Talara**, US$2, 2 hrs, with **Eppo**. To **Máncora**, US$3.15, 3 hrs, with **Eppo**. To **Tumbes**, 282 km, 4½ hrs, US$4.80, several buses daily, eg **Cruz del Sur** (also to Lima), **Cial** and **Emtrafesa** (also to Chiclayo and Trujillo); also *colectivos*, US$5.75. To **Paita**, **Trans Dora**, every 20 mins, 1 hr, US$0.75; also from Paita terminal on Av Gullman, just off Sánchez Cerro. All services drop off and collect passengers in the market area in Paita. To **Catacaos**, *colectivos* leave Piura from the far side of Puente San Miguel, US$0.20, 15-20 mins; also combis from the bus terminal, block 12 Av Sánchez Cerro, US$0.25. For **Chulucanas** combis from Piura charge US$1.50.

To **Ecuador** **Trans Loja**, 4 daily to **Loja**. **Unión Cariamanga**, 2 daily to **Loja**, both via Sullana, La Tina and Macará, 8 hrs, US$8. There are connecting *colectivos* to **Vilcabamba** from Loja. **CIFA** to **Machala** US$6, 6 hrs, and **Guayaquil** US$10, 9 hrs, via Tumbes, 5 a day. Otherwise go to Tumbes and travel on from there for the **Aguas Verdes crossing to Ecuador**.

Bus companies **Cial**, Bolognesi 817, T073-304250. **CIFA**, Los Naranjos y Sánchez Cerro (cuadra 11-12) opposite Emtrafesa, T073-305925. **Cruz del Sur**, La Libertad 1176, T073-337094. **Emtrafesa**, Los Naranjos 235, T073-337093. **Eppo**, T073-331160. **Flores**, Av Libertad 1210, T073-306664 (helpful staff). **Ittsa**, Sánchez Cerro 1142, T073-333982. **Línea**, Sánchez Cerro 1215, T073-327821. **Tepsa**, Loreto 1195, T073-323721. **Trans Dora**, Sánchez Cerro 1391. **Trans Loja**, Sánchez Cerro 1480, T073-309407. **Unión Cariamanga**, Sánchez Cerro y Av Vice, Urb Santa Ana, T073-990 0135 (mob).

Car rental

At the air port: **Servitours**, T073-342008, www.servitourspiura.com; **Vicús**, T073-342051, www.vicusrentacar.com. US$50 per day for a small vehicle; they also provide transfers to Punta Sal US$80.

Taxis

Radio Taxis, T073-324509 or 324630.

Huancabamba amd Las Guaringas *p420*

To get to **Huancabamba**, take a bus from Piura to Canchaque and Huancabamba, which leaves daily at 0900 and 1000 (at least 10 hrs, US$9), from Av Ramón Castilla 196. Buy your ticket early on the day before travelling. It returns from Huancabamba at 0700 and 1000. A truck costs US$11.50. If driving, take the Pan-American Highway south of Piura for 66 km where there is a signpost to Huancabamba. Buses to **Las Guaringas** lakes leave at 0400 from the main plaza in Huancabamba.

Sullana to Ecuador *p422, map p422*

There are frequent buses from Piura to **Sullana**, 38 km, 30 mins (US$0.45), **Eppo**, **Sullana Express** and **Turismo del Norte**, all on 1100 block of Sánchez Cerro; also *colectivos* (US$1). To **La Tina** on the Ecuadorean frontier, is a further 128 km, 1¾ hrs, US$2.85. It's best to take an early bus to Sullana (start at 0430, leave when full), then a *colectivo* (see under Sullana). Try not to arrive in Sullana or Piura after dark, it's unsafe.

Sullana

Several bus companies, including **Ormeño** use a new Terminal Terrestre. There are several daily buses to and from **Tumbes**, 244 km, 4-5 hrs US$5. If you have time, it is worth continuing to Piura rather than staying in Sullana. To **Chiclayo** and **Trujillo** see under Piura. To **Lima**, 1076 km, 14-16 hrs, US$9-18, several buses daily, most coming from Tumbes or Talara. A luxury overnight bus via Trujillo with **Ittsa** (T073-503705) is US$18; also with **Cruz del Sur** and **Ormeño**. To **Paita** *colectivos* leave from the market, 2 blocks from Av Lama, US$1, 1 hr. To **Talara**, Eppo and Emtrafesa, C Comercio, 1 block from Av Lama, each leave hourly. Eppo are faster but more expensive, 1 hr, US$1.25. To **Máncora**, Eppo, 5 a day, 2½ hrs, US$3, or travel to Talara and then on from there via Los Organos.

Taxi Mototaxis in Sullana charge US$0.30 around town. Radio Taxis, T073-502210/504354.

Border at La Tina-Macará

From Sullana to the border combis leave from Terminal Terrestre La Capullana, off Av Buenos Aires, several blocks beyond the canal, to the international bridge. They leave when full, US$2.85 per person, 1¾ hrs. It's best to take a taxi or mototaxi to and from the terminal. From the border to Macará is 4 km: walk over the bridge and take one of the pickups which run from the border (10 mins, US$0.30, or US$1.25 for whole car). Frequent buses leave the Ecuadorean side for Loja (5-6 hrs, US$5), so if you are not taking the through bus (see under Piura), you can go from Sullana to Loja in a day. From the border to Sullana, cars may leave before they are full.

To Ecuador via Ayabaca

From Piura to Ayabaca, Trans Vegas is recommended, Av Panamericana frente al cementerio, Urb San Ramón, T073-308729, daily 0830, 1500, plus Sat 0800, Sun 2300. Also Poderoso Cautivo, Av Sullana Norte next to Iglesia Cristo Rey, T073-309888, daily 0900, 1500, Sun also 2300. To Piura, both companies are on Cáceres at Plaza de Armas. Vegas, T073-471080, Tue-Sun 0830, 1500, Mon 0800, 0900, 1500. Poderoso Cautivo, T073-471247, daily 0830, 1500, Fri also 1530, 1630. To **Espíndola and border** from Ayabaca, station wagons and pickups leave when full from L Prado y Bolognesi, near the market, 1 or 2 a day, so go early, US$3 pp, US$18 to hire the vehicle, 3½ hrs, beware over- charging. Arrange for driver to take you to the international bridge and preferably on to Jimbura. To Ayabaca, a pickup truck leaves Espíndola about 0500 daily; if staying in Jimbura, go to Espíndola and let the driver know, he will pick you up in the morning. There is no fixed schedule during the day, be patient.

Border at Alamor

From Zapotillo, buses go to **Loja**, 7 hrs, and **Quito**.

Directory

Piura *p419, map p421*

Banks BCP, Grau y Tacna. Cash and Visa and Amex TCs (US$12 commission), cheques changed in the mornings only, has ATM. Banco Continental, Plaza de Armas. Changes Amex TCs with US$10 commission. Interbank, Grau 170, changes Visa TCs, ATM for Visa, MasterCard and AmEx. *Casas de cambio* are at Arequipa 600 block and 722, and Ica 366, 456 and 460. Street changers can be found on Grau outside BCP. **Consulates** Honorary British Consul, c/o American Airlines, Huancavelica 223, T073-305990. Honorary German Consul, Jutta Moritz de Irazola, Las Amapolas K6, Urb Miraflores, Casilla 76, T073-332920. **Internet** Several in the centre. 10 machines in the Biblioteca Municipal, Urb Grau, US$0.60 per hr, clean. **Laundry** Lavandería Liz-to, Tacna 785. Charges by weight. **Post** On the corner of Libertad and Ayacucho on Plaza de Armas is not too helpful, Mon-Sat, 0800-1600. Perhaps it's better going to Hotel Los Portales. **Telephone** Loreto 259, national and international phone and fax. Also at Ovalo Grau 483. **Useful addresses** Dirección Regional de Turismo, Av Fortunato Chirichigno, Urb San Eduardo, T073-308229, at the north end of town; Indecopi is also here, T073-304045, helpful when there are problems. Touring y Automóvil Club del Perú, Sánchez Cerro 1237, T073-325641, has little information.

Sullana *p422, map p422*

Banks BCP, San Martín 685. Changes cash and TCs. There are *casas de cambio* and street changers on San Martín by Tarapacá. **Immigration** Grau 939. **Internet** Several in the centre, on San Martín and Av Lama. **Post** San Martín 778, Mon-Sat 0800-1930, Sun 0800-1300. **Telephone** Telephone and fax at Miró Quesada 213.

Coastal route to Ecuador

Although it leads to the tiresome border crossing of Aguas Verdes/Huaquillas, this road passes some of Peru's best and most popular beaches and to the area around Tumbes. The region also has national parks protecting habitats not found anywhere else in the country. ▸▸ *For Sleeping, Eating and other listings, see pages 432-436.*

Talara and around ▸▸ *pp432-436. Colour map 1, B1.*

→ *Phone code: 073.*

Talara is the main centre of the coastal oil area, with a state-owned 60,000 barrel-a-day oil refinery and a fertilizer plant. Set in a desert oasis 5 km west of the Panamericana, the city is a triumph over formidable natural difficulties, with water piped 40 km from the Río Chira. A couple of kilometres from the town is La Peña beach, which is unspoilt. Other attractions in the area can be reached via paved highways which connect the town with the Negritos, Lagunitos, La Brea and other oilfields.

Of historical interest are the old tarpits at **La Brea**, 21 km inland from Punta Pariñas, south of Talara, and near the foot of the Amotape mountains. Here the Spaniards boiled the tar to get pitch for caulking their ships. Surfers will love the empty swell north and south of town, especially near Negritos where a gentle beach break and rolling thunder are separated by Punta Balcones, the westernmost point of South America. The impressive sea lion colony and the occasional dolphin make this an interesting spot.

Some 31 km north of Talara, is the small port of **Cabo Blanco**, famous for its excellent sea-fishing and surfing. The scenery has, unfortunately, been spoilt by numerous oil installations. The turn-off from the Pan-American Highway is at the town of **El Alto**, where many oil workers are housed. There are several basic hotels here. Camping is permitted free of charge at Cabo Blanco, on the beach or by the **Fishing Club** overlooking the sea, at least in the off-season, June to December. The film of Ernest Hemingway's *The Old Man and the Sea* was shot here. Marlin grew scarce in the late 1960s owing to commercial fishing and to climatic and maritime factors but in the last few years the marlin have returned. The old **Fishing Club** in Cabo Blanco, built in the 1950s, has been remodelled in the shape of the **Fishing Club Lodge Hotel**, which has a restaurant, pool, and offers watersports (it's likely to be full in the New Year period). A launch also provides all the necessary facilities for deep-sea fishing. Now, would-be Ernest Hemingways can return to Cabo Blanco in search of their dream catch.

Los Organos, a small town and fishing port with a fine long sandy beach and easy surfing at its southern end, provides a quieter and cheaper alternative to Máncora. For those looking to relax, it's especially suitable at peak periods.

Máncora and around ▸▸ *pp432-436. Colour map 1, B1.*

A small resort stretching along 3 km of the highway, Máncora is parallel to a long, attractive, sandy beach with safe bathing. It is a popular stop-off for travellers on the Peru-Ecuador route, even more so with young *limeños* who arrive at weekends and holiday times. Consequently it has a very lively feel with numerous bars and music playing all night. The water here is warm enough for bathing and the town has some of the friendliest local surfers on the planet. Surfing is best November to March (boards and suits can be hired from several places along the southern blocks of Avenida Piura, US$1.50 each per hour). This stretch of coast is famous for its excellent *mero* (grouper).

The Pan-American Highway runs through the centre of town and is the main street, called Avenida Piura. Most of the tourist facilities are south of the town centre and *artesanía* stalls line the avenue between the centre and south end. At peak times youngsters spill out from the conentration of bars bringing traffic to a complete standstill. At the north end of town the beach is inaccessible and dirty, and this is not a safe area. South of Máncora along the coastal road (old Pan-American Highway) are some excellent beaches which are being developed, for example **Las Pocitas**, a resort ideal for families, or just for relaxing.

Fresh water is piped into the area, producing the incongruous but welcome sight of green lawns and lush gardens between the sea and desert cliffs. There is a line of rocks parallel to the beach, which form interesting bathing pools at low tide, though these can be dangerous at high tide.

At **Las Arenas** resort, 4 km south of Máncora, the beach is completely unspoiled, with armies of small crabs and abundant bird life, including frigates and masked and brown pelicans.

East of Máncora are hot mud baths (*baños de barro*), which are nice after a day in the surf. There is no infrastructure, but the landscape, desert foothills and shrub lands, is beautiful. The access is north of town, at Km 1168, from where you head for Quebrada Fernández. Beyond is **El Angolo game reserve**, which extends as far south as the Río Chira. Take a mototaxi from Máncora, 20 minutes, and pay US$5.75 for the return journey and an hour's wait while you bathe.

North of Máncora » pp432-436.

At Km 1182 is an enormous customs house for checking southbound traffic. Twenty-two kilometres north of Máncora, at Km 1187 (El Arco – or arch), is the turn-off for **Punta Sal Grande**, a posh resort town at the southern end of beautiful Playa Punta Sal, a 10-km-long sandy beach, with calm surf. It's a favourite of well-to-do Lima businessmen and politicians, but in the low season is almost deserted and hotel rates are significantly lower. The beach offers kilometres of golden sand, relatively warm turquoise water, interesting sea-life in the rock pools and huge schools of whales passing on the distant horizon at dusk. A pleasant walk can be made along the beach to **Punta Sal Chica**, allow at least three hours for the round trip and carry water with you.

The fishing village of **Cancas** has a few shops, restaurants and a gas station. From Punta Mero (Km 1204) north, the beach is used by *larveros*, extracting shrimp larvae from the ocean for use in the shrimp industry, and is no longer considered safe for camping. Several new resorts are being built between Punta Mero and Tumbes.

Zorritos, 27 km south of Tumbes (US$0.55 by combi), is an important fishing centre, with a good beach. Several new hotels and resorts have been built. At **Caleta La Cruz** is the only part of the Peruvian coast where the sea is warm all year. There are two good beaches near Tumbes, one is at Caleta La Cruz 16 km southwest, where Pizarro landed in 1532. The original Cruz de Conquista was taken to Lima. Regular *colectivos* run back and forth from Tumbes, US$0.30 each way.

Tumbes » pp432-436. Colour map 1, A1.

→ *Phone code: 072. Population: 34,000.*

Tumbes, about 141 km north of Talara, and 265 km north of Piura, is the most northerly of Peru's provincial capitals. It is not the most beautiful, but it does have some interesting historic wooden buildings in the centre. Tumbes is also a garrison town, so watch where you point your camera. Mosquito repellent is a must for the Tumbes area.

Ins and outs

Getting there A taxi to the airport costs US$4, 20 minutes. Combis charge US$1.50. Taxis meet flights to take passengers to the border for US$7-9. There are no combis from the airport to the border. Beware of overcharging. All bus companies have offices on Avenida Tumbes.

Getting around Everything is fairly conveniently located close to the Plaza de Armas, although transport to the Ecuadorean border is a little bit further out. Hotels are mostly central to the north of the river either side of Avenida Tumbes and Bolívar.

Tourist information **Centro Cívico** ⓘ *Bolognesi 194, 2nd level, on the plaza, T072-524940, irntum@yahoo.com, 0730-1300, 1400-1630*. Helpful.

Sights

The long promenade, the **Malecón Benavides**, beside the high banks of the Río Tumbes, gives good views of the river. It is decorated with arches and a monstrous statue called *El Beso* (the Kiss), has several cafés, but is rather dilapidated. Old houses are best seen on **Calle Grau**, particularly at the junction with Calle Los Andes, and a colonial public library with a small museum stands in the **Plaza de Armas**. The **cathedral,** dating in its present incarnation from 1903, was restored in 1985. There are two pedestrian malls, arranged with benches and plants, Paseo de Los Libertadores on Bolívar and Paseo de la Concordia on San Martín, both leading north from the Plaza de Armas. In the main plaza and the Paseo de la Concordia there are several ornate, brightly coloured mosaic statues giving the city a slightly more exotic, tropical feel than anywhere else on the Peruvian coast.

The Río Tumbes forms a significant boundary between the dry, scrubby desert vegetation to the south and the more lush green landscape north of the river. The river was only bridged in 1930 and the long-term isolation of Tumbes from the rest of Peru is still reflected in the people and their approach to life today.

Around Tumbes

» pp432-436.

The remains of the Cabeza de Vaca cult centre of the Tumpis people can be found at **Corrales**, 5 km south of Tumbes, but were heavily damaged by the 1983 and 1997/1998 rains. The Incas built their fort of San Pedro on the site of the Tumpis settlement. The fort was visited by Pizarro on his way from the coast along the Inca coastal highway up to Cajamarca.

Three protected areas consisting of three distinct environments form the UNESCO Biosphere Reserve of northwest Peru. It is an area rich in wildlife and flora, but is little visited by travellers passing by en route between Peru and Ecuador. In a single day it is possible to visit all three areas and sample the rainforest, dry scrub and mangrove swamps.

Santuario Nacional los Manglares de Tumbes

This national reserve was created to protect the mangrove ecosystem in the northernmost part of the Peruvian coast. It extends between the border with Ecuador in the north and Puerto Pizarro (see below) in the south. Of the 4750 remaining hectares, 2988 are protected. There are five species of mangrove, the main one being the red mangrove on whose roots the *conchas negras* live. At least 200 bird species have been recorded, eight of which are endemic, including the mangrove eagle. The mangroves are under threat from fresh water brought down by the rivers during El Niño and the expanding shrimp farming industry, though at 3000 ha it's small compared to that of Ecuador. The mangrove swamps are full of pelicans; it's best to visit them at high tide. A few tame birds beg for fish on the beaches.

Puerto Pizarro

Puerto Pizarro, a small, rubbish-strewn fishing port 13 km northeast of Tumbes, is another access point for the mangroves. Worth visiting from here is the research station where the **Río Tumbes crocodile**, a UN Red-data species, is protected. The crocodile is found at the river's mouth, threatened by shrimp farming, and in the Río Tumbes' upper reaches, threatened by gold-mining. Boats from **Comité de Transporte Acuático** ⓘ *Malecón Turístico, T072-543019*, go to: **Isla de Amor** (bars, restaurants, camping, windsurfing, hammocks for rent, overnighting 'homeless lovers', US$4.30); **Isla Hueso de Ballena** (open ocean and quiet bay, swimming, no services, US$5.75); **crocodile farm** (US$7.15), **Isla de los Pájaros** (best to see birds 1700-1800, US$8.55); full tour including mangroves, two hours, US$12.85 (price per boat, maximum eight people). **Festival of San Pedro y San Pablo** takes place on 29-30 June.

Parque Nacional Cerros de Amotape

The Parque Nacional Cerros de Amotape was created to protect an area representative of the equatorial forest. It extends southeast from the south bank of the Tumbes river, towards the El Angolo game preserve northeast of Máncora. It covers 90,700 ha comprising seven different habitats, including the best-preserved area of dry forest on the Pacific coast. Some of the endemic species are the Tumbes crocodile, the river otter and white-winged turkeys. Other species to be seen are black parrot, puma, deer, tigrillo and white-backed squirrels. Permission to enter is needed from Inrena, which Pronaturaleza can arrange. There is no entrance fee. All water must be carried which is why most visitors choose to visit by tour.

Tumbes

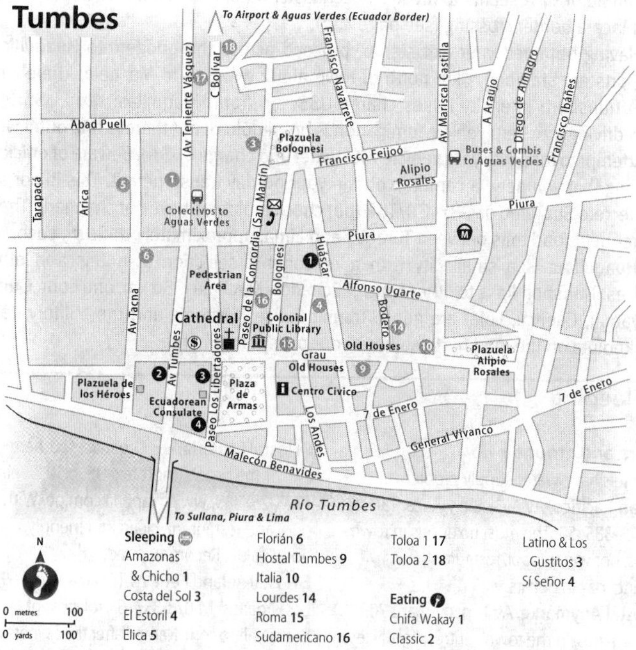

Sleeping
Amazonas & Chicho 1
Costa del Sol 3
El Estoril 4
Elica 5
Florián 6
Hostal Tumbes 9
Italia 10
Lourdes 14
Roma 15
Sudamericano 16
Toloa 1 17
Toloa 2 18

Eating
Chifa Wakay 1
Classic 2
Latino & Los Gustitos 3
Sí Señor 4

Amazonas Explorer, see page 170, organizes commercial descents of the Río Tumbes once a year around Christmas time, to take advantage of the best weather. It involves the chance to see the rare wildlife, with 4WD, trekking and rafting through a spectacular canyon in the heart of Amotape. The expedition ends just a few hours from the beach at Máncora.

Zona Reservada de Tumbes

The Zona Reservada de Tumbes, formerly Bosque Nacional de Tumbes (75,000 ha), lies to the northeast of Tumbes, between the Ecuadorean border and Cerros de Amotape National Park. It was created to protect dry equatorial forest and tropical rainforest. The wildlife includes monkeys, otters, wild boars, small cats and crocodiles. Access from Tumbes is via Cabuyal, Pampas de Hospital and El Caucho to the Quebrada Faical research station or via Zarumilla and Matapalo. The best accessible forest is around El Narango, which lies beyond the research station.

Border at Aguas Verdes (Ecuador)

The main Peruvian immigration and customs complex is outside Zarumilla, about 4 km before the international bridge. The frontier is open 24 hours a day and passports can be stamped on either side of the border at any time. There are virtually no customs formalities at the border for passengers crossing on foot, but spot-checks sometimes take place.

This border has a terrible reputation for scams: police officers on either side of the international bridge sometimes ask for bribes. Try to avoid them if possible but if approached be courteous but firm. Porters on either side of the border charge exorbitant prices; don't be bullied. Taxi drivers try to rip passengers off, or rob them. People offer to expedite formalities for US$20, without saying how they will help you. Money changers give out fake currency. And so on. Travelling on a through bus such as **Ormeño** or **CIFA** seems to involve less hassle, but it is much better to use the La Tina-Macará border crossing (see page 422).

Having obtained your exit stamp, proceed across the bridge into Huaquillas. Passports are stamped 3 km north of town along the road to Machala. There's no urban transport; inter-city buses charge US$0.20 from Huaquillas; taxis US$1.50. When driving into Peru vehicle fumigation is not required, but there is one outfit who will attempt to fumigate your vehicle with water and charge US$10. Beware of officials claiming that you need a carnet to obtain your 90-day transit permit. This is not so; cite Decreto Supremo 015-87-ICTI/TUR (but check that rules have not changed). There are frequent road tolls between Tumbes and Lima, approximately US$0.75 each.

Huaquillas is a small city with a reasonable selection of hotels and other services. Transport links to other parts of Ecuador (Machala – 80 km, one hour, Quito, Guayaquil, Cuenca, Loja) are good. Transit Police, Customs and the Military have checkpoints on the road north so keep your passport to hand.

Sleeping

Talara and around *p428*

All hotels have water-supply problems.

B **Gran Pacífico**, Av Aviación y Arica, Talara, T/F073-385450. The most luxurious in town, suites, hot water, pool, restaurant, bar, parking, pay in dollars.

E **Hostal Anymarke**, Av Túpac Amaru 709, Los Organos. In the town centre, slightly less well kept than Roland Kent.

E **Hostal La Perla**, Los Organos, southern end of the beach (mototaxi US$0.50, 5 mins), T073-257389, www.elaperla.com.pe. With pool and restaurant, clean and friendly, good value. Recommended.

E **Hostal Roland Kent**, Av Túpac Amaru 769, Los Organos, T/F073-857163, rolandkent peru@yahoo.com. Named after the owner and his favourite brand of cigarettes! Clean, friendly, TV, good value, best restaurant in town.

E Hostal Talara, Av del Ejército 217, Talara, T073-382186. Clean and comfortable.
E Residencial Grau, Av Grau 77, Talara, T073-382841, near the main plaza. Clean, friendly, possible to park one motor bike, owner changes dollars.

Máncora and around *p428*

All places to stay are to be found along the Panamericana between the main plaza at the north end of Máncora town and the bridge at the south end. The better hotels are at the southern end of Máncora. Prices can double in high season (Dec-Mar).
AL Las Arenas, 3.5 km south of Máncora, T073-258240, hotellasarenasdemancora@terra.com. Full board, 8 luxury bungalows, pool, lush gardens, trampoline, playground, kayaks, free transport from Tumbes airport.
C Puerto Palos, along the old Panamericana south of town (10 mins by moto-taxi, US$1.45), T073-258199, www.puerto palos.com. Excellent, small, nice pool over- looking the ocean, lots of activities available. Restaurant is good but expensive. Recommended.
C-D Las Olas on the beach in block 1 of Av Piura, Máncora, T073-258109. Smart, cabin-style rooms with bath, hammocks and gardens, half and full-board rates. **El Mar** in the same area has the same prices and facilties.
D Punta Ballenas, south of Cabo Blanco bridge at the south entrance to town, T073-258136. **C** in high season, lovely setting on beach, garden with small pool, price includes breakfast, expensive restaurant. Recommended.
E Hosal Casa Azul del Turista, Av Piura 224, Máncora, T073-258126. Clean, friendly, family-run, with bath and TV, and roof terraces giving sea views. Recommended (but not at week- ends or holiday times due to its proximity to the **Sol y Mar** disco.
E Sausalito, Piura block 4, Máncora, T073-258058. Comfortable, quieter rooms at back, some rooms without windows, breakfast included.
F Sol y Mar, Piura block 2, on beach, Máncora, T073-258106 (ask for Coqui Quiroga), hsolymar@hotmail.com. With bath, fan and mosquito repellent extra, basic, restaurant, shop, internet café (very slow connection), occasionally host parties, noisy disco till 0600 at weekends and holidays blights even its neighbours.
F-G Hospedaje Crillon, Paita 168, 1 block back from Panamericana in Máncora centre, T073-258001. Basic rooms with 4 or more beds, shared bath, plenty of water, recommended.

North of Máncora *p429*

A Punta Sal Club Hotel, north end of beach at Punta Sal Chica, access road at Km 1193, T072-540088, www.puntasal.com.pe. Price per person. 18 bungalows, 12 rooms, solar-heated water, relaxing, private beach, water-sports, pool, horse riding, deep-sea fishing, transport to Tumbes airport US$10 per person. Recommended. **B** without full board (**AL/A** in high season). With bathroom, all rooms have ocean view, comfortable, friendly, pool, excellent restaurant. Recommended.
B Caballito de Mar, Playa Punta Sal, 500 m along at the southern end of the bay, T072-540058, www.hotelcaballitodemar.com.
B Hotel Punta Camarón, at Km 1235, T072-247 2737, puntacamaron@terra.com.pe. With secluded private beach, swimming pool, restaurant. Recommended.
D Hospedaje El Bucanero, at the entrance to Playa Punta Sal, set back from the beach, T072-381125, www.elbucaneropunta sal.com. Price per person With a variety of rooms, pool, restaurant, bar, gardens and billiards, popular with travellers, great view.
D Hotel Playa Florida, at Km 1222, T/F072-968 8088, www.playa-florida.com. Pleasant bungalows on the ocean (look for the red roofs), food available.
D Los Delfines, near the beach at the entrance to Playa Punta Sal, T072-617804, angelicaborja@hotmail.com. Shared bathroom, clean, nice rooms, restaurant open in high season, meals on request in low season, vegetarian available, Canadian-run, very friendly, full board **AL** (more during high season); **A** for a room only in high season.
D per person **Sunset Punta Sal**, 500 m south along the beach, T072-807702, puntasunset@hotmail.com. **B** in high season, full board, wonderful place overlooking the sea, small, with pool, restaurant, popular with travellers.
E Huá, on the beach at the entrance to Playa Punta Sal, T072-540023, www.huapuntasal.com. **C** in the high season. A rustic old wooden building, rooms with bath, pleasant terrace overlooking ocean, discount for IYHF card holders, camping permitted on the beach beside the hotel, meals available.

E Las Terrazas, opposite Sunset Punta Sal, T072-964 0353, lasterrazaspuntasal@yahoo.com. Price per person. Basic and cheap, but friendly, restaurant has sea view, some rooms better than others, not all with own bath.
F Casa Grillo Centro Ecoturistico Naturista, Los Pinos 563, between Bocapán and Los Pinos, 30 km from Tumbes, T/F072-544222, casagrillo@hotmail.com. Price per person. To get there take a *colectivo* from Tumbes market to Los Pinos, or get off bus on Panamericana at Km 1236.5. Youth hostel with excellent restaurant including vegetarian meals, very friendly, great place to relax, 6 rustic-style rooms for up to 4 people, shared bath, hot water, laundry, also surfing, scuba diving, fishing, cycling, trekking, horse riding (US$4 per hr), camping available. Recommended.

Tumbes *p429, map p431*

The water supply is poor. There are many cheap hotels by the market. At holiday times it can be very difficult to find a vacant room.
B Costa del Sol, San Martín 275, Plazuela Bolognesi, T072-523991, ventastumbes@costadelsolperu.com. Clean, hot water, minibar, fan, front rooms noisy, restaurant has good food and service (US$5.75-7), parking extra, has nice garden with swimming pool, racquetball court, provides some tourist information.
E Chicho, Tumbes 327, T/F072-523696. With bathroom, fan, mosquito net, TV, clean, quieter rooms at the back.
E Florián, Piura 414 near El Dorado buses, T072-522464. Clean, private bath, fan.
E Lourdes, Mayor Bodero 118, T072-522966. With bathroom, fan, clean, friendly, roof restaurant, slow service. Recommended.
E Roma, Bolognesi 425 Plaza de Armas, T072-524137. With bathroom, fan, pleasant, convenient.
F Amazonas, Av Tumbes 317, T072-525266. With bathroom, fan, clean, friendly, water supply in the mornings is unreliable, noisy.
F El Estoril, Huáscar 317, 2 blocks from the main plaza, T072-521360. With bathroom, good, clean, friendly, discount for long stay.
F Elica, Tacna 319, T072-523870. With bathroom, clean, fan, quiet, good.
F Hostal Tumbes, Grau 614, T072-522203. With bathroom, cold water, fan, friendly, clean, good value. Recommended.
F Italia, Grau 733, T072-523396. Cold showers, friendly, also good value.
F Toloa 1, Av Tumbes 436, T072-523771. With bathroom, fan, clean, safe, helpful.
F Toloa 2, Bolívar 458, T072-524135. With bathroom, fan, OK.
G Sudamericano, San Martín 130, Paseo de la Concordia. Shared bathroom, basic but good value.

Around Tumbes *p430*

F Hospedaje Bayside, by the Malecón, Puerto Pizarro, T072-543045. Price per person. Bungalows with bath, pool, food available.
F Hostal Francis, Av República del Perú 220, Aguas Verdes, T072-561177. An OK option if you are stuck overnight in the border area.
F Imperio, plaza, Zarumilla, Km 1290 on the Panamericana, 5 km south of Aguas Verdes, There is a signpost on the highway and the main plaza is only a few blocks away from the turn-off, T072-565178. Small, modern, basic, very clean, very friendly. Cold water turned off at night, mosquito nets. Recommended.

Eating

Talara and around *p428*

The better restaurants are in the main hotels; cheaper restaurants are on the main plaza.

Several restaurants overlook the beach in Los Organos: **Bambú** is clean and prepares an excellent *ceviche* with fish freshly caught by the fishing boats bobbing in the bay.

Máncora and around *p428*

There are many small restaurants and surprisingly trendy bars lining the Panamericana. Among the good ones are La Espada and Don Pedro, on the highway, both offer excellent value lobster dishes.
ΨΨ Laguna Camp, 100 m from the sea near the new breakwater, T9401 5628, www.vivamancora.com/lagunacamp. Thatched roofs, hammocks, delicious food, breakfast, lunch and dinner, pizza and barbeque nights, has cabins sleeping up to 6 people, helpful. Recommended.
Ψ Stephanie's, café adjoining Sol y Mar overlooking beach. Serves *fuentes*, huge plates big enough for 2 people.
Ψ Café La Bajadita, Máncora. The best place in the evening to hang out, eat chocolate cake or *manjarblanco* and listen to rock and reggae.

North of Máncora *p429*
Good restaurants in Zorritos include **El Brujo**; **Sunset Beach**, Km 1245, T072-542243, good for seafood; **Zuco Zuco**, for pizza.

Tumbes *p429, map p431*
There are cheap restaurants on Plaza de Armas, Paseo de la Concordia and near the markets.
ΨΨ-Ψ Chifa Wakay, Huáscar 413. Smart Chinese, good, recommended.
ΨΨ-Ψ Classic, Tumbes 185. Popular and recommended for local food.
ΨΨ-Ψ Latino, Bolívar 163, on Plaza de Armas. Good set meals and à la carte, also *peña* most evenings.
ΨΨ-Ψ Los Gustitos, Bolívar 148. Excellent set menus and à la carte.
Ψ Pizzería Studio on the plaza. Good pizza and desserts.

Cafés
Heladería La Suprema, Paseo Libertadores 298. Good ice cream, sweets and cold drinks.
Sí Señor, Bolívar 119, on plaza. Good snacks.

Activities and tours

Tumbes *p429, map p431*
Most companies offer day tours of the local area for US$20 per person, minimum 2, and US$35-50 per person to the hinterland.
Preference Tours, Grau 427, T072-525518. Knowledgeable and friendly.
Rosillo Tours, Tumbes 293, T/F072-523892. Information, tickets, Western Union agents.

Transport

Talara and around *p428*
Air WayraPerú (Parque 23-7, T073-382011) flies from **Lima** via Trujillo 3 times a week.
Bus See under Sullana. To and from **Tumbes**, 171 km, 3 hrs, US$3.50, several daily. Most come from Piura and most stop at major towns going north. To **Piura**, 111 km, 2 hrs, US$1.75. To **El Alto** (Cabo Blanco), 32 km, 30 mins, US$0.75. To **Máncora** take a combi from beside the Tepsa terminal (Av Iw Merino F21, Pariñas) to Los Organos (an oil workers town on the Panamericana with a windy beach and good seafood restaurants on the plaza), US$1, 1 hr; change combis there and continue to Máncora, 28 km, 20 mins, US$0.50. **Los Organos to/from Piura**, Eppo 3 hrs, US$3.50, and **Dorado**, 2½ hrs, US$4. *Colectivos* leave when full for **Máncora**, 15 mins, US$0.40, and **Tumbes**, 2½ hrs, US$1.80. All transport leaves from the Panamericana in the town centre.

Máncora and around *p428*
To **Sullana and Piura** with **EPPO**, Grau 470, 1 block north of plaza, and **Dorado** both offer hourly service, just over 3 hrs, US$4, and just under 3 hrs, US$5, respectively. Other buses stop en route from Tumbes in the main plaza. To **Tumbes** (and points in between), combis tour the length of Av Piura all day as far as the bridge until full, US$1.50, 2 hrs.

North of Máncora *p429*
A taxi from Máncora is the quickest and easiest way to get to Punta Sal Grande, 20 mins, US$9. Mototaxis are also prepared to make the trip, 40 mins, US$6. Alternatively, take a combi from Máncora heading for Tumbes which can drop you at El Arco, 15 mins, US$0.50, as can buses from Tumbes or the south. A mototaxi to/from El Arco and the hotels costs US$1.50, up to 10 mins, or 30 mins' walk. However, if popping in to Máncora for anything while staying at Punta Sal, it is best not to use passing buses for the short journey as they can be held up at the Customs checkpoint; use combis instead.

Tumbes *p429, map p431*
Air Daily flights to **Lima** with **WayraPerú**, Av Tumbes Norte 270, T072-525020.

Bus Daily buses to and from **Lima**, 1320 km, 18-20hrs, US$12 (normal service), US$25 (**Cruz del Sur**), US$34 (**Cruz del Sur** VIP service). Most bus companies have offices on Av Tumbes. Cheaper buses usually leave 1600-2100, and more expensive ones 1200-1400. Except for luxury service, most buses to Lima stop at major cities en route. Tickets to anywhere between Tumbes and Lima sell quickly, so if arriving from Ecuador you may have to stay overnight. Piura is a good place for connections in the daytime. To **Talara**, 171 km, US$3.50, 3 hrs. To **Sullana**, 244 km, 3-4 hrs, US$4.50, several buses daily. To **Piura**, 4-5 hrs, 282 km, US$4.50; with **Trans Chiclayo, Cruz del Sur, El Dorado**, also to Máncora and Trujillo) 8 a day. **Comité**

Tumbles/Piura *colectivos* costs US$5.75, fast cars, leave when full, 3½ hrs. To **Chiclayo**, 552 km, 6 hrs, US$5.75, several each day with **Cruz del Sur**, **El Dorado**. To **Trujillo**, 769 km, 10-11 hrs, US$7.15-14.35, **Ormeño**, **Cruz del Sur**, **El Dorado** and **Emtrafesa**. To **Chimbote**, 889 km, 13-14 hrs, US$10. For transport to the border, see page 432.

Bus companies Civa, Av Tumbes 518, T072-525120. **Comité Tumbes/Piura** *colectivos*, Tumbes 308, T072-525977. **Cruz del Sur**, Tumbes Norte 319, T072-896163. **El Dorado**, Piura 459, T072-523480. **Emtrafesa**, Tumbes 596, T072-522894. **Ormeño**, Av Tumbes s/n, T072-522228. **Tepsa**, Av Tumbes 195-199, T072-522428. **Trans Chiclayo**, 466, T072-525260.

Around Tumbes *p430*

The best access to **Santuario Nacional los Manglares de Tumbes** is via the Panamericana north as far as Zarumilla. Combis leave every few mins from Tumbes, US$0.50, 30 mins. Then hire a motorbike in Zarumilla to go to CEDECOM (Centro de Conservación para el Desarrollo de los Manglares), 7 km, US$1.50 each way but you must arrange for the bike to return to collect you. Standard tour price is US$12 for a boat taking up to 6 passengers, 2½ hrs, and includes the mangrove walkway and a trip up several creeks, subject to tide levels. Book with **Pronaturaleza**, in Tumbes, who can also arrange a sanctuary visitors permit from Inrena. There is no entry fee.

For **Puerto Pizarro**, take *colectivo* No 6 from the small plaza on C Piura in Tumbes; US$0.50, 20 mins.

Access to **Parque Nacional Cerros de Amotape** is via the road which goes south-east from the Panamericana at Bocapán (Km 1233) to Casitas and Huásimo, it takes 2 hrs by car from Tumbes, and is best done in the dry season (Jul-Nov). Also access via Quebrada Fernández from Máncora and via Querecotilo and Los Encuentros from Sullana.

From **Tumbes to the border** *colectivos* leave from block 3 of Av Tumbes. US$1 per person or US$6 to hire a car, but overcharging of gringos is very common, especially from the border to Tumbes. Make sure the driver takes you all the way to the border and not just as far as the complex 4 km south of the bridge. Combis leave from the market area along Mcal Castilla across the C Alipio Rosales, US$0.50 (luggage on the roof). Run-down city buses ply the same route as combis, US$0.40, but are slower. All vehicles only leave when full, 30-45 mins to Aguas Verdes on the Peruvian side of the international bridge. They pass the turn-off for the airport from which it is a 500-m walk to the terminal. *Colectivos* to the airport charge US$1.50 per person, but often ask for much more. Mototaxi from the border to Zarumilla costs US$0.50 per person. *Colectivos* can cross the bridge, taxis cannot (so don't hire a Peruvian taxi to take you into Ecuador).

Directory

Máncora and around *p428*

Banks Tienda Marlón, Piura 613. Changes US$ cash at poor rates. **Internet** Several internet cafés on the highway. **Telephone** Piura 509, opposite the church.

Tumbes *p429, map p431*

Banks BCP, Paseo de los Libertadores 261, for cash only, poor rates. **Banco Continental**, Bolívar 121, changes cash and Amex TCs only, US$5 commission. **Cambios Internacionales**, Av Bolívar 161, Plaza de Armas. Cash only, good rates. Money changers on the street (on Bolívar, left of the cathedral), some of whom are unscrupulous, give a much better rate than the banks or *cambios*, but don't accept the first offer you are given. Street changers don't change cheques. All banks close for lunch. Rates offered at the airport are bad. If you are travelling on to Ecuador, it is better to change your soles at the border as the rate is higher. **Consulates** Ecuadorean Consulate, Bolívar 155, Plaza de Armas, T072-523022, Mon-Fri 0900-1300 and 1400-1630. **Internet** Widely available in many cheap cafés and major hotels. **Laundry** Lavandería Flash, Piura 1000. Pay by weight. **Post** San Martín 208, on Paseo de la Concordia. **Telephone** San Martín 210, on Paseo de la Concordia. **Useful adresses** Pronaturaleza, Av Tarapacá 4-16, Urb Fonavi, T072-523412. **Touring y Automóvil Club**, Huáscar 330, T072-523475, tumbes@touringperu.com.pe.

Around Tumbes *p430*

Banks Money can be changed on either side of the border. Ecuador uses the dollar as currency. Do not change money on the minibus in Aguas Verdes, very poor rates.

Northern Highlands

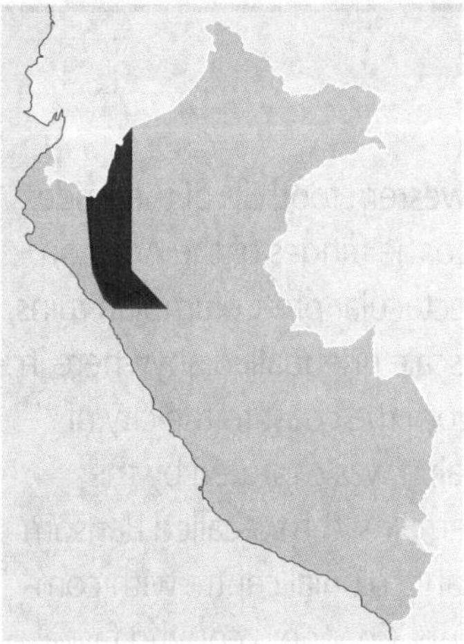

Footprint features

Introduction

This vast area stretches from the western foothills of the Andes across the mountains and down to the fringes of the Amazon jungle. It contains Peru's most spectacular pre-Columbian ruins, some of them built on a massive scale unequalled anywhere in the Americas. A good road rises from the coast to the city of Cajamarca, where the Inca Atahualpa was captured by the Spanish. Only one Inca building remains, the so-called Ransom Chamber, but the city has a pleasant colonial centre with comfortable hotels and good restaurants. Change is coming fast as a huge gold mine is bringing new investment, but also conflict, to the area. Close by are the hot springs where Atahualpa used to bathe, still very much in use today, and a number of pre-Inca sites. Beyond Cajamarca, a tortuous road winds its way east to the functional town of Chachapoyas. This is a friendly place, opening its doors to visitors as it lies at the centre of a region full of fantastic archaeological treasures whose mysteries are just being uncovered. There are fortresses, mysterious cities and strange burial sites replete with mummies and giant sarcophagi.

From Chachapoyas there are three options: carry on eastwards on one of Peru's most beautiful roads to the tropical lowland town of Tarapoto passing waterfalls and high moors before dropping down to the jungle zone; return to the coast at Chiclayo; or you can head north to Ecuador on a new route via Jaén and San Ignacio for the crossing to Zumba and Vilcabamba. With new roads and bridges in operation, a great adventure is opening up. It's now possible to travel from Ecuador, through Chachapoyas and Cajamarca on to the Cordillera Blanca, even to Cuzco, without touching the coast, and all by public transport. It may be a slow route, but it will take some beating. All these possibilities are getting easier as the area becomes the focus of tourism development to rival the Lima-Cuzco-Arequipa axis.

★ Don't miss...

1 **Marca Huamachuco** For an out-of-the-way archaeological experience, go to this ancient site, in its strategic location overlooking all the surrounding valleys, page 441.

2 **Los Baños del Inca** Fancy an invigorating swim? More like a quick dip, as the waters are so potent you are advised not to stay in for long, page 449.

3 **Heladería Holanda** If you are in need of refreshment, try one of the exotic fruit-flavoured ice creams on the plaza in Cajamarca, page 453.

4 **Kuélap** Hike up to the vast fortress of the Chachapoyans. Seeing it in sunshine gives the clearest view, but on a misty day the Cloud People's citadel is truly atmospheric, page 459.

5 **Tarapoto** From the high passes, follow the waters as they rush down towards the gateway to the jungle, page 477.

The coast to Cajamarca

Cajamarca can be reached from the coast, directly northeast from Trujillo on an improving road (see below), or via a much faster road, from the port of Pacasmayo, midway between Trujillo and Chiclayo. The paved 180-km road branches off the Pan-American Highway soon after it crosses the Río Jequetepeque at Madre de Dios. However, it still takes a couple of days by bus via Huamachuco and Cajabamba, as opposed to seven hours on the paved road from either Trujillo or Chiclayo. The old road is more interesting, passing through sierra towns and over the bare puna before dropping into the Huamachuco Valley, where the archaeological site of Marca Huamachuco is one of the main attractions.

▸▸ *For Sleeping, Eating and other listings, see pages 443-446.*

Chilete and Kuntur Wasi → *Colour map 1, C3.*

Some 103 km east of Pacasmayo is the mining town of **Chilete**. Some 21 km from Chilete, on the road north to San Pablo, are the pyramid and stone monoliths of **Kuntur Wasi**. If you are rushing along the paved road, do try to pause here, it is a very fine pre-Inca site. Devoted to a feline cult, it is undergoing new development under a Japanese archaeological team. It now has an excellent on-site museum, making a visit worthwhile. There are a couple of hotels at Chilete but rooms are hard to find on Tuesday because of the Wednesday market. Further along the road to Cajamarca is Yonán, where there are petroglyphs.

Trujillo to Huamachuco

The road is paved to **Otusco**, arguably the most accessible sierra town, in terms of proximity to the coast, anywhere in Peru. Being 1½ hours from Trujillo, it makes a pleasant half-day excursion. 'La Ciudad de la Fe', as it is known, is an attractive Andean town at 2200 m with some narrow cobbled streets. The modern church houses the important **Virgen de la Puerta**, which attracts devotees from all over Peru, especially during the big **festival** on 15 December. Adjoining it, in the old colonial church, is an amazing **museum** ⓘ *Mon and Wed-Sat 0830-1230, 1400-1800, Sun 0830-1700, US$0.30*, filled with public gifts for the Virgen, including endless cabinets displaying elaborately embroidered capes, cheap jewellery and even shoes.

From the Otusco turn-off, the road is being improved as far the mining towns of **Shorey** and **Quiruvilca**. The pollution in these mining towns is shocking. About 8 km east of Quiruvilca, Alto Chicama (the second largest opencast gold mine in Peru) is about to enter production. When this happens, there will be great changes in the Trujillo-Huamachuco area. In Shorey a road branches off to **Santiago de Chuco**, birthplace of the poet César Vallejo (see Literature, page 599), where there is the annual festival of Santiago El Mayor in the second half of July. The main procession is on 25 July, when the image is carried through the streets. Two hours beyond Santiago de Chuco is **Cachicadan**, where there are good hot baths. Theresa Siess (Germany) advises that "it is possible to walk, in five days, to Sihuas at the northern end of the Cordillera Blanca via the villages of Angasmarca, Mollepata, Pampa and Conchucos, staying in basic *hostales* in each village."

A spectacular but rough road, with a superb *balcón andino* (viewpoint, after the Pass) looking down in to the Alto Chicama valley, continues beyond Otusco to **Usquil** (two hours). It then descends steeply down to **Coina** at 1200 m (two hours). Crowded combis pass through from Trujillo, US$2.50. Hikes can be made through fields of barley and *limón* orchards around Coina and along the picturesque Chicama valley. Beyond Coina is **Chuquizongo** (one hour), famed for its fighting bulls, and **Huaranchal** (another hour), which has good thermal baths (US$0.50). There are a couple of combis each day from Coina.

Huamachuco → *Phone code: 044. Colour map 3, A2. Altitude: 3180 m.*

The main road runs on to this colonial town, which was formerly on the Royal Inca road coming from Cajabamba. The centre of the town follows the original Inca town plan. The plaza was once twice the size with an *usnu* (platform) in the centre. The old church of San José now sits on top of the *usnu*. The main reason for visiting Huamachuco is to see the spectacular, but little known ruins of **Marca Huamachuco**, which are located on the summit (3600 m) of one of the mountains northwest of town. The town also has the largest main plaza in Peru, with fine topiary, and a controversial modern **cathedral**, likened by some to an aeroplane hangar, sitting on top of the remains of an Inca palace. There is a colourful **Sunday market** and **Museo Municipal Wamachuko** ⓘ *Sucre 195, Mon-Sat 0900-1300, 1500-1900, Sun 0900-1200, free*, displays artefacts found at Cerro Amaru and Marca Huamachuco, plus aerial photos of the latter.

Marca Huamachuco

ⓘ *No entry fee. A minimum of 2 hrs is needed, 4 hrs to really explore. Carry all food and drink with you. Access is along a poor vehicle road, off the road to Sanagorán. There is an archway at the turn-off, about 5 km from Huamachuco. In dry weather, 4WDs can make it to the top. It is much faster to walk on the mule trail that starts just after the archway. A mototaxi to the turn-off costs US$2. There are also combis to Sanagorán in the morning.*

The Marca Huamachuco ruins surely rank in the top 10 archaeological sites in Peru. It is an extensive site, 3 km long, dating back to at least 300 BC though many structures were added later. Its most impressive features are: **El Castillo**, a remarkable circular structure with walls up to 8 m high located at the highest point of the site. This and other structures are the oldest-known buildings in Peru to extend to more than two storeys and may have reached five storeys. The outer defensive wall, which is accessible where it bisects the hill halfway along, also reaches up to 8 m in height. It consists of two parallel walls with gallery rooms in between. **El Convento** complex consists of five circular structures of varying sizes located towards the northern end of the hill. These are later constructions dating back to AD 600-800. The largest one has been partially reconstructed by the INC and provides an interesting insight into how they must once have appeared, with two or three parallel outer walls, gallery rooms between them and several other internal structures. It has been suggested that these buildings housed the privileged members of an elite class. (The guardian should be tipped, US$1.)

Some 3 km before the ruins you will pass the remarkable **Cerro Amaru** on the left. It would seem that the whole of this relatively small hilltop was adapted to store water by placing an impermeable layer of clay around it. Wells (**Los Chiles**) on the summit, which can still be viewed, then provided access to the water within. Almost certainly the hill acquired major religious and cultural significance within the Huari-Tiahuanaco empire and became a place of pilgrimage and sacrifice in times of drought.

It seems likely that Marca Huamachuco existed for many centuries as the centre of an autonomous religious cult, separate from the activities of the Chachapoyans to the north and east. The site was certainly used as much as a ceremonial centre as it was for defensive purposes. Latest theories suggest that the Huari-Tiahuanaco culture (AD 600-1100) may have developed from the north out of places such as Marca Huamachuco and Yaino and then spread south, rather than the other way round. Apparently, the chronology of sites fits much better on this basis, but, if correct, this would require a complete reassessment of the Huari-Tiahuanuco culture.

Around Huamachuco

Wiracochapampa is an extensive Huari site, 3 km away, a 45-minute walk, to the north of the town. Much of the site is overgrown and poorly conserved, but walls up to 3 m high can still be found. It is believed that the complex was never completed, possibly because the principal builder was taken south to construct Piquillacta, near Cuzco, with which it has many similarities.

Also worth seeing is **Laguna Sausacocha** (3150 m), a beautiful spot surrounded by low hills, along the road to Cajabamba. Here are **Hospedaje Piscis** and several simple *comedores* (try *ceviche de trucha*). It is possible to go rowing on the lake.

The **Yanasara thermal baths** are a 30-minute walk from the village of El Pallar set in a beautiful valley at 2300 m. The hot, clean baths consist of a pool and four individual baths, all US$0.30 per person. Thermal baths can also be found at **El Edén** ⓘ *free, 1½ hrs south of Huamachuco, take a combi for Sarin, US$1.50*. An open-air complex of four pools, you can sit beneath a mini-waterfall in one of them, and a warm river set among rock cliffs. Take food and drink.

Cushuro (4000 m), 3 km south of Huamachuco, is a vicuña-breeding centre with a good stretch of the Royal Inca highway passing nearby.

A pleasant two-hour walk can be made up the Río Grande valley to the hacienda of **Cochabamba**, once the Andean retreat of the owners of the Laredo sugar plantation.

South from Huamachuco → *Colour map 3, A2.*

It is now possible to travel, via Retamas and Tayabamba (see below), to Sihuas and the Cordillera Blanca along a road which is very poor in places and involves crossing the Río Marañón twice. The building of a new bridge over the river means that it is feasible to go from Cuzco to Quito entirely by public transport without going down to the Pacific coast, though few travellers have made this journey. The route from Cajamarca to Huaraz via Huamachuco and the upper Marañón Valley is considerably longer, more difficult and more expensive than going via Trujillo and Chimbote on the coast. The rewards, however, are incomparable views and a glimpse of everyday life in some of the country's most tranquil highland villages as well as its grimiest mining camps. For those with plenty of time, the route provides access to the wilds of Río Abiseo National Park. Along the way, vertiginous roads repeatedly traverse altitudes ranging from 4200 m to 1450 m, with vast changes in temperatures between the *puna* and Marañón valley, and vertical drops of 1000 m from hair-pin bends. The road may be impassable in the wet season.

From Huamachuco, follow the main road to Cajabamba as far as Sausacocha, where a turn-off goes down to Yanasara (see above). The Río Grande is then crossed before climbing to Chugay (3400 m, Hospedaje Pérez and basic *comedores*) and on to a pass at 3900 m. From here the road plummets 2450 m to **Chahual** (1450 m), a small hot settlement where a bridge spans the Río Marañón. The hillsides are covered in cactuses, mango and avocado trees.

At Chahual, right after the bridge, the road forks: left to Pataz, and right to climb 1000 m to the **Balcón del Diablo**, overlooking **Laguna Pías**. The town of Pías, down by the lake and reached via a turn-off from the main road, has an office for **Parque Nacional Río Abiseo** and a landing strip (for charter flights to Lima for mining companies; spare seats may be available). **Pataz** is a small gold-mining town, about 100 km from Huamachuco. From here you can reach the World Heritage site of **Pajatén**, with its circular pre-Inca ruins (it requires a 10-day trip with mules from Los Alisos, near Pataz). The ruins lie within the Río Abiseo National Park, and both INRENA and INC permits are needed to visit. These are issued to archaeologists, researchers and 'adventure' tourists, though day passes to enter the park can also be obtained (check with both institutes). Pataz is one hour by road from Chahual. Your best chance of finding a *camioneta* going up is early in the morning.

The road continues to **Retamas** (2700 m), a rough-and-tumble mining town. To avoid sleeping in Retamas, take a shared taxi to **Llacuabamba** (15 minutes, US$0.60), which is more tranquil. You must return to Retamas for onward transport. Near Retamas is **Parcoy**, the original settlement in the area with a colonial church. After Retamasare more hectic and scarred mining communities, Marsa and Buldibuyo, bordering the Río Abiseo National Park. The road then drops down to **Tayabamba** (3300 m). This small, chilly Andean town is surrounded by scenic countryside. It has a large church and a rotating bronze angel in the neat plaza. The interesting annual fiesta is held in honour of **Santo Toribio**, 24-31 April.

North from Huamachuco

From Huamachuco the gravel road runs on 55 km past Laguna Sausacocha through some small highland villages, where roof tiles are baked in round ovens, to **Cajabamba,** which sits on a balcony overlooking the sugar-producing Condebamba valley. The climate is mild for its altitude because of influence from this large warm valley. Founded in 1572, this is an especially friendly town with an attractive Plaza de Armas. The annual festival is **Virgen del Rosario,** starting the first weekend of October and featuring the *Danza de los Diablos*. The surrounding countryside offers good walking amid lakes, waterfalls and Inca road remnants, well worth taking a few days to explore. An excellent source of information is **Sr Miguel Rodríguez** ⓘ *Bolgnesi 849 Yachayhuasi, T044-851329, ccyachayhusic@hotmail.com*. He has a small private museum (donations appreciated), sells local crafts and can arrange for guides to nearby attractions.

The road continues from Cajabamba, much of it newly asphalted, through **San Marcos** (2400 m) to Cajamarca. There is a short section of asphalt road to the south of San Marcos, which is important for its Sunday cattle market. Both it and Cajabamba are on the Inca road. From San Marcos to Cajamarca (124 km) the road is paved and excellent (three hours by bus, US$2.50).

Sleeping

Chilete and Kuntur Wasi *p440*

F-G Hospedaje Caribe, Miraflores 241, Chilete, T076-554103.

F-G Hospedaje Miraflores, Miraflores 232, Chilete, T076-554057.

Trujillo to Huamachuco *p440*

All hotels are full in mid-Dec.

F Hostal Silita Star, in Cachicadan. Attractive and rustic with hot water, TV and restaurant. Recommended.

F Hostería El Sol, 500 m above the town (before you enter arriving from Otusco), Coina, T044-231933, www.coina-andes-hostel.info (website due in 2007). Meals are prepared in the adjoining hospital canteen. Bungalows set among pines and palms, pool. Camping possible. Being renovated in 2007. The original owner of the *hostal* – Dr Kaufmann – also founded the hospital.

F Los Portales, Santa Rosa 680, Otusco. Hot water, with bath, TV, clean, good value.

G Hospedaje San José, Tacna 672, Otusco, T044-323550. With hot water and TV.

G Hostal Coina, Av 28 de Julio s/n, Coina. Basic but clean and friendly.

Huamachuco *p441*

C-E Real, Bolívar 250, T044-441402, www.hotelrealperu.com. New, clean, with bath, TV, sauna, internet, many of the fittings are of wood. Recommended.

D-F Hostal Santa Fe, San Martín 297, T044-441019, hs_turistico_santafe@hotmail.com. New, clean, TV, hot water. Recommended.

E Hospedaje Colonial Plaza, Castilla 208, on the plaza, T044-441760. An old colonial house with beautiful patios, some of the rooms retain original furniture, hot water, laundry facilities. Can arrange horse-riding.

E Hostal Gran Colonial, Castilla 537, T044-511101, grancolonialhostal@hotmail.com. An attractive old colonial house, with bath, hot water, TV. Its restaurant is clean and good value. Recommended.

F Hostal Noche Buena, San Román 401 on the main plaza, T044-441435. Clean with hot showers, TV, laundry, overlooking the plaza.

F Huamachuco, Castilla 354, on the plaza, T044-441393. Clean, with hot showers (**G** without), friendly, good value, has parking.

Around Huamachuco *p441*

F Hotel Yanasara, Yanasara, T044-441245. A large new hotel set among meadows and a 5-min walk from the thermal baths, with restaurant and a pool, booking may be required in peak periods. Camping is also permitted within the grounds.

South from Huamachuco *p442*

F Hostal Morillo, Llacuabamba. With private bath, hot water, parking, basic, some short stay couples, but OK for where it is.

F Hostal Caballero, Bolognesi 649, Tayabamba, T044-330024. With private bath, hot water, basic but OK, suffers from water shortages.

F Hostal Gemiles, Bolognesi 656, Tayabamba. New, clean, with private bath, hot water all day. Recommended.

G Hostal El Triunfo, Salaverry 227, Tayabamba. Near bus agencies. With private bath and electric shower, cheaper without, small rooms, basic and friendly, suffers from water shortages.

G Hostal El Triunfo, Salaverry 227, Tayabamba. Near bus agencies. With private bath and electric shower, cheaper without, small rooms, basic and friendly, suffers from water shortages.

G Hostal Imperial Class, Retamas. Shared bath, basic, caters to short-stay couples.

G Hostal Oasis, Chahual. Clean and friendly and has a restaurant. There are a couple of simple *comedores* by the bridge.

G Hostal Paraíso, Huancaspata. Possibly best in town, but rustic, rooms around a courtyard, shared bath, hot water.

G Hostal Roldán, Huancaspata. Also rustic with rooms around a courtyard, cold water and shared bath.

North from Huamachuco *p443*

F Hostal La Casona, Jr Alfonso Ugarte 586, Plaza de Armas, Cajabamba, T076-848385. Small rooms, electric shower, clean and friendly, with restaurant.

F Jhoel, Jr Grau 633, Cajabamba, T076-551653. Private bath with electric shower, patio, clean and pleasant, good value.

G Hostal Flores, Leoncio Prado 137, on the Plaza de Armas, Cajabamba, T076-551086. With electric shower, cheaper without bath, friendly and clean but rooms are gloomy, nice patio; no breakfast.

E Sol Naciente, Jr Inclán 485, 1 block from Plaza de Armas, San Marcos, T076-558191. With bath and hot water, cheaper without.

Eating

Trujillo to Huamachuco *p440*

Milagros, Tacna 790, Otusco. Good for *cuy*.

Sagitario, Tacna 769, Otusco. The best place in town for the delicious local speciality of *jamón con yuca*.

Huamachuco *p441*

El Túnel, on the Trujillo road at the entrance to town. With tables outside, good for typical dishes and a game of 'sapo'.

La Casona, Sánchez Carrión 294. Daily 0700-0900, 1200-1430, 1900-2030. Serves good-value and quality set meals and local dishes, popular.

Salud y Vida, L Prado 1082. Offers simple vegetarian meals.

Café Doña Emilia, Sánchez Carrión esq San Ramón, on Plaza de Armas. For pastries and coffee.

South of Huamachuco

La Huanuqueña, Llacuabamba. Serves an adequate *menú*.

Juan Baptista, Bolognesi 461, Tayabamba. The only proper restaurant in town but has a limited menu. Closes at 2100, like most places in town. There's also an unnamed *comedor* at Bolognesi y Sucre. Good home cooking.

Cosas Dulces, next to church on the Plaza de Armas, Tayabamba. For sweets and hot drinks.

Restaurant Kananga, in Huancaspata. Apparently named after a Japanese cartoon character, this is the best place to eat and it serves an excellent *caldo*.

North from Huamachuco *p443*

Cafetería La Otuscana, Grau 929, Cajabamba. Good bakery, sweets and sandwiches, daily 0730-2200.

Don Lucho, Jr Leoncio Prado 227, Cajabamba. Good local trout and other à la carte dishes.

Fuente de soda Grau, Grau 832, Cajabamba. Serving big fresh fruit salads and cakes.

La Casona, in hotel of same name in Cajabamba. *Menú* and à la carte, opens early, good meals.

Quengococha, Bolognesi 790, Cajabamba. Tasty local dishes served in earthenware pots.

Bars and clubs

Huamachuco *p441*

Bar Michi Wasi, San Román 461, on the plaza. An attractive, atmospheric bar and a good place to meet locals who know the area. Recommended.

Café La Nonna, Balta 569. Evenings only for snacks; the atmospheric rear room has sofas and candles.

Festivals and events

Huamachuco *p441*
2nd Sun in Aug Waman Raymi, a major festival held in the ruins of Wiracochapampa (see page 441), a northern version of Inti Raymi in Cuzco.
10 Aug Los Wamachucos, another colourful festival, is held in the neighbourhood above the centre.
15 Aug Beginning of a week of festivities to mark the **founding of Huamacucho** which features spectacular fireworks and the remarkable Turcos – aggressive male dancers from a nearby village who wear at least 10 layered skirts when dancing. Huamachuco (founded in 1553) has made an effort to rescue its pre-Hispanic and pre-Inca traditions. Celebrations include many native themes and dances.

Transport

Trujillo to Huamachuco *p440*
Bus
To **Otusco** from Trujillo, **Emp Pacífico**, Prolongación Unión 1888, buses leave when full, 2 hrs, US$1.50. Car combis leave from opposite the **Pacífico** terminal when full, 1½ hrs, US$2.50. From Otusco to **Trujillo**, *colectivos* leave when full from the south side of town. To **Coina** from Trujillo with **Turismo Express**, Unión 1888, or **Coina Express**, Unión 1557, 6 hrs, US$4. Buses to **Santiago de Chuco from Trujillo**, Horna, N de Piérola 1279, T044-294880, 2100, 6 hrs, US$4.55, only at night; they continue to **Cachicadan**.Combis depart frequently, when full, from **Santiago de Chuco to Cachicadan**, US$1.50, 1½ hrs.

Huamachuco *p441*
Air
Charter flights only.

Bus
To **Trujillo**, 170 km, improved road, 6 hrs: **Tunesa (Turismo Negreiros)**; Balta y Suárez, 0900 and 1300. Recommended. **Trans Horna**, San Martín 875, T044-441070, 4 a day including bus *cama* service. Recommended. Also **Mercedes**, Av 10 de Julio 766, T044-441582. To **Cajabamba**, **Trans Los Andes**, Pasaje Hospital 109, have combis at 0430, 1230, 1600, 3 hrs, US$2.50. **Horna** also has daily departues at 1600 and 2000, 3 hrs, US$1.90. To **Retamas**, **Trans Garrincha**, Garcilazo de la Vega s/n esquina Román, T044-441594, Sun, Wed, Fri at 0600, 12 hrs, US$7.50. The bus passes through from Trujillo but seats may sometimes be booked in Huamachuco. Enquire in advance. Combis leave from near the hospital daily 0200-0600, depending on demand, 10 hrs, US$10. They are less comfortable than the bus but faster, and have an easier time negotiating the narrow winding road.

Around Huamachuco *p441*
To **Laguna Sausacocha**, combis take 30 mins, US$0.60. Combis and shared taxis go directly from Huamachuco to **Yanasara** (1½ hrs, US$1.20), from which the baths are a 15-min walk.

South from Huamachuco *p442*
Air
For **Chahual**, there is a small airport 5 km down the valley. **Air Líder** has flights to **Lima**, Mon-Sat, US$90, 1 hr.

Bus Buses also arrive in **Chahual** after 8 hrs from Huamachuco, US$7.

From **Retamas**, **Garrincha** travel to **Huamachuco** Mon 0800, Thu 2000, Sat 0400, 12 hrs, US$7.50, continuing to **Trujillo** 19 hrs, US$13.50. To Retamas from **Trujillo**, Garrincha (Prolongación Vallejo 1250, T044-441594), Tue and Sat 2100, 22 hrs, US$18. You can also take combis to **Huamachuco** starting 1800 daily, 10 hrs, US$10. Combis and shared taxis to **Tayabamba**, 6 a day 0500-1700, 3 hrs, US$4.50; Tayabamba-Retamas 6 a day 0700-1630.

Most transport in **Tayabamba** leaves from Salaverry corner Cahuide (behind the church), where their agencies are located, except as noted below. To **Sihuas** for the Cordillera Blanca: **La Perla de Alto Mayo**, Grau y Sucre, Mon, Wed, Sat at 1930; **Andía**, Mon, Wed, Sat at 1900; **Garrincha**, Mon and Thu at 0800; **San Antonio de Padua**, Fri at 1900; all 7-8 hrs, US$6. Most buses continue to **Chimbote** (17 hrs, US$13.50) and some to **Trujillo** (20 hrs, US$15) or **Lima** (24 hrs, US$16.50).

North from Huamachuco *p443*
From **Cajabamba** to **Huamachuco**: Trans Los Andes, Grau 1170, buses leave from police station below the market, 3 a day, 3 hrs, US$2.50; **Horna**, Av L Martínez 405, at 0430 and 0900, 3 hrs, US$1.90. From **Cajabamba** to **Cajamarca**, combis 3 hrs, US$3.50. Bus companies include **Rojas** and **Perú Bus**, several daily, 4 hrs, US$3. Some continue to **Trujillo**, 10 hrs, US$7.50, and to **Lima**, 18 hrs, US$13.70.

Directory

Huamachuco *p441*
Banks Caja Norperuano, Sánchez Carrión on Plaza de Armas, has good rates; cash only. Obtain soles elsewhere if relying on ATMs or TCs. **Casas de cambio** on Sánchez Carrión, block 7, offer poor rates. **Internet** All over town. Best places are in Castilla, block 3, in the plaza. **Post Office** Grau 454, Mon-Fri 0830-1230, 1400-1700.

Cajamarca and around

Cajamarca is a beautiful colonial town and the most important in the northern highlands. It sits at the edge of a green valley which is ideal for dairy farming. Around the Plaza de Armas are many fine old houses, which are being converted into tasteful hotels, restaurants and galleries to cater for engineers and incomers from the adjacent Yanacocha mining project. The airport has been expanded to cater for the mining personnel, but tourism has yet to catch on to this facility. The mine, now that it is fully operational and looking to expand, has provoked opposition from farmers and created worries over pollution, intruding on the provincial calm of a city once closely tied to its pastoral surroundings. It remains, though, a great place to buy handicrafts, but lest you forget where the money now lies, you can find soapstone carvings of miners with power drills alongside more traditional figures. Outside town are several good haciendas which offer bed, board and rural pursuits, while at the Baños del Inca, just up the road, you can unwind as the steam from the thermal waters meets the cool mountain air. ▸▸ *For Sleeping, Eating and other listings, see pages 451-455.*

Ins and outs

Getting there The airport is 3 km northeast of town (take the Cerillo road); taxi US$1.50, mototaxi US$0.75. The bus offices are to the southeast of the centre, on the Baños del Inca road past La Recoleta church; a 20-minute walk from the Plaza de Armas.

Getting around All the main sights are clustered around the Plaza de Armas. With its many old colonial buildings it is an interesting town to wander around although the climb up Santa Apolonia hill is quite demanding. The district around Plaza Francia (Amazonas y José Gálvez), the market area and east of Amazonas are not safe at night (prostitution and drugs). Buses in town charge US$0.15. Taxis US$0.60 within city limits. Mototaxis US$0.30. Combis run to the main places outside town, like Baños del Inca. Others, like Cumbemayo, are best reached on a tour, while still others make good day walks.

Best time to visit Cajamarca has a pleasant climate the year round, with warm days and chilly nights. The wettest months are December to March. Depending on your point of view, Carnival (February or March) is the time to be there, or the time to avoid – it is a riotous, messy affair. Hotels are also booked up at this time. More sedate festivals are Holy Week, especially Palm Sunday at nearby Porcón, and Corpus Christi in May. During October and November there are numerous school trips to this area, so most of the budget hotels are full at this time.

Tourist information **Dirección Regional de Turismo** and **Instituto Nacional de Cultura** ⓘ *Belén 631, T076-362997, cajamarca@ mincetur.gob.pe, Mon-Fri 0730-1300, 1430-1800; www.inccajamarca.org*. **University tourist school's office** ⓘ *Del Batán 289, T076-361546, Mon-Fri 0830-1300, 1500-2200*, voluntary donation requested.

Background

Before Cajamarca became an Inca religious centre and favoured haunt of the nobility in 1456, it had been at the heart of a culture known as Caxamarca, which flourished from AD 500 to 1000. The violent events of 1532-1533 are today belied by the city's provincial calm. It was named provincial capital in 1855 and Patrimonio Histórico y Cultural de las Américas by the Organization of American States in 1986. It is now seeking UNESCO World Heritage status. In addition to its historical associations, Cajamarca is best known for its dairy industry, textiles and intricately worked mirrors (see Shopping, page 454). Change is coming, though, in the form of the Circuito Turístico Nororiental, which is opening up the Chiclayo-Cajamarca-Chachapoyas tourist route, and in the effect on the town from the Yanacocha gold mine. This has brought many foreign mining engineers and economic benefits, but also serious debates and protests over ecological impact, compensation to *campesinos* and threats to the city's drinking water supply. Only groups are allowed to visit the mine, which has a **public relations office** ⓘ *Av Evitamiento 540/563, T076-584000 anexo 23735, www.yanacocha.com.pe.*

Cajamarca

» *pp451-455. Colour map 1, C3.*

→ *Phone code: 076. Population: 117,500. Altitude: 2750 m.*

Plaza de Armas

The main Plaza de Armas, where Atahualpa was executed, has a 350-year-old fountain, topiary and gardens. It was remodelled in 2006. The impressive **cathedral**, opened in 1776, is still missing its belfry, but the façade has beautiful baroque carving in stone. The altar is covered in original gold leaf.

On the opposite side of the plaza is the 17th-century **San Francisco Church**, older than the cathedral and with more interior stone carving and elaborate altars. A side chapel has an ornate ceiling. **Museo de Arte Colonial** ⓘ *Mon-Sat 1430-1800. US$0.85, entrance is unmarked on far left corner of church.* Tickets are sold from an unmarked office on the right of courtyard as you walk towards the church. Attached to San Francisco, the museum is filled with colonial paintings and icons. The guided tour of the museum includes entry to the church's spooky catacombs.

Complejo Belén

ⓘ *Mon-Sat 0900-1300, 1500-1730, Sat-Sun 0900-1230, US$1.20, valid for more than one day. A ticket is also valid for the Cuarto de Rescate. A guide in Spanish for all the sites costs US$2.85 (US$5.75-8.50 for guides in other languages).*

This group of buildings comprises the **tourist office** and **Institute of Culture**, a beautifully ornate church, considered the city's finest, and two museums. The arches, pillars and walls of the nave of Belén church are covered in lozenges (*rombos*), a design picked out in the gold tracery of the altar. See the inside of the dome, where eight giant cherubs support an intricate flowering centrepiece. The carved pulpit has a spiral staircase and the doors are intricately worked in wood. In the same courtyard is the **Museo Médico Belén**, which has a collection of medical instruments. Across the street is a maternity hospital from the colonial era, now the **Archaeological and Ethnological Museum** ⓘ *Junín y Belén*. It has a wide range of ceramics from all regions and civilizations of Peru.

Many belfries were left half-finished in protest against a Spanish tax levied on the completion of a church.

Cuarto de Rescate

ⓘ *Entrance is at Amalia Puga 750, Mon-Sat 0900-1250, 1500-1750, Sun 0900-1250.* The Cuarto de Rescate shown to tourists is not the actual ransom chamber but in fact the room where Atahualpa was held prisoner. A red line on the wall is said to indicate where Atahualpa reached up and drew a mark, agreeing to have his subjects fill the room to the line with gold treasures. The chamber is roped off and can only be viewed from the outside. Pollution and weather have had a detrimental effect on the stone.

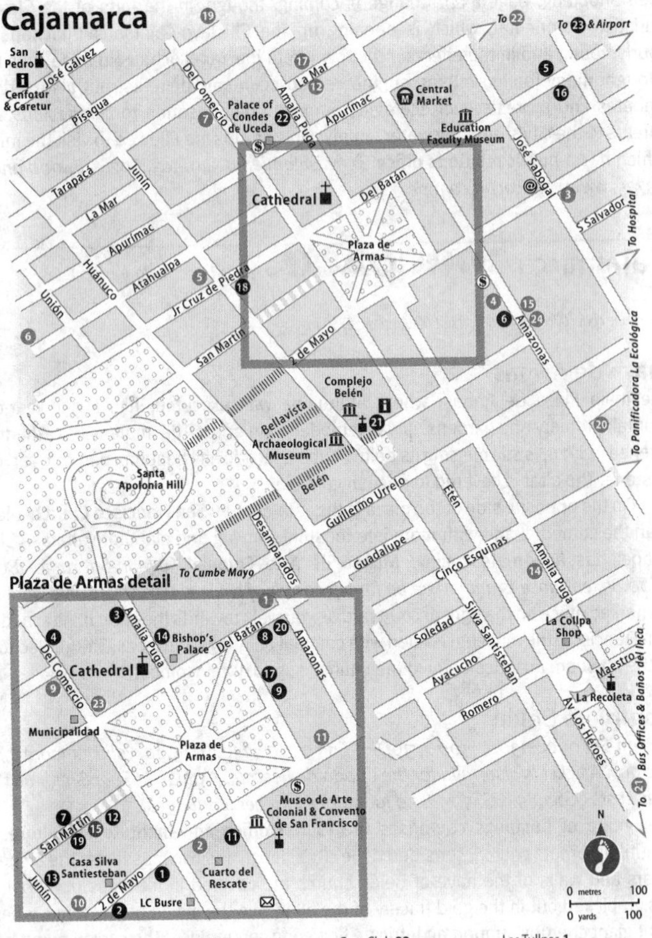

Sleeping
Casa Blanca 2
Casa Pensión 3
Clarín 20
Colonial Inn 21
Continental 4
Costa del Sol 23
El Cabildo 5
El Cumbe Inn 6
El Ingenio 22
Gran Continental 24
Hospedaje Los Jasmines 15
Hostal Atahualpa 9
Hostal Becerra 1
Hostal Cajamarca 10
Hostal Dos de Mayo 11
Hostal El Portal del Marqués 7
Hostal Los Pinos 17
Hostal Portada del Sol 19
La Hispana 12
Los Balcones de la Recoleta 14

Eating
Akaesh 2
Casa Club 22
Cascanuez Café Bar 3
Christian 4
Donde Octavio 20
Don Paco 11
El Batán Gran Bufet de Arte 5
El Cajamarqués 6
El Capulí 21
El Pez Loco 7
El Zarco 8
El Zarco Campestre 23
Heladería Holanda 9
Las Tullpas 1
Om-Gri 12
Pizzería El Marengo 13
Pizzería Vaca Loca 19
Querubino 14
Rosana D'Avila 16
Salas 17
Sanguchón.com 18

Bars & clubs
Rodeo Video 15

Other sights

Also worth seeing are **La Recoleta Church** ⓘ *Maestro y Av Los Héroes*, and **San Pedro** ⓘ *Gálvez y Junín*. The city has many old colonial houses with garden patios, and 104 elaborately carved doorways: see the **Bishop's Palace** across the street from the cathedral; the **Palace of the Condes de Uceda** ⓘ *Jr Apurímac 719*, now occupied by BCP bank; and the **Casa Silva Santiesteban** ⓘ *Junín y 2 de Mayo*.

Museo Arqueológico Horacio H Urteaga ⓘ *Del Batán 289, Mon-Fri 0700-1445, free, donations accepted*, of the Universidad Nacional de Cajamarca, has objects of the pre-Inca Cajamarca and other cultures. The university maintains an experimental arboretum and agricultural station, the **Museo Silvo-agropecuario** ⓘ *Km 2.5 on the road to Baños del Inca*, with a lovely mural at the entrance.

You can also visit the plaza where Atahualpa was ambushed and the stone altar set high on **Santa Apolonia hill** ⓘ *US$0.60*. To get there, take bus marked Santa Apolonia/Fonavi, or micro 'A' or combis on Sabogal or Tarapacá. Here the Inca is said to have reviewed his subjects. There is a road to the top or, if you are fit, you can walk up from Calle 2 de Mayo, using the stairway. The view from the top, over red-tiled roofs and green fields, is worth the effort, especially very early in the morning for the beautiful sunrises.

Around Cajamarca

»pp 451-455. Colour map 1, C3.

Los Baños del Inca

ⓘ *0500-1945, entry US$0.60, T076-348385, www.inkatermas.com.pe. The main baths are divided into 5 categories; prices range from US$1 to US$1.50, all with private tubs and no pool. Sauna US$3, massage US$6-9 (take your own towel; soaps are sold outside). Only spend 20 mins maximum in the water; obey instructions; many of the facilities allow bathers in shifts, divided by time and/or sex. Combis marked Baños del Inca cost US$0.20, microbuses US$0.15, 15 mins, ask driver where to get off. Transport returns to Cajamarca from the plaza, in front of Hostal José Gálvez. Taxis US$1.80 minimum.*

Six kilometres southeast are the sulphurous thermal springs known as Los Baños del Inca, where there are baths whose water temperature is 78°C. They have several medicinal benefits, including dermatological, gastric and anti-stress. Atahualpa tried the effect of these waters on a festering war wound and his bath is still there. The best time to bathe is first thing in the morning. The complex is regularly renewed, with gardens, recreational centres and two types of accommodation, detailed in Sleeping below. The Piscina Municipal (US$0.60, operates in shifts of 1¾ hours with 15 minutes celaning between each) is a large pool with tepid water, best for swimming laps. The construction of luxury homes for upper echelon mining personnel has given Baños del Inca an increasingly suburban feel, complete with commuter traffic.

Cumbe Mayo

ⓘ *A guided tour costs US$7.55 per person and runs from 0930-1430, and a taxi US$15 (no buses). It may be possible to go with the milk truck leaving at 0400 from C Revilla 170; ask Sr Segundo Malca, Jr Pisagua 482. There's a small charge, dress warmly. To walk up takes 3-4 hrs (take a guide or tour, best time May-Sep). See below for details.*

Cumbe Mayo (3600 m), a pampa on a mountain range, is 20 km southwest of Cajamarca. It is famous for its extraordinary, well-engineered pre-Inca channels, running for 9 km across the mountain tops. It is said to be the oldest man-made construction in South America. The sheer scale of the scene is impressive and the huge rock formations of **Los Frailones** ('big monks') and others with fanciful names are strange indeed. It is worth taking a guided tour since the area has a lot of petroglyphs, altars and sacrificial stones from pre-Inca cultures. On the way to Cumbe Mayo is the **Layzón ceremonial centre** from 500-200 BC (7 km).

The trail to the site starts from the hill of Santa Apolonia (Silla del Inca), and goes to Cumbe Mayo, straight through the village and up the hill. At the top of the mountain, leave the trail and take the road to the right to the canal. The walk is not difficult and you do not need hiking boots. Take a good torch/flashlight. The locals use the trail to bring their goods to market.

Other sights near Cajamarca

Llacanora is a typical Andean village in beautiful scenery (13 km southeast). Nearby is **La Collpa**, a hacienda which is now a cooperative farm of the Ministry of Agriculture which breeds bulls and has a lake and gardens. The cows are handmilked at 1400, not a particularly inspiring spectacle in itself, but the difference here is that the cows are called by name and respond accordingly.

Ventanillas de Otusco ⓘ *0800-1800, US$1*, part of an old pre-Inca cemetery, has a gallery of secondary burial niches. A one-day round trip can be made: take a bus from Del Batán to Ventanillas de Otusco (30 minutes) or a *colectivo* leaving hourly from Revilla 170, US$0.15, then walk to Baños del Inca (1½ hours, 6 km). You can either follow the east shore of the Río Chonta, or take a higher route with better views through the village of Puylucana. Ask for directions often and take a stick to fend off dogs. From Baños del Inca walk to Llacanora (one hour, 7 km), passing the caves and rock art at Callacpuma, and then a further hour to La Collpa.

Another typical Andean village from which you can walk to Baños del Inca is **Pariamarca.** Take a micro from Ovalo Bolognesi heading towards the coast. Ask to be let out at the turn-off to Pariamarca and walk from there.

A road goes to **Ventanillas de Combayo**, some 20 km past the burial niches of Otusco. These are more numerous and more spectacular, being located in a rather isolated, mountainous area, and are distributed over the face of a steep 200-m high hillside. There are occasional combis on weekdays, but more transport to the site on Sunday when a market is held nearby, one hour.

Porcón, at 3400 m, a rural cooperative with its evangelical faith expressed on billboards, is a popular excursion, 30 km northwest of Cajamarca. It is tightly organized and has a bakery, cheese- and yoghurt-making, zoo and vicuñas. Its carpentry uses wood from extensive pine plantations. A good guide helps to explain everything. If not taking a tour, contact **Cooperativa Agraria Atahualpa-Jerusalén** ⓘ *Chanchamayo 1355, Fonavi 1, T/F076-825631, granjaporcon@yahoo.com.*

Around Cajamarca

Sleeping

Cajamarca *p447, map p448*

AL **Posada del Puruay**, 5 km north of the city, T076-367928, postmast@p-puruay.com.pe. A 17th-century hacienda which has been converted into a 'hotel museum' with all rooms appointed to a high standard and containing beautiful pieces of colonial furniture. All rooms en suite. Recommended.

A Costa del Sol, Cruz de la Piedra 707, T076-343434, ventascajamarca@costadelsol peru.com. New hotel on the Plaza de Armas, part of a Peruvian chain, with breakfast, airport transfer, welcome drink; restaurant, café and bars, pool.

B Continental, Jr Amazonas 760, T076-363063, and **Gran Continental**, Amazonas 781, T076-341030, www.hoteles continental peru.com. Price includes breakfast. Very clean, hot water, modern, good restaurant (popular for lunch, specializes in *cuy frito*). The former caters more for the tourist market, while the **Gran**, a bit pricier, is aimed more at mining personnel.

B-C El Ingenio, Av Vía de Evitamiento 1611-1709, T/F076-367121, www.elingenio.com. 1½ blocks from new El Quinde shopping mall. With bathroom, solar-powered hot water, spacious, very relaxed, internet in rooms, helpful, good restaurant, bar, parking. Highly recommended.

C Clarín, Amazonas 1025, T076-341275, Hotel_clarin@hotmail.com. A modern hotel with pleasant decoration, rooms with bath, good beds, laptop connection, car park, restaurant, *panadería* next door.

C El Cumbe Inn, Pasaje Atahualpa 345, T076-366858, www.elcumbeinn.com. Includes breakfast, ask for discount in low season. Comfortable, bright rooms, with bath, hot water, cable TV and internet connection, personal service, 2 patios, small gym, well kept, will arrange taxis and tours, restaurant. Frequently recommended.

C Hostal El Portal del Marqués, Del Comercio 644, T/F076-368464, portalmarques@terra.com.pe. Price includes breakfast. Located in an attractive converted colonial house, all rooms carpeted, en suite, with TV, internet connection, laundry, safe, parking, tourist restaurant **El Mesón Gourmet** also has lunchtime *menú*. Recommended.

C La Hispana, Jr La Mar 542, T076-364225. Small, quiet, modern and very comfortable. Recommended.

C Casa Blanca, 2 de Mayo 446, Plaza de Armas, T/F076-822141. Price includes breakfast. Room service, clean, safe, nice old building with garden, good restaurant. Also has disco-bar.

D El Cabildo, Junín 1062, T/F076-367025, cabildoh@latinmail.com. Includes breakfast. In a historic monument with patio and modern fountain, full of character, elegant, local decorations, comfortable, breakfast served, gym, massage if booked in advance. Recommended.

D Hostal Cajamarca, 2 de Mayo 311, T076-362532, hostalcajamarca@hotmail. com. Sizeable rooms in a colonial house, clean, hot water, food excellent in **Los Faroles** restaurant, **Cajamarca Tours** next door. Recommended.

D Los Balcones de la Recoleta, Amalia Puga 1050, T076-363302, luchi9200@ yahoo.com.pe. A beautifully restored 19th-century house, with a pleasant courtyard full of flowers; some rooms with period furniture but all are en suite with internet access, breakfast extra, use of kitchen, helpful staff, some English spoken. Recommended.

D Hostal Los Pinos, Jr La Mar 521, T/F076-365992, pinoshostal@yahoo.com. Price includes small breakfast. Lovely colonial house with a new extension, comfortable and secure, helpful staff, expensive laundry, lunch menu available for US$3.

D Hostal Portada del Sol, Pisagua 731, T076-363395, PortadadelSol@terra.com.pe. Good rooms, tastefully decorated, with bath, hot water, comfortable beds, internet access. Also has **Portada del Sol Hacienda** at Km 6 on road to Cumbe Mayo (**C**). Good choice.

E Colonial Inn, Av Los Héroes 350, T076-313551, www.colonialprado.com. Hot water, cheaper with shared bath, English spoken, 24-hr attention, meals extra, convenient for buses, mainly for groups.

E Hostal Becerra, Del Batán 195, T076-367867. With bath, hot water and TV, modern, pleasant, clean and friendly, but front rooms can be noisy, they'll let you leave your luggage until late buses depart.

E Hospedaje Los Jasmines, Amazonas 775, T076-361812, hospedajelosjasmines@ yahoo.com. In a converted colonial house with a pleasant courtyard and café serving good cakes, 10 rooms with bath, 2 without, all funds go to disabled children, some staff are disabled, guests can visit the project's school and help. Owner Christa Stark from Germany also has **Fundo Ecológico El Porongo** on the road to Baños del Inca, bunk beds, **G** per person. Recommended.

E Hostal Pepe, Av Atahualpa 343, T076-361887. The most convenient for bus offices on Atahualpa. Cheaper without bath, hot water, no breakfast, noisy from all-night traffic. Better than **San Carlos**, opposite.

F Hostal Atahualpa, Pasaje Atahualpa 686, T076-342629. Hot water 0600-1100, a bit run-down but clean, meals extra, restaurant open 0800-2200.

F Hostal Dos de Mayo, 2 de Mayo 585, T076-362527. With bath, hot water, basic, quite dark, friendly and helpful, internet cabins, good-value menú in the restaurant.

F Casa Pensión, 2 de Mayo 712, T076-369888. Full board, shared rooms, some with bath.

Around Cajamarca *p449*

L-AL Laguna Seca, Av Manco Cápac 1098, Los Baños del Inca, T076-594600, www.lagunaseca.com.pe. In pleasant surroundings with thermal streams (atmospheric misty mornings), private hot thermal baths in rooms, swimming pool with thermal water, good restaurant, bar, health spa with a variety of treatments (US$10-48), horses for hire. Recommended.

B Hostal Fundo Campero San Antonio, is 2 km off the Baños road (turn off at Km 5 from Cajamarca), T/F076-348237, jc_luna@viabcp.com. An old hacienda, wonderfully restored, with open fireplaces and gardens, 15 mins' walk along the river to Baños del Inca. All rooms en suite. The price includes breakfast and a ride on the hotel's *caballos de paso*. Restaurant serves the hotel's own dairy produce, fruit and vegetables, catch your own trout for supper; try the *licor de sauco* (elderberry). Recommended.

B-E Los Baños del Inca, see page 449, T076-348385, www.inkatermas.com.pe. Various levels of accommodation: **B** bungalows for 2 to 4 with thermal water, TV, fridge; **E** per person **Albergue Juvenil**, not IYFH, rooms with 3 bunk beds, private bath, caters to groups, basic and overpriced. Camping possible.

There are a few more *hostales* and *hospedajes* in **Baños del Inca** (eg Hostal José Gálvez, Manco Capac 552, T076-348396), but some cater for mining company personnel, others for hourly clients.

Eating

Cajamarca *p447, map p448*

There are cheap eating places on Del Comercio and 2 de Mayo y Sabogal.

TTT El Batán Gran Bufet de Arte, Del Batán 369, T076-366025, elbatanrestaurant@yahoo.com.mx. International dishes and nouvelle cuisine, good wine list and wide choice of drinks, local dishes on non-tourist menu, live music on Sat, art gallery on the 2nd floor.

TTT Paskana, Av Atahualpa Km 2, road to Baños del Inca, T076-344217, www.paskana.com. Expensive by top quality, seafood and meat dishes, also has **Taberna El Diablo** (TTT). Open 1100-1500, 1900-2300, parking.

TTT Querubino, Amalia Puga 589. Mediterranean-style decoration with American and French influence in the cooking, specializes in fish, but lots of choice, breakfasts, cocktails, coffees, expensive wines.

TT Casa Club, Amalia Puga 458-A, T076-340198. Open 0800-2300. Set menu, including vegetarian, and extensive selection à la carte, family atmosphere, slow but attentive service.

TT Don Paco, Amalia Puga 390, T076-362655. Opposite Sn Francisco. Typical, including *novo andino*, and international dishes, tasty food, desserts and drinks.

TT El Cajamarqués, Amazonas 770, T076-362128. Has good value set menus available after 1300, elegant colonial building with garden full of exotic birds, nice place for families.

TT El Pez Loco, San Martín 333. Recommended for fish, also on road to Baños del Inca.

TT Las Tullpas, 2 de Mayo 930. Open 0730-2300. Local and international dishes, à la carte and *menú ejecutivo*.

TT Om-Gri, San Martín 360, near the Plaza de Armas. Good Italian dishes, small, friendly, French spoken, opens at 1300 (1830 Sun).

TT Pizzería El Marengo, Junín 1201, T076-368045. Good pizzas and warm atmosphere. Phone for delivery.

TT Salas, Amalia Puga 637, on the main plaza, T076-362867. A Cajamarca tradition, daily 0700-2200. Fast service but can get very busy, excellent local food (try their *cuy* frito), best *tamales* in town; also has a branch in Baños del Inca (Fri-Sun 1100-1600 and holidays). Both serve the same food at same prices, own production. Recommended.

TT-T **El Zarco**, Jr Del Batán 170, T076-363421. Sun-Fri 0700-2300. Very popular with local residents, good vegetarian dishes, excellent fish, popular for breakfast.

TT-T **El Zarco Campestre**, off road to airport, open daily. Both **El Zarco's** use own produce, recommended for pork.

T **Christian**, Del Comercio 719. Snacks, juices, set lunch for US$1.10.

T **Donde Octavio**, Jr Del Batán 190-196 corner Amazonas. Recommended for *tamales* and *humitas*.

T **Natur's Center**, Amalia Puga 409. New vegetarian place with a good selection of dishes.

T **Pizzería Vaca Loca**, San Martín 330. Popular, the name doesn't seem to put the locals off.

T **Rosana D'Avila's** restaurant, Del Batán 368. Good value, tasty buffet, set lunches, open for dinner too. For early breakfasts go to the market.

Cafés

Akaesh, 2 de Mayo 334, T076-368108. Café with couches, also has a bar, live music Fri night, closed Sun.

Cascanuez Café Bar, Amalia Puga 554, near the cathedral. Great cakes, extensive menu including *humitas*, breakfasts, ice creams and coffees. Recommended.

El Capulí, Jr Junín, in the Complejo Belén. Mon-Thu 0900-1300, 1500-2000 (Fri-Sat 2400). Coffee, drinks, sandwiches and snacks. Lovely atmosphere for a quiet coffee, reading your Handbook and planning your next activity.

Heladería Holanda, Amalia Puga 657 on the Plaza de Armas, T076-340113. Dutch-owned, easily the best ice creams in Cajamarca, 50 flavours (but not all on at the same time), try *poro poro*, *lúcuma* or *sauco*, also serves coffee. Also has a branch in Baños del Inca.

Panadería Campos, Jr del Comercio 661. Good for local cookies, *rosquitas*. Also sells postcards by well-known local photographer, Sr Campos.

Panadería La Ideal, Amalia Puga 307. Good for bread.

Sanguchón.com, Junín 1137. Best burgers in town, sandwiches, also popular bar.

Around Cajamarca *p449*

There are several cheap restaurants at or near the thermal complex at Los Baños del Inca, as well as the **Salas** restaurant (see above). Many people, after a bathe, go to the **Pastelería** (at the bus stop, opposite **Heladería Holanda**) for a good selection of cakes at great prices.

Bars and clubs

Cajamarca *p447, map p448*

Embrujo, Apurímac 519. Disco bar, popular with younger set.

Mamba, Av Atahualpa 493, on road to Baños del Inca. Disco and grill, good varied programmes, opens 2100, live music and dancing Fri and Sat.

Rodeo Video, San Martín 352. Pub/disco.

Festivals and events

Cajamarca *p447, map p448*

Feb Cajamarca is known as the Carnival capital of Peru. **Carnival week**, with many processions and dances, is a messy, raucous affair – the level of water, motor oil and paint-throwing would put Laurel and Hardy to shame. This is not for the faint-hearted. You have been warned!

May/Jun Corpus Christi is a solemn religious affair.

24 Jun San Juan in Cajamarca, Chota, Llacanora, San Juan and Cutervo.

First Sun in Oct Festival Folklórico in Cajamarca.

Second week Oct The city's **'Tourist Week'**.

Around Cajamarca *p449*

22-20 Jul An agricultural fair, **Feria Fongal**, is held at Baños del Inca. It coincides with **Fiestas Patrias** and besides agricultural displays, has *artesanía* and *caballos de paso*.

7-8 Sep **Fiesta de Huanchaco** in Baños del Inca, a festival organized by the local campesinos.

Mar/Apr **Domingo de Ramos** (Palm Sun) processions in Porcón are worth seeing.

Shopping

Cajamarca *p447, map p448*

Food and drink

The area is renowned for its dairy produce. Many shops sell cheese, butter, honey, etc. Look out for *queso ahumado* (smoked cheese), sold at shops on 2 de Mayo, block 5, and Amazonas, blocks 5-8. Eucalyptus honey is sold in the market on Amazonas, block 7, and is said to be a cure for rheumatism. Also look out for local jams, especially *mermelada de sauco* (elderberry).

El Porcón, Cooperative Atahualpa-Jerusalén, Chanchamayo 1355 (1 block from Vía Evitamiento, 'Fonavi' combis, No 19, and micros 'A' pass). It sells excellent *queso suizo*.

La Collpa, see page 450, has a shop at Romero 124, sells some of the best cheese and butter. Try the *queso mantecoso*, which is full-cream cheese, or sweet *manjar blanco*.

Los Alpes, Junín 965. Recommended for quality and variety, Swiss-run, pricey but excellent.

Handicrafts

Cajamarca is famous for its gilded mirrors. The Cajamarquiña frames are not carved but decorated with patterns transferred onto pieces of glass using the silkscreen process. This tradition lapsed during the post-colonial period and present production goes back less than 20 years.

Cajamarca is also an excellent place to buy cheap, good-quality handicrafts. Specialities include cotton and wool saddlebags (*alforjas*), found at the San Antonio market, at the north end of Jr Apurímac. Handwoven woollen items can be made to order. Other items include painted ceramic masks and soapstone figures (including miners with power drills). The market on Amazonas is good for *artesanía*. There are stalls in the street on block 7 of Belén every day. There are several shops on 300 block of 2 de Mayo. All offer a good range of local crafts.

Textiles y Artesanías Paredes, 2 de Mayo 264, up the steps. Has a different selection from what you find in the streets.

Supermarkets

El Quinde, Av Hoyos Rubio, blocks 6 and 7, Fonavi. New shopping centre on the road to airport, with well-stocked supermarket.

Activites and tours

Cajamarca *p447, map p448*

Several travel agencies around the Plaza de Armas offer trips to local sites and further afield (eg Kuntur Wasi, Kuélap), trekking on Inca and other trails, riding *caballos de paso* and handicraft tours. Average prices of local tours: city tour, US$7.55, Cumbe Mayo, US$7.55, Ventanillas de Otusco US$6, Porcón US$6, Combayo US$30 (full day), Kuntur Wasi US$30, Kuélap US$260 (3-5 days). Recommended are:

Asociación Civil para el Rescate del Ecosistema de Cajamarca, Aprec, Av Manco Cápac 1098, Baños del Inca, T076-894600, www.aprec.org. The association, sponsored by **Pro Aves Perú, Hotel Laguna Seca** and **Yanacocha** mines, aims to "restore the ecological health" of the Cajamarca region. Four Inca trail loops have been made accessible to hikers, including one, to Sangal, which passes the hummingbird's habitat.

Atahualpa Inca Tours, La Mar 435, T076-367014 (in **Hostal El Mirador**), www.nunura.com/elmirador.

Cajamarca Tours, 2 de Mayo 323, T/F076-362813 (also DHL, Western Union and flight reconfirmations).

Clarín Tours, Del Batán 161, T/F076-366829, www.clarintours.com.

Cumbemayo Tours, Amalia Puga 635 on the plaza, T076-362938, cumbemayotours@usa.net. Guides in English and French.

Inca Baths Tours, Amalia Puga 667, T076-364310, incablaz@hotmail.com.

Socio Adventures, Ben Eastwood, Pje Chota 123, Dpto 1A, Urb Ramón Castilla, Cajamarca, T076-341118, www.socioadventures.com. They offer a Stove Trek Tour, where you donate materials and help a local family build a cooking stove while taking a 5-day, 5-night guided tour of the area. You stay at their lodge called the **Blur Poncho** near Chota, excellent food and accommodation.

Transport

Cajamarca *p447, map p448*

Air

To **Lima** (about US$120) daily with **Aero Cóndor**, and **LC Busre**, Sun-Fri. **Aero Cóndor**, 2 de Mayo 323, T076-365674. **LC Busre**, Comercio 1024, T076-361098.

Bus

To **Lima**, 856 km, 12-14 hrs, económico US$9-12, to US$21-24.25 on **Civa's** double-deckers, to US$27-33.35 for **Cruz del Sur's** luxury service (includes taxi to your lodging in Lima), several buses daily. The road is paved. To **Pacasmayo**, 189 km, 5-6 hrs, US$7, several buses and hourly *colectivos*. To **Trujillo**, 296 km, 6½ hrs, US$4.55-10, regular buses 0900- 2230 most continue to Lima. To **Chiclayo**, 260 km, 6 hrs, US$4.55-9, several buses daily; change buses to go on to Piura and Tumbes. To **Celendín**, 112 km, 4 hrs, US$3, **Atahualpa** at 0700 and 1300, **Royal Palace's** 0900 (poor minibuses). Also combis from Av Atahualpa cuadra 3, leave when full 0400-1800, 3½ hrs, US$3. The route follows a fairly good dirt road through beautiful country. **Perú Bus**, **Rojas** and others go to **Cajabamba**, 75 km, US$3, 4 hrs, several daily; also combis, US$3.50, 3 hrs. These buses, and **Royal Palace's**, also go to **Bambamarca**, **Chota** and **Cutervo.**

Bus companies: Atahualpa, Atahualpa 299, T076-363060; **Civa**, Ayacucho 753, T076-361460; **Cruz del Sur**, Atahualpa 600, T076-361737; **El Cumbe**, Sucre 594, T076-363068; **Emtrafesa**, Atahualpa 299, T369663; **Línea**, Atahualpa 318, T076-363956; **Rojas**, Atahualpa 405, T076-340548; **Royal Palace's**, Atahualpa 339, T076-365855; **Tepsa**, Sucre 594, T076-363306. **Turismo Días**, Sucre 422, T076-368289.

Taxi

Radio taxi: **El Sol**, T076-368897, 24 hrs.

Directory

Cajamarca *p447, map p448*

Banks BCP, Apurímac 719. Open 1000-1800. Changes Amex TCs without commission, cash advance on Visa, MasterCard and Amex, 0.5% commission, Visa and MasterCard ATM. **Banco Continental**, Tarapacá 721. Visa and MasterCard ATM. **Banco Wiese**, Amazonas 750. Accepts Amex TCs, 0.5% commission, cash advance and ATM for Visa and MasterCard. **Interbank**, 2 de Mayo 546, on plaza. Closed 1300-1600. Accepts Vias TCs without commission if paid in soles, US$5 for dollars, Visa, MasterCard, AmEx ATM. There is a **Telebanco 24 Horas** ATM (Visa) at the gas station next to Cial buses on Av Atahualpa. Dollars can be changed in most banks and travel agencies on east side of plaza, but euros are hard to change. Casa de cambio in **Casa del Artefacto** musical and electrical store at Amazonas 537. Good rates, cash only. Casas de cambio also at Jr del Comercio y Apurímac and at Amalia Puga 673. **Street changers** on Jr Del Batán by the Plaza de Armas and at Del Batán y Amazonas. **Hospitals** **Clínica Limatambo**, Puno 265, T076-364241. Private, recommended. Doctor Gurmandi speaks English. **Clínica San Francisco**, Av Grau 851, T076-362050. Private, recommended. Hospital at Av Mario Urteaga. **Internet** There are internet cabins everywhere; rates are US$0.35 per hr. **Laundry** **Lavandería Dandy**, Jr Amalia Puga 545. Pay by weight. **Lava Express**, Jr Belén 678. Good service, US$1.50 per kg. **Post** Serpost, Jr Amalia Puga 778. 0800-2045. **Telephone** Public phone offices cn be found all over the centre. **Useful addresses** Indecopi, Tarapacá 815, p 2, T076-363315, inguzman@indecopi.gob.pe. The place to go if you have a complaint about tourist services.

Chachapoyas Region

The Chachapoyas Region contains so many archaeological riches that you need at least a week to begin to appreciate the remarkable legacy of the Chachapoyans, also known as 'The Cloud People'. Great pre-Inca cities, immense fortresses such as Kuélap and ancient effigies which gaze over a dramatic landscape reward the visitor to a region which is due to become a major tourist destination as soon as regular air service begins. There are many cities and burial sites scattered around the cloud-covered mountain slopes, often in inaccessible places. To reach them is an adventure in itself. ▸▸ *For Sleeping, Eating and other listings, see pages 468-473.*

Ins and outs

Getting there The city of Chachapoyas is the best base for visiting this region. As there are no scheduled flights, it has to be reached overland from Chiclayo, Cajamarca or Tarapoto. **Móvil Tours** offer reasonably comfortable bus services from Lima, travelling Chiclayo-Chachapoyas by day. Bus schedules starting from Chiclayo all involve an overnight journey, missing the fine scenery along the way. An alternative is to go by bus from Chiclayo to Jaén, continuing the next day to Chachapoyas, via Bagua Grande and Pedro Ruiz, using combis. From Cajamarca, you can go first to Celendín (see page 457) and then on to Chachapoyas, crossing the Marañón at Balsas between descents and climbs of thousands of vertical metres. The journey is an entirely unforgettable experience in its own right, but half of it is done at night. Also beautiful is the route from Tarapoto via Moyobamba and Pedro Ruiz, especially since the highway has been paved. It is possible to do this journey in one day, leaving Tarapoto at 0800 or 0900, but the last part will be done in darkness. Break the journey in Moyobamba or Pedro Ruiz and take combis on some stretches.

Best time to visit The dry season is preferable (normally May to September), but the seasons are less stable than in the past; in the last few years it has been sunny and dry well into December. During the rains, roads may become impassable due to landslides and access to the more remote areas may be impossible, or involve weeks of delay. Likewise, trekking in the area can be very pleasant in the dry season, but may involve wading through waist-deep mud on some routes during the rainy season. Other places are still accessible in the wet, but rubber boots are essential. Good hiking gear is always a must, as well as a sleeping bag, tent and canned goods.

Tourist information iperú ⓘ *Jr Ortiz 588, Plaza de Armas, Chachapoyas, T041-477292, iperuchachapoyas@promperu.gob.pe, Mon-Sat 0800-1300, 1500-1900.* **Dircetur** (Dirección Regional de Turismo) ⓘ *Grau 640, T041-478355.* Websites: www.chachapoyasonline.com, www.regionamazonas.gob.pe.

Background

Theories about the Chachapoyan Empire show that their cities, highways, terracing, irrigation, massive stonework and metalcraft were all fully developed. The culture began about AD 800 and covered an area bounded by the rivers Marañón and Huallaga, as far as Pataz in the south and Bagua in the north. Socially the Chachapoya were organized into chiefdoms, which formed war-alliances in the case of external aggression. Archaeologists claim that this region overwhelms even Machu-Picchu and its neighbouring Inca sites in grandeur and mystery. By some counts, its 'lost' and uncharted cities, such as Pueblo Alto, near the village of Pueblo Nuevo (25 km from Kuélap) and Saposoa in the northeast of San Martín department, exceed three dozen. By far the majority of these cities, fortresses and villages were never discovered by the Spanish. In fact many had already returned to the jungle by the time they arrived in 1532.

This region is called La Ceja de la Selva (the eyebrow of the jungle), whose beautiful scenery includes a good deal of virgin cloudforest (although other sections are sadly deforested), as well as endless deep dry canyons traversed by hair-raisingly dangerous roads. The temperature is always in the 20°s during the day, but the nights are cool at around 3000 m. Many ruins are overgrown with ferns, bromeliads and orchids and easily missed.

The central geographic feature of the department, and its boundary with neighbouring Cajamarca, is the great Río Marañón, one of the major tributaries of the Amazon. Running roughly parallel to the mighty Marañón, one range to the east, is the gentler valley of the Utcubamba, home to much of the area's ancient and present population. Over yet another cordillera to the east, lie the isolated subtropical valleys of the province of Rodríguez de Mendoza, the origin of whose inhabitants, has been the source of much debate (see page 466).

The German ethnologist, Doctor Peter Lerche, of the **Camayoc Foundation** ⓘ *http://camayocperu.com/lerche.htm*, is the resident expert regarding Chachapoyan cultures and trekking. He is very knowledgeable, speaks English, sometimes guides groups and may be contacted for information on anthropology and history. In an article in National Geographic, September 2000, "Quest for the Lost Tombs of the Peruvian Cloud People", Doctor Lerche writes about the discovery of a Chachapoya tomb named the 'White House' and gives a good general introduction to the history and archaeology of the region (he has also provided information for this section). The **Camayoc Foundation** website is also a good source of information.

Cajamarca to Chachapoyas » pp468-473.

East from Cajamarca, the first town of note is **Celendín**, whose residents are known as Shilicos. It is a clean and tranquil place, with warm friendly people but a decidedly chilly climate. The plaza and cathedral are both appealing. There is also an interesting local market on Sunday. Walk up the hill to the chapel of San Isidro Labrador for views of town and surroundings. Note the huge hats worn by the townsfolk. These are woven from fine straw and can be bought, along with other straw handicrafts, at **Artesanías San José de Pilco** ⓘ *2 de Mayo 319*.

The rough road from Celendín to Chachapoyas (226 km) follows a winding course, crossing the wide and deep canyon of the Río Marañón at Balsas, at 950 m. It then climbs steeply, over countless hair-raising hairpin bends, with superb views of the mountains and the valleys below, to reach the Barro Negro pass at 3680 m, before descending to Leymebamba in the upper Utcubamba valley (see page 463). The journey takes 12-14 hours in the dry season. It can be much longer and more dangerous when it rains. Take warm clothing, food and water. Paving of the road to Chachapoyas will shorten the journey time. The route is generally safe but vehicle robberies are not unknown.

Chachapoyas and around » pp468-473. Colour map 1, C4.

→ *Phone code: 041. Population: 25,000. Altitude: 2335 m.*

Chachapoyas, or 'Chacha', as it is known among locals, is the capital of the Department of Amazonas. It was founded on 5 September 1538, but retains only some of its colonial character, in the form of large old homes with their typical patios and wooden balconies. The city's importance as a crossroads between the coast and jungle began to decline in the late 1940s, with the building of the road through Pedro Ruiz. However, archaeological and ecological tourism have grown gradually since the 1990s and there are hopes that these will bring increasing economic benefits to the region.

Chachapoyas

The modern cathedral faces a spacious plaza which fills with locals for the evening paseo. Other interesting churches are the **Capilla de la Virgen Asunta**, the city's patroness, at Asunción y Puno, and **Señor de Burgos**, at Amazonas y Santa Lucía. The **Instituto Nacional de Cultura** (INC) has a small **museum** ⓘ *Ayacucho 904, Mon-Fri 0800-1300, 1400-1645, free*. It contains a few artefacts and mummies in display cases, with explanations in Spanish.

The **Mirador Guayamil** offers fine views of the city, especially at early dusk. Nearby is the **Pozo de Yanayacu**, also known as the *fuente del amor*, at the west end of Avenida Salamanca. Legend has it that those who visit this well will fall in love and remain in Chachapoyas. A decisive battle for independence from Spain took place at the **Pampas de Higos Urco**, at the east end of town, a 20-minute walk, with great views of lush Andes to the east.

Huancas

Huancas, a picturesque village, stands on a hilltop north of Chacha. It's a two-hour walk starting on the airport road. The town is developing a reputation as an artisans' centre and local pottery can be bought. Walk uphill from Huancas for a magnificent view into the deep **canyon** of the Río Sonche. There is good walking in the area, which also has Inca and pre-Inca ruins. *Colectivos* for Huancas leave from Jirón Ortiz Arrieta y Libertad; 20 minutes, 0700-1800, US$0.60. A large prison complex has been built nearby and all *colectivos* go there on the way to the village.

Levanto → *Colour map 1, C4.*

The Spaniards built this, their first capital of the area, in 1538, directly on top of the previous Chachapoyan structures. Although the capital was moved to Chachapoyas a few years later, Levanto still retained its importance, at least for a while, as it had been one of the seven great cities of the Chachapoyans as described by Cieza de León

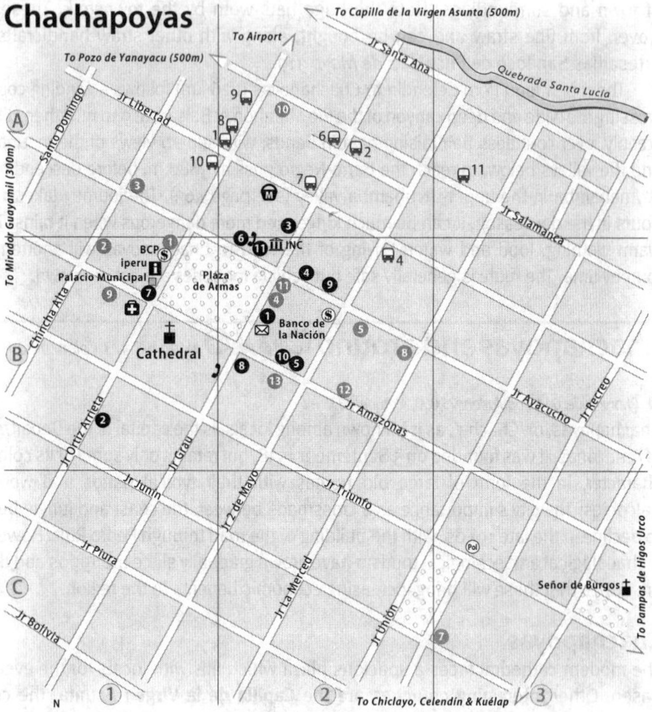

Sleeping
Belén 1 *B1*
Casa Vieja 2 *B1*
Casona Monsante 12 *B2*
El Dorado 3 *A1*
El Tejado & Restaurant 4 *B2*
Gran Vilaya & Café de Guías 5 *B2*
Hostal El Danubio 7 *C3*
Hostal Johumaji 8 *B2*
Hostal Kuélap 9 *B1*
Laguna de los Cóndores 10 *A2*
Puma Urcu & Café Café 13 *B2*
Revash 11 *B2*

Eating
Chacha 1 *B2*
Chifa Chuy Xien 10 *B2*
Dulcería Santa Helena 5 *B2*
El Edén 3 *A2*
Kuélap 4 *B2*
La Tushpa 2 *B1*
Las Rocas 6 *B2*
Mari Pizza 11 *B2*
Mass Burger 7 *B1*
Matalache 8 *B2*
Panadería San José 9 *B2*

Transport
Cars to Bagua Grande 7 *A2*
Cars to Pedro Ruiz 2 *A2*
Colectivos to Huancas 1 *A2*
Combis to Leymebamba 4 *B2*
Comité Interprovincial Santo Tomás & Trans Rollers Combis 6 *A2*
San Juan de Luya Combis 8 *A2*
Trans Zelada 9 *A2*
Turismo Kuélap 10 *A1*
Virgen del Carmen 11 *A3*

and Garcilaso de la Vega. Nowadays Levanto is a small, unspoilt colonial village set on flat ground overlooking the massive canyon of the Utcubamba River. Kuélap can, on a clear day, be seen on the other side of the rift. The town is a good centre for exploring the many ruins around.

The Kuélap east-west Highway starts at Levanto and links with the Inca military highway at Jalca Grande (see page 462). Levanto was about midway on the north-south route from Colombia to the Huari, then Inca hub, at Huánuco. This stone road crosses the modern vehicle road at La Molina, about 5 km from Chachapoyas. The nicest way to get to Levanto from Chachapoyas is by the Inca road, four to five hours. Take the heavy transit road out of Chachapoyas for 40 minutes, then take the stone path on the left. It is in pretty good shape, with one 15-m-long stone stairway in excellent condition. A taxi from Chachapoyas to Levanto and back, including driver waiting while you look around, is US$14.50. » *See also Transport, page 472.*

Yalape

About five minutes' drive, or a pleasant 30-minute walk, from Levanto on the road to Chachapoyas are the partly cleared ruins of Yalape. The local people are helpful and will guide you to the ruins which can be easily seen from the road (look for the three, linked curving walls above the road, opposite a solitary modern building). Yalape seems to have been a massive residential complex extending over many hectares. The majority of the walls visible from the road are of white limestone and there are well-preserved examples of typical Chachapoyan architecture and masonry with elaborate friezes. It is easy to climb up to the ruins, but many of the structures are overgrown.

Near Yalape is the site of **San Pedro de Wushpu**: coming from Chachapoyas, at the point where the road drops over the crest, is a fork in the road. Take the left branch (right goes to Levanto). The ruins are similar to Yalape but easier to get to; ask at the first house on the left on the side road.

Morgan Davis has reconstructed an Inca building at **Colla Cruz**, about 20 minutes' walk from Levanto. On a classic Inca stone terrace, a regional-style round building has been constructed, with a three-storey high-thatched roof. This garrison guarded the road which ran past Colcamar, over the Cordillera Oriental on a 1.5-km-staircase, through Gran Vilaya, to Cajamarca's central north-south road and on to the coastal highway.

Kuélap and Tingo → *Phone code: 041. Colour map 1, C4. Altitude: 1800 m.*

ⓘ *0800-1700, US$3, 50% discount for students with identification. A small Centro de Interpretaciones is open 0800-1630; it has a good model of the site. There is a toilet block. The ruins are locked. The guardian, Gabriel Portocarrero, has the keys and accompanies visitors. He's very informative and friendly. Guides are available; pay them what you think appropriate. There is a drinks and snacks stall.*

The undisputed highlight among the archaeological riches around Chachapoyas is **Kuélap** (3000 m), a spectacular pre-Inca walled city which was rediscovered in 1843 by Juan Crisótomo Nieto. Even the most exaggerated descriptions fail to do justice to the sheer scale of this site great fortress.

Kuélap was built over a period of 200 years, from AD 900-1100 and contained three times more stone than the Great Pyramid at Giza in Egypt.The site lies sprawled along the summit of a mountain crest, more than a kilometre in length. It is divided into three parts: at the northwest end is a small outpost; at the southeast end of the ridge is a spread-out village in total ruin; and the cigar-shaped fortress lies between the two, 585 m long by 110 m wide at its widest. The walls are as formidable as those of any pre-Columbian city. They vary in height between 8 and 17 m and were constructed in 40 courses of stone block, each one weighing between 100 and 200 kg. It has been estimated that 100,000 such blocks went into the completion of this massive structure.

The majority of the main walls on all four levels are original. Also original is the inverted, cone-shaped structure, long assumed to be a dungeon, although recent studies claim it to be a giant solar calendar, known as *el tintero* (the inkwell). There are a number of defensive walls and passageways as well as many houses. Some reconstruction has taken place, mostly of small houses and walls, but only one building has been completely restored. The remainder have been left in their cloudforest setting, the trees covered in bromeliads and moss, the flowers visited by hummingbirds. Although there are no carvings, some structures are adorned

Sites around Chachapoyas

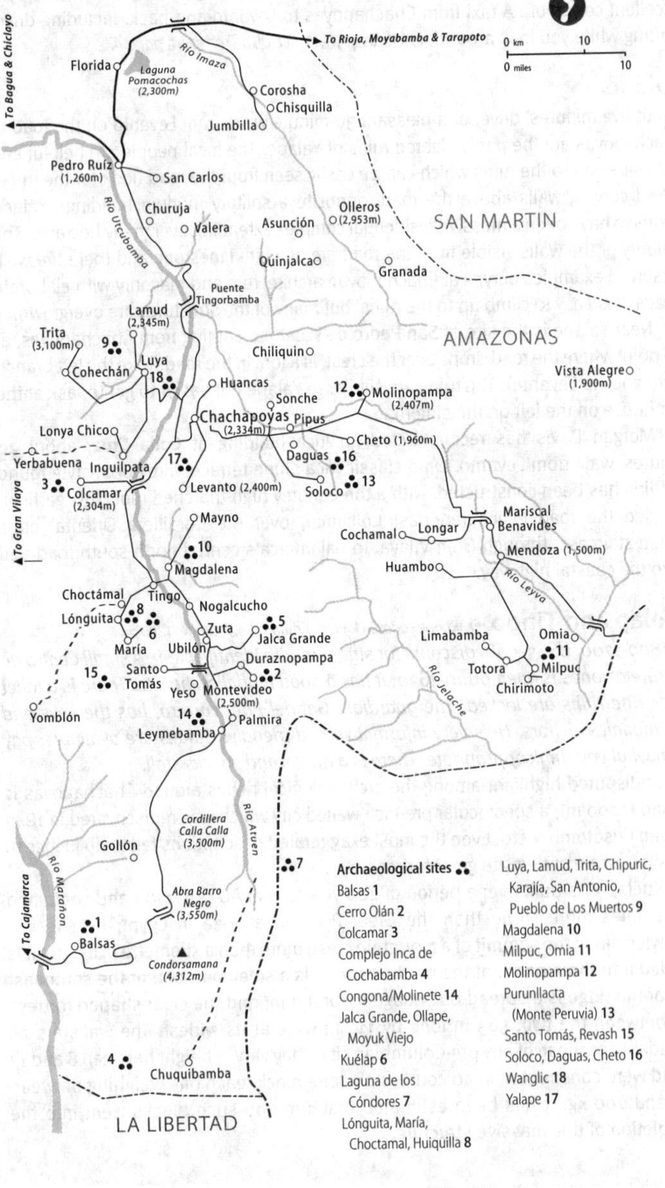

with simple geometric friezes which represent the eyes of animals and birds. An interesting feature is that almost all the buildings (about 420 in number) are circular. Recent archaeological findings indicate that they were public spaces and served as kitchens, toilets and storage areas, rather than warriors' barracks as was first thought. It is estimated that up to 3500 people lived in Kuélap at its zenith. The site was never mentioned in Inca chronicles, meaning that by the time of the Inca invasion in the 1470s, it was of little significance to the Chachas.The five rectangular structures indicate that the Incas occupied the fortress.

Public transport is not plentiful in this region. Most journeys are done by *colectivo* and combi, starting their routes in Chachapoyas. To reach the more remote archaeological sites you will have to do some walking, in one or two cases for several days. Tours can also be arranged.

Tingo, about 37 km by road south of Chachapoyas, is the village from which to reach Kuélap. Much of the village was washed away in the floods of 1993. In the hills above Tingo, 3.5 km away, is **Tingo Nuevo**, with its plaza of flowers and topiary in front of the church. Market day is Sunday.

There are four options to get from Tingo to Kuélap: **1** Take a tour from Chachapoyas with one of the agencies (see page 471). Most hotels will organize tours to Kuélap and other archaeological sites when there are sufficient people. Expect to pay around US$12-20 per person for a full-day trip to Kuélap, including guide and lunch. When booking a tour, request a guide who speaks English, if you so wish. Tours leave at 0800 and, after a spectacular, if not disconcerting, three-hour drive, you arrive at Kuélap. The tours usually allow a sufficient three to four hours for exploration before returning to Chachapoyas, with a possible stop along the way for a late lunch. **2** Hire your own vehicle with driver in Chachapoyas, US$35 per vehicle. **3** A less expensive option and, in many ways, the recommended one since it allows you to see Kuélap wrapped in early-morning mist, is to take the local combi to Choctámal, María or Quisongo (see Chachapoyas Transport, page 472). You can spend the night in Choctámal village or at María (see Sleeping, page 469). The next day, it is a relatively gentle 19 km, four- to five-hour walk along the vehicle road to Kuélap. It's best to visit the site at your leisure and spend the night here (see Sleeping, page 469), then walk down the steep path (three to four hours) to Tingo the next day. **4** Take a combi from Chachapoyas to Tingo (see Transport, page 472). Either spend the night in Tingo and start climbing at dawn the next day, or hike straight up and spend the night in María. The strenuous 3½- to four-hour hike (with a 1200 m vertical gain) to Kuélap begins on the right-hand side of the bridge, past the police station. At first the track follows the west bank of the Utcubamba, before turning right and climbing steeply into the mountains. The route is intermittently marked with red arrows painted on the rocks. It can get very hot and there

Kuélap

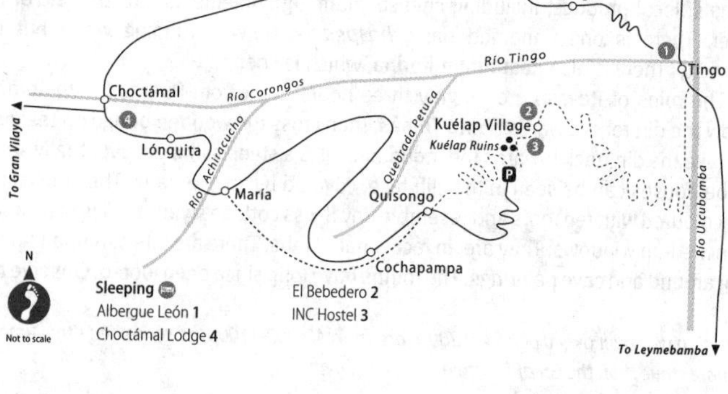

 is no water whatsoever until the top, but the trail may be muddy in the rainy season. Take water, food, adequate clothing and footwear, etc. You reach the small village of Kuélap first, the walls of the fortress become visible only at the very end of the climb. To walk down takes about three hours.

Between Tingo and Leymebamba

» pp468-473.

South of Tingo and Kuélap there are many sights of interest on either bank of the Río Utcubamba. To visit the sites south of Chacha, you have to descend to the road in the Río Utcubamba valley, cross the bridge to the west bank and head to Tingo. At Shipamarca there is a Sunday *feria* of handicrafts. Before Tingo is a sign to Kuélap, but this is a poor road. It's better to continue to Tingo itself where the new road to Kuélap starts beside the river. Between these two roads, look for the ruins of Macros above the east bank of the river.

Jalca Grande

The town of Jalca Grande (or La Jalca as it is known locally), at 2800 m, lies between Montevideo and Tingo, up on the east side of the main valley. There is a market on Saturday. In the town itself, one block west of the Plaza de Armas, is the **Choza Redonda**, the remains of a Chachapoyan roundhouse which was inhabited until 1964. Half an hour west of the town are the ruins of **Ollape**, a series of platforms with intricate fretwork designs and wide balconies. A much larger site, though more primitive, is **Moyuk Viejo**, a 2½-hour walk to the north.

A strenuous but rewarding three- to four-day trek can be made from La Jalca to Huambo or Limabamba (see page 466), over the cordillera and through cloudforests to the subtropical valleys. Part of the route follows an ancient road and there are undeveloped ruins along the way. Trekking experience and self-sufficiency are indispensable.

Ubilón

Jalca Grande can also be reached from Ubilón, on the main road north to Tingo. Lots of transport passes Ubilón, but there is only one daily bus direct to the village. It's a strenuous three-hour walk uphill to La Jalca. There is not much in Ubilón itself, save for a few shops selling next to nothing. Cheap, basic accommodation is available at **Bodega Irmita**.

Revash

Further south are the towns of **Yerbabuena** and **Puente Santo Tomás**, which is at the turn-off for the vivid burial *chullpas* of **Revash**, belonging to the Revash culture (around AD 1250). In Yerbabuena the Sunday market is the largest in the area, with animals, local produce, including cheeses, farming implements, etc, on sale or for barter. There is one unnamed basic *hospedaje*, G, with running water but no electricity. There is also **Restaurant Karina**, which is cheap.

The ruins of **Revash** are roughly three hours' walk from Puente Santo Tomás. Follow the dirt road towards **Santo Tomás**, then cross the wooden bridge on the right and take the dirt track towards the mountains; it is a steep climb up. Eventually small adobe houses can be seen in the cliff face, covered by an overhang. The houses are buff coloured with red roofs and resemble tiny Swiss cottages with crosses in the form of bricked-up windows. They are, in fact, small tombs. There are lots of human bones lying around and cave paintings. The tombs have long since been looted. Observe the

Kuélap was built over a period of 200 years, from AD 900-1100, and contained three times more stone than the Great Pyramid at Giza in Egypt.

structures from below. Please do not climb on the houses as they are incredibly fragile. Examine the cliff face to the left of the houses and you'll notice several more tombs, peeking out from the limestone face. It is about an hour's walk back downhill from Santo Tomás to Puente Santo Tomás, from where there is transport north towards Chachapoyas.

Cerro Olán

Another Chachapoyan site is Cerro Olán, reached by *colectivo* to **San Pedro de Utac**, a small village beyond Montevideo, then a 30 minutes' walk. From the plaza a clear trail rises directly into the hills east of town to the ruins, which can be seen from the village. Here are the remains of towers which some archaeologists claim had roofs like mediaeval European castles. According to Morgan Davis this was essentially a military installation and once a small city of considerable luxury, similar in construction to La Congona (see page 464) but on a grander scale. Ask the alcalde for accommodation. The road south from Chachapoyas crosses the Utcubamba River then passes through **Palmira** and heads to Leymebamba.

Leymebamba → *Colour map 1, C4.*

This pleasant town derives its name from a visit in around 1475, by the Inca Túpac Yupanqui, who stayed to celebrate the **Fiesta de Inti-Raymi**. From that moment, the town came to be known as the Field of the Festival of The Sun, or **Raymi-Pampa**, which in turn became Leymebamba. The city was moved from its original location, 3 km south, following an epidemic of yellow fever in the 1600s. The local fiesta is held in honour of the Virgen del Carmen on the week preceeding 16 July.

The town's market is very limited; try the one at Yerbabuena on Sunday morning (see above). The young Spanish priest, Padre Diego, is very helpful. He is involved in the new museum project (see below). Water is sporadic and should be boiled to within an inch of its life. The Centro de Salud is helpful and will even visit your hotel if you're too ill to move. The **Comité Turístico** on the plaza is the place to go for all information on how to reach sites, including Laguna de los Cóndores (see below), for guides and horse hire. See www.leymebamba.org.

Laguna de los Cóndores

In 1996 a spectacular site consisting of six burial *chullpas*, containing 219 mummies and vast quantities of ceramics, textiles, woodwork, *quipus* and everyday utensils from the late Inca period, was discovered at Laguna de los Cóndores, a beautiful lake in a jungle setting, south of Leymebamba.

> *In addition to those at hotels (see Sleeping, page 469), there are a couple of phone lines in town, T041-770209 and T041-770264, which are shared.*

In order to protect this major discovery from *huaqueros*, who had already done considerable damage, all the material was moved to a spectacular new **museum** ⓘ *Tue-Sun 0930-1630, entry fee US$4.35, but anything over that amount is most welcome.* From the town it's a 30- to 40-minute walk, take the footpath and ask directions constantly, the road is much longer. It was opened in 2001, with Austrian financial assistance, at San Miguel (3 km south), the site of the original Leymebamba town. A proportion of over 5000 artefacts discovered are on display, the great majority of them saved from the Laguna de los Cóndores site. The museum and its materials were entirely made by hand, a true artisan construction. There is a café, a great place to admire the architecture and lush surroundings. For further information contact Dr Sonia Guillén ⓘ *Centro Mallqui Bioanthropology Foundation, http://centromallqui.org.pe.*

The trip to Laguna de los Cóndores from Leymebamba takes 10 to 12 hours on foot and horseback, nine hours return (three days in all). It is not for the faint-hearted, but is generally agreed to be one of the trips of a lifetime. The route climbs to 3700 m before descending to the laguna where there is a basic lodge, US$5. Bring all food and cook it there or pay the family to prepare it. Make sure your horse is in good condition as the track is often knee deep in mud. Also take food and warm clothes. It is best done during the dry season (May to September); hire a local guide and horses. Three-day tours cost about US$70 per person. Unfortunately, the impressive funerary site overlooking the river has been stripped of artefacts and even some of its colourful plaster. Please do not climb on the houses or remove anything from the site.

La Congona

There are numerous ruins around Leymebamba, many of which are covered in vegetation. The most spectacular is the Chachapoyan site of La Congona.

The site is a brisk three-hour walk along a clear trail which starts at the lower end of 16 de Julio. The path climbs steeply from the town, then levels off before descending to a large flat pasture. Turn left at the end of the pasture and follow the white sand, then bear right where the trail divides, to reach the middle of three peaks, identified by a white limestone cliff. The ruins are clustered in a small area, impossible to see until you are right among them. The views are stupendous and the ruins worth the effort. This is the best preserved of three sites, with 30 decorated round stone houses and a watch tower. It is supposed to be the only site displaying all three Chacha friezes – zigzag, rhomboid and Greek stepped.

There are two other sites, **El Molinete** and **Pumahuanyuna**, nearby. All three can be visited in a day but a guide is essential to explain the area and show the way to the ruins as it is easy to get lost.

Northwest of Chachapoyas » pp468-473.

There are more extraordinary archaeological remains, including strange sarcophagi in cliffs, with rewarding trekking possibilities in this area.

Luya, Karajía, Lamud and Pueblo de los Muertos

The village of **Luya** is on a turn-off from the road north to Pedro Ruiz (see below). In a lush canyon, 1½ hours' walk from the road to Luya is **Wanglic** (also spelled Huanglic), a funeral site with large circular structures built under a ledge. Nearby is a beautiful waterfall, a worthwhile excursion. Three kilometres or 1½ hours' walk from Luya is **Chipuric**, a residential complex belonging to the Chachapoyas culture. The site consists of burial tombs set in a cliff face on a high ledge with circular stone buildings on the hill above. The tombs, which are 1 m high and look like beehives, have all been looted. Continue along the dirt road from Luya until it forks; take the higher road with the irrigation canal. At **Pueblo Molino** (a small cluster of houses and one shop), the cliff face and the burial tombs are visible. On the lower road which passes below the cliff on the other side of the river, is Chipuric town. The cliff is steep but it's possible to climb up to the tombs with some difficulty and quite a few scratches from the thorn bushes. There are great views from the top, though.

Karajía, also known as Solmol, is 2½ hours' walk from Luya but more accessible from **Trita**. A short walk from Trita, in the valley behind the village, are the remarkable, 2.5-m high sarcophagi, which date from AD 1200, set into an impressive cliff face. Just below these inscrutable figures are plenty of human bones, if you look carefully. Study the cliff face for a dozen more, smaller sarcophagi. The main figures have been looted long ago by grave robbers who at least broke in via holes in the back, thus preserving the striking effigies. Ask for directions in Luya. Expect to pay around US$3.50-5 a day with a local guide. In dry weather a short way to get there is from Luya or Cohechán (see below) to Cruzpata (*colectivos* run from Luya to Cruzpata). At other times the road can be very muddy.

A good way to get to know the local people and to appreciate fully the magnificent scenery of this region is a three- to four-day trek starting from Luya. Walk two to 2½ hours to **Shipata** and from there to Karajía (30-40 minutes). Ask around for directions. You cannot get to the sarcophagi, but can view them from the other side of the valley (the same viewpoint as from Trita), with binoculars preferably. At Shipata you can stay with Sra Rosa Zota, who will cook you dinner and breakfast. A better option, however, is to continue one to 1½ hours to **Cohechán**. To get there from Karajía, you have to go back to Shipata. Continue from Cohechán to **Belén** (four to five hours) and **Vista Hermosa**, thence to Yumal and Choctámal (see under Gran Vilaya, below).

Ten minutes north of Luya, 37 km northwest of Chachapoyas, is **Lamud**, a convenient base for several interesting archaeological sites. The local fiesta of **Señor de Gualamita** on 14 September is well-attended.

At **San Antonio**, half an hour from Lamud, is a sandstone cliff face with several groups of burial tombs high on a ledge. They are difficult to see unless you know what you're looking for (there are sarcophogi and other tombs, but you need binoculars to see them). The ruins, set on the hill above, are a residential complex, thought to form part of a group of people belonging to the Chipuric. The main nucleus is almost completely ruined, but the ruins are unusual in that the stucco is still in place. A guide is not necessary, but ask for directions. On the bottom of the hill, where the road ends, a colonial-era tunnel and water-wheel can be explored.

Ten kilometres from Lamud are the mind-boggling ruins of **Pueblo de los Muertos**, circular stone houses overlooking the valley a thousand metres below. A road goes to within 40 minutes of the site and then you have a steep, 40-minute walk on loose rock. The view is spectacular and the ruins are difficult to find as they are

Gran Vilaya Region

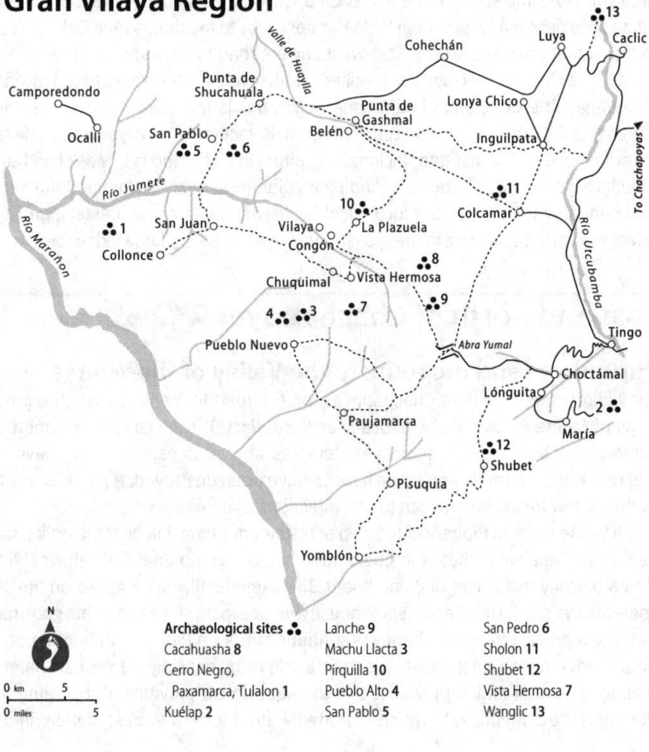

overgrown. Since being brought to public attention by Gene Savoy in the mid-1960s, the site has been largely destroyed by local grave robbers. Despite this, it is unmatched for location and scenery in the area. Ask directions before setting out.

Gran Vilaya → *Colour map 1, C4.*

The name Gran Vilaya was created by US explorer, Gene Savoy, one of the candidates for the original 'Indiana Jones', who discovered this extensive set of ruined complexes in 1985. There are about 30 sites spread over this vast area, 15 of which are considered significant. Among the sites are **Pueblo Alto**, **Pueblo Nuevo**, **Paxamarca** and **Machu Llacta**.

To get to this area, head north from Tingo or south from Chachapoyas as far as the Huinchuco bridge across the Río Utcubamba. On the west bank of the river a road leads to the left, if heading north, to the town of Colcamar, which is the starting point for exploring the area. A road from Choctámal to the Yumal pass into the Gran Vilaya region facilitates access but also places the area's cloudforests at considerable risk.

The whole area stretches west from the Río Utcubamba to the Río Marañón. Moist air pushing up from the Amazon Basin creates a unique biosphere of clouds and mist in which bromeliads and orchids thrive. Being near to the equator and over 3000 m above sea level, the daytime temperature is a constant 22°C. While the Marañón valley is a desert, the peaks are always misted from June to September and drenched in rain the rest of the year. This creates a huge variety of mini-ecological zones, each with its own flora and fauna, depending on altitude and which flank of the mountain they are on.

The Inca roads in this region make for incredible trekking. Three villages are possible starting points, Cohechán, Inguilpata or Colcamar. Trails all lead to Belén, a gigantic silted-in glacial tarn with a spectacular panorama of the river meandering below. This is above the nightly freeze line and the only large flat spot in the zone. From here you cross the spine of the Andes on a 1.6-km Inca stairway, dropping into Gran Vilaya. You pass many ruins near Vista Hermosa (3½ to four hours from Belén). You can lodge with Sr Cruz. The Kuélap East-West ancient road takes you over the Abra Yumal pass with a climb of 1600-1700 m ('a killer'), from where the trail thankfully descends to Choctámal. The **Choctámal Lodge** (see page 469) is therefore a good finishing (or starting) point for treks in the Gran Vilaya. It is recommended you take a letter of introduction from the Instituto Nacional de Cultura in Chachapoyas, or ask **Los Tambos Chachapoyanos** for assistance in finding a guide (essential), accommodation, meals and perhaps horses. Also ask local *alcaldes* for help. Padre Juan Castelli, an English priest who has been living in the area for many years, is very knowledgeable.

East and north of Chachapoyas » *pp468-473.*

Purunllacta and the route to the Valley of the Whites

Forty kilometres east from Chachapoyas, on the road to Mendoza, are the pre-Inca ruins of **Monte Peruvia** (known locally as **Purunllacta**). They consist of hundreds of white stone houses with staircases, temples and palaces. The ruins have been cleared by local farmers and some houses have been destroyed. A guide is useful as there are few locals from whom to ask directions.

If you're stuck in **Pipus**, ask to sleep at restaurant **Huaracina** or at the police station next door. There are no hotels in **Cheto** but a house high up on the hill above the town with a balcony has cheap bed and board. The same family has a house on the plaza. There are two small shops and a small house with one room serves basic but good meals.

The road east from Chachapoyas continues through Pipus to **Molinopampa**, two hours' drive from Chachapoyas, it then carries on, passing a forest of palms, to **Mendoza**, capital and supply centre of the subtropical province of the same name (Rodríguez de Mendoza), which reportedly produces the best coffee in Peru.

The Valley of the Whites

The tiny villages in the Guayabamba valley could be any other sleepy, sub- tropical settlements. A collection of wooden houses on a fertile plain where oranges, bananas, guava and yucca grow. But the people of this remote region are very different from your average jungle dweller. They are blond-haired, blue-eyed and fair- skinned and could easily have just stepped off the 1700 flight from Stockholm.

The people of the Guayabamba valley themselves don't know where they came from and opinions among experts vary. Some posit the theory that they originate from warring conquistador factions in the early 16th century. This view hasn't satisfied those who point to the rarity of this phenomenon. It's true that the Spanish chronicler Garcilaso de la Vega described the fair-skinned people resisting the Incas before the conquest, but evidence tends to show that it is unlikely that the people of Guayamba have anything to do with the Chachapoyas cloud people.

Dr Jacques de Mahieu of Buenos Aires believes the cloud people to be descendants of the Vikings, who came to Peru in the 11th century. He supports such a theory with evidence on Easter Island, west of Chile, of drawings showing Viking longships, as well as linguistic parallels between the Quechua language and Scandinavian tongues.

The romantic theories are countered by research showing that the pre-conquest peoples did not speak Quechua in this region and that the Spanish chroniclers have been misunderstood: the phrase "the Chachapoyas were of fair complexion" has been taken to mean, wrongly, that they were blond. Perhaps the mystery will be solved by investigation into the DNA of the mummies found at Laguna de Cóndores and Scandinavian bog people and other European mummies. Moreover, in Guayamba DNA samples can be traced to one Spanish family who lived in the region for a long time and there is evidence that the people of Chirimoto were originally Italian and Spanish settlers in the 1820s.

Whatever the explanation, the incongruous presence of these fair-skinned people in such a remote part of Peru will continue to attract the attention of ethnologists.

Organically grown coffee from the area is exported directly to Europe. There are several simple restaurants on Rodríguez de Mendoza.

Mendoza is also the starting point for an ethnologically interesting area in the Guayabamba Valley where there is a high incidence of fair-skinned people (see box, page 467). There are roads and public transport to the small towns of Huambo, Santa Rosa, Totora, Limabamba, Chirimoto Viejo and Milpuc; and horse trails to other remote villages. Visitors going beyond Mendoza should be self sufficient.

North of Chachapoyas

The road north from Chachapoyas, paved for 13 km, heads through the beautiful Utcubamba River canyon with steep mountains on either side. In places the road is cut into the canyon wall. In the rainy season landslides may occur. **Pedro Ruiz** is the town at the crossroads, where you can either head west to Chiclayo on the coast or east to Tarapoto, Yurimaguas and the jungle. This is a small but important junction at the confluence of the Río Ingenio and the Utucubamba.

There are many interesting options for walking in the surrounding hills, covered with patches of cloudforest and a good deal of undeveloped archaeology. **Catarata Chinata** is a lovely 150-m waterfall which can be reached by walking along the trail to

How high?

In 2002 the German explorer Stefan Ziemendorff came across a waterfall in Amazonas department, near the Pedro Ruiz-Chachapoyas road, called Gocta. Its whereabouts was not revealed by locals who feared that a mermaid living in the waters below the fall would curse whoever disclosed its location. Ziemendorff has not been so timid, but there is no agreement on where the falls rank in the world's waterfall hierarchy. At 771 m (2530 feet), it could be the third highest, or the fifth, or the 14th, but Miles Buesst of South American Explorers in Lima is certain of one thing: they are "utterly spectacular and well worth the visit: at one lookout there are eight separate waterfalls visible and The World Waterfall Database gives Gocta itself a 'scenic rating' of 96%, which I think is ungenerous!" SAE can advise on how to get there, or contact local tour operators (but beware of overcharging).

the village of San Carlos, about two hours uphill. Continue uphill past San Carlos then turn left along a smaller track to the waterfall, a further two hours. Ask the locals for directions. It's a very nice full-day hike through sections of cloudforest.

Pomacochas lake, 2150 m above sea level, is near the town of Florida. The blue-green water is surrounded by totora reeds. Take a combi to Florida or Balsapata along the road to Rioja (one hour, US$1.75); there are good views of the lake from the road. Where the buses stop in Florida, women sell cheese and bread spread with *dulce/manjar*. There are a couple of hotels in the town and it is a popular day excursion from Chachapoyas.

Near Florida is the **Río Chido** trail, a famous birdwatching site with some rare species, including the marvellous spatula-tail hummingbird. Access is five minutes before the high point on the road to Florida, at San Ignacio. A highly recommended guide is Dilberto Faustino, who is very enthusiastic and knowledgeable.

Sleeping

Cajamarca to Chachapoyas *p457*

F Hostal Celendín, Jr Unión 305, Plaza de Armas, Celendín, T076-555041. Colonial, with bathroom, hot water, patio, pleasant, good restaurant.

F Loyer's, José Gálvez 410, Celendín, T076-555210. With bathroom, cheaper without, patio, nice.

F Naranja Mecánica (Orange), Jr Unión 217, T076-555640, Celendín, www.celendinperu.com. New Dutch-Peruvian owned *hostal* in the centre, small, B&B, shared bath, café with a set-price menu (Wed-Sun 1500-2100, vegetarians catered for), book exchange.

G Maxmar, 2 de Mayo 349, Celendín. With bathroom, cheaper without, hot shower extra, basic, clean, parking, good value, owner Francisco is very helpful.

G Raymi Wasi, Jr José Gálvez, Celendín, beside La Reserve (same owner), T076-555374. With bath, hot water, TV, large rooms, has patio, quiet, clean, parking, good value.

Chachapoyas and around *p457*

C Gran Vilaya, Ayacucho 755, T041-477664, http://granhotelvilaya.com. The best in town, comfortable rooms, firm beds, parking, English spoken, all services. Gumercindo Zegarra, the proprietor, is knowledgeable about happenings in and around Chachapoyas.

D Casa Vieja, Chincha Alta 569, T041-477353, www.casaviejaperu.com. In a converted old house, very nicely decorated, all rooms different, family atmosphere, hot water, cable TV, living room and *comedor* with open fire, continental breakfast, internet and library. Repeatedly recommended.

D Casona Monsante, Jr Amazonas 746, T041-477702, www.lacasonamonsante.com.

Rooms in a converted colonial house have cable TV, patio, there is a cafeteria, breakfast costs US$1.50.

E Belén, Jr Ortiz Arrieta 540, T041-477830, www.hostalbelen.com.pe. On the plaza next to the bank. With bath, hot water, nicely furnished.

E Kuélap, Amazonas 1057, T041-477136, www.hotelkuelap.com. With private bathroom, hot water and TV, cheaper without TV, cheaper still with shared bathroom and cold water, parking. Recommended.

E Puma Urcu, Jr Amazonas 833, T041-477871, hotelpumaurcu@peru.com. Carpeted rooms, hot water, cable TV, **Café Café** next door, both hotel and café receive good reports.

E Revash, Grau 517, Plaza de Armas, T041-477391. With private bathroom, plenty of hot water, patio, friendly, helpful, laundry, good local information, restaurant. Recommended.

F El Dorado, Ayacucho 1062, T041-477047. With bathroom, hot water, clean, helpful.

F El Tejado, Grau 534, Plaza de Armas, T041-477654. On first floor, same entrance as restaurant, good, laundry.

F Levanto Lodge, Levanto, kuelap@msn.com. Price per person. 2 circular buildings with tall thatched roofs, stand behind Levanto's church; they can accommodate 12 people (**G** per person with own sleeping bag) and have bathroom, basic but with hot shower, lounge with fireplace and kitchen, meals US$1.

G Hostal El Danubio, Tres Esquinas 193 y Junín 584, Plazuela Belén, some distance from centre, T041-477337. With private bathroom, hot water, cheaper with shared bath and cold water, clean, friendly, meals can be ordered in advance.

G Hostal Johumaji, Ayacucho 711, T041-477279, olvacha@ddm.com.pe. With bathroom, hot water, TV, cheaper without TV, meals extra.

G Laguna de los Cóndores, Salamanca 941, T041-477492. Very basic, shared bathroom, cold water.

Kuélap and Tingo *p459, map p461*

F Albergue León, Jr Saenz Peña s/n, Tingo, no sign, walk 50 m from the police checkpoint to the corner and turn left, it's the third house on the left (right-hand door), T041-999 9390. Price per person. Basic, shared bathroom, cold water, friendly, run by Lucho León, who is very knowledgeable.

F Valle Kuélap. A new hotel in Tingo, with bungalows.

When walking up to Kuélap from Tingo, the last house to the right of the track (**El Bebedero**, just above a small spring) offers accommodation: bed, breakfast and evening meal for US$6; good meals, friendly and helpful. A bit further, on the left, 100 m below the ruins, is the **Instituto Nacional de Cultura (INC)** hostel. It's a clean dormitory with room for about 12 people, in a lovely setting, US$1.75 per person, no running water (please conserve the rainwater in the buckets), simple meals may be available from the caretaker for US$1. There is free camping outside the hostel.

Leymebamba *p463*

D Hostal La Casona, Jr Amazonas 223, Leymebamba, T041-830106, www.lacasonadeleymebamba.com. With bath, hot water, breakfast available on request.

E Hostal La Petaca, Jr Amazonas 461, Leymebamba, opposite the church, T041-770288. With bath, hot water.

E Laguna de los Cóndores, Jr Amazonas 320, Leymebamba, half a block from the plaza, T041-770208, www.chachapoyasperu.com.pe/hostallagunadeloscondores.htm. Cheaper without bath, warm water, a good choice.

There is a *hostal* in La Jalca, one block from the plaza, passing the church, where the phone is, very basic. You may be able to find a room through the Alcaldía. Don't expect too much privacy, however, as it is used until 2200, after which time there is no electricity. So bring a torch (and a pack of cards; there isn't much in the way of nightlife, other than drinking).

F Escobedo, 16 de Julio 514, Leymebamba. Cold water, very basic, doors locked at 2130.

F Mirita, 16 de Julio 539, Leymebamba. Basic, warm water in shared bathroom.

Northwest of Chachapoyas *p464*

E Hostal Kuélap, Garcilaso de la Vega 452, Lamud, on the plaza. Clean, basic, friendly, hot water, **F** with cold water and shared bathroom.

F-G Choctámal Lodge, 3 km outside Choctámal, known locally as 'el hotel', kuelap@msn.com. Price per person. The facilities are not always open. Check beforehand at **Chachapoyas Tours**, address below, or ask in Choctámal for Norma Cruz. Most expensive rooms have hot tub, cheaper for room with just sheets and towels, and cheaper if you have a sleeping bag. Breakfast included. Meals start at US$1. It's in a lovely setting with great views, but cold at night.

G **Hostal Jucusbamba**, in Luya. Basic accommodation.

Choctámal village has no hotels, but accommodation may be available in local homes.

In **María**, 8 small *hospedajes* all charge US$3 per night, comfortable, friendly, big meals.

East and north of Chachapoyas *p466*

E **Casablanca**, Pedro Ruiz, on the main road, close to the Chachapoyas turning. Private bathroom, comfortable, the best in town.

F **Amazonense**, Pedro Ruiz, near Policía Nacional on the main road. Cheaper with shared bathroom, basic, clean, friendly, helpful. Recommended.

G **Altiplano**, Rodríguez de Mendoza 321, Mendoza. With bathroom, cheaper without, cold water, very basic.

G **Grandez**, Pje Hilario López 110, Mendoza. With bathroom, cheaper without, cold water, very basic.

Eating

Cajamarca to Chachapoyas *p457*

¥¥-¥ **La Reserve**, José Gálvez 313, Celendín. Good quality and value. Recommended.

¥ **Bella Aurora**, Grau 485, Celendín. Good.

¥ **Jalisco**, Jr Unión, Plaza de Armas, Celendín. Good value breakfasts and other meals, but beware of overcharging.

¥ **Santa Isabel**, Jr José Gálvez 512, Celendín. Clean, OK.

Chachapoyas and around *p457*

¥¥-¥ **El Tejado**, upstairs at Grau 534, Plaza de Armas, T041-777654. Good quality, slightly upscale, nice view and atmosphere. Recommended.

¥ **Chacha**, Grau 541, Plaza de Armas. Popular with locals, clean, but average food.

¥ **Chifa Chuy Xien**, Jr Amazonas 848, opposite Hotel Puma Urcu. Authentic Chinese cooking, daily specials and à la carte.

¥ **El Edén**, Grau y Ayacucho. Very good vegetarian, large helpings, open by 0830, closed Sat afternoon/evening.

¥ **La Tushpa**, Jr Ortiz Arrieta 753. The best in town, excellent meat and *platos criollos*, very clean kitchen, attentive service, open for lunch and dinner. Recommended.

¥ **Las Rocas**, Ayacucho 932 on Plaza. Popular, good local dishes, open daily (and Sun evening when many others are shut)).

¥ **Kuélap**, Ayacucho 832. Good, friendly. Recommended.

¥ **Mari Pizza**, Ayacucho 912. Good pizza.

¥ **Matalache**, corner of Amazonas and Grau. Good and very popular. Serves huge portions. After a hard trek, try the massive *bistec a lo pobre* (tenderized steak piled high with fried plantains, fries and egg). Recommended.

¥ **Panadería San José**, Ayacucho 816. Does good breakfasts and other meals throughout the day, also regional snacks. Closed Sun.

¥ **Tinkuy Wasi**, Prolongación Jr Kuélap, Barrio Santa Rosa, above El Mirador del Colorado. Very good *cecina* served with chips and *mote*, in a country setting above town, lovely views.

Cafés

Café de Guías, in **Hotel Gran Vilaya**. Serves snacks, meals and organic coffee from the area, also has lots of local information, good.

Dulcería Santa Helena, Amazonas 800. Try here for sweets.

Mass Burger, Ortiz Arrieta, Plaza de Armas. Excellent juices, cakes, fruit salads.

There are 2 small bar-*bodegas* in Levanto selling drinks, but little food.

Kuélap and Tingo *p459, map p461*

Kuélap, at the junction of the main road with the road on the south bank of the Río Tingo. Clean and OK. There are 2 other eating places in Kuélap.

Sites between Tingo and Leymebamba *p462*

¥ **Cely Pizza's**, Jr La Verdad 530, Leymebamba, 2 blocks from Plaza de Armas, opposite the health centre. Good value,

There is some very tasty local cuisine in this area. Try the tropical fruits, the local sausage (chorizo) *and fried green bananas* (tocacho).

2-course set meals for US$2.50, pizzas take 20 mins unless you book in advance, will cook vegetarian meals at 24 hrs notice, great for breakfast, very clean, has fridge for cold beer, friendly. Recommended.

El Sabor Tropical, 16 de Julio, Leymebamba. Good chicken and chips, friendly.

Northwest of Chachapoyas *p464*

María, Lamud, down from **Hostal Kuélap**. Cheap, friendly and obliging, steak and chips is recommended, ask for *pensión* which is 3 meals for US$1.80, excellent value, popular.

East and north of Chachapoyas *p466*

Some simple cheap little places in Pedro Ruiz:

Aleidita, on the road to Chachapoyas.

Puerta de Kuélap on the Marginal towards Chiclayo.

Chilico, on the Marginal, towards Moyobamba.

Festivals and events

Cajamarca to Chachapoyas *p457*

16-29 Jul Celendín hosts its **Virgen del Carmen** festival. Bullfights with matadores from Spain and cock fighting are all part of the well-attended celebrations.

Chachapoyas and around *p457*

First week of Jun Among the town's festivals are **Semana Turística de Amazonas**.

Aug Virgen Asunta.

Activities and tours

Chachapoyas and around *p457*

Tours in the surrounding area include: city tour, Levanto, Yalape (0800-1530, US$8.65), Kuélap (see page 459), Karajía, La Jalca, Leymebamba (all full day, US$12-20, depending on distance and number of passengers, including guide and food), Revash (by vehicle to Santo Tomás, then 2-hr hike), Gran Vilaya or Laguna de los Cóndores (4-5 days each, depending on size of group), Mendoza (groups of 6 to 8).

Andes Tours, contact information same as Hostal Revash. Daily trips to Kuélap, other conventional tours to ruins and caves in the area and trekking trips to Gran Vilaya, Laguna de los Cóndores and other destinations. These trips combine travel by car, on horseback and walking.

Chachapoyas Tours SAC, Grau 534, Plaza de Armas (**Hotel El Tejado**), T041-478838 www.kuelapperu.com, or in the USA T(1) 866-396 9582, international T407-5836786. Reliable, English-speaking guide, good service. Recommended. Related to this company is Charles Motley's **Los Tambos Chachapoyanos** (LTC) programme, www.kuelap.org, with the lodges at Levanto and Choctámal (see page 469).

Vilaya Tours, c/o **Gran Hotel Vilaya**, Jr Grau 624, T041-477506, www.vilayatours.com. All-inclusive area treks throughout northern Peru catering to international clientele. Excellent guides. Robert Dover is one of the founders and is British, contact him through **Vilaya Tours**, or the **Café de Guías** (see Eating, page 470). They have a regular newsletter and also work in conjunction with community projects. Recommended.

Kuélap and Tingo *p459, map p461*

Oscar Arce Cáceres, based at 'El Chillo' near the Río Utcubamba, 4½ km outside Tingo. Oscar owns a farm and knows the area very well. He is a very reliable guide but only speaks Spanish. He also has accommodation with bath, provides good meals and stores luggage. The trek into this area, like the walk up to Kuélap, starts from Tingo – the way is all mule track. The walk from El Chillo to Kuélap is shorter than from Tingo. The return to El Chillo can be made via the village of Nogalcucho (ask for directions). El Chillo is one of the places where the marvellous spatule-tail hummingbird, unique to the Río Utcubamba, may be seen.

Leo Cobina, G Prada y 2 de Mayo, Leymebamba, recommended guide.

Lázaro Mostanza Lozano, San Martín y 2 de Mayo, or through Hotel Laguna de los Cóndores.

Northwest of Chachapoyas *p464*

Angel Mestanza Bobadilla, Garcilaso de la Vega 458, Lamud, near the hotel on the plaza, T041-780213/780223, amesbo@latinmail.com. He is a photographer and is recommended. His prices are reasonable. One trip is to local caves (be prepared to get muddy; take a torch); also to waterfalls.

East and north of Chachapoyas *p466*

Augustus Grandez Loja, Mendoza, a local guide, can take travellers around the little-known environs of Mendoza. He can provide horses for longer treks. Ask for him in town.

Transport

Cajamarca to Chachapoyas *p457*

Bus

Celendín to Cajamarca, 107 km, 4-5 hrs (or 3½-4 hrs in a combi) : with **Atahualpa**, 2 de Mayo 707, Plaza de Armas, T076-555256, at 0700 and 1300 daily, US$3; **Royal Palace's**, Jr Unión 333, Plaza de Armas, at 0645 and 1300 daily, poor minibuses, US$3. **Celendín to Chachapoyas** via Balsas and Leymebamba, 12-14 hrs (may be much longer in the rainy season, take warm clothing, food and water): **Virgen del Carmen**, Cáceres 117, on Sun and Thu at 1100, US$11. Other local transport leaves from the market area.

Chachapoyas and around *p457*

Bus

To **Chiclayo** with **Móvil Tours**, US$10.60, en route to Trujillo, 2000, US$12, and Lima, 1230, 22 hrs, US$24. **Civa**, to Chiclayo at 0600 daily, 11½ hrs (may be longer in the rainy season), US$9-10.60; to **Lima** 1230, 24 hrs, US$16.65- 27.25; **Turismo Kuélap**, at 1700 daily, US$9 to Chiclayo. To **Celendín**, from which there are connections to Cajamarca: with **Virgen del Carmen**, Tue and Fri at 0600, 14-15 hrs (may be much longer in the rainy season, an unforgettable journey, take warm clothing, food and water), US$11. To **Pedro Ruiz**, for connections to Chiclayo or Tarapoto, combis (US$2.15, 2 hrs, 0800-1800) and cars/*colectivos* – more common (US$3, 1¾ hrs) leave from Grau y Salamanca, also from Ortiz Arrieta y Libertad. To **Bagua Grande**, 0430-1800, cars US$6, 3 hrs, from Grau 355 y Libertad. To **Mendoza** (86 km), **Trans Zelada** buses leave 1600 daily from Ortiz Arrieta 310, US$3.65, 3½ hrs (also to Chiclayo, Trujillo and Lima, 1100, US$20); cars 0400-2000, from Ortiz Arrieta, cuadra 3 (uphill from **Zelada**), US$4,55, 3 hrs.

For **Kuélap**, **Roller's**, combis or cars, at 0500 and 1400, from Kuélap to Chachapoyas at 1200 and 1700, US$3.65, 3 hrs; **Yumal** US$3.65, 3 hrs; **María** US$3, 2½ hrs; **Lónguita** US$2.42, 2 hrs; **Tingo** US$1.50, 1½ hrs. Combis to Tingo from Grau y Salamanca, US$2.25, 1½ hrs. To **Santo Tomás**, **Comité Interprovincial Santo Tomás**, 0800-1600, US$2.75, 3 hrs; **Cruce de Revash**, US$2.75, 2½ hrs; **Tingo** US$2.25, 1½ hrs. To **Leymebamba**, combis and small buses from 2 de Mayo y Libertad, 1200, 1600 (also from cuadra 8 of Libertad), US$3, 2½ hrs. To **Jalca Grande**, Comité Interprovincial Santo Tomás, departures about 1300 onwards (few if any on Sat), US$3.65 (return in morning). To **Luya** and **Lamud**, from **San Juan de Luya**, Ortiz Arrieta 364, cars 0400-2000, US$2.25, 1 hr to Lamud, same price to Luya. Taxis may be hired from the plaza for any local destination.

Levanto is 2 hrs by truck. Trucks leave from the market in Chachapoyas most days at 0600, US$0.90, and there are trucks and combis (2 hrs, US$1) from outside **Bodega El Amigo** on Jr Hermosura at 1400. To walk to Levanto, see page 458.

Bus companies Civa, San Juan de la Libertad 956, T041-478048. **Comité Interprovincial Santo Tomás**, Grau, by the cul-de-sac between Salamanca and Libertad. **Móvil Tours**, Jr Libertad 464, T041-478545.

Roller's, Grau 302.**Trans Zelada**, Ortiz Arrieta 310. **Turismo Kuélap**, Ortiz Arrieta 412, T041-478128. **Virgen del Carmen**, Av Salamanca 650.

Car

If driving your own vehicle, there is a petrol station in Tingo, the last on the route to Celendín. Otherwise there is fuel in Chacha (84 octane only).

Kuélap and Tingo *p459, map p461*

There are several combis (from 0500) daily from Tingo to **Chachapoyas**. Tingo to **Leymebamba** takes 2 hrs, US$1.75.

Sites between Tingo and Leymebamba *p462*

Jalca Grande: Comité Interprovincial Santo Tomás combis from Chachapoyas, see above for details. They return from La Jalca to Chachapoyas at 0500 daily.

Leymebamba: buses from Chachapoyas to **Celendín** (see page 472) pass through Leymebamba 3½ hrs after departure and make a lunch stop here. There's no guarantee of a seat, but you might have a better chance if you purchase your ticket in advance in Chachapoyas, informing that you will get on in Leymebamba. Combis run direct to Celendín on Sun and Tue, 1100. Combis to **Chachapoyas** leave the plaza regularly. The road between Chachapoyas and Leymebamba takes 2½-3½ hrs by car, but both car and bus take longer in the rainy season.

Northwest of Chachapoyas *p464*

For transport to **Luya** and **Lamud** see Chachapoyas Transport, page 472. The road is unpaved but in reasonable condition.

East and north of Chachapoyas *p466*

There is no direct transport from Chachapoyas to **Cheto** for Purunllacta. Take a combi at 0930 and 1500 from Jr Salamanca, fourth block down from the market, to Pipus, which stands at the turn-off to Cheto; 1½ hrs, US$1.35. You may have a long wait in Pipus for transport to Cheto; a *camioneta* leaves early in the morning, US$0.90; or it's a 2-hr walk on a rough road.

From **Mendoza**, Trans Zelada buses run to **Chachapoyas**, 1100 daily, US$3.65, 3½ hrs. Cars US$4.55, 3 hrs. To **Limabamba**, 3 daily between 1300 and 1500, 2 hrs, US$1.20.

To and from **Pedro Ruiz** there are many buses on the **Chiclayo**, **Tarapoto** (8-9 hrs) and **Chachapoyas** routes. All pass through town, day and night. There is no way to reserve a seat and buses are usually full. **Móvil**, Av Marginal 123, T041-780238, is the company for buses to **Lima** and **Tarapoto**. To **Bagua Grande**, cars US$2.75, 1 hr. To **Chachapoyas**, combis US$2.15, 2 hrs; cars US$3, 1¾ hrs. To **Nuevo Cajamarca**, combis US$4.55, 2 hrs. Combis to **Moyobamba**, US$5.75, 4 hrs. One side of the junction for Chachapoyas, by the bridge, is the **Trans Kuélap** office. Opposite the turning, in **Restaurante Gissela** (breakfasts and lunches) is the **Civa** office. Cars to Bagua Grande stop outside the restaurant. For cars and combis to Chachapoyas, from the junction walk down the main road towards Bagua and turn left a short way down a side street.

Directory

Cajamarca to Chachapoyas *p457*

Banks There are banks or *cambios* for exchange in Celendín, but try the local shops. **Post** Jr Unión 415, Celendín. **Telephone** José Gálvez 600 y Pardo, Plaza de Armas, Celendín.

Chachapoyas and around *p457*

Banks BCP, Ortiz Arrieta 576, Plaza de Armas. Gives cash on Visa card, changes cash and TCs, ATM (Visa/Plus). There are 2 well-signed places on Ayacucho, Plaza de Armas, which change cash. **Internet** Many places around the plaza and elsewhere, US$0.45 per hr. **Laundry** Lavandería Speed Clean, Ayacucho 964 on plaza (ask at the appliance store at the same address), T041-777665. Clean, Amazonas 817. **Post** Grau on Plaza de Armas. **Telephone** Ayacucho 926, Plaza de Armas. Also at Grau 608.

East and north of Chachapoyas *p466*

Banks Banco de la Nación, in Pedro Ruiz, changes cash only. **Post and telephone** Rodríguez de Mendoza in Mendoza. Telephone on the main road in Pedro Ruiz between Casablanca and Policía Nacional.

To Ecuador and to the Amazon

The road from Pedro Ruiz (see page 467) goes west for 65 km to Bagua Grande, at first through a narrow gorge, the ridges covered with lush cloudforest, then along the broad and fertile lower Utcubamba valley. It then crosses the Marañón at Corral Quemado. From the confluence of the Marañón with the Río Chamaya, the road follows the latter, past bare cliffs covered by dry scrub, towering over the deep river canyons. ▸▸ *For Sleeping, Eating and other listings, see pages 478-482.*

To Ecuador ▸▸ *pp478-482.*

The Baguas and Chamaya

With the opening of a bridge at Balsas on the Peru-Ecuador border, this route is becoming a worthwhile route for those who do not want to leave the highlands. The first town of note heading west from Pedro Ruiz is **Bagua Grande** (phone code 041). It's a hot and dusty place, sprawled along its main street, Avenida Chachapoyas, where most hotels and restaurants are located. Bagua Grande is not very safe and suffers water shortages. If arriving late, ask to sleep on the bus until daybreak. Police may ask to see travellers' documents here. The town celebrates the **Fiesta de Santiago** over the last week in July and tourist week festivities in September. There are internet cafés by the Plaza de Armas. **BCP** changes cash and Amex traveller's cheques.

Near Bagua Grande, along a side road to Sarameriza is **Bagua Chica**, also referred to as just Bagua, a garrison. Pay careful attention to the names when arranging transport, so you are not taken to the wrong Bagua. Between the turning for Bagua Chica and the turning for Jaén is a toll post (US$0.75 for cars). By the 24 de Julio bridge over the Río Marañón is a forestry control post. From Bagua Grande the main road continues northwest, then forks: southwest to **Chamaya** (50 km from Bagua Grande, one basic hostel, **El Volante**), for Jaén and the coast; and northeast to Sarameriza, the first port on the Marañón. From Chamaya it's 15 minutes to Jaén, the best place to break the journey from Chachapoyas or the jungle to Ecuador or Chiclayo and vice-versa.

Jaén and around → *Phone code: 076. Colour map 1, B3. Population: 25,000. Altitude: 740 m.*

Although it was founded in 1536, Jaén retains little of its colonial character. Rather, it is the modern and prosperous centre of a rich agricultural region producing rice, coffee, and cocoa (also, reputedly, opium poppies). From 1563 to 1789 it was governed by the Real Audiencia de Quito and it is close to territory that used to be disputed by the two countries, hence its former designation 'Corazón de la Peruanidad'. The local festival of **Señor de Huamantanga** on 14 September is widely attended. It is a friendly place and there is a **Dircetur office** ⓘ *Jr Zarumilla 1345, T076-431188.*

A colourful modern **cathedral** dominates the large plaza around which most services of interest to the visitor are clustered. A **museum** ⓘ *Instituto 4 de Junio, Hermógenes Mejía s/n,* displays pre-Columbian artifacts from the Pakamuros culture.

To bathe in the **Marañón,** take a combi from the corner of Cajamarca and Eloy Ureta to Bellavista (40 minutes, US$0.50). From here it is a 45-minute walk beside rice paddies to the river, ask for directions. Swimming is possible but mind the strong current. Many locals go there on Sundays. A motorboat across the Marañón costs US$0.45 one way.

Jaén to the border→ *Colour map 1, B3.*

A pleasant road runs north from Jaén through rice fields, then alongside the Río Chinchipe to Puerto Ciruelos, where the road leaves the river and climbs through forested hills to **San Ignacio** (phone code 076), near the border with Ecuador. It is a nice town with steep streets and a modern plaza in the centre of a coffee-growing area. The **Fiesta de San Ignacio Loyola** is celebrated on 30 July; the **Semana Turística** is the third week in September. You can take excursions to waterfalls, lakes, petroglyphs and ancient ruins in the nearby hills. From San Ignacio the narrow, unpaved road runs 45 km through green hills to **Namballe**. Just to the north a dirt road goes west to the **Santuario Tabaconas-Namballe** ⓘ *reserve office at San Martín 332, Jaén, T076-846166, snntabaconasnamballe@yahoo.es*, a 29,500-ha reserve, between 1200 and 3800 m protecting several Andean ecosystems. The border is 15 minutes from town at **La Balsa**, where a few shops sell drinks and basic items and there are money changers, but no lodgings. To leave Peru head directly to immigration (0800-1300, 1500-2000). (When entering Peru, stop at the PNP after immigration.) The Ecuadorean immigration service is supposedly open 24 hours, knock on the door or ask for the officer if he is not in sight. Once through Ecuadorean immigration, you can take a *ranchera* to Zumba, 1½ hours, from where buses run to Vilcabamba (six-seven hours) and Loja, a further 1½ hours, many minibuses daily, US$1. To get to Vilcabamba in one day, you need to leave Jaén by 0700, a tiring journey but the road Jaén-Loja is being improved, with paving in progress in each country. You may have to stay in Zumba.

To the coast

Heading west from Chamaya (see above), the highway reaches the Abra de Porculla (at 2150 m, the lowest pass through the Peruvian Andes) in 60 km, before descending to join the old Pan-American Highway at Olmos (see page 413). From here you can go southwest to Chiclayo, or northwest to Piura. The road from Pedro Ruiz west to Olmos is paved, but prone to landslides in the rainy season.

Northeast to Sarameriza → *Colour map 1, B4.*

The road from Bagua Grande to **Sarameriza** first passes through **Aramango** and **Chiriaco** and continues to another fork, northeast to **Oracuza** and **Santa María de Nieve**, and east to Sarameriza and **Puerto Delfus**, both on the Río Marañón.

Santa María de Nieve is a welcoming place, typical of a small riverside town with a mixed community. It has a zoo, good swimming in the river, fishing and trips to indigenous villages and downriver to the Pongo de Manseriche.

Travelling beyond Bagua Chica, even though some birdwatching groups do go here, is not recommended unless you have permission from the Aguaruna communities and take local guides who know each community that you will pass through. There have been robberies and sexual assaults on desolate parts of road.

East to the Amazon » pp478-482.

The eastern branch of the road at Pedro Ruiz runs all the way to Yurimaguas. The road has been paved as far as Tarapoto. All sections are still prone to landslides in the wet season. This is a very beautiful journey, first passing Laguna Pomacochas (see page 468), then leading to where the high Andes tumble into the Amazon Basin before your eyes.

Nuevo Cajamarca → *Phone code: 042. Colour map 1, B4. Altitude: 940 m.*

After Florida, the road winds down then up through Buenos Aires to a cultivated zone around the villages of La Esperanza, El Progreso and Oso Perdido. A further forested descent leads to the town of Nuevo Cajamarca, 152 km east of Pedro Ruiz. There is a market and accommodation on the main road (F **Continental** is the best).

Rioja → *Phone code: 042. Colour map 1, B5. Altitude: 900 m.*

Beyond Nuevo Cajamarca, 22 km, is Rioja. Nearby there are a number of caves (Diamante, Cascayunga) and river sources (Tioyacu, Negro), as *complejos* and *recreos turísticos*, which have accommodation, swimming pools and local foods. The best is the **Yacumama Lodge**, where the owner gives guests tours of his property and can arrange local excursions.

Moyobamba → *Phone code 042. Colour map 1, B5. Population: 14,000. Altitude: 915 m.*

Moyobamba, a pleasant town in the attractive Río Mayo valley, was founded in 1540 as the original capital of Maynas. It then became capital of Loreto before the establishment of the department of San Martín, of which it became capital in 1906. This area has to cope with lots of rain in the wet season and in some years the whole area is flooded. At the end of June the town celebrates its annual tourist week festival (**San Juan**); the **Fiesta de Santiago** is late July and for three days around 1 November is the **Festival de la Orquídea**. The valley is renowned for its orchids. There are three places where you can see orchids around Moyobamba: **Jardín Botánico San Francisco** ⓘ *Barrio Lluyllucucha, follow Jr Arequipa to the south, daily 0800-1700, US$0.30*, a park at the west end of town; **Orquideario Wakanki** ⓘ *just before you get to the San Mateo thermal baths, open 0900-1700, US$0.60*, where the orchids have been placed on the trees; and **Viveros AgrOriente** ⓘ *Jr Reyes Guerra 900, by Punta de Tahuishco, Tue-Sun 0900-1300, 1600-2000, US$0.30*, a commercial orchid and tropical fruit nursery which also has a small zoo with regional animals and birds.

A pleasant promenade with nice views of the Río Mayo valley is **Punta de Tahuishco** (from the town centre follow Jirón Reyes Guerra seven blocks north). A steep path goes down from here to **Puerto Tahuishco**, the town's harbour on the Río Mayo. Boats can be hired for excursions on the river and a passenger boat serves communities upriver, going as far as Nueva Piura, returning the next day. From **Morro de Calzada**, 10 km west along the road to Rioja, there is a good view. Take a truck to Calzada (20 minutes), then walk up for 20 minutes. There are Baños Termales at **San Mateo** ⓘ *5 km to the southeast, off the road to Jepelacio, open 0500-2200, US$0.30*, which are hot and worth a visit at weekends when the entire town seems to be there, and sulphur baths at **Oromina** ⓘ *6.5 km west, open 0500-1800, US$0.30*.

For the **Paccha waterfalls** ⓘ *US$0.30 payable in Nuevo San Miguel, insist on a receipt*, in a beautiful, unspoilt setting, take a *colectivo* or combi to Nuevo San Miguel. Walk past town for 15 minutes; just before a bridge is a sign for the falls to the right. A

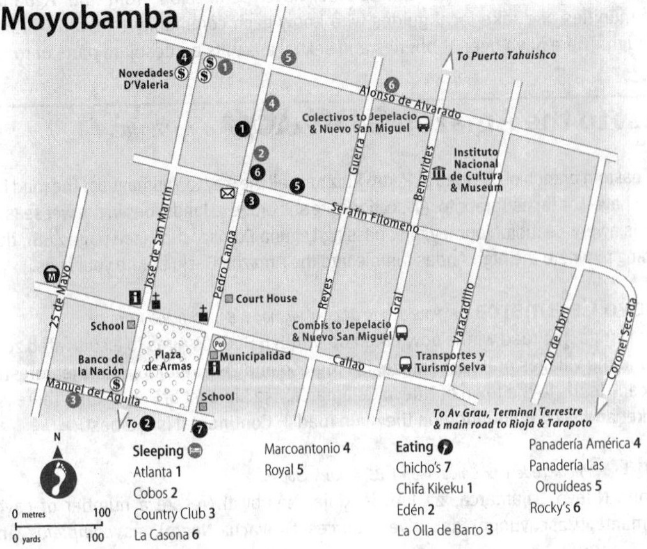

trail follows the river upstream through lovely forest, the first falls are only five minutes away. Getting to the other four falls requires crossing some log bridges. At the house by the trailhead there is a small orchid nursery which can be visited.

The tourist office, **Dircetur** ⓘ *Jr San Martín 301, T042-562043, www.turismosanmartin.com*, is on the plaza. **Oficina Municipal de Información** ⓘ *Jr Pedro Canga 262, T042-562191, www.munimoyobamba.gob.pe, Tue-Sun 0900-1300, 1600-2000*, is very helpful. Information on excursions and hikes is available from the **Instituto Nacional de Cultura** ⓘ *Jr Benavides 352*, which also has a small departmental **museum** ⓘ *Mon-Fri 0800-1300, 1400-1700.*

Tarapoto → *Phone code: 042. Colour map 1, C5. Altitude: 500 m.*

Rioja, Moyobamba and Tarapoto are growing centres of population, with much forest clearance beside the Carretera Marginal de la Selva. The 109 km from Moyobamba to Tarapoto is fully paved. It is heavily used by trucks, with fuel and meals available. You can stop at Tabalosas to buy fresh fruit from women at the roadside. Tarapoto is a busy town, founded in 1782, with a good local market 1½ blocks from the Plaza Mayor on Avenida Raimondi. It is a very friendly place, eager to embrace tourism and agricultural development now that the threat of terrorism and drug-trafficking has receded from the area. It competes with Iquitos for the record number of motorcycle taxis per square metre of road. There are three parts to the town: Tarapoto itself, Morales to the west and La Banda de Shilcayo to the east. The **Museo Regional de la Universidad Nacional de San Martín** ⓘ *Maynas, half a block from the plaza, behind the church, Mon-Fri 0800-1200, 1230-2000, US$0.35*, contains a little of everything: paleontology, geology, ethnography, stuffed animals, and so on, but it's rather faded and dusty. In the second week of July is the town's rowdy **tourist week festival, Santa Cruz de los Motilones**, but between May and September, it seems like every weekend celebrates something. It doesn't take much for the Tarapoteños to party. Tourist

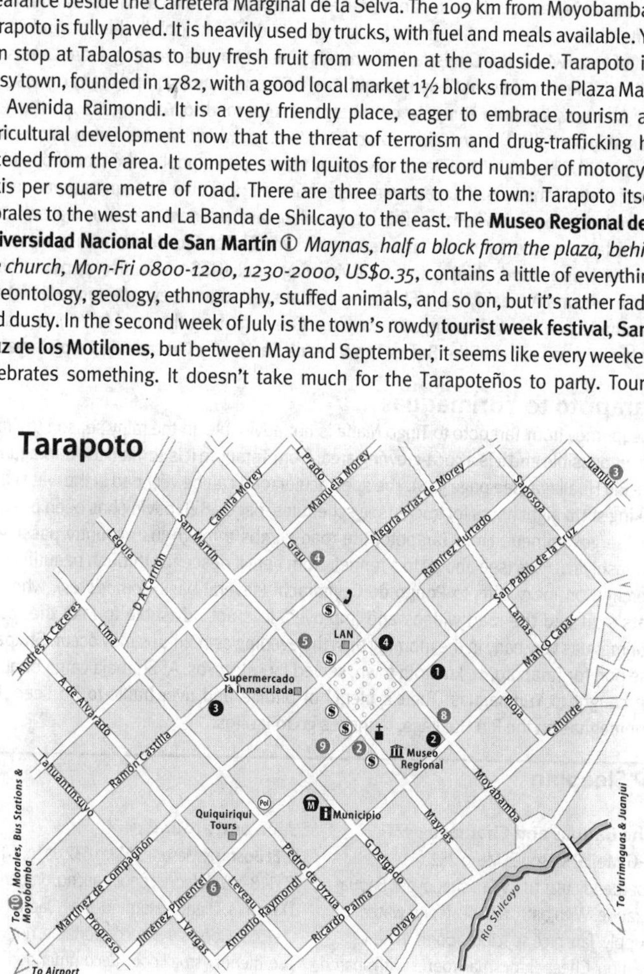

Sleeping
Alojamiento Santa Juanita 10
Edinson 2
El Mirador 3
July 4
La Posada 5
Lily 6
Nilas 8
San Antonio 9

Eating
Chifa Lug Ming 1
El Maguaré 2
Helados Regionales La Muyuna 3
Real 4

 information is available at **Dircetur** ⓘ *Jr Angel Delgado Morey, cuadra 1, T042-522567, tarapoto@mincetur.gob.pe*. There is a tourist information office at the **Municipalidad** ⓘ *Jr Gregorio Delgado 260, open 0730-1330, 1500-1800*.

Around Tarapoto

There are petroglyphs at **Demor** and **Pólish** east of the city, 4 and 5 km respectively. **Laguna Azul** (or Laguna Sauce as it is also known) is a big lake 52 km south of Tarapoto, with *cabañas* for rent on the shore. They cost US$80 per night for four beds and a shower. They are very basic and no fresh water or food is available. You can go river rafting on the Río Mayo for US$10 per person.

On the road to Moyobamba, 22 km from Tarapoto, a road leads off to **Lamas** where there is a small but highly recommended **museum** ⓘ *US$0.60*. The custodian will show you round in garbled Spanish, and there are exhibits on the local Lamista community. Turn right out of the museum and walk a couple of blocks uphill, then down into the part of town where the Lamistas live. There's a market in the morning. From Lamas you can visit the waterfalls at **Chapawanqui** (taxi US$7, 15 minutes) and many others.

About 14 km from Tarapoto on the spectacular road to Yurimaguas are the 50-m **Ahuashiyacu Falls** ⓘ *entry US$0.30 (toilets US$0.15)*, which can be visited by tour from Tarapoto (US$14.50 by mototaxi). A walkway leads up to a pool at the foot of one of the lower parts of the falls. You can swim here, but wait until after the sun has warmed the water; before 0900 it's freezing. This is a popular place at lunchtimes and weekends. The entire falls can be seen from the *recreo turístico* **El Paraíso Verde**, with a restaurant serving typical food, drinks, toilets, swimming pool (US$0.60), also popular. About 300 m beyond Ahuashiyacu is **El Mono y La Gata** restaurant, beyond which is **El Pozo**, a manmade pool for swimming and washing. Carry on along the road to Yurimaguas for 22 km and you come to the **Baños Termales de San José y Cascada de Carpishoyacu**.

Tarapoto to Yurimaguas

The journey from Tarapoto to Tingo María is not advisable. In the rainy season the roads are impossible and it is a coca-growing area. From Tarapoto it is 129 km to Yurimaguas on the Río Huallaga (see page 528). The spectacular road can be very bad in the wet season, taking six to eight hours for trucks (see schedules, page 482); paving has been promised by the government. From Tarapoto, the road climbs through lush country passing the Ahuashiyacu Falls (see above) to a tunnel. From here it descends through beautiful forest perched on rocky cliffs to **Pongo de Caynarachi** (several basic *comedores*), where the flats start and the road widens and improves. It is not advisable to take the road to Yurimaguas very early in the morning or in the evening as hold-ups may occur. **Shapaja** is the port for Tarapoto, 14 km from town, served by *colectivos*. At Shapaja cargo boats can be caught to Yurimaguas. There's plenty of birdlife and river traffic to be seen. From Yurimaguas on the Río Huallaga, launches go to Iquitos.

Sleeping

The Baguas and Chamaya *p474*

E-G Mejía, Mesones Muro 282 (perpendicular to Av Chachapoyas), Bagua Grande. With bath, reliable (cold) water supply, fan, nice spacious rooms in new section. Cheaper for small rooms with shared bath.

F Iris, Av Chachapoyas 2390, Bagua Grande, T041-774115. Cheaper with shared bath, cold water, fan, simple, clean.

Jaén and around *p474*

C El Bosque, Mesones Muro 632, Jaén, T/F076-731184. With fridge, pool, parking, gardens.

D Prim's, Diego Palomino 1341, Jaén, T076-731039. Good service, comfortable, hot water, a/c, friendly, small pool. Recommended.

D-E Hostal Valle Verde, Mcal Castilla 203, Plaza de Armas, T/F 076-732201, hostal valleverde@hotmail.com. Very clean and modern, large comfortable rooms and beds,

a/c (cheaper with fan), hot water, frigobar, parking, includes breakfast. Recommended.
E **Cancún**, Diego Palomino 1413, Jaén, T076-733511. Clean and pleasant, with bath, hot water, fan, restaurant, pool. Recommended.
E **Hostal César**, Mesones Muro 168, Jaén, T076-731277, F731491. Spacious rooms, comfortable, fan, phone, TV, parking.
F **Hostal Diego**, Diego Palomino 1267, T076-8031225. Private bath, fan, TV, views over the river, good value.
G **Santa Elena**, Sánchez Carrión 142, T076-803020. Private bath, cold water, fan, simple, nice, good value.

Jaén to the border *p474*

E **Sol de la Frontera**, 1.5 km north of Namballe, 5 km from La Balsa, isabelayub@yahoo.es. Being built by a British woman, Isabel Wood. Some rooms open, bath tubs with plugs, gas water heaters, continental breakfast included, rural setting in 2.5 ha of countryside.
F-G **El Olivar**, Av San Ignacio 145, San Ignacio, T076-8446052. Cheaper with shared bath, cold water, basic, restaurant.
F-G **La Posada**, Jr Porvenir 218, San Ignacio, T/F 076-8846180. Best in town, some rooms with hot water (cheaper with shared bath), simple, pleasant, helpful, decent restaurant.
F-G **Paraíso**, at the entrance to Namballe from San Ignacio. With bath (cheaper without), fan, basic, changes dollars.
G **Hostal Maldonado**, near the plaza, Namballe, T076-330011 (community phone). Shared bath, cold water, basic.

Northeast to Sarameriza *p475*

G **The Torres family**, Santa María de Nieve, luidelrio@hotmail.com. Ask to be taken to Inigo's house, contact the Torres who offer rooms, meals, laundry and guiding. The house, with garden and hammocks on the balcony, has great views of the river.

Rioja *p475*

Hostal San Martín, Grau 540; **San Ramón**, Jr Faustino Maldonado 840; and **Carranza**, Jr Huallanga. All basic (**G**).

Moyobamba *p476, map p476*

B **Puerto Mirador**, Jr Sucre, 1 km from the centre, T/F042-562050, www.barrioperu.terra.com.pe/pmirador. Includes breakfast, lovely grounds and views overlooking the river valley, pool, good restaurant.
C-D **Marcoantonio**, Jr Pedro Canga 488, T/F042-562045, www.altomayoperu.com. Smartest in town centre, with breakfast, bath and hot water, TV, restaurant.
D **La Casona**, Alonso de Alvarado 682, T042-563858. Nicely refurbushed old home, lovely courtyard with orchids, comfortable rooms, private bath, includes breakfast. Recommended.
E-F **Hostal Atlanta**, Alonso de Alvarado 865, T042-562063. With bathroom, hot water (cheaper without), TV, fan, clean, good but noisy, no breakfast.
F **Hostal Cobos**, Jr Pedro Canga 404, T042-562153. With bathroom, cold water, simple but good, friendly.
F **Hostal Country Club**, Manuel del Aguila 667, T042-562110. With bath, hot water, clean, comfortable, friendly, nice garden, also travel agency sells airline tickets and can arrange transport for touring. Recommended.
F **Hostal Royal**, Alonso de Alvarado 784, T042-562662, F562564. With bath, hot water, TV (cheaper without), laundry, cafeteria.

Tarapoto *p477, map p477*

B **Nilas**, Jr Moyobamba 173, T042-527331, http://linkaweb.tripod.com/nilas.html. Modern, the best in the centre, with bath, hot water, breakfast included, a/c, TV, fridge, internet access, pool, jacuzzi, gym, airport transfer, very well appointed, also has conference facilities.
B **Río Shilcayo**, Pasaje Las Flores 224, 1 km east of town in La Banda de Shilcayo, T042-522225, (in Lima T01-447 9359). With bathroom, excellent meals, non-residents can use the swimming pool for a fee.
C **Lily**, Jiménez Pimentel 405-407, T042-523154. With bath, a/c, TV, breakfast and tax included, laundry, sauna, restaurant.
D **La Posada Inn**, San Martín 146, T042-522234, laposada@ terra.com.pe. Another good central hotel, comfortable, with bath, hot water, fridge, TV, some rooms with a/c, nice atmosphere, breakfast and lunch, small library of books in Spanish on the region.
E **El Mirador**, Jr San Pablo de la Cruz 517, T042-522177. 5 blocks uphill from the plaza, with bath, cold water, fan, TV, very welcoming, clean, laundry facilities, breakfast (US$2) and hammocks on rooftop terrace with good views, also offers tours. Recommended.

F Edinson, Av Raimondi y Maynas, 10 m from Plaza Mayor, T042-523997, T/F524010. With bathroom, a/c, cheaper without, cold water, breakfast, clean and comfortable, also has karaoke bars and disco.

F July, Jr Alegría Arias de Morey 205, T042-522087. With bath, cold water, TV, fridge.

G Hostal San Antonio, Jr Jiménez Pimentel 126, T042-522226. With private bathroom and TV, fan, courtyard, no breakfast. Noisy but recommended.

G Misti 1, Leoncio Prado 341, 3 blocks from the plaza. Rooms with bath, cold shower, quiet, with small garden, snacks and fruit juices on offer for US$1, very helpful (**Misti 2** on the plaza is not as good and is noisy, but they'll tell you how to get to No 1).

G pp **Alojamiento Santa Juanita**, Av Salaverry 602, Morales (20 mins from centre). Good beds, fan, spotless, family-run, owner speaks English, safe.

Eating

Jaén and around *p474*

ℽ **Cloudy Chicken**, Diego Palomino 1284. Selection of set meals (*comida criolla*) at midday, Chinese in the evening, *pollo a la brasa*.

ℽ **Lactobac**, Bolívar 1382 at Plaza de Armas. Variety of à la carte dishes, snacks, desserts, very popular, also open for breakfast. Recommended.

Jaén to the border *p474*

In San Ignacio, both *hostales* have restaurants. There are a couple of internet cafés here and in Namballe, which also has basic eateries.

ℽ **El Tundal**, Av San Ignacio 140, San Ignacio. Regional dishes, à la carte only.

Pastelería Díaz, Av San Ignacio 167, San Ignacio. For bread and sweets.

Rioja *p475*

ℽ **Restaurante Los Olivos**. Recommended.

Moyobamba *p476, map p476*

ℽℽ **La Tullpa de Mamá**, at Punta de Tahuishco. With nice views, same owners and menu as **Olla de Barro**.

ℽℽ-ℽ **La Olla de Barro**, Pedro Canga y S Filomeno. Typical food, expensive compared with other places in town but still good value. It opens for breakfast.

ℽ **Chicho's**, Manuel del Aguila y Pedro Canga, Plaza de Armas. For pizza, pasta, hamburguers, snacks.

ℽ **Chifa Kikeku**, Pedro Canga 451. Chinese-Peruvian food.

ℽ **Edén**, down the stairs at the end of Jr San Martín, 1 block from the Plaza de Armas. Vegetarian.

ℽ **La Buena Salud**, on a lane off Jr Callao, block 8. Opposite the market, vegetarian set meals and à la carte.

ℽ **Rocky's**, Pedro Canga 402. Typical food, good, has cheap *menú*. Open for breakfast.

Tarapoto *p477, map p477*

Regional specialities include *cecina* (dried pork) and *chorizo*, both usually served with *tocacho* (fried green bananas), also *juanes*, *inchicapi* and *ensalada de chonta* as in Iquitos (see page 540). Interesting juices are *cocona*, made with cloves and cinnamon, and *aguajina*, from the aguaje fruit (deep purple skin, orange inside, sold on street corners). Regional fruits include grapes and pineapples.

ℽℽ **Real**, on Moyobamba on the plaza. One of the best restaurants in town and more expensive than elsewhere.

ℽ **El Maguaré**, Jr Moyobamba corner Manco Cápac. Choice of set meals and à la carte, good food and service.

ℽ **Helados Regionales La Muyuna**, Jr Ramón Castilla 271. Good ice cream and drinks made with jungle fruits. Open 0900-2300 except closed Fri from 1800 and Sat until 1815.

Around Tarapoto *p478*

ℽ **Rolly's**, San Martín 925, just off the plaza in Lamas. Serves good food.

Bars and clubs

Tarapoto *p477, map p477*

For local clubs, check out the neighbourhood of Morales, about 10 mins west of town on the highway. Two popular ones are **El Papillón** and **Las Pumas**. They sometimes charge a US$1.50 cover at weekends.

Activities and tours

Moyobamba *p476, map p476*

Ecotours Moyobamba, Callao 878, T042-563363, www.altomayo.com. Tours throughout the region.

Tarapoto *p477, map p477*
Quiquiriqui Tours, Jiménez Pimentel 314, T042-527863. Sells flight tickets, **Turismo Tarapoto** bus tickets (see below) and tours.

Transport

The Baguas and Chamaya *p474*

Bus Many buses pass through Bagua Grande en route from Chiclayo to Tarapoto and Chachapoyas and vice versa, by day or night. You can book for Lima (US$15.15-27.30) or Chiclayo (US$5.45), but for Tarapoto (US$7.60) or Chachapoyas (US$4.55) you must wait and see if there is space and they are often full. A better bet is to take a car or combi. Cars and combis to **Jaén** and **Bagua Chica** leave from Mcal Castilla y Angamos at the west end of town: to Jaén, cars US$1.80, 1 hr; combis US$1.50, 1¼ hrs. From Jr B Alcedo at the east end of town, cars (US$2.75, 1 hr) leave to **Pedro Ruiz**, to **Chachapoyas**, cars US$6, 3 hrs. Taking a mototaxi (US$0.30) between the 2 stops is a good alternative to walking in the heat.

Marañón or **Cenepa** buses Chiclayo-Bagua Chica, 6 hrs, US$4.50, at 1030, 2100 or 2130.

From Bagua Chica, take a car or combi to **Imaza** (also called Imacita), 6 hrs, US$8.60. From Imaza boats go to **Santa María de Nieve**, 4 hrs, US$13 (**Civan** or **Riomar** companies, none after 1500).

Jaén and around *p474*

Bus Arrange bus transport at Mesones Muro, block 4. Enquire which address the bus actually leaves from, some companies also have ticket offices in the centre of town. Eg **Móvil Tours**, Av Mesones Muro 422 (next to terminal with other bus companies); **Civa** has an office at the terminal on Mesones Muro block 4, in addition to an office Mcal Ureta 1300 y V Pinillos and terminal at Bolívar 936. To **Chiclayo**: Móvil *bus cama* at 1700, US$7.60, 5½ hrs; regular service at 2330, US$6.66. **Civa**, 1330 and 2230, US$4.55, 6 hrs. **Transcade**, 1000 and 2100, US$4.55, 6 hrs. In front of the bus terminal at Mesones Muro are cars to Chiclayo US$9, 5 hrs. To **Lima**: Móvil *bus cama* at 1700, US$21.20, 15½ hrs; regular service at 2330, US$18.20. **Civa**, 1700, US$18.20, 16 hrs. Service to Lima also goes through **Trujillo**. To **Piura**: Tarapoto Tours at 2200, US$7.60, 8 hrs. **Sol Peruano**, at 2230, US$7.60, 8 hrs. To **Tarapoto**: US$7.60, 9 hrs, **Jaén Express** at 1730, **Tarapoto Tours** at 1930, **Sol Peruano** at 2030. To **Moyobamba**: US$5.45, 7 hrs, same service as Tarapoto, likewise to **Pedro Ruiz**: US$4.55, 3hrs. To **Bagua Grande**: cars US$1.80, 1hr; combis US$1.50, 1¼ hrs. To **Bagua Chica**: combis US$1.50, 1¼ hrs. To **San Ignacio**, combis from Av Pinillos 638, 0400-1900, US$3.65, 3 hrs.

Jaén to the border *p474*

Bus From San Ignacio to **Chiclayo**, daily with **Turismo Adriazén**, Av San Ignacio 406, and **Ramírez Tours**, Cajamarca 179. To **Jaén**, combis from Av Mariano Melgar, block 3, US$3.65, 3 hrs. To **Namballe** and **La Balsa** (border with Ecuador), cars from Jr Santa Rosa corner Progreso: Namballe US$2.45 1¾ hrs; La Balsa US$3, 2 hrs. Ranchera from La Balsa to **Zumba** at 1230 and 1730, US$1.75. There are no pickups to Zumba. If it has not been raining and the road is passable, there is one bus (**Transportes Nambija**) which goes from La Balsa directly to Loja at 2030, US$7.50, 8-9 hrs. There are miltary controls at Pucapamba, 20 mins north of La Balsa and just north of Zumba; keep passport to hand.

Nuevo Cajamarca *p475*

Be careful travelling at night in this region; buses tend to travel in convoy.

There are 2 small bus terminals at the eastern and western edges of town. Buses from/to Chiclayo and Tarapoto stop here (except express services such as **Móvil Tours**). There are frequent *colectivos* to **Rioja**, US$0.90, 20 mins, and to **Pedro Ruiz**, US$4.55, 2 hrs. Cars to **Bagua Grande**, US$6, 3½ hrs; combis US$4.55, 5 hrs. Cars to **Moyobamba**, US$1.50, 40 mins.

Rioja *p475*

Bus Buses from/to Chiclayo and Tarapoto (except express services) stop here. Regular combis go to **Moyobamba**, US$0.90, 20 mins.

Moyobamba *p476, map p476*

Bus

Local *Colectivos* from General Benavides y Alonso de Alvarado to **Jepelacio**, 30 mins, US$0.90 or US$4.55 as a taxi; to **Nuevo San Miguel**, 1½-2 hrs, US$2; also combis from General Benavides y Callao. If stuck in Jepelacio or Nuevo San Miguel, there are simple *comedores* and you can arrange for very basic accommodation.

Long distance Buses leave from the Terminal Terrestre, about 12 blocks from the centre on Av Grau, which leads out of town to the main highway (mototaxi to the centre US$0.30). Several companies to **Tarapoto** (eg **Tarapoto Tours**, T042-563539, **Paredes Estrella, Sol Peruano, Móvil Tours**), US$3.60, 2 hrs. To **Yurimaguas**, US$7.60, 8 hrs. Buses heading west, en route from Tarapoto to **Pedro Ruiz** (US$6-US$7.60, 3½-4 hrs), **Chiclayo** (US$7.60-US$15, 12 hrs), **Trujillo** (US$12-US$18, 12-14 hrs) and **Lima** (US$21-US$29, 21-24 hrs), arrive at about 1030 and later. They will not sell you a ticket the day before if you are going to an intermediate destination such as Pedro Ruiz, but they do take you if they have room when the bus arrives (Ejetur will sell tickets to Pedro Ruiz, but they are the worst company on this route).

Colectivos

Transportes y Turismo Cajamarca, Serafín Filomeno y Benavides, and **Empresa San Martín**, Benavides 276; to **Tarapoto**, US$6, 2 hrs, to **Rioja** US$0.90, 20 mins, to **Nuevo Cajamarca**, US$1.50, 40 mins. There is no service direct to Pedro Ruiz or Yurimaguas unless you have enough people to fill a car. Combis leave from **Transportes y Turismo** Selva terminal, Jr Callao between **Benavides** and **Varacadillo**. To **Tarapoto** US$3, 2½ hrs, **Rioja** US$0.85, **Pedro Ruiz** US$5.75; departures between 0530 and 1900, leave when full.

Tarapoto *p477, map p477*

Air

Flights to **Lima** with **Lan** (Ramírez Hurtado, on the plaza), daily, and **Star Perú** (San Pablo de la Cruz 100, T042-528765). **Wayra Perú** (Plaza Mayor 195, T042-531991) flies to Lima and Iquitos daily. Book flights in advance, particularly in the rainy season. A taxi to the airport is US$3, mototaxi US$1.50. There's no bus service, but it's no problem to walk.

Bus

Buses to destinations to the west all leave from Av Salaverry, Morales, about 10 mins by mototaxi from the plaza. There are buses to **Moyobamba**, 116 km, US$3.65, 2 hrs; **Pedro Ruiz**, US$7.20 (US$8.65 **Tarapoto Tours** and Paredes Estrella), 9 hrs; **Chiclayo**, 690 km, 12 hrs, US$18.20; **Trujillo**, US$21.20, 15 hrs; and **Lima**, US$32 (*bus semi-cama*), US$27.30, 24 hrs (regular service, **Móvil**, slightly less with other companies). To **Jaén**, US$9.10, 9 hrs, **Tarapoto Tours** and **Transportes Jaén**. Combis to Moyobamba leave from **Turismo La Selva**, Av Salaverry, closer to the centre than the bus offices. Cars also run to **Moyobamba**, US$5.75.

To **Yurimaguas**, from La Banda de Shilcayo, bus US$3.65, 7-8 hrs; combi US$3.65, 5 hrs; pickup US$4.55 in front, US$2.50 in the back, 5 hrs; cars US$7.50, 4 hrs.

From Tarapoto to **Laguna Azul**, a *colectivo* takes 2½ hrs and costs US$3.45.

To **Lamas**, *colectivo* from Tarapoto, 30 mins, US$0.85, from Paradero Lamas on road to Moyobamba (take mototaxi from centre, US$0.45). There are infrequent combis.

Bus companies Móvil, Av Salaverry 858 (T042-563539); **Paredes Estrella** (T042-523681) at 0800 and 1400, **Tarapoto Tours** (T042-525240), at 1230 and 1300, **Sol Peruano** at 1100, **Expreso Huamanga** at 1230 and 1400.

Directory

Jaén and around *p474*

Banks BCP, Bolívar y V Pinillos. Cash only; ATM (Visa/Plus). **Banco Continental**, Ramón Castilla y San Martín. Cash, US$5 commission for TCs. **Cambios Coronel**, V Pinillos 360 (Coronel 2 across the street at 339). Cash only, good rates. **Ceymar** and **John Lennon**, V Pinillos on the plaza, next to public phones. Cash only. **Internet** Foto center Erick, Pardo Miguel 425. US$1.15 per hr. **Post** Pardo Miguel y Bolívar. **Telephone** V Pinillos, on the plaza.

Moyobamba *p476, map p476*

Banks BCP, Alonso de Alvarado 903 y San Martín. ATM (Visa/Plus). **BBV Continental**, San Martín 494. **Novedades D'Valeria**, San Martín 481. Good rates for cash.

Tarapoto *p477, map p477*

Banks BCP, Maynas 134. Changes TCs, ATM for Plus/Visa. **BBV Continental**, Ramírez Hurtado, Plaza Mayor, with Visa/Plus ATM. **Interbank**, Grau 119, near the plaza. No commission on changing TCs for soles, handles MasterCard. Street changers near Maynas and Jiménez Pimentel, on Plaza Mayor. **Internet** Several places in the centre.

Central Highlands

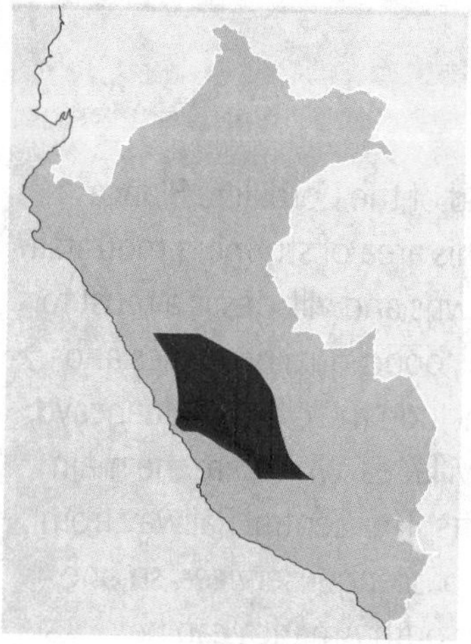

Footprint features

Introduction

Stretching from the southern end of the Cordillera Blanca right up to Cuzco department, this area of stunning mountain scenery and timeless Andean towns and villages is a must for those who appreciate traditional, good-quality textiles and ceramics. The main highlights include the cities of Huancayo, Ayacucho and the surrounding villages, which are the main production centres for handicrafts. The Central Railway from Lima to Huancayo has restarted passenger services, so one of the outstanding train rides in South America can be experienced once more. But the service is intermittent and Huancayo is still a little off the tourist compass. Meanwhile, Ayacucho hosts one of the largest and most impressive Holy Week celebrations in Latin America and at that time becomes a real focus of attention.

If you are seeking refuge from the Andean chill, the road through Tarma to the Selva Central is one of the most beautiful in Peru, leading to a relatively unexplored region of the country. More than just fabulous landscapes, this area also hides important pre-Inca sites, such as Kótosh (near Huánuco) and Huari (outside Ayacucho), two early examples of Andean urban civilizations. Stretches of the Royal Inca Road run from the temple fortress of Huánuco Viejo and up the Yanahuanca Valley, serving as reminders of this great imperial causeway. The Spaniards, too, have left their mark, with fine churches and mansions in Ayacucho.

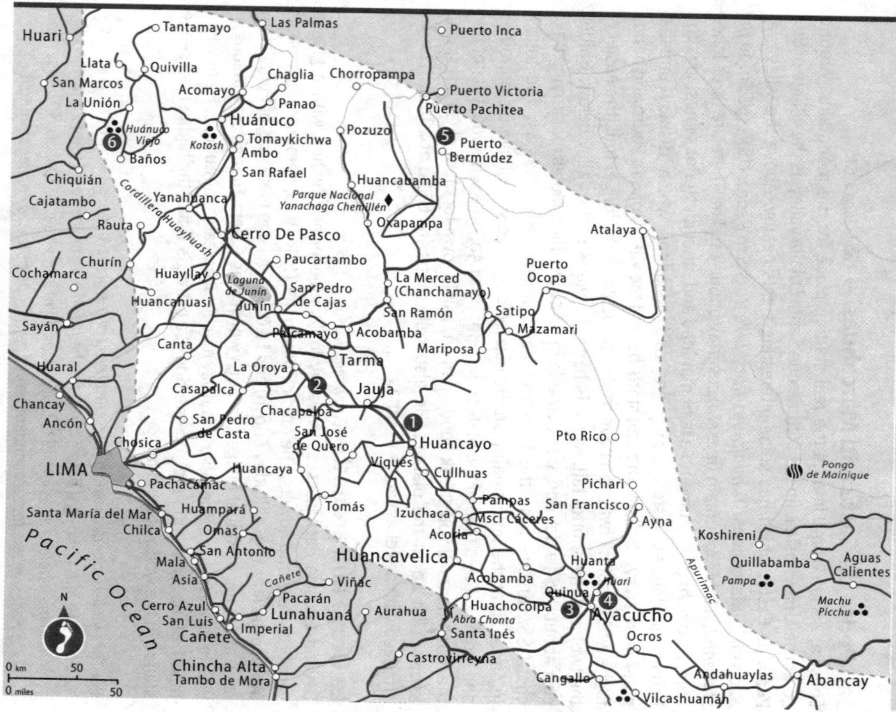

★ Don't miss...

1. **Mantaro Valley** Go shopping in this souvenir-hunter's paradise. Each village specializes in its very own variety of artesania, page 489.
2. **Train from Lima to Huancayo** Time your arrival (or departure) with the occasional running of one of the the engineering marvels of South America, page 486.
3. **Ayacucho** Don't miss the fine array of colonial churches, spectacular processions with carpets of flowers decorating the streets and the artists' quarter of Santa Ana, page 497.
4. **Quinua** Above this charming town with its handicraft shops is a telling, 44-m high obelisk commemorating South America's struggle for independence, page 501.
5. **The Selva Central** Puerto Bermúdez is the popular starting place for the central jungles, approachable by car from Lima, but far enough away for real rainforest experience, page 512.
6. **Capaq Ñan (Royal Inca Road)** Hike the route which will lead you back to times before the Spaniards arrived. One fine section goes to the temple-fortress of Huánuco Viejo near La Unión, page 520.

Lima to Ayacucho

The Central Highway and the famous Central Railway take you up from the coast to the thin air of the metal-smelting zone of La Oroya. To get there you have to pass over some of the highest routes in the continent. Beyond La Oroya are traditional towns and remains of prehispanic cultures on the altiplano. Huancayo is the commercial centre of the region and the heart of a valley whose villages concentrate on making handicrafts and holding festivals. Head south towards Ayachucho on difficult roads, either via the departmental capital of Huancavelica, or through more remote but magnificent scenery. » *For Sleeping, Eating and other listings, see pages 490-496.*

Ins and outs

Getting there There are flights from Lima to Ayacucho. The Central Highway between Lima and Huancayo more or less parallels the course of the railway. At La Oroya (see page 487) it divides, with its southern branch following the valley of the Río Mantaro to Huancayo and on to Huancavelica or Ayacucho. Buses serve all the main towns. Note that, although the main roads from Lima to Huancayo and Pisco to Ayacucho are paved, all other roads in this region are in poor condition, especially when wet.

San Pedro de Casta and Marcahuasi → *Colour map 3, C4.*

Chosica, 40 km from Lima, is the real starting place for the mountains. Around 40 km beyond Chosica, up the picturesque Santa Eulalia valley, is the village of **San Pedro de Casta**, which has some interesting sights nearby. Above the village, at 4200 m, is **Marcahuasi** ⓘ *minimum 3 hrs' hike from San Pedro, US$3 (US$0.90 for students)*, a table mountain (*meseta*) covering about 3 sq km. There are three lakes here, a 40-m high Monumento a la humanidad and other mysterious lines, gigantic figures, sculptures, astrological signs and megaliths which display unusual non-American symbolism. The trail starts behind the village of San Pedro and bends to the left. About halfway you have to choose between the longer trail (the easier of the two) and the shorter tail, which is better for views of the valley below. Guides cost about US$3 a day and are advisable in misty weather. Mules for carrying bags cost US$4 to hire from the tourist office; a horse costs US$4.45. The tourist information at the municipality on the plaza (T01-571 2087) will advise on routes and lodging; buy a map of the plateau here for US$1.50, otherwise you will not find the monuments. If you speak good Spanish, ask in town for Manuel Olivares, who knows a lot about the plateau. He also sells maps for US$0.20. Tours can be arranged with travel agencies in Lima.

La Oroya and around → *Colour map 3, C4.*

Beyond Chosica each successive valley looks greener and lusher, with a greater variety of trees and flowers. The road climbs to the **Ticlio Pass**, before the descent to **Morococha** (Km 169, altitude 4600 m) and **La Oroya**. A large metal flag of Peru can be seen at the top of Mount Meiggs, through which runs **Galera Tunnel**, 1175 m long, in which the main line of the Central Railway reaches its greatest altitude, 4782 m. At the mouth of the tunnel (Km 132), on one side of a crater, is **Ticlio**, the highest passenger station in the world at 4758 m.

The Lima–Huancayo railway, was the project of the great American railway engineer, Henry Meiggs (who died before it was finished) and built by the Pole Ernesto Malinowski. Along the whole of its length (335 km to Huancayo) it traverses 66 tunnels, 59 bridges and 22 zig-zags, where the steep mountainside permits no other way of negotiating it.

La Oroya (3755 m), the main smelting centre for the region's mining industry, can seem a dreary place with its slag heaps and appalling air pollution, but is nevertheless full of vitality. It stands at the fork of the Yauli and Mantaro rivers, 196 km from Lima by a road. » *For places to the east and north of La Oroya, see pages 510 and 517.*

Jauja and around

→ *Colour map 3, C5.* *Altitude: 3330 m.*

Some 80 km southeast of La Oroya is Jauja, a friendly, unspoilt town in the middle of a good area for walking. There is a good **archaeological museum** ⓘ *free, but donations welcome*, with artefacts from the Huari culture. On a hill above Jauja is a fine line of Inca storehouses and, on hills nearby, are the ruins of hundreds of circular stone buildings from the Huanca culture. There are also ruins near the **Laguna de Paca** ⓘ *3½ km away, colectivos leave regularly from Av Pizarro, 10 mins, US$0.30*. The western side of the lake is lined with restaurants which are good for lunch; try the delicious *ceviche de trucha* and, at weekends, *pachamanca*. It is possible to walk around the lake in about three hours. Many restaurants have launches offering half-hour boat trips at weekends, US$0.75 per person.

From Concepción, 18 km south of Jauja, a branch road leads for 6 km to the **Convent of Santa Rosa de Ocopa** ⓘ *Wed-Mon 0900-1200 and 1500-1800, tours start on the hour and last 45 mins, US$1.10, colectivos run from the market in Concepción, 15 mins, US$0.25*. This Franciscan monastery, set in beautiful surroundings, was established in 1725 for training missionaries for the jungle. It contains a fine library with over 20,000 volumes and a biological museum with animals and insects from the jungle. The convent also contains a large collection of paintings, including copies by the priests of many works by masters such as Murillo and Ribera. On the walls are paintings of Huancayo by the contemporary painter, Josue Sánchez.

Huancayo and around

» *pp490-496.*

→ *Colour map 3, C5.* *Altitude: 3271 m.*

The large, sprawling departmental capital of Huancayo is a functional kind of place. As the main commercial centre for inland Peru it has had to eschew tourist trappings in favour of the no-nonsense comings and goings of everyday trade. Huancayo's attractions are beyond the city boundaries. It lies in the beautiful Mantaro Valley, surrounded by villages that produce their own original crafts and celebrate festivals all year round, see page 493. The city has its own important festivals, however, when people flock from far and wide with an incredible range of food, crafts and music. At this height, nights are chilly and altitude can be a problem for those arriving straight from the coast.

Ins and outs

Huancayo is not on an air route but is served, if a bit haphazardly, by train to and from Lima and Huancavelica. Bus services are good and, as elsewhere in the Andes, serve the entire region. **Dircetur** ⓘ *Av Libertad 204, Huayucachi, opposite the Electroandes plant, T064-433007, Mon-Fri 0800-1300 and 1400-1700*, has information about the area and is helpful. Beware of theft if arriving early in the morning. » *For further information, see Transport, page 494.*

Sights

The Plaza de Armas is called **Plaza Constitución**. The main sights, though, as well as the Sunday market, are quite a way from the centre. The **Sunday market** gets going after 0900 every week and provides little taste of Huancayo at festival time. The stalls on Jirón Huancavelica, 3 km long, still sell typical clothes, fruit, vegetables, hardware, handicrafts and, especially, traditional medicines and goods for witchcraft. However, the market has been described as expensive and offering little choice; it is better to go to the villages for local handicrafts. There is also an impressive daily market behind the railway station.

Parque de Identidad Wanka ⓘ *Jr San Jorge, Barrio San Carlos, northeast of the city (35 mins' walk from Plaza), free but contributions are appreciated*, is a fascinating mixture of surrealistic construction, interwoven with indigenous plants and trees and the cultural history of the Mantaro Valley. It can get crowded at weekends. Opposite are the **Misti Wasi** and **Pacaywasi** restaurants serving traditional meals; there are about six others in the area.

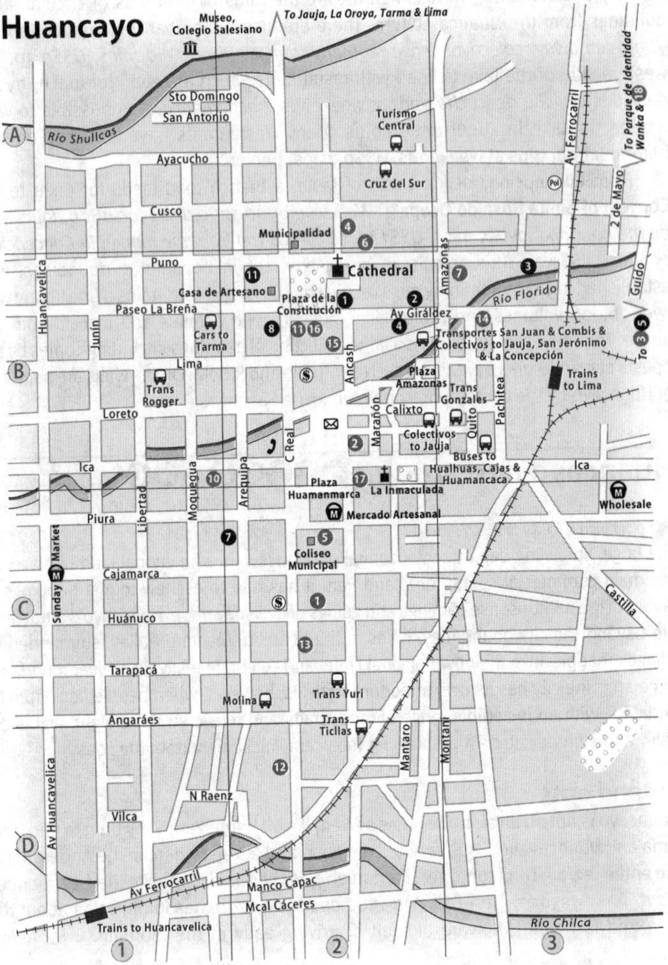

Sleeping

Casa Alojamiento de Aldo y Soledad Bonilla **1** *C2*
Casa Hospedaje **2** *B2*
Confort **4** *A2*
El Dorado **5** *C2*
El Marquez **6** *B2*
Hostal Baldeón **7** *B3*
Hostal Santo Domingo **10** *B1*
Kiya **11** *B2*
La Casa de la Abuela **3** *B3*
Percy's **12** *D2*
Peru Andino Lodging & Excursions **18** *A3*
Presidente **13** *C2*
Pussy Cat **14** *B3*
Roger **15** *B2*
Santa Felicita **16** *B2*
Turismo **17** *B2*

Eating

Berisso **2** *B2*
Café El Parque **1** *B2*
Chez Viena **3** *B3*
Chifa El Centro **4** *B2*
El Paraíso **7** *C2*
El Pino **8** *B2*
La Cabaña **5** *B3*
Pizzería Antojitos **11** *B2*

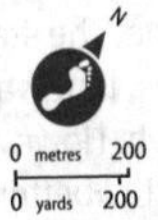

Mantaro Valley → *Colour map 3, C5.*

The main attraction in the area is the Mantaro Valley, which is rich in culture, music, local food, dances and handicrafts and plays host to numerous festivals. To the west of the Río Mantaro, 19 km from Huancayo, is **Viques**, which is known for the production of belts and blankets. **Sra María Magdalena Huzco**, Calle San Martín, two blocks from the Plaza Principal, offers **weaving lessons**, US$34 for 15 hours, plus the cost of materials. Other weavers may also give lessons. It's a worthwhile experience, not just for learning how to weave, but also for an insight into the life of this part of Peru. **Huayucachi**, 7 km away, organizes festivals with dancing and impressive costumes in January and February and also makes embroidery.

The ruins of **Warivilca** ⓘ *15 km from Huancayo, daily 1000-1200 and 1500-1700, US$0.15; to get here take one of the micros for Chilca, which leave from Calle Real*, feature the remains of a pre-Inca temple of the Huanca culture. There is a museum in the plaza (open in the morning only), with deformed skulls, and modelled and painted pottery of successive Huanca and Inca occupations of the shrine. The ruins and museum are under the supervision of a local archaeologist and are slowly being restored.

The villages of **Cochas Chico** and **Cochas Grande**, 11 km from Huancayo on the east side of the river, are both well worth visiting. Micros leave from Plaza Hunamarco or by the market near the railway line, US$0.25. This is where the famous *mate burilado*, or gourd carving, is done (see page 596). You can buy the gourds cheaply direct from the manufacturers, but ask around. You can also enjoy beautiful views of the Valle de Mantaro and Huancayo.

In the village of **Hualhuas**, 12 km from Huancayo, you can find fine alpaca weavings, which you can watch being made. The weavers take special orders; small items can be finished in a day. Negotiate a price. One particularly recommended place to buy them is **Tahuantisuyo**, run by Familia Faustino Maldonado y Agripina, on a side road on the way to the San Jerónimo junction.

The town of **San Jerónimo** is renowned for the making of silver filigree jewellery, on sale at the Wednesday market. A major fiesta is held in the town on the third Saturday in August, when one of the two plazas is converted into a temporary bullring.

Izcuchaca

On the railway line between Huancayo and Huancavelica, **Izcuchaca** is the site of a bridge over the Río Mantaro. On the edge of town is a fascinating pottery workshop whose machinery is driven by a water turbine. There is also a small shop. The town celebrates the **Fiesta de la Virgen de Cocharcas** from 5th to 10th October. It's a nice hike to the chapel on a hill overlooking the valley (one to 1½ hours each way). Heading towards Ayacucho, there is a good road from Izcuchaca to the Quichuas hydroelectric scheme, but thereafter it is narrow with hair-raising bends and spectacular bridges. The scenery, however, is staggering.

Huancavelica and around » pp490-496.

→ *Colour map 3, C5. Altitude: 3660 m.*

Huancavelica, capital of the next department south, is a friendly and attractive town, surrounded by huge, rocky mountains. It's not really geared up for tourism, owing to its remoteness. Founded in the 16th century by the Spanish to exploit rich deposits of mercury and silver, Huancavelica has very few mines open now. It is predominantly an indigenous town, where people still wear traditional costume.

Ins and outs

Like Huancaya, Huancavelica is not on an air route and bus services are limited but, mechanical problems aside, the Huancayo–Huancavelica train service should run daily. Buses and *colectivos* serve the entire region. The **Dircetur** office ⓘ *Victoria Garma 444, p 2, T067-452938, dircetur_hcv@hotmail.com, Mon-Fri 0800-1300, 1415-1730*, is very helpful. Don't wander around the surrounding hills alone. ➤➤ *For further information, see Transport, page 494.*

Sights

The **cathedral** on the Plaza de Armas has an altar considered to be one of the finest examples of colonial art in Peru. Bisecting the town is the Río Huancavelica. South of the river is the main commercial centre. North of the river, on the hillside, are the **thermal baths** ⓘ *0600-1500, US$0.15 for private rooms (water is not very hot), US$0.10 for the hot public pool.* There are also hot showers but take a lock for the doors. The **handicraft sellers** congregate in front of the Municipalidad on M Muñoz and the Biblioteco on the Plaza de Armas (V Toledo). The regional **INC office** ⓘ *Plazoleta San Juan de Dios s/n, T067-453420, inc_huancavelica@yahoo.es*, is a good source of information on festivals, archaeological sites, history, and more. The institute also runs courses on music and dancing, and hosts lectures some evenings. There is an interesting but small **Museo Regional** ⓘ *Arica y Raimondi, Mon-Sat 1000-1300 and 1500-1900.*

Routes to Ayacucho → *Colour map 3, C5/6.*

If driving to Ayacucho and beyond, roads are amazingly rough. Don't go alone and count kilometres diligently to keep a record of where you are as road signs are poor. The direct route from Huancavelica to Ayacucho (247 km) goes via **Santa Inés** (4650 m) at Km 78. Out of Huancavelica, the road climbs steeply with switchbacks between herds of llamas and alpacas grazing on rocky perches. Around Pucapampa (Km 43) is one of the highest habitable *altiplanos* (4500 m), where the rare and highly prized ash-grey alpaca can be seen. Snow-covered mountains are seen as the road climbs to 4853 m at the **Abra Chonta** pass, 23 km before Santa Inés. By taking the turn-off to Huachocolpa at Abra Chonta and continuing for 3 km you'll reach the highest drivable pass in the world, at 5059 m. Nearby are two lakes (Laguna Choclacocha), which can be visited in 2½ hours. Beyond Santa Inés at the **Abra de Apacheta** (4750 m), 98 km from Ayacucho, the rocks have oxidized into all the colours of the rainbow, with a violet river running through the fabulous scenery.

An alternative is to travel from Huancavelica to **Lircay**, a small village with accommodation. From here, catch a bus to **Julcamarca**, which has a colonial church, and a minibus from Julcamarca plaza to Ayacucho; beautiful scenery all the way.

There is another route to Ayacucho from Huancayo, little used by buses, which involves less climbing for cyclists. Cross the pass into the Mantaro valley on the road to **Quichuas**. Then continue to **Anco** and **Mayocc**, where you'll find accommodation. From here the road crosses a bridge after 10 km and in another 20 km reaches **Huanta** (see page 501). A paved road in poor condition runs from here to Ayacucho. ➤➤ *For further information, see Transport, page 494.*

Sleeping

San Pedro de Casta and Marcahuasi *p486*

F Marcahuasi, just off the plaza. The best hotel in San Pedro (**G** per person without bath), clean, has a restaurant.

La Oroya and around *p486*

G Hostal Inti, Arequipa 117, La Oroya, T064-391098. Shared bathroom, warm water, clean but basic.

G Hostal Chavín, Tarma 281, La Oroya. Shared bathroom, cheap restaurant.

Jauja and around *p487*

F per person **Hostal Manco Cápac**, Jr Manco Cápac 575, T064-361620, niegemann ilse@hotmail.com. Central, with good rooms and a beautiful patio, pleasant, relaxing, good breakfast and coffee. Book ahead at weekends and holiday periods. Recommended.

F Hostal María Nieves, Jr Gálvez 491, 1 block from the Plaza de Armas, T064-362543. Clean, safe, helpful, friendly, price includes large breakfast, hot water all day. Good choice.
G Hostal Los Algarrobos, Huancayo 264, T064-362633. Shared bathroom, hot water in the morning, very clean, good value.

Huancayo and around *p487, map p488*
The places listed below are all in Huancayo. Prices may rise in Holy Week.
C El Marquez, Puno 294, T064-219026, www.elmarquezhuancayo.com. Rooms with bath and TV, free internet access, good value and efficient, safe parking.
C Presidente, C Real 1138, T064-231275, same email address as Turismo. With bathroom, clean, friendly, helpful, safe, breakfast only. Recommended.
C Turismo, Ancash 729, T064-231072, hotelhyo@correo.dnet.com.pe. In an old building. Rooms with bathroom, some rooms are small, quiet. Restaurant serves good meals for US$3.50.
D Kiya, Giráldez 107, Plaza Constitución, T064-214955. With bath, hot water, restaurant does not serve breakfast, avoid noisy rooms on Av Real.
D Santa Felicita, Giráldez 145, Plaza Constitución, T064-235285. With bathroom, hot water, good.
E per person **Casa Alojamiento de Aldo y Soledad Bonilla**, Huánuco 332, no sign, half a block from Mcal Cáceres bus station, T064-232103. Prices are for full board, beautiful colonial house, some hot water, owners speak English, laundry, secure, relaxing, nice courtyard, they can arrange local tours, book ahead to guarantee a room.
E El Dorado, Piura 452, T064-223947. With bathroom, hot water, friendly, clean, some rooms with TV are in the **D** category.
E Hospedaje César Ada, Pasaje Santa Teresa 294, El Tambo-3 Esquinas, Vilcacoto, 5 km from centre, T064-253646 for pickup, wadaycesar@hotmail.com. Quiet, shared bath, garden, meals available, use of kitchen, breakfast included.
E La Casa de la Abuela, Av Giráldez 691, T064-223303. **G** pp in dorms. Comfortable hostel with a warm atmosphere and plenty of services. Some rooms with antique beds, good hot showers, breakfast included, meals available, games room, internet, laundry services, sociable staff. Good place to meet other backpackers. Free taxi pickup from the bus station if requested in advance.
E Roger, Ancash 460, T064-233488. With bathroom, hot water, basic, clean.
F Confort, Ancash 231, 1 block from the main plaza, T064-233601. All rooms are good value with hot water, very clean, spacious, ask for a room not facing the street for peace and quiet, safe for bikes, car parking US$1.
F Percy's, Real 1399, T064-231208. Shared bathroom, hot water in morning, TV, basic but clean and good value.
F Pussy Cat, Giráldez 359, T064-231565. Not what the name might suggest, **G** with shared bathroom, hot water, safe, friendly, luggage stored, comfortable beds.
G per person **Casa hospedaje**, Huamanmarca 125, T064-219980. Central, small, comfortable, hot water, shared showers, family run, nice atmosphere.
G per person **Hostal Baldeón**, Amazonas 543, T064-231634. Friendly, kitchen and laundry facilities, nice patio, good hot shower on request, basic rooms with poor beds, security-conscious.
G Hostal Santo Domingo, Ica 655, T064-235461. Set around two pleasant patios, clean, basic, good value.
G per person **Peru Andino Lodging and Excursions**, Pasaje San Antonio 113-115, San Carlos, on Av Centenario go 3 blocks from 2 de Mayo to San José, then 3 blocks north (left), 10-15 mins' walk from the centre, T064-223956; if taking a taxi, stress that it's Pasaje San Antonio). Price includes breakfast, clean rooms with hot showers, several with private bathroom, safe area, cosy atmosphere, run by Sra Juana, her daughter speaks some English, friendly. Organize trekking and mountain bike tours, Spanish classes, cooking and laundry facilities. Highly recommended.

Mantaro Valley *p489*
E Hostal La Llamita, Jr Huancayo 445, Hualhuas. 30 rooms with bath, hot water, also dormitories (**G** per person with shared bath and cold water), friendly owner,

For an explanation of sleeping and eating price codes used in this guide, see inside the front cover. Other relevant information is found in Essentials, pages 53-58.

swimming pool, laundry and restaurant. It also has a handicraft shop.

Huancavelica and around *p489, map p492*

D Presidente, Plaza de Armas, T067-952760. Lovely colonial building, cheaper without bathroom, price includes breakfast and bath, very clean but not a warm building, hot water a 'hit and miss' affair, overpriced.

F Camacho, Jr Carabaya 481, T067-753298. Best of the cheap hotels, room with toilet, cheaper without, shared hot shower in morning and early evening, clean and well maintained, excellent value.

F San José, Jr Huancayo, at top of Barranca (past Santo Domingo), T067-752958. With bath, hot water 1700-1900, **G** without bath, clean, comfortable beds, helpful.

G Santo Domingo, Av Barranca 336, T067-753086. Cheap, very basic, with shared bathroom and cold water.

Routes to Ayacucho *p490*

The following are all **G**. In **Santa Inés**, you can sleep at **Alojamiento Andino**, and there's a very friendly restaurant called **El Favorito**; several others. **Lircay** has an unnamed hostal at Sucre y La Unión, with bath and hot water. It's much better than **Hostal El Paraíso**, opposite, also with bath. **Hostal Villa Julcamarca**, near the plaza in **Julcamarca** has no tap water and is really basic. In **Quichas**, try **Hostal Recreo Sol y Sombra**, which is basic but helpful and charming, with a small courtyard. The **Hostal Gabi** in **Anco** is appalling but better than anything else.

Eating

La Oroya and around *p486*

🍴🍴 **El Tambo**, 2 km outside La Oroya on t he road to Lima. Good trout and frogs. The Chanchamayo bus stops here en route Lima–Tarma.

🍴 **La Caracocha**, Lima 168, La Oroya. Cheap, good menu.

Jauja and around *p487*

🍴 **Centro Naturista**, Huarancayo 138. Serves fruit salad, yoghurt, granola, etc.

🍴 **El Paraíso**, Ayacucho 915. Just off the plaza, this is a good place for chicken and Andean dishes.

🍴 **Ganso de Oro**, R Palma 249. Good restaurant in hotel of same name, US$2-4 per meal, the best in town.

🍴 **La Rotunda**, Tarapacá 415. Tables in a pleasant courtyard or dining rooms, good lunch menu and pizzas in the evening.

🍴 **Marychris**, Jr Bolívar 1166, T362386. For lunch only, *menú* US$1.55, excellent food.

Huancayo and around *p487, map p488*

🍴🍴 **La Cabaña**, Av Giraldez 652. Pizzas, ice-cream, *calentitos* and other dishes, roast New Zealand lamb, folk music at weekends (see **Incas del Perú** under Tour operators, below).

🍴🍴 **Pizzería Antojitos**, Puno 599. Attractive, atmospheric pizzeria, live music some nights.

🍴 **Chifa El Centro**, Giráldez 245. Chinese food, good service, excellent value and atmosphere (waterfall and rainforest).

🍴 **El Pino**, Real 539. Serves typical food for about US$2-3 a dish, and fixed-price *menú*.

Huancavelica

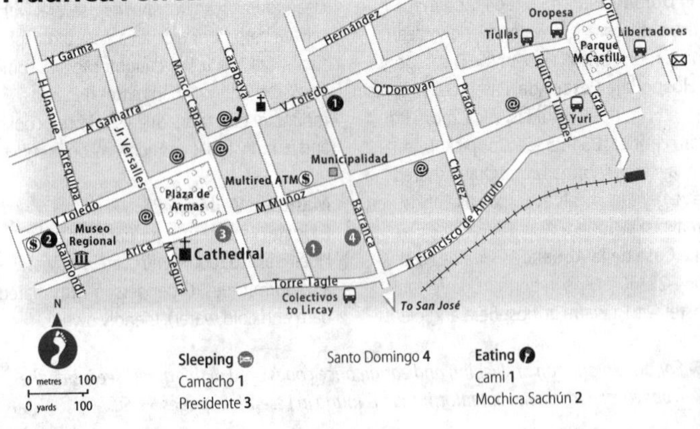

Cafés

Berisso, Giráldez 258. Good for cakes and quiche, friendly.

Café El Parque, Giráldez y Ancash, main plaza. Smart place to take coffee and cake.

Chez Viena, Puno 125. Another posh place for coffee and cakes.

El Paraíso, Arequipa 929, very good vegetarian food, good value and service.

ImaginArte, Jr Ancash 260. An interesting contemporary art gallery, often displaying work based on ethnic Peruvian culture. Good coffee and cakes add to the appeal.

Panadería Koky, Ancash y Puno. Good for breakfasts and pastries, pricey.

Huancavelica and around

p489, map p492

There are lots of cheap, basic restaurants on C Muñoz and Jr Virrey Toledo. All serve typical food, mostly with a set menu for around US$1.50. There area also *chifas* on Toledo.

¶¶ **La Casona**, Jr Virrey Toledo 230. Good-value *menú* and *peña*.

¶¶ **Mochica Sachún**, Av Virrey Toledo 303. Great *menú* for US$1.50, otherwise expensive, popular.

¶ **Cami**, Barranca y Toledo. No sign, small, lively, good set menus and juices.

Bars and clubs

Huancayo and around *p487, map p488*

All the *peñas* have folklore shows with dancing, normally Fri, Sat and Sun 1300-2200. Entrance is about US$2 per person. Try **Ollantaytambo**, Puno, block 2, or **Taki Wasi**, Huancavelica y 13 de Noviembre. Most discos are open 2000-0200; some charge an entrance fee of US$3-4.

Festivals and events

Huancayo *p487, map p488*

19-31 Jan Festividad del Tayta Niño

8 Sep Festividad de la Virgen de Cocharcas.

30 Sep Festividad de San Jerónimo de Tunan.

Oct San Francisco de Asís, San Lucas. The culmination of month-long celebrations for El Señor de los Milagros.

16 Nov The beginning of Semana Turística de Huancayo.

Mantaro Valley *p489*

There are so many festivals in the Mantaro Valley that it is impossible to list them all. Practically every day of the year there is a celebration of some sort in one of the villages. We list a selection below.

19-31 Jan Festividad del Tayta Niño, in Huayucachi.

Feb Carnival celebrations for the whole of the month, with highlights on 2, **Virgen de la Candelaria**, and 17-19, **Concurso de Carnaval**.

Mar/Apr Semana Santa is impressive throughout the valley, especially the **Good Fri** processions.

1 May Fiesta de la Cruz also takes place throughout the valley.

24-30 Jul Fiesta de Santiago.

8 Sep La Virgen de Cocharcas is held in Concepción, Jauja and, more famously, in Sapallanga, 8 km south of Huancayo.

Sep The Semana Turística del Valle del Mantaro is held on different dates.

Huancavelica and around

p489, map p492

The whole area is rich in culture with many festivals and dances.

4-8 Jan Fiesta de los Reyes Magos y los Pastores.

2nd Sun in Jan Fiesta del Niño Perdido. Pukllaylay Carnavales.

20 Jan-mid Mar Celebration of the first fruits from the ground (harvest).

Mar/Apr Semana Santa, Holy Week.

End May-beginning Jun Toro Pukllay.

May and Aug Fiesta de Santiago.

22-28 Dec Los Laygas.

Shopping

Huancayo and around *p487, map p488*

All handicrafts are made outside Huancayo in the many villages of the Mantaro Valley (see page 489). The villages are worth a visit to learn how the items are made.

Casa de Artesano, corner of Real and Paseo La Breña, Plaza Constitución, has a wide selection of good quality crafts.

There is also a large market between Ancash and Real, block 7, offering a wide selection of local handicrafts. Watch out for pickpockets. There are 2 supermarkets on Real between Breña and Lima.

Activities and tours

Huancayo and around *p487, map p488*

Guides

Marco Jurado Ames, andinismo_peru @yahoo.es. Organizes long-distance treks on the 'hidden paths of Peru'. Many of these include Huancayo, such as a two-week trip from Lima to Machu Picchu via Huancayo, the Amazon lowlands and Vilcabamba.

Tour operators

American Travel & Service, Plaza Constitución 122, of 2 (next to the cathedral), T064-211181, T932 5767 (mob), www.traveltourshuancayo.com. Wide range of classical and more adventurous tours in the Mantaro Valley and in the Central Jungle. Transport and equipment rental possible. Most group based day tours start at US$8-10 per person.

Andina Tours, C Real 455, of 2, T064-253434, T999 8168 (mob), andinatours_hyo @hotmail.com. Professional tour organizer.

Incas del Perú, Av Giráldez 652, T064-223303, www.incasdelperu.org. Associated with the **La Cabaña/Otra Lado** restaurants and **La Casa de la Abuela**. Jungle, biking and riding trips throughout the region, as well as language and volunteer programs. Very popular with travellers in the region.

Peruvian Tours, Plaza Constitución 122, p 2, of 1, T064-213069, T966 1044 (mob). Next to the cathedral and American Travel & Service. Classic tours of the Mantaro Valley, plus day trips up to the Huaytapallana Nevados above Huancayo, plus long, 16-hr excursions to Cerro de Pasco and Tarma.

Transport

San Pedro de Casta and Marcahuasi *p486*

Colectivo minibuses for **Chosica** leave from Av Grau, Lima, when full, 0600-2100, US$0.60. *Colectivo* taxis leave from the **Sheraton Hotel**, behind the Centro Cívico on Av Garcilaso de la Vega, US$1.50 for a seat or US$6 for the whole car. A regular taxi will charge US$6-10 Lima–Chosica. Most buses on the Lima–La Oroya route are full so take a *colectivo* taxi from Chosica to reach **La Oroya**, US$3.60, 3 hrs, very scenic, passing the second highest railway in the world. For **San Pedro de Casta**, buses leave **Chosica** from Parque Echenique, opposite the market, at 0900 and 1500, 4 hrs, US$2; return 0700 and 1400. The road is in a reasonable condition until the Callahuanca hydroelectric station.

La Oroya and around *p486*

To **Lima** from La Oroya, 4½ hrs, US$5.20. To **Jauja** (80 km), 1½ hrs, US$1. To **Tarma**, 1½ hrs, US$1.35. To **Cerro de Pasco**, 131 km, 3 hrs, US$2.20. To **Huánuco**, 236 km, 6 hrs, US$4.35. *Colectivos* also run on all routes; they are quicker but only leave when full and prices are double that of the bus fares.

Jauja and around *p487*

Bus

To **Lima**, **Cruz del Sur**, Pizarro 220, direct, 5 hrs, US$8. To **Huancayo**, 44 km, 1 hr, US$1.25; continuous combis and *colectivos* leave from Av Pizarro y Junín. To **Cerro de Pasco**, **Oriental** from 28 de Julio 156, and **Turismo Central** from 28 de Julio 150, 5 hrs, US$3.55. **Oriental** and **Turismo Central** also to **Huánuco**, 7 hrs, US$5.35. To **Tarma**, **Trans Muruhuay**, hourly, 0600-1900, 2 hrs, US$2. Also **ET San Juan**, both from Jr Tarma; the latter continues to **Chanchamayo**, 4 hrs, US$4.50. To **Satipo**, with **Turismo Central**, 12 hrs, US$6.25.

Huancayo and around *p487, map p488*

Bus

Most of the bus offices of the better companies running to Lima are 2-3 blocks north of the main plaza, while those of the cheaper companies are located to the north of the Río Shullcas, a 10-15 min walk from the centre. Bus companies to destinations south of Huancayo, eg Huancavelica and Ayacucho, are 4-5 blocks south of the main plaza. A new bus terminal for all buses to all destinations is being planned, 3 km north of the centre.

To **Lima**, 7 hrs on a good paved road, US$10. Travel by day for fantastic views and, of course, for safety. If you must travel by night, take warm clothing. Recommended are **Ormeño**, Av Mcal Castilla 1379, El Tambo; **Cruz del Sur**, Ayacucho 281, T064-235650; **Trans Turismo Central**, Jr Ayacucho 274, T064-223128 (double-decker *bus cama*), and

Transportes Rogger, Lima 561, T064-212687, *cama* and *semi-cama* at 1300 and 2330, *comercial* at 2230.

To **Huancavelica**, 147 km, 5 hrs, US$2.85. Many buses leave daily, eg **Transportes Yuri**, Ancash 1220, 3 a day. The road is being improved but takes longer when wet. The scenery is spectacular.

To **Ayacucho**, 319 km , 9-10 hrs, US$6.65-7.55. **Molina**, C Angaráes 334, T064-224501, 3 a day, recommended. The road is paved for the first 70 km, then in poor condition and is very difficult in the wet. Take warm clothing.

To **Cerro de Pasco**, 255 km, 5 hrs, US$4, several departures. Alternatively, take a bus to **La Oroya** (every 20 mins, from Av Real about 10 blocks north of the main plaza) and change (see above). The road to La Oroya and on to Cerro is in good condition. To **Huánuco**, 7 hrs, **Turismo Central** have a direct bus at 2115, US$6, good service.

To **Chanchamayo**, **Empresa San Juan**, Ferrocarril 161 and Plaza Amazonas, and **Trans Muruhuay** each have an hourly service via Jauja to **Tarma**, 3 hrs, US$2.50, some of which continue on to **La Merced**, 5 hrs, US$4. The only company with a direct daytime service to **Satipo** is **Selva Tours**, Giráldez block 3, at 0800, US$6, 229 km, 12 hrs, on a very difficult road, which is impossible in the wet.

ETAS/Angoma, Loreto 744, T064-215424, travels to **Cañete** on the coast (see page 284), 289 km, 10 hrs, US$4. Tickets are best bought the day before; the office is usually open until about 1930. It is a poor road though the stunning Cañete valley, with beautiful mountain landscapes (best views on the right). The bus passes through **Llapay**, US$4.55 any time from 1130 in the dry season to 1500 in the wet season, **Yauyos** (2 hrs from Llapay), **Chavín** (3 hrs) and **Catahuasi** (3½hrs) arriving in **Cañete** from 1930 onwards.

Local To **Jauja**, 44 km, 1 hr. *Colectivos* and combis leave every few mins from Huamanmarca y Amazonas, and Plaza Amazonas, US$1.50. Ones via San Jerónimo and Concepción have 'Izquierda' on the front. Most buses to the **Mantaro Valley** leave from several places around the market area. Buses to **Hualhuas, Cajas** and **Huamancaca** leave from block 3 of Pachitea. Buses to **Cochas** leave from Amazonas y Giráldez.

Train

There are 2 unconnected railway stations. The **Central station** (Av Ferrocarril 461, T064-217724/216662) serves **Lima**, via **La Oroya** (298 km). Service on this railway with trains at certain weekends is run by **Ferrocarril Centro Andino**, T01-361 2828, ext 222, www.ferroviasperu.com. The fare is US$48 return. The train leaves Lima Fri 0700, arrives Huancayo 1800, returns Sun 1800, arrives Lima 0500. Coaches have reclining seats, heating, restaurant, tourist information, toilets and nurse with first aid and oxygen. Information on forthcoming departures can be obtained from **Incas del Perú**, see Activities and tours, page 494.

From the small station in Chilca suburb (15 mins by taxi, US$1), trains run 128.7 km to **Huancavelica**, on a narrow gauge track (3 ft). There are 2 trains: the *autovagón* leaves at 1300 daily. It costs US$4 and has 1st class and buffet carriages. The journey takes 7 hrs, and is a spectacular one with fine views, passing through typical mountain villages. There are 38 tunnels and the line reaches 3676 m. Meals, drinks and snacks are served on the train, and vendors sell food and crafts at the village stations. The local train leaves at 0630 daily and takes 5 hrs. There are 1st, US$2.55, 2nd, US$2.20, and buffet, US$3.70, classes. Tickets can only be bought on the day of travel; get in the queue at 0600 at the latest. Services are often suspended, especially when rainy; the trains frequently suffer technical problems.

Izuchaca *p489*

Trains to **Huancavelica** pass at around 0900 and 1600. To **Huancayo**, the *autovagón* reaches Izcuchaca at 0800; the local train at 1400-1430. The direct bus from Huancayo to **Ayacucho** passes at 0800, alternatively take a truck – about 8 hrs to Ayacucho.

Huancavelica and around

p489, map p492

Bus

All bus companies are at the east end of town, around Parque M Castilla, on Muñoz, Iquitos, Tumbes and O'Donovan. To **Huancayo**, 147 km, 5 hrs, US$2.85, rough road. **Transportes Yuri** at 2200 and **Transportes Ticllas**, 6 a day. To go only as far as **Izcuchaca** costs US$1.45. To **Lima** there are 2 routes: one is via Huancayo, 445 km, 13 hrs minimum, US$5.70. **Libertadores** buses to Huancayo at 1830 go on to Lima, also **Ticllas** at 1700. The other route is via **Pisco**, 269 km, 12 hrs, US$7 and **Ica**, US$8, at 1730 daily, with **Oropesa**, O'Donovon 599. Buy your ticket 1 day in advance. The road is poor until it joins the Ayacucho–Pisco road, where it improves. The views are spectacular, but most of the journey is done at night.

The only direct transport from Huancavelica to **Ayacucho**, is 0430 Sat with **San Juan Bautista**, Plaza Túpac Amaru 107, T067-803062, US$5.70. On other days you have to catch a **San Juan Bautista** bus at 0430 to **Rumichaca** on the paved Pisco–Ayacucho road, just beyond Santa Inés, 4 hrs, then wait for a passing bus to Ayacucho, 1500, 3 hrs, US$2, or take a truck. (There's nothing in Rumichaca other than a couple of foodstalls and some filthy toilets.) From Rumichaca it's a spectacular but cold journey to Ayacucho on the paved road, which rarely drops below 4000 m for 150 km. The best alternative is to take a *colectivo* from Huancavelica to **Lircay**, and continue with the same company from Lircay Terminal Terrestre hourly from 0430 to **Julcamarca**, 2½ hrs, US$3. Minibuses run from Julcamarca plaza to Ayacucho, US$2, 2 hrs. The final option is to travel by bus or train from Huacavelica to **Izucacha** and change for services to Ayacucho there. A taxi between Huancavelica and Izcuchaca costs US$22 minimum.

Train

Just a little beyond the bus stations and about 500m from the Plaza de Armas is the train station. The *autovagón* leaves daily at 0630, arrives in **Izcuchaca** at 0800, US$1.70, then continues to **Huancayo**. It tends to be very crowded. The local train leaves at 1300 daily and passes Izcuchaca at 1400-1430. Sit on the left for the best views. For further details, see Huancayo Transport, page 494.

Directory

Jauja and around *p487*

Banks No TCs are accepted at the BCP, Junín 790. **Banco de la Nación**, Bolívar 821. **Dollar Exchange Huarancayo**, on Jr Huarancayo, gives a much better rate than BCP. **Internet** All along Junín blocks 9 to 12. **Post** Jr Bolívar. **Telephone** Telefónica at Bolognesi 546. Also at Ricardo Palma, opposite the Hotel Ganso de Oro, gives better service and prices.

Huancayo and around *p487, map p488*

Banks BCP, Real 1039. Changes TCs with no commission, cash advance on Visa. **Banco Wiese**, Real casi Ica. ATM does not accept international cards, poor rates for TCs. **Interbank** and **Banco Continental** are on block 6 of Real. There are several *casas de cambio* on Ancash and on Av Lima between Ancash and Real. Street changers hang out in front of Hotel Kiya. **Hospital** Daniel A Carrión, Av Daniel A Carrión 1552, T064-222157/232222. **Internet** Numerous places round Plaza Constitución on Giráldez, Paseo La Breña. Average price under US$0.75 per hr. **Language classes** Katia Cerna is a recommended teacher, T064-225332, katiacerna@hotmail .com She can arrange home stays; her sister works in adventure tourism. **Incas del Perú** (see page 494) organize Spanish courses for beginners, US$100 per week, 3 hrs a day, including 5 nights' accommodation at **La Casa de La Abuela** and all meals, also homestays, and classes in weaving, Quechua, traditional music and gourd carving. See also Peru Andino Lodging above. **Laundry** Good *lavandería* on Paseo La Breña behind Casa de Artesano. **Post** On Plaza Huamanmarca. **Useful addresses** Police, Av Ferrocaril 555, T064-211653. **Tourist Police**, Av Ferrocarril 580, T064-219851. **Touring y Automóvil Club del Perú**, Jr Lima 355, T064-231204, huancayo@touringperu.com.pe.

Huancavelica and around *p489, map p492*

Banks BCP, Virrey Toledo 300 block, west of Plaza. There is a Multired ATM on M Muñoz in the arches of the Municipalidad. **Internet** Despite what they say, internet places open around 0900 till 2100-2200. There are places on V Toledo and M Muñoz. Also **Librería Municipal**, Plaza de Armas, US$0.60 per hr. **Post** On Ferrua Jos, at block 8 of M Muñoz. **Telephone** Carabaya y Virrey Toledo.

Ayacucho and its hinterland

➔ *Colour map 5, A4. Altitude: 2748 m .*

The city of Ayacucho, the capital of its Department, is famous for its hugely impressive Semana Santa celebrations, its splendid market and, not least, a plethora of churches – 33 of them no less – giving the city its alternative name La Ciudad de las Iglesias. A week can easily be spent enjoying Ayacucho and its hinterland. The climate is lovely, with warm, sunny days and pleasant balmy evenings. It is a hospitable, tranquil place, where the inhabitants are eager to promote tourism. It also boasts a large, active student population. » *For Sleeping, Eating and other listings, see pages 503-509.*

Ins and outs

Getting there and around The airport is to the east of the city along Av Castilla. A taxi to the centre costs US$2. Walk half a block down the street from the airport for a bus or *colectivo* to the Plaza Mayor. Most of the bus offices are much nearer the centre of town, in the north and northeast. This is a large city but the interesting churches and colonial houses are all fairly close to the Plaza Mayor. Barrio Santa Ana is further away to the south and you will probably want to take a taxi to get to it (US$1; it's easy to walk back). Taxis are cheap and mototaxis are plentiful. » *For further information, see Transport, page 507.*

Tourist information iperú ⓘ *Portal Municipal 48, on the Plaza, T066-318305, iperuayacucho@promperu.gob.pe, Mon-Sat 0830-1930, Sun 0830-1430*, is very helpful. Ask Smith Pariona Medina here for guides who work with the **Asociación de Guías e Turismo - Ayacucho (Agotur-A)**. There is a desk at the airport to meet incoming flights. **Dircetur** ⓘ *Asamblea 481, T066-312548. Mon-Fri 0745-1700*, is also friendly and helpful.

Background

The city was founded on 9 January 1539 by the invading Spaniards, who named it San Juan de la Frontera. This was changed to San Juan de la Victoria after the Battle of Chupas, when the king's forces finally defeated the rival Almagrist power. Despite these Spanish titles, the city always kept its original name of Huamanga. It became an important base for the army of the Liberator Simón Bolívar in his triumphant sweep south from the Battle of Junín. It was here, on the Pampa de Quinua, on 9 December 1824, that the decisive Battle of Ayacucho was fought, bringing Spanish rule in Peru to an end. Huamanga was, therefore, the first city on the continent to celebrate its liberty. In the midst of the massive festivities, the Liberator decreed that the city be named Ayacucho, meaning 'City of Blood'. For much of the 1980s and early 1990s, this title seemed appropriate as the Shining Path terrorized the local populace, severely punishing anyone they suspected of siding with the military. Now, though, peace has returned to this beautiful colonial Andean city.

Sights » *pp503-509.*

The construction of Ayacucho's many colonial religious buildings is said to have been financed by wealthy Spanish mine-owners and governors. Unfortunately many have fallen into disrepair and are closed to the public.

Plaza Mayor and north

Ayacucho is built round the Plaza Mayor in the centre of which is a statue of Independence hero Antonio José de Sucre. Facing onto the plaza are the cathedral,

Ayacucho

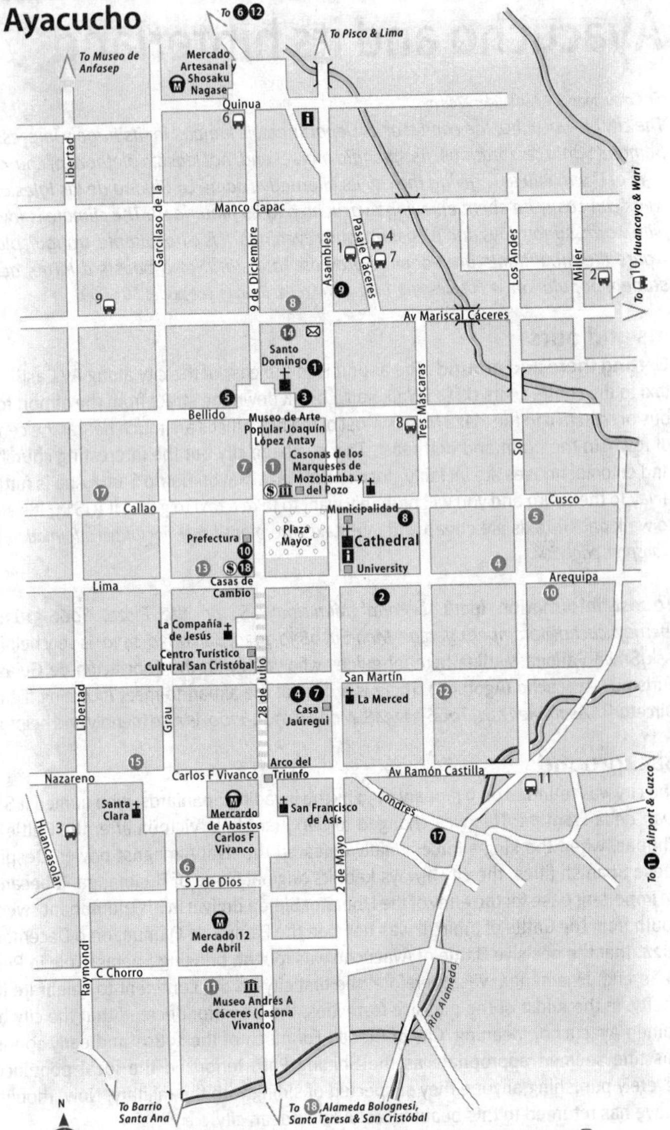

N

0 metres 100
0 yards 100

Sleeping
Ayacucho Hotel Plaza **1**
El Mesón **4**
Florida **5**
Grau **6**
Hospedaje El Centro **8**
Hostal 3 Máscaras **12**
Hostal El Marqués de Valdelirios **18**
Hostal San Blas & La Posada de Santa Inés **11**
La Crillonesa **15**
Marcos **7**
San Francisco **17**
Santa María **10**
Santa Rosa **13**

Eating
Brasa Roja **8**
Cabo Blanco **6**
Café Dorado **9**
Cameycar & Chifa Hua Lin **1**
La Casona **3**
La Miel **10**
La Pradera **2**
Los Flores **11**
Los Manglares de Tumbes **12**
Mia Pizza **4**
Nino **5**
Portal 1 **18**
Tradición **7**
Urpicha **17**

Bars & clubs
Punto Caliente **14**

Transport
Colectivos to Julcamarca **2**
Combis for Huari, Qinua & Huanta **10**
Combis to Vilcashuamán **11**
Cruz del Sur **9**
Libertadores **8**
Molina **6**
Ormeño **3**
Reybus **4**
Turismo Los Chankas **7**
Wari **1**

Municipalidad, the Prefectura and the Supreme Court, housed in fine colonial buildings within the Plaza's arcades. The **cathedral** ① *1700-1900, Sun 0900-1700*, was built in 1612. The two towers are in green stone, while the portal is pink. It has three strong, solid naves of simple architecture, in contrast to the elegant decoration of the interior, particularly the superb gold-leaf altars. The cathedral is beautifully lit at night. Next to the cathedral is the **Universidad Nacional de San Cristóbal de Huamanga**, UNSCH, in the Casona de Castilla y Zamora. It has a small courtyard in which grows a fig tree, after which the university café, **La Higuera**, is named.

On the north side of the Plaza Mayor, on the corner of Portal de la Unión and Asamblea, are the **Casonas de los Marqueses de Mozobamba y del Pozo**, also called Velarde-Alvarez. The **Museo de Arte Popular Joaquín López Antay** ① *Portal de la Unión 28, in the BCP building, museo@unsch.edu.pe, Tue-Fri 1030-1700, Sat 1030-1230*, displays local craft work. Leading north from the Plaza is Jr Asamblea, full of eating places, internet cafés and discos. On a parallel street, one of the city's most notable churches is **Santo Domingo** (1548) ① *9 de Diciembre, block 2, open for Mass daily 0700-0800*. Its fine façade has triple Roman arches and Byzantine towers.

North of the centre, **Museo de Anfasep** (Asociación Nacional de Familiares de Secuestrados Detenidos y Desaparecidos del Perú) ① *Prol Libertad 1226, www.dhperu.org/anfasep, 15 mins' walk fro Mercado Artesanal Shosake Nagase, or mototaxi, entry free but give a donation*, provides an insight into the recent history of this region during the violence surrounding the Sendero Luminoso campaign and the government's attempts to counter it.

South of Plaza Mayor

A stroll down Jr 28 de Julio towards the prominent **Arco del Triunfo** (1910), which commemorates victory over the Spaniards, passes **La Compañía de Jesús** (1605) ① *open only for Mass*. It has one of the most important façades of Viceregal architecture. It is of baroque style and guarded by two impressive 18th-century towers. Its altar is covered in gold leaf and large paintings of saints adorn the nave.

Go through the arch to the church of **San Francisco de Asís** ① *28 de Julio, block 3, open daily for morning mass and 1730-1830*. It dates from 1552 and has an elaborate gilt main altar and several others. It claims the largest bell in the city in its tower. Across 28 de Julio from San Francisco is the **Mercado de Abastos Carlos F Vivanco**, the packed central market. As well as all the household items, meat and other local produce, look for the cheese sellers, the breads and the section dedicated to fruit juices.

Santa Clara de Asís ① *Jr Grau, block 3, open for Mass*, is renowned for its beautifully delicate coffered ceiling. It is open for the sale of sweets and cakes made by the nuns (go to the door at Nazarenas 184, it's usually open). On the 5th block of 28 de Julio is the late 16th-century **Casona Vivanco**, which houses the **Museo Andrés A Cáceres** ① *Jr 28 de Julio 508, T066-812360, Mon-Sat 0900-1300, 1400-1800. US$1.25*. The museum has a collection of baroque paintings and colonial furniture, some republican and contemporary art, and exhibits on Mariscal Cáceres' battles in the War of the Pacific.

Further south still, on a pretty plazuela, is **Santa Teresa** ① *28 de Julio, block 6, open daily for Mass 1600*, with its monastery dating from 1683. It has magnificent gold-leafed altars, heavily brocaded and carved in the churrigueresque style. Opposite is tiny **San Cristóbal** ① *Jr 28 de Julio, block 6, rarely open*, with its single tower. This was the first church to be founded in the city (1540) and is one of the oldest in South America.

Back near the centre, the 16th-century church of **La Merced** ① *2 de Mayo, block, open for Mass*, is the second oldest in the city. The high choir is a good example of the simplicity of the churches of the early period of the Viceroyalty. In 1886 a flagstone was discovered with the sculpted image of a sleeping warrior, known popularly as the 'Chejo-Pacheco'. **Casa Jáuregui** ① *opposite La Merced on 2 de Mayo, Mon-Fri 0800-1700*, also called **Ruiz de Ochoa**, was built in the second half of the 18th century and became the Jáuregui family home, until Peruvian banks restored it in 1974-97. Its oustanding feature is its doorway, which has a blue balcony supported by two fierce beasts with erect penises.

Barrio Santa Ana

For a fascinating insight into Inca and pre-Inca art and culture, a visit to **Barrio Santa Ana** is a must. Here, about 200 families have workshops making *artesanías*: textiles, *retablos*, ceramics and work in stone. Their work is distributed through the galleries in the Barrio. **Galería de Arte Latina** ⓘ *Plazuela de Santa Ana 105, T066-528315, wari39@hotmail.com*, is especially recommended. The owner, Alejandro Gallardo Llacctahuamán, and his son, Alexander, are very friendly and have lots of information on weaving techniques and the preservation of their culture. They plan to open a textile museum soon and Alexander is working with local communities and orphans. Also visit **Wari Art Gallery** ⓘ *Jr Mcal Cáceres 302, Santa Ana, T066-312529*, run by Gregorio Sulca and his family, who will explain the Quechua legends, weaving and iconography. Next door is the Sulcas' **Instituto de Cultura Quechua**, which affords wonderful views of the city and surrounding hills from its roof. Both the Gallardos and the Sulcas are renowned internationally. A good grasp of Spanish is essential to appreciate the galleries fully.

Galleries in the barrio are closed on Sunday.

Around Ayacucho » pp503-509.

Vilcashuamán and Vischongo

The impressive Inca ruins of **Vilcashuamán** are four hours to the south of Ayacucho (120 km), beyond Cangallo. According to John Hemming, Vilcashuamán was an important provincial capital, the crossroads where the road from Cuzco to the Pacific met the empire's north–south highway. The tourist office on the Plaza in Ayacucho has a guidebook, in Spanish, which can be consulted. Near Vilcashuamán is the village of **Vischongo**, which has a market on Wednesday. About an hour's walk uphill from the village are the Inca baths of **Intihuatana**, which are worth seeing as much for their superb location on a beautiful lake as for the ruins themselves.

It is possible to see both ruins in a day, though it's more relaxing to spend the night in Vilcashuamán, or better still, camp at the lake near Vischongo. Tours to Vilcashuamán from Ayacucho include both Vischongo and Intihuatana. » *For further details, see Activities and tours and Transport, page 507.*

Huari

ⓘ *22 km from Ayacucho, daily 0800-1700, US$0.90.*

A good road going north from Ayacucho leads to Huari (frequently spelt Wari), dating from the 'Middle Horizon' (AD 600-1000), when the Huari culture spread across most of Peru. This was the first urban walled centre in the Andes and was used for political, administrative, ceremonial, residential and productive purposes. The huge irregular stone walls are up to 4 m high (although many are long and low) and rectangular houses and streets can be made out. There are large areas of flat stone, which may have been for religious purposes, and there are tomb complexes and subterranean canals and tunnels.

The most important activity here was artistic production. High temperature ovens were used to mass produce ceramics of many different colours. The Huari also worked with gold, silver, metal and alloys such as bronze, which was used for weapons and decorative objects. The ruins now lie in an extensive tuna cactus forest. There is a small museum at the site, but very little direction and the few explanations are only in Spanish. Tombs of the Huari nobles are being excavated along the road from Ayacucho to Quinua.

The Huari influence

The city of Huari had a population of 50,000 and reached its apogee in AD 900. Its influence spread throughout much of Peru: north to Cajamarca; along the north coast to Lambayeque; south along the coast to Moquegua; and south across the sierra to Cuzco. Before the Inca invasion, the Huari formed a *chanca* – a confederation of ethnic groups – and populated the Pampas river and an area west of the Apurímac. This political agreement between the peoples of Ayacucho, Andahuaylas, Junín and Huancavelica was seen by the Incas in Cuzco as a threat. The Incas fought back around 1440 with a bloody attack on the Huari on the Pampa de Ayacucho, and so began a period of Inca domination. The scene of this massacre is still known as *Rincón de los Muertos*.

Quinua

This village, 37 km northeast of Ayacucho, has a charming cobbled main plaza and many of the buildings have been restored. There is a small market on Sunday. Nearby, on the Pampa de Quinua, a huge obelisk commemorates the battle of Ayacucho. The obelisk is 44 m high, representing 44 years of struggle for independence.

The village's handicrafts are recommended, especially ceramics, which range from model churches and nativity figures to humorous groups of musicians and gossiping women. The rich red local clay is modelled mainly by hand and decorated with local mineral earth colours. Traditionally, the model churches are set on the roofs of newly occupied houses to ward off evil spirits. Virtually every roof in the village has a church on it – including the church itself. **San Pedro Ceramics**, at the foot of the hill leading to the monument, and **Mamerto Sánchez**, Jr Sucre, are good places to find typical pieces but there are many others. By the *paradero* are several *recreos*, tourist restaurants serving typical food.

Huanta Valley → *Colour map 5, A4.*

The town of **Huanta**, one hour from Ayacucho on the road to Huancayo, overlooks the valley and has a pleasant plaza with palms and other trees. It was in Huanta that the Pokras and Chancas warriors put up their last, brave fight against the Inca invasion. Huanta celebrates the **Fiesta de la Cruz** during the first week of May, with much music and dancing. Its Sunday market is large and interesting, while the permanent daily market covers quite an area. There are many places to eat around town.

The **valley of Luricocha**, 5 km away, can be visited. It has a lovely, warm climate. The *recreos* (tourist restaurants) at Luricocha are famous for their *platos típicos*. Take a combi from Parque Hospital in Huanta (US$0.15).

The area is notable as the site of perhaps the oldest known culture in South America, 20,000 years old, evidence of which was found in the cave of **Pikimachay**. The cave is 24 km from Ayacucho, on the road to Huanta. It is a 30-minute walk from the road. The remains are now in Lima's museums.

Ayacucho to Cuzco » pp503-509.

Andahuaylas and around → *Colour map 5, A4.*

About 240 km from Ayacucho, in a fertile, temperate valley of lush meadows, cornfields and groves of eucalyptus, alder and willow, stands Andahuaylas (2980 m). The town offers few exotic crafts, but it has a good market on Sunday and the surrounding scenery is beautiful. The church of **San Pedro** ⓘ *daily 1600-1670*, takes up the south side of the plaza, which has tulip and other trees, flowers and statues. On the north side is the Municipalidad, with a small **Museo Arqueológico**, which has a good collection of pre-Columbian objects, including mummies. The **Andahuaylas Archaeological Project** is based at the museum and there's also an office of **Dircetur** ⓘ *Av Túpac Amaru 374, T083-421627, diturandahuaylas@hotmail.com.*

A good nearby excursion is to the **Laguna de Pacucha**, beautifully set among the hills. On the shore is the town of Pacucha and various places to eat. A road follows the north shore of the lake and a turn-off climbs to **Sóndor** ⓘ *US$0.60 (beware overcharging by the guardian)*, an Inca archaeological site at 3300 m. Various buildings and small plazas lead up to a conical hill surrounded by concentric stone walls or terracing. At the summit is a large rock said to be an *intihuatana* (hitching post of the sun). There are wonderful views back to Pachuca and over the surrounding valleys and mountains. Each 18-19 June Sóndor Raymi is celebrated.

Abancay and around → *Colour map 5, A5.*

Nestled between mountains in the upper reaches of a glacial valley at 2378 m, this friendly town is first glimpsed after about two hours on the bus from Andahuaylas. The last few kilometres are on the paved highway from Nazca, a relief after the rough, tortuous descent from the high sierra. The town is a functional, commercial centre, growing in importance now that the paved Lima–Nazca–Cuzco road passes through. It also hopes to benefit from the tourist trade to Choquequirao; there is much investment in building hotels and generally improving the town. For information visit the **tourist office** ⓘ *Lima 206, T083-321664, open 0800-1430*, or **Dircetur** ⓘ *Av Arenas 121, p 1, T083-321664, apurimac@mincetur.gob.pe.*

Half-day tours are run to nearby sites such as the former haciendas of **Yaca** and **Illanya**. Near Yaca is a place where silk worms are bred. Also included is the colonial bridge at **Pachachaca** (which can be seen from any bus going to Andahuaylas), the **Mirador at Taraccasa**, for views over the city, and the thermal baths of **Santo Tomás.**

Santuario Nacional de Ampay ⓘ *US$1.50*, north of town, encompasses lagoons, called Angasccocha (3200 m) and Uspaccocha (3820 m), a glacier on Ampay mountain at 5235 m and flora and fauna typical of these altitudes. By public transport, take a *colectivo* to Tamburco and ask the driver where to get off. It takes two days of trekking to get to the glacier, with overnight camping.

One hour out of Abancay, at a place called **Carbonera**, a road to the left goes to **Huanipaca** (40 minutes, US$15.15 in car, lodging available, and guides). It continues

Sleeping
Hostal Apurímac Tours 1
Hostal Arenas 2
Hostal El Dorado 3
Hostal Victoria 5
Imperial 4
Kavaxio Palace 6
Turistas 7

Eating
Café Mundial 1
Chifa Shanghai 2
Dulce & Salad 3
Focarela Pizzería 4
La Delicia 5
La Valera 6
Natur Center 7
Panadería Buen Gusto 8
Panadería Cynthia 9
Pizzería Napolitana 10

Bars & clubs
El Pato Video Pub 11

N
0 metres 50
0 yards 50

to Ccenhualla, from where Choquequirao is visible. You descend 1½ hours to **Hacienda San Ignacio** by the Río Apurímac, then climb 14 hours up to **Choquequirao** (much steeper than the Cachora route). Shortly after Carbonera is the turn to Cachora.

For Cachora and the route to Choquequirao, see West from Cuzco, page 214.

Three kilometres from the main road to Cuzco, at 3000 m, is the **Saywite stone** ⓘ *Km 49 from Abancay, well-signed, allow 1-2 hours to see the whole site. US$3, students US$1.* This large carved rock and its surroundings is a UNESCO World Heritage site. The principal monolith is said to represent the three regions of jungle, sierra and coast, with the associated animals and Inca sacred sites of each. The holes around the perimeter suggest that it was covered in gold. It is said to have been defaced when a cast was made, breaking off many of the animals' heads; ask the guardian for a closer look. Six main areas spread away from the stone and its neighbouring group of buildings. Look out for a staircase beside an elegant watercourse of channels and pools; a group of buildings around a stone (split by lightning), called the Casa de Piedra (or Rumi Huasi), an *usnu* platform and another monolith, called the Intihuatana.

About 20 minutes from Saywite is **Curahuasi** (126 km from Cuzco), famous for its aromatic anise herb, which has several roadside restaurants and *hospedajes*. A good two-hour walk takes you up Cerro San Cristóbal to **Capitán Rumi**, a huge rock overlooking the Apurímac canyon. The views are staggering, particularly if Salkantay and its snowy neighbours are free of cloud. Ask for directions, especially at the start.

Not far from the new road bridge over the Apurímac are the thermal baths of **Cconoc** ⓘ *US$1.80*. An unmade road twists down to the river's edge where several pools and spouts are fed by warm water coming out of the cliffs. They are fairly clean, but watch out for the biting midges.

Sleeping

Ayacucho *p497, map p498*

B Ayacucho Hotel Plaza, 9 de Diciembre 184, T066-312202, hplaza@derrama.org.pe. Beautiful colonial building but the rooms don't match up to the palatial splendour of the reception. It's comfortable, has TV, and some rooms overlook the plaza.

C-D Santa María, Arequipa 328, T066-314988, santamariayac@latinmail.com. A modern hotel with suites and huge rooms, some on two floors (the stairs are a bit flimsy), price includes breakfast. Bedrooms are comfortable, with a proper bath, large TV and good fixtures and furnishings. There is a restaurant/bar, a garage in the basement and a great view from the roof.

D Marcos, 9 de Diciembre 143, T066-316867. A comfortable, modern hotel in a cul-de-sac 1/2 block from the Plaza. It's quiet, clean and rooms have bath, hot water and TV. The price includes breakfast in the cafetería.

D Santa Rosa, Jr Lima 166, T066-314614, www.hotel-santarosa.com. Lovely colonial courtyard in th Casona Gutiérrez (1630); the Monja Alferez lived here for a while. It also served as the press HQ during the terrorist years. There is a roof terrace. Rooms are very clean and warm, hot water all day, friendly, attntive staff, car parking, good restaurant (🍴) with good value menu. Recommended.

E Hostal El Marqués de Valdelirios, Alameda Bolognesi 720, T066-318944. Go through the arch below Santa Teresa to the broad Alameda for this lovely colonial-style mansion, beautifully furnished, with blue flower pots, pickup from the airport for US$3, reserve at least 24 hrs in advance. Price includes breakfast, hot water, bar. Recommended.

E Hostal Tres Máscaras, Jr 3 Máscaras 194, T066-314107, hoteltresmascaras@yahoo.com. New rooms with bath are better, but with less character, than the old ones, some of which have shared bathroom (**F**), in this nice colonial building, which has a deep red patio with plants and caged parrots. Clean, basic rooms, hot water, breakfast extra, car park.

E San Francisco, Jr Callao 290, T066-312353, www.sanfranciscohotel.cjb.net. Rather like an old museum with a nice patio, this is a friendly hotel and a popular choice. Breakfast is extra (US$1 - none on Sun), hot water, TV, comfortable rooms and some suites. Recommended. Will book El Encanto de Oro in Andahuaylas.

E-F Florida, Jr Cusco 310, T066-312565, F316029. Small and pleasant: a leafy courtyard leads to a modern block with clean, quiet rooms with bath and TV, hot water from electric showers. There are caged birds in the patio.

F El Mesón, Jr Arequipa 273, T066-312938. A nice, clean, friendly *hostal*, hot water on request, laundry service, disco close by.

F Hospedaje El Centro, Av Cáceres 1048, T313556. Rooms without bath and TV are **G**, large rooms, hot water, very clean, good value, but on a busy avenue.

F Grau, Jr San Juan de Dios 192, T066-312695. On the third floor (the second is a separate *hospedaje*), by the markets. With bath (**G** without, but with TV), hot water in all bathrooms, clean, clothes washing facilities and laundry service, good value, safe, friendly, noisy, breakfast extra. Recommended.

G Hostal San Blas, Jr Chorro 167, T066-312712. Special tourist price represents good value, nice rooms with bath (cheaper without), hot water all day, clean, friendly, kitchen facilities and laundry service, cheap meals available, bicycles to lend, tourist information. Recommended.

G La Crillonesa, El Nazareno 165, T066-312350, hotelcrillonesa@hotmail.com. A big blue and white building just up from Santa Clara and the market, with colourful, locally made decorations and excellent services. The price, set specially for tourists, includes bath, hot water in the basins as well as the shower, 1-hour free internet, kitchen and laundry facilities, discount for longer stay, great views from roof terrace. English and Italian spoken, clean, friendly, lots of tourist information. Carlos will act as a local tour guide and knows everyone. Recommended.

G La Posada de Santa Inés, Jr Chorro 139, T066-319544, posada_staines@hotmail.com. Opposite Mercado 12 de Abril, with bath, hot water morning and evening, TV, terrace with small swimming pool (ask in advance for it to be cleaned), clean, very good value.

Andahuaylas and around *p501*

E El Encanto de Oro, Av Pedro Casafranca 424, T083-723066, www.encantodeoro.4t.com. A large modern hotel, 1 block from the market, 2 from the Plaza, with spacious, comfortable rooms, well decorated and good facilities. Discount available making for excellent value, breakfast included, TV, hot water 24 hrs, laundry service, restaurant with mirador, internet across the street, organizes trips on request. Advisable to reserve 15 days in advance.

E Sol de Oro, Jr Juan A Trelles 164, T083-721152, soldeorohotel@hotmail.com. A tall blue building, with lift to upper floors, near the bus stations. Price includes breakfast, hot water 24 hrs, plain rooms, TV, clean, laundry service, garage and tourist information. El Dorado Inn restaurant alongside.

F El Encanto de Apurímac, Jr Juan Francisco Ramos 401, T083-723527. Close to Los Chankas and other bus stations, with bath, TV, hot water, clean, very friendly and helpful.

G Hostal Waliman, Av Andahuaylas 266. Cold water in the shared bathrooms, very basic but clean and helpful.

G La Pradera, Jr Ramos 409, T083-801942. Also convenient for buses, plain rooms but OK, with bath, cheaper without TV, hot water, no breakfast.

G Las Américas, Jr Ramos 410, T721646. Near the bus stations. A bit gloomy in the public areas, but rooms are fine if basic. Cheaper without bath, **G** per person with shared bath, hot water, clean, friendly. Recommended.

Abancay and around *p502*

C-D Turistas, Av Díaz Bárcenas 500, T083-321017, hotursa@terra.com.pe. With bathroom, breakfast included. The original building is in colonial style, rooms (**D**) a bit gloomy, breakfast not included. Newer rooms on top floor (best) and in new block (**C**), including breakfast. Good restaurant (🍴), enjoy a pisco sour over a game of billiards in the wood panelled bar. Internet (US$0.60 per hour), parking space.

E Imperial, Díaz Bárcenas 517, T083-321538. Rooms are around the central parking space

For an explanation of sleeping and eating price codes used in this guide, see inside the front cover. Other relevant information is found in Essentials, pages 53-58.

in this hospitable, efficient and spotless hotel. Rooms have great beds,TV and hot water (also in the shared bathrooms). The price of rooms without bath does not include breakfast. Helpful and good value.

E **Kavaxio Palace**, Díaz Bárcenas 1112, at El Olivo, T083-803050. New, rooms with bath have hot water, TV; hot water also in the shared bathrooms. Breakfast extra. Good service, welcoming.

E-F **Hostal El Dorado**, Av Arenas 131, T083-322005. This is an excellent choice. You go down to a little garden with a lemon tree, around which are the clean, comfortable rooms with an oriental feel. With bath, hot water, TV, breakfast extra.

F **Hostal Arenas**, Av Arenas 192, T083-322107. A brand new hotel is being built beside the old one, with plain but well-appointed rooms, good beds, big showers, hot water, TV, new restaurants, internet, parking, lift to top floor, which has good views. The old part has rooms without bath and cold water. Hospitable.

F **Hostal Victoria**, Arequipa 309. Clean, modern, central, TV, hot water.

G **Hostal Apurímac Tours**, Jr Cusco 421, T083-321446. Another new building, with rooms upstairs, with bath and hot water. The comedor in the courtyard serves breakfast and lunch, pay extra for either.

Eating

Ayacucho *p497, map p498*

Those wishing to try *cuy* should do so in Ayacucho as it's a lot cheaper than Cuzco. Also try *mondongo*, a soup made from intestines, maize and mint. Many restaurants include this and *puca picante* (beef in a thick spicy sauce, rather like Indian curry) on their Fri lunch menu. You can also find *mondongo* at the **central market** in the Sección Comidas in the main building, or at Pasajes 2 and 3 outside; make sure the food is piping hot.

For a cheap, healthy breakfast try *maca*, a drink of maca (see page 517), apple and quinoa. It is sold opposite **Santa Clara** between 0600 and 0800. There are countless small, unnamed eating places around the centre. Few vegetarian options in town, so if required, buy food in the market and prepare it yourself in *hostales* such as **La Crillonesa** or **San Blas**.

TTT **Las Flores**, Jr José Olaya 106, Plaza Conchopata, east of city. Specializes in *cuy*, with *chicharrón, ccapchi* and beer, bougainvillea-filled patios, rustic. Similar restaurants on the plaza, boys guard cars, taxi US$1 from centre. Open 0900-1900.

TT **Tradición**, San Martín 406. Another popular place, specializing in local food, also has a good cheap *menú*.

TT **Urpicha**, Jr Londres 272. Recommended for typical food, which is its only cuisine. The dish called *urpicha* includes something of everything.

TT-T **La Casona**, Jr Bellido 463. Open 1200-2200. Dining under the arches and in dining room, regional specialities, try *puca picante* and *cuy*, and a wide menu. Recommended for food, service and cleanliness.

TT-T **Los Manglares de Tumbes**, Av 26 de Enero, Asoc UNSCH, mz B lote 2. Open 0900-1600/1700 daily, big, smart place, for ceviches and seafood, à la carte, very good.

TT-T **Nino**, Jr 9 de Diciembre 205, on small plaza opposite **Santo Domingo** church, T066-814537. Open Sun evening, very nice dining rooms with pleasant decor, terrace and garden (look for the owls in the trees); chicken, pastas and pizzas, including take-away, friendly.

T **Brasa Roja**, Jr Cusco block 1. Relatively upmarket chicken place with food cooked *a la leña*, salads, very good.

T **Cabo Blanco**, Av Maravillas 198, close to **Shosaku Nagase** market (see Shopping). Ceviches, seafood and fish dishes, small place with friendly personal service.

T **Café Dorado**, Jr Asamblea 310. Excellent value set menu and chicken dishes in a long, cavernous dining room, mirrors and wood oven.

T **Chifa Hua Lin**, Asamblea 257. Very popular Chinese, said to be the best in town.

T **Mía Pizza**, San Martín 420-424. Open 1800-2400, for pizzas, pastas and karaoke (also has a bar to get you in the mood for singing).

Cafés

Centro Turístico Cultural San Cristóbal, 28 de Julio 178, has some expensive cafés (eg **Lalo's**, No 115, open 0900-2100, and **New York**, No 114) as well as other restaurants; all have tables in the pleasant courtyard.

La Higuera, in UNSCH, next to cathedral on Plaza. Off pretty courtyard, Mon-Sat 0700-2100 for breakfasts; lunch specials Mon-Fri.
La Miel, Portal Constitución 11-12, two locations. Good coffee, hot drinks, juices, shakes, cakes and snacks, also ice creams.
Portal 1, Portal Constitución 1. A good café on the corner of the plaza serving snacks, light meals and ice cream.

Huanta Valley *p501*

¥ **La Casona**, Gral Córdoba 162. A huge place on the plaza in Huanta serving traditional dishes, chicken and good value *menú*.

Andahuaylas and around *p501*

¥ **La Casona**, Jr R Castilla 259 and Av Perú 260. A relatively upmarket pair of chicken restaurants, also *parrilladas*.
¥ **El Dragón**, Jr Juan A Trellas 279. A recommended chifa serving huge portions, excellent value (same owner as Hotel El Encanto de Apurímac).
¥ **Il Gatto**, Jr G Cáceres 334. A warm pizzería, with wooden furniture, pizzas (generous toppings, not thin cust) cooked in a wood-burning oven, very friendly.
¥ **Napolitano**, Jr R Castilla 431. A small pizzería which also sells *macerados* (fuit steeped in *pisco*) and has a cambio.
¥ **Nuevo Horizonte**, Jr Constitución 426. Vegetarian and health food restaurant, clean, open for breakfast.

Abancay and around *p502*

¥¥-¥ **La Valera**, Arenas 150. An Argentinian-style steak house.
¥ **Chifa Shanghai**, Arenas 129. Large helpings, popular with locals.
¥ **Focarela Pizzería**, Díaz Bárcenas 521, T083-322036. Simple but pleasant decor, pizza from a wood-burning oven, fresh, generous toppings, popular (ask for 'vino de la casa'!).
¥ **Pizzería Napolitana**, Diaz Barcenas 208. With a wood-fired clay oven and wide choice of toppings.

Cafés

Café Mundial, Arequipa 301. Open early for breakfast and also for evening snacks.
Dulce & Salad, Arequipa y 2 de Mayo. A pleasant café and heladería, four type of breakfast, daily salad specials, sandwiches, hot and cold drinks, cakes and a bar.
La Delicia, Díaz Bárcenas 210. A small vegetarian place serving breakfast, lunch buffet, juices, yoghurts and other products.
Natur Center, Díaz Bárcenas 211. An equally small vegetarian café with breakfast, lunch *menú*, juices and treatments.
Panadería Cynthia, Huancavelica 311. With Café serving enormous croissants.
Panadería Buen Gusto, Núñez 209. Good breads and cakes baked on the premises, also has a café.

Bars and clubs

Ayacucho *p497, map p498*

There are many discos on Jr Asamblea, but their names and locations change frequently, owing to non-compliance with safety laws.
Punto Caliente, Cáceres 1045. Pizzas, drinks and music videos, same owner as Mía Pizza.

Andahuaylas and around *p501*

El Garabato, on main plaza beside Municipalidad. Video and music club, with tables from tree trunks, animal skins on the wall, woollen seat covers, expensive drinks, popular. There are many others around the plaza.

Abancay and around *p502*

Av Arenas has many *peñas turísticas*, bars and clubs. The best place for a beer is **El Pato Video Pub**, Arenas 176.

Festivals and events

Ayacucho *p497, map p498*

This area is well known for its festivals throughout the year. Almost every day there is a celebration in one of the surrounding villages, even in Ayacucho itself. Check with the tourist office.
6 Jan Bajada de Reyes, when people pay to take gifts from an adorned Baby Jesus.
Feb and Mar Festival Internacional de la Tuna y Cochinilla (date varies, lasts for 15 days), for real 'dye' hards.
Feb/Mar **Carnival** has a respectable side and a riotous side, the *comparas urbanas* and the *comparsas rurales*; ask Carlos at Hotel La Crillonesa about taking part.
Mar/Apr Ayacucho is famous for its Semana Santa which begins on the Fri

before Holy Week. There follows one of the world's finest Holy Week celebrations, with candle-lit nightly processions, floral 'paintings' on the streets, daily fairs (the biggest on Easter Sat), horse races and contests among peoples from all over central Peru. All accommodation is fully booked for months in advance of Holy Week. Many people offer beds in their homes during the week. Look out for notices on the doors, especially on Jr Libertad.

30 Aug One of the main festivals in Barrio Santa Ana, with processions and bull running in the plaza.

Shopping

Ayacucho *p497, map p498*

Ayacucho is a good place to buy local crafts including filigree silver, which often uses mudéjar patterns. Also look out for little painted altars which show the nativity scene, carvings in local alabaster, harps, or the pre-Inca tradition of carving dried gourds. The most famous goods are carpets and *retablos*. In both weaving and *retablos*, scenes of recent political strife have been added to more traditional motifs. Even the newspaper stands on the Plaza, along with the Coca Cola emblems, are painted like *retablos*. For carpets, go to Barrio Santa Ana, page 500. See also Arts and crafts page 592.

Centro Turístico Cultural San Cristóbal, Jr 28 de Julio 178. Complex with a quiet courtyard, art galleries, shops and restaurants, etc.

Familia Pizarro, Jr San Cristóbal 215, Barrio Belén. Good-quality textiles, masks for Carnaval and *piedra de huamanga* (local alabaster).

Shosaku Nagase, a large new Mercado Artesanal y Centro de Capacitación, on Jr Quinua. Some of the same goods can be found in the Mercado Carlos Vivanco (see Sights, above).

Taller y Galería de Arte Robert Torre, Mz 0, lote 5, Urb César Mujica Cacho-Yanamilla, T066-970 7511, rotma4@hotmail.com. Sculpture, painting, see Robert's work in progress, full explanations in Spanish, public art as well as his own styles (not artesanal), works for sale.

Activities and tours

Ayacucho *p497, map p498*

Tours to **Vilcashuamán** with travel agencies include Intihuatana, full day US$13, but they only run with 8 passengers. Alternatively stay overnight. Trips to **Huari**, **Quinua** village and the battlefield with travel agencies, US$7.55 per person, minimum 4 people.

Orlando Román, T066-960-1982, orlandoyabish@starmedia.com. English-speaking guide, also gives Spanish classes (at La Crillonesa if you wish), reliable.

Urpillay Tours, Portal Independencia 62, T066-315074, urpillaytours@terra.com. All local tours and flight tickets.

Wari Tours, Portal Independencia 70, T066-311415. Local tours. Also handles Ormeño bus tickets and Western Union.

Warpa Picchu, Portal Independencia 66, T066-315191. All the regular tours, but with an ecotourism angle.

Willy Tours, Jr 9 de Diciembre 107, T066-314075. Personal guide, also handles flight and bus tickets.

Abancay and around *p502*

Local tour prices US$32-28 per person, depending on numbers.

Apurimak Tours, at Hotel Turistas, see Sleeping. Run local tours and 1- and 2-day trips to Santuario Nacional de Ampay: one-day, 7 hours, US$40 per person for 1-2 people (cheaper for more people). Also a 3-day trip to Choquequirao including transport, guide, horses, tents and food, just bring your sleeping-bag, US$60 pp.

Carlos Valer, guide in Abancay – ask for him at Hotel Turistas – very knowledgeable and kind.

Transport

Ayacucho *p497, map p498*

Air

To **Lima**, with **Aero Cóndor**, Tue, Thu, Sun, US$83, 55 mins, via **Andahuaylas**, 30 mins. LC Busre daily from **Lima** (US$70).

Airline offices Aero Cóndor, 9 de Diciembre 123, T066-313060, daily 0900-2100. LC Busre, Jr Lima 178, T066-316012. Most travel agents also sell tickets.

Bus

To **Lima**, 9-10 hrs on a good paved road, via **Ica** (7 hrs). For **Pisco**, 332 km, you have to take a Ica/Lima bus and get out at San Clemente, 10 mins from Pisco, and take a bus or combi (same fare to San Clemente as for Ica). Companies include **Wari**, Pasaje Cáceres 177, T066-326323, US$5.15 at 1800, and **ReyBus**, Pasaje Cáceres 166 (opposite Wari), US$5.80. More expensive are **Cruz del Sur**, Av Mcal Cáceres 1264, T066-812813, US$15.15 to Lima, **Libertadores**, Tres Máscaras 493, T066-313614, and **Ormeño**, Jr Libertad 257, T066-312495 (ticket office at Asamblea 354), US$7.55 to Lima at 0730 and US$12 at 2030 (with video, toilet, heating, a/c), good meal stops, US$6.65 to San Clemente for Pisco; also to Ica at 2100, 7 hrs, US$7.55.

To **Huancayo**, 319 km, 9-10 hrs, US$6.65-7.55, with **Molina**, Jr 9 de Diciembre 458, T066-312984, 3 a day. The road is paved as far as **Huanta**, thereafter it is rough, especially in the wet season, but the views are breathtaking.

For **Huancavelica**, take an **Ormeño** 0730 bus as far as **Rumichaca**, US$2, where combis wait at 1030 for **Huancavelica**, 4 hrs. Otherwise take a Huancayo bus as far as **Izcuchaca**, then take another bus; this is a longer route.

To **Andahuaylas**, 261 km, 10-11 hrs (more in the rainy season), the road is unpaved but in good condition when dry. Daytime buses stop for lunch at **Chumbes** (4½ hrs), which has a few eateries, a shop selling fruit, bread and refrescos, and some grim toilets. Departures are **Wari** at 0400, **ReyBus** at 1830 (not Sun), and **Los Chankas**, Pasaje Cáceres 144, T066-312391, at 0630 (good) and 1900, all US$6.

Although you still have to change buses in Andahuaylas, **Los Chankas**' 1900 service has a direct connection (no waiting) through to **Cuzco**, US$12. To get to **Abancay**, a further 138 km, 5 hrs, you must change buses and then go on to Cuzco, a further 195 km, 5 hrs. It takes 24 hrs to Cuzco. There are no direct buses. Road conditions are quite good, given the terrain crossed, but landslides a common occurrence in the wet season. The scenery, though, is stunning and makes up for it.

Local Combis to **Vilcashuamán** run from Av Ramón Castilla, daily 0400-1500 whenever full, 4 hrs, US$3. From Vilcashuamán to **Vischongo** costs US$0.45. The return journey from Vischongo to Ayacucho takes a little under 4 hrs, and costs US$2.70. Combis to **Huari**, 40 mins, US$0.75, and **Quinua**, a further 25 mins (US$0.50, US$1 from Ayacucho) leave from Paradero below the Ovalo de la Magdalena, at the corner of Jr Ciro Alegría and Jr Salvador Cavero, when full from 0700 onwards. Ask the driver to go all the way to the Obelisco in Quinua for an extra 50 ¢, then walk back to the town. Combis and cars to **Huanta** leave from the same place, US$1.35.

Huanta Valley *p501*

The *paradero* in Huanta is at R Castlla y Amazonas. **Expreso Huamanga**, Amazonas 404, and **Molina**, G Santillana at Parque Alameda, have night buses to **Lima**, US$7.55. **Molina** and **Turismo Central**, G Santillana 464, run daily to **Huancayo**, US$6.60.

Andahuaylas and around *p501*

Air

Aero Cóndor, Jr R Palma 330, T083-422877, to **Lima**, Tue, Thu, Sun, 1 hr 10 mins, US$83.

Bus

Daily buses to **Ayacucho**, minimum of 10 hrs, US$6, with Wari, Av José María Arguedas opposite El Piloto petrol station, at 0800; **Los Chankas**, Av José María Arguedas y Jr Trelles, T083-722441, at 0600 and 1800 or 1840. To **Lima**, buses go via Ayacucho or Pampachiri and Puquio; **Wari** take the latter route, 3 a day, US$15.15. On all night buses, take a blanket.

To **Abancay**, 5 hrs, **Señor de Huanca**, Av Martinelli 170, T083-721218, at 0600, 1300 and 2000 daily, US$3.40; **Los Chankas** at 0630, US$3.60. To **Cuzco**, **San Jerónimo**, Av José María Arguedas 425, T083-801767, via Abancay, 1800 or 1830, also 1900 Sun, US$6, and **Los Chankas**. **Molina**, Av José María Arguedas y Av Lázaro Castilla, over the bridge, also goes to Abancay and Cuzco at 1900.

Local *Colectivo* from Av Los Chankas y Av Andahuaylas, at the back of the market, to **Pacucha**, US$0.75, about 40 mins. To get to **Sóndor**, take a taxi from Andahuaylas, US$10, or catch the *colectivo* to Pacucha, then walk 8-10 km. *Colectivos* to **Argama**

(also from behind Andahuaylas market), pass the entrance. With any form of public transport you will have to walk back to Pacucha, unless very lucky.

Abancay and around *p502*
All interprovincial buses leave from the **Terminal Terrestre**, on Av Pachacútec, on the west side of town. It has a restaurant, internet and phones, a cambio, toilets and shops. Taxi to centre US$0.60, otherwise it's a steep 5 blocks up Av Juan Pablo Castro to Jr Lima. Several companies also have offices on or near the El Olivo roundabout at Av Díaz Bárcenas y Gamarra.

All buses on the **Lima–Nazca–Cuzco** route, via Chalhuanca and Puquio, pass through Abancay at about midnight. Abancay–Lima bus companies such as **Wari** always reserve a few seats for **Puquio**, US$5.50, and **Nazca**, 464 km, US$7.50, if you wish to break the journey. The journey to **Cuzco** takes 4½ hrs and costs US$3.65. The scenery en route is dramatic, especially as it descends into the Apurímac valley and climbs out again. The road is paved and in good condition. (Coming from Cuzco, after the pass it takes 1 hr to zig-zag down to Abancay.)

Buses to **Cachora** (for Choquequirao) depart from the terminal at Jr Prado Alto, between Huancavelica and Núñez (5 blocks uphill from Díaz Bárcenas; it's not the first Jr Prado you come to), daily 0500 and 1400, 2 hrs, US$1.50. Cars from the Curahuasi terminal on Av Arenas, next to the Wari office, charge US$10.

Bus company offices Bredde, Gamarra 423, T083-321643, and Av Arenas 210, 5 daily to Cuzco, including at 0600 and 1300. **Cruz del Sur**, Díaz Bárcenas 1151, T083- 323028, serving the whole country. **Los Chankas**, Díaz Bárcenas 1011, El Olivo, T083-321485, to Andahuaylas and Cuzco. **Molina**, Gamarra 422, T083-322646, 3 daily to Cuzco, also to Andahuaylas at 2330, US$4.25. **San Jerónimo**, to Cuzco at 2130 and Andahuaylas at 2130. **Señor de Huanca**, Av Arenas 198, T083-322377, to Andahuaylas at 0600, 1300, 2000, US$3.40. **Wari**, Av Arenas 200 block, 5 daily to Lima, also to Andahuaylas. Several others to Lima and Cuzco.

Directory

Ayacucho *p497, map p498*
Banks BCP, Portal Unión 28. No commission on cheques, cash advance on Visa, AmEx and Visa ATM. **Interbank**, opposite Hotel Ayacucho, Jr 9 de Diciembre 183, has ATM for Visa, Mastercard/Cirrus and AmEx. 0915-1315, 1630-1830, Sat 0930-1230. Many street changers and casas de cambio can be found at Portal Constitución Nos 2, 3 and 5 on the plaza, they offer a good rate for cash, another on same side as BCP. **Chemists** Farmacia del Pino, 28 de Julio 123. **Inka Farma**, 28 de Julio 250. **Internet** All over the centre. Connections and machines are good, average price is US$0.60 per hr, some charge US$0.90 at night. All 0800-2300 daily. **Internet El Hueco**, Portal Constitución 9, inside, downstairs. Open 0700-2400, has plug-in for laptops, printers, phone cabins, even a playpen. **Post office** Asamblea 293. **Telephone** Many phone offices in the centre. **Useful addresses** Tourist Police at 2 de Mayo y Arequipa.

Andahuaylas and around *p501*
Banks BCP, Av Perú, 6th block east of the Plaza. Multi-Red ATM on north side of Plaza. **Cambio Machi**, Jr R Castilla 371, closes 1800. Another cambio in **Pizzería Napolitana**. **Internet** J F Ramos 317, US$0.45 per hr, also has phone cabins. **FutureNet**, Constitución 445, also has phones. Many others around town, all the same price.

Abancay and around *p502*
Banks BCP, Jr Arequipa 218, has ATM outside, Visa and AmEx. There are several cambios on Jr Arequipa, opposite the Mercado Central, including **Machi**, No 202 (also at Díaz Bárcenas 105) and **Oro Verde**. **Internet** The town is full of internet places. Some have phone cabins. **Post office** Junín y Arequipa. Mon-Sat 0800-2000, and Sun 0800-1500.

East of La Oroya and La Selva Central

From La Oroya, a paved road heads north towards Cerro de Pasco and Huánuco. After 25 km a turn-off branches east and drops 600 m before it reaches Tarma, which is 30 km off the Carretera Central. Beyond Tarma the road continues its steep descent. In the 80 km between Tarma and La Merced the road, passing by great overhanging cliffs, drops 2450 m and the vegetation changes dramatically from temperate to tropical. This is a really beautiful run, leading to Peru's central jungle area which, until recently, has received scant attention compared with the Iquitos and southeastern areas. All this is about to change. ▸▸ *For Sleeping, Eating and other listings, see pages 513-517.*

Ins and outs

The main city of this region, Tarma, is easily reached by road from Lima in six hours, and from Huancayo in three hours. From Tarma, roads descend the eastern flanks of the Andes to the Selva Central. Tourist information is available in Tarma ⓘ *2 de Mayo 775 on the plaza, T064-321010, turistarma@hotmail.com, Mon-Fri 0800-1300, 1600-1800*. The office is very helpful and has good displays on the walls about the surrounding area.

Tarma and around ▸▸ *pp513-517.*

→ *Colour map 3, C4. Altitude: 3050 m.*

Tarma, 'the Pearl of the Andes', was founded in 1538 and is one of the oldest towns in Peru. Though this small, flat-roofed place, with plenty of trees, is now growing with garish modern buildings, it still has a lot of charm. The **Semana Santa** celebrations are spectacular, with a very colourful Easter Sunday morning procession in the main

Tarma

plaza. With its beautiful surrounding countryside, the town is also notable for its locally made fine **flower-carpets**. In 1999 it recorded the largest flower carpet in the world. » *For further details, see Festivals, page 515.*

The **Odria Museum** ⓘ *2 de Mayo 755, Mon-Sat 0900-1300, 1530-2100, free,* celebrates the life of Tarma's most famous son, General Manuel Odria, who became president of Peru in the 1930s. The museum contains personal memorabilia. There is a large *artesanía* market at Lima 548.

Around Tarma

About 8 km south of Tarma on the road to Huancayo, at **Tarmatambo**, is the start of a good section of Inca road which runs 3 km to Huasqui on the Tarma–La Oroya road. There are also ruins and caves and a spectacular view of terrace farming and of Tarma itself. It's 20 minutes by car from Tarma. Some 30 km from Tarma on the Huancayo road is **El Santuario Rupestre Pintish Machay,** near Huairicolca. Here is the largest site of cave paintings in Peru, some 600 pictures dating back 4000 to 10,000 years.

To the north, some 8 km from Tarma, the small hillside town of **Acobamba** has some attractive old buildings. There are festivities during May, see page 515. Some 2 km up beyond the town is the futuristic **Santuario de Muruhuay,** with a venerated picture painted on the rock behind the altar. Its design was inspired by Le Corbusier's work. It also has fine *tapices* made in San Pedro de Cajas which depict the Crucifixion.

The **Grutas de Huagapo,** also known as 'La gruta que llora' (the cave that weeps), is 4 km from the town of **Palcamayo,** which is 15 km northwest of Acobamba. The caves can be entered for about 100 m, at which point it is up to 30 m high and 20 m wide. Guides with torches and ropes can be hired near the entrance to reach 300 m. Beyond that wet suits and simple caving gear are needed. Even without a guide you can penetrate the cave for some way with a torch. The cave is the deepest in South America and investigations, which have penetrated up to 2800 m, suggest that the system extends over 30 km underground. There is a small but impressive gorge, **Cañón de Ushtu,** 10 minutes walk down river from the cave.

Northwest beyond Palcamayo, the road climbs steeply for 14 km to **San Pedro de Cajas,** a large village which is famed for its coloured sheep-wool weavings. The principal shops are on the central plaza and the road to Palcamayo. (This road joins up with the main road from La Oroya to Cerro de Pasco below Junín.) The town holds the **Festival de La Pukcha** (Hilado) on 28-30 June. There is accommodation in the village and a couple of restaurants.

Three kilometres beyond San Pedro on the road to La Oroya is a **vicuña reserve** and co-operative, which is the best place to see vicuña at close range. The animals are accustomed to people and roam near the road. Every August they are sheared and the money from the sale of the fleece goes to the reserve.

Chanchamayo and further east » *pp513-517.*

➔ *Colour map 3, B5.*

The towns of San Ramón and La Merced, collectively known as Chanchamayo, are some 73 km east of Tarma. **San Ramón** is 11 km before La Merced on the banks of the Río Tarma. It is a busy, attractive town in the lower foothills of the Andes, where the temperature is noticeably higher than in Tarma. For information, visit **Dircetur** ⓘ *Pardo 110, San Ramón, T064-331265.* The surrounding hills are covered in coffee plantations.

La Merced lies in the fertile Chanchamayo Valley, famous for its citrus and coffee production. Campa people can usually be found around the central plaza selling bows, arrows, necklaces and trinkets. La Merced has two central **markets,** the Mercado Nuevo and the Mercado Viejo. At the latter you can usually find Campa articles, exotic herbs and jungle medicines such as *uña de gato* and *sangre de grado.*

 The hill behind the town can be climbed up to **La Cruz** for a wonderful view of the entire Chanchamayo Valley, or you can hire a mototaxi for US$1. There is a restaurant and small recreation area here. At holiday times prices double as the area is full of Limeños seeking tropical warmth.

East of Chanchamayo

A 123-km paved road leads from Chanchamayo to **Satipo**. At Km 20, the confluence of the Chanchamayo and Paucartambo rivers forms the Río Perené. The road follows the river, winding through lush jungle and Asháninka villages, where indigenous artefacts are often for sale. At Km 70, palm-thatched huts signals the outskirts of **Pichinaki.**

A few years ago this village represented the remotest of Peruvian outposts, but its fertile lands and warm climate were ideal for coffee, bananas and citrus. Tens of thousands of Andean *campesinos* flocked to the region in search of jobs and land. A paved road reached the town in 1999 and it is now the commercial hub of the region. Its long sandy beaches on the Río Perené make an ideal retreat from the encircling jungle and a jumping-off point to visit the waterfalls, lakes and remote indigenous villages in the area. During the dry season (April-August), the town's plaza and streets are covered with drying coffee beans. Most of the good restaurants are at **Playa Pescadora** (El Puerto Pichinaki) and serve the local delicacy, *doncella* fish (**El Bambú** is recommended).

Beyond Pichinaki the paved road pulls away from the Río Perené and goes to the noisy, semi-modern jungle town of **Satipo**, the main centre of this region. One kilometre from town is **Isla de Fantasía** and **El Lagarto**, with restaurant, nightclub and swimming in the river.

A dirt road continues east to **Mazamari** and **Puerto Ocopa** near the confluence of the Satipo and Perené rivers. Some 10 km along this road are the **Arcoiris waterfalls.** From here you can take a boat down the Río Tambo to its confluence with the Urubamba at **Atalaya,** where it forms the Ucayali. It used to be a centre of the drugs trade, but now it is safe to visit with an army base on the outskirts. It has become a regional centre for commerce and travel, with several *hostales*, a market and a tourist office on the plaza which will help with day trips.

North of Chanchamayo » *pp513-517.*

Puerto Bermúdez

The road has been extended from **San Luis de Shuaro** over an intervening mountain range. A turn-off east leads north to **Puerto Bermúdez** on the Río Neguachi. This is a great base for exploring further into the Selva Central Peruana, with trips upriver to the Asháninka community. Boat passages are possible from passing traders and there is an eating house opposite the airstrip.

Oxapampa → *Colour map 3, B4. Altitude: 1794 m.*

Oxapampa is set on a fertile plain on the Río Huancabamba, a tributary of the Ucayali, 81 km from La Merced. A third of the inhabitants are descendants of a German-Austrian community of 70 families which settled in 1859 at **Pozuzo** (www.munipozuzo.gob.pe), 80 km downstream, and spread later to Oxapampa. There is much livestock farming here, and coffee is planted on land cleared by the timber trade. On 5 August the town hosts a festival, the **Virgen de Las Nieves.** The tourist office ⓘ *Bolívar 466, 2nd floor, T063-462375, www.oxapampaonline.com, Mon-Fri 0800-1230, 1400-1700*, sells maps and guidebooks.

North of Oxapampa

On the main road to Pozuzo, at the end of Oxapampa, go to **Inrena** for authorization to visit the **Yanachaga Chemillén National Park**, where there is good birdwatching very early in the morning and camping is possible for US$1.50. The staff are extremely helpful and will give you trekking information.

Some 25 km from Oxapampa is **Huancabamba**, from where it is 55 km to **Pozuzo**. The whole road between La Merced and Pozuzo is very rough, depending on the season, and crosses no less than 30 rivers. Downstream, 40 km from Pozuzo, is **Nuevo Pozuzo**; there is no transport between the two so it's a two-day walk. There is an interesting museum opposite the church in the town centre ⓘ *US$0.75*. The town celebrates the **Semana Turística de Pozuzo** during the last week in July.

Sleeping

Tarma and around *p510, map p510*
Accommodation is hard to find at Easter but you can apply to the Municipalidad for rooms with local families. Also contact the tourist information office (address above).

B **Los Portales**, Av Castilla 512, T064-321411, www.hoteleslosportales.com. Out of town, with bathroom, hot water, heating, quiet, secluded, price includes breakfast, very good restaurant, but expensive.

C **Hacienda La Florida**, 6 km from Tarma, T064-341041, www.haciendalaflorida.com. 18th-century working hacienda, 12 rooms, some furnished with antiques, with bath, hot water, price includes breakfast but US$5 extra for lunch and dinner, owned by German-Peruvian couple Inge and Pepe who arrange excursions. Great for kids as you can milk cows and ride tractors. Recommended. Also camping for US$3 and new backpacker rooms under construction.

C **Hacienda Santa María**, 2 km out of town at Sacsamarca 1249, T064-321232 (Lima 01-445 1214), www.haciendasantamaria.com. A beautiful (non-working) 17th-century hacienda, has less land than La Florida but beautiful gardens and antique furniture, great fireplace. Includes breakfast and light evening meal. Excellent guides will arrange local day trips for you. Recommended.

D-E **El Caporal**, Lima 616, T064-323636, hostalelcaporal@yahoo.es. Includes breakfast, very clean, good location, rooms with large new bathrooms, hot water, cable TV. Recommended.

E **Hostal Campestre Auberge Normandie**, beside the Santuario de Muruhuay, Acobamba, T064-349 5440, www.normandie.com.pe. 16 cabins with bath and hot water, TV, bar, restaurant, parking, fine views over the valley.

E **Hostal Internacional**, Dos de Mayo 307, T064-321830. With bathroom and hot water, clean. The owner is a dentist, whose practice is next to the *hostal*.

F **Albania**, Amazonas 534, T064-321399. Clean, small rooms with bath and hot water.

F **Hostal Central**, Huánuco 614, T064-310149. Shared bathroom, hot water, friendly, laundry facilities, a bit rundown but popular with gringos, has an observatory which opens Fri at 2000.

F **Hostal El Márquez**, Huaraz 389, T064-321060. An old building with character, with bathroom but shared shower, hot water.

F **La Colmena**, Jauja 618, T064-321157. An old building with character, even if a bit rundown, with bath, clean, convenient for Lima and Huancayo buses.

F **Vargas**, Dos de Mayo 627, T064-321460. With bath, hot water in morning, clean, large rooms, cable TV.

G **Hostal El Dorado**, Huánuco 488, T064-321598. Cheaper without bath, hot water, rooms set round a patio, first floor rooms better, clean.

Chanchamayo *p511*
There are many places to stay just outside San Ramón, off the main road to La Merced.

B **El Refugio**, Ejército 490, San Ramón, T/F064-331082, www.hotelelrefugio.com.pe. Bungalows set in a beautiful tropical garden, with pool, run down but friendly staff, price includes breakfast, good value.

B **Río Grande Inn**, Km 97, San Ramón, T064-332193, www.riograndebungalows.com. Price includes breakfast, bungalows, swimming pool, very good service, overlooking river.

C **Coco's**, Km 102.5 on road to La Merced, T064-337874, cocosinn@hotmail.com. Price includes breakfast. Bungalows ideal for families or groups, great garden, swimming pool, friendly staff.

D El Rancho, Playa Hermosa, San Ramón, T064-331076, www.geocities.com/elrancho peru. Bungalows, which are basic, large grounds, camping US$6 per tent.
D Residencial Rey, Junín 103, La Merced, T064-531185. Same owner as Reyna, which is slightly more expensive, private bathroom, cable TV, brightly lit.
D Reyna, Palca 259, La Merced, T064-531780. Clean rooms with private bath, cable TV and, like its partner, brightly lit.
E Conquistador, Progreso 298, San Ramón, T064-331771, conquistador@viabcp.com. Modern, hot water, TV, parking, has a good *chifa* downstairs.
E El Parral, Uriate 355-361, San Ramón, T064-331128. Modern, with hot water, TV, clean, good restaurant serving local specialities, especially meat.
E Los Portales, Jiménez 119, La Merced, T064-531283. Hot water, with bathroom, TV, comfortable, friendly.
E Primavera, Arequipa 175, La Merced, T064-531433. Friendly, rooms with TV, private bathroom, hot water. Recommended.
F Chanchamayo, Progreso 291, San Ramón, T064-809659, hotel-chanchamayo_7@hotmail.com. With hot water, TV, rooms without bathroom half the price.
G Hospedaje Los Víctor, Jr Tarma 373, on Plaza de Armas, La Merced, T064-809550. With bath, cold water, good, clean and friendly.
G Santa Rosa, 2 de Mayo 447, La Merced, T064-531012. With private bath, clean, cheaper than many others.

East of Chanchamayo *p512*

E Hostal Majestic, on the plaza, Jr Fundadores 408, Satipo, T064-545015. With bathroom, electricity 1900-2300 only, noisy.
E Hostal Brando, Ene 120, Atalaya, T064-461128. New, tiled building, comfortable beds, TV, fan, cold water, helpful staff.
E Hostal Denis, Jr Raymondy 144, Atalaya, T064-461087. New building across from Plaza de Armas, quiet, TV, fan, cold water.

Puerto Bermúdez *p512*

F Hostal Pinto, Oxapampa s/n, T063-720212. Basic but has rooms with own bathroom.
G per person **Albergue Cultural Humboldt**, by the Río Pacitea at La Rampa, 4 mins' walk from the centre, T063-830020, www.geocities.com/puerto_bermudez, alberguehumboldt.free.fr/en/index.htm. US$5 extra for 3 meals a day. The owner, Basque writer Jesús, has created a real haven for backpackers, with maps, library and book exchange. Recommended. Jesús will arrange tours, from day trips to camping and trekking in the primary forest. He has a good relationship with many Asháninka communities that you can visit. Ask him about volunteering at a local Asháninka school.

Oxapampa *p512*

D D'Palma Lodge, Prolongación Thomas Schauss, T063-462123, www.depalmalodge.com. Price includes breakfast. Bungalows set in a spacious area, friendly. Permits camping at US$3 per tent.
E Albergue Turístico Bottger, Jr Mcal Castilla 6th block, T063-462377, www.oxapampaonline.com/bottger/. Very popular, in a quiet area, serves good meals.
E Posada Edelweiss, Carretera Central, Lote 58-Miraflores, T063-462567, www.romaperu.com/posada. Buffet kreakfast and lunch included, very nice owner. Recommended.
F Don Calucho, San Martín 411, T063-462109, doncalucho_oxa@yahoo.com. Rooms with private bath, quiet, pleasant, a good option.

North of Oxapampa *p512*

E Albergue Turístico Frau Maria Egg, Los Colonos, Pozuzo, T01-444 9927 (Lima), fraumariaegg@pozuzo.com. Includes breakfast, nice garden, swimming pool. Recommended.
E Hostal Tirol, Pozuzo. Price includes meals. Clean. Recommended.

Eating

Tarma and around *p510, map p510*

Several eating places on Lima, including a vegetarian restaurant. Tarma's *manjarblanco* is famous, as is *pachamanca*, *mondongo* and *picante de cuyes*. In the central market try *cachanga* – fried bread with cinnamon. Good places to buy local produce such as *manjar blanco* and honey are **El Tarmenito**, Lima 149, or **La Pastora**, Arequipa 656, open since 1902.

Café Picaflor, Lima 306. A small place opposite the cathedral, good for snacks.
Chifa Roberto Siu, Lima 557, T064-704025. A good option for Chinese food, popular with locals.
Comedor Vegetariano, Arequipa 695. Open 0700-2100, vegetarian, small and cheap, sells great bread.
El Sabor Criollo, Huaraz 296. A pleasant local restaurant, try *aji de gallina*, cheap and friendly.
Lo Mejorcito de Tarma, Arequipa 501, T064-321766. Open 0700-2300, offers a good set *menú* with choices at US$1.50, good for local specialities, popular, also has tourist information.
Salud y Vida, Arequipa 677. Open 0730-2000, a small vegetarian place, good value.
Señorial/Pollería Braserita, Huánuco 138-140, T064-323334. Good *menú*, extensive choice, excellent *sopa criolla*, open late.

Chanchamayo *p511*
Boris, Tarma 376 interior, Plaza de Armas, La Merced. Great food, very extensive menu, and very helpful and informative owner, Boris Rojas.
Rincón Gaucho, Junín 234, La Merced, T064-337966. Best place for steak, anticuchos and other meat dishes.
Shambari-Campa, on the Plaza de Armas, La Merced. It has an extensive menu, an excellent set *menú* at US$3, and hundreds of interesting old photos, some dating back to the start of the century, of the local area cover the walls. Highly recommended.
Café Prisci, Progreso 256, San Ramón. Good for snacks, home-made lemon pie.
Chifa Felipe Siu, Progreso 440, San Ramón. One of the most popular restaurants in town, along with **Chifa Conquistador**, see Sleeping.
Chipipizzas, Junín 234, La Merced, T064-337966. Pizzas, burgers, pasta, sandwiches. Good service and clean.

Oxapampa *p512*
La Casa de Baco, Carretera Central, Miraflores Oxapampa. Typical food, good for meats.
Oasis, Jr Bolognesi 120, T063-762206. This is a highly recommended restaurant.
Típico Oxapampino, Plaza de Armas. Very popular, good food, nice owner.

North of Oxapampa *p512*
Guten Appetit, Av los Colonos, Pozuzo. A very popular restaurant in the town.
Típico Pozucino, Av Los Colonos s/n, La Colonia-Pozuzo, T063-707001. Good, cheap food, try *albondigas de carne* or potato salad.

Bars and clubs

Tarma and around *p510, map p510*
La Calesa, Arequipa 433. An old, quiet pub-style bar.
La Esquina del Recuerdo, Huánuco 998. Good for drinks.

Festivals and events

Tarma and around *p510, map p510*
20-25 Feb Carnaval Tarmeño.
Mar/Apr Semana Santa and the Concurso de Alfombras de Flores (flower carpet competition).
May Festividad Señor de Muruhuay.
23-24 Jun Circuito Turístico de Ciclismo de Montaña in Huasihuasi.
23-27 Jun Festival de la Papa.
24 Jun Tayta Inti ceremony is held in Tarmatambo.
23-29 Jul Semana Turística.
28-30 Sep Fiesta de la Siembra del Maíz in Tarma as well as Acobamba.
Oct Señor de Los Milagros processions.
1-2 Nov Festival del Pan Tarmeño 'La Wawa' (the same time as All Saints).

Activities and tours

Tarma and around *p510, map p510*
For the local guides association, email taruma84@hotmail.com, or ask at the tourist office on the main plaza. Many tour operators come and go, especially during the holidays. They offer a variety of day trips to local sites, leaving around 0930 and returning at 1800, average cost US$7.

Chanchamayo *p511*
There are a number of informal tour operators on the main plaza in La Merced catering to Lima weekenders; they are often

closed in low season. Check on safety record before taking part in any adventure sports.

Impala Tours, Jr Tarma 290, La Merced, T064-532476, gadc28@yahoo.com, also Jr Progreso 290, San Ramón. Owner Gustavo de Madariaga is very helpful. They offer a number of day trips to surrounding area, costing around US$10 per person.

Luis Cornejo Silva, Pje San Pablo 151, La Merced, T064-962 8149 (mob), luchoteguia @hotmail.com. Very reliable and helpful local guide. Fee from US$15/day.

Transport

Tarma and around *p510, map p510*

Direct buses leave daily to **Lima**, 231 km, 6 hrs, US$5.50; **Transportes Chanchamayo**, Callao 1002, T064-321882, is recommended as the most reliable, departs 0900, 1400 en route from Chanchamayo. Also **Transportes Junín**, Amazonas 667, 3 daily, *bus cama* at night; **Transportes La Merced**, Vienrich 420, 3 daily, and **Trans Muruhuay**, Huaraz y Amazonas, several daily, starting in Tarma. There is a good lunch stop at El Tambo before La Oroya, with superb fried trout. *Colectivos* to Lima leave from Castilla y Vienrich, wait till full, US$11 per person, 4 hrs. The road is paved for the entire route.

To **Jauja**, 2 hrs, US$2, and **Huancayo**, 3 hrs, US$3, with **Transportes San Juan** from the stadium every hr on the ½ hr, en route from Chanchamayo; also **Trans Muruhuay**, 0500-1800 (leave when full). *Colectivos* (cars) depart when full from Callao y Jauja, 2 hrs, US$4 to Jauja, or 3 hrs, US$6, to Huancayo.

Buses to **La Oroya** leave regularly from opposite the petrol station on Av Castilla block 2, 1 hr, US$1.25, while *colectivos* leave from the petrol station itself, 45 mins, US$2.

To **Chanchamayo**, **Transportes San Juan** from the stadium every hr on the half ½ hr, **Trans Angelitos** every hr on the hr, and **Empresa Junín**, 3 daily direct, 1½ hrs, US$1.50 to **San Ramón**, and 2 hrs, US$1.75 to **La Merced**. Also, **Selva Tours** *colectivos*, 1¼-1½ hrs, US$3 and US$3.50 respectively.

Local *Colectivos* and **Canary Tours** buses run from the centre of Tarma to **Acobamba** and up to **Muruhuay** every 10 mins, US$0.35. *Colectivos* for **San Pedro**, which pass the cave, depart from 2 de Mayo y Puno in Tarma, 40 mins, US$1. Combis, 1 hr, US$0.50, and *colectivos*, 30 mins, US$0.75, go from Paucartambo y Otero, Tarma, to **Palcamayo**, a 30-min walk down river from the cave.

Chanchamayo *p511*

Air

There is a small airstrip in San Ramón where Aero Montaña, T064-339191, rfmamsa @hotmail.com, has air taxis that can be chartered (*viaje especial*) to the jungle towns, including **Puerto Bermúdez**, 33 mins, with a maximum of 3 people. Flights cost US$250 per hr and you have to pay for the pilot's return to base. You can also just go to the air base, across the river, on the east side of town.

Bus

San Ramón To **Lima**, **Transportes La Merced**, Paucartambo y Alvariño, 5 daily, 7 hrs, US$6. To **Huánuco**, **Transportes León de Huánuco**, Paucartambo 380, departs 2200, 6-7 hrs, US$7. To **Tarma**, **Transportes San Juan**, Progreso 105, or **Trans Angelitos**, hourly, 2 hrs, US$1.50, or **Selva Tours** *colectivos*, 1 hr, US$3.

La Merced There is a large bus station on the east side of town, from which most buses arrive and depart. To **Satipo**, **Transportes Lobato**, 1130 and 2330, 2½ hrs, US$3; other buses passing through from Huancayo and Lima may also have room. To **Oxapampa**, **Empresa Santa Rosa**, every ½ hr, 3 hrs, US$3; there are also regular *colectivos*, 2 hrs, US$5. To **Pozuzo**, **Empresa Santa Rosa**, 0430 and 0830, 6 hrs, US$4.50; the condition of the road improves after Oxapampa. To **Puerto Bermúdez**, **Empresa Transdife**, **Villarrica** and **Servicio Especial** all have 4WD pickups (US$7 standing or US$10 seated) and minibuses (US$8.80), departing at 0330 and 0430 (or when full). You can buy your tickets in advance at the bus terminal. This is not a paved road and takes around 8 hrs in the dry season. To **Lima**, **Expreso Satipo**, **Transportes Lobato**, **Junín**, **La Merced** and **Chanchamayo** (recommended) each have several buses during the day, 8 hrs, US$6.50. To **Tarma**, **Transportes San Juan**, hourly, 2½ hrs, US$1.75, or **Selva Tours** *colectivos*, just over 1 hr, US$3.50.

Local There is a flow of combis and *colectivos* between San Ramón market and main plaza and Arica y Junín in La Merced, 15 mins, US$0.20 and US$0.30 respectively.

East of Chanchamayo *p512*
To reach **Atalaya**, catch a bus to **Satipo** (originating from La Victoria in Lima), 2 daily, 9 hrs, US$8.30; then take a *colectivo* to **Puerto Ocopa** (2½ hrs, US$5), and *lancha* to **Atalaya** (6 hrs downstream, 9 hrs upstream on Río Tambo, US$10). Buses to **Huancayo** and **Lima** depart from Satipo at night, a very cold journey, 12 hrs, US$9.50, with **Apóstol** San Pedro (more expensive but no better), Expreso Satipo and Lobato.

From Atalaya there are boats to **Pucallpa**, several a week, basic, hammock space, 36 hrs, US$16. They stop at all main towns, food is usually available, but take your own snacks, fruit and drinks. Hammocks can be bought in Sepahua or Atalaya. There are also flights from Atalaya to Pucallpa when demand is sufficient, usually several a week.

North of Chanchamayo *p512*
From Puerto Bermúdez you can either go to **La Merced** (8 hrs) or **Pucallpa** (12 hrs) by public transport.

Oxapampa *p512*
Empresa Santa Rosa, Kennedy y Loaechle, T063-762582, to **La Merced**, US$2.50, 3 hrs. Combis to **Pozuzo**, 3-5 per day, US$3, 3-4 hrs. Direct buses to **Lima** take 11-12 hrs.

Directory

Tarma and around *p510, map p510*
Banks BCP, Lima 407. Changes Amex TCs, ATM. Banco del Trabajo, Lima and Jauja, also has an ATM. Various casas de cambio will change dollars and euros. **Internet** Internet offices can be found all along Av Lima or Malecón José Gálvez just off Lima. **Telephone** Telefónica, Plaza de Armas.

Chanchamayo *p511*
Banks Banco de la Nación, Ancash y Lima. BCP, Junín y Tarma. **Internet** Over a dozen internet cafés in La Merced. SoftService, Palca 279, and Selva net, Junín 210, are good. Next to El Parral on Uriate, San Ramón. **Post office** Progreso 402, San Ramón.

North of La Oroya and the Huallaga Valley

A paved road runs 130 km north from La Oroya to Cerro de Pasco. It runs up the Mantaro valley through narrow canyons to the wet and mournful Junín pampa; at over 4250 m, it's one of the world's largest high-altitude plains. Blue peaks line the pampa in a distant wall. This windswept sheet of yellow grass is bitterly cold and the only signs of life are the young herders with their sheep and llamas. The road passes the eastern shores of the Lago de Junín, which is famous for its birdlife. From Junín to Cerro de Pasco the landscape is dominated by the cultivation of maca, through the Sierra Verde project; since it was declared that this tuber has strong nutritional value demand has soared. Maca juice, cake, bread, liquor, etc, is sold from roadside stalls all around the lake. It is even claimed to have aphrodisiac properties.

The Central Highway from Cerro de Pasco continues northeast another 528 km to Pucallpa, the limit of navigation for large Amazon river boats. The western part of this road (Cerro de Pasco–Huánuco) is a good paved highway and the descent along the Río Huallaga is dramatic. The road drops 2436 m in the 100 km from Cerro de Pasco to Huánuco; most of it is in the first 32 km. From the bleak vistas of the high ranges the road plunges below the tree line into another world of tropical beauty. » *For Sleeping, Eating and other listings, see pages 522-524.*

Ins and outs

There are good roads all the way down to Huánuco, with bus services from the capital. There is also a road connection from the Callejón de Huaylas to Huánuco, so if you wish you stay in the sierra, you do not have to backtrack to the coast. For information, contact the department of tourism in Junín (T063-200550/51, junin@mit inci.gob.pe), **Dircetur Pasco** ⓘ *Edif Estatal No 3, San Juan Pampa, Cerro de Pasco, T063-421029, www.mincetur.gob.pe*, in Cerro de Pasco, or **Dircetur** in Huánuco ⓘ *Bolívar 381, T062-512980, www.mincetur.gob.pe*. A useful website is www.webhuanuco.com.

Pampas de Junín » *pp522-524.*

Junín → *Colour map 3, B4. Altitude 4135 m.*

The town of Junín lies some distance south of Lago de Junín and has the desolate feel of a high puna town, bisected by the railway. Although small, it is typical of the lifestyle of the Peruvian Andes, with 16th-century architecture, strong local traditions and distinctive cuisine. It is a good starting point for seeing Andean wildlife and, as such, is becoming increasingly popular with birdwatchers and photographers.

The town has two plazas, one old, one new, called La Libertad. In the latter is a small underground museum with memorabilia from the battle. There is a large handicrafts centre at the southern entrance to the town. The Municpalidad is a few blocks from Plaza La Libertad; just behind is the **Inrena**, where you can buy tickets for the Sanctuary of Chacamarca and the National Reserve of Junín. Staff are very friendly.

Chacamarca

Three kilometres south of Junín, the **Chacamarca Historical Sanctuary** covers 2500 ha and includes the site of one of the most important battles of independence, at which the Peruvians under Bolívar defeated the Spaniards in 1824. An obelisk marks the battlefield. There's also an interesting underground museum and the remains of the pre-Inca citadel of Chacamarca. The wildlife of the high puna includes vicuña and foxes and there are springs at Yaropuquio. A taxi from the main street will cost you US$1.50-2.

Lago Junín National Reserve

ⓘ *US$5, ticket from Inrena in Junín.*

Peru's largest lake after Titicaca at 30 km by 14 km, Lago Junín protects one of the best birdwatching sites in the central Andes, where all the highland waterbirds and raptors may be seen. The surrounding fields abound with sierra-finches and ground-tyrants. Giant coot and even flamingos may be seen and, if you are really lucky, you can spot the diademed sandpiper and white-bellied cinclodes. Note that the *zambullidor de Junín*, Junin grebe, is in danger of extinction but can still be found here. In total, about 131 different species of birds can be found on the lake, 20% of which depend entirely on the lake's specific conditions for survival. Birdwatchers should sail around the lake; local fishermen are usually around to take visitors out.

There are several ways to get to the lake. The easiest is from the village of Huayre, 5 km south of **Carhuamayo** on the east side, from where it is a 20-minute walk down to the shore. Carhuamayo is the best place to stay near the lake, 50 minutes north of Junín. Nearby are Lago Shalipaico, the Minahuaraco fortress and Chuyroc caves. Another good viewing point is close to the village of **Ondores** on the west side of the lake; no paved roads here. Nearby are the interesting caves of Pachamachay with prehistoric paintings and El Mirador de Canoc lookout point. Beyond Ondores is San Pedro de Pari. On the way you can stop to see some outstanding geological formations, ancient paintings on the rocks, the church of San Pedro and the Mirador de Comac Punta, with breathtaking views.

The deep canyon of Goyllarisquisga (the 'place where a star fell'), 42 km north of Cerro de Pasco, is the highest coal mine in the world.

Cerro de Pasco and around » pp522-524.

→ *Colour map 3, B4. Altitude: 4330 m.*.

This long-established mining centre, 130 km from La Oroya by road, lies 8 km off the Carretera Central between Lago Patarcocha and the huge abyss of the mine above which its buildings and streets cling precariously. Not surprisingly for a place that claims to be the highest city in the world, nights are bitterly cold. Cerro de Pasco is famous as the site of a battle in the War of Independence. On 6 December 1820, local hero, Antonio Alvarez de Arenales, defeated Diego de O'Reilly's royalist troops at Cerro Uliachin (1 km from town). Although Cerro de Pasco is not an attractive place, the old corrugated iron buildings have a certain charm and it is very friendly.

Huayllay

Forty kilometres southwest of Cerro de Pasco is the **Santuario Nacional de Huayllay** (aka Bosque de Piedras) ⓘ *visits are recommended Apr-Aug, US$1, payable only if the guides Ernesto and Christian are there*, which has unique weathered limestone formations in the shape of a tortoise, elephant, alpaca, etc. Four tourist circuits, at 4100 to 4600 m, pass spectacular rock formations, archeological remains, rock paintings, springs and beautiful high Andean landscapes. This is another great place for birdwatching. Camping is permitted within the Sanctuary but be warned that nights become bitterly cold. The village of **Huallay**, is 20 minutes beyond the sanctuary entrance.

Also near Huallay are the ruins of an Inca community centre, **Bon Bón Marca**, which marks the course of a good section of Inca road, and the thermal springs of **Calera** ⓘ *10 mins beyond the sanctuary entrance, daily 0700-2200, US$0.75*. The new individual baths, which can take up to four people, are the cleanest. Take a swimsuit; the baths are very hot and clean, ideal for a splash after a tiring day.

Yanahuanca Valley → *Colour map 3, B4.*

Some 65 km northwest of Cerro de Pasco, **Yanahuanca** is situated in the beautiful valley of the same name, with good **hot baths** nearby. From the village you can reach one of the longest surviving stretches of Inca road by heading 2 km up the valley to where a lesser valley cuts northwards between the towering crags. The Inca road, its paving uneven and disturbed by countless horse and donkey convoys, leads up the smaller valley, its course sometimes shared by a stream, to the village of **Huarautambo**, about 4 km away, which is surrounded by many pre-Inca remains. The **Capaq Ñan** (Royal Inca road) is not only almost unbroken for more than 150 km from the Yanahuanca Valley, but it is also shown on the map issued by the **Instituto Geográfico Militar**. The clearest stretch ends at Huari in Ancash (see page 520).

Huánuco and the route to Huaraz

» *pp522-524. Colour map 3, B4.*

Huánuco is an attractive Andean town on the Upper Huallaga at 1894 m. The city was founded in 1539, by Gómez de Alvarado, and is one of the oldest in Peru. It was originally known as 'Los Caballeros de León de Huánuco'. Its most famous son is Leoncio Prado, who refused to surrender to the Chileans at the Battle of Huamachuco in 1882 and is commemorated all over the city. There is a large main plaza fringed by enormous ficus trees, which are much more attractive than the modern cathedral. The natural history museum, **Museo de Ciencias** ⓘ *Gen Prado 495, Mon-Fri 0900-1200, 1500-1800, Sat-Sun 1000-1200, US$0.50*, claims to have 10,000 exhibits of fauna from Peru's three regions, plus a good collection of shells and minerals. Many of the displays have multiple language signs. The town also holds an interesting market.

From Huánuco, a spectacular but very poor dirt road, impassable at times in the wet season, leads all the way to La Unión, capital of Dos de Mayo district (137 km). From Huánuco it climbs out of the Higueras Valley to **La Corona del Inca** (the 'Crown of the Inca'), also known as Lacsahuarina, meaning 'Two Princesses' in Quechua. This distinctive rock formation is at the pass before the descent into the upper canyon of the Río Marañón. The route then follows the Marañón to its confluence with the Río Vizcarra.

Kótosh

ⓘ *5 km from Huánuco on the road west to La Unión. Admission US$0.75, including a guide (in Spanish). Taxi from Huánuco, US$5 including a 30-min wait.*

Investigations suggest that this archaeological site, at an altitude of 1912 m, was occupied for over 2000 years. Six distinct phases of occupation have been identified the oldest of which dates back 4000 years. The Temple of Crossed Hands, the earliest evidence of a complex society and of pottery in Peru, dates from 2000 BC; it is said to be the 'oldest temple in the Americas'. There are three main temple buildings, some of which have been partly reconstructed, though the original 'crossed hands' sculpture is now in the Archaeology Museum in Lima. The site has a new access bridge, is in good condition and has a small museum which gives clear explanations of Kótosh. A guide will take you around a marked circuit, which also passes through a small botanical garden of desert plants.

Tantamayo and around → *Colour map 3, B3. Altitude: 3600 m.*

Tantamayo 50 km beyond the turn off to La Unión is a farming village surrounded by pre-Columbian ruins from the Yarowillca culture. **Japallan** is perhaps the most scenically sited, guarding the entrance to the valley leading from the spectacular Marañón canyon. To get there, cross the river from Tantamayo and walk west to San Pedro de Pariarca; at the start of the village take the path to the right to Pariash (Upper Pariarca), and head for the ruins silhouetted on a ridge. The ruins of **Selinin** are just above Pariash. The most elaborate are **Piruru** – which was occupied continuously for 1700 years, from 3000 BC as a ceremonial, and later, a ceramics centre – and **Susupillu**. Both sites have high-rise stone dwellings. To reach Susupillu head northeast through the tiny village of La Florida. There are other ruins further afield.

All the above mentioned ruins are visible from Tantamayo and can be reached on foot in about three to four hours; guides are available to visit the sites. The walks to the ruins are arduous, so take warm clothing, a hat and suntan lotion, but the scenery is stunning. Pictures and information on the sites are available from Huánuco post office. In Tantamayo there are four basic hotels and one restaurant, Ortega, on the corner of the plaza. For details of transport, see under Huánuco page 523.

La Unión → *Colour map 3, B3. Altitude: 3204 m.*

La Unión is a very friendly, fast-developing town which straddles the Río Vizcarra. Electricity can be a problem and it gets very cold at night but there are good **hot baths** at Tauripampa, 5 km up the Vizcarra valley, US$0.50 per person. A section of the **Royal Inca Road**, just upriver from the baths on the north side of the valley, runs on towards Huari.

You can hike to the **Cordillera Raura** from **Laguna Lauricocha**. To reach the lake from La Unión take a *camioneta* to **Baños**, then take another *camioneta* from there to **Antacolpa**. It's half a day's walk to the lake from here. In 1959, caves were discovered by the lake, containing 9500-year-old human remains and some paintings. This is where the Río Marañón rises, eventually becoming the Ucayali and then Amazon rivers, before spilling into the Atlantic Ocean, 5800 km away to the east.

Huánuco Viejo

ⓘ *2½ hrs' walk from La Unión. Admission US$1.50; a local farmer may be available to act as a guide (US$1).*

On the pampa above La Unión are the Inca ruins of Huánuco Viejo, a great temple-fortress with residential quarters. To get there, take the very steep path starting behind the market and climb towards the cross, which is at the edge of a plateau (this takes one hour). Continue straight through the village on the wide path. Note that, though the locals are friendly, some of their dogs are not always well disposed to strangers. The views of the pampa, surrounded on all sides by mountains, are beautiful. Seemingly at the foot of a mountain, in front and to your right, is the silvery metallic roof of a little chapel, behind which are the ruins, 4 km from the plateau's edge.

Huánuco Viejo was a major Inca settlement on the royal highway from Cuzco to Quito. The site has examples of very fine Inca stonework comparable with anything to be seen in Cuzco. This includes an *usnu*, measuring 30 m by 50 m and 4 m high, encased with superb stone blocks and with carved monkeys adorning the entrance and at one corner. An *usnu* was a ceremonial or judging platform, though its exact function is still uncertain. The *usnu* is surrounded by a huge central plaza, 547 m by 370 m, which, possibly, had to accommodate huge herds of animals. On the east side of the plaza are two *kallankas* (barracks), 84 m and 75 m long, nearly 10 m wide and two-storeys high, with thatched roofs. Running from the *kallankas* down to the royal Inca quarters and Inca bath are a series of six fine stone gateways adorned with beautifully carved pumas. Illa Tupac used the site as his stronghold from which he mounted resistance against the Spanish from 1536 until at least 1542. The site was then largely forgotten by the outside world and left untouched until the mid-20th century.

Allow at least one hour to visit the main part of the site and at least two hours for the whole site, which covers over 2 sq km and contains the remains of over 3500 structures. You should take warm clothing and be prepared for some violent

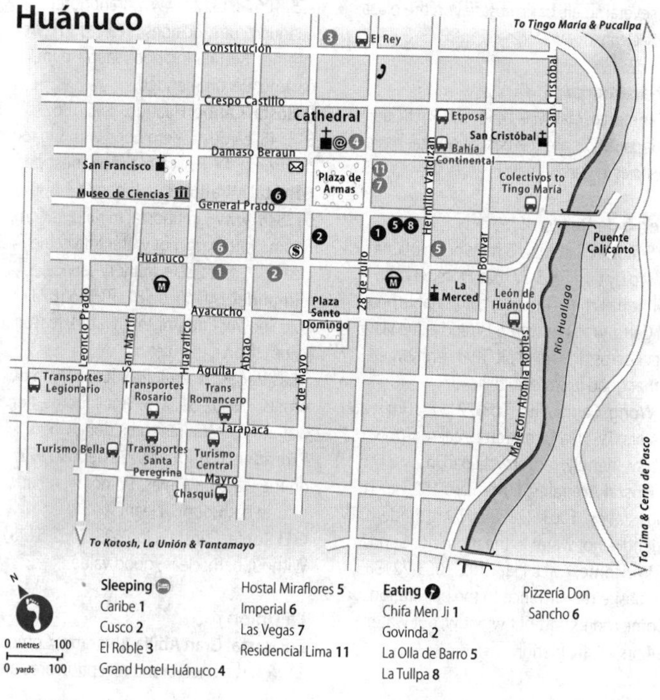

Sleeping
Caribe 1
Cusco 2
El Roble 3
Grand Hotel Huánuco 4
Hostal Miraflores 5
Imperial 6
Las Vegas 7
Residencial Lima 11

Eating
Chifa Men Ji 1
Govinda 2
La Olla de Barro 5
La Tullpa 8
Pizzería Don Sancho 6

 thunderstorms. A major festival, **Fiesta del Sol**, is held at the site on 27 July each year, but lodgings in the town are almost impossible to find at this time.

One of the finest stretches of the Royal Inca Road, or Capaq Ñan, runs southwest from the site to the **Callejón de Conchucos**. The **Mountain Institute** has set up a six-day trek, known as the **Inka Naani** (www.mountain.org/work/andes/tourism/incanani.cfm) between Huánuco Viejo and the Pomachaca bridge, near San Marcos (see page 364; also see page 355 for the **Mountain Institute**'s project at Vicos). The project, based on the work of Ricardo Espinosa (see page 616), involves conservation of the Road and community tourism with villages along the route, which usually starts at Pomachaca. Apply to the Mountain Institute via the website for prices, departure dates, etc.

Huallanca (Huánuco) and on to Huaraz → *Colour map 3, B3.*

It is possible to get to the **Cordillera Blanca** from La Unión. Take a *colectivo* to **Huallanca** and from there take **El Rápido** bus to Huaraz via **Chiquián** (see page 330). The route from La Unión to Huallanca is a poor dirt road, following the attractive and, in places, very narrow Vizcarra gorge for most of the journey. Paving starts in Huansala and continues all the way to **Huaraz**.

! It's best to travel this route by day.

Often known as Huallanca (Huánuco) to distinguish it from the settlement of the same name in the Cañón del Pato (see page 348), this is an attractive, unspoilt small town set between four hills in the Vizcarra valley. Large-scale mining projects in the area are likely to bring rapid change to the town and are polluting the Río Vizcarra.

Sleeping

Junín *p518*

G Hostal Leo, on Plaza La Libertad. The best of several small, basic *hostales* on the plaza, very clean, hot water, nice.

Chacamarca *p518*

Gianmarco, Maravillas 454, and **Patricia**, Tarapacá 862, are the best of several basic *hostales* in Carhuamayo.

Cerro de Pasco *p519*

D Señorial, San Juan, 5 mins north of Cerro de Pasco by taxi, T063-721026, hotelsenorial @hotmail.com. The most comfortable hotel in Cerro, with hot water, TV, and a fine view back across the mine pit. There are some other good *hostales* in this district.

E Wong, Carrión 99, T063-721515. Hot water 24 hrs, TV, clean, comfortable if run-down, noisy, friendly, motorcycle parking.

F Hostal Arenales, Jr Arenales 162, near the bus station, T063-723088. Clean, modern, TV, friendly, hot water in the morning. Good.

F Welcome, Av La Plata 125, T063-721883, opposite the entrance to the bus station. Some rooms without window, hot water 24 hrs, clean, friendly.

Huánuco *p519, map p521*

B Grand Hotel Huánuco, Damaso Beraun 775, T062-514222, www.grandhotel huanuco.com. Includes breakfast, TV, free internet. Restaurant, pool, sauna, gym, parking. Recommended.

D Hostal Caribe, Huánuco 546, T062-513645. Large modern hotel with big rooms, bathroom, TV. **Hostal Mariño** is next door.

E Hostal Miraflores, Valdizan 564, T062-512848, www.granhostal miraflores.com. Rooms with bath, hot water and cable TV, clean, TV, quiet, safe, laundry service.

F Imperial, Huánuco 581, T062-518737. With cold shower (intermittent water), reasonable value, clean and quiet.

F Las Vegas, 28 de Julio 936, on Plaza de Armas, T/F062-512315. Small rooms, hot water, TV. Restaurant next door. Good.

F Residencial Lima, Av. 28 de Julio 922, on the Plaza de Armas. TV, hot water and private bathrooms, clean.

G El Roble, Constitución 629, T062-512515. Without bath, clean, good value.

La Unión *p520*

E-F Hostal Gran Abilia Alvarado, Comercio 1196, has a once-grand reception area and a

nice garden. Rooms are small and basic but clean, some private bathrooms. Breakfast extra before 0700; good restaurant. Helpful owners provide some information about visiting Huánuco Viejo. Camping possible.
G **Hostal Paraíso**, near the bus station just off the main road, signed. Cheap, basic and pleasant.

Huallanca (Huánuco) *p522*
E **Hotel Milán**, 28 de Julio 107, Huallanca (Huánuco). Modern, TV and hot water in all rooms, best in town. The restaurant in Hotel Milán is good and serves trout caught in lakes high above the town.
G **Hostal Yesica**, L Prado 507, Huallanca (Huánuco). Hot water, shared bathroom, the best of the basic ones.

Eating

Lago Junín National Reserve *p518*
There are numerous restaurants along the main road in Carhuamayo. The best is **Savoy**. You can also find locals selling *pachamanca*, fried frogs' legs and maca products.
San Ignacio de Loyola, corner of Plaza La Libertad, Junín. Perhaps the best place to try as most restaurants are unreliable.

Cerro de Pasco *p519*
Local specialities are trout, fried frog, *ferrocarril* (which is known elsewhere as *bistec a lo pobre*) and *maca*, the tuber, see page 517.
Los Angeles, Jr Libertad, near the market. Excellent *menú* for US$1.50.
San Fernando bakery in the plaza. First-rate hot chocolate, bread and pastries.
Tito's, on the Plaza de Armas. The best place in Cerro for chicken.

Huánuco *p519, map p521*
Chifa Men Ji, 28 de Julio, block 8. Good prices, nice Chinese food, clean.
Govinda, 2 de Mayo 1044. Reckoned to be the best vegetarian in town.
La Olla de Barro, Gral Prado 852, close to main plaza. Serves typical food, good value.
La Tullpa, Gral Prado 819. Regional food. Recommended.
Pizzería Don Sancho, Prado 645. For the best pizzas in town.

La Unión *p520*
Chifa Khon Wa, 2 de Mayo 611. The best Chinese in town, serving authentic chifa.
Vizcarra, beside the old bridge over the river. The best of the local restaurants.

Huallanca (Huánuco)
El Norteño, Comercio 441, Huallanca (Huánuco). Apart from the Hotel Millán, this is the most popular place to eat.

Festivals and events

Cerro de Pasco *p519*
May Festival de La Chonguinada Cerreña is celebrated in the 1st wk.
May/Jun Semana Turística de Huarica.
5 Aug Virgen de Las Nieves.
Nov Semana Turística de Pasco (last wk).

Huánuco *p519, map p521*
20-25 Jan Carnaval Huanuqueño.
21 Mar Festival de las Cataratas.
1 May Festival of El Señor de Chacos in San Rafael, in the province of Ambo.
3 May La Cruz de Mayo, in Huánuco.
16 Jul Fiesta de la Virgen del Carmen.
Last week of Jul Festival de la Perricholi.
12-18 Aug Tourist Week in Huánuco.
15 Aug Founding of the city.
25-27 Sep Festival del Cóndor Pasa.
28-29 Oct Fiesta del Rey y del Señor de Burgos, the patron of Huánuco.
25 Dec Fiesta de los Negritos.

Transport

Junín *p518*
To **Carhuamayo**, taxi *colectivos* charge US$1.50. To **Ondores**, US$0.90-1.50 for a 30-min ride. To **San Pedro de Pari**, US$1.50.

Carhuamayo *p518*
To **Cerro de Pasco**, 40 min, *colectivos* charge US$1.50.

Cerro de Pasco *p519*
All services use the large, enclosed bus station. To **Lima**, several companies including Carhuamayo and Transportes Apóstol San Pedro, hourly 0800-1200, plus 4 departures 2030-2130, 8 hrs, US$4-5. If there are no convenient daytime buses, you could change buses in La Oroya. Buses to **Carhuamayo**,

1 hr, US$1; **Junín**, 1½ hrs, US$1, and **La Oroya**, 2½ hrs, US$2, leave when full, about every 20-30 mins. *Colectivos* (cars) also depart with a similar frequency to all places, eg, 1½ hrs, US$2.50, to La Oroya. To **Tarma**, **Empresa Junín** at 0600 and 1500, 3 hrs, $2.50. *Colectivos* hourly, 1½ hrs, US$4. To **Huancayo**, various companies throughout the day, 5 hrs, US$4. To **Oyón, Transportes Javier**, 1230, 5 hrs, US$3.50; there is also a bus to the mine at **Raura**, 1100, 7 hrs, US$5. To **Yanahuanca**, **Transportes Javier**, 0500, 1230, 1445, 3 hrs, US$2; also US$2 by taxi, 45 mins. Minibuses to **Huayllay** leave throughout the day, about 1 hr, US$1; they return until 1800-1900. Taxis to the **Calera** thermal baths run throughout the day, US$1.50, 45 mins, or pickup a Huayllay combi, US$1.20, about 1 hr. To **Huánuco**, buses and cars leave when full, 2½ hrs and 1½ hrs, US$2 and US$4 respectively.

Huánuco *p519, map p521*

Air

Airport T062-513066. To **Lima**, **LC Busre** (2 de Mayo 1355, T062-518113), daily, 55 mins.

Bus

To **Lima**, US$9, 8 hrs, various companies: **León de Huánuco**, Malecón Alomía Robles 821, at 1000, 2030, 2130; **Bahía Continental**, Valdizan 718, T062-519999, at 2100, 2200, recommended; also **Etposa**, Crespo Castillo 800, T062-512903; **Pillkobuss**, Jr 28 de Julio 535, T064-519770, www.geocities.com /gminternacional, and **Transportes El Rey**, 28 de Julio 1215. Most buses leave 2030-2200, most companies also have a bus at 0900-1000. *Colectivo* to Lima, US$20, 0400, 10 hrs; book the night before at Gen Prado 607, 1 block from the plaza. Recommended.

Bus to **Cerro de Pasco**, 3 hrs, US$2; *colectivos* less than 2 hrs, US$4. All leave when full from the roundabout, Ovalo Carhuayna, on the north side of the city, 3 km from the centre. To **Huancayo**, 6 hrs, US$5, with **Turismo Central**, Tarapacá 530, at 2130, or with **Trans Rey** at 2215, from depot on 28 de Julio, US$5.70, 7 hrs.

Colectivos run to **Tingo María**, from block 1 of Prado close to Puente Calicanto, 2½ hrs, US$5. Also **Etnasa**, 3-4 hrs, US2. For **Pucallpa**, take a *colectivo* to Tingo María, then a bus from there. This route has many checkpoints and robberies can occur. Travel by day and check on the current safety situation.

To **La Unión**, **Transportes El Niño**, Aguilar 530, is a *colectivo* service, departs when full, 5 hrs, US$7.15. Old buses also run on this rough road: **Transportes Santa Peregrina**, Tarapacá 448, and **Transportes Rosario**, Tarapacá 400 block, 0730, 6 hrs, US$5.70, are the most reliable. To **Tantamayo**, **Turismo Bella**, San Martín 571, at 0630 and 0730, operate old buses on this rough route, but is recommend by locals, 8 hrs, US$6; also **Chasqui**, Mayro 572. To **Baños**, **Transportes Legionario**, Independencia 656, run buses and truck-buses on alternate days, 0830; also **Transportes Romancero**, Tarapacá 500 block, 0900, 4 hrs, US$3.50.

La Unión *p520*

To **Huánuco**, **Transportes El Niño**, *colectivo* service from Jr Comercio 12, T062-515952; **Transportes Santa Peregrina** and **Rosario** buses leave at 0630, prices and journey times as above. (Note that if you don't take a night bus from Huaraz to La Unión, you will have to spend the night in La Unión.) To **Tantamayo**, several combis and buses daily, 5-6 hrs, US$4. However, it may be easier to take a combi to Tingo Chico at the Vizcarra/Marañón confluence, 1 hr, US$0.75, then wait for the bus services from Huánuco to Tantamayo.

Combis run about hourly, to **El Cruce** from where it is a 30-min walk to **Huánuco Viejo**; the last return combi leaves El Cruce at 1800. To **Huallanca (Huánuco)**, combis leave from the market, about half hourly, when full and follow the attractive Vizcarra valley, 1 hr, US$0.75; they return from the corner of Comercio y 28 de Julio in Huallanca.

Directory

Cerro de Pasco *p519*

Banks BCP, Jr Bolognesi. Money changers on Jr Bolognesi between the market and the cathedral.

Huánuco *p519, map p521*

Banks BCP, at Dos de Mayo 1005. Casa de cambio at Gral Prado 635. **Internet** Several in the centre. **Post** 2 de Mayo on the Plaza. 0800-2000 Mon-Sat, 0800-1400 Sun. **Telephone** Telefónica del Perú, 28 de Julio 1170.

Amazon Basin

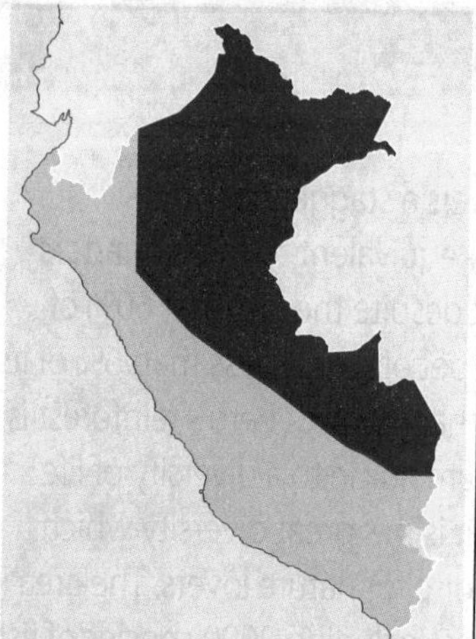

Footprint features

Introduction

The immense Amazon Basin covers a staggering 4,000,000 sq km, an area roughly equivalent to three quarters the size of the United States. But despite the fact that 60% of Peru is covered by this green carpet of jungle, less than 6% of its population lives here, meaning that much of Peru's rainforest is still intact. The Peruvian jungles are home to a diversity of life unequalled anywhere on Earth. It is this great diversity which makes the Amazon Basin a paradise for nature lovers. The area is home to 10,000,000 living species, including 2000 species of fish and 300 mammals. It also has over 10% of the world's 8600 bird species and, together with the adjacent Andean foothills, 4000 butterfly species. This incredible biological diversity, however, brings with it an acute ecological fragility. Ecologists consider the Amazon rainforest to be the lungs of the earth – producing 20% of the Earth's oxygen – and any fundamental change could have disastrous implications for our future on this planet.

The two major tourist areas in the Peruvian Amazon Basin are the northern and southern jungles. They share many characteristics, but the main difference is that the northern tourist area is based on the River Amazon itself, with Iquitos at its centre. Although it has lost its rubber-boom dynamism, the city is still at the heart of life on the river. There are jungle lodges upstream and down, none more than half a day away by fast boat. To get right into the wilds from here, head for Peru's largest national reserve, Pacaya-Samiria. In the south the Manu Biosphere Reserve and Tambopata National Reserve are also far removed from the modern world. Most of Manu is in fact off limits to tourists but, where access is possible, there are unparalleled opportunities for wildlife spotting. Many lodges in the area are close to the river port of Puerto Maldonado and include local communities as part of the jungle experience.

★ Don't miss...

1 **Pacaya-Samiria** The wildlife of endless waterways and wetlands is the latest jungle hotspot for nature tourism, page 529.

2 **Iquitos** Amid the buzz of a thousand motorcycle taxis, look at the Iron House, or any other old mansion, and try to imagine the days of the rubber barons, when this city was closer to Paris than Lima, page 532.

3 **Canopy walkway** Watch the bird and animal life in the forest canopy at first or last light from the highest possible level, page 539.

4 **Jungle lodges** Your days will be filled with brand new sights, smells, sounds and things to touch (with care!), thanks to the sharp eyes of your guide and boatman, pages 535 and 555.

5 **Manu** Make an early start to visit a *collpa* (macaw lick) to see the multitude of macaws and parrots getting their essential minerals, page 548.

6 **Tambopata** Take your patience to an oxbow lake and hope to see giant river otters, page 553.

Northern Jungle

From the heights of the Andes down to the Amazonian lowlands a road runs to Pucallpa, the second city of this region of Peru. It passes through the Huallaga Valley, not the safest part of the country owing to the narcotics trade, but if you stick to the main route you should be OK. From Pucallpa and Yurimaguas, further north, you can venture into the jungle if you want to continue beyond, the only way is to spend several days in a boat, getting to know the rivers and their traffic.

Standing on the banks of the Amazon itself the city of Iquitos still retains something of a frontier feel. It became famous during the rubber boom of the late 19th century and is now the main tourist attraction in this part of the country. For jungle visits there are many lodges to choose from and two fine protected areas, Pacaya-Samiria and Allpahuayo-Mishana. ▸▸ *For Sleeping, Eating and other listings, see pages 536-547.*

Tingo María to Iquitos ▸▸ *pp536-547.*

The overland route from the central Andes to Pucallpa runs from Huánuco east to Tingo María on a paved road, and gives the first views of the vast green carpet of jungle. Beyond Huánuco the road begins a sharp climb to the heights of Carpish (3023 m). A descent over 58 km brings it to the Huallaga river again; the road continues along the river to Tingo María. Landslides along this section are frequent and construction work causes delays. This route is periodically disrupted by violence related to drug cultivation and trafficking. Robberies also occur and it is advisable to travel only by day. Seek local advice.

Tingo María → *Phone code: 062. Colour map 3, A4. Altitude: 655 m.*

Tingo María is on the Middle Huallaga, in the Ceja de Montaña, or edge (literally, eyebrow) of the mountains. The meeting here of *sierra* and *selva* makes the landscape striking. Bananas, sugar cane, cocoa, rubber, tea and coffee are grown. The main crop of the area, though, is coca, grown on the *chacras* (smallholdings) in the countryside, and sold legitimately (and otherwise) in Tingo María. These crops thrive in the tropical climate, with an annual rainfall of 2642 mm. In the height of the rainy season the town can be isolated for days. The altitude, however, prevents the climate from being oppressive: the maximum temperature is 34°C, minimum 18°C, with a relative humidity of 77.5%. **Dircetur tourist office** ⓘ *Av Ericson 162, T062-562310, cataperu10@hotmail.com.*

On a rough road, 6.5 km from Tingo, is a fascinating cave, the **Cueva de las Lechuzas** ⓘ *US$0.90*. Take a motorcycle-taxi from town, US$1.75, then pay US$0.45 for the ferry to cross the Río Monzón just before the cave. Take a torch, and do not wear open shoes. The cave can be reached by boat when the river is high. There are many oilbirds in the cave and parakeets near the entrance. The cave is in the 18,000-ha **Parque Nacional de Tingo María** ⓘ *US$1.75*, the second national park created in Peru. A mototaxi to the entrance costs US$0.60.

North to Yurimaguas → *Colour map 1, B5.*

The Río Huallaga winds northwards for 930 km from its source to the confluence with the Marañón. The Upper Huallaga flows fast and furiously, but by the time it becomes the Lower Huallaga it moves slowly through a flat landscape. The main port of the Lower Huallaga, **Yurimaguas,** is below the last rapids and only 150 m above the Atlantic Ocean, yet distant from that ocean by over a month's voyage. Between the Upper and Lower lies the Middle Huallaga: that third of the river which is downstream from Tingo María and upstream from Yurimaguas.

At **Tulumayo**, soon after leaving Tingo María, a road runs north down the Huallaga past **La Morada** to **Aucayacu**, which has a couple of poor hotels, and **Tocache**, which also has a couple of hotels, plus an airport. The road has been pushed north from Tocache to join another built south from Tarapoto and has now been joined at Tarapoto (see page 475) to the Olmos–Bagua–Yurimaguas Transandean Highway to the coast at Chiclayo. The road is paved to 20 km past Aucayacu, thereafter it is gravel.

Yurimaguas → *Phone code: 065. Colour map 1, B5. Population: 25,700. Altitude: 160 m.*

Yurimaguas is a very friendly, relaxed jungle town. It is the road head on the lower Río Huallaga, an ideal starting point for river travel in the Peruvian Amazon. The town has a fine church of the Passionist Fathers, based on the Cathedral of Burgos in Spain. A colourful market is held from 0600-0800, full of fruit and animals. In addition to the **tourist information office** ⓘ *T065-352676, Mon-Fri 0800-1600*, there is a small **Museo Arqueológico** (same hours) in the Consejo Regional building. There are some interesting excursions in the area too, including the gorge of **Shanusi** and the lakes of **Mushuyacu** and **Sanango**. Tours can also be made to meet local people in the villages of **Balsapuerto** (70 km west) and **Puerto Libre**.

Lagunas → *Colour map 1, B6.*

The river journey to Iquitos can be broken at Lagunas, 12 hours from Yurimaguas; all *lanchas* stop here. This is a good access point for Pacaya-Samiria Reserve. There are several local tour operators in the village, eg Manuel Rojas, T065-401116, and Gamaniel Valles, T065-401007.

Reserva Nacional Pacaya-Samiria → *Colour map 2, C2.*

ⓘ *Reserve office in Iquitos, Ricardo Palma 113, p 4, T065-232980, Mon-Fri 0800-1300, 1500-1800, has general information and an up-to-date list of tour operators. You must go here to obtain proof of payment for the park entry fee (US$33); payment itself must be made at Banco de la Nación.*

Pacaya-Samiria Reserve, at 2,080,000 ha, is the country's largest such protected area. It is bounded by the rivers Marañón and Ucuyali – and a tributary of it, the Canal de Puinahua – narrowing to their confluence near the town of **Nauta**. The reserve's waterways, lakes and swamps provide habitat for mammals such as the manatee, tapir, river dolphins and giant river otters, as well as black caiman, boas and the *charapa* (yellow-headed river turtle), 193 species of fish and some 330 bird species. Many of the animals found here are in danger of extinction. Trips are mostly on the river, sleeping in hammocks. Iquitos operators enter through Nauta to Yarina where there is a shelter, also through Requena. Other entry points are the village of **Maipuco**, 18-20 hours from Yurimaguas, and **Leoncio Prado**, on the Marañón, opposite the outflow of the Río Samiria (*hospedajes* **5 Hermanitos** and **Ruiz**).

The main part of the reserve is off-limits to tourists, who may only be taken to surrounding forest. Some guides, however, penetrate Pacaya-Samiria illegally: if caught, you may face stiff penalties for trespassing. You must make sure that your tour will not do anything that will endanger the wildlife in the reserve. Above all, do not join a tour that involves living off the land. When arranging a guide and boat from Lagunas, make sure the boat has enough fuel. Take bottled water, or purifier, and mosquito repellent.

Tingo María to Pucallpa → *Colour map 3, A4/5.*

From Tingo María to the end of the road at Pucallpa is 255 km, with a climb over the watershed – the Cordillera Azul – between the Huallaga and Ucayali rivers. The road is in poor shape for most of the journey, but paving around Aguaytía and the last stretch to Pucallpa is in progress. It is affected by mud and landslides in the rainy season. Apart

Androgynous Amazonians

The Amazon is the longest river in the world. It rises high up in the Andes as the Marañón, then joins the Ucayali and winds its way east to disgorge itself finally into the Atlantic, over 6000 km from its source. At its mouth, the Amazon is 300 km wide. This mighty waterway was named by the Spaniard Francisco de Orellana during his epic voyage in 1542, following an encounter with a hostile, long-haired indigenous group which he took to be the fearsome women warriors of Greek legend.

from its insecurity, another reason not to travel this road at night is that you will miss the tremendous views as you go from the high jungle to the Amazon Basin. Sit on the right side of the bus to appreciate the landscape and the hairpin bends and sheer drops. When the road was being surveyed it was thought that the lowest pass over the Cordillera Azul was more that 3650 m high, but an old document stating that a Father Abad had found a pass through these mountains in 1757 was rediscovered, and the road now goes through the pass of Father Abad, a gigantic gap 4 km long and 2000 m deep. At the top of the pass is a Peruvian customs house; the jungle land to the east is a free zone. Concrete stairs and metal handrails have been built for viewing the waterfalls. Coming down from the pass the roadbed runs along the floor of a magnificent canyon, the **Boquerón Abad**. It is a beautiful trip through luxuriant jungle, with ferns and sheer walls of bare rock punctuated by occasional waterfalls plunging into the roaring torrent below. East of the foot of the pass the road goes over the flat pampa, with few bends, to the village of **Aguaytía**. Here you'll find a narcotics police outpost, petrol, accommodation (see Sleeping, page 536), and two restaurants. Nearby is the 20-m high **Velo de la Novia** waterfall, in a beautiful setting. From Aguaytía the road continues for 161 km to Pucallpa – five hours by bus. There is a fuel station three hours before Pucallpa.

To make the most of the park, stay for a minimum of five days.

Pucallpa → *Phone code: 061. Colour map 3, A5. Population: 400,000.*

The capital of the department of Ucayali is a rapidly expanding jungle town on the Río Ucayali, navigable by vessels of 3000 tons from Iquitos, 533 nautical miles away. The town's newer sections have paved streets, sewers and lights, but much of the frontier atmosphere still exists. The climate is tropical. The dry season is from June to October when it's hot and dusty. The rainy seasons are October to November and February to March and the town is muddy through to May.

There is narcotics activity in the area. The city itself is safe enough to visit, but don't travel at night. The tourist office is the **Dirección Regional de Turismo** ⓘ *Jr 2 de Mayo 111, T061-571303, ucayali@mincetur.gob.pe, Mon-Fri 0800-1300, 1400-1645*. Information is also available at **Consejo Transitorio de Administración Regional (CTAR-Ucayali)** ⓘ *Raymondi 220, T061-575018, oppto-ucayali@pres.gob.pe.*

The **Museo Regional** ⓘ *Jr Inmaculada 999, 0800-1200 and 1600-1800, US$0.90*, has some good examples of Shibipo ceramics, as well as some delightful pickled snakes and other reptiles. You will probably want to take a taxi or mototaxi to visit it. **Usko Ayar Amazonian School of Painting** ⓘ *Jr LM Sánchez Cerro 465-467, Pucallpa, www.egallery.com/coll/amazon.php*, is in the house of artist Pablo Amaringo, a former *vegetalista* (healer). The school provides art classes for local people and is financially dependent upon selling their work. The internationally renowned school welcomes overseas visitors for short or long stays to study painting and learn Spanish and/or teach English with Peruvian students. The painting is oriented around the Amazonian cultures, in particular the healing and hallucinogenic effects of ayahuasca. For more information see the book, *Wizard of the Upper Amazon*.

The floating ports of **La Hoyada** and **Puerto Italia** are about 5 km away and worth a visit to see the canoe traffic and open-air markets. Both are reached by dirt roads. When river levels are low, boats leave from a different port, **Pucallpillo**, five minutes from the centre. The economy of the area includes sawmills, plywood factories, a paper mill, oil refinery, fishing and boat building; timber is trucked out to the highlands and the coast. Large discoveries of oil and gas are being explored, and gold-mining is underway nearby. **Ganso Azul oilfield** has a 75-km pipeline to the Pucallpa refinery.

Lago Yarinacocha

The main tourist attraction of the area, especially with Peruvians, is the picturesque Lake Yarinacocha, where you can see river dolphins. On the lake are the **Hospital Amazónico Albert Schweitzer**, which serves the local people, and the **Summer School of Linguistics** for the study of indigenous languages (callers by appointment only). A good place to swim is at **San José**; take the road out behind the power station round the lake beyond the Summer School of Linguistics. Certain sections of Lake Yarinacocha have been designated as a reserve. The beautifully located **Jardín Botánico Chullachaqui** can be reached by boat from Puerto Callao to Pueblo Nueva Luz de Fátima. It's a 45-minute trip, then an hour's walk to the garden; entry is free. For information about traditional medicine contact **Mateo Arevalomayna** ⓘ *San Francisco de Yarinacocha, T061-573152*, or ask at **Moroti-Shobo**, an organization which is working to re-establish the use of traditional remedies.

San Francisco and **Santa Clara** can be visited at the far end of the lake on its western arm. Both are Shibipo villages still practising traditional ceramic and textile crafts. A canal near Santa Clara links Lake Yarinacocha with the Río Ucayali. There are a

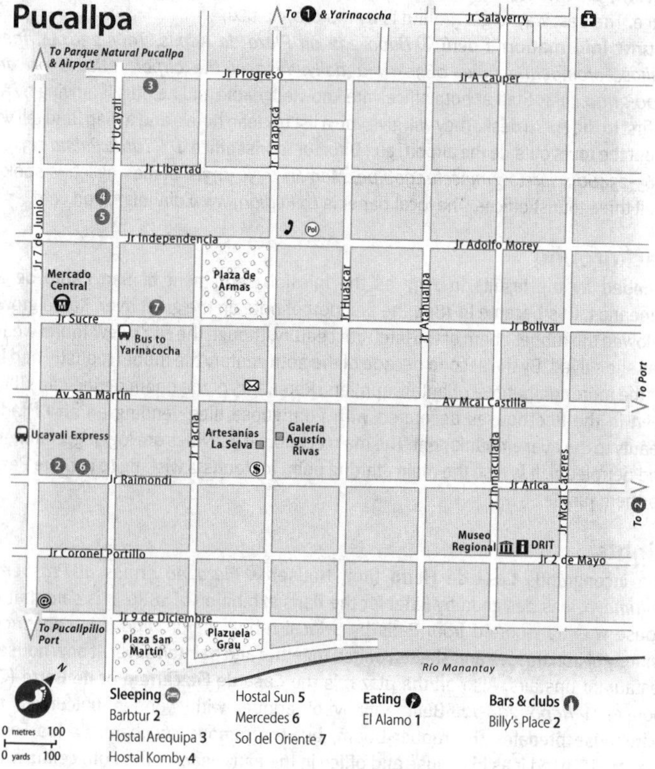

 few other villages nearby, such as **Nuevo Destino** and **Santa Marta**, which are within an hour's walk. The Shibipo people are very kind and friendly and a visit is recommended. To reach these villages take one of the motorized canoes, or *peke-pekes*, which leave from Puerto Callao when full, US$0.90.

Iquitos

» *pp536-547. Colour map 2, B4.*

→ *Phone code: 065. Population: 600,000.*

Capital of the Department of Loreto and chief town of Peru's jungle region, Iquitos is some 800 km downstream from Pucallpa and 3646 km from the mouth of the Amazon. It is an urban oasis, completely isolated except by air and river, and while retaining something of a frontier feel, it is a pleasant tropical city. It's active, friendly and generally safe. The central area is always busy with traders' shops up and down the streets leading north and south. It may seem, too, that Iquitos is attempting a new world record for the highest concentration of motorcycles in a built-up area. As a result of the motorcycle noise, the city suffers from collective hearing loss and televisions and music are played at top volume, making the din even worse.

Ins and outs

Getting there Francisco Secada Vigneta airport is in the southwest, T065-260147. There are several ports in Iquitos, but the main one for all long-haul service in large vessels is Masusa, 2 km north of the centre. The rise and fall of the river is such that the islands off Iquitos are constantly moving.

Getting around Iquitos is well spread out. Hotels are dotted about all over the place. The best way to get around is by motorcycle taxi.

Tourist information i perú ⓘ *Napo 232 on Plaza de Armas, T065-236144, iperu iquitos@promperu.gob.pe, 0830-1930 daily; also at the airport 0800-1300 and 1600-2000 daily*. Staff at both offices are knowledgeable and helpful. If arriving by air, go first to the **i perú** desk. They will give you a list of clean hotels and a map, and tell you about the touts outside the airport, etc. **Dircetur tourist office** ⓘ *Ricardo Palma 113, p 5, T065-234609, loreto@mincetur.gob.pe, Mon-Fri 0730-1430*. Some English is spoken in all three tourist offices. The local paper is *La Región*, www.diariolaregion.com.

Background

Founded by the Jesuits in 1757 as the mission settlement of San Pablo de los Napeanos, this became in 1864 the first port of note on the great river. Rapid growth followed the rubber boom of the late 19th century, though the city's new-found wealth was short lived. By the second decade of the 20th century the rubber industry had left for the more competitive oriental suppliers. Remnants of the boom period can still be seen in the fine houses decorated with Portuguese tiles, lending an air of faded beauty to the river embankment. The main economic activities are logging, commerce and petroleum. It is also the main starting point for tourists wishing to explore Peru's northern jungle.

Sights

The incongruous **Casa de Fierro** (Iron House) ⓘ *Plaza de Armas at Próspero y Putumayo*, was designed by Eiffel for the Paris exhibition of 1889. It is said that the house was transported from Paris by a local rubber baron, and it is constructed entirely of iron trusses and sheets, bolted together and painted silver. It now houses a restaurant upstairs. Also on the plaza, is the **Casa de Fitzcarrald** or **de Barro** (Clay House) ⓘ *Napo 200-12*. Built entirely of adobe, with wooden balconies, this warehouse predates the rubber boom, but the famous *cauchero*, Carlos Fermín Fitzcarrald, used it as his house and office in the early years of the 20th century. This is now a *Cuaracao* appliance store; descendants of Fitzcarrald still live upstairs. Werner Herzog's film *Fitzcarraldo* is a cause célèbre in the town. Next door to the tourist office on the plaza is a **Museo Municipal** ⓘ *Napo 224, T065-234272, Mon-Fri 0700-1445, free*, with stuffed animals and woodcarvings of local native peoples.

Also worth seeing is the old **Hotel Palace** ⓘ *on the corner of Malecón Tarapacá and Putumayo*, now the army barracks. Of special interest are the older buildings, faced with *azulejos* (glazed tiles). Many are along the Malecón. They date from the boom of 1890-1912, when the rubber barons imported the tiles from Portugal and Italy and ironwork from England to embellish their homes. **Museo Amazónico** ⓘ *on the corner of*

Iquitos

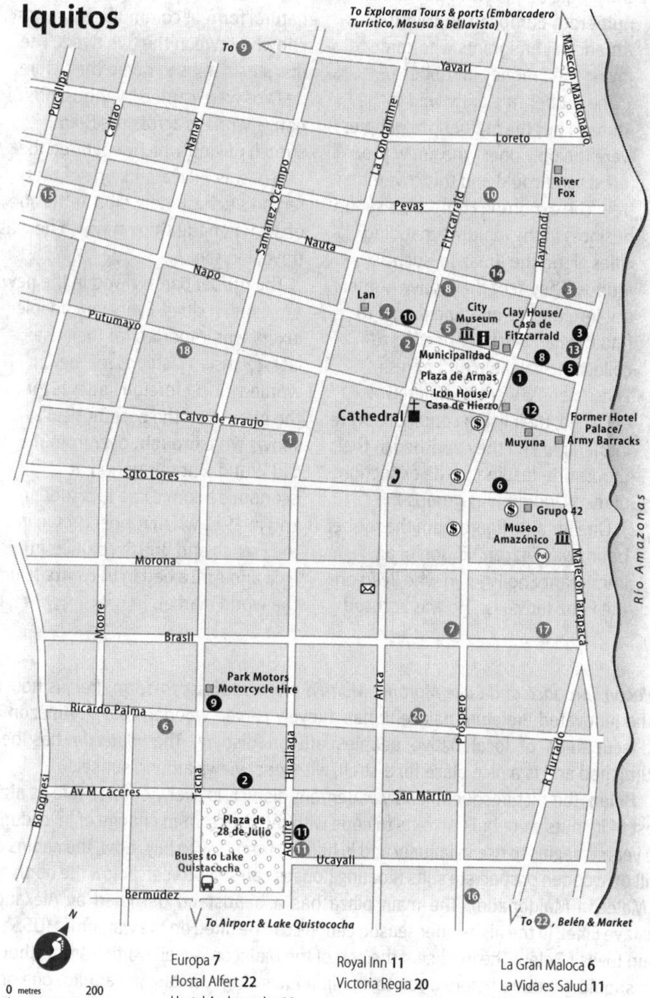

0 metres 200
0 yards 200

Sleeping
Acosta 1
Amazonas 2
El Dorado 4
El Dorado Plaza 5
El Sitio 6
Europa 7
Hostal Alfert 22
Hostal Ambassador 10
Hostal Colibrí 3
Internacional 16
Isabel 17
Jhuliana 18
La Casa de Samantha 15
Marañón 8
Posada de Lobo 9
Royal Inn 11
Victoria Regia 20

Eating
Ari's Burger 1
Chifa Long Fung 2
El Nuevo Mesón 3
Fitzcarrald 5
Heladería 1
Huasaí 10
La Gran Maloca 6
La Vida es Salud 11
Montecarlo 8
Paulina 9
Pollón 1
Yellow Rose of Texas 12

Bars & clubs
Arandú 13
Teatro Café Amauta 14

Rubber barons

The conquest and colonization of the vast Amazon Basin was consolidated by the end of the 19th century with the invention of the process of vulcanizing rubber. Many and varied uses were found for this new product and demand was such that the jungle began to be populated by numerous European and North American immigrants who came to invest their money in rubber.

The rubber tree grew wild in the Amazon but the indigenous peoples were the only ones who knew the forests and could find this coveted tree. The exporting companies set up business in the rapidly expanding cities along the Amazon, such as Iquitos. They sent their 'slave hunters' out into the surrounding jungle to find the native labour needed to collect the valuable rubber resin. These people were completely enslaved, their living conditions were intolerable and they perished in their thousands, leading to the extinction of many indigenous groups.

One notable figure from the rubber boom was Fitzcarrald, son of an immigrant Englishman who lived on the Peruvian coast. He was accused of spying during the 1879 war between Peru and Chile and fled to the Amazon where he lived for many years among the indigenous people.

Thanks to Fitzcarrald, the isthmus between the basin of the Ucayali river and that of the Madre de Dios was discovered. Before this, no natural form of communication was known between the two rivers. The first steamships to go up the Madre de Dios were carried by thousands of native workers across the 8-km stretch of land which separated the two basins. Fitzcarrald, one of the region's richest men, died at the age of 36 when the ship on which he was travelling sank.

The rubber barons lived in the new Amazonian cities. Every imaginable luxury was imported for their use: latest Parisian fashions for the women; finest foreign liqueurs for the men; even the best musical shows were brought over from the Old World. But this period of economic boom came to a sudden end in 1912 when rubber grown in the French and British colonies in Asia and Africa began to compete on the world market.

Malecón Tarapacá and Calle Morona, Mon-Fri 0830-1200, 1530-1800, free, is housed in the renovated Prefetura palace. It has a lovely carved wooden ceiling. Amazon art and scupltures of local native peoples are on display. The *malecón* has been refurbished and is a nice place for a stroll, with great views around sunset.

Belén, the picturesque, friendly waterfront district, is lively, but not safe at night. Most of its huts were built on rafts to cope with the river's 10-m change of level during the year: it begins to rise in January and is highest from May to July. Now, the cabins are built on wooden or concrete stilts (floating houses can still be seen below the north end of Malecón Maldonado). The main plaza has a bandstand designed by Alexandre Gustave Eiffel. In the high-water season canoes can be hired on the waterfront (US$3 an hour) to visit Belén. The market at the end of the Malecón is well worth visiting, though you should get there before 0900 to see it in full swing. On Pasaje Paquito, one of its side streets, vendors sell local medicinal herbs and potions.

Around Iquitos

Allpahuayo-Mishana Reserve ⓘ *Instituto de Investigaciones de la Amazonía Peruana (IIAP), Av Quiñones on the way to the airport, T065-265515*. Some 22 km south of Iquitos by road or two to three hours by boat from Bellavista, this reserve protects the largest concentration of white-sand jungle (*varillales*) in Peru. Part of the Napo ecoregion, biodiversity here is among the highest in the Amazon Basin, with many birds and several endangered species including two primates and some endemic species.

There is a beach at **Bellavista**, a suburb of Iquitos, which is safe for swimming and very popular at weekends in summer. Boats can be hired from here to see the meeting of the Nanay and Amazon rivers, and to visit beaches and villages en route. There are lots of food stalls selling typical local dishes. Take a bus from Jirón Próspero to 'Bellavista Nanay'. It takes around 15 minutes and costs US$0.40.

Boats leave Iquitos for the village of **Indiana**. A road leads from Indiana to the village of Mazán through the secondary jungle. It's about a two-hour walk or a US$0.80 mototaxi ride. If the hotel in Indiana is full, ask at the mission or municipality for a tent for the night. From Indiana you can do several hikes of between two and four hours to little villages along the Napo River.

Some 4 km south of the city, **Lake Quistococha** is beautifully situated in lush jungle, with a fish hatchery at the lakeside. On the lake, **Parque Zoológico de Quistococha** ⓘ *0900-1700, US$1.30*, gives an insight into the local wildlife, though conditions are squalid. At the entrance are interesting pictures and texts of local legends. The ticket office will supply a map of the lake and environs. There's a good two-hour walk through the surrounding jungle on a clearly marked trail. See particularly the paiche, a huge Amazonian fish whose steaks (*paiche a la loretana*) you can eat in Iquitos' restaurants. There are also bars and restaurants on the lakeside and a small beach. Boats are for hire on the lake and swimming is safe but the sandflies are vicious, so take insect repellent.

On the road to Quistococha is the turn-off to the village of **Santo Tomás**. Take a left turn just before the airport, and then another left 300 m further on. Then it's about 4 km to the village. There are restaurants open on Sunday and dugout canoes can be hired. The village hosts a fiesta on 22-25 September. Trucks go there, taking passengers.

Pilpintuhuasi Butterfly Farm ⓘ *near the village of Padre Cocha, T065-232665, www.amazonanimalorphanage.org, Tue-Sun 0900-1600, US$5*. As well as butterflies, it also has a small well-kept zoo, Austrian-Peruvian run. It is a 20-minute walk from Padre Cocha to the butterfly farm.

Iquitos to the Brazilian/Colombian border

» *pp536-547. Colour map 2, B5/6.*

The village of **Pebas**, on the north bank, is three hours from Iquitos. **Pituayac**, a part of Pebas, is a military area. One of the greatest of Peru's abstract painters, Francisco Grippa, lives in Pebas. His house overlooks the river and you can stay there if you are interested in his work and art in general. Anyone in town will tell you where he lives. If you want to see his paintings, but don't want to stop in Pebas, there are several on display in the **Hotel El Dorado** in Iquitos.

San Pablo, a further three hours downstream, is a refuelling stop, where children swim next to the jetty. You can buy crackers and drinks during the five-minute halt; the boat will wait for you. After another hour you reach **Chimbote**, where there is a police and customs point. Your passport will be stamped and your bags checked. Food can be bought, but it's not that hygienic.

Caballococha, 45 minutes from Chimbote, is the kind of town you always imagined when reading the books of García Márquez: lost in the jungle and in time, hot, humid and nostalgic. It is built on a small arm of the river, surrounded by lush green tropical vegetation.

Between Caballococha and Santa Rosa, the journey is beautiful, taking about two hours. To your left are the rolling green hills of Colombia's Amacayacu National Park. The Iquitos–Tabatinga *rápidos* usually take the narrow, southern arm of the river, which does not give views of Colombia, so ask before you buy your ticket which route it will take. Otherwise you must take a Leticia–Caballococha boat.

Santa Rosa is the small Peruvian military base across the river from **Leticia** (Colombia) and **Tabatinga** (Brazil), in the region known as the 'tri-border'. It is the only place with a good beach, so it gets busy at weekends. It only has one very basic *hostal* next to the jetty and the large, pleasant café on the waterfront only sells *refrescos*, no water or coffee. There are no money changers.

Crossing the border

The border is open 24 hours a day. When leaving Peru, check procedures in Iquitos first at Immigration (see page 547) or with the Capitanía at the port. Travelling by *rápido*, you get your exit stamp at the police station in Santa Rosa in front of the jetty. After clearing customs and getting your exit stamp, the *rápido* will take you to Tabatinga across the river (five minutes).

If you go to Brazil or Colombia from Santa Rosa, you will need a Peruvian exit stamp, which means that you will need an entry and exit stamp from either Colombia or Brazil if you want to re-enter Peru. There is an immigration office in the port of Tabatinga. Your best bet is to take a taxi and ask the driver to take you to the Polícia Federal, whose office is on the main road, some 2 km from the port. The process is straightforward; Brazilian immigration is friendly and there is always somebody who speaks English. If you intend to stay in the border region, choose Brazilian immigration formalities over Colombian, which take longer, with more questions asked. All immigration services are free of charge. Once you have a Brazilian or Colombian entry stamp, you can move freely between Leticia and Tabatinga as there is no border between the two. Nobody will check your passport if you just walk or drive (if you take a boat – for which there is no need – between Tabatinga and Leticia, the Colombians may give you a hard time). US citizens need a Brazilian visa; if who don't have one, enter via Colombia. If you go to any other destination in Brazil, you will have to get a Brazilian entry stamp. The same goes for Colombia. Peruvian immigration will give you a 30-day entry stamp in Santa Rosa. The officer is friendly and he will usually ask if you need more days.

Sleeping

Tingo María *p528*

Hotels are often fully booked.

C **Madera Verde**, Av Universitaria s/n, a way out of Tingo María on the road to Huánuco, near the university, T/F062-561800, maverde@ terra.com.pe. Several chalets set in beautiful surroundings, with and without bathroom, restaurant, swimming pool.

E **Hospedaje Agroturístico Villa Jennifer**, Km 3.4 Carretera a Castillo Grande, 10 mins from Tingo María, T062-960 3509, www.villajennifer.es.vg. This Danish- Peruvian-owned hotel offers breakfast in the price, weekend packages and tours to local sites, restaurant, laundry service. Surrounded by local flora, with lots of birdlife.

F **Hostal Marco Antonio**, Jr Monzón 364, T062-562201. Quiet, restaurant of the same name next door.

F **Nueva York**, Av Alameda Perú 553, T062-562406. With bath and TV, cheaper without, hot water, restaurant, laundry, good value.

G **Hostal Central**, Av Tito Jaime 440. Central, as the names suggests, OK.

G **Hostal Cusco**, Raimondi 671. Basic, but very cheap.

G **Viena**, Jr Lamas. With bathroom, good value, clean.

Yurimaguas *p529*

D **Hostal Residencial El Naranjo**, Arica 318, T065-351560, hotel_elnaranjo@hotmail.com. Best in town, with bath, a/c (**E** with fan), hot water, clean, comfortable, small pool, good restaurant. Recommended.

E **Luis Antonio**, Av Jáuregui 407, T065-352061, antonio@vibcp.com. With fan and bath, **D** with a/c, cold water, balconies overlooking pool, clean, friendly and helpful. Recommended.

F Hostal El Caballito, Av Jáuregui 403, T065-352427. With bath, cold water, fan, clean and pleasant, good value.
F Leo's Palace, Sargento Lores 106, Plaza de Armas, T065-351499. Good, **D** with a/c, friendly, reasonably priced, restaurant.
G Hostal El Cisne, Mcal Castilla 419, T065-351234. Shared bath, cold water, basic. There are several other hotels near the intersection of Jáuregui and Tacna.

Lagunas *p529*
G Hostal Isabel, Calle Miraflores 1 block from plaza. Shared bath, cold water, basic, meals available.
G Hostal La Sombra, Jr Vásquez 1121. Shared bathroom, basic, friendly, good food.

Pucallpa *p530, map p531*
A Sol del Oriente, Av San Martín 552, T061-575154, hsoloriente@qnet.com.pe. Price includes breakfast and taxes. With bathroom, pool and good restaurant. The hotel also has a mini zoo.
B Divina Montaña, Carretera Federico Basadre Km 11.3, outside Pucallpa on the road to Tingo María, T061-574027, Divina-montana@terra.com.pe. Bungalows for rent, restaurant, swimming pool, sports facilities.
E Hostal Arequipa, Jr Progreso 573, T061-571348. With bathroom but no a/c, good, comfortable rooms with safe, cable TV, clean, restaurant, friendly staff.
E Mercedes, Raimondi 601, T061-575120. Good but noisy, with good bar and restaurant attached, swimming pool.
F Barbtur, Raimondi 670, T061-572532. With bathroom, **F** without, friendly, clean, good beds.
F Hostal Komby, Ucayali 360, T061-571184. Comfortable, pool, excellent value.
F Hostal Sun, Ucayali 380, next to Komby. With bathroom, cheaper without, clean, good value.

Lago Yarinacocha *p531*
C La Cabaña Lodge, T061-616679. Prices include all meals and transport to and from Yarinacocha harbour, run by Ruth and Leroy from the USA, great food, jungle trips from US$50 per day including boat, guide and food.
C-D La Perla, next door to **La Cabaña Lodge**. Price (per person) includes all meals, German-Peruvian owned, English and German spoken, no electricity after 2100, good, jungle tours organized.
D Jana Shobo Amazonian Lodge, T061-596943, www.janashobo.tk. Owned by the Ugarte family, this small lodge is set in 10 ha of forest on the lake shore. Price includes meals and airport transfer, packages and tours available. Camping possible, living room, reading room and kitchen.
E-F Los Delfines, T061-571129. Rooms with bathroom, fan, fridge, some with TV, clean.
G Casa Artesanal Shibipo, San Francisco. A good place to spend the night, in the house of Alberto Sánchez Ríos, very friendly and warmly recommended.
G Don José's Alojamiento, Puerto Inca. Clean, safe, laundry, big rooms. Recommended.
G El Pescador, Puerto Callao. The cheapest place in town, friendly, restaurant, 20 rooms and an extension.

Iquitos *p532, map p533*
Around Independence Day (27 and 28 Jul) and Easter, Iquitos gets crowded. Prices rise at this time. At all times, hotels are more expensive than the rest of the country, but discounts can be negotiated in the low season (Jan-Apr). Taxi drivers and touts at the airport are paid commission by some hotels, insist on being taken where you want to go.
AL El Dorado Plaza, Napo 258 on main plaza, T065-222555, www.eldoradoplazahotel.com. 5 stars, very good accommo- dation and restaurant, excellent service, friendly, bar, internet access, prices include service charge, breakfast, welcome drink and transfer to/from airport. The hotel offers special 3-day/2-night packages from Lima in conjunction with some of the Amazon lodges. Recommended.
A El Dorado, Napo 362, T065-232574, dorado@eldoradoplazahotel.com. Same ownership as **El Dorado Plaza**, pool (open to restaurant users), cable TV, bar and restaurant, prices include service and airport transfer. Highly recommended.
A Victoria Regia, Ricardo Palma 252, T065-231983, www.victoriaregiahotel.com. Regarded as the second best in the city. Price includes breakfast and airport transfer, a/c, fridge, cable TV, free map of city, safe deposit boxes in rooms, good restaurant and pool. Has own internet next door. Recommended.
C Acosta, Calvo de Araujo y Huallaga, T065-235974, www.hotelacosta.com. Price includes

breakfast and airport transfer, a/c, fridge, cable TV, safety deposit boxes, good restaurant.

C Amazonas, Plaza de Armas, Arica 108, T065-242431. Modern, a/c, phone, fridge bar, TV.

C Europa, Próspero 494, T065-231123, rcpowerv@terra.com.pe. A/c, cable TV, phone and fridge in every room, pleasant café/bar, good views from 5th floor.

C Jhuliana, Putumayo 521, T/F065-233154. Includes tax and breakfast, friendly, nice pool, restaurant. Recommended.

C La Posada de Lobo, Pantoja 417 with Yavari, T065-236140. A/c, hot water, TV, fridge, swimming pool, jacuzzi, gym, laundry, email service, price includes breakfast, relaxed atmosphere, pleasant and good value.

D Hostal Ambassador, Pevas 260, T065-233110, www.paseosamazonicos.com. Includes breakfast, a/c, transport to and from airport, member of Peruvian YHA, cafeteria, owns **Sinchicuy Lodge**. Recommended.

D Internacional, Próspero 835, T/F065-234684. A/c, with bathroom, cable TV, fridge, phone, friendly, secure, medium-priced restaurant, good value. Recommended.

D Marañón, Nauta 285, T065-242673, hotel maranon@terra.com.pe. Includes breakfast and airport transfers, small pool, a/c, frigobar, hot water, comfortable. Recommended.

D Royal Inn, Aguirre 793, T065-224244, royalinn_casinohotel@terra.com. Includes breakfast, a/c, frigobar, hot water, bidet, modern and comfortable.

E Hospedaje Yacuruna, Pevas 225, T065-223801, yacurunalodge@hotmail.com. A small place with private bath, cold water and fan.

F El Sitio, Ricardo Palma 545 (no sign), T065-234932. With bathroom, very clean, fan, good value. Highly recommended.

F Hospedaje Mi Selvita, Av Quiñonez Km 3.5, Pasaje Roma No 14, near the airport, T065-260165, raxafe@operamail.com. A charming *hostal* in lovely gardens, run by travel agent Aydee Ríos Cárdenas (who speaks some English). Clean, simple rooms with cool shower, fan, TV, meals.

F Hostal Alfert, García Sanz 01, T065-234105. Hard beds, check fan, friendly, good views to the river, safe but in the market area, arranges jungle trips, but not an authorized operator.

F Hostal Colibrí, Nauta 172, T065-241737. One block from plaza and 50 m from river, new building, TV, fan, hot water, secure, good value, helpful, a/c rooms are more expensive.

G Isabel, Brasil 164, T065-234901. In 1910 building, with bathroom, basic, clean, but plug the holes in the walls, secure, often full.

G La Casa de Samantha, Jr Nauta 787, T065-231005. Shared bath, cold water, small place, family-run, friendly and helpful.

Jungle lodges

See Activities and tours, page 541, for general hints on booking tours. Note especially the advice on checking credentials.

Amazon Lodge and Safaris, Av La Marina 592A, T065-251078. 48 km downriver from Iquitos. Friendly and comfortable; 3 days/2 nights, US$200 per person for 2-4 people, US$50 per person for additional nights.

Amazon Wilderness Expeditions, Jr Putumayo 163, altos 202, T065-234565. Good tours to Emerald Forest Camp, on Río Yanayacu, 185 km from Iquitos, US$65 per day. Comfortable, simple accommodation (no shower – wash in river), clean, good food. Ask for guide Juan Carlos Palomino Berndt, T065-993 5472 (mob).

Amazon Yarapa River Lodge, Av La Marina 124, T065-993 1172, www.yarapariverlodge.com. On Río Yarapa, tributary of the Amazon, in a pristine location, this award- winning lodge has a field laboratory in conjunction with Cornell University. It uses ecofriendly resources and local materials, and works with nearby villages. Flexible and responsible.

Cumaceba Lodge and Expeditions, Putumayo 184 in the Iron House, T/F065-232229, www.cumaceba.com. Tours of 2-8 days to their lodges on the Amazon and Yarapa rivers, good birdwatching guides, 3 days/2 nights. Very good all round.

Explorama Tours, by the riverside docks on Av La Marina 340, PO Box 446, T065-252530, www.explorama.com, are highly recommended as the most efficient and, with over 40 years experience, certainly the biggest and most established. The following 4 sites are run by them: **Ceiba Tops**, 40 km (1½ hrs) from Iquitos, is a resort providing 'an adventure in luxury', 75 a/c rooms with electricity, hot showers, pool with hydromassage, beautiful gardens. The food is good and, as in all Explorama's properties, is served communally. There are attractive walks and other excursions, a recommended jungle experience for those who want their creature comforts, US$200 per person for 1 night/2 days, US$98 for each additional night (1-2 people). **Explorama Lodge** at Yanamono, 80 km (2½ hrs) from Iquitos, has palm-thatched accommodation with separate bathroom and shower facilities connected by covered walkways, cold water, no electricity, good food and service. US$285 for 3 days/2 nights and US$85 for each additional day (1-2 people). **Explornapo Lodge** at Llachapa on the Sucusai creek (a tributary of the Napo), is in the same style as **Explorama Lodge**, but is further away from Iquitos, 160 km (4 hrs), and is set in 105,000 ha of primary rainforest, so is better for seeing wildlife, US$820 for 5 days/4 nights (other packages are available). Nearby is the impressive **canopy walkway** 35 m above the forest floor and 500 m long, 'a magnificent experience and not to be missed'. It is associated with the **Amazon Center for Tropical Studies (ACTS)**, a scientific station, only 10 mins from the canopy walkway. **Explor Tambos**, 2 hrs from **Explornapo**, offer more primitive accommodation, 8 shelters for 16 campers, bathing in the river, offers the best chance to see rare fauna. Close to Explornapo is the **ReNuPeRu** medicinal plant garden, run by a *curandero*. Members of **South American Explorers** are offered 15% discount.

Heliconia Lodge, Ricardo Palma 242, T065-231959, www.amazonriverexpeditions.com. On the Río Amazonas, 1½ hrs from Iquitos, the lodge has hot water, electricity for 3 hrs a day, good guiding and staff; rustic yet comfortable, 3 days/2 nights trips. Under same management as hotels **Victoria Regia** and **Acosta**, see above. They organize trips to Allpahuayo-Mishana and Pacaya-Samiria with **Amazon Tours and Cruises**, see Activities and tours, page 541, and to the ACTS canopy walkway.

Jacamar Amazon Jungle Lodge, 5079 Mariana Lane, Tega Cay, SC 29708, USA, T1-803-548 6738, www.jacamarlodge.com. In the Reserva Comunal de Tamshiyacu-Tahuayo. Do as much or as little as you please, plenty of activities, remote, great food and attentive staff. Fully screened rooms, no electricity, flushing toilets, capacity for 24 guests. Recommended.

Muyuna Amazon Lodge, Putumayo 163, T065-242858, T065 993 4424 (mob), www.muyuna.com. 140 km from Iquitos, on the Yanayacu, before San Juan village. Packages from 1-5 nights available, 2 nights/3 days US$300; users of this guidebook should make reservations in person for discounted price (similarly SAE members, 10%). Everything is included in the price. Good guides, accommodation, food and service, well organized and professional, flexible, radio contact, will collect passengers from airport if requested in advance. They offer a 7-day birdwatching trip, combining several areas including Allpahuayo-Mishana Reserve; also have a new underwater micro- phone for listening to dolphins. Highly recommended.

Paseos Amazónicos Ambassador, Pevas 246, T/F065-231618, www.paseosamazonicos.com, operate the **Amazonas Sinchicuy Lodge**. The lodge is 1½ hrs from Iquitos on the Sinchicuy river, 25 mins by boat from the Amazon river. It consists of several wooden buildings with thatched roofs on stilts, cabins with bathroom, no electricity but paraffin lamps are provided, good food, and plenty of activities, disabled facilities, includes visits to local villages. Recommended. They also have **Tambo Yanayacu** and **Tambo Amazónico** lodges, organize visits to Pacaya-Samiria and local tours.

Tahuayo Lodge, Amazonia Expeditions, 10305 Riverburn Dr, Tampa, FL 33647, toll free T+1 800-262 9669, www.peru jungle.com. Near the Reserva Comunal de Tamshiyacu-Tahuayo on the Río Tahuayo, 145 km upriver from Iquitos, clean, comfortable cabins with cold shower, buffet meals, good food, laundry service, wide range of excursions, excellent staff. A 7-day programme costs US$1295, all inclusive, extra days US$100. Recommended. The lodge is associated with the **Rainforest Conservation Fund** (www.rainforestconservation.org), which works in Tamshiyacu-Tahuayo, one of the world's richest areas for primate species and for amphibians (there is a poison dart frog management programme), birds, other animals and plants.

Iquitos to the Brazilian/Colombian border *p535*

There are several very basic *hostales* in Caballococha, including **G Hostal Internacional** (shared facilities).

Eating

Tingo María *p528*

¥ **El Antojito 2**, Jr Chiclayo 458. Good local food.

¥ **Girasol**, Av Raimondi 253, T062-562065. Chicken, burgers, cakes, juices.

¥ **La Cabaña**, Raimondi 600 block. A good restaurant with fairly clean **F** rooms.

Yurimaguas *p529*

¥¥ **Pizzería**, Jáuregui at Plaza de Armas. Pizza, snacks and drinks.

¥ **Prosperidad**, Jáuregui y Próspero. *Pollo a la brasa* and fruit juices.

There are several other simple *comedores*. On the 2nd block of Jáuregui is a small juice bar serving cold drinks and home-made jungle fruit ice cream.

Pucallpa *p530, map p531*

¥¥ **El Alamo**, Carretera Yarinacocha 2650, T061-571510. Here you can find good local food, such as *patarashca*, barbecued fish wrapped in bijao leaves, and *zarapatera*, a spicy soup made with turtle meat served in its shell, *chonta* salad, made with palm shoots, and *juanes*, rice with chicken or fish served during the San Juan festival.

Lago Yarinacocha *p531*

Around Lake Yarinacocha there are many restaurants and bars on the waterfront and near the plaza, and also stalls selling barbecued fresh fish and local dishes.

Iquitos *p532, map p533*

Try palm heart salad (*chonta*), or a *la loretana* dish; also try *inchicapi* (chicken, corn and peanut soup), *cecina* (fried dried pork), *tacacho* (fried green banana and pork, mashed into balls and eaten for breakfast or tea), *juanes* (chicken, rice, olive and egg, seasoned and wrapped in bijao leaves and sold in restaurants). Many jungle species such as deer and wild boar still figure prominently in Iquitos restaurants. Please be responsible. Try the local drink *chuchuhuasi*, made from the bark of a tree, which is supposed to have aphrodisiac properties but tastes like fortified cough tincture (for sale at Arica 1046), and *jugo de cocona*, the alcoholic *cola de mono* and *siete raices* (aguardiente mixed with the bark of 7 trees and wild honey), sold at **Exquisita Amazónica**, Abtao 590. *Camu-camu* is an interesting but acquired taste, said to have one of the highest vitamin C concentrations in the world. Many private homes offer set lunch, look for the board outside.

¥¥¥ **Fitzcarrald**, Malecón Maldonado 103 y Napo. Smart, best pizza in town, also good pastas and salads.

¥¥¥ **La Gran Maloca**, Sargento Lores 170, opposite **Banco Continental**. A/c, high class.

¥¥¥ **Montecarlo**, Napo 140. Next to the casino, "best food in town".

¥¥ **Ari's Burger**, Plaza de Armas, Próspero 127. Fast food, good breakfasts, popular with tourists.

¥¥ **El Nuevo Mesón**, Malecón Maldonado 153. Local specialities include wild boar, alligator, turtle, tapir and other endangered species, has lots of regular dishes, too. Avoid.

¥¥ **Long Fung**, San Martín at Plaza 28 de Julio. Good Chinese if a little expensive, a/c dining room, daily 1200-1500, 1900-2400 .

¥¥ **Pollón**, on the plaza next to **Ari's Burger**. For chicken and chips, open in the daytime.

¥¥ **The Regal**, in the Casa de Hierro, Plaza de Armas, Próspero y Putumayo, 2nd floor. Nice location, good set lunch for US$2.30, other meals more expensive.

¥¥ **Yellow Rose of Texas**, Putumayo 180. Run by the ex-director of the tourist office, Gerald W Mayeaux. Varied food, Texan atmosphere. Open 24 hrs so you can wait here if arriving late at night, huge breakfasts, lots of information, also has a bar, Sky TV and Texan saddle seats. Often recommended.

¥ **Huasaí**, Napo 326. Varied and innovative menu, popular and recommended, 0730-1600 daily.

¥ **La Vida es Salud**, Aguirre 759 on Plaza 28 de Julio. Vegetarian, simple little place, good value, open daily.

¥ **Paulina**, Tacna 591.Good set lunch, popular with locals and tourists, very noisy.

Cafés

Heladería, Próspero 415. Excellent ice cream, several local flavours including *aguaje* and *camu-camu*. Highly recommended.

Juguería Paladar, Próspero 245. Excellent juices.

Iquitos to the Brazilian/Colombian border *p535*
Restaurant El Sabroso, next to the port, in Caballococha. This is the best place to eat here, good sandwiches for about US$1. There are several cheap *comedores* around the main plaza, which is also next to the port.

Bars and clubs

Pucallpa *p530, map p531*
Billy's Place, on Arica, on the street east of Jr Mcal Cáceres. A decent bar run by an American called Rick (Billy is his pet jaguar). He only sells beer, has TV and pinball. All the locals know it; the area is very dark late at night.

Iquitos *p532, map p533*
La Ribereña, Raymondi 453. With terraced seats on a nice plaza.
Noa Noa, Pevas y Fitzcarrald. Disco, popular with locals and tourists, varied music, open Tue-Sun.
Snack Bar Arandú, Malecón Maldonado. Good views of the Amazon river.
Teatro Café Amauta, Nauta 248. Live music, open 2200-2400, good atmosphere, popular, small exhibition hall.
Tuspa, Raymondi block 2. Light rock, lively, good place to listen to music.

Festivals and events

Pucallpa *p530, map p531*
24 Jun Fiesta de San Juan.
5-20 Oct Pucallpa's **Aniversario Político** and the **Ucayali regional fair**.

Iquitos *p532, map p533*
5 Jan Anniversary of the **Founding of Iquitos**.
Feb/Mar During **Carnival** you can see the local dance La Pandilla.
24 Jun **Festival of San Juan**, patron saint of Loreto. **Tourist week**, with regional music, held in the Mercado Artesanal de San Juan, is celebrated around the same time.
28-30 Aug **Santa Rosa de Lima** is celebrated in Rumococha.
22-25 Sep **Santo Tomás** is celebrated in the village of the same name (see also page 535).
8 Dec **La Purísima**, celebrated in Punchana, near the docks.

Shopping

Pucallpa *p530, map p531*
Many Shibipo women carry and sell their products around Pucallpa and Yarinacocha.
Agustín Rivas, at Jr Tarapacá 861, above a small restaurant whose entrance is at No 863 (ask for it), Pucallpa. For local woodcarvings visit the workshop of this sculptor. His work is made from huge tree roots and when Sr Rivas is in town he is happy to chat over a cup of tea. His family runs the gallery when he is in Iquitos.
Artesanías La Selva, Jr Tarapacá 868, Pucallpa, has a reasonable selection of indigenous craftwork.

Iquitos *p532, map p533*
Good hammocks in the markets in Iquitos cost about US$5.75.
For arts and crafts: **Amazon Arts and Crafts**, Napo block 100; **Artesanías de la Selva**, R Palma 190; **Mercado Artesanal de Productores**, 4 km from the centre in the San Juan district, on the road to the airport (take a *colectivo*). Cheapest in town with more choice than elsewhere.
Mad Mick's Trading Post, next to the Iron House. Hires out rubber boots for those going to the jungle.

Activities and tours

Tingo María *p528*
Tingo María Travel Tours, Av Raimondi 460, Tingo María, T064-562501. Local excursions.

Yurimaguas *p529*
There are some small tour operators in town, offering trips into the jungle: eg **Nilo Hidalgo**, Jr Elena Pardo 115, T065-352832, www.nilotour.cjb.net, US$70-100 per person per day. Also **Manguares Expeditions**, Sargento Lores 126, near Plaza de Armas.

Reserva Nacional Pacaya-Samiria *p529*
For Pacaya-Samiria Reserve, there are 5 registered operators in Lagunas. Guides charge US$15 per day. Trips to Pacaya-Samiria can also be arranged in Iquitos. Expeditions must be booked in advance, all equipment and food is provided.
Asiendes (Asociación Indígena en Defensa de la Ecología Samiria), asiendesperu@hot

mail.com, or contact through **Yellow Rose of Texas** restaurant in Iquitos, see Eating above. A local association which runs trips into Pacaya-Samiria, promoting the jungle and benefiting the community, 4-7 days, US$50 per day, all-inclusive except boat passage from Iquitos and price of entry to the park. You stay at rangers' stations or can camp, very good experience, respectful of wildlife, knowledgeable and accommodating guides. Recommended.

Pucallpa *p530, map p531*

Jungle tours from Pucallpa are not very well organized. You can negotiate a price for a group with the boatmen on the waterfront. Expect to pay around US$30 per day per person and use only accredited guides. Ask the tourist office (see page 530) for advice about visiting the Río Piski area, which has authentic Shibipo culture. There is no passenger traffic, so the trip may be pricey.

Laser Viajes y Turismo, Raimondi 470, T061-571120. Recommended as helpful for planning a jungle trip.

Iquitos *p532, map p533*

See Sleeping above for jungle lodges and the trips that they offer. All agencies are under the control of the local Chamber of Tourism. They arrange 1-day or longer trips to places of interest with guides speaking some English. Package tours booked in Lima or abroad are much more expensive than those booked in Iquitos and personal approaches to lodge operators will often yield better prices than booking through an agency or the internet. Take your time before making a decision and don't be bullied by the hustlers at the airport (they get paid a hefty commission). You must make sure your tour operator or guide has a proper licence (the Municipalidad's *Iquitos Guía Turística* gives a full list). Do not go with a company which does not have legal authorization; there are many unscrupulous people about. Find out all the details of the trip and food arrangements before paying (a minimum of US$45 per day). Speed boats for river trips can be hired by the hour or day at the Embarcadero Turístico, at the intersection of Av de la Marina and Samánez Ocampo in

Punchana. Prices vary greatly, usually US$10-20 per hr, and are negotiable. In fact, all prices are negotiable, except **Muyuna**, who do not take commissions.

Take a long-sleeved shirt, waterproof coat and shoes or light boots on jungle trips and a good torch, as well as *espirales* to ward off the mosquitoes at night – they can be bought from pharmacies in Iquitos. Premier is the most effective local insect repellent. The dry season is from Jul-Sep (Sep is the best month to see flowers and butterflies).

Amazon Tours and Cruises, Requena 336, T065-231611, www.amazontours.net. An American-owned company offering a variety of cruises, many for nature watching, from 1-7 days on *Dawn of the Amazon I* and the luxury *Dawn of the Amazon III*. Also peacock bass fishing, trips to villages (including Pevas), jungle cabin at Llachama and more. Conscientious and efficient.

Blue Morpho, Centre for Shamanic Studies and Workshops, C Moore 144, T065-231168, www.bluemorphotours.com. For reservation information, schedule and pricing, see website.

Transport

Tingo María *p528*

Buses to **Huánuco**, 119 km, 3-4 hrs, US$2 with **Etnasa** (but this company is not recommended because of theft and drug-trafficking). Better to take one of the several micros daily, US$2 per seat, or *colectivos*, US$3.50, 2 hrs. Direct buses continue to **Lima**, 12 hrs, with **Trans Rey** (T01-431 9808 in Lima), US$15 bus cama, **León de Huánuco** and **Bahía** (T01-424 1539), US$11. From Lima to Tingo María, **León de Huánuco** buses leave at 1900, so if continuing to Pucallpa, there is time to grab breakfast on Raimondi and then take another **León** bus, or a *colectivo* onwards. To **Pucallpa**, 255 km, 12 hrs, US$4.30-8.50. **Ucayali Express** *colectivos* leave from the corner of Raimondi and Callao. There are other *colectivos* and taxis, which all leave in the early morning in convoy.

North to Yurimaguas *p528*

Colectivos run from Tingo María to **Tocache** US$13, 4½ hrs; or bus US$9.50, 6 hrs. **Tarapoto**–Tocache, US$7.50 by *colectivo*. *Colectivos* and taxis run from Tocache to **Yurimaguas**. A daily *camioneta* runs from Tarapoto to Yurimaguas, US$7-9, 6-8 hrs. The **Juanjui**–Tocache road has 4 bridges and a ferry just before Juanjui (US$9.20 per vehicle). Juanjui–Tarapoto by *colectivo* US$12.50.

For the river journey, start early if you do not wish to spend a night at the river village of **Sión**. There are no facilities, but the nights are not cold. The river runs through marvellous jungle with high cliffs. Boats sometimes run aground in the river near Sión. Take food and bottled water. Balsa wood rafts also ply this stretch of river.

Yurimaguas *p529*

To/from **Tarapoto** (a beautiful journey, but not safe at night), *colectivos*, 4 hrs, US$7.50, pickups, 5 hrs, US$4.55 in cab, US$2.50 in back, and combis, 5 hrs, US$3.65. You can also hire a car for the ride (US$30), allowing you to stop and sight-see en route. **Paredes Estrella**, on 5th block of Mcal Cáceres (recommended), 0700 daily to **Tarapoto** (8 hrs, US$3.65), **Moyobamba** (10 hrs, US7.50), **Perdo Ruiz** (for Chachapoyas,

16 hrs, US$10.50), **Chiclayo** (24 hrs, US$15), **Trujillo** (28 hrs, US$18), and **Lima** (34 hrs, US$24). Also **Huamanga** and **Sol Peruano**, offices on same street.

By *lancha* to **Iquitos** takes 2 days and 2 nights, take a hammock, mosquito net, bottled water – or purification, fruit and drinks. There are police inspections at each end of the trip. Fares usually include meals, US$18 2nd-class hammock, US$25 1st class hammock, US$35 for 1 bunk in a cabin. **Eduardo**, Elena Pardo 114, T065-351270, is the best company. To buy a hammock costs US$5.75-8.50 in Yurimaguas, on Jáuregui (make sure to buy string to tie it up with). Arriving bus passengers are surrounded by touts trying to sell boat tickets to Iquitos. It is not wise to go to the docks at night to find a boat. Check into a hotel and ask advice in town, then go to the docks next day. The trip is a great experience, but you should take care of your belongings, especially at embarkation and disembarkation, and all travellers should be wary of unwanted attention from the crew.

Pucallpa *p530, map p531*

The airport is to the northwest of the town. Bus from the airport to town, US$0.25; motos US$1; taxi US$2-3. Daily flights to/from **Lima** (1 hr), with **Star Perú** (7 de Junio 865, T061-590585) and **WayraPerú** (Jr Coronel Portillo 522, T061-592715). **Aero Andino** (Jr Bolívar 252, T061-590084) to **Atalaya**, **Contamaná**, **Orellana**, **Papa Hermosa**, **Sepahua**, **Tarapoto** and **Purús**. 9-seater planes depart when a minimum of 6 passengers arrive, several times a week.

The ticket office of **Ucayali Express** as well as the depot for buses to Yarinacocha are in blocks south of the Plaza de Armas. There are regular bus services to **Lima**, 812 km, 18-20 hrs (longer in the rainy season, Nov-Mar), US$11. To **Tingo María**, 255 km, 7-9 hrs, US$4.30-8.50, combis leave at 0600, 0700 and 0800 with **Ucayali Express** (7 de Junio y San Martín). All buses have police guard and go in convoy. Take blankets as the crossing of the Cordillera at night is bitterly cold.

By river to **Atalaya**, several per week 1½ days, US$16. To **Iquitos**, the trip takes 3-5 days, and costs US$20 per person for hammock space, or US$30 for a bed in a cabin. You can go to Puerto La Hoyada, 5 km northeast of the town, Puerto Italia and Pucallpillo to find boats going to Iquitos. A mototaxi to any of the ports costs US$0.75 from the Plaza de Armas, but strap all your bags on tight as things can fall off on the bumpy roads. Taxis charge US$3. Pucallpillo is the low-water port, but there are times when all ports are in use. The large boats to Iquitos and beyond will all be docked at one of them, so you must ask around. The Capitanía on the waterfront may give you information about sailings, but this is seldom reliable. There are usually 2-3 boats in port at any given time. Quality varies, so talking to the staff can help you get a feel for the atmosphere aboard. Departure times are marked on chalk boards on the deck. Schedules seem to change almost hourly, which means that you need to keep a close eye on developments and for Peruvians in the know starting to embark.

Do not pay for your trip before you board the vessel, and only pay the captain. Some boat captains may allow you to live on board a couple of days before sailing. It's safer to club together and pay for a cabin in which to lock your belongings, even if you sleep outside in a hammock. There's a risk of illness as the river water is used for cooking and drinking. Bottled drinking water can be bought in Pucallpa, but not cheaply. You can buy crackers, toilet paper and some sweets on board at inflated prices; warm beer is reasonable at US$1.45 for a big bottle. Vegetarians must take their own supplies. Also take lots of insect repellent, long sleeves and long trousers for the night-time.

Boats going upstream on the Amazon and its tributaries stay closer to the bank than boats going down, which stay in midstream. Further down the Río Ucayali are **Contamaná**, with a frontier-town atmosphere, and **Requena**, from which launches sail to Iquitos, taking 12 hrs. Unlike most other villages, which are mestizo, **Roroboya**, about 12 hrs downstream from Pucallpa, is Shipibo Indian.

Travellers to Iquitos may need confirmation from the PNP that their documents are in order, this must then be signed by the Capitanía otherwise no passenger can be accepted on a trip leaving Pucallpa. No such clearance is necessary when returning to Pucallpa.

Lago Yarinacocha *p531*
Yarinacocha is 20 mins by *colectivo* or bus from the market in Pucallpa, US$0.30, or 15 mins by taxi, US$2.

Iquitos *p532, map p533*
Air
Iquitos flights are frequently delayed; be sure to reconfirm your flight in Iquitos, as they are often overbooked, especially over Christmas. Check times in advance as itineraries frequently change. A taxi to the airport costs US$2.85 per car (T065-241284). A motocarro (motorcycle with 2 seats) is US$2. To take a city bus from the airport, walk out to the main road; most bus lines run through the centre of town, US$0.20. **Lan, Star Perú** and **WayraPerú** have daily flights to **Lima**. **Grupo 42** (military) has one flight a week in a Twin Otter to **Lagunas** (US$50, for Reserva Nacional Pacaya-Samiria), **Yurimaguas** (US$55), **Tarapoto** (US$80) and **Pucallpa** (US$60). Irregular flights with **Aviaselva** are sometimes available to **Leticia** (Colombia), ask around Iquitos travel agencies.

Airline offices Grupo 42, Sargento Lores 127, T065-233224, Mon-Fri 0800-1300 and 1400-1800. **Lan**, Napo 374, T065-232421, Mon-Sat 0900-1900, Sun and holidays 0900-1200. **Star Perú**, Próspero 428, T065-236208. **WayraPerú**, Napo 374, T065-221047.

Bus
To get to **Lake Quistococha**, combis leave every hour until 1500 from Plaza 28 de Julio. The last one back leaves at 1700. Alternatively take a mototaxi there and back with a 1-hour wait, which costs US$6. Another option is to hire a motorbike and spend the day there.

Boat
Both the quality of river boats and frequency of service are much better than they used to be. Large passenger and cargo vessels are called *lanchas*, smaller faster craft are called *rápidos* or *deslizadores* (speedboats). You can find information on boats and tickets at **Bellavista**, Malecón Tarapacá 596; or in the Puerto Masusa district of Puchana, at Av La Marina with Masusa (take a bus from the centre, 10 mins).

Local A *rápido* boat to **Indiana** costs US$3 from the Embarcadero Turístico, at the intersection of Av de la Marina and Samánez Ocampo in Punchana. To **Pilpintuhuasi Butterfly Farm** take a *colectivo* boat from Bellavista to Padre Cocha (US$0.30, leave when full) or hire a boat for US$2.50; US$10 with 2-hr wait.

Long distance All *lanchas* leave from Masusa, 2 km north of the centre, a dangerous area at night. All sailings around 1800-2000, the first night's meal is not included. Always deal directly with boat owners or managers, avoid touts and middlemen. All fares are negotiable.
You can buy a ticket either to sling your hammock on deck, or for a berth in a cabin sleeping 4 people. There are adequate washing and toilet facilities, but the food is rice, meat and beans (and whatever can be picked up en route) cooked in river water. There is a good cheap bar on board. If arriving in Iquitos on a regular, slow boat, take extreme care when disembarking. Things get very chaotic at this time and theft and pickpocketing is rife.
Lanchas serve all of the following destinations: **Pucallpa**, 3-5 days upriver along the Amazon and Ucayali, hammock US$22, berth US$35. *Baylon I* is an OK vessel. To **Yurimaguas**, 3-4 days up river along the Amazon, Marañón and Huallaga, 2nd class hammock space US$18, 1st class hammock space US$25, berth US$35. **Eduardo** company is recommended, *Eduardo IV* and *Eduardo V* are their newest vessels. **Islandia** for **Leticia** (Colombia) and **Tabatinga** (Brazil), 2-3 days downriver on the Amazon, hammock space US$15, berth US$22. *Gran Diego* is a nice vessel. Passengers disembark in Peru for immigration formalities (no exchange facilities), then take another US$1 boat to **Marco**, the port for **Tabatinga**. Most boats for **Manaus** depart from Marco.

If you plan to stop off along the way at small villages on the river in Peru (see Iquitos to the Brazilian/Colombian border, page 535), you can usually get a passing boat to make an unscheduled stop and pick you up. The best way to do this is to flag it down with a white sheet. Note that this method doesn't work on the Brazilian part of the river, where boats don't make unscheduled stops. The only way to board a Brazilian boat between stops is to hire a canoe to take you out to meet it in mid-river then flag it down.

Pantoja (for Ecuador), 5-7 days upriver on the Napo, hammock space US$30, no berths. There are 4 boats – all basic – operating on this route: the *Victor* and the Camila (same owner, T065-242082) as well as the *Jeisawell* and the *Siempre Adelante* (same owner, T065-266159, T065-9613049, mob). Each sails twice a month, but will not go all the way to Pantoja unless there is cargo. To make this long and arduous voyage a day shorter, you can take a small boat to **Indiana** (see local boat transport, above) and cross to Mazán to catch the *lancha* on the Napo, but there may not be much space left on board. Alternatively, you can take a *rápido* from Mazán to **Santa Clotilde** (5 hrs, US$24), less than halfway to Pantoja. In Santa Clotilde is **G Alojamiento El Cielo**, shared bath, cold water, OK; from here you can either board a *lancha* from Iquitos to Pantoja when it calls, or look for a smaller boat sailing from Santa Clotilde to Pantoja. The trip requires plenty of time and patience.

Rápidos for **Tabatinga** (Brazil) leave from the Embarcadero Turístico, Tue-Sun 0600, 10-12 hrs journey, US$60. There are no boats direct to Manaus. Boats go to **Santa Rosa** on the border, opposite Tabatinga. They leave most days at 0600-0615; be at the port at 0445 for customs check. They go to Santa Rosa for immigration formalities then take passengers across to Tabatinga. Purchase tickets in advance from company offices: **Brastur**, Arica 46, **Trans Turismo Amazonas**, Av La Marina 135, or **River Fox**, Raymondi 344, T065-243404 (which is not recommended). All include a small breakfast of a sandwich and coffee, a passable lunch and mineral water (ask for it). All carry life jackets and have clean bathrooms. Luggage limit is 15 kg. Most travel agencies sell tickets. Hotels have details of sailings; ask around which boats are reliable. *Rápidos* leave Tabatinga for Iquitos every morning at 0600: the same price and almost the same time, 11-12 hrs.

See page 63 for general tips on river travel.

Motorcycle hire

Park Motors, Tacna 579, T/F065-231688. The tourist office has details of other companies. Expect to pay US$2.50 per hr, US$25 for 24 hrs; remember that traffic in town is chaotic.

Iquitos to the Brazilian/Colombian border *p535*

Air

Grupo 42 (the Peruvian Air Force) flights between **Santa Rosa** and **Iquitos** were suspended in 2004. Ask in any travel agency in Iquitos about resumption of this service. In Tabatinga, ask at **Blue Moon**, T92-97-412 2227; andyturismo@yahoo. com.br.

There are flights 3 days per week from **Tabatinga** to **Manaus** with Varig, and others with Rico (expensive, so ask about discounts). Aero República flies 4 days a week from **Leticia** to **Bogotá**.

Boat

Details of ferry services from Iquitos to the border are given above. Slow boats between **Iquitos** and **Santa Rosa** stop in **Caballococha**. *Rápidos* between **Iquitos** and **Tabatinga** only make a brief stop, so to see the town, take a *rápido* boat from **Leticia** (Colombia), 2-3 hrs depending on the number of stops, then catch a flight out or a rápido the next day. Small boats between **Tabatinga** and **Santa Rosa**, or **Leticia** and Santa Rosa are readily available and charge US$1.75 per passenger.

Directory

Tingo María *p528*

Internet Several places on Raimondi and in the streets near the Plaza de Armas, fast and cheap. **Telephone** Catel, Av Raimondi 272, Tingo María, T062-562551, phone, fax and internet.

Pucallpa *p530, map p531*

Banks It is easy to change dollars (cash) at the banks, travel agencies, the better hotels and bigger stores. There are also lots of street changers (watch them carefully). BCP, Raimondi y Tarapacá, is the only place to change TCs. Cash advances can be made on Visa at BCP and Interbank. **Police** Policía Nacional, Jr Independencia 3rd block, T061-575211. **Post** Tarapacá y San Martín.

Iquitos *p532, map p533*

Banks Don't change money on the streets. Visit the tourist office and obtain a list with the names of reliable money changers. BCP, Plaza de Armas. For Visa, also cash and TCs at good rates, has a Visa ATM around the corner on Próspero. BBV Continental, Sargento Lores 171, for Visa, 1% commission on TCs. Banco de la Nación, Condamine 478, good rates. Banco Wiese Sudameris, Próspero 282. Banco del Trabajo, Próspero 223, has Unicard ATM for Visa/Plus and MasterCard/Cirrus. **Casa de cambio** at Tienda Wing Kong, Próspero 312, Mon-Sat 0800-1300 and 1500-2000, Sun 0900-1200. Western Union, Napo 359, T065-235182. **Consulates** Britain, Casa de Hierro (Iron House), Putumayo 189, T065-22273 2, Mon-Fri 1100-1200. Colombia, Calvo de Araujo 431, T065-231461. There are no Brazilian or Ecuadorean consulates. If you need a visa for either of these countries and plan to travel there from Iquitos, you must get the visa beforehand at home or in Lima. **Hospitals** Clínica Loreto, Morona 471, T065-233752, 24-hr attention. Recommended, but only Spanish spoken. **Immigration** Mcal Cáceres 18th block, T065-235371, quick service. **Internet** There are internet places every- where, US$0.80 per hr. **Laundry** At Ricardo Palma, blocks 4 and 5, and at Putumayo, block 1. **Police** Tourist police, Sargento Lores 834, T065-231851. Helpful with complaints against tour operators. In emergency T065-241000/241001. **Post** On the corner of C Arica with Morona, near the Plaza de Armas, 0700-2000. **Telephone** Telefónica, Arica 276. Locutorio at Próspero 523, private cabins, cheap national and international calls, helpful staff. **Useful addresses** Indecopi, C Huallaga 325, T065-243490, ameza@ indecopi.gob.pe, for the tourism protection service.

Iquitos to the Brazilian/Colombian border *p535*

Banks There is no exchange office in Santa Rosa, but you can pay in reais. You can use Colombian pesos in Brazil and reais in Colombia. Peruvian soles are not accepted in Colombia, but sometimes you pay with soles in Brazil. There are no exchange facilities in Tabatinga port, but there are several *casas de cambio* in Leticia, the best place to change money, even for reais into soles. US dollars are accepted everywhere. **Internet** The only place with internet is Leticia. Connection is very slow.

Southern Jungle

Both the Manu Biosphere Reserve and Tambopata National Park offer amazing wildlife spotting, large parts being remote and pristine, with such highlights as macaw clay licks and birdwatching on undisturbed lakes. The southern selva is found mostly within the Department of Madre de Dios, created in 1902, and contains the Manu National Biosphere Reserve (2.2 million ha), the Tambopata National Reserve (254,358 ha) and the Bahuaja-Sonene National Park (1.1 million ha). ▸▸ *For Sleeping, Eating and other listings, see pages 555-566.*

Background

The forest of this lowland region is technically called subtropical moist forest, which means that it receives less rainfall than tropical forest and is dominated by the flood plains of its meandering rivers. One of the most striking features is the former river channels that have become isolated as oxbow lakes (*cochas*). These are home to black caiman and giant otter and a host of other species. Other rare species living in the forest are jaguar, puma, ocelot and tapir. There are also capybara, thirteen species of primate and many hundreds of bird species. If you include the cloudforests and highlands of the Manu Biosphere Reserve, the bird count almost totals 1000.

The relative proximity to Cuzco of Manu in particular has made it one of the prime nature watching destinations in South America. Despite its reputation, Manu is heavily protected, with visitor numbers limited and a large percentage of the park inaccessible to tourists. Nevertheless, there is no need to worry that this level of management is going to diminish your pleasure. There is more than enough in the way of birds, animals and plants to satisfy the most ardent wildlife enthusiast. Tambopata does have a town in the vicinity, Puerto Maldonado, and the area is under threat from exploitation and settlement. The suspension of oil exploration in 2000 led to a change of status for a large tract of this area, giving immediate protection to another of Peru's zones of record-breaking diversity.

Since 2003 the new emerging threat to the forests of Madre de Dios is the planned construction of the Transoceánica, a road linking the Atlantic and Pacific Oceans via Puerto Maldonado and Brazil. The paving of this road system, creating a high-speed link between the two countries, will certainly bring more uncontrolled colonization in the area, placing the forests of the Tambopata region under further pressure. The uncontrolled colonization of the Bahuaja-Sonene's southern border, in the Tambopata headwaters area is another cause for concern. On top of that is illegal logging and the issue of new oil exploration contracts for most of Madre de Dios outside of the conservation concessions. This, in spite of the fact that they overlap heavily with the indigenous territories concession, including the lands of indigenous peoples living in voluntary isolation.

A pair of binoculars is essential for wildlife viewing and insect repellent is a must.

Manu Biosphere Reserve » *pp555-566. Colour map 4, C4.*

No other rainforest can compare with Manu for the diversity of its life forms. It is one of the world's great wilderness experiences, with the best birdwatching as well as offering the best chance of seeing giant otters, jaguars, ocelots and several of the 13 species of primate which abound in this pristine tropical wilderness. The more remote areas of the reserve are home to uncontacted indigenous tribes and many other indigenous groups with very little knowledge of the outside world. Covering an area of 1,881,000 ha, Manu Biosphere Reserve is also one of the largest conservation units on Earth, encompassing the complete drainage of the Manu river, with an altitudinal range of 200-4100 m above sea level.

Ins and outs

Getting there and around To visit Manu you must go as part of a tour leaving from Cuzco, either by road or by air. The frontier town of Puerto Maldonado is the starting point for expeditions to the Tambopata National Reserve and is only a 30-minute flight from Cuzco. » *For further details see Activities and tours, page 560 and Transport page 564.*

Best time to visit The climate is warm and humid, with a rainy season from November to March and a dry season from April to October. A cool air mass descending from the Andes, called a *friaje*, is characteristic of the dry season, when temperatures drop to 15-16°C during the day, and 13°C at night. Always bring a sweater at this time. The best time to visit is during the dry season when there are fewer mosquitoes and the rivers are low, exposing the beaches. This is also a good time to see birds nesting and to view the animals at close range, as they stay close to the rivers.

Information **Manu National Park Office** ⓘ *Av Micaela Bastidas 310, Cuzco, T084-240898, pqnmanu@terra.com.pe, casilla postal 591, 0800-1400*. They issue a permit for the former Reserved Zone, costing S/.150 per person (about US$40). This is included in package tour prices. For information on conservation issues: **Asociación Peruana para la Conservación de la Naturaleza (Apeco)** ⓘ *Parque José Acosta 187, p 2,*

Magdalena del Mar, Lima 17, T01-264 0094, www.apeco.org.pe; and **Pronaturaleza** ⓘ *Av Alberto de Campo 417, Lima 17, T01-264 2736 and Jr Cajamarca, cuadra 1 s/n, Puerto Maldonado, T082-571585, www.pronaturaleza.org*. **Perú Verde** ⓘ *Ricaldo Palma J-1, Santa Mónica, Cuzco, T084-226392, www.peruverde.org*, is a local NGO that can help with information and has free video shows about Manu National Park and Tambopata National Reserve. Staff are friendly and helpful and also have information on programmes and research in the jungle area of Río Madre de Dios.

The park areas

The biosphere reserve formerly comprised the **Manu National Park** (1,692,137 ha), where only government-sponsored biologists and anthropologists may visit with permits from the Ministry of Agriculture in Lima, the **Manu Reserved Zone** (257,000 ha), set aside for applied scientific research and ecotourism, and the **Cultural Zone** (92,000 ha), containing acculturated native groups and colonists, where the locals still employ their traditional way of life. In 2003 the Manu Reserved Zone was absorbed into the

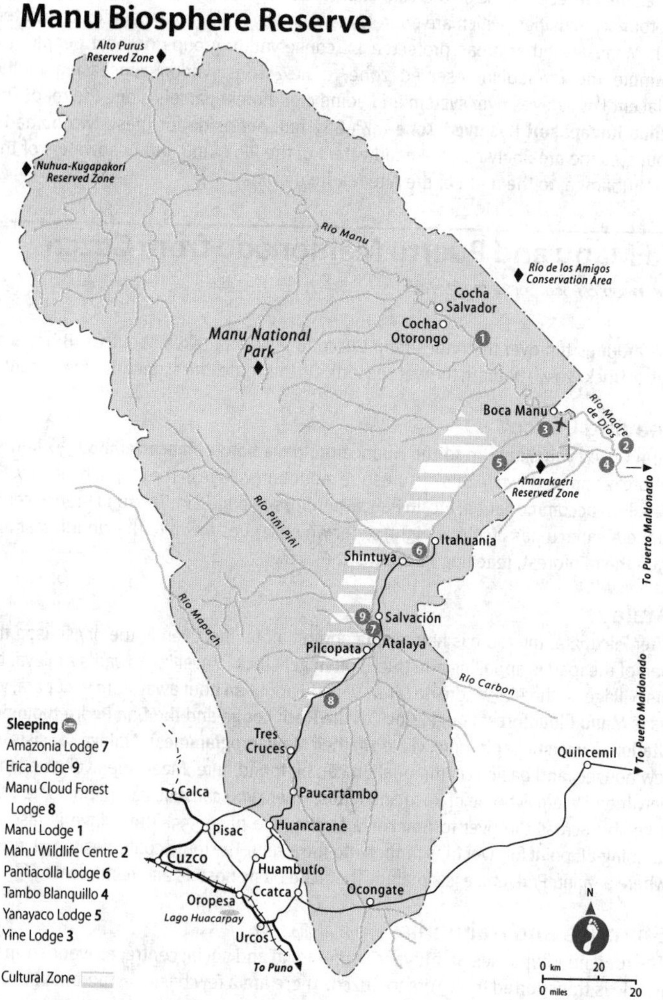

 Manu National Park, increasing its protected status. Ecotourism activities have been allowed to continue in specially designated tourism and recreational zones along the course of the Lower Manu River. These tourism and recreational areas are accessible by permit only. Entry is strictly controlled and visitors must visit the area under the auspices of an authorized operator with an authorized guide. Permits are limited and reservations should be made well in advance, though it is possible to book a place on a trip at the last minute in Cuzco. In the former Reserved Zone there are two lodges, the rustic **Casa Machiguenga** run by the Machiguenga communities of Tayakome and Yomibato with the help of a German NGO, and the upmarket **Manu Lodge.** In the Cocha Salvador area, several companies have tented safari camp infrastructures, some with shower and dining facilities, but all visitors sleep in tents. Some companies have installed walk-in tents with cots and bedding.

The Cultural and Multiple Use Zones are accessible to anyone and several lodges exist in the area. It is possible to visit these lodges under your own steam. Among the ethnic groups in the Multiple Use Zone (a system of buffer areas surrounding the core Manu area) are the Harakmbut, Machiguenga and Yine in the Amarakaeri Reserved Zone, on the east bank of the Alto Madre de Dios. They have set up their own ecotourism activities, which are entirely managed by indigenous people. Associated with Manu are other areas protected by conservation groups or local people, for example the Blanquillo reserved zone, a new conservation concession in the adjacent Los Amigos river system and some cloudforest parcels along the road. The **Nuhua-Kugapakori Reserved Zone** (443,887 ha), set aside for these two nomadic groups, is the area between the headwaters of the Río Manu and headwaters of the Río Urubamba, to the north of the Alto Madre de Dios.

To Manu and Puerto Maldonado from Cuzco

» *pp555-566. Colour map 5, A5/6.*

The arduous trip over the Andes from Cuzco to Pilcopata takes about 16-18 hours by bus or truck (20-40 hours in the wet season). On this route, the scenery is magnificent.

Leaving Cuzco

From Cuzco you climb up to the Huancarani pass before **Paucartambo** (3½ hours), before dropping down to this picturesque mountain village in the Mapacho Valley. For details of accommodation, etc, in Paucartambo, see page 213. The road then ascends to the Ajcanacu pass (cold at night), after which it goes down to the cloudforest and then the rainforest, reaching **Pilcopata** at 650 m.

Atalaya

After Pilcopata, the route is hair-raising and breathtaking. Even in the dry season this part of the road is appalling and trucks often get stuck. Travelling towards Atalaya, the first village on the Alto Madre de Dios river and about an hour away from Pilcopata, you pass **Manu Cloudforest Lodge, Cock of the Rock Lodge** and the **San Pedro Biological Station** (owned by Tapir Tours, visited in their Manu programmes). Atalaya consists of a few houses, and basic accommodation can be found here. Meals are available at the very friendly family home of Rosa and Klaus, where you can also camp. Boats here will take you across the river to **Amazonia Lodge,** see page 555. The village is also the jumping-off point for river trips further into the Manu. The route continues to **Salvación,** where a Manu Park office is situated. There are basic hostels and restaurants.

Shintuya and Itahuania → *Colour map 5, A6.*

The road now bypasses Shintuya, a commercial and social centre, as wood from the jungle is transported from here to Cuzco. There are a few basic restaurants and you can camp (beware of thieves). The priest will let you stay in the dormitory rooms at the mission. Supplies are expensive. There are two Shintuyas: one is the port and mission and the other is the indigenous village. The end of the road is **Itahuania**, the starting point for river transport. It won't be long before the port moves down river as the road is being built to Nuevo Edén, 11 km away, and there are plans to extend to Diamante by early 2007, with the road one day planned to reach Boca Colorado. **Note**: It is not possible to arrange trips to the Reserved Zone of the National Park from Itahuania, owing to park regulations; all arrangements must be made in Cuzco.

Boca Manu

Boca Manu is the connecting point between the rivers Alto Madre de Dios, Manu and Madre de Dios. It has a few houses, an airstrip and some well-stocked shops. It is also the entrance to the Manu Reserve and to go further you must be part of an organized group. The park ranger station is located in **Limonal**, 20 minutes by boat from Boca Manu. You need to show your permit here; camping is allowed if you have a permit.

To the Reserved Zone

Upstream on the Río Manu you pass the **Manu Lodge** (see page 555) on the Cocha Juárez, three to four hours by boat. You can continue to Cocha Otorongo, 2½ hours, and Cocha Salvador, 30 minutes, the biggest lake with plenty of wildlife where the **Casa Machiguenga Lodge** is located and several companies have safari camp concessions. From here it is one hour to **Pakitza,** the entrance to the National Park Zone. This is only for biologists and others with a special permit.

Boca Colorado

From Itahuania infrequent cargo boats sail to the gold-mining centre of Boca Colorado on the Río Madre de Dios, via Boca Manu, passing several ecotourism lodges including **Pantiacolla Lodge** and **Manu Wildlife Centre**, see page 555. The trip takes around nine hours, and costs US$15. Basic accommodation can be found here and is not recommended for lone women travellers. From Boca Colorado a road now runs to Puerto Maldonado, three hours by *colectivo*. Some lodges in the Manu area now use this route: flight to Puerto Maldonado, a vehicle to Boca Colorado and then a boat upstream to the lodge.

Between Boca Manu and Colorado is **Blanquillo**, a private reserve (10,000 ha). Bring a good tent with you and all food if you want to camp and do it yourself, or alternatively accommodation is available at the **Tambo Blanquillo** (full board or accommodation only). Wildlife is abundant, especially macaws and parrots at the macaw lick near Manu Wildlife Centre (see above). There are occasional boats to Blanquillo from Shintuya, six to eight hours.

Puerto Maldonado

» *pp555-566. Colour map 6, A3.*

→ *Phone code: 082. Population: over 60,000. Altitude: 250 m.*

Puerto Maldonado is an important starting point for visiting the rainforest, or for departing to Brazil or Bolivia. Still, most visitors won't see much of the place because they are whisked through town on their way to a lodge on the Río Madre de Dios or the Río Tambopata. The city dwellers aren't too pleased about this and would like tourists to spend some time in town, which is a major timber, gold mining and tourism centre, expanding rapidly. It's a safe place, with *chicha* music blaring out from most street corners. **Dircetur tourist office** ⓘ *Urb Fonavi, F20, Pasaje 12 de Septiembre, T082-571164, 082-9703987 (mob), carloagpe@yahoo.com.*

Ins and outs

The road from Cuzco to Puerto Maldonado is being improved, with regular bus services. The road is passable in the wet season but takes a lot longer than in the dry. In its pre-upgrading state it was expertly described in Matthew Parris' book *Inka-Cola*. The road passes through Ocongate and Marcapata before reaching **Quincemil**, 240 km from Urcos, a centre for alluvial gold-mining. Quincemil marks the halfway point and the end of the all-weather road. Petrol is scarce here because most vehicles continue on 70 km to **Mazuko**, where it's cheaper. The journey is very rough, but the changing scenery is magnificent. This road is rarely passable in the wet season. Take warm clothing for travelling through the sierra. For an alternative route, see page 550.

Sights

Overlooking the confluence of the rivers Tambopata and Madre de Dios, Puerto Maldonado is a major logging and brazil-nut processing centre. From the park at the end of Jirón Arequipa, across from the Capitanía, you get a good view of the two rivers, the ferries across the Madre de Dios and the stacks of lumber at the dockside. The brazil-nut harvest is from December to February and the crop tends to be good on alternate years. Nuts are sold on the street, plain or coated in sugar or chocolate. **El Mirador** ⓘ *at the junction of Av Fitzcarrald and Av Madre de Dios, Mon-Sat*

Puerto Maldonado

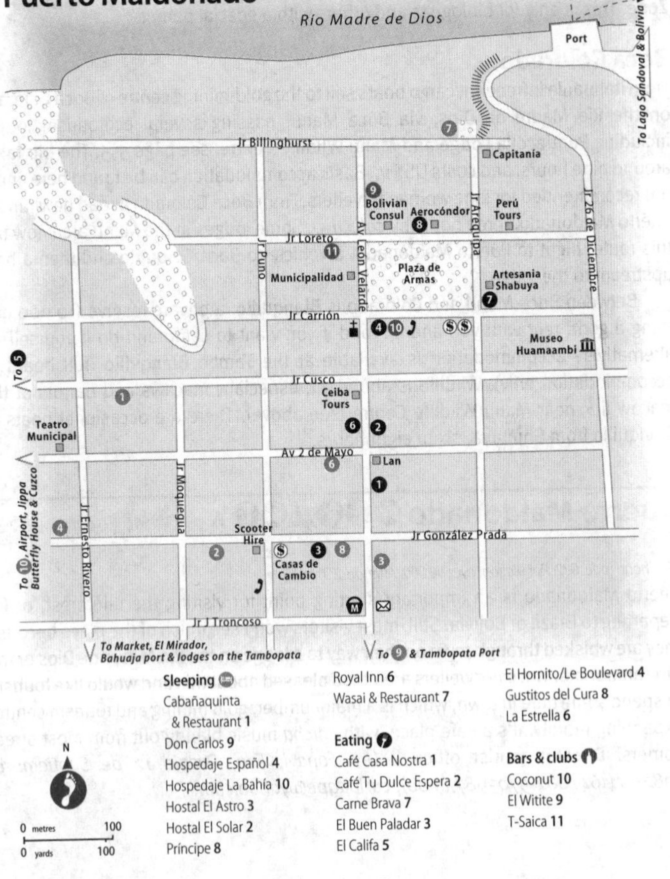

0900-1700, Sun 1200-1700, US$0.60, is a 47-m-high tower with 250 steps and three platforms giving fine views over the city and surrounding rainforest. There is also a toilet at the top – no curtains – from which there is an equally fine view over the city! **Museo Huamaambi** ⓘ *26 de Diciembre 360, US$1*, contains photos and artefacts pertaining to the Harakmbut culture of central Madre de Dios. **Jippa Butterfly House** ⓘ *adjoining the airport entrance (a 5-min walk from the terminal building), open 0800-1330, www.butterflyhouse.com.pe, US$3*, breeds butterflies as part of a sustainable development project and offers guided tours. Worth a visit if you arrive early for your flight or if it is delayed. **El Serpentario** snake house is next door.

Around Puerto Maldonado

The beautiful and tranquil **Lago Sandoval** ⓘ *US$9.50, you must go with a guide (see page 560); this can be arranged by the boat driver*, is a one-hour boat ride along the Río Madre de Dios from Puerto Maldonado, and then a 5-km walk into the jungle. There is an interpretation centre at the start of the trail and a 35-m-high observation tower overlooking the lake. It is possible to see giant river otters early in the morning and several species of monkeys, macaws and hoatzin. There are two jungle lodges at the lake, see Sleeping. At weekends, especially on Sundays, the lake gets quite busy.

Upstream from Lago Sandoval, towards Puerto Maldonado, is the wreck of the *Fitzcarrald*. The steamer (a replica of Fitzcarrald's boat) lies a few metres from the Madre de Dios in the bed of a small stream. The German director, Werner Herzog, was inspired to make his famous film, *Fitzcarraldo*, by the story of Fitzcarrald's attempt to haul a boat from the Ucuyali to the Madre de Dios drainage basins (in what is now the Manu National Park).

For those interested in seeing a gold-rush town, a trip to **Laberinto** is suggested. There is one hotel and several poor restaurants. At Km 13 on the Cuzco road is a pleasant recreational centre with a restaurant and natural pools where it's possible to swim. It gets busy at weekends. It's US$2 each way by *mototaxi* from town. Trips can be made to **Lago Valencia**, 60 km away near the Bolivian border; four hours there, eight hours back. It is an oxbow lake with lots of wildlife, and many excellent beaches and islands are located within an hour's boat ride.

Tambopata National Reserve (TNR)

▸▸ *pp555-566. Colour map 6, A3.*

From Puerto Maldonado you can visit the Tambopata National Reserve by travelling up the Tambopata river or down the Madre de Dios. The area was first declared a reserve in 1990 and is a very reasonable alternative for those who do not have the time or money to visit Manu. It is a close rival in terms of seeing wildlife and boasts some superb oxbow lakes. There are a number of lodges here which are excellent for lowland rainforest birding. **Explorers' Inn** is perhaps the most famous, but the **Posada Amazonas/Tambopata Research Centre** and **Libertador Tambopata Lodge** are also good. In an effort to ensure that more tourism income stays in the area, a few local families have established their own small-scale *casas de hospedaje*, which offer more basic facilities and make use of the nearby forest.

Ins and outs

The fee to enter the TNR is US$9.50 for a one-day visit to anywhere between Lago Sandoval and Chuncho Collpa; US$20 for up to five days, including one re-entry; and US$31.25 for up to five days, including a visit to the Tambopata Collpa. If staying at a lodge, they will organize the payment of the fee, otherwise you need to visit the **INRENA office** ⓘ *Av 28 de Julio s/n, block 8, T082-573278, Mon-Fri 0830-1300, 1430-1800, Sat 0900-1200.* ▸▸ *For Transport details, see page 564.*

The park areas

The **Bahuaja-Sonene National Park** runs from the Río Heath, which forms the Bolivian border, across to the Río Tambopata, 50-80 km upstream from Puerto Maldonado. It was expanded to 1,091,416 ha in August 2000, with the Tambopata National Reserve (254,358 ha) created to form a buffer zone. The park is closed to visitors though those visiting the *collpa* (macaw lick) on the Tambopata or river rafting down the Tambopata will travel through it.

Río Las Piedras

Lying to the northeast of, and running roughly parallel to the Río Manu, this drainage runs some 700 km from remote rainforest headwaters in the Alto Purús region. The lower, more easily accessible section of the river, closer to Puerto Maldonado and currently outside state protection, runs through rich tropical forests, very similar to those in the Manu and Tambopata areas. Close to 600 species of birds, at least eight primate species and some of the Amazon's larger mammals, jaguar, puma, tapir and giant anteater, are all present. Healthy populations of giant otters exist in the rivers and oxbow lakes, and there are several clay licks that attract parrots, macaws and, in some cases, larger mammals as well. Due to its lack of protected status it's also fairly straightforward to tailor your own itinerary in this part of the forest. The only real downside is that hunting pressure has resulted in wildlife being somewhat shyer and more secretive than in Manu or Tambopata. Nevertheless this remains an excellent wildlife destination.

Tambopata National Reserve & Bahuaja-Sonene National Park

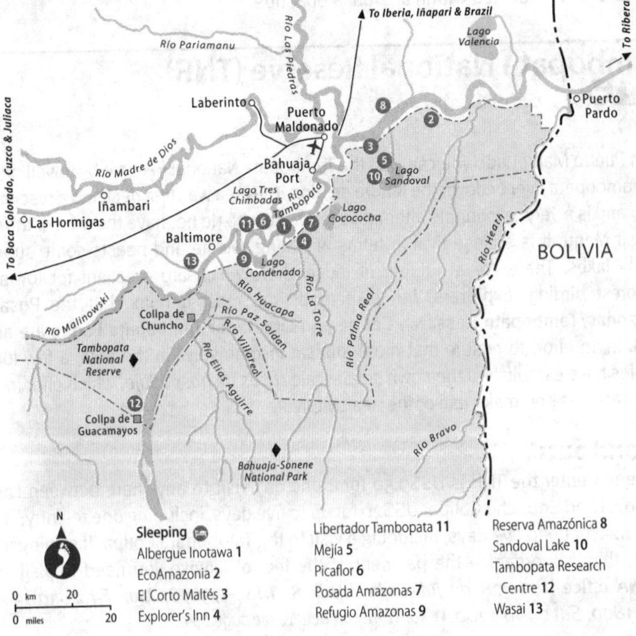

To Iberia and Iñapari

» pp555-566. Colour map 4, C6.

Daily public transport runs on the improved dirt road which begins across the Río Madre de Dios and runs to Iberia and Iñapari on the border with Brazil. Take one of the frequent ferries which crosses from Puerto Maldonado (a bridge is about to be built). In the dry, it is a fast road and dangerous for motorcyclists because of passing traffic. Along the road there remains no primary forest, only secondary growth and small *chacras* (farms). There are also picturesque *caseríos* (settlements) that serve as collecting and processing centres for the brazil nut industry. Approximately 70% of the inhabitants in the Madre de Dios are involved in the collection of the prized nut.

Iberia, at Km 168, has accommodation. Just outside the town the local rubber tappers' association has set up a reserve with an information centre and a swimming pool (US$0.50). **Iñapari**, at the end of the road, Km 235, has two accommodation options, but **Assis Brasil** across the border is more attractive. A bridge from Iñapari to Assis Brasil now links the two countries. Peruvian immigration is in Iñapari. Exit stamps can be obtained between 0800-1830. Walk across the bridge over the Rio Acre to Assis Brasil, where there is no Policía Federal office. Travel on to **Brasiléia** to obtain your Brazil entry stamp at Policía Federal. You must have a yellow fever certificate to enter Brazil. Officials in Iñapari are reported to be obstructive to foreign travellers entering Peru, giving only 30 days' entry.

Check in advance that you do not need a consular visa for Brazil or Bolivia; they are not issued at the border.

There is a road from Assis Brasil to Brasiléia in Brazil (120 km, buses run in the dry season, 2½ hours, US$3.60; 4WD vehicles in the wet season), from where a new bridge has been opened to Cobija in Bolivia. There are no exchange facilities en route and poor exchange rates for Brazilian currency at Iñapari.

Sleeping

Manu Biosphere Reserve *p548, map p549*

Amazonia Lodge, in Cuzco at Matará 334, T/F084-231370, amazonia1@correo.dnet.com.pe. On the Río Alto Madre de Dios just across the river from Atalaya, an old tea hacienda run by the Yabar family, famous for its bird diversity and fine hospitality, a great place to relax, contact Santiago in advance and he'll arrange a pickup.

Casa Machiguenga, contact Manu Expeditions or the Apeco NGO, T084-225595. Near Cocha Salvador, upriver from Manu Lodge, Machiguenga-style cabins run by the local community of Tayakome with NGO help.

Cock of the Rock Lodge, run by the Perú Verde group. On the road from Paucartambo to Atalaya at San Pedro, at 1500 m, next to a Cock of the Rock lek, double rooms with shared bath and 7 private cabins with en-suite bath.

Erika Lodge, contact Aventuras Ecológicas Manu, Plateros 356, Cuzco; or Ernesto Yallico, Casilla 560, Cuzco, T084-227765. On the Alto Madre de Dios, 25 mins from Atalaya. Like Amazonia Lodge, this is good place for birds. It offers basic facilities and is cheaper than the other, more luxurious lodges.

Manu Cloud Forest Lodge, owned by Manu Nature Tours (see Tours and activities, page 560). Located at Unión at 1800 m on the road from Paucartambo to Atalaya, 6 rooms with 4 beds.

Manu Lodge, run by **Manu Nature Tours** (see Tours and activities, page 560) and only bookable as part of a full package deal with transport. Situated on the Manu river, 3 hrs upriver from Boca Manu towards Cocha Salvador, It's a fine location overlooking Cocha Juárez, an oxbox lake, which often plays host to a family of giant otters. The lodge has an extensive trail system, and stands of mauritia palms near the lake provide nesting sites for colonies of blue and yellow macaws.

Manu Wildlife Centre, book through **Manu Expeditions** or **InkaNatura**. 2 hrs down the Río Madre de Dios from Boca Manu, near the Blanquillo macaw lick. 22 double cabins, all with private bathroom and hot water. It also has a tapir lick and canopy tower for birdwatching.

Pantiacolla Lodge, book through Pantiacolla Tours. 30 mins downriver from Shintuya. Owned by the Moscoso family. This lodge is located at the foot of the Pantiacolla Mountains, which boasts vast biological diversity, particularly with birds. There are good trail system. Also managed by Pantiacolla is the **Yine Lodge**, see below, and the **Posada San Pedro Cloud Forest Lodge**, with 14 rooms, before Pilcopata.

Yanayaco Lodge, Procuradores 46, Cuzco, T084-248122, 084-960 6368 (mob), www.yanayacolodge.com. A relatively new lodge approximately 1 hr by boat above Diamante village on the southern bank of the Madre de Dios, close to a small parrot *collpa* (mineral lick); claims to offer frequent sightings of large mammals. Using local river transport to arrive at the lodge rates are very reasonable, US$35 including food and board in double room. The lodge also offers several different itineraries in Manu.

To Manu and Puerto Maldonado from Cuzco *p550*

Turismo Indígena Wanamei, T084-254033, T084-965 2520 (mob), or Av 26 de Diciembre 276, Puerto Maldonado, T082-572539, www.ecoturismowanamei.com. A new initiative of the Harakmbut indigenous people to introduce visitors to their ancestral lands, the Amarakaeri Communal Reserve, located between Manu and Tambopata. They offer 4- to 9-day trips starting and ending in Cuzco. Accommodation includes lodges, communities and camping. The trips aim to offer not only excellent wildlife viewing opportunities but also an insight into the daily life of indigenous peoples in the early 21st century. To gain the most from this unusual experience you need to speak Spanish (or Harakmbut!). The 5-day/4-night trip costs US$200 and includes all transport, meals, lodging and a guide.

D Boca Manu Lodge, book through **Emperadores Tours**, Procuradores 190, Cuzco, T084-239987. Run by long-standing Manu resident Juan de Dios Carpio. Juan owns a general store in Boca, so if you're stranded in Boca Manu and you're looking for a reasonably priced place to stay this could be an option – just ask at the store.

G Hostal, Boca Manu, run by the community. Basic accommodation.

G The Mission, Shintuya. The priest will let you stay in the dormitory rooms. There are a few basic restaurants and you can camp (beware of thieves). Supplies are expensive.

G Sra Rubella, Pilcopata. This unnamed place is very basic, but friendly.

Lodges

Yine Lodge, next to the airstrip, Boca Manu. A smart cooperative project between **Pantiacolla Tours** and the native Yine community of Diamante.

Puerto Maldonado *p551, map p551*

B Wasai, Billinghurst, opposite the Capitanía, T082-572290, www.wasai.com. Price includes breakfast, a/c, TV, shower. In a beautiful location overlooking the Madre de Dios, with forest surrounding cabin-style rooms which are built on a slope down to the river, small pool with waterfall, good restaurant if slightly expensive. Recommended, although service can be stretched if hotel is full. They run local tours and have a lodge on the Tambopata River (see page 553).

C Cabañaquinta, Cusco 535, T082-571045, www.hotelcabanaquinta.com. With buffet breakfast, bathroom, a/c, small pool, sauna, good restaurant, friendly, lovely garden, very comfortable, price includes airport transfer if needed. Recommended.

D Don Carlos, Av León Velarde 1271, T082-571029. Nice view over the Río Tambopata, a/c, restaurant, TV, phone, good.

E Amarumayo, Libertad 433, 10 mins from centre, T082-573860, residenciamarumayo @hotmail.com. Price includes breakfast. Comfortable, with pool and garden, good restaurant. Recommended.

E Hospedaje Español, González Prada 670, T082-572381. Garden setting, clean, friendly.

E Hospedaje La Bahía, 2 de Mayo 710, T082-572127. Cheaper without bath or TV, large rooms, clean. Best of cheaper options.

E Hostal El Solar, González Prada 445, T082-571571. With bath (cheaper without), basic but clean, fan.

E Príncipe, Jr González Prada 355, T082-572838. With bathroom, basic.

E Royal Inn, Av 2 de Mayo 333, T082-571048. Modern and clean, rooms at back are less noisy.

F Hostal El Astro, Velarde 617, T082-572128. Clean, safe, family-run.
F Hotel Toni, in Quincemil, on the road from Cuzco to Puerto Maldonado. Friendly, clean, cold shower, good meals.

Tambopata National Reserve (TNR)

p553, map p554

Most of the lodges in the Tambopata area use the term 'ecotourism', or something similar, in their publicity material, but it is applied pretty loosely. **Posada Amazonas'** collaboration with the local community is unique in the area, but fortunately no lodge offers trips where guests hunt for their meals. See page 43 for points to note. Prices are given only for standard 3-day/2-night packages which include all transport links, accommodation on a full-board basis and guiding. Lodges on the Tambopata are reached by vehicle to Bahuaja port, 15 km upriver from Puerto Maldonado, by the community of Infierno, then by boat. Some of the lodges mentioned above also offer guiding and research placements to biology and environmental science graduates. For more details send an SAE to **TReeS: UK**, c/o J Forrest, PO Box 33153, London NW3 4DR. Long-term visitors should be aware that leishmaniasis exists in this area.

Río Madre de Dios

C Casa de Hospedaje Mejía, book via **Ceiba Tours** in Puerto Maldonado (see Activities and tours, page 560). A small, family-run, rustic lodge close to Lago Sandoval, with 10 double rooms, none en suite. Canoes available to explore the lake. An English-speaking guide can be arranged. 3 days/2 nights costs US$70, one of the cheapest options.
Eco Amazonia Lodge, book through their office in Lima: Av 1083, of 408, Miraflores, T01-242 2708; in Cuzco T083-225068, www.ecoamazonia.com.pe. On the Madre de Dios, 1 hr downriver from Puerto Maldonado. Accommodation for up to 80 in basic bungalows and dormitories, good for birdwatching with viewing platforms and tree canopy access, has a pool and its own Monkey Island with animals taken from the forest, US$160 for 3 days/2 nights.
El Corto Maltés, Billinghurst 229, Puerto Maldonado, T/F082-573831, cortomaltes @terra.com.pe. On the south side of the Madre de Dios river, one of the closest to Puerto Maldonado, halfway to Sandoval, the focus of most visits. Bungalows are very well spaced out and all have a river view. Hot water, huge dining room, well run, pool planned. Ayahuasca sessions can be arranged. US$180 for 3 days/2 nights.
Estancia Bello Horizonte, 20 km northwest of Puerto Maldonado, office in Puerto Maldonado, Loreto 258, T082-572748 (in **Heladería Gustitos del Cura**), www.estancia bellohorizonte.com. In a nice stretch of forest overlooking the Madre de Dios, a small lodge with bungalows for 25 people, with private bath, hammock and pool. 3 days/2 nights US$95-140, depending on the package. It is part of the scheme to train and employ young people. Suitable for those wanting to avoid a river trip.
Reserva Amazónica Lodge, 45 mins by boat down the Río Madre de Dios. To book: **Inkaterra**, Andalucía 174, Lima 18, T01-610 0400, Cuzco T084- 245314, Puerto Maldonado T082-572283, www.inkaterra. com. A hotel in the jungle with 6 suites with electricity and hot water, and 38 rustic bungalows, solar power, good food. Caters mainly for large groups. Jungle tours available with multilingual guides, the lodge is surrounded by its own 10,000-ha reserve but most tours go to Lago Sandoval, US$120 per person (double occupancy) for 2 days/1 night package, rising to US$370 for 5 days/ 4 nights, a naturalists programme is also provided, negotiable out of season. Has the largest number of ant species recorded in a single location, 362. The lodge has a 350-m canopy walkway, two 30-m canopy viewing towers and a Monkey Island (Isla Rolín).
Sandoval Lake Lodge, to book, **InkaNatura**, Manuel Bañón 461, San Isidro, Lima, T01-440 2022, www.inkanatura.com. Also have an office in Cuzco. 1 km beyond Mejía on Lago Sandoval, usually accessed by canoe across the lake after a 3-km walk or rickshaw ride along the trail, this lodge, on a *cocha*, is part-owned by local brazil-nut collectors. It can accommodate 50 people in 25 rooms, bar and dining area, electricity, hot water. There is a system of trails nearby, guides are available in several languages. Price for 3 days/2 nights is US$215.

Río Tambopata

Albergue Inotawa, T082-572511, www.inotawaexpeditions.com. On the Tambopata, just downstream from **Explorer's Inn**, visits are made to the nearby Lago Tres Chimbadas. It is part of the scheme to show visitors the life of long-term colonists in the Tambopata area; facilities are quite basic. Most rooms have bath, food, mosquito net, English- and Spanish-speaking guides. 3 days/2 nights costs US$160.

Casa de Hospedaje Picaflor, Casilla 105, Puerto Maldonado, picaflor_rc@yahoo.com. A small (4 rooms), family-run guesthouse with solar lighting, a good library, great cakes and fresh bread baked daily. It's located just downriver from **Libertador Tambopata Lodge**, guiding in English/Spanish, good trail system, visits also made to Lake Condenados. Suited to birders and backpackers wanting a more intimate rainforest experience, US$20 per person per night plus TNR fee and transport. Special arrangements also for researchers and volunteers wanting to stay 4 or more weeks.

Casas de Hospedaje Baltimore, several families in the community of Baltimore on the banks of the Río Tambopata, 60 km upriver, www.baltimoreperu.com. They are developing accommodation for visitors (with EU funding), 4-12 tourists per home. They offer the opportunity to experience the forest close-up, and an insight into daily life in the forest at a more economical price. Prices vary depending on method of access: about US$120, 3 days/2 nights. Guiding in Spanish; English-speaking guide can be arranged. Researchers and volunteers also welcomed by arrangement.

Explorer's Inn, book through **Peruvian Safaris**, Alcanfores 459, Miraflores, Lima, T01-447 8888, or Plateros 365, T084-235342 Cuzco, www.peruviansafaris.com. The office in Puerto Maldonado is at Fonavi H15, T/F082-572078. The lodge is located adjoining the TNR, in the part where most research work has been done, 58 km from Puerto Maldonado. It's a 2½-hr ride up the Río Tambopata (1½ hrs return, in the early morning, so take warm clothes and rain gear), one of the best places in Peru for seeing jungle birds (more than 580 species have been recorded here), butterflies (more than 1230 species), also giant river otters, but you probably need more than a 2-day tour to benefit fully from the location. Offers tours through the adjoining community of La Torre to meet local people and find out about their farms (*chacras*) and handicrafts. The guides are biologists and naturalists from around the world who undertake research in the reserve in return for acting as guides. They provide interesting wildlife treks, including to the macaw lick (*collpa*), 5 days/4 nights costing US$450.

Libertador Tambopata Lodge, on the Río Tambopata, make reservations at Suecia 343, Cuzco, T084-245695, www.tambopatalodge.com. Associated with the **Libertador** hotel chain, the lodge has rooms with solar-heated water, accommodates 60. Good guides, excellent food. Trips go to Lake Condenado, some to Lake Sachavacayoc, and to the Collpa de Chuncho, guiding mainly in English and Spanish, package US$200 per person for 3 days/2 nights. Naturalists programme provided.

Posada Amazonas Lodge, on the Tambopata river, 2 hrs upriver from Puerto Maldonado. Book through **Rainforest Expeditions**, Aramburú 166, of 4B, Miraflores, Lima 18, T01-421 8347, or Portal de Carnes 236, Cuzco, T084-246243, www.perunature.com. A unique collaboration between a tour agency and the local community of Infierno. 24 large attractive rooms with bathroom, cold showers, visits to Lake Tres Chimbadas, with good birdwatching opportunities including the Tambopata Collpa. Offers trips to a nearby indigenous primary health care project where a native healer gives guided tours of the medicinal plant garden. Tourist income has helped the centre become self-funding. Service and guiding is very good. Recommended. Prices start at US$190 for a 3 day/2 night package.

They also offer 5 days/4 nights for US$690, staying at the **Tambopata Research Centre**. Rooms are smaller than those at the **Posada Amazonas**, shared showers, cold water (the TRC has had to be renewed because of river encroachment, but it's as good as ever). The lodge is next to the famous Tambopata macaw clay lick. Tapir are often seen here on the bank opposite the *collpa*.

Refugio Amazonas, was opened in 2005 close to Lago Condenados. It is the usual stopover for those visiting the *collpa*. 3 bungalows accommodate 70 people in en suite rooms, large, kerosene-lit, open bedrooms with mosquito nets, well-designed and run, atmospheric. Prices as for **Posada Amazonas Lodge** (see above).

Wasai Lodge, on the Río Tambopata, 120 km (4½ hrs) upriver from Puerto Maldonado, T082-572290, 3 hrs return, same owners as **Hotel Wasai** in town; www.wasai.com. Small lodge with 7 bungalows for 40 people, 20 km of trails around the lodge, guides in English and Spanish. 3 days/2 nights costs US$300; including 1 night in **Hotel Wasai**; 5 days/4 nights costs US$400, including 1 night in the hotel and a visit to Collpa de Chuncho.

See also Activities and tours, page 564.

Río Las Piedras

Amazon Rainforest Conservation Centre, contact Pepe Moscoso, Jr Los Cedros B-17, Los Castaños, Puerto Maldonado, T082-573655, www.laspiedrasamazon.com. Roughly 8 hrs up Río Las Piedras, in a magnificent location overlooking Lago Soledad, a beautiful oxbow lake, which has a family of giant otters. Surrounding the lodge is a 7000-ha private reserve. 8 comfortable bungalows, with bath, hot water, small balcony. Activities include a viewing platform 35 m up an ironwood tree, a hide overlooking a macaw lick, and walks on the extensive trail network. Most trips break the river journey half way at Tipishca Camp, overlooking an oxbow lake with a family of otters. A 6-day/5-night programme with 5-7 people costs US$985.

Las Piedras Biodiversity Station is, in effect, a *casa de hospedaje*, T/F082-573922, www.rainforestresearch.netfirms.com. A small lodge in a 4000-ha concession of 'primary' rainforest 90 km up the Río Las Piedras. Visitors camp en route to the lodge. With only 20 beds in 10 rooms the lodge looks to offer a more personalized experience of the rainforest. Central dining room, shared bath, no electricity, library, guiding in English/ Spanish. Owing to the remoteness of the lodge the minimum package is for 4 days/3 nights, US$470 per person based on a group of 4 people. Special rates offered for those wanting to stay longer than 2 weeks.

To Iberia and Iñapari *p555*

G **Hostal Aquino**, Iberia, Km 168. The better of the 2 hotels here. Basic, cold shower.

G **Hostal Milagros**, Iñapari, at the end of the road, Km 235. Of the 2 basic hotels here, this is the better. With restaurant.

G In Assis Brasil, across the border, there are 3 hotels, and a good *churrascaría*.

Eating

Puerto Maldonado *p551, map p552*

The best restaurant in town is at the **Hotel Wasai**, the best lunchtime menu is at the **Cabañaquinta**.

¥¥-¥ **Carne Brava**, on the Plaza de Armas. One of the smart new joints for a steak and chips. Similar, also on the Plaza, is **Vaka Loca**.

¥¥-¥ **El Califa**, Piura 266. Often has bushmeat, mashed banana and palm hearts on the menu. Recommended.

¥¥-¥ **El Hornito/Chez Maggy**, on the plaza. Cosy atmosphere, good pizzas, but pasta dishes are not such good value.

El Buen Paladar, González Prada 365. Good-value lunch menu.

La Casa Nostra, Av León Velarde 515. The best place for snacks and cakes.

La Estrella, Av León Velarde 474. The smartest and best of the *pollo a la brasa* places.

Cafés

Gustitos del Cura, Loreto 258, Plaza de Armas. An ice cream parlour run by a project for homeless teenagers, offering delicious and unusual flavours such as lúcuma and brazil nut, only US$0.30 for a large cone!

Tu Dulce Espera, Av L Velarde 475. Good for evening juices and snacks.

Bars and clubs

Puerto Maldonado *p551, map p552*

Coconut, east side of the plaza. Disco.

El Witite, Av León Velarde 153. A popular, good disco, latin music, open Fri and Sat.

Le Boulevard, behind El Hornito. Live music, popular.

T-Saica, Loreto 335. An atmospheric bar with live music at weekends.

There is a billiard hall at **Puno 520**.

Activities and tours

Manu Biosphere Reserve *p548, map p549*

The tour operators listed below are situated in Cuzco, the gateway to the reserve.

Amazon Trails Peru, Tandapata 660, Cuzco (aso at Triunfo 342), T084-437499, T084-974 1735 (mob), www.amazontrailsperu.com. Small agency operated by Abraham Huaman León who has many years' experience guiding in the region. Mainly offers interesting itineraries in the buffer zones surrounding Manu, but trips to the former Reserved Zone (now part of the National Park) are possible. Well organized and recommended.

Expediciones Vilca, Plateros 363, T084-251872, www.cbc.org.pe/manuvilca/. Manu jungle tours: 8 days/7 nights, other lengths of stay are available. Will supply sleeping bags at no extra cost. Minimum 5 people, maximum 10 per guide. This is the only economical tour which camps at the Otorongo camp, which is supposedly quieter than Salvador where many agencies camp. There are discounts for students and SAE members. Very efficient, good service.

InkaNatura Travel, Gran Hotel Chiclayo (lobby), Chiclayo, T074-209948 (Plateros 361, Cuzco, T084-255255; Manuel Bañón 461, San Isidro, Lima, T01-4402022), www.inkanatura.com. A non-profit organization with proceeds directed back into projects on sustainable tourism and conservation. Arranges trips to the Manu Reserved Zone, Manu Wildlife Centre, The Biotrip, 6 days/ 5 nights, which takes you through the Andes to lowland jungle, and Sandoval Lake Lodge in

Tambopata. They sell a book called *Peru's Amazonian Eden – Manu*, US$80, proceeds go to the projects. The same title can be found in other bookshops at a much inflated price. 10% discount on all trips for **Footprint** readers.

Manu Ecological Adventures, Plateros 356, T084-261640, www.manuadventures.com. Manu jungle tours, either economical tour in and out overland, or in by land and out by plane, giving you longer in the jungle, both leave on Sun. Other lengths of stay are available leaving on Mon and Tue. Options include a mountain biking descent through the cloudforest and 3 hrs of whitewater rafting on the way to **Erika Lodge** on the upper Río Madre de Dios. They operate with a minimum of 4 people and a maximum of 10 people per guide.

Manu Expeditions, Humberto Vidal Unda G-5, p 2, Urb Magisterial, T084-226671, www.manuexpeditions.com. English spoken, Mon-Fri 0900-1300, 1500-1900; Sat 0900-1300. Run by ornithologist and British Consul Barry Walker of the **Cross Keys Pub**. 3 trips available to the reserve and Manu Wildlife Centre. 2 of the trips on 1st Sun of every month visit a lodge run by Machiguenga people and cost an extra US$150.

Manu Nature Tours, Av Pardo 1046, T084-252721, www.manuperu.com. Owned by Boris Gómez Luna, English spoken. This company aims more for the luxury end of the market and owns 2 comfortable lodges in the cloudforest and Reserved Zone. Tours are very much based around these sites, thus entailing less travel between different areas. **Manu Lodge** has an extensive trail system and also offers canopy climbing for an additional US$45 per person. In the cloudforest zone a novel 'llama taxi' service is run by the local community of Jajahuana.

Oropéndola, Santa Teresa 379, interior p 2, T084-241428, www.oropendolaperu.org. Guide Walter Mancilla is an expert on flora and fauna. A new company for Manu, using lodges run by indigenous communities. Good reports of attention to detail and to the needs of clients.

Pantiacolla Tours, Saphi 554, T084-238323, www.pantiacolla.com. Manu jungle tours: 5- and 7-day trips include return flights, the 9-day trip is an overland return. Prices do not include park entrance fee. Guaranteed departure dates regardless of number, maximum 10 people per guide. The trips involve a combination of camping, platform camping and lodges. All clients are given a booklet entitled *Talking About Manu*, written by the Dutch owner, Marianne van Vlaardingen, who is a biologist. She is extremely friendly and helpful. Marianne and her Peruvian husband Gustavo have recently opened an ecotourism lodge in conjunction with the Yine native community of Diamante. Yine guides are used and community members are being trained in the various aspects of running the project.

Puerto Maldonado *p551, map p552*

The usual price for trips to Lago Sandoval is US$25 per person per day (minimum of 2 people), and US$35 per person per day for longer trips lasting 2-4 days (minimum of 4-6 people). All guides should have a carnet issued by the Ministry of Tourism (DIRCETUR), which also verifies them as suitable guides for trips to other places and confirms their identity. Check that the carnet has not expired. Reputable guides are **Hernán Llave Cortez, Romel Nacimiento** and the **Mejía** brothers, all of whom can be contacted on arrival at the airport, if available. Also recommended: **Víctor Yohamona**, T082-968 6279 (mob), victorguideperu@hotmail.com. Speaks English, French and German. Boat hire can be arranged through the Capitanía del Puerto (Río Madre de Dios), T082-573003, about US$10 (beware overcharging).

Ceiba Tours, Av L Velarde 420, T082-573567, turismomejia@hotmail.com. Organize local trips, including to their own lodge at Lago Sandoval.

Perú Tours, Loreto 176, T082-573244, perutoursytravel@hotmail. Com. Organize local trips.

Tambopata National Reserve (TNR)
p553, map p554

Peruvian Safaris, Plateros 365, T084-235342, www.peruviansafaris.com. For reservations for the **Explorer's Inn** – excluding park entrance fees and flights.

Tambo Tours, 20919 Coral Bridge Lane, Suite 225-A, Spring, TX, 77388, USA, T 1-888-2-GO-PERU (246-7378), T001-281 528 9448, www.2GOPERU.com. See page 168.

Wasai Lodge and Expeditions, contact Las Higueras 257, Residencial Monterrico, La Molina, Lima 12, T01-436 8792, www.wasai.com. River trips. Wildlife observation, birdwatching, canoing, volunteer work, etc. For lodge, see page 559.

Transport

Manu Biosphere Reserve *p548, map p549*

Air

There is an airstrip at **Boca Manu**, but no regular flights from Cuzco. These are arranged the day before, usually by Manu tour operators, if there are enough passengers. If you want to arrange a private flight this will set you back around US$750 one way (this cost can be divided between the number of passengers). Contact **Transandes**, T084-224638, or **Aerocóndor**, T084-252774. Both airlines have offices in the Cuzco airport terminal. Flights, which use small prop-engined aircraft, are sometimes delayed by bad weather.

Road

From the Coliseo Cerrado in Cuzco 3 bus companies run to **Pilcopata** Mon, Wed, Fri, returning same night, US$10. They are fully booked even in low season. Trucks to Pilcopata run on same days, returning Tue, Thu, Sat, 10 hrs in wet season, less in the dry. Only basic supplies are available after leaving

Cuzco, so take all your camping and food essentials, including insect repellent. Transport can be disrupted in the wet season because the road is in poor condition (tour companies have latest details). *Camioneta* service runs between Pilcopata and **Salvación** to connect with the buses, Mon, Wed, Fri. The same *camionetas* run **Itahuania–Shintuya– Salvación** regularly, when there are sufficient passengers, probably once a day, and 2 trucks a day. On Sun, there is no traffic whatsoever. To **Boca Manu** you can hire a boat in Atalaya, US$212 for a *peke peke*, or US$400 for a motorboat. It's cheaper to wait or hope for a boat going empty up to Boca Manu to pick up passengers, when the fare will be US$12.50 per passenger. Itahuania–Boca Manu in a shared boat with other passengers is US$6.25. A private chartered boat would be US$105. From Itahuania, cargo boats leave for **Boca Colorado** via Boca Manu, but only when the boat is fully laden; about 6-8 a week, 9 hrs, US$15. From Boca Colorado *colectivos* run to **Puerto Maldonado**, 3 hrs. Tour operators usually use their own vehicles for the overland trip from Cuzco to Manu.

Puerto Maldonado *p551, map p552*

Air

To **Lima**, daily with **Lan** and **Aerocóndor**. Both fly via Cuzco. Combis to the airport run along Av 2 de Mayo, 10-15 mins, US$0.60. A mototaxi from town to the airport is US$2. If on the last flight of the day into Puerto Maldonado, usually Lan, don't hang around as most vehicles return to town quickly. A yellow fever vaccination is offered free, but check that a new needle is used.

Airline offices Lan, Av León Velarde y 2 de Mayo, T082-573677. **Aerocóndor**, Loreto 222, T082-571733.

Bus

There are daily buses from the Terminal Terrestre in **Cuzco** with **Transportes Iguazú** and **Mendivil**. Both on Av Tambopata, blocks 3 and 5 in Puerto Maldonado. 19 hrs (potentially much longer in the wet), US$15, depart 1400 from Puerto Maldonado. Another option is to go from Cuzco to **Urcos**, 1 hr, US$2.25, then look for the **Transportes Juan Carlos** bus in Urcos' main plaza. This is a Volvo truck modified with seats and windows. In the dry season this takes 26 hrs to Puerto Maldonado, US$13; it leaves about 1500 daily. There are also daily buses from **Mazuko** to Puerto Maldonado with **Transportes Bolpebra** and **Transportes Señor de la Cumbre**, 4 hrs, US$3. **Turismo Boca Colorado**, Tacna 342, T082-573435 operate *colectivos* to **Boca Colorado**, depart when full, 3 hrs, US$9.50. To **Laberinto**, combis take 50 mins, US$1.50, uncomfortable (return in the afternoon daily – see Around Puerto Maldonado, page 553). To **Juliaca**, **Transportes Madre de Dios**, Av Tambopata 1000, and **Transportes Tahuamanu**, Fizcarrald 609, daily services via San Gabán, at 1700 and 1900 respectively, 18 hrs, US$15.

Motorcycles/taxis

Scooters and mopeds can be hired from **San Francisco**, and others, on the corner of Puno and G Prada for US$1.15 per hr or US$10 per day. No deposit is required but your passport and driving licence need to be shown. Mototaxis around town charge US$0.60; riding pillion on a bike is US$0.30.

Boat

For **Boca Manu** and **Itahuania** take a *colectivo* to **Boca Colorado** (see above) and then take a cargo boat (no fixed schedule). From Itahuania there is transport to **Pilcopata** and **Cuzco** (see above under Manu Biosphere Reserve).

Tambopata National Reserve (TNR) *p553, map p554*

Boat A river taxi makes 2 journeys a week, Mon and Thu upriver, Tue and Fri down, up to 10 hrs, US$5 to travel as far as **Wasai Lodge.** It leaves Puerto Maldonado between 0600 and 0900.

To Iberia and Iñapari *p555*

The easiest way to reach the border with **Brazil** is to take one of the car *colectivos* (3 companies) that leave for the border from C Piura, 1 block from the market in **Puerto Maldonado** between 0700-0800, 4 hrs, US$10. **Transportes Bolpebra**, Av E Rivero 850, have a bus at 0900 daily, 5 hrs, US$4.50.

Directory

Puerto Maldonado *p551, map p552*

Banks BCP, cash advances with Visa, no commission on TCs (Amex only). Banco de la Nación, cash on MasterCard, quite good rates for TCs. Both are on the south side of the plaza. The best rates for cash are at the casas de cambio/gold shops on Puno 6th block, eg Cárdenas Hermanos, Puno 605. **Consulates** Bolivia, on the north side of the plaza. **Immigration** Peruvian immigration is at 26 de Diciembre 356, 1 block from the plaza, get your exit stamp here. **Internet** All over town, along Av León Velarde and most main streets. **Post** Serpost, Av León Velarde 6th block. **Telephone** Telefónica, west side of plaza, adjoining the Municipalidad. A phone office on the plaza, next to El Hornito, sells phone cards for national and international calls.

Background

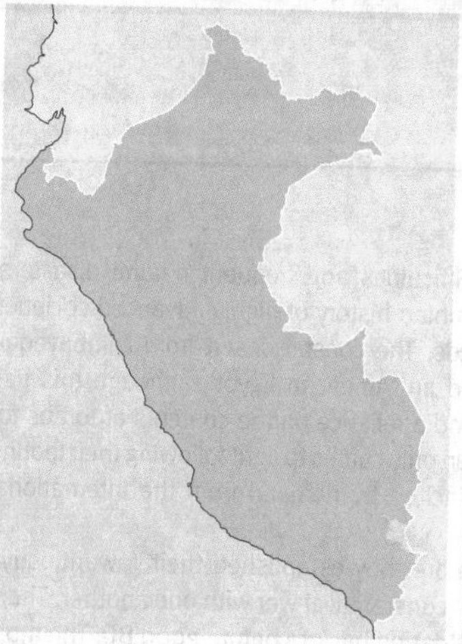

Footprint features

History

Pre-Columbian history

Despite Peru's formidable geographical difficulties and frequent natural disasters, archaeologists have uncovered a pre-Columbian history of highly advanced societies that prevailed against these awesome odds. The coastal desert from Lambayeque department south to Paracas has revealed an 'American Egypt', although this has meant a bias towards the coastal region and a reliance on the contents of tombs for information. Knowledge of these tombs often only comes to light following their looting by gangs of huaqueros (grave robbers), incited by demand from the international antiquities market.

The Incas told the Spaniards that before they established their Tawantinsuyo Empire, the land was overrun by primitives constantly at war with one another. There were, in fact, many other civilized cultures dating back to before 2000 BC. The most accomplished of these were the Chavín and Sechín (circa 900-200 BC), the Paracas-Nazca (circa 200 BC-AD 500), the Huari-Tiahuanaco (circa 750 BC-AD 1000), and the Moche-Chimú (200 BC-AD 1400).

Early settlement

It is generally accepted that the earliest settlers in Peru were related to people who had crossed the Bering Straits from Asia and drifted through the Americas from about 20,000 BC. However, theories of early migrations from across the Pacific and Atlantic have been rife since Thor Heyerdahl's raft expeditions in 1947 and 1969-1970, see also under Túcume page 410.

The earliest evidence of human presence has been found at three sites: Pikimachay near Ayacucho, Pachamachay in Junín and the Guitarrero Cave in the Callejón de Huaylas. All have a radiocarbon date prior to 9000 BC. It had been thought that village settlement in Peru, on the central coast at Pampa, dated from 2500 BC. The theory was that, between these two dates, people lived nomadically in small groups, mainly hunting and gathering but also cultivating some plants seasonally. Domestication of llamas, alpacas and guinea pigs also began at this time, particularly important for the highland people around the Titicaca basin. Caral, however, has overturned many of the accepted tenets of Peruvian archaeology for this period. Caral is a city, 20 km from the coast in the Supe Valley whose date is about 2600 BC. It is a monumental construction and appears to be easily the oldest city in South America, flourishing for some 500 years. The evidence points to complex urban society beginning much earlier than previously thought and the city seems to have had a primarily religious, rather than warlike purpose. If these deductions are correct, they also upset some long-held beliefs about city-building worldwide being principally bellicose rather than peaceful.

The abundant wealth of marine life produced by the Humboldt Current, especially along the north coast, boosted population growth and settlement in this area. Around 2000 BC climatic change dried up the lomas ('fog meadows'), and drove sea shoals to deeper water. People turned to farming and began to spread inland along river valleys.

Origins of Andean civilization

From the second millennium BC to around the first century BC is known as the Formative Period (also called Preceramic Period VI and Initial Period) when the first signs of the high culture of Andean society appeared. During this period sophisticated irrigation and canal systems were developed, farming productivity increased and communities had more time to devote to building and producing ceramics and textiles. The development of pottery also led to trade and cultural links with other communities. Distribution of land and water to the farmers was probably organized by a corporate authority, and this may have led to the later 'Mit'a' labour system developed by the Incas.

Above all, this period is characterized by the construction of centres of urban concentration (Caral notwithstanding) that promoted labour specialization and the development of cultural expression. The earliest buildings built were huacas, adobe platform mounds, centres of cult or sacred power. Huaca Florida was the largest example of this period, near the Río Rimac, later replaced by Huaca Garagay as a major centre for the area. Similar centres spread along the north coast, such as El Aspero and Piedra Parada.

During this period, however, much more advanced architecture was being built at Kotosh, in the central Andes near Huánuco. Japanese archaeological excavations there in the 1960s revealed a temple with ornamental niches and friezes. Some of the earliest pottery was also found here, showing signs of influence from southern Ecuador and the tropical lowlands, adding weight to theories of Andean culture originating in the Amazon. Radiocarbon dates of some Kotosh remains are as early as 1850 BC.

Chavín and Sechín

For the next 1000 years or so up to c 900 BC, communities grew and spread inland from the north coast and south along the northern highlands. Farmers still lived in simple adobe or rough stone houses but built increasingly large and complex ceremonial centres, such as at Las Haldas in the Casma Valley (dated at 1700 BC). As farming became more productive and pottery more advanced, commerce grew and states began to develop throughout central and North-central Peru, with the associated signs of social structure and hierarchies.

Around 900 BC a new era was marked by the rise of two important centres; **Chavín de Huantar** in the central Andes and **Sechín Alto**, inland from Casma on the north coast (some date the latter from 1600 BC).

Chavín takes its name from the site of Chavín de Huantar in the northern highlands. This was the first of several 'horizon styles' that were of the greatest importance in Peru and had very widespread influence. The other later ones, the Huari-Tiahuanaco and the Inca, were pan-Peruvian, affecting all parts of the country. The chief importance of Chavín de Huantar was not so much in its highly advanced architecture as in the influence of its cult coupled with the artistic style of its ceramics and other artefacts. The founders of Chavín may have originated in the tropical lowlands as some of its carved monoliths show representations of monkeys and felines.

Objects with Chavín traits have been found all along the coast from Piura to the Lurin valley south of Lima, and its cult ideology spread to temples around the same area. Richard L Burger of Yale University has argued that the extent of Chavín influence has been exaggerated. Many sites on the coast already had their own cult practices and the Chavín idols may have been simply added alongside. There is evidence of an El Niño flood that devastated the north coast around 500 BC. Local cults fell from grace as social order was disrupted and the Chavín cult was snatched up as a timely new alternative.

Chavín cult

The Chavín cult was paralleled by the great advances made at this time in textile production and in some of the earliest examples of metallurgy (whose origins have been attributed to some gold, silver and copper ornaments found in graves in Chongoyape, near Chiclayo, which show Chavín-style features). But earlier evidence has been discovered in the Andahuaylas region, dating from 1800-900 BC. The religious symbolism of gold and other precious metals and stones is thought to have been an inspiration behind some of the beautiful artefacts found in the central Andean area. The emergence of social hierarchies also created a demand for luxury goods as status symbols.

The cultural brilliance of Chavín de Huántar was complemented by its contemporary, **Sechín**. This huge granite-faced complex near Casma, 370 km north of Lima, was described by JC Tello as the biggest structure of its kind in the Andes. According to Michael Moseley of Harvard University, Chavín and Sechín may have combined forces, with Sechín as the military power that spread the cultural word of Chavín, but their influence did not reach far to the south where the Paracas and Tiahuanaco cultures held sway.

Upper Formative Period

The Chavín hegemony, which is also known as the Middle Formative Period (or Early Horizon), broke up around 300 BC. The 'unity' of this period was broken and the initial phase of the regional diversification of Andean cultures began. The process of domestication of plants and animals culminated in the Upper Formative Period. Agricultural technology progressed leading to an economic security that permitted a considerable growth in the centres of population. Among the many diverse stylistic/cultural groups of this period are: the Vicus on the north coast; Salinar in the Chicama valley; Paracas Necrópolis on the south coast; and Huarás in the Ancash highlands.

Paracas Necrópolis was the early phase of the Nazca culture and is renowned for the superb technical quality and stylistic variety in its weaving and pottery. The mantos (large, decorated cloth) rank amongst the world's best, and many of the finest examples can be seen in the museums of Lima. The extreme dryness of the desert here has preserved the textiles and ceramics in the mummies' tombs which have been excavated.

Paracas Necrópolis is, in fact, a cemetery located on the slopes of Cerro Colorado, in the Department of Ica, from which 429 funerary bundles were excavated (see page 290). Each bundle is a mummy wrapped in many fine and rough textiles. Paracas Necrópolis corresponds to the last of the 10 phases into which Paracas ceramics have been divided. The previous ones, known as Paracas Cavernas, relate to the Middle Formative Period and were influenced by the Chavín cult.

Nazca culture

The Regional Development Period up to about AD 500, was a time of great social and cultural development. Sizable towns of 5-10,000 inhabitants grew on the south coast, populated by artisans, merchants, government administrators and religious officials.

One of the most famous cultures of this period, or indeed of pre-Columbian history was the Nazca. The Nazca Lines are a feature of the region. Straight lines, abstract designs and outlines of animals are scratched in the desert surface forming a lighter contrast that can be seen clearly from the air. There are many theories of how and why the lines were made but no explanation has yet been able definitively to establish their place in Peruvian history (see Nazca Lines, page 301). There are similarities between the style of some of the line patterns and that of the pottery and textiles of the same period. It is clear from the scale of the lines and quality of the work that they were important to the Nazca culture.

In contrast to the quantity and quality of the Nazca artefacts found, relatively few major buildings belonging to this period have been uncovered in the southern desert. Dos Palmas is a complex of rooms and courtyards in the Pisco Valley, while Cahuachi in the Nazca Valley is a large area including adobe platforms, pyramids and a 'wooden Stonehenge' cluster of preserved tree trunks. Most recently excavated are the architectural complex of Los Molinos, with large buildings, patios and passages, and the necropolis of La Muña, both near Palpa. As most of the archaeological evidence of the Nazca culture came from their desert cemeteries, little is known about the lives and social organization of the people. Alpaca hair found in Nazca textiles, however, indicates that there must have been strong trade links with highland people.

Moche culture

Nazca's contemporaries on the north coast were the militaristic Moche who, from about AD 100-800 built up an empire whose traces stretch from Piura in the north to Casma, beyond Chimbote, in the south. The Moche built their capital in the middle of the desert, outside present day Trujillo. It features the pyramid temples of the Huaca del Sol and Huaca de la Luna (see page 390). The Moche roads and system of way stations are thought to have been an early inspiration for the Inca network. The Moche increased the coastal population with intensive irrigation projects. Skillful engineering works were carried out, such as the La Cumbre canal, still in use today, and the Ascope aqueduct.

The Moche's greatest achievement, however, was its artistic genius. Exquisite ornaments in gold, silver and precious stones were made by its craftsmen. Moche pottery progressed through five stylistic periods, most notable for the stunningly lifelike portrait vases. A wide variety of ceremonial and everyday scenes were created in naturalistic ceramics, telling us more about Moche life than is known about other earlier cultures, and perhaps used by them as 'visual aids' to compensate for the lack of a written language (see also page 393).

A spectacular discovery of a Moche royal tomb at **Sipán** was made in February 1987 by Walter Alva, director of the Brüning Archaeological Museum, Lambayeque. Reports of the excavation in the National Geographic magazine (October 1988 and June 1990), talked of the richest unlooted tomb in the New World (see page 409). The find included semi-precious stones brought from Chile and Argentina, and seashells from Ecuador (the Moche were also great navigators).

The cause of the collapse of the Moche Empire around AD 600-700 is unknown, but it may have been started by a 30-year drought at the end of the sixth century, followed by one of the periodic El Niño flash floods (identified by meteorologists from ice thickness in the Andes) and finished by the encroaching forces of the Huari Empire. The decline of the Moche signalled a general tipping of the balance of power in Peru from the north coast to the southern sierra.

Huari-Tiahuanaco

The ascendant Huari-Tiahuanaco movement, from circa AD 600-1000, combined the religious cult of the Tiahuanaco site in the Titicaca basin, with the military dynamism of the Huari, based in the central highlands. The two cultures developed independently but, as had occurred with the Chavín-Sechín association, they are generally thought to have merged compatibly.

Up until their own demise around AD 1440, the Huari-Tiahuanaco had spread their empire and influence from Cajamarca and Lambayeque in the north and across much of southern Peru, northern Bolivia and Argentina. The Huari introduced a new concept in urban life, the great walled urban centre, the best example of which is their capital city, 22 km north of Ayacucho (see page 501). They also made considerable gains in art and technology, building roads, terraces and irrigation canals across the country.

The Huari-Tiahuanaco ran their empire with efficient labour and administrative systems that were later adopted and refined by the Incas. Labour tribute for state projects had been practised by the Moche and was further developed now. But the empire could not contain regional kingdoms who began to fight for land and power. As control broke down, rivalry and coalitions emerged, and the system collapsed.

Chimú culture

After the decline of the Huari Empire, the unity that had been imposed on the Andes was broken. A new stage of autonomous regional or local political organizations began. Among the cultures corresponding to this period were the Kuélap, centred in the Chachapoyas region (see page 455), and the Chimú.

The Chimú culture had two centres. To the north was Lambayeque, near Chiclayo, while to the south, in the Moche valley near present-day Trujillo, was the great adobe walled city of Chan Chán. Covering 20 sq km, this was the largest prehispanic Peruvian city (see page 391).

Chimú has been classified as a despotic state that based its power on wars of conquest. Rigid social stratification existed and power rested in the hands of the great lord Siquic and the lord Alaec. These lords were followed in social scale by a group of urban couriers who enjoyed a certain degree of economic power. At the bottom were the peasants and slaves. In 1450, the Chimú kingdom was conquered by the Inca Túpac Yupanqui, the son and heir of the Inca ruler Pachacuti Inca Yupanqui.

Inca Dynasty

The origins of the Inca Dynasty are shrouded in mythology. The best known story reported by the Spanish chroniclers talks about Manco Cápac and his sister rising out of Lake Titicaca, created by the Sun as divine founders of a chosen race. This was in approximately AD 1200. Over the next 300 years the small tribe grew to supremacy as leaders of the largest empire ever known in the Americas, the four territories of Tawantinsuyo, united by Cuzco as the umbilicus of the Universe. The four quarters of Tawantinsuyo, all radiating out from Cuzco, were: 1 Chinchaysuyo, north and northwest; 2 Cuntisuyo, south and west; 3 Collasuyo, south and east; 4 Antisuyo, east.

At its peak, just before the Spanish Conquest, the Inca Empire stretched from the Río Maule in central Chile, north to the present Ecuador-Colombia border, containing most of Ecuador, Peru, western Bolivia, northern Chile and northwest Argentina. The area was roughly equivalent to France, Belgium, Holland, Luxembourg, Italy and Switzerland combined (980,000 sq km).

The first Inca ruler, Manco Cápac, moved to the fertile Cuzco region, and established Cuzco as his capital. Successive generations of rulers were fully occupied with local conquests of rivals, such as the Colla and Lupaca to the south, and the Chanca to the northwest. At the end of Inca Viracocha's reign the hated Chanca were finally defeated, largely thanks to the heroism of one of his sons, Pachacútec Inca Yupanqui, who was subsequently crowned as the new ruler.

From the start of Pachacútec's own reign in 1438, imperial expansion grew in earnest. With the help of his son and heir, Topa Inca, territory was conquered from the Titicaca basin south into Chile, and all the north and central coast down to the Lurin Valley. The Incas also subjugated the Chimú, their highly sophisticated rivals on the coast (see above). Typical of the Inca method of government, some of the Chimú skills were assimilated into their own political and administrative system, and some Chimú nobles were even given positions in Cuzco.

Perhaps the pivotal event in Inca history came in 1527 with the death of the ruler, Huayna Capac. Civil war broke out in the confusion over his rightful successor. One of his legitimate sons, Huáscar, ruled the southern part of the empire from Cuzco. Atahualpa, Huáscar's half-brother, governed Quito, the capital of Chinchaysuyo. In 1532, soon after Atahualpa had won the civil war, Francisco Pizarro arrived in Tumbes

According to legend, the Incas were a small group who originally lived near Lake Titicaca. They later moved to Cuzco, from where they expanded to create their empire of Tawantinsuyo.

with 179 conquistadores, many on horseback. Atahualpa's army was marching south, probably for the first time, when he clashed with Pizarro at Cajamarca.

Francisco Pizarro's only chance against the formidable imperial army he encountered at Cajamarca was a bold stroke. He drew Atahualpa into an ambush, slaughtered his guards, promised him liberty if a certain room were filled with treasure, and finally killed him after receiving news that another Inca army was on its way to free him. Pushing on to Cuzco, he was at first hailed as the executioner of a traitor: Atahualpa had ordered the death of Huáscar in 1533, while himself a captive of Pizarro, and his victorious generals were bringing the defeated Huáscar to see his half-brother. Panic followed when the conquistadores set about sacking the city, and they fought off with difficulty an attempt by Manco Inca to recapture Cuzco in 1536.

Inca society

The Incas were a small aristocracy numbering only a few thousand, centred in the highland city of Cuzco, at 3400 m. They rose gradually as a small regional dynasty, similar to others in the Andes of that period, starting around AD 1200. Then in the mid-1400s, they began to expand explosively under Pachacútec, a sort of Andean Alexander the Great, and later his son, Topa. Under a hundred years later, they fell before the rapacious warriors of Spain. The Incas were not the first dynasty in Andean history to dominate their neighbours, but they did it more thoroughly and went further than anyone before them.

Empire building

Enough remains today of their astounding highways, cities and agricultural terracing for people to marvel and wonder how they accomplished so much in so short a time. They seem to have been amazingly energetic, industrious and efficient – and the reports of their Spanish conquerors confirm this hypothesis.

They must also have had the willing cooperation of most of their subject peoples, most of the time. In fact, the Incas were master diplomats and alliance-builders first, and military conquerors only second, if the first method of expansion failed. The Inca skill at generating wealth by means of highly efficient agriculture and distribution brought them enormous prestige and enabled them to 'out-gift' neighbouring chiefs in huge royal feasts involving ritual outpourings of generosity, often in the form of vast gifts of textiles, exotic products from distant regions, and perhaps wives to add blood ties to the alliance. The 'out-gifted' chief was required by the Andean laws of reciprocity to provide something in return, and this would usually be his loyalty, as well as a levy of manpower from his own chiefdom.

Thus, with each new alliance the Incas wielded greater labour forces and their mighty public works programmes surged ahead. These were administered through an institution known as mit'a, a form of taxation through labour. The state provided the materials, such as wool and cotton for making textiles, and the communities provided skills and labour.

Mit'a contingents worked royal mines, royal plantations for producing coca leaves, royal quarries and so on. The system strove to be equitable, and workers in such hardship posts as high altitude mines and lowland coca plantations were given correspondingly shorter terms of service.

Organization

Huge administrative centres were built in different parts of the empire, where people and supplies were gathered. Articles such as textiles and pottery were produced there in large workshops. Work in these places was carried out in a festive manner, with plentiful food, drink and music. Here was Andean reciprocity at work: the subject supplied his labour, and the ruler was expected to provide generously while he did so.

Aside from mit'a contributions there were also royal lands claimed by the Inca as his portion in every conquered province, and worked for his benefit by the local population. Thus, the contribution of each citizen to the state was quite large, but apparently, the imperial economy was productive enough to sustain this.

Another institution was the practice of moving populations around: inserting loyal groups into restive areas, and removing recalcitrant populations to loyal areas. These movements of *mitmakuna*, as they were called, were also used to introduce skilled farmers and engineers into areas where productivity needed to be raised.

Communications

The huge empire was held together by an extensive and highly efficient highway system. There were an estimated 30,000 km of major highway, most of it neatly paved and drained, stringing together the major Inca sites. Two parallel highways ran north to south, along the coastal desert strip and the mountains, and dozens of east-west roads crossing from the coast to the Amazon fringes. These roadways took the most direct routes, with wide stone stairways zig-zagging up the steepest mountain slopes and rope suspension bridges crossing the many narrow gorges of the Andes. The north-south roads formed a great axis which eventually came to be known as **Capaq Ñan** – "Royal, or Principal Road", in Quechua – which exceeded in grandeur not only the other roads, but also their utilitarian concept. They became the Incas' symbol of power over men and over the sacred forces of nature. So marvellous were these roads that the Spaniards who saw them at the height of their glory said that there was nothing comparable in all Christendom.

Every 12 km or so there was a tambo, or way station, where goods could be stored and travellers lodged. The tambos were also control points, where the Inca state's accountants tallied movements of goods and people. Even more numerous than tambos, were the huts of the chasquis, or relay runners, who continually sped royal and military messages along these highways.

The Inca state kept records and transmitted information in various ways. Accounting and statistical records were kept on skeins of knotted strings known as quipus. Numbers employed the decimal system (although Italian engineer Nicolino De Pasquale claimed in 2006 the number system was based on 40), and colours indicated the categories being recorded. An entire class of people, known as quipucamayocs, existed whose job was to create and interpret these. Neither the Incas nor their Andean predecessors had a system of writing as we understand it, but there may have been a system of encoding language into quipus. Archaeologists are studying this problem today. History and other forms of knowledge were transmitted via songs and poetry. Music and dancing, full of encoded information which could be read by the educated elite, were part of every major ceremony and public event information was also carried in textiles, which had for millennia been the most vital expression of Andean culture.

Textiles

Clothing carried insignia of status, ethnic origin, age and so on. Special garments were made and worn for various rites of passage. It has been calculated that, after agriculture, no activity was more important to Inca civilization than weaving. Vast stores of textiles were maintained to sustain the Inca system of ritual giving. Armies and mit'a workers were partly paid in textiles. The finest materials were reserved for the nobility, and the Inca emperor himself displayed his status by changing into new clothes every day and having the previous day's burned.

Most weaving was done by women, and the Incas kept large numbers of 'chosen women' in female-only houses all over the empire, partly for the purpose of supplying textiles to the elite and for the many deities, to whom they were frequently given as burned offerings. These women had other duties, such as making *chicha* – the Inca corn beer which was consumed and sacrificed in vast quantities on ceremonial occasions. They also became wives and concubines to the Inca elite and loyal nobilities. And some may have served as priestesses of the moon, in parallel to the male priesthood of the sun.

Religious worship

The Incas have always been portrayed as sun-worshippers, but it now seems that they were mountain-worshippers too. Recent research has shown that Machu Picchu was at least partly dedicated to the worship of the surrounding mountains, and Inca sacrificial victims have been excavated on frozen Andean peaks at 6700 m. In fact, until technical climbing was invented, the Incas held the world altitude record for humans.

Human sacrifice was not common, but every other kind was, and ritual attended every event in the Inca calendar. The main temple of Cuzco was dedicated to the numerous deities: the Sun, the Moon, Venus, the Pleiades, the Rainbow, Thunder and Lightning, and the countless religious icons of subject peoples which had been brought to Cuzco, partly in homage, partly as hostage. Here, worship was continuous and the fabulous opulence included gold cladding on the walls, and a famous garden filled with life-size objects of gold and silver. Despite this pantheism, the Incas acknowledged an overall Creator God, whom they called Viracocha. A special temple was dedicated to him, at Raqchi, about 100 km southeast of Cuzco. Part of it still stands today.

Military forces

The conquering Spaniards noted with admiration the Inca storehouse system, still well-stocked when they found it, despite several years of civil war among the Incas. Besides textiles, military equipment, and ritual objects, they found huge quantities of food. Like most Inca endeavours, the food stores served a multiple purpose: to supply feasts, to provide during lean times, to feed travelling work parties, and to supply armies on the march.

Inca armies were able to travel light and move fast because of this system. Every major Inca settlement also incorporated great halls where large numbers of people could be accommodated, or feasts and gatherings held, and large squares or esplanades for public assemblies.

Inca technology is usually deemed inferior to that of contemporary Europe. Their military technology certainly was. They had not invented iron-smelting, and basically fought with clubs, palmwood spears, slings, wooden shields, cotton armour and straw-stuffed helmets. They did not even make much use of the bow and arrow, a weapon they were well aware of. Military tactics, too, were primitive. The disciplined formations of the Inca armies quickly dissolved into melees of unbridled individualism once battle was joined. This, presumably, was because warfare constituted a theatre of manly prowess, but was not the main priority of Inca life. Its form was ritualistic. Battles were suspended by both sides for religious observance. Negotiation, combined with displays of superior Inca strength, usually achieved victory, and total annihilation of the enemy was not on the agenda.

Architecture

Other technologies, however, were superior in every way to their 16th century counterparts: textiles; settlement planning; and agriculture in particular with its sophisticated irrigation and soil conservation systems, ecological sensitivity, specialized crop strains and high productivity under the harshest conditions. The Incas fell short of their Andean predecessors in the better-known arts of ancient America – ceramics, textiles and metalwork – but it could be argued that their supreme efforts were made in architecture, stoneworking, landscaping, roadbuilding, and the harmonious combination of these elements.

These are the outstanding survivals of Inca civilization, which still remain to fascinate the visitor: the huge, exotically close-fit blocks of stone, cut in graceful, almost sensual curves; the astoundingly craggy and inaccessible sites encircled by great sweeps of Andean scenery; the rhythmic layers of farm terracing that provided land and food to this still-enigmatic people. The finest examples of Inca architecture can be seen in the city of Cuzco and throughout the Sacred Valley. As more evidence of Inca society is uncovered each year, our knowledge of these remarkable people can only improve: in 2002 alone two new cities in the Vilcabamba region were revealed, as well as the huge cemetery at Purucucho (see Excursions from Lima section, page 99) and a mummy at Machu Picchu.

Ruling elite

The ruling elite lived privileged lives in their capital at Cuzco. They reserved for themselves and privileged insiders certain luxuries, such as the chewing of coca, the wearing of fine vicuña wool, and the practice of polygamy. But they were an austere people, too. Everyone had work to do, and the nobility were constantly being posted to state business throughout the empire. Young nobles were expected to learn martial skills, besides being able to read the quipus, speak both Quechua and the southern language of Aymara, and know the epic poems.

The Inca elite belonged to royal clans known as panacas, which each had the unusual feature of being united around veneration of the mummy of their founding ancestor – a previous Inca emperor, unless they happened to belong to the panaca founded by the Inca emperor who was alive at the time. Each new emperor built his own palace in Cuzco and amassed his own wealth rather than inheriting it from his forebears, which perhaps helps to account for the urge to unlimited expansion.

This urge ultimately led the Incas to overreach themselves. Techniques of diplomacy and incorporation no longer worked as they journeyed farther from the homeland and met ever-increasing resistance from people less familiar with their ways. During the reign of Wayna Cápac, the last emperor before the Spanish invasion, the Incas had to establish a northern capital at Quito in order to cope with permanent war on their northern frontier. Following Wayna Cápac's death came a devastating civil war between Cuzco and Quito, and immediately thereafter came the Spanish invasion. Tawantisuyo, the empire of the four quarters, collapsed with dizzying suddenness.

Conquest and after

Peruvian history after the arrival of the Spaniards was not just a matter of conquistadores versus Incas. The vast majority of the huge empire remained unaware of the conquest for many years. The Chimú and the Chachapoyas cultures were powerful enemies of the Incas. The Chimú developed a highly sophisticated culture and a powerful empire stretching for 560 km along the coast from Tumbes south to present-day Lima. Their history was well-recorded by the Spanish chroniclers and continued through the conquest possibly up to about 1600. The Kuélap/ Chachapoyas people were not so much an empire as a loose-knit 'confederation of ethnic groups with no recognized capital' (Morgan Davis *Chachapoyas: The Cloud People*, Ontario, 1988). But the culture did develop into an advanced society with great skill in roads and monument building. Their fortress at Kuélap was known as the most impregnable in Tawantinsuyo. It remained intact against Inca attack and Manco Inca even tried, unsuccessfully, to gain refuge here against the Spaniards.

In 1535, wishing to secure his communications with Spain, Pizarro founded Lima, near the ocean, as his capital. The same year Diego de Almagro set out to conquer Chile. Unsuccessful, he returned to Peru, quarrelled with Pizarro, and in 1538 fought a pitched battle with Pizarro's men at the Salt Pits, near Cuzco. He was defeated and put to death. Pizarro, who had not been at the battle, was assassinated in his palace in Lima by Almagro's son three years later.

For the next 27 years each succeeding representative of the Kingdom of Spain sought to subdue the Inca successor state of Vilcabamba, north of Cuzco, and to unify the fierce Spanish factions. Francisco de Toledo (appointed 1568) solved both problems during his 14 years in office: Vilcabamba was crushed in 1572 and the last reigning Inca, Túpac Amaru, put to death.

For the next 200 years the Viceroys closely followed Toledo's system, if not his methods. The Major Government – the Viceroy, the Audiencia (High Court), and corregidores (administrators) – ruled through the Minor Government – indigenous chiefs put in charge of large groups of natives – a rough approximation to the original Inca system.

Towards independence

There was an indigenous rising in 1780, under the leadership of an Inca noble who called himself Túpac Amaru II. He and many of his lieutenants were captured and put to death under torture at Cuzco. Another indigenous leader in revolt suffered the same fate in 1814, but this last flare-up had the sympathy of many of the locally born Spanish, who resented their status, inferior to the Spaniards born in Spain, the refusal to give them any but the lowest offices, the high taxation imposed by the home government, and the severe restrictions upon trade with any country but Spain.

Help came to them from the outside world. José de San Martín's Argentine troops, convoyed from Chile under the protection of Lord Cochrane's squadron, landed in southern Peru on 7 September 1820. San Martín proclaimed Peruvian independence at Lima on 28 July 1821, though most of the country was still in the hands of the Viceroy, José de La Serna. Bolívar, who had already freed Venezuela and Colombia, sent Antonio José de Sucre to Ecuador where, on 24 May 1822, he gained a victory over La Serna at Pichincha.

San Martín, after a meeting with Bolívar at Guayaquil, left for Argentina and a self-imposed exile in France, while Bolívar and Sucre completed the conquest of Peru by defeating La Serna at the battle of Junín (6 August 1824) and the decisive battle of Ayacucho (9 December 1824). For over a year there was a last stand in the Real Felipe fortress at Callao by the Spanish troops under General Rodil before they capitulated on 22 January 1826. Bolívar was invited to stay in Peru, but left for Colombia in 1826.

Post-independence Peru

Following independence Peru attempted a confederation with Bolivia in the 1830s but this proved temporary. Then, in 1879 came the disastrous War of the Pacific, in which Peru and Bolivia were defeated by Chile and Peru lost its southern territory.

Economic change

Peru's economic development since independence has been based upon the export of minerals and foodstuffs to Europe and the United States. Guano, a traditional fertilizer in Peru and derived from the manure of seabirds, was first shipped to Europe in 1841. In the three decades that followed it became an important fertilizer in Europe and by the early 1860s over 80% of the Peruvian government's revenues were derived from its export. Much of this income, though, went to pay off interest on the spiralling national debt. By the 1870s the richer deposits were exhausted and cheaper alternatives to guano were being discovered. One of these was nitrates, discovered in the Atacama desert, but Peru's defeat by Chile in the War of the Pacific ensured that she would lose her share of this wealth.

War of the Pacific

One of the major international wars in Latin America since independence, this conflict has its roots in a border dispute between Chile and Bolivia. The frontier between the two in the Atacama desert was ill-defined.

There had already been one conflict, in 1836-1839, when Chile defeated Peru and Bolivia, putting an end to a confederation of the two states. The discovery of nitrates in the Atacama only complicated relations, for in the Bolivian Atacama province of Antofagasta nitrates were exploited by Anglo-Chilean companies.

In 1878 the Bolivian government, short of revenue, attempted to tax the Chilean-owned Antofagasta Railroad and Nitrate Company. When the company refused to pay, the Bolivians seized the company's assets. The Chilean government claimed that the Bolivian action broke an 1874 agreement between the two states. When Peru announced that it would honour a secret alliance with Bolivia by supporting her, the Chilean president, Aníbal Pinto, declared war on both states.

Control of the sea was vital, and this was where Chile concentrated her efforts. Following a successful naval campaign, the Chileans invaded the southern Peruvian province of Tarapacá and then landed troops north of Tacna, seizing the town in May 1880 before capturing Arica, further south. The Chilean armies were hot stuff, and in January 1881 they seized control of Lima.

Despite these defeats and the loss of their capital, Peru did not sue for peace, although Bolivia had already signed a ceasefire, giving up her coastal province. Under the 1883 peace settlement Peru gave up Tarapacá to Chile. Although the provinces of Tacna and Arica were to be occupied by Chile for 10 years, it was not until 1929 that an agreement was reached under which Tacna was returned to Peru, while Chile kept Arica. Apart from souring relations between Chile and her two northern neighbours to this day, the War gave Chile a monopoly over the world's supply of nitrates and enabled her to dominate the southern Pacific coast.

After the decline of guano, Peru developed several new exports. In the 1890s the demand in Europe and USA for Amazonian rubber for tyres and for use in electrical components led to a brief boom in both the Brazilian and Peruvian Amazon. The Peruvian industry was based around the port of Iquitos. This boom was short-lived as cheaper rubber was soon being produced from plantations in the East Indies. Peru's colonial mineral exports, gold and silver, were replaced by copper, although ownership was mainly under control of foreign companies, particularly the US-based Cerro de Pasco Copper Corporation and Northern Peru Mining. Oil became another important product, amounting to 30% of Peruvian exports by 1930. Further exports came from sugar and cotton, which were produced on coastal plantations, see also page 585.

Social change

Independence from Spanish rule meant that power passed into the hands of the Creole elite with no immediate alternation of the colonial social system. The contribución de indíginas, the colonial tribute collected from the native peoples was not abolished until 1854, the same year as the ending of slavery.

Until the 1970s land relations in the sierra changed very little, as the older landholding families continued to exert their traditional influence over 'their' peones. The traditional elite, the so-called '44 families', were still very powerful, though increasingly divided between the coastal aristocracy with their interests in plantation agriculture and trade, and the serrano elite, more conservative and inward looking.

The pattern of export growth did, however, have major social effects on the coast. The expansion of plantation agriculture and mining led to the growth of a new labour force; this was supplied partially by Chinese indentured labourers, about 100,000 of whom arrived between 1855 and 1875, partly by the migration of indigenous people from the sierra and partly by the descendants of black slaves.

Political developments

19th century

For much of the period since independence Peruvian political life has been dominated by the traditional elites. Political parties have been slow to develop and the roots of much of the political conflict and instability which have marked the country's history lie in personal ambitions and in regional and other rivalries within the elite.

The early years after independence were particularly chaotic as rival caudillos (political bosses) who had fought in the independence wars vied with each other for power. The increased wealth brought about by the guano boom led to greater stability, though political corruption became a serious problem under the presidency of José Rufino Echenique (1851-1854) who paid out large sums of the guano revenues as compensation to upper class families for their (alleged) losses in the Wars of Independence. Defeat by Chile in the War of the Pacific discredited civilian politicians even further and led to a period of military rule in the 1880s.

Early 20th century

Even though the voting system was changed in 1898, this did little to change the dominance of the elite. Voting was not secret so landowners herded their workers to the polls and watched to make sure they voted correctly. Yet voters were also lured by promises as well as threats. One of the more unusual presidents was Guillermo Billinghurst (1912-1914) who campaigned on the promise of a larger loaf of bread for five cents, thus gaining the nickname of "Big Bread Billinghurst". As president he proposed a publicly funded housing programme, supported the introduction of an eight hour day and was eventually overthrown by the military who, along with the elite, were alarmed at his growing popularity among the urban population.

The 1920s This decade was dominated by Augusto Leguía. After winning the 1919 elections Leguía claimed that Congress was plotting to prevent him from becoming president and induced the military to help him close Congress. Backed by the armed forces, Leguía introduced a new constitution which gave him greater powers and enabled him to be re-elected in 1924 and 1929. Claiming his goal was to prevent the rise of communism, he proposed to build a partnership between business and labour. A large programme of public works, particularly involving building roads, bridges and railways, was begun, the work being carried out by poor rural men who were forced into unpaid building work. The Leguía regime dealt harshly with critics: opposition newspapers were closed and opposition leaders arrested and deported. His overthrow in 1930 ended what Peruvians call the *Oncenio* or 11 year period.

The 1920s also saw the emergence of a political thinker who would have great influence in the future, not only in Peru but elsewhere in Latin America. Juan Carlos Mariátegui, a socialist writer and journalist, argued that the solution to Peru's problems lay in the reintegration of the indigenous people through land reform and the breaking up of the great landed estates. See also page 599.

The formation of APRA Another influential thinker of this period was Víctor Raúl Haya de la Torre, a student exiled by Leguía in 1924. He returned after the latter's fall to create the Alianza Popular Revolucionaria Americana, a political party which called for state control of the economy, nationalization of key industries and protection of the middle classes, which, Haya de la Torre argued, were threatened by foreign economic interests.

In 1932 APRA seized control of Trujillo; when the army arrived to deal with the rising, the rebels murdered about 50 hostages, including 10 army officers. In reprisal the army murdered about 1000 local residents suspected of sympathizing with APRA. APRA eventually became the largest and easily the best-organized political party in Peru, but the distrust of the military and the upper class for Haya de la Torre ensured that he never became president.

A turning point in Peruvian history occurred in 1948 with the seizure of power by General Manuel Odría, backed by the coastal elite. Odría outlawed APRA and went on to win the 1950 election in which he was the only candidate. He pursued policies of encouraging export earnings and also tried to build up working class support by public works projects in Lima. Faced with a decline in export earnings and the fall in world market prices after 1953, plus increasing unemployment, Odría was forced to stand down in 1956.

In 1962 Haya de la Torre was at last permitted to run for the presidency. But although he won the largest percentage of votes he was prevented from taking office by the armed forces who seized power and organized fresh elections for 1963. In these the military obtained the desired result: Haya de la Torre came second to Fernando Belaúnde Terry. Belaúnde attempted to introduce reforms, particularly in the landholding structure of the sierra; when these reforms were weakened by landowner opposition in Congress, peasant groups began invading landholdings in protest.

At the same time, under the influence of the Cuban revolution, terrorist groups began operating in the sierra. Military action to deal with this led to the deaths of an estimated 8000 people. Meanwhile Belaúnde's attempts to solve a long-running dispute with the International Petroleum Company (a subsidiary of Standard Oil) resulted in him being attacked for selling out to the unpopular oil company and contributed to the armed forces' decision to seize power in 1968.

The 1968 coup

This was a major landmark in Peruvian history. Led by General Juan Velasco Alvarado, the Junta had no intention of handing power back to the civilians. A manifesto issued on the day of the coup attacked the 'unjust social and economic order' and argued for its replacement by a new economic system 'neither capitalist nor communist'. Partly as a result of their experiences in dealing with the insurgency, the coup leaders concluded that agrarian reform was a priority.

Wide-ranging land reform was launched in 1969, during which large estates were taken over and reorganized into cooperatives. By the mid-1970s, 75% of productive land was under cooperative management. The government also tried to improve the lives of shanty-town dwellers around Lima, as well as attempting to increase the influence of workers in industrial companies. At the same time efforts were made to reduce the influence of foreign companies. Soon after the coup, IPC was nationalized, to be followed by other transnationals including ITT, Chase Manhattan Bank and the two mining giants Cerro de Pasco and Marcona Mining. After a dispute with the US government, compensation was agreed.

Understandably, opposition to the Velasco government came from the business and landholding elite. The government's crack-down on expressions of dissent, the seizure of newspapers and taking over of TV and radio stations all offended sections of the urban middle class. Trade unions and peasant movements found that, although they agreed with many of the regime's policies, it refused to listen and expected their passive and unqualified support. As world sugar and copper prices dropped, inflation rose and strikes increased. Velasco's problems were further increased by opposition within the armed forces and by his own ill-health. In August 1975 he was replaced by General Francisco Morales Bermúdez, a more conservative officer, who dismantled some of Velasco's policies and led the way to a restoration of civilian rule.

Belaúnde returned to power in 1980 by winning the first elections after military rule. His government was badly affected by the 1982 debt crisis and the 1981-1983 world recession, and inflation reached over 100% a year in 1983-1984. His term was also marked by the growth of the Maoist movement Sendero Luminoso (Shining Path) and the smaller, Marxist **Túpac Amaru** (MRTA) – see box page, 583.

Initially conceived in the University of Ayacucho, Shining Path gained most support for its goal of overthrowing the whole system of Lima-based government from highland indigenous and migrants to urban shanty towns. The activities of Sendero Luminoso and Túpac Amaru (MRTA) were effectively curtailed after the arrest of both their leaders in 1992. Víctor Polay of MRTA was arrested in June and Abimael Guzmán of Sendero Luminoso was captured in September. Although Sendero did not capitulate, many of its members in 1994-1995 took advantage of the Law of Repentance, which guaranteed lighter sentences in return for surrender, and freedom in exchange for valuable information. Meanwhile, Túpac Amaru was thought to have ceased operations (see below).

In 1985 APRA, in opposition for over 50 years, finally came to power. With Haya de la Torre dead, the APRA candidate Alan García Pérez won the elections and was allowed to take office by the armed forces. García attempted to implement an ambitious economic programme intended to solve many of Peru's deep-seated economic and social problems. He cut taxes, reduced interest rates, froze prices and devalued the currency. However, the economic boom which this produced in 1986-1987 stored up problems as increased incomes were spent on imports. Moreover, the government's refusal to pay more than 10% of its foreign debt meant that it was unable to borrow. In 1988 inflation hit 3000% and unemployment soared. By the time his term of office ended in 1990 Peru was bankrupt and García and APRA were discredited.

Modern Peru

Peru under Fujimori

In presidential elections held over two rounds in 1990, **Alberto Fujimori** of the Cambio 90 movement defeated the novelist **Mario Vargas Llosa**, who belonged to the Fredemo (Democratic Front) coalition. Fujimori, without an established political network behind him, failed to win a majority in either the senate or the lower house. Lack of congressional support was one of the reasons behind the dissolution of congress and the suspension of the constitution on 5 April 1992. The president declared that he needed a freer hand to introduce market reforms and combat terrorism and drug trafficking, at the same time as rooting out corruption.

In elections to a new, 80-member Democratic Constituent Congress (CCD) in November 1992, Fujimori's Cambio 90/Nueva Mayoría coalition won a majority of seats. Though three major political parties, APRA, Acción Popular and the Movimiento de Libertad, boycotted the elections, they satisfied many aid donor's requirements for the resumption of financial assistance.

A new constitution drawn up by the CCD was approved by a narrow majority of the electorate in October 1993. Among the new articles were the immediate re-election of the president (previously prohibited for one presidential term), the establishment of a single-chamber congress, the designation of Peru as a market economy and the favouring of foreign investment. As expected, Fujimori stood for re-election on 9 April 1995 and the opposition chose as an independent to stand against him former UN General Secretary, Javier Pérez de Cuéllar. Fujimori was re-elected by a resounding margin, winning about 65% of the votes cast. The coalition that supported him also won a majority in Congress.

The government's success in most economic areas did not appear to accelerate the distribution of foreign funds for social projects. Rising unemployment and the austerity imposed by economic policy continued to cause hardship for many, despite the government's stated aim of alleviating poverty.

Dramatic events on 17 December 1996 thrust several of these issues into sharper focus: 14 Túpac Amaru terrorists infiltrated a reception at the Japanese Embassy in Lima, taking 490 hostages. Among the rebel's demands were the release of their imprisoned colleagues, better treatment for prisoners and new measures to raise living standards. Most of the hostages were released and negotiations were pursued during a stalemate that lasted until 22 April 1997. The president took sole responsibility for the successful, but risky assault which freed all the hostages (one died of heart failure) and killed all the terrorists. By not yielding to Túpac Amaru, Fujimori regained much popularity.

But this masked the fact that no steps had been taken to ease social problems. It also deflected attention from Fujimori's plans to stand for a third term following his unpopular manipulation of the law to persuade Congress that the new constitution did not apply to his first period in office. His chances of winning looked remote as demands grew for a more open, democratic approach, though opposition to his standing for a third term of office remained fragmented. Ultimately, his chances hinged on the economy, which looked to be improving until the worst El Niño of the 20th century hit Peru in late 1997, causing chaos, many deaths and devasting damage.

Fujimori's unpopularity was further driven home by Shell-Mobil's withdrawal from the multi-million dollar Camisea natural gas project, which was supposed to pull Peru out of its energy deficit. In July 1998, a 1.4 million-name petition was presented to the National Electoral Authority, requesting a referendum on whether Fujimori should be allowed to stand for a third term. In spite of the amendment to the constitution following Fujimori's auto golpe in 1993, allowing presidents to run for only two successive terms, the president had, in 1996, pushed through congress a law of 'authentic interpretation' of the constitution, allowing him to run for election once more on the grounds that the new constitution did not apply to his first term. All the same, until the last month of campaigning for the 2000 presidential elections, Fujimori had a clear lead over his rivals, who insisted that he should not stand. Moreover, local and international observers voiced increasing concern over the state domination of the media. Meanwhile, the popularity of a fourth candidate, Alejandro Toledo, a former World Bank official of humble origins, surged to such an extent that he and Fujimori were neck and neck in the first poll. Toledo, a pro-marketeer given to left-wing rhetoric, and his supporters claimed that Fujimori's slim majority was the result of fraud, a view echoed in the pressure put on the president, by the US government among others, to allow a second ballot. The run-off election, on 28 May 2000, was also contentious since foreign observers, including the Organization of American States, said the electoral system was unprepared and flawed, proposing a postponement. The authorities refused to delay. Toledo boycotted the election and Fujimori was returned unopposed, but with scant approval. Having won, he proposed "to strengthen democracy".

Revolutionary movements – until the final victory

Officially speaking, the Peruvian civil war ended in 1992. On 12 September of that year, leader of the Shining Path, Abimael Guzmán, stood after his arrest in front of the television cameras, reduced from "National Enemy Number One" to "Prisoner Number 1509". Nobody knows how many people died in the carnage that lasted for more than a decade, but the most conservative estimates speak of 35,000.

The Maoist Shining Path was officially fighting for the resurrection of the Inca state and against Western imperialism and white supremacy in this racially and economically divided society. However, its methods were brutal and counter- productive. They included intimidation and the killing of several progressive leaders and hundreds of members of other revolutionary movements (including the contemporaneous Movimiento Revolucionario Túpac Amaru – MRTA). The plan was to reduce Peru's economy to ashes by destroying its infrastructure, military and police posts, power plants, tourism and other 'strategic targets'.

Both the army and the Shining Path were responsible for the eradication of countless towns and villages in the jungle and Andes, mass executions and torture of civilians. Sandwiched between these opposing forces, villagers in the mountains were forced to migrate to the coast, settling in enormous shantytowns, doubling the population of Lima in little more than a decade. Both sides forcibly recruited children from poor neighbourhoods and both controlled the traffic in drugs (they took it in turns to "tax" the same airstrips used by Colombian drug cartels).

During his term of office ex-president Fujimori did remove terrorism from Peru, however questionable the methods now appear. Evidence has recently come to light that many war crimes initially blamed on the Shining Path were in fact committed by the armed forces, even though it suited the terrorists to claim responsibility at the time. And investigations into the web of intrigue surrounding Fujimori's henchman, Vladimiro Montesinos, indicate some form of 'working relationship' with Sendero Luminoso. The Fujimori-Montesinos propaganda machine managed to discredit the entire Peruvian Left by comparing it to the Shining Path. Consequently, when the war ended, there was almost no legitimate opposition in the country from this end of the political spectrum.

Both Professor Guzmán (yes, he graduated from the Philosophy Department of the University of Arequipa and was a respected expert on the German philosopher Kant) and Víctor Polay (leader of the Marxist MRTA) are now locked away in underwater cells in the navy bunker on the island of San Lorenzo (Callao). They were condemned to life imprisonment by military tribunal. Nevertheless, many Peruvian and foreign analysts believe that both Shining Path and MRTA are recruiting again, albeit with softer methods, gaining support in the jungle, the Andes and in Lima. Unless the gap between the rich and poor can be narrowed, this period of relative peace in Peru may be at risk.

This pledge proved to be utterly worthless following the airing of a secretly shot video on 14 September 2000 of Fujimori's close aide and head of the National Intelligence Service (SIN), Vladimiro Montesinos, allegedly handing US$15,000 to a congressman, Alberto Kouri, to persuade him to switch allegiances to Fujimori's coalition. Fujimori's demise was swift. His initial reaction was to close down SIN and announce new elections, eventually set for 8 April 2001, at which he would not stand. Montesinos was declared a wanted man and he fled to Panama, where he was denied asylum. He returned to Peru in October and Fujimori personally led the search parties to find his former ally. Peruvians watched in amazement as this game of cat-and-mouse was played out on their TV screens. While Montesinos himself successfully evaded capture, investigators began to uncover the extent of his empire, which held hundreds of senior figures in its web. His activities encompassed extortion, money-laundering, bribery, intimidation, alleged arms and drugs dealing and possible links with the CIA and death squads. Swiss bank accounts in his name were found to contain about US$70 million, while other millions were discovered in accounts in the Cayman Islands and elsewhere. In early 2001 he was eventually captured in Venezuela and returned to Peru where he is now being tried on, and convicted of, a multitude of charges. Fujimori, on the other hand, fled to Japan from where, on 20 November 2000, he sent Congress an email announcing his resignation. Congress rejected this, firing him instead on charges of being "morally unfit" to govern. An interim president, Valentín Paniagua, was sworn in, with ex-UN Secretary General Javier Pérez de Cuéllar as Prime Minister, and the government set about uncovering the depth of corruption associated with Montesinos and Fujimori. In 2004, prosecutors sought to charge exiled Fujimori with ordering the deaths of 25 people in 1991 and 1992. This followed the Truth and Reconciliation Committee's report (2003) into the civil war of the 1980s-1990s, which stated that over 69,000 Peruvians had been killed. With attempts to extradite Fujimori from Japan coming to nothing, prosecution could not proceed. Meanwhile Fujimori declared that he would be exonerated and stand again for the presidency in 2006. To this end he flew to Chile in November 2005 with a view to entering Peru, but the Chilean authorities jailed him for seven months and then did not allow him to leave for Peru.

Post-Fujimori In the run-up to the 2001 elections, the front-runner was Alejandro Toledo, but with far from a clear majority. Ex-President Alan García emerged as Toledo's main opponent, forcing a second ballot on 3 June. This was won by Toledo with 52% of the vote. He pledged to heal the wounds that had opened in Peru since his first electoral battle with the disgraced Fujimori, but his presidency was marked by slow progress on both the political and economic fronts. With the poverty levels still high, few jobs created and a variety of scandals, Toledo's popularity plummeted. A series of major confrontations and damaging strikes forced the president to declare a state of emergency in May 2003 to restore order. Nor could Toledo escape charges of corruption being laid at his own door; accusations that he and his sister orchestrated voter fraud in 2000 were upheld by a congressional commission in May 2005, but no action was agreed.

The April 2006 elections were contested by Alan García, the conservative Lourdes Flores and Ollanta Humala, a former military officer and unsuccessful coup leader who claimed support from Venezuela's Hugo Chávez and Evo Morales of Bolivia. García and Humala won through to the second round, which García won, in part because many were suspicious, even critical of the "Chávez factor" and the latter's interference in Peruvian affairs. Many were equally suspicious of García's ability to overcome his past record as president, but prior to taking office he pledged to rein in public spending and not squander the benefits of an economy that had shown strong growth in 2005 (GDP grew by 6.4%, with a further 6% forecast for 2006). Humala's Unión por el Perú-Partido Nacionalista Peruano (UPP-PNP) won 45 seats in Congress, compared with 36 for APRA, forcing García to forge allies with right-leaning parties in order to sustain a majority for his policies. His cabinet included APRA members and independents, as well as an unprecedented number of women (six), to help tackle social problems. But much would depend upon García's ability to succeed where no previous government seems to have made significant progrees, namely alleviating poverty.

Constitution and government

Peru has a single chamber, 120-seat congress. Men and women over 18 are eligible to vote, and registration and voting is compulsory until the age of 60. Those who do not vote are fined. The President, to whom is entrusted the Executive Power, is elected for five years and may be re-elected for a second term. Peru is divided into 24 Departments (divided into 150 Provinces, subdivided into 1321 Districts).

Economy

Structure of production

Agriculture, forestry and **fishing** account for about 15% of GDP and employ about a third of the labour force. The coastal region is the most productive area of the country and has traditionally been the dominant economic region. Occupying 11% of the total land area, most of the export crops are grown here: cotton, rice, sugar, artichokes, asparagus and fruit where the coastal desert is irrigated. Most food production is in the sierra, where revitalization of agriculture, with the aim of returning to the self-sufficiency of Inca times, has been a long-term goal. There have been improvements in living standards, but two-thirds of the inhabitants of the sierra still live in poverty and prices for many crops remain very low. Peru has the potential to be the world's leading exporter of fishmeal, as in 2001-02, but the industry is susceptible to the Niño current forcing the main catch, anchovy, out of Peruvian waters. When this happens, as for instance in 1983 and 1997-1998, fishing suffers a dramatic decline.

The government estimates that the **illegal drugs** trade generates some US$600 million a year. It is believed that Peru accounts for a third of world cocaine production, being the second-largest grower of coca leaf after Colombia. Following efforts to curb the cultivation of coca for the production of cocaine, United Nations officials recorded a 5% drop in coca production in 2003 to 44,200 ha. The trend reversed dramatically in 2004, with a 14% increase to 50,300 ha, largely because of a lack of development of alternative crops in just two areas where the government has little influence through the rule of law.

Manufacturing and **mining**contribute 26% of GDP. Food processing, fishmeal, oil refining, metals and transport equipment are important sectors. Mining has traditionally been important in Peru since pre-Conquest times. The sector contracted sharply in the 1980s because of poor world prices, strikes and terrorist activity in mining areas, but a new Mining Law in 1992 encouraged domestic and foreign investment and the sector has since boomed. Copper and iron deposits are found on the south coast, but the sierra is the principal mining area for all minerals, including silver, gold, lead and zinc. The largest gold mine in Latin America, Yanacocha, is in Cajamarca, contributing the majority of Peru's annual production of 130 tonnes. Another major project is the Antamina in Ancash, the world's leading combined copper and zinc mine.

Oil production comes from the northeast jungle, although some is produced on and off the northwest coast. No major new reserves of oil have been found since 1976 and proven reserves have declined to 370 million barrels. Peru is a net importer of oil. However, the Camisea gas and condensates field in the southeast jungle is huge, with reserves in two deposits estimated at 11 trillion cu ft of natural gas and 600 million barrels of condensates, equivalent to more than six times current reserves of oil. The project and its associated pipeline and processing facilities on the coast is also hugely controversial, primarily for environmental and humanitarian reasons.

Since the early 1990s, when the threat of terrorism had receded, numbers of foreign **tourists** to Peru have grown steadily. The total number of visitors in 2005 was 1.5 million, with revenues of US$1.2 billion. Most visitors come from the USA (over 45%), followed by the UK, Spain, France, Germany, Canada and Japan.

A way of life

Coca leaves have long been used by the people of the Andes as a tonic. As casual as a coffee-break and as sacred as Communion, coca chewing is an ancient ritual.

The coca leaves are chewed with a piece of *cal*, or lime, which activates with the saliva. Some cocaine is absorbed into the bloodstream through the mouth, providing a slight numbing of cheek and tongue and more is absorbed in the stomach and intestinal tract. The desired effect is to numb the senses, which helps stave off hunger pangs and exhaustion, and to help people live at high altitude with no ill-effects.

As well as being a prerequisite for manual workers, such as miners, coca is also taken in a social context. The native population used to deny this because, in the eyes of their Spanish bosses and clergy, an increase in labour productivity was the only permissible reason for tolerating consumption of 'the devil's leaf'. The only places where coca is not chewed is in church and in the marital bed. The masticated leaves are spat out at the bedside.

Coca is also used in various rites, such as in offerings to Pachamama, or Mother Earth, to feed her when she gets hungry. Various items such as flowers and sweets, along with the coca leaves, are put together in bundles called *pagos* and burned on the mountains at midnight. In Andean markets different *pagos* are sold for different purposes: to put into the foundation of a new house; for help in matters of health, business or love; or for magic, white or black. The leaves are also used for fortune-telling.

Society

The most remarkable thing about Peru is its people. For most Peruvians life is a daily struggle to survive in the face of seemingly insurmountable problems. Most people do get by, through a combination of ingenuity, determination and sheer hard work. Many work full time and study at night school. Those without work (and employment opportunities are few and far between) invent their own jobs.

Peru may not be the poorest country in South America, but recent estimates put the number of poor at just over 50% of the population, while almost a fifth of people live in extreme poverty. Over a third of homes have no electricity or running water and a third of children suffer from chronic malnutrition.

Health

There have been major improvements in health care in recent years, but almost a third of the population has no access to public health services. The infant mortality rate is high – 33.4 deaths per 1000 births – and the figure rises steeply in some rural areas where 1 in 10 infants dies within a year of birth. Life expectancy is 69.8 years (2000-2005, UN figures).

As only a small percentage of the population contributes to social security schemes, medical consultations are not necessarily free. People also have to pay for prescribed medicines, which are very expensive, and so rarely finish a course of treatment. As with other areas, there is a huge gulf between those who can afford to pay for health care and those who cannot. Lack of health education and limited primary health care also means that many women die in childbirth. Abortion is illegal in Peru, but those with cash can always find a private doctor. Those without the means to pay for a doctor run the risk of death or infection from botched abortions.

Education

Education is free and compulsory for both sexes between six and 14. There are public and private secondary schools and private elementary schools. There are 32 state and private universities, and two Catholic universities. But resources are extremely limited and teachers earn a pittance. Poorer schoolchildren don't have money to buy pencils and notebooks and textbooks are few and far between in state schools. Furthermore, many children have to work instead of attending school; a quarter of those who start primary school don't finish. This is also due to the fact that classes are taught in Spanish and those whose native tongue is Quechua, Aymara or one of the Amazonian languages find it difficult and give up.

Migration

The structure of Peruvian society, especially in the coastal cities, has been radically altered by internal migration. This movement began most significantly in the 1950s and 1960s as people from all parts of Peru sought urban jobs in place of work on the land. It was a time of great upheaval as the old system of labour on large estates was threatened by the peasant majority's growing awareness of the imbalances between the wealthy cities and impoverished sierra. The process culminated in the agrarian reforms of the government of General Juan Velasco (1968-1975). Province-to-city migration was given renewed impetus during the war between the state and Sendero Luminoso in the 1980s. Many communities which were depopulated in that decade are now beginning to come alive again.

Culture

People

Peruvian society today is a melting pot of Native Andeans, Afro-Peruvians, Spanish, immigrant Chinese, Japanese, Italians, Germans and, to a lesser extent, indigenous Amazon tribes, who have lived together for so long that many Peruvians can claim to have mixed blood. The total population in 2005 was 28.0 million, with an annual average growth rate of 1.5%. Forecast growth rate for 2010-2015 is 1.36% (2000-2005, UN statistics). The urban population represents 72.3% of the total.

Criollos and mestizos

The first immigrants were the Spaniards who followed Pizarro's expeditionary force. Their effect, demographically, politically and culturally, has been enormous. They intermarried with the indigenous population and the children of mixed parentage were called mestizos. The Peruvian-born children of Spanish parents were known as criollos, though this word is now used to describe people who live on the coast, regardless of their ancestory, and coastal culture in general.

Afro-Peruvians

Peru's black community is based on the coast, mainly in Chincha, south of Lima, and also in some working-class districts of the capital. Their forefathers were originally imported into Peru in the 16th century as slaves to work on the sugar and cotton plantations on the coast. The black community represents between 2-5% of the total population.

Asian immigrants

There are two main Asian communities in Peru, the Japanese and Chinese. Large numbers of poor Chinese labourers were brought to Peru in the mid-19th century to work in virtual slavery on the guano reserves on the Pacific coast and to build the railroads in the central Andes. The culinary influence of the Chinese can be seen in the many chifas found throughout the country.

The Japanese community, now numbering some 100,000, established itself in the first half of the 20th century. The normally reclusive community gained prominence when Alberto Fujimori, one of its members, became the first president of Japanese descent outside Japan anywhere in the world. During Fujimori's presidency, many other Japanese Peruvians took prominent positions in business, central and local government. The nickname 'chino' is applied to anyone of Oriental origin.

Europeans

Like most of Latin America, Peru received many emigrés from Europe seeking land and opportunities in the late 19th century. The country's wealth and political power remains concentrated in the hands of this small and exclusive class of whites, which also consists of the descendants of the first Spanish families. There still exists a deep divide between people of European descent and the old colonial snobbery persists.

Peru's indigenous people

Peru has a substantial indigenous population, only smaller as a percentage of the total than Bolivia and Guatemala of the Latin American republics. The literacy rate of the indigenous population is the lowest of any comparable group in South America and their diet is 50% below acceptable levels. The highland communities bore the brunt of the conflict between Sendero Luminoso and the security forces, which caused thousands of deaths and mass migration from the countryside to provincial cities or to Lima. Many indigenous groups are also under threat from colonization, development and road-building projects. Long after the end of Spanish rule, discrimination, dispossession and exploitation are still a fact of life for many native Peruvians.

Quechua

Predominantly an agricultural society, growing potatoes and corn as their basic diet, they are largely outside the money economy. Today, there remain two enduring legacies of Inca rule; their magnificent architecture and their language, Quechua, which, although predating the Incas themselves, has become synonymous with the descendants of their subjects. Quechua is one of the key channels of continuity with the captivating pre-European past and indigenous identity of the Andes. Sadly, that continuity still takes the form of a distinctly underprivileged status in relation to the dominant Spanish and it is only the remoteness of many Quechua speakers which has preserved the language in rural areas. This isolation has also helped preserve many of their ancient traditions and beliefs. Most speakers today are bilingual in Spanish and Quechua is still losing ground fast. It remains primarily a spoken, in-group language, strongly bound up with the distinct indigenous identity, but unlike the Aymara (see below), the seven million or so Quechua-speakers have generally been much less successful in asserting themselves. There is no real sense of unity between the disparate groups of speakers scattered through Ecuador, Peru and Bolivia. Some recent developments in these three countries have at last been more positive. The language is now increasingly written and is being fitfully introduced in primary education, though the impact of Spanish, and polemics about standardisation, continue to have a very disruptive effect. At least some Quechua-speaking

Consult www.comunidadandina.org, for information in Spanish and English on the Andean community.

The Afro-Peruvian experience since 1532

The first person of African descent to arrive in the Americas came in 1492 with Christopher Columbus. He was a mulatto from Spain, and a free man. During the next three centuries an estimated 15 million Africans arrived in the Americas as slaves. Francisco Pizarro brought the first black slaves to Peru. They were present at the capture of Atahualpa in Cajamarca in 1532 and saved the Spanish during Manco Inca's siege of Cuzco in 1536, when they put out the fire engulfing the great hall of Sunturwasi, where the *conquistadores* had taken refuge.

When Hernando de Soto returned to Spain in 1534 bearing Atahualpa's gold and silver ransom, he asked the crown for permission to take 100 slaves back to Peru. By 1550, their number had risen to 3000 – half of whom lived in Lima – and by 1640 to 30,000. In total, between 1532 and 1816, an estimated 100,000 African slaves were transported to Peru.

They were sent to replace an indigenous labour force ravaged by the destruction of its sociopolitical infrastructure and by European diseases. Some worked in the cities as servants, artisans or porters, others in the mines of Huancavelica or Potosí and the majority toiled on the coast in sugar cane plantations, cotton fields and vineyards.

Indigenous and African workers transformed Peru into the richest of all the Spanish colonies in the 16th and 17th centuries. Many fortunes, including that amassed by the Jesuits, were made using slave labour. The ownership of black slaves was a status symbol and became such a powerful measure of social mobility that even some Afro-Peruvians who had achieved their own freedom subsequently acquired slaves.

The location of Afro-Peruvian communities today reflects the colonial distribution of black labour. They are concentrated in the coastal areas once dominated by the great haciendas: Chincha, Cañete and Ica, the northern departments of Lambayeque and Piura, and the cities, especially Lima. Here, the vibrant culture created by slaves from diverse African heritages lives on in local art, music, dance, religioun, folklore and food (see pages 596 and 55).

The wars of independence spread the libertarian ideal of emancipation. Promised their freedom, hundreds of Afro-Peruvians joined the republican armies, only to find their situation little changed in 1821 under the fledgling government. In 1854, Generals Ramón Castilla and José Rufino Echenique engaged in civil war and were in need of troops. To attract black recruits Echenique offered freedom to those who would join him and, in reply, Castilla announced the abolition of slavery, paying off landowners with awards raised from guano exports.

The 25,000 black slaves freed in 1854 were received by society with contempt and remained oppressed by labour laws. Racism lives on in Peru today. Colour is still identified with inferiority in everyday attitudes and in the poverty and marginalization of black communities and their lack of representation in government. One hundred and fifty years after abolition, those who shared the hardships of the *conquistadores* have still not shared in their glory or wealth.

communities are gradually recovering a long-deserved semblance of pride in their native tongue and culture, such as the successful Otavalo traders in Ecuador, or the Jalq'a and Tarabuco peoples around Sucre in Bolivia thanks to their beautiful weaving traditions. See also Festivals, on page 598.

Aymara

High up in the Andes, in the southern part of Peru, lies a wide, barren and hostile plateau, the *altiplano*. Prior to Inca rule Tiahuanaco on Lake Titicaca was a highly organized centre for one the greatest cultures South America has ever witnessed: the Aymara people. Today, the shores of this lake and the plains that surround it remain the homeland of the Aymara. The majority live in Bolivia, the rest are scattered on the southwestern side of Peru and northern Chile. The climate is so harsh on the *altiplano* that, though they are extremely hard-working, their lives are very poor. They speak their own unwritten language, Aymara. More so than the scattered group of different peoples that speak Quechua, the Altiplano Aymara people form a compact group with a clear sense of their own distinct identity and in many respects have been able to preserve more of their indigenous traditions and belief system.

The Aymaras are a deeply religious people whose culture is permeated with the idea of the sacred. They believe that God, the Supreme Being, gives them security in their daily lives and this God of Life manifests him/herself through the deities, such as those of the mountains, the water, wind, sun, moon and *wa'qas* (sacred places).

As a sign of gratitude, the Aymara give wax'ta (offerings), wilancha (llama sacrifices) and ch'alla (sprinkling alcohol on the ground) to the achachilas (the protecting spirits of the family and community), the Pachamama (Mother Earth), Kuntur Mamani and Uywiri (protecting spirits of the home).

The remote mountains of the bleak *altiplano* are of particular importance for the Aymara. The most sacred places are these high mountains, far from human problems. It is here that the people have built their altars to offer worship, to communicate with their God and ask forgiveness. The community is also held important in the lives of the Aymara. The achachila is the great-great grandfather of the family as well as the protector of the community, and as such is God's representative on earth.

The offerings to the sacred mountains take place for the most part in August and are community celebrations. Many different rituals are celebrated: there are those within the family; in the mountains; for the planting and the harvest; rites to ask for rain or to ask for protection against hailstorms and frosts; and ceremonies for Mother Earth.

All such rituals are led by Aymara Yatiris, who are male or female priests. The Yatiri is a wise person – someone who knows – and the community's spiritual and moral guide. Through a method of divination that involves the reading of coca leaves, they guide individuals in their personal decision-making.

Amazonian peoples

Before the arrival of the Europeans, an estimated six million people inhabited the Amazon Basin, comprising more than 2000 tribes or ethnic-linguistic groups who managed to adapt to their surroundings through the domestication of a great variety of animals and plants, and to benefit from the numerous nutritional, curative, narcotic and hallucinogenic properties of thousands of wild plants.

It's not easy to determine the precise origin of these aboriginal people. What is known, however, is that since the beginning of colonial times this population slowly but constantly decreased, mainly because of the effect of western diseases such as influenza and measles. This demographic decline reached dramatic levels during the rubber boom of the late 19th and early 20th centuries, due to forced labour and slavery.

Today, at the basin level, the population is calculated at no more than two million inhabitants making up 400 ethnic groups, of which approximately 200-250,000 live in the Peruvian jungle. Within the basin it is possible to distinguish at least three large conglomerates of aboriginal societies: the inhabitants of the varzea, or seasonally flooded lands alongside the large rivers (such as the Omagua, Cocama and Shipibo people); the people in the interfluvial zones or firm lands (such as the Amahuaca, Cashibo and Yaminahua) and those living in the Andean foothills (such as the Amuesha, Asháninka and Machiguenga).

Andean mysticism

Since the 1990s Andean shamanism and mysticism have attracted increasing attention, though they have always played an important part in the lives of indigenous people.

In highland cities, especially, it is common to engage a ritual specialist, called an altomisayoq, to perform a pago, or offering, when laying the foundations of a house or starting a business venture. Ritual objects for use in these ceremonies are sold at specialized stands in the local markets. Another type of ritualist, called a curandero, is summoned when someone is ill.

Some of these healers are experts in the use of dozens of medicinal plants, while others invoke spirit powers to expel illness. Sometimes eggs or guinea pigs are passed over the patient's body, and then cracked, or killed, in order to read the innards and diagnose the illness. Inevitably this field has its share of charlatans, but there are also curanderos who have many attested cures to their credit.

One thing shamans from all the Andean regions have in common is the use of a mesa – a layout of ceremonial power objects – which is thought to attract spirit power and channel it to the shaman. Another feature running through all strains of Andean mysticism, despite the usual presence of Christian elements, is a living connection, via innumerable practices and associations, to Peru's pre-Columbian past.

Those ritualists who seek to communicate with 'the other side' in their ceremonies often use psychoactive plants. These vary according to the region. On the coast, curanderos often take an infusion of the San Pedro cactus, a form of mescaline. The highland shamans invariably chew coca leaf, a much milder psychoactive, but with broader uses. Coca is burned with every offering, and many ritualists cast the leaves to read the fortunes of their clients. These shamans usually invoke the power of the mountain deities in their ceremonies. In the rainforest regions shamans use the powerful psychedelic vine, ayahuasca (vine of the dead – so called because it is believed to transport the user to the spirit world), as they have for millenia.

The Amazonian natives began to be decimated in the 16th century, and so were the first endangered species of the jungle. These communities still face threats to their traditional lifestyles, notably from timber companies, gold miners and multinational oil and gas companies. There appears to be little effective control of deforestation and the intrusion of colonists who have taken over native lands to establish small farms. And though oil companies have reached compensation agreements with local communities, previous oil exploration has contaminated many jungle rivers, as well as exposing natives to risk from diseases against which they have no immunity.

Religion

The Inca religion (described on page 575) was displaced by Roman Catholicism from the 16th century onwards, the conversion of the inhabitants of the 'New World' to Christianity being one of the stated aims of the Spanish conquistadores. Today, statistics vary between 81 and 89% of the population declaring itself Catholic.

One of the first exponents of Liberation Theology, under which the Conference of Latin American Bishops in 1968 committed themselves to the 'option for the poor', was Gustavo Gutiérrez, from Huánuco. This doctrine caused much consternation to orthodox Catholics, particularly those members of the Latin American church who had traditionally aligned themselves with the oligarchy. Gutiérrez, however, traced the church's duty to the voiceless and the marginalized back to Fray Bartolomé de las Casas (see *The Peru Reader*, pages 293-296; reference under Books, page 615).

The Catholic Church faced a further challenge to its authority when President Fujimori won the battle over family planning and the need to slow down the rate of population growth. Its greatest threat, however, comes from the proliferation of evangelical Protestant groups throughout the country. Some 6% of the population now declare themselves Protestant and one million or more people belong to some 27 different non-Catholic denominations.

Although the vast majority of the population ostensibly belongs to the Roman Catholic religion, in reality religious life for many Peruvians is a mix of Catholic beliefs imported from Europe and indigenous traditions based on animism, the worship of deities from the natural world such as mountains, animals and plants. Some of these ancient indigenous traditions and beliefs are described throughout this section.

Arts and crafts

Peru has a rich variety of handicrafts. Its geographic division into four distinct regions – coast, mountains, valleys and Amazon Basin – coupled with cultural differences, has resulted in numerous variations in technique and design. Each province, even each community, has developed its own style of weaving or carving.

The Incas inherited 3000 years of skills and traditions: gold, metal and precious stonework from the Chimú; feather textiles from the Nazca; and the elaborate textiles of the Paracas. All of these played important roles in political, social and religious ceremonies. Though much of this artistic heritage was destroyed by the Spanish conquest, the traditions adapted and evolved in numerous ways, absorbing new methods, concepts and materials from Europe while maintaining ancient techniques and symbols.

Textiles and costumes

Woven cloth was the most highly prized possession and sought after trading commodity in the Andes in pre-Columbian times. It is, therefore, not surprising that ancient weaving traditions have survived. In the ninth century BC camelid fibre was introduced into weaving on the south coast. This allowed the development of the textiles of the Paracas culture which consist of intricate patterns of animalistic, supernatural and human forms embroidered onto dark backgrounds. The culture of the Chancay valleys cultivated cotton for white and beige dyed patterned cloth in preference to the camelid fibres used by the Paracas and Nazca cultures. The Incas inherited this rich weaving tradition. They forced the Aymaras to work in mit'as or textile workshops. The ruins of some enormous mit'as can be seen at the temple of Raqchi, south of Cuzco (see page 212). Inca textiles are of high quality and very different from coastal textiles, being warp-faced, closely woven and without embroidery. The largest quantities of the finest textiles were made specifically to be burned as ritual offerings – a tradition which still survives. The Spanish, too, exploited this wealth and skill by using the mitas and exporting the cloth to Europe.

Prior to Inca rule Aymara men wore a tunic (*llahua*) and a mantle (*llacata*) and carried a bag for coca leaves (*huallquepo*). The women wore a wrapped dress (*urku*) and mantle (*iscayo*) and a belt (*huaka*); their coca bag was called an *istalla*. The *urku* was fastened at shoulder level with a pair of metal *tupu*, the traditional Andean dress-pins. Inca men had tunics (*unkus*) and a bag for coca leaves called a *ch'uspa*. The women wore a blouse (*huguna*), skirts (*aksu*) and belts (*chumpis*), and carried

A belt for every occasion

The belt plays a particularly important role in the lives of the indigenous peoples. The Incas developed a range of belts, or *chumpis*, of ritual and spiritual significance which are still used today.

Chumpis are believed to have protective and purifying qualities. In the Cuzco area, some communities place *chumpis* on sacred mountain tops, or *apus*, in order to communicate with the gods.

Traditionally women give birth lying on a *chumpi* and the baby is wrapped in a softer version, known as a *walt'ana*, which ensures he or she will grow up properly. From adolescence, women wear a *chumpi* under their skirt to encourage a lover or deter an unwanted suitor. It is even common practice for the bridegroom to lasso his bride with one. And the age-old tradition of burying the dead with the family *chumpi* is still occasionally observed.

foodstuffs in large, rectangular cloths called *lliclla*s, which were fastened at the chest with a single pin or a smaller clasp called a *ttipqui*. Women of the Sacred Valley now wear a layered, gathered skirt called a *pollera* and a *montera*, a large, round, red Spanish type of hat. Textiles continue to play an important part in society. They are still used specifically for ritual ceremonies and some even held to possess magical powers. One of the most enduring of these traditions is found among the Aymara people of Taquile island on Lake Titicaca.

Textile materials and techniques

The Andean people used mainly alpaca or llama wool. The former can be spun into fine, shining yarn when woven and has a lustre similar to that of silk, though sheep's wool came to be widely used following the Spanish conquest. A commonly used technique is the drop spindle. A stick is weighted with a wooden wheel and the raw material is fed through one hand. A sudden twist and drop in the spindle spins the yarn. This very sensitive art can be seen practised by women while herding animals in the fields.

Spinning wheels were introduced by Europeans and are now prevalent owing to increased demand. In Ayacucho and San Pedro de Cajas, centres of the cottage textile industry, the wheel is the most common form of spinning. Pre-Columbian looms were often portable and those in use today are generally similar. A woman will herd her animals while making a piece of costume, perhaps on a backstrap loom, or waist loom, so-called because the weaver controls the tension on one side with her waist with the other side tied to an upright or tree. The pre-Columbian looms are usually used for personal costume while the treadle loom is used by men for more commercial pieces.

The skills of dyeing were still practised virtually unchanged even after the arrival of the Spanish. Nowadays, the word *makhnu* refers to any natural dye, but originally was the name for cochineal, an insect which lives on the leaves of the nopal cactus. These dyes were used widely by pre-Columbian weavers. Today, the biggest centre of production in South America is the valleys around Ayacucho. Vegetable dyes are also used, made from the leaves, fruit and seeds of shrubs and flowers and from lichen, tree bark and roots.

Symbolism

Symbolism plays an important role in weaving. Traditionally every piece of textile from a particular community had identical symbols and colours which were a source of identity as well as carrying specific symbols and telling a story. One example is on the island of Taquile where the Inti (sun) and Chaska (Venus) symbols are employed as well as motifs such as fish and birds, unique to the island.

Animal figures dominated the motifs of the Chavín culture and were commonly used in Paracas textiles. Specimens of cotton and wool embroidery found in Paracas graves often show a puma as a central motif. Today, this and other pre-Columbian motifs are found on many rugs and wall-hangings from the Ayacucho region. Other symbols include Spanish figures such as horses and scenes depicting the execution of Túpac Amaru.

Pottery

The most spectacular archaeological finds in South America have been made in Peru. The Nazca culture (100 BC-AD 900) excelled in polychrome painting of vessels with motifs of supernatural beings, often with strong feline characteristics, as well as birds, fish and animals. Many of the Nazca ceramic motifs are similar to those found in Paracas textiles.

Moche or Mochica vessels combined modelling and painting to depict details of Moche daily life. Human forms are modelled on stirrup spout vessels with such precision that they suggest personal portraits. The Moche also excelled in intricate linear painting often using brown on a cream base. See also page 290.

Inca ceramic decoration consists mainly of small-scale geometric and usually symmetrical designs. One distinctive form of vessel which continues to be made and used is the arybola. This pot is designed to carry liquid, especially *chicha*, and is secured with a rope on the bearer's back. It is believed that arybolas were used mainly by the governing Inca élite and became important status symbols. Today, Inca-style is very popular in Cuzco and Pisac.

With the Spanish invasion many indigenous communities lost their artistic traditions, others remained relatively untouched, while others still combined Hispanic and indigenous traditions and techniques. The Spanish brought three innovations: the potter's wheel, which gave greater speed and uniformity; knowledge of the enclosed kiln; and the technique of lead glazes. The enclosed kiln made temperature regulation easier and allowed higher temperatures to be maintained, producing stronger pieces. Today, many communities continue to apply prehispanic techniques, while others use more modern processes.

Jewellery and metalwork

Some of the earliest goldwork originates from the Chavín culture – eg the Tumi knife found in Lambayeque. These first appeared in the Moche culture, when they were associated with human sacrifice. Five centuries later, the Incas used Tumis for surgical operations such as trepanning skulls. Today, they are a common motif.

The Incas associated gold with the Sun. However, very few examples remain as the Spanish melted down their amassed gold and silver objects. They then went on to send millions of indigenous people to their deaths in gold and silver mines.

During the colonial period gold and silver pieces were made to decorate the altars of churches and houses of the élite. Metalworkers came from Spain and Italy to develop the industry. The Spanish preferred silver and strongly influenced the evolution of silverwork during the colonial period. A style known as Andean baroque developed around Cuzco embracing both indigenous and European elements. Silver bowls in this style – cochas – are still used in Andean ceremonies.

False filigree This was practised by some prehispanic cultures. The effect of filigree was obtained with the use of droplets or beads of gold. True filigree work developed in the colonial period. Today, there are a number of centres. Originally popular in Ayacucho, the tradition continues in the small community of San Jerónimo de Tunan,

From pagan ritual to folk art

Retablos – or St Mark's boxes, as they were originally known – were introduced to Latin America by the Spanish in the 16th century. These simple, portable altars containing religious images were intended to aid in the task of converting the native population to Catholicism. Early examples often contained images of St James, patron saint of the Spanish army.

The *retablos* were made from a variety of materials and two distinct styles evolved to suit different needs. Those of clay, leather and plaster were destined for the native rural population, while those for use by the colonial hierarchy were made of gold and silver, or the famous alabaster of Ayacucho, known as Huamanga stone.

Traditional *retablos* had 2 floors inside a box. On the top floor were the patron saints of animals: St Mark, patron saint of bulls; St Agnes, patron saint of goats; and St Anthony, patron saint of mules, among others. On the lower floor was a scene of a cattle thief being reprimanded by a landowner.

From the 17th century onwards, the native rural population used the *retablo* in ceremonies accompanying cattle branding. During August, a ritual believed to have its roots in pagan fertility festivals took place in which the *retablo* was placed on a table and surrounded by offerings of food and coca leaves. People danced round and sang in front of the box, asking for protection for their animals and celebrating their well-being.

In the 1940s the first *retablo* reached Lima, by which time the art of making them had virtually disappeared. However, with the new-found outside interest a revival began. The traditional elements began to be varied and the magical or ritualistic value was lost as they became a manifestation of folk art. The artist Joaquín López and his family created the early examples, but today they are made in many workshops.

The figures are made from a mixture of plaster and mashed potato, modelled or made in moulds, sealed with glue, then painted and positioned inside the brightly painted box. Some miniature versions are made in chiclet boxes or egg shells, while, at the other end of the scale, some have five floors and take months to complete.

Extracted from *Arts and Crafts of South America*, by Lucy Davies and Mo Fini,Tumi.

near Huancayo. Here, silversmiths produce intricate filigree earrings, spoons and jewellery boxes. Catacaos near Piura also has a long tradition of filigree work in silver and gold.

Seeds, flowers and feathers These continue to be used as jewellery by many Amazonian peoples. Prehispanic cultures also favoured particular natural materials; eg the sea shell spondylus was highly revered by the Chavín and Moche. It was found only along part of the Ecuadorean coast and must have been acquired through trade. The western fashion for natural or ethnic jewellery has encouraged production, using brightly coloured feathers, fish bones, seeds or animal teeth.

Woodcarving

Wood is one of the most commonly used materials. Carved ceremonial objects include drums, carved sticks with healing properties, masks and the Incas' keros – wooden vessels for drinking *chicha*. Keros come in all shapes and sizes and were traditionally decorated with scenes of war, local dances, or harvesting coca leaves. The Chancay, who lived along the coast between 100 BC and AD 1200, used keros carved with sea birds and fish. Today, they are used in some Andean ceremonies, especially during Fiesta de la Cruz, the Andean May festival.

Glass mirrors were introduced by the Spanish, although the Chimú and Lambayeque cultures used obsidian and silver plates, and Inca *chasquis* (messengers) used reflective stones to communicate between hilltop forts. Transporting mirrors was costly so they were produced in Lima and Quito. Cuzco and Cajamarca then became centres of production. In Cuzco the frames were carved, covered in gold leaf and decorated with tiny pieces of cut mirror. Cajamarca artisans, meanwhile, incorporated painted glass into the frames.

Gourd-carving

Gourd-carving, or *máte burilado*, as it is known, is one of Peru's most popular and traditional handicrafts. It is thought even to predate pottery – engraved gourds found on the coast have been dated to some 4500 years ago. During the Inca empire gourd-carving became a valued art form and workshops were set up and supported by the state. Gourds were used in rituals and ceremonies and to make poporos – containers for the lime used while chewing coca leaves. Today, gourd-carving is centred around the small communities of Cochas Grande and Chico, near Huancayo.

The information on arts and crafts in this Handbook has been adapted from *Arts and Crafts of South America*, by Lucy Davies and Mo Fini, published by Tumi, 1994. Tumi, the Latin American Craft Centre, specializes in Andean and Mexican products and produces cultural and educational videos for schools: at 8/9 New Bond Street Place, Bath BA1 1BH, T01225-446025, www.tumi.co.uk. Tumi (Music) Ltd specializes in different rhythms of Latin America.

Music and dance

The music of Peru can be described as the very heartbeat of the country. Peruvians see music as something in which to participate, and not as a spectacle. Just about everyone, it seems, can play a musical instrument or sing. Just as music is the heartbeat of the country, so dance conveys the rich and ancient heritage that typifies much of the national spirit. Peruvians are tireless dancers and dancing is the most popular form of entertainment. Unsuspecting travellers should note that once they make that first wavering step there will be no respite until they collapse from exhaustion.

Each region has its own distinctive music and dance that reflects its particular lifestyle, its mood and its physical surroundings. The music of the sierra, for example, is played in a minor key and tends to be sad and mournful, while the music of the lowlands is more up-tempo and generally happier. Peruvian music divides at a very basic level into that of the highlands (Andina) and that of the coast (Criolla).

Highlands

When people talk of Peruvian music they are almost certainly referring to the music of the Quechua- and Aymara-speaking people of the highlands which provides the most distinctive Peruvian sound. The highlands themselves can be very roughly subdivided into some half dozen major musical regions, of which perhaps the most characteristic are Ancash and the north, the Mantaro Valley, Cuzco, Puno and the Altiplano, Ayacucho and Parinacochas.

Musical instruments Before the arrival of the Spanish in Latin America, the only instruments were wind and percussion. Although it is a popular misconception that Andean music is based on the panpipes, guitar and charango, anyone who travels through the Andes will realize that these instruments only represent a small aspect of Andean music. The highland instrumentation varies from region to region, although the harp and violin are ubiquitous. In the Mantaro area the harp is backed by brass and wind instruments, notably the clarinet. In Cuzco it is the charango and quena and on the *altiplano* the sicu panpipes.

The Quena is a flute, usually made of reed, characterized by not having a mouthpiece to blow through. As with all Andean instruments, there is a family of quenas varying in length from around 15-50 cm. The sicu is the Aymara name for the zampoña, or panpipes. It is the most important prehispanic Andean instrument, formed by several reed tubes of different sizes held together by knotted string. Virtually the only instrument of European origin is the Charango. When stringed instruments were first introduced by the Spanish, the indigenous people liked them but wanted something that was their own and so the charango was born. Originally, they were made of clay, condor skeletons and armadillo or tortoise shells.

Highland dances The highlands are immensely rich in terms of music and dance, with over 200 dances recorded. Every village has its fiestas and every fiesta has its communal and religious dances.

Comparsas are organized groups of dancers who perform for spectators dances following a set pattern of movements to a particular musical accompaniment, wearing a specific costume. They have a long tradition, having mostly originated from certain contexts and circumstances and some of them still parody the ex-Spanish colonial masters.

One of the most notable is the comical Auqui Auqui (auqui is Aymara for old man). The dance satirizes the solemnity and pomposity of Spanish gentlemen from the colonial period. Because of their dignified dress and manners they could appear old, and a humped back is added to the dancers to emphasize age. These little old men have long pointed noses, flowing beards and carry crooked walking sticks. They dance stooped, regularly pausing to complain and rub aching backs, at times even stumbling and falling. Another dance parody is the Contradanza, performed in the highlands of La Libertad.

Many dances for couples and/or groups are danced spontaneously at fiestas throughout Peru. These include indigenous dances which have originated in a specific region and ballroom dances that reflect the Spanish influence. One of the most popular of the indigenous dances is the **Huayno**, which originated on the *altiplano* but is now danced throughout the country. It involves numerous couples, who whirl around or advance down the street arm-in-arm, in a Pandilla. During fiestas, and especially after a few drinks, this can develop into a kind of uncontrolled frenzy.

Two of the most spectacular dances to be seen are the **Baile de las Tijeras** (scissor dance) from the Ayacucho/Huancavelica area, for men only, and the pounding, stamping **Huaylas** for both sexes. Huaylas competitions are held annually in Lima and should not be missed. Also very popular among indigenous and/or mestizo people are the Marinera, Carnaval, Pasacalle, Chuscada (from Ancash), Huaylas, Santiago and Chonguinada (all from the Mantaro) and Huayllacha (from Parinacochas).

Urban and other styles Owing to the overwhelming migration of peasants into the barrios of Lima, most types of Andean music and dance can be seen in the capital, notably on Sundays at the so-called 'Coliseos', which exist for that purpose. This flood of migration to the cities has also meant that the distinct styles of regional and ethnic groups have become blurred. One example is **Chicha music**, which comes from the pueblos jóvenes, and was once the favourite dance music of Peru's urban working class. Chicha is a hybrid of Huayno music and the Colombian Cumbia rhythm – a meeting of the highlands and the tropical coast.

Tecno-cumbia originated in the jungle region with groups such as Rossy War, from Puerto Maldonado, and Euforia, from Iquitos. It is a vibrant dance music which has gained much greater popularity across Peruvian society than *chicha* music ever managed. There are now also many exponents on the coast such as Agua Marina and Armonía 10. Many of the songs comment on political issues and Fujimori used to join Rossy War on stage. Tecno-cumbia has evolved into a more sophisticated form with wider appeal across Peruvian society. Grupo 5, from Chiclayo, are currently the most popular exponents. For singing only, the mestizo Muliza, are popular in the Central Region, and the soulful lament of the Yaraví, originally Indian, but developed early in the 19th century by the Arequipan hero of independence Mariano Melgar, see page 601.

Coast

Música Criolla The music from the coast, could not be more different from that of the sierra. Here the roots are Spanish and African. The immensely popular **Valsesito** is a syncopated waltz that would certainly be looked at askance in Vienna and the **Polca** has also undergone an attractive sea change. Reigning over all is the **Marinera**, Peru's national dance, a splendidly rhythmic and graceful courting encounter and a close cousin of Chile's and Bolivia's Cueca and the Argentine Zamba, all of them descended from the Zamacueca. The Marinera has its 'Limeña' and 'Norteña' versions and a more syncopated relative, the Tondero, found in the northern coastal regions, is said to have been influenced by slaves brought from Madagascar. All these dances are accompanied by guitars and frequently the cajón, a resonant wooden box on which the player sits, pounding it with his hands. Some of the great names of 'Música Criolla' are the singer/composers Chabuca Granda and Alicia Maguiña, the female singer Jesús Vásquez and the groups Los Morochucos and Hermanos Zañartu.

Afro-Peruvian Also on the coast is the music of the small but influential black community, the 'Música Negroide' or 'Afro-Peruano', which had virtually died out when it was resuscitated in the 1950s, but has since gone from strength to strength, thanks to Nicomedes and Victoria Santa Cruz who have been largely responsible for popularizing this black music and making it an essential ingredient in contemporary Peruvian popular music. It has all the qualities to be found in black music from the Caribbean – a powerful, charismatic beat, rhythmic and lively dancing, and strong percussion provided by the cajón and the quijada de burro, a donkey's jaw with the teeth loosened. Its greatest star is the Afro-Peruvian diva Susana Baca. Her incredible, passionate voice inspired Talking Head's David Byrne to explore this genre further and release a compilation album in 1995, thus bringing Afro-Peruvian music to the attention of the world. Other notable exponents are the excellent Perú Negro, one of the best music and dance groups in Latin America, and the singer Eva Ayllón. In the footsteps of the dynamic Gotan Project (Argentine musicians who have taken a radical approach to the interpretation of the tango), Novalima, a group of internationally based Peruvian musicians, have produced new arrangements of many classic Afro-Peruvian tracks (see www.novalima.net). Some of the classic dances in the black repertoire are the Festejo, Son del Diablo, Toro Mata, Landó and Alcatraz. In the last named one of the partners dances behind the other with a candle, trying to set light to a piece of paper tucked into the rear of the other partner's waist.

Festivals

Fiestas (festivals) are a fundamental part of life for most Peruvians, taking place the length and breadth of the country and with such frequency that it would be hard to miss one, even during the briefest of stays. This is fortunate, because arriving in any town or village during these frenetic celebrations is a great Peruvian experience.

While Peru's festivals can't rival those of Brazil for fame or colour, the quantity of alcohol consumed and the partying run them pretty close. What this means is that, at some point, you will fall over, through inebriation or exhaustion, or both. After several days of this, you will awake with a hangover the size of the Amazon rainforest and probably have no recollection of what you did with your backpack.

Peruvian festivals also involve widespread balloons-filled-with-water fights, bags of flour and any other missile guaranteed to cause a mess. In the Amazon region various petroleum by-products are favoured ingredients, which can be bad news for smokers. Some travellers complain that they are being picked on, but to someone from the *altiplano*, a 6-ft tall, blond-haired gringo makes an easier target. So, don't wear your best clothes, do arm yourself with plenty of water bombs, and get into the spirit and have some fun! With over 3000 fiestas, there are too many to mention them all. The main national ones are described in Holidays and festivals, on page 20, and details of local fiestas are given under the listings for each town.

Among the most notable celebrations are Carnival week in Cajamarca – a raucous and messy affair, even by Peruvian standards – and the fiesta of the Virgen de la Candelaria, which takes place in the first week in February along the shores of Lake Titicaca near the Bolivian border and features dance groups from all around the region. The most famous Holy Week is held in Ayacucho, when many thousands of fervent devotees participate in daily processions. On the coast, the Marinera festival in January and the Spring festival in September in Trujillo are opportunities to see the Marinera dancers, while in the black communities of Chincha, south of Lima, you can enjoy the best of Afro-Peruvian music and dance (see Music and dance above).

Meaning of fiestas

It is only when they don their extravagant costumes and masks and drink, eat and dance to excess that the indigenous Peruvians show their true character. The rest of the time they hide behind a metaphorical mask of stony indifference as a form of protection against the alien reality in which they are forced to live. When they consume alcohol and coca and start dancing, the pride in their origins resurfaces. This allows them to forget the reality of poverty, unemployment and oppression and reaffirms their will to live as well as their unity with the world around them.

The object of the fiesta is a practical one, such as the success of the coming harvest or the fertility of animals. Thus the constant eating, drinking and dancing serves the purpose of giving thanks for the sun and rain that makes things grow and for the fertility of the soil and livestock, gifts from Pachamama, or Mother Earth, the most sacred of all gods. So, when you see the Aymara spill a little *chicha* (maize beer) every time they refill, it's not because they're sloppy but because they're offering a *ch'alla* (sacrifice) to Pachamama.

The participants in the dances that are the central part of the fiesta are dressed in garish, outlandish costumes and elaborate masks, each one depicting a character from popular myth. Some of these originate in the colonial period, others survive from the Inca Empire or even further back. Often the costumes caricature the Spanish. In this way, the indigenous people mock those who erased their heritage.

Literature

Quechua

The fact that the Incas had no written texts in the conventional European sense and that the Spaniards were keen to suppress their conquest's culture means that there is little evidence today of what poetry and theatre was performed in pre-conquest times. It is known that the Incas had two types of poet, the amautas, historians, poets and teachers who composed works that celebrated the ruling class' gods, heroes and

Day of the Dead

One of the most important dates in the indigenous people's calendar is the 2 November, the 'Day of the Dead'. This tradition has been practised since time immemorial. In the Incaic calendar, November was the eighth month and meant Ayamarca, or land of the dead. This celebration, or 'All Saints' as it is also known, is just one example of religious adaptation in which the ancient beliefs of ethnic cultures are mixed with the rites of the Catholic Church.

According to Aymara belief, the spirit (*athun ajayu*) visits its relatives at this time of the year and is fed in order to continue its journey before its reincarnation. The relatives of the dead prepare for the arrival of the spirit days in advance. Among the many items necessary for these meticulous preparations are little bread dolls, each one of which has a particular significance. A ladder is needed for the spirit to descend from the other world to the terrestrial one. There are other figures which represent the grandparents, great grandparents and loved ones of the person who has 'passed into a better life'. Horse-shaped breads are prepared that will serve as a means of transport for the soul in order to avoid fatigue.

Inside the home, the relatives construct a tomb supported by boxes over which is laid a black cloth. Here they put the bread, along with sweets, flowers, onions and sugar cane. This latter item is an indispensable part of the table as it symbolizes the invigorating element which prevents the spirit from becoming tired on its journey towards the Earth. The union of the flowers with the onion is called *tojoro* and is a vital part of the preparations. It ensures that the dead one does not become disoriented and arrives in the correct house.

The tomb is also adorned with the dead relative's favourite food and drink, not forgetting the all-important glass of beer as, according to popular tradition, this is the first nourishment taken by the souls when they arrive at their houses. Once the spirit has arrived and feasted with its living relatives, the entire ceremony is then transported to the graveside in the local cemetery, where it is carried out again, beside the many other mourning families.

This meeting of the living and their dead relatives is re-enacted the following year, though less ostentatiously, and again for the final time in the third year, the year of the farewell. It does not continue after this; just as well as the costs can be crippling for the family concerned.

events, and haravecs, who expressed popular sentiments. There is strong evidence also that drama was important in Inca society.

Written Quechua even today is far less common than works in the oral tradition. Although Spanish culture has had some influence on Quechua, the native stories, lyrics and fables retain their own identity. Not until the 19th century did Peruvian writers begin seriously to incorporate indigenous ideas into their art, but their audience was limited. Nevertheless, the influence of Quechua on Peruvian literature in Spanish continues to grow.

Colonial Period

In 16th-century Lima, headquarters of the Viceroyalty of Peru, the Spanish officials concentrated their efforts on the religious education of the new territories and literary output was limited to mainly histories and letters.

Chroniclers such as Pedro Cieza de León (*Crónica del Perú*, published from 1553) and Agustín de Zárate (*Historia del descubrimiento y conquista del Perú*, 1555) were written from the point of view that Spanish domination was right. Their most renowned successors, though, took a different stance. Inca Garcilaso de la Vega was a mestizo, whose *Comentarios reales que tratan del origen de los Incas* (1609) were at pains to justify the achievements, religion and culture of the Inca Empire. He also commented on Spanish society in the colony. A later work, Historia general del Perú (1617) went further in condemning Viceroy Toledo's suppression of Inca culture. Through his work, written in Spain, many aspects of Inca society, plus poems and prayers have survived.

Writing at about the same time as Inca Garcilaso was Felipe Guaman Poma de Ayala, whose *El primer nueva corónica y buen gobierno* (1613-15) is possibly one of the most reproduced of Latin American texts (eg on T-shirts, CDs, posters and carrier bags). Guaman Poma was a minor provincial Inca chief from Ayacucho province whose writings and illustrations, addressed to King Felipe III of Spain, offer a view of a stable pre-conquest Andean society (not uniquely Inca), in contrast with the unsympathetic colonial society that usurped it.

In the years up to Independence, the growth of an intellectual elite in Lima spawned more poetry than anything else. As criollo discontent grew, satire increased both in poetry and in the sketches which accompanied dramas imported from Spain. The poet Mariano Melgar (1791-1815) wrote in a variety of styles, including the yaraví, the love-song derived from the pre-Columbian harawi (from haravek). Melgar died in an uprising against the Spanish but played an important part in the Peruvian struggle from freedom from the colonial imagination.

After Independence

After Independence, Peruvian writers imitated Spanish costumbrismo, sketches of characters and life-styles from the new Republic. The first author to transcend this fashion was Ricardo Palma (1833-1919), whose inspiration, the tradición, fused costumbrismo and Peru's rich oral traditions. Palma's hugely popular Tradiciones peruanas is a collection of pieces which celebrate the people, history and customs of Peru through sayings, small incidents in mainly colonial history and gentle irony.

Much soul-searching was to follow Peru's defeat in the War of the Pacific. Manuel González Prada (1844-1918), for instance, wrote essays fiercely critical of the state of the nation: *Páginas libres* (1894), *Horas de lucha* (1908). José Carlos Mariátegui, the foremost Peruvian political thinker of the early 20th century, said that González Prada represented the first lucid instant of Peruvian consciousness. He also wrote poetry, some Romantic, some, like his *Baladas peruanas*, an evocation of indigenous and colonial history, very pro-Indian, very anti-White.

20th century

Mariátegui himself (1895-1930), after a visit to Europe in 1919, considered deeply the question of Peruvian identity. His opinion was that it could only be seen in a global context and that the answer lay in Marxism. With this perspective he wrote about politics, economics, literature and the indigenous question (see *Siete ensayos de interpretación de la realidad peruana*, 1928).

Other writers had continued this theme. For instance Clorinda Matto de Turner (1854-1909) intended to express in *Aves sin nido* (1889) her "tender love for the indigenous people" and hoped to improve their lot. Regardless of the debate over whether the novel achieves these aims, she was the forerunner by several years of the 'indigenist' genre in Peru and the most popular of those who took up González Prada's cause.

 Other prose writers continued in this vein at the beginning of the 20th century, but it was Ciro Alegría (1909-1967) who gave major, fictional impetus to the racial question. Like Mariátegui, Alegría was politically committed, but to the APRA party, rather than Marxism. Of his first three novels, *La serpiente de oro* (1935), *Los perros hambrientos* (1938) and *El mundo es ancho y ajeno* (1941), the latter is his most famous.

Contemporary with Alegría was José María Arguedas (1911-1969), whose novels, stories and politics were also deeply rooted in the ethnic question. Arguedas, though not Indian, had a largely Quechua upbringing and tried to reconcile this with the hispanic world in which he worked. This inner conflict was one of the main causes of his suicide. His books include *Agua* (short stories, 1935), *Yawar fiesta* (1941), *Los ríos profundos* (1958) and *Todas las sangres* (1964). They portray different aspects of the confrontation of indigenous society with the changing outside world that impinges on it.

In the 1950s and 1960s, there was a move away from the predominantly rural and indigenist to an urban setting. At the forefront were, among others, Mario Vargas Llosa, Julio Ramón Ribeyro, Enrique Congrains Martín, Oswaldo Reynoso, Luis Loayza, Sebastián Salazar Bondy and Carlos E Zavaleta. Taking their cue from a phrase used by both poet César Mora and Salazar Bondy (in an essay of 1964), "Lima, la horrible", they explored all aspects of the city, including the influx of people from the sierra. These writers incorporated new narrative techniques in the urban novel, which presented a world where popular culture and speech were rich sources of literary material, despite the difficulty in transcribing them.

Many writers, such as Vargas Llosa, broadened their horizons beyond the capital. His novels after La ciudad y los perros encompassed many different parts of the country. An additional factor was that several writers spent many years abroad, Vargas Llosa himself, for instance, and Ribeyro (1929-1994). The latter's short stories, though mostly set in Lima, embrace universal themes of delusion and frustration. The title story of *Los gallinazos sin pluma* (1955), a tale of squalor and greed amid the city's rubbish tips, has become a classic, even though it does not contain the irony, pathos and humour of many of his other stories or novels.

Other writers of this period include Manuel Scorza (1928-1983), who wrote a series of five novels under the general title of *La guerra silenciosa* (including *Redoble por Rancas*, *El jinete insomne*, *La tumba del relámpago*) which follow the tradition of the indigenist struggle, and also emphasize the need to defend indigenous society with growing militancy if necessary.

Alfredo Bryce Echenique (born 1939) has enjoyed much popularity following the success of *Un mundo para Julius* (1970), a brilliant satire on the upper and middle classes of Lima. His other novels include *Tantas veces Pedro* (1977), *La última mudanza de Felipe Carrillo* (1988), *No me esperen en abril* (1995), *Dos señoras conversan* (1990), *La amigdalitis de Tarzan* (2000) and *El huerto de mi amada*, which won the Premio Planeta (Barcelona) in 2002. Other contemporary writers of note are: Jaime Bayly (born 1965), who is also a journalist and TV presenter. His novels include *Fue ayer y no me acuerdo*, *Los últimos días de la prensa*, *No se lo digas a nadie* and *La noche es virgen*. The last named is typical of his style, full of irony and slang, dealing with the lives the young and affluent in Lima, gay/bisexual, bored, dope-smoking rock-music fans. His most recent novel is *Y de repente, un ángel* (2005). A highly rated short-story writer is Pilar Dughi (born 1956), for instance *Ave de la noche* (1996). See also Rodolfo Hinostroza (born 1941), novelist, playwright and poet, whose books include *Cuentos de Contranatura* (1972) and *Extremo occidente* (2002); Fernando Ampuero (born 1949), whose books include *Miraflores Melody* (1979), *Malos modales* (1994), *Bicho raro* (1996), *Cuentos escogidos* (1998) and *El enano, historia de una enemistad* (2001); Alonso Cueto (born 1954), *La batalla del pasado*, *El tigre blanco* and *El otro amor de Diana*

Abril; Mario Bellatín (born 1960 in Mexico but educated in Peru), among whose works are the excellent short novels *Salón de belleza* (1994) and *Damas chinas* (1995); and Ivan Thays (born 1968), *Escena de caza* (1996) and *Viaje interior*, as well as short stories. A new voice is Daniel Alarcón, born in Lima but brought up in Birmingham, Alabama, whose first collection of stories, *War by Candlelight* (*Guerra en la penumbra* – 2005) is set almost entirely in Lima but is written in English. He is editor of the arts magazine *Etiqueta negra*.

20th-century poetry

At the end of the 19th century, the term Modernism was introduced in Latin America by the Nicaraguan Rubén Darío, not to define a precise school of poetry, but to indicate a break with both Romanticism and Realism. In Peru one major exponent was José Santos Chocano (1875-1934), who labelled his poetry "mundonovismo" (New Worldism), claiming for himself the role of Poet of South America. He won international fame (see, for example, *Alma América*, 1906), but his star soon waned.

A much less assuming character was José María Eguren (1874-1942) who, feeling alienated from the society around him, sought spiritual reality in the natural world (*Simbólicas*, 1911; *La canción de las figuras*, 1916; Poesías, 1929). It has been said that with Eguren the flourishing of Peruvian 20th century poetry began.

Without doubt, the most important poet in Peru, if not Latin America, in the first half of the 20th century, was César Vallejo. Born in 1892 in Santiago de Chuco (Libertad), Vallejo left Peru in 1923 after being framed and briefly jailed in Trujillo for a political crime. In 1928 he was a founder of the Peruvian Socialist Party, then he joined the Communist Party in 1931 in Madrid. From 1936 to his death in Paris in 1938 he opposed the fascist takeover in Spain. His first volume was *Los heraldos negros* in which the dominating theme of all his work, a sense of confusion and inadequacy in the face of the unpredictability of life, first surfaces. *Trilce* (1922), his second work, is unlike anything before it in the Spanish language. The poems contain (among other things) made-up words, distortions of syntax, their own internal logic and rhythm, graphic devices and innovative uses of sounds, clichés and alliterations. *Poemas humanos* and *España, aparta de mí este cáliz* (written as a result of Vallejo's experiences in the Spanish Civil War) were both published posthumously, in 1939.

In the 1960s writers began to reflect the broadening horizons of that increasingly liberal decade, politically and socially, which followed the Cuban Revolution. One poet who embraced the revolutionary fervour was Javier Heraud (born Miraflores 1942). His early volumes, *El río* (1960) and *El viaje* (1961) are apparently simple in conception and expression, but display a transition from embarking on the adventure of life (the river) to autumnal imagery of solitude. In 1961 he went to the USSR, Asia, Paris and Madrid, then in 1962 to Cuba to study cinema. He returned to Peru in 1963 and joined the Ejército de Liberación Nacional. On 15 May 1963 he was shot by government forces near Puerto Maldonado. Heraud's friend César Calvo, now living in Cuba, is a poet and essayist worth reading.

Other major poets born in the early 20th century are Emilio Adolfo Westphalen (1911) and Jorge Eduardo Eielson (see his book *Celebración*). Others who began to publish in the 1960s were Luis Hernández (1941-1977), Antonio Cisneros (born 1942) and Marco Martos (born 1942).

In the 1970s, during the social changes propelled by the Velasco regime (1968-1975), new voices arose, many from outside Lima, eg the Hora Zero group (1970-1973 – Enrique Verástegui, Jorge Pimentel, Juan Ramírez Ruiz), whose energetic poetry employed slang, obscenities and other means to challenge preconceptions. Other poets of the 1970s and after: José Watanabe (born 1946), a film-maker as well as poet, with *Album de familia* (1971) and *Historia natural* (1996); Giovanna Pollarolo (poet, short story writer and screenwriter, born 1952) whose collections include *Huerto de olivos*, 1982, *Entre mujeres solas*, 1996, *La ceremonia de adios*, 1997 and Atado de nervios, 1999, and Rocio Silva Santiesteban (born 1967) who has published short stories as well as the poetry collections *Asuntos circunstanciales* (1984), *Este oficio no me gusta* (1987) and *Mariposa negra* (1996). Younger poets of note are: Ericka Ghersi (born 1972), *Zenobia y el anciano* (1994), *Contra la ausencia* (2002), Renato Cisneros (born 1976), *Ritual de los prójimos* (1998) and *Maquina fantasma* (2002), Rosella di Paolo (born 1960), *Piel alzada* (1993), *Tablillas de San Lázaro* (2001) among other collections, and Marita Troiano, whose works include *Mortal in puribus* (1996) and *Secreto a veces* (2003).

Fine art and sculpture

The Catholic Church was the main patron of the arts during the colonial period. The churches and monasteries that sprang up in the newly conquered territories created a demand for paintings and sculptures, met initially by imports from Europe of both works of art and of skilled craftsmen, and later by home- grown products.

Colonial period

An essential requirement for the inauguration of any new church was an image for the altar and many churches in Lima preserve fine examples of sculptures imported from Seville during the 16th and 17th centuries. Not surprisingly, among the earliest of these are figures of the crucified Christ, such as those in the Cathedral and the church of La Merced by Juan Martínez Montañés, one of the foremost Spanish sculptors of the day, and that in San Pedro, by his pupil Juan de Mesa of 1625. Statues of the Virgin and Child were also imported to Lima from an early date, and examples from the mid-16th century survive in the Cathedral and in Santo Domingo by Roque de Balduque, also from Seville although Flemish by birth.

Sculptures were expensive and difficult to import, and as part of their policy of relative frugality the Franciscan monks tended to favour paintings. In Lima, the museum of San Francisco now houses an excellent collection of paintings imported from Europe, including a powerful series of saints by Zubarán, as well as other works from his studio, a series of paintings of the life of Christ from Ruben's workshop and works from the circles of Ribera and Murillo, see page 86.

The Jesuits commissioned the Sevillian artist Juan de Valdés Leal to paint a series of the life of St Ignatius Loyola (1660s) which still hangs in San Pedro. The Cathedral museum has a curious series from the Bassano workshop of Venice representing the labours of the monks and dating from the early 17th century. Another interesting artistic import from Europe that can still be seen in San Pedro (see Lima Churches) are the gloriously colourful painted tile decorations (*azulejos*) on the walls of Dominican monastery, produced to order by Sevillian workshops in 1586 and 1604.

Painters and sculptors soon made their way to Peru in search of lucrative commissions including several Italians who arrived during the later 16th century. The Jesuit Bernardo Bitti (1548-1610), for example, trained in Rome before working in Lima, Cuzco, Juli and Arequipa, where examples of his elegantly Mannerist paintings are preserved in the Jesuit church of the Compañia, see Arequipa page 250.

Another Italian, Mateo Pérez de Alesio worked in the Sistine Chapel in Rome before settling in Peru. In Lima the Sevillian sculptor Pedro de Noguera (1592-1655) won the contract for the choirstalls of the Cathedral in 1623 and, together with other Spanish craftsmen, produced a set of cedar stalls decorated with vigorous figures of saints and Biblical characters, an outstanding work unmatched elsewhere in the Viceroyalty.

Native artists

European imports, however, could not keep up with demand and local workshops of creole, mestizo and indigenous craftsmen flourished from the latter part of the 16th century. As the Viceregal capital and the point of arrival into Peru, the art of Lima was always strongly influenced by European, especially Spanish models, but the old Inca capital of Cuzco became the centre of a regional school of painting which developed its own characteristics.

A series of paintings of the 1660s, now hanging in the Museo de Arte Religioso, see Cuzco page 141, commemorate the colourful Corpus Christi procession of statues of the local patron saints through the streets of Cuzco. These paintings document the appearance of the city and local populace, including Spanish and Inca nobility, priests and laity, rich and poor, Spaniard, Indian, African and mestizo. Many of the statues represented in this series are still venerated in the local parish churches. They are periodically painted and dressed in new robes, but underneath are the original sculptures, executed by native craftsmen. Some are of carved wood while others use the pre-conquest technique of maguey cactus covered in sized cloth.

A remarkable example of an indigenous Andean who acquired European skills was Felipe Guaman Poma de Ayala whose 1000-page letter to the King of Spain celebrating the Andean past and condemning the colonial present contained a visual history of colonial and precolonial life in the Andes, see also page 601.

One of the most successful native painters was Diego Quispe Tito (1611-1681) who claimed descent from the Inca nobility and whose large canvases, often based on Flemish engravings, demonstrate the wide range of European sources that were available to Andean artists in the 17th century. But the Cuzco School is best known for the anonymous devotional works where the painted contours of the figures are overlaid with flat patterns in gold, creating highly decorative images with an underlying tension between the two- and three-dimensional aspects of the work. The taste for richly decorated surfaces can also be seen in the 17th and 18th century frescoed interiors of many Andean churches, as in Chinchero, Andahuaylillas and Huaro, and in the ornate carving on altarpieces and pulpits throughout Peru.

Andean content creeps into colonial religious art in a number of ways, most simply by the inclusion of elements of indigenous flora and fauna, or, as in the case of the Corpus Christi paintings, by the use of a specific setting, with recognizable buildings and individuals.

Changes to traditional Christian iconography include the representation of one of the Magi as an Inca, as in the painting of the Adoration of the Magi in San Pedro in Juli (see Puno Excursions, page 222). Another example is that to commemorate his miraculous intervention in the conquest of Cuzco in 1534, Santiago is often depicted triumphing over indigenous people instead of the more familiar Moors. Among the most remarkable 'inventions' of colonial art are the fantastically over-dressed archangels carrying muskets which were so popular in the 18th century. There is no direct European source for these archangels, but in the Andes they seem to have served as a painted guard of honour to the image of Christ or the Virgin on the high altar.

Independence and after

Political independence from Spain in 1824 had little immediate impact on the arts of Peru except to create a demand for portraits of the new national and continental heroes such as Simón Bolívar and San Martín, many of the best of them produced by the mulatto artist José Gil de Castro (died Lima 1841). Later in the century another mulatto, Pancho Fierro (1810-1879) mocked the rigidity and pretentiousness of Lima society in lively satirical watercolours, while Francisco Laso (1823-1860), an active campaigner for political reform, made the Andean people into respectable subjects for oil paintings.

It was not until the latter part of the 19th century that events from colonial history became popular. The Museo de Arte in Lima (see Lima page 84) has examples of grandiose paintings by Ignacio Merino (1817-1876) glorifying Columbus, as well as the gigantic romanticized 'Funeral of Atahualpa' by Luis Montero (1826-1869). A curious late flowering of this celebration of colonial history is the chapel commemorating Francisco Pizarro in Lima cathedral which was redecorated in 1928 with garish mosaic pictures of the conqueror's exploits.

Impressionism arrived late and had a limited impact in Peru. Teofilo Castillo (1857-1922), instead of using the technique to capture contemporary reality, created frothy visions of an idealized colonial past. Typical of his work is the large 'Funeral Procession of Santa Rosa' of 1918, with everything bathed in clouds of incense and rose petals, which hangs in the Museo de Arte, in Lima. Daniel Hernández (1856-1932), founder of Peru's first Art School, used a similar style for his portraits of Lima notables past and present.

20th century to today

During the first half of the 20th century, Peruvian art was dominated by figurative styles and local subject matter. Political theories of the 1920s recognized the importance of Andean indigenous culture to Peruvian identity and created a climate which encouraged a figurative indigenista school of painting, derived in part from the socialist realism of the Mexican muralists. The movement flourished after the founding of the Escuela de Bellas Artes in 1920. José Sabogal (1888-1956) is the best known exponent of the group which also included Mario Urteaga (1875-1957), Jorge Vinatea Reinoso (1900-1931), Enrique Camino Brent (1909-1960), Camilo Blas (1903-1984) and Alejandro González (1900-1984). Their work can be seen in the Museo de Arte and the Museo Banco Central de Reserva in Lima.

The Mexican muralist tradition persisted into the 1960s with Manuel Ugarte Eléspuru (1911) and Teodoro Núñez Ureta (1914), both of whom undertook large-scale commissions in public buildings in Lima. Examples of public sculpture in the indigenist mode can be seen in plazas and parks throughout Peru, but it was in photography that indigenism found its most powerful expression. From the beginning of the century photographic studios flourished even in smaller towns. Martín Chambi (1891-1973) is the best known of the early 20th century Peruvian photographers but there were many others, including Miguel Chani (1860-1951) who maintained the grandly named Fotografía Universal studios in Cuzco, Puno and Arequipa.

From the middle of the century artists have experimented with a variety of predominantly abstract styles and the best-known contemporary Peruvian painter, Fernando de Szyszlo (1925) has created a visual language of his own, borrowing from Abstract Expressionism on the one hand and from pre-Columbian iconography on the other. His strong images, which suggest rather than represent mythical beings and cosmic forces, have influenced a whole generation of younger Peruvian artists. Look for his monument, Intihuatana 2000, near the sea in Miraflores.

Other leading figures whose work can be seen in public and commercial galleries in Lima include Venancio Shinki, Tilsa Tsuchiya, José Tola, Ricardo Weisse, Ramiro Llona and Leoncio Villanueva. Carlos Revilla, whose wife is his muse and principal subject of his painting, is clearly influenced by Hieronymous Bosch, while Bill Caro is an important exponent of hyperrealism. Víctor Delfín, a painter and sculptor (with beautiful work in iron) can be visited at his house in Barranco (Domeyko 366). His piece, The Kiss (El beso), is in the Parque del Amor in Lima. Pedro Azabache (from Trujillo) is a disciple of José Sabogal; his work is much broader in scope than the indigenism of his mentor. There are many other new artists whose work could be mentioned (Luz Letts, Eduardo Tokeshi, Carlos Enrique Polanco, Bruno Zepilli, Christian Bendayan – try to contact him in Iquitos, Flavia Gandolfo, Claudia Coca) and there are plenty of galleries in Lima with representative

Viringo

If you go to a Peruvian museum at a coastal archaeological site, you will probably see an elegant dog, with a long, thin nose and arched neck prowling around the entrance. It may be a bit shy, and, if the weather is cold, it may be waring a little woollen jacket. This is because the dog has no hair.

The Peruvian Hairless, or viringo, is a rare breed today, but in Inca times was a companion animal whose main job was to warm his master's bed. The Chavín, Moche and Chimú cultures represented it on their ceramics, but its origins are unknown. The most likely theory is that it accompanied the first migrants to the Amercian continent from Asia. In its most common, hairless form, it has no fleas and no smell.

Breeders note that it needs protecting against the sun and the cold, but there is also a coated variety (called 'powder puff' in the dog world).

In recognition of the importance of this dog in its history, the Peruvian government decreed in Law number 27537 that every site museum on the coast must have at least one viringo on the premises.

In 2006 archaeologists announced the discovery of over 40 mummified dogs at tombs of the Chiribaya people in the Ilo valley, dating from 900-1350 AD. They weren't viringos, though, but a distinct breed, christened 'Chiribaya shepherds' as it is supposed that they herded llamas.

exhibitions. A new foundation is working towards opening a museum of contemporary art in Barranco, Lima, which is long overdue in a country where art is constantly changing. One striking modern piece outside Lima is the mosaic mural at the Ciudad Universitaria UNT in Trujillo, which, at several kilometres long, will be the longest work of art in the world when complete.

Land and environment

Geography

Peru is the third largest South American country, the size of France, Spain and the United Kingdom combined, and presents formidable difficulties to human habitation. Virtually all of the 2250 km of its Pacific coast is desert. From the narrow coastal shelf the Andes rise steeply to a high plateau dominated by massive ranges of snow-capped peaks and gouged with deep canyons. The heavily forested and deeply ravined Andean slopes are more gradual to the east. Further east, towards Brazil and Colombia, begin the vast jungles of the Amazon Basin.

Geology

The geological structure of Peru is dominated by the Nazca Plate beneath the Pacific Ocean, which stretches from Colombia in the north southwards to mid Chile. Along the coastline, this Plate meets and dives below the mass of the South American Plate which has been moving westwards for much of the Earth's geological history. Prior to the middle of the Tertiary Period, say 40 million years ago, marine sediments suggest that the Amazon Basin drained west to the Pacific, but from that time to the present, tectonic forces have created the Andes range the length of the continent, forming the highest peaks outside the Himalayas. The process continues today as shown by the earthquakes and active volcanoes and, in spite of erosion, the mountains still grow higher.

Coast

The coastal region, a narrow ribbon of desert 2250 km long, takes up 11% of the country and holds 44% of the population. It is the economic heart of Peru, consuming most of the imports and supplying half of the exports. When irrigated, the river valleys are extremely fertile, creating oases which grow cotton throughout the country, sugar-cane, rice and asparagus in the north, and grapes, fruit and olives in the south. At the same time, the coastal current teems with fish, and Peru has on occasion had the largest catch in the world.

Not far beyond the border with Ecuador in the north, there are mangrove swamps and tropical rainforest, but southwards this quickly changes to drier and eventually desert conditions. South of Piura is the desert of Sechura, followed by the dry barren land or shifting sands to Chimbote. However, several rivers draining the high mountains to the east more or less reach the sea and water the highly productive 'oases' of Piura, Trujillo, Cajamarca and Chimbote.

South of Chimbote, the Andes reach the sea, and apart from a thin strip of coastland north of Lima, the coastal mountains continue to the Chilean border at Arica. This area receives less rain than the Sahara, but because of the high Andes inland, over 50 Peruvian rivers reach the sea, or would do naturally for at least part of the year. As in the north, there are oases in the south, but mostly inland at the foot of the mountains where the river flow is greatest and high sunshine levels ensure good crop production.

The climate of this region depends almost entirely on the ocean currents along the Pacific coast. Two bodies of water drift northwards, the one closest to the shore, known as the Humboldt Current, is the colder, following the deep sea trench along the edge of the Pacific Plate. The basic wind systems here are the South-East Trades crossing the continent from the Atlantic, but the strong tropical sun over the land draws air into Peru from the Pacific. Being cool, this air does no more than condense into mist (known as the garúa) over the coastal mountains. This is sufficient to provide moisture for some unusual flora but virtually never produces rain, hence the desert conditions. The mixing of the two cold ocean currents, and the cloud cover which protects the water from the strongest sunlight, creates the unique conditions favourable to fish, notably sardines and anchovy, giving Peru an enormous economic resource. In turn, the fish support vast numbers of seabirds whose deposits of guano have been another very successful export for the country. This is the normal situation; every few years, however, it is disrupted by the phenomenon known as 'El Niño', see page 610.

Highlands

The highlands, or la sierra, extend inland from the coastal strip some 250 km in the north, increasing to 400 km in the south. The average altitude is about 3000 m and 50% of Peruvians live there. Essentially it is a plateau dissected by dramatic canyons and dominated by some of the most spectacular mountain ranges in the world.

Mountains

The tallest peaks are in the Cordillera Blanca (Huascarán; 6768 m) and the neighbouring Cordillera Huayhuash (Yerupajá; 6634 m). Huascarán is often quoted as the second highest point in South America after Aconcagua, but this is not so; there are some five other peaks on or near the Argentina-Chile border over 6770 m. The snowline here, at 9° south, is between 4500 m and 5000 m, much lower than further south. For example, at 16° south, permanent snow starts at 6000 m on

Coropuna (6425 m). Peru has more tropical glaciers than any other country in South America, but in recent years scientists have recorded rapid shrinkage of snow and glaciers from Peruvian peaks. This loss is blamed on global warming.

The reasons for this anomaly can be traced again to the Humboldt current. The Cordillera Blanca is less than 100 km from the coast, and the cool air drawn in depresses temperatures at high altitudes. Precipitation comes also from the east and falls as snow. Constant high winds and temperatures well below freezing at night create an unusual microclimate and with it spectacular mountain scenery, making it a mecca for snow and ice mountaineers. Dangers are heightened by the quite frequent earthquakes causing avalanches and landslides which have brought heavy loss of life to the valleys of the region. In 1970, 20,000 people lost their lives when Yungay, immediately west of Huascarán, was overwhelmed.

Canyons

Equally dramatic are the deep canyons taking water from the high mountains to the Pacific. The Colca Canyon, about 100 km north of Arequipa, has been measured at 3200 m from the lower rim to the river, more than twice as deep as the Grand Canyon. At one point it is overlooked by the 5227 m Señal Yajirhua peak, a stupendous 4150 m above the water level. Deeper even than Colca is the Cotahuasi Canyon, also in Arequipa Department, whose deepest point is 3354 m. Other canyons have been found in this remote area yet to be measured and documented.

In spite of these ups and downs which cause great communications difficulties, the presence of water and a more temperate climate on the plateau has attracted people throughout the ages. Present day important population centres in the Highlands include Cajamarca in the north, Huancayo in central Peru and Cuzco in the south, all at around 3000 m. Above this, at around 4000 m, is the 'high steppe' or puna, with constant winds and wide day/night temperature fluctuations. Nevertheless, fruit and potatoes (which originally came from the puna of Peru and Bolivia) are grown at this altitude and the meagre grasslands are home to the ubiquitous llama.

Volcanoes

Although hot springs and evidence of ancient volcanic activity can be seen almost anywhere in Peru, the southern part of the sierra is the only area where there are active volcanoes. These represent the northernmost of a line of volcanoes which stretch 1500 km south along the Chile-Bolivia border to Argentina. Sabancaya (5977 m), just south of the Colca canyon, is currently active, often with a dark plume downwind from the summit. Beyond the Colca canyon is the Valle de los Volcanes, with 80 cinder cones rising 50-250 m above a desolate floor of lava and ash. There are other dormant or recently active volcanoes near the western side of Lake Titicaca – for example Ubinas – but the most notable is El Misti (5822 m) which overlooks Arequipa. It is perfectly shaped, indicating its status as active in the recent geologic past. Some experts believe it is one of the most potentially dangerous volcanoes in South America. Certainly a major eruption would be a catastrophe for the nearby city.

Lake Titicaca

The southeastern border with Bolivia passes through Titicaca, with about half of the lake in each country. It is the largest lake in South America (ignoring Lake Maracaibo in Venezuela which is linked to the sea) and at 3812 m, the highest navigable body of water in the world. It covers about 8300 sq km, running 190 km northwest to southeast, and is 80 km across. It lies in a 60,000 sq km basin between the coastal and eastern Andes which spread out southwards to their widest point at latitude 18° south.

The average depth is over 100 m, with the deepest point recorded at 281 m. Twenty-five rivers, most from Peru, flow into the lake and a small outlet leaves the

When the winds blow

Anyone who tuned into a weather forecast during late 1997 now knows about the climatic effect called El Niño, which means "Christ child". El Niño was so named by Peruvian fishermen who noticed the warming of the waters of the eastern Pacific around Christmas time.

Every three to seven years, for some as yet unexplained reason, the trade winds that usually blow west from South America subside. So the warm waters of the Pacific – a giant pool the size of Canada – drift eastwards towards South America. The result is worldwide weather chaos.

In 1997 El Niño made its third visit of the decade. The eastern Pacific heated faster than at any time in recorded history to become the most devastating climatic event of the century, surpassing even the 1982-83 El Niño, which killed thousands and caused almost US$14 billion in damage.

The 1997 El Niño caused drought in Australia, New Zealand, Thailand, Malaysia and Papua New Guinea, forest fires in Indonesia, famine in North Korea, hurricanes along the US Pacific coast and the failure of the fish harvest in Peru. El Niño also sparked epidemics of cholera, encephalitis and bubonic plague.

The 1997-1998 event, the worst for 50 years, was the last in a rapid succession in the 1990s. Since then there has another event in 2002-03. Scientists still appear to know little about El Niño, but monitoring and research continue around the globe.

lake at Desaguadero on the Bolivia-Peru border. This takes no more than 5% of the inflow, the rest is lost through evaporation and hence the waters of the lake are slightly brackish, producing the totora reeds used to make the mats and balsa boats for which the lake dwellers are famed.

The lake is the remnant of a vast area of water formed in the Ice Age known as Lake Ballivián. This extended at least 600 km to the south into Bolivia and included what is now Lake Poopó and the Salar de Uyuni. Now the lake level fluctuates seasonally, normally rising from December to March and receding for the rest of the year but extremes of 5 m between high and low levels have been recorded. This can cause problems and high levels in the late 1980s disrupted transport links near the shoreline. The night temperature can fall as low as -25°C but high daytime temperatures ensure that the surface average is about 14°C.

Eastern Andes and Amazon Basin

Almost half of Peru is on the eastern side of the Andes and about 90% of the country's drainage is into the Amazon system. It is an area of heavy rainfall with cloudforest above 3500 m and tropical rainforest lower down. There is little savanna, or natural grasslands, characteristic of other parts of the Amazon Basin.

There is some dispute on the Amazon's source. Officially, the mighty river begins as the Marañón, whose longest tributary rises just east of the Cordillera Huayhuash. However, the longest journey for the proverbial raindrop, some 6400 km, probably starts in southern Peru, where the headwaters of the Apurímac (Ucayali) flow from the snows on the northern side of the Nevado Mismi, near Cailloma.

With much more rainfall on the eastern side of the Andes, rivers are turbulent and erosion dramatic. Although vertical drops are not as great – there is a whole continent to cross to the Atlantic – valleys are deep, ridges narrow and jagged and there is forest below 3000 m. At 1500 m the Amazon jungle begins and water is the only means of surface transport available, apart from three roads which reach Borja (on the Marañón),

Yurimaguas (on the Huallaga) and Pucallpa (on the Ucayali), all at about 300 m above the Atlantic which is still 4000 km or so downstream. The vastness of the Amazon lowlands becomes apparent and it is here that Peru bulges 650 km northeast past Iquitos to the point where it meets Colombia and Brazil at Leticia. Oil and gas have recently been found in the Amazon, and new finds are made every year, which means that new pipelines and roads will eventually link more places to the Pacific coast.

Climate

Coast

On the coast summertime is from December-April, when temperatures range from 25° to 35°C and it is hot and dry. Wintertime is May-November, when the temperature drops a bit and it is cloudy.

The coastal climate is determined by the cold sea-water adjoining deserts. Prevailing inshore winds pick up so little moisture over the cold Humboldt current, which flows from Antarctica, that only from May to November does it condense. The resultant blanket of sea-mist (called garúa) extends from the south to about 200 km north of Lima. It is thickest to the south as far as Chincha and to the north as far as Huarmey, beyond which it thins and the sun can be expected to break through.

Sierra

From April-October is the dry season. It is hot and dry during the day, around 20°-25°C, and cold and dry at night, often below freezing. From November-April is the wet season, when it is dry and clear most mornings, with some rainfall in the afternoon. There is a small temperature drop (18°C) and not much difference at night (15°C).

Selva

April to October is the dry season, with temperatures up to 35°C. In the jungle areas of the south, a cold front can pass through at night. November to April is the wet season. It is humid and hot, with heavy rainfall at any time.

Flora and fauna

Peru is a country of great biological diversity. The fauna and flora are to a large extent determined by the influence of the Andes, the longest uninterrupted mountain chain in the world, and the mighty Amazon river, which has the largest volume of any river in the world. Of Earth's 32 known climate zones Peru has 28, and of the 117 recognized micro-climates Peru has 84. Throughout the country there are 61 protected natural areas.

Natural history

This diversity arises not only from the wide range of habitats available, but also from the history of the continent. South America has essentially been an island for some 70 million years joined only by a narrow isthmus to Central and North America. Land passage played a significant role in the gradual colonization of South America by species from the north. When the land-link closed these colonists evolved to a wide variety of forms free from the competitive pressures that prevailed elsewhere. When the land-bridge was re-established some four million years ago a new invasion of species took place from North America, adding to the diversity but also leading to numerous extinctions. Comparative stability has ensued since then and has guaranteed the survival of many primitive groups like the opossums.

Coast

The coastal region of Peru is extremely arid, partly as a result of the cold Humboldt current (see Climate above). The paucity of animal life in the area between the coast and the mountains is obviously due to this lack of rain, though in some areas intermittent lomas, which are areas of sparse scrubby vegetation caused by moisture in the sea mist. The plants which survive provide ideal living conditions for insects which attract insectivorous birds and humming birds to feed on their nectar. Cactuses are abundant in northern Peru and provide a wooded landscape of trees and shrubs including the huarango (*Prosopis juliflora*). Also common in the north is the algorrobo tree – 250,000 ha were planted in 1997 to take advantage of the El Niño rains. Algorrobo forests (*algorrobales*), scrub thicket (*matorrales*) and coastal wetlands each provide habitat for some 30 species of birds. Mammals include foxes, three species of deer and six species of dogs from pre-Columbian times.

Andes

From the desert rise the steep Andean slopes. In the deeply incised valleys Andean fox and deer may occasionally be spotted. Herds of llamas and alpacas graze the steep hillsides. Mountain caracara and Andean lapwing are frequently observed soaring, and there is always the possibility of spotting flocks of mitred parrots or even the biggest species of hummingbird in the world (Patagonia gigas).

The Andean zone has many lakes and rivers and countless swamps. Exclusive to this area short-winged grebe and the torrent duck which feeds in the fast flowing rivers, and giant and horned coots. Chilean flamingo frequent the shallow soda lakes. The puna, a habitat characterized by tussock grass and pockets of stunted alpine flowers, gives way to relict elfin forest and tangled bamboo thicket in this inhospitable windswept and frost-prone region. Occasionally the dissected remains of a Puya plant can be found; the result of the nocturnal foraging of the rare spectacled bear. There are quite a number of endemic species of rodent including the viscacha, and it is the last stronghold of the chinchilla. Here pumas roam preying on the herbivores which frequent these mountain – pudu, a tiny Andean deer or guemal and the mountain tapir.

Tropical Andes

The elfin forest gradually grades into mist enshrouded cloudforest at about 3500 m. In the tropical zones of the Andes, the humidity in the cloudforests stimulates the growth of a vast variety of plants particularly mosses and lichens. The cloudforests are found in a narrow strip that runs along the eastern slopes of the spine of the Andes. It is these dense, often impenetrable, forests clothing the steep slopes that are important in protecting the headwaters of all the streams and rivers that cascade from the Andes to form the mighty Amazon as it begins its long journey to the sea. This is a verdant world of dripping epiphytic mosses, lichens, ferns and orchids which grow in profusion despite the plummeting overnight temperatures. The high humidity resulting from the 2 m of rain that can fall in a year is responsible for the maintenance of the forest and it accumulates in puddles and leaks from the ground in a constant trickle that combines to form myriad icy, crystal-clear streams that cascade over precipitous waterfalls. In secluded areas, orange Andean Cock-of-the-Rock give their spectacular display to females in the early morning mists. Woolly monkeys are also occasionally sighted as they descend the wooded slopes. Mixed flocks of colourful tanagers are commonly encountered as are the golden-headed quetzal and Amazon umbrella bird.

Amazon Basin

At about 1500 m there is a gradual transition to the vast lowland forests of the Amazon Basin, which are warmer and more equable than the cloudforests clothing the mountains above. The daily temperature varies little during the year with a high

The debonair dolphin

Two species of dolphin live in the Amazon, the pink *Inia geoffrensis* and the grey *Sotalia fluvialis*.The pink dolphin is mainly solitary, but small groups are often found. Instead of a dorsal fin, it has a hump on its back and it also has a long bottle nose but because of its surfacing habits, you are unlikely to see its nose. The grey dolphin swims in groups and is a more 'conventional' shape, with a dorsal fin and shorter snout. When surfacing it often jumps right out of the water. For centuries the dolphins have lived peacefully with man on the river and, as a result, many myths have grown up around them. Sadly, destruction of habitat and pollution have threatened this harmonious coexistence.

The best-known legend concerns the night-time exploits of the pink dolphin. Indigenous people of the Amazon call it the 'bufeo' and believe that it lives in an underwater city in Lake Caballococha, near the Peru-Colombia border. By night, the *bufeo* transforms himself into a suave gentleman in a white linen suit and, in this guise, he preys on local women. Even today, unwanted pregnancies are sometimes blamed on this magical animal.

For some communities the dolphin is a semi-divine being, for others a untrustworthy witchdoctor. Its teeth, says Alex Shoumatoff in *The Rivers Amazon, are claimed to cure children's diarrhoea, its ear to grant a long-lasting erection and its "grated left eye is an aphrodisiac powder."*

In scientific circles, the pink river dolphins were, until recently, a forgotten species, considered extinct. All that remained was the skeleton of one in Paris, brought back from South America as a gift to Napoleon, and a few vague scientific papers dating from the 19th century in the Natural History Museum in London. The *bufeo* was rediscovered by a British expedition in 1956, then forgotten again until 1987, when Jacques Cousteau astounded TV viewers around the world with the first-ever pictures of pink dolphins frolicking in Amazon.

Now many Amazon lodges take travellers on dolphin-spotting expeditions. With some patience you can see one, or both types of dolphin in the flesh. The more curious pink ones circle quite close to the boat, while the grey will be further away, plunging into the river in unison – a fantastic sight. Back on land, however, female travellers should beware a charming, smartly dressed gentleman who doesn't raise his hat (it covers his blowhole).

of 23-32°C falling slightly to 20-26°C overnight. This lowland region receives some 2 m of rainfall per year most of it falling from November to April. The rest of the year is sufficiently dry, at least in the lowland areas to inhibit the growth of epiphytes and orchids which are so characteristic of the highland areas. For a week or two in the rainy season the rivers flood the forest. The zone immediately surrounding this seasonally flooded forest is referred to as terre firme forest.

The vast river basin of the Amazon is home to an immense variety of species. The environment has largely dictated the lifestyle. Life in or around rivers, lakes, swamps and forest depend on the ability to swim and climb and amphibious and tree-dwelling animals are common. Once the entire Amazon Basin was a great inland sea and the river still contains mammals more typical of the coast, eg manatees and dolphins.

Here in the relatively constant climatic conditions animal and plant life has evolved to an amazing diversity over the millennia. It has been estimated that 3.9 sq km of forest can harbour some 1200 vascular plants, 600 species of tree, and 120 woody plants. Here, in these relatively flat lands, a soaring canopy some 50 m overhead is the power- house of the forest. It is a habitat choked with strangling vines and philodendrons among which mixed troupes of squirrel monkeys and brown capuchins forage. In the high canopy small groups of spider monkeys perform their lazy aerial acrobatics, whilst lower down, cling to epiphyte-clad trunks and branches, groups of saddle-backed and emperor tamarins forage for blossom, fruit and the occasional insect prey.

The most accessible part of the jungle is on or near the many meandering rivers. At each bend of the river the forest is undermined by the currents during the seasonal floods at the rate of some 10-20 m per year leaving a sheer mud and clay bank, whilst on the opposite bend new land is laid down as broad beaches of fine sand and silt.

A succession of vegetation can be seen. The fast growing willow-like Tessaria first stabilizes the ground enabling the tall stands of caña brava Gynerium to become established. Within these dense almost impenetrable stands the seeds of rainforest trees germinate and over a few years thrust their way towards the light. The fastest growing is a species of Cercropia which forms a canopy 15-18 m over the caña but even this is relatively short-lived. The gap in the canopy is quickly filled by other species. Two types of mahogany outgrow the other trees forming a closed canopy at 40 m with a lush understory of shade tolerant Heliconia and ginger. Eventually even the long-lived trees die off to be replaced by others providing a forest of great diversity.

Jungle wildlife

The meandering course of the river provides many excellent opportunities to see herds of russet-brown capybara – a sheep-sized rodent – peccaries and brocket deer. Of considerable ecological interest are the presence of ox-bow lakes, or *cochas*, since these provide an abundance of wildlife which can easily be seen around the lake margins.

The best way to see the wildlife, however, is to get above the canopy. Ridges provide elevated view points from which you can enjoy excellent views. From here, it is possible to look across the lowland flood plain to the foothills of the Andes, some 200 km away. Flocks of parrots and macaws can be seen flying between fruiting trees and troupes of squirrel monkeys and brown capuchins come very close.

The lowland rainforest of Peru is particularly famous for its primates and giant otters. Giant otters were once widespread in Amazonia but came close to extinction in the 1960s owing to persecution by the fur trade. The giant otter population in Peru has since recovered and is now estimated to be at least several hundred. Jaguar and other predators are also much in evidence. Although rarely seen their paw marks are commonly found along the forest trails. Rare bird species are also much in evidence, including fasciated tiger-heron and primitive hoatzins.

The (very) early-morning is the best time to see peccaries, brocket deer and tapir at mineral licks (collpa). Macaw and parrot licks are found along the banks of the river. Here at dawn a dazzling display arrives and clambers around in the branches overhanging the clay-lick. At its peak there may be 600 birds of up to six species (including red and green macaws, and blue-headed parrots) clamouring to begin their descent to the riverbank where they jostle for access to the mineral rich clay. A necessary addition to their diet which may also neutralize the toxins present in the leaf and seed diet. Rare game birds such as razor billed curassows and piping guans may also be seen.

A list of over 600 species has been compiled. Noteworthy are the black-faced cotinga, crested eagle, and the Harpy eagle, the world's most impressive raptor, easily capable of taking an adult monkey. Mixed species flocks are commonly observed containing from 25 to 100-plus birds of perhaps 30 species including blue dacnis, blue-tailed emerald, bananaquit, thick-billed euphoria and the paradise tanager. Each species occupies a slightly different niche, and since there are few individuals of each species in the flock, competition is avoided. Mixed flocks foraging in the canopy are often led by a white-winged shrike, whereas flocks in the understorey are often led by the bluish-slate antshrike. For more information, see page 59.

Books

History and culture

Alden Mason, J *The Ancient Civilizations of Peru* (1991).

Cáceres Macedo, Justo *The Prehispanic Cultures of Peru* (1988).

Hemming, John *The Conquest of the Incas* (1970). The one, invaluable book on the period of the Conquest.

Kendall, Ann *Everyday Life of the Incas* (1978) Batsford.

Mosely, Michael E *The Incas and their Ancestors: The Archaeology of Peru*.

Portal Cabellos, Manuel, *Oro y tragedia de los Incas*, excellent on the division of the empire, civil war and huaqueros.

Peru Explorer, a new bi-monthly investigative archaeology magazine (US$1.50) is published by Consorcio Gráfico del Pacífico.

Bowen, Sally *The Fujimori File. Peru and its President 1990-2000* (2000). A very readable account of the last decade of the 20th century; it ends at the election of that year so the final momentous events of Fujimori's term happened after publication. Bowen has also written, with **Jane Holligan**, *The Imperfect Spy: the Many Lives of Vladimiro Montesinos* (2003), Peisa.

Cuzco and Machu Picchu

See Footprint's *Cuzco and the Inca Heartland*.

Bingham, Hiram *Lost City of the Incas* (2002), Weidenfeld & Nicolson. A new illustrated edition, with an introduction by Hugh Thomson.

Frost, Peter *Exploring Cusco*. On Cuzco, the Sacred Valley, Inca Trail, Machu Picchu and other ruins.

Frost, Peter *The Machu Picchu Historical Sanctuary*, Nuevas Imagenes. Recommended book on Machu Picchu, with colour photos.

Milligan, Max *In the Realm of the Incas* (2001) Harper Collins. A beautiful book with photographs and text.

Morrison, Tony *Qosqo. The Navel of the World* (1997) Condor Books. Cuzco's past and present with an extensive section of photographs of the city and its surroundings.

Reinhard, Johan *The Sacred Center* explains Machu Picchu in archaeological terms.

Thomson, Hugh *The White Rock* (2002), Phoenix, describes Thomson's own travels in the Inca heartland, as well as the journeys of earlier explorers and the history of the region. Also by Thompson is *Cochineal Red: Travels through Ancient Peru* (2006), Weidenfeld & Nicolson. Exploration of the cultures that precede the Incas.

Nazca

Hadingham, E *Lines to the Mountain Gods: Nasca and the Mysteries of Peru* (1987) Random House.

Morrison, Tony *Pathways to the Gods: The Mystery of the Andes Lines* (1978), Michael Russell, obtainable in Lima; and *The Mystery of the Nasca Lines* (1987), nonesuch Expeditions, with an intro by Marie Reiche.

Reinhard, Dr Johan *The Nasca Lines – a new perspective on their origin and meaning*, Editorial Los Pinos, Lima 18.

Woodman, Jim *Nasca, the flight of Condor 1* (1980) Pocket Books, NY. An account of the balloon flight project over the lines.

Chachapoyas area

Muscutt, Keith *Warriors of the Clouds: A Lost Civilization in the Upper Amazon of Peru* (1998) New Mexico Press. Excellent coffee table book and Chachapoyas memoir; also refer to its website (www.chachapoyas.com).

The following **novels** are recommended **Matthiessen, Peter** *At Play in the Fields of the Lord* (1965); **Shakespeare, Nicholas** *The Vision of Elena Silves* (1989); **Thubron, Colin** *To the Last City* (2002) Chatto & Windus; **Wilder, Thornton** *The Bridge of San Luis Rey* (1941) Penguin; **Vltchek, Andre** *Point of No Return* (2005) Mainstay Press. Good **travel books** are: **Murphy, Dervla** *Eight Feet in the Andes* (1994); **Parris, Matthew** *Inca-Kola* (1990); **Shah, Tahir** *Trail of Feathers* (2001) Phoenix; **Wright, Ronald** *Cut Stones and Crossroads: a Journey in Peru* (1984) Viking.

Climbing, trekking and cycling

Biggar, John *The Andes. A Guide for Climbers* (1999) Andes Publishing.
Bartle, Jim *Parque Nacional Huascarán*, photo collection in English and Spanish.
Díaz, Felipe *Callejón de Huaylas y Cordillera Blanca* (Spanish, English and German editions), available locally.
Gómez, Antonio, and Tomé, Juan José *La Cordillera Blanca de Los Andes* (1998) Desnivel, Spanish only, climbing guide with some trekking and general information, available locally. Also *Escaladas en los Andes. Guía de la Cordillera Blanca* (1999) Desnivel (Spanish only), a climbing guide.
Kolff, Helen and Kees *Flores silvestres de la Cordillera Blanca/Wildflowers of the Cordillera Blanca* (1997) El Instituto Montaña, is a bilingual guide, fully illustrated.
Ricker, John F *Yuraq Janka, Cordilleras Blanca and Rosko* (1977), The Alpine Club of Canada, The American Alpine CLub.
Sharman, David *Climbs of the Cordillera Blanca of Peru* (1995) Whizzo. Another climbing guide, available locally, from South American Explorers, as well as from Cordee in the UK and Alpenbooks in the USA.
Simpson, Joe *Touching the Void* (1997) Vintage. A nail-biting account of Simpson's accident in the Cordillera Huayhuasah.

Capaq Ñan, the Royal Inca Road

Espinosa, Ricardo, *La Gran Ruta Inca, The Great Inca Route* (2002), Petróleos del Perú. A photographic and textual record of Espinosa's walk the length of the Camino Real de los Incas, in Spanish and English. He has also walked the length of Peru's coast, described in *El Perú a toda Costa* (1997) Editur. The same company has published *Zarzar, Omar, Por los Caminos del Perú en Bicicleta.*
Muller, Karin *Along the Inca Road. A Woman's Journey into an Ancient Empire* (2000), National Geographic.
Portway, Christopher *Journey Along the Andes* (1993) Impact Books. An account of the Andean Inca road.

Wildlife and environment

Frost, Peter et al (Edited by Jim Bartle), *Machu Picchu Historical Sanctuary*, with superb text and photos on all aspects of the Inca Trail and the endangered ecosystem.
Clements, James F and Shany, Noam *A Field Guide to the Birds of Peru* (2001) Ibis.
Emmons, Louise H *Neotropical Rainforest Mammals*. A field guide.
Hilty, Steve, and Brown, William *A guide to the Birds of Colombia* (1986), covers the vast majority of Amazonian species.
Koepcke, Maria *The Birds of the Department of Lima* (1983), is useful for the coast.
Krabbe, Nils and Fjeldsa, Jon *Birds of the High Andes* (1990) University of Copenhagen, which covers all Peruvian birds that occur above 3000 m.
MacQuarrie, Kim, and André and Cornelia Bartschi, *Manu National Park*, is a large, expensive book, with beautiful photographs.
Parker, Ted, Parker, Susan, and Plenge, Manuel *An Annotated checklist of Peruvian Birds* (1982), slightly outdated but useful, it lists all Peruvian birds by habitat type.
Person, David L and Beletsky, Les *Ecotraveller's Wildlife Guide: Peru* (2001) Academic Press, is recommended.
Ridgely, Robert, and Tudor, Guy *Birds of South America Volumes 1 & 2* (1989 and 1994) helps with the passerines, especially vol 2.
TReeS (see under Tambopata National Reserve for address) publish *The Ecology of Tropical Rainforests, Tambopata – A Bird Checklist, Tambopata – Mammal, Amphibian & Reptile Checklist and Reporte Tambopata*; they also produce tapes and CDs of Jungle Sounds and Birds of Southeast Peru.
Valqui, Thomas, *Where to Watch Birds in Peru* (2004), www.granperu.com/bird watchingbook/. Describes 151 sites, how to get there and what to expect once there.
Walker, Barry, and Jon Fjeldsa *Birds of Machu Picchu*.

Footnotes

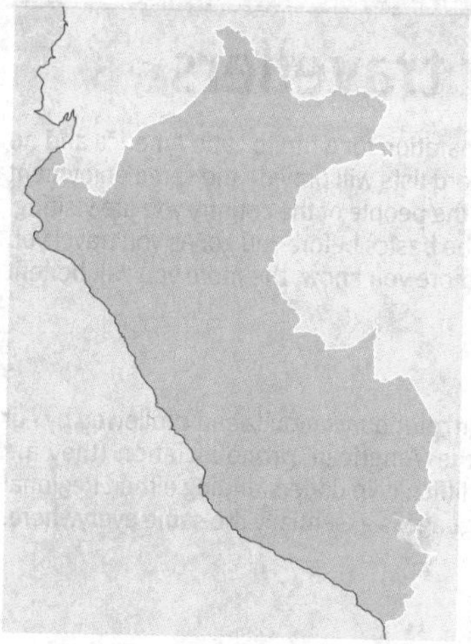

Basic Spanish for travellers

Learning Spanish is a useful part of the preparation for a trip to Latin America and no volumes of dictionaries, phrase books or word lists will provide the same enjoyment as being able to communicate directly with the people of the country you are visiting. It is a good idea to make an effort to grasp the basics before you go. As you travel you will pick up more of the language and the more you know, the more you will benefit from your stay.

General pronunciation

Whether you have been taught the 'Castilian' pronounciation (*z* and *c* followed by *i* or *e* are pronounced as the *th* in think) or the 'American' pronounciation (they are pronounced as *s*), you will encounter little difficulty in understanding either. Regional accents and usages vary, but the basic language is essentially the same everywhere.

Vowels

a	as in English *cat*
e	as in English *best*
i	as the *ee* in English *feet*
o	as in English *shop*
u	as the *oo* in English *food*
ai	as the *i* in English *ride*
ei	as *ey* in English *they*
oi	as *oy* in English *toy*

Consonants

Most consonants can be pronounced more or less as they are in English. The exceptions are:

	before *e* or *i* is the same as *j*
h	is always silent (except in *ch* as in *chair*)
j	as the *ch* in Scottish *loch*
ll	as the *y* in *yellow*
ñ	as the *ni* in English *onion*
rr	trilled much more than in English
x	depending on its location, pronounced *x, s, sh* or *j*

Spanish words and phrases

Greetings, courtesies

hello	*hola*
good morning	*buenos días*
good afternoon/evening/night	*buenas tardes/noches*
goodbye	*adiós/chao*
pleased to meet you	*mucho gusto*
see you later	*hasta luego*
how are you?	*¿cómo está?¿cómo estás?*
I'm fine, thanks	*estoy muy bien, gracias*
I'm called...	*me llamo...*
what is your name?	*¿cómo se llama? ¿cómo te llamas?*
yes/no	*sí/no*
please	*por favor*
thank you (very much)	*(muchas) gracias*
I speak Spanish	*hablo español*
I don't speak Spanish	*no hablo español*
do you speak English?	*¿habla inglés?*
I don't understand	*no entiendo/no comprendo*
please speak slowly	*hable despacio por favor*
I am very sorry	*lo siento mucho/disculpe*
what do you want?	*¿qué quiere? ¿qué quieres?*
I want	*quiero*
I don't want it	*no lo quiero*
leave me alone	*déjeme en paz/no me moleste*
good/bad	*bueno/malo*

Basic questions and requests

have you got a room for two people?	*¿tiene una habitación para dos personas?*
how do I get to_?	*¿cómo llego a_?*
how much does it cost?	*¿cuánto cuesta? ¿cuánto es?*
I'd like to make a long-distance phone call	*quisiera hacer una llamada de larga distancia*
is service included?	*¿está incluido el servicio?*
is tax included?	*¿están incluidos los impuestos?*
when does the bus leave (arrive)?	*¿a qué hora sale (llega) el autobús?*
when?	*¿cuándo?*
where is_?	*¿dónde está_?*
where can I buy tickets?	*¿dónde puedo comprar boletos?*
where is the nearest petrol station?	*¿dónde está la gasolinera más cercana?*
why?	*¿por qué?*

Basic words and phrases

bank	*el banco*
bathroom/toilet	*el baño*
to be	*ser, estar*
bill	*la factura/la cuenta*
cash	*el efectivo*
cheap	*barato/a*
credit card	*la tarjeta de crédito*
exchange house	*la casa de cambio*
exchange rate	*el tipo de cambio*
expensive	*caro/a*
to go	*ir*
to have	*tener, haber*
market	*el mercado*
note/coin	*el billete/la moneda*
police (policeman)	*la policía (el policía)*
post office	*el correo*
public telephone	*el teléfono público*
shop	*la tienda*
supermarket	*el supermercado*
there is/are	*hay*
there isn't/aren't	*no hay*
ticket office	*la taquilla*
travellers' cheques	*los cheques de viajero/los travelers*

Getting around

aeroplane	*el avión*
airport	*el aeropuerto*
arrival/departure	*la llegada/salida*
avenue	*la avenida*
block	*la cuadra*
border	*la frontera*
bus station	*la terminal de autobuses/camiones*
bus	*el bus/el autobús/el camión*
collective/fixed-route taxi	*el colectivo*
corner	*la esquina*
customs	*la aduana*
first/second class	*la primera/segunda clase*
left/right	*izquierda/derecha*
ticket	*el boleto*
empty/full	*vacío/lleno*
highway, main road	*la carretera*
immigration	*la inmigración*
insurance	*el seguro*
insured person	*el asegurado/la asegurada*

to insure yourself against	*asegurarse contra*
luggage	*el equipaje*
motorway, freeway	*el autopista/la carretera*
north, south, west, east	*el norte, el sur, el oeste (occidente), el este (oriente)*
oil	*el aceite*
to park	*estacionarse*
passport	*el pasaporte*
petrol/gasoline	*la gasolina*
puncture	*el pinchazo/la ponchadura*
street	*la calle*
that way	*por allí/por allá*
this way	*por aquí/por acá*
tourist card/visa	*la tarjeta de turista/visa*
tyre	*la llanta*
unleaded	*sin plomo*
waiting room	*la sala de espera*
to walk	*caminar/andar*

Accommodation

air conditioning	*el aire acondicionado*
all-inclusive	*todo incluido*
bathroom, private	*el baño privado*
bed, double/single	*la cama matrimonial/sencilla*
blankets	*las cobijas/mantas*
to clean	*limpiar*
dining room	*el comedor*
guesthouse	*la casa de huéspedes*
hotel	*el hotel*
noisy	*ruidoso*
pillows	*las almohadas*
power cut	*el apagón/corte*
restaurant	*el restaurante*
room/bedroom	*el cuarto/la habitación*
sheets	*las sábanas*
shower	*la ducha/regadera*
soap	*el jabón*
toilet	*el sanitario/excusado*
toilet paper	*el papel higiénico*
towels, clean/dirty	*las toallas limpias/sucias*
water, hot/cold	*el agua caliente/fría*

Health

aspirin	*la aspirina*
blood	*la sangre*
chemist	*la farmacia*
condoms	*los preservativos, los condones*
contact lenses	*los lentes de contacto*
contraceptives	*los anticonceptivos*
contraceptive pill	*la píldora anticonceptiva*
diarrhoea	*la diarrea*
doctor	*el médico*
fever/sweat	*la fiebre/el sudor*
pain	*el dolor*
head	*la cabeza*
period/sanitary towels	*la regla/las toallas femininas*
stomach	*el estómago*
altitude sickness	*el soroche*

Family

family	*la familia*
brother/sister	*el hermano/la hermana*
daughter/son	*la hija/el hijo*
father/mother	*el padre/la madre*
husband/wife	*el esposo (marido)/la esposa*
boyfriend/girlfriend	*el novio/la novia*
friend	*el amigo/la amiga*
married	*casado/a*
single/unmarried	*soltero/a*

Months, days and time

January	*enero*
February	*febrero*
March	*marzo*
April	*abril*
May	*mayo*
June	*junio*
July	*julio*
August	*agosto*
September	*septiembre*
October	*octubre*
November	*noviembre*
December	*diciembre*
Monday	*lunes*
Tuesday	*martes*
Wednesday	*miércoles*
Thursday	*jueves*
Friday	*viernes*
Saturday	*sábado*
Sunday	*domingo*
at one o'clock	*a la una*
at half past two	*a las dos y media*
at a quarter to three	*a cuarto para las tres/a las tres menos quince*
it's one o'clock	*es la una*
it's seven o'clock	*son las siete*
it's six twenty	*son las seis y veinte*
it's five to nine	*son cinco para las nueve/las nueve menos cinco*
in ten minutes	*en diez minutos*
five hours	*cinco horas*
does it take long?	*¿tarda mucho?*

Numbers

one	*uno/una*
two	*dos*
three	*tres*
four	*cuatro*
five	*cinco*
six	*seis*
seven	*siete*
eight	*ocho*
nine	*nueve*
ten	*diez*
eleven	*once*
twelve	*doce*
thirteen	*trece*
fourteen	*catorce*

fifteen	*quince*
sixteen	*dieciséis*
seventeen	*diecisiete*
eighteen	*dieciocho*
nineteen	*diecinueve*
twenty	*veinte*
twenty-one	*veintiuno*
thirty	*treinta*
forty	*cuarenta*
fifty	*cincuenta*
sixty	*sesenta*
seventy	*setenta*
eighty	*ochenta*
ninety	*noventa*
hundred	*cien/ciento*
thousand	*mil*

Food

avocado	*el aguacate*
baked	*al horno*
bakery	*la panadería*
banana	*el plátano*
beans	*los frijoles/las habichuelas*
beef	*la carne de res*
beef steak or pork fillet	*el bistec*
boiled rice	*el arroz blanco*
bread	*el pan*
breakfast	*el desayuno*
butter	*la mantequilla*
cake	*el pastel*
chewing gum	*el chicle*
chicken	*el pollo*
chilli pepper or green pepper	*el ají/el chile/el pimiento*
clear soup, stock	*el caldo*
cooked	*cocido*
dining room	*el comedor*
egg	*el huevo*
fish	*el pescado*
fork	*el tenedor*
fried	*frito*
garlic	*el ajo*
goat	*el chivo*
grapefruit	*la toronja/el pomelo*
grill	*la parrilla*
guava	*la guayaba*
ham	*el jamón*
hamburger	*la hamburguesa*
hot, spicy	*picante*
ice cream	*el helado*
jam	*la mermelada*
knife	*el cuchillo*
lime	*el limón*
lobster	*la langosta*
lunch	*el almuerzo/la comida*
meal	*la comida*
meat	*la carne*
minced meat	*el picadillo*
onion	*la cebolla*
orange	*la naranja*

pepper	*el pimiento*
pasty, turnover	*la empanada/el pastelito*
pork	*el cerdo*
potato	*la papa*
prawns	*los camarones*
raw	*crudo*
restaurant	*el restaurante*
salad	*la ensalada*
salt	*la sal*
sandwich	*el bocadillo*
sauce	*la salsa*
sausage	*la longaniza/el chorizo*
scrambled eggs	*los huevos revueltos*
seafood	*los mariscos*
soup	*la sopa*
spoon	*la cuchara*
squash	*la calabaza*
squid	*los calamares*
supper	*la cena*
sweet	*dulce*
to eat	*comer*
toasted	*tostado*
turkey	*el pavo*
vegetables	*los legumbres/vegetales*
without meat	*sin carne*
yam	*el camote*

Drink

beer	*la cerveza*
boiled	*hervido/a*
bottled	*en botella*
camomile tea	*té de manzanilla*
canned	*en lata*
coffee	*el café*
coffee, white	*el café con leche*
cold	*frío*
cup	*la taza*
drink	*la bebida*
drunk	*borracho/a*
firewater	*el aguardiente*
fruit milkshake	*el batido/licuado*
glass	*el vaso*
hot	*caliente*
ice/without ice	*el hielo/sin hielo*
juice	*el jugo*
lemonade	*la limonada*
milk	*la leche*
mint	*la menta/la hierbabuena*
rum	*el ron*
soft drink	*el refresco*
sugar	*el azúcar*
tea	*el té*
to drink	*beber/tomar*
water	*el agua*
water, carbonated	*el agua mineral con gas*
water, still mineral	*el agua mineral sin gas*
wine, red	*el vino tinto*
wine, white	*el vino blanco*

Food glossary

Food has always played an important role in Peruvian culture. The country's range of climates has made it internationally recognized for its diverse cuisine.

Ají (hot pepper) Ají is found in many varieties and is used to add 'spice' to everything from soup to fish to vegetable dishes. It is a staple in Peruvian kitchens from the coast to the most remote jungle villages. They can be extremely spicy, so take care!
Ají de Gallina A rich mix of creamed, spicy chicken over rice and boiled potatoes. A wonderfully tasty dish, see the recipe for details of how to make it.
Anticuchos (beef heart kebabs) Beef heart barbecued and served with cold potato and a wonderful assortment of spicy sauces. A must for all meat lovers.
Arrebosado Refers to something cooked in an omelette.
Arroz (rice) A staple of Peruvian cooking.
Arroz con leche Rice pudding.
Arroz con pato (duck with rice) Originally from the north coast but found everywhere.
Cau Cau Tripe and potatoes.
Causa A casserole served cold with a base of yellow potato and mixed with hot peppers, onion, avocado, with either chicken, crab or meat. A fantastic starter.
Ceviche The national dish of Peru. Raw fish or seafood marinated in a mixture of lime juice, red onions and hot peppers served with a boiled yam (*camote*) and corn. Ceviche is a dish served for lunch. Most *cevicherías* (ceviche restaurants) close around 1600.
Choclo (corn) Another staple. The large kernels are great with fresh cheese.
Chicha de Jora A strong fermented beverage mostly found in mountain communities. The people who make it use their saliva to aid in the fermenting process.
Cuy (guinea pig) Prepared in a variety of ways, from stewed to fried.
Estofado A mild chicken stew, with lots of potatoes and vegetables, served with rice.
Granos (grains) Kiwicha and Quinoa are very high sources of protein and staples of the Inca diet. Quinoa is wonderful in soups and Kiwicha is a common breakfast food for children throughout the country.
Lomo saltado Strips of sirloin sautéed with tomato, onion, ají amarillo (a spicy orange pepper) and french fried potatoes served with rice.
Maíz morado (purple corn) This type of corn is not edible for humans. It's boiled and the liquid is used to make *chicha*, a sweet and very traditional Peruvian refreshment.
Manjar blanco A caramel sweet made from boiled milk and sugar.
Pachamanca Typical mountain cuisine, so popular it's now prepared everywhere. Beef, pork and chicken mixed with a variety of vegetables, and cooked together over heated stones in a hole in the ground.
Papa (potato) The potato is as Peruvian as the Inca himself. There are more than 2000 varieties of tubers although only a fraction are edible. The International Potato Institute is located on the outskirts of Lima. The *papa amarilla* (yellow potato) is by far the best-tasting of the lot.
Papa ocopa A typical dish from the Arequipa region. A spicy peanut sauce served over cold potatoes with a slice of hard boiled egg.
Papa a la Huancaína Originated in the department of Huancayo, this creamy cheese sauce served over cold potatoes is a common starter for set menus everywhere.
Papa rellena (stuffed potato) First baked then fried, the potato is stuffed with meat, onions, olives, boiled egg and raisins. *Camote* (yams) can be substituted for potatoes.
Picarones Deep-fried doughnut batter, bathed in a honey sauce.
Rocoto relleno (stuffed hot peppers) Stuffed with meat and potatoes, then baked.
Seco de cabrito A favourite dish from the north coast. Roasted goat marinated with *chicha*, served with beans and rice.
Suspiro a la limeña Manjar blanco with baked egg-white.
Turrón Popular sweet shortbread, covered in molasses or honey, sold during the Oct celebration of Señor de los Milagros (Lord of Miracles) in Lima.

Index

Map index

Advertisers' index

Acknowledgements

This edition would not have been possible without the help of a number of people. The authors are most grateful to the Footprint team, Felicity Laughton, Sophie Blacksell, Alan Murphy, Sarah Sorensen, Rob Lunn and Kevin Feeney for their support.

Steve would like to thank Chris Benway of Café Andino/La Cima Logistics for his valued advice and support throughout my time in Huaraz. Mellan Leiva Pariachi (and four legged friends) for his excellent work on the Alpamayo North trek. Thanks to Carlos Zárate of Carlos Zárate Adventuras and also to Charlie Bird and the crew of Crossing the Line Films for their invaluable assistance up on the chilly slopes of Nevado Mismi. Simon Cross and climbing friends Scott and Ben were a mine of information in the mountains of the Cordillera Blanca and great partners while climbing Pisco. Pablo Tour and the Cabrera family provided assistance in both Arequipa and the Colca Canyon region, as did Walter and Pepi of Kuntur Wassi in Cabanaconde.

For work in the Cuzco and Madre del Dios regions I'd like to thank some longstanding and special friends: Marianne Van Vlaardingen for her knowledge of the region's wild places and indigenous people. Jane of Jack's Café, Fiona and David of Ecotrek Peru and Simon Leishman, biking extraordinaire, all deserve a place here for their friendship and constant finger on the pulse of the Cuzco tourism scene. Similarly Lucy and Heather of South American Explorers have always been helpful beyond the call of duty. Thanks to Katie Powell for her info on 'roughing it' through the depths of the rainforest, and of course, for many very special memories. Finally thanks to Kay Isbell for vast amounts of wisdom and guidance over the years.

For their help with updating the book, our warmest thanks go to: Robert and Daisy Kunstaetter, who updated the Titicaca region, the South coast and routes from Piura to Ecuador.
John Forrest and Julia Porturas, who travelled in La Libertad and the route from the Pacific coast to Cajamarca, the route south from Lima to Abancay and on to the Scared Valley, and in Tambopata.
Walter Eberhart, for a detailed report on Cajamarca, Huanchaco and Trujillo.
Lucy Bertenshaw and Heather MacBrayne of South American Explorers in Cuzco and Miles Buesst of South American Explorers in Lima, for answering so many questions and for providing updates.
Michael White, Clara Bravo and Delicia Andrés for updates on the coast north of Lima, especially the Trujillo area
Mariella Bernasconi for more news from Lima and Cuzco
Marthe Zeldenrust for new information on the Cañete Valley
Alberto Cafferrata for news from Caraz and elsewhere.

Specialist help has come from Prof Larry Goodyear, head of the Leicester School of Pharmacy and director of Nomad Medical (Health), Paul Cripps (Rafting), PromPerú (many areas, but especially birdwatching) and, of course, all the experts and contributors who helped to put the first editions of this book together.

Travellers' letters

Many thanks to the following travellers for sending in their comments:

Chris Alger (UK); Tomer Alpert (Israel); Alvaro Alliende (Chile); Michael Anderson (UK); Ignacio Ballen (Peru); Julien Barber (UK); Adrian Beck; Hope Becker and Adrian (UK); Paul Beckitt (UK); Eva Berger (Germany); Diana Blair (USA); Claudine Blum (Switzerland); Peter Boers (The Netherlands); John Boyd (Eire); Timothy Brignall (UK); Astrid Brucker (Germany); Jayne Burrage Churchill (UK); Leen Buysrogge; Edward Cahill; Jocelyn Cai (Singapore); Susan Cannon (Peru); Michael Carlton; Francis Chambers; Ursula Chan (USA); Teleri Cousins (UK); Juan d'Ornellas (UK); Jeroen Decuyper (Belgium); Petra Deen (The Netherlands); Richard Desomme and Catherine Koch; Hessel Dokkum; Shannon Donovan (New Zealand); Reid Dusenberry (USA); Ben Eastwood (Australia); Pam Elliott (Canada); Wolfram Engelhardt (Germany); Aoife Farrelly with Eileen and Trish (Eire); Sunita, Shane and Sheldon Ferrao (Canada); Jo Fowler and Robert Dickson (UK); Eva Gengenbach (Germany); Joachim Götz (Germany); Oliver Greenall (UK); Thomas Gut (Switzerland); Jochen Hager (US); Petri Hännikäinen (Finland); Anne Hay (UK); Beata Hemer (Sweden); Valerie Hooper (US); Clarisa Hopkins (Australia); Bea Huber (Switzerland); David Huerta (Chile); Ricardo G Huerta Niño (USA); Vicky Jacobs (UK); Mr and Mrs Katz; Alex and Janette Kernitsky and Kfar Ilan (Israel); Angelene Kiel (US); Bernadette Kurte (Peru); Laurie Lakin; Jodie Larson (USA); David Latham and Jo; Dan Lauritsen; Edna Lazar (US); Irving Levinson (USA); Vicky Locke (UK); Henry Long; Chris Lotz (South Africa); Michael Lubin (USA); Jonnie Lyle (UK); Bonnie McAlister (USA); Sasha McInnes (Canada); Sandra and Fraser McIver (UK); Andrea McNeal (US); Ciara Maguire (Eire); Rebecca Martin (Eire); Jean-Pierre Mélon (Belgium); Anna Molenaar (The Netherlands); Sean Morris; Naomi Paget (UK); Jean-Paul Penrose (UK); Jan Peters (US); Daniel Plewman (Eire); John Polt (USA); Babette Prick (The Netherlands); Giorgio Raschio (Italy); Ranjan Raychowdhury (UK); I N Roy (Canada); Kathrin Reinke (Germany); David Rutkowski (US); Jaime Salinas (Bolivia); Philipp Schaab (Germany); Angela and Axel Schmitz (Germany); Oliver Schuetz; Susanne Schuster (UK); David Schwartz (USA); Steve Scott (UK); Peter Selley (UK); Avi Shua; Karen Siegel (Ecuador); Ole Skjerven (Norway); Cath Smith (UK); Rick Smith (USA); David Snashall (UK); Josh Snyder (US); Michael Spindler (USA); Martin Steer (Ireland); Steph Steph (Switzerland); Alma Stephenson and Jennifer Dean (Australia); Nina Strandkjaer (Denmark); Pamela Suing (USA); Ariana Svenson (Australia); Matt Swainson (Australia); Lior Tal (Peru); Andrew Tester (New Zealand); David Thovson (US); Fabian Toonen (Netherlands); Terhi Tuominen and Teija Vaha (Finland); Volker T Umpfenbach (Germany); Bernie Upjohn and Eric Potter (Australia); Patterson Molina Vale (Brazil); Guy Vanackeren (Peru); Dineke Veerman (the Netherlands); Tim Wade (Australia); John Walker (USA); Brian and Ruth Whiting (US); Graham Williams (UK); Rudolf Winkler (Germany); Amelia Wix; Hin Kyeol Woo (USA); Susan Wright; Elad Z; Austin Zeiderman (US); Paola Zimmermann (Germany); Roland Zimmermann (Germany)

We should also like to thank all those contributors to the 3rd edition of Footprint's Cuzco and the Inca Heartland.

Complete title listing

Footprint publishes travel guides to over 150 destinations worldwide. Each guide is packed with practical, concise and colourful information for everybody from first-time travellers to travel aficionados. The list is growing fast and current titles are noted below. Available from all good bookshops and online Www.footprintbooks.com

(P) denotes pocket guide

Latin America & Caribbean

Antigua & Leeward Islands (P)
Argentina
Barbados (P)
Bolivia
Brazil
Caribbean Islands
Mexico & Central America
Chile
Colombia
Costa Rica
Cuba
Cuzco & the Inca heartland
Discover Belize, Guatemala & Southern Mexico
Discover Patagonia
Discover Peru, Bolivia & Ecuador
Dominican Republic (P)
Ecuador & Galápagos
Havana (P)
Jamaica (P)
Nicaragua
Peru
Rio de Janeiro (P)
St Lucia (P)
South American Handbook
Venezuela

North America

Discover Western Canada
New York (P)
Vancouver (P)

Africa

Cape Town (P)
East Africa
Egypt
Kenya
Libya
Marrakech (P)
Morocco
Namibia
South Africa
Tanzania
Tunisia
Uganda

Middle East

Dubai (P)
Israel
Jordan
Syria & Lebanon

Australasia
Australia
Discover East Coast Australia
New Zealand
Sydney (P)
West Coast Australia

Asia
Bali
Bangkok & the Beaches
Bhutan
Borneo
Cambodia
Discover Vietnam, Cambodia & Laos
Goa
Hong Kong (P)
India
Indonesia
Laos
Malaysia & Singapore
Nepal
Northern Pakistan
Rajasthan
South India
Sri Lanka
Sumatra
Thailand
Tibet
Vietnam

Europe
Andalucía
Barcelona (P)
Belfast & the north of Ireland (P)
Berlin (P)
Bilbao (P)
Bologna (P)
Britain
Cardiff (P)
Copenhagen (P)
Costa de la Luz (P)
Croatia
Dublin (P)
Edinburgh (P)
England
European City Breaks
Glasgow (P)
Ireland
Lisbon (P)
London
London (P)
Madrid (P)
Naples & the Amalfi Coast (P)
Northern Spain
Paris (P)
Reykjavík (P)
Scotland
Scotland Highlands & Islands
Seville (P)
Siena & the heart of Tuscany (P)
Spain
Tallinn (P)
Turin (P)
Turkey
Valencia (P)
Verona (P)
Wales

Lifestyle guides
Diving the World
Snowboarding the World
Surfing Britain
Surfing Europe
Surfing the World
Wine Travel Guide to the World

Also available
Traveller's Handbook (WEXAS)
Traveller's Healthbook (WEXAS)
Traveller's Internet Guide (WEXAS)

Credits

Footprint credits
Editors: Felicity Laughton, Sophie Blacksell
Map editor: Sarah Sorensen
Picture editor: Rob Lunn

Publisher: Patrick Dawson
Editorial: Alan Murphy, Nicola Gibbs
Cartography: Robert Lunn, Kevin Feeney
Design: Mytton Williams
Sales and marketing: Andy Riddle
Advertising: Debbie Wylde
Finance and administration:
Elizabeth Taylor, Vassia Efstathiou

Photography credits
Front cover: Index Stock Imagery/Photolibrary (Sacsayhuaman)
Back cover: Jamie Marshall/Alamy (masked dancers)
Inside colour section: age fotostock/ Superstock, Jamie Marshall/Alamy, Roger Rowland/Travel Ink, Sue Cunningham Photographic/Alamy.

Print
Manufactured in Italy by LegoPrint
Pulp from sustainable forests

Footprint feedback

We try as hard as we can to make each Footprint guide as up to date as possible but, of course, things always change. If you want to let us know about your experiences – good, bad or ugly – then don't delay, go to **www.footprintbooks.com** and send in your comments.

Publishing information
Footprint Peru
6th edition

January 2007

ISBN 1 904777 88 0
CIP DATA: A catalogue record for this book is available from the British Library

Published by Footprint
6 Riverside Court
Lower Bristol Road
Bath BA2 3DZ, UK
T +44 (0)1225 469141
F +44 (0)1225 469461
discover@footprintbooks.com
www.footprintbooks.com

Distributed in the USA by
Publishers Group West

Neither the black and white nor coloured maps are intended to have any political significance.
Every effort has been made to ensure that the facts in this guidebook are accurate. However, travellers should still obtain advice from consulates, airlines etc about travel and visa requirements before travelling. The authors and publishers cannot accept responsibility for any loss, injury or inconvenience however caused.

Notes

Take
Sunglasses
insurance booklet.
passport copies.
water bottle.

buy
towels?

?

To do - notify credit card cos etc

Map symbols

Administration

- Capital city
- Other city, town
- International border
- Regional border
- Disputed border

Roads and travel

- National highway, motorway
- Main road
- Minor road
- Track
- Footpath
- Railway with station
- Airport
- Bus station
- Metro station
- Cable car
- Funicular
- Ferry

Water features

- River, canal
- Lake, ocean
- Seasonal marshland
- Beach, sandbank
- Waterfall
- Reef

Topographical features

- Contours (approx)
- Mountain, volcano
- Mountain pass
- Escarpment
- Gorge
- Glacier
- Salt flat
- Rocks

Cities and towns

- Main through route
- Main street
- Minor street
- Pedestrianized street
- Tunnel
- One way-street
- Steps
- Bridge
- Fortified wall
- Park, garden, stadium
- Sleeping
- Eating
- Bars & clubs
- Building
- Sight
- Cathedral, church
- Chinese temple
- Hindu temple
- Meru
- Mosque
- Stupa
- Synagogue
- Tourist office
- Museum
- Post office
- Police
- Bank
- Internet
- Telephone
- Market
- Medical services
- Parking
- Petrol
- Golf
- Detail map
- Related map

Other symbols

- Archaeological site
- National park, wildlife reserve
- Viewing point
- Campsite
- Refuge, lodge
- Castle, fort
- Diving
- Deciduous, coniferous, palm trees
- Hide
- Vineyard, winery
- Distillery
- Shipwreck
- Historic battlefield

No necesitamos enseñarle más...
MIRAFLORES PARK
HOTEL
ORIENT-EXPRESS HOTELS
TRAINS & CRUISES
Av. Malecón de la Reserva,
1035 Miraflores, Lima – Perú
www.mira-park.com
MACHU
PICCHU
SANCTUARY LODGE
ORIENT-EXPRESS HOTELS
TRAINS & CRUISES
Machu Picchu
Cusco - Perú
www.sanctuarylodge.net
HOTEL
MONASTERIO
ORIENT-EXPRESS HOTELS
TRAINS & CRUISES
Calle Palacio 136, Plazoleta Nazarenas
Cusco – Perú
www.monasterio.orient-express.com
El Parador del Colca
Valle del Colca
Arequipa - Perú
www.paradordelcolca.com
www.365publicidad.com

PERURAIL

Exploring the Land of the Incas

Cusco - Lake Titicaca

A stunning rail journey beginning in Cusco and running south to the historic city of Puno and the famed Lake Titicaca. The gentle climb is breathtaking, with the first half of the journey dominated by magnificent Andean mountains, which slowly give way to the gentler, rolling Andean plains with their herds of vicuña and alpaca. There is a scenic stop at La Raya, the highest point of the journey.

An extraordinary destination deserves an extraordinary passage of way
Welcome aboard the Perurail's train services

Cusco - Machu Picchu

"In the variety of its charms and the power of its spell, I know of no place in the world which can compare with it. Not only has it great snow peaks looming above the clouds... it has also in striking contrast, orchids and ferns, the delectable beauty of luxurious vegetation, and the mysterious witchery of the jungle..."
Hiram Bingham ("Machu Picchu, The Lost City of the Incas")

reservas@perurail.com
Phone: 084-238722
Fax: 084-222114
www.perurail.com

"Let Yourself Go!"
Go Peru For Less.
Peru for Less
BUILDING MAGICAL MEMORIES
Go to www.peruforless.com/footprint for a chance to win a trip to and around Peru.
1 US Based with Local Operations
2 Tour Package and Hotel Variety
3 Price Guarantee
Lake Titicaca. 3,812 m above sea level.
USA (Toll free) 1-877-269-0309
UK 44-203-002-0571
Lima 51-1-272-0542
Cusco 51-84-23-1641
www.peruforless.com

Patients travel from around the world to Lima in search of the perfect smile!
Take advantage of our 45 minute ZOOM! Whitening System or a full cosmetic smile makeover in just 48 hours!
Travel and Smile.net
World Class Cosmetic Dentistry
Dr. Enrique Yuen
Cosmetic Dentist
www.travelandsmile.net
+511-99445647
Private, world-class dentistry at a fraction of the cost you'd pay in Europe or the USA.
Conveniently located in Miraflores, Lima's No. 1 tourist district!

JOURNEY
PERU
See the true colours of Peru; from condors in the Colca Canyon to Amazon rainforest lodges; from trekking the Inca Trail to exploring Andean markets. Let us show you the Peru we know and love.
• Flights & Airpasses • Select hotels • Language courses
• Tailor-made travel • Small group tours • Honeymoons
Call the UK's No 1 specialist to Latin America.
London 020 8747 3108
Manchester 0161 832 1441
www.journeylatinamerica.co.uk
JOURNEY LATIN AMERICA
ATOL Protected 2828 ABTA (V2522) IATA AITO

Map 1

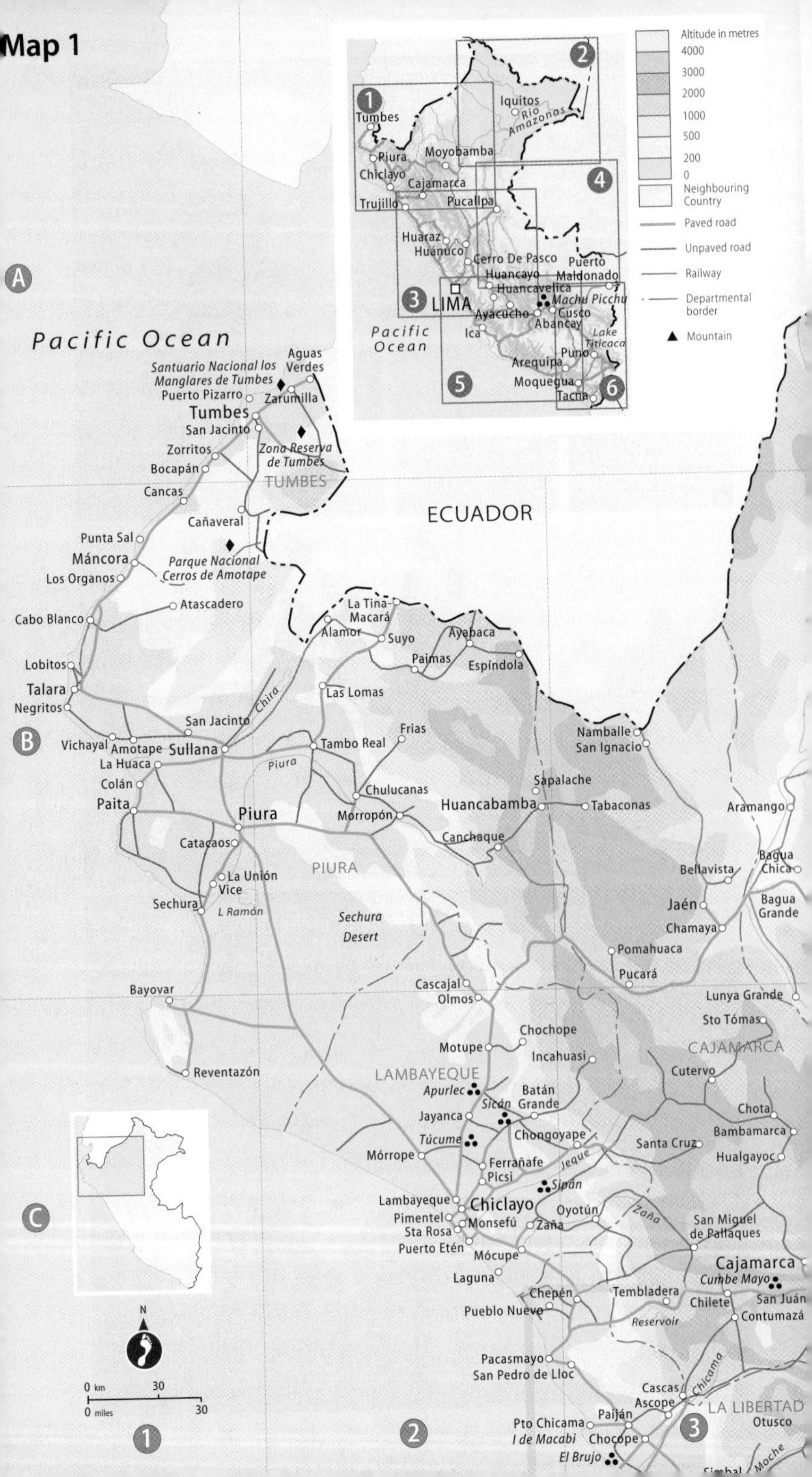
Altitude in metres
4000
3000
2000
1000
500
200
0
Neighbouring Country
Paved road
Unpaved road
Railway
Departmental border
Mountain
Tumbes
Iquitos
Rio Amazonas
Piura
Moyobamba
Chiclayo
Cajamarca
Trujillo
Pucallpa
Huaraz
Huánuco
Cerro De Pasco
Puerto Maldonado
Huancayo
Huancavelica
LIMA
Machu Picchu
Ayacucho
Cusco
Abancay
Pacific Ocean
Ica
Lake Titicaca
Puno
Arequipa
Moquegua
Tacna
Pacific Ocean
Aguas Verdes
Santuario Nacional los Manglares de Tumbes
Puerto Pizarro
Zarumilla
Tumbes
San Jacinto
Zorritos
Zona Reserva de Tumbes
Bocapán
TUMBES
Cancas
ECUADOR
Cañaveral
Punta Sal
Máncora
Parque Nacional Cerros de Amotape
Los Organos
Atascadero
La Tina-Macará
Cabo Blanco
Alamor
Suyo
Ayabaca
Paimas
Lobitos
Espíndola
Talara
Negritos
Las Lomas
Chira
San Jacinto
Frias
Namballe
San Ignacio
Vichayal
Amotape
Sullana
Tambo Real
La Huaca
Piura
Sapalache
Colán
Chulucanas
Paita
Huancabamba
Tabaconas
Aramango
Piura
Morropón
Catacaos
Canchaque
La Unión
PIURA
Bellavista
Bagua Chica
Vice
Sechura
L Ramón
Jaén
Bagua Grande
Sechura Desert
Chamaya
Pomahuaca
Pucará
Bayovar
Cascajal
Olmos
Lunya Grande
Sto Tómas
Chochope
CAJAMARCA
Motupe
Incahuasi
Reventazón
LAMBAYEQUE
Cutervo
Apurlec
Batán Grande
Sicán
Chota
Jayanca
Chongoyape
Bambamarca
Túcume
Santa Cruz
Mórrope
Ferrañafe
Hualgayoc
Jeque
Picsi
Sipán
Lambayeque
Chiclayo
Oyotún
Zaña
San Miguel de Pallaques
Pimentel
Monsefú
Sta Rosa
Zaña
Puerto Etén
Mócupe
Cajamarca
Cumbe Mayo
Laguna
Chepén
Tembladera
Chilete
San Juán
Pueblo Nuevo
Contumazá
Reservoir
Pacasmayo
San Pedro de Lloc
Cascas
Chicama
Ascope
LA LIBERTAD
Otusco
Pto Chicama
Paiján
I de Macabi
Chocope
El Brujo
Moche
A
B
C
1
2
3
4
5
6
N
0 km 30
0 miles 30

Marsella
Soldado Bartra
San Jacinto
Andoas
Tambo
Map 2
Tigre
A
Trompeteros
Pastaza
Morona
Cenepa
LORETO
Borja
Santa María de Nieve
Sameriza
Orellana
Oracuza
Marañon
Pto América
Barranca
San Ramón
La Libertad
Marañon
B
Chiriaco
Jeberos
Lagunas
Sta Cruz
AMAZONAS
Balsapuertos
Yurimaguas
Nuevo Cajamarca
Shucushuyacu
Pedro Ruíz
Florida
Jumbilla
Rioja
Moyobamba
Shanusi
Churuja
Papa Playa
Lamud
Molinopampa
San Antonio
Chachapoyas
Pipus
Cheto
Navarro
2 de Mayo
Gran Vilaya
Levanto
Mcl Benavides
Tabalosas
Huimbayoc
Tingo
Mendoza
Lamas
Map 4
Kuélap
Ubilón
Chazuta
Palmira
Tarapoto
Shapaja
Sta Catallina
Leymebamba
Laguna Azul
Sisa
Sta Rosa
Buenos Aires
Orellana
Huallabamba
Balsas
Saposoa
Celendín
Shamboyacu
Sacanche
Bellavista
Pampa Hermosa
SAN MARTIN
Juanjuí
C
Pampas de Sacramento
Bolívar
Llacanora
San Marcos
Biabo
Map 3
Campanilla
Marañon
Cajabamba
Parque Nacional Ríp Abiseo
Marca Huamachuco
Yanasara
Huamachuco
4
Pataz
5
6
Chahual
Retamas
Puerto Pizarro
Mollepata

Map 2

Güeppi
ECUADOR
Pantoja
A
Campuya
Curaray
Copal Urco
Sta Clotilde
Vidal
Marsella
Soldado
Bartra
Map 1
Napo
San
Jacinto
Andoas
Tambo
B
Tigre
Intuto
Trompeteros
Pastaza
LORETO
San Fernando
Nauta
Miraflores
Concordia
Parinari
Bagazán
Marañon
Yanayacu
Requena
ca
C
Reserva Nacional
Pacaya-Samiria
San Ramón
La Libertad
Bretaña
Flor de Punga
Lagunas
Jeberos
Tapiche
Iberia
Sta Cruz
Tamanco
Ucuyali
Sta Isabel
Nva Alejandria
1
2
3

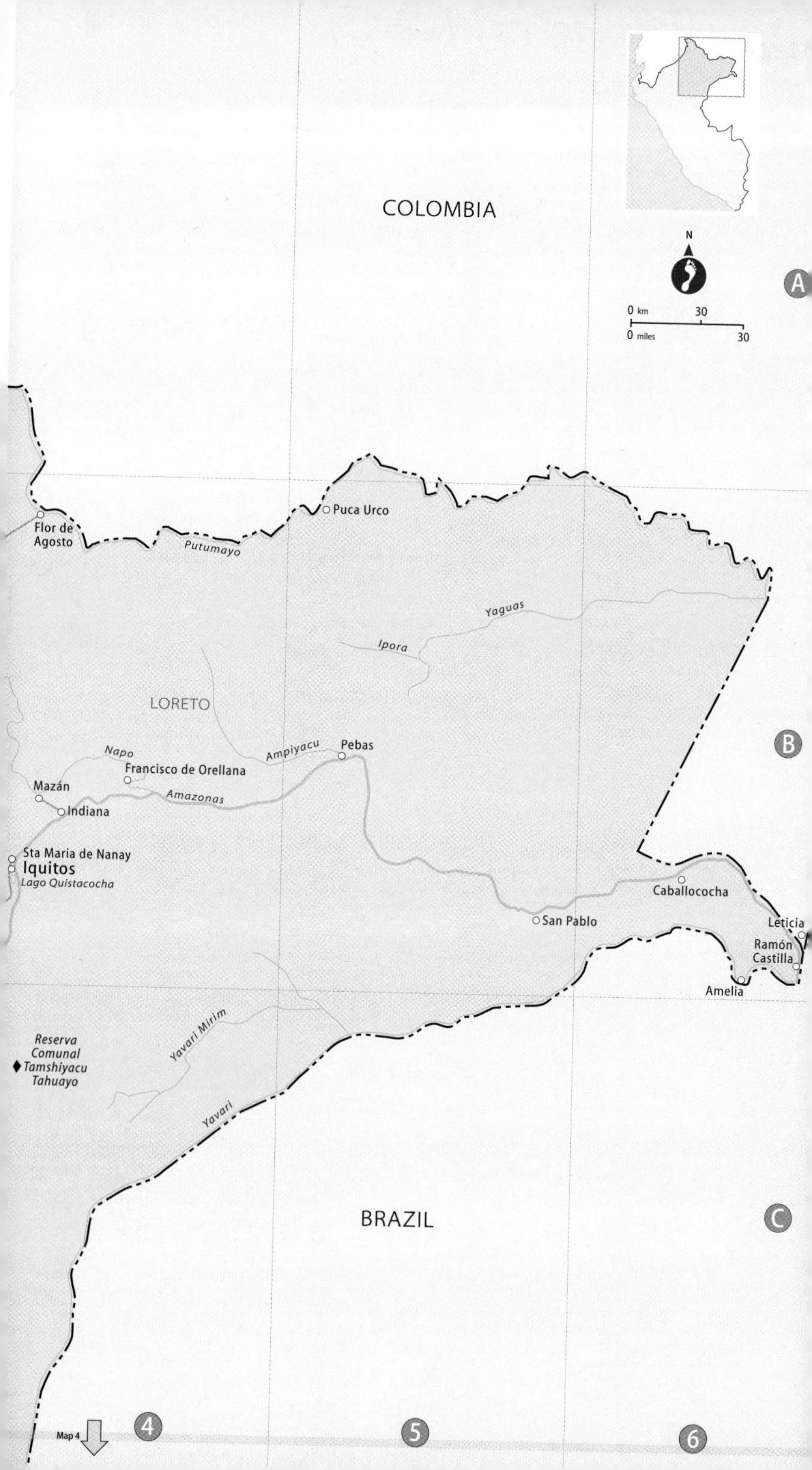

COLOMBIA
N
0 km
30
0 miles
30
A
Flor de Agosto
Putumayo
Puca Urco
Yaguas
Ipora
LORETO
B
Napo
Ampiyacu
Pebas
Francisco de Orellana
Mazán
Amazonas
Indiana
Sta Maria de Nanay
Iquitos
Lago Quistacocha
Caballococha
San Pablo
Leticia
Ramón Castilla
Amelia
Reserva Comunal Tamshiyacu Tahuayo
Yavari Mirim
Yavari
BRAZIL
C
4
Map 4
5
6

Map 3
de Pallaques
San Juan
Llacanora
San Marcos
Campanilla
Tembladera
Contumazá
LAMBAYEQUE
SAN MARTIN
Pacasmayo
San Pedro de Lloc
Chicama
Cajabamba
Cascas
Ascope
Coina
Parque Nacional Río Abiseo
Pataz
Pto
Paiján
Huamachuco
Retamas
Chocope
Otusco
Chahual
Puerto Pizarro
Tocache Nuevo
El Brujo
Simbal
Moche
Quiruvilca
Parcoy
Marsa
Shorey
Cachicadan
Buldibuyo
Huanchaco
Laredo
LA LIBERTAD
Chan Chán
Huacas del Sol & de la Luna
Santiago de Chuco
Mollepata
Tayabamba
Trujillo
Salaverry
Pallasca
Virú
Cabana
Huancaspata
Tauca
Pto Morin
Sihuas
Huacrachuco
San Pedro de Chonta
El Carmelo
Corongo
Tarica
Pasacancha
Santa
Tres Cruces
Tanguche
Chuquicara
Alpamayo (5,947m)
Pomabamba
Piscobamba
Cordillera Blanca
Huallanca
Cañon del Pato
Cashapampa
Yanama
Llamellín
Santa
Pamparomas
Caraz
Huascarán
San Luis
Chimbote
Yungay (6,768m)
Pueblo Libre
Chacas
Tantamayo
Mancos
Chavín de Pariarca
Nepeña
Moro
Carhuaz
Chancos
Marcará
Huascarán NP
Huari
Samanco
Anta
Sechín
ANCASH
Llata
Playa Tortugas
Monterrey
Pariacoto
Huaraz
San Marcos
Quivilla
Casma
Sechín
Chavín
Yaután
Casma
Olleros
Chavín de Huantar
Recuay
Chavinillo
Catac
Huansala
La Unión
Huánuco Viejo
La Merced
Culebras
Pacific Ocean
Pachacato
Huallanca
Aija
Carpa
Culebras
Huayán
Baños
Huayllapampa
Aquia
Huarmey
Huarmey
Marca
Chiquián
Yerupajá (6,634m)
Pampa Mata Caballos
Conococha (4,100m)
Cordillera Huayhuash
Chasqitambo
Cajatambo
Raura
Fortaleza
Pativilca
Oyón
Paramongá
Cochas
Pativilca
Churín
Barranca
Supe
Cochamarca
Huaura
Pto Supe
Caral
Huancahuasi
Végueta
Huaura
Sayán
Huacho
Reserva Nacional Loma de Lachay
Paraíso
Chancay
Las Salinas
Huaral
Santa Rosa de Quives
Chancay
Aucallama
Yangas
Chillón
Ancón
Puente Piedra
LIMA
Sta Rosa
Ventanilla
Comas
Chosica
Callao
Cieneguilla
LIMA
Miraflores
Pachacámac
Chorrillos
Lurín
Pántanos de Villa
Sta María del Mar
Pucusana
Chilca
N
0 km
30
0 miles
30
A
B
C
1
2
3

LORETO
BRAZIL
Sierra Contamana
Biabo
Map 1
Map 4
Abuja
L Yarinacocha
San Francisco
Pucallpa
Uchiza
Progreso
Masisea
Díaz
Honoria
L Chauya Cocha
San Alejandro
Ganzo Azul
L Inuria
Pachitea
Tournavista
Aucayacu
Aguaytía
La Morada
Monzón
Tingo María
Las Palmas
Puerto Inca
HUANUCO
UCAYALI
Chorropampa
Chaglia
Churubamba
Puerto Victoria
Acomayo
Panao
Puerto Pachitea
Yarumayo
Pozuzo
Huánuco
Kotosh
Tomaykichwa
Ucayali
Ambo
Puerto Bermúdez
Palcazú
San Rafael
PASCO
Huancabamba
Parque Nacional Yanachaga Chemillén
Neguachi
Yanahuanca
Oxapampa
San Juan de Pampa
Atalaya
Cerro De Pasco
Villa Rica
Shelby
Urubamba
Paucartambo
L Punrún
San Luis de Shuaro
Huayllay
Carhuamayo
Laguna de Junín
La Merced (Chanchamayo)
Pichanaki
Puerto Ocopa
Ulcumayo
Santuario Bosque de Piedras
San Pedro de Cajas
San Ramón
Ondores
Junín
Tambo
Satipo
Palcamayo
Mazamari
Acobamba
JUNIN
Canta
Mariposa
Tarma
La Oroya
Huairicolca
Casapalca
Morococha
San Mateo
Rimac
Chacapalpa
Jauja
Comas
Map 5
San Pedro de Casta
Concepción
Matucana
Ricardo Palma
Huancayo
Chupaca
Pto Rico
San José de Quero
Viques
Sapallanga
Antioquia
Langa
Huancaya
Cullhuas
Pázos
Salcabamba
Tomás
Pichari
CUSCO
Huampará
Pampas
San Francisco
Yauyos
Vilca
Izuchaca
Mscl Cáceres
Ayna
Mala
Omas
Acoria
San Antonio
Mala
Huancavelica
Mayocc
APURIMAC
Omas
Huanta
Ayamachay
Acobamba
Asia
Cañete
Viñac
HUANCAVELICA
Lircay
Julcamarca
Quinua
Pacarán
San Juan
Huari
San Miguel
Quilmaná
Abra Chonta
Huachocolpa
Apurimac
Cerro Azul
Lunahuaná
Aurahua
Ayacucho
San Luis
Imperial
L Orococha
Chiquinturca
Cañete
Santa Inés
Chiara
Ocros
A
B
C
4
5
6

Map 4

Map 2
Map 1
Map 3
LORETO
Orellana
A
Conamaná
Cerro do Canchyauya
Pampas de Sacramento
Sierra Contamana
Abuja
L Yarinacocha
Pucallpa
Masisea
Honoria
L Chauya Cocha
San Alejandro
Ganzo Azul
L Inuria
Tournavista
Pachitea
B
HUANUCO
Puerto Inca
UCAYALI
Puerto Victoria
Puerto Pachitea
Curanja
Palcazú
Puerto Bermúdez
PASCO
Huancabamba
Neguachi
Ucayali
Atalaya
Oxapampa
San Luis de Shuaro
C
La Merced (Chanchamayo)
San Ramón
Pichanaki
Puerto Ocopa
Shepahua
Tambo
Satipo
Mazamari
JUNIN
Acobamba
CUSCO
Mariposa
Jauja
Comas
Concepción
Camisea
1
2
3

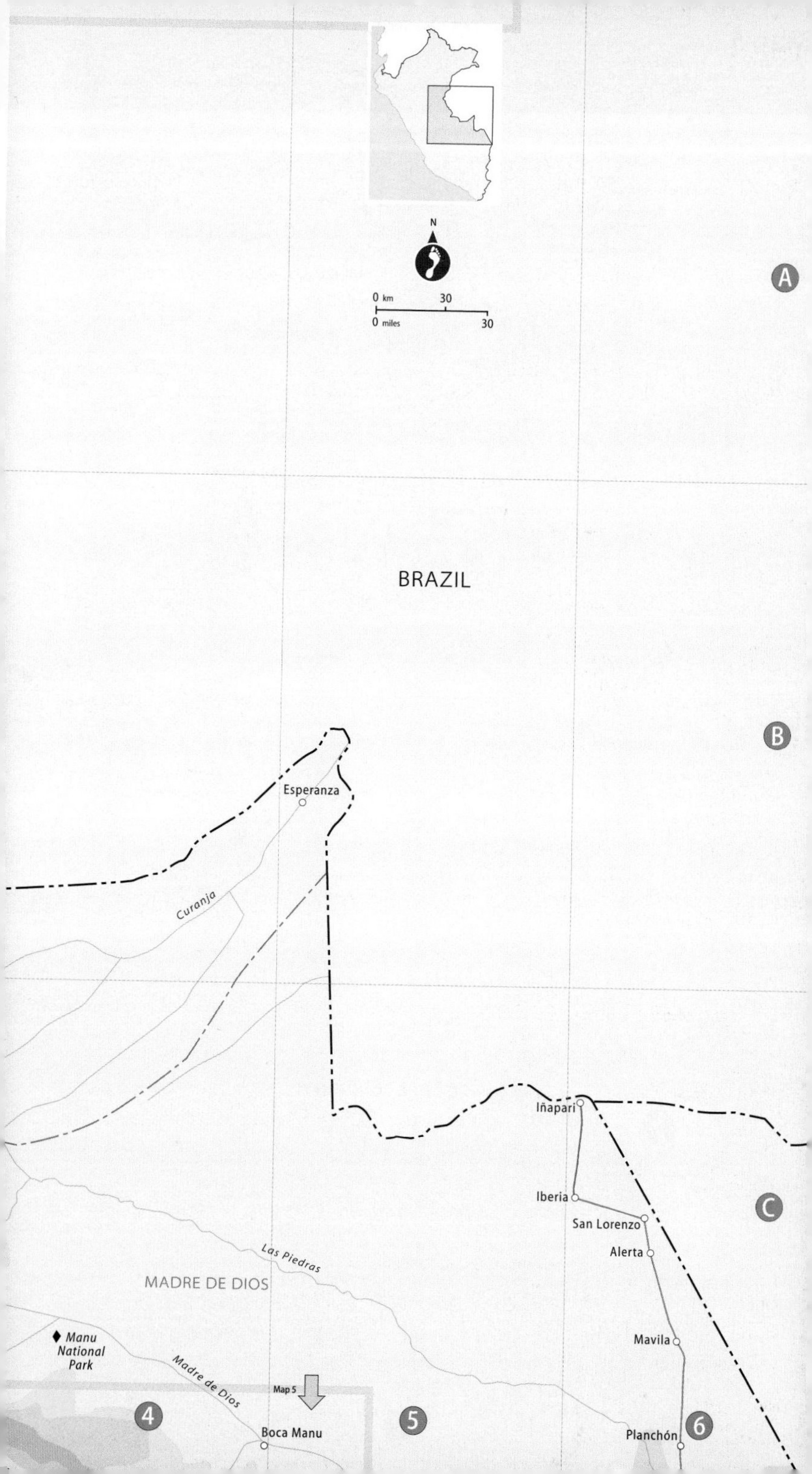
N
0 km
30
0 miles
30
A
BRAZIL
B
Esperanza
Curanja
Iñapari
Iberia
San Lorenzo
Alerta
C
Las Piedras
MADRE DE DIOS
Manu National Park
Madre de Dios
Mavila
Map 5
4
Boca Manu
5
Planchón
6

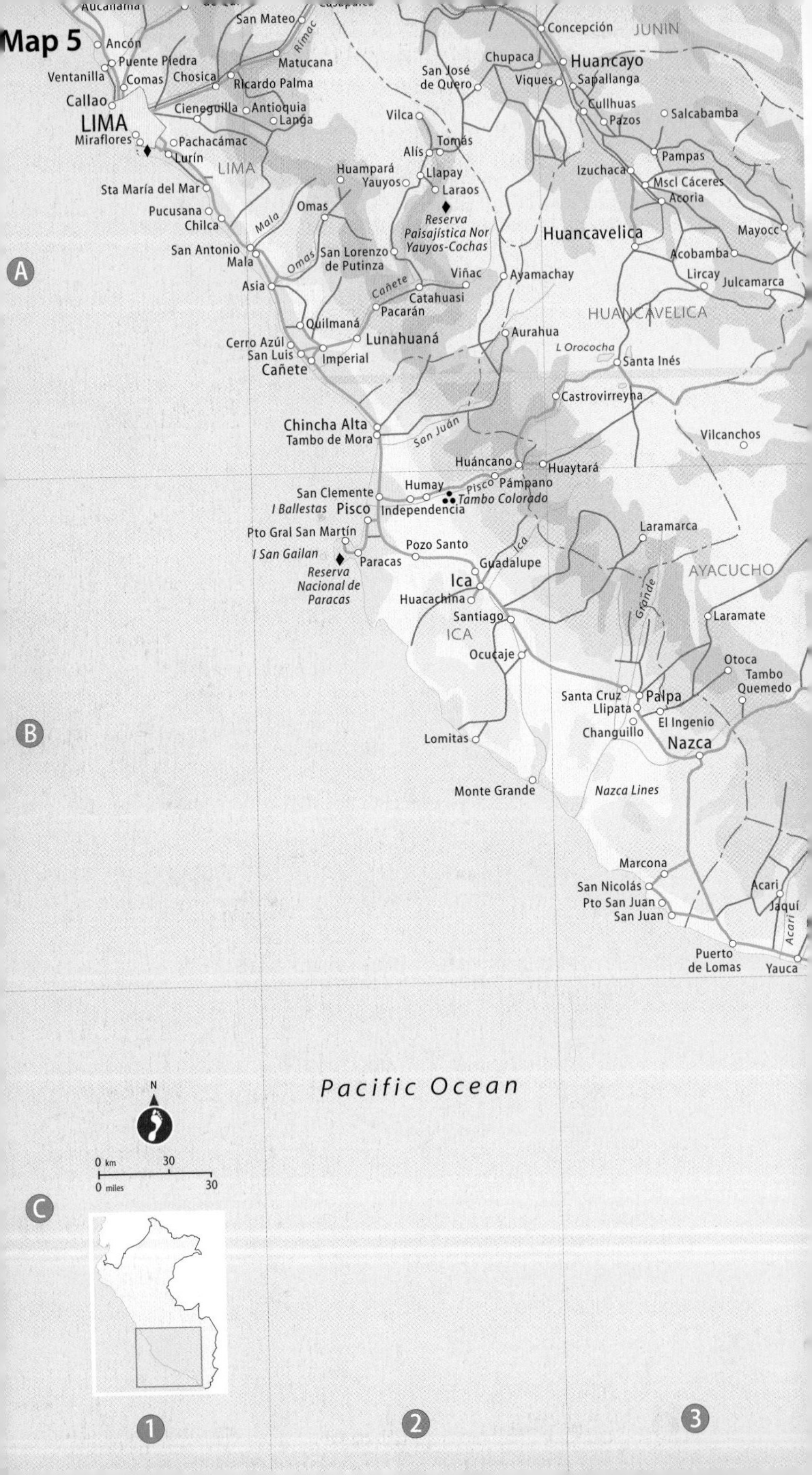

Map 5
San Mateo
Rimac
Concepción
JUNIN
Ancón
Puente Piedra
Matucana
Chupaca
Huancayo
Ventanilla
Comas
Chosica
San José de Quero
Viques
Sapallanga
Ricardo Palma
Callao
Cieneguilla
Antioquia
Cullhuas
Langa
Vilca
Pazos
Salcabamba
LIMA
Miraflores
Pachacámac
Tomás
Lurín
Alís
Pampas
LIMA
Huampará
Llapay
Izuchaca
Yauyos
Laraos
Mscl Cáceres
Sta María del Mar
Acoria
Omas
Reserva Paisajística Nor Yauyos-Cochas
Pucusana
Mala
Chilca
Huancavelica
Mayocc
San Antonio
Mala
San Lorenzo de Putinza
Omas
Acobamba
Viñac
Ayamachay
Lircay
Julcamarca
Asia
Cañete
Catahuasi
Pacarán
HUANCAVELICA
Quilmaná
Aurahua
Lunahuaná
Cerro Azúl
L Orococha
San Luis
Imperial
Santa Inés
Cañete
Castrovirreyna
Chincha Alta
San Juán
Vilcanchos
Tambo de Mora
Huáncano
Huaytará
Humay
Pisco
Pámpano
San Clemente
Tambo Colorado
I Ballestas
Pisco
Independencia
Laramarca
Pto Gral San Martín
Ica
Pozo Santo
I San Gailan
Paracas
Guadalupe
AYACUCHO
Reserva Nacional de Paracas
Ica
Grande
Huacachina
Laramate
Santiago
ICA
Ocucaje
Otoca
Tambo Quemedo
Santa Cruz
Palpa
Llipata
El Ingenio
Changuillo
Nazca
Lomitas
Monte Grande
Nazca Lines
Marcona
San Nicolás
Acari
Pto San Juan
Jaquí
San Juan
Acari
Puerto de Lomas
Yauca
Pacific Ocean
N
0 km 30
0 miles 30
A
B
C
1
2
3

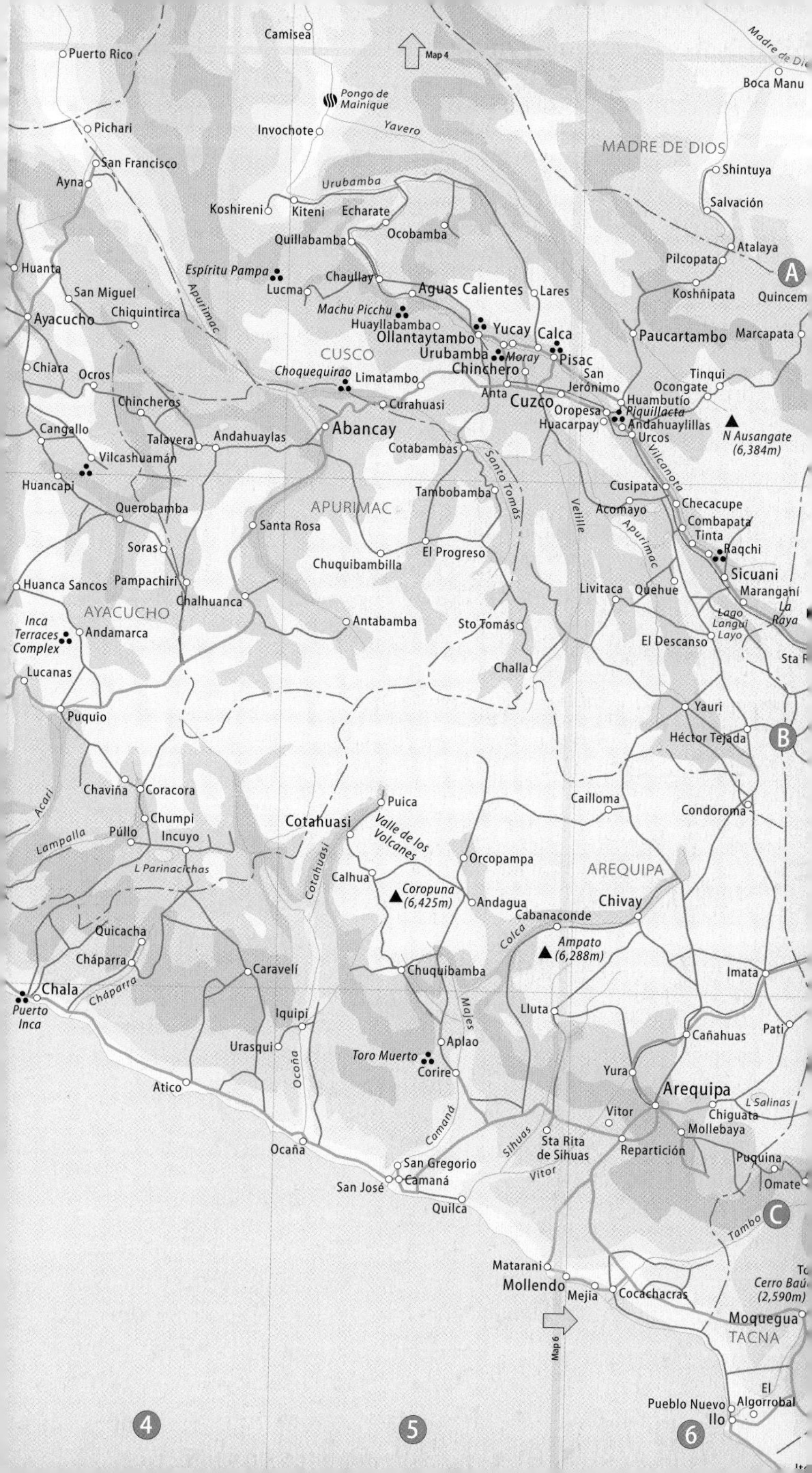

Camisea
Map 4
Puerto Rico
Madre de Dios
Boca Manu
Pongo de Mainique
Pichari
Invochote
Yavero
MADRE DE DIOS
San Francisco
Shintuya
Ayna
Urubamba
Koshireni
Kiteni
Echarate
Salvación
Quillabamba
Ocobamba
Atalaya
Pilcopata
Huanta
Espíritu Pampa
A
Lucma
Chaullay
Aguas Calientes
Lares
Koshñipata
Quincem
San Miguel
Apurimac
Machu Picchu
Ayacucho
Chiquintirca
Huayllabamba
Yucay
Calca
Paucartambo
Marcapata
Ollantaytambo
CUSCO
Urubamba
Moray
Pisac
Chiara
Choquequirao
Chinchero
San Jerónimo
Tinqui
Ocros
Limatambo
Anta
Ocongate
Chincheros
Curahuasi
Cuzco
Huambutío
Oropesa
Piquillacta
Cangallo
Abancay
Huacarpay
Andahuaylillas
N Ausangate (6,384m)
Talavera
Andahuaylas
Urcos
Vilcashuamán
Cotabambas
Santo Tomás
Vilcanota
Huancapi
Tambobamba
Cusipata
Checacupe
Querobamba
APURIMAC
Velille
Acomayo
Combapata
Santa Rosa
Tinta
Soras
El Progreso
Raqchi
Chuquibambilla
Sicuani
Huanca Sancos
Pampachiri
Livitaca
Quehue
Marangani
Chalhuanca
La Raya
AYACUCHO
Lago Langui Layo
Inca Terraces Complex
Andamarca
Antabamba
Sto Tomás
El Descanso
Sta R
Lucanas
Challa
Yauri
Puquio
Héctor Tejada
B
Chaviña
Coracora
Cailloma
Puica
Condoroma
Acari
Chumpi
Cotahuasi
Valle de los Volcanes
Lampalla
Púllo
Incuyo
Orcopampa
L Parinacichas
AREQUIPA
Calhua
Cotahuasi
Coropuna (6,425m)
Andagua
Chivay
Cabanaconde
Quicacha
Colca
Ampato (6,288m)
Cháparra
Caravelí
Chuquibamba
Imata
Chala
Cháparra
Majes
Puerto Inca
Iquipi
Lluta
Pati
Urasqui
Aplao
Cañahuas
Toro Muerto
Ocoña
Corire
Yura
Atico
Arequipa
L Salinas
Vitor
Chiguata
Camaná
Sihuas
Mollebaya
Sta Rita de Sihuas
Repartición
Ocaña
San Gregorio
Vitor
Puquina
Omate
San José
Camaná
Quilca
C
Tambo
Matarani
Mollendo
Mejia
Cocachacras
Cerro Baú (2,590m)
Moquegua
Map 6
TACNA
El Algorrobal
Pueblo Nuevo
Ilo
4
5
6

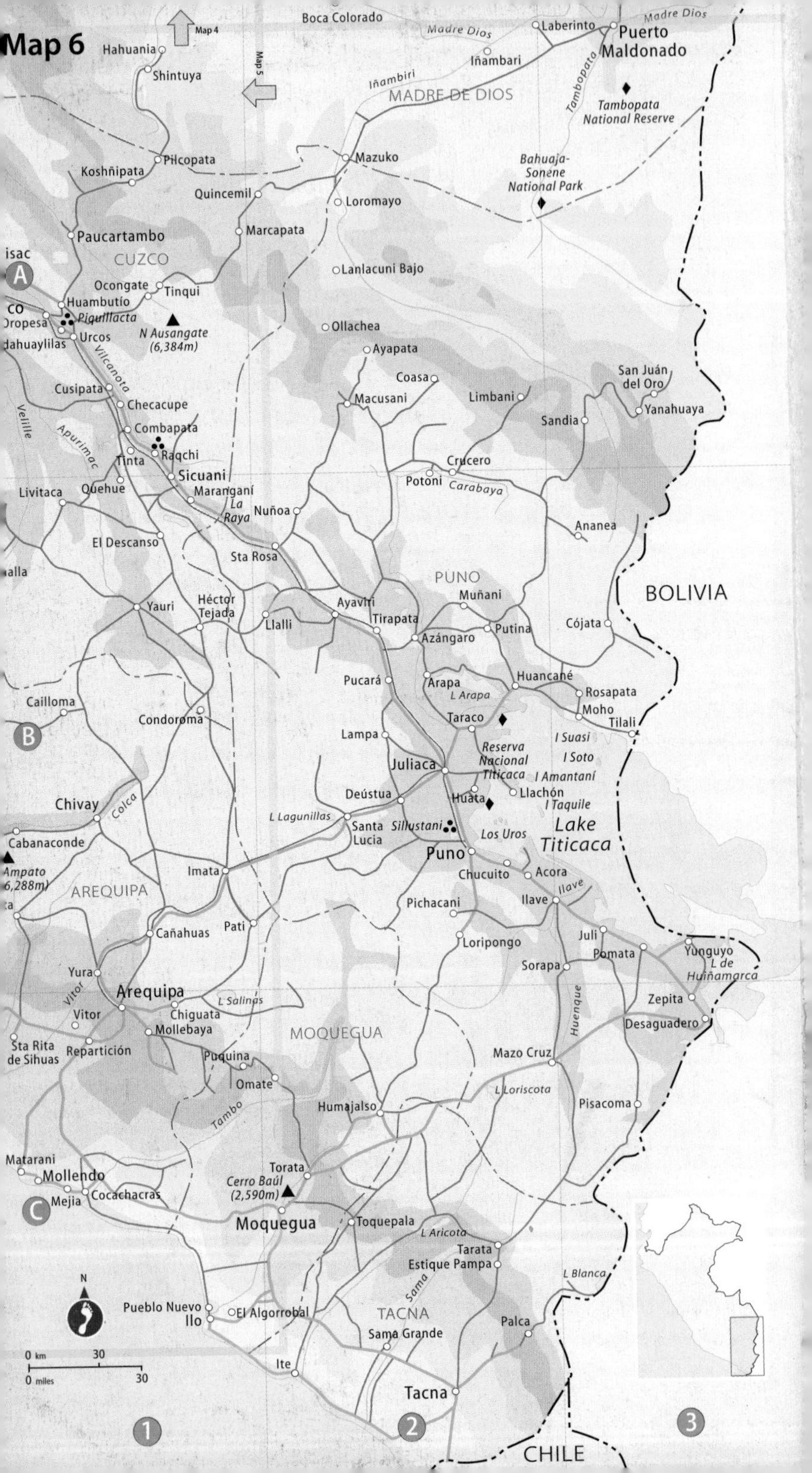
Map 6
Map 4
Map 5
Boca Colorado
Madre Dios
Laberinto
Puerto Maldonado
Iñambari
Tambopata
Tambopata National Reserve
Iñambiri
MADRE DE DIOS
Hahuania
Shintuya
Pilcopata
Koshñipata
Mazuko
Bahuaja-Sonene National Park
Quincemil
Loromayo
Paucartambo
Marcapata
CUZCO
Lanlacuni Bajo
Ocongate
Tinqui
Huambutío
Piquillacta
N Ausangate (6,384m)
Urcos
Ollachea
Ayapata
Coasa
Vilcanota
Cusipata
Checacupe
Macusani
Limbani
San Juán del Oro
Yanahuaya
Sandia
Velille
Apurimac
Combapata
Raqchi
Tinta
Sicuani
Crucero
Potoni
Carabaya
Livitaca
Quehue
Marangani
La Raya
Nuñoa
Ananea
El Descanso
Sta Rosa
PUNO
BOLIVIA
Muñani
Yauri
Héctor Tejada
Llalli
Ayaviri
Tirapata
Azángaro
Putina
Cójata
Pucará
Arapa
L Arapa
Huancané
Rosapata
Moho
Tilali
Cailloma
Condoroma
Taraco
Lampa
Reserva Nacional Titicaca
I Suasi
I Soto
Juliaca
I Amantaní
Llachón
Chivay
Colca
Deústua
Huata
I Taquile
L Lagunillas
Santa Lucia
Sillustani
Los Uros
Lake Titicaca
Cabanaconde
Puno
Ampato (6,288m)
Imata
Chucuito
Acora
AREQUIPA
Ilave
Pichacani
Pati
Cañahuas
Loripongo
Juli
Pomata
Yunguyo
L de Huiñamarca
Sorapa
Yura
Vitor
Arequipa
L Salinas
Chiguata
Huenque
Zepita
Desaguadero
Mollebaya
MOQUEGUA
Sta Rita de Sihuas
Repartición
Mazo Cruz
Puquina
Omate
L Loriscota
Tambo
Humajalso
Pisacoma
Matarani
Torata
Mollendo
Cerro Baúl (2,590m)
Mejia
Cocachacras
Moquegua
Toquepala
L Aricota
Tarata
Estique Pampa
L Blanca
Sama
N
Pueblo Nuevo
El Algorrobal
Ilo
TACNA
Palca
Sama Grande
0 km 30
0 miles 30
Ite
Tacna
A
B
C
1
2
3
CHILE